HANDBOOK OF
PHONOLOGICAL
DEVELOPMENT

HANDBOOK OF
PHONOLOGICAL
DEVELOPMENT
From the Perspective of
Constraint-Based Nonlinear Phonology

BARBARA HANDFORD BERNHARDT
University of British Columbia, Vancouver, British Columbia

JOSEPH PAUL STEMBERGER
Department of Communication Disorders
University of Minnesota, Minneapolis, Minnesota

ACADEMIC PRESS

San Diego   London   Boston   New York   Sydney   Tokyo   Toronto

Copyright © 1998 by ACADEMIC PRESS

Academic Press
a division of Harcourt Brace & Company
525 B Street, Suite 1900, San Diego, California 92101-4495, USA
http://www.apnet.com

Academic Press Limited
24-28 Oval Road, London NW1 7DX, UK
http://www.hbuk.co.uk/ap/

Library of Congress Card Catalog Number: 97-80298

International Standard Book Number: 0-12-092830-2

PRINTED IN THE UNITED STATES OF AMERICA
97 98 99 00 01 02 BB 9 8 7 6 5 4 3 2 1

To Gwendolyn, Morgan, and Larissa Stemberger
and
To Carmine and Travis Bernhardt

CONTENTS

3

PHONOLOGICAL REPRESENTATIONS AND PROCESSES

4

CONSTRAINTS

5

SEGMENTAL DEVELOPMENT

6

PROSODIC DEVELOPMENT

7

SEQUENCES OF ELEMENTS

8

THEORY AND APPLICATION:
NOT JUST FOR THE CLINICIAN

9

ACQUISITION OF ADULT ALTERNATIONS

10

DISCUSSION AND CONCLUSIONS

PREFACE

Sometimes in life an opportunity comes along to team up with someone who has similar and complementary interests for a common purpose. Technology has facilitated such a collaboration, in spite of an international border and 2000 miles distance. This book is the culmination of that collaboration and represents an integration of knowledge from linguistics, psycholinguistics, and speech–language pathology as they relate to phonological development. Because of the blend of information and the varying perspectives, the book is aimed at a variety of audiences—linguists, developmental psychologists, and speech–language pathologists—who have an interest in both phonology and acquisition. Utilizing data from our own work and from the literature, we have attempted to address the full range of phonological patterns observed in children's speech, as well as developmental patterns as the child's system changes over time. The data are examined from the perspectives of current linguistic and psycholinguistic theories, particularly multilinear (nonlinear) and constraint-based theories. This book covers a far greater range of phenomena than previous books and papers on phonological development and is, to our knowledge, the first attempt to provide a single framework for all of it.

The book focuses primarily on speech production rather than on perception. In terms of developmental periods, prelinguistic data are discussed, but the majority of the data come from the period of real words. Although we give equal weight to segmental and syllable–word structure phenomena, we do not address intonation or other suprasegmental aspects of speech production (except in passing); this partly reflects our feeling that not much is known about these areas and also the fact that such aspects of speech cannot be accurately transcribed using the human ear. We begin with a general exploration of issues in nonlinear (multilinear) constraint-based theories (Chapters 1–4) and then examine phonological acquisition data in light of those theories (Chapters 5–10). Major current perspectives in phonology and phonological development are discussed: the mechanisms accounting for the differences between adult and child forms (rules/processes versus constraints), the nature of the lexicon, the feature as the basic unit of analysis, and the innateness issue. We present information about what phonological patterns may be present in the child's speech and how to account for those patterns. We also address how learning takes place (leading to changes in the child's system).

We assume that readers possess a general introductory background in phonological theory and phonetics and some familiarity with phonological features and phonological processes. We assume no knowledge of multilinear phonological or constraint-based theories, as one of our purposes is to provide an introduction to (our versions of) those theories. Nor do we assume any previous background in phonological development. The book presents the range of known and possible (but often unknown) phenomena in developmental phonology, and thus serves as a comprehensive overview for both the novice and the specialist in this area.

Different chapters will have greater meaning than others for different sorts of readers. The phonologist may choose to skim Chapter 3 (an introduction to non-linear/multilinear phonology), merely to ascertain our theoretical perspectives, and may wish to scan Chapter 2 for those sections that are especially relevant to acquisition rather than to linguistic theory. The speech–language pathologist and psychologist may wish to devote more time to those tutorial chapters. Chapter 4 and Appendixes C and D are addressed to all readers, because they describe our version of constraint-based (Optimality) theory, and are a basis for the data chapters. (Appendixes C and D support Chapter 4. Appendix C lists the constraints, and Appendix D gives some guidance on how to determine which constraints are relevant for a given phonological pattern in the data.) Chapters 5–9 are the meat of the book for all readers: data in light of the theories, and theories in light of the data. The data chapters begin with the small units: features and speech sounds (segments). We then proceed to larger units: syllables and word structures in Chapter 6, and sequences of elements in Chapter 7. Chapter 8 examines several sets of data from children with phonological disorders. It will be of particular interest to the speech–language pathologist, but the phenomena and issues will be of interest to all readers. The final data chapter (Chapter 9) focuses on the child's acquisition of alternations that are present in adult speech. The data chapters are organized in terms of various parts of the phonological system, constraints on these parts of the system, and the repair processes that accommodate those constraints. We have attempted to cross-reference as many sections as possible, so that a reader may follow up on various aspects of development or data sets from a particular child.

This book is meant to contribute to the convergence and reconciliation of various perspectives in phonology. We emphasize the ideas of multilinear phonology and constraint-based analysis and their applicability to developmental data. We argue that current linguistic theories provide useful insights that not only explain developmental patterns better, but also can provide useful clinical techniques to accelerate development in children with phonological disorders. At the same time, we examine those current theories in light of the data, seeing whether the data can supply useful information bearing on alternative analyses proposed in the literature.

We thank our colleagues and students in developmental phonology (many of whom are cited in this book) and at our respective universities for their enthusiastic encouragement and helpful feedback during the writing process. To our students who told us which parts were clear and which parts were not, we are grateful. Funding provided by the British Columbia Medical Services Foundation (to the first author), by the National Science Foundation (Research Grant DBS-9209642 to the second author), by the University of British Columbia summer grants program, and by our departments has enabled us to collect and analyze data for this book, and we gratefully acknowledge those financial contributions. This book is a by-product of the technological age, and we acknowledge those amazing inventors of computers, electronic mail (and ftp-ing!), airplanes, and the telephone. Above all, we acknowledge and thank our own families, and the families and children in the various phonological projects in British Columbia, without whose words, there would have been no stories to tell.

1

INTRODUCTION

"The Child is Father of the Man."
—*W. Wordsworth: "My heart leaps up." (1807)*

William Wordsworth was not thinking about child phonology when he penned the line: "The Child is Father of the Man." But his insight does pertain to child phonology. Many constraints on phonological content and processing that are present in babbling continue into adulthood. Thus, the child is "parent" to the adult, even though the "adult parent" transmits the ambient language to the child. This relational paradox provides the two main objectives for this book: (1) to examine acquisition data in the light of phonological theories developed to account for the adult/parent language, and (2) to examine those adult theories in the context of child/parent language.

With respect to the first objective, new interpretations of child data are possible because of significant changes in phonological and psycholinguistic theories and models. Changes in theory do not necessarily create opportunities for better insights in related fields. However, from our perspectives in psycholinguistics and speech-language pathology, the recent theories do provide more interesting, testable, and applicable ideas for psychological processing and children's phonological acquisition than any previous ones. In phonology, changes have affected all aspects of theory: the issues, the analyses, and even the way that linguists think about phonological patterns. The earlier sequential ("linear") theory, with its arbitrary and often complex set of rules and processes (Chomsky & Halle, 1968), has been replaced with a constraint-based representational theory (e.g., Goldsmith, 1976; Kenstowicz, 1994). In psychology, advances in computer simulation have accelerated development of acquisition theories, and developmental models have benefited from the development of connectionist theories and models (e.g.,

Rumelhart & McClelland, 1986; Stemberger, 1985, 1992b). These two streams of thought and research have recently converged in a phonological theory called Optimality Theory (McCarthy & Prince, 1993; Prince & Smolensky, 1993). The first half of the book is a tutorial on multilinear and constraint-based phonological theory, tailored to the needs of work on acquisition. The second half examines acquisition data in detail, from the feature to the word, in the light of both general multilinear (nonlinear) theory and Optimality Theory (OT).

The examination of acquisition data in the context of current theories also provides an opportunity to evaluate the theories, our second objective. What is known about phonological acquisition has often not filtered through to linguists who are developing phonological theories. In our view, the ultimate theory of phonological behavior will account for all phonological data, whether diachronic or synchronic, from adults or children, or from first or second language acquisition. Phonologists often work with many competing proposals. Developmental data may support one of those proposals more than the others, and thus provide additional information with which to choose between competing hypotheses. Throughout this book, we indicate where such is the case, with the claim that such data are fundamental to theory development.

This chapter begins with discussion of the general relationship between acquisition data and phonological theory. The subsequent sections delineate specific theoretical issues addressed in the book, and the types of data utilized.

1.1. PHONOLOGICAL THEORIES
AND ACQUISITION DATA

In the introductory statement, we indicated the two major purposes of this book: (1) to examine acquisition data in the light of current phonological theories, and (2) to evaluate the ability of those phonological theories to account for acquisition data. The rationale for those objectives is elaborated in the following subsections.

1.1.1. ACQUISITION DATA IN THE LIGHT
OF PHONOLOGICAL THEORY

Application of phonological theories to child data is not a new enterprise in the study of phonological acquisition. As we discuss below, a number of assumptions underlie this application, principally,

1. that developed (adult) and developing (child) systems are sufficiently similar to allow such an enterprise,
2. that the language(s) on which the theory is based are sufficiently similar to the child's ambient language, and
3. that data from children are interpretable in the context of abstract phonological theories.

Jakobson (1968/1941), an early advocate of this approach, asserted that phonological acquisition follows an innately determined order, from unmarked to marked universal features, structures, and contrasts of adult phonology. Some acquisition research continues in the Jakobsonian (structuralist) tradition today (e.g., Ingram, 1988a,b; Dinnsen, 1992; Beers, 1995). Similarly, Stampe (1969) suggested that children come to the language learning process with innate limitations on phonetic capacity and a number of natural phonological processes to deal with those limitations. Over time, exposure to the ambient language results in suppression of the innate processes. Stampe's (1969) theory of natural phonology has had a strong impact on approaches to the assessment and remediation of phonological disorders (e.g., Edwards & Bernhardt, 1973a; Ingram, 1981; Grunwell, 1985; Hodson & Paden, 1991). Thus, the application of phonological theory to acquisition data has been a fruitful enterprise, both in research and clinical work.

Some developmental phonologists have not been in total agreement, however, about the validity or at least the sufficiency of applying adult phonological theory to child data (e.g., Waterson, 1971; Macken & Ferguson, 1983; Menn, 1976, 1983). Such researchers advocate a more developmentally oriented research approach, in order to account for differences among children, and between adult and child data. Variability in acquisition across children is not something to be ignored, and we address it frequently throughout the book.

Variability notwithstanding, child phonology does not appear at any point to be otherworldly. Rather, differences between child and adult phonology generally reflect the relative frequency of particular patterns or features. Consonant harmony (in which /tɪk/ may be realized as [kɪk], for example) and default onset use (frequent use of one speech sound in syllable-initial position) are two examples where frequency and features may differ. Consonant harmony is relatively common in early child phonology, but rare in adult phonology (Vihman, 1978; Stemberger & Stoel-Gammon, 1991). Default onsets (particularly glottal stop or [t]) are found in many adult languages. Many children also use default onsets such as glottal stops, but some use other types of default onsets, such as nasals or oral glides (see §6.1.3, §7.4.4.3, and §8.3). To our knowledge, however, no child phonologist has reported any segment or feature that does not occur somewhere in a language of the world. Moreover, just as children become adults without an identifiable demarcation between childhood and adulthood (puberty rites notwithstanding), so does child phonology become adult phonology gradually, over time. There is no developmental point where child phonology is transformed into adult phonology. As we discuss in §1.2.1, development is assumed to be a continuous process. Although developmental continuity does not *dictate* the use of adult frameworks for child data, we suggest that the utilization of one framework allows us to describe more exactly the gradual transition from child to adult phonology. How much adult-like *underlying* structure one can infer at any given point is a different issue, but, then, the nature of underlying representation and the lexicon are also issues for adult phonology (see §2.3, §3.11).

There are other potentially more deleterious factors for the application enterprise. We outline these in detail in §5.3, in our discussion of the order of acquisition of features. False assumptions can be made about what a theory entails, how it can be applied, and how the application can be evaluated. A particular (abstract) theory may be irrelevant to the real-time process of acquisition, even if it has the semblance of relevance at first. Assumed implications of a particular theory for acquisition may be invalid or at least debatable. The procedures used in application may be flawed in terms of experimental design. Finally, evaluation of the application may be based on false premises or methods.

We wrote this book because we have found the new concepts and formalism of multilinear and constraint-based theory to be useful and elucidating, both for psycholinguistic research and for speech-language pathology applications. We present data and examples throughout to support this assertion. There are instances where the theories or their implications are unclear and/or do not account for the data. We indicate this as it arises, and then present a concentrated discussion on data that fall outside the scope of the theories (for good or ill) in Chapter 10. As we discuss in the next section, benefits can accrue to phonological theory from both the supporting and disconfirming child data.

1.1.2. TESTING PHONOLOGICAL THEORY
WITH ACQUISITION DATA

Theory construction in linguistics utilizes adult synchronic data as its primary source of information. This modus operandi grew out of structuralist methods early in the twentieth century, when the basic goal of phonology was to develop procedures for analyzing corpora of utterances, rather than to account for a speaker's knowledge of the language (Kenstowicz & Kisseberth, 1979:174). In the second half of the century, there has been more interest in speakers' intuitions about language and even the learnability of certain aspects of language. However, the primary data for theory development remain adult synchronic data. Data from acquisition (first or second), historical change, or phonological processing are still considered "external" evidence (Kenstowicz & Kisseberth, 1979). Most phonologists do not alter theories when noncorroborative patterns are found in a "secondary" set of evidence, such as child data. This stems in part from historical practices in linguistics, and in part from uncertainty regarding the influence of external (in this case, maturational and learning) factors on phonological patterns.

While we acknowledge the importance and "impurity" of developmental factors, we submit that adult synchronic data are also imperfect for the following reasons:

1. Adult phonology is the end product of a learning process, and thus reflects limits on what can be learned, rather than on what may be inherent in the phonological system. Because children are at the beginning of the learning process, their phonology is less bound by the constraints on what can be learned and more bound by the limits on what is possible in phonology.

2. Adult phonology is subject to historical change, and may not be a good indicator of what is possible in human phonological systems. All synchronic phonological patterns are the result of historical sound change. As a result, synchronic patterns reflect diachronic constraints on sound change. This fact has its greatest ramifications for research on universals. Phonologists take note of phonological patterns that do or do not appear in the languages of the world, and construct phonological theories in such a way that such "impossible" patterns cannot be handled by the theory.

However, phonological patterns that are not found in adult languages may be absent for one of two reasons. The patterns may be impossible in human phonology (as is generally assumed in theory development). However, they may be absent solely because there is no plausible historical source for them. (See Stemberger, 1996a, for an extensive discussion of this topic.) They might be perfectly compatible with human phonology, but be absent due to historical accident. Child phonological patterns are not subject to the same constraints on diachronic sound changes, and consequently may be a purer reflection of the range of phenomena that are possible in human phonological systems.

By giving equal weight to child data in theory construction and evaluation, we suggest that phonological theory will reflect what is possible in human phonology (1) before, during, *and* after learning, (2) with *less* mature and *more* mature mechanisms, and (3) with and *without* reference to the influence of diachrony. With this book, we attempt to present developmental data in a form in which they can be useful for testing phonological theories. We also present positions on a number of theoretical issues which take child data into account.

1.2. DEVELOPMENTAL ISSUES

Developmental issues concern the learning process, and the differences and similarities between adult and child phonology and between perception and production. General issues are as follows:

1. The origin of phonological phenomena and the learning process (including the innateness issue). Development involves a learning process. What and how much does the child bring through genetic programming to the language learning process? Does the child have built-in constraints on phonetic output, or are some learned? If there are phonological processes, are they 'natural,' that is, phonetically or neurologically determined? Is there a predetermined pathway for development which is predictable from phonological universals, or are children more individual in their learning patterns? Is the process continuous or discontinuous?

2. The nature of the child's phonological representations in perception and production. The child's output is often different from the adult target form. Does this imply that the child's underlying forms are therefore different from adult targets and underlying forms? Or are adult-like representations converted through

processes or rules into child outputs? Or do constraints on output inhibit the production of certain patterns, without the active effect of processes?

3. The number and type of lexicon(s) in which representations are stored. Discussion of underlying representation (UR) leads to a consideration of how the child's underlying forms are stored, that is, in one lexicon, or in different lexicons. What is the nature of the lexicon(s)? Are perceptual forms stored differently from production forms? If there is more than one lexicon, how are the two (or more) related?

These issues (except the continuity issue) are discussed in depth in Chapters 2–4, in the context of presenting the theoretical foundations for the book. Our perspective on the continuity issue is independent of the theoretical frameworks presented in the subsequent chapters, and thus is elaborated in the next subsection. Other developmental issues that concern the development of syllable and word structure and the feature system are presented in the Chapters 5–9.

1.2.1. THE CONTINUITY HYPOTHESIS

A general developmental debate concerns the relationship between adult and child systems. Is development best viewed as a continuous process, in which each period in acquisition is a natural outgrowth of the previous period, and the beginning and end-states are parts of a coherent whole? Or is each period of acquisition so different from every other period and from the adult end-state, that moving from one period ("stage") to the next is best viewed as a set of discontinuous maturational leaps, with different mechanisms or organizing principles at each period ("stage")?

Before presenting the arguments for and against continuity, a few comments are necessary about the word *stage*. This word is often used in developmental research and argumentation, particularly by researchers who subscribe to the discontinuity hypothesis, but also by researchers who subscribe to the continuity hypothesis. Stage has as many definitions as there are authors, some more rigid than others. In the loosest sense, stage is synonymous with "period" or "point" of acquisition. Thus, a stage has no prescribed set of behaviors, and is not a necessary step in an invariant sequence. This loose definition is most compatible with variability in child language, and the continuity perspective. Sets of behaviors merge into other sets independently and in a relatively free sequence. Were we to use the word in this book, we would use it in that way. (We time-reference longitudinal data only, speaking of points of acquisition.) In the most rigid sense, a stage is a necessary step in an invariant sequence of discrete steps, and is definable in terms of particular (expected, required, ?innate?) behaviors. This rigid definition is most compatible with the discontinuity hypothesis. In between, there are softer or harder views on the invariant nature, the necessary steps, or the prescribed behaviors, that allow different perspectives on continuity. Fikkert (1994), for example, posits that there are stages with an invariant order, but (a) a child may skip a particular stage, and (b) transitions between stages are variable, so that a child may vacillate between two or even three stages in the course of a few utterances. An unfortunate aspect of developmental research is that researchers too frequently neglect to define the term "stage" in their writings. Thus, when they are talking about continuity or discontinuity, it can be difficult to interpret their claims.

Although the concept of stage may not be defined, the continuity debate is often discussed in the context of other developmental topics: (a) the origin of language, (b) the nature of representation, or (c) cognitive development. Proponents of the continuity hypothesis do not necessarily agree on these other topics, suggesting that it is an independent issue.

Within the nativist "camp," there are both perspectives. Proponents of the discontinuity view assert that periods ("stages") of language development are qualitatively different and a result of genetically predetermined maturational breakthroughs. For syntactic development, Gleitman and Wanner (1982) dubbed this the "tadpole to frog" hypothesis. For phonological development, Jakobson (1968/1941) called the transition from babbling to speech a developmental discontinuity. Other proponents of the innateness hypothesis espouse the continuity view, whether for syntax (Pinker, 1984) or phonology (Stampe, 1969, 1973; Dresher, 1994). In studies of *learnability*, the principles and parameters model of Chomsky (1986) is often adopted (Wexler & Culicover, 1980). This perspective assumes that a child's system represents the universal (innate) endowment for languages. Thus, this view holds that child phonology is continuous with universal aspects of adult phonology. Parameter settings for the phonology of the target language are presumed to be "set" early on in response to "positive evidence" from linguistic input. Continuity with the specific target adult language is created through parametric convergence. "Intermediate stage" grammars are considered to fall within the range of variation in (innately endowed) Universal Grammar (UG), and to be natural steps in a continuous process, playing no crucial role in determining the outcome (Dresher, 1994:1).

Theoreticians with less of a nativist view also differ on the continuity issue. Different perspectives on the nature of representation, individual differences, and factors specific to learning can lead to alternative views on innateness and continuity. One discontinuity that has been proposed concerns representation. Some theorists hypothesize that children first have holistic representations of words, only later moving to segment-based or feature-based representations (Waterson, 1971; Ferguson & Farwell, 1975; Iverson & Wheeler, 1987; Levelt, 1994; Velleman & Vihman, 1994). Can such a change be gradual and continuous? Or is there a sudden shift suggesting a discontinuity? Researchers with this perspective on representation ironically tend to support the continuity hypothesis (e.g., Vihman, 1992), citing the segmental and syllabic similarities between babbling and speech output, for example. How can this dichotomous view about continuity and representational metamorphosis be rationalized? Is it possible for representation to have discontinuities, while output shows gradual continuous change? Theoreticians sometimes suggest that nonlinguistic rather than linguistic factors are responsible for apparent linguistic discontinuities, for example, the learner's lack of skill, or the actual process of change itself. Such proposals are made both by "cognitive" theorists working with nonnativist perspectives (e.g., Menn, 1992: 4–5) and learnability theorists working with nativist perspectives (e.g., Dresher, 1994:1). If apparent linguistic discontinuities are a result of changes in nonlinguistic factors, then phonological development *per se* can still be considered a *continuous developmental linguistic process.*

The current state of knowledge and methods of enquiry make it impossible to confirm that child phonology is continuous or discontinuous with adult phonology in any strictly empirical sense. Furthermore, assumptions about development may influence methodologies and data interpretation. If researchers begin with an assumption of discontinuity, they may focus on major dissimilarities between developmental phonological periods, but, at least from the point of view of those assuming continuity, miss small but crucial details. If researchers begin with an assumption of continuity, they may focus on similarities between linguistic "stages" and small incremental changes, but, at least from the point of view of those assuming discontinuity, miss critical qualitative differences.

Testing the continuity perspective will require both methodological rigor and the construction of phonological theories that account for both child and adult phonological phenomena. In terms of methodology, *many* longitudinal data sets will be needed, sampled at intervals of less than a month. These data will need to be examined for evidence of small incremental changes versus major breakthroughs, and for similarities versus differences over time. Careful study of other nonphonological factors, both internal and external to the child, will be needed to assess how/when/if they influence change. Theory construction will require a cooperative venture between those working with adult data and those working with developmental data. Developmental data provide a valuable window into what is *possible* in phonology, *before* too much learning takes place. Adult phonology is, after all, the end-state of "learned" phonology. If we *can* construct theories that are based on both types of data, we have more support for the continuity assumption. As we indicated above, often there are a variety of proposals for a given phonological pattern in adult phonology. Where child data support one of those alternatives, there is reason to favor that alternative over others. In §3.4.3, we discuss the representation of consonants and vowels and theories of adjacency. We will observe that the frequencies of different harmony patterns in adult versus child phonology give reason to choose Odden's (1994) proposal of adjacency over Archangeli and Pulleyblank's (1987) proposal. This alternative accounts for data in both adult and child phonology and is thus preferred on those grounds.[1] Thus,

---

[1] Interestingly, Levelt (1994) adopted the Archangeli and Pulleyblank (1987) view of consonant and vowel representation, and in so doing, was led to adopt the view of word-based representation for early child phonology. As we discussed above, the concept of early word-based representation leads to positing of a discontinuity in representational development. Odden's (1994) proposal allows us to handle consonant harmony in child phonology without word-based representation, a preferred solution (see §7.4 for details).

both methodological changes and changes in theory construction may help confirm or disconfirm the continuity hypothesis.

Is there a best assumption to make, given that the current state of knowledge does not permit us to verify claims easily? Pinker (1984) states that the "most explanatory theory will posit the fewest developmental changes in the mechanisms of the virtual machine, attributing developmental changes, where necessary, to increases in the child's knowledge base, increasing access of computational procedures to the knowledge base, and quantitative changes in parameters like the size of working memory" (1984:6–7). He suggests that the "best approach . . . is to assume that there are no qualitative maturational changes until the theory positing constant computational mechanisms cannot account for the data" (1984:9). We, too, adopt a continuity perspective in this book, acknowledging where data may not support that perspective.

1.3. PHONOLOGICAL THEORY ISSUES

Issues for adult phonological theory are also issues for child phonology. In Chapters 2–4, we outline the basic worldviews and frameworks in question, and indicate which views and frameworks we adopt. We stay primarily in the mainstream of phonological theory, because those theories are more widely used and tested. The major concepts examined in the phonological theory sections include the following:

1. structural hierarchy and autonomy
2. feature geometry, including special feature issues: binary versus privative designation; consonants and vowels; affricates
3. underspecification of default features
4. syllable and word structure theories: timing units, onset-rime and mora theories, feet, words, and templates
5. constraint-based versus process-based analysis
6. adjacency

Current views of phonology include a much richer description of representational structure than previous theories. Key to this structure are the concepts of structural hierarchy and autonomy. A number of autonomous "levels" or "tiers" are posited to account for phonological form. Currently, many phonologists consider these levels to be hierarchically arranged, both at the macrolevel (words being "higher" than syllables, syllables being "higher" than segments or phonemes) and at the microlevel (syllables having internal structure, segments being divided into hierarchically arranged features). Although the phonological levels are autonomous, and can have their own set of operations, hierarchical arrangement constrains the type of operations that can occur. Elements that are nonadjacent in the hierarchy are unlikely to interact with each other in phonological phenomena. In this book, we operate with the concepts of autonomy and hierarchy, and examine their relevance for the acquisition of sound sequences (see especially Chapters 5 and 7).

In current standard theory, features are considered to be the minimal and basic units of representation, organized into a geometric hierarchy with groupings that reflect the phenomena that occur and the various articulators. Place, manner, and voicing features are considered to have separate locations in the hierarchy. In Chapter 3, we discuss issues regarding feature definition and organization. For this book, we have adopted a fairly standard feature framework, although we discuss variants where data warrant such discussion. In Chapter 5, we discuss child data that suggest that different children may be working with different definitions of features.

Another concept which concerns both features and higher level prosodic (syllable and word) structure is underspecification. Proponents of underspecification claim that redundant feature and word structure information is absent from underlying representations. Redundant (default) information is "filled in" where necessary for pronounceability. In Chapters 4 and 5, we address theories of underspecification, including our own perspective, default underspecification.

The description of syllable and word (prosodic) structure has changed extensively in the past 20 years. A variety of prosodic structure levels have been proposed. The closest level of structure to the segment is considered to be the "timing unit" level. Timing units "commit" real time to the realization of the segments with which they are associated. Timing unit theories vary in the degree of separateness of representation for consonants and vowels, and in their description of stress-related and non-stress-related units. Syllable and word structure is generally considered to be predictable on the basis of the segments and timing units present. However, the internal structure of the syllable is debated. Is the timing unit (or *mora*) the basic structure? Do all parts of the syllable have equal status, that is, the initial consonants (onset), the vowel (nucleus), the final consonants (coda)? Or is there a hierarchical structure of subsyllabic units? Are some units extrasyllabic? Syllables are incorporated into word structure, possibly through the mediation of a "foot" level (incorporating strong and weak syllables). How does the "foot" interact with the syllable and the higher level structure, the prosodic word? We examine these structures and theories in the light of developmental phenomena in Chapters 6 and 7.

Representations limit the type of phenomena that can occur. As views on representation have changed, so have descriptions of phonological phenomena. The three main views in current phonology are: rules/processes, constraints plus rules/processes, and constraints only. Rules in current phonology are limited to operations of addition or deletion, either at the macrolevel (addition or deletion of syllables or segments) or microlevel (addition or deletion of features or feature values); see §3.3.2. Advocates of one current theory (OT) argue that such rules are only descriptors; nothing is actually added or deleted. Constraints on output merely inhibit the production of certain structures; nothing "happens" to phonological elements. They either appear, or fail to appear. Throughout the book, we operate with a constraint-based perspective (outlined in detail in Chapter 4, and in Appendices C and D). Analyses are presented with both constraints and rules/processes, in order to make the text readable to people who have had little exposure to OT; however, our basic view is that the constraints-only perspective is a better analysis in the end, and can account particularly well for child data. Over the years, theories of phonological development have assumed either a constraint-based or process-based view of phonology. We discuss the alternate developmental views in Chapter 2, with further discussion of phonological learning in a constraint-based system in Chapter 4.

1.4. DEVELOPMENTAL DATA

In the previous sections, we have given an overview of theoretical issues discussed in the book. But the other half of the enterprise is to examine developmental data. In this section we first outline major developmental phenomena, and then comment on the type of data used, and give caveats about the data collection and analysis process.

1.4.1. GENERAL DEVELOPMENTAL PHONOLOGICAL PHENOMENA

Phonological and developmental theories need to account for the following noncontroversial facts:

1. Children's words typically differ systematically from adult target words, generally (but not always) in the direction of simplification. During development, the child's pronunciation of many words differs from the adult's pronunciations. In general, systematic patterns can be identified which account for the differences (but see our discussion of variability below). Differences are most frequently in the direction of simplification. The child's productions are usually within the bounds of the adult system, but with fewer elements, at both the segmental and prosodic levels. For example, glottal stops may substitute for a variety of segments with oral place of articulation. Syllable structure may be simplified through deletion of consonants.

Occasionally, the child's inability to produce adult targets results in more complex pronunciations (although presumably to the child, they are in some way "easier"). In terms of word structure, a child may produce clusters in place of target singleton consonants (e.g., replacement of /v/ or /z/ with [bz], see §7.3.1.9). Noninventory phones may appear as substitutions for target segments, for example, voiceless nasals (Edwards & Bernhardt, 1973a; §5.5.3.4) or clicks (Bedore, Leonard, & Gandour, 1994; §5.5.1.2.1) in the speech of English-learning children. These unusual examples are exceptions to the rule, both for a given child's system, and across children. Most of the time, the child's forms are identifiably simpler and less marked than the adult targets.

2. Children's productions change over time, either quickly or slowly depending on the normalcy of the system. Children begin the learning process with limited segmental inventories and syllable/word structure, and, in the normal acquisition process, have acquired *most* aspects of the adult phonological system by age 6;0. Thus, hundreds of changes occur (at least in most languages) in a relatively short time span, the system rarely going for longer than a month without some change. Children with phonological disorders have more protracted development, with longer-lasting learning plateaus (Stoel-Gammon & Dunn, 1985).

Most developmental change is positive, and in the direction of the adult form. Occasionally, regressions occur, in which some aspect of the child's output becomes less like the adult target than it had been previously (see §4.12.2). However, regressions are infrequent in development. Development is usually a positive progression.

3. Although some general developmental trends and patterns can be described, variability is a notable aspect of phonological acquisition. Variability is observable both across children, and for individuals.

(a) Between-child variability: Between-child variability is observable in the order of acquisition of segments and structures, and in simplification patterns, both across and within languages. Characteristically, early words have minimal structural complexity (CV syllables and combinations), and are composed of vowels, stops, glides, and nasals (Edwards & Shriberg, 1983). Liquids, fricatives, and clusters tend to be later acquired elements. Across children, however, there is variation in the acquisition order for specific segments and structures, and in the way that adult target forms are modified. In the data chapters, we outline examples of such variation both for order of acquisition and for types of simplification patterns.

(b) Within-child variability: Within-child variability can be observable for single lexical items, or for certain segments or syllable structures. Ferguson & Farwell (1975) noted that some words can have several pronunciations at the same point in time. Regressions, advanced forms (individual words or groups of words that appear to be "ahead" of general patterns), overgeneralizations or undergeneralizations of patterns, and chain shifts (phones appearing as substitutions but not as matches with the adult targets) can result in within-child variability for words or segments. When development proceeds in an item-by-item fashion (lexical diffusion) rather than in an across-the-board fashion, there tends to be variable accuracy in production of certain segments or word structures. This variability can be random, or may result from contextual influences.

Context (word position or sequences) may affect production of segments and structures. For example, certain consonants, such as velars or fricatives, may appear *only* in syllable codas (§6.1.12), or only with certain vowels (§7.3.4). Sequence constraints may prohibit the appearance of one sound class before another, for example, labials before coronals (§7.4.1.3). Coda consonants may be produced only if they are nasal, etc. (§6.1.12). Clusters may be produced only if they are made up of stops and glides (§7.3.1).

A researcher's analysis methodologies and theoretical perspectives can lead to an emphasis or de-emphasis on variability in acquisition. The "cognitive" theorists have tended to focus on *phonetic output* and the child's *creative construction* of a phonological system. Thus, their discussions tend to stress the importance of variability (Ferguson & Farwell, 1975; Macken & Ferguson, 1983). Theorists with more of a universalist perspective (Jakobson, 1968/1941; Dresher, 1994) tend to focus less on phonetics and more on *phonology, phonemic representation,* and *contrasts*; thus, their discussions tend to emphasize general trends and systematicity. In this book, we attempt to identify general trends and tendencies wherever possible, while addressing the range of individual difference.

4. Children generally perceive words accurately before they produce them accurately. Although children may occasionally misperceive words or phones (Macken, 1980), they generally understand more than they can produce accurately (Jusczyk, 1992). In fact, there is evidence that at least some children avoid words they cannot pronounce, suggesting that those children have very good perception and self-awareness (Schwartz & Leonard, 1982). Misperceptions that do occur include confusions of phones with similar formant structure and intensity, such as [f]-[θ] in English (Velleman, 1988), and segmentation errors (e.g., *another* perceived as *a "nother"*; *this morning* perceived as *the "smorning"*).

Some researchers have asserted that phonemic discrimination is an ability that develops over time (Garnica, 1973; Barton, 1980). This claim is not easily falsifiable or verifiable, because it is difficult to construct phonemic discrimination tasks that young children can/will do. Charles (Bernhardt, 1992b), a 6-year-old subject with a phonological disorder, exemplifies the task bias problem. Charles used [θ] or [ð] for sibilants. During a discrimination task involving similarity judgments, he was asked if [ʃiːp] and [siːp] were the same or different. He responded, "[θiːp], [θiːp], they're the same." When the experimenter pointed out that he was accurate about his own pronunciations, but that the task required him to comment on the adult productions, he completed the remainder of the test with 100% accuracy. Because this 6-year-old audibly vocalized his response strategy, the experimenter was able to redirect him on the task. Such testing luxuries are usually not possible with younger preschoolers and toddlers, the preferred age group for testing in terms of evaluating the notion of developing phonemic discrimination. Thus, the facts about development of phonemic discrimination are still unknown. We are assuming in this book that, overall, children's perception of the adult targets is not only advanced in comparison with their production, but essentially adult-like early in the acquisition process (see also Ingram, 1992; Vihman, 1996). Thus, if the child has normal hearing, mispronunciations are largely due to production factors rather than perceptual factors.

Occasional studies have argued that children accurately perceive adult pronunciations, but may not be aware that their own pronunciations differ from those of adults. This is often termed the "fis phenomenon," after an early prominent report (Berko & Brown, 1960). We would like to note that children must generally be aware of their own "mispronunciations." (a) There are also anecdotes of children admitting that they cannot pronounce something ("Only Daddy can say that"). (b) Children may avoid using words with sounds that they cannot pronounce (Schwartz & Leonard, 1982). (c) Children notice when they produce slips of the tongue. Stemberger (1989) notes that children detect and self-correct errors:

That *Founds*–Sounds funny.

Stemberger (p. 181) reports that adults in his study corrected 85.7% of perseveration errors, whereas the two children self-corrected fewer errors (37.1% for Gwendolyn; 72.6% for Morgan). But to self-correct any errors, children must be aware of when their pronunciation differs from that of adults. Not only must they be aware of mispronunciations, they must be aware of their own systematic mispronunciations, which they do not attempt to self-correct (because they can do no better).

5. Phonological development appears to have many similarities with development in other linguistic and nonlinguistic domains, although specific comparisons have yet to be made. The general facts of phonological acquisition are similar to developmental facts for other domains. Simple elements appear before complex ones. General trends can be described, but individual differences are also noticeable. Regressions can occur while the system advances at a reasonably rapid rate. Comprehension precedes production. Some aspects of phonological acquisition are unreported in other domains, for example, the "chain shift," but it is not clear whether they are merely unreported, or are in fact infrequent.[2] Specific aspects of phonological acquisition which pertain to the sound system may have parallels in other domains or vary greatly because of the mechanisms and material to be learned, but those convergences and divergences are largely unexplored as of yet.

1.4.2. WHAT COUNTS AS DATA: TYPICAL VERSUS PROTRACTED DEVELOPMENT

In the past 20 years, analysis in child phonology has been based on data from children with normal development and from children with protracted development. Children in the latter group are often called "phonologically delayed" or "disordered." The delay may be concomitant with other developmental delays, or may specifically concern phonological acquisition. Although we always note in this book when the data presented come from children with protracted development, we contend that data from both sources are valid and useful for testing and application of phonological theory. Studies conducted by a number of researchers indicate that children with phonological delay show similar phonological patterns to those of younger typically developing children (e.g., Ingram, 1980; Schwartz et al., 1980; Grunwell, 1987; Beers, 1995). For example, Beers (1995) compared the phonologies of 15 children with protracted development and 45 younger typically developing children, and noted that the proportion of "normal" processes exceeded that of unusual processes for both groups, and that any differences be-

---

[2] We are unsure what a chain shift would be in syntax or if there are any such phenomena.

tween the groups were not significant. Where the two groups do differ is in *age* of acquisition for various components of the phonological system, and *degree of prevalence* of patterns and constraints. Grunwell (1987) noted that the longer period for development can result in the phenomenon of "chronological mismatch." A child with a general phonological delay (in, for example, syllable structure) may nonetheless produce typically late segments (liquids or fricatives). She also noted that children with protracted development may also show greater variability than children with typically developing speech. Some children with protracted development may have one or two idiosyncratic productions that occur rarely in the typically developing population. For example, phenomena such as nasal snorts (Edwards & Bernhardt, 1973a), ingressive airstream use (Ingram & Terselic, 1983), and metathesis in initial clusters (Bernhardt, 1994a; Lorentz, 1976) are rare in typical development. With the possible exception of the nasal snort, such phenomena are not outside the bounds of phonology, however.

The data from children with protracted development can often provide us with a better window on phonological constraints and processes than data from the typically developing child. There are more patterns to observe, giving a broader research perspective. Furthermore, patterns persist for longer, with the result that changes are more noticeable when they occur. We include both types of data throughout Chapters 5–7, noting what kind of data they are, but treating them as equally valid. Chapter 8 focuses solely on protracted development, in order to discuss clinical applications.

1.4.3. WHAT COUNTS AS DATA: HOW MUCH AND WHAT KIND OF DATA DO WE NEED?

The study of language presents an interesting research problem in terms of subject sample size. In most research domains, we are looking for patterns that are true of populations rather than individuals. If an individual's performance is at the tail-end of a normal distribution, that performance is essentially ignored for the acceptance or rejection of a hypothesis. In language research, in contrast, we are interested in discovering the "universals" of grammar: not just the most frequent patterns for the human population, but also the full range of what is possible. Probabilistic data are not sufficient for discovering the range of possibilities for language. Rare or individual language patterns or structures still fall within the range of possibilities, and affect our interpretation of universals. Thus, both individual and large sample studies are needed, from a wide variety of languages. Language acquisition research has included both individual and group studies, and we refer to both types in this book.

Research on phonological development has a number of additional methodological challenges concerning frequency of sampling, type of data collected, methods of analysis, and the concept of "acquired." When analyzing data, it is important to know the conditions in which data were collected, in order to evaluate their validity and reliability.

1.4.3.1. Frequency of Sampling

Because development is a process of change, we want to know what happens over time. The more frequent and more comprehensive the sampling points, the more precise the description of that process of change. Frequent sampling points are possible in longitudinal studies of individuals. But generalizability is compromised. Less frequent sampling points are necessary with cross-sectional group studies, but details of the process of change are lost (and often insufficient exemplars are collected to make definitive statements about the phonological patterns that are present). What is needed are detailed longitudinal records of many subjects (single subject designs multiply replicated).

1.4.3.2. Type of Data

Developmental data can be collected in controlled or naturalistic settings, with advantages and disadvantages to each type of collection method. Laboratory data typically are collected in quiet settings, making transcription or acoustic analysis more reliable. Furthermore, laboratory research often uses a set list of stimuli, allowing researchers to compare behaviors more systematically across time and across children. On the other hand, naturalistic conversational samples may be more typical of a child's performance (Morrison & Shriberg, 1992).

In terms of analysis, a number of other challenges face the developmental phonologist or speech-language pathologist. Phonetic transcription or acoustic analysis are usually based on methodologies designed for study of adult phonetics and phonology. These may or may not be appropriate for child speech, and are very time-consuming, which limits the size of the samples that can be studied. The narrowness of phonetic transcription is another concern. Phonetic details are often critical to the analysis. Unfortunately, the narrower the transcription, the worse the reliability among transcribers (Shriberg & Lof, 1991). Even trained listeners often have difficulty transcribing sounds that are not phonemic in their own language or dialect. For English speakers, this includes, for example, glottal stops, unaspirated voiceless stops, and dentalized sibilants–sounds which children often produce, and which can be very important for the phonological analysis. Thus, it is critical that researchers learn to transcribe phonetic detail reliably, and that they indicate the level of detail and reliability in their reports. Another issue relating to analysis is the difference between phonetic and phonological data. Phonetic data are what we collect from the child through the various sampling methods. But phonological data are abstract interpretations of the data. Even assuming reliable transcriptions of the phonetic data, which analysis frameworks are best employed? As we proceed throughout the book, we will indicate where the child data suggest the utility of particular multilinear and constraint-based frameworks for analysis.

1.4.3.3. What "Acquired" Means

One of the other methodological and learning issues in acquisition research concerns what it means to have "learned" or "acquired" something. How frequently does a segment or structure or word have to be present in obligatory contexts before it can be said to have been "acquired?"

Different researchers have different operational definitions regarding "acquisition." Cazden (1968), in studying the morphological development of Adam, Eve, and Sarah, used a criterion of 90% correct in obligatory context over three sampling sessions. She chose this criterion, because, after this level was attained, fluctuation in performance stabilized (ceiling effect). Fey (1986) notes that many researchers and speech-language pathologists have adopted this criterion.

But other researchers have different criteria. Stemberger (1992c) defines "mastery" as 100% correct usage, in a diary study report. Olswang and Bain (1985) and Diedrich and Bangert (1980) suggest that 75% correct might be a sufficient level of mastery for the purposes of phonological intervention. In some large-sample normative studies of development, consonantal phonemes were said to be mastered when a certain percentage of children (often 75%) used a segment once in a word. Sander (1972), reanalyzing early samples of Wellman et al. (1931), Poole (1934), and Templin (1957), suggested that there need to be two types of acquisition data: *customary production* (a level at which the group average was over 50% correct), and *mastery* (a level at which the group average was 90% correct).

Different sampling and analysis methodologies used by different researchers often make it very difficult (or even invalid) to generalize across the studies. Throughout the book, we indicate where data are scarce or suspect, with suggestions for future research. Many of the data we use are from individuals, rather than groups, because we are interested in the range of possible patterns and developmental processes. In addition to using examples from the literature, we rely extensively on previously unpublished data from our own studies: assessment and treatment samples from many older children collected by Bernhardt and her colleagues; and extensive diary studies by Stemberger of his three children Gwendolyn, Morgan, and Larissa, using standard diary methodology (as in Smith, 1973). We use these data because of the fine detail and the broad range of phenomena that they include. We denote these data with the abbreviation "p.u.d.:" previously unpublished data. More detailed studies, of large numbers of children, are required. The compilation of longitudinal data from increasingly larger numbers of individuals will enable us to make stronger claims about many of the questions in phonological acquisition.

1.5. LOOKING FORWARD

This book presents concepts of multilinear phonology and constraint-based analysis and their applicability to developmental data. We argue that current linguistic theories provide useful insights, insights that not only explain developmental patterns better, but that can also provide useful clinical techniques to accelerate development in children with phonological disorders. Reciprocally, the developmental data in many instances points to alternatives for theory-building. Thus, data and theory converge in a way to reconcile various perspectives in phonology.

2

WORLDVIEWS
FOR PHONOLOGY

The pronunciations of words reveal many consistent patterns, patterns which differ in their details in particular languages and for particular speakers (especially in language acquisition). In most instances, variations in pronunciation are predictable from the particular set of phonological elements that are present. Any adequate theory of language must be able to account for such variation and for its phonological predictability. Many accounts have been put forward, each representing a particular view of the world. In this chapter, we focus on four issues which reflect different linguistic worldviews.

The first issue concerns the derivation of variations in pronunciation. The three main views that are current in phonological theory are: rules; constraints plus rules; and constraints only. In discussing these three approaches, we show how each leads to different expectations about the phenomena found in human languages, both in adult grammars and in phonological development in children. We argue that constraints are important, and that the most useful worldview is one in which there are only constraints, with no processes or rules. In §2.1.1.1, we also address the issue of whether child phonology is in fact phonology (and not "just" phonetics).

The second issue pertains to the nature of the units that are considered to be basic in phonology. Most researchers agree that there are segments, which are composed of features and which are grouped together into syllables. But which unit is basic? Modern phonological theory treats the feature as the basic unit, leading to expectations about phonological behavior that are different from segment-based expectations.

The third issue concerns storage of information about words. All aspects of the pronunciation of a word could be stored in the word's lexical representation. However, information could also be stored in a way that is independent of particular words, in the form of general rules or constraints, rather than as a part of particular words or morphemes. We are most sympathetic to the latter position.

A related issue can be found specifically in the developmental literature. Some researchers have argued that there are two separate lexicons, one for storing the perceived form of a word, and one for storing the form of the word as it is actually pronounced by the child. This is related to the issue of where information is stored, because it holds that information about the child's pronunciation of a particular word must be stored in the word's lexical representation, rather than as rules or constraints in the general processing system. Other researchers posit a single lexicon, used for both perception and production, with information about the child's pronunciation of a word being stored in the system as rules or constraints, rather than in the word's lexical representation. We believe that information about the child's pronunciation is stored only in the system (on psychological grounds).

The fourth issue involves the developmental origin of the language system: whether it is innate or derives from general properties of cognition. Most approaches to development that derive from linguistic theory emphasize the role of innateness, in the form of Universal Grammar (UG). Bound up in this issue is the general question of where constraints come from, and whether constraints should be positive (stating what is allowed) or negative (stating what is not allowed). We argue that innateness and UG are separate issues, and that the concepts of linguistic theory are interesting and useful regardless of one's views on this issue. We also suggest that it is unlikely that some of the concepts posited within linguistic theory (in particular phonetic grounding) are innate.

2.1. ISSUE 1:
THE MECHANISMS OF PHONOLOGY

Words and morphemes often show variations in pronunciation. To account for the variations, phonologists have posited three different types of mechanisms: rules (or processes), constraints, or a combination of rules and constraints. The choice of mechanisms has a large impact on our expectations about the types of phenomena that occur in phonological development.

Readers familiar with recent developments in syntax will be aware that this issue has also been prominent there. Early work in generative syntax was based entirely on rules (e.g., Chomsky, 1965). It soon became clear that such an approach was too powerful. Rules could be posited for anything, but some changes to syntactic structures appeared to be systematically excluded from human languages. There appeared to be constraints on rules. In more recent work (e.g., Chomsky, 1986), rules have been subordinated to constraints. Many syntacticians hold that there is only a single rule (*Move-α*: "move something somewhere"), and that the details of what is moved and where it can (and cannot) be moved are provided by constraints. Bromberger and Halle (1989) argued that phonology is intrinsically different from syntax, and that rules are required in phonology. Recent developments within phonological theory suggest that constraints are extremely important. We argue here that the most useful point of view is that there are no rules or processes in phonology, only constraints on phonological representations.

The terms "rule" and "process" have often been used interchangeably in phonological theory, although some approaches distinguish between them. When a distinction is made, both terms refer to procedures that change the pronunciation of the word. Stampe (1973) uses "process" to refer to procedures that are universal (and innate, and which therefore do not have to be learned) and uses "rule" to refer to language-specific procedures that must be learned. Most phonologists do not make such a distinction, and we do not feel that such a distinction is needed. We use the two terms interchangeably, but most often use the term "process."

We focus our discussion here around phenomena in English that are familiar to anyone who has studied the phonology of English: the allomorphy of the English -s (plural in nouns, possessive in noun phrases, third-person present singular in verbs) and -ed (past tense, perfect aspect, passive modality) suffixes. The -s affixes have three allomorphs: /əz/[1] after sibilant fricatives and affricates (/s, z, ʃ, ʒ, tʃ, dʒ/, as in (a) below), /s/ after other voiceless consonants (/p, t, k, f, θ/, as in (b)), and /z/ after all other voiced segments (the consonants /b, d, g, v, ð, m, n, ŋ, ɹ, l/ and all vowels, as in (c)).

a. glasses   /glæs-əz/
   bushes   /bʊʃ-əz/
   bridges   /bɹɪdʒ-əz/
b. cups   /kʌp-s/
   cats   /kæt-s/
   myths   /mɪθ-s/
c. bugs   /bʌg-z/
   caves   /keɪv-z/
   cows   /kaʊ-z/

Similarly, the past tense -ed suffix has three allomorphs: /əd/ after /t, d/ (a), /t/ after other voiceless consonants (b), and /d/ after all other voiced phones (c).

a. acted   /ækt-əd/
   needed   /niːd-əd/
b. laughed   /læf-t/
   bumped   /bʌmp-t/
   missed   /mɪs-t/
c. buzzed   /bʌz-d/
   grabbed   /gɹæb-d/
   fried   /fɹaɪ-d/

[1] The vowel is different in different dialects. Instead of [ə], the vowel can be [ɨ] or [ɪ].

This allomorphy is productive in English. New words that are coined that generally follow these patterns, even in experimental situations (Berko, 1958; Derwing & Baker, 1980): *wugs* /wʌg-z/, *mooked* /mʊk-t/. When adults and children commit errors in which irregular plurals and past tense forms are regularized, they use the appropriate allomorph (e.g., Bybee & Slobin, 1982):

a. /əz/:	*gooses	/guːs-əz/	(for *geese*)
/s/:	*foots	/fʊt-s/	(for *feet*)
/z/:	*mans	/mæn-z/	(for *men*)
b. /əd/:	*sitted	/sɪt-əd/	(for *sat*)
/t/:	*sinked	/sɪŋk-t/	(for *sank* or *sunk*)
/d/:	*choosed	/tʃuːz-d/	(for *chose*)

Thus, this allomorphy is present in the pronunciations of known words, of novel words, and of errors. We must be able to account for it. The mechanisms needed to account for it are the basic mechanisms of phonology.

2.1.1. THE FIRST WORLDVIEW: RULES/PROCESSES

One way to account for these patterns is to assume that they are created via rules or processes. Rules are special procedures that alter the pronunciations of words whenever certain conditions are present (such as the existence of /z/ at the end of a word after a voiceless consonant).[2] In a rule-based system, we assume that the *-s* and *-ed* suffixes each have a basic, or *underlying*, pronunciation, which surfaces unchanged in many words, but which is changed by the rules in words that have some particular phonological environment. For *-s* and *-ed*, it is usually assumed that the underlying pronunciations are /z/ and /d/. This is because any of the three allomorphs could appear after vowels and be perfectly pronounceable. We find monomorphemic words such as:

a.	seat	/siːt/
b.	seed	/siːd/
c.	period	/pɪɹiəd/

After the vowel /iː/, we find words that have /t/ or /d/ or /əd/, but in past tense forms, only /d/ appears (as in *ski-ed* /skiːd/). After other phonemes, however, there are restrictions. In English, no word may end in */kd/ or */gt/, for example. In fact, all three allomorphs cannot be pronounced after the majority of consonants in English. But they all could in principle be pronounced after vowels, and it is

---

[2] Some nonpsychologically-based approaches to linguistics have viewed rules as well-formedness statements between two representations. But it is clear that in actual practice linguists have never accepted this idea.

/z/ and /d/ that appear there. Consequently, we conclude that /z/ and /d/ are the basic pronunciations. This gives us underlying forms like:

a. rubbed   /ɹʌb—d/
b. picked   /pɪk—d/
c. patted   /pæt—d/

The word *rubbed* in (a) has the correct pronunciation in its underlying form, and thus it remains unchanged. However, the other words have underlying forms that do not match their actual pronunciations, and therefore rules are needed to alter the pronunciations. For *picked* in (b), we need to change /d/ into [t]; the consonant is changed from voiced to voiceless. The rule can be stated informally as:

Make the -*d* voiceless after a voiceless consonant.

When this rule applies, it alters the pronunciation to /pɪkt/, which is the actual pronunciation. For *patted* in (c) above, we need to add the vowel /ə/ between the /t/ and the /d/, via the rule:

Add /ə/ between /t/ (or /d/) and /d/ at the end of the word.

When this rule applies, it alters the pronunciation to /pætəd/, which is the actual pronunciation. Similar rules derive the different allomorphs for the -*s* suffixes.

From the standpoint of the phonological system of the language, rules in a purely rule-based system like standard generative phonology (e.g., Chomsky & Halle, 1968) are arbitrary procedures for altering the pronunciations of words. There is no particular reason why phonological rules exist; they just do. Kaye (1988) has proposed that phonological rules exist for reasons that are external to phonology but rooted within communication. He suggests that phonological rules can be used by listeners to help segment the speech stream into words and morphemes. While this may sometimes be the case, there are many instances in which phonological rules obscure the boundaries between words. The motivation for the rules, even if external, remains unclear.

Were it not for the fact that allomorphy exists and is common, we would not want to have phonological rules in a purely rule-based system, because rules add complexity to a language. The simplest language would be one in which morphemes and words are combined and then pronounced without alteration; there would be no phonological rules at all. Such a language would be easier to learn. It is probably for this reason that play languages like Klingon (Okrand, 1992) have no allomorphy or phonological rules (thus making them more marketable). Every phonological rule that is added to a language increases its complexity.

The complexity introduced by rules was something of an embarrassment to phonological theory. Linguistics is dedicated to the principle that grammars should be simple, and that theories should account for what is common or uncommon in human languages. A purely rule-based theory predicts that many human languages will have no phonological rules, and that those (few) languages that do have phonological rules will not have many. However, all languages have alternations requiring phonological rules, and some languages have large numbers of them. Classical generative phonology had no explanation for this, and was forced to stipulate that rules were a natural part of human languages. This was not a desirable explanation.

The rule-based approach to phonology spawned theories of child phonological development (Stampe, 1969, 1973; N. Smith, 1973). Stampe (1969, 1973) proposed that humans are born with a set of innate phonological processes. These processes alter underlying representations (URs), so that the child's production differs notably from the adult target pronunciation.[3] For example, the process of Final Devoicing alters final voiced obstruents so that they become voiceless; the words *dog* (adult [dɑg]) and *dad* (adult [dæd]) are altered to [dɑk] and [dæt]. Additional processes convert velars into alveolars (so *key* might be pronounced [diː]), voice initial consonants, delete unstressed syllables, etc. Stampe proposed that acquisition of an adult phonological system consists of learning to suppress the processes that are not part of the adult language. When a process is suppressed, the speaker then has the capability of pronouncing the former target of that process correctly. Thus, speakers of English learn to suppress Final Devoicing, and in so doing acquire the ability to produce word-final voiced obstruents. Speakers of German, Russian, and Cambodian, however, never learn to suppress Final Devoicing; consequently, obstruents are always devoiced in final position, even in the adult language.

Stampe's approach went somewhat beyond the phonological theory of Chomsky and Halle (1968): it attempted to account for why certain processes are common crosslinguistically, and why those same processes appear frequently in the speech of young children learning a first language, and of adults acquiring a second language. However, it suffers from the same major conceptual flaw as standard generative phonology, in that the innate processes make the grammar more complex. Why can a child not pronounce a final voiced obstruent like [d]? Because an innate process prevents the child from pronouncing it accurately. If only the child lacked that innate process, the correct (adult-like) pronunciation of [d] would be possible. We might hope that some child would have a genetic mutation that would disable the innate processes, allowing the child to pronounce words with adult-like competence from the beginning, without passing through a period in which pronunciations are highly inaccurate. In this worldview, our genetic inheritance has saddled us with a set of innate processes without which acquisition would be easier and faster. There is no explanation for the existence of the processes.[4]

Another possible problem with this view is that processes are goal-oriented: a process has a purpose, such as devoicing final obstruents. In adult speech, the processes are an intended part of the grammar, such that a failure to apply a pro-

---

[3]Because Stampe's theory focused on the relationship between the adult pronunciation and the child pronunciation, it involves what is usually called a *relational* analysis in speech-language pathology (e.g., Stoel-Gammon & Dunn, 1985).

[4]Stampe did claim that processes have a phonetic basis, but was vague about what that basis was and, if there was such a basis, why innateness was required. See §2.4.4.

cess leads to an incorrect pronunciation of words. Processes in child phonological development must be viewed the same way: they are goal-oriented procedures that alter the intended output of the phonological system. When viewing inaccurate articulation in the context of language, this seems plausible enough.

But consider a parallel analysis for the acquisition of any other motor skill, such as walking. (We address below whether this is a fair comparison.)

> Children are born with innate processes such as falling down. The reason a young child cannot walk is that this process is active, and changes the goal of walking into the goal of falling down.[5] Only when the child learns to suppress the goal of falling down does the child begin to walk; indeed, walking is automatic once the falling down process is suppressed.[6]

Such an explanation is very unsatisfying. We view the acquisition of walking as involving the learning of motor skills needed in walking. Reflexes (?processes?) may be involved, but learning to walk involves suppression of some reflexes and coordination of others. Falling down is not a process, but is merely what happens when the child attempts to walk without all the necessary subskills for walking. Falling down is not the intended output of some procedure that applies when walking is the child's goal; it is an accident that happens when a child attempts to walk, and walking is impossible for some reason.

For the acquisition of most motor skills, we do not take a rule-based worldview. Some might conclude that the acquisition of the ability to pronounce words should also lead us to a different worldview. Others might protest that speech is special and involves mechanisms that are inappropriate for the acquisition of other motor skills; they might interpret our analogy to walking as a *reductio ad absurdum*.[7] But, as we will see in §2.1.3, there are other worldviews in which the acquisition of speech and walking are entirely parallel. It is a legitimate question whether they should be parallel, and a potential cost to any theory in which they must be nonparallel.

For readers who would like a different example, consider how children learn to draw. Details are often left out of pictures, and replaced by "squiggles." In a rule-based approach, there might be a process of "Squiggle-ization" (or "Detail Deletion") that causes the child to replace details with squiggles. When this process is eventually suppressed by the child, the details become possible and are drawn in clearly.[8] We assume that no one would want to take such an approach, although it is entirely parallel to a rule-based approach to phonological development.

---

[5] We use the term "goal" in a procedural sense: "the output that the system is designed to produce." We do not mean to imply that the child is consciously or intentionally altering those goals.

[6] But adults can still fall down on occasion, especially if too much attention is devoted to some concurrent task. By the same token, suppressed phonological processes might reemerge during second language acquisition.

[7] Just because a result is absurd does not mean that the argument is a *reductio ad absurdum*. There are things that are inherently absurd, and so cannot be reduced to absurdity.

[8] More or less, depending on the success of the suppression, of course.

2.1.1.1. Modularity: Phonetics versus Phonology

Another issue is raised by these comments: the possible difference between the acquisition of output representations versus the acquisition of motor skills. Could the child have accurate output representations, which are then altered because of the lack of motor skills? This is the position of Hale and Reiss (1995) and Reiss and Hale (1996). It presupposes that the language system is compartmentalized into several modules, each of which is responsible for different aspects of the system. Some aspects of the pronunciation of a word are due to the phonology, but other aspects are due to the phonetics. Perhaps child phonology is really due to phonetics, not to phonology.

The problem with this idea is that it is equally applicable to adult speech: alternations could be due to alteration by the motor system. Perhaps there is no such thing as epenthesis or assimilation in adult language competence. Stemberger (1996a) argues that if this point of view is taken, modern phonology must be abandoned as insufficiently supported by empirical data or logical argumentation. The phenomena of child phonology are by-and-large the same as the phenomena of adult phonology. If child phonology may be done in the phonetic component, then so can most of adult phonology. There are presently no criteria that allow phonologists to continue to deal with the phenomena that have traditionally been handled by phonology, if we reject the notion that child phonology is phonology. We thus reject Hale and Reiss's proposal. We favor a broad interpretation of what is phonological.

2.1.2. THE SECOND WORLDVIEW: CONSTRAINTS PLUS RULES

There is another way to conceptualize the allomorphy of -*s* and -*ed* discussed above. Hockett (1955) noted that the variation in pronunciation of -*ed* is not entirely arbitrary. If we assume that the underlying pronunciation is /d/, then we would expect the past tense forms of the words *walk* and *need* to be *[wɑkd] and *[niːdd]. These pronunciations are problematic, however, because they involve word-final sequences like *[kd] and *[dd] that otherwise do not occur in English. The problematic sequences must be altered into something that English speakers can pronounce.

For English, we can make the following generalizations:

No word may end with a voiceless consonant followed by a voiced obstruent.
No word may end in two identical consonants.

Greenberg (1965) reports that the first statement is true of almost all languages. McCarthy (1986) takes the second statement to be the most common situation across languages. Such generalizations (or *constraints*) state that certain things are either impossible in a language or are required in a language. When a word *violates* a constraint, the word is impossible (or at least difficult) for speakers of the language to pronounce. A pronunciation like */wɑkd/ violates the first constraint above, and is *ill formed*. In order to convert the word into something that is *well formed* (i.e., pronounceable), a rule applies to resolve the violation. Paradis (1988, 1993) refers to rules as *repair strategies* to highlight their function of "repairing" ill-formed words so that they can be pronounced. In the case of */wɑkd/, devoicing would be the repair strategy that English speakers use: by changing */wɑkd/ into [wɑkt], we no longer violate the constraint. Further, word-final [kt] violates no constraints in English, as witnessed by such words as *act* /ækt/. In the word */niːdd/, which violates the second constraint above, we can resolve the violation by separating the two /d/'s. If we employ the repair strategy of Schwa Insertion to insert /ə/ between the two /d/'s, we get [niːdəd], which no longer violates the constraint. The two processes of Devoicing and Schwa Insertion are motivated by the need to make all words in English abide by constraints on sequences of consonants.

Phonologists have long talked about constraints on phonological representations. Constraints played a limited role in early generative phonology (Chomsky & Halle, 1968), where they were used only to constrain the forms stored in lexical entries (explaining why no English word like */bnɪk/ is possible). Kisseberth (1970) expanded the use of constraints, arguing that some rules existed solely to repair sequences that were prohibited by constraints. He further argued that some rules could fail to apply in certain contexts, because a sequence would be created that would violate a constraint. This point of view became standard (e.g., Goldsmith, 1976; Clements & Keyser, 1983; McCarthy, 1986; Yip, 1988). Paradis (1988, 1993) proposed that *all* phonological rules are repair strategies motivated by constraints.

In this worldview, rules are not entirely arbitrary. They are motivated by ill-formedness in words, and are needed by the speaker in order to pronounce the word at all. Without question, phonological patterns can be imagined that no human being can pronounce; to take an extreme example, a single syllable like [gnstgkxzjm]. Furthermore, it is a reasonable viewpoint that young children begin life with fewer abilities than adults, so that there are more things that are impossible for them to pronounce than for adults; consequently, children might reasonably have more repair strategies than adults.

There is still some arbitrariness to these processes, however. While Devoicing and Schwa Insertion repair violations of the constraints above, there are other ways to repair those violations. For example, the final /d/ could be deleted in both words, so */wɑkd/ and */niːdd/ would be pronounced [wɑk] and [niːd]. Or the /k/ in */wɑkd/ could be voiced to yield [wɑgd]; word-final [gd] does not violate the constraints, and appears in words like *hugged* [hʌgd]. Or the final /d/ in */niːdd/ could be altered to [z], yielding [niːdz]; this does not violate the constraints, and occurs as the pronunciation of the present tense form *needs*. A particular language picks a particular repair strategy to resolve the violation of a particular constraint. But a different language might employ a different repair strategy to resolve violations of the same constraint.

Before this worldview became common in linguistics, it was proposed as a theory of phonological development.[9] Menn (1978) proposed that child pronunciations were subject to severe constraints (such as allowing no word-final voiced obstruents), and that processes were created by the child in order to alter the word into something that the child could pronounce. This viewpoint was developed further by Menn (1983), Macken and Ferguson (1983), and Macken (1987). As in Paradis's theory, constraint violations could be resolved in many ways, with differences across children (and languages). The details of the origin of a given child's repair strategies were not made explicit, but a type of problem solving (not necessarily conscious problem solving) was assumed. For this reason, this was called the *cognitive* approach to phonological development. Stampe's (1969, 1973) theory of processes could be modified to include this worldview, and some Stampeans may in fact have viewed processes as motivated by constraints (Geoff Nathan, p.c.). (This is perhaps what Stampe, 1973, intended when he emphasized that processes are inherent in the human vocal tract.)

This worldview is more satisfying than the rules-only worldview, in that it explains why rules are present, and why all languages and all children have processes. One drawback is that learners must determine how to resolve constraint violations. Another is that we might have to assume that children apply a large number of processes every time a word is pronounced, often making extensive alterations, leading to a consistent alteration from, for example, underlying *locket* /lɑkət/ to surface [jatə]. Menn (1983) attempted to avoid this on-line application of processes by proposing that most processes are done to a word only once, and that the results are stored permanently in a production lexicon. (This is addressed further below.)

Any approach which uses processes still has the same kind of drawbacks discussed above for rules-only theory: a certain amount of arbitrariness (as discussed above), and a goal orientation for processes. Processes alter the intended output of the system from one thing to another. While this is superficially plausible for language, it is implausible for other motor activities such as learning to walk; there cannot be a process that takes an attempt to walk (where walking violates a constraint on motor activity in the child's system) and converts it into an attempt to fall down (which repairs the constraint violation). Only in a system without processes can this be avoided.

2.1.3. THE THIRD WORLDVIEW: CONSTRAINTS ONLY

The remaining point of view is that rules and processes do not exist. There are constraints, and only constraints. Two hypotheses make this worldview possible. First, the constraints themselves are involved in altering the pronunciation of a

---

[9] Because constraints focus on what is possible in the surface pronunciation, and repair strategies address the relationship between the adult pronunciation and the child's pronunciation, this approach combines a relational analysis of children's phonology with an *independent* analysis (to use a term from speech-language pathology; e.g., Stoel-Gammon & Dunn, 1985).

word that violates a constraint. Second, it is possible to violate constraints: when two constraints conflict, one constraint "wins," and the other is violated. This point of view has been put forward within linguistic theory in the form of Optimality Theory (OT, as in Prince & Smolensky, 1993; McCarthy & Prince, 1993a; see Archangeli & Langendoen, 1997, for the best introduction), and outside of linguistic theory by connectionists (for phonological acquisition, see Stemberger, 1992a).

Consider how to deal with the ill-formed pronunciation */wɑkd/ in OT, which we follow in this book. There is a type of constraint that was implicit within phonological theory and within the "cognitive" approach to language acquisition, but which is made overt within OT as constraints on "faithfulness." In a sense, the underlying pronunciation of a word constitutes a set of constraints on the surface pronunciation of a word. The surface pronunciation tends to be as "faithful" to the underlying representation as possible; that is, there are as few changes as are consistent with the constraints of the language. The single most important determinant of the surface pronunciation is the underlying representation. "Faithfulness" to the underlying representation induces a speaker to pronounce a given word the same way every time, and to pronounce different words differently. We can state "faithfulness" informally as follows:

> The surface pronunciation should include *all* the information in the underlying pronunciation, and *only* that information.

Without "faithfulness," listeners would not be able to determine which word was intended. Faithfulness serves a communicative purpose.

Speakers are constrained to pronounce a word exactly as it is within the underlying representation, *unless* that is impossible because of other constraints. This was taken for granted in earlier theory, and indeed is a principle of phonological analysis within linguistic theory dating back more than two thousand years (to Panini's grammar of Sanskrit).

In OT, this principle is made explicit. Faithfulness is instantiated as two constraints: one to prevent deletion, and one to prevent insertion. We present a full discussion of the constraints that we use in this book in Chapter 4. We present a partial analysis here, using our constraint names. These two constraints work together to ensure that all parts of the underlying representation are pronounced and that nothing is added that is not a part of the underlying representation:

> **Survived**: the surface pronunciation should include each piece of information present in the underlying representation.
> *No deletion.*
>
> **Not(Syllable)**: the surface representation should include as few syllables as possible.
> *No insertion of vowels.*

Survived is violated if something in the underlying representation is deleted. **Not(Syllable)** is violated whenever there is a syllable present; since one syllable must always be present for any word, this constraint is often used to prevent the addition of new vowels, which cause a new syllable to be created. Deletion and insertion are not due to a rule, but are violations of these faithfulness constraints. Instead of rules or processes, we have only constraints and violations of constraints. The only way that **Survived** can be violated is by deleting an element: violating **Survived** thus *requires* deletion. If **Survived** is violated, then some element is deleted. The only way that **Not(Syllable)** can be violated in a way that is relevant here is if a vowel is inserted. All changes in the pronunciation are viewed as violations of these constraints; no mechanism is needed to change the pronunciation *other than* some mechanism that will force the speaker to violate these two constraints.[10]

These two constraints are obviously in conflict with any constraint that makes an underlying pronunciation ill formed. Consider the constraint above against voiced obstruents after voiceless obstruents:

NoSequence(-voiced . . . + voiced):   A voiced phone may not follow a voiceless phone (at the end of a syllable).

This constraint makes it ill formed to have a voiced obstruent after a voiceless obstruent. In the underlying form of *walked*, /wɑk-d/, this constraint should prevent us from pronouncing either the [-voiced] of /k/ or the [+voiced] of /d/, unless we separate the two consonants with a vowel (so that [-voiced] and [+voiced] are no longer in adjacent consonants). However, **Survived** requires that both [-voiced] and [+voiced] be pronounced. **Not(Syllable)** prevents the addition of a vowel between the two consonants. Thus, there is an absolute conflict: unless the faithfulness constraints are violated, then the constraint against */kd/ must be violated. This is the usual situation within OT: constraints conflict for every word (and every sound in every word) that a speaker ever produces. Nothing can be produced without violating *some* constraint.

The theory needs a way to resolve these conflicts between constraints: a way of determining which constraints a speaker will violate when constraints conflict. In OT, this is done by ranking the constraints from most important (highest ranked, least subject to violation, most constraining) to least important (lowest ranked, most subject to violation, least constraining). The highest-ranked constraint is *never* violated, while the lowest-ranked constraint is *usually* violated.

Constraints, and their relative ranking (importance) can be viewed as an online filter through which words are passed during production. Consider an analogy with a filter that has four sides made of different substances (wood, plastic, paper, metal) and a screen at the bottom made of wire mesh. If fine-grained sand is placed in this filter and pressure is applied, all the sand passes out through the wire mesh.

---

[10]For those readers who feel that this sounds like nothing more than a different perspective on the same concepts, we call attention to the fact that this chapter is entitled "worldviews." There are many conceptual similarities between "rules" and "constraint violations," but they lead to different ways of looking at the world, as is discussed further in the text.

However, if stones (too big to fit through the holes in the wire mesh) are placed in this filter and pressure is applied, one of the sides might give way (e.g., the one made of paper), and the stones would pass out though the side rather than through the wire mesh at the bottom. One absolute constraint is that *something* must pass through the filter, but that can happen in different ways, depending on which constraint is the "weak-link" that gives way under pressure.

The pronunciation of a word is molded (on-line) in an analogous fashion. The speaker attempts to reproduce the word's underlying representation. However, the constraints only allow some of the characteristics of the underlying representation to pass through unaltered. Some constraints put more pressure on the phonological form than others, and can force less important constraints to be violated. Whichever constraint is ranked the lowest is the "weak link" that gives way: the lowest-ranked constraint is the least constraining and is the one constraint that is violated, if *some* constraint *must* be violated.

We portray the ranking of one constraint higher than another constraint via a *constraint list*; the higher-ranked constraints are on the left, separated from the lower-ranked constraints by a 3-line border.[11] If it does not matter which of two constraints is ranked higher, they are placed in the same column; this is often the case with the higher-ranked constraints, when we are considering three or more constraints at one time. Each constraint is found on a single line in the list.

For an underlying form like */wɑkd/, there are a number of possible rankings of the constraint. Thus, there are three different patterns that are observed, depending on the (significant) rankings. We begin with the rankings that do *not* work for English.

In the first constraint ranking below, the two faithfulness constraints **Not(Syllable)** and **Survived** are ranked highest, so the speaker must be faithful (regardless of the order of the two faithfulness constraints); the speaker violates **NoSequence(-voiced . . . + voiced)**, and produces [wɑkd].

Survived	‖	**NoSequence(-voiced . . . + voiced)**	*[wɑkd]
Not(Syllable)	‖		

This, of course, is not how the constraint violation is repaired in (adult) English.

Consider a second constraint ranking below. In this case, the speaker must produce all the underlying features but must also obey **NoSequence(-voiced . . . + voiced)**. S/he does so at the cost of violating the lowest-ranked constraint, **Not(Syllable)**. Consequently, the two consonants are separated by inserting a vowel, which is schwa in the case of English: [wɑkəd].

Survived	‖	**Not(Syllable)**	*[wɑkəd]
NoSequence(-voiced . . . + voiced)	‖		

[11] In the literature (e.g., Prince & Smolensky, 1993), the symbol "»" is placed between two constraints to denote that the constraint on the left is higher-ranked. We do not make use of that here, because it is not visually salient enough to be processed easily.

Note that [wɑkəd] does not violate **NoSequence(-voiced . . . + voiced)**, since the word-final /d/ is preceded by a vowel, and does not violate **Survived**, since all the material in the underlying pronunciation is present in the surface pronunciation. This, of course, is not how the constraint violation is repaired in (adult) English.

Consider a third ranking. In the following case, the speaker cannot add any new elements and also must abide by **NoSequence(-voiced . . . + voiced)**.

| **Not(Syllable)** ||| **Survived**   [wɑkt] OR *[wɑk] |
| **NoSequence(-voiced . . . + voiced)** ||| |

The actual pronunciation will violate the lowest-ranked constraint, **Survived**, with two possibilities, depending on which element we fail to include in the surface pronunciation. If we fail to include the entire segment /d/, then /d/ is deleted, and the surface pronunciation is *[wɑk]. If we fail only to include the feature [+voiced] (which is the feature that is making the */kd/ sequence ill-formed), then a voiceless consonant appears,[12] and the surface pronunciation is [wɑkt]. Clearly, this last result is what happens in (adult) English. This last constraint ranking must be correct. The particular **Survived** constraint that is violated is the one that requires the survival of the feature [+voiced].

For the word *needed* */niːdd/, both **Survived** and **Not(Syllable)** are relevant, but in addition, a **NotTwice** constraint is needed to rule out a sequence of two identical segments (such as /dd/). Again starting with what does not happen in adult English, consider the following ranking.

| **Survived** ||| **NotTwice**   *[niːdd] |
| **Not(Syllable)** ||| |

If the two faithfulness constraints **Not(Syllable)** and **Survived** are ranked highest, the speaker must violate **NotTwice** and pronounce the word as [niːdd]. This, of course, is not what speakers of adult English do.

If **Survived** is ranked lowest, as in the following ranking, the entire allomorph deletes (since *[dt] is also ill-formed in English).

| **Not(Syllable)** ||| **Survived**   *[niːd] |
| **NotTwice** ||| |

This, of course, is also not what happens in (adult) English.

In the actual constraint ranking for adult English, **Not(Syllable)** is violated.

| **Survived** ||| **Not(Syllable)**   [niːdəd] |
| **NotTwice** ||| |

When **Not(Syllable)** is violated, segments can be inserted. A vowel is filled in between the two consonants, and [niːdəd] results.

Interestingly, in the speech of many young children, the *-ed* is simply deleted after /t/ and /d/ (Berko, 1958; MacWhinney, 1978; Bybee & Slobin, 1982), which

---

[12] See our discussion of underspecification and default feature values in Chapters 3 and 4.

is the result that is expected from the second ranking, in which **Survived** is ranked lowest. Young children can have constraint rankings that differ from that of adults, often with the faithfulness constraints ranked too low and other constraints ranked too high. This leads to massive unfaithfulness in the pronunciations of words, as compared to the adult pronunciations. Most of this book is devoted to exploring the differences in constraint rankings between adult and child speech.

In a sense, we are using the word "constraint" very differently here than in the previous section, where we dealt with rules and constraints together. In the view of rules as repair strategies, constraints do not tolerate violations, and violations must be repaired via rules (Paradis, 1993); constraints represent things that are *absolutely impossible* for a speaker. In OT, constraints can be violated; they represent things that are *relatively difficult*. Violations of constraints are avoided only if there is a choice; if there is no choice, the speaker produces the word with the violation. In this view, constraints constitute difficulties but not impossibilities. This is one of the major ways in which the constraints-only worldview differs from the rules-plus-constraints worldview. The other major difference in this point of view is that alterations of the pronunciation derive from violations of the faithfulness constraints, rather than from the application of processes.

The view that a constraint can be violated (and only represents a point of difficulty rather than something that is impossible) can be viewed as a readjustment of the boundary between competence and performance. Performance models such as connectionist models have always viewed constraints as violable, under the right circumstances; see Stemberger (1992) for an explicit discussion of this in the context of phonological development. All modern psychological models view performance as gradient, with elements more accessible or less accessible, but with few absolutes; see Levelt (1989) for speech production. In performance, information is gathered from numerous sources; a given piece of information may have an effect in combination with certain information but have no effect when combined with other information. Such cue-trading is common in the perception of speech segments (e.g., McClelland & Elman, 1986) and is evident in how listeners interpret the syntactic role of nouns in sentences (Bates & MacWhinney, 1987). In contrast, linguistic competence models other than OT all treat constraints as absolute and unviolable. In our opinion, the violability of constraints in OT represents a shift of a characteristic from performance into competence. The line that separates competence and performance has been redrawn at a different location than it had been drawn previously. This is not a problem. The exact boundary between competence and performance has never had any form of empirical support; the location of the boundary has been arbitrary. It can and should be redrawn when that is useful for theories of language.

In one sense, a constraints-only worldview does not constitute a big change from a rules-plus-constraints worldview. The same alterations of the pronunciation occur. One could even object that we are just calling "process" by a new name: "constraint violation." The change is primarily a change in worldview.

Looking at the types of analyses in OT, it is clearly a large change in world-view. With processes, one is tempted to create complex processes that make multiple changes in complex environments. With constraints, one is tempted towards simplicity: complex behavior most often results when many simple constraints are simultaneously violated. Furthermore, it is possible to describe a process on the basis of very little general information about the phonological system. With constraints, one is often forced into a much broader and more detailed analysis of the phonological system and of the interaction of different constraints.

Note that simplicity in the phonological system does not necessarily make the theory simple for the researcher to use. Constraints are simpler than processes in terms of how they work. However, determining the constraint rankings and analyzing data using constraints requires more knowledge about the language, or (in the case of developmental phonology) a given child's system.

Accounting for the alteration of pronunciations via constraints has an interesting benefit. In a rule-based system, as noted above, the system actively alters the "intended" output from something that is impossible to something that can be pronounced, in a goal-oriented fashion that seems inappropriate when applied to learning other motor activities such as walking. It also requires some form of complex problem solving on the part of the child in order to create some repair strategy that will alter an unpronounceable word into something pronounceable. In a constraint-based system, no problem solving is required; given that the constraints exist, the constraint system automatically alters the form into something that is consistent with the constraint system. The child tries to reproduce a word accurately, but fails to do so because of inappropriate constraint rankings that are present due to lack of time or skill needed to learn the rankings for the adult language.

Consider learning to walk in a constraint-based system. In order to walk, certain constraints on movement must be overcome; they must become "less important" by being reranked lower than the child's "underlying form": the intention to walk. If the constraints are not overcome, some constraint will prevent the child from walking: the child will fail to walk. What actually results is something that automatically derives from the failure to overcome that constraint. Falling down is not done by altering the intended output of the system, but is an accidental by-product of an inadequately controlled set of constraints on movement. Although we cannot prove that the acquisition of speech and the acquisition of other motor skills should be parallel, it is simpler to assume a single type of mechanism underlying all learning than to assume different learning mechanisms in different domains. A constraints-only worldview allows this.

In the remainder of this book, we assume that constraints are important. We present both current viewpoints, however: purely constraint-based systems, and systems that use both constraints and rules. Although we view a purely constraint-based system as preferable, both worldviews are still common and of value for developing an understanding of phonological phenomena.

2.1.4. WHAT RULES AND CONSTRAINTS
HAVE IN COMMON

In previous sections, we discussed differences between rules and constraints. They also have some conceptual similarities, however. In our view, the main difference is that constraints unpack rules into their component parts. A constraint can help explain what a rule is doing, in a way that integrates that rule into the rest of the phonological system.

As noted above, the typical view of rules is that they are procedures. Application of a rule might require the following steps:

Step 1:   Locate the rule where it is stored in the language system.

Step 2:   Compare the structural description of the rule (the part of the rule that is changed, plus the environment) to the word that is being produced.

Step 3a: If the structural description matches the word, apply the rule.

Step 3b: If the structural description does not match the word, do not apply the rule.

Step 4:   Go on to the next rule, or exit the phonological system.

This procedure is how a computer program would implement a phonological rule. In this view, rules work quite differently from the way that constraints work.

One problem with the most common approach to rules in the 1970s was their serial application, leading to lengthy derivations. This runs afoul of the "100-step problem" (Touretzky, 1986): given the speed of reaction times and the speed of processing in neural tissue, there can be no more than 100 steps in the processing for any action or perception. Common models for rule systems (e.g., Chomsky & Halle, 1968) required thousands of steps for the production of every word. This is clearly not acceptable for any model that strives for relevance to human cognition. However, there are other approaches to rules (e.g., Koutsoudas, Sanders, & Noll, 1974; Hooper, 1978) in which derivations are much shorter, with only a few levels needed; the 100-step problem might not be an issue (depending on how many steps are needed for the semantic and lexical processing). Constraints allow for even shorter derivations (e.g., Goldsmith, 1993; Wheeler & Touretzky, 1993; Prince & Smolensky, 1993), and this is one of the differences between rules and constraints.

The above procedure-based description of rules is not the only view of rules. Hooper (1978) proposed that rules should be viewed as a type of constraint, and that constraints and rules should be stated in exactly the same way. Consider, for example, the following:

$$[\text{-sonorant}] \rightarrow [\text{-voiced}] \, / \, \underline{\hspace{1cm}}_\sigma]$$

This rule ensures that any syllable-final obstruent ([-sonorant]) is voiceless. Hooper suggested that this rule could serve two functions. First, it makes a true surface generalization about the language. This "rule" would be a part of a language in which all word-final obstruents are voiceless in the underlying representations of all words, even if there are no actual alternations converting underlying voiced obstruents into voiceless ones word-finally. It states a constraint on surface pronunciations. However, as stated, it also accounts for alternations: if a voiced obstruent *does* show up in this environment, the rule can change it so that it becomes voiceless. In Hooper's view, rules and constraints can be described in the same way and have the same outcome.

There are differences between rules as envisioned by Hooper and constraints as envisioned by OT, however. In OT, rules can be viewed, not as procedures, but as a *bundle* of simple constraints. We can break down the syllable-final devoicing rule into the following parts:

1. Output constraint: Syllable-final voiced obstruents are not allowed.
2. Faithfulness constraint: Be faithful to all features in the underlying representation, including [+voiced].
3. Ranking: When the constraint in (1) conflicts with the constraint in (2), the constraint in (1) has priority. Violate faithfulness.

Thus, the rule takes two constraints that are ranked in a specific order, and packages them as a single statement about the language. In OT, rules are unpacked into their component parts.

There is an advantage to unpacking rules into their parts. If the parts are independent of each other, they will hold true more generally for the language, not *just* for a specific rule (as in Hooper's, 1978, perspective above). Systems using rules have a great deal of redundancy, because the same constraint often has to be made a part of two or more rules (which enforce the constraint in different environments). By unpacking the rules, constraints need to be stated only once. Bundling constraints together into a rule provides the flexibility to manipulate the ranking of each *token* of a constraint. Constraint A might be ranked higher than Constraint B when they are bundled together in Rule A, but the ranking might be reversed when they are bundled together in Rule B. Furthermore, unpacking the rules leads us to a more constrained theory. For example, a general ranking of constraints on place of articulation leads us to expect that epenthetic consonants should always have the same place of articulation, regardless of manner of articulation. But if rules are used to insert a nasal consonant in one environment but an oral stop in a different environment, the two rules could supply different places of articulation (e.g., nasal [m] but oral stop [t]), because the rules do not embody a single set of constraints on place of articulation. In OT, in contrast, all rankings must refer to a single token of a constraint, and there is less flexibility. This leads to a simpler system, which is to be preferred (as long as it is empirically adequate).

Lastly, by unpacking a rule into its components, we derive a more explicit picture of the particular phonological phenomenon. In a sense, this view of rules holds that rules and constraints are not that different, except that a purely constraint-based theory provides a different way of thinking about the phonological patterns that is in many ways more explicit.

Rules and constraints are also similar in that a mechanism is needed to designate which rule or constraint is more important, when they conflict. In rule-based theories, this mechanism is *rule ordering*: Rule A is done before Rule B. Depending on the nature of the rules, this often means that one rule has priority over the other. In "bleeding" orderings, Rule A changes the environment so that Rule B cannot apply. Although the term "ordering" was used, in fact there was no temporal order between the two rules, because only Rule A applied. Koutsoudas et al. (1974) introduced the term *precedence*: Rule A takes precedence over Rule B when they conflict, so that only Rule A applies. In "counterfeeding" orderings, in contrast, Rule A states that some output X is impossible, but Rule B creates X in the output. There is a conflict between the two rules, and the second rule is given priority, so that it can create a violation to Rule A. Although this terminology has never been used in relation to rule ordering, we could say that Rule A could be violated, but only when Rule B has priority. In OT, the mechanism that designates which constraint is more important is constraint ranking. In many ways, rule ordering and constraint ranking are similar and reflect the same basic concept about priority.

We believe that a purely constraint-based phonology is different from a purely rule-based theory, or a theory that mixes constraints and rules. However, there are many parallels. Most of the concepts are similar, and there are mechanisms with similar functions. Rules can be viewed as bundles of constraints, with a specific ranking between the bundled constraints. Phonologists have *not* previously viewed rules in that way, but some (such as Hooper) have approached that perspective. In our view, the main difference between rules and constraints is in terms of the worldview that each entails. That difference in worldview can make a difference in the types of phonological phenomena that might be predicted. We contend that the constraints-only worldview gives interesting and valuable insights into phonology, both in general and relative to phonological development.

2.2. ISSUE 2: THE BASIC UNIT OF ANALYSIS

Most people (at least in European-derived cultures) view the segment as the basic unit of phonological representations.[13] A word such as *cat* is viewed as a sequence of three elements: /k/, /æ/, and /t/. However, there are other levels of representation, including syllables and features (and higher units such as feet and phonological words). The word *cat* is a single syllable /kæt/: a single element, not three. Each of the segments is actually a grouping of many phonological features: /æ/ is [+low], [-high], [-back], etc.[14] The word *cat* can be viewed as one element (a syllable), as three elements (segments), or as more than 50 elements (features).

---

[13] This may derive from the fact that European languages are written alphabetically, with segment-sized graphemes.

[14] See Appendix B for a full set of the features used in this book, with definitions and commentary.

These three levels are not mutually exclusive. We take for granted that *all three levels* are needed for different purposes. It is nevertheless an important issue as to which level of representation is viewed as "basic." There are three possibilities.

1. The syllable is the basic unit. Syllables contain segments and features, but syllables are the basic unit, and the unit with the greatest import for phonological processes and for acquisition. Some developmentalists assume that the syllable is the basic level for young children (Treiman & Breaux, 1982; Vihman, 1992).

2. The segment is the basic unit. Segments are grouped into syllables, and also contain features, but segments are the units with the greatest import for phonological processes and for acquisition. This seems to be the view held by most Westerners without training in linguistics, and was the dominant view within linguistics as recently as the 1950s.

3. The feature is the basic unit. Features are grouped into segments and syllables, but features are the units that have the greatest import for processes and for acquisition. This is currently the dominant view within phonology.

In principle, it makes little difference which unit we view as the most basic one, since we can always make reference to the other levels of analysis. In practice, this does matter, because it leads us to think in certain ways, to expect certain types of phenomena (but not others), and to entertain certain types of hypotheses (but not others).

A similar question of levels arises in physics. Consider three "levels" of matter: molecules, atoms, and subatomic particles. Matter can generally be described at all three levels, and all three are important for different purposes. Molecules are the appropriate level of description for chemical reactions and the physical size needed for filters. Atoms are the appropriate level of description for heaviness and determining which elements will combine with which other ones. Subatomic particles are the appropriate level for determining whether a given token of an element will react chemically, and so on.

Research on language has not been in full agreement as to which level of analysis is basic in phonology: the syllable, the segment, or the feature. In this book, we follow multilinear phonology in assuming that the feature is the basic unit of analysis, but that segments and syllables also exist and are important. This viewpoint has many consequences for the way that we analyze phonological phenomena.

Until the 1950s, the major focus in linguistics was on the segment: the phonemes and allophones of the language and the contrasts that they allowed. Phonemes and allophones were treated as indivisible atoms of representation, with no internal parts. Although segments had phonetic properties (such as the use of the tip of the tongue in /t/), these properties were not viewed as isolable parts of segments, but as inherent properties (like color). Phonological alternations were discussed in terms of those phonetic properties, but the focus was on the changes in the segments. Jakobson's (1931) theories of phonological change and language acquisition (1968/1941) focus on whole segments and their relationships to each other, rather than on their phonetic characteristics.

This point of view began to change in the early 1950s, when Jakobson, Fant, and Halle (1951) proposed the first theory of phonological features. This may at first have been only a codification of the phonetic properties of words, without the implication that a segment was simply a collection of features, but it allowed a shift in focus to the features themselves. The feature came to be viewed not as a characteristic of a larger unit, but as a unit in its own right: a command to the motor system. A particular phoneme came to be viewed as a particular set of features; the segment was not important in and of itself. Early generative phonology (e.g., Halle, 1959) stated alternations and sound changes in terms of how the *features* change, ignoring the effects on the segments of which the features are a part. This shift in focus ultimately led to multilinear phonology (Goldsmith, 1976).

This change in the way that we conceptualize phonology cannot be overemphasized. In the viewpoint in which segments are basic, only segments are independently manipulable. You can delete, insert, or reorder segments, but you cannot delete, insert, or reorder features, because features are just inherent properties of segments. You can only *change* the inherent properties. In contrast, in the viewpoint in which features are basic, features can be treated in the same way that segments can be treated: they can be deleted, inserted, and reordered independently of the segments containing them. Archangeli and Pulleyblank's (1994) theory of *combinatorial specification* is the most radical position possible: only the features are real elements, and segments are nothing more than the set of features that happen to be present at any given moment in time. Archangeli and Pulleyblank argue that this change in viewpoint is extensive enough that it is misleading to use the term "segment"; they replace the term "segment" with the term *path*. There has only been a change in focus, but it is a major change: it implies that features should have the same properties that we have always attributed to segments, and must be treated as independent of each other.

Consider the way that segments have always been viewed. The words *two* and *true* contrast in that the word *true* has exactly the same segments as *two* (/tuː/) *plus* the additional segment /ɹ/ between the /t/ and the /uː/ (/tɹuː/). The /ɹ/ happens to appear in an environment after a /t/ and before an /uː/, but it does not *have to* be there, and we can delete it without affecting the other elements. Further, we do not represent directly that there is no /ɹ/ in /tuː/. We could in principle have a null segment /Ø/ that encodes the fact that there is no segment present; we might have *strew* /stɹuː/, *true* /Øtɹuː/, *stew* /stØuː/, and *two* /ØtØuː/. But we do not view this as necessary. When segments are absent from a given location in the word, they are simply absent. In some cases, constraints might require that a segment be present: syllables might be required to begin with a consonant. In that case, we can insert a consonant, such as [ʔ]. We can delete consonants as units. And we can combine deletion and insertion: if for some reason we must delete a syllable-initial consonant (say, the /z/ in *zoo*), we might then insert [ʔ] so that the syllable still starts with a consonant ([ʔuː]).

Now consider treating features in exactly the same way. In /d/, the feature [+voiced] occurs at the same time as the features [-sonorant] and [-continuant]. But [+voiced] does not *have to* be there, and we can delete it without affecting the other features. Of course, the segment would then have no feature [voiced], and there may be a constraint that all consonants must have a [voiced] feature. We can repair the violation of that constraint by inserting a [voiced] feature, such as [-voiced]. This deletion of [+voiced] followed by the insertion of [-voiced] is entirely parallel to the example above, with the deletion of the whole segment /z/ followed by the insertion of the whole segment [?]. Features and segments are parallel in terms of their behavior. Further, a given feature can in principle be a part of two segments, in the same way that an electron can be a part of two atoms in a molecule. As discussed in Chapter 3, this is useful in describing assimilations; if /gt/ is pronounced [gd], we can say that [gd] has a single token of [+voiced] that is shared by the two segments. The parallelism between features and segments has been forcefully drawn by Archangeli and Pulleyblank (1994) for linguistic theory, and by Stemberger (1991a, 1991b, 1992b) for psycholinguistics.

The focus on features explains much of the behavior of speech sounds in language acquisition and in psycholinguistic performance, and we assume it here. We want to emphasize, however, that segments do exist (as groups of features) and can have their own special properties. For example, there are strong restrictions on exactly which features may be combined within a single segment, and many phonologists feel that minimal contrasts between segments (where a single feature distinguishes two segments) lead to special properties (Steriade, 1987; Mester & Itô, 1989). Stemberger (1991a, 1991b, 1992b) has shown that speakers are sensitive to the frequency of segments, meaning that segments are important enough in psycholinguistic representations that they are tracked somehow in speech processing. We are not abandoning segments, but shifting our focus such that features are more important.

The change in worldview from the *segment as the basic unit* to the *feature as the basic unit* made multilinear phonology possible and is arguably the most important assumption of multilinear phonology, even though it may be one of the least intuitive of modern phonology. We demonstrate in later chapters how this worldview leads to productive approaches to phonological development.

2.2.1. SEGMENT VERSUS WORD AS THE BASIC UNIT

In Chapter 1, we alluded to a discontinuity assumption relating to representation. A number of child phonologists differentiate between children's early words (up to 50 or 75) and words acquired after that point (Fee, 1995a; Ferguson & Farwell, 1975; Macken, 1979; Vihman, Velleman, & McCune, 1994), claiming that early words are stored as unorganized wholes, rather than as sequences of segments. Only later do segments and features become the basic units, when the system has too many words to encode holistically; storage capacity needs then to be maximized by a change to feature-based and segment-based representation.

Vihman et al. (1994) suggest that a child's hierarchical structure may lack levels of the adult phonology. Features are then assigned directly to the word level (see also Iverson & Wheeler, 1987). Features thus assigned can be realized in both consonants and vowels: for example, Word=Labial ([bu], where both the consonant and the vowel are labial), and Word=Coronal ([di], where both the consonant and vowel are coronal). Levelt (1994) argues that this was the case in early words for several Dutch-learning children.

There are a number of problems with a word-based perspective. First of all, examples given usually only refer to place features. In most early words, stop or nasal consonants combine with vowels. Contrasting manner features must be encoded, even if place features are similar. Furthermore, many children produce words with different places of articulation for consonants and vowels. If a child's first word is *up* (as was the case for Stemberger's daughter Morgan) or *mama* (a common early word), does this mean that these children begin with segment/feature-based representation for place and manner of articulation? It is more parsimonious to suggest that children who show identical place features in early words show evidence of assimilation between the two segments.

Another problem for the word-based-representation perspective concerns the point of reorganization into segment/feature-based representation. The word-based-representation hypothesis predicts that children should have a wide variety of phones in early words, because each word is unique and independent of all others. Then, at the representational conversion point, a discontinuous and massive regression might be expected, as the system tries to consolidate itself with a few general patterns. The frequent words might not change (according to Macken's, 1980b, hypothesis), but many others might. Such massive regression has never been reported, however. Development appears to be much more gradual and continuous.

The word-based hypothesis has little empirical support and appears to have more to do with place features than others. Segment-based representations work even for early words, but constraints on sequences, especially for place features, may highly restrict the range of possible outputs. Given its complexity, the word-based approach to representation is insufficiently motivated. We return to this issue in Chapter 7, in the discussion of consonant-vowel interactions and consonant harmony.

2.3. ISSUE 3: LEXICAL STORAGE
VERSUS SYSTEM STORAGE

The pronunciation of a word can be stored in different ways in the human language system. Information can be stored as part of the representation of a particular word (or morpheme) in the lexicon; in essence, the pronunciation is "memorized" for each word, individually. Information can also be stored in a way that is independent of any particular lexical item, however; the information can be filled in via rules or constraints when the speaker processes the word through the speech production system. Almost everyone agrees that some information must be stored in each of these ways. One major difference in viewpoint hinges on the relative balance between the two alternatives.

Some information about the pronunciation of a word (or morpheme) is usually idiosyncratic to that word (or morpheme) (except in the case of homonyms). If this were not the case, all words would be pronounced identically. The information that in principle cannot be predicted in any fashion must be stored in the lexical entry of each word (or morpheme). It must be in the underlying or input representation for the word (or morpheme).

Some information about the pronunciation of the word (or morpheme) is predictable in some fashion, however. Predictable information could in principle be left out of the lexical representation of the word, and filled in during processing. We say that such information is stored in the system rather than in the lexical item. We can identify three kinds of information that could in principle be stored in the system: redundancies, information assimilated from elsewhere, and default information.

Redundant information can be predicted from other information that must be present in the lexical representation. Features are often predictable from other features within the segment, because no language allows all possible combinations of all features. For example, in most languages, sonorant segments (vowels, glides, liquids, and nasals) are obligatorily voiced. Thus, the value of the [voiced] feature for sonorant segments could be stored in the system. A rule or constraint could fill in [+voiced], ensuring that sonorants are pronounced as [+voiced]. Similar redundancies may occur within specific languages. In English, velar consonants include only oral and nasal stops; [k], [g], and [ŋ] are possible, but the fricatives [x] and [ɣ] are not. The feature [-continuant] is thus predictable (redundant) for velar consonants. This information could be left out of lexical storage and filled in by the (English) system. (On the other hand, [-continuant] is not redundant for alveolar consonants, since the fricatives [s] and [z] are possible in English. Thus, some information relative to [continuant] needs to be stored for at least some alveolar consonants in English.)

Information can also be redundant on the basis of other segments. Often, the information can be viewed as assimilated from another segment. For example, the vowel in the English word *ban* [bæ̃ːn] is nasalized, because it precedes a nasal consonant. If a vowel does not precede a nasal consonant, on the other hand, it is oral: *bat* [bæːt]. Since the orality or nasality of a vowel is always predictable from context, that aspect of the pronunciation could be left out of the lexical representation, and filled in via a rule or a constraint.

Finally, default (redundant) information could be supplied by the processing system. Default information will surface if there is no lexical information to the contrary. It has been argued that defaults are usually the most frequent alternative (e.g., Stemberger, 1991a, 1992b). For example, in English morphology, the most common past tense form is *-ed*: *jumped*, *walked*, *squealed*, *crunched*, etc. Such past tense forms could be created entirely within the processing system, with no consideration of the particular lexical items involved. In contrast, less common ("irregular") patterns, involving vowel change, for example, *sang* (*cf.* base *sing*) and *fell* (*cf.* base *fall*) must be (at least partially) stored as an idiosyncratic aspect of those particular lexical items. With respect to particular features, the alveolar place of articulation for consonants is by far the most frequent place of articulation in English, and could be considered a default place feature. It may therefore be absent in lexical entries for segments like /t/ and /n/, and filled in via a rule or constraint.

Although predictable information can *in principle* be left out of the lexical representation and filled in via a rule or constraint during processing, that is not the only possibility. Predictable information could in principle be stored in the lexical entry, along with the unpredictable information. In a word such as *ban* [bæ̃ːn], the voicing and nasality (and length) of the vowel /æ/ could be stored in the lexical entry of the word, as well as the alveolar place of articulation of the nasal /n/.

Different researchers have taken different stands on this issue, which has led to different expectations about the nature of lexical representations, learning, and processes/constraints. Although there have been attempts to address the issue empirically, no one has yet provided empirical data that are viewed as compelling enough to induce all researchers to abandon one approach or the other. Furthermore, some researchers take different stands on the issue depending on what type of information is involved.

Chomsky and Halle (1968) took the point of view that as little information as possible should be present in the lexical representation. This has long been the dominant position within Generative Phonology (e.g., Archangeli, 1988).

Prince and Smolensky (1993), in the initial treatise on OT, proposed that there were two competing principles:

*Spec:	As little information as possible should be stored in the lexicon.
Lexicon optimization:	As few constraints as possible should be violated in the processing of input representations into output representations.

The first principle represents the earlier dominant position within phonology. The second principle requires that as much information as possible be stored in lexical entries, since the best way to avoid the violation of (high-ranked) constraints is for the input and output to be identical. If information is left out of the lexical representation, that automatically entails an increase in the number of constraint violations (since the constraints that require some value of a particular feature are automatically violated). *Spec has received little attention in the OT literature. Lexicon optimization, however, has received much attention (Smolensky, 1993; Inkelas, 1994; Yip, 1995). Currently, the dominant position within OT seems to be that as much information as possible should be stored lexically. No explicit reasons have been given for why this position has been taken, however.

Although we have contrasted two extreme positions, most researchers have a more moderate view. Archangeli and Pulleyblank (1994) argue that most commonly, predictable information (of all sorts) is absent from the lexical representation, but sometimes, such information can be present. Itô, Mester, and Padgett (1995) assume that *redundant* features are not present in lexical representations but *default* information *is* present in lexical representations. McCarthy and Prince (1994) note that the basic shape of reduplicative affixes in an adult language could be handled lexically or within the processing system, and opt to store the information solely within the processing system (thus ignoring lexicon optimization, at least in the context of reduplicative affixation).

Our worldview leans toward minimal lexical storage because of our assumptions about learning. We believe that the most plausible learning mechanisms are error-driven: that the system learns only enough to correct errors. Such learning mechanisms tend to minimize the amount of information that is stored in the lexicon. In particular, default information will tend not to be stored in lexical representations. However, the predictions about redundant features are more complex. We expect that redundant features sometimes *will* be present in lexical representations. We return to these issues in later chapters.

2.3.1. TYPE OF STORAGE IN MODELS OF LANGUAGE ACQUISITION

This same issue has arisen within the language acquisition literature, focusing specifically on the best way to capture generalizations about the child's non-adult pronunciations of words. The issue seems more complex for children, because we must account for both the adult and child pronunciations. There is often evidence that the child can adequately perceive the adult pronunciation, but cannot faithfully reproduce it in production. This implies that the adult phonological form must be stored somewhere in the child's language system. But what is the best way to capture the child's pronunciations? Information about the child's pronunciations could be stored entirely within the system (as rules or constraints). In this view, all words have just one lexical representation: the adult pronunciation (as perceived by the child). Alternatively, information about the child's system could be stored permanently in the lexicon. In this view, all words have two lexical representations: one for perception (adult pronunciation) and one for production (child pronunciation). Different researchers within child phonology have taken different positions on this issue.

2.3.1.1. Early Single-Lexicon Models

One approach to child phonology is to assume that most of the differences between the child and adult pronunciations are stored in the system, rather than in the lexicon. The underlying representation then reflects the adult pronunciation, and the child's pronunciation is derived through the action of processes or constraints. Because each word has a single lexical representation, such models are called "single-lexicon" models. Because only one lexical entry is generally posited for adult language, this approach is consistent with the continuity hypothesis (see §1.2.1).

Early developmental models of the lexicon were single-lexicon models, including Stampe's (1969, 1973) natural phonology theory and Smith's (1973) generative phonology diary study. The structure of these models is presented in Figure 2.1 (including a level of "low-level" phonetic rules that create the final phonetic output). Key assumptions for the relationship between adult and child phonology were as follows:

1. Children have adult-like representations, based on generally accurate perception of words.
2. Rules/processes can be postulated to account for differences between underlying forms and the child's productions.
3. These rules/processes operate in real time (on-line), every time a child pronounces a word (Menn, 1983:9).

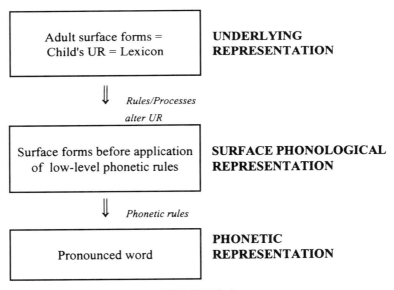

FIGURE 2.1

This type of model accounts for the majority of words a child produces. Information about the child's pronunciations is stored only in the system.

However, there are some aspects of child pronunciations that are not necessarily handled well. As discussed in Chapter 4, child pronunciations are often variable, in one of two ways:

1. Different tokens of a word can be pronounced in different ways.
2. A given phoneme can be pronounced differently in different words.

A number of child phonologists have felt that a single-lexicon model does not handle variability well (e.g., Menn, 1978, 1983; Straight, 1980; Dinnsen & Elbert, 1984; Spencer, 1988). In particular, the second type of variability, in which some words are pronounced in a more adult-like fashion than others, has been viewed as problematic.

In a single-lexicon model, some words must be tagged as lexical exceptions (see also §4.10), so that the word either does not undergo a given process that it would be expected to undergo, or so that it will undergo a process that most similar words do not undergo. Tagging words as lexical exceptions is cumbersome, however, especially if the number of exceptions is high. Ferguson and Farwell (1975) and Straight (1980) comment that learning for some children appears to proceed slowly, item by item, rather than "across-the-board." In such cases, which words would be categorized as exceptional?

The designation of learning as item-by-item versus across-the-board reflects one's opinion on rate of acquisition. For example, if all of a child's words with /l/ become pronounced with [l] rather than glides within a week (as was the case for Bernhardt's son, previously unpublished data, [p.u.d.]), we tend to assume across-the-board learning, even though each lexical item has to undergo the change as it is pronounced. If this change takes several weeks or longer, we may be more inclined to focus on the item-by-item aspect rather than the general pattern. We still have to account for variable rates of learning in a theory of phonological development, however, no matter what our perspective.

Macken (1980b) proposed a more flexible single-lexicon model. Her model allowed for two sources of lexical storage for a child's particular pronunciations of certain words:

1. Misperceptions of the adult input form resulting in divergent underlying forms (a possibility assumed by all researchers)
2. Frequency: Words that a child uses frequently might be stored with two pronunciations: the adult one *and* the child one.

This proposal suggests that frequent exceptional forms do not have to be re-created with on-line constraints/processes each time they are produced. Once stored in this way, these exceptional words ("regressive idioms") may become resistant to modification because of the power of habit (frequency effects). Menn suggests that a child may be capable of changing the word, but has "temporarily stopped monitoring, stopped really listening to himself and/or to the adult model. He expects that he is correct and does not bother to check up" (1983:11).

2.3.1.2. Early Two-Lexicon Models

For some developmental phonologists, the degree of exceptionality in child speech suggested that even the revised single-lexicon model of Macken (1980b) was inadequate (Menn, 1983; Dinnsen & Elbert, 1984). The two-lexicon model of representation was one attempt to account for the various types of exceptionality (Ingram, 1974; Kiparsky & Menn, 1977; Menn, 1983). Two lexicons were

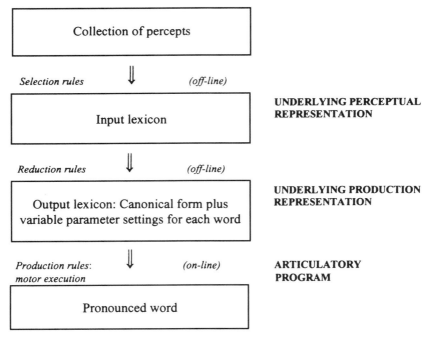

FIGURE 2.2

assumed: the "input" or "recognition lexicon" (for perceived forms), and the "output" or "active lexicon" (for storage of the child's own productions). (See Figure 2.2.)

Both of the child's lexicons refer to the same semantic information (Menn & Matthei, 1992). Thus, the concept of double entry proposed in Macken's (1980b) model extends to the whole lexicon.

In the two-lexicon model, a word is first subject to selection "rules," "which characterize . . . those aspects of the adult word that the child preserves" (Menn & Matthei, 1992:217). These percepts are then stored in an input lexicon. Transduction processes or constraints modify the perceptual representation, but *only once*, during the creation of an entry in the *output lexicon*. Thus, transduction is off-line, and not part of on-line production as in single-lexicon models. When the child utters the target word even for the second time, it is accessed from the output lexicon. Menn suggests that off-line processing and storage is more parsimonious than real-time on-line processing (1983:9), in which processes have to affect a word *each* time it is pronounced.

Early two-lexicon models assumed that the output and input lexicons "(almost) coincide" over time, as the child's productions become equivalent to the adult productions (Menn & Matthei, 1992:222). (Menn & Matthei, 1992, allow for the possibility that adults may have slight variation between perception and production of some words, to handle perception of dialectal variants, etc.)

By having a separate lexicon for stored child output forms, the two-lexicon model provides an easy way to account for exceptional words; any word can be altered to have an adult-like form before others are, or remain child-like after others have become adult-like. There must be mechanisms that change the representations in the output lexicon over the course of acquisition, and there is no reason to expect that every word would be changed simultaneously by that mechanism. Indeed, it seems more likely that changing all the entries would take time, so that word-by-word change would be predicted as basic.

The early two-lexicon model accounts for certain types of variability and accessibility of words. It raises some concerns, however. It not only allows for item-by-item learning, but *requires* that changes take place in that way. There are a number of additional issues that are difficult for the early two-lexicon model (see Menn and Matthei, 1992; Stemberger, 1992a, 1993b; Chiat, 1994). One problem is vagueness: the model did not sufficiently instantiate or explain phonological processing issues, such as how entries are revised, how long revision takes, what mechanism identifies what can be changed, what the search procedures are, etc. Another issue is speed of change: we doubt that there are any psychologically plausible mechanisms that can find and alter stored forms as rapidly as change may occur in the child's system. Other issues concern single lexical item variability, frequency effects, the continuity hypothesis, and processes between morphemes or words (multimorphemic processes). With some adjustments, the early two-lexicon model could handle some of these concerns, but fails primarily with respect to multimorphemic processes, as we discuss below.

2.3.1.2.1. Single Lexical Item Variability

As children learn new structures and features, single lexical items will often be produced with old and new pronunciations in the same time period. Variability at the point of change is the most common type of variability in phonological development. The two-lexicon model does not explain how a child would select one versus the other form from the output lexicon, or whether two forms can coexist (Menn, 1978), or if or when an old form is deleted.

When there are two or more stored forms for a single item, some type of competition is implied. Menn and Matthei suggest that competition is "a strange notion for a linguist's lexicon" (1992:224), but a full accounting of child language development must include notions from performance. Competition is a basic principle in most serial models of processing (see Levelt, 1989, for an overview), and could be incorporated into the two-lexicon model. Competition models predict that each variant of a word will surface with a certain probability on any given trial. This works, but is less appealing if there is variability for most words, or if many words have five or six variants. We return to this issue below in our discussion of connectionist models.

2.3.1.2.2. Frequency Effects

Another issue concerns the effect of frequency. Frequency can account for a variety of types of exceptions. Regressive and progressive idioms are sometimes the high-frequency words (Menn & Matthei, 1992). Item-by-item learning can reflect frequency factors: some words may show changes earlier than others because they are used more often. For example, during speech therapy, low-frequency words are sometimes more resistant to change, presumably because of less practice with new patterns. Further, if a child has just learned to produce velars, for example, the stability of that articulation may not be such as to allow all new words to be produced with velars; the child may still be using the off-line reduction rule that eliminates velars in the creation of entries in the output lexicon.

Frequency is a probabilistic notion, and generative linguistic theories have been built more on absolutes than probabilities. Menn and Matthei comment that "generative-based boxologies are deterministic, and there is no straightforward way to graft probabilistic processes onto them" (1992: 228). However, performance models deal with probabilistic data, and two-lexicon models could also do so, if revised.

2.3.1.2.3. The Continuity Hypothesis

If children have two-lexicon models, but adults have only one lexicon, a notable discontinuity is introduced between adult and child phonology. Acceptance of the early two-lexicon model means acceptance of this type of representational discontinuity, something that may not be desirable, as we have discussed in Chapter 1. Alternatively, we might accept that adults also have two lexicons, one for perception and one for production. Smolensky (1996a) has recently suggested that adults may have entirely separate grammars for perception and production. Thus, continuity may not be a problem here.

2.3.1.2.4. Multimorphemic Processes

The major difficulty for two-lexicon models concerns their inability to account for between-word and other "postlexical" (multimorphemic) processes. A number of researchers have noted the occurrence of such assimilation or deletion processes when words are combined into phrases (Scollon, 1976; Donahue, 1986; Matthei, 1989; Stemberger, 1988). If the child's pronunciation is dealt with off-line and stored in the output lexicon, then aspects of the adult pronunciation should not emerge in two-word combinations; and they sometimes do.

Stemberger (1993b) provides data that are challenging for a two-lexicon approach. At 2;10, Gwendolyn generally formed the past tense of vowel-final words by adding [d], as in adult English. There were two exceptions to this, however. First, forms that are irregular in adult speech, such as *threw*, could be produced correctly as irregulars or could be regularized (*throwed*), as is common in child language. Second, words that are consonant-final in adult speech but were vowel-final in the child's speech, such as *kiss* /kɪs/ [tʰiː], did not have *-d* added in the past tense:

Words:	*pee*	*sew*	*throw*	*kiss*
Two-Lexicon Child				
Representation:	/piː/	/soʊ/	/soʊ/	/tiː/
Past Tense Formation:	piː+d	soʊ+d	soʊ+d	tiː+d
Predicted Output:	[pʰiːd]	[soʊd]	[soʊd]	*[tʰiːd]
				[tʰiː]

The two-lexicon approach seems to predict that all words that are vowel-final in the child's speech should be treated the same for the creation of past tense forms. Since a final /d/ is added to words like *pee*, it should also be added to words like *kiss* /tiː/. This prediction fails, suggesting that the two-lexicon approach is inadequate.

The two-lexicon approach can be salvaged if this prediction can be side-stepped in some way. We see two ways in which this can be attempted, but both fail. First is the memorization of a few forms. Perhaps the formation of past tense forms was not productive at this age, and the child simply memorized a few forms. Thus, final [d] would not appear in any past tense form in which it was not present in the adult form. This is incorrect, since the child produced regularizations like *throwed*, which must presumably be produced on-line and not stored in the lexicon. (Marcus et al., 1992, argue that regularizations in child language are not in fact produced by the grammar, but are performance errors, so they could not be stored in the lexicon.) Thus, final [d] could also have been added to *kiss*, and it was not.

The second way to salvage the two-lexicon approach is with input and output lexicon storage. The past tense form *kissed* may have been stored in the input lexicon as /kɪst/ and in the output lexicon as /tiː/. In production, the child simply used the stored form; since a stored past tense form was available, *-d* was not added on-line to create a new one. However, this child was variable on irregular past tense forms, sometimes producing them correctly and sometimes incorrectly. This means that the child had difficulty accessing past tense forms stored in the lexicon, and, when she was unable to locate the stored form, created a past tense form on-line. Presumably, this difficulty should affect *all* stored forms, whether irregular (*threw*) or regular (*kissed*). We thus predict that *kissed* should have been variable between [tʰiː] and *[tʰiːd]. This prediction is incorrect.

The two-lexicon approach thus makes the wrong predictions about this child's inflectional morphology. We must conclude that the phonological representation of *kiss* in the output lexicon was *not* vowel-final, but was consonant-final, as in adult speech. This is a rejection of the most fundamental assumption of the two-lexicon approach: the fact that [tʰiː] was vowel-final is not stored in a lexical representation, but rather in the phonological system (as a rule or constraint that caused the deletion of the final /s/).

For all "postlexical" examples (i.e., involving morphological additions or embedding of the word in phrases), the same problem exists. Some of the reduction processes of child phonology must apply *after* the output lexicon. The same processes can sometimes mediate between the perceptual lexicon and the production lexicon (applying off-line) and sometimes follow the production lexicon (applying on-line). But if *some* processes *must* apply on-line, what evidence is there that any apply off-line? Further, all available data from morphology and phrases suggest that the relevant processes are *usually* on-line. To salvage the two-lexicon approach, we would have to assume that, for some unknown reason, processes are shifted from applying off-line before the production lexicon to applying on-line after the production lexicon *just before* relevant inflectional affixes and phrases appear, so that the form stored in the production lexicon is more adult-like. Until a good explanation can be offered for why such restructuring would always take place just before relevant data become available, we must assume that the early two-lexicon approach is flawed. A single-lexicon approach is thus preferable to the standard two-lexicon approach. Below, we develop a revised variant of the two-lexicon approach that may be more adequate, however.

2.3.1.3. Connectionism and Two Lexicons

Above, we discussed frequency effects, on-line processing, and competition between levels of phonological structure. These are also a part of phonological processing in adults, and are key to the development of models of the lexicon. (See speech error accounts of Dell, 1986; Stemberger, 1985, 1990, 1991a.) Major assumptions of the Dell and Stemberger phonological processing models are as follows:

1. Information is encoded in terms of *units* with various *activation levels* (measures of the amount of activity). When not active, a unit returns to its basic *resting* level. (Resting levels also differ across units.)

2. The system is made up of *connected* units that can be both mutually enhancing or inhibitory. These connections and their interactive effects are present at the level of units, words, and major linguistic components of the language processor. The system is incapable of processing one word discretely from other words in the lexicon. Accessing of one word activates many nontarget words also, due to their similarity to the target word in either meaning or sound. These gangs of nontarget words can have considerable effects on processing, especially in small lexicons.

3. Random fluctuations are present for resting levels and the amount of activation that is passed between units. Such *noise* can result in increased activation for the wrong unit, and in errors in accessing (retrieving) the intended unit for production.

In terms of learning, there are two basic generalizations (for Stemberger's model):

1. Resting levels become higher each time a unit is accessed. High-frequency targets thus become more accessible.

2. Mapping between units on adjacent levels must be learned. If insufficient activation is passed from one level to the next, faithfulness to the perceived form will not be maintained, and adjustments will need to be made to the activation levels for subsequent attempts at the target. Generally, these adjustments are small, and it will therefore take time for noticeable changes in output to occur.

With the above assumptions, it is not necessary to use two lexicons to account for differences between perception and production. The child attempts to be faithful to the perceptually based representation of the lexical item. The child's production will be wildly or minimally divergent from the perceptually based representation, depending on how readily a child can access a given unit for production purposes. Accessibility will vary depending on a variety of factors, such as output capacity constraints, activation levels for various units, noise in the system, gang effects, and interactive competitions between various levels of the phonology. Resting levels for various units will increase with practice, resulting in frequency effects. Lexical exceptions are predicted: some words have high resting levels and are pronounced more accurately; some words have low resting levels and are pronounced less accurately. Communication breakdowns and noticing a lack of faithfulness to the perceptual representation will drive the child to change the system, bit by bit, as the activation of units changes.

Variability between different outputs is encoded via random fluctuations of activation levels, such that the most activated output is different on different trials. Differences in resting levels lead to differences between lexical items.

The main reasons for replacing the linguistically based single-lexicon model with a two-lexicon model were

1. to have a model that accounted for lexical variability, and
2. to have an economical model that did not require on-line processing each time a child produced a variant of the adult form.

Connectionism allows for a two-lexicon model that operates without underlying *phonological* representations. All of the previous models (whether single-lexicon or two-lexicon models) have assumed underlying phonological representations. There is one variant of the two-lexicon approach that may be psychologically plausible. Until recently, this variant was possible only within a connectionist approach to cognition (e.g., Dell, Juliano, & Govindjee, 1993). It is also possible within an OT framework, which has borrowed many of its characteristics from connectionism (as in Hammond, 1995). What makes this variant plausible is its assumed absence of underlying *phonological* representations for morphemes or words. In standard single-lexicon models (especially in linguistic theory), a morpheme is assumed to have a single representation that is used in all aspects of lexical processing. (See Figure 2.3.)

During speech perception and comprehension, the underlying representation is compared to the (processed) auditory input, to determine which word/morpheme

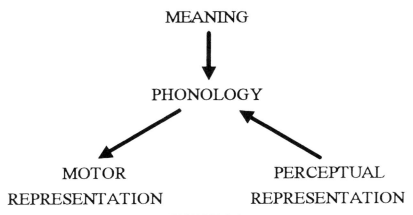

FIGURE 2.3

has been heard. In speech production, the underlying representation provides input into the phonological system and serves as the basis for constructing the surface pronunciation of the morpheme/word. Such single-lexicon models were found lacking by many developmental phonologists, but current two-lexicon models also have serious problems. Because a connectionist-inspired two-lexicon model does not assume underlying phonological representations, it may escape some of the problems of both types of previous models. The new approach (see Figure 2.4) assumes that only a meaning-based representation is used for both production and perception/comprehension.

There is no single phonological representation that is used for all tasks. A stored form is used during perception/comprehension to access the word's meaning. During production, a phonological form is produced *on the basis of the word's meaning*. These two representations are separate, but related. Mechanisms of learning guarantee identity between the perceptual form and the production form. In production, phonological output is created on the basis of a meaning-based representation for a morpheme/word. Initially, this output is very inaccurate, and does not match the perceptual form. The output form arises as it does

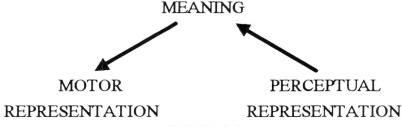

FIGURE 2.4

because of certain inherent biases in the phonological system (which exist even before any words are learned) and certain inherent, although probably random, mappings from meaning to sound. The learner must learn how to map the meaning-based input pattern onto the appropriate sound-based (articulation-based) output pattern for each morpheme/word. In a connectionist model, this is accomplished by altering the weights in the connections between units in the input representation and units in the output representation, so that, on the next attempt, that particular meaning-based input pattern will be more likely to give rise to that particular sound-based output pattern (e.g., Rumelhart & McClelland, 1986). The exact mechanism for this in an OT model is less clear, but may be analogous; it involves (in all probability) reranking constraints so that particular features are likely to be output (and these features are the ones that are supported by the faithfulness constraints).

This approach allows us to uncouple the representations used for perception and production. The perceived form is driven by auditory input, and includes fine details (such as subphonemic duration and pitch differences). With earlier approaches, much of this information had to be discarded. Since syllable structure, allophonic features, etc., were not present in underlying representations, all that information would have to be either deleted or ignored for the purposes of lexical access. But that seems implausible. The speech signal is highly redundant for a reason: redundancy makes it easier to determine which word was heard. Why would a perceptual system ignore allophonic information as irrelevant for lexical access, rather than exploit it to make the task easier? In a two-lexicon approach without underlying representations, no information needs to be ignored. A highly redundant, fully specified, and perceptually based phonological form is used to access a meaning-based representation directly.

In production, processing is quite different. The pronunciation is not driven by faithfulness to a real-world event (the acoustic signal), but must be constructed on the basis of a nonphonological input pattern. The phonological system has constraints on output, however, with inherent biases determining what is easy to produce, what is difficult to produce, and what is impossible to produce. The mapping from a meaning based representation to a sound-based representation needs to provide only enough information to alter the inherent biases of the system so that the output matches the form stored in the perceptual lexicon. Any aspect of the pronunciation that arises automatically through the inherent biases in the production phonological system does not need to be learned for production. It is not necessarily a lexical fact about the word *map* that the /m/ and the /æ/ are voiced. That fact may be derived automatically via biases in the phonological system, and does not have to be learned as a phonologically unpredictable characteristic of the word *map*. Only phonologically unpredictable information needs to be learned in the mapping. In the production lexicon, then, the output form is determined through the interaction of three independent sources of information: (a) the mapping between the meaning-based input representation and the sound-based output representation, (b) inherent biases within the output phonological system, and

(c) a communicatively grounded constraint that the produced form should sound (roughly) like what the speaker hears other people producing (the perceptual form).

This approach is plausible psychologically in a number of ways. First, it assumes that all perceptual information can be used in accessing a word in perception/comprehension. Second, it assumes that the speaker goes directly from a meaning-based representation of the morpheme/word to the surface pronunciation of the word. There is abundant evidence for the reality of meaning and of surface phonological representations, but no psychological evidence that requires intermediate phonological representations. There is no psychological evidence that the surface representation must be derived through a sequence of steps, each of which is a full phonological representation of the morpheme/word.

We would like to emphasize that perception and production have different phonological systems in this model. Perceptual phonology is driven solely by perceptual input and is fully specified. Production phonology is driven jointly by meaning and articulation; some aspects of the output must be attributed to lexical information and other aspects must be attributed to the phonological system. This means that the lexical input does not specify all the information in the output. Phonologically predictable information never has any lexical specification. This is true not only of allophonic features and syllable structure, but also of all default features and feature values. Thus, underspecification holds true of the mapping from the morpheme/word to the production phonology, but not of the mapping from the perception phonology to the morpheme/word.

We suggest that this revised version of the two-lexicon approach has greater promise than previous models. Production is done on-line, each time, and reflects biases of the phonological system. Thus, the model can handle multimorphemic processes and constraints, which the previous two-lexicon model could not. As we discussed in §2.1.3, we do not believe that production processing involves the alteration of underlying representations of words by "real" rules or processes, as assumed in the previous models. A two-lexicon model without phonological representations bypasses this "alteration" model, but still accounts for differences between perception and production processing, which was a goal of the original two-lexicon model.

The approach taken in this book is compatible with such an updated two-lexicon model, but does not require it. Analyses in this book may be interpreted either within a single-lexicon approach, or within this updated two-lexicon approach. The differences between them are subtle enough that we know of no empirical information that would allow us to choose between them at the present time. We thus assume that the adult pronunciation is encoded in the mapping from a meaning-based input to a sound-based output, and that information about the child's pronunciation is stored in the constraint rankings of the child's phonological system. Only in relatively rare instances is information about the child's form stored in the lexicon: when the child has misperceived the adult form, or if the child happens to learn his/her own pronunciation as an acceptable output (especially if adults start imitating the pronunciation; Priestly, 1977, reports an instance of this).

Because it fits in better with previous work, we will phrase our proposals in terms of a model with underlying representations. However, by "underlying representation," we mean only "the set of elements (and connections between them) that are determined primarily by activation from the lexical item." The input is solely meaning-based, and it activates phonological elements in the output. We regard this updated two-lexicon model as the most likely way to represent human language.

2.4. ISSUE 4: INNATENESS

The origin of human language and its characteristics is a topic of perennial interest. There are two extreme positions. One is that language derives from independent properties of human cognition. Humans purportedly learn and use a complex communication system because they have such flexible general skills of memory and learning. Language has the characteristics that it has because of the characteristics of those other cognitive mechanisms, combined with general functional constraints on communication and (for phonology) basic properties of the vocal tract and of perception. Different human languages share common properties because all humans have essentially the same cognitive and perceptual systems and vocal-tract anatomy. There is a sense in which the properties of language are "innate," but only in a derivative fashion: human memory innately has certain characteristics, and memory imposes those characteristics on language. For example, Hopper and Thompson (1984) argue that languages have nouns and verbs for functional reasons, because the distinction encodes a pragmatic difference in real-world objects/events/states that humans find important and useful. (See Elman et al., 1996, for a recent statement of this "emergentist" position.)

The second position is that language derives from special innate mechanisms that are specific to human language. For example, without the appropriate genes, a speaker would not have nouns and verbs, though the speaker might be normal in all other aspects of human cognition. In this view, the characteristics of language cannot be derived from independent characteristics of human cognition. (See Lightfoot, 1992, and Pinker, 1991, for recent statements.)

This is a very contentious issue, and we do not attempt to resolve it here. Indeed the answer to this question is not known. Disagreements as sharp as are found on this issue simply do not arise when there is clear, unambiguous, compelling evidence one way or the other.

Instead, we address another important issue. To what extent do the ideas of modern linguistics, including the ideas that we use in this book, depend on the view that the major characteristics of language are innate? It is rare to find a major work in modern formal linguistics that does not mention innateness prominently at some point. Prince and Smolensky (1993), in their presentation of OT, mention this on the first page of their monograph. Works in developmental phonology that assume a modern linguistic framework frequently assume at least some degree of innateness (e.g., Ingram, 1989a; Levelt, 1994). Researchers in other fields may have the impression that innateness is an integral part of the package of ideas used in modern linguistics, and may have even rejected linguistic theories, assuming that they necessarily imply adherence to a nativist worldview.

We do not believe that the concepts used by modern phonology require the nativist hypothesis. For most purposes, it does not matter whether language is innate or not. The same constraints and representations can arise and hold true of human languages whether they are innate or derivable from independent aspects of cognition or communication. As a result, modern phonological theory has some interesting things to say and should be examined, regardless of one's position on innateness.

We begin with a discussion of what we think the relevant issues have been in the innateness debate, and then go on to discuss constraints and the ways in which they can be viewed. We sketch a way that the same constraints that we discuss here can be thought of in a system in which nothing specific to phonology is innate (except insofar as the vocal tract and general constraints on memory systems are innate). Part of this sketch addresses where constraints come from, and the role of normal (and abnormal) vocal tract anatomy on those constraints.

2.4.1. A QUESTION OF DEFAULTS

The myriad articles on the subject of innateness seldom discuss what underlies the major differences in worldview. This major division in the field derives at least in part from an individual researcher's short-term and long-term goals regarding the research process, and which worldview s/he believes will likely be fruitful immediately, or over time.

The position that there is no innateness specific to language cannot yet provide details about how to derive many of the specific characteristics of human language. This approach presupposes that all aspects of human language can eventually be derived from independent aspects of cognition or from functional constraints on communication and on the vocal tract. With that presupposition comes the responsibility to say explicitly which independent aspect of cognition underlies each particular property of human language. How do we guarantee that all speakers of all languages have features, segments, and syllables, and that all speakers of all languages draw on exactly the same set of features?[15] How do we account for the fact that the same phonological constraints are observed in many different languages? These are difficult questions. As yet, there are few detailed answers. But those who take this point of view are optimistic that answers will eventually be found.

One default position is that all similar human skills should derive from the same cognitive mechanisms. There must be general procedures for learning skills, since no one would argue that there are genes that are specific to learning how to program computers, and yet people can learn that skill. It is simplest to assume

---

[15] We should note that it is a presupposition that all speakers of all languages *do* have segments and syllables, and use exactly the same set of features. If they do not, then there is less to account for in linguistic theory.

that general learning procedures can account for the acquisition of all skills, until such time as it can be demonstrated that this is false. One assumes the simplest theory (that there is a single learning mechanism that underlies all learning) until it is proven that a more complex theory (with domain-specific learning mechanisms) must be assumed. This is the default position taken by many researchers. As the default position, it is assumed *in the absence* of compelling evidence bearing on the issue. Many (but by no means all) psychologists and speech-language pathologists take this position.

Proponents of language-specific innateness are skeptical that we will ever be able to derive the major characteristics of human language from independent aspects of cognition. They maintain that we know that innateness is powerful enough that it could in theory derive all the properties of human languages independently of all other cognitive systems. As a result, we should assume language-specific innateness until it is demonstrated that it is not necessary. This is in many ways an act of pessimism, a view that the basic characteristics of language are so unique that they cannot be successfully derived from independent principles. If that is the case, why not work with language-specific innateness now, since we will ultimately be left with that position after all attempts to derive the properties of language from independent principles have failed. This is the default position taken by many researchers. As the default position, it is assumed *in the absence* of compelling evidence bearing on the issue. Many (but by no means all) theoretical linguists take this position.

The choice between these two worldviews is thus made on theoretical grounds, reflecting what a given researcher views as the default position (to be held until there is compelling evidence to the contrary), and reflecting a pragmatic decision about which line of research is likely to prove fruitful. Although many researchers have attempted to find clear empirical evidence, none has yet been found.

It is important to make the topic of this argument clear. It is *not* a disagreement about data. Many properties are common to all or almost all human languages: so-called "universals." Researchers on both sides of the issue agree that our theories need to account for these universal properties. The sole point of disagreement is about why these properties are present, focusing in particular on *how the properties develop*. Nativists hold that the properties are stored in human genes, and become available at the appropriate point in development, as those genes are expressed. Emergentists hold that those properties derive from independent characteristics, and become available after those independent characteristics develop.

The point of disagreement is thus on the issue of *development*, rather than on the properties of human language. This point is rarely made clear in the literature, but it is at the heart of whether the innateness issue matters for our purposes in this book.

2.4.2. INNATENESS DOES NOT MATTER (FOR MOST PURPOSES)

It is unclear whether innateness matters for any linguistic description of any adult human language, and it is adult human languages that constitute the database on which linguistic theory has been developed. Innateness is a question about how universal properties of human languages *develop*. Adult systems are past the developmental stage. It is important for adult systems that language have certain characteristics, restricting what must be present, what cannot be present, and what range of options can be used to express a particular linguistic function. For the purposes of describing adult languages, the origin of those properties should not matter. No one has ever provided an overt argument that proves that the source of those universal properties affects linguistic analyses of adult human languages.

Even for acquisition, there is a level of description where one's stand on this issue does not matter. A particular developmental pattern is present, regardless of whether it derives from an innate genetic program that is specific to language, or derives from constraints imposed by other cognitive systems. In this book, we are concerned about the phonological patterns that arise in child language and about how to describe them. Constraints on output play a large role in shaping those phonological patterns. But it does not matter in any of our data chapters whether those constraints are innate in a way that is specific to language, or whether they derive from physical properties of the vocal tract combined with general properties of information processing in the human cognitive system. It only matters that there are constraints, and that the constraints seem to be of a certain type.

Ultimately, of course, the source of the patterns does matter. The developmental story will be very different if all the developmental patterns can be firmly rooted in general properties of cognition and learning, than if they derive from genetic programs specific to language. For the acquisition of phonology, those independent principles presumably involve general constraints on motor activity, memory, and cognition, and specific constraints on the vocal tract. We wish only to point out that for many purposes, one's stand on the issue does not matter. We address below one instance where it *does* matter (phonetic grounding).

2.4.3. THE POSSIBLE ORIGIN OF CONSTRAINTS

For constraint-based views of phonology, one important question concerns the origin of constraints. If they are innate in a way that is specific to language, we account for the fact that the same constraints are observed in many different languages (and in children learning target adult languages that do not show any effects of that particular constraint). Prince and Smolensky (1993) appear to take this point of view. However, when the functions of constraints are considered, there is an alternative account that does not require innateness.

The key observation is Prince and Smolensky's suggestion that some of the more important constraints are designed to limit complexity (their *Complex, but especially their *Struc, which holds that all structure should be avoided). This certainly seems to be true of human language. For example, words tend to be short (Zipf, 1935). Similarly, languages tend to avoid complex onsets, nuclei, and codas. Even when the language allows more than one consonant in an onset, most words begin with just a single consonant (for English, see French, Carter, & Koenig, 1930; Stemberger, 1990).

Stampe (1973) observed that there are two opposite forces at work in the shaping of phonological forms. First, from the point of view of the speaker, producing any information at all is difficult, because it requires cognitive resources, and so on. The less content and the less the diversity of features and feature combinations, the better. If the speaker could communicate telepathically (silently), the "speaker" might view that as optimal (because less effort would presumably be required). Second, from the point of view of the listener, words should be as distinct as possible, to facilitate lexical access and avoid ambiguity. This requires longer and more diverse outputs, with many feature contrasts. Stampe suggested that phonological systems find a happy medium, providing enough complexity to make perceptual processing acceptably efficient, while not requiring too much effort from the speaker.

Faithfulness constraints are motivated by consideration of the listener. They require that the phonological characteristics of a particular lexical item will always be present when that lexical item is produced.

Negative constraints are motivated by the difficulty that speakers have in any production (or motor) task. Any element that is produced has a cost (an inherent level of difficulty), and some elements have more cost (more difficulty) than others. The phonological system attempts to minimize cost (difficulty). This often leads to unfaithfulness.

In Chapter 4, we provide a full discussion of the negative constraints that we use in this book. In essence, they boil down to the following generalizations:

1. No element can be produced.
2. Insofar as an element *can* be produced,
   (a) it cannot be combined with any other element,
       (i) either at the same time, or
       (ii) in sequence, and
   (b) it cannot be produced
       (i) twice in a row, or
       (ii) for an extended period of time.

We propose constraints to handle each one of these aspects of difficulty.

These are not *general* constraints, however, since some elements and combinations of elements are more difficult than others. As an example, consider that combining frication and alveolar place (in [s]) appears to be far easier than combining frication and velar place (in [x]), at least for English speakers. Each negative constraint must have a variant for each element: **Not(+ voiced)** governs the difficulty of producing a voiced segment, and **Not(-voiced)** governs the difficulty of producing a voiceless segment. In general, a different level of difficulty is involved with every element; two elements are seldom equally difficult to produce. In the next two subsections, we consider sources of relative difficulty for different elements (and combinations of elements). For now, we address the sources of these basic constraints and whether they must be innate.

Note that the constraints as we have phrased them are negative: they *prohibit* elements and combinations of elements:

Not(Anything):   The child cannot do anything.

Stated in this way, the constraints probably are innate. If they were not, why would there be explicit negative constraints against each particular feature, etc.? It is difficult to imagine how the constraints might arise.

However, constraints do not have to be stated in a negative fashion. Constraints can also be stated positively: something is *required*. OT and other constraint-based linguistic theories tend to have some positive and some negative constraints. However, *all* constraints can, in principle, be stated in a positive fashion:

Possible(Nothing):   One thing that is possible is: (nothing).

A constraint such as **Possible** focuses on what the speaker *can* do rather than on what the speaker *cannot* do. If an element is not covered by a **Possible** constraint, then it is, of course, not possible. Further, we can rank these **Possible** constraints by level of difficulty. Some elements or combinations of elements are possible but extremely difficult to produce. Other elements or combinations of elements are not just possible, but are also very easy to produce.

In language development, there might initially be no **Possible** constraints: nothing would be possible. At some point, as the child attempts to produce speech, **Possible** constraints develop and gradually increase in strength so that some elements and combinations of elements become easy, while other elements remain difficult or impossible.

Every negative constraint can be recast into one or more positive constraints. Consider this negative constraint:

Not(Coda):   Codas are prohibited.

The same effect (no codas anywhere in the language) can be achieved via the following two positive constraints:

Possible(Onset):   Onsets are possible.
Possible(Nucleus):   Nuclei are possible.

We do not require an explicit statement that codas are prohibited. In the absence of a positive statement that codas are possible, codas are impossible. For every negative constraint, we can make a set of positive constraints that encode the same information. The choice between positive and negative constraints does not matter for some purposes.

For other purposes, however, the difference between positive and negative constraints is very important. With negative constraints, it is difficult to see how innateness can be avoided. As learning proceeds, some constraints can be "overcome;" in OT this involves reranking of constraints. With positive constraints, in contrast, we can start out with no constraints at all. Learning proceeds by learning how to do things: adding positive constraints that state that something is possible.

With practice, the number of positive constraints increases, and a greater variety of outputs is observed. It is not difficult to imagine an emergentist version of learning. The child merely has to learn how to manipulate the vocal tract, and learning is parallel to learning how to manipulate *any* part of the body for *any* motor task (including walking, dancing, playing tennis, etc.).

We explore here a version of OT in which all constraints are positive, and in which initially the child has no positive constraints (and can do nothing). As the child learns to control the vocal apparatus for speech, the number of positive constraints increases. Some positive constraints relate to features like [+nasal]. Others relate to stringing segments together into words: coordinating different places of articulation within the same word, for example.

The first issue that must be addressed is how to deal with the constraint ranking of OT. What does a constraint ranking like this mean?

Possible(Nucleus) ||| **Possible(Onset)** ||| **Possible(Coda)**

It means that some things are more "possible" than others: that some things are easier than others. Adopting an algorithm whereby easier things are preferred to harder things, this ranking would mean that, given a choice between producing a consonant as an onset or as a coda, it would be easier (preferable) to produce it as an onset, and thus it would be produced as an onset. Intervocalic consonants would therefore be syllable-initial. Pronunciations that involve only high-ranked constraints are more optimal than pronunciations that involve only low-ranked constraints. The algorithm maximizes optimality. The main thing that has changed from standard views of OT is how optimality is measured.

The faithfulness constraints would still play as important a role as before. Some elements might be so optimal that they would be present even if they were not in the input (a violation of **Not**); this would include default features and segments. Other elements would be lower-ranked, and would be possible only when they are present in the underlying representation of the lexical item. Some elements would be impossible even when they are in the underlying representation (a violation of **Survived**).

This approach may have a hard time dealing with the elements themselves, however. The constraint **Possible(Coda)** says that codas can be produced, but why should there be codas in the first place? In an innatist approach, we simply stipulate (in human genetic material) what the basic elements of phonology are. In a strictly emergentist approach, we must explain their origin. If the basic elements of phonology are learned, rather than innate, what guarantee do we have that all speakers (and all languages) will arrive at exactly the same set of features, for example?

One possible answer is that there is no exact match between the units of one person's phonological system and another person's phonological system. Different languages might define features in slightly different ways. We note in Appendix B that there is some disagreement about the exact definition of features, and perhaps that is because different languages use different features. If so, then why do different languages have nearly identical sets of features? The answer is probably that all normal adults have very similar vocal tracts and have learned similar adult target languages. As a result, all speakers develop feature systems that are approximately the same, but with minor variations that are generally unimportant within a given language community. Our present state of knowledge suggests that features and other elements of phonology may be learned rather than innate.

We have presented a sketch of an emergentist version of OT because we want to convince readers that OT is a worthwhile theory to pursue, regardless of one's stand on innateness. Readers who prefer innate systems can simply accept the work on OT at face value. Readers who prefer emergentist systems should realize that there is a possible emergentist variant of OT that will work on very simple principles, using positively stated versions of the negative constraints. We believe that, should the emergentist version prove to be superior, most of the analyses within OT will transfer over to the emergentist framework, with little effect on the *concepts* that are involved and the *types of information* that are used to explain particular phonological patterns. As such, work on OT should contribute to the development of reasonable theories of human language and of language acquisition, under a broad range of theoretical assumptions.

The innateness issue often leads to heated interactions between theoreticians. We do not feel that the current state of knowledge justifies anything other than pursuing all options. OT sees the world in a general way, and innateness is not a *necessary* part of that viewpoint. However, working with OT as if innateness were a required part does not necessarily do any harm. Consequently, we argue that OT is worth pursuing.

2.4.4. NOT INNATE I: PHONETIC GROUNDING

Numerous recent works have argued that constraints on phonological form should be phonetically grounded: they should be derivable from physical constraints on the vocal tract or from characteristics of speech perception. Archangeli and Pulleyblank (1994) devote a chapter to this idea, and it is often echoed in the literature (e.g.,, Cole & Kisseberth, 1994; Hayes, 1996). We suggest that this point of view is unlikely to be compatible with a view that constraints are innate. The consequences of innateness are implausible for phonetic grounding. We also suggest that it is not the constraints themselves that are phonetically grounded, but only the *ranking* of those constraints.

Chomsky's (1965) arguments for innateness include as crucial the idea that constraints on human language are arbitrary and cannot be derived from independent principles. He argues first that the constraints cannot be derived from the linguistic input to the child. He then argues that the constraints are unusual and strange-looking, and that they cannot be derived from any other known facts about human cognition. This is a *crucial* component of the argument. If the constraints made perfect sense relative to independently known facts, no one would ever have suggested that they have to be innate.

Pinker and Bloom (1990) have since described how a set of innate arbitrary constraints could be spread to all human beings during evolutionary development. They argue that all people in a community must speak a language with the same characteristics, in order to communicate (efficiently). It does not matter what those characteristics are, providing they are the same for all individuals. This constitutes an evolutionary pressure that selects against individuals with a different set of arbitrary constraints that prevents them from having the same language system as everyone else.[16] Individuals with a different innate system communicate more poorly and do less well in life (on average); they wind up having fewer offspring and thus do not pass on their genes to as many individuals in the next generation. Over generations, individuals with the less common innate system are outcompeted by individuals with the more common innate system. Eventually, everyone has the same innate system, even though all the constraints imposed on language are arbitrary.[17]

An important component of these arguments is arbitrariness. If the constraints can be independently derived, we have little reason to assume that they are innate. They are present for other reasons, and do not have to be favored by evolutionary pressure.

Phonetic grounding is demonstrably *functional*. It can be derived from independent characteristics of the vocal tract or the perceptual system. There is thus little reason to posit that phonetic grounding is innate. Further, for phonetically grounded constraints to be innate in a language-specific way requires the following evolutionary scenario:

> People whose genes provide constraints that are phonetically grounded learn language better and more efficiently than people whose genes provide constraints that are not phonetically grounded. People with phonetically grounded constraints do better in life than people with constraints that are not phonetically grounded, and tend to have more children, who then pass on the genes for phonetically grounded constraints. Over time, people with phonetically grounded constraints outcompete people with ungrounded constraints, and everyone comes to have phonetically grounded constraints.

---

[16] We presuppose here that the reader has some familiarity with evolutionary theory. If an innate characteristic allows an individual to have a greater than average number of offspring, that characteristic tends to become more widespread in later generations. For example, if most individuals have 5 offspring but an individual with a certain characteristic has 10 offspring, differences escalate rapidly. Three generations later, most individuals will have 125 descendants (5*5*5), but individuals with the special characteristic will have 1000 (10*10*10). If the original population had 9 regular individuals and 1 special individual (only 10% "special"), the population three generations later would have 1125 regular individuals (125*9) and 1000 special individuals (47.1% "special"). In this way, characteristics that lead to a greater than average number of offspring eventually spread to the entire population. The characteristic could increase the number of surviving offspring by making it less likely that the individual will die young or by making the individual healthier and thus more capable of producing and rearing more offspring.

[17] Pinker and Bloom (1990) do not actually provide any empirical evidence that having a different language system imposes a cost in terms of number of offspring, however. As a result, we do not know whether their argument is valid.

To take an example, consider the feature [ATR] (Advanced Tongue Root). Archangeli and Pulleyblank note that [-ATR] high vowels are relatively uncommon across languages, because it is relatively difficult to combine a high tongue position with a nonadvanced position of the tongue root. They also note that, in the vowel harmony of some languages with [-ATR] high vowels, [-ATR] nevertheless fails to spread onto high vowels. They argue that there is a constraint against the co-occurrence of [-ATR] and [+high] (which in our constraint system would be **NotCo-occurring(-ATR, +high)**), and that this constraint is firmly grounded in articulation. For this constraint to be innate, we would have to assume that languages with [-ATR] high vowels (such as Isoko) impose a cost on their speakers. Communication would be poorer, the speakers would do less well in life, and the speakers ultimately would have fewer offspring. That is the clearest way that a functionally based *innate* constraint could become universal among humans. The only alternative would be to assume that the innate constraint is universal among humans by accident. For some reason, the constraint arose and, via many random accidents, has spread to all humans. The only problem with this perspective is that it also means that the phonetic grounding of the constraint is accidental. The possibility that *all* constraints are phonetically grounded *by chance* is too remote to consider. However, this perspective leaves us with the idea that [-ATR] high vowels in a language must lower the speakers' biological fitness so that the speakers will have, on average, fewer offspring than the speakers of a language which has only [+ATR] high vowels. Languages with [-ATR] high vowels (like Isoko) are thus genetically harmful to the people who speak them. It has long been a tenet of linguistics that all natural languages are equally functional (Boas, 1911), but this viewpoint must reject that tenet.

A similar argument can be mounted on the basis of any other phonetically grounded constraint. Southern Paiute is an inferior language and harms the biological fitness of speakers because it has voiceless vowels. Burmese is inferior because it has voiceless nasals. And so on.

We assume that no one would view this scenario as likely. Further, it is not based on any form of empirical data. We have no reason to believe that speakers of Southern Paiute or Burmese really have fewer offspring than speakers of other languages (or if they do, that this difference derives from characteristics of the phonologies of the languages). It seems intuitively unlikely that such minor details of the phonology could have such large impacts on reproductive fitness.

If constraints are phonetically grounded, the only plausible point of view is that the grounding is not innate, but is derived directly from constraints on the vocal tract and on perception. Learners attempt to reproduce what they hear. Certain elements and combinations of elements are more difficult than others. The more difficult elements and combinations of elements are less prone to arise through historical change, and are more likely to be eliminated through historical change. It is *phonetic difficulty* that restricts elements and combinations of elements, not constraints stored in human genes.

We should note, however, that we do not believe that the constraints themselves are phonetically grounded. If the constraints are stated in negative terms, *every-thing* is ruled out: all elements and all combinations of elements. Phonetic ground-ing comes into play only in the *rankings* of the constraints. When phonetic grounding makes a particular combination more difficult, that particular constraint must be ranked higher. When phonetic grounding makes something easier, that particular negative constraint must be ranked lower. Constraints rule out *every-thing*. Phonetic grounding is expressed in the rankings.

2.4.5. NOT INNATE II: ABNORMAL VOCAL TRACTS

Most discussions of constraints, especially of phonetic grounding, have as-sumed that the speakers in question have normal adult vocal tracts (and normal brains). All normal adults have vocal tracts with variation that falls within certain limits. By and large (and ignoring the effects of practice), what one normal adult human finds relatively difficult to articulate, all normal adult humans find rela-tively difficult to articulate. This is not to say that all humans actually have equal skill levels, only that the relative difficulty of different articulations is similar across normal vocal tracts.

Not all human beings have normal adult vocal tracts. First, young children have vocal tracts that differ in certain significant ways from the vocal tracts of adults. Secondly, some speakers have vocal tracts with anatomical or physiological dif-ferences: cleft palate, poor velopharyngeal control, tongue thrusting, muscular weakness, etc. We address here the possible effects of some of these differences on phonetic grounding. In such cases, constraint rankings will not necessarily be the same in young children as in adults, and constraint rankings may be especially different in persons with anatomical or physiological disorders affecting the per-ceptual and production mechanisms.

When a child has a cleft palate, there is no way to isolate the oral and nasal cavities. If air moves through the oral cavity, it also moves through the nasal cavity. Even after palatal repair surgery, there is often velopharyngeal incompe-tence, in which the child is not able to close off the nasal cavity efficiently (e.g., Stengelhofen, 1989). This leads to a reversal of the usual difficulty for oral and nasal phones. In normals, oral phones are easier than nasal phones, and some children denasalize nasal stops like /n/ into oral stops like [d]. With cleft palate, nasalized phones are easier than purely oral phones, and some children nasalize oral stops like [d] into nasal stops like [n]. In order to prevent nasalization, some children with cleft palate substitute glottal stop [ʔ] for oral stops, since preventing air from moving through both cavities is the only way the child can prevent air from moving through the nasal cavity. The inability to seal off the nasal cavity makes it even harder for the child to build up the pressure necessary to produce fricatives, which consequently are even more difficult than they are for normal children. In Chapter 8, we return to this discussion, showing that phonological patterns in cleft palate speech can be analyzed with the same set of constraints that are used for persons with normal oral structures. However, the ranking of the constraints (which determines relative difficulty, and also determines which features act as defaults) often differs from that of people with normal structures, because of the differences in phonetic grounding.

Cleft palate speech is noticeably different in terms of phonetic grounding, but even children with normal vocal tracts show phonetically grounded differences. For example, all young children have smaller vocal tracts than adults do, and furthermore, the relative sizes of the various parts of the vocal tract differ from those of adults. In particular, the tongue is much larger relative to the oral cavity in children than in adults. This difference may mean that it is relatively more difficult for the child to produce dorsal consonants and small differences in vowel height. It also explains why children produce anterior coronals as dentals rather than as alveolars: with the relatively large tongue size, it is more difficult to retract the tongue to the alveolar ridge than in adult speech. The relative contribution of differences between the child and adult vocal tracts to differences in phonological patterning has not been extensively explored. We note here that those differences can in principle have effects on phonetic grounding. This can affect the constraint rankings, which can lead to differences in phonological patterns. Extreme differences like cleft palate are most noticeable, but more subtle effects are also undoubtedly present.

2.5. SUMMARY AND CONCLUSIONS

Phonology can be approached with different worldviews, each of which gives the researcher particular expectations about the types of phenomena that will be present. We have reviewed the worldviews for four issues that play an important role in modern phonological theory, particularly for theories of acquisition. We have argued that constraints are important, and that the most promising theory is one that lacks rules and processes altogether. We have argued that features can profitably be viewed as the basic unit of phonology, a viewpoint that leads us to expect that features will show the same set of phenomena that have always been attributed to segments. We have argued that much predictable information should be stored in the system, not in lexical representations. In terms of development and the origin of language, we have argued that the innateness issue does not matter for our purposes here, although certain aspects of the theory (in particular the ranking of constraints to reflect phonetic grounding) are unlikely to be innate. We hope that this overview of worldviews has helped to clarify the viewpoints of modern phonology. It will serve as a foundation for the chapters that follow.

3

PHONOLOGICAL REPRESENTATIONS AND PROCESSES

This chapter provides an overview of concepts in modern phonological theory that are needed for addressing issues of acquisition. Those readers with a good knowledge of phonological theory over the past decade may wish to merely skim this chapter to see the stands that we have taken on some of the controversial issues within phonological theory today. Readers less familiar with modern phonology will want to read it more closely. This chapter addresses only basic representations and processes; constraints are discussed in Chapter 4.

Phonological theory has come to focus far more on representations than it did in early generative phonology. The representations should be such that we can explain the types of patterns (processes and restrictions on segmental inventories and words) that are common in the languages of the world, and explain why other conceivable patterns (processes or restrictions) either do not occur in human languages or are uncommon. Halle (1962) originally proposed this criterion, using it to argue that phonological features are needed. Chomsky and Halle (1968) used it as a guide for deciding which features should be used in phonology. However, when it came to accounting for which processes were common vs. uncommon in the languages of the world, a very different style of explanation was used: ad hoc stipulations were made (in the form of *naturalness* and *markedness*):

Marked: If a marked segment is present in a language, then the unmarked segment is also present.
If an unmarked segment is present, the marked segment is not necessarily present.
Unmarked segments are higher in frequency than marked.

Natural: A process that is very frequent across languages.
Unnatural processes are infrequent or unattested.

Markedness is for segments and features, while naturalness is for processes. Both effectively say that what was common should be common. Since there was no independent evidence for markedness or naturalness, the concepts were circular: a given process is common because it is natural, and we know that it is natural because it is common. Phonologists now generally prefer to account for statistical properties of processes across languages by manipulating the representations so that what is common is easy to state but what is uncommon is difficult and awkward to state (e.g., McCarthy, 1988).

This chapter is organized in terms of the various phonological units, from the smallest to the largest. It seems appropriate to begin with features, given the worldview discussed in Chapter 2 that features should be a basic unit of phonology. We then proceed "up" the phonological hierarchy, from features to segments, to timing units, syllables, feet, and, finally, prosodic words.

We address points of disagreement that have arisen in the phonology literature. In some cases, we adopt a particular stand on the issue. In other cases, we employ two or more alternatives in our discussion of acquisition phenomena, discussing which alternative is more useful and working out the different ramifications of each alternative (even for treatment, in disordered development).

There are many variants of modern phonological theory. We follow the "mainstream" North American approach to phonology. We do not address variants such as Government and Charm Theory (Kaye, Lowenstamm, & Vergnaud, 1990), Dependency Phonology (Anderson & Durand, 1987), or Particle Phonology (Schane, 1984). Nor can we hope to cover the full range of ideas currently being discussed. This chapter is meant to give a basic overview of multilinear phonology, comprehensible even for those previously unfamiliar with the theory. We stress concepts over formalism. Formalism has a way of changing. Concepts are more enduring, and are often preserved when theories change, but packaged in a different formalism.

3.1. PHONOLOGICAL FEATURES

All speech sounds are composed of smaller units called *features* that encode the phonetic information of the segment. There is currently some disagreement over the optimal set of features for human languages. In Appendix B, we provide details of the feature set used here. These features are close to those of Chomsky and Halle (1968), except for the features for place of articulation, which follow Sagey (1986). We use the following features:

[voiced]
[spread-glottis] ([s.g.])
[constricted-glottis] ([c.g.])
[sonorant]
[consonantal]
[continuant]
[nasal]

[lateral]
[tense]
[Labial]
  [round]
  [labiodental]   (=[distributed])
[Coronal]
  [anterior]
  [distributed]
  [grooved]   (=[strident])
[Dorsal]
  [back]
  [high]
  [low]
[Radical]
  [AdvancedTongueRoot] ([ATR])
  [RetractedTongueRoot] ([RTR])

We have adopted certain orthographic conventions relating to features. If a feature is cited directly as a noun, it is enclosed in square brackets, whether a value ([+sonorant], [-voiced]) is included or not. If no value is included ([back]), it means that we are referring to all instances of that feature, whether [+back] or [-back]. Most features are written with the first letter in lower case. However, the articulator "nodes" are written with a capital letter. We follow the convention (used in Stemberger, 1993b) that the articulator nodes both have a capital letter *and* are enclosed in square brackets ([Coronal]). The reader should be aware that many other phonologists capitalize the names of articulator nodes, but do not enclose them in brackets (Coronal, Labial). We use brackets because the articulator nodes have phonetic content, whereas all other nodes that are capitalized without brackets lack inherent phonetic content (see §3.4, on feature geometry). We follow these same conventions if the feature is used as an adjective, and a specific value is included (*all [-back] vowels*). The features can also be used as adjectives or nouns without brackets, capitalization, or ± values if reference is being made to a segment with the + value (*all back vowels*; *most coronal consonants*; *most sonorants are voiced*). It is general practice to abbreviate feature names when they appear in brackets: [+son]=[+sonorant], [+cons]=[+consonantal]. We generally give full feature names, for clarity, using abbreviations only when space on the page is a primary consideration.

It is often convenient to be able to refer to all the articulator nodes as a class. For this purpose, we use the variable [Artic] (for "articulator node"). It has no separate status, but merely stands as an abbreviation for "[Labial] or [Coronal] or [Dorsal] or [Radical]," so that we are not forced to write out the whole list of articulator nodes.

In the rest of §3.1, we address subsidiary issues related to features: how to characterize affricates, whether features are binary, and which features are active.

3.1.1. THE PROBLEM OF AFFRICATES

The features that we present above (like those in Chomsky & Halle, 1968) do a reasonable job of representing all manners of articulation except one: affricates. Research on affricates has led to disagreements about the proper way to represent affricates. Affricates have been represented in at least four different ways, and the ultimate solution is unclear.

Jakobson et al. (1951) proposed that the affricates [ʧ] and [ʤ] are [+strident] stops ([+grooved] in our terminology). They argued that this was enough to distinguish the affricates from other segments, since stops are otherwise [-strident]: no feature should represent the apparent change during the segment from a stop-like articulation to a fricative-like articulation. The apparent change in manner was viewed to result from the way that strident stops are implemented phonetically.

Chomsky and Halle (1968) treated affricates as stops with an extra manner feature: [delayed-release] derived from an analysis whereby the release of the stop is very slow, with a fricative-like element produced during the (slow) release gesture. This feature is no longer used.

Within multilinear phonology, a new possibility arose. Clements and Keyser (1983) proposed that affricates were made up of two segments. For example, /ʧ/ is really /t/ followed by /ʃ/. (The /t/ and /ʃ/ are abnormally short, however, because they have only one timing unit rather than two; see §3.6.) Goldsmith (1990) and Kenstowicz (1994) show that this analysis fails in several ways. As a result, this analysis has been abandoned.

A second possibility within multilinear phonology is that affricates are a single segment, but they are specified as both [-continuant] (at the beginning) and [+continuant] (at the end). This analysis also has drawbacks. For example, it presupposes that an affricate will behave like a stop at the beginning of the affricate, but like a fricative at the end. Goldsmith (1990) and Kenstowicz (1994) show that this is rarely the case. As a result, this analysis has also largely been abandoned. Lombardi (1990) argued for a variant in which [-continuant] and [+continuant] are unordered with respect to one another (except phonetically), but this violates our assumption that a tier is a line of (ordered) elements.

Shaw (1991), LaCharité (1993), and Rubach (1994) came full circle, and proposed that affricates are [+strident] ([+grooved]) stops. However, this implies that nonstrident segments can never be affricates. An interdental affricate [tθ] is [-grooved]; if the definition of an affricate is that it is a [+grooved] stop, then the affricate /tθ/ cannot exist. Labial affricates like [pf] and [pɸ] also could not be represented, since [grooved] is not defined for labials. Unfortunately, affricates like [tθ] and [pf] occur both in adult languages and in the speech of young English-learning children. Thus, the analysis of affricates as [+grooved] (strident) stops does not allow us to represent all affricates, which is clearly a problem.

The final word has not yet been said about the representation of affricates. We make use of two positions: (a) that some affricates are [+grooved] stops, and (b) that some affricates are [-continuant] at the beginning and [+continuant] at the end. In later chapters, we discuss developmental evidence that bears on this issue.

3.1.2. BINARY VERSUS PRIVATIVE FEATURES

In Chomsky and Halle (1968), all features were binary. That is, they had two overt values: [+F] (meaning that the segment had the characteristic defined by the feature) and [-F] (meaning that the segment lacked the feature defined by the feature). There is nothing about features per se that requires binarity. In theory, features could have many values; there could be a scale for lip-rounding, for example, that went from [round] (completely spread lips), to [99round] (with very rounded lips). While this has been suggested for phonetics (see Ladefoged, 1993), few phonologists have found it useful (partly because the exact value of rounding in natural speech is highly variable from utterance to utterance).

There is a variation on binary (two-valued) features that has been commonly employed since the 1960s: single-valued features. These have been variously called "unary," "simplex," or "monovalent" features, but we adopt the term that is in most widespread usage today: *privative* features. A privative feature has only one value: [+F] (meaning that the segment has the characteristic defined by the feature). If a segment lacks the phonetic characteristic defined by the feature, then it is simply blank for that feature; there is no [-F] value. In a sense, a privative feature does have two values: present vs. absent. Privativeness is modeled after properties of objects in the real world. An object such as a car is a tangible thing when it exists. But the lack of a car is not represented in the real world via an object that is [-car]; the car is simply absent. Parking lots are filled with cars or spaces, never with [-car]'s. A privative feature is a mental object; when it is absent, it is not represented at all. Lamb (1966), Sanders (1974), and Rice and Avery (1995) treated all features as privative. However, this is not the dominant view.

The most common position within phonological theory is that some features are binary, but that others are privative. Most phonologists use privative features for the major places of articulation: [Labial], [Coronal], [Dorsal], and [Radical]. Many have also suggested that [round] and [voiced] are privative. In this book, we take a relatively conservative position: the major place features are privative, but all other features are binary—at least for the surface representations of speech sounds. As we will see in §3.11, our position is that all features are underlyingly privative, but are binary on the surface: they have only one value ([+F] or [-F]) in underlying representations, and the other value is filled in during the course of the derivation (or, in actual language production, during processing). For now, we deal with the surface representations, which have both values of all binary features (but of course only one value of privative features).

3.1.3. DISTINCTIVE AND ACTIVE FEATURES

All the features in a segment are not equally important. The features used in phonology are called *distinctive* features, because, ideally, the features only encode enough of the phonetic detail of the segment so that it can be distinguished from other segments. Distinguishing the segment from other segments can be interpreted in two very different ways.

First, we might reference the distinctiveness of segments to the set of segments that appear in human languages, as encoded in the International Phonetic Alphabet (Appendix A), for example. If a language has a simple voiced bilabial stop [b], we need to use the full set of features that are necessary to distinguish it from a voiced aspirated (breathy voiced) stop like [bʰ], so [b] would be represented as [-spread-glottis] ([-s.g.]).

Alternatively, we might reference the distinctiveness of segments just to the set of segments within the particular language. In that case, we need fewer features to show the contrasts between the segments. For example, Spanish has the voiceless stop [p] and the voiced stop [b], but lacks the aspirated stops *[bʰ] and *[pʰ]. For Spanish, if we were to characterize /b/ as [+voiced], without any mention of [-s.g.], we would not confuse /b/ with any other segment *within Spanish*. As a result, there is a possibility that [-s.g.] should not be included in underlying representations. It should instead be added late in the derivation, or possibly not at all; we could merely say that in Spanish, stops are phonetically unaspirated.

There would be only one reason to include the feature [-s.g.] in underlying representations in Spanish: if the feature was necessary to describe phonological patterns within the language (such as in alternations). This turns out not to be the case, and we simply leave this feature out of underlying representations.

When a feature plays a role within the phonology of a language, either by being necessary to allow us to distinguish between two segments in the language, or by playing some role in processes, we say that the feature is *active*.[1] If the feature plays no role, it is not active. Only active features are included in underlying representations.

In some cases, features might be active only for certain classes of segments. For example, obstruents can contrast on the feature [voiced], as with [t] and [d]. On the other hand, in most languages, sonorants are voiced, and they do not contrast with voiceless sonorants. Because they are predictably voiced, it has been proposed that the feature [+voiced] is not active for sonorants, and is therefore absent from underlying representations. In those few languages in which sonorants necessarily behave as voiced in phonological phenomena, the feature [voiced] must be active for sonorants, at least at the point in the derivation where those phenomena occur. We further assume that a feature may be active if it is used in perception; thus, a feature that never appears in the output of child speech can still be active, if it is active in adult speech. The activeness of features interacts with the notion of phonological underspecification that we address in §3.11.

Given the assumptions to this point, the (full) representation of the consonants and vowels of English can be as given in Tables 3.1 and 3.2. We list the inactive features here, but do not state any plus or minus values, because there is no guarantee that the features that are inactive in adult English will be inactive in the speech of children learning English. We include [ʔ] because some children may interpret it as a phoneme of English. We treat [h] and [ʔ] as [+sonorant] (see

---

[1] Some phonologists use the term *activated* instead. We avoid this term because it is used differently within connectionist theory (see §2.3.1.3).

TABLE 3.1. Fully specified consonant feature matrix for adult English

	p	t	tʃ	k	b	d	dʒ	g	f	θ	s	ʃ	v	ð	z	ʒ	m	n	ŋ	l	ɹ	w	j	h	ʔ
sonorant	−	−	−	−	−	−	−	−	−	−	−	−	−	−	−	−	+	+	+	+	+	+	+	+	+
consonantal	+	+	+	+	+	+	+	+	+	+	+	+	+	+	+	+	+	+	+	+	+	−	−	−	−
continuant	−	−	−	−	−	−	−	−	+	+	+	+	+	+	+	+	−	−	−	+	+	+	+	+	−
nasal[a]	−	−	−	−	−	−	−	−	−	−	−	−	−	−	−	−	+	+	+	−	−	−	−	−	−
lateral																				+					
tense																									
Laryngeal	√	√	√	√	√	√	√	√	√	√	√	√	√	√	√	√	√	√	√	√	√	√	√	√	√
voiced	−	−	−	−	+	+	+	+	−	−	−	−	+	+	+	+	+	+	+	+	+	+	+	−	−
spread-glottis	+/−	+/−	+/−	+/−					+	+	+	+												+	
constricted-glottis.	+/−	+/−	+/−	+/−																					+
Place	√	√	√	√	√	√	√	√	√	√	√	√	√	√	√	√	√	√	√	√	√	√	√		
Labial	√				√				√				√				√					√			
round																					+	+			
labiodental									+				+												
Coronal		√	√			√	√			√	√	√		√	√	√		√		√	√		√		
anterior		+	−			+	−			+	+	−		+	+	−		+		+	−		−		
distributed		−	+			−	+			+	−	+		+	−	+		−		−	+		+		
grooved[b]		−	+			−	+			−	+	+		−	+	+									
Dorsal				√				√											√			√	√		
back				+				+											+			+	−		
high				+				+											+			+	+		
low				−				−											−			−	−		

[a]We include [-nasal] as active because of the oral-nasal distinction.
[b][grooved] is included for obstruents only, where it is contrastive.

TABLE 3.2.   Fully Specified Vowel Feature Matrix for Adult English

	i	ɪ	e	ɛ	æ	u	ʊ	o	ɔ	ɨ	ə	ʌ	ɑ/a
sonorant	+	+	+	+	+	+	+	+	+	+	+	+	+
consonantal	–	–	–	–	–	–	–	–	–	–	–	–	–
continuant	+	+	+	+	+	+	+	+	+	+	+	+	+
nasal													
lateral													
tense	+	–	+	–	?	+	–	+	?	–	–	–	?
voiced	+	+	+	+	+	+	+	+	+	+	+	+	+
spread glottis													
constricted glottis													
Labial						√	√	√	√				
round						+	+	+	+				
labiodental													
Coronal	√	√	√	√	√								
anterior	–	–	–	–	–								
distributed													
grooved													
Dorsal	√	√	√	√	√	√	√	√	√	√	√	√	√
back	–	–	–	–	–	+	+	+	+	+	+	+	+
high	+	+	–	–	–	+	+	–	–	+	–	–	–
low	–	–	–	–	+	–	–	–	+/–	–	–	–	+

Appendix B and §5.5.3.1). We treat [l] as [+continuant] (see Appendix B). We treat English [ɹ] as a glide ([-consonantal]); see Kahn (1976) and Ladefoged (1993). Voiceless stops are given as [+/-s.g.] and [+/-c.g.], because they can appear allophonically as aspirated, unaspirated, or glottalized, in different environments. We give /ɔ/ as [+/-low] because it is sometimes [+low] (as in U.S. *dog* [dɔːg]) and sometimes [-low] (as in British *all* [ɔːl] or in the diphthong [ɔɪ] as in *boy*).

We treat /ɹ/ as [Labial]. This is reasonable, since [ɹ] is rounded in onsets (*red* [ɹɛd]) and when syllabic and stressed (*bird* [bɹ̩ːd]). However, /ɹ/ is also unrounded in codas after unrounded vowels (*fair* [fɛɹ]) and when syllabic and unstressed (*wicker* [wɪkɹ̩]). We believe that /ɹ/ is underlyingly rounded because it shows an affinity for rounding. It is rounded in codas after rounded vowels (*four* [fɔɹ]). Historically, /ɑ/ has become rounded when it comes between rounded /w/ and /ɹ/ (*swarm* /swɔɹm/); this assimilation may have been a way to supply the coda /ɹ/

with rounding. Rounding is deleted in codas after unrounded vowels and in un-stressed syllables; see Chapter 4 for further discussion.

We treat /l/ as underlyingly [Coronal]. However, there is a nonapical allophone of /l/ in codas and when syllabic, in words such as *milk* and *supple*. This allophone is not [Coronal], and may possibly not be [+consonantal]. We treat /l/ as under-lyingly nonvelarized; it becomes velarized in codas, when syllabic, and in onsets before [+back] vowels. In §5.5.1.5.3, we note that some children may take the phoneme to be underlyingly velarized /ɫ/, and develarize it in onsets before front vowels.

3.2. THE RELATIONSHIP BETWEEN FEATURES: PHONOLOGY WITH TIERS

In early generative phonology, as segments came to be viewed as groups of features, the prevailing view was that the features were unordered with respect to each other; segments were just a bundle of simultaneously occurring features. This is no longer held to be true. Features are integrated into a hierarchical struc-ture, such that there is one location for every feature and a feature can appear only in that location, but see below. We start by defining the basic notions of *tier* and *association lines*, and then address the structure of the segment in more detail.

Every feature is independent of every other feature; we refer to this property as *feature autonomy*. Further, as we look across the different segments in a word, the same feature in each segment can be found at the same location, so that all the tokens of that feature seem to create a line (or string) of their own. Each string is called a *tier*. We refer to each tier by using the name of the feature on that tier: the coronal tier, the continuant tier, the voicing tier, the sonorant tier, etc. The ap-proach to phonology in which different features appear on different tiers has been given many names. Goldsmith (1976), emphasizing that each feature constituted an autonomous chunk (or "segment") unto itself, called it *autosegmental* pho-nology. More recently, researchers have stressed that what is important is that there is not a single "line" of segments, but rather a large group of lines (strings), and have proposed the name *nonlinear phonology*. This is misleading, however, because the term implies that there are no lines of elements, and there are in fact many lines; the words "planar" or "multidimensional" would better express the intended meaning, but are not widely used. Recently, phonologists have begun to use the term *multilinear*. This expresses the nature of this approach better than the other terms, and we thus use the term multilinear phonology in this book.

It is not enough to have just the feature tiers. We also need to capture the notion of the segment: that features on different tiers occur at the same time. Simultane-ous occurrence of elements on different tiers is expressed via the *association line*: a link between elements on two tiers. Two elements are simultaneous if they are connected via an association line, or if they are linked to elements connected by an association line. For example, consider some tiers containing place features.

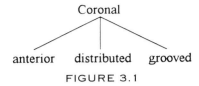

FIGURE 3.1

The features [anterior] and [Coronal] are simultaneous, and consequently are linked together. The same is true of [Coronal] and [distributed], and [Coronal] and [grooved]. However, there are no direct links between the subsidiary features [anterior], [distributed], and [grooved]. Because the subsidiary features are all simultaneous with [Coronal], all are also simultaneous with each other. In a moment, we will return to the issue of which features are linked together directly, and which are linked only indirectly through their mutual association with another feature.[2]

Just because elements on different tiers are independent of each other, there is no reason why they must appear in a simple one-to-one relationship with each other. The relationship can also be many-to-one. For example, both of the following situations are possible.

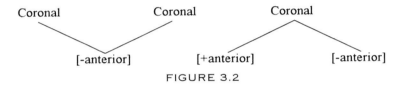

FIGURE 3.2

On the left, there are two different tokens of the feature [Coronal] in sequence; this arises when there are two coronal consonants in a row. There is a single feature [-anterior] that is linked to both instances of [Coronal], meaning that this feature is simultaneous with both consonants; both consonants are [-anterior], as in the sequence [ʃtʃ] in the word *question*.[3] On the right, we have a hypothetical

[2] The association line is just one of several ways of indicating that two elements occur at the same point in time. Another mechanism would be *indexing*. Each element could have a code associated with it that indicates the timing of that element relative to other elements. For example, all elements in the first segment could be indexed with the code "T1" (for "time 1"); all elements in the second segment could be indexed with the code "T2," and so on. Looking at the elements $[+\text{sonorant}]_{T1}$, $[+\text{voiced}]_{T1}$, and $[\text{Labial}]_{T2}$, we know that the first and second features occur at the same point in time, but the third feature occurs at a different point in time. Functionally, this is equivalent to using an association line. One difference is in the way one is inclined to think of association lines vs. indexes. An association line seems to be an element, and one is tempted to think of it as having an existence separate from the elements that it links together. Indexes, however, clearly have no independent existence, but are an annotation on the element. This difference is not a real one. Association lines do not have an independent existence; it is impossible to have an association line that is not linked to elements at both ends. We use association lines here, but note that indexing also can do the job.

[3] Note that the representation of this sequence of consonants is ambiguous, since we get an adequate phonetic description if there is one [-anterior] feature linked to both segments, or if there are two tokens of the feature [-anterior], each linked to a single segment. We address this ambiguity below, and note ways in which the two possibilities can be disambiguated.

situation in which the place of articulation changes during a single segment, starting as alveolar or dental and ending as palatoalveolar, for example. While this is possible, it is unlikely with place features.[4]

The main use for having a feature change its value during a segment has been for describing affricates. As discussed above, it has been proposed that affricates begin as stops and end as fricatives. This could be represented by having the segment dominate two tokens of the feature [continuant] (see §3.1.2):

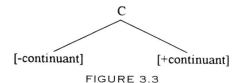

FIGURE 3.3

We address developmental data in later chapters for which such a representation is quite useful.

These representations entail something that has been stressed in phonetics for many years: it is impossible to slice speech into discrete segment-sized units. Hockett (1955) noted that segments overlap; he provided the following analogy: the segments of phonological theory are like Easter eggs, each discrete and with a unique pattern, that pass through a machine that smashes them, after which it is difficult to tell which bit of yolk, egg white, or shell came from which egg. Öhman (1966), Fowler (1980), and Browman and Goldstein (1986) emphasize the extent of phonetic coarticulation in speech, and note that coarticulation can extend over many segments. Long after phoneticians had rejected the notion that speech could be divided into a sequence of discrete segments, phonologists were still assuming discrete segments, suggesting that discreteness was a property of phonological representations, but not of phonetics. In multilinear phonology, however, it is frequently the case that one cannot divide representations into discrete segments, because individual features can extend over a sequence of two or more segments.

Because association lines encode the notion of simultaneity, there are constraints on the way that association lines can link elements together. The following constraint has been assumed since Goldsmith (1976):

Line Crossing Constraint: Association lines may not cross.

An example of crossing association lines would be the following.

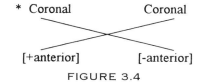

FIGURE 3.4

---

[4] In [tʃ] and [dʒ], place of articulation does not change during the affricate. Even though the stop portion of the affricate is represented with the symbols [t] or [d], the stop portion is a palatoalveolar, just like the fricative portion.

The first [Coronal] is attached to [-anterior], which is second on the anteriority tier. The second [Coronal] is linked to [+anterior], which is first on the anteriority tier. It was noted early on that such representations never occur in human languages, and so it was assumed that any such representation was ill formed, and could never arise.

Sagey (1988) pointed out that the Line Crossing Constraint is directly derivable from two facts: (a) that linear (left-to-right) order within a tier encodes temporal order (elements on the left precede elements on the right, in time) and (b) that association lines encode simultaneity. Consider four statements about the temporal relationship between the [Coronal] and [anterior] elements above.

1. The first [Coronal] precedes the second [Coronal] in time.
2. [+anterior] precedes [-anterior] in time.
3. The first [Coronal] and [-anterior] occur at the same point in time.
4. The second [Coronal] and [+anterior] occur at the same point in time.

From these statements, we can derive two others.

5. If the first [Coronal] occurs at the same time as [-anterior], and if the first [Coronal] precedes the second [Coronal], then [-anterior] also precedes the second [Coronal].
6. If [-anterior] precedes the second [Coronal], and if the second [Coronal] occurs at the same time as [+anterior], then [-anterior] precedes [+anterior].

But there is a problem here. By (2), we know that [+anterior] precedes [-anterior], but by (6), we know that [-anterior] precedes [+anterior]. We have a situation where a single element occurs both before and after another element, without being either simultaneous or discontinuous. In the real world, such a temporal relationship is impossible. The Line Crossing Constraint simply enforces constraints on time in the real world. It is not specifically language-related.

As we link together elements on different tiers, we are guided by a number of considerations.

1. There should be a consistent relationship between two elements, so that two tiers always link with each other in all segments, and never link directly to other tiers.[5]
2. There should be as few association lines as possible. It would become very complicated if every feature had a link directly to every other feature with which it was simultaneous.
3. Once we limit the number of association lines, we introduce a *dependency* relation between some features. Consider the following:

[5] A few phonologists (e.g., Piggott, 1992) have suggested that a given feature might appear in different locations in different languages. This position is not strongly supported as yet.

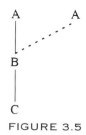

FIGURE 3.5

Suppose that we were to add a link between B and the second A. Automatically, C would become simultaneous with the second A, even though we did not overtly change the link between B and C. Similarly, if we were to delete B, C would no longer be linked, and it would also be deleted. By limiting the number of association lines between tiers, we introduce dependencies, whereby we predict that *groups* of features should behave as chunks, deleting together, etc. In essence, we derive a representation where a segment is made up of "subsegments" of different groups of features. This is a desirable result, because different groups of features tend to act as units relative to processes like deletion or assimilation.

We have reached a point where we can no longer focus just on representations. We must take a detour into the types of processes found in multilinear phonology. This is necessary, because groupings of features are motivated by processes: features that regularly are affected together in processes should be grouped together via association lines. In order to discuss the processes that motivate feature groupings, we must first discuss the nature of processes in general. We can then return to the question of feature groupings.

3.3. PROCESSES

In this section, we review the types of processes that are used in multilinear phonology. We prefer a purely constraint-based approach such as Optimality Theory (OT). However, purely constraint-based approaches are relatively difficult to start out with, conceptually. It is often easier, at first, to conceive of something in terms of processes that alter pronunciations, rather than in terms of the constraints that motivate those processes. We discuss in Chapter 4 how to reconceptualize those changes as due to constraints.

We begin by reviewing what is wrong with old-style linear rules, and then introduce the basics of multilinear rules. Throughout this chapter, our focus will still be largely on adult phonology, although we foreshadow phenomena of child phonology at a number of places. Indeed, we give particular examples of processes and constraints to facilitate the transfer to developmental phenomena.

3.3.1. RULES/PROCESSES IN
EARLY GENERATIVE PHONOLOGY

Within early generative phonology, rules were always of the form:

$$A \rightarrow B / C \underline{\hspace{1cm}} D$$

where A is the focus of the rule, B is what changes, and C and D are the elements in the surrounding environment. Rules of this form could change features, or insert or delete whole segments:

Rule A: [-consonantal] → [+nasal] / ____ [+nasal]
Rule B: V → Ø / ____ V
Rule C: Ø → e / # ____ CCC

Rule A changes the value of the feature [nasal] in vowels and glides to [+nasal] before a [+nasal] segment; if the focus of the rule is already [+nasal], the rule deletes the original value and makes it [+nasal] in any case, thus applying *vacuously*. Rule B deletes the first of two vowels in a sequence. Rule C inserts the vowel /e/ at the beginning of a word if that word starts with (at least) three consonants.

This way of stating rules allowed us to state most of the processes that we observe in human languages, but there were problems. The biggest problem was that there was no way to explain why certain processes are common across languages while others are not. A second problem was that changes to more than one segment could not be described.

For feature-changing rules like Rule A, there is no explanation for differences in frequency for various types of feature changes across languages. Rather than Rule A, which is relatively common and has the motivation of assimilation, we could imagine Rule A'.

Rule A':   [-consonantal] → [+s.g.] / ____ [+nasal]

In Rule A, vowels and glides become voiceless (aspirated) before nasals, a rule that, to our knowledge, occurs in no human language and has never been observed in phonological development. The formalism treats these two rules as parallel. They differ only in that the change part of Rule A contains a feature value that is present in the environment, while this is not the case in Rule A'. It was accidental in this theory that the same feature occurred in both parts of the rule. There was no special status for rules in which the two features were the same, versus rules in which the two features were different. Instead, we had to appeal to the circular notions of naturalness and markedness to explain what is common or uncommon across languages.

Second, there are changes involving more than one segment. A prototypical example is *compensatory lengthening* (addressed in more detail below), in which a segment is deleted, and a neighboring segment becomes long, as in this example from Choctaw (Nicklas, 1972).

$$/\text{tiw-li}/ \rightarrow [\text{tiwːi}]$$

In order to handle such changes, the theory was forced to do one of two things. First, two rules could be used:

Rule D: C → [+long] / _____ [+lateral]
Rule E: [+lateral] → Ø/ C: _____

Rule D makes any consonant long before /l/, and Rule E deletes /l/ after a long consonant. This works, but only by breaking what appears to be a single process down into two steps. Further, those two steps fail to capture the insight contained in the name "compensatory lengthening": that a segment becomes long to "compensate" the word for the lost segment, to make up for the deleted segment's duration. Rule D actually just says that consonants are long before /l/, and it is just an accident that /l/ is later deleted. Rule D occurs only in languages in which the /l/ is later deleted, suggesting that the two changes are integrally connected.

In order to capture compensatory lengthening as a single operation, we would have to use an entirely different formalism that is capable of changing multiple segments:

$$C \quad [+\text{lateral}] \quad \Rightarrow \quad C: \quad \emptyset$$

But this makes any number of undesirable processes possible, because we can change any number of segments in any way we want, including, as an extreme case, reordering sequences of segments:

$$[+\text{lateral}] \quad [+\text{syllabic}, +\text{low}, +\text{round}] \quad [+\text{continuant}] \Rightarrow 3\ 2\ 1$$

Sequences like /lɔf/, /lɔz/, and /lɔʃ/ would become [fɔl], [zɔl], and [ʃɔl], but this would not happen with any other vowel, not even low unrounded /ɑ/. We recognize this to be a crazy rule, but we can still state it easily. In early theory, there was no way to change more than one segment in a single operation, without opening the door to complicated processes that never occur in human language.

Linear rules (though they are still often employed in work on phonological development) have problems. For this reason, phonologists no longer write rules in this fashion. These defects provided some of the impetus behind developing multilinear phonology.

3.3.2. BASIC PROCESSES: SPREADING, DELINKING, DELETION, INSERTION

The types of processes that are used in multilinear phonology reflect the differences in worldview from linear phonology. Since features are independent elements, processes focus on features rather than segments. There are only two possible operations in multilinear phonology: addition and deletion. The material that is added or deleted can either be a phonological element (a feature, node, timing unit, etc.) or an association line. Given these two operations (insertion and deletion) and the two objects that these operations may be done on (elements and association lines), we have four different combinations (Archangeli & Pulleyblank, 1994):

1. Add an association line to an existing element *(spreading)*.
2. Delete an association line from an existing element *(delinking)*.
3. Insert an element that had not been there before and add an association line to it.
4. Delete an existing element (and its association lines).

Note that there is no possibility of changing an element that is already present into something else. In order to change, for example, [-nasal] into [+nasal], we must break it down into two operations: delete [-nasal], and insert (and link up) [+nasal]. One might think that this would cause problems and lead to complex analyses, given the extent to which feature-changing rules were used in early generative phonology. In actual practice, however, breaking down rules into components like this is advantageous. Rules that were feature-changing in earlier phonology now involve one of two situations: assimilations (the spreading of features) or replacement of a nondefault feature with a default feature (which is simple and automatic; see below and Chapter 4).

The operation that is most prototypically nonlinear in nature (and that could not be stated within linear theories) is the addition of association lines between two existing elements: spreading. The addition of the association line realigns two elements in time: two elements that do not occur at the same point in time in the underlying representation are realigned so that they occur at the same point in time on the surface. All assimilations are analyzed as spreading.

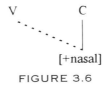

$$V \qquad C$$

[+nasal]

FIGURE 3.6

Although the formalism is very different from that of linear phonology, this is a formal rule within multilinear phonology. The solid lines denote existing association lines. The dashed line represents the addition of an association line; the dashing makes up the "change" part of the rule. This rule adds an association line between the feature [+nasal] in a consonant and spreads it to the preceding vowel; since the vowel thereby becomes simultaneous with the feature [+nasal], the vowel is now nasalized.

When elements spread, we need to consider the direction in which they spread. Spreading is leftward (or *right-to-left*; R-to-L) if the element is linked up so that it now begins earlier in time than it otherwise would have. Spreading is (*rightward left-to-right*; L-to-R) if the element ends later in time than it otherwise would have. In some processes, a feature might spread *bidirectionally*: both leftward and rightward. However, spreading is usually in just one direction.

Note that we did not mention the feature [-nasal] in the vowel, even though the vowel was presumably oral until this rule applied. That is because the feature [-nasal] is absent for vowels in underlying representations, and we consequently can ignore it. If the feature had been specified (present in underlying representation), we would have had to do an additional operation to delete it; if we were to spread [+nasal] from the consonant to the vowel without deleting [-nasal], we would have the following.

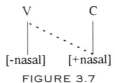

FIGURE 3.7

This would be interpreted phonetically as a vowel that changes from [-nasal] to [+nasal] in the middle. If in fact the entire vowel is nasalized, we would have to delete [-nasal]:

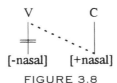

FIGURE 3.8

Notice that we did not actually remove the feature [-nasal]; we delinked it. This means that the feature is no longer attached to any Root node; it is now *floating*.[6] This is a problem because floating elements are not well formed (see Chapter 4): all elements must be linked. There is a reason for this. Association lines make explicit at what point in time an element occurs. Without an association line, we do not know when the element should be produced in the word, and that is impossible in the real world: elements must be produced at some point in time. Therefore, floating elements must be eliminated from the representations. There are three ways to do this:

1. Link the floating element to some other existing element.
2. Insert a new element to which the floating feature can attach.
3. Delete the floating element *(Stray Erasure)*.

There are two restrictions on linking up floating elements. First, they may not attach to anything that is already specified for that feature. In this instance, [-nasal] may not attach to the vowel, because the vowel is linked to [+nasal]. Second, a

---

[6] If indexes are used instead of association lines, a floating element would be one with a unique index, such that it does not co-occur with a higher element (such as a segment or a syllable).

feature may not reattach to the same element from which it was delinked. This also would prohibit [-nasal] from linking to the vowel. Thus, we either must insert another segment to which [-nasal] can attach, or attach [-nasal] to some existing segment. While both of these things can happen to floating features (even in phonological development, as we will see in later chapters), if no such process exists in the language, the floating element is deleted. Deletion is the most common process when an element is delinked in a rule.

Note that this complexity was caused by the assumption that [-nasal] was present in the vowel to begin with. If we instead assume that the vowel has no specification for [nasal], then we can simply spread [+nasal]. We do not need to worry about [-nasal], because it is not present.

This view of assimilation as spreading has eliminated one aspect of rules in the old linear framework: vacuous application is no longer possible. A linear rule of vowel nasalization would take the underlying sequence /ãn/, in which the vowel is already nasalized, and change the vowel's [+nasal] feature to [+nasal]; the rule applied, but there was no observable change in the representation of the vowel. With spreading, "vacuous" application *does* make a change:

FIGURE 3.9

Via spreading and delinking, we go from two independent (adjacent) [+nasal] tokens, each of which is linked to a single segment, to a single [+nasal] token that is linked to two (adjacent) segments. The underlying and surface representations would have the same surface pronunciation, but they are not identical representations. We note in later chapters the ramifications of this difference in representation for child phonology.

Spreading (with the concomitant delinking of any feature that was already there) is pervasive in human language, whether adult or child phonological systems. Unlike linear rules for assimilation, spreading captures the fact that the rules are assimilations. Rather than merely changing one feature in the environment of another (such that repetition of the feature accidentally arises), we adjust the temporal characteristics of the feature; we realign it, so that it appears earlier or later than it otherwise would have. The maximum similarity between two segments derives from making the two segments share the same element. Note that if we were to introduce some other feature, such as [+s.g.], into the vowel before a nasal, it would be an entirely unrelated operation; vowel nasalization involves adding an association line between elements in different segments, while adding

[+s.g.] would involve inserting a new element. Assimilations make up a unique class of processes, involving one particular formal operation: spreading.

3.3.3. A QUESTION OF LEVELS: DOMAIN OF A RULE OR PROCESS

We have been discussing processes as if they were *always* applicable to a particular sequence of elements whenever it arises. This is not the case. Processes can be restricted to specific morphosyntactic or phonological categories. The category that a process or constraint is restricted to is known as the *domain* of the rule or constraint. This could be viewed as a special instantiation of the environment portion of a rule, though it is one that is often awkward to state formally in a rule.

Morphological domains are common and in many ways intuitive. The bulk of phonological processes and constraints apply just to the word, for example. A particular sequence of phonemes, such as /st/, might be impossible within a word (in an adult language like Arabic or in the speech of some child). Nonetheless, [st] may arise freely at word boundaries, where the first word ends in /s/ and the second word begins with /t/. Some processes have entire phrases or even sentences as their domains, and therefore affect sequences of phonemes at word boundaries as well as within words. Other processes may be more restricted, being applicable only within morphemes. Processes are sometimes limited to particular morphosyntactic word classes, such as nouns or verbs.

Phonological domains refer to suprasegmental structure. The domain may be as low in the phonological hierarchy as part of a syllable (onset, coda, rime), or may be higher (a whole syllable, a foot, a prosodic word). For example, Seri does not tolerate two glottal stops within the same syllable. There are no syllables like *[.ʔaʔ.].[7] However, the constraint holds only within the syllable, and sequences of syllables like [.ʔa.ʔa.] are possible (Marlett & Stemberger, 1983). It is relatively common for a sequence to be allowed in one domain but not in another. In other cases, however, a sequence may be disallowed in all domains, but different processes may be used in different domains to eliminate the sequence. Some domains are weaker than others and more prone to restriction and processes; see §4.7.1.5, §6.1.12, and §6.2.5.3.

3.3.4. A QUESTION OF LEVELS: STRATA

In a different meaning of the word "level," it has been suggested that morphological and phonological rules need to be grouped together into two or more discrete subgroups, ordered one after the other. The theory of lexical phonology (Kiparsky, 1982, 1985; Mohanan, 1986; Kaisse & Shaw, 1985) refers to these levels as *strata*.

---

[7] We follow the International Phonetic Association (IPA) practice of placing periods at the edges of syllables.

Within each stratum, morphological and phonological rules are intermixed. The main characteristics of the strata are usually defined in terms of the morphological rules. Mohanan (1986) argues that English has five strata:

Stratum 1: irregular morphology
Stratum 2: regular derivational morphology
Stratum 3: compounding
Stratum 4: regular inflectional morphology
Postlexical stratum: anything crossing word-boundaries; most allophonic rules

The postlexical stratum is special: it follows the insertion of words into sentences; processes at that level may cross word boundaries. All earlier strata are "lexical," and occur before the word is inserted into the sentence; processes on these lexical strata cannot extend beyond the edge of the word, and may be restricted to certain types of words (such as those involving inflectional morphology).

The different strata are strictly ordered. All processes at Stratum 1 are completed before any processes at Stratum 2 are applied. All processes at Stratum 2 are completed before any processes at Stratum 3 are applied, and so on. This can have important consequences for the output of the phonological system. Often, a process that affects some sequence on an earlier stratum may have no effect on that same sequence if it is created on a later stratum.

On some strata, processes are restricted to apply only in "derived" environments, that is, environments that are created at that stratum, that were not present in earlier strata. An environment is derived if (a) it involves an affix or phonological structure added at that stratum, or (b) it involves phonological changes made via other processes or constraints at that stratum. However, only certain strata may have processes restricted in this way. We will not discuss the restrictions further here, because it seems unlikely that a language system with essentially no morphology (such as we find in the speech of very young children) will have processes restricted to derived environments in this way.

The actual number of strata that are needed is in dispute within phonological theory. Mohanan (1986) argued that English has five strata, but that other languages can have more or fewer. Kiparsky (1982) originally argued that English has four strata, but later Kiparsky (1985) argued that only three strata are needed. McCarthy and Prince (1993) are silent about the criteria to determine how many levels are needed and what is on each level. Goldsmith (1993), Lakoff (1993), and Wheeler and Touretzky (1993) argue that only two levels are needed (not counting the lexical representation).

Stemberger (1993b) points out that lexical phonology posits an organization of phonology that is similar to the two-lexicon approach for child phonology. One could begin with underlying representations that encode the child's perception of the adult pronunciation. At Stratum 1 a large number of processes apply, reducing the word to the child's basic pronunciation. At Stratum 2 (which is possibly postlexical), a small number of additional processes might occur.

3.3.5. MISCELLANEOUS

We have not discussed the concept of *ordering*: rules or processes may have to apply to words in a particular order. Rule ordering was an important issue in phonological theory in the 1960s and 1970s, but is less important today. Typologies were developed, laying out the types of rule orderings that were possible, and their consequences. We will not discuss this issue here. Current phonological theory holds that processes are not strictly ordered, except in ways that are derivable from other characteristics of the rules involved. In approaches that do not use processes, the constraints all have their effects simultaneously, not in sequence, although as we discussed in §2.1.4, constraint ranking and rule ordering have some overlap as concepts.

We have introduced several notational conventions used in the statement of rules (and in showing how forms change). We review them here, and add some others:

| | A solid line denotes an existing connection.
┊ | A dashed line denotes a new connection being created.
ǂ | A solid line with a double bar through it denotes an existing connection being deleted.
ẋ | A solid line with an 'x' through it denotes the lack of an existing connection.
Ⓔ | A "floating" (unassociated) element is encircled.

We have seen the first three of these in use. The fourth (an x-ed out association line) is used when it is crucial that no existing link appear in that position, but many phonologists believe that rules cannot refer to "blanks" in this way. The last convention is used primarily with elements that are written orthographically with only one letter.

Note that spreading is subject to the Line Crossing Constraint discussed above: association lines may not cross. A typical example of this occurs with tone in languages in which tone is distinctive; "H" is a high tone, "L" is a low tone.

FIGURE 3.10

The presence of any feature on any tier blocks the spread of a feature past it. We will see many instances of this in this book.

An element can be called "floating" for two reasons. First, it is floating if it is not linked upward to the next higher element. An example would be a feature [+nasal] that is not linked up into a segment. Second, it is floating if it is not linked downward to the next lower element. An example would be a segment that has no specification for the feature [nasal]. The term "floating" thus means "un-linked with reference to the level (higher or lower) that is being addressed."

An element can be deleted outright if necessary, but only by using a formal statement of rules that is reminiscent of nonlinear phonological rules. Suppose that obstruents become voiceless at the end of a syllable. We could simply delink the feature:

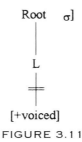

FIGURE 3.11

Unless the floating [+voiced] feature can link up to some other segment, it will be deleted automatically via Stray Erasure. However, if it would not work to delete it automatically, we could use the following notation:

FIGURE 3.12

The "zero" notation here means that we are deleting only the feature that is the focus of the rule; the rest of the segment remains intact. Once [+voiced] is deleted, the obstruent shows up as voiceless, either because a feature-filling rule supplies [-voiced], or because [voiced] is a privative feature and [-voiced] simply does not exist.

This type of rule notation is used for the deletion or insertion of elements. Note that it is not usable for spreading or delinking, because there is no way to indicate association lines in the focus or change part of the rule. This notation can be used for the insertion of features:

[ ] → [-nasal]   ([Ønasal] is realized as [-nasal].)

This rule fills in the feature value [-nasal] in any segment (vowel or consonant) that is not specified as [+nasal]. Such insertions always involve the addition of an association line, but this is usually taken to be automatic and is never shown. It should be stressed that any element in the representation can be involved in such rules, whether a feature, an organizing node, or one of the higher "prosodic" nodes to be discussed below: a timing unit, a syllable node, a foot node, or a prosodic word node. The term *prosodic* refers to elements that are outside of the segment and generally extend for a longer period of time than a single segment. If the environment for the insertion is a complex one involving syllable position, for example, the association line is drawn in solidly, even though technically it is being added. For example, if we were to aspirate a voiceless stop in syllable-initial position, we could state the rule as follows:

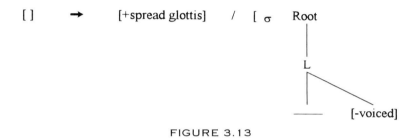

FIGURE 3.13

Thus, we can use two different formal ways to state rules in multilinear phonology. When we delete or insert elements, we use rules that resemble those used in nonlinear generative phonology. When we spread or delink, we simply give the necessary parts of the environment, and add or delete association lines. All rules in multilinear phonology are stated in one of these two ways.

3.4. FEATURE GEOMETRY

Now that we have reviewed the processes of multilinear phonology, we can return to the way that features are grouped together. The structural grouping of features within the segment is known as *feature geometry*. Feature geometry is motivated by both spreading and deletion.

3.4.1. SPREADING AND FEATURE GEOMETRY

The spreading of multiple features is one of the main arguments for feature geometry. There are some features that often assimilate together. There are others that never assimilate together. We could simply stipulate that it is "natural" for certain features to assimilate together, but this is not the best explanation. The preference is to predict the facts directly. Phonologists assume that most (or possibly all) assimilations involve the spread of a single element. When groups of features spread, it is because they are all dependent on the same higher element.

Place of articulation features often spread together. For example, in English it is common to find colloquial pronunciations like the following:

ten pounds	[tʰɛm pʰaʊndz]
ten kids	[tʰɛŋ kʰɪdz]
ten ducks	[tʰɛn dʌks]
ten chains	[tʰɛɲ ʧeɪnz]
ten things	[tʰɛŋ̟ θɪŋz]
ten flocks	[tʰɛɱ flɑːks]

We see that different pronunciations of the word *ten* have a final nasal with different places of articulation, assimilated from the following consonant. Note that every place feature changes, not just one or two.[8]

We can capture such "natural" groupings of features by linking them all together. If done in the right way, the deletion or spreading of one element can affect many features indirectly. Other, "unnatural," groupings of features are not linked together as a group, so that deleting them or adding association lines requires one operation for each feature; processes that require many operations should be uncommon. The groupings thus express directly which features act together and which do not. The presence of clear instances where several features spread as a group drives our ideas about these groupings. The lack of clear instances of features spreading as a group makes us uncomfortable positing that they are grouped.

We can express the dependencies in one of two ways. First, we can link one feature directly to another, as done above. Second, both features can be linked to some third element (a third feature, or some other type of element). Both alternatives have been taken in recent phonological theory. The features we have been dealing with are now called *content nodes*, because they have inherent phonetic content. The features that have dependent features (the privative articulator nodes) are *primary* content nodes.[9] Features that themselves never have dependent features are *secondary* content nodes, also known as *terminal features*. The other nodes in the geometry have no phonetic content, and exist for the sole purpose of organizing features into groups; they are *organizing* nodes.

Consider the example of nasal place assimilation in English. All place features are dependent on one organizing node: the Place node. The assimilation can be analyzed as the spreading of the Place node, with the delinking of the /n/'s original Place node.

---

[8] There is some indication that there is a very weak coronal articulation in this /n/, with a small constriction that does not even approach contact with the alveolar ridge (Browman & Goldstein, 1986). What is of greatest importance here is the spread of the place features from the following consonant, which is beyond question.

[9] The feature [sonorant] is viewed as a primary content node by some researchers, for example, Rice and Avery (1989).

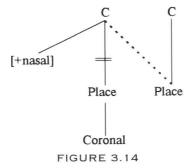

FIGURE 3.14

This rule states that a coronal nasal consonant loses its Place node before any consonant, and that the Place node of that following consonant spreads leftward to the nasal. Note that all features that are dependent on the organizing node are "dragged along" when the organizing node spreads.

It has often been observed that such assimilation is generally between adjacent consonants (e.g., Archangeli & Pulleyblank, 1987). When there is a vowel between the nasal and the consonant, this spreading is not possible, since association lines would cross with the Place node of the vowel:

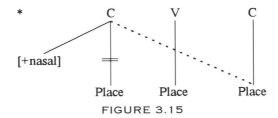

FIGURE 3.15

Many researchers have suggested that this explains why consonants rarely assimilate the place of articulation of distant consonants in adult grammars; the Place node cannot spread, because the vowel's Place node prevents spreading.

There are other natural groupings of features. All the laryngeal features of a segment can spread together: in classical Greek, sequences like /btʰ/ show up as [pʰtʰ]. This is evidence that all laryngeal features are linked to an organizing node: the Laryngeal node. It is also clear that all of the features in a segment may spread together. A sequence of two consonants can be converted into a single long consonant. A common example in child language is *donkey* [dakːi]. All features are grouped together under a single organizing node: the Root node.

Phonologists who subscribe to this theory agree on the existence of these three organizing nodes: Root, Laryngeal, Place. The Place node groups together place of articulation features. The Laryngeal node groups together features that represent the state of the larynx. The Root node groups together all the features of the segment, and is involved in any process that involves whole segments.[10] Clements (1985) tentatively proposed that all the manner features should be grouped under a Manner node. He also argued that the Manner node and the Place node should be further grouped together under the SupraLaryngeal node. However, linguists have found little evidence that all manner features spread together, to the exclusion of voicing and place features (as the Manner node predicts), or that all manner and place features spread together to the exclusion of voicing (as the SupraLaryngeal node predicts). Technically, there is no direct evidence against the Manner and SupraLaryngeal nodes: it is not necessarily the case that something *has* to spread just because it exists. However, the lack of spreading means that there is little use for these nodes. Because they have not turned out to be useful, the SupraLaryngeal node and the Manner node have been eliminated from the feature geometry.[11] Beyond these points, there is little agreement as to the exact details of the feature geometry. The following is a common view of feature geometry in recent theory:

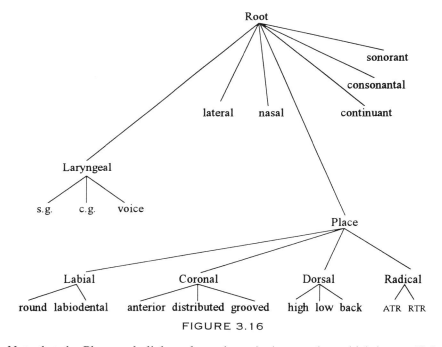

FIGURE 3.16

Note that the Place node links only to the articulator nodes, which in turn link only to the subsidiary features that are defined for each articulator, as presented in

---

[10] The name is semantically similar to the term *Root Directory* used with computers. The root directory is the highest directory, from which all subdirectories depend (either directly, or mediated via another subdirectory).

[11] We return to this issue briefly in Chapter 5, with some relevant data from phonological development.

Appendix B. The Laryngeal node links directly to each laryngeal feature, with no further substructure. At the top is the Root node, linking together all features, either directly or indirectly. All the manner features are on separate tiers that link directly to the Root node, with no further substructure.[12]

One class of segments lacks a Place node: the glottals [h] and [ʔ]. These segments often behave as if they have no place features. This is reasonable phonetically, since glottals involve the larynx (just as all segments do), but what is going on above the larynx does not seem to be important: the supralaryngeal vocal tract takes on whatever configuration is needed for surrounding segments. For example, /h/ is a voiceless version of the following vowel: /hɪt/ [ɪ̥ɪt], /hæt/ [æ̥æːt], /huːt/ [u̥uːt], /hɑt/ [ɑ̥ɑːt]. The lack of a Place node in glottals makes certain types of processes possible near glottals that would not be possible near other consonants. In some languages, vowels assimilate completely to each other if they have contiguous Root nodes, but no such total assimilation takes place if consonants separate the two vowels. This can be interpreted as the spreading of Place nodes. Consonants block the spread because their Place nodes intervene. However, glottal consonants usually allow the total assimilation to take place. Steriade (1987) uses this to argue that glottals have no Place nodes; if they had Place nodes, we would expect glottals to block total vowel assimilation, but they do not.

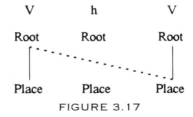

FIGURE 3.17

The Place node also spreads from consonants and vowels to the glottals /h/ and /ʔ/; when consonantal Place spreads, we get phenomena like Toba Batak /iphɑ/ being realized as [ipːhɑ]; when vowel Place spreads, we get [h] as a voiceless version of the following vowel, as in /hɑt/ [ɑ̥ɑːt] (Goldsmith, 1976):

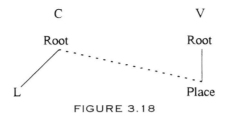

FIGURE 3.18

[12] Note that [grooved] and [distributed] are treated as place features rather than as manner features. Because they are relevant just for [Coronal] consonants, providing further detail about tongue shape, in the same way that [round] and [labiodental] provide further detail about lip shape, this is phonetically reasonable. In contrast, a manner feature such as [continuant] refers to airflow independent of any place of articulation. It is possible that [lateral] could also be interpreted as further information

Manner features are still unclear. Avery and Rice (1989) have proposed that the features [nasal] and [lateral] should be dependent on the feature [sonorant] (which they rename the "Spontaneous Voicing" or "SV" node):

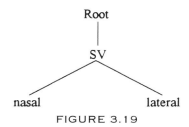

FIGURE 3.19

They base this proposal on several facts. One fact involves the spreading of the features [+nasal] and [+lateral] onto stops, which then become [+sonorant]; for example, /bn/ becomes [mn]. Such assimilations are often thought of as the assimilation of nasality, but more than just [+nasal] changes; the underlying stop is an obstruent, but the surface nasal is a sonorant. This could be evidence that the features [sonorant,nasal,lateral] make up a grouping in the feature geometry. Given that [nasal] and [lateral] are dependents of [sonorant], we further predict that [sonorant] cannot spread by itself: the dependent features [nasal] and [lateral] must spread with it. McCarthy (1988) had previously observed that processes rarely seem to affect the features [sonorant] and [consonantal] by themselves, and suggested that these features may not be on separate tiers of their own. He proposed that [sonorant] and [consonantal] are properties of the Root node, rather than independent elements. However, Rice and Avery's SV node (=[sonorant]) also explains this fact. Kaisse (1992) argued that there are processes in which [consonantal] is involved, and thus [consonantal] is on a separate tier. We accept the point of view that both [sonorant] and [consonantal] are on separate tiers under the Root node. We reject the hypothesis that [nasal] and [lateral] are dependents of [sonorant], but we believe that the final word is not yet in (see §5.5.3.1).

3.4.2. DELETION AND FEATURE GEOMETRY

Deletion is also used to argue for feature geometry. Consider the deletion of a segment. If features were not grouped into segments, we would have to delete each feature independently. We predict that such a complex process should not be common in human languages. In contrast, if all features are dominated by a Root node, we can achieve deletion of every feature in a segment simply by deleting the Root node. We predict (correctly) that such a simple process should be common.

Deletion provides evidence for several organizing nodes. As just noted, there

---

about tongue shape and should also be a dependent of [Coronal]. We feel that it is more useful for phonological patterns to assume that [lateral] links to the Root node, but for most purposes it would work as well if [lateral] linked to [Coronal].

is evidence for the Root node. There is evidence that the Laryngeal node might be delinked as a unit, since in some languages (Greek, Sanskrit, Cambodian) all laryngeal features are deleted in coda position. The Place node commonly deletes in a process known as *Debuccalization*, whereby true consonants become the glottals [h] or [ʔ]. This can be accomplished by the delinking of the Place node:

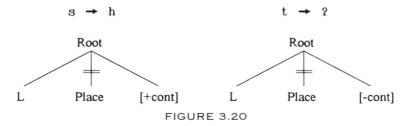

FIGURE 3.20

Debuccalization results in a consonant with no Place node: a glottal. The glottal [h] tends to result from voiceless fricatives, either because they are redundantly [+spread-glottis] or because they are [+continuant]. The glottal [h] also tends to result from aspirated stops, since they are [+s.g.]. From unaspirated stops, which are neither [+continuant] nor [+s.g.], the glottal [ʔ] tends to result. There is evidence from deletion for the organizing nodes Root, Laryngeal, and Place. There is no solid evidence for any other putative organizing nodes.

3.4.3. THE PROBLEM OF CONSONANTS VERSUS VOWELS

The place features of consonants and vowels seem to be insulated from each other in some way: consonants can be invisible to vowels, and vowels can be invisible to consonants. Unfortunately, the data are complicated. A number of different proposals can handle part of the observed data, and it is unclear whether any one proposal fully accounts for all the data. This area is the least settled area of feature geometry. We cannot do this topic justice in this chapter. Instead, we merely lay out two options, and express our preference. In later chapters, we discuss which options are better at accounting for phenomena from phonological development.

The basic facts that must be accounted for are the following:

1. Two vowels can interact (assimilate or dissimilate), ignoring the consonants between them.
2. Two consonants can interact, ignoring the vowels between them.
3. Two vowels can interact, but the interaction can be blocked if they are separated by (a) any consonant, or (b) a particular type of consonant.
4. Two consonants can interact, but the interaction can be blocked if they are separated by (a) any vowel, or (b) a particular type of vowel.
5. Vowels can interact with consonants.
6. Consonants can interact with vowels.

We find several conflicting patterns. Sometimes consonants and vowels are invisible to each other, and sometimes they are not. Trying to account for both the invisibility *and* the lack of invisibility has proven to be a difficult problem.

One way to achieve invisibility is to assume that consonants and vowels are on different *planes* in the representation (McCarthy, 1981; 1989). This would involve putting the Root nodes of consonants on a different tier than the Root nodes of vowels:

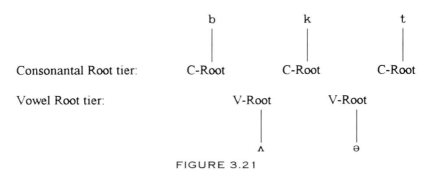

FIGURE 3.21

The Root nodes of consonants, and all features under them, would be on a different plane than the Root nodes (and all features) of vowels; we encode this by differentiating the Root nodes into C-Root and V-Root. As a result, there is a sense in which any two consecutive consonants are next to each other, even when a vowel "separates" them. Similarly, any two consecutive vowels are next to each other, even when "separated" by a consonant. The order of consonants is determined by the order of the Root nodes on the C-Root tier. The order of the vowels is determined by the order of the Root nodes on the V-Root tier. However, the order of consonants relative to vowels is not determined by the order of the Root nodes. Whether a given consonant is before or after a given vowel must be determined in some other way. We discuss how this is done in §3.6. For child phonology (§7.3.4), we find it very useful to put consonants and vowels on different planes. There is a problem, however, in that it is difficult to account for how consonants and vowels assimilate to each other, or for instances in which interactions between vowels are blocked by the presence of (particular types of) consonants.

McCarthy (1989) argues that such segregation of consonants and vowels is only possible if the order of the consonants and vowels is predictable in the language. This holds true in only two situations. First, the morphology could determine the order of the consonants and vowels (as in Semitic languages). Second, the syllable structure could be so simple that the order of the consonants relative to the vowels would be predictable (for example, if every syllable is CV, with a single consonant in the onset followed by a single short vowel). We believe, however, that such segregation may be true for all human languages (see §3.4.3.1).

Given two planes, it must be determined what characteristic causes a segment to be on a particular plane. It is clear that true consonants ([+consonantal] segments: liquids, nasals, and obstruents) should be on the C-plane. All syllabic vow-els, in contrast, should be on the V-plane. We believe that glottals ([h] and [ʔ]) should be on the C-plane, because they pattern with consonants. Glides ([w] and [j]) are unclear to us. If [syllabic] is the relevant feature, then glides should be on the C-plane. But glides often pattern with vowels, which suggests that they should be on the V-plane. It is possible that it might be variable across languages (adult or child) which plane glides are on; see Stemberger (1993a) for some relevant discussion. We leave the question of glides unsettled, but generally assume that they have V-Place, not C-Place.

The existence of the two planes has ramifications for the feature [consonantal]. In most respects, all elements on the C-plane can be viewed as a fusion of a feature such as [Labial] or [+sonorant] with the feature [+consonantal]. All elements on the V-plane can be viewed as a fusion of a feature such as [Labial] or [+sonorant] with the feature [-consonantal]. Why, then, would the feature [consonantal] be needed independently? Cho and Inkelas (1995) argue that [consonantal] can be dispensed with, on theoretical grounds, and that no empirical evidence prevents us from doing that. The sole sort of data that would prevent us from doing so would be evidence for the glottals /h/ and /ʔ/ patterning with vowels and glides; this would implicate [-consonantal]. Cho and Inkelas claim that there are no clear examples of this sort known at the moment. We retain the feature [consonantal] here, but note that it may not exist as an independent feature.

An alternative way to achieve invisibility is to assume that consonants and vowels have different representations just for place features. In this approach, the Root nodes of consonants and vowels lie within a single plane. Consonants and vowels both have Place nodes, which are also on a single plane. However, there are different tiers for consonant and vowel place information. One straightforward way to do this is to assume that the Place node dominates one subnode for con-sonantal place (C-Place) and one subnode for vowel place (V-Place).

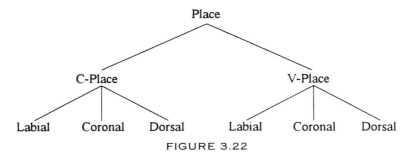

FIGURE 3.22

This was suggested as a possibility by Clements (1985) and followed up by Cle-ments (1989), McCarthy (1991), and Stemberger (1993a). Although we use the same label "Labial" for both consonant and vowel place features, note that there are two distinct Labial tiers: one under the C-Place node, and one under the V-Place node. There are many variants of this approach. Some lack a C-Place node; the Place node dominates consonant articulator nodes and the V-Place node. In some approaches, vowels are assumed not to have articulator nodes, but only the features [back], [high], [low], and [round]. But all variants have in common that consonant place features are on different tiers than vowel place features. This approach has difficulty with two facts: consonants and vowels can assimilate to each other, and interactions between vowels can be blocked by intervening consonants.

Various means have been introduced to account for the lack of invisibility. Here we discuss just the way that we find most convincing: separate planes for consonants and vowels. In later chapters addressing data from child phonology, we address additional alternatives.

Assimilation between consonants and vowels can be handled if we allow *transplanar* spreading. A [Labial] node, whether consonantal or vocalic, can spread to any Place node, whether consonantal or vocalic. For example, consider the syllable /do/ being pronounced [bo] (as sometimes happens in phonological development; see §7.3.4.2):[13]

FIGURE 3.23

In order for this to be possible, a single type of element, [Labial], must be able to attach to two different places in the geometry: the C-Place node, or the V-Place node. Since this element can attach to either type of node, it should be able to spread to either type of node, without regard for its original place of attachment. However, there is a tendency for an articulator node to spread to the same type of node to which it originally was attached. Thus, vocalic [Labial] tends to spread to vowels (not consonants), and consonantal [Labial] tends to spread to consonants (not vowels).

Note also that the whole V-Place node can spread to a consonant:

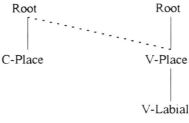

FIGURE 3.24

---

[13] We ignore here the fact that the consonant is a coronal. As discussed below, we believe that /d/ has no specification for place of articulation in the underlying representation. Alternatively, we could make the rule more complex, so that it deletes an underlying [Coronal] node.

Here, [Labial] remains a vocalic articulation, and is therefore phonetically realized as lip rounding. Rounded dorsals ([kʷ]), coronals ([tʷ]), and labials ([pʷ]) result. Similarly, spreading a V-Place node that contains [Dorsal] results in a velarized consonant (like [ɫ]), and spreading V-Place that contains [Coronal] results in a palatalized consonant ([pʲ]).

This view of assimilation can account for the transparency of intervening segments. If a [V-Labial] node spreads to a preceding V-Place node, then an intervening labial consonant does not block the spread; the consonantal [C-Labial] node is on a different tier.

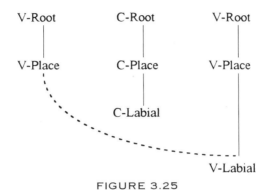

FIGURE 3.25

Association lines do not cross. Thus, we account for transparency.

When an intervening labial consonant blocks the spread of [Labial] from vowel to vowel, however, the situation is more confusing. There is one way to analyze this in which a line-crossing violation would arise. Suppose that the [Labial] can spread only to the preceding *segment*; in order to spread to the preceding vowel, [Labial] must first attach to any intervening consonant, attaching to whatever place subnode is present (C-Place or V-Place). This is possible with an intervening /k/:

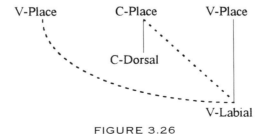

FIGURE 3.26

[Labial] and [Dorsal] both occur in the same segment, which is quite common (e.g., in [u]); we have, for example, /iku/ pronounced [ukʷu]. Although the /k/ may not be transcribed as rounded, it probably is; in English, all consonants that lie between two rounded vowels are as rounded as the vowels (as in *cocoa*).[14] This does not happen with intervening /p/ for an interesting reason. In order for [V-Labial] to spread to /p/, the resulting [pʷ] must be specified for [Labial] twice: one [C-Labial] and one [V-Labial]. Ordinarily, no segment has two tokens of the same feature with the same value; for example, /i/ is not *[+high, +high]. In order for a labial consonant to participate in the spreading of [V-Labial], this constraint must be violated. In at least some languages, no segment may be specified twice for [Labial], even if one is [C-Labial] and the other is [V-Labial]. It is not the crossing of association lines that causes the lack of transparency, but the inability of the intervening consonant to participate in the assimilation.

We are less certain about the invisibility of a consonant to dissimilation between vowels. Suppose that the first of two rounded vowels becomes unrounded, so that /u . . . u/ becomes [i . . . u]. Can an intervening labial consonant block the dissimilation, when an intervening dorsal consonant allows the dissimilation? Can we define the domain of the dissimilation such that /uku/ becomes [iku], but /upu/ remains [upu]? We are unsure of how to do that. However, we are also unsure whether any such data actually occurs in any language.[15]

Dissimilation between a consonant and a vowel needs a further elaboration of the theory. In some languages (e.g., Chinese: Yip 1988), rounded vowels may not be adjacent to a labial consonant.[16] If [C-Labial] and [V-Labial] are on different tiers, this is not a simple Obligatory Contour Principle (OCP) effect: the OCP usually prevents repetition of an element on a particular tier (see §4.7.2.1). We must assume here that the OCP can hold in a different way: there may not be two separate tokens of [Labial] under adjacent Place nodes. This characterization of the OCP effect does not require that the two tokens of [Labial] be on the same tier. Thus, consonantal place features can cause dissimilation of vocalic place features, and vice versa.

We have accounted for the six facts that we listed above. We relist them here, along with our explanation.

1. Two vowels can interact (assimilate or dissimilate), ignoring the consonants between them.
   Explanation: Only features under the V-Place node are involved.
2. Two consonants can interact, ignoring the vowels between them.
   Explanation: Only features under the C-Place node are involved.

---

[14] Ni Chiósann and Padgett (1993) express skepticism that the intervening consonants are rounded, but they have no relevant data.

[15] It should be noted that data of this sort could be accounted for in a different way. In /upu/, each segment has a [Labial] node. The OCP can motivate the fusion of the three [Labial] nodes into a single [Labial] node that is linked to all three segments. Dissimilation is no longer possible, since there is only one [Labial] node present; [upʷu] results. With /uku/, the /k/ does not have a [Labial] node. We cannot fuse the two [Labial] nodes of the vowels without either (a) having [Labial] linked to the first and third segments, but not to the middle segment, or (b) spreading the [Labial] to the intervening /k/. If neither option is allowed, then fusion will not take place. Instead, dissimilation occurs, with the first [Labial] node deleted; /uku/ is realized as [iku].

[16] The facts of Chinese are actually more complicated than this. See Yip (1988) for details.

3. Two vowels can interact, but the interaction can be blocked if they are separated by (a) any consonant, or (b) a particular type of consonant.
   Explanation: The intervening consonant must participate in the assimilation. If no consonant may be specified for V-Place, all intervening consonants block assimilation. If particular C-Place and V-Place features may not be combined, then particular intervening consonants block assimilation.
4. Two consonants can interact, but the interaction can be blocked if they are separated by (a) any vowel, or (b) a particular type of vowel.
   Explanation: The intervening vowel must participate in the assimilation. If no vowel may be specified for C-Place, all intervening vowels block assimilation. If particular C-Place and V-Place features may not be combined, then particular intervening vowels block assimilation.
5. Vowels can interact with consonants.
   Explanation: For assimilation, [V-Labial] spreads to the consonant's C-Place node. For dissimilation, the OCP is defined with reference to adjacent Place nodes, not in terms of V-Place.
6. Consonants can interact with vowels.
   Explanation: For assimilation, [C-Labial] spreads to the vowel's V-Place node. For dissimilation, the OCP is defined with reference to adjacent Place nodes, not in terms of C-Place.

This analysis of consonants and vowels works essentially the same way whether consonants and vowels have their Root nodes on separate planes, or whether there is a distinction between V-Place and C-Place nodes.

We emphasize that the data are complex and diverse, and that there is little agreement in the phonology literature. The reader will encounter many other ways to handle the data. We will not discuss other alternatives in this book, except where they are relevant for acquisition data.

3.4.3.1. Phonetic Justification for Separate Planes

It may seem odd to posit that consonants and vowels are on separate planes. We perceive the consonants and vowels as occurring in a fixed order relative to each other, and it is natural to think of speech as a stream of segments: a single line of root nodes. However, phoneticians have long posited a separation of consonants and vowels of this sort. McCarthy (1989) did not cite that literature as support for his ideas, but it is difficult to ignore the parallels between the proposals.

Research during the past three decades has shown that the linear and sequential view of consonants versus vowels is not supported by observation. In an acoustic study of Swedish, Öhman (1966) discovered a phenomenon known as *vowel-to-vowel coarticulation*. He compared nonsense words with the same initial vowel and following consonant, but with different final vowels, such as /aba/ vs. /abi/ vs. /abu/. The linear view of consonants and vowels predicts that the three words should diverge acoustically at the end of the medial /b/. Öhman discovered that the three words actually diverge just *before* the /b/. The transitions from the /a/ into the /b/ are different for all three words, because the transitions are changing partly in the direction of the acoustic formants of the final vowel. The only way to explain this divergence is to assume that the change from the first vowel to the second occurs simultaneously with the consonant, and that the consonant is *superimposed* on the vowels, rather than occurring between the two vowels. Öhman proposed that there are two separate output channels in the motor system, one for vowels and one for consonants, executed in parallel. The changeover from the /a/ articulation to the following vowel ignores the consonant; it is the same regardless of the particular consonant (or even if there is no consonant at all). Instrumental work in articulatory phonetics (e.g., Gay, 1977) has confirmed this proposal many times over. Fowler (1980) built a detailed theory of articulation out of this concept, with the idea that vowels are continuous and consonants are superimposed on top of them. She envisions two channels, in which vowels are of long duration, and the superimposed consonants take up some of the vowels' duration. Vowels are adjacent in the vowel channel. Consonants are adjacent in the consonant channel.

On the basis of these phonetic models, it is actually possible to consider it an odd proposal that consonants and vowels are on the *same* plane. A single-plane analysis is a complex one. In the phonological system, the consonants and vowels are on a single plane, but they must be split apart into two distinct channels in the phonetic system. In languages such as Arabic, which, McCarthy (1981) argues, initially have consonants and vowels on separate planes, it is even more complex: consonants and vowels start out on different planes, are merged into a single plane within the phonology, and finally are split back apart into two channels in the phonetic system. In contrast, if we assume that consonants and vowels are on separate planes in all languages, there is no need to split them apart in the phonetic system. Any model that requires consonants and vowels to be on a single plane is more complex, and this requires additional justification.

We take these phonetic models as reasonable justification for assuming that consonants and vowels are on separate planes. Assuming separate planes is also useful for accounting for phonological patterns. In later chapters where we address data from child phonology, we rely on this C-V separation into two planes.

3.5. ADJACENCY

An additional concept that is of some importance is the concept of *adjacency*, which plays a large role both in the statement of processes and in the motivation for certain types of (dissimilatory) processes.

Two elements are adjacent if

1. they are on the same tier, and
2. they are "next to" each other in some sense.

Given (1), it makes sense to ask whether two instances of [+voiced] are adjacent, because they are on the same tier. It makes no sense to ask whether an instance of [+voiced] is adjacent to an instance of [Coronal]; for this question to make sense, we have to rephrase it in terms of elements on a single tier, such as whether a Root node dominating [+voiced] is adjacent to a Root node dominating [Coronal]. The part of the definition of adjacency in (2) is vague, since we must define what we mean by "next to," and there are many different ways that this might be done:

Two elements on the same tier are "next to" each other, if

1. there is nothing between them on that tier;
2. there is nothing between the elements on the next higher tier to which the elements link;
3. there is nothing between the elements on the tier above the one to which the two elements are associated (through the intermediate tier);
4. there is nothing between the two Root nodes which dominate the two elements; and
5. there is nothing between the two syllable nodes which dominate the two elements.

These five ways to define adjacency are not exhaustive. We could ask the same question about any two tiers that dominate the elements in question.

It seems that a single definition of adjacency is impossible; more than one "level" of adjacency is important. Phonologists have sought to limit the number of levels, however. Archangeli and Pulleyblank (1987) argued that there are only two important levels of adjacency:

1. *Minimal* adjacency: Looking one tier up from the two elements, there is nothing between the elements on that tier to which the two elements attach.
2. *Maximal* adjacency: Looking up to the highest level in the representations that has an element that preserves some phonetic information about individual segments, there is nothing between the elements that dominates the two elements in question.
   Consonants: The tier for maximal adjacency is the timing unit tier.
   Vowels: The tier for maximal adjacency is the syllable tier (since syllables presuppose vowels).

Consider place features for the consonants in the word *shoddy*:

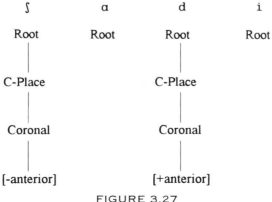

FIGURE 3.27

By minimal adjacency, the feature [-anterior] of /ʃ/ and the feature [+anterior] of /d/ are adjacent because, when we look at the next highest tier ([Coronal]), there is nothing between those two [Coronal] nodes. By maximal adjacency, in contrast, the two [anterior] features are not adjacent, because their Root nodes are separated by other Root nodes. In contrast, the two vowels /ɑ/ and /i/ are adjacent by maximal adjacency, because they are in adjacent syllables.

The usefulness of two different notions of adjacency will perhaps be clearer given an analogy with objects in the world. Consider a parking lot in which some spaces are filled with cars, but some are empty. If two cars are in adjacent spaces, the cars are clearly adjacent for all purposes: it is impossible to put another car between them, and "assimilation" (banging the other car with a door) treats them as adjacent. If two cars are separated by an empty space, however, they are not adjacent for some purposes: another car can be placed between them, and they are too far apart for a door to bang the other car. However, an object thrown from one car may go through the empty space and hit the other car, so the two cars are adjacent for that purpose. Whether we want to consider two cars separated by an empty space to be adjacent depends on our purpose. But two cars in adjacent spaces are adjacent for all purposes. Similarly, adjacency in phonology depends on the purpose.

Odden (1994) argues that there are three levels of adjacency (though we use our own terms for the levels here):

Tier adjacency:	there is nothing between the two elements on the tier where they are situated.
Root adjacency:	there is nothing between the two Root nodes that dominate the two elements.
Syllable adjacency:	there is nothing between the two elements on the tier that they are on, *and* they are in adjacent syllables.

In our judgment, these three levels of adjacency work well. For all three levels, two elements are adjacent only if they are on the same tier and have nothing between them on that tier. Tier adjacency consists just of those two conditions. The other two levels add additional conditions: either that the two elements are in adjacent segments (Root adjacency) or that they are in adjacent syllables (syllable adjacency). The three levels of adjacency differ in terms of how limited a sequence of segments and syllables is allowed: tier adjacency allows the two elements to be separated by unlimited numbers of segments and syllables; syllable adjacency allows no intervening syllables but does allow intervening segments; and Root adjacency allows no intervening segments.

Our decision to place consonants and vowels on separate planes requires us to add one additional type of adjacency (timing unit adjacency). We have yet to discuss how to specify the order of consonants relative to vowels, and thus how to determine which consonants are next to which vowels. We turn to that issue now.

3.6. TIMING UNITS

The Root node unites all the features of a segment into one group, but this is not entirely sufficient to handle all instances in which the features of a segment act as a unit. It is necessary to distinguish between the phonetic content of the segment and an element that simply indicates that a segment is present. We refer to these additional elements as *timing units*. There are several competing proposals about the exact details of these timing units and whether all segments have them, or only a subset of segments. In this section, we lay out four proposals and explain our practice in the later chapters of this book.

Timing units can be thought of in several ways. First, they are "enablers," which allow the phonetic content of the segment to be expressed. Second, they commit some amount of real time during speech production to the realization of the segments with which they are associated. Third, like all phonological elements, they are independent of the segments to which they are attached. This has several consequences. (a) There can be more timing units than segments. (b) There can be more segments than timing units. (c) A segment can be deleted without affecting the associated timing unit, leaving that timing unit free to link to some other segment (compensatory lengthening). (d) Morphological affixes can in principle add timing units to the word without adding any segments.

The earliest proposal for timing units was made by McCarthy (1979, 1981). He assumed that the timing unit encoded not only the presence of a segment but also whether it was [+syllabic] (C) or [-syllabic] (V). The word *dip* is an example of a word with one timing unit for every segment:

FIGURE 3.28

When two timing units are linked to a single segment, that segment takes up two consecutive units of time. As a result, the segment is long. There is some argument about whether long vowels have two syllabic timing units (VV), or whether the second timing unit is a nonsyllabic one (VC); we address this issue further below. The word *deep* is an example of a word in which the vowel has two timing units:

FIGURE 3.29

The long vowels of "standard" English are [iː] and [uː], and arguably [æː], [ɑː], and [ɔː] (since the low vowels are phonetically the longest vowels of English; Peterson & Lehiste, 1960).

There is some psychological support for this view of long segments. Rumelhart and Norman (1983) reported that "doubled letters" in the spelling of words (such as in b*OO*k and ha*MM*er) behave unusually in typing. When typists make errors, they usually replace both letters together (e.g., ha*PP*er for 'hammer'), or they double the wrong letter (e.g., bo*KK* for 'book'), producing letter substitutions that are otherwise very rare. This is also true of handwriting errors (Badecker, 1988; Tainturier & Caramazza, 1994). Stemberger (1984) reported for speech errors in German, Swedish, and Choctaw that vowels and consonants tend to move about while their length remains unchanged, though on occasion the length moves without otherwise affecting the segments; this has since been replicated for German (Berg, 1988) and also reported for Italian (Magno Caldognetto & Tonelli, 1985), Japanese (Kamio & Terao, 1986), and other languages:

1. German: ypigə vyːzə–viːzə   'a luxurious meadow'
2. Choctaw: haθːak–hatːak ãːθiːt   'there are honest men'

In (1), the speaker mispronounced the target vowel /iː/ of the word /viːzə/ as a long /yː/, perseverating the /y/ from the previous word /ypigə/; but the short /y/ of /ypigə/ became long when it replaced the long /iː/ of /viːzə/. In (2), the consonant /θ/ was anticipated from the word /ãːθiːt/, where it is short, to replace the long consonant /tː/ in /hatːak/, thereby taking on the length of /tː/ and becoming long /θː/. Length is only rarely misordered in terms of vowels or consonants. Length is relatively independent of the segments with which it is associated, a fact that is captured nicely by encoding length as two timing units attached to a single segment.

The diphthongs of English (/eɪ/, /oʊ/, /aɪ/, /aʊ/, and /ɔɪ/) also have two timing units; we assume that they are VV. Unlike long vowels, diphthongs contain two segments, each of which is linked to a single timing unit, as in the word *wipe*:

FIGURE 3.30

Adult English does not contrast long and short consonants. Many languages (e.g., Swedish, Italian, Arabic, Japanese, Choctaw) do contrast long and short consonants, however (where they are often represented orthographically as two identical letters in sequence, such as {tt}). The Swedish word *sitta* is represented in the following way:

FIGURE 3.31

English-learning children sometimes produce long consonants (e.g., *monkey* [mʌkːi]).

A variant of the CV tier was proposed several years later (Levin, 1985). It was identical, except that the feature [syllabic] was not a part of the timing unit. The timing unit was a pure unit of time, and was called "X." Representations using the X tier for *dip*, *deep*, and *sitta* are:

FIGURE 3.32

Note that long vowels are always just XX, as are long consonants. Hayes (1989) maintains that this approach makes wrong predictions about the types of compensatory lengthening that are possible in human language, and makes generalization about stress systems overly complicated.

A more radical view of timing units is moraic theory (Hyman, 1985; McCarthy & Prince, 1988; Hayes, 1989). The timing unit is called a *mora*, represented with the symbol "μ." This approach differs from CV theory and X theory in that not all segments have moras. All vowels have moras, and long vowels and diphthongs have two moras. A syllable with a coda has an additional mora for the coda in some languages (including adult English). Onsets never have moras. Languages rarely allow more than two moras in a syllable, but some do (see Hayes, 1989). A long vowel has two moras. A long consonant links to one mora (and directly to a syllable node; see below). The words *dip*, *deep*, and *sitta* would be represented as follows.

FIGURE 3.33

This approach predicts that consonants in onsets and consonants in codas will behave very differently from each other. This has become the most popular approach within phonological theory. However, moraic theory cannot handle all the facts of stress systems (Tranel, 1991) or compensatory lengthening (Rubach, 1993).

The fourth and last approach that we will address here is one that has recently been developed by one of the authors (Stemberger, 1994a). It is a compromise position between all three of these approaches. Like CV theory, it distinguishes between two types of timing units. Like X theory, some of the timing units are pure timing units with no additional information encoded; we use "X" to represent such timing units. Like moraic theory, some of the timing units encode the feature [+moraic] (a privative feature); we represent such timing units as "μ." The words *dip*, *deep*, and *sitta* would be represented as follows.

FIGURE 3.34

Stemberger argues that this approach has the strengths of the other three approaches without any of the weaknesses. We presuppose this approach here, but note that, for our purposes, consequences are often similar to moraic theory. (Shaw, 1992, approaches moraic theory in a similar fashion.) In general, we will use either the CV approach or the moraic approach. We will note where the data suit one approach better than the other.

To summarize, the four symbols that are used for timing units are:

X: a pure timing unit, unspecified for [syllabic] or [moraic]
C: a timing unit that is specified as [-syllabic]
V: a timing unit that is specified as [+syllabic]
μ: a timing unit that is specified as [+moraic]

We will not usually make reference to the features [syllabic] or [moraic], but will when the need arises.

Now that we have the concept of timing units, we can return to the issue of the consonant-vowel separation raised above. We can represent consonants and vowels as being on different planes:

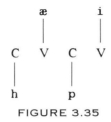

FIGURE 3.35

The two vowels /æ/ and /i/ are adjacent to each other on the vowel plane; no segment intervenes between /æ/ and /i/. The two consonants /h/ and /p/ are adjacent to each other on the consonant plane; no segment intervenes between /h/ and /p/. Because the two vowels are adjacent, the intervening consonants can be ignored for some purposes. Because the two consonants are adjacent, the intervening vowels can be ignored for some purposes.

Now that consonants and vowels are on different planes, we must also introduce another level of adjacency. In our discussion above, Root node adjacency restricted a phonological process or constraint to adjacent Root nodes, in such a way that the consonants between two vowels made the two vowels non-adjacent (because the consonant's Root node separated the two vowel Root nodes). If consonants and vowels are on different planes, however, Root node adjacency is not relevant for telling if a consonant and a vowel are adjacent. Consider the word *bouquets* /buːkeɪz/:

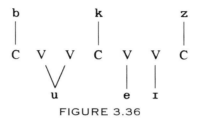

FIGURE 3.36

By Root adjacency, the /b/ is adjacent to /k/, but not to /z/ or to any of the vowels. Since the Root nodes of the /b/ and the /uː/ are on different planes, they cannot be adjacent by Root node adjacency. In order to have a way to refer to the adjacency of /b/ and /uː/, we have to refer to the timing units to which they are linked. Because the C timing unit that is linked to /b/ is adjacent on the Timing Unit tier to the V timing unit of the /uː/, the /b/ and the /uː/ are adjacent via Timing Unit adjacency:

Timing Unit adjacency: there is nothing between the two timing units
                             which dominate the two elements.

This level of adjacency is needed *solely* because we have separate planes for C-Root nodes and V-Root nodes. Timing Unit adjacency allows us to refer to consonants and vowels as adjacent, even though they are on different planes.

3.7. SYLLABLES

The segments of a word do not appear in isolation. There is generally more than one segment in a word. Further, segments group together in systematic ways. For consonants to appear, at least one vowel (or syllabic consonant) must be present: the consonants group around it. Further, the consonants group in predictable ways, across languages, within a language, and in the speech of young children acquiring a language. The smallest major grouping of segments that all phonologists agree on is the *syllable*. There is fair agreement among linguists on what constitutes a syllable, and native speakers of a language can generally say how many syllables are in a word and where the boundaries between syllables lie (though native speakers may find some syllabification tasks difficult).

Syllables were not a part of early generative phonology (Chomsky & Halle, 1968), although many researchers argued that they were needed (e.g., Fudge, 1969; Vennemann, 1972; Hooper, 1978). Chomsky and Halle (1968) believed that any generalization that could be stated in terms of syllables could also be stated in terms of consonants and vowels, and thus syllables were not needed. However, Kahn (1976) showed that syllables can only be avoided at the cost of great complexity and the obscuring of simple generalizations. Consider how to determine whether voiceless stops in English are aspirated or not. The words in the left column have aspirated stops, while those in the right column have unaspirated stops.[17]

Aspirated		*Unaspirated*	
pin	[pʰĩn]	spot	[spɑːt]
play	[pʰleɪ] [17]	supper	[ˈsʌpɹ̩]
report	[ɹəˈpʰɔːɹt]	happy	[ˈhæːpi]
potato	[pʰəˈtʰeɪɾoʊ]	sip	[sɪp]
acquaint	[ʔəˈkʰwẽĩnt]	mistake	[məsteɪk]
repress	[ɹiːˈpʰɹɛs]	display	[dəˈspleɪ]
complain	[kʰm̩ˈpʰlẽĩn]	shpiel	[ʃpiːɫ]
ectopic	[ʔɛkˈtʰɑːpɪk]	acknowledge	[ʔæːkˈnɑːɫəʤ]
*ifkana	[ʔɪfˈkʰɑːnə]		
*ithkana	[ʔɪθˈkʰɑːnə]		

In purely linear terms, voiceless stops are aspirated at the beginning of a word (whether the vowel after it is stressed or not), or when it precedes a stressed syllable (with an optional liquid or glide between the stop and the stressed vowel, but not if a nasal intervenes), *and* if the preceding segment is a sonorant, a stop, or a [-grooved] fricative (but not if the preceding segment is /s/ or /ʃ/):

$$\begin{bmatrix}-\text{cont}\\-\text{vcd}\end{bmatrix} \rightarrow [+\text{s.g.}] \;/\; \left\{ \begin{array}{l} \#\;__ \\ \left\{\begin{array}{c}[+\text{son}]\\[-\text{cont}]\\ \begin{bmatrix}+\text{cont}\\-\text{strid}\end{bmatrix}\end{array}\right\}__\left(\begin{bmatrix}-\text{syl}\\+\text{son}\\-\text{nas}\end{bmatrix}\right)\quad \begin{array}{c}\text{V}\\ [+\text{stress}]\end{array} \end{array} \right\}$$

FIGURE 3.37A

[17] We use [pʰl] rather than the [p̥] that is sometimes used. These are two phonetically equivalent representations of the same articulation. We prefer the former, because it reflects the fact that the aspiration is a property of the /p/.

This is a complicated description for what strikes English speakers as a simple phenomenon. Kahn observed that all the complex conditions here merely state in linear terms all the situations in which the voiceless stop is at the beginning of a syllable, and proposed that the rule could be stated simply as: syllable-initial voiceless stops are [+s.g.]:[18]

$$[\text{-cont}] \rightarrow \quad [\text{+s.g.}] / \quad [_\sigma \underline{\hspace{2cm}}$$
$$[\text{-vcd}]$$

While this is an extreme example of the amount of simplification that syllables can provide, it is generally the case that syllables simplify the statement of phonological patterns. Syllables are now taken for granted.

The peak of a syllable (also referred to as the *head* of the syllable), is generally a vowel. Indeed, most vowels are heads of syllables; the sole exceptions are those vowels (commonly called "glides") that are adjacent to the head vowel in the same syllable, such as the second vowel in the diphthong [aɪ]. Consonants are usually not heads of syllables; the sole exceptions are syllabic consonants, which are generally not allowed to occur next to vowels (see discussion in Prince & Smolensky, 1993). In general, given a sequence of vowels and consonants, the syllable structure is entirely predictable: we can identify which vowels will be heads, which will instead be glides, and which consonants will be syllabic. For every syllabic element, whether a consonant or a vowel, there is one syllable (by definition).

Nonsyllabic elements (whether true consonants, or glides), can appear either before the head of the syllable or after it. Consonants that appear before the head of the syllable make up the *onset*; all languages allow syllables to have onsets, and a few languages require every syllable to have an onset. Consonants that appear after the head of the syllable make up the *coda*; all languages allow syllables to lack a coda, and some languages do not allow a syllable to have a coda. Syllables that have no coda are referred to as *open* syllables; syllables that do have codas are referred to as *closed* syllables. Languages prefer open syllables over closed syllables.

There is a debate going on within phonological theory about the exact status of the notions "onset" and "coda." There are two possibilities. First, the concepts might be defined solely in terms of the side of the head on which a segment appears: onsets on the left side, codas on the right side. The representations themselves would not *label* a segment as being in the onset or in the coda, but that information would be *derivable* from the representations. This is referred to as *flat* syllable structure. Second, the representations themselves could contain a unit that is labeled either "onset" or "coda"; these would be "organizing nodes" at a high level of representation, grouping segments together in the same way that the Root node groups features together. This is referred to as *hierarchical* syllable structure.

---

[18]This assumes that the /p/ of *supper* is actually *ambisyllabic*, belonging both to the first syllable ([sʌp]) and to the second syllable ([pɹ̩]). Ambisyllabic stops are not aspirated, though ambisyllabic /t/ and /d/ become [ɾ].

Phonologists who argue for hierarchical structure generally also include another organizing node, called a *rime* (or sometimes *rhyme*), which groups together the nucleus (containing the head of the syllable) and the coda. The two opposing proposals are thus:

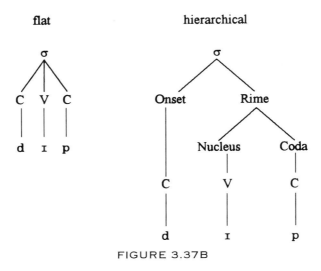

FIGURE 3.37B

The final word is not yet in on this debate. There is evidence that the nucleus and coda have an affinity for each other, both within adult grammars and in psycholinguistic tasks (see Treiman, 1988, for review). However, placing organizing nodes in the representation is awkward, and the organizing nodes frequently get in the way of expressing phonological processes. We will follow the practice of not putting these organizing nodes between the segments and the syllable nodes, because of the awkwardness. However, we believe that such structure is present, and will discuss language acquisition evidence in favor of such representations.

Many linguists assume that there is an additional subgrouping: the *appendix* (see Goldsmith, 1990, for discussion). The appendix is a special element that is not present in all languages. When it is present, it appears only at the edges of words: word-finally in some languages, word-initially in other languages, or at both edges. The appendix allows for one or more additional consonants than would be allowed in the onset or coda. Because it is a subgrouping (either an appendix to the syllable or to the word) and not a syllable in its own right, appendices lead to extra-long consonant sequences at the edges of words. For example, Borowsky (1989) argued that word-internal syllables in English have at most two elements in the rime, as in the first syllables of the words *simple* /.sɪm.pl̩./ and *lighten* /.laɪ.tn̩./; words with three elements in the rime, such as *Arctic* /.ɑɹk.tɪk./ are unusual, and subject to simplifying historical changes (/.ɑɹ.tɪk./). However, word-final syllables often have three elements, as in *dump* /.dʌmp./, or even more if the final elements are coronal, as in *coax* /.koʊks./ and *lynx* /.lɪŋks./. Borowsky argued that the rime allows only two elements, and that all additional elements are a part of a word-final appendix. Others have argued that the /s/ of /s/+stop clusters is part of a word-initial appendix, thus allowing us to say that all consonant sequences in the onset abide by the sonority hierarchy (see below). See Goldsmith (1990) for a thorough review of these proposals. We do not believe that there is sufficient evidence to include such a concept in phonological theory. There are other reasons why consonant sequences at word edges can be longer than consonant sequences within the word. In following chapters, we note that constraints on sequences routinely have greater effects word-internally than either word-finally or word-initially. However, we discuss some acquisition data in §6.1.10.1 that many phonologists would take as evidence for an appendix.

The representation of monosyllabic words is more straightforward than that of bisyllabic or multisyllabic words. With a single-syllable word, once we identify the head, all segments before the head are in the onset, and all segments after the head are in the coda. With two-syllable words, however, this clarity is restricted to segments at the edges of the word. All segments at the beginning of the word before the head of the first syllable are in the onset of the first syllable. All segments at the end of the word after the head of the second syllable are in the coda of the second syllable. But the status of consonants in the middle of the word, between the two heads, is unclear. In principle, intervocalic consonants could either make up the onset of the second syllable or the coda of the first syllable.

In almost all adult languages, the division of consonants between the two syllables is simple and predictable. If there is only one intervocalic consonant, it makes up the onset of the second syllable, rather than the coda of the first syllable. A word like /pani/ would be [.pa.ni.], never *[.pan.i.]. This arises because onsets are often obligatory (and thus preferred) and codas optional (and thus avoided). This preference/avoidance is obvious in languages that never allow codas in any syllable, but is subtly present in most languages in the syllabification of intervocalic consonants as onsets rather than as codas.[19]

If there is more than one intervocalic consonant, the result depends on the particular sequence of consonants that is present. As many consonants are placed in the onset as possible, given the sequences of consonants that are allowed within onsets in the language in question. Some languages allow only a single consonant in an onset. In that case, given the words /pegsa/ and /pebri/, they would be syllabified [.peg.sa.] and [.peb.ri.]. However, many languages allow two or more consonants within an onset, with the second consonant often restricted to a glide or liquid. In such a language, these two words would be syllabified [.peg.sa.] (because a syllable cannot begin with *[gs]) and [.pe.bri.] (because a syllable is allowed to begin with [br]). Given the sequences of consonants that are allowed in

---

[19]There may be one exception to this: vowels seem to prefer to be in rimes rather than in onsets. When a vowel is nonsyllabic (i.e., is a glide), it may still prefer to be in a rime, and thus would be part of the coda. In an English word like *flower*, the syllabification seems to be [.flaʊ.ɻ.] rather than *[.fla.wɻ.], reflecting this preference. For all true consonants, however, the consonant generally prefers to go into the onset of the second syllable.

a word-initial onset, and the sequences of consonants that are allowed within a word-final coda, we can accurately divide all sequences of intervocalic consonants into their respective syllables, in almost all languages.

In a few languages, the treatment of intervocalic consonants is unclear. In English and other Germanic languages, for example, phonologists and native speakers in general are uncertain about what to do with segments such as /p/ in the word *happy*. Is /hæpi/ syllabified as [.hæ.pi.] (as it would be in most languages) or as [.hæp.i.] (which would be impossible in most languages)? People tend to be uncertain of the answer. As a result, it has been suggested that intervocalic consonants in English belong to *both* syllables, making up both the coda of the first syllable and the onset of the second syllable. A consonant that belongs to two syllables in this way is called *ambisyllabic*, and is represented as in the following figure:

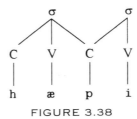

FIGURE 3.38

Kahn (1976) presents phonological arguments that intervocalic consonants are ambisyllabic in English, and Treiman (1988) reviews pertinent psycholinguistic evidence. Kahn proposed that /t/ and /d/ become taps in English ([ɾ]) only when ambisyllabic. However, other alternatives have been put forward to handle the same information (e.g., Kiparsky, 1979), and psycholinguists have also split on this issue (Treiman, 1988). We further address this issue for child language in §6.1.13 (see also Bernhardt & Stemberger, in prep.).

It should be noted that ambisyllabic consonants are impossible within the moraic approach to timing units. A long consonant is represented as one that links to both a mora (in the first syllable) and a syllable node (in the second syllable):

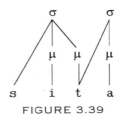

FIGURE 3.39

Long consonants belong to both syllables. There is no way to link a consonant to two syllables without making it long. Short ambisyllabic consonants such as have been proposed for English are simply not possible.

The order of consonants within an onset or within a coda generally is governed by the *sonority hierarchy*, a scale based on the "sonority" of a segment. Sonority is not well defined, but seems to correspond to how similar a segment is to the most prototypical segment with high sonority: a vowel.[20] The scale is, roughly:

vowel
glide
liquid
nasal
voiced fricative
voiceless fricative
voiced stop
voiceless stop

The head of the syllable is usually the "peak" of sonority, and sonority tends to decrease towards the edges of the syllable. Thus, the first consonant in the onset is low in sonority, the second consonant is higher in sonority than the first, the head of the syllable is highest, the first consonant in the coda is lower in sonority than the head of the syllable, and the second consonant in the coda is lower yet. A typical syllable would be *drink* /dɹɪŋk/: stop-glide-vowel-nasal-stop.

There are exceptions to this generalization. The most common one cross-linguistically involves /s/. /s/ is higher in sonority than stops, but often precedes stops in onsets (in words like *stand* /stænd/) and follows them in codas (in words like *ax* /æks/). We do not know why this is the case, but /s/ creates sequences in onsets and codas with unusual sonority relationships. Some phonologists argue that /s/ is part of an appendix in such contexts, (S. Davis, 1991; Fikkert, 1994).

3.7.1. BUILDING SYLLABLES

The syllable structure of a word is entirely predictable from the segments and timing units that are present. As a result, phonologists assume that no structure is present in underlying representations above the timing unit tier. Syllables (as well as higher-level units like feet and prosodic words) are constructed on the basis of the segments that are present.

The process of syllabification proceeds as follows. The underlying representation of a word like *donkeys* consists of the timing unit tier, the Root tier, and all dependent tiers. For the purposes of higher-level structure, we do not need to worry about the details of segmental geometry. Here we will simply use the phonetic symbols to denote the segments that are present. We will also ignore the fact that consonants and vowels are on separate planes, since that detail does not affect the linking of syllable nodes to timing units.

---

[20] Ladefoged (1993) suggests that sonority is determined by the amplitude of the segment, but this is not universally accepted.

FIGURE 3.40

The syllable tier is constructed on top of the timing unit nodes. First, syllable nodes are inserted and linked to V timing units.

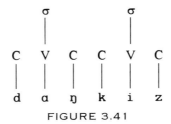

FIGURE 3.41

Onsets are then linked to the syllable nodes. As many consonants link to the onset as are allowed in the language as long as the onsets created are "legal" sequences of consonants.

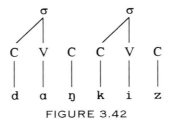

FIGURE 3.42

In this case, only the /k/ of the intervocalic consonant cluster /ŋk/ can link to the onset of the second syllable, because English does not allow onsets with the sequence /ŋk/ (because /ŋ/ is higher in sonority than /k/). Since onsets are constructed first, any singleton intervocalic consonant will belong to the onset of the second syllable. The word *bucket*, for example, will be syllabified [.bʌ.kət.]. The next step is to add consonants to the coda: as many as are allowed in codas in the language (which might be zero, if the language does not allow codas) as long as the resulting consonant sequences make legal codas in the language.

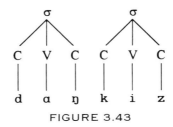

FIGURE 3.43

At this point, all the segments in the word *donkeys* have been linked to a syllable node. The word is well formed.

In some instances, not all consonants are syllabified; some remain floating, or *extrasyllabic*. In English, this may happen with words that end in syllabic /ɹ/, /l/, /m/, and /n/. In Chomsky and Halle (1968) it was proposed that English has no underlyingly syllabic consonants, and that surface syllabic consonants are derived from extrasyllabic consonants. For example, with the morpheme *algorithm*, the word-final /m/ is syllabic in the word *algorithm* itself, but is nonsyllabic in the derived form *algorithmic*, where the /m/ precedes a vowel. Many phonologists assume that the /m/ is underlyingly nonsyllabic, and that syllabification proceeds as follows; here we focus just on the final syllable:

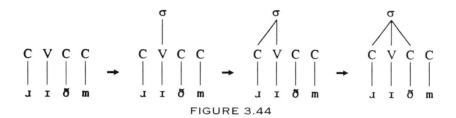

FIGURE 3.44

The /m/ is still floating at this point. It cannot be added to the coda, because the sequence /ðm/ is not allowed within a coda in English (because the /m/ is higher in sonority than the /ð/). Because the /m/ is floating, it will be deleted via Stray Erasure unless some way can be found to rescue it. One way to rescue the /m/ would be to insert a vowel either before or after it. Some languages do take this option, which can be used with any consonant. However, because the /m/ is a sonorant consonant, English allows it to be syllabic. As a result, English makes the /m/ syllabic; this option also derives syllabic /l/, /n/, and /ɹ/.[21]

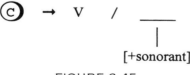

FIGURE 3.45

Once the /m/ gains a [+syllabic] feature/status, we can construct a syllable on top of it. Any consonant immediately before it that has been linked to the preceding coda is automatically resyllabified, so that as many consonants as possible are in the onset of the now-syllabic /m/.

---

[21] See Stemberger (1983) for arguments that syllabic /ɹ/ as in *bird* is a syllabic consonant and not a vowel (/ɝ/) in adult English. Whether children treat them as consonants or vowels is less clear.

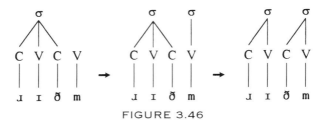

FIGURE 3.46

Note that no problem ever arises in the derived form *algorithmic*. Because a vowel follows the /m/, the /m/ automatically becomes part of the onset of the second vowel, and is never extrasyllabic.

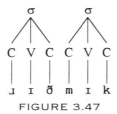

FIGURE 3.47

Extrasyllabic consonants arise in the construction of syllables in many languages. The three options for dealing with them are as follows:

1. Insert a vowel before or after the extrasyllabic consonant.
2. Make the extrasyllabic consonant syllabic.
3. Delete the extrasyllabic consonant. (Stray Erasure)

English-learning children have much more restricted syllable structure than adult English speakers, frequently resulting in extrasyllabic consonants. All three of these options have been observed (§6.1).

3.8. FEET

In English and many other languages, some syllables are more prominent than others, because they are stressed (that is, longer, louder, and of higher pitch), while other syllables are unstressed. Further, some stressed syllables are more prominent (that is, have greater stress) than others. There are a number of approaches towards stress in modern phonological theory (see Goldsmith, 1990, for a detailed discussion). One approach treats stress as being fundamentally different from all other aspects of phonology, with a unique representation (the "grid"). The other approach simply extends the notions that we have been discussing in this chapter, by introducing a higher-order organizing node that groups together two or more syllables; the *foot*. There is only one stressed syllable in a foot, and that syllable is the *head* of the foot.[22] We follow the common convention of placing the stressed syllable (the head) directly beneath the Foot node in multilinear representations;[23] unstressed syllables are linked up with a slanted line. We illustrate feet with the words *happy* (with stress on the first syllable) and *balloon* (with stress on the second syllable). A foot with stress on the first syllable is *left-prominent* (or *trochaic*, or *left-headed*). A foot with stress on the second syllable is *right-prominent* (or *iambic*, or *right-headed*).

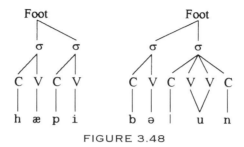

FIGURE 3.48

Most feet in most languages have only two syllables: feet are usually *binary*. In English, almost all two-syllable words are left-prominent (i.e., have stress on the first syllable), but there are unpredictable exceptions.

We make use of feet instead of the grid. Recent work by Prince and Smolensky (1993) and McCarthy and Prince (1993a) show that the foot is a useful concept for describing the size of words and for capturing which portions of words tend to undergo processes. There is a hybrid model based on the grid that groups grid marks into feet (see Kenstowicz, 1994, for an extensive overview and discussion). There has been little argumentation in the literature to justify the extra complexity, and most of that revolves around issues that are not relevant to language acquisition. For simplicity, we make use of a purely foot-based approach.

It has been claimed that feet must universally have at least two moras (McCarthy & Prince, 1993a; Mester, 1994); those moras can be either in two syllables or in a single syllable. Adult English is such a language: no word can be made up of a single open syllable with a short vowel (*/bɛ/, */sɪ/, */gʊ/, */mʌ/), unless the word is unstressed (e.g., *the* /ðə/), and thus part of some larger foot. However, as long as the foot has two moras, it does not matter whether it is made up of a single syllable that has a long vowel (as in *see*) or a coda (as in *sit*), or of two short open syllables (as in *city*). In some languages, however, feet are required to have two syllables rather than just two moras.

---

[22] The terms go together in a somewhat infelicitous way here, leading to a fair amount of humor in introductory classes until people tire of the obvious jokes.

[23] Some phonologists abbreviate the word "Foot" with "F" or the Greek letter "Φ." We write the word out in full, for clarity.

The basic foot has at most two syllables. However, feet can have three or more syllables, and when this happens, stress can be on the middle syllable rather than on one of the edge syllables. In the English word *ballooning*, for example, there is a single foot with stress on the middle syllable. Such feet are viewed as derived. In English, the inflectional affixes (*-ing*, *-s*, *-ed*) can never serve as the head of a foot, and are added as extra syllables to the last foot of the base word (when they are syllabic). First, a foot is built with just two syllables, and stress is on either the left or the right syllable. This basic foot is constructed before the *-ing* suffix is added to the word. When the *-ing* is added, it is later adjoined to the basic foot, producing an odd configuration: an extra-large foot with stress in the middle.

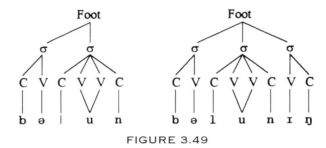

FIGURE 3.49

Such feet also arise in words like *banana* /bə'nænə/ because schwa may not be stressed in English (see §6.2).[24]

Feet are generally predictable from the syllables that they group together. Phonologists often assume that feet are not present in underlying forms; but Levelt (1989) argues on the basis of psycholinguistic evidence that they are present underlyingly in English and Dutch, at least. There are also many words with unpredictable stress. Nevertheless, we can make the following observations about the vowel in an unstressed syllable in English. (a) The unstressed vowel may not be long or diphthongal, unless it is in an open syllable, and even then only [iː], [uː], and [oʊ] are possible. Further, the unstressed tense vowels [i] and [u] are short in many dialects (e.g., Halle & Mohanan, 1985). (b) Short lax vowels other than [ə] may not be unstressed. (c) The low vowels [æ], [ɑ], [ɒ], and [ɔ] may not be unstressed. The restrictions on vowels in unstressed syllables derive from the status of unstressed syllables as weak prosodic domains (see §4.7.1.5 and §6.2.5.3). The odd placement of stress in *banana* and *balloon* probably is related to these restrictions on unstressed vowels. However, some words have unpredictable stress. For the purposes of the acquisition of English, it works best if we assume that the child

[24] Many phonologists assume that the initial unstressed syllable of *balloon* and *banana* are not part of any foot, but link directly to a higher-level element (the prosodic word). We do not regard that analysis as sufficiently motivated.

knows where the stressed syllable is in the adult pronunciation and adjoins non-head syllables according to general principles (see §6.2).

3.9. PROSODIC WORDS

Feet are further grouped under one ultimate organizing node, into a constituent known as the *prosodic* word. The head of the prosodic word is the foot that contains the syllable with the greatest level of stress: the *primary* stress. Other (non-head) feet contain *secondary* stress. A word generally constitutes one prosodic word, no matter how long it is, and has only one primary stress.[25] An example of a prosodic word with two feet would be *demonstration* (with the nonhead foot /dɛmən/ followed by the head foot /stɹeɪʃn/).

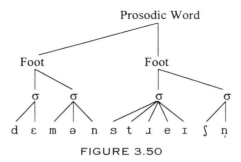

FIGURE 3.50

Prosodic words in English are often right-prominent in this way. However, if the second foot has only one syllable, the prosodic word is generally left-prominent: in *demonstrate*, primary stress falls on the syllable /dɛm/, and secondary stress on the syllable /stɹeɪt/.

A minimal (prosodic) word in most languages has one foot. Since a foot has at least two moras or two syllables, the minimal word in most languages has at least two moras, and in some languages must have at least two syllables. In some languages, the size of the minimal word depends on the part of speech of the word. In Choctaw, nouns can be monosyllabic (with two moras), but verbs must be at least bisyllabic (e.g., Nicklas, 1972).

Some languages also have a maximal word: an absolute upper bound on the length of a word. If a language has such a fixed length, words tend to be relatively short: either two syllables (limited to a single foot) or four syllables (limited to two feet). Young children often have maximal words, sometimes limited to a single foot (§6.3.2).

---

[25] An exception in English is that function words like articles and prepositions are generally part of some larger prosodic word. Words like *a* and *the* are unstressed, and become part of a nearby foot, such as the following noun in *the dog*.

3.9.1. TEMPLATES

The characteristics of syllables, feet, and prosodic words within a language can have a large impact on the processes that are present in the language. In particular, they can conspire to make all words in the language very similar to each other.

Suppose a language has the following characteristics:

1. A prosodic word can have only one foot.
2. A foot must have two syllables.
3. A syllable allows
   (a) no coda, and
   (b) only one consonant in the onset.

Given these constraints on the prosodic units, all words in the language must be CVCV: two open syllables with a single consonant in the onset of each. If some word underlyingly differs from CVCV (because it has an odd underlying form, or is borrowed from another language, etc.), processes may alter the word to fit: by deleting extra syllables and extra consonants if the word is too long; by inserting a syllable if the input is too short; or by inserting consonants if one is missing.

McCarthy (1981) and Marantz (1982) originally proposed that such restrictions on the form of a word should be encoded by supplying a standard CV-tier representation for all words: CVCV. This was called a *template*. The segments of the word (or morpheme) would link up to this template, and appropriate changes would be made if the template and the segments did not match up exactly. Macken (1992) follows this proposal in accounting for patterns in phonological development (especially in early development).

Current constraint-based views of "templates" hold that they are not an explicit part of the phonological system, but are instead derivable from constraints placed on the various prosodic units involved (McCarthy & Prince, 1993a). The prosodic units can require that a syllable be open, that it have just one mora or that it have two, that there should be a single syllable, or a single foot, etc. The constraints impose a certain shape on the segmental material in the word or morpheme. Similar phenomena occur in the basic shapes of words in phonological development: "templates" arise through the interaction of constraints on syllables, feet, and prosodic words with the segmental material of the word.

3.10. WHAT IS SPECIFIED
IN UNDERLYING FORMS

In several places in this chapter, we have mentioned underlying representation. In this section, we consider which of the elements we have discussed need to be stored in underlying forms and which can be supplied by the phonological system. As discussed in §2.3, one issue that divides different approaches in phonology is the extent to which information should be stored in lexical representations versus the extent to which they should be supplied by the system. This issue affects both structure and the features themselves. We first address timing units, and suggest that timing units are present in underlying representations. We then address features and organizing nodes, and argue that organizing nodes are always present in underlying representations, but as few features (content nodes) are present in underlying representations as is possible.

Phonologists who work within CV-theory, X-theory, and Xμ-theory have always assumed that all timing units are present in underlying representations. This is viewed as necessary for several reasons. First, there can be two timing units attached to a single segment; thus, the number of timing units is not predictable. Second, in some languages there are timing units with no segments; thus, those timing units must be present in underlying representations. When such floating timing units are present, the other timing units of the word must also be present, or else we would have no idea where in the word the free timing unit should go.[26] Third, in some languages the timing unit tier is determined by the morphology of the language (see Goldsmith, 1990, for an overview for several languages), and so must be present underlyingly. Fourth, Stemberger (1990) presents a model of psychological processing in which the timing unit tier provides information about whether a segment is present at all; if the timing unit is not present, then the speaker does not know that a segment should be produced in that part of the word. Finally, even in child phonological development, segments often leave behind their timing units when they delete, and it is convenient to assume that the timing units were present underlyingly.

Within moraic phonology, Hyman (1985) assumed that timing units are present underlyingly, as did Hayes (1989) and McCarthy and Prince (1993a). McCarthy (1989) pointed out that moras are usually predictable, and suggested that they are not present underlyingly. A process could insert a mora for each vowel; if the vowel already has an underlying mora, this would result in two moras being attached to the vowel (a long vowel); but if the vowel has no underlying mora, it would have only a single mora and be short. Long consonants would also have to have a mora specified underlyingly. In some languages, an additional mora would be inserted for consonants in the coda. One problem with this is that it cannot handle the difference between syllabic vowels (vowels) and nonsyllabic vowels (glides); the obvious solution would be to have a mora attached to true vowels in the underlying representation, but no mora attached to glides. Further, McCarthy's solution is only possible if we use processes. If we instead account for alternations

---

[26] If there is only one element on a tier, and it is unattached, we have no way of determining the temporal relationship between that element and elements on other tiers. There are only two ways to determine temporal relationships. When there are two elements on one tier, we know their sequential order. When there is an association line between two elements, we know that they are simultaneous. If there is a single unattached timing unit in the underlying form of the word, neither of these two ways hold, and so the timing unit could in principle wind up anywhere in the word. But free timing units are in fact always consistently in one place in the word, and so the other timing units of the word must also be underlying.

via constraints, his solution is untenable: if a constraint says that a vowel must have at least one mora, then a vowel with one underlying mora already abides by the constraint and will not change. It is difficult in a constraint-based system to insert a mora in every vowel in order to avoid a constraint violation. Lexical storage is needed for the moras of vowels and geminate consonants. However, the mora of a coda consonant is entirely predictable, and thus can be left out of underlying representations and inserted via a process or constraint called *Weight by Position*.

Regardless of the approach to timing units, most phonologists are in agreement that they should be in the underlying representation. We will therefore work under the assumption that all timing units are present in the underlying representation, with the exception that in moraic phonology, the mora in codas can be derived via Weight by Position.

Archangeli and Pulleyblank (1994) have recently argued that in some languages all of the vowel features are floating, and that they link up to the segments linked to V timing units, beginning with the leftmost vowel. In such languages, there are severe restrictions on the order of vowels in a word. For example, in Tiv, the first syllable can contain any vowel in the language, but all other syllables must be /e/, unless a feature from the first vowel spreads to the later vowels. Archangeli and Pulleyblank account for this by assuming that all vowel features are floating, and that /e/ has no features; the floating features link up to the first vowel, so that all later vowels must have no features (and so surface as /e/) unless they derive those features via spreading from the first vowel.

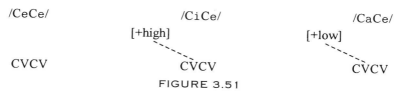

FIGURE 3.51

Archangeli and Pulleyblank illustrate floating features of this sort only with vowels. In §5.5.3.2, we address whether data from child phonological development involves floating consonantal features (Vellemann, 1992).

The most extreme instances where association lines are absent in underlying forms occur when the basic shape of a word is determined by general principles, rather than lexically. In Arabic and other Semitic languages, for example, the CV tier is a morpheme in its own right, related to verbal aspect or noun number, and the vowels and the consonants also make up separate morphemes. McCarthy (1981) proposed that consonants and vowels are underlyingly unassociated with timing units. The consonants of the base verb or noun link up to the C timing units, one-to-one and L-to-R; the vowels link up to the V timing units in the same way (but there are some complexities with the vowels that we will not address here):

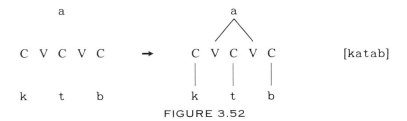

FIGURE 3.52

In this case, the CV template has three consonant positions, allowing the three consonants of the base verb to become linked. In some cases, however, the base verb has only two consonants. When this happens, the final consonant is spread to the third C timing unit, and ultimately shows up twice:

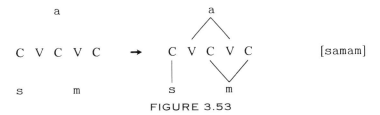

FIGURE 3.53

The two halves of the /m/ are separated by an /a/. This leads to the gestures for /m/ being interrupted, and separated by vowel gestures.

In some languages, the shape of all words is predictable. In Sierra Miwok (Goldsmith, 1990), base words have one of three CV tier patterns. Words can be lexically marked to take a particular pattern in the base form. The segments map onto the CV template, L-to-R, one-to-one, with spreading of the final timing unit or segment if there are different numbers of segments and timing units. As in Arabic, many inflected forms take a different CV template, and these are the same for all words in the language. Different stems have the CV templates: CVCVVC and CVCCV. In later chapters, we address proposals that some young English-learning children impose CV templates on words in this way (Macken, 1992; Vellemann, 1992).

3.11. DEFAULTS AND FEATURE UNDERSPECIFICATION

Researchers have argued whether all of the features of segments are present in underlying representations. Four positions have been previously proposed: full specification, contrastive specification, radical underspecification, and combinatorial specification. In §4.4.2.2, we propose an alternative variant: default under-specification. In a process-based theory, the positions make distinguishable empirical predictions. However, in purely constraint-based theories like OT, it is difficult to distinguish empirically between the positions. Most phonologists, working without any theory of learning, have thus assumed that full specification is the best alternative. We prefer to adopt a theory with radical or default underspecification, because we believe that any adequate theory of learning will lead to such an outcome automatically (see Stemberger, 1991a, 1993a, 1996c, for discussion). No one has yet articulated a theory of learning that would lead to any of the other positions.

In all positions on underspecification, there are some features and feature values that are treated in a special fashion that is distinct from the way that other features and feature values are treated. These special features and feature values can be referred to using two neutral terms that can be used with all positions: *default* features and feature values, or *unmarked* features and feature values. We prefer the term "default." The term "unmarked" has a long usage within linguistic theory, denoting those features and feature values that are most common cross-linguistically. For example, voiceless obstruents are found in all languages, but some languages lack voiced obstruents; and in those languages with voiced obstruents, there are generally fewer voiced obstruent phonemes than voiceless obstruent phonemes. We say that [-voiced] is *unmarked* for obstruents. The term "default" does not necessarily imply any consistency across languages, however. Different languages may have different defaults (Archangeli, 1984, 1988). Thus, "default" is the best neutral term to use.

In the next section, we first introduce the five approaches. We then discuss the evidence that has been used to justify underspecification, showing that the default features and feature values take part in special phonological patterns that are distinct from the patterns of nondefault features and feature values. In this chapter, which is process-oriented, we argue that radical underspecification (or combinatorial specification) handle the data best. In §4.4.2.2, we return to this issue within OT. OT allows a version of full specification (default underspecification) that incorporates the main insights and explanations of radical underspecification, in a way that is impossible within a process-based theory. We stress again that the choice between the positions within an OT framework depends on the theory of learning that is assumed, not (at the moment) on the basis of empirical differences. We will also show the value of default underspecification for phonological pattern analysis within OT.

3.11.1. THE FIVE APPROACHES
TO FEATURE SPECIFICATION

Full specification means that all active features are specified in underlying representations. Chomsky and Halle (1968) ultimately argued for this position, and it has been raised more recently by Mohanan (1991) and Smolensky (1993). Smolensky (1993) and McCarthy and Prince (1994) argue that constraint rankings can derive statistical properties of processes across languages, even with full specification.

Contrastive specification (Steriade, 1987; Clements, 1988; Mester & Itô, 1989), in contrast, includes in underlying representations only those features that are *contrastive*, that is, that are necessary to distinguish between different underlying segments. For example, in English vowels, the feature [high] is contrastive and must be present in underlying representations, because it is the only feature that distinguishes high [ɪ] from mid [ɛ]. Similarly, [low] is necessary to distinguish [ɛ] from [æ]. However, the features [high] and [low] are sometimes predictable, and are not needed to distinguish between segments in those contexts. For example, all non-syllabic dorsal segments in English, whether glides or velar consonants, are [+high]; there are no [-high] dorsals in English. Further, in all languages, high vowels are automatically [-low] and low vowels are [-high], because no segment can be both [+high] and [+low] simultaneously. In contrastive specification, these predictable values of [high] and [low] are left blank in underlying representations and filled in later via a *feature-filling rule*; the contrastive values of [high] and [low] are present in underlying representations, however. The feature [tense], in contrast, is entirely predictable in English. If the vowel is [-low] and has only a single timing unit (e.g., is short and monophthongal), it is [-tense]: [ɪ], [ɛ], [ɨ], [ə], [ʌ], [ʊ]. If the vowel is [-low] and has two timing units (i.e., is long or diphthongal), then the vowel is [+tense]: [iː], [eɪ], [uː], [oʊ]. Since [tense] is predictable for all vowels in English (and in all consonants as well), we can leave it out of underlying representations.[27]

Similarly, all vowels (like all sonorants) in English are [+voiced], and their value of [nasal] is predictable (because they are [-nasal] unless they are near a [+nasal] segment); thus, neither [+voiced] nor [-nasal] would be specified underlyingly for vowels in English. For consonants, [+voiced] and [-voiced] would be specified for obstruents, since they are the only features that distinguish stops such as /t/ and /d/; but voicing is predictable for sonorant consonants and would not be present in underlying representations. Contrastive specification leads us to leave many features out of underlying representations, and fill them in by rule.

Radical underspecification (Archangeli, 1984; 1988) goes further in terms of what is considered to be "predictable." Because features have at most two values, we can in principle predict one value of the feature from the other value. For

---

[27] Alternatively, one could say that the length of a vowel is predictable from tenseness. Tense vowels in English are all long or diphthongal, and thus must have two timing units. Nonlow lax vowels must be short, with a single timing unit. In principle, one could specify all vowels for tenseness, and leave out the second timing unit of long vowels and diphthongs. Linguists tend to leave [tense] underspecified, and place all timing units in the underlying representation. Within speech-language pathology, transcriptions generally reflect tenseness and leave out length (e.g., /i/ for [iː] and /ɪ/ for [ɪ]). No one has contrasted the two positions to see which works best. This raises the problem of ambiguity for contrastive specification: if two features are predictable from each other, which one is underlying and which is derived? No one has provided an answer to this question.

example, if we know that a segment is [+voiced], then we know that it is not [-voiced]. Suppose we assume that only [+voiced] is specified in underlying representations for obstruents in English. For /d/, we see [+voiced], and consequently know that it is voiced. If we look at /t/, we see no specification for [voiced]. The lack of a specification for [voiced] in /t/ tells us that /t/ is *not* [+voiced]; consequently, we know that it is [-voiced], because that is the only other possibility. We fill in the value [-voiced] for obstruents without a specification for [voiced]. We need two rules for voicing in English:

a. [] → [−voiced] / [_____]
             [−son]
b. [] → [+voiced] / [_____]
             [+son]

The "[]" in the target part of the rule means that there is no specification on the tier on which a feature is inserted. Consequently, the rule can never apply to voiced obstruents, which already have [+voiced] on that tier. In this way, we can eliminate one value of every feature from underlying representations. In essence, every feature is privative in underlying representations. Most features, however, are made binary when the other feature value is inserted via a feature-filling rule.

Combinatorial specification (Archangeli & Pulleyblank, 1994) is a less radical variant of radical underspecification. It holds that radical underspecification is the usual situation. However, predictable features are sometimes present in underlying representations. The default value of a feature could be present underlyingly. A redundant feature could be present underlyingly. A predictable feature might be present underlyingly in some words but absent in others. In most instances, radical underspecification and combinatorial underspecification use identical analyses. We do not explore the differences between them in this book.

Default underspecification is an alternative position that we present in §4.4.2.2, which derives from properties of OT and our view of learning. Like combinatorial specification, it is a variant of radical underspecification in which some predictable features may be specified. Unlike combinatorial specification, default features cannot be specified in underlying representations (except in very specific circumstances). However, predictable nondefault features may or may not be specified in underlying representations. A given redundant nondefault feature must be either specified or underspecified in all words, but languages (and children) will differ in terms of which features are specified and which are underspecified. For example, [-voiced] is the general default feature that is underspecified. Sonorants, however, have the redundant nondefault feature [+voiced], which may be specified in underlying representations in some languages. For most purposes, this approach makes the same predictions as radical underspecification. For redundant nondefault features, however, it does a more adequate job of accounting for some phonological patterns in child phonology (see §5.5.3.3, §5.5.3.6, and §6.1.6.4).

3.11.2. WHICH FEATURES ARE THE DEFAULTS?

Archangeli (1984) noted that consonants and vowels seem to differ across languages in terms of exactly which features and feature values are the defaults. In general, the same feature values for consonants are the defaults in all languages. The default, or "maximally underspecified," consonant seems to be [t], with the following feature values being defaults (or underspecified):

Place: Coronal, +anterior
Manner: -sonorant, +consonantal, -continuant, -nasal, -lateral
Voicing: -voiced

These values seem to be the default values for consonants in most languages. (See Paradis & Prunet, 1991b, for a focus on place of articulation, with arguments that anterior coronals are underspecified for place features.) Vowels, in contrast, seem to vary; Archangeli (1984) argues that any vowel in the language might be the default. The patterns of the vowels in processes would tell us which one was default (maximally underspecified). Yip (1987) argued that /ɪ/ is the default vowel of English, but Stemberger (1992b, 1993a) provides psycholinguistic evidence that the default vowel of English (in stressed syllables) is /ɛ/.

There is no reason to believe that all speakers of all languages have the same default features and feature values. When we examine data from language acquisition, we find that most English-learning children have similar defaults, but there is variation across children. At times, it is useful to assume that the default place of articulation is labial or dorsal, or that the default manner of articulation is a fricative. (See §5.5.4.3 and §8.3-§8.5.)

3.11.3. MOTIVATING UNDERSPECIFICATION

The original motivation for leaving out predictable features was to simplify underlying representations and extract generalizations about the segmental inventory of a language (Chomsky & Halle, 1968; Kiparsky, 1982). These are no longer considered to be important motivations. Underspecification of features is motivated instead by phonological patterns (including processes). An underspecified feature is not part of the representation, and hence cannot be linked to anything else and is not adjacent to any other element. Thus, the underspecified feature behaves as if it were not present, for some purposes. Further, the lack of a feature specification makes the segment ill formed: some process must apply to supply a feature. An alternative to the appropriate default feature-filling rule would be to "fill in" the feature from context, via assimilation from a nearby segment. Thus, underspecification predicts that one value of a feature should tend to assimilate to the other value: the blank value should assimilate to the specified value. None of these arguments are iron-clad. See §4.4.2.1 for alternatives within OT.

3.11.3.1. Asymmetries in Assimilation

Spreading involves the addition of an association line from one element that is already present in the representation to another already-present element. Although there *can* be an element already present, spreading usually involves linking a specified nondefault feature to a segment with an underspecified default feature. The vowel nasalization rule discussed in §3.4 is a good example.

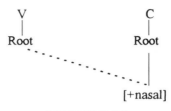

FIGURE 3.54

In this case, the vowel is underspecified for the feature [nasal]. Because under-specification makes the vowel ill formed, something must be done to resolve the situation. Barring deleting the vowel (which no language does), the situation must be resolved by linking [nasal] to the vowel. One common resolution is to insert [-nasal] into the vowel, via a default feature-filling rule. However, spreading a feature from a nearby segment is another way to fill in [nasal] on the vowel, if a token of [nasal] is nearby. English typically spreads [+nasal] right-to-left. Words like *ban* /bæn/ are pronounced [bæ̃:n]; but the vowel in *nab* /næb/ is oral ([næ:b]), because [+nasal] does not generally spread rightwards.

In contrast, suppose that a nasalized vowel appeared before an oral stop (in some language other than English, of course). We would have the following representation:

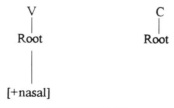

FIGURE 3.55

If this vowel were to become [-nasal] before a [-nasal] segment, no feature-filling would be going on. Instead, the specified feature [+nasal] would delink before a consonant underspecified for [nasal], thus increasing the degree of ill-formedness of the representation. While this is technically possible (and can happen), there is less motivation for it. Feature-filling provides a drive both to spread specified features to segments that are underspecified for that feature and a reason not to delete specified features. In the most common case, then, we find asymmetries: specified features spread, and the underspecified values do not. Underspecification accounts for these asymmetries directly.

Asymmetries of assimilation are quite common (see Avery & Rice, 1989). Voiceless obstruents tend to become voiced or aspirated next to voiced or aspirated obstruents more than the reverse. Anterior coronal consonants tend to take on other places of articulation more than the reverse. Oral stops tend to become nasals more than the reverse. Other aspects of manner features are less clear, because manner features are less often involved in assimilations (McCarthy, 1988; Kaisse, 1992).

3.11.3.2. Transparency to Assimilation and Dissimilation

Phonological underspecification is also motivated by the phenomenon of *transparency*. In some cases, spreading skips over an intervening segment. The intervening segment is transparent to the spreading. Transparency requires that the intervening segment not be specified for the feature that is spreading, or else line-crossing would occur. It should be noted that this is uncommon. Further, it turns out that these arguments fail to work within OT. We thus will not review them here.

Transparency is also relevant to dissimilatory phenomena. Sometimes, when there are two adjacent identical elements, one deletes. This is only possible when the two elements are adjacent in the sense of having no element between them on the same tier. Dissimilations sometimes provide evidence that an intervening segment is underspecified for the relevant feature. Mester and Itô (1989) provide such an example from Japanese. In one type of noun compounding, if the first segment of the word is an obstruent, it becomes [+voiced], unless there is a later voiced obstruent in the word, in which case it remains voiceless:

1. ori - kami ⇒ ori-gami
2. onːa - kotoba ⇒ onːa-kotoba (*onːa-gotoba)

The two voiced obstruents do not have adjacent Root nodes; they are always separated by at least one vowel, and they can additionally be separated by other consonants. If the intervening consonant is a voiceless obstruent (as in *kotoba*) and specified as [-voiced], then the two tokens of [+voiced] would not be adjacent, and so should be allowable:

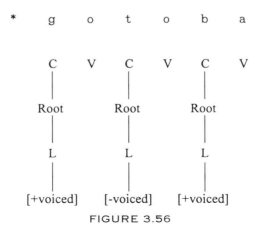

FIGURE 3.56

That the first [+voiced] is disallowed can be taken as evidence that the two tokens of [+voiced] are in fact adjacent, and that the intervening voiceless obstruent is underspecified for the feature [voiced]; it is also evidence that the vowels are not [+voiced] in underlying representations.

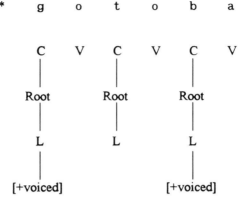

FIGURE 3.57

3.11.3.3. Less Tendency to Dissimilate

It has also been suggested that unspecified features might be less subject to dissimilation. S. Davis (1991) notes that there are constraints on place of articulation in stops in a word where the first stop follows an /s/. We do not find English words like *spep or *skick. However, we do find words like *stats*, *astute*, *stout*, and so on. We can assume that English does not allow a repetition of articulator nodes in this environment (between the second consonant in a cluster and a later coda consonant). But since alveolars are underspecified for place features, they have no articulator nodes: there is no repetition of articulator nodes, and two coronals are consequently allowed:

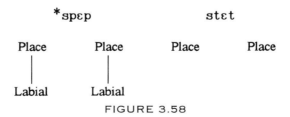

FIGURE 3.58

Yip (1991) argues for underspecification based on the complexity of sequences of consonants. In many languages, including English, there can be only one specified place of articulation in a sequence of consonants. Thus, one does not find words like *apker or *akper, even if manner of articulation is different: *afker, *afper*.[28] This holds even for marked coronals like /ʃ/ and /θ/: *ashker*, *athker*. In contrast, alveolars can co-occur with other places of articulation, and also with other alveolars: *actor*, *apt*, *sister*. Yip argues that there is a constraint that there can be only one specified articulator node in a sequence of consonants, and that alveolars are not bound by this restriction because they do not have any specified articulator nodes.

However, this could instead reflect constraints that disfavor sequences with two nondefaults, but allow sequences with one or two defaults. The pattern does not necessarily reflect underspecification (Smolensky, 1993).

3.11.3.4. Feature Adjustments after Assimilation

One last argument for underspecification is that sometimes assimilations lead to other feature changes. Consider the colloquial pronunciation of the sequence /vn̩/ in English:

seven /sɛvn̩/ [sɛbm̩]

This at first appears to be a straight-forward assimilation. First, the redundant feature [-continuant] spreads from the nasal to the fricative. Second, the Place node spreads from the /v/ to the /n/. But there is an oddity here: the resulting sequence is not labiodental, like the /v/, but bilabial, as one would expect of labial stops and nasals. If we assume that the /v/ is specified for the feature [+labiodental], then we need to change that feature after the assimilation. However, if we assume that /v/ is underspecified for [labiodental] (because the value of that feature is always predictable in English), the late-applying default feature-filling rules automatically fill in [-labiodental] for /bm/, since that is the default value for stops and nasals. It is common to find "automatic" adjustments of features after rules have either spread or delinked features. Chomsky and Halle (1968) suggested that we need special "clean-up rules" to make these adjustments. No special rules are needed if underspecification is assumed, however, because the redundant features were never present; once the change is made, a different set of feature-filling rules apply, whichever rules are appropriate to the surface segment. However, in OT, redundant features are enforced by constraints that can cause underlying features to delete and be replaced by the redundant features. These data thus do not uniquely implicate underspecification.

3.11.3.5. Summary of Grammar-Internal Evidence for Underspecification

Phonological underspecification is thus motivated:

1. by asymmetries in assimilation;
2. by transparency to assimilation;
3. by transparency to dissimilation;
4. by failure to undergo dissimilation;
5. by restrictions on the occurrence of specified articulator nodes; and

---

[28] There are a small number of words and names borrowed from other languages that violate this constraint: *Afghan*, *segment*, *atmosphere*, *Apgar*, etc.

6. because underspecification allows for automatic adjustments of predictable features after spreading or delinking.

Underspecification is still controversial within phonological theory. However, it accounts for so many patterns that we feel it is a workable hypothesis and use it in this book.

3.11.4. PSYCHOLINGUISTIC EVIDENCE FOR UNDERSPECIFICATION

There are additional arguments for phonological underspecification. Underspecification has been shown to be useful in accounting for data external to phonological theory: errors in speech production. Since such evidence provides convergent evidence for underspecification, we review it here. No one has yet addressed the data from an OT point of view assuming full specification, and it is unclear whether that point of view can account for all the data (though it can clearly account for *some* of it.)

Stemberger (1991a, 1991b, 1992b) has argued that evidence from speech errors by adult native speakers of English (in natural speech, and in psycholinguistic experiments) implies radical underspecification. Stemberger found two different patterns of asymmetry in errors for English monosyllables, whereby some segment A tends to be mispronounced as segment B. One pattern was entirely reasonable from a psychological point of view: speakers tended to mispronounce relatively low-frequency (uncommon) segments as relatively high-frequency (common) segments, but were less likely to mispronounce a high-frequency element as a low-frequency element. This type of frequency effect is observed in many other aspects of language processing and in other cognitive activities; it is reasonable that low-frequency elements, with which the speaker has had relatively less practice, will be more likely to undergo an error than a better-practiced high-frequency item. For example, speakers are more likely to mispronounce low-frequency velar /g/ as high-frequency labial /b/ than the reverse. In contrast, labial /p/ is lower in frequency than velar /k/, and speakers are more likely to mispronounce /p/ as /k/ than the reverse. Thus we see opposite patterns with voiced versus voiceless labial and velar stops, depending on the frequencies of the phonemes involved. Similarly, the relatively low-frequency low front vowel /æ/ tends to be mispronounced as the higher-frequency high front vowel /iː/ more than the reverse, but the relatively low-frequency high back vowel /uː/ tends to be mispronounced as the higher-frequency low back vowel /ɑ/ more than the reverse. These frequency-based errors are pervasive and noticeable (at least in experimental situations), and are consistent with the fact that frequency effects are found in many other aspects of language processing.

The second pattern of asymmetry found in the studies was not as expected. The most frequent feature value along some phonetic dimension (place, manner, or voicing), which we might expect to be the most resistant to error, actually had the highest error rate of all. For example, alveolar /t/ was far more frequent than either velar /k/ or labial /p/, but speakers were more likely to mispronounce /t/ as /k/ or /p/ than the reverse. Similarly, voiceless /t/ was more frequent than voiced /d/, but /t/ was more likely to be mispronounced as /d/ than the reverse. The stop /d/ was more frequent than the fricative /z/, but /d/ was more likely to be mispronounced as /z/ than the reverse. The most prominent asymmetry was originally reported by Shattuck-Hufnagel and Klatt (1979): alveolar /t/, /d/, and /s/ (among the most frequent phonemes of English) are more likely to be mispronounced as /tʃ/, /dʒ/, and /ʃ/ (among the least frequent phonemes of English) than the reverse. Thus, there seems to be an *antifrequency effect*, with more errors on the more frequent phoneme, the opposite of the expected frequency effect. But we cannot have frequency effects and antifrequency effects within a single processing component in speech production. Something else must underlie the apparent antifrequency effects.

The theory of underspecification can explain the antifrequency asymmetries. If /t/ is blank for all features, then those features are at risk to be replaced by specified features from the context. Thus, /t/ tends to be replaced by /k/ (specified for [Dorsal]), /p/ (specified for [Labial]), /d/ (specified for [+voiced]), /s/ (specified for [+continuant]), and /n/ (specified for [+nasal]). Segments with nondefault (specified) features, in contrast, do not tend to lose their specifications and so are more resistant to error. Hence, an asymmetry arises.

Stemberger (1993b) predicted that these same asymmetries would be relevant to morphological errors, such as those in which irregular verbs like *got* and *fell* are regularized to *getted* and *falled*. The hypothesis was that, for reasons of psychological processing, the vowels of the base form and past tense should be in competition for production in the same way that they are in phonological speech errors, and that the competition between the base vowel and the past tense vowel should be resolved in the same way. Further, if the base vowel were erroneously produced, the system should tend to make a further error and regularize the verb, resulting in an addition of -ed to the base form. If the vowel of the past tense was underspecified relative to the vowel of the base (like the /ɛ/ of *fell* is underspecified relative to the /a/ of *fall*), then the underspecified vowel should tend to be replaced by the specified vowel, and a regularization (*falled*) should be relatively likely. However, if the vowel of the base form was underspecified relative to the vowel of the past tense (like the /a/ of *got* relative to the /ɛ/ of *get*), then the past tense vowel should tend to prevail, and regularizations (*getted*) should be relatively unlikely. If neither vowel was underspecified relative to the other, however, the most frequent vowel should tend to win; regularizations would be relatively likely when the more frequent vowel was in the base form, and relatively unlikely when the more frequent vowel was in the past tense form. These predictions hold true for regularizations in child speech (Stemberger, 1993a). Stemberger and Setchell (1994) replicated this for adult errors, and showed that the same effect can also be observed in other types of inflectional errors. Morphological errors combine frequency effects and apparent antifrequency effects. Phonological underspecification nicely predicts the results. We conclude that there are interesting patterns of psychological performance that implicate radical underspecification in phonological representations, patterns which have yet to be accounted for if contrastive specification or full specification are assumed.

Stemberger (1991a, 1992b) further argues that learners derive underspecification from phoneme frequency. The most frequent feature or feature value along a phonetic dimension (place, manner, or voicing) is the underspecified value. Stemberger describes a processing model in which the most frequent value can arise by default, but less frequent values must be specified in the lexical entry in order to be produced accurately. As will be discussed below and in Chapter 4, this claim has interesting ramifications for phonological development, because phone frequency changes during the course of acquisition, suggesting that underspecification may also change over the course of acquisition.

There is some evidence for underspecification in aphasic speech. Béland and Favreau (1991) demonstrate that there is an asymmetry in nonassimilatory phonological paraphasias, such that nondefault places of articulation are generally replaced by the default place of articulation (anterior coronal). Béland, Paradis, and Bois (1993) show that error rates are greatest in words which contain two nondefault places of articulation, intermediate when one nondefault place is combined with the default place, and least when all consonants have default place of articulation. These results suggest that there is a difficulty with nondefault features, especially when several are combined in a single word.

The psycholinguistic evidence suggests that one feature (the default) is special, and that all nondefaults are equivalent. It is not clear that the full specification account can account for the fact that all nondefaults are equivalent, even within OT. We return to this issue in §4.4.2.2.

3.11.5. FURTHER ISSUES FOR UNDERSPECIFICATION

Given that some features may be absent, what about the organizing nodes that dominate those features? For example, if /t/ has no place or laryngeal features, does it have a Place node or a Laryngeal node? Clements (1985), Pulleyblank (1988), and Paradis and Prunet (1989) assume that organizing nodes are present only when there are specified features beneath them, and are otherwise underspecified because they are predictable. Pulleyblank (1988) goes as far as possible with this proposal, arguing that the Root node is predictable given that a V timing unit is present, so that the maximally underspecified vowel should have no features and no organizing nodes, only a timing unit. Avery and Rice (1989) and Stemberger (1993a), in contrast, assume that all organizing nodes are present in the underlying representation. At this point, however, there is little relevant empirical evidence. We assume that all organizing nodes are present, and note acquisition data that are easiest to account for if that is the case.

The underspecified feature matrices for adult English consonants and vowel are given in Tables 3.3 and 3.4. Note that /ɔ/ is the only vowel for which [V-Labial] is unpredictable. The vowel /ɔ/ is not present in many dialects, and rounding

TABLE 3.3. Underspecified Consonant Feature Matrix for Adult English (/t/ Underspecified)

	p	t	tʃ	k	b	d	dʒ	g	f	θ	s	ʃ	v	ð	z	ʒ	m	n	ŋ	l	ɹ	w	j	h	ʔ
sonorant																									
consonantal[a]																					−	−	−		
continuant									+	+	+	+	+	+	+	+									
nasal																	+	+	+						
lateral																				+					
tense																									
Laryngeal	√	√	√	√	√	√	√	√	√	√	√	√	√	√	√	√									√
voiced					+	+	+	+					+	+	+	+									
spread-glottis																								+	
constricted-glottis																									
Place	√	√	√	√	√	√	√	√	√	√	√	√	√	√	√	√	√	√	√	√	√	√	√		
Labial	√				√				√				√				√					√			
round																						√			
labiodental																									
Coronal		√	√			√	√			√	√	√		√	√	√		√		√	√		√		
anterior			−				−					−				−					−				
distributed										−				−											
grooved										−				−											
Dorsal				√				√											√			√	√		
back																						√			
high																						√	√		
low																									

[a]Because /h/ and /ʔ/ have no place, they are *predictably* [−consonantal].

TABLE 3.4.   Underspecified Vowel Feature Matrix for Adult English (/ɛ/Underspecified)

	i	ɪ	e	ɛ	æ	u	ʊ	o	ɔ	ɨ	ə	ʌ	ɑ/a
sonorant													
consonantal													
continuant													
nasal													
lateral													
tense													
voiced													
spread glottis													
constricted glottis													
Labial									√				
round													
labiodental													
Coronal													
anterior													
distributed													
grooved													
Dorsal	√	√	√	√	√	√	√	√	√	√	√	√	√
back						+	+	+	+	+	+	+	+
high	+	+				+	+			+			
low					+								+

is entirely predictable in those dialects.[29] We view the rounding of vowels as a nondefault feature (since most vowels are unrounded) that is redundant with other features and therefore *may* be left underspecified. However, we remind the reader that our position on underspecification (default underspecification) allows redundant nondefault features to be specified underlyingly. The values for consonants seem to be useful for most English-learning children. The reader is cautioned that the values for vowels may not hold for the early stages of acquisition, and may not be established until the child has acquired the entire vowel system of adult English.

[29] In /ɔɹ/ and /ɔɪ/, we believe that the /ɔ/ is a mid vowel. Long and diphthongal [+back] mid vowels are predictably [+round]. Stemberger (1983) and Shattuck-Hufnagel (1986) note for speech errors that there is a relationship between the diphthong /oʊ/ and the sequence /ɔɹ/, such that they appear to start with the same vowel.

3.12. SUMMARY AND CONCLUSIONS

We have reviewed the basic assumptions about phonological representations in recent phonological theory: the features, their organization with respect to each other (feature geometry), and how the various levels of the phonological hierarchy are associated with each other. We have noted points of controversy, in some cases controversies that we view as unresolved within phonological theory and have made clear our own stand on these controversies. We have also discussed concepts such as underspecification and the related concepts of active features and privative features. The types of processes that are used in multilinear phonology, and the types of formalisms that are used to state these processes have been reviewed, with a particular focus on how assimilation and dissimilation work within multilinear theory. We have not covered all the necessary concepts, however. In Chapter 4, we address constraints in detail. Minimally, constraints are used to motivate processes. In the approach that we adopt in this book, constraints are more extensive, and take the place of processes.

4

CONSTRAINTS

In this chapter, we provide an in-depth discussion of constraints. We begin with a discussion of the role of constraints in recent phonological theory and a brief discussion of theories that have only constraints, without processes. We then turn to Optimality Theory (OT), some conventions for presenting information within that theory, and an extensive discussion of the constraints used in this book. We caution the reader that OT is still under development and that there are currently many different versions of the theory. We discuss some of the variants, and propose a set of constraints that we find useful. Last, we explore several issues relating to language acquisition, and how OT deals with them.

4.1. THE ROLE OF CONSTRAINTS
IN RECENT THEORY

As noted in §2.1, constraints have come to play an active role in most phonological theories. Violations of constraints are ill formed. Processes are repair strategies that resolve the violations, so that constraints are not violated in surface pronunciations. Constraints are also used to motivate exceptions to processes. A process fails to apply to a form that it might be expected to apply to, if the application of the process would create a violation of some constraint.

The role of constraints in phonological theory is best illustrated with a constraint proposed by Goldsmith (1976):

Obligatory Contour Principle (OCP):   **A sequence of two identical elements is prohibited.**

The repetition of any element on any tier is considered an OCP violation. McCarthy (1986) and Yip (1988) argued that the OCP was a powerful force relative to phonological rules. Some rules existed primarily to resolve OCP violations. Other rules were restricted so that they would not apply if the result of the application was an OCP violation.

Yip argued that OCP violations can be resolved via deletion of one of the repeated elements, but in ways that are often rather surprising. Suppose, for example, that the OCP prevents the feature [Labial] from appearing in two adjacent consonants, but two tokens of [Labial] arise for some reason. This OCP violation can be resolved in a number of ways.

1. Delete one of the [Labial] features (either the left one or the right one). Since all consonants must have some articulator node, fill in the default feature [Coronal].

The violation is resolved by turning one of the labials into a coronal.

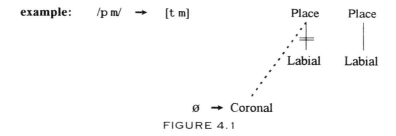

example: /p m/ ➞ [t m]

FIGURE 4.1

2. Delete one of the segments containing the feature [Labial] (either the left one or the right one).

The violation is resolved at a level higher than the feature that causes the OCP violation, but deleting the element that contains the [Labial] also repairs the violation.

example: /pm/ ➞ [m]

3. Delete one of the [Labial] features, and spread the other [Labial] feature to take its place.

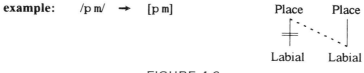

example: /p m/ ➞ [p m]

FIGURE 4.2

Since only one instance of [Labial] remains, this solves the OCP violation.

In most instances, this last repair would not be detectable phonetically; the sequence /pm/ is still pronounced [pm]; but the representation has changed, from two (singly-linked) tokens of [Labial] to one (doubly-linked) token. When one [Labial] has a dependent feature, however, the assimilation can be detected:

example: /p mʷ/ → [pʷ mʷ]

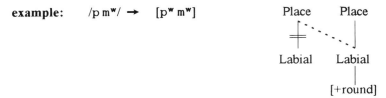

FIGURE 4.3

This could be described as the spreading of [+round] from one labial to another. But the motivation for the process might be to avoid sequences of two [Labial] nodes, and the assimilation occurs to resolve that violation. Here, the OCP violation has been resolved at the level of the feature that is causing the violation. However, Yip also proposes that the violation can occur at a higher level, up to and including the entire segment that is causing the violation:

4. Delete one of the segments that contains the [Labial] feature (either the left one or the right one), and spread the other segment to take the place of the deleted segment.

example: /m fʷ/ → [fʷ:]

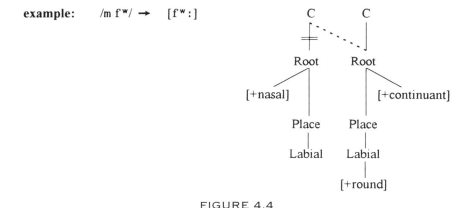

FIGURE 4.4

This repairs the OCP violation, but only at the cost of being unfaithful to other features (such as [+nasal], which is deleted from the first segment). Yip's insight is that assimilations can be motivated by a constraint that prevents the repetition of identical elements. Assimilation can be used as an alternative to dissimilation, and thus can occur for the same reasons that dissimilation occurs.

This discussion of the OCP highlights the way that constraints are used in modern phonological theory. A constraint leads to ill-formedness for some sequence or combination of elements. This constraint violation can be repaired in many different ways, including ways that we think of as opposites (such as assimilation vs. dissimilation). Further, the repair can involve different levels in the phonological hierarchy: from the level on which the violation occurs (such as [Labial]) to much higher levels.

LaCharité and Paradis (1993) argue that there is some predictability to the type of repair that is made to resolve constraint violations. They propose that repairs follow the *Minimal Principle*: the repair is made as low as possible in the phonological structure (where terminal features are at the bottom and prosodic words are at the top). For example, if a sequence of two tokens of [Labial] is prohibited, the lowest location in the representation where this can be resolved is on the [Labial] tier: by delinking [Labial] (deriving a default coronal consonant). All other alternatives (such as deleting the entire segment, or inserting a vowel between the two labials so that they are not adjacent) involve changes at a higher level in the hierarchy. Thus, languages with this constraint should delete one token of [Labial]. We show in later chapters that there are counterexamples to this proposal in phonological development. This proposal is best interpreted as a prediction about what processes are statistically most likely to occur, across languages and across children. To refer to processes that affect a higher-than-necessary level in the phonological hierarchy, we use the term *nonminimal repairs*.[1]

Constraints lead us to search for and locate motivations common to processes that are (at first appearance) very different from each other. They allow us to begin to decompose processes (which can be very complex) into simpler parts. In the example above, there are many different processes which we can reduce to the same environment (a sequence of two [Labial] features), all of which have changes that include a specific component (a surface form with only one [Labial] in it). Other aspects of the processes vary, but we have simplified our description of the different processes by extracting these common characteristics.

Several recent theories propose that all processes can be decomposed into common parts that are shared with other processes. All aspects of a process can be motivated by a set of independent constraints. These constraints determine whether it is the left or right instance of [Labial] (or the segment that contains it) that is deleted (or spread). They determine whether it is just the offending feature that is affected, or the entire segment (or syllable, or foot) that contains it. They determine whether it is simple deletion that occurs, or also spreading. In this view, any process, no matter how complex-looking, can be decomposed into smaller, simpler parts. Phonologists are looking for a universal set of simple constraints that, in combination, can account for all the processes that occur in the grammars of all (adult) human languages.

---

[1] We do not use the term "maximal," because the repair can be at different levels: Root node, timing unit, syllable, foot, etc. A "maximal" repair would presumably be one where the entire prosodic word is deleted.

In this book, we take the point of view that all processes can be decomposed into parts in this way. All processes derive from the combination of simple constraints. Later chapters explore child phonological development from this point of view, covering both common and uncommon combinations of constraints. In the remainder of this chapter, we present an overview of OT, and the constraints that are currently our best guess about what is needed. In later chapters, we also discuss the data in terms of repair processes, as a way of focusing the reader on the pattern involved.

4.2. CONSTRAINTS ALL THE WAY DOWN

As discussed in §2.1.3, it is possible to dispense with the notion of rule and process, and deal solely with constraints. There are two main approaches within phonological theory today that take this approach: OT (Prince & Smolensky, 1993; McCarthy & Prince, 1993a; see Archangeli & Langendoen, 1997, for introduction) and Declarative Phonology (DP; Scobbie, 1993). The two approaches share several crucial assumptions, but differ on others. Both approaches assume that there are only constraints and no processes, and that the underlying representation (UR) constitutes the most important constraint of all. We operate with the OT framework in this book. Declarative Phonology works for adult grammars, but seems ill-suited for language acquisition, and we will do little more than review the basic way that it works.

DP makes two additional assumptions. First, like earlier rule-based phonological theories, constraints are absolute and can never be violated. Second, all alternations are coded into the underlying representation for the morphemes involved. Constraints act to select out the particular variant that must appear in a given phonological environment (as also in Hockett, 1958; Lamb, 1966; Hudson, 1980, 1986.) For example, the *-ed* suffixes of English have a lexical entry along the following lines:

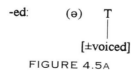

FIGURE 4.5A

The schwa is notated as variable; thus, it appears only when its absence would violate some constraint, such as the OCP in *[niːd-d]. Both values of [voiced] are listed, with some mechanism for giving [+voiced] priority in environments where either [+voiced] or [-voiced] is possible (such as after a vowel). In environments where [+voiced] is impossible, as in *[wɑk-d], constraints select out [-voiced]. It is possible to take all alternations observed in adult speech, code them into lexical entries in this way, and then allow constraints to select out the necessary variant. In DP, the necessity of coding all the variant pronunciations into the underlying representation derives from the other two assumptions: the underlying representation is a set of constraints on the pronunciation, and constraints can never be violated. The only way to be faithful to the underlying representations without violating any of the constraints imposed by the underlying representation is to note directly which elements are required and which elements are allowed to vary.

However, for language acquisition, coding variation into the lexical entry is a drawback, because it requires two things. First, the differences between adult and child pronunciations have to be directly coded into lexical entries. Selection is then made on the basis of the child's phonological constraints. As the child's phonological constraints change, the lexical entries must be restructured every time, in order to reflect the new constraints. This is a complex and cumbersome way to view change in the child's system. Furthermore, the mechanisms needed to determine which changes to make in the underlying representations are both complex and unknown. We do not believe that any plausible psychological mechanisms exist for the restructuring of lexical representations as rapidly as changes can occur in a child's phonological system.

OT is more flexible, because it assumes that constraints can be violated. It is thus not necessary to encode all alternations directly into underlying representations. The underlying representation can be a single invariant form which accurately reflects the adult pronunciation (insofar as the child has perceived the form correctly). This is then changed into different surface variants by the constraints of the language. Because the ranking of the constraints can change over the course of development, the child's pronunciation changes over the course of development. This provides a more reasonable account of development.

4.2.1. SOME FORMALISM: CONSTRAINT TABLES

In §2.1.3, we discussed some of the basic concepts of OT but did not introduce much of the formalism. OT uses a notational device that we call a *constraint table*: a table that lists the constraints in different rows, and the possible pronunciations and the particular constraints they violate in different columns.[2] The underlying representation is given in the upper left corner of the constraint table. Solid lines between rows denote that the higher row is ranked higher than the row below it; a dashed line means that the constraints are ranked as equally important or that it does not matter for our purposes which is ranked higher. Asterisks denote constraint violations. If a constraint is violated more than once, there is one asterisk

---

[2] The standard OT jargon is "*tableau*," with the French plural *tableaux*. "Constraint table" is simpler and semantically more transparent.

for each violation. The best candidate is the one that violates only low-ranked constraints; it is denoted in the table by enclosing it in a box.

The layout of the tables differs from the general practice of the literature. We have reversed the standard layout of the tables, which is to place constraints in columns and candidate pronunciations in rows. The standard layout has a problem: when there are many constraints, physical limitations on the page make it difficult to list all the constraints, without (a) switching to a much smaller font, or (b) using abbreviations for constraint names. Although it is standard to use (often extreme) abbreviations, we feel that this makes it more difficult to read and process the information. By placing constraints in rows, it becomes far easier to include all the necessary information. Our use of special borders to draw attention to important cells is also not standard.

Constraint tables may at first seem very intimidating, especially to the nonlinguist. However, they represent a clear graphical presentation of constraint hierarchies and constraint violations. Once the reader becomes familiar with them, they allow the reader to understand the situation much more quickly than if the same information were packaged only in prose. Constraint tables are no more complex than charts commonly used for the organization and presentation of data in speech-language pathology, audiology, or psychology, and are very useful, since the information they contain is easy to assimilate visually. To achieve the greatest clarity, we will discuss each constraint table in the text, explicitly pointing out the crucial information.

For illustrative purposes, we return to the phenomenon of Final Devoicing that we discussed in §2.1.3 Consider just two constraints:[3]

> **Survived**:   All elements in the underlying representation must be present in the output.
> **Not(+ voiced)**:   [+voiced] is not allowed in the output (in codas).

Consider what happens if **Not(+voiced)** is ranked higher than **Survived (+ voiced)**. Note that the first (leftmost) candidate is the adult pronunciation, and that the last (rightmost) candidate is the child's actual pronunciation; this is a general convention that we follow in this book, to the extent possible. (See Table 4.1.)

TABLE 4.1

/bɛd/	bɛd	bɛt
Not(+voiced)	*!	
Survived(+voiced)		*

[3] Actually, [+voiced] survives in onsets but not in codas. See §4.7.1.4 for a discussion of the effect of strong versus weak prosodic positions on survival.

Both of these pronunciations violate one constraint. The candidate [bɛd] violates **Not(+voiced)**, since [+voiced] appears in a coda; but it does not violate **Survived(+voiced)**, since all elements in the underlying representation are present on the surface. The candidate [bɛt] does not violate **Not(+voiced)**, since the final consonant is voiceless; but it violates **Survived(+voiced)**, since the underlying feature [+voiced] is not present on the surface. Since the higher-ranked constraint is **Not(+voiced)**, that constraint will not be violated: [+voiced] is not allowed in codas under any circumstances. The lower-ranked constraint is **Survived (+voiced)**, which is therefore violated by deleting [+voiced]. The exclamation point after the asterisk in the "bɛd" column in Table 4.1 above denotes a "fatal" violation: the violation that makes this pronunciation worse than others. We also draw attention to cells with fatal violations by giving them a different border. Further, all cells in Table 4.2 below that point are irrelevant, and we denote this by lightly shading them; it does not matter whether there are any violations of lower constraints, because there is a violation of a high-ranked constraint. The optimal candidate, [bɛt], is marked with a double-line border.[4]

If the constraints are in the opposite order, the results are different.

TABLE 4.2

/bɛd/	bɛd	bɛt
Survived(+voiced)		*!
Not(+voiced)	*	

Since **Survived(+voiced)** gives the fatal violation, the optimal pronunciation is [bɛd], even though it contains [+voiced] in a coda. If the two constraints are ranked in this way, there may not be any evidence that the language has the **Not(+voiced)** constraint, because **Survived(+voiced)** will always force underlying [+voiced] elements to be pronounced, even when they are in codas. If the language contains evidence for the constraint, it will be of a more subtle nature (such as not allowing [+voiced] to *spread* into a coda).

This brings up an important assumption of OT: all constraints are universal, and are present in every language (and in every speaker, whether adult or child). High-ranked constraints can directly affect phonological forms. Low-ranked constraints often have no effect on phonological form, since they are easily violated. This universality is reasonable whether constraints are innate or derive from in-

---

[4]Violations in low-ranked constraints are irrelevant because OT assumes a strict ranking of constraints, where degree of violation is not important. If, in fact, two violations of a low-ranked constraint are worse than one violation of a high-ranked constraint, then violations of low-ranked constraints would *not* be irrelevant. We believe that this is the case, but that it rarely actually matters.

dependent characteristics of human cognition and human anatomy (see §2.4). Even though some constraints are too low-ranked to have much effect, they still are constraints on the system. We discuss this possibility further below.

The phonological system is far more complex than this example with final devoicing reflects, however. There are many additional constraints. If we add in the constraint **Not(V-Root)**, we end up with six possible constraint tables:

Not(V-Root):   Vowels should not be present in the output.
       Note: As discussed in §4.4.2, one consequence of this constraint is
               that elements that are not present in underlying
               representations may not be inserted.

In each constraint table, all three output candidates violate one of the constraints. Which output candidate is optimal is determined entirely by which constraint is ranked lowest: it is always the lowest-ranked constraint that is violated. If **Not(+ voiced)** is ranked lowest, then it is **Not(+ voiced)** that is violated. Since **Not(+ voiced)** is violated only when the feature [+voiced] appears in the coda, then [+voiced] appears in the coda. The relative ranking of the two higher-ranked constraints does not matter here; the optimal candidate is determined solely by the lowest-ranked constraint. To save space, when the relative ranking of two constraints does not matter, those two rows in the table are separated by a dashed line; if the order *does* matter, a solid line separates the two rows.[5] (See Table 4.3.)

TABLE 4.3

/bɛd/	bɛd	bɛt	bɛdə
Survived(+voiced)		*!	
Not(V-Root)			*!
NotCo-occurring(Coda,+voiced)	*		

The optimal output is different if **Survived(+ voiced)** is the lowest-ranked constraint. **Survived(+ voiced)** is violated if an input element does not appear in the output. If the feature [+voiced] is deleted (with the consequent insertion of the default feature [-voiced]), then we avoid a violation of **Not(+ voiced)**. Thus, when **Survived(+ voiced)** is ranked lowest, we observe Final Devoicing of obstruents. It does not matter whether **Not(+ voiced)** is ranked higher or lower than **Not(V-Root)**, since it is the lowest-ranked constraint that determines which candidate is optimal. (See Table 4.4.)

---

[5] The dashed line between constraints can also be used to denote that the constraints are ranked as equals. The consequences of equally ranked constraints are discussed in §4.11.

TABLE 4.4

/bɛd/	bɛd	bɛt	bɛdə
Not(V-Root)			*!
Not(+voiced)	*!		
Survived(+voiced)		*	

Finally, the third output candidate is optimal if **Not(V-Root)** is the lowest-ranked constraint. **Not(V-Root)** is violated when a segment is inserted that is not present in the underlying representation. The insertion of a word-final schwa allows the final /d/ of *bed* to appear in the onset of the syllable that the schwa creates. Since the [+voiced] of the /d/ is not in a coda, there is no violation of **Not(+voiced)**. The /d/ can be faithfully pronounced as [d], but only if there is epenthesis. It does not matter whether **Not(+voiced)** is ranked higher or lower than **Survived(+voiced)**; the optimal candidate is determined solely by the low ranking of **Not(V-Root)**. (See Table 4.5.)

TABLE 4.5

/bɛd/	bɛd	bɛt	bɛdə
Survived(+voiced)		*!	
Not(+voiced)	*!		
Not(V-Root)			*

These three pronunciations do not exhaust the possibilities, since there are additional relevant constraints. The faithfulness constraints are not single constraints, but *families* of constraints. There is one **Survived** and **Not** constraint for every element in the phonological representation: **Survived(+voiced)**, **Survived (Labial)**, etc.; **Not(+voiced)**, **Not(Labial)**, etc. Consider the following:

Survived(Root):   An underlying Root node must be present in the output.

Survived(+voiced):   An underlying [+voiced] must be present in the output.

This raises an additional possibility for the pronunciation of *bed*: [bɛ], in which the entire final consonant is deleted, a violation of **Survived(C-Root)**. We consider here only the two constraint tables (Tables 4.6a and 4.6b) in which the two **Survived** constraints are the lowest-ranked constraints.

TABLE 4.6A

/bɛd/	bɛd	bɛt	bɛ	bɛdə
Not(+voiced)	*!			
Not(V-Root)				*!
Survived(C-Root)			*!	
Survived(+voiced)		*		

TABLE 4.6B

/bɛd/	bɛd	bɛt	bɛ	bɛdə
Not(+voiced)	*!			
Not(V-Root)				*!
Survived(+voiced)		*!		
Survived(C-Root)			*	

Note that a violation of **Not(+voiced)** is avoided in [bɛ]: since there is no coda at all, it cannot contain the feature [+voiced]. Which **Survived** constraint is violated depends on which one is ranked lower. If **Survived(+voiced)** is lower-ranked, then it is the one that is violated: the Root node survives but [+voiced] does not, and a voiceless stop results. If **Survived(Root)** is lower-ranked, then it is the one that is violated: the entire final voiced obstruent is deleted, resulting in [bɛ]. Note that this is a nonminimal repair: it resolves a constraint violation involving [+voiced] by deleting at a higher level (the Root node) than would be necessary to resolve the violation.[6]

OT is currently in its infancy, and there are still many things that are unclear. The exact set of constraints in human languages has yet to be worked out in detail. Thus far, researchers working with particular phenomena in particular languages posit the constraints needed to derive those phenomena. Consequently, many constraints are postulated ad hoc to account for specific phenomena in particular languages. Reasoning is often circular: we need Constraint X to derive the patterns in this language, and the patterns in this language constitute the evidence for Constraint X. This circularity will lessen as constraints are replicated for additional

---

[6]The astute reader may wonder why this is not also a violation of **Survived(+voiced)**. We are oversimplifying here. It is actually **LinkedUpwards(Root)** that is violated as is discussed in the text.

languages (and children). Currently, we do not know what the constraints of human language are, nor whether there are any limits as to which constraints are possible. For now, we must posit the constraints that are necessary to account for the observed patterns. The value of this endeavor rests partly in the identification of the motivation behind the phonological patterns that we observe. Like any theory, a constraint-based view is valuable only insofar as it provides us with useful insights about behavior.

In the remainder of this chapter, we provide an overview of the constraints that we use in this book. We have not strived for absolute completeness. We focus on the constraints needed for the phenomena encountered in phonological development, especially in English-learning children. This covers most of the phonological constraints needed for adult languages, but not many of the morphologically related ones.

Although OT uses no rules or processes, most current versions of OT assume the same representations as previous nonlinear theories. The difference lies mainly in the way that dynamic changes to those representations occur. Changes in terms of the number of association lines can still be described as "spreading" or "de-linking," etc. OT does not represent a new theory about phonological representations. It replaces only the theory of how those nonlinear representations are built and altered. It replaces the theory of *phonological processes* without addressing the theory of *phonological representations*.

In the following chapters, we often refer to "repair processes" motivated by constraints, but also provide constraint rankings or tables. Processes are in many ways easier to understand, because the interaction of constraints can become very complex. In our view, a fully constraint-based phonology is more likely to be psychologically valid, and provides a more reasonable description of phonological development. It does, however, have the drawback of requiring far more problem solving on the part of the practitioner to derive the necessary constraint-ranking from a complex set of data; easily seen processes can be hard-to-see constraint rankings. We thus talk about patterns in terms of both processes and constraints.

In our experience, the most difficult task in building a constraint table is determining which constraints are relevant to the phenomenon at hand. In Appendix D, we provide some tips to follow: given a certain surface phenomenon, certain constraints are the most likely ones to be involved. We also provide some tips about which output candidates to consider. Anyone applying OT to their own work will find these two tasks to be the most challenging.

4.2.2. HOW DO WE KNOW WHAT THE CONSTRAINTS ARE?

Having decided to use constraints, we are faced with the problem of determining what the constraints are. There has been little research on this question within OT. Most of the work has been devoted to working out the basic principles: how the theory should be structured, independent of the particular constraints that are used. Most work uses an ad hoc set of constraints. In this section, we lay out the philosophy behind the set of constraints that we use in this book.

We believe that constraints should have the following characteristics:

1. They should be simple and nonredundant.
2. They should be grounded, reflecting constraints on cognition, articulation, perception, and communication.

The constraints used by most practitioners of OT have neither characteristic.

All constraints should be simple. Ideally, a given constraint should refer to only a single type of information. Consider the following three types of information:

1. The element is present in the underlying representation.
2. The element is linked up in the output.
3. The element is in a coda.

We could deal with all three types of information via separate simple constraints as follows:

1. Elements in the input should be in the output.
2. Elements should be linked up.
3. There should not be a coda.

We could then use the interaction of these three constraints to determine whether an underlying element would surface in a coda, or whether it would be deleted. Alternatively, we could combine all three types of information into a single complex constraint:

Elements in the input should not be in a coda in the output.

If this constraint is violated, then the segment might be deleted rather than being produced as part of a coda. We would additionally have similar constraints of similar complexity, including:

1. Elements in the input should be in an onset in the output.
2. Elements in the input should be in a nucleus in the output.
3. Inserted elements should be in an onset in the output.

We would have many constraints that are all quite similar, each subsuming the same types of information.

We believe that all constraints should be simple (in the sense of uncomplicated). They should have as few parts and as few degrees of freedom as possible. Partly this is because science values simplicity in general. Partly this is because of the way that constraints differ from processes, as discussed in §2.1.4. In OT, processes are unpacked into a set of independent constraints. By using simple constraints, the unpacking of processes is taken as far as it can go, and the resulting theory is very different from a process-based theory. If complex constraints are used, the constraints come closer to packaging the same information that processes do, and the theory more closely resembles a process-based theory. If unpacking processes into sets of constraints is a desirable thing, we should unpack them fully. Finally, we feel that simple constraints are compatible with any point of view on the issue of innateness. Simple constraints could be innate, or could reasonably derive from independent aspects of cognition, phonetics, etc. Complex constraints probably require that the constraints be innate. Since we do not have a definitive answer to that issue (see §2.4), it is best to pursue an approach that is compatible with either resolution of the issue. For these reasons, we use simple constraints.

We also believe that constraints need to be grounded in cognition, articulation, perception, and communication. Nothing should be mysterious. If it is impossible to provide a reasonable explanation for the existence of a particular constraint, it is a suspect constraint. The constraints that we use in this book fall into three main categories:

1. FAITHFULNESS: *Input-to-Output Correspondence Constraints*
   "Be true to your word."
   Pronounce everything in the lexical entry, without change.
2. NEGATIVE CONSTRAINTS: *Output Constraints*
   An element such as [+voiced]
   a. is not allowed at all: **NOT(+voiced)**
   b. cannot be combined with other features at the same time:
      NotCo-occurring(+voiced,X)
   c. cannot be used in a sequence with anything else:
      NoSequence(+voiced...X)
   d. cannot be done twice in a row: **NotTwice(+voiced)**, and
   e. cannot be extended beyond its basic inherent duration
      (can be linked upwards to only a single element):
      SinglyLinked(+voiced)

For elements that dominate other elements, we also restrict the number of dependent elements to a minimum:

   f. The element can link downwards to only a single element:
      NotComplex(Onset)
3. STRUCTURE: *Output Constraints*
   Segments are grouped into syllables, which have certain optimal characteristics.
   Syllables are grouped into feet, which have certain optimal characteristics.

Faithfulness is clearly a reasonable type of constraint to have. Without it, there would be no way to ensure that different words are pronounced differently. McCarthy and Prince (1994) coin the term *correspondence* for constraints on the relationship between the input and the output. For added clarity, we refer to them as *input-to-output correspondence* constraints. We feel that it is desirable to keep such constraints to a minimum. In our system, the only such constraints are **Survived** (preventing deletion) and **Contiguity** (preventing reordering and separation); no correspondence constraint is needed to prevent insertion of elements (see below).

All other constraints are purely constraints on output. Elements in the output are subject to these constraints (if they are ranked high enough), whether the element is in the input or is inserted in the output.

Constraints that create structure are in principle suspect, since one could question why structure is needed at all. However, certain patterns in the data do show that some segments "cohere" more than others. Structure is used to explain such cohesiveness, but some alternative concept might also account for it. It is to be hoped that the structural constraints can be adapted to whatever concept is used to account for cohesiveness, if they are simple enough. Some of the structural constraints may be grounded in articulation and perception (involving rhythms) or in communicative functions (such as making word boundaries easier for a listener to detect).

The negative constraints are firmly grounded in cognition, and are true of all human performance, whether motor or perceptual. Any articulation requires some degree of effort: it has some level of difficulty (however small) and requires some amount of cognitive resources. Since cognitive resources are limited, this sets an upper limit on what a speaker is capable of producing. If an element takes too many resources to produce, it may instead be deleted or avoided. Further, if given a choice between an articulation that uses many resources (difficult) versus an articulation that uses few resources (easy), it is reasonable that the speaker might choose the easy articulation:

Ease of articulation: Try to use as few resources as possible.

Given that an activity is possible, combining several activities at the same time requires enough resources to do both. Concurrent tasks can decrease accuracy on each task individually. Performing two different actions in sequence is always more difficult than performing the actions separately (until the sequence is well learned, in any event). Performing an action twice can cause special difficulty (e.g., Norman, 1981). All cognitive activities are constrained in this way.

OT can thus be viewed as a modern instantiation of ease-of-articulation theories (see also Hayes, 1996). However, it differs from earlier theories in a crucial way. Earlier theories assume that it is possible to characterize what is easy versus what is difficult *for all speakers, regardless of age or language*; what is difficult for one person is equally difficult for another. OT instead posits that the difficulty of a particular action can be different for different people, depending on experience and on chance factors. For reasons that are not well understood, any given task can be hard for one person but easy for another. Further, particular actions become easier with practice (while unpracticed actions remain difficult). We assume that different individuals start with different constraint rankings (so that there is variation across individuals as to what is easy and what is difficult), and that constraints are reranked in the course of development, reflecting practice with particular elements, combinations, sequences, etc. Since reranking will be different for speakers of different languages, what is difficult and what is easy will vary across languages (to some degree). Older ease-of-articulation theories do not recognize the role of individual variation or practice.

Some types of grounding are expressed in the constraint rankings, and not in the constraints themselves. For example, general cognitive constraints on combining features make a cost to the combination of [-sonorant] with either [+voiced] or [-voiced]; there are constraints against both combinations of features. However, facts specific to *articulation* make it more difficult to combine [-sonorant] with [+voiced] than with [-voiced]: voiced obstruents are more difficult than voiceless obstruents. During voicing, supralaryngeal pressure constantly increases, and voicing becomes difficult to sustain as pressure rises; but a wider range of pressures are possible for voiceless obstruents. This difference in difficulty is reflected in the relative ranking of the two constraints, which is firmly grounded in phonetics. In general, it appears that:

1. The constraints *themselves* are *cognitively* (and communicatively) grounded.
2. The constraint *rankings* are *phonetically* grounded.

We believe that input-to-output correspondence constraints should be kept to a minimum, for two reasons. First, all such constraints other than faithfulness constraints probably have no grounding. Second, such constraints greatly increase the power of the system, bringing us back conceptually to rules. There are two logically possible types of input-to-output constraints in addition to faithfulness:

UNFAITHFULNESS: The output must be different from the input in some specific way.

CO-OCCURRENCE: If some element is present in the input, then some particular element/characteristic must be present in the output.[7]

Unfaithfulness constraints have not (yet) been used within OT, but a possible example would arise if McCarthy's (1989) analysis of the moras of vowels were to be adopted in OT. McCarthy assumed that as few moras are present underlyingly as possible, and that moras are inserted by rule: every vowel receives one additional mora, regardless of how many moras the vowel has in the input:

Inserted(Mora):   A vowel must be linked to a mora that is not present in the input.

This would require the representation to change: unfaithfulness. There are input-to-output co-occurrence constraints of this sorts that at first seem reasonable:

Co-occurring(Input[+low]→Output[-high]):   If a vowel is [+low] in the input, it must be [-high] in the output.

---

[7] Note that this differs from our usual use of the term "co-occurrence," which refers to the co-occurrence of two elements in the output. These correspondence co-occurrence constraints are closely related, however, as will be made clear below.

This seems reasonable at first. The features [+low] and [+high] both cannot be present in the same segment, since they are phonetically incompatible. However, this constraint could have an effect even if [+low] fails to survive in the output. Thus, an underlying low vowel could surface as any [-high] vowel, whether low ([æ]) or mid ([e]), but could not surface as high ([i]). Underlying mid vowels, in contrast, could surface as [+high]. The co-occurrence restriction is phonetically grounded if it holds entirely on the output; it is not phonetically grounded if it holds only on the correspondence between input and output.

We believe that input-to-output correspondence constraints must be avoided, to the extent possible, because they make virtually anything possible. A system that allows only faithfulness constraints and output constraints is far less powerful. It is an empirical question as to whether our highly constrained approach will succeed, but we feel that it is necessary to try. More complex theories (such as McCarthy and Prince, 1994, and most current variants of OT) should be used only if the simpler variants fail.

4.2.3. GEN (THE GENERATOR) AND EVAL (THE EVALUATOR)

There are two components of OT that we rarely mention in this book. In addition to the set of ranked constraints, there is *Gen*: a component that supplies a set of output candidates from which the optimal candidate is selected for production. There is also *Eval*: a component that evaluates each output candidate against the set of ranked constraints, and determines which candidate is the optimal one. Eval is integral to the system; it is the component that determines the actual output within the system. But it operates silently in the background and supplies the answers that are needed to select the best output candidate.

We rarely mention Gen because very little is known about it (Prince & Smolensky, 1993). If there are types of outputs that Gen never generates and provides for evaluation, then those outputs represent patterns that can never appear in human language. Any restrictions within Gen would constitute constraints that could never be violated under any circumstances (as opposed to the rankable constraints, which can be violated). Possible candidates for such nonviolable constraints would be basic feature geometry and syllable structure. However, since we know nothing about Gen, we do not place any constraints within Gen in this book. We explicitly discuss all constraints that we need, with the understanding that some of them may be a part of Gen and thus can never be violated.

The way that we envision Gen is that it supplies all possible output forms in the language on the basis of any input. The constraints quickly winnow out most of these forms, and narrow the set of *likely* outputs to a relatively small number. In practice, researchers working within OT have treated Gen in this way.

Note that there are always far more output candidates that are "likely" than we could possibly present in any constraint table. In practice, only those candidates that are relevant to the particular issue under examination (the final consonant, the feature [+voiced], the stress pattern, etc.) are presented. In some constraint tables, we present a set of candidates that represent everything that is likely to happen across languages (or across children). In other instances, we tailor the candidates that we present to the particular language system under examination, showing how that particular system rules out particular alternatives that are likely in that system. There are no guidelines about which candidates to present, however. The reader is reminded that constraint tables are for illustrative purposes only. There are always more constraints and more output candidates than can be presented in a single table, and no reader would ever be able to make sense of that full complexity.

Prince and Smolensky (1993) conceive of Gen as generating an infinite number of candidates. This, of course, would make it impossible to instantiate OT within a human being, since a finite creature cannot generate an infinite number of candidates in a finite time. Indeed, a human being must be able to decide on the output candidate within about 200 or 250 msec, so the total candidate set must not only be finite, but small. There is currently no proof that there is a possible Gen function that can be instantiated within a human being. This is a point where OT makes a promissory note: to prove some day that there is a variant of Gen that will fit inside a human being and still generate for a given input all the candidates necessary to derive every pronunciation that could arise in all languages. Although the theory is vague on this point, we believe that it is a worthwhile gamble to pursue the theory. (For discussion, see Golston, 1996, and Hammond, 1995.)

4.3. THE CONSTRAINTS OF OPTIMALITY THEORY

In the next sections of this chapter, we provide an overview of the constraints of OT. We would like to emphasize at the outset that the number of constraints is *very* large. We would estimate that there are thousands of constraints, of both a positive nature (requiring that something be present) and a negative nature (ruling something out). This is true for the adult language whether we assume that the constraints are innate or learned.

A second point that we would like to emphasize is that constraint ranking does most of the work that rule ordering did in earlier theories. In process-based theories, it is often held that the processes must apply in a particular temporal order, to derive the correct pronunciation. In OT, the constraints are not temporally ordered in this way. All the constraints have their effects simultaneously, in parallel. Requiring that constraints be satisfied in parallel often has the same results as a feeding order (where Process A creates the environment for Process B, which then applies) in process-based accounts. For example, consider two hypothetical processes that alter syllable-final /n/ to [tʰ]:

Process A: Change nasals in codas into oral stops.
Process B: Make oral stops in codas aspirated ([+s.g.]).

Process B cannot apply to /n/ in a word like *pan*, because /n/ is not an oral stop. But Process A converts the /n/ into the oral stop [t]. Process B *can* apply to [t], changing it to [tʰ], so Process B applies in the word *pan*, yielding [pʰætʰ]. In a process-based model, Process A must first apply, then Process B can apply. Without that ordering, the final consonant of *pan* would surface as an unaspirated oral stop. In OT, however, the constraints are satisfied in parallel, at the same time. One constraint prevents [+sonorant, +nasal] in a coda; the other constraint requires that oral stops in codas be [+s.g.]:

[n]: violates constraint on nasals in codas
[t]: violates constraint requiring [+s.g.] in oral stops in codas
[tʰ]: violates neither constraint

[tʰ] is the optimal output, because it violates neither of the constraints, whereas the other possibilities violate at least one of the constraints. There is no need for ordering. In this way, almost all instances in which ordering has been posited for process-based accounts can be derived without any (temporal) ordering.

The constraints can be thought of as falling into five natural groupings:

Faithfulness: ensuring that the surface and UR are the same
Structure: building prosodic structure
Features: requiring certain co-occurrences of features
preventing certain co-occurrences of features
preventing sequences of elements, based on their feature content
Alignment: requiring that certain elements (usually one morphological, one phonological) co-occur in a particular way
Morphology: governing the presence of affixes

There is some artificiality to this division, but we believe that the reader will find it useful. We stress that the groupings are entirely pedagogical in nature: they have no important status within OT itself. Indeed, a particular constraint may sometimes enforce faithfulness and sometimes prevent faithfulness.

We have renamed most of the constraints that are used in OT. In one sense, the name that is used for a particular constraint does not matter; only the constraint's effects on phonology matters. However, names that do not clearly reflect the content of the constraint are difficult to learn and remember. Unfortunately, many constraint names in OT (and in phonology in general) are relatively opaque: from the label placed on the constraint, it is not always possible to tell what the constraint does. A good example is the OCP. The acronym "OCP" has no inherent meaning until it is memorized. Further, even the words for which "OCP" stands are rather unclear: in "the Obligatory Contour Principle," the constraint is not obligatory (since no constraints are obligatory in OT, but can be violated under certain circumstances), and the word "contour" is not commonly used to refer to the types of multiattachment that the OCP favors. Further, linguists tend to use abbreviations in the names of constraints that nonlinguists may find daunting. For example, Itô, Mester, and Padgett (1995) take the relatively transparent name **RedundancyCondition** (which addresses which features are redundant relative to which other features) and abbreviate it as **R-Cond**, which is much less transparent. Another tendency that decreases transparency is the use of mathematical notation such as "*" as a negator, so that ***Struc** (leading to the unfortunate pronunciation, "star-struck") means "no structure (is allowed)." Although linguists are accustomed to such opaque terms, they can be a significant barrier for nonlinguists (especially if "unusual" pronunciations, such as "star-struck," are used). Speech-language pathologists and psychologists may react negatively to such terms, decide that they require too great an effort to learn and use, and subsequently lose interest in learning the theory .

An additional problem is that some constraints are given names more appropriate for processes. For example, Prince and Smolensky (1993) introduce the constraints **Parse** and **Fill**, and Itô et al. (1995) introduce the constraints ***Insert** and ***Spread**. All four of these constraints have a verb as their name, which conjures up a process: to parse segments, to fill in material, to insert, and to spread. But the constraints are actually constraints on output representations, and we feel that it is misleading and confusing to use such names. Constraint names should not tempt the reader to think in terms of processes.

In order to solve these problems with the names of constraints, we have decided to rename the vast majority of constraints. We have chosen names that we feel are transparent: the reader can remember the name by knowing the content of the constraint, and will generally know the content of the constraint by knowing the name. Although this will facilitate the learning of OT by the novice, there are costs. Because the labels that we use for constraints differ from the labels found more generally in the field, readers may find it more difficult to read the general OT literature. We provide the reader with other names that are found in the literature. To differentiate old and new names, we make use of two icons placed before the constraint name. The new name is marked by a pencil icon when we first define the constraint: ✑. The old name (that we recommend against using) will be marked by a scissors icon, meant only to mean that the *name* should *be cut out* (with no further judgment). To illustrate a small change of name:

OLD NAME: ✂**NoCoda**
NEW NAME: ✑**Not(Coda)**

The reader will thus know the name we use for the constraint in this book, along with other names used in the literature. For easy reference, Appendix C contains a list of the old and new names of the constraints.

We emphasize that the change of names is for ease of learning and ease of use. In many cases, we accept the definition of the constraints as originally proposed, but have simply changed the name. Labels are never important to a theory; only the concepts are important. Renaming constraints makes no substantive change to the theory. However, it can make learning and using the theory more pleasant, and that is one of our goals.

There is, however, a cost to using only transparent names: they can be quite long. Although they facilitate learning, they can be cumbersome once the system is mastered. After mastery, opaque names are no longer a barrier, and may be preferable because they can be used more quickly. We encourage the reader to use abbreviations once the constraints are mastered. However, we feel strongly that abbreviations should not be used in the published literature, and do not use abbreviations in this book.

4.4. FAITHFULNESS CONSTRAINTS

By "faithfulness," we mean that the information in the UR should surface without change. Prince and Smolensky (1993) break faithfulness down into three separate properties:

1. All elements and association lines in the UR should also be present on the surface. *Do not delete anything.*
2. No elements or association lines should be present on the surface unless they were in the UR. *Do not add anything.*
3. Elements should be in the same order with respect to each other on the surface as they were in the UR. *Do not change the order of elements.*

We discuss the faithfulness constraints in that order. We caution the reader that our system differs from that of Prince and Smolensky in a number of ways, which we will discuss and motivate.

4.4.1. DELETING ELEMENTS AND AVOIDING DELETION

The first aspect of faithfulness requires that all elements and association lines that are present in the UR must also be present on the surface. No deletion is allowed. Constraints are violated when some element or association line is deleted.

In order to be pronounced, an element must be integrated into the phonological structure (thus anchoring it in time), with links through higher elements all the way up to a prosodic word node (which is necessary for actual pronunciation). This is represented by linking the element to an element on the tier above it, via an association line. It is a very important constraint on output that all elements should be linked upwards:

✏️**LinkedUpwards**: An element must be linked to an element on the tier above it. (An element must be anchored in time relative to other elements.)

    violation: an unlinked (floating) element[8]

---

[8] Recall that a floating element is one that has not been integrated into the temporal structure of the word. Consequently, it is not anchored in time and cannot be produced in real time.

grounding: Since speech occurs in real time, with certain temporal properties, all elements must be anchored in time relative to each other.

old name: ✄Parse

One consequence of this constraint is that all elements in the underlying representation must be linked in the surface pronunciation. This usually leads to faithfulness, but not always. If a feature is floating (unlinked) in the underlying representation, linking that feature up is unfaithful to the underlying form. Further, this constraint does not refer just to underlying elements. It constrains *all* elements; if an element is inserted (see §4.4.2), that element must also be linked upwards (and thus anchored in time) in order to be produced.

The **LinkedUpwards** constraint is not in and of itself sufficient to ensure that underlying elements are pronounced, however. **LinkedUpwards** requires that an element must be linked *IF* it is present in the output. Such linkage can be avoided if the feature is simply deleted, so that it is not part of the representation. We need some additional constraint or principle to prevent such deletion. Prince and Smolensky (1993) assume a principle that they call *containment*, which holds *absolutely* that no underlying element can be deleted; this was viewed as a part of Gen, and thus could not be violated. McCarthy and Prince (1995), however, suggest that this leads to problems. We thus assume that "containment" is a violable constraint:

✏Survived: An element in the underlying representation must be present in the output.

violation: a deleted element

grounding: For communicative purposes, to distinguish lexical items from each other, underlying elements must be present in the output. The greater the number of deleted elements, the greater the number of homophonous lexical items, and the greater the difficulty of lexical access in perception.

old names: ✄Containment; ✄MAX; ✄Corr$_{io}$; ✄Ident; ✄Match

Any deletion of an underlying element violates this constraint. If **Survived** is not violated, then **LinkedUpwards** requires the element to be linked. Thus, the underlying element may be pronounced.

The **Survived** and **LinkedUpwards** constraints are not single constraints. Rather, each one is a *family* of constraints. There is one member of the family for each element in the phonological representation. **Survived(Root)** and **Linked-Upwards(Root)** require an underlying Root node to be present in the output and linked up. **Survived(+ voiced)** and **LinkedUpwards(+ voiced)** require any underlying [+voiced] feature to be present in the output and linked up, and so on. The sole exception is that there is no **LinkedUpwards** constraint for the highest structural node, which cannot be linked in the way required by the constraint. We follow the general practice of using the family name for all members of the constraint, modified with the name of the particular element that is relevant to a particular constraint. There are a variety of ways that the particular element could be added to the name. Conventions that have appeared in the literature include: capitalized (≪**LinkedUpwardsVoice**), hyphenated (≪**LinkedUpwards-Voice**), slashed (≪**LinkedUpwards/Voice**), and superscripted (≪**LinkedUpwards** ^Voice^). We place the particular element in parentheses:

☞**LinkedUpwards(Foot)**
☞**LinkedUpwards(σ)**
☞**LinkedUpwards(Onset)**   (plus other syllable components)
☞**LinkedUpwards(μ)**   (plus other timing units)
☞**LinkedUpwards(Root)**
☞**LinkedUpwards(Place)**   (plus other organizing nodes)
☞**LinkedUpwards(+ sonorant)**
☞**LinkedUpwards(-sonorant)**
☞**LinkedUpwards(+ continuant)**
☞**LinkedUpwards(-continuant)**
    etc. (one for each value of each feature)
    Note: No known inherent ranking within the family.

Which of these family members is relevant depends on which element is involved in the deletion (or is prevented from being deleted). If a consonant *and* its timing unit are deleted, **LinkedUpwards(C)** is involved. If the timing unit is not deleted, but the consonant is, **LinkedUpwards(Root)** is involved; the timing unit will then be expressed phonetically (through compensatory lengthening, for example). If the consonant is produced, but loses its Place node (becoming a glottal consonant), **LinkedUpwards(Place)** is involved. If [Dorsal] is deleted, **Linked-Upwards(Dorsal)** is involved, and so on.

Similarly, there is a **Survived** constraint for each of these elements. Note, however, that **Survived** is only relevant if the element is actually in the underlying representation. Any element that is not specified underlyingly (such as [Coronal], [-voiced], or syllables and feet; see §3.11) cannot be subject to a **Survived** constraint.

In addition to its use with content elements, **Survived** also has a family member that deals with association lines:

☞**Survived(Link)**:   An underlying association line must be present in the
                       output.
    violation: An underlying link is deleted.
    old name: ≪Parse(Link)

This constraint is violated if an underlyingly linked feature is (a) deleted, (b) made floating, or (c) flopped onto another segment (so that it delinks from the segment to which it was originally attached).

In some instances, the system takes two input elements that are in conflict, and deletes one. For example, if a vowel cannot be adjacent to another vowel, one of the vowels is deleted. Although one could imagine a special survived constraint that selects which element survives (such as ✂Survived(First)), this is not an attractive option. It would be best to have a constraint that gives preference to material early in the word versus another constraint that gives preference to material late in the word:

✏**Priority(Left,X)**:	Element X early in the word has priority.
grounding:	PRIMACY EFFECT
✏**Priority(Right,X)**:	Element X late in the word has priority.
grounding:	RECENCY EFFECT

When some negative constraint makes it possible for only one of two elements to link up, the relative ranking of these two constraints will determine which links up (unless some constraint that is ranked even higher also has an effect on which element links up). If **Priority(Left,X)** is ranked higher, then the element on the left links up. If **Priority(Right,X)** is ranked higher, then the element on the right links up. It is not sufficient to establish priority once and for all, for all features/ elements in a language. Consequently, we use constraint families, with one family member for each element in the system.

In some instances, two singly linked tokens of an element can be converted into one doubly linked token of the element:

FIGURE 4.5B

We do not view this as involving deletion. Both segments are linked to a token of [Labial] in both the input and the output; the single token of [Labial] in the output represents (corresponds to) both tokens in the input. This is instead a violation of the following constraint:

✏**Distinct(<element>)**:	Elements that are distinct in the input should be distinct in the output.
old names:	✂*MultipleCorrespondence; OCP

This constraint is also of great importance for morphology (see §4.9). This is not (and should not) be a violation of **Survived**. The system can tell that a token of [Labial] is linked to the first segment in both input and output, and has no way of determining whether the token in the output is different from the token in the input. Extra association lines are ignored (as they are for assimilation). The same is true for the second segment. No token of [Labial] has been deleted; two tokens have been merged into a single token. Only if **Distinct** is ranked high can this merger be prevented. It has often been assumed that such mergers are obligatory in the output (e.g., Archangeli, 1984), but there is no evidence to support such a assumption.

4.4.1.1. Ranking Survived Relative to LinkedUpwards

As noted above, it is often difficult to determine whether a violation of **Survived** or **LinkedUpwards** underlies a given pattern. If they are ranked as equals or very close, there is no way to differentiate between them. But if they are ranked in certain ways relative to other constraints, they can be differentiated. There are four basic patterns.

Pattern 1:   Survived,LinkedUpwards » negative constraint

If both constraints are ranked higher than the relevant negative constraint, then the feature is linked upwards in the output, and the feature is pronounced.

Pattern 2:   negative constraint » Survived
             (*ranking of LinkedUpwards irrelevant*)

If **Survived** is ranked lower than a relevant negative constraint, and no other positive constraint can rescue the feature in question, then the feature is deleted. It is not present in the output, and hence is not pronounced. The ranking of **LinkedUpwards** does not matter, since that constraint is only relevant when the feature is present.

Pattern 3:   Survived » negative constraint » LinkedUpwards

If **Survived** is ranked so high that it cannot be violated, but **LinkedUpwards** is ranked so low that it can be violated, the results are quite different. The feature survives in the output, but it does so as an unlinked (floating) feature. This means that it is not pronounced. The resulting lack of pronunciation is phonetically indistinguishable from deletion (a **Survived** violation). In general, this ranking is indistinguishable from a ranking in which **Survived** is ranked very low. Faced with inconclusive data, we sometimes pick one constraint, sometimes the other, but most often list both in the same row of the constraint table, to show that it is unclear which constraint is violated.

On occasion, there *is* a way to determine whether an element is deleted outright or is floating, thereby providing evidence about which of the two constraints is violated. In all instances, the data involve two elements that are at different levels in the phonological hierarchy. For example, both the feature [+nasal] and the Root node that it attaches to may be involved. By observing the behavior of one element, we can sometimes find evidence concerning whether the *other* element is deleted or floating. This is the subject of Pattern 4.

Pattern 4:   Survived,LinkedUpwards » negative constraint » Not(Link)

This ranking sometimes has a very interesting result. The high ranking of **Survived** means that the feature must be present in the output, even under very adverse circumstances, such as the deletion of the entire segment which contains the feature. The low ranking of **Not(Link)** allows an association line to be added between the feature and another segment that is not deleted. This allows the feature to survive and be pronounced. We could say that spreading is used to rescue a feature with a high-ranked **Survived** constraint.

It is common both in adult grammars and in phonological development for a feature to spread from a segment that is otherwise deleted. For example, a vowel might be oral when there is a following nasal consonant in the output, but nasalized when an underlying nasal consonant is deleted from a coda: /pana/ [pana] versus /pan/ [pã] (French: Kenstowicz, 1994:523; Choctaw: Niklas, 1973). The feature [+nasal] is *flopped* from the deleted segment onto a linked-up segment.

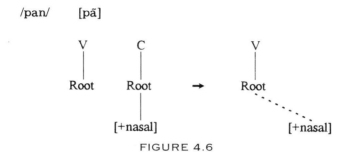

FIGURE 4.6

After deletion of the second consonant (a **Survived(Root)** violation), the surviving feature [+nasal] links to the preceding vowel. In Table 4.7 the final consonant is deleted because **Survived(Root)** is low-ranked. **Survived(+nasal)** prevents the feature [+nasal] from being deleted. Because of the low ranking of **Not(Link)**, an association line is inserted and links [+nasal] up to the preceding vowel: a nasalized vowel results. In this way, the deletion of an element is prevented even when a higher element is deleted. Note that the vowel here is short. This means that the C timing unit of the /n/ is also deleted. If **Survived(C-TimingUnit)** is also ranked high, the timing unit will survive, and may link to the vowel, making the vowel long; this is known as compensatory lengthening. For compensatory lengthening to occur, **SinglyLinked(V-Root)** must also be low-ranked; see §4.4.3.

TABLE 4.7

/pan/	pan	pana	pa	pã
Not(Coda)	*!			
Not(V-Root)		*!		
Survived(+nasal)			*!	
Survived(Root)			*	*
LinkedUpwards(Root)				
Not(Link)				*

The above analysis requires that the nasal consonant's Root node be *deleted* outright. Consider what would happen if it were floating, as in Table 4.8 and Figure 4.7:

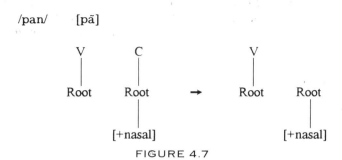

/pan/   [pã]

FIGURE 4.7

TABLE 4.8

/pan/	pan	pana	pa	pã
Not(Coda)	*!			
Not(V-Root)		*!		
Survived(+nasal) LinkedUpwards(+nasal)				
Not(Link)				*!
Survived(Root)				
Linked Upwards(Root)			*	*

In this second case, [+nasal] is present and linked to a floating Root node. Thus, there is no violation of either **Survived(+ nasal)** or **LinkedUpwards(+ nasal)**. However, **LinkedUpwards(Root)** is violated by both candidates in which deletion occurs, and cannot choose between them. The deciding constraint is **Not(Link)**: no association lines can be added; therefore, no assimilation occurs.

Above, in Table 4.7, in contrast, the Root node was deleted, thus violating **Survived(Root)** but not **LinkedUpwards(Root)**. The feature [+nasal] was floating, and had to spread to a nearby segment in order to satisfy **LinkedUpwards(+ nasal)**. Assimilation occurred because the feature [+nasal] was locally ill formed.

Thus, we can distinguish between **Survived** and **LinkedUpwards** violations when a higher-level element is deleted. Unfortunately, when only one level is involved in the repair, **Survived** and **LinkedUpwards** violations are indistinguishable, because they lead to identical pronunciations.

4.4.1.2. Nonminimal Repairs via LinkedUpwards

Given our discussion so far, we have only two options when a feature causes an ill-formedness:

1. Repair the ill-formedness: delete the feature
2. Permit the ill-formedness: pronounce the feature

If the ill-formedness is repaired, it must be repaired by deleting just the offending feature. If a higher element (such as a Root node) were to be deleted, we would repair the violation, but only at the cost of violating faithfulness for every other element within the Root node, even though those elements might not violate any high-ranked constraints. Thus, repairs must be as low in the phonological hierarchy as possible. But there must be some way to derive nonminimal repairs, where a deletion is made at a higher level, such as delinking the Root node (and all elements that it contains).

We can derive nonminimal repairs via **LinkedUpwards**, because **Linked-Upwards** refers just to linkage and does not mean that the feature is actually pronounced. As discussed above, a feature is well formed if it is linked to an element on the next tier up, even if that higher element is floating. This leads us to a mechanism for deriving nonminimal repairs. Consider the repair in which the /d/ of *bed* is deleted because [+voiced] is prohibited in codas (as in Table 4.9). If **LinkedUpwards(+voiced)** is high-ranked, [+voiced] must be linked up. If **Not(+voiced)** is also high-ranked, [+voiced] may not appear in a coda. This conflict can be resolved if the Root node is not linked up: [+voiced] is linked up, but is not in the coda:

TABLE 4.9

/bɛd/	bɛd	bɛt	bɛ	bɛdə
Not(+voiced) <in coda>	*!			
Not(Root)				*!
LinkedUpwards(+voiced) Survived(+voiced)		*!		
LinkedUpwards(Root)			*	

Ranking different **LinkedUpwards** constraints in this way provides a way to derive the nonminimal repair. The Root node deletes, even though it is the feature [+voiced] that is causing the problem. Since the individual feature must be linked, the break in the chain anchoring [+voiced] to a prosodic word must be at a higher level.

In a sense, using **LinkedUpwards(+voiced)** in this way removes the independence of [+voiced] and Laryngeal that arises from placing the elements on two tiers. It fuses them, so that they now must have the same fate. It removes the possibility of deleting or delinking just the feature [+voiced]. In order to delete or delink [+voiced], we must delete or delink the higher element as well. Only by removing the independence of elements on different tiers can we account for non-minimal repairs.

4.4.1.3. Nonminimal Repairs via MAX and Ident

McCarthy and Prince (1995) draw a distinction between the survival of whole segments and the survival of individual features. They use two constraints: **MAX** (similar to **Survived(Root)**) and **Ident(Feature)** (similar to **Survived(Feature)**; Orgun, 1995, uses a slightly different but related constraint, **Match(Feature)**). There is a crucial difference between **Survived(Feature)** and **Ident(Feature)**, however. **Ident** is defined in a way that is contingent on the survival of the segment:

Ident(Feature): *If two segments correspond to each other*, then they must be identical for the feature [Feature].

Ident does not require that underlying features appear in the output, *unless* the segment that contains them is present in the output.

Alderete et al. (1996) explicitly note that this allows a mechanism for nonminimal repairs. Consider the constraint that prohibits a voiced obstruent in a coda. The problematical feature in the /d/ of *bed* is [+voiced], and the coda-voicing constraint will not be violated if [+voiced] is deleted: [bɛt]. However, the [t] in the output corresponds to the /d/ in the input, and **Ident** does not allow them to have different features. We can avoid violations of both coda-voicing and **Ident** if we delete the whole /d/: [bɛ]. The deletion of the whole segment does not violate **Ident**, because the /d/ in the input does not correspond to any segment in the output, and **Ident** is only relevant if the input segment corresponds to an output segment. This contingent definition of **Ident** thus provides a mechanism for nonminimal deletions, given the following rankings:

| Ident | ‖ | MAX |
| <Negative Constraint> | ‖ | |

In contrast, **Survived(Feature)** is not defined contingently and makes it more difficult to derive nonminimal deletions. As noted in §4.4.1.2, if the whole segment is deleted, **Survived(Feature)** is violated. The only solution available to us is to force the whole segment to be present in the output but floating. It turns out that this works for deletions that interact with the segment's position in the word or syllable. However, it may *not* work if the problem is the combination of two features; for example, if voiced fricatives are ruled out absolutely, but voiced stops and voiceless fricatives are possible. In our system, a nonminimal deletion of all voiced fricatives involves a floating voiced fricative; as a result, the constraint that rules out voiced fricatives still seems to be violated.[9] Interestingly, the sorts of

---

[9] This would be true, unless we adopt a definition of the **NotCo-occurring** constraint, such that it is not violated in floating segments. We opt for this possibility.

nonminimal deletions that cause us problems never occur in adult phonology; they involve "impossible segments," which Prince and Smolensky (1993) note never appear in input representations in adult languages. Our use of **Survived** runs into difficulties only with child phonology.

We are uncomfortable about adopting the constraint **Ident**, however. The function of **Ident** is almost the same as the function of **Survived**. One of our goals is to have as few constraints as possible, with minimal overlap in function between different constraints. We think it is highly suspect for a system to have both **Ident** and **Survived**. **Survived** is more general and is needed for other purposes, and thus we prefer it to **Ident**. In later chapters, we note which deletions are handled more elegantly by **Ident** (which we will refer to using the unabbreviated name **Identical**). We leave it as an open question whether **Identical** is needed.

4.4.2. ADDING ELEMENTS AND AVOIDING INSERTION

A second aspect of faithfulness is that no elements should be present on the surface unless they are present in the underlying representation. The relevant constraint family could directly prevent insertion as such ($\ll$*Insert), but this label is process-oriented and hence should be avoided. A better label would not refer to the insertion process, but to the presence of a feature in the output that is not in the input. Names in the literature include $\ll$RecF , $\ll$DEP, $\ll$LexFeat, and $\ll$Corr$_{oi}$(X) (e.g., Archangeli & Pulleyblank , 1994; McCarthy & Prince, 1995; Orgun, 1995). Given our conventions for constraint names, we would use the name **Lexical:**

$\ll$**Lexical**:   Elements in the output must be present in the input (in the underlying lexical representation).

   violation: An element is in the output without being in the input (i.e., an element is added/epenthesized).

However, we are not certain that a constraint that specifically prevents the insertion of elements is needed, and do not make use of such a constraint in this book.

There is a need for a constraint that prevents elements from occurring in the output. This is needed to motivate the deletion of underlying elements. Every element has a cost in terms of resources used; the fewer the elements in the output, the fewer the resources consumed, and the easier it is to produce the word. This constraint is not (entirely) a faithfulness constraint, since it often forces unfaithfulness. This is accomplished via the following constraint family:

   ✏**Not**:   An element must not appear in the output.

   violation: The element is present in the output, *whether it is floating or linked.*

   grounding: In cognitive processing, all elements make use of resources. The relative ranking of **Not** constraints reflects the resources needed.

   old names: $\ll$*(Feature); *Struc

We would like to emphasize that the constraint is violated whenever an element is present in the output, whether that element is linked up or not. **Not** can be satisfied only if an element is entirely deleted.

An element is possible only if there is a constraint that requires that the element be present in the output, ranked higher than **Not**. Most commonly, this higher-ranked constraint is **Survived**. If **Survived** is ranked higher than **Not**, then the element is (generally) possible in the output and will be produced (unless prevented by another constraint). If **Survived** is ranked lower than **Not**, then the element is (generally) not possible in the output and will not be produced (unless required by another constraint).

Not provides us with a mechanism for deleting an element. This is a constraint family, with one member for every element in the phonological hierarchy, plus a member for association lines:

☞**Not(ProsodicWord)**
☞**Not(Foot)**
☞**Not(σ)**
☞**Not(Onset)**   (plus other syllable components)
☞**Not(Coda)**   (≫**NoCoda**, ≫***Coda**)
☞**Not(μ)**   (plus other timing units)
☞**Not(Root)**
☞**Not(Place)**   (plus other organizing nodes)
☞**Not(+sonorant)**
☞**Not(-sonorant)**
☞**Not(+nasal)**
☞**Not(-nasal)**
   etc., one for both values of every feature
☞**Not(Link)**:   Association lines may not be present in the output.

Following a suggestion by Prince and Smolensky (1993) about a related constraint, we assume that there is some predictability about the ranking of some of the members of this constraint family. Specifically, the members that deal with a specific feature constraint are ranked by markedness. For place of articulation, for example, **Not(Dorsal)** is ranked highest (assuming that velars are the most marked consonants), **Not(Labial)** is intermediate, and **Not(Coronal)** is ranked lowest (since coronals are the least marked place of articulation). (See below for further discussion.)

These **Not** constraints rule out all features. To avoid violations, the only output would be null: phonetically realized as silence. Having any element or association line violates these constraints. Only if there is a higher-ranked constraint that requires that the element be present can it be present. If the element is present in the lexical representation, **Survived** is the higher-ranked constraint that does this. We follow Stampe (1973) here. He noted that the optimal output for a speaker would be the output that requires the least effort (silence), but that the optimal output for the listener would be the one that maintains all underlying lexical distinctions (faithfulness). Other constraints (such as **Co-occurring**; see §4.7.1.1) can also motivate violations of **Not**.

However, **Not** also prevents the insertion of elements that are not present in the underlying representation. Insertion of elements is possible only if some higher-ranked constraint requires the element to be present (such as **LinkedDownwards**, discussed below). In fact, this constraint does everything that a putative constraint like **Lexical** does, and more. **Lexical** would only prevent insertion. **Not** prevents insertion and *additionally* allows deletion to occur. We cannot do without **Not**, but we can do without **Lexical** (we think). Note that an inserted element, because it is not part of the lexical representation, has no **Survived** constraint to require that it be present in the output. Inserted elements must be required by some other constraint. The interaction between **Survived** and **Not** prevents the deletion of an element, while also preventing the insertion of new elements.

Note that **Not** partly enforces faithfulness (by preventing insertion) but partly causes unfaithfulness (by causing underlying elements to delete). As noted above, although faithfulness is a useful concept, there are few constraints that only enforce faithfulness; most can lead to unfaithfulness in some circumstances.

Prince and Smolensky (1993) were unable to have a constraint against the presence of elements, because they assumed that no underlying element could ever be deleted (containment). They had to assume a constraint that would not be violated if a feature was present in the output but floating. That constraint was a constraint on linking elements:

✂***Struc**: No structure is allowed.

This was a constraint family, instantiated in members that ruled out the presence of association lines between two elements on different tiers:

✂***Pl/Dor**: Place may not dominate a [Dorsal] node.
violation: A velar or uvular consonant; (labio)velarization.

Their system holds that elements may be present, but not linked up. In their system, then, there is no way to prevent the insertion of floating elements; the following are equally good outputs:

1. output identical to input
2. output identical to input, plus a floating [Labial]
3. output identical to input, plus eight floating [Labial]'s
4. output identical to input, plus 963 floating [Labial]'s

Without an additional constraint, all of these outputs are equally optimal. The floating [Labial]'s will not be pronounced, because they are not linked (and are thus not anchored in time). Thus, all of these outputs are phonetically equivalent. A particular output would be chosen at random, so that the exact number of floating inserted elements (from zero to many) would vary on every trial. Although there can in principle be no empirical evidence against this proposition, we view it as unsatisfying. It is unlikely that the language system would be set up to consume limited cognitive resources in such a way. Such variability of output should be accepted only if there is some empirical evidence for it. Negative constraints should refer to presence of elements, not to linkage.

4.4.2.1. Deriving Default Status by Ranking Not Constraints

Smolensky (1993) points out that the relative ranking of the members of the **Not** constraint family derives the default value used for resolving underspecification.[10] Given any ranking of competing features or feature values, the lowest-ranked one will be the one that is violated. Smolensky proposes the following ranking for place of articulation features:

   Not(Dorsal) ||| **Not(Labial)** ||| **Not(Coronal)**

It is more optimal to have a coronal consonant than to have a labial or dorsal consonant, and it is more optimal to have a labial consonant than to have a dorsal consonant. This constraint ranking tends to make all consonants appear as coronals, since changing /k/ and /p/ into [t] would remove violations of high-ranked constraints, at the (smaller) cost of a violation of the lowest-ranked constraint in this set. Whether this actually happens depends on the relative rankings of **Survived(Dorsal)** and **Survived(Labial)**. If these constraints are ranked higher than the **Not** constraints, then underlying dorsals and labials will surface as dorsals and labials, not as coronals. But if the **Survived** constraints are ranked lower than these **Not** constraints, then the consonants will surface as coronals. The articulator node with the lowest-ranked **Not** constraint acts as the default, and may replace articulator nodes with higher-ranked **Not** constraints.

When there is no underlying articulator node (or when the underlying articulator node cannot surface in the output), the articulator node with the lowest-ranked **Not** constraint should be the one that is inserted. For example, if an epenthetic consonant is added so that a syllable will have an onset, it should be a coronal (unless it has no Place node, in which case it will be a glottal). Using constraint-ranking in this way is the best way to derive the defaults that are used for feature-filling. In order to resolve underspecification with binary features, the **Not** constraints must cover both values of a feature. For example:

   Not(+ nasal) ||| **Not(-nasal)**

This constraint ranking leads to [-nasal] being the default value, filled in whenever there is a **LinkedDownwards** violation because [nasal] is not specified. Oral stops and oral vowels are the default, not nasal stops and nasalized vowels. If there were a single **Not(nasal)** constraint that did not mention the value of the feature, there would be nothing to determine which value is the default. There must be one **Not**

---

[10] Smolensky additionally argues that underspecification arises in only a few restricted situations, and argues that lexical representations might be fully specified.

constraint for each value of each feature. The ranking within the **Not** constraint family is the way that default feature-filling rules are implemented within OT.

We note here one important fact about default features. If underspecification is assumed, then the default feature values ([Coronal], [-continuant], [-nasal], etc.) are not present in underlying representations. As a result, these feature values are not helped by any **Survived** constraints (since **Survived** is only relevant to elements that are present in the input). The default feature values are present in the output only because some other high-ranked constraint requires them to be present. The lack of relevance of **Survived(Coronal)** to the segment /t/, however, can sometimes lead to the default feature being at a disadvantage relative to nondefault features (which are helped by **Survived(Labial)** and **Survived(Dorsal)**). We discuss this possibility below and in later chapters.

The default status of the lowest-ranked **Not** constraint accounts for some of the same facts as underspecification. Smolensky argued that underspecification was not needed, although he was unable to account for key facts about assimilation (that default features are replaced by nondefaults). More recent work has provided a solution to the assimilation facts (see §4.6.1). However, this does not mean that underspecification is wrong. Whether there is underspecification or not depends on the model of learning that is assumed. Since OT does not yet have a full theory of learning, no conclusions can yet be drawn about underspecification.

Psycholinguistic work by Stemberger (1991a, 1991b, 1992, 1993a) reported patterns of errors in performance that can be accounted for via underspecification, but which are mysterious with full specification, even within OT. In general, the studies showed that, when there is a processing conflict between two phonemes, an error is made on the phoneme *of lower frequency*. For example, when the contrast involves two nondefault features (such as [Labial] versus [Dorsal]), the error rate is highest on the phoneme that is *lower* in frequency. However, when the contrast is between a nondefault feature and a default feature ([Labial]/[Dorsal] versus [Coronal]), the error is on the segment with the default feature, *even though* the default segment is almost always the phoneme with the *higher* frequency. Stemberger and Stoel-Gammon (1991) explicitly address whether markedness can account for these results, and conclude that it cannot. Markedness does not predict that errors between segments with two nondefaults will be qualitatively different from errors between a default and a nondefault segment. Smolensky's (1993) analysis makes this same false prediction. Because the OT analysis is not (yet) compatible with the psycholinguistic facts, we continue to use underspecification in this book.

4.4.2.2. Default Underspecification

One consequence of Smolensky's (1993) analysis of default feature insertion is that there can be only one default. It makes no sense to talk of [+F] as the default for one class of segments and [-F] as the default for another class of segments. There is only one lowest-ranked **Not** constraint.

We must modify that conclusion slightly for our version of OT, in which consonants and vowels are on different planes. It is possible to have different defaults for consonants and vowels, because they have different features. In theory, we could have the following rankings:

Not(V-[− cont]) ‖ **Not(V-[+ cont])**
Not(C-[+ cont]) ‖ **Not(C-[− cont])**

This ranking leads to [-continuant] as the default value for consonants, but [+continuant] as the default value for vowels. Within the class of (true) consonants, however, there can be only one default value of [continuant], and that value will be the default regardless of place or manner of articulation. The evidence (see §3.11) suggests that the default features for consonants are:

[-continuant]
[-sonorant]
[-nasal]
[+consonantal]
[-voiced]
[-s.g.]
[Coronal]
[+anterior]
[-distributed]
[-strident]

When a segment has a nondefault feature on the surface, there are two different ways in which it can be derived.

First, the nondefault feature may be underlying. This is certainly how *contrastive* nondefault features (such as [+voiced] in voiced obstruents and [+continuant] in fricatives) are derived. The underlying feature then appears on the surface because some positive constraint such as **Survived(+ continuant)** is ranked higher than **Not(+ continuant)**. In principle, *redundant* nondefault features, which can be predicted from other elements in the phonological representation, could also be derived in this way (via specification in the underlying representation). Full specification assumes that all nondefault features are stored in lexical entries. Radical underspecification assumes that only contrastive nondefault features are stored.

Second, the nondefault feature need not be underlying, but may be derived through constraints on feature co-occurrence, whether positive or negative:

Co-occurring(+ sonorant→ + voiced)
NotCo-occurring(+ sonorant,-voiced)

If either of these constraints is ranked high enough, [+voiced] is inserted in the output rather than the general default [-voiced]. Note that this is only possible with *redundant* nondefault features. This is the standard assumption within radical underspecification.

If the co-occurrence constraints are too low-ranked, it is impossible to insert any feature other than the general default. Note that the following constraint list is not presented in the usual horizontal fashion, due to space limitations on the width of the page:

Survived(+ voiced)

Not(+ voiced)

Not(-voiced)

NotCo-occurring(+ son,-voiced)
Co-occurring(+ son→ + voiced)

This ranking allows any underlyingly [+voiced] consonant to surface as voiced, but prevents the insertion of [+voiced] (higher ranking of **Not(+ voiced)** than **Not(-voiced)**). If sonorant consonants such as /n/ and /l/ are underlyingly underspecified for [voiced], [-voiced] would be inserted, leading to voiceless sonorants: [n̥] and [l̥]. Given this ranking, voiced sonorants would only appear in the output if [+voiced] were specified in the underlying representation for sonorants. However, if the co-occurrence constraints were high-ranked, then the nondefault feature [+voiced] could be inserted; only then would it be possible for sonorants to be underspecified for voicing in the underlying representation.

OT thus leads us to a new variant of underspecification. The general default feature may not be present in the underlying representation. Nondefault features, *even when redundant*, must be present in the underlying representation, whenever co-occurrence constraints are ranked too low to allow insertion of nondefault features. However, when co-occurrence constraints are high-ranked, then the redundant nondefault feature need not be specified underlyingly. The ranking of the relevant co-occurrence constraints is not predictable in advance. Thus, it is impossible to predict which redundant nondefault features (if any) will be specified underlyingly. We refer to this new version of underspecification as *default underspecification*, since we only know for certain that the defaults are underspecified.

Default underspecification bears some resemblance to combinatorial specification (Archangeli & Pulleyblank, 1994), but differs in some respects. In both approaches, predictable features can be specified in underlying representations. However, combinatorial specification also allows default features to be specified (impossible in default underspecification). If data can be found that require default features to be specified in lexical representations, that would constitute evidence against default underspecification, and evidence in favor of combinatorial specification (or full specification). Combinatorial specification also allows different lexical items to vary as to whether the predictable feature is specified or not. For example, they posit that a language might have two /i/'s: one specified as [Coronal] and one with no features. It is a property of lexical items as to which /i/ is present. In contrast, default underspecification requires the feature to be either specified or underspecified for all words. In combinatorial specification, the specification of predictable features was viewed as arbitrary. In default underspecification, specification arises only when the co-occurrence constraints that underlie the insertion of the redundant default feature are low-ranked. In our version of OT, the initial state of the system, before learning, is semirandom. Thus, the co-occurrence constraints must sometimes be low-ranked, allowing the underlying specification of the feature to develop during learning.

Stemberger (1991a, 1996c) provides a learning model which utilizes this theory, as follows. Underspecification implies that there is no lexical component to the presence of a default feature in the output: the feature is present solely because it is supplied by the phonology. If an error-driven learning scheme is assumed, there is no reason to learn a lexical component for default features, since they will appear in the output in any case. Because they will always appear in the output, errors will not occur, and there is hence no motivation to learn (because learning is driven by error). If co-occurrence constraints are ranked high enough, there is no need for a lexical component for redundant nondefault features, because such features will also be supplied without error by the phonology. However, if the co-occurrence constraints are ranked too low, such features will not be supplied by the phonology, errors will occur, and learning will take place. Two types of learning are possible: reranking the co-occurrence constraints upwards, or learning a lexical component for redundant nondefault features. We know of no reason why the latter possibility is in principle ruled out. In Chapters 5–9, we will see data from child phonology in which redundant nondefault features seem to be specified.

4.4.2.3. Requiring Insertion

Prince and Smolensky (1993) introduced a very different constraint to prevent the insertion of entire segments. They proposed that the epenthesis of entire segments should occur when the following constraint is violated:

✂**Fill**:   Syllable positions are filled with segmental material.

This constraint requires that if an onset is present, for example, it must dominate a Root node (a segment). This does not obviously have anything to do with epenthesis. To make it relevant to epenthesis, Prince and Smolensky proposed a particular analysis of epenthesis, but provided few details. They argued that epenthesis does not involve the addition of a segment, but rather the addition of an onset node, a nucleus node, or a higher node such as a mora, a syllable, or a foot. If an onset node is epenthesized, but no segmental material is added *on the same stratum*, then this violates the **Fill** constraint.

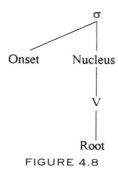

FIGURE 4.8

But there must be more to this story, because an onset without segmental material would not be classified as epenthesis: no listener would be able to detect that epenthesis had occurred, since an empty onset has no phonetic realization.[11] In order to be classified as epenthesis, segmental material must be inserted. But if that insertion occurs on the same stratum in which the Onset node is inserted, then the Onset node is filled with segmental material and **Fill** is not violated. In order for **Fill** to prevent epenthesis, segmental material must be inserted into the empty onset *at a later stratum* (or in the phonetic component). Prince and Smolensky's analysis of epenthesis thus requires that epenthesis occur in two serial steps: add an empty onset at an early stratum, then insert segmental material at a later stratum.

This analysis has theoretical problems. If constraints can be ranked at late strata in such a way as to lead to the insertion of segmental material, why is it impossible for them to be ranked that way in an early stratum? Why is it that segmental material cannot be inserted at the same time that the onset is inserted, so that the inserted onset is never empty, dominates segmental material from the start, and does not violate **Fill**? Further, when the epenthesis occurs on the last stratum, on which segmental material is filled in, there is no **Fill** violation at that level. As a result, Prince and Smolensky are left with no constraint against epenthesis on the last stratum (or in the phonetic component). An alternative account of epenthesis is needed, and discussed below: **Not(Root)**.

Nonetheless, the **Fill** constraint is useful. A more transparent term would be **LinkedDownwards**: an element must be linked to appropriate elements on the next tier down. It is thus a close counterpart to **LinkedUpwards**, which requires that an element be linked up to the next tier. This is a constraint that must be present for any reasonable system. Without it, it would be possible to have syllables (and even prosodic words) with no segmental material at all: silent words, feet, and syllables. Further, the constraint can be used at the segmental level to

---

[11] Recall that the word "empty" denotes a node that dominates no other elements. It is used only with those nodes that normally do dominate other elements, such as a syllable node or a Root node or a Place node.

require that an element be inserted. For example, if Place nodes must be filled with specified material, then an empty Place node (as found in the underlying representation of alveolar consonants in English) violates the constraint, and the [Coronal] articulator node is inserted in order to avoid the violation of **Linked-Downwards**. We thus adopt this constraint. Again, this is a family of constraints. Members of this family refer to any node in the feature geometry or in prosodic structure, as long as that node can dominate other material. There is no **LinkedDownwards** constraint for terminal features, which by definition cannot be linked to an element on a lower tier.

☞**LinkedDownwards**:	Elements must be linked to an element on the appropriate lower tier.
	☞**LinkedDownwards(ProsodicWord)**
	☞**LinkedDownwards(Foot)**
	☞**LinkedDownwards(σ)**
	☞**LinkedDownwards(μ)** (plus other timing units)
	μ must link to a Root node.
	μ must link to tone in tone languages.[12]
	☞**LinkedDownwards(Onset)** (plus other syllable components)
	☞**LinkedDownwards(Root)**
	☞**LinkedDownwards(Place)** (plus other organizing nodes)
	☞**LinkedDownwards(Coronal)** (plus other articulator nodes)
violation:	an element that does not dominate **all** required elements on tiers below it
	(The elements that are required are determined by Downwards Structure constraints.) *Note: No known inherent ranking within the family.*
grounding:	The phonological representation must contain all the specifications required for the motor system to construct the word's motor pattern.
repairs:	for nodes above the Root node: *epenthesis* of feet, syllables, timing units, segments
	for Root nodes and below: *insertion of default features*

The **LinkedDownwards** constraint family does not prevent the insertion of material, and often requires the insertion of elements.

As noted in §3.4.1, when a feature spreads, it is sometimes necessary to generate all the structure that would be needed to support that segment. This is known as the **Node Generation Convention**. One might naively think that there should

---

[12] In some languages, all moras must be linked to a tone. In others, only the head mora of the syllable may link to a tone (Kisseberth, 1993).

be a constraint that specifically accounts for this. However, that is not necessary. Node generation is a combination of several things: requirements that a feature such as [+round] survive and link to [Labial], that [Labial] link to Place, that Place link to Root, and that Root link to V (for a vowel). If [Labial] is present in a segment that is being deleted, it will not survive and be linked up unless something happens: [Labial] must spread to another segment. If no segment is there, then a Root node and a Place node must be inserted (violating **Not(Root)** and **Not(Place)**), to serve as an anchor to which the [Labial] node can be linked. Node Generation results from a high ranking of **Survived** or other constraints that cause spreading, along with a (relatively) low ranking of the **Not** constraints.

4.4.2.4 To Insert or Not to Insert?

LinkedDownwards and **Not** inherently conflict. For example, **LinkedDownwards(Place)** requires that an articulator node be present. Given underspecification, anterior coronals, which have no underlying articulator nodes, violate **LinkedDownwards(Place)**. In order to avoid a **LinkedDownwards(Place)** violation, the default articulator node [Coronal] is inserted. However, the insertion of [Coronal] leads to a violation of **Not(Coronal)**. In most languages, **LinkedDownwards(Place)** is ranked higher than **Not(Coronal)**, and so [Coronal] is inserted. But the opposite ranking, **Not(Coronal)** higher than **LinkedDownwards(Place)**, would prevent the insertion of [Coronal], which would cause problems. To make the possibilities clearer, consider the following constraint ranking (see Table 4.10):

TABLE 4.10

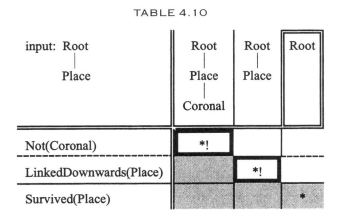

Since **Not(Coronal)** is ranked higher than **LinkedDownwards(Place)**, it is more optimal to have an empty Place node than to have a coronal articulator node. But *some* articulator node must be present for a consonant to be pronounced with an oral articulation. There is a problem: an articulator node cannot be inserted, but one must be present. Recall from above that **Not(Labial)** and **Not(Dorsal)** are ranked even higher than **Not(Coronal)**, so those articulator nodes cannot serve as alternative defaults to be inserted here. One way around the problem is to produce a consonant with no Place node. If **LinkedUpwards(Place)** is ranked low, we can delete the Place node. By definition, a consonant with no Place node is a glottal: [ʔ] or [h]. The ranking below accounts for this common process in adult languages (Debuccalization) and child phonology (Glottal Replacement):

Survived(Root)		LinkedDownwards(Place)		Survived(Place)
LinkedUpwards(Root)	‖	Not(Coronal)	‖	LinkedUpwards(Place)
Not(Dorsal)				
Not(Labial)				

(Note that, as much as possible, particularly for these long lists, competing constraints are placed across from each other in the lists, in order to make more obvious their relative ranking.) Another option would be to delete the segment; this would happen if **LinkedUpwards(Root)** or **Survived(Root)** were the lowest-ranked constraints, as in the following ranking:

Survived(Place)		LinkedDownwards(Place)		Survived(Root)
LinkedUpwards(Place)	‖	Not(Coronal)	‖	LinkedUpwards(Root)
Not(Dorsal)				
Not(Labial)				

The above ranking leads to a nonminimal repair. As noted above, we are forced to treat the consonant as floating. As always, what deletes depends on which of the relevant constraints is the lowest-ranked. In later chapters, we discuss instances of such ranking in child phonology.

4.4.2.5. Preventing Multiple Expression

The previous section dealt with the need to fill prosodic slots with segmental material. There must also be constraints that prevent or allow multiple copies of an element:

SinglyExpressed(X):   An element X in the input will be expressed only once in the output.

Bock (1982) proposed this as a property of the access of lexical items in the construction of sentences: a given piece of semantics tends to be packaged in only one lexical item. The constraint can, of course, be violated if it is ranked low enough. This constraint is violated when an affix is expressed twice; Stemberger (1995) reports on a child who doubly expressed the *-ed* suffix in order to create an extra syllable, so that final clusters could be avoided (*breakeded* [veɪktəd]); see also §9.1.3.1. At the phonological level, a phoneme might be doubly expressed to provide an onset to another syllable, for example: *apple* [bapu]. The underlying /p/ is expressed twice, so that there can be a word-initial onset. Note that the multiple expression of phonological elements (two tokens of the element) is often ambiguous with the double linking of that element (a single token); we note possible uses of this constraint in later chapters.

4.4.2.6. Output-to-Output Faithfulness

We have been dealing solely with faithfulness between the input (lexical representation) and the output (surface pronunciation). It is also possible to posit relationships of an analogous sort between two parts of the output, or between two outputs.

McCarthy and Prince (1994, 1995) rely heavily on the notion of output-to-output correspondence for morphological reduplication in adult languages. From an input such as /fla/, the reduplicated output might be /fa-fla/. The prefix is a copy of the base form, and is governed by constraints (MAX and R=B) that the prefix correspond to the base. However, segments (and features) in the base can be dropped in the prefix if there are phonological constraints that are ranked higher than the output-to-output correspondence constraints. If **NotComplex(Onset)** is ranked higher than the correspondence constraint, then the cluster is simplified: the output is [fa-fla]; [fla-fla] results only if the correspondence constraints are ranked higher than negative phonological constraints.

For English and similar languages, child phonology does not appear to have any phenomena that require output-to-output correspondence, and we will not make use of such constraints here. It should be noted that reduplication does not require such constraints for the basic phenomena. In [fa-fla], the prefix [fa] corresponds to the /fla/ of the input (just as the [fla] of the base corresponds to the /fla/ of the input), but constraint rankings deal with the prefix differently from the way that they deal with the base. We discuss this in §4.7.1.4.

McCarthy (1995) uses a different sort of output-to-output constraint. He maintains that a plural form might be constrained to correspond to a singular form, for example. This is the instantiation of what was once called *transderivational constraints* (e.g., Chung, 1983). This is a radical departure from anything that we have discussed so far. In order to determine what the plural form should look like, the system first has to generate the singular form, then generate the plural form, comparing it to the singular form. We do find occasional uses for such constraints, in relation to inflected forms in English-learning children, and we will call attention to them when needed.

It should be noted that such constraints have the potential to lead to a theory that is very different from the one that is laid out here: a prototype-based theory of phonology. There could be a prototypical word, representing the "perfect" word. This prototypical word might be universal (the same for all children), but would more likely reflect the statistical properties of the target language. It would be the prototypical length and contain the default vowels and consonants of the language; for adult English, it would likely be ['tʰɛɾə]. Correspondence constraints could require that all outputs be identical to the prototype. If faithfulness constraints are ranked higher, the prototype is overridden, and nondefault structures and segments are output. If the prototype correspondence constraints are

higher-ranked, then the output is altered in the direction of default structures, segments, and features. In theory, we could eliminate almost all the constraints
discussed in this chapter: **NotComplex(Onset)** could be replaced by **Corre-
sponding(Base→Prototype, Onset)**, since the prototype has a simple onset. We
will not pursue such a theory, because of its generality. We think that it is a drawback of the concept of output-to-output correspondence constraints that such a
theory is possible.[13]

4.4.3. BASIC DURATION: SINGLE VERSUS LONG

In underlying representations, most elements are singly linked (short). To be
faithful to the input, elements should not gain any new links to other elements.
The constraint **Not(Link)** partly addresses this aspect of faithfulness, but not entirely. There are instances (especially in assimilation) in which it is necessary to
have a constraint that explicitly prevents an element from spreading. We believe
that the most appropriate constraint is the following:

☞**SinglyLinked**:   An element can be linked upwards to only a single higher
                   element.
    violation: a doubly-linked element
  grounding: Extension of a gesture beyond its basic duration requires
                   additional resources.

SinglyLinked refers only to linkage to the next higher tier. It does not address
whether some element on an even higher tier is doubly linked. For example,
SinglyLinked(Labial) is not violated if it is linked to a single Place node, even if
the Root node is linked to two timing units (/pː/):

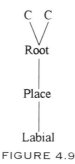

FIGURE 4.9

If constraints are ranked appropriately, this constraint prevents assimilation as
a means of filling in features. Consider the following constraint ranking.

LinkedDownwards(Place) ‖‖ **Not(Coronal)**
SinglyLinked(Labial)

----

[13]However, this resembles the notion of "templates," used by Macken (1992) and Vellemann
(1992).

Given the following representation (which could be underlying, if underspecification is assumed, or could be derived, if an underlying [Dorsal] node, for example, is impossible in the input), assimilation would not be possible:

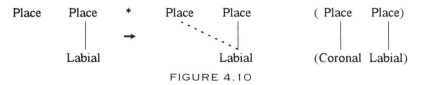

FIGURE 4.10

[Labial] cannot spread here, because **SinglyLinked(Labial)** is high-ranked. Because **LinkedDownwards(Place)** requires that an articulator node be present, the default articulator feature [Coronal] is inserted. The opposite ranking will lead to assimilation:

LinkedDownwards(Place) ||| **SinglyLinked(Labial)**
Not(Coronal)

The above ranking prevents the default feature [Coronal] from being inserted; it is more optimal to spread the feature [Labial] from the following segment.

This constraint also has some applicability to the segmental inventory of the language. Some segments can surface as long, but others must be short. In English, for example, long vowels occur (*seat* /siːt/), but long consonants are not permitted (**sitty* [sɪtːi]). **SinglyLinked(C-Root)** is high-ranked, but **SinglyLinked(V-Root)** is low-ranked.

4.4.4. KEEPING ELEMENTS TOGETHER AND IN ORDER

The third faithfulness constraint is Contiguity:

✏️**Contiguity**: Elements next to each other (contiguous) in the UR must be contiguous on the surface.

   violation: (a) In associating segments to syllables, a segment is skipped, so that underlyingly noncontiguous consonants become contiguous on the surface.

          (b) In associating segments to syllables, a segment is epenthesized between two underlying segments, so that underlyingly contiguous segments are noncontiguous on the surface.

          (c) metathesis

   grounding: Preserving lexical information (as with **Survived**).

McCarthy and Prince (1993a, 1994) propose this constraint for reduplicative affixes. They do not treat it as a basic constraint on phonological form in general. However, in basic syllabification in adult phonology, consonants do not tend to be "skipped." When there are more consonants than can be put in an onset or in a coda, the consonant that usually links up is the one that is closest to the vowel. We do not (often) find the deletion of the consonant that is contiguous to the nucleus. Contiguity is an important part of basic syllabification. Like any constraint, it can be violated.

In basic syllabification in child phonology, contiguity is frequently violated, in ways that are quite similar to contiguity violations in adults' reduplicative affixes. We treat contiguity as a basic faithfulness constraint, and make extensive use of it in later chapters.

It is not clear whether we need any constraint that specifically refers to the linear order of elements. Consider, for example, a word such as *past* /pæst/. If we were to reorder any of the segments (for example, as [spæt]), there would be **Contiguity** violations. The /s/ would be contiguous to the /p/, and no longer contiguous to either the /æ/ or the /t/. This will always be the case when there are three or more phonemes in the word. In a word with only two segments, however, reordering does not violate a **Contiguity**; if *up* /ʌp/ is reordered to [pʰʌ], the /p/ and /ʌ/ are still contiguous. McCarthy and Prince (1994) rule out such reordering with a constraint called **Anchoring**: segments at the edges in the input should also be at the edges in the output. Together, **Contiguity** and **Anchoring** prevent any sort of reordering. It appears that no special constraints are needed to preserve the underlying order of elements, and we do not use any.

4.4.5. AVOIDING UNFAITHFULNESS: SEMPER FIDELIS

One additional way to avoid unfaithfulness is possible, and it does not involve constraints. A speaker may use only those words that have underlying representations that are compatible with the constraint rankings of the phonological system. If a word has some element that would violate one or more faithfulness constraints, the speaker can choose to never use the word, on the grounds that it cannot be pronounced faithfully. This is not a phonological phenomenon per se, but represents a different type of communicative strategy.

Avoidance of "unpronounceable" words is a documented property of the speech of young children (e.g., Ferguson & Farwell, 1975; Schwartz & Leonard, 1982; Matthei, 1989). Children sometimes pick and choose the words that they are willing to use. Words are avoided when they contain segments or structures that are not possible outputs of the child's phonological system.

Avoidance may also be a property of adult speech. English has no base morphemes that begin with sequences of consonants that are prohibited in a syllable onset in English. It would have been reasonable for there to be morphemes like */mspleɪ/, which might be pronounced faithfully after vowel-final words like *a* and *the* (*a msplay* /.əm.spleɪ./), but which would show vowel epenthesis after consonants or a pause (*that msplay* /.ðæt.mə.spleɪ./, *Msplays!* /.mə.spleɪz./). In English, as in most languages, most base morphemes have phonological forms that do not bring them into conflict with the constraint rankings of the adult grammar. In a sense, this is a type of avoidance: new words that violate high-ranked constraints are neither coined nor borrowed from other languages, unless their lexical representations are altered to conform to the constraints of the language.

4.5. BUILDING STRUCTURE

There are constraints that concern structural linkage: features to segments, segments to syllables, syllables to feet, and feet to prosodic words. In this section, we review these constraints.

We could view these constraints as *absolute* constraints on phonological form. A feature such as [+anterior] can link to [Coronal] and nowhere else; the only other option is not linking at all. These structure constraints could *in principle* be nonviolable, and perhaps should not be included in any constraint ranking. They may be a part of **Gen**. Nevertheless, it is important that the researcher be aware that such constraints are being assumed, and so we list them here.

4.5.1. BUILDING SYLLABLES

4.5.1.1. Linkage

One basic constraint is that syllables must exist: all segmental elements must be dominated by a syllable node. This sort of dependency needs to be reflected in our notation, in such a way that the relation is unambiguously differentiated from other types of relations. We will use the symbol " ◄ " for this dependency relation, with the following syntax:

(name of the affected element) ◄(name of the required element)
    violation: element linked to some other higher element
    grounding: Unknown. No one has provided grounding for why there is
                structure at all.

The requirement that all segments be dominated by a syllable could be stated in the following way:

    ✺**Root◄σ**: Every Root node must be dominated by a syllable node.

This is inaccurate, however, because Root nodes are separated from syllable nodes by timing units (at least in rimes, even in moraic theory), and (more controversially) by onset, nucleus, coda, and rime nodes. The constraints that we use should reflect these intermediate units:

    ☞**Root◄X**
    ☞**X◄Onset** versus ☞**X◄Nucleus** versus ☞**X◄Coda**
    ☞**Onset◄σ**
    ☞**Nucleus◄Rime**
    ☞**Coda◄Rime**
    ☞**Rime◄σ**
    ☞**σ◄Foot**
    ☞**Foot◄PrWd**

These constraints define the higher units to which an element must be linked, in order to satisfy **LinkedUpwards**.

Upwards structure constraints are also needed to account for feature geometry. For every element, there is a constraint that addresses where that feature links in the feature geometry.

☞**[continuant]◄Root**   (one for all features that link to the Root)
☞**Laryngeal◄Root**
☞**[voiced]◄Laryngeal** (one for all laryngeal features)
☞**Place◄Root**
☞**[Dorsal]◄Place**   (one for all articulator nodes)
☞**[high]◄[Dorsal]**   (for every feature that links to [Dorsal])
   etc.
   violation: linking to the wrong higher element

These constraints are universally high-ranked. For example, [Coronal] does not link to the Laryngeal or Place nodes, or to [Labial]. These constraints enforce feature geometry.

One might question whether we need *both* the **LinkedUpwards** constraints and the upwards structure constraints. In theory, the upwards structure constraints would be sufficient, since they are violated when an element is not linked upwards. If the constraint states that [Labial] links to a Place node, then that constraint should be violated if (a) [Labial] links to a Root node, or (b) [Labial] links to nothing at all (is floating). Perhaps the upwards structure constraint can also do the duty of **LinkedUpwards**. However, we think that there is a qualitative difference between a floating feature (which happens commonly) and a feature that is linked to the wrong place in the feature geometry (which never happens). If a single constraint rules out both these things, we cannot explain why failure to link is common, but linkage to an incorrect element is impossible. Consequently, we use two constraint families.

We have been assuming that feature geometry is the same in all human languages. In theory, languages could vary, with several constraints that govern where a feature may link. If this is possible, the following are likely competing constraints:

[nasal]◄[sonorant] versus **[nasal]◄Root**
[lateral]◄[sonorant] versus **[lateral]◄Root**

There would be two places for [nasal] and [sonorant] to link. If **[nasal]◄Root** is ranked higher, then [nasal] links to the Root node. But if **[nasal]◄[sonorant]** is ranked higher, then [nasal] links to the [sonorant] node (Rice & Avery, 1995). We leave this possibility of variation in feature geometry across languages for future research. (See §5.5.3.1 for discussion of this possibility in child phonology.)

Another possible instance of ambiguity of attachment has been proposed for syllables and feet, as discussed in §3.8 and §3.9. For words such as *balloon*, some phonologists have proposed that the initial unstressed syllable attaches to the prosodic word rather than the foot (see Hayes, 1995; Kenstowicz, 1994), implying the existence of the following upwards structure constraint:

σ◄**PrWd**:   A syllable links to a prosodic word.

This constraint would be ranked lower than σ◄**Foot**, so that most syllables would be part of a foot. Only if a higher-ranked constraint prevented a syllable from being part of a foot would the syllable attach to the prosodic word; in this instance, because all feet in English would have to be left-prominent, putting [bə] into a foot would create a right-prominent foot. As noted in §3.8, we do not follow that analysis here, but assume that all syllables are part of a foot.

Root nodes also have this ambiguity of attachment in moraic theory. Hayes (1989) suggested that segments within the rime attach to mora units, but that onset consonants link directly to syllable nodes. This implies the presence of both of the following constraints:

Root◄μ: A Root node links to a mora.
Root◄σ: A Root node links to a syllable.

Depending on which is ranked higher (and on interactions with co-occurrence constraints that are sensitive to position in the syllable, which we discuss in §4.7.1.3), a Root node will attach either to a mora (in rimes) or to a syllable node (in onsets, and possibly in codas).

4.5.1.2. Downwards Structure

A second structural relationship involves which elements a particular element dominates; this involves elements that are *lower* in the phonological hierarchy: downwards structure. Such constraints define the elements to which the target element is linked in order to satisfy the **LinkedDownwards** constraint. In theory, one could state exactly the same information using both types of constraints. Having two sets of exactly identical constraints would not be very useful, however; they would more profitably be viewed as a single constraint. Instead, we will use these downwards structure constraints to encode which elements *must* be dominated by an element (without being violated). We will use the symbol "►" for this type of dependency relation, with the following syntax:

(name of the affected element)►(name of the required element)

A good example of this type of constraint comes from syllable structure. We assume that syllables have two parts: onsets and rimes. Further, rimes have two parts: nuclei and codas. Every syllable must have a rime, and every rime must have a nucleus. However, the onset is often absent (even though it is most optimal for a syllable to have an onset), and codas are often prohibited. For the required and preferred parts of the syllable, Prince and Smolensky (1993) use the following constraints:

✂**ONS**:   A syllable must have an onset.
✂**Nuc**:   A syllable must have a nucleus.

We rename these constraints as follows:

☞σ►**Onset**:   A syllable must immediately dominate an onset.
violation: There is no onset.

☞σ►**Rime**:   A syllable must immediately dominate a rime.
violation: A syllable without a rime
                 A head-less syllable with only an onset

☞**Rime►Nucleus**:   A rime must immediately dominate a nucleus.
violation: A rime without a nucleus
                 A head-less syllable

σ►**Rime** and **Rime►Nucleus** are ranked so high that all syllables have these parts, in all languages.[14] In contrast, σ►**Onset** is ranked lower, and onsetless syllables are possible (though not preferred) in most languages.

The Upwards Structure and Downwards Structure constraints are similar in many ways, but do different jobs. Consider the onset constraints, **Onset◄σ** and σ►**Onset**. The first constraint requires that, if an onset is present, it must attach to a syllable node; the constraint says nothing about whether the onset node is present. The second constraint requires that a syllable, if present, must link to an onset node; it requires that the onset node be present. This difference is especially clear with the coda constraints. There is a **Coda◄Rime** constraint, since a coda, if present, must link to a rime. But there is no **Rime►Coda** constraint, since rimes are not required to have codas. Similarly, a Place node must link upwards to a Root node, but a Root node does not have to link downwards to a Place node (since glottals [h] and [ʔ] have no Place nodes).

The downwards structure constraints also extend to structure lower in the phonological hierarchy:

☞**Place►Artic**

A Place node must dominate some articulator node, though it does not matter *which* articulator node it dominates. Similar Downwards Structure constraints are found for all elements in the phonological hierarchy that can dominate other elements.

4.5.1.3. Putting Segments into Syllables, Part I: Whole Segments

The constraints presented so far derive the presence of syllables and the parts of a syllable, but this is not enough. We need something to tell us which segments are allowed in which parts of a syllable. A syllable such as */.ato./, where the /t/ is syllabic and the /a/ and /o/ are nonsyllabic, is universally disallowed. We must have constraints on syllable structure that tell us what can be syllabic, what can appear in onsets, and what can appear in codas. In this section, we present one way to do this: the analysis of Prince and Smolensky (1993). The greatest drawback to this analysis is that the constraints refer to whole segments, thereby missing the many feature-based generalizations that are apparent in the data. We lay out this analysis here, and return to the issue in §4.7.1, where we derive the effects through constraints on features.

---

[14] Shaw (1996) argues that rimes may lack a nucleus in a some languages, implying that the constraint is ranked lower in those languages.

Prince and Smolensky (1993) put segments into syllables via the following two constraints: [15]

✄***M/X**:   The segment X may not associate to Margin nodes (Onset or Coda).
violation: The segment X is in an onset or coda.

✄***P/X**:   X may not associate to Nucleus nodes.
violation: The segment X is syllabic.

These are both families of constraints. There is one constraint in each family for each segment that is a possible segment in any human language. Within each family, the ranking is determined universally, as a function of sonority. The highest-ranked ***M** constraint (***M/a**) rules out the most sonorant vowel ([a]) from being in an onset or coda; the lowest-ranked ***M** constraint (***M/t**) rules out the least sonorous consonant ([t]) from being in an onset or coda. This means that [t] (subject to the lowest-ranked constraint) will be easy to put in an onset or coda, while [a] (subject to the highest-ranked constraint) will be hard to put in an onset or coda. The ***P** constraint family is universally ranked but in the opposite order: ***P/t** is highest-ranked (so that syllabic [t] is highly unusual) and ***P/a** is lowest-ranked (so that syllabic [a] is the norm). In the interest of transparent and consistent constraint names, we would rename them: ☞**Notσ-Peak(t)**, ☞**Notσ-Margin(a)**.

The **Notσ-Margin** constraint family presumes that onsets and codas are governed by the same set of preferences. As we discuss in §4.7.1.3, however, codas are additionally covered by other constraints, so that the preferences for onsets and codas are not identical.

Prince and Smolensky (1993) demonstrate that these constraints determine what is a possible segment in a language. If the constraints against, for example, /u/ as a head or as a margin are ranked higher than **Survived** and **Linked-Upwards**, then it is more optimal to delete the /u/ than to put it in a syllable. (See Table 4.11.)

TABLE 4.11

/u/	u	w	∅
Notσ-Peak(u)	*!		
Notσ-Margin(u)		*!	
Survived(u) LinkedUpwards(u)			*

---

[15] In the early chapters of their book, Prince and Smolensky (1993) use a variety of constraints, including HNUC, Pk-Prom, Poss-Nuc, Poss-Mar, and Poss-Cod, which were superseded in later chapters.

Prince and Smolensky rightly note that "impossible" segments would not actually be present in the underlying forms of words in adult speech; since no one would ever pronounce them, a learner would never know that they were present, and hence would not put them in the underlying representation. However, impossible segments are commonly present in the underlying representations of words in early child language: not all the sounds of the adult language are possible for a child, but the child can observe them in adult speech and put them in the underlying representation on that basis. (See §8.3 and §8.5.)

Only if **Survived** and **LinkedUpwards** are higher-ranked than these constraints will a segment be possible in a language. If **Notσ-Peak** is ranked higher, then the segment is nonsyllabic (see Table 4.12):

TABLE 4.12

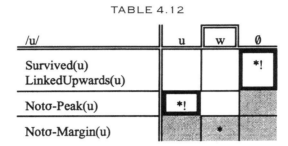

If **Notσ-Margin** is ranked higher, then the segment will be syllabic (see Table 4.13):

TABLE 4.13

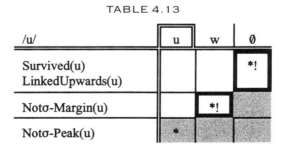

Prince and Smolensky discuss "coercible" margins and nuclei. A coercible margin is a segment that is optimally syllabic, but which can be nonsyllabic for syllable structure reasons. The vowel /u/ is generally syllabic, but can be nonsyllabic ([w]) if the next syllable would otherwise have no onset (see Table 4.14):

TABLE 4.14

/uap/	uap	wap	ap
Survived(u) LinkedUpwards(u)			*!
σ▸Onset	**!		*
Notσ-Margin(u)		*	
Notσ-Peak(u)	*		

The ranking of **Notσ-Margin(u)** over **Notσ-Peak(u)** means that it is more optimal for the segment to be syllabic (violating the lower-ranked constraint) than to
be nonsyllabic (violating the higher-ranked constraint). However, the constraint
that requires that a syllable have an onset is ranked even higher. By making the
/u/ nonsyllabic, we avoid two violations of that constraint. Thus, even though /u/
is more optimally syllabic than nonsyllabic, it can be coerced into being nonsyllabic when that leads to a more optimal syllable structure.

Similarly, segments that are more optimally nonsyllabic can be made syllabic
if the alternative is to delete the segment. In English, /n/ is generally an onset or
coda, but it can be syllabic in words such as *bacon* [beɪkn̩]. Because a coda may
not contain a [kn] cluster in English, the /n/ cannot be a part of the first syllable
of the word. Rather than insert a vowel (prevented by a high ranking of **Not(V-
Root)**), the /n/ is made syllabic (thus violating the lower-ranked **Notσ-Peak(n)**
constraint). In most languages, syllabic consonants are possible only when there
are no vowels nearby and the consonant could not otherwise be made part of any
syllable.

We regard these constraints as inherently in conflict with the general assumptions of multilinear phonology. Multilinear phonology stresses that segments are
made up of features. These constraints, in contrast, involve whole segments as if
they had no internal content. We will not make use of these constraints in this
book (see §4.7.1).

4.5.1.4. Complexity

The constraints to this point only derive onsets, nuclei, and codas. But languages (and children) can differ in terms of how complex onsets, nuclei, and codas
are allowed to be. Any part of the syllable can be limited to one segment, to two,
or to more than two. This is done via the constraint **NotComplex** (called ✂*Complex** by Prince & Smolensky, 1993):

✏**NotComplex**:   No more than one dependent element may associate to any
                   anchoring node. ("Singly linked downwards")

> **violation**:   Consonant clusters within an onset
>   Consonant clusters within a coda
>   Diphthongs (complex nuclei)
>   Two articulator nodes under a single Place node
>   Affricates (two tokens of [continuant] under a single Root
>   node)
> **grounding**:   More complex structure takes greater resources, both
>   because of the resource demands of the additional
>   elements, and because clusters are less frequent than single
>   segments. Lower frequency entails greater resource
>   demands.

This is a family of constraints:

☞**NotComplex(Onset)**
☞**NotComplex(Nucleus)**
☞**NotComplex(Coda)**
☞**NotComplex(μ)**
☞**NotComplex(Root)**
☞**NotComplex(Place)**
Note: No known universal ranking within the family.

Violation of this constraint is gradient: one element (no violation) versus two elements (1 violation) versus three elements (2 violations) versus four elements (3 violations), etc. How many elements are allowed in an onset, nucleus, or coda depends on interactions with the sequence constraints **NoSequence** and **NotTwice** discussed in §4.7.2.

Not all uses of **NotComplex** involve syllable structure. **NotComplex(Place)** allows a segment to have only one articulator node; a segment such as English [ɹ] that is both [Coronal] and [Labial] would be prohibited. **NotComplex(Root)** prohibits a Root node from linking to two tokens of [continuant]; affricates are prohibited (if they are treated as [-continuant . . . +continuant]). **NotComplex(μ)** allows a mora to link to just a single segment, ruling out structures where a mora links to both a vowel and a coda consonant:

FIGURE 4.11

Note that **NotComplex** is defined over a particular constituent of the syllable. Consonant clusters are *not* a violation of **NotComplex** if the first consonant is in a coda and the second consonant is in an onset. Such clusters are instead subject to constraints on sequences, such as **NoSequence** (see §4.7.2.2 and §7.3.1).

This constraint could be extended to the rime:

NotComplex(Rime)

Such a constraint would limit a rime to a single constituent: a nucleus or a coda. If the nucleus is required in every syllable (and see Shaw, 1996, for arguments to the contrary), the result of this constraint would be to prohibit the occurrence of codas, as an alternative to **Not(Coda)**.

4.5.1.5. Restrictions on Codas, Part I: The Coda Condition

We also find strong limitations on features that may appear in a coda. We discuss one alternative here, but return to the issue with a different analysis (that we find preferable) in §4.7.1.3.

Itô et al. (1995) assume the following constraint:

✂**CodaCond**: Coda Condition
A coda consonant can have only Coronal place, or else no place specification of its own.
violation: The coda consonant has an articulator node of its own.

This limits coda consonants to a coronal place of articulation, unless the consonant is a glide or a glottal consonant, or unless the consonant assimilates its place of articulation from a following consonant (as in a cluster such as [mp]).

This constraint is probably unnecessary. Prince and Smolensky argue that by ranking **Not(Coda)** higher than **Notσ-Peak(X)** and **Notσ-Margin(X)** for a particular consonant, the consonant is not a possible coda; this leads either to deletion, or to insertion of a vowel so that the consonant may be in an onset. Since negative constraints against [Coronal] tend to be ranked lower than negative constraints against other articulator nodes (see §4.7.1.7), we derive the fact that [Coronal] may be the only permissible articulator node. We return to this issue below.

4.5.2. BUILDING FEET AND PROSODIC WORDS

Syllables must be grouped into feet, and feet must be grouped into prosodic words, via the Upwards Structure constraints discussed in §4.5.1.1. In this section, we turn to additional constraints on the form of feet and prosodic words.

4.5.2.1. Prominent Syllables

Not all the syllables of a word are equally prominent. Some are stressed and some are unstressed. If a word contains more than one stressed syllable, one tends to be more prominent than the others.

There are two basic kinds of feet: left-prominent (trochaic) feet (with the stressed head syllable on the left), and right-prominent (iambic) feet (with the stressed head stressed syllable on the right). Prince and Smolensky (1993) propose two constraints, one for each type of foot.

✂**RhType = I**: Rhythm type is iambic (right-prominent).
violation: Trochaic rhythm, or no feet at all.

✂**RhType = T**: Rhythm type is trochaic (left-prominent).
violation: Iambic rhythm, or no feet at all.

These two constraints define whether the language is iambic (highest-ranked constraint: RhType = I) or trochaic (highest-ranked constraint: RhType=T). McCarthy and Prince (1993a) give these constraints different names: ✂**FtForm (Iambic)** and ✂**FtForm(Trochaic)**. More recent analyses hold that the head of the foot is aligned with the left versus right edge of the foot (see §4.6 for alignment constraints). The terms "trochaic" and "iambic" are opaque terms, which are defined in terms of whether the prominent syllable is at the left or right edge of the foot. We use the following more-transparent constraint names instead:

✏**Prominent(Foot,Left)**: The foot's stressed syllable is on the left. (The foot is trochaic.)
✏**Prominent(Foot,Right)**: The foot's stressed syllable is on the right. (The foot is iambic.)

If a prosodic word contains two or more feet, one foot (or at least, the stressed syllable within one foot) is more prominent than the other foot (or feet). The most prominent foot is either the leftmost or the rightmost foot:

✏**Prominent(PrWd,Left)**: The syllable with the greatest level of stress is in the leftmost foot.
✏**Prominent(PrWd,Right)**: The syllable with the greatest level of stress is in the rightmost foot.

Note that there is no provision for a foot or word where the most prominent syllable is in the *middle* of a sequence of syllables. Although such feet arguably do occur (as in the word *bananas*), they arise only through the violation of constraints that require the prominent syllable or foot to be on the left or on the right.

4.5.2.2. Binary Feet and Prosodic Words

A basic characteristic of feet is that they are binary in most languages.[16] Prince and Smolensky (1993) propose the following constraint.

✂**FtBin**: Foot Binarity
Feet are binary at some level of analysis (μ, σ).
violation: Foot has a single light syllable.
Foot has three or more syllables.
grounding: Unknown.

Keeping the same content, but with a more transparent name, we use

✏**Binary(Foot)**

---

[16]Ternary feet, which must have at least three syllables, have been reported for some languages. See Hayes (1995) for discussion.

Note that the definition of binarity can be either in terms of moras or of syllables. This is in some ways nonoptimal. It is reasonable to posit two separate constraints:

☞**Binary(Foot,μ)**:   A foot has two moras.
☞**Binary(Foot,σ)**:   A foot has two syllables.

Depending on the constraint rankings, all feet may have two moras, all feet may have two syllables, or feet may either have two moras or two syllables.

Violations of **Binary(Foot)** arise when there are either too many syllables or too few syllables in the word. If the faithfulness constraints are ranked higher than **Binary(Foot)**, then the output contains a foot that either is too light (a single short vowel with no coda) or is too heavy (three or more moras). The high ranking of faithfulness precludes making any changes in the elements that are present. However, if **Binary(Foot)** is ranked higher than faithfulness, then the foot will be binary, with the relevant faithfulness constraints violated. Consider a word like *syllable* that has three syllables but only one foot, thus violating **Binary(Foot)**. To avoid violating **Binary**, the segmental material of the third syllable could be deleted, either by deleting the segment /l/ outright (*[sɪləb], violating **Survived(Root)**), or by leaving the final syllable floating in the output (*[sɪlə], violating **LinkedUpwards(σ)**) and hence not being pronounced:

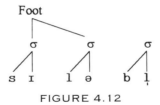

FIGURE 4.12

Consider a word made up of a single light syllable, which also violates **Binary(Foot)**. If **Not(μ)** is violated, a mora is inserted that was not present in the underlying representation, so that the foot is binary (with two moras). The vowel is consequently made long: input /si/ (one mora on the vowel), output [siː] (two moras on the vowel). If **Not(σ)** is violated, in contrast, a whole syllable is added, so that the foot is binary by virtue of having two syllables. The added syllable could contain all default elements (McCarthy & Prince, 1993a, for Axininca Campa: input /si/, output [sita]) or could be a reduplication of the underlying syllable. The feature content of the inserted syllable is fully determined by independent constraints on default phonological elements and whether insertion or assimilation is more optimal.

There has been less research on the size of prosodic words. However, it is likely that prosodic words can sometimes be limited to two feet:

☞**Binary(PrWd)**:   A prosodic word can have *at most* two feet.

Note that this definition differs slightly from the definition of binarity for feet. A foot that is not binary is nonoptimal, whether it has just a single mora (too small) or three syllables (too large). But a prosodic word with just one foot is always well formed. Binarity places limits *only* on the upper size limit of prosodic words.

4.5.2.3. Complexity of Feet and Prosodic Words

Feet and prosodic words can sometimes be severely limited in size. The following two constraints are needed:

> ☞**NotComplex(Foot)**:   A foot may contain only one syllable.
> ☞**NotComplex(PrWd)**:   A prosodic word may contain only one foot.

The first constraint limits a foot to a single syllable. The second constraint limits a prosodic word to a single foot. This means that there may be only a single stressed syllable in a word. Inputs with extra syllables and feet would be problematic. These constraints are often important in early child phonology.[17]

4.5.2.4. Syllable Weight

Heavy syllables tend to be stressed, a property that is called *quantity sensitivity*. A general statement of quantity-sensitivity is given by this constraint, from McCarthy and Prince (1993a):

> ✂**WSP**:   *Weight-to-Stress Principle*:
>   Heavy syllables are prominent in foot structure . . .
>   *A heavy syllable is stressed.*
> **violation**:   A heavy syllable is unstressed.
> **grounding**:   One of the phonetic cues for stress is that the vowel is
>   phonetically longer in duration (e.g., Ladefoged, 1993).
>   Underlying long vowels already have one of the cues for stress,
>   so can be perceived as stressed. For syllables that are heavy
>   because they have a coda, a similar argument can be couched in
>   terms of "phonetic duration of the rime."

If **WSP** is ranked high, stress is quantity-sensitive: no heavy syllable can be unstressed. In a word in which all the syllables are heavy, all feet will be monosyllabic, even though that violates (lower-ranked) **Binary(Foot,σ)**. However, if **WSP** is ranked lower than **Binary(Foot)**, the language is not quantity-sensitive, and unstressed syllables can be either heavy or light: a foot must be binary even if that means that the stressed syllable is light and the unstressed syllable is heavy.

A second characteristic of heaviness is the *Stress-to-Weight Principle*: stressed syllables tend to become heavy. Goldsmith (1990) noted that a short vowel in a light syllable lengthens in some languages; or, alternatively, that the following medial consonant geminates (providing a coda for the stressed syllable). Myers

---

[17] A foot may also be limited to a single syllable via **Aligned(σ,L,Foot,L)**, which requires all syllables to be at the beginning of the foot. Since only one syllable can actually begin the foot, a high ranking of this constraint leads to feet with just one syllable. We do not make use of alignment constraints in this book.

(1987) proposed that a medial consonant might be syllabified as a coda rather than an onset, to make the stressed syllable heavy. We suggest two constraints:

☞**Light(Unstressed)**: Unstressed syllables should be light.
violation: a heavy unstressed syllable
Old name: Weight-to-Stress Principle

☞**Heavy(Stressed)**: Stressed syllables should be heavy.
violation: a light stressed syllable
Old Name: Stress-to-Weight Principle

English is usually described as a language with quantity-sensitive stress, and we will see the effects of **Light(Unstressed)** in the phonological development of English-learning children. We suggest in §6.2.4.2 that **Heavy(Stressed)** may play a role in child English, by affecting the syllabification of medial consonants.

Codas make syllables heavy in some languages but not in others. In process terms, this is done via Weight-by-Position, which inserts a mora into a coda. Previous work in OT has used a Weight-by-Position constraint. We use the following constraint:

☞**Co-occurring(Rime→μ)**: A rime must co-occur with a mora. (If a segment is dominated by a rime, it must be moraic.)

We discuss the **Co-occurring** constraint family in §4.7.1.

Note that syllables tend to be limited to at most two moras, however (Hayes, 1989). Thus **Co-occurring(Rime→μ)** must introduce at most one nonunderlying mora into the syllable. To prevent, for example, a syllable like /anst/ from having four moras, we must have a constraint limiting a syllable to two moras.

☞**Binary(σ,μ)**: A syllable is limited to two moras.
violation: a syllable with three or more moras

Note that we are interpreting the **Binary** constraint with syllables as we did for prosodic words (but not for feet): a syllable with only one mora is not a violation of **Binary**.

The **Co-occurring(Rime→μ)** constraint requires that a mora be present if a coda is present. However, the constraint does not actually provide a mechanism for the mora to be present. That mechanism is provided by:

☞**Not(μ)**: Moras are not allowed in the output.
violation: any mora in the output

With the ranking **Survived(μ)** ≫ **Not(μ)**, only underlying moras are permitted, unless some higher-ranked constraint forces a mora to be inserted. If **Not(μ)** is ranked higher than **Co-occurring(Rime→μ)**, then no mora is inserted, and syllables with codas are light; codas are not moraic. If **Not(μ)** is ranked lower than **Co-occurring(Rime→μ)**, a mora is inserted, and codas make syllables heavy; codas are moraic.

4.5.2.5. Minimal and Maximal Words

Researchers often refer to the "minimal" and "maximal" size of a word. These can be useful notions, but no special constraints are needed to derive them. They can be derived from other constraints that are independently needed.

Given **Binary(Foot)** (a foot must have two moras or two syllables), and the fact that a Prosodic Word must have at least one foot, a word must have at least two moras or two syllables. This conjunction of constraints is abbreviated as ✂MinWd. We will sometimes use the term *minimal word*, but will not use this "constraint." We consider it to be a phenomenon that results from the interaction of several constraints, not a constraint in and for itself. Note that the minimal word can be different in different language systems. If a foot must be binary in terms of *syllables*, then a minimal word will have two syllables.

Similarly, phonologists sometimes refer to the *maximal word*: an upper limit to the size of a word. This also derives from the interaction of constraints. If a prosodic word is limited to one foot (**NotComplex(PrWd)**) and a foot is limited to two syllables (**Binary(Foot,σ)**), then a prosodic word is limited to two syllables. If, however, the prosodic word may have two feet, then the maximal word has four syllables. Again, we refer to the concept of the maximal word on occasion, but suggest that it, too, is not a constraint. The maximum size of a word derives from the interaction of constraints.

4.5.2.6. Word-Final Consonants and Extrametrical Syllables

McCarthy and Prince (1994) note that in some languages, all word-final syllables must end in a coda. They propose a constraint that aligns the right edge of a prosodic word with a consonant: **Align(PrWd,R,C,R)**; any word that ends in a vowel violates this constraint. Although this works, one must ask what the grounding for such a constraint might be, given that the **Not(Coda)** constraint has such a strong effect in so many languages. Stemberger (1996b) notes that this is similar to one phenomenon observed with stress: in some stress languages, the last syllable of the word is always unstressed, leading to unusual stress patterns. For example, if feet are left-prominent, all feet in the word are disyllabic (stressed-unstressed), but word-final feet appear to be trisyllabic (stressed-unstressed-unstressed). The standard process analysis (see Kenstowicz, 1994; Hayes, 1995) is that the last syllable is "extrametrical" and cannot be placed in a foot by the usual foot-building processes. In OT, a constraint is usually assumed that forces the last foot to be nonfinal (e.g., Prince & Smolensky, 1993), with the consequence that a syllable separates the foot from the end of the word. But why should a language have both **Align** and **DoNotAlign** constraints?

Stemberger (1996b) proposes a possible grounding, based on phonetic studies of speech, such as Fowler (1980). There is a low-level phonetic effect known as *word-final lengthening*, whereby the final syllable of a word is longer in duration than that same syllable would be if it were in nonfinal position. Stemberger suggests that there is a phonological equivalent to word-final lengthening: the end of the word must be "more massive." This serves a communicative goal: by making the end of the word more distinctive, a listener may better be able to determine where one word ends and the next begins, which is a very challenging task (see discussion in McClelland & Elman, 1986). There is the following constraint:

☞**WordFinalMassiveness**: Words end with extra *nonprominent* elements.
            violation: a vowel-final word [18]
                       a word ending in a stressed syllable
                       a word ending in one unstressed syllable in a
                       left-prominent binary foot

This makes the end of the word more massive in some way than other constraints would normally allow. That massiveness can take two forms: a final consonant or a final unstressed syllable. If the constraint is relatively low-ranked, a final coda or unstressed syllable might be allowed if one is underlying, but words without such codas or unstressed syllables would be tolerated. If the constraint is high-ranked, then *all* words would have to abide by them. If **Not(Coda)** is ranked higher than **Not(σ)**, the constraint is satisfied via an extra unstressed syllable at the end of the word: an "extrametrical" syllable; words may end in one unstressed syllable if the dominant foot pattern in the language is right-prominent (unstressed-stressed), or may end in two unstressed syllables if the dominant foot pattern is left prominent (stressed-unstressed).If **Not(σ)** is ranked higher than **Not(Coda)**, then **WordFinalMassiveness** is satisfied by requiring all words to end in a coda.

This constraint allows word-final syllables to be more massive than nonfinal syllables. For example, in Arabic, nonfinal syllables may contain either a coda (VC) or a long vowel (V:), but not both (*V:C); but in word-final syllables, V:C and VCC sequences are allowed (e.g., Goldsmith, 1990). Goldsmith (1990) also notes that English allows word-final sequences that would never be tolerated word-internally. He suggests that the extra material is allowed because there is a special word-final appendix in which the extra consonants are placed, but we are not convinced that appendices exist. We suggest instead that **WordFinalMassiveness** allows codas in final syllables to be larger than in other syllables.

4.6. ALIGNMENT AND PLACEMENT

Alignment constraints are of a novel sort, reflecting a concept that has been discussed in one form or another for many years. We feel that alignment constraints are too powerful, and will not make use of them in this book. They are, however, commonly used even in the acquisition literature (Levelt, 1996; Demuth, 1996a).

Consider the following observation:

In English, word boundaries generally coincide with syllable boundaries.

---

[18] This may possibly include "aspiration" of a voiceless stop, which can be viewed as a voiceless vowel.

For example, the sequence /st/ is syllable-initial at the beginning of a word (as in *the stone* /.ðə.stoʊn/), but is split between two syllables if the /s/ ends a word and the /t/ begins a word (as in *pulse tone* /.pʌls.toʊn./). One way to express the relationship would be:

The edge of a word is also the edge of a syllable.

We could also say that it is necessary to align the edges of words with the edges of syllables:

Align the left edge of a word with the left edge of a syllable.
Align the right edge of a word with the right edge of a syllable.

These two statements say that when a speaker begins a new word, s/he will also begin a new syllable.

We find similar effects at higher prosodic levels. The phrase *my balloon* has two stressed syllables and hence two feet. The feet are /maɪ/ and /bəluːn/, not */maɪbə/ and */luːn/. This is the case even though most feet in English are left-prominent (as with the incorrect */maɪbə/) and not right-prominent (as with the correct /bəluːn/). The edges of words tend to be aligned with the edges of feet, even if less marked feet would be created by violating the constraint.

Similarly, it is often necessary in morphology to place material at either the left or right edge of the word. A prefix (such as *re-* in *re-do*) is added to a word at the left edge. A suffix (such as *-s* as in *cat-s*) is added to the right edge. We can characterize a prefix in one of two ways:

1. **Align the left edge of the affix with the left edge of the word.**
2. **Align the right edge of the affix with the left edge of the base.**

In (1), we are saying that the left edge (beginning) of the affix begins the word. In (2), we are saying that the right edge (end) of the affix is immediately followed by the left edge (beginning) of the base. (See §4.9.) Similarly, we can characterize a suffix in one of two ways:

3. **Align the right edge of the affix with the right edge of the word.**
4. **Align the left edge of the affix with the right edge of the base.**

In (3), we are saying that the right edge (end) of the affix ends the word. In (4), we are saying that the left edge (beginning) of the affix immediately follows the right edge (end) of the base. The statements in (1–4) are what we mean when we say that an affix is a prefix or a suffix.

Such statements are necessary to define the relationship between syllables and word boundaries, and between prefixes and base forms, and they share an important property. They (arguably) say that the edge of one element coincides with the edge of another element. McCarthy and Prince (1993b) argue that statements of this sort are far more frequent than you might expect by chance. They suggest that this type of relationship should be formalized as a general property of *alignment*:

An edge (L or R) of any element can be aligned with an edge (L or R) of any other element.

The constraint that accomplishes this is:

✄**Align(Category, Edge, Category, Edge)**:   *Generalized Alignment*
Align the left or right edge of one category (morphological or phonological) with the left or right edge of another category.

This is a large family of constraints. Anything may be aligned with anything else. In keeping with our restriction that constraint names may not be verbs, we use the passive form of the word *Align*:

🖙**Aligned(Category, Edge, Category, Edge)**

Itô and Mester (1994) have proposed that **Aligned** can be used to derive some of the basic syllable constraints that we discussed above. It is possible to replace σ▸**Onset** and **Not(Coda)** with versions of **Aligned**:

Aligned(σ,L,C,L):   The left edge of a syllable must be aligned with the left edge of a consonant.[19]

      violation: The left edge of a syllable is aligned with the left edge of a vowel.

This constraint requires that a syllable start with a consonant, which is exactly the σ▸**Onset** constraint.

Aligned(C,L,σ,L):   The left edge of every consonant must be aligned with the left edge of a syllable.

      violation: a consonant anywhere except at the left edge of a syllable

Since a coda contains a consonant that is not at the left edge of a syllable, by definition, a coda consonant automatically violates this constraint, and this constraint could be used instead of **Not(Coda)**. This constraint *also* rules out complex onsets. For example, the /l/ of the word *play* /.pleɪ./ is not at the left edge of a syllable, and thus this constraint could replace **NotComplex(Onset)**.[20] An

---

[19] These constraints do not appear to work unless C and V timing units are assumed (rather than moras). The constraints are not violated if a glide (a nonsyllabic vowel) appears at the edge of the syllable, but *are* violated if a syllabic consonant begins the syllable. We know of no definition of "C" that accounts for the role in syllable structure played by nonsyllabic vowels and syllabic consonants, other than "C timing unit."

[20] Some languages allow complex onsets without allowing codas, while others allow codas without allowing complex onsets. These differences can be derived by the interaction between **Aligned** and other constraints. High ranking of **Not(V-Root)** prevents a vowel from being inserted to eliminate clusters and codas.

Aligned constraint that aligns the right edge of a syllable with a vowel could also be used to rule out codas:

Aligned(σ,R,V,R):   The right edge of every syllable must be aligned with the right edge of a vowel.

     violation: a syllable with a coda

There are undoubtedly many constraints that refer to the location of elements at edges of other elements. We do not believe, however, that it is necessary or desirable to have a general constraint that can align any element or category with any other element or category. McCarthy and Prince (1993b) note that the work of generalized alignment can be done with many specific constraints, and with restrictions on the domain of constraints that must be available to the theory of phonology independently. Generalized alignment predicts the possibility of many phenomena that have never been observed in human languages (adult or child). We discuss an example of this excessive power below, in §4.9.

In the history of phonological theory, there are instances where a theoretical mechanism has been introduced that was later abandoned because of excessive power. It is instructive to consider one of them. Transformations were introduced in early generative phonology. Chomsky and Halle (1968) and other early works provide numerous examples that demonstrated that transformations could be used to provide analyses of many difficult-to-analyze phonological patterns. After a few years of entirely positive work, researchers began to focus on the fact that transformations could do anything at all, with no limits. There was no explanation for why certain patterns *never* occurred in any human language. More and more restrictions were placed on the power of transformations, so that many of the early analyses using transformations were no longer possible. With OT, transformations have now been abandoned. We believe that generalized alignment should be abandoned for similar reasons.

We have other conceptual and empirical objections to generalized alignment. In addition to the excessive power of the constraint, there are consequences for the analysis of morphology that make incorrect predictions for language acquisition (see §4.9 below). For purely phonological constraints, we see the following drawbacks.

1. There is no known grounding for most **Aligned** constraints. Why should a constraint such as **Aligned(Labial,Left,ProsodicWord,Left)** (used for assimilation by Levelt, 1996) be present? According to Cole and Kisseberth (1994), the grounding for this constraint is simplicity: it restricts a word to a single feature. However, the **Aligned** constraint does *not* have that effect. Preventing any other place feature in the word is achieved rather via **NotComplex(Place)**, not via alignment. We believe that all constraints should be grounded, and that constraints with no obvious grounding are suspect, and should be avoided.

2. Many **Aligned** constraints are violated in *all* their uses. In vowel harmony, for example, the feature [+back] spreads to vowels, not to consonants. If

Aligned(+ back,L,PrWd,L) causes the input /tiko/ to yield the output [tuko], the left edge of the feature [+back] is *not* aligned with the left edge of the prosodic word, because [t] is at the left edge, and [+back] is not linked to [t]. It is true that [tiko] violates the **Aligned** constraint to a greater degree, since the left edge of [+back] is three segments from the left edge of the word, whereas the left edge of [+back] is only one segment from the left edge of the word in [tuko]. But **Aligned** is still violated. Basically, **Aligned** is being used only to say that the feature [+back] should spread left as far as it can. There is no evidence at all that the edges of [+back] and the prosodic word are or should be aligned. Although the alignment analysis works, there is no direct evidence for it.

3. There are known instances of harmony where there is no clear alignment with an edge.

This occurs, for example, in word-internal assimilation in child phonology. Stemberger and Stoel-Gammon (1991) give the example of *Canada geese* /kænədə giːs/ [kʰænəgə giːs], where [Dorsal] spreads to a preceding /d/ but not to the earlier /n/. Such assimilations must be accounted for via other mechanisms. It is necessary to prove that those other mechanisms are insufficient to account for all assimilations, in order to prove that **Aligned** is needed in addition. That argument has yet to be made.

4. There is no evidence that affixes or feet have their *edges* lined up with the *edges* of words. There is ample evidence that a foot or affix is *located* at one edge of a word. No one has yet made an empirical argument that the *edges* must be aligned.

Because argumentation and empirical evidence do not sufficiently show the need for an alignment constraint, we will not make use of it in this book. There are data from phonological development where one might be tempted to use **Aligned**. However, we will conclude that **Aligned** is unnecessary. In all instances in which **Aligned** might be used, we find that some other constraint (such as **Contiguity**) explains the patterns better. The reader should be aware, however, that **Aligned** is heavily used in phonological theory at the moment, and is considered by many to be one of the more basic constraints on phonological form.

4.6.1. HOW TO ACCOUNT FOR ASSIMILATION, PART I: SPREADING FOR THE SAKE OF SPREADING

In recent process-based versions of multilinear phonology, assimilation is driven by some ill-formedness in the word (Yip, 1988; Archangeli & Pulleyblank, 1994). A violation of **LinkedDownwards** or **Not** or constraints on sequences (such as **NotCo-occurring** or **NoSequence** or **NotTwice**, discussed in §4.7.2) is resolved by spreading a feature from the source segment (sometimes with the deletion of a feature in the target segment). No constraint has the explicit purpose of causing assimilation. Further, assimilation occurs in a purely *local* fashion: the interaction of two nearby segments determines whether spreading occurs or not.

In contrast, some analyses within OT assume a constraint which has the sole purpose of causing assimilation. Itô et al. (1995) proposed the following constraint:

✂*Spread: Do not spread an element (i.e., elements should be linked only to what they are linked to in the UR).
Do not add additional association lines.

If this constraint is violated, assimilation occurs. Note that spreading is still local, in that whether spreading happens or not is determined by the two segments (target and source) that are involved. This constraint is too process-oriented. Further, there are already constraints that prevent the insertion of association lines: **Not(Link)** and **SinglyLinked**, and an additional constraint like ***Spread** is not needed.

A second alternative, which is probably now the dominant approach within OT, additionally abandons the view that assimilation is determined locally. It was originally proposed by Cole and Kisseberth (1994), and is a central part of their optimal domains theory (ODT). We will not give full details of their theory here, but address just the core concept of how to account for assimilation. Assimilation is determined by a *global* consideration that is not sensitive to the nature of the target segment or the relation between the target and source segments. This alternative involves aligning a feature with the left or right edge of a phonological or morphological unit. For example, consider the following constraint:

Aligned(Labial,L,PrWd,L): The left edge of the feature Labial should coincide with the left edge of the prosodic word.

If a [Labial] element is present, it must occur at the beginning of the prosodic word; if no [Labial] element is present, then the constraint is irrelevant. In a word such as *pot*, this constraint is met, since [Labial] occurs at the beginning of the prosodic word. However, in the word *top*, the constraint is violated, since [Labial] occurs only at the end of the word, not at the beginning. In order to satisfy this **Aligned** constraint, some change must be made so that [Labial] occurs at the beginning of the prosodic word (or is deleted). One solution is to spread [Labial] so that it is linked to both the first and the second consonants (see Table 4.15):

TABLE 4.15

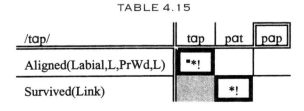

If **Aligned(Labial,L,PrWd,L)** is highest-ranked, the optimal output must begin with a labial ([p]). This can be accomplished by spreading the [Labial], so that it is linked to both the source (final) and target (initial) consonants: the harmonized output [pɑp]. Alternatively, it can be accomplished by flopping the [Labial] element from the final consonant onto the first consonant, so that it remains singly-linked (but violates **Survived(Link)**); the final consonant would receive the default place feature [Coronal], yielding the output [pɑt]. If **Survived(Link)** is ranked high (higher than any constraint that would cause it to be deleted), then harmony results, not flop.

One important aspect of assimilation is that it is often directional. Often a feature may spread only in one direction: to the left but not to the right; or to the right but not to the left. Yip (1988) and Archangeli and Pulleyblank (1994), working within process-based theories, propose that all spreading rules have a parameter that determines the direction of spreading. Alignment encodes directionality. **Aligned(Left)** spreads from right-to-left. **Aligned(Right)** spreads from left-to-right.

Several **Aligned** constraints can be combined in one analysis. Assume that the following constraint is ranked slightly lower:

Aligned(Dorsal,L,PrWd,L):   The left edge of the feature Dorsal should coincide with the left edge of the prosodic word.

This constraint would lead to Velar harmony in words like *dog* (in the same way as shown with [Labial] in Table 4.15). When both [Labial] and [Dorsal] are present, the interactions are interesting.[21] (See Table 4.16.)

TABLE 4.16

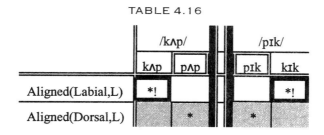

	/kʌp/		/pɪk/	
	kʌp	pʌp	pɪk	kɪk
Aligned(Labial,L)	*!			*!
Aligned(Dorsal,L)		*	*	

Because **Aligned(Labial,L,Prwd,L)** is ranked highest, it has priority. Labial Harmony is observed if the word starts with a dorsal, but Velar Harmony is not possible if the word starts with a labial. An initial alveolar is replaced by a labial or velar (but never vice versa), and a velar is replaced by a labial. If the other constraint, **Aligned(Dorsal,L,PrWd,L)**, is ranked highest, of course, the output is the reverse (see Table 4.17):

---

[21] Note that we have merged two constraint tables together here. We do this to save space. It is possible only when both tables have the same constraint rankings, but different input forms.

TABLE 4.17

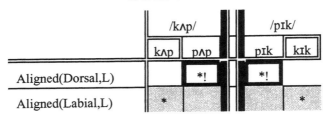

	/kʌp/			/pɪk/	
	kʌp	pʌp		pɪk	kɪk
Aligned(Dorsal,L)		*!		*!	
Aligned(Labial,L)	*				*

These two **Aligned** constraints align the feature with the left edge of the word, but the right edges can also be aligned. Interactions would be identical to what we have discussed so far, except that the direction of spreading would be left-to-right, rather than right-to-left.

If a left-edge and a right-edge constraint are combined, it is possible to reverse the order of the features involved:

Aligned(Labial,L,PrWd,L): The left edge of the feature Labial should coincide with the left edge of the prosodic word.

Aligned(Dorsal,R,PrWd,R): The right edge of the feature Dorsal should coincide with the right edge of the prosodic word. (See Table 4.18.)

TABLE 4.18

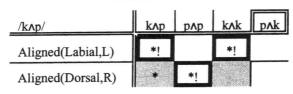

/kʌp/	kʌp	pʌp	kʌk	pʌk
Aligned(Labial,L)	*!		*!	
Aligned(Dorsal,R)	*	*!		

These **Aligned** constraints, then, do more than just cause assimilation. In combination with other constraints, they can cause the flopping of features from one segment into another, even to the extent of reversing the order of the features. Only if **Survived(Link)** were ranked higher than the **Aligned** constraints would assimilation be impossible.

Although she does not use these terms, this analysis is essentially that of Levelt (1994) for consonant harmony in child language. Alignment analyses of consonant harmony and flop in child language are now common (e.g., Vellemann, 1996; Goad, 1996b).

Aligned is a family of constraints. Presumably, there are such **Aligned** constraints for every single phonological feature, aligning the left or right edge with every phonological and morphological category that is allowed in the theory.

There is no known grounding for such constraints, and we are consequently unexcited about them. We prefer attributing assimilation to the repair of ill-formedness due to constraints on underspecification, feature occurrence, sequences, etc. (See §4.7.3.)

Before leaving assimilation, we must address one important characteristic of assimilation: the effect of default versus nondefault status of a feature. As noted in §4.4.2.1, the lowest-ranked **Not** constraint along a given dimension acts as the default, since the negative constraints against it are the least constraining. Thus, if a feature must be inserted, it is the default feature. However, it has long been noted that assimilations favor the *nondefault* value: defaults tend to be replaced by nondefault features, and default features less often spread to replace nondefault features. As noted in §3.11.3.1, this has been used as an argument for underspecification (see Paradis & Prunet, 1991, for review). Smolensky (1993) was unable to account for this fact in his analyses, which assumed full specification of features. Because negative constraints were lower on default features than on nondefault features, he predicted, incorrectly, that default features should also be favored in assimilations (as did Jakobson, 1968/1941). This problem has now been solved in OT, with two possibilities.

A particular ranking of the faithfulness constraints can derive this asymmetry (Gnanadesikan, 1995). The following ranking for the **Not** constraints tends to prevent the occurrence of nondefault features:

Not(Dorsal) ||| **Not(Labial)** ||| **Not(Coronal)**

If only one feature is possible, it will be the default feature. In contrast, the following ranking for the **Survived** constraints favors nondefault features:

Survived(Dorsal) ||| **Survived(Labial)** ||| **Survived(Coronal)**

If any feature survives in the output, it will be a nondefault feature. This ranking of **Survived** constraints follows the general principle that the ranking of constraints involving nondefaults is predictably higher than the ranking of constraints involving defaults. Consider how this impacts on assimilation (see Table 4.19):

TABLE 4.19

/dʌk/	dʌk	gʌk
Survived(Dorsal)		
Aligned(Dorsal,L,PrWd,L)	*!	
Survived(Coronal)		*

Because **Survived(Coronal)** is lowest-ranked, [Dorsal] may replace it in this assimilation. Contrast what happens if [Coronal] spreads via alignment as in Table 4.20:

TABLE 4.20

/kʌt/	kʌt	dʌt
Survived(Dorsal)		*!
Aligned(Coronal,L,PrWd,L)	*	
Survived(Coronal)		

Because **Survived(Dorsal)** is so high-ranked, [Coronal] is prevented from spreading. The high ranking of **Survived(Dorsal)** does not absolutely prevent [Coronal] from spreading, because the **Aligned** constraint can be ranked even higher than the **Survived(Dorsal)** constraint. But it makes a statistical prediction that spreading of the default [Coronal] will be less common than the spreading of the nondefaults [Dorsal] and [Labial]. In this way, the asymmetry involving defaults is predicted: defaults are at an advantage with respect to all negative constraints, but at a disadvantage in assimilation. In this book, we on occasion make use of the rankings of the **Survived** constraints suggested here.

In many ways, this analysis captures the same insights as underspecification. By ranking **Survived(Coronal)** low, we are essentially saying that there is little lexical motivation behind the appearance of [Coronal] in the output: [Coronal] appears because it is the default feature, not because it is present in the underlying representation. In fact, it does not matter at all which of these two rankings we have:

LinkedDownwards(Place) ||| **Survived(Coronal)** ||| **Not(Coronal)**

or:

 LinkedDownwards(Place) ||| **Not(Coronal)** ||| **Survived(Coronal)**

Given that *some* articulator node must be present, and given that **Not(Coronal)** is the lowest-ranked **Not** constraint, [Coronal] will be present in the output no matter what. Putting [Coronal] in the input (full specification) or leaving it out (radical underspecification) makes no difference. In contrast, for nondefault features, **Survived** must be ranked above **Not**, or else the nondefault feature will be replaced by the default feature: /k/ will become [t] (as in Velar Fronting in child phonology). One could say that the full-specification analysis of OT actually instantiates the radical underspecification analysis of earlier process-based theories (in which [Coronal] is present in the output because it is the default), not the full-specification analysis within earlier theories (in which [Coronal] is present in the output because it is present underlyingly).

Kiparsky (1994) has a different way to predict the asymmetry. He maintains that constraints may never refer to the default features. Thus, there are a set of constraints such as (using our constraint names):

      Survived(Artic):   All articulator nodes must survive.
Survived(Dorsal):   [Dorsal] must survive.
Survived(Labial):   [Labial] must survive.

If **Survived(Artic)** is high-ranked, all articulator nodes must survive in the output, and no assimilation of place features is possible. If **Survived(Artic)** is ranked low, but **Survived(Dorsal)** and **Survived(Labial)** are ranked high, then only [Coronal] may be deleted. Assimilations may spread [Dorsal] and [Labial] to replace [Coronal], but no feature may spread to replace [Dorsal] or [Labial]. Note that this proposal uses redundancy. Faithfulness constraints always appear in multiple variants, one that refers to a general case ([Artic], [nasal], [voiced]), and ones that refer to specific nondefault features ([Dorsal], [Labial], [+nasal], [+voiced]). Although this works, we are unhappy with the redundancy involved. We think that it is better to have constraints referring only to the specific features (including the defaults). We do not follow this alternative in this book. We make use of default underspecification in the input, but assume that all features are present (full specification) in the output.

We believe that assimilation also occurs for other reasons. We return to a discussion of assimilation in §4.7.3, after discussing sequence constraints.

4.7. OTHER CONSTRAINTS ON SEGMENTAL FEATURES

There are several constraint families that prevent a feature from appearing, or that require a feature to appear. We draw a basic division between two groups of constraints. The first group of constraints affects features within a segment: **co-occurrence** constraints. The second group affects features that appear in sequences of segments: **sequence** constraints. This section ends with discussions of the import of co-occurrence constraints for analyses of the "complexity" that arises when multiple nondefault features are present in a single segment, and for assimilation between consonants and vowels.

4.7.1. CO-OCCURRENCE CONSTRAINTS

We can break down constraints on the co-occurrence of features into two groups, depending on whether they are stated in a positive way or a negative way. We make use of both positive and negative constraints, because that allows more straightforward analyses of the effects involved; but everything could be restated solely in terms of negative constraints. We begin with the positive constraints. After discussing basic co-occurrence constraints, we discuss co-occurrence constraints that have an impact on features that are allowed to occur in different parts of the syllable (onsets versus rimes). The last several subsections of this section readdress the issue of constraints on putting segments into syllables (raised initially in §4.5.1).

4.7.1.1. Redundancies (Positive Co-Occurrence)

Positive co-occurrence constraints require that two (or more) elements be present at the same point in time. We name this constraint **Co-occurring**, and list which features must co-occur. In general, such constraints are part of a phenomenon that is standardly referred to as *redundancy*: one feature implies the existence of another. This implication is usually one-sided: if Feature A is present, then Feature B must also be present; but if Feature B is present, Feature A need not be present. For example, all nasals are voiced: [+nasal] implies [+voiced]. But not all voiced segments are nasals, since some are oral vowels, or liquids, or voiced obstruents: [+voiced] does not imply [+nasal]. Itô et al. (1995) refer to this constraint as the Redundancy Condition (abbreviated to ✂**R-Cond**), and refer to individual members of the family with specific names such as ✂**NasVoi** (nasals are voiced). We do not use such names, both because names are abbreviated and because the names of specific constraints do not include the name of the constraint family. We use the following type of name:

✏**Co-occurring(+ nasal→ + voiced)**:   The feature [+nasal] must co-occur
                                     with the feature [+voiced].
                    violation: [+nasal] without [+voiced] (a nasal
                                     that is voiceless or underspecified
                                     for voicing)

The elements in parentheses are *crucially ordered*. [+nasal] must co-occur with [+voiced], but [+voiced] does not have to co-occur with [+nasal]. This implicational relationship is reflected by our use of the "→" arrow in the name.

There are many redundancies in human languages, and it would be impossible to list all the members of the **Co-occurring** constraint family. An additional example:

✏**Co-occurring(-consonantal, + back, -low→V-Labial)**
                                     :   High and mid back vowels and
                                           glides are rounded.
                    violation: unrounded high and mid back
                                           vowels and glides

These constraints capture the well-known redundancy (see §3.11.5, Tables 3.3 and 3.4) that in most languages the rounding of the vowel is predictable. High and mid back vowels are rounded in most languages, and all other vowels (whether front, or low back) are unrounded.

We present here one last example that we will address in §5.5.1.3. All labials in English are predictable for the feature [labiodental]: fricatives are [+labiodental]; stops and nasals are [-labiodental]; vowels and glides are [-labiodental]. The following constraints are involved:

✏**Co-occurring(-sonorant,Labial, + continuant→ + labiodental)**
                                     :   Labial fricatives are
                                           labiodental.
                    violation: bilabial fricatives

✏**Co-occurring(Labial→-labiodental)**:   Labials are bilabial.
                                    violation: labiodentals

The second constraint simply says that all labials are bilabial. If the first constraint is ranked higher than the second, then fricatives are labiodental. If the first constraint is ranked lower than the second, then even the fricatives are bilabial. In our discussion of defaults in phonological development, we will discuss other variants of these constraints, to account for the fact that the labial glide /w/ surfaces as a labiodental glide [ʋ] in the speech of some children.

There are many more members of the **Co-occurring** constraint family. They are all straightforward statements of feature redundancies, where one feature is predictable from another. We will introduce others as needed. All members of the **Co-occurring** constraint family are positive co-occurrence constraints: Feature A requires that Feature B be present.

4.7.1.2. Incompatibilities (Negative Co-Occurrences)

Co-occurrence constraints can be negative: two features may not occur at the same point in time (such as within the same segment). Archangeli and Pulleyblank (1994) call these *Path Conditions*, and do not include the constraint family name in each constraint name (e.g., ✄*Lo, +ATR**). Our formulation of the constraint resembles **Co-occurring**:

NotCo-occurring(A,B):   A & B may not occur at the same point in time.
         violation: the features occur at the same point in time.
        grounding: in cognitive processing, coordinating two elements
                           at the same time requires additional resources.

The order of A and B in the parentheses does not matter; this is reflected by the comma between them in the name. A constraint on co-occurrence is a symmetrical relationship: the two (or more) elements may not all occur at the same time. (If one feature survives and the other does not, priority for survival is determined by other constraints, such as the relative ranking of the **Survived** constraints for the two elements.) The following are some specific members of this constraint family:

✏**NotCo-occurring(+low, +ATR)**:   [+low] and [+ATR] may not
                                       occur at the same point in time.
                   violation: a [+ATR] low vowel

✏**NotCo-occurring(+nasal,-sonorant)**:   Obstruents may not be [+nasal].
                       violation: a nasal obstruent (such as a
                                          prenasalized stop)

✏**NotCo-occurring(+cons,Cor,Lab)**:   Consonants may not be both
                                          coronal and labial.
                   violation: a labiocoronal (such as [pʲ])

The elements that may not co-occur can include elements that are outside the segment, such as timing units and rimes. For example, in most dialects of English, high vowels may be long ([iː], [uː]), but mid vowels must be diphthongal rather than long ([eɪ] not *[eː], [oʊ] not *[oː]). This would be accounted for via the following constraint (unviolated in most dialects):

☞**NotCo-occurring(μμ,-high,-low)**:   Mid vowels cannot be long.
                                 violation: the long vowels [eː] and [oː]

Archangeli and Pulleyblank (1994) argue that all **NotCo-occurring** constraints should be phonetically grounded, in order to explain why the two features cannot co-occur. They concentrate on constraints that involve the feature Advanced Tongue Root ([ATR]). They argue that it is articulatorily difficult to produce [-ATR] high vowels, since the raising of the tongue tends to pull the tongue root forward; and that it is articulatorily difficult to produce [+ATR] low vowels, since the lowering of the tongue pushes the tongue root back. But the phonetic grounding of some of the constraints that have been proposed is unclear. We believe that the constraints themselves are not phonetically grounded, but rule out all possible co-occurrences between elements. The grounding is cognitive (in that resources are required to coordinate features, during information processing). However, the constraint *rankings* are phonetically grounded, so that some co-occurrences are less optimal than others, universally; see the discussion in §2.4.4.

In general, the ranking of **NotCo-occurring** constraints is correlated with the ranking of **Not** constraints. It is more difficult to combine a nondefault feature with another nondefault feature than to combine it with a default feature:

NotCo-occurring(Labial, + voiced) ||| NotCo-occurring(Coronal, + voiced)

This expresses the basic insight of combinatorial specification (Archangeli & Pulleyblank, 1994). See §4.7.1.7 for discussion.

4.7.1.3. Putting Segments into Syllables, Part II

According to Jakobson (1968/1941), one main characteristic of speech is the existence of a rhythm that alternates between relatively "closed" and relatively "open" states of the vocal tract. Optimally, the speaker begins with the closed state. The closed versus open states are maximally different in articulation and in acoustic realization. As a result, alternating between them is perceptually easier and more salient than alternating between two different closed positions or two different open positions. Furthermore, the articulations of the open and closed states are maximally different. Producing the two states involves less motoric interference than between two open states or two closed states. Jakobson proposed that children begin with only this much ability, and thus begin with maximal contrasts between the open and closed states. We adopt this proposal in two ways: via syllable structure and via constraints on what appears in different parts of the syllable. Clements (1990) and Everett (1995) have recently echoed Jakobson's proposals, stating them in terms of sonority rather than openness of the vocal tract; we will point out the few ways in which our proposal differs from theirs empirically.

The major division between closed versus open states is encoded via syllable structure: the syllable has an onset and a rime. But this is not sufficient in and of itself. The onset and rime can have very similar articulatory and acoustic states, such as when the palatal glide [j] precedes the vowel [i] in [ji]: there is only a minimal change in articulation. To make it likely that the onset and the rime are more distinct, there should be constraints on which elements are allowed in the onset and in the rime. Consonants in the onset are instances of the syllable-margin; for reasons that will become clear below, we state our constraints in terms of the syllable margin rather than of the onset. We do not, however, state any constraints in terms of the syllable nucleus, but only in terms of the rime. In the universally unmarked type of syllable, the rime has only a vowel within it, so that constraints on the rime are equivalent to constraints on the vowel. This may seem to be a "trick," but the appearance of a trick partly derives from the fact that we are calling the second constituent of the syllable the "rime"; had we called it the "peak," it would seem reasonable.

The optimal syllable margin and the optimal rime should have opposite characteristics, derived from the rhythms inherent in syllables. The degree of openness of the vocal tract should be the main determinant. There are a number of features that relate to degree of openness of the vocal tract:

Optimal Syllable-Margin	Optimal Rime
-sonorant	+sonorant
+consonantal	-consonantal
-continuant	+continuant
C-Place	no C-Place
no V-Place	V-Place
	Dorsal
	-high
	+low

The feature [sonorant] is related to the openness of the vocal tract, since closed vocal tracts affect pressure in a way that makes voicing difficult and leads to [-sonorant] segments. The feature [consonantal] reflects the openness of the vocal tract, since it is directly related to the degree of constriction. [continuant] specifically refers to full closure in the oral and pharyngeal cavities. One defining characteristic of C-Place versus V-Place is the degree of constriction. Segments may have both, in which case the C-Place features represent closure or close approximation, while the V-Place features involve more distance between the articulators. We also list [Dorsal] for the optimal rime, since it is the case that the vocal tract can most easily be made open in that region. We have *not* said that the optimal syllable-margin is a nondorsal, because we know of no evidence that this is the case, but leave the possibility open.

We have not listed any laryngeal features here, although the greatest acoustic differentiation is for the syllable-margin to be voiceless and the rime to be voiced. This fact can be derived from other characteristics: the optimal obstruent is voiceless, and the optimal *sonorant* is voiced. We account for this via the following two constraints:

>   **Co-occurring(+ sonorant→ + voiced)**:   Sonorants must be voiced.
>   **NotCo-occurring(-sonorant, + voiced)**:   Obstruents must be voiceless.

Of course, both of these constraints can be overridden. Voiceless ([+s.g.]) sonorants are possible, either because they are underlying (as with the initial glide in *which* [ʍɪtʃ] in some dialects) or because [+s.g.] is spread from another segment (as in the common realization of the word-initial cluster /sm/ as [m̥] in early child phonology: *smile* [m̥ɑɪo]). Voiced obstruents are also possible, because [+voiced] is underlying or assimilated from elsewhere. The constraints on syllable-margins and rimes do not override these constraints. In no language (or child) is the optimal sonorant consonant in an onset voiceless. Nor is it ever the case in any language (or child) that the optimal obstruent in a coda is voiced.

There is, however, some indication that the optimal syllabic segment is voiced. In those unusual languages that allow obstruents to be syllabic, voiced obstruents make better syllabic consonants than voiceless obstruents (as implied for Berber by Prince & Smolensky, 1993). We may simply be wrong in attributing effects to the openness of the vocal tract rather than to sonority, since sonority predicts that voicing makes something a better nucleus. We leave this issue unresolved here, but note that a constraint such as **Co-occurring(V→ + voiced)** could account for the relation between voicing and the syllabic status of an element. There is no evidence that voicing is in general preferred within a rime. Below, we discuss the crosslinguistic tendency for devoicing in codas.

The optimal syllable margin and optimal rime can be derived via constraint families that are needed for other purposes: **Co-occurring** and **NotCo-occurring**. Basically, a syllable margin must co-occur (or cannot co-occur) with some features (unless another constraint overrides them), and a rime must co-occur (or cannot co-occur) with a complementary set of features. For syllable margins, the constraints are:

>   ☞**Co-occurring(σ-Margin→-sonorant)**
>   ☞**Co-occurring(σ-Margin→ + consonantal)**
>   ☞**Co-occurring(σ-Margin→-continuant)**
>   ☞**Co-occurring(σ-Margin→C-Place)**
>   ☞**NotCo-occurring(σ-Margin,V-Place)**

For rimes, the constraints include all the features that refer to openness in the vocal tract (including [+low]):

>   ☞**Co-occurring(Rime→ + sonorant)**
>   ☞**Co-occurring(Rime→-consonantal)**
>   ☞**Co-occurring(Rime→ + continuant)**
>   ☞**Co-occurring(Rime→V-Place)**
>   ☞**Co-occurring(Rime→Dorsal)**
>   ☞**Co-occurring(Rime→-high)**

☞**Co-occurring(Rime→ + low)**
☞**Co-occurring(Rime→μ)**
☞**NotCo-occurring(Rime,C-Place)**

For onsets, only the **Co-occurring(σ-Margin)** constraints are relevant, so these constraints represent an absolute "pressure" on the form of onset consonants to be as non-vowel-like as possible. Similarly, for syllabic segments, only the **Co-occurring(Rime)** constraints are relevant, so these constraints represent a "pressure" on the form of syllabic elements to be as vowel-like as possible.

For codas, however, both sets of constraints are relevant. This means that coda consonants are subject to two opposite "pressures": one "pressure" drives coda consonants to be vowel-like, but the other drives coda consonants to be non-vowel-like. If one whole set of constraints is ranked above the other whole set, then coda consonants will either be as vowel-like as possible (the rime constraints are ranked higher) or as obstruent-like as possible (the syllable margin constraints are ranked higher). If the two are interspersed, a complex pattern will emerge. Stops and nasals may be possible (both [-continuant]), but fricatives and liquids ([+continuant]) may not be. This would result from:

Co-occurring(σ-Margin→-continuant) ‖	**Co-occurring(σ-Margin→-sonorant)**
Co-occurring(Rime→ + sonorant) ‖	**Co-occurring(Rime→ + continuant)**

In contrast, with the reverse ranking, fricatives and liquids would be possible in codas, but stops and nasals would not be. Many different patterns would be possible, depending on exactly the way that the individual constraints are ranked relative to each other. Prince (1984) noted the existence of languages with strong restrictions on coda consonants that reflect the rime-related constraints that we have proposed here. See Goldsmith (1990) for additional discussion.

Note the constraint **Co-occurring(Rime→μ)**, which requires that elements within the rime be moraic. The effect on syllabic elements is obvious, since they are always moraic. The effect on codas is interesting. If this constraint is ranked high enough, a coda consonant becomes moraic: weight-by-position, as discussed above. If the constraint is ranked lower than **Not(μ)**, however, then no mora can be inserted, and the coda consonant remains nonmoraic. This accounts for the variation across languages as to whether coda consonants are moraic, and does so in a way that unifies that variation with other asymmetries between the onset and the coda.

Note that **NotCo-occurring(Rime,C-Place)** requires that coda consonants not have consonantal place features.[22] If this is ranked higher than **Linked-Upwards(C-Place)**, an underlying C-Place node is deleted, resulting in a consonant with no Place node: [ʔ] or [h]. Although such Glottal Replacement (or Debuccalization) can occur in any position in the word or syllable in child language, it is most common in codas; see Dylan's data in §8.6.1.2.

---

[22] This is not redundant with the requirement that the syllabic element have V-Place. When a language has palatalized consonants, they are still poor nuclei, even though they have V-Place.

The affinity of codas for [Dorsal] has been reported in several contexts. Trigo (1988) even proposed that [Dorsal] is the unmarked articulator node in codas, based on the fact that the velar nasal [ŋ] is restricted to codas in many languages (including English). Velarized laterals (as in *pill* [pʰɪɫ]) are often restricted to codas. It has also been observed for child phonological development (e.g., Stoel-Gammon, 1985) that velars may appear in codas before they appear in onsets. This can be derived using the **Co-occurring(Rime→Dorsal)** constraint. We take for granted that there must be a general constraint against all elements, including **Not(Dorsal)**. If **Survived(Dorsal)** (**LinkedUpwards(Dorsal)**) is the highest-ranked constraint, then velars are possible outputs. If **Not(Dorsal)** is the highest-ranked constraint, then the feature [Dorsal] never appears in any surface form. Instead, [Dorsal] is deleted, and the default articulator node [Coronal] is inserted; in developmental studies, this is referred to as *Velar Fronting*. However, consider what happens if **Co-occurring(Rime→Dorsal)** is the highest-ranked constraint, for coda versus onset positions. (See Table 4.21.)

TABLE 4.21

	/pɪk/		/kaʊ/	
	pɪk	pɪt	kʰaʊ	tʰaʊ
Co-occurring(Rime→Dorsal)		*!		
Not(Dorsal)	*		*!	
Survived(Dorsal)		*		*

Velar Fronting is ruled out for the final velar, because that would violate **Co-occurring(Rime→Dorsal)**. The velar correctly surfaces. However, because there is no special constraint requiring [Dorsal] to be in an onset, [Dorsal] is impossible in onsets, and Velar Fronting occurs. We discuss such interactions in child phonology in §6.1.12.2.1.

These constraints can in principle lead to different default features in onsets versus codas. Consider this ranking:

Co-occurring(Rime→Dorsal) ||| **Not(Dorsal)** ||| **Not(Coronal)**

The high ranking of the **Co-occurring** constraint makes it optimal to have a dorsal consonant in the coda. If the default [Coronal] is filled in, this **Co-occurring** constraint would be violated. Consequently, the apparent default feature in coda position will be [Dorsal], not [Coronal] (as in onsets). We note in §6.1.12.2 and §8.4 that young children can in fact have apparent defaults in codas that reflect the **Co-occurring(Rime)** constraints.

We have not yet provided a satisfactory account of why [+voiced] is often avoided in codas, even when voiced obstruents occur in onsets. The constraints discussed so far do not address any laryngeal feature relative to position in the syllable. Further, if we were to introduce a constraint that said that rime segments should be voiced (since vowels are), we would predict a tendency for obstruent consonants to be voiced when they appear in codas, which is the opposite of the actual facts. We believe this derives from the general fact that faithfulness is ranked lower in codas than in onsets (see §4.7.1.5). An alternative possibility is the following constraint:

✏**NotCo-occurring(Coda, + voiced)**:   Coda consonants may not be voiced.

This constraint is ranked lower than **Co-occurring(+ sonorant→ + voiced)**, so that sonorant consonants are not devoiced in codas (in any language).

Though this constraint appears to be ad hoc, we believe that it is grounded in a difference in the production and perception of voicing in different syllable positions. Stops are rarely voiced throughout, since it is difficult to maintain a sufficiently low oral pressure to maintain voicing during the entire closure. In word-initial position, generally only the last portion of the stop is voiced, and listeners perceive a stop as (pre)voiced if there is as little as 10 msec of prevoicing. Further, it is possible to begin voicing quite sharply: instantaneously with the release of closure, the high oral pressure of a voiceless stop is neutralized, and voicing begins with essentially no delay. The situation is quite different in codas. After vowels, it takes a pitch period or two for the oral pressure of a voiceless stop to build up sufficiently to prevent voicing; "voiceless" stops routinely show one or two pitch-periods of vocal-cord vibration (e.g., Dinnsen & Charles-Luce, 1984). The perceiver ignores this very brief period of voicing, and perceives the consonant as "voiceless." For a voiced stop, if adequate accommodation is not made to the rise in pressure that comes from voicing during closure, the oral pressure rapidly becomes too high, and voicing ceases. The problem here is that even voiceless stops have a few pitch periods of voicing, so that voiced stops must maintain voicing for even longer in order to be perceived as "voiced." There is thus an asymmetry between onset and coda position: if there is vocal cord vibration during the last 10 msec of the stop in an onset, the stop is perceived as voiced; but if there is vocal cord vibration during the first 10 msec of the stop in a coda, the stop is perceived as voiceless. It follows that it is articulatorily more difficult to produce an acceptable-sounding voiced stop in a coda than in an onset: voicing must be maintained for a longer period of time to be perceived in a coda than in an onset. This asymmetry is reflected in our **NotCo-occurring(Coda, + voiced)** constraint (but see §4.7.1.5 for another possibility).

The constraints that we have laid out concern a language's preferences for what should be syllabic and what should be nonsyllabic. Syllabic elements should have as many of the properties demanded by the rime constraints as possible. Onset elements should have as many of the properties demanded by the syllable margin constraints as possible. Coda elements can show a wide variety of patterns, depending on the ranking. Given a choice between making /ɑ/ and /i/ syllabic, [ɑ] will be made syllabic, because it is [+low] (optimal, via **Co-occurring (Rime→ +low)**). Given a choice between making /d/ or /n/ syllabic, [n] will be syllabic, because it is [+sonorant] (**Co-occurring(Rime→ +sonorant)**). These preferences can take a set of consonants and vowels and derive which are syllabic and which are not, in combination with constraints on how many consonants can be in an onset, etc.

In §4.5.1.3, we discussed Prince and Smolensky's (1993) proposal to derive preferences as to what is syllabic and what is not, which involved constraints such as **Notσ-Peak(t)** and **Notσ-Margin(ɑ)**. By ranking these constraints in the right way, a preference is established for a segment to be either nonsyllabic (a margin) or syllabic (a head). One thing that makes us uncomfortable about these constraints is that they deal with entire segments. For every possible segment in human language, there is one constraint of each type; within each constraint family, the individual constraints are ranked by sonority, with no possibility of language-particular reranking. This analysis entirely misses the fact that sonority is related to (and possibly derivable from) the individual features that make up a segment (see Clements, 1990, for discussion). We avoid constraints that refer to whole segments, because *features* are the basic unit of phonology. In §6.1.6.1.2, we present child data that suggest that the relevant constraints can be ranked differently for different children, providing support for our feature-based approach and against a whole-segment sonority-based approach.

4.7.1.4. Putting Segments into Syllables, Part III: Strong and Weak Prosodic Positions

The constraints that we have just discussed predict two basic patterns in relation to what can appear as an onset versus a coda, if there can be a coda at all:

1. Onsets and codas allow the same set of segments.
2. Onsets allow low-sonority segments, but codas allow high-sonority segments.

These constraints do *not* predict the following pattern:

3. Codas allow only a subset of the features allowed in onsets.

This third pattern is also attested; see Goldsmith (1990) for discussion, and §6.1.12.1 for data from child phonology. For example, when the onset allows voiceless stops, voiced stops, voiceless fricatives, nasals, and glides, the coda may allow only voiceless stops. Itô and Mester (1993) argue that there must be constraints that restrict codas to just [Coronal] if consonantal place features are present (unless the place feature is doubly-linked to both a coda consonant and an onset consonant). Itô and Mester (1993), Itô et al. (1995), and Goldsmith (1990) argue for a concept called *licensing*, which determines which features may appear in a coda versus an onset.

Prince and Smolensky (1993) suggest that licensing is not necessary, and that the restrictions on coda consonants can be derived through interactions between independently needed constraints. Consider Table 4.22, and the way that /p/ is allowed in an onset but not in a coda:

TABLE 4.22

	/pa/			/ap/			/ta/		/at/	
	pa	ta	a	ap	at	a	ta	a	at	a
σ▸Onset			*!	*	*	*		*	*	*
Survived(Labial) LinkedUp(Labial)		*!			*!					
Notσ-Margin(p)	*			*!						
Survived(Root)			*			*		*		*
Not(Coda)					*				*	
Notσ-Margin(t)							*		*	

Merely by ranking the **Notσ-Margin** constraint over **Survived(Root)**, [p] is prohibited in the output except when it is required to give a syllable an onset. The high-ranking of **Survived(Labial)** and **LinkedUpwards(Labial)** (and **Survived (Place)** and **LinkedUpwards(Place)**) prevents the feature [Labial] from being deleted, with the concomitant insertion of default [Coronal]; this ranking causes a nonminimal repair, in which a whole segment is deleted, not just one offending feature. Note that /t/ surfaces in both onset and coda position, but /p/ survives only in a onset.

If **Survived(Labial)** and **LinkedUpwards(Labial)** are ranked low, just the feature [Labial] is deleted, leading to substitution of [t] for [p] as in Table 4.23:

TABLE 4.23

	/pa/			/ap/			/ta/		/at/	
	pa	ta	a	ap	at	a	ta	a	at	a
σ▸Onset			*!	*	*	*		*!	*	*
Notσ-Margin(p)	*!			*!						
Survived(Root)			*			*!		*		*!
Not(Coda)					*				*	
Notσ-Margin(t)		*			*		*		*	
Survived(Labial)		*			*					

Unfortunately, this ranking does not capture an asymmetry between onsets and codas, but predicts that onsets and codas will be parallel. Deletions are blocked in onset position, but substitutions are allowed, because an onset is still *present* when there is a substitution. Patterns commonly occur in child language in which place, manner, and voicing features are allowed in onsets but prohibited from coda position. For example, a child may have fricatives in onset position ([s], [f]), but substitute stops for fricatives in coda position ([t], [p]). We cannot see how to derive such a pattern through the simple interaction of constraints of this sort.

Itô and Mester (1993) also stress that a labial may be allowed in a coda, but only if it is the first half of a geminate consonant, or if the articulator node is doubly linked to onset and coda position. This interaction is not predicted, even by the ranking that successfully derives the onset/coda asymmetry with regard to deletion (see Table 4.24):

TABLE 4.24

napːa	napːa	natːa	napa
σ▸Onset			
Survived(Labial) LinkedUpwards(Labial)		*!	
Notσ-Margin(p)	**!		*
Survived(Root)			
Not(Coda)	*	*	
Notσ-Margin(t)		**	

Because the geminate consonant is a part of both onset and coda, it violates **Notσ-Margin(p)** twice, and so is less optimal than an output in which the /p/ is short. One way to ensure that [napːa] is the optimal output is to require that all underlying timing units survive in the output, thus preventing shortening to [napa]. However, this would also prevent deletion of the coda in [ap], so it is not a possibility. With these constraints, /p/ is deleted from a coda, whether it is an independent consonant, or the first part of a geminate consonant. Clearly, something additional is needed to account for these facts.

Cole and Kisseberth (1994) suggest a solution to this and related problems. They note that this difficulty also occurs with unstressed syllables: elements that are possible in stressed syllables are not always possible in unstressed syllables. In English, for example, a full range of vowels is allowed in stressed syllables, but far fewer vowel contrasts are allowed in unstressed syllables; stressed /bɪt/ versus /bɛt/ versus /bʌt/ versus /bʊt/ are all possible, but not unstressed /ˈræbɪt/ versus /ˈræbɛt/ versus /ˈræbʌt/ versus /ˈræbʊt/. We note also that word-final unstressed syllables statistically tend to have very restricted coda consonants; English has many words in which the coda in the final unstressed syllable is /t, s, n, k/, but very few in which it is /d/ (*naked*; inflected forms are not counted here), /p/

(*ketchup*), /b/ (*cherub*), /f/ (*sheriff*), or /g/ (??no examples??). Although most consonants are technically allowed in this environment, few lexical items include marked coda consonants. Cole and Kisseberth further note that some positions in the word are "strong" positions that allow many contrasts (such as word-initial syllables), while other positions in the word are "weak" and allow a narrower range of contrasts (such as word-final syllables). They propose that the faithfulness constraints should occur in multiple families, one for each prosodic position. Thus, there would be one set of **Survived** constraints for onsets, but a different set of **Survived** constraints for codas. By having separate constraints for different phonological environments, one gains flexibility. **Survived$_{\text{Onset}}$(Labial)** can be ranked higher than **Survived$_{\text{Coda}}$(Labial)**, leading to a greater degree of faithfulness in onsets than in codas; having a single faithfulness constraint that covers both onsets and codas is much more restrictive and links faithfulness in the two syllable positions in a way that can make things difficult. To see how this solves the problem, consider Table 4.25:

TABLE 4.25

	/pa/			/ap/			/ta/		/at/	
	pa	ta	a	ap	at	a	ta	a	at	a
σ▸Onset			*!	*	*	*		*!	*	*
Survived$_{\text{Onset}}$(Labial)		*!								
Notσ-Margin(p)	*			*!						
Survived(Root)			*			*!		*		*!
Not(Coda)				*	*				*	
Notσ-Margin(t)		*			*		*		*	
Survived$_{\text{Coda}}$(Labial)					*					

By ranking the **Survived$_{\text{Onset}}$** constraints high, we guarantee that survival is optimal in onsets, and that negative constraints will be violated: the output of /pa/ is [pa], not *[ta]. By ranking the **Survived$_{\text{Coda}}$** constraints low, we guarantee that the negative constraints are highly constraining, and that survival is violated: the output of [ap] is [at], not *[ap].

For this analysis, it is no longer crucial that the negative constraints refer to whole segments. In fact, we can assume the following ranking:

Survived$_{\text{Onset}}$(Labial) ||| **Not(Labial)** ||| **Survived$_{\text{Coda}}$(Labial)**

Recall that a feature in general survives if the **Survived** constraint is ranked higher than **Not**, but does not survive if the **Not** constraint is ranked higher than **Sur-**

vived. This ranking leads to survival of underlying features in onsets but not in codas.

This proposal also solves the problem of doubly linked elements in codas. If [Labial] is singly linked and in a short segment, it is entirely within the coda and so is subject only to **Survived$_{Coda}$(Labial)**; the low ranking of that constraint makes it impossible to have [Labial] in a coda. If the [Labial] is doubly linked (as in /mp/) or in a doubly linked segment (as in /pː/), in contrast, the feature [Labial] is both in a coda *and* in an onset, and so is subject to both **Survived$_{Coda}$(Labial)** *and* **Survived$_{Onset}$(Labial)**. Since **Survived$_{Onset}$(Labial)** is high-ranked, [Labial] survives. Because there is no constraint that *prevents* [Labial] in a coda, and **Survived$_{Onset}$(Labial)** prevents deletion of [Labial], [Labial] is allowed to surface in the coda. Thus, [nampa] and [napːa] are possible outputs, even if *[nam] and *[nap] are not possible outputs. This captures the insights behind licensing (see Goldsmith, 1990), without needing licensing as an separate concept; one could say that licensing is an emergent property of the constraints and their ranking. In this respect, the feature-based analysis taken here is superior to a whole-segment-based analysis employing **Notσ-Margin(p)** and **Notσ-Margin(m)**, since the codas in /nampa/ and /napːa/ violate those constraints just as surely as the codas in /nam/ and /nap/, and so should be equally impossible. A feature-based approach is superior.

Similarly, these data suggest that the negative constraints optimally should refer to the *presence* of features (as with our **Not** constraints). Prince and Smolensky (1993) use negative constraints such as ***Pl/Lab** (a variant of ***Struc**), that refer to *linkage* of [Labial]. Since the coda portions of /nampa/ and /napːa/ both incur a violation of these linkage-based constraints, they should rule out the coda portion. The **Not** constraints used here are superior, since they refer to presence, and not to linkage.

If there are even more families of constraints, each constraining elements in particular prosodic positions, we can account for differences in faithfulness in other strong positions (stressed syllables, word-initial syllables, etc.) versus weak positions (unstressed syllables, word-final syllables, etc.). Since the effects of strong and weak prosodic positions are widespread in human languages (see Cole & Kisseberth, 1994), this is a useful modification of the theory. (Alderete et al., 1996, assume a similar analysis.)

This proposal impacts on the sorts of phenomena that occur at word boundaries. In many languages, when two vowels come together at word boundaries, one deletes (Archangeli & Pulleyblank, 1988; Goldsmith, 1990:52). Since **Survived$_{WordInitial}$(V-Root)** is ranked higher than **Survived$_{WordFinal}$(V-Root)**, the word-initial vowel should survive, and the word-final vowel should delete. This is generally the case. Note that we do not need any special constraint (such as **Priority(WordInitial)** to derive this result); the rankings of the **Survived** constraints derive the result directly.

There is a price for this modification of the theory, however. It vastly increases the number of constraints in the system. It loosens the empirical testability of the theory. It seems to require stipulating what constitutes "strong" and "weak" positions, with no necessarily independent justification for why a given position is strong or weak. Although we might be willing to pay this price, it would be preferable not to have to make such stipulations.

4.7.1.5. The Sliding Scale of Faithfulness

An alternative to this duplication of constraints is possible. We can question one of the assumptions of the theory: a single ranking for constraints. We believe that faithfulness constraints can be involved in more than one ranking. There is a single ranking for all **Survived** constraints relative to each other, within a particular person's phonological system (barring minor instabilities needed to account for variability; see §4.11). But the ranking of the **Survived** constraints relative to other constraints is not always the same.

Kirchner (1994) and Nathan (1996) make an interesting proposal regarding faithfulness constraints. In their studies of fast-speech phenomena, they remarked that faithfulness is greater in slow, careful speech than in fast speech. Although one could attempt to account for fast speech by saying that the constraint rankings are different than in slow speech, that would fail to capture this predictable relationship between the two speech variants. Both authors propose independently that faithfulness constraints, as a group, can be shifted higher or lower in the rankings as a function of speech style (and possibly also as a function of such extragrammatical factors as fatigue, attention, etc.). This proposal can be adapted to account for strong versus weak prosodic positions without multiplying the number of constraints involved, in a way that makes the relationship between OT and cognitive models more explicit.

It is currently taken for granted in models of psychological processing that elements have activation levels (which are a measure of activity or strength), and that the inherent activation level of an element determines whether that element can be successfully accessed. This is true both for connectionist models (Dell, 1986; Stemberger, 1984, 1992b) and for symbolic models (Levelt, 1989). Successful access translates into faithfulness. High activation levels lead to greater accessibility (greater faithfulness), and low activation levels lead to lesser accessibility (lesser faithfulness). The psycholinguistics literature contains numerous proposals concerning the relationship between activation levels and position in the word. For example, word-initial position gives an element higher levels of activation (Brown & McNeill, 1966; Stemberger, Elman, & Haden, 1985; Dell, 1986; Levelt, 1989), both in perception and in production. Marslen-Wilson and Tyler (1978) and Cole, Jakimik, and Cooper (1978) suggest that word-initial position is stronger because it plays a greater role than word-final position in lexical access in auditory language processing. It has been proposed that stressed syllables have higher levels of activation than unstressed syllables (Berg, 1990). The differences that have been proposed bear a striking similarity to the examples of strong versus weak prosodic positions discussed by Cole and Kisseberth (1994) and Beckman (1995).

We propose that the ranking of the **Survived** constraints is directly related to activation levels. **Survived** is ranked higher if activation levels are high, but lower if activation levels are low. Given our knowledge of activation levels in different positions in the word, **Survived** should be ranked higher in syllable onsets than in syllable codas;[23] higher in word-initial position than in word-final position; and higher in stressed syllables than in unstressed syllables. There is a single constraint, but it is not ranked the same in all positions in the word. This is roughly equivalent to having multiple constraints, one for each position, but there are differences. (a) With different **Survived** subfamilies for each position, the rankings within each subfamily are independent, allowing for different rankings (and defaults) in each position in the word. With a sliding scale for faithfulness, there is a single ranking of **Survived** constraints relative to each other, in all positions in the word. (b) There is an independent characteristic that determines strong versus weak positions in the word. There is thus far less arbitrariness involved in claiming that a particular position is weak or strong. (c) The relationship between the theory of phonology and psycholinguistic processing becomes more straightforward. The characteristic that we index faithfulness to (activation level) has been viewed as related to faithfulness in psycholinguistic processing.

There are many additional consequences to this proposal, since there are many other ways in which the activation level can be increased or decreased. For example, faithfulness might be greater in high-frequency words than in low-frequency words. In specific situations in which elements compete, activation levels can be lowered. Elements that are active at the same time can influence the activation levels of other elements, via spreading activation (Dell, 1985). In later chapters, we note phenomena in child phonology that can be analyzed via reference to activation levels and their consequent effects on faithfulness.

We believe that there are additional strong and weak domains of a less phonological nature: base morphemes (open class lexical items) versus affixes, clitics, and other closed class lexical items. (See also Alderete et al., 1996.) Steriade (1988) observes that the base morphemes of a language exhibit the full range of segments, syllable structures, foot structures, and prosodic word structures that the language allows. She also observes that affixes are generally highly reduced, often constituting a single syllable or less, lacking consonant clusters and diphthongs, and even being restricted to default features. She suggests that affixes are more subject to constraints on markedness. In our terms, base morphemes are a strong domain, while affixes are weak domains. Closed class lexical items (such as articles and pronouns) are also often restricted in the same ways. Further, closed class lexical items are prone to cliticization, wherein they lose stress and often lose segments (e.g., *her* [hɝ] may be reduced to [ɚ] in phrases like *saw her*). We believe that it may even be predictable that affixes and closed class lexical items are weak domains. Lexical items are selected on the basis of meaning. In a con-

---

[23] In the typical case, at any rate. Some children seem to have more difficulty with onsets than with codas.

nectionist system (such as that of Dell, 1986, or Stemberger, 1985), lexical items are activated on the basis of activation from semantic features. The more semantic features that a word reflects, the more activation the lexical item should receive. Base morphemes have rich meanings, and thus should receive a great deal of activation. Affixes and closed class lexical items have very impoverished meanings, and thus should receive less activation. To illustrate the contrast in meaning, consider *her* (a female, where "female" is a relatively simple concept) versus *woman* (a female human being, where "human being" is a more complex concept) or *lioness*. Indeed, some nouns with minimal semantic content show unusual phrasal stress patterns. For example, phrasal stress within a noun phrase generally falls on the noun (*the big **dog***), but generally falls on the adjective if the noun is *one* (*the **big** one*); the word *one* is almost pronoun-like in its semantic impoverishment, and it also fails to attract main phrasal stress. Similarly, in the word *dogs*, the base morpheme *dog* carries more information than the plural morpheme *-s*. We suggest that the low semantic content of affixes and closed class lexical items lead to them being weak domains for phonology. The **Survived** constraints are ranked higher for base morphemes than for affixes and closed class lexical items.

Treating base morphemes as strong domains has consequences for phonologically based reductions in child phonology. If **NotComplex(Coda)** is high-ranked, so that all word-final clusters are reduced to a single consonant, consonants within the base morpheme should tend to survive and consonants within suffixes to delete. (See Stemberger & Bernhardt, 1997; and §6.4.1.1 and §9.1.3.1).

Treating affixes as weak domains also leads us to a new possible analysis of reduplication. McCarthy and Prince (1994) argue that a reduplicative affix corresponds to the base morpheme in the output, and low ranking of the output-to-output correspondence constraints leads to a reduction of the affix towards unmarked elements. We can accomplish the same reduction using prosodic domains, if the reduplicative affix corresponds to the input. An input string such as /flat/ would be realized as two output strings: the reduplicative prefix and the base morpheme. Since the prefix is in a weak domain, faithfulness is ranked lower than for base morphemes. This raises the possibility that the prefix will be subject to phonological constraints and be reduced (to [fa]), even though the base morpheme is not reduced (and surfaces faithfully as [flat]). Thus, the core phenomena of reduplication can be handled via input-to-output correspondence constraints. Whether this is a better solution than using output-to-output constraints remains to be explored.

Many practitioners of OT might object strenuously to having a sliding scale for faithfulness indexed to activation levels. They might suggest that it mixes performance concepts with competence concepts, in an unacceptable fashion. However, OT is itself based on a redrawing of the boundary between competence and performance. Violable constraints have been commonplace in performance models for a long time, but were not a part of linguistic competence models. If we can redraw the boundary between competence and performance to start a new theory, as we have done for OT, why is it not acceptable to redraw that boundary again, and talk of activation levels? Until a coherent argument is made that this is illegitimate, objections have no empirical (or even theoretical) basis.

We have been discussing **Survived** constraints, but we also suspect that **Co-occurring** constraints should be ranked high in prosodically strong positions and low in prosodically weak positions. Because elements are of lower activation levels (and hence more marginal) in weak positions, elements that they require to be present should also be more marginal. Making this assumption can allow us to capture some of the phonological patterns that are observed in human languages. For example, consider the fact that voiceless stops in English are allophonically aspirated ([+s.g.]) in word-initial position and as the first consonant in a stressed syllable, but are usually [-s.g.] elsewhere. We attribute the aspiration to the following constraint:

Co-occurring(-voiced⟶ + s.g.)

This is ranked high (higher than **Not(+s.g.)**) in stressed syllables and in word-initial position (hence the two aspirated stops in *potato* /pəteɪtoʊ/ [pʰətʰeɪɾoʊ]), both of which are in strong domains; it is more optimal to obey the **Co-occurring** constraint than to insert the default [-s.g.]. It is ranked low (lower than **Not(+s.g.)**) in other domains (hence the unaspirated stops in *happy* and *soup*); it is more optimal to insert the default feature [-s.g.] than to obey the **Co-occurring** constraint.[24]

Even the lack of aspiration in /sp/, /st/, and /sk/ clusters (*spot* /spɑt/ [spɑːt], never *[spʰɑːt]) can be attributed to low ranking of **Co-occurring** in a weak domain. There is evidence that the second consonant of an onset is in a weak domain in English. Stemberger and Treiman (1986) base that argument on speech errors; they show that the second consonant in a word-initial consonant cluster has a much higher error rate than the first consonant (both in naturally occurring errors and in experimentally induced errors), even controlling for segmental content. Clements and Keyser (1983) and S. Davis (1991) discuss restrictions on place and manner features on the second consonant in a word-initial cluster. The stop in an /s/-stop cluster may not have a nondefault articulator node if that would create a **NotTwice** violation, even though there is no such restriction on the stop if it is word-initial:

kick /kɪk/   vs.   **spop* /spɑp/

pop /pɑp/   vs.   **spop* /spɑp/

It appears that **NotTwice(Labial)** and **NotTwice(Dorsal)** are ranked high enough to prevent [Labial] and [Dorsal] from appearing in the second position in a cluster,

---

[24] An alternative to account for such aspiration would be to use generalized alignment. **Aligned (Foot,L, +s.g.,L)** would ensure that the left edge of a foot begins with [+s.g.]; if one is not present underlyingly, it must be inserted. **Survived(+ voiced)** and **NotCo-occurring(+ voiced, + s.g.)** would prevent aspiration in voiced segments. Note that any violation of alignment prevents aspiration, so that the stop in an /st/ cluster is not aspirated. It is unclear which constraint ranking would yield the lack of aspiration in stops that are not in foot-initial position, however. Given that the constraint requires [+s.g.] in every foot, it is expected that a token of [+s.g.] that is not properly aligned would be more optimal than no [+s.g.] at all. This analysis predicts *[bʌmpʰi].

but they are *not* ranked high enough to have an effect on a syllable-initial consonant. Only /t/ is possible in this environment, because **NotTwice(Coronal)** is ranked lower than the other two negative constraints (as expected for a default feature; see below). Similarly, **NotTwice(+ nasal)** prevents a nasal in the second position in a cluster if a nasal follows:

> *man* /mæn/   vs.   **sman* /smæn/

But note that two stops are allowed (*spat* /spæt/), due to the lower ranking of **NotTwice(-continuant)**. Likewise, /ɹ/ and /l/ are prevented in this environment:

> *rare* /ɹɛɹ/   vs.   **grare* /gɹɛɹ/
> *lull*   /lʌl/   vs.   **clull* /klʌl/

The fact that **NotTwice** has an affect only in the second consonant in a cluster (regardless of the manner of articulation of the second consonant) suggests that we are dealing with a weak prosodic position. As a result, **Co-occurring(-voiced→ + s.g.)** might also be ranked below **Not(+ s.g.)** in this environment, so that the stop in an /s/-stop cluster is unaspirated.

Adult English also provides an interaction between **NotComplex(Place)** and prosodic positions. In most North American dialects, the glide /ɹ/ is [Coronal, -anterior] in all environments. In codas (after an unrounded vowel; e.g., *hear*) and when an unstressed syllabic (e.g., *butter*), /ɹ/ is not rounded; its only articulator feature is [Coronal]. However, in onsets (e.g., *ray*, *gray*) and when a stressed syllabic (e.g., *herd*), /ɹ/ is rounded ([Labial]). In §3.1.3, we suggested that /ɹ/ is underlyingly [Labial,Coronal]: it has two articulator nodes, thereby violating **NotComplex(Place)**. In strong prosodic positions, **Survived(Labial)** is ranked higher than **NotComplex**; /ɹ/ is rounded. In weak prosodic positions, **Survived(Labial)** is ranked lower than **NotComplex**; [Labial] deletes, and /ɹ/ is unrounded. In general, *any* negative constraint may be ranked higher than **Survived** in weak positions (but lower than **Survived** in strong positions).

This subsection makes a number of claims.

1. It is better to have constraints that reflect features rather than whole segments (and that refer to *presence* of features in the output, rather than only to *linkage* of those features).

2. It is not necessary to have a concept such as licensing. The effects that licensing was meant to account for can be derived via constraint ranking and constraint interactions.

3. We need to distinguish between faithfulness in strong versus weak prosodic positions, with faithfulness being greater in strong positions.

4. It is better to avoid positing separate faithfulness constraints in different prosodic positions. Instead, we index the ranking of **Survived** to activation levels (the concept used to address faithfulness in psycholinguistic processing models), which allows us to derive which positions are strong versus weak in an independent fashion.

5. Base morphemes constitute strong prosodic domains, but affixes and other closed class lexical items constitute weak prosodic domains.

4.7.1.6. Putting Segments into Syllables, Part IV:
Sonority within Onsets and Codas

We have yet to account for one last aspect of syllable structure: the role of sonority in the ordering of segments within an onset or within a coda (see Vennemann, 1972; Hooper, 1976; Steriade, 1981; Goldsmith, 1990). The consonants within an onset are generally ordered from low sonority to high sonority: /tra/ and /pla/, not *[rta], *[lpa]. Similarly, the consonants within a coda are generally ordered from high sonority to low sonority: [art] and [alp], not *[atr] and *[apl]. We have not yet introduced constraints to handle these facts.

One possible solution would be to make use of alignment constraints. **Aligned (σ,L,{low-sonority-features},L)** entails that it is more optimal for a syllable to begin with low-sonority features than with high-sonority features. Consequently, if there are two consonants in the onset, it is more optimal to put the low-sonority consonant first, since it does not violate the alignment constraint; [tra] is more optimal than *[rta]. Similarly, **Aligned(σ,R,{low-sonority-features},R)** entails that it is more optimal for a syllable to end with low-sonority features than with high-sonority features; [art] is more optimal than *[atr]. As noted previously, generalized alignment is not a desirable constraint.

Another solution would be to make use of **NoSequence** constraints with domains that are specific to onsets and to codas. **NoSequence$_{Onset}$** constraints would favor low-sonority elements in first position, and **NoSequence$_{Coda}$** constraints would favor low-sonority elements in second position. The grounding for such constraints would be rhythmical in nature. We take the Jakobsonian point of view that syllables establish a rhythm between open and closed states of the vocal tract. If there are consonant clusters, the consonants are generally ordered to disturb this rhythm as little as possible: Closed-PartiallyOpen-Open-PartiallyOpen-Closed in *Clark* /klɑɹk/. Consequently, special **NoSequence** constraints are needed to enforce the rhythm of the syllables. We assume that this is the best solution.

4.7.1.7. Co-Occurrence and "Complexity" within the Segment

In child phonology (and more rarely in adult speech), patterns might occasionally be attributed to "complexity" within the segment. When examining segmental inventories, or the set of consonants permitted within codas, it appears that at most one nondefault feature is permitted:

allowed:	Ø	+nas	+cont	+vcd	Labial	Dorsal
	t	n	s	d	p	k

not allowed:	+nas	+cont	+vcd	+nas	+vcd	+cont
	Labial	Labial	Labial	Dorsal	Dorsal	+vcd
	m	f	b	ŋ	g	z

Using underspecification, we could say that no more than one specified feature is allowed (Archangeli & Pulleyblank, 1994). We could then use a constraint such as **NotComplex(Segment)** to express that only one (specified) element is allowed within the segment (at most). The constraint would be violated if there were more than one specified feature. This constraint could then be used to motivate deletion of features or whole segments.

However, this is not possible in OT, since all constraints refer to outputs, in which all surface features have been filled in. Although input representations can be underspecified, output representations cannot be. Thus, [Coronal], [Labial], and [Dorsal] are all present, and all three articulator nodes should contribute equally to complexity. There is no way for [Coronal] to contribute less to complexity. Some other mechanism must be found to account for such effects.

The default status of [Coronal], [-nasal], [-continuant], etc., must be responsible for the special behavior of these features. Recall that the **Not** constraints are ranked in such a way that the default feature in any contrast is the lowest-ranked: **Not(+ voiced)** over **Not(-voiced)**; **Not(Dorsal)** over **Not(Labial)** over **Not(Coronal)**. Smolensky (1993) suggests that other constraints may be ranked in such a way as to reflect this same hierarchy: all constraints against [Coronal] are ranked lower than all (equivalent) constraints against [Labial], etc.:

NotCo-occurring(Labial, + continuant) ||| **NotCo-occurring(Coronal, + continuant)**

NotCo-occurring(Labial, + nasal) ||| **NotCo-occurring(Coronal, + nasal)**

NotCo-occurring(Labial, + voiced) ||| **NotCo-occurring(Coronal, + voiced)**

Thus, [s] is less constrained than [f], [n] is less constrained than [m], and [d] is less constrained than [b]. This is important, because other constraints can be ordered between these constraints. Consequently, combinations of nondefault elements might be impossible (the constraints on the left here), but combinations of one nondefault element with default elements would still be possible (the constraints on the right here). Consider Table 4.26:

TABLE 4.26

	t	s	p	f
NotCo-occurring(Labial,+cont)				*
Survived(+continuant)				
Survived(Labial)				
Not(+continuant)		*		*
Not(Labial)			*	*
NotCo-occurring(Coronal,+cont)		*		
NotCo-occurring(Labial,-cont)			*	
Not(-continuant)	*		*	
Not(Coronal)	*	*		

This does not show optimal outputs of a single input, but merely which constraints are violated by particular outputs. Only /f/ (combining two nondefault elements) violates the highest-ranked constraint. Due to the high ranking of **Survived(+ continuant)** and **Survived(Labial)**, both [s] and [p] will be possible outputs. Only [f] will not be possible here. This pattern arises because the ranking of the **NotCo-occurring** constraints is correlated with the ranking of the **Not** constraints: the default value is always ranked lower than the nondefault values.

This correlation between **Not** and **NotCo-occurring** is plausible. The default feature is the easiest to produce. It should thus use fewer resources and be the easiest to combine with other elements. Given that the lowest-ranked **Not** constraint also tends to be the most frequent feature value, the correlation means that it is easier to combine a particular element with another element of high frequency than with another element of low frequency. This correlation is grounded in the effects of practice: well-practiced items are easier to combine with other items. Complexity is not involved in such effects.

However, this correlation may be broken. In child phonology, it is often the case that the only fricative is [f], suggesting that it is easier to combine nondefault [+continuant] with nondefault [Labial] than with default [Coronal] (§5.5.4.3):

NotCo-occurring(Labial, + cont) ||| **NotCo-occurring(Coronal, + cont)**

This is probably due to the facilitative effect of visual information, which allows the child to observe how [f] is made (but not how [s] is made).

4.7.1.8. Nonminimal Repairs via NotCo-Occurring, Conjoined Constraints, and Sliding Scales

We discussed nonminimal repairs in §4.4.1.2 and §4.4.1.3 above, and the mechanisms through which they can be derived. Nonminimal repairs can involve a whole segment being deleted in order to avoid the violation of a **NotCo-occurring** constraint, even if both of the offending features are allowed to appear individually. Consider the following constraint table, which examines the realization of /f/. Table 4.27 presupposes a particular definition of **NotCo-occurring**: since the constraint requires that two elements not occur at the same point in time, the elements must be linked up to a timing unit (or syllable) in order to violate it; if a segment is not anchored in time, then the two elements do not occur at the same point in time, and **NotCo-occurring** is consequently not violated.

This analysis presumes that the C timing unit of the coda is not deleted but rather is delinked, and that [t] is inserted to replace the /f/, as seen in Figure 4.13. The /f/ is floating, and [t] is inserted as a default consonant, in order to fill the /f/'s stranded timing unit. Given the high ranking of **LinkedDownwards(C)**, the C element must link to a Root node. If the **Survived** and **LinkedUpwards** constraints for the individual elements are ranked high enough, they cannot be deleted or delinked individually, but **NotCo-occurring(Labial, + cont)** prevents [Labial] and [+continuant] from being produced at the same point in time. In this instance, the entire Root node is left floating. In contrast, when there is only one nondefault

TABLE 4.27

/f/	f	Ø	p	s	h	t
NotCo-occurring(Labial,+cont)	*!					
LinkedDownwards(C) Survived(Root)		*!				
Survived(+continuant) LinkedUpwards(+continuant)			*!			
Survived(Labial) LinkedUpwards(Labial)				*!		
Survived(Place) LinkedUpwards(Place)					*!	
LinkedUpwards(Root)						*
Not(Root)						*

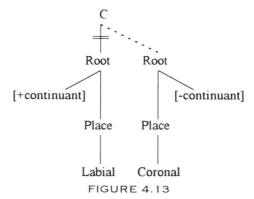

FIGURE 4.13

feature, it is not subject to the **NotCo-occurring** constraint, and thus it is accurately produced (as [s] or [p]). In this way, both of the nondefault features are lost when the segment has two nondefault features. A nonminimal repair is achieved: the constraint violation is due to [Labial] and [+continuant], but the repair is at a higher level (the Root node).

This explanation presupposes that **NotCo-occurring** is violated only when a Root node is linked to a timing unit or syllable. We are uncomfortable with that presupposition. It seems more straightforward for **NotCo-occurring(A,B)** to be violated whenever [A] and [B] are dominated by the same higher node. If [Labial] and [+continuant] are dominated by the same Root node, shouldn't **NotCo-occurring(Labial, +continuant)** be violated? If that is the case, treating the /f/ as a floating segment will not avoid violating the constraint. Alternative ways to do so have been discussed above in §4.4.1.3 and §4.5.1.3: **Ident** and **Notσ-Margin(f)**. They are less satisfactory, and therefore we will use **NotCo-occurring** for nonminimal repairs.

Another alternative to handle such repairs would be to make use of conjoined constraints of a particular type: involving an "exclusive-or" relationship. An exclusive-or relationship is one which is "true" if A and B are both true or both false, but is false if one is true and the other is false. In terms of constraints, a constraint such as **Survived(Labial& +continuant)** would be violated if [Labial] survived but [+continuant] did not, or if [+continuant] survived and [Labial] did not; but it would not be violated if both features survived or if both features deleted. Such a conjoined constraint essentially fuses the features into one unit, making it impossible to treat the features autonomously (for the purpose of survival). We prefer to avoid complex constraints. Further, an exclusive-or relationship seems out of step with the way that constraints work in OT, although we do not believe that it can be ruled out in principle.

A last way to handle nonminimal repairs can be derived from considerations of activation levels (with the concept of a *threshold*, or minimal necessary level of activation), using the sliding scale for faithfulness. Dell (1985) proposed that the different features in a segment reinforce each other, giving activation to each other. This entails a certain amount of dependence between different features. If two features have high activation levels, this reinforcing activation is probably not needed; the features can be accessed in any event. However, if both features have only marginal activation levels, the reinforcing activation may be crucial for the successful access of both features. Suppose that [Labial] and [+continuant] are both of marginal activation levels. If one of those features falls below a crucial minimal activation level and is deleted, that removes the reinforcing activation from the lost feature, dropping the other feature below the threshold, so that it too is deleted. In this way, we can account for the deletion of *both* features. In order for both features to be possible when they occur separately (as with [Labial] in [p] and [+continuant] in [s]), we must assume that activation levels in segments with two nondefault features are overall slightly lower than when there is just one nondefault feature; this follows from our assumption that combining two features takes extra resources. Any effect that lowers activation levels also lowers the ranking of **Survived**. Here, we would say that combining two nondefault features lowers the ranking of the **Survived** constraints for both features, making it possible for both features to be deleted, if the **Survived** constraints come to be ranked lower than relevant negative constraints (such as **NotCo-occurring** or **Not**). We will not use this explanation here, but find that it has a certain appeal.

It is not always the case that two nondefaults are impossible. Children sometimes can combine two nondefaults ([Labial] and [+nasal] in [m]), but cannot combine the nondefault with a default ([Labial] and [-nasal] in [p]) (§5.5.4.3). It would seem that the more "complex" segment is preferred over the simpler segment that has fewer nondefaults. One way to account for this would be to assume that the rankings of the **NotCo-occurring** constraints do *not* have to be correlated with the rankings of the **Not** constraints. We have been assuming that if **Not(Labial)** is ranked higher than **Not(Coronal)**, then **NotCo-occurring** constraints involving [Labial] should be ranked higher than those involving [Coronal]. But consider the following constraint ranking:

Survived(+ nasal)

Not(+ nasal)
NotCo-occurring(Labial,-nasal)

Survived(Labial)

NotCo-occurring(Labial, + nasal)

Not(Coronal)
Not(-nasal)

Since the **Survived** constraints for both [Labial] and [+nasal] are ranked above the **NotCo-occurring** constraint that prevents us from combining these two features, /m/ surfaces as [m], with both features present. However, since **Survived (Labial)** is ranked lower than the **NotCo-occurring** constraint that prevents [Labial] from being combined with the default [-nasal], that combination is ruled out. The high ranking of **Not(+ nasal)** prevents the insertion of [+nasal] to avoid the violation of this constraint. Instead, [Labial] must delete; /p/ surfaces as default coronal [t].

This analysis is possible if the ranking of the ranking of the **NotCo-occurring** constraints does not have to be correlated with the ranking of the **Not** constraints. We believe that such a correlated ranking normally is present. But if we take that as a strong tendency rather than as an absolute, analyses such as this are possible.

We would like to note that an alternative possibility derives from consideration of activation levels. Dell (1986) argued that the different features in a segment reinforce each other. If we assume underspecification, we have the following underlying representations:

/p/:   [Labial]
/m/:   [Labial,+nasal]

In /m/, the features [Labial] and [+nasal] reinforce each other, via spreading activation. If [+nasal] is of high activation (equivalent to a high ranking of **Survived(+ nasal)**), this increases the activation level of [Labial]. If [Labial] is of marginal activation, such that it usually does not have enough activation to be accessed in the output representation, then the extra activation from [+nasal] may give it *just enough* activation to be accessible in the output. In contrast, /p/ has no other lexical features to reinforce [Labial]. On its own, [Labial] does not have enough activation to be accessed, and so [Labial] is deleted; the default [Coronal] is accessed in its place. As a result, [Labial] cannot be combined with default features (which are absent in underlying representations and hence supply less reinforcing activation), but can be combined with the lexically specified nondefault features. It is not that [-nasal] actively *hurts* [Labial] (as in the constraint ranking above), but rather that it does not *help* [Labial]. Since we believe that the ranking of **Survived(Labial)** is indexed to the activation level of [Labial], this means that **Survived(Labial)** is ranked higher for /m/ than for /p/. Note that combining a marginal nondefault feature with another nondefault feature *helps* if the other feature is of high activation level, but *hurts* if the other feature is of marginal activation level. We believe that this type of explanation is more explanatory than the constraint ranking given above. But both explanations work, and we recognize that others may have different preferences.

4.7.1.9. Assimilation between the C and V Places

Prince and Smolensky (1993) address one additional complexity that concerns Place information. We have been assuming that consonants and vowels have the same features for place of articulation (Labial, Coronal, Dorsal), but that the features are under the C-Place node for consonants and under the V-Place node for vowels. But since [Labial] is allowed to link to both C-Place and to V-Place, in theory a [C-Labial] node could link to V-Place, and a [V-Labial] node could link to C-Place. Prince and Smolensky propose the following constraints (translated into our system):

☞**V-Artic◀V-Place**:   A vocalic articulator node must link to V-Place.
      violation: A vowel place feature that is the main place of
                     articulation of a consonant.

☞**C-Artic◀**C-Place: A consonantal articulator node must link to C-Place.
      violation: A consonant place feature that is the main place of
                     articulation of a vowel.

This will tend to prevent vowels from assimilating to consonants and consonants from assimilating to vowels. But violations are possible, and consequently consonants and vowels can assimilate to each other:

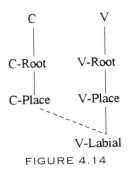

FIGURE 4.14

The doubly linked feature would be interpreted as a consonantal labial articulation in the consonant, but as a vocalic labial articulation (lip-rounding) in the vowel. An example of this would be /tu/ being pronounced [pu]. In §7.4.2, we discuss such assimilations in child phonology.

In contrast, if V-Place links directly to the C-Root node, it is not interpreted as a consonantal articulation. If there is also a C-Place node, then V-Place is interpreted phonetically as a secondary place of articulation: palatalization, velarization, etc. If there is no C-Place node, then V-Place attached to C-Root yields a glide.

4.7.2. SEQUENCE CONSTRAINTS

Thus far, we have dealt with constraints on the elements themselves and on combinations of elements within the same segment. We now turn to constraints on sequences of elements. There are two families of constraints that restrict sequences of elements. One constraint family, which was called "the OCP" in earlier theory, prohibits a sequence of two identical elements. The other constraint family, which Yip (1991) has termed "the Cluster Condition," puts strong constraints on the distribution of features across sequences of segments. We propose alternative names for both.

4.7.2.1. Sequences of Identical Elements: NotTwice

There is a constraint on sequences of identical elements:

☞**NotTwice**: An element may not appear twice if the two tokens are adjacent.

  violation: two adjacent tokens of an element

   Note: *Constraints affecting nondefault features are ranked higher than constraints affecting default features.*

There is one **NotTwice** constraint for every element in the phonological hierarchy: **NotTwice(Labial)**, **NotTwice(Place)**, **NotTwice(Root)**, etc. On occasion in later chapters, we find the need for a complex constraint such as **NotTwice(Labial, +continuant)**, which prohibits sequences like *[fw] while allowing [sw] (two [+continuant] segments) and [pw] (two labials). However, we dislike such complexity and feel that it constitutes a (mild) failure of our system; we try to avoid such complex constraints.

In general, constraints affecting nondefaults are ranked higher than constraints affecting defaults; for example, **NotTwice(Labial)** has an affect more often than **NotTwice(Coronal)** (S. Davis, 1991). Kenstowicz (1994) argues for several African tone languages that the default low tone is not subject to **NotTwice** (and so sequences of low tones occur), but that nondefault high tone is subject to **Not-Twice** (so that sequences of high tones are not tolerated).

There appear to be two variants of **NotTwice**, differing in terms of how identity of elements is defined. In one variant, the mere presence of a feature or node is sufficient: if there are two identical elements on the relevant tier, then **NotTwice** is violated. In the other variant, two elements are identical only if they dominate absolutely identical material. **NotTwice(σ)** is an excellent example: it does not rule out two adjacent syllable nodes, but rather two adjacent syllable nodes that dominate exactly identical segmental material. Similarly, **NotTwice(Root)** does not rule out adjacent Root nodes, unless those Root nodes dominate exactly identical sets of features and nodes; adjacent identical segments (e.g., /bb/) are disallowed, but two segments are allowed as long as some single feature is different (e.g., /bv/). On the other hand, **NotTwice(Place)** might rule out two adjacent Place nodes whether they dominate identical articulator nodes or not, *or* might be restricted to Place nodes that dominate identical material. **NotTwice(Coronal)** might rule out two adjacent coronal consonants regardless of subsidiary features, *or* might be restricted to those coronals that have the same value of [anterior], [distributed], and [grooved]. In addition to the general **NotTwice** constraints that rule out two identical elements on any tier, we need the following constraint family:

☞**NotTwice**_{Dependents}:   An element may not appear twice if the two tokens are adjacent, if both tokens of the element also have identical dependents.

NotTwice also appears in four variants depending on the level of adjacency (see §3.5) that is relevant: tier adjacency, Root adjacency, syllable adjacency, or timing unit adjacency. As an example involving Root adjacency, Yip (1988) proposed for English that two consonants that violate **NotTwice(Coronal)** can be made nonadjacent by epenthesizing a vowel (schwa) between them, even though the epenthesized segment contains no element on the Coronal tier. This works with Root adjacency and timing unit adjacency, because the epenthesized vowel puts a Root node and a timing unit between the two consonants. This does not work with tier adjacency, because the vowel does not put anything between the two consonants on the Coronal tier. Nor does it work with syllable adjacency, because the two consonants are still in adjacent syllables. Odden (1994) takes tier adjacency to be the default type of adjacency. We assume that tier adjacency is what is generally relevant to the **NotTwice** constraint family. If other adjacency levels are relevant, we note that in our statement of the constraint.

In total, there are eight different families of NotTwice constraints (and possibly twelve), depending on the effects of dependent features and on the adjacency level that is involved:

NotTwice_{TierAdj}
NotTwice_{RootAdj}
NotTwice_{TimingUnitAdj}
NotTwice_{RootσAdj}
NotTwice_{Dependents,TierAdj}
NotTwice_{Dependents,RootAdj}
NotTwice_{Dependents,TimingUnitAdj}
NotTwice_{Dependents,σAdj}

We generally just refer to **NotTwice**, without specifying which subfamily is involved. We make clear in the text which subfamily is relevant.

4.7.2.2. Sequences of Nonidentical Elements: NoSequence

The second family of constraints, which, in a narrower context, Yip (1991) called "the Cluster Condition," places constraints on the distribution of features across segments. Certain sequences are prohibited:

☞**NoSequence(A...B)**: Given two segments, A cannot be in the first segment if B is in the second segment.

       violation: The sequence A...B is present.

       Note: *the ordering of different family members is correlated with the ordering of **Not** constraints.*

Note the notation used here: "..." (to denote that something follows, adapted from the orthographic convention in quotations, where "..." can denote that something follows, but will not necessarily be reported: "Eric came in, grabbed the milk, and..."); please note that it is often the case that *nothing* comes between [A] and [B], but "..." is still used in the convention employed here. Here, we must spell out exactly what relevant element follows. A violation of this constraint can be repaired (a) by deleting one of the two elements (A or B) or a higher element that contains A or B, or (b) by separating A and B so that they are no longer adjacent, or (c) by re-ordering the elements so that they are no longer in the prohibited sequence (metathesis).

Yip (1991) uses this type of constraint to restrict where articulator nodes may go. First, at most one nondefault articulator node is allowed in a set of adjacent consonants. The general form of the constraints on articulator nodes would be:

☞**NoSequence(Artic...Artic)**

Kiparsky (1995) calls such constraints a generalized form of the OCP (**NotTwice**). **NotTwice** is violated only if there are two tokens of a feature with the same value: two tokens of [+nasal], two tokens of [-nasal], two tokens of [Labial], etc. A generalized form of **NotTwice** would rule out two tokens regardless of value: two tokens of [nasal] (even if one is [+nasal] and the other is [-nasal]) or two articulator nodes (even if one is [Coronal] and one is [Labial]). On the other hand, **NotTwice** could be viewed as a special instance of **NoSequence**, in which the prohibited elements just happen to be the same:

NotTwice(Labial) = NoSequence(Labial...Labial)

However, we use two constraint families for three reasons. (a) It is clear that repetition of an element incurs a special cost in speech production (e.g., Stemberger, 1991a) and in the performance of actions in general (e.g., Norman, 1981). It is likely that the repetition of elements is also special within phonology. (b) **NotTwice** seems to be defined mostly in terms of tier adjacency but **NoSequence** seems to be defined mostly in terms of Root adjacency. (c) **NotTwice** has a variant in which identity is defined over that element plus all dependent elements. **No-Sequence** is defined only in terms of a single element; the dependents of that element do not seem to matter. Despite some similarities, the two constraints cannot be easily collapsed into a single constraint family.

NoSequence constraints can be restricted to different levels of adjacency. They could hold on adjacent timing units, in which case only Root-adjacent consonants would be affected: consonants in clusters. They could hold on adjacent C-Place nodes, in which case the two consonants could be separated by a vowel or by glottal consonants. Usually, **NoSequence** constraints are defined on adjacent Root nodes. These Root nodes can be truly adjacent, or they may be adjacent C-Root nodes on the consonant plane (see §3.5 and §7.1).

The ordering of particular **NoSequence** constraints is partially predictable, because the ordering is correlated with the ordering of the **Not** constraint family. Since **Not(Coronal)** is the lowest-ranked **Not** constraint that affects articulator features, the **NoSequence** constraints affecting [Coronal] are lower-ranked than the **NoSequence** constraints that differ only in that they affect a nondefault articulator feature. It is predictable for all languages that the following "high-ranked" constraints will be ranked higher than the following "low-ranked" constraints: [25]

> high-ranked: **NoSequence(Dorsal...Labial)**
>   **NoSequence(Labial...Dorsal)**
>
> lower-ranked: **NoSequence(Coronal...Labial)**
>   **NoSequence(Coronal...Dorsal)**
>   **NoSequence(Dorsal...Coronal)**
>   **NoSequence(Labial...Coronal)**

We can predict that the **NoSequence** constraints that affect two nondefault features are ranked higher than the **NoSequence** constraints that affect one default and one nondefault feature.[26] However, there is no reason why a constraint with [Labial] on the left should be ranked higher or lower than a constraint with [Labial] on the right; that must be determined in a language-specific fashion. Although this is the unmarked case, we find instances in child phonology where it is useful to have constraints in other orders that are *not* correlated with the rankings of the related **Not** constraints.

Yip (1991) discusses intervocalic and word-final consonant clusters in English relative to the occurrence of different places of articulation. She reports that the

---

[25] The constraints within the "high-ranked" and "low-ranked" sets will be ranked relative to each other in a particular language. For English (§7.4.1.3), **NoSequence(Coronal...Labial)** and **No-Sequence(Coronal...Dorsal)** are ranked higher than **NoSequence(Labial...Coronal)** and **No-Sequence(Dorsal...Coronal)**. As far as we know, this further ranking is unpredictable across languages.

[26] Béland, Paradis, and Bois (1993) report the effects of such constraint rankings in the speech of French-speaking aphasics.

two predictably high-ranked constraints are not violated except in a few foreign words: English does not generally permit clusters like */pk/ or */kp/ (or */fk/, */kf/, etc.). Further, if both segments are stops, the nondefault feature must occur in the first stop, and the default [Coronal] must appear in the second stop: /pt/ (*helicopter*) and /kt/ (*act*) versus */tp/ and */tk/. In English, the **NoSequence** constraints with the default [Coronal] on the left are ranked higher than the ones with the [Coronal] on the right; consequently, [Coronal] can only appear on the right. It should be noted that these constraints do not lead to alternations in adult English,[27] but English words obey the constraints. If a word or name is borrowed from another language that has a different ranking of these constraints (as in names like *Apgar* and nouns like *magma*), **Survived** and **LinkedUpwards** ensure that they are pronounced faithfully.

When one of the consonants in an English medial or final cluster is a fricative, the pattern is more complex. If one of the segments is [Dorsal], it is the stop, and the fricative is consequently [Coronal]. That is because the velar fricative [x] is not permitted in English, due to the constraint:

NotCo-occurring(Dorsal,-sonorant, + continuant)

But [+continuant] is allowed in either segment; both /sk/ (*ask*) and /ks/ (*box*) occur. If the nondefault articulator is [Labial], it can either occur in the fricative (in which case it must be first: /ft/ as in *lift* versus */tf/) or the stop (in which case it can be in either segment: /sp/ as in *whisper* or /ps/ as in *Gypsy*). Note that /f/ follows the same pattern as the stops, due to the same constraint rankings. Note also that /s/ partly follows this general pattern, since /ps/ is possible. However, /s/ is also exceptional, in that the other order (/sp/) is also allowed. The exceptional behavior of /s/ in codas derives from the fact that /sp/ is the only order allowed in syllable onsets (where both */ft/ and */tf/ are impossible); there must be exceptional rankings to allow /sp/ in onsets, and these rankings also permit /sp/ in codas.

Although we have illustrated **NoSequence** with place features, all features are affected by members of this constraint family. There could be constraints that mix features of different types: [Labial] in the first segment cannot be followed by [+continuant] in the second segment. However, we have not found any uses for such mixed-feature constraints. Further, **NoSequence** constraints most often affect two place features. It is somewhat less common for two voicing features to be affected. Manner features are affected least of all.

Violations of these constraints on articulator features can be resolved in several ways:

1. by deleting one of the features (in association with the insertion of default [Coronal] or the spreading of the other feature);
2. by deleting a higher element such as the Place node (in which case Debuccalization would occur, resulting in [h] or [ʔ]);

---

[27] See Chapters 7 and 9 for the role of these constraints in child English.

3. by deleting one of the segments, but not its timing unit (with spreading of the other Root node, yielding a long consonant);

4. by deleting one of the segments *and* its timing unit; or

5. by inserting a segment between the two relevant features, so that they are no longer adjacent.

The **NoSequence** constraints mark a particular sequence as ill formed, but do not say which element to affect. Other constraints, including **Priority(Left)** and **Priority(Right)**, determine which segment is affected.

4.7.3. HOW TO ACCOUNT FOR ASSIMILATION, PART II: SPREADING TO RESOLVE VIOLATIONS OF SEQUENCE CONSTRAINTS

In §4.6.1, we showed how **Aligned** can be used to handle assimilation. We argue here that no special constraints are needed to deal with assimilation. Spreading is motivated by the sequence constraints that we have already discussed. Spreading occurs as a way to resolve violations of sequence constraints such as **NoSequence** and/or other constraints such as **LinkedDownwards(Place)**. Our approach follows the main approach to assimilation within multilinear phonology, before OT. Kiparsky (1995) also takes this approach to assimilation. We view this analysis as superior to the alignment analysis of assimilation, discussed in §4.6.1.

Spreading involves the addition of association lines to an element. We have already discussed two faithfulness constraints that deal with association lines:

☞**Survived(Link)**
☞**Not(Link)**

The first constraint requires that all links that are present underlyingly also be present on the surface. The second constraint minimizes the number of association lines, preventing the insertion of association lines (among other things). Together, if unviolated, these two constraints keep elements linked up in the same way as in underlying representations, and do not allow those elements to spread. **Not(Link)**, if ranked high enough, prevents the insertion of default features (which require a link to be added, so that they can be linked upwards) and in some instances also prevents assimilation (if there is no element already associated to the element on the higher tier). However, **Not(Link)** cannot prevent assimilation if the number of association lines is the same in all likely outputs:

FIGURE 4.15

On the left, [Coronal] has been inserted; on the right, assimilation has occurred. In both outputs, there are two association lines between Place nodes and articulator features. Thus, the two candidates are equal with relation to **Not(Link)**. Some other constraint must prevent assimilation.

SinglyLinked is designed partly to prevent assimilation. There is a violation for every association line more than one; a doubly linked feature violates the constraint once; a triply linked feature violates the constraint twice, and so on. Extending the duration of an element takes resources, and the greater the extension, the more resources are required. **SinglyLinked** is high-ranked if a lot of resources are required, but low-ranked if few resources are required. By ranking **Singly-Linked** relative to other constraints, assimilation can be required or prevented. Because assimilation violates this constraint, assimilation never occurs unless the spreading allows the system to avoid violating a higher-ranked constraint.

Assimilations can occur for a number of reasons. Each motivation reflects the high-ranking of a particular constraint. Spreading can occur to fill in a feature that is missing, thus resolving a violation of **LinkedDownwards**. Spreading can also occur to resolve a **NoSequence** or **NotTwice** violation.

Spreading as feature-filling can be illustrated by the spreading of [+nasal] from the final consonant to the vowel in the English word *ban* [bæ̃n]. The vowel /æ/ is underspecified for the feature [nasal], but **LinkedDownwards** is high-ranked and requires that [nasal] be filled in. The filling in of the feature can be accomplished by insertion, violating **Not(-nasal)**. This is illustrated in Table 4.28 (where [æ] represents an oral vowel and [Æ] represents a vowel unspecified for [nasal]); note that this is not the ranking needed for adult English:

TABLE 4.28

/pÆːn/	pʰæ̃ːn	pʰÆːn	pʰæːn
LinkedDownwards(Root)		*!	
SinglyLinked(+nasal)	*!		
Not(-nasal)			*

The lowest-ranked constraint is violated: [-nasal] is filled in and the vowel is oral. With a different ranking (that of adult English), as in Table 4.29:

TABLE 4.29

/pÆːn/	pʰæ̃ːn	pʰÆːn	pʰæːn
LinkedDownwards(Root)		*!	
Not(-nasal)			*!
SinglyLinked(+nasal)	*		

The lowest-ranked constraint is violated: a link is added between [+nasal] and the vowel; the vowel becomes nasalized via assimilation, and the feature [+nasal] becomes doubly linked. It does not matter for **LinkedDownwards** which method is used to link the Root node to [nasal], just as long as [nasal] is linked up in some way to the Root node. Spreading and feature insertion represent two alternative ways to satisfy the **LinkedDownwards** constraint.

The constraints discussed so far do not explain one aspect of nasality spreading in English: the direction. It has often been observed (e.g., Ladefoged, 1993) that [+nasal] spreads only from right-to-left, as in *pan* [pʰæn]; it cannot spread left-to-right as in *nap* [næp] (never *[næp]). Leftward spreading is caused by **Priority(Right,nasal)**. When the system could spread either a feature on the left or on the right, **Priority** determines which feature. This constraint corresponds to the rule parameter in Archangeli and Pulleyblank (1994) and Yip (1988) that determined the direction of spread: left-to-right versus right-to-left.

Of course, if there is no consonant on the right, then the **Priority** constraint becomes irrelevant. In that case, spreading from left-to-right becomes possible. In many English dialects, the vowel is optionally nasalized after a nasal consonant if there is no following oral consonant: *no* /noʊ/ [nõʊ̃], *me* /miː/ [mĩː], *more* /moɹ/ [mɔ̃ɹ̃]. The vowels will be nasal if **Not(-nasal)** is ranked higher than **SinglyLinked(+nasal)**, so that it is preferable to spread [+nasal] than to insert default [-nasal].

The following properties hold for spreading that is motivated purely by feature-filling:

1. **SinglyLinked** is low-ranked.
2. Without assimilation, a high-ranked constraint would be violated.
3. A link is inserted (violating **SinglyLinked**), to avoid the violation of that high-ranked constraint.
4. Spreading is often left-to-right or right-to-left, reflecting which **Priority** constraint is high-ranked.
5. When the preferred direction of spreading is impossible, spreading may occur from the other direction
6. Assimilation is entirely a local interaction of elements.

LinkedDownwards is involved: *some* token of the element involved must be present. If there is no underlying element present, then some element must be filled in, and assimilation is one way to accomplish that result.

We emphasize again that there is no need to mention where the inserted association line goes (*which two elements* the link is added between). A link is added only when the insertion of the link would repair a constraint violation. Adding a link that repairs no violation is a pure constraint violation in and of itself, and thus is less optimal than *not* inserting the link. A link is inserted between two elements if it resolves a constraint violation involving one of those elements or both. A link is added to a floating feature in order to avoid violating **LinkedUpwards**. A link is added between [Dorsal] and an empty Place node in order to avoid a

LinkedDownwards violation. There is no need to say *where* the link should be added. The place where the link is added is determined by other constraints.

The particular high-ranked constraint can vary, and there may be several high-ranked constraints involved. Feature constraints are often involved: **Not**, **Co-occurring**, **NotCo-occurring**, **NotTwice**, or **NoSequence**. Syllable-related constraints (including **Co-occurring(Rime→ +sonorant)**) may be implicated. **Survived** may be involved, if spreading is the only way for an element to link upwards. Any constraint that (a) requires an element to be present or (b) prevents an element from being present can cause spreading to occur, as long as **Singly-Linked** is ranked low enough.

When spreading occurs to resolve a **NoSequence** constraint, there are some differences from the above example. **NoSequence** constraints specify that two elements are impossible *in a particular order*. Thus, it can be the case that no assimilation will occur if the features are in one order, but assimilation will occur if the features are in the opposite order. This often is the case with assimilations in adult phonology. In Korean, for example, /kp/ surfaces faithfully as [kp], but /pk/ surfaces as [kː], with the feature [Labial] deleted and the feature [Dorsal] doubly linked (Avery & Rice, 1989). The feature [Dorsal] can spread right-to-left, but not left-to-right. In our system, this derives from the following ranking:

> **NoSequence(Labial...Dorsal)**
> **Survived(Dorsal)**
> **LinkedDownwards(Place)**
>
> ═══════════════════════
>
> **Survived(Labial)**
>
> ═══════════════════════
>
> **NoSequence(Dorsal...Labial)**
> **Not(Coronal)**
>
> ═══════════════════════
>
> **SinglyLinked(Dorsal)**
> **SinglyLinked(Labial)**

The low ranking of **NoSequence(Dorsal . . . Labial)**, below both of the **Survived** constraints, allows /kp/ to surface faithfully as [kp]. In contrast, the high ranking of **NoSequence(Labial . . . Dorsal)** makes *[pk] an impossible output. Since only one of the two articulator nodes is allowed, one must be deleted. Since **Survived(Dorsal)** is the higher-ranked **Survived** constraint, [Dorsal] survives and [Labial] is deleted. The high ranking of **LinkedDownwards(Place)** requires that *some* articulator node must be present; the low ranking of **SinglyLinked(Dorsal)** (below **Not(Coronal)**) leads to the double linking of [Dorsal] (rather than the insertion of default [Coronal]—which is prohibited in this environment in the output in any event).

In some instances, assimilation cannot occur if an impossible output segment would be created. Archangeli and Pulleyblank (1994) discuss an instance of this in Yoruba. The feature [-ATR] spreads from right-to-left; /oCa/ [ɔCa], with

[-ATR] spreading from the /a/ to the earlier mid vowel. Spreading is only right-to-left (so that /aCo/ is unassimilated [aCo]). This directionality entails that the assimilation is due to a **NoSequence** constraint, and is not just the result of a feature-filling operation. The fact that it is [-ATR] that spreads rather than [+ATR] derives from the fact that [-ATR] is the nondefault feature (see below). The basic constraints and rankings are just like those for Korean above, but with [+ATR] substituted for [Labial] and [-ATR] substituted for [Dorsal]. **NoSequence(+ATR...-ATR)** is high-ranked; thus, assimilation occurs. **NoSequence(-ATR... +ATR)** is ranked low enough for that sequence to be tolerated. Thus far, this example is exactly like the one in Korean above. However, high vowels may not be [-ATR] in Yoruba, and do not undergo assimilation: /uCa/ [uCa]. This derives from the following two constraints, ranked higher than the list above:

NotCo-occurring(+high,-ATR)
Survived(-ATR) [28]

The **NotCo-occurring** constraint prevents the usual resolution, with [-ATR] spreading from left-to-right. The high ranking of **Survived(-ATR)** prevents [-ATR] from being deleted. Since [-ATR] cannot be deleted, but the /u/ must be [+ATR], there is no option but to violate **NoSequence(+ATR...-ATR)**.

A further complexity arises in words with three syllables, with a high vowel as the first vowel and a [-ATR] vowel as the third vowel. There are two possible outputs here:

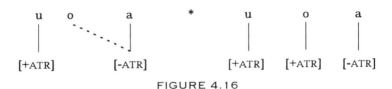

FIGURE 4.16

On the right, the second vowel is [+ATR], creating a violation of **NoSequence(+ATR...-ATR)**. On the right, the [-ATR] of /a/ spreads to the /o/, thereby avoiding a violation of the **NoSequence** constraint between the /o/ and the /a/, but *creating* a violation of the **NoSequence** constraint between the /u/ and the following vowels. Since **NoSequence** is violated by both outputs, what determines that the output on the left is the correct one: [uCɔCa]? **Priority (Right,ATR)** chooses the output on the left as the more optimal one: when a choice is possible, priority is given to the [ATR] element on the right.

There is one final complexity of the Yoruba data. If the second vowel is a high vowel, spreading of [-ATR] to the first vowel is blocked: /oCuCa/ [oCuCa] (never

---

[28] Or, alternatively, **Co-occurring(+low→-ATR)**, which fills in [-ATR] predictably in the low vowel [a] in Yoruba, as Archangeli and Pulleyblank argue.

*[ɔCuCa]). Consider the following representation (with the [ATR] specification of /u/ ignored for illustrative purposes):

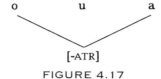

FIGURE 4.17

The [-ATR] element is attached to the first and third vowels, but not to the middle vowel. Several researchers have recently proposed that such structures are impossible. ✄***Gapped** is another common name for this constraint, but we call it:

☞**Uninterrupted**

The [-ATR] gesture begins in [ɔ], is interrupted in [u] (which is [+ATR]), and then resumes in [a]. This is nonoptimal. It is best for gestures to be continuous, and not interrupted in the middle. This constraint can be used to prevent spreading when any element intervenes between the target and source segments.

Uninterrupted is also relevant in one additional type of assimilation, which Goldsmith (1990) calls *plateauing*. This has the following effect:

FIGURE 4.18

When there are two adjacent tokens of the same feature (tier adjacency), but they are separated by a segment that is underspecified for that feature, the feature spreads to the intervening segment (thus creating a "plateau" for the feature, rather than two peaks separated by a valley). One example of this is Intervocalic Voicing: an obstruent becomes voiced when it is surrounded by voiced segments. We analyze this in one of two ways, both resolved through the merger of the two B elements: as an effect of **NotTwice**, where the repetition of the B elements is a violation, or as an effect of **Not**, minimizing the number of tokens of a feature in the output. This could result in the following representation:

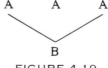

FIGURE 4.19

This would violate **Uninterrupted**; thus, the feature also spreads to the intervening segment.

One last property of spreading is that features often spread between segments that have other features in common. A frequently cited example (see Archangeli, 1984; Itô et al., 1995; Odden, 1991) is the relation between vowel height and rounding: the feature [+round] often spreads from one high vowel to another, or from one mid vowel to another, but frequently will not spread from a mid vowel to a high vowel, or from a high vowel to a mid vowel. Itô et al. (1995) propose the following specific constraint:

✂**Shared Height Harmony**:   Two vowels of the same height must have the same value of [round].

However, there are instances of the effects of such shared features that go far beyond height and rounding, and it would be desirable to have a more general principle from which to derive the effects of shared features. Yip (1988) would say that this is an effect of **NotTwice(high)**: to prevent a repetition of either [+high] or [-high], a higher node in the feature geometry spreads, to ensure that there is only one instance of [high] in the pronunciation. We suspect that Yip's solution will ultimately prove unworkable. We do not believe that phonological theory has yet provided an adequate explanation for the effects of shared features on spreading (although see the next subsection). We will return to this issue in §10.2.2, where we address other phenomena that we believe are not adequately accounted for by the theory.

This discussion has provided the basic reasons for spreading. We return to the topic in §7.3.1.8 and §7.4.2, when we discuss assimilation in child phonology in detail.

4.8. DOMAINS

We noted in §3.3.3 that processes often had to be restricted to particular domains, such as the prosodic word or the syllable. The word "domain" has recently developed another additional interpretation. In this section, we address both types of "domain."

4.8.1. DOMAIN OF THE CONSTRAINTS

Just as processes might apply only within a particular domain, so constraints may hold only within a particular domain. The domain may be phonological (onset, syllable, foot, prosodic word, etc.), morphological (root, stem, word), or syntactic (phrase, sentence, etc.). All the constraints that deal with sequences (**Sequence**, **NoSequence**, **NotTwice**) must occur in multiple variants, one for each domain that is possible. This represents a massive explosion of constraints, but it is unclear how to avoid it, given the sorts of data that occur in adult grammars and in child language acquisition. We will not normally include the domain of the constraint in the constraint name, but will note in the text what the domain of the constraint is, if we know that it is restricted.

4.8.2. FEATURE DOMAINS

One additional concept within OT is relevant to features; the concept of the *feature domain*. A given feature extends over a particular sequence of segments, from one to many. This is referred to as the domain of the feature. Kisseberth (1993) and Cole and Kisseberth (1994) have explored the characteristics of feature domains, developing a subarea of OT that they refer to as *optimal domains theory* (ODT).

Feature domains differ from "the set of segments to which a feature is linked" in only a few ways. Assimilation is handled by aligning the edge of the feature domain with the edge of a category such as a phonological word (rather than actually aligning the feature itself).

☞**Aligned(LabialDomain,L,PrWd,L):**   The left edge of the feature domain
                                                                      for Labial should coincide with the
                                                                      left edge of the prosodic word.
            ✂**Expression:**   Every segment within a domain
                                                must be linked to the feature
                                                required by the domain.

This second constraint, ✂**Expression**, is equivalent to our **Uninterrupted** constraint; Smolensky (1993) refers to it as ✂***Embed**. The reader who wishes to use domains within our framework should use the constraint name:

☞**UninterruptedDomain**

This is a constraint family. There is one constraint for every element: feature, node in the feature geometry, or node in suprasegmental structure.

The main new aspect of this analysis is in terms of whether assimilation involves spreading. If we align the feature [Labial] itself, then the edge of that feature must be at the left edge of the word. But if we align the feature *domain*, all we are saying is that the leftmost segment must be a labial. We can satisfy this constraint by *inserting* [Labial]:

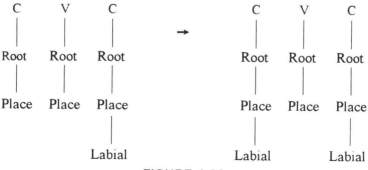

FIGURE 4.20

Cole and Kisseberth state that they know of no empirical reason to prefer inserting a feature rather than spreading, but note that feature domains allow this as an alternative to spreading. We will not make use of feature domains in our analyses of assimilation, since we view it as more straightforward to spread the feature.

A second new aspect of this analysis is Smolensky's (1993) interpretation of **UninterruptedDomain**. One way to have an interrupted domain is to have the opposite feature value in the middle of it:

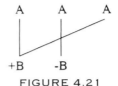

FIGURE 4.21

This is an example of an embedded (interrupted) domain: there is a wide B-Domain (with the value [+]), and a narrow B-Domain (with the value [-]) inside it; Smolensky emphasizes that in principle the embedded B-Domain could have the same value ([+] or [-]) as the higher B-Domain. Note that association lines may cross. Although the prohibition against crossing association lines was an absolute constraint in earlier theory, constraints in OT are violable. The ramifications of this proposal have yet to be worked out in detail. We will not follow this analysis here.

Cole and Kisseberth propose a new concept known as *parasitic alignment* that addresses the issue of similarity effects within assimilations. We have noted that assimilations can sometimes be restricted to two segments that share some feature that is not involved with the assimilation. A common example is that the assimilation of the feature [round] is limited to vowels of the same height; in Yawelmani (Archangeli, 1984), /i/ becomes [u] after /u/ but not after /o/ (effect of shared [+high]), and /a/ becomes [o] after /o/ but not after /u/ (effect of shared [-high]). In parasitic alignment, the edges of two domains are aligned:

Aligned(RoundDomain,R,HighDomain,R)

This means that the right edge of the rounding domain must occur in the same vowel as the right edge of the high domain. If a word of the shape /uCi/ has a single high domain (stipulating that both vowels must be [+high]), then the right edge of the rounding domain of the /u/ must be moved to the right, to be aligned with the right edge of the high domain; /i/ becomes rounded to [u]. Similarly for the two [-high] vowels in /oCa/. If the vowels differ in height, however, there must be two high domains. Since the two vowels in /oCi/ are in different high domains, there will be no assimilation; the right edge of the rounding domain of the /o/ is aligned with the right edge of the high domain of the /o/, which extends only over the vowel /o/, and does not include the following /i/. This provides a resolution to the problem of why shared features can lead to assimilation. We do not make much use of feature domains in this book, but note that feature domains plus parasitic alignment do provide an analysis of similarity effects in assimilation, which are still problematical for the approach that we take in this book.

4.9. MORPHOLOGICAL CONSTRAINTS

Many constraints within OT are designed specifically to account for constraints on the shape of affixes. Most often, the shape of reduplicative affixes is addressed. There are, however, other more general constraints. We will not address reduplicative constraints here, since true grammatical reduplication is not a part of English or most other languages for which acquisition has been studied (although there are phenomena that resemble it in an occasional English-learning or Polish-learning child, as reported by Munson & Ingram, 1986; Stemberger, 1988a; Smoczyńska, 1985). In this section, we address the few constraints that are needed for phonological development.

We should note that the phonological constraints that we have already discussed can in theory affect the realization of the phonological material of affixes. For example, a constraint ranking that leads to the deletion of word-final /z/ will often affect all instances of /z/, whether that /z/ is part of a base morpheme (as in the word *pose*) or the plural suffix (as in the word *toes*). If morphology is not explicitly relevant, then the phonological form of affixes is treated like any equivalent phonological form. However, morphology *can* play a more dominant role in the phonological form of a word.

One general constraint on morphology is that all the morphosyntactic features (governing number, gender, case, tense, aspect, etc.) that should be expressed in the word must be expressed in some way. We use the following constraint (called ✂**M-Parse** by Prince & Smolensky, 1993, and ✂**Subcat** by McHugh, 1994):

Expressed: An output form expresses a particular morphological feature
              contained in the input.
  violation: A morphological feature is not overtly expressed.

This requires that a word that is supposed to be produced as a plural form, for example, is actually produced as a plural form, rather than (incorrectly) as a singular form.

McHugh (1994) and Samek-Lodovici (1992) propose that this expression is only possible if there is overt phonological material for the affix. We use the following constraint (called ✂**Recov-MCat** by McHugh, and ✂**Afx** by Samek-Lodovici):

Distinct: The inflected form must lead to at least one phonological element
              that is not part of the base morpheme's input representation.
  violation: The inflected form is identical to the base's input.

If all of a morpheme's segmental material is deleted (as can happen in adult grammars, and which we will see in §6.4 and §9.1.3.1 for phonological development), then a violation ensues. This constraint predicts that the segmental material of affixes may lead to sequences that could never occur in monomorphemic forms (see §6.4 and §9.1.3.2). Although most uses of this constraint are morphological, it may also have one phonological use: preventing the merger of two adjacent identical elements. If the underlying form has two tokens of /n/ in *unknown*

/ʌnnoʊn/, then the output should also have two (short) tokens of /n/, not one (long) token: [ʔʌnnoʌn], not *[ʔʌnːoʊn]. This would be due to a high ranking for **Distinct(Root)**; see §6.1.6.4.5.

In addition, we will treat each affix as a constraint that imposes certain constraints on the phonological form of the word:

☞**Plural(/z/,PrWd,R)**: The prosodic word must end in /z/.

More precisely, the word must end in a segment with all the features that are present underlyingly in /z/. The notation here implies that different affixes can be attached to different morphological units (bases, stems, prosodic words, etc.), at either the right edge (R) or the left edge (L). This constraint is fully violated only if *all* the phonetic material of the /z/ is absent in the output. This constraint may be high-ranked at all times, but may only be relevant if the feature [plural] is in the input.

There can be interactions between phonological and morphological constraints, affecting the way that affixes are expressed and their phonological shape. Such interactions are the main focus of McCarthy and Prince (1993a). They use the term *prosodic morphology* to describe the situation in which phonological constraints are ranked higher than morphological constraints.

High ranking guarantees that candidates that end in /z/ will be strong candidates for output. Consider the plural of the English word *bee*, if **Plural(/z/, PrWd,R)** is ranked higher than negative constraints (see Table 4.30):

TABLE 4.30

/biː/ - [+plural]	biːz	biː
Plural(/z/,PrWd,R)		*!
Not(Coda)	*	

In contrast, if the negative constraints are ranked higher than **Plural(z)**, it is the base form that is output, not the plural (see Table 4.31):

TABLE 4.31

/biː/ - [+plural]	biːz	biː
Not(Coda)	*!	
Plural(/z/,PrWd,R)		*

Thus, phonological constraints can prevent a morpheme from being expressed in the word. (See §6.4 for extensive discussion.)

This constraint, even if high-ranked, is insufficient to derive the correct pronunciation in many instances, however, since it just requires that the plural end in /z/. If the base form ends in /z/, as in the word *cause* /kɑːz/, then the plural will be *cause* (without any overt change), rather than *causes*: the output [kʰɑːz] ends in [z], and thus does not violate **Plural(/z/,PrWd,R)**. As Stemberger (1981), Menn and MacWhinney (1984), and Yip (1995) discuss, affixes sometimes make no overt change when the near part of the stem is identical to the affix, even in adult grammars. In child language it is common for a word like *cause* to be used without change as a plural form. In order to derive the adult pronunciation [kʰɑːzəz], with two tokens of [z], **Distinct(Plural)** must be high-ranked, so that the /z/ of the base cannot satisfy that **Plural(/z/)** constraint. (See Table 4.32.)

TABLE 4.32

/kɑːz/ - [+plural]	kɑːzəz	kɑːz
Plural(/z/,PrWd,R)		
Distinct(Plural)		*!
Not(Root)	*****	***

Neither output violates the **Plural** constraint, but an additional /z/ is added, in order to satisfy **Distinct**, even though this comes at the cost of additional violations of the lower-ranked **Not(Root)** constraint. **Distinct** must be high-ranked in order to have such an affect. If it is ranked lower than the negative constraints, the affix is not overtly added (see Table 4.33):

TABLE 4.33

/kɑːz/ - [+plural]	kɑːzəz	kɑːz
Plural(/z/,PrWd,R)		
Not(Root)	*****!	***
Distinct		*

Because the **Plural** constraint is not violated by either output, it cannot help choose between them. The fatal violation is a phonological one, and no affixal material is added. This analysis captures the long-held intuition that plurals like *cause* occur because the base form already "looks like" it is inflected as a plural (Berko, 1958; MacWhinney, 1978; Bybee & Slobin, 1982; Stemberger, 1981; etc.)

McCarthy and Prince (1993b) separate out the affix constraints into two parts. One part determines the phonological material in the affix (/z/ for the English Plural), without specifying where it goes in the word. The other involves alignment:

Aligned(PluralAffix, R, PrWd, R):   The right edge of the plural affix
                                            should coincide with the right edge of
                                            the prosodic word.

Since the right edges are aligned, the affix is a suffix. If the left edges are aligned, the affix is a prefix. McCarthy and Prince show that such an approach can provide an account of infixes as well: infixes are prefixes or suffixes that cannot actually begin or end the word because of other constraints. Suppose, for example, that [+voiced] is disallowed in codas, and that high ranking of **LinkedUpwards** (**+voiced**) and **Survived(+voiced)** prevents us from delinking it. It would be impossible for a plural to end in /z/. If the /z/ is deleted, however, that violates **Plural(/z/)**. But if the /z/ is realized earlier in the word, plurality is still overtly expressed (see Table 4.34):

TABLE 4.34

/laɪən/-[+plural]	laɪənz	laɪəz	laɪən	laɪzən
NotCo-occurring(Coda,+voiced)	*!	*!		
Plural(z)			*!	
Aligned				**

While infixes clearly occur in some languages, they do not occur in (adult) English. We are uncomfortable with a theory that predicts that they should occur in English child language. No such data have ever been reported. Alignment also predicts that the plural -z can be a prefix in some words (see Table 4.35):

TABLE 4.35

/æpəl/-[+plural]	apuz	apu	apzu	azpu	zapu
Not(Coda)	*!		*!	*!	
Plural(/z/)		*!			
Aligned(Affix,R)			*	**	***

Given an analysis of affixes using **Aligned**, there is no way to prevent such rankings from occurring in development. Since there is no evidence that such data ever occur, we regard this as a failure of the alignment analysis. As a result, we do not follow the alignment analysis here, but include placement of the affix as a characteristic of the affix constraint itself. The way that we defined our constraints above (e.g., **Plural(/z/,PrWd,R)**), the constraint will be violated if the /z/ is added anywhere but at the end of the prosodic word, to the same degree that it is violated if no affix is added at all. Since the addition of a segment will always violate some negative constraint, this situation is resolved by adding no affix at all.

Nevertheless, the alignment analysis of affixation does yield an intriguing analysis of infixes. According to McCarthy and Prince (1994), infixes generally occur close to the left or right edge of a morphological unit. In at least some instances, a phonological constraint forces a prefix or suffix to occur as an infix. In Tagalog, the prefix *um-* appears as a true prefix when the base begins with a vowel, but as an infix positioned after the onset of the first syllable if the base begins with a consonant: for /gradwet/, we see [gr-um-adwet]. They argue that the constraints that syllables must have onsets and must not have codas would be violated if *um-* was prefixed (in *[um-gradwet]), and that the correct [gr-um-adwet] reflects the leftmost positioning of [um] in which all syllables have an onset and in which no codas are created. This is an interesting analysis. In order to maintain the analysis in our system, we would require a modification of the positioning portion of our affix constraints:

Affix("Left"um"Left",PrWd,"Left")

This introduces a vagueness to the constraint: it should be somewhere at or near the left edge of the word, but exactly where it should occur is not specified. If it occurs at exactly the left edge, it is a prefix. If it is not exactly at the left edge, but is infixed, this affix constraint is not violated, but **Contiguity** *is* violated. In [gr-um-adwet], the /r/ and /a/ or /gradwet/ are no longer contiguous. If **Contiguity** is low-ranked (and thus violable), and some other constraint (such as **Not(Coda)** or σ▸**Onset**) is also high-ranked, then the affix will be an infix. If **Contiguity** is ranked highest, however, the affix will be a prefix. Indeed, if we considered it desirable, we could propose that *all* affixes are vague about exactly where they are placed, and that only **Contiguity** forces them to be true prefixes and suffixes. However, we have doubts about the wisdom of this, since young English-learning children never convert suffixes into infixes, as this analysis would predict. Tentatively, we suggest that there are two types of affixes: ones which specify their positioning precisely, and ones which specify their positioning vaguely. In this book, we have no need to refer to infixation again, and consequently leave this issue unresolved.

McCarthy and Prince (1993a) argue that constraints can require a certain morphological category to be of a certain size: a syllable, a foot, a prosodic word, etc. (✄**Mcat**≈**PCat**). We will have little need of this constraint in this book, but recommend:

✍**Size** (⟨**morph**⟩ = ⟨**phon**⟩):	A particular morphological category is always of a certain phonological size.
✍**Size(Stem** = **PrWd**):	A stem is always a prosodic word.

It is unclear whether such a constraint is actually needed. Independently needed constraints such as **Binary(Foot,σ)** also restrict the allowable size of words. If such a constraint holds only in a particular *morphological* domain (such as verb stems), it has the same effect as the **Size** constraint.

Because our focus in this book is not on morphology, we will not address these constraints in detail. For our purposes here, we do not need most of the morphological constraints that have been addressed in the literature, especially those governing morphological reduplication and infixation, and we refer the interested reader to McCarthy and Prince (1993a; 1994). We have discussed those aspects of morphology that are relevant to language acquisition, and return to them in §6.4 and Chapter 9.

4.10. LEXICAL EXCEPTIONS

Up to this point, we have been making the assumption that all words are subject to the same constraint rankings. This assumption turns out to be untenable. Sometimes lexical items are exceptions, in that a violation of a constraint might be tolerated (although in most words the violation is not tolerated) or the violation might be resolved in a way that is different from the way it is resolved in most words. Any given word with a word-initial fricative in adult speech might have a single consistent pronunciation, but the fricative might be dealt with in different ways in different words (Deletion versus Stopping versus Gliding, etc.), in ways that cannot be predicted from the phonological environment. Menn (1983) discusses an instance in child phonology in which word-initial stops assimilated nasality from later in the word: *dance* [næns]. However, for phonologically unpredictable reasons, the word *down* [daʊn] did not undergo Nasal Assimilation. All theories must have a way to deal with exceptions.

In OT, lexical exceptions can be dealt with in a variety of ways. In some instances, the "exceptions" are just lexical items with unusual underlying representations, which are subject to the same constraint rankings as other words. In other instances, however, lexical exceptions represent a reranking of one or more constraints for an individual lexical item.

Selkirk (1982) provided an example of unusual underlying representations. She observed that there is a constraint against starting a syllable with two fricatives. Almost all English words abide by this constraint, with a few exceptions such as *sphere* and *sphinx*. Such words are among the few words in English with lexical entries that would lead to violations of this constraint. Faithfulness constraints, including **LinkedUpwards**, **Survived(Root)**, and **Not(V-Root)**, prevent either the deletion of one of the fricatives (or the feature [+continuant]) or the insertion of an epenthetic vowel adjacent to the /s/. Faithfulness requires that these words have onsets that otherwise are not permitted in English. The words have unusual underlying forms, but pronunciations that are faithful to those unusual underlying forms. **NotTwice(-sonorant, + continuant)** is ranked high enough that such words sound odd, however, and new words of that sort are never coined.

In other instances, however, underlying forms of two words might be comparable, with both words apparently violating some constraint, but with the two words treated differently. For example, the violation might be tolerated in one word, but resolved via deletion in the other word. This has often been reported for language acquisition (Smith, 1973; Ferguson & Farwell, 1975; Menn, 1983; Menn & Matthei, 1992). Leopold (1947) reports that his daughter Hildegard reduced all word-initial /pɹ/ clusters to [p], except the word *pretty*, which was consistently produced with [pɹ]; no phonological factors in the rest of the word could account for the exceptional production of [pɹ] in this word.

In OT, lexical exceptions could be handled by allowing individual lexical items to rerank constraints *for that one word* (e.g., in Golston's, 1996, approach). For example, suppose that the standard ranking is:

> **NotComplex(Onset)**   ‖‖   **Survived(Root)**
> **LinkedUpwards(Root)**

Then the speaker might delete the /ɹ/ from /pɹ/ to yield [p] (a **Survived(Root)** violation) rather than produce both consonants in the onset (a **NotComplex (Onset)** violation). However, suppose the two constraints are reranked:

> **Survived(Root)**   ‖‖   **NotComplex(Onset)**
> **LinkedUpwards(Root)**

Both members of the cluster must be linked into the onset ([pɹ]), even though there is a **NotComplex(Onset)** violation, because otherwise a **Survived(Root)/ LinkedUpwards(Root)** violation arises.

For the child discussed above, the standard ranking is with **NotComplex (Onset)** ranked higher than **Survived(Root)/LinkedUpwards(Root)**. For the word *pretty*, however, the constraints are reranked so that **Survived(Root)** and **LinkedUpwards(Root)** are ranked higher, and both members of the cluster are produced. Although in this case the exception allows for more possibilities than the standard ranking, it is also possible that the reranking would lead to something being impossible that generally is allowed.

Some readers may view this reranking as ad hoc and undesirable. However, it must be kept in mind that all words are always subject to all constraints, and the rankings must reflect what actually happens to the word. We can describe what the theory is claiming about exceptions in the following way:

> "X is generally impossible, but *is* possible in this one word."
> "X is generally possible, but is *not* possible in this one word."

Lexically determined reranking has only this meaning, and it seems an entirely reasonable way to go about it. (We have a difficult time imagining any mechanism to handle exceptions that does not boil down to these same concepts.)

Menn and Matthei (1992) maintain that lexical exceptions are at least partly predictable. *If* there are any lexical exceptions at all (and there often are not), it is the most frequent words in the child's speech that are exceptional (whether because they are more faithful to the adult pronunciation, or because they are less faithful).

Our version of OT predicts that high-frequency words can be more faithful than low-frequency words. Tyler and Edwards (1993) report that this can happen. They report that English-learning children acquire aspiration in word-initial voiceless stops (as in *pot*>[pʰɑt]) first in frequent words, and only later in infrequent words and new words. We can account for this because **Survived** is on a sliding scale, indexed to activation levels. High-frequency words have higher activation levels than low-frequency words (e.g., Brown & McNeill, 1966; Stemberger & Mac-Whinney, 1986; Dell, 1990; Stemberger, 1992a). If a word inherently has a low activation level, **Survived** constraints will be ranked lower than usual for that word. If the word has an inherently high activation level, **Survived** constraints will be ranked higher than usual for that word. In some instances, **Survived** will be ranked differently relative to some other critical constraint, and consequently different words will resolve violations of the same constraint in different ways. This derives instances in which high-frequency words are more faithful than other words.

Stemberger (1992a) notes that it may not be as easy to account for instances in which high-frequency words are *less* faithful than other words, without adding additional principles. Menn and Matthei (1992) suggest that children may store their own pronunciations for high-frequency words and so be less prone to change them as the system matures. There is no way to account for such effects within the system as we have laid it out, however. If we ignore the problem of predicting *which* words will be exceptional, and focus just on the mechanism, it is clear that when different words have different inherent activation levels, they can differ in faithfulness. This can be derived by assuming that the **Survived** constraints are ranked differently for the two words, as a function of the differences in activation levels. What is unclear is whether we can *predict* which words have high activation levels; it may be that in some cases we must simply *stipulate* that a word has a high or a low activation level. Such stipulation is undesirable, but it remains to be seen whether it can be avoided.

4.11. VARIABILITY THAT IS NOT LEXICALLY IDIOSYNCRATIC

Not all variability is lexically idiosyncratic. In many instances, there are two or more pronunciations of a given word, determined solely by the phonological characteristics of the word; all words with those phonological characteristics show two or more pronunciations. A commonly cited example in adult English is the variability between syllabic /ɹ̩/ and nonsyllabic /ɹ/ in words like *celery*; many speakers vary between pronouncing the word with two syllables ([sɛɫɹi]) or with three syllables ([sɛɫɹ̩i]). On one occasion the word will be pronounced one way, but on another occasion (possibly even the next sentence) the pronunciation will be different.

Such variability is common in the speech of young children. Ferguson and Farwell (1975) take variability to be the rule in early child speech. Others (e.g., Smith, 1973) have reported that pronunciations are often stable, with most words having a single pronunciation. We believe that most words are pronounced with a single pronunciation at most points during development for most children. However, in times of change (as the child's pronunciation changes, generally in the direction of being closer to the adult target pronunciation, but not always), variability can arise. This seems to be especially true of disordered speech during treatment: treatment tends to lead to variability between the old pronunciation and the taught pronunciation, rather than a direct replacement (Stoel-Gammon & Dunn, 1985). We take the following as the most common pattern of change, using an example from Morgan (*mouse*, at 1;8) and a hypothetical example (*bite*) that is similar to Gwendolyn's variability at 2;5:

Point A:	the word has a single stable pronunciation
	bite [baɪ] *mouse* [maʊh]
Point B:	the old pronunciation varies with a new pronunciation
	[baɪ]~[baɪt] [maʊh]~[maʊtʰ]
Point C:	the word stabilizes to a new nonvariable pronunciation; the old pronunciation disappears
	[baɪt] [maʊtʰ]

Point B can last for a very short period of time, or for a very long period (and no one understands why changes sometimes are fast, and sometimes are slow). Sometimes, the next change in the system appears before the child has stabilized the new nonvariable pronunciation, so that the word has three variant pronunciations. It is unusual for a new pronunciation to arise abruptly, with no period of variability.

There are two possible ways that nonlexical variability can be encoded within OT. First (and the way that we prefer), the ranking of a particular constraint may be unstable. If the constraint is sometimes ranked fairly high, but at other times is ranked fairly low, then different pronunciations result. It is unclear why some constraints are ranked stably, while others are ranked unstably. In theory, the unstable ranking can be probabilistic, so that the constraint is more often ranked at one place in the ranking than at the other. Thus, the variants do not have to be equally frequent. Variant A could occur 50% of the time or 95%. We prefer this explanation, because it can derive any frequency of occurrence for the variants.

Second, two or more constraints may be ranked equally. In that case, violations of the two constraints count as "ties": neither violation is worse than the other, and both variants are equally optimal. For example, suppose that **Survived(Root)** and **Not(Coda)** are equally ranked. If the final consonant of the word *bed* is linked up, that violates **Not(Coda)**. To avoid a violation of **Not(Coda)**, the final /d/ could be deleted, but that would violate **Survived(Root)**. If one of the constraints is ranked higher than the other, then the consonant will either always be deleted or always be linked up. But if the two constraints are ranked as equals, then the pronunciation with the /d/ linked up is no better (and no worse) than the pronunciation in which the /d/ is deleted. As a result, both pronunciations are acceptable. The system chooses one of the outputs at random: the /d/ is pronounced on half of all trials, but deleted on the other half. One drawback is that this seems to predict that variant pronunciations will always be of equal frequency, and that is not always the case (e.g., Guy, 1991). It is unclear how this mechanism can be structured to allow for the variants to have different probabilities of occurrence. We thus do not use equal rankings to derive variability.

4.12. LEARNING ISSUES AND CURRENT THEORY

In this section, we focus on two aspects of phonology based on current theory and our hypotheses for development: constraint rankings, and underspecification. As suggested in §2.4.3, output constraints do not depend on representational analysis, but do undergo changes as learning proceeds.

We assume throughout an additive learning perspective. One of the assumptions of rule/process-based theory was that children have to unlearn the rules or suppress the processes so that they can learn: a negative progression. Representational and constraint-based theories suggest that development is a more positive progression, a conceptually more appealing perspective on growth and development. Representations are built up until they are adult-like in terms of specification and content. The high-ranked negative constraints of early development (**Not** constraints) become low-ranked, as the child becomes capable of doing things. In some cases, a child will proceed down a developmental path that does not lead quickly to the adult system. In such cases, a negative progression might be involved for that part of the system. In general, however, learning appears to proceed from the impossible to the possible.

4.12.1. SETTING THE CONSTRAINT RANKINGS IN ACQUISITION

In a book that explores the acquisition of phonology, something must be said about how the adult phonological system is acquired by the child. This issue has been addressed by several researchers. However, the research has been of an abstract formal nature, and has not attempted to account for children's phonological development. We review two approaches, and then lay out a proposal of our own.

Tesar and Smolensky (in press) propose the following. Initially, all constraints are equally ranked. On the basis of input, it can be seen that some constraints must be ranked higher than others. Whenever there is positive evidence for rankings that are not equal, the constraints are reranked in the necessary way. The mechanism for reranking is *constraint demotion*: constraints can be reranked lower, never higher. Reranking is *goal-oriented*: the adult data require a certain ranking, and the constraints are reranked so that they (ultimately) have that ranking. When the adult target candidate loses (so that the child alters the pronunciation), the system can identify which constraint was responsible: the highest-ranked constraint that is fatally violated is ranked too high. By ranking that constraint lower, so that it is not violated on the next trial with that word, the child's pronunciation comes to more closely approximate the adult pronunciation. However, there may now be another constraint that is ranked too high, and is fatally violated. This second constraint is demoted. This reranking process continues until the adult pronunciation is attained. If there is no evidence in the target adult language about how two particular constraints are ranked, no reranking occurs; those constraints are ranked as equals even in the mature system. All adults (who speak the same dialect) are predicted to have identical constraint rankings.

Tesar and Smolensky (in press) argue that constraints must be demoted, never promoted (ranked higher). With constraint demotion, the misranked constraint can always be identified. However, with constraint promotion, there is a problem. It is usually difficult to determine which of several low-ranked constraints is the one that is misranked. How can we guarantee that a learner will always pick the correct constraint to rerank? With constraint demotion, it is possible to prove that the learning mechanism will ultimately converge on the appropriate ranking for the target language. With constraint promotion, that cannot be proven: by promoting the wrong constraints, the system may never converge on the target ranking. Tesar and Smolensky argue that constraint demotion is a necessary part of learning. However, this approach fails to account for the most common type of regressions in phonological development; see §4.12.2.

This basic approach makes the wrong predictions about child phonological development, provided that variability arises whenever constraints are equally ranked (see §4.11). The initial equal ranking of all constraints predicts massive variability in the pronunciations of all words, with a large number of variant pronunciations for all words. Although variability is present in child phonology, rampant variability is highly unusual: there are usually two or three variant pronunciations at most, and variability usually arises only at times of change in the child's phonological system. Since massive variability is not present, this approach is not appropriate for modeling child language acquisition.

The basic approach also incorrectly predicts that constraint rankings, when not equal, are always the correct rankings for the target language that is being learned. As we discuss in later chapters, this is not true of young children. Children often have clear constraint rankings that are markedly different from the rankings of adult English and do not appear to be learned by the child on the basis of adult English words. Some alternative learning mechanism is needed that allows constraints to be ranked (one higher, one lower) in a way that is quite different from that of the adult target language.

Tesar and Smolensky (in press) are aware that the simplest approach cannot account for child phonological development. They also explore the proposals of developmentalists (e.g., Stemberger, 1996a, 1996b; Levelt, 1996; Gnanadesikan, 1995) that the initial state has constraints ranked in a partially random fashion, but with **Survived** generally low-ranked. They show that constraint demotion should still be expected to find the correct constraint ranking for the language. However, they neglect one important aspect of acquisition: the nature of the underlying representation. Their learning algorithms give no details of how the underlying representations are learned. Tesar (1995) and Smolensky (1996b) propose that the underlying form is constantly being revised, as the constraint ranking gradually begins to approximate the ranking needed for the adult language. However, full details have not been worked out. It also fails to capture the fact that faithfulness is sometimes ranked higher in the child's speech than it is in the adult target language; see §9.1.1.

One very interesting effect can be derived, however (though Tesar and Smolensky do not point this out). We assume that learning takes place gradually, and that the child reranks constraints often, as evidence is noted for different rankings. Many learning trials are needed before the correct ranking is finally achieved. Frequent elements are encountered more often than infrequent elements, both in perception and production, and we would expect that learning trials will consequently be more frequent with high-frequency elements than with low-frequency elements. This means that the learner more often reranks constraints for high-frequency elements than for low-frequency elements, which leads to a frequency effect: there will be a tendency for high-frequency elements to be mastered before low-frequency elements, all other things being equal. This last qualification is important, because all other things are often not equal: some constraint rankings are easier to achieve than others, independently of frequency, and the frequency of learning trials will not necessarily lead to a hard-to-achieve ranking for a frequent element being acquired before an easy-to-achieve ranking for an infrequent element. However, this tendency does lead to the expectation that frequency can affect how early an element is mastered. For example, if palatoalveolar affricates are very frequent (as in Quiche Mayan), we predict that children will master them earlier than in languages in which affricates are infrequent (as in English). Such crosslinguistic frequency effects have been reported (Pye, Ingram, & List, 1987; Ingram, 1988a,b).

Pulleyblank and Turkel (1995) propose an alternative, involving genetic learning algorithms. At any given time, a learner has multiple grammars. Initially, these grammars are set up with all constraints ranked in a hierarchy (with little or no equal ranking of constraints); these initial rankings are either random or semi-random. Unlike Tesar and Smolensky's system, reranking is *not* goal-oriented. Reranking occurs only as the result of random mutations in the grammar. Mutations that lead to a better ranking of constraints confer greater optimality on the grammar, and that mutated grammar is more likely to survive as the learner modifies the phonological system. Mutations that lead to a worse ranking of constraints decrease the optimality of the grammar, and that mutated grammar is less likely to survive as the learner modifies the phonological system. This learning algorithm is closely based on genetic systems used for evolutionary biology. In evolutionary biology, mutations of the genes (the grammar that underlies the organism) occur at random: some mutations are good (and tend to survive into later generations) and some are bad (and tend not to be passed on to later generations). Pulleyblank and Turkel have adopted a preexisting learning algorithm for use with OT. It should be noted that when the language provides no information about the relative ranking of two constraints, then there is no pressure for the grammar to have one ranking or the other. It is predicted that different adults will have identical constraint rankings where there are data to require those rankings, but will have different constraint rankings when there are no relevant data in the language.

The appropriateness of using a genetic learning algorithm of learning is questionable. Across generations of organisms, changes in characteristics are initially random and must be shaped via natural selection. The changes themselves are not goal-oriented: to take a famous example, the offspring of giraffes do not have longer necks just because the parents spend a lot of time stretching their necks to reach leaves high up in trees. It is the *selection* of those characteristics (once they have a genetic basis) that is goal-oriented. In contrast, changes within an organism during development *can* be goal-oriented. If an individual stretches his/her neck throughout development, the neck can in fact wind up longer than it would otherwise have been, by affecting the development of muscles and joints. Changes within an individual can easily be made, and can be goal-oriented. (Practice can lead to the mastery of a skill: goal-oriented learning. But mastering that skill does not mean that offspring will be born with the skill: non-goal-oriented evolution.)

Learning is more likely to be goal-oriented. Performance includes errors. Cognitive systems are altered in order to make errors less likely: *error-driven learning*. Connectionist models of cognition make use of goal-oriented error-driven learning algorithms (e.g., Rumelhart & McClelland, 1986). Such learning is the most efficient way to learn. We do not have a fully elaborated theory of the learning of constraint rankings by young children. The following sketch reflects our current thinking about what a full model could look like.

First, the child must begin with some ranking of constraints. Because variability is limited, most constraints are ranked stably, and there are few equally ranked constraints. Furthermore, because each child appears to have a unique phonological system, different children must begin with different constraint rankings. There is a randomness in a given child's initial constraint rankings. However, there is also consistency across children: some things are almost universal across children, while other things are rare. In general, **Survived/LinkedUpwards** constraints are ranked fairly low, and **Not** constraints are ranked fairly high. As a result, segments and features (and syllables and even feet) tend to be deleted. Constraints tend to be ranked so that the insertion of segments is not common. Other negative constraints that restrict the presence and linkage of elements (such as **NoSequence, NotTwice, NotComplex**) also tend to be high-ranked. These initial constraint rankings tend to lead to great unfaithfulness, with a limited syllable structure and far fewer feature contrasts than in adult speech.

We assume that some learning of constraint rankings begins during the babbling period (Locke, 1983; Vihman, 1992). The initial rankings are modified during this period. Even though the child's utterances are not meaningful during the babbling period, children do imitate adults. The child can thus learn what constraint rankings are necessary in order to produce some structure or segment. Further, phone frequencies during this period can lead to rankings in which the most frequent output is ranked as the default (Stemberger, 1991b; below). The rankings that result from learning during this period serve for the child's first words. Consequently, the child's first words frequently bear a close phonological similarity to the child's babbling utterances.

These early constraint rankings must be altered in order for the child to acquire the target adult language. Some component of the language system must have access to the correct (adult) pronunciation, compare the child's actual pronunciation, and be able to determine where these two pronunciations are different. This component figures out which constraints are ranked incorrectly, and re-ranks the constraints accordingly.[29]

The details of this reranking are unclear. It might be that the ranking of the relevant constraint can be changed by only a single position (higher or lower) in the ranking. In that case, the constraint might have to be reranked many times before its position in the ranking changes enough to have an effect on the output. This would imply that changes tend to be small and take a long time to achieve. This seems plausible, looking at what happens in acquisition. Making very large changes in the ranking could lead to massive changes in output (some good, some bad). Large changes would probably lead to many changes in which the child's pronunciations become *less* adult-like (the opposite of the desired sort of change). But we are unsure how large the changes in ranking can be.

To account for the variability that usually accompanies change in the child's system, we must assume that the constraint is initially reranked unstably. Eventually, a constraint ranking is reached that allows the child to reproduce the adult pronunciation faithfully. Note that, as with Pulleyblank and Turkel's algorithm, this mature constraint ranking will not be identical for all speakers: where the relative ranking of two constraints makes no difference for the adult language, some speakers will have one ranking and other speakers will have the other ranking. Although this has no effect on current English, it does mean that different speakers will react differently to words borrowed from other languages and may show different tendencies for sound change.

The trickiest part for this view of learning is determining which constraint is at fault, and which should be reranked. It should be possible to narrow the choice of constraints to just a few, and to know exactly how to deal with the constraint that is incorrectly ranked. We believe that constraints can sometimes be reranked lower, but that the main type of reranking is upward. In particular, the main problem is that faithfulness is ranked too low in the child's speech. When some element fails to survive, **Survived** is generally reranked higher. However, it may be that other constraints are reranked, sometimes higher, sometimes lower.

For concreteness, we return to our example of the word *bed* [bɛd] from §4.2.1, and the different possible pronunciations that we addressed. We list the child's output, how the child's output differs from the adult target pronunciation, which

---

[29] In the connectionist literature, this component is usually called the *teacher* (e.g., Rumelhart & McClelland, 1986). However, since this term has generally been misunderstood as referring to another human being who overtly corrects the learner (e.g., Pinker & Prince, 1988; Lachter & Bever, 1988), some other term should be found.

constraint is improperly ranked (as given in the relevant constraint table that the OT system uses in determining which output is optimal), and what reranking is required. In most cases, two options are possible, and we list them both.

Output: [bɛ]
   Discrepancy: Failed to link up final C.
   Resolution: Rank **Survived/LinkedUpwards(C)** higher.
             OR
             Rank **Not(Coda)** lower.

Output: [bɛʔ]
   Discrepancy: Failed to link up Place node.
   Resolution: Rank **Survived/LinkedUpwards(Place)** higher.
             OR
             Rank **Not(Place)** lower.
             OR
             Rank **Not(Coronal)** lower.
             OR
             Rank **NoSequence** constraints lower.

Output: [bɛt]
   Discrepancy: Failed to link up [+voiced].
   Resolution: Rank **Survived/LinkedUpwards(+voiced)** higher.
             OR
             Rank **Not(+voiced)** lower.

Output: [bɛdə]
   Discrepancy: Inserted a final vowel.
   Resolution: Rank **Not(V-Root)** higher.
             OR
             Rank **Not(Coda)** lower.

Output: [bɛd]
   Discrepancy: None.
   Resolution: Do not change the ranking.

Of course, sometimes the constraint that is at fault is not immediately apparent to the observer, on the basis of the surface pronunciation. Violations of many different constraints can be avoided by failing to link up an element in the output. However, note that the ambiguity is partly our problem as observers. We do not have access to the child's internal representations used during the process of generating the optimal output. According to OT, information about which high-ranked constraint is the constraint that is fatally ranked too high is included in that internal (cognitive) representation (i.e., **Not, NotTwice, NoSequence, Not(Coda)**, etc.) Thus, the child would have an easier task determining which constraint is at fault than we do, as outside observers.

4.12.2. REGRESSIONS AND CONSTRAINT RANKINGS

In §4.12.1, we talked about the reranking of constraints during the acquisition process. Note that constraints do not "disappear" from the system. All that happens is a change in their relative ranking. If a negative constraint is ranked low enough, it will not prevent certain types of output, given that the rankings remain stable. The constraints may appear to have "disappeared." But even in adults, if the system is stressed, or the brain is injured, or another language is learned, "regressive" patterns may appear which indicate additional rerankings.[30] Children sometimes show regressive patterns during development, and we need to explain how regressions can arise.

When reranking occurs as intended, the child's pronunciation changes so that it is closer to the target adult pronunciation. If only one constraint is ranked improperly, this might in fact always be the case. However, many constraints are ranked differently than in adult speech. When a constraint is reranked relative to a constraint that is distant in the constraint ranking, reranking relative to all intervening constraints will also occur. As that reranking happens, there may be unanticipated changes in output.

For example, suppose that the child pronounces *bed* as [bɛdə], with epenthesis of a final vowel (see Table 4.36):

TABLE 4.36

/bɛd/	bɛd	bɛ	bɛdə
Not(Coda)	*!		
LinkedUpwards(Root) Survived(C-Root)		*!	
Not(V-Root)			*

Suppose also that the child learns to avoid this unfaithfulness by reranking **Not(V-Root)** higher so that epenthesis becomes impossible (see Table 4.37):

TABLE 4.37

/bɛd/	bɛd	bɛ	bɛdə
Not(Coda)	*!		
Not(V-Root)			*!
LinkedUpwards(Root) Survived(C-Root)		*	

[30] Stampe (1969) talked about *suppression* of phonological processes as learning takes place, an analogous concept to reranking of constraints. Processes did not disappear, but were merely suppressed, inhibited, or reordered so they did not affect output. However, they might reappear during second language learning, aphasic language breakdown, etc.

If the motivation behind epenthesis was to avoid having a coda, and **Not(Coda)** is still ranked higher than **LinkedUpwards(Root)** and **Survived(Root)**, the child will now delete the final consonant: [bɛ]. In one respect (relative to epenthesis), the child's pronunciation has become closer to the adult pronunciation. But in another respect (relative to the presence versus absence of the /d/), the child's pronunciation has become less faithful. Solving one problem has led to another, because of the way that the constraints were ranked. Of course, a different reranking would not lead to this problem. If **Not(Coda)** is instead ranked lower, at first no change is apparent (see Table 4.38):

TABLE 4.38

/bɛd/	bɛd	bɛ	bɛdə
LinkedUpwards(Root) Survived(C-Root)		*!	
Not(Coda)	*!		
Not(V-Root)			*

The reranking has been too small to achieve a change in output. But if **Not(Coda)** is reranked downwards again, the adult form is achieved (see Table 4.39):

TABLE 4.39

/bɛd/	bɛd	bɛ	bɛdə
LinkedUpwards(Root) Survived(C-Root)		*!	
Not(V-Root)			*!
Not(Coda)	*		

If the right constraint is reranked relative to all other constraints, no regression will occur. But if the wrong constraint is reranked, or an incorrect intermediate ranking is achieved, regressions occur.

Regressions of this sort, in which the pronunciation becomes more adult-like in one respect but less adult-like in another respect, are not uncommon during phonological development. They are probably the most common form of regression. They all have the following general characteristics:

1. The constraint that is responsible for the child's mispronunciation is ranked too high, both before and after the reranking.
2. Two lower-ranked constraints are reranked with respect to each other.

3. The high-ranked constraint is unviolated at both Point 1 and Point 2, but different "repair strategies" are used to avoid that violation.

We refer to these as "trade-off" regressions. With respect to the adult pronunciation of a particular word, the child improves along one dimension, but worsens along a second dimension. There is a trade-off with respect to faithfulness. It should be noted that our approach to learning, which allows constraints to be ranked upwards, allows such regressions to occur. However, the Tesar and Smolensky (in press) approach, which allows only constraint demotion, is intrinsically incapable of accounting for most such regressions. Their approach was *designed* to rerank only the constraint that was causing the problem in the first place. Trade-off regressions involve the reranking of a different constraint that was *not* causing the problem. Constraint demotion was designed to *prevent* such regressions from occurring. Since such regressions occur, we know that constraint demotion is the wrong approach for child phonological development.

Some regressions are a bit different, in that the pronunciation of a given word does not simultaneously improve in one respect and worsen in another respect. In some regressions, the pronunciations of some words improve, but the pronunciations of other words worsen. A clear hypothetical example would be the following. The child reduces all words to a monosyllable due to an excessively high ranking of **Not(σ)**: *bucket* [bʌ]. In order to allow longer words, **Binary(Foot,σ)** might be reranked higher than **Not(σ)**, thereby forcing the parsing of the second syllable. While this would be one way to make, for example, *bucket* be pronounced [bʌkə], it might also force *all* feet to have two syllables. Suddenly, the child would have to pronounce words like *duck* (previously [dʌ]) with two syllables: [dʌkə]. This problem would have to be resolved via the reranking of one of two constraints (**Binary(Foot,σ)** or **Not(V-Root)**) relative to the other constraint. In some cases, this type of regression might occur because the "wrong" constraint was reranked. In other cases, the right constraint may have been reranked, but some other constraint is improperly ranked, and thus interacts with the newly reranked constraint in the wrong way.

Consider the following regression, which one of us (Bernhardt) has often observed during therapy. The child initially shows Velar Fronting, wherein all dorsals are pronounced as (anterior) coronals: *cup* [tʰʌp]. Consider Table 4.40, showing how the pronunciations of *cup* and *top* are derived:

TABLE 4.40

	/kʌp/		/tɑp/	
	kʌp	tʌp	tɑp	kɑp
Not(Dorsal)	*!			*!
Survived(Dorsal)		*		
Not(Coronal)		*	*	

Because **Not(Dorsal)** is ranked higher than **Survived(Dorsal)**, [Dorsal] is never possible in the output. The low ranking of **Not(Coronal)** means that [Coronal] acts as the default feature; underlying velar consonants surface as coronals. Note that underlyingly underspecified consonants also surface as coronals (since the default place is [Coronal]). Note also that **Survived(Coronal)** plays no role here; because [Coronal] is not present in the underlying representation, **Survived** is irrelevant. Now, suppose that **Not(Dorsal)** is reranked lower to correct Velar Fronting errors, so that it is now the lowest-ranked in this set of constraints (see Table 4.41):

TABLE 4.41

	/kʌp/			/tɑp/	
	kʌp	tʌp		tɑp	kɑp
Survived(Dorsal)		*!			
Not(Coronal)		*		*!	
Not(Dorsal)	*				*

By ranking **Not(Dorsal)** so low, underlying [Dorsal] now survives. However, **Not(Dorsal)** is now the lowest-ranked constraint against articulator features and now acts as the default. Underlyingly underspecified consonants incorrectly surface as velars rather than as coronals. Note that this is possible *only* because the **Survived(Coronal)** constraint cannot ensure that a [Coronal] feature is present in the output.[31] Default features rely entirely on the ranking of the relevant **Not** constraints to derive the correct feature in the output; as a result, underspecified features should be especially prone to such regressions. Other underlying nondefault features, such as [Labial], should be stable and should not be replaced with [Dorsal], because **Survived(Labial)** protects [Labial] and ensures that [Labial] is in the output.

The reranking has simultaneously led to an improvement in the pronunciation of velars, but to a worsening in the pronunciation of coronals. Note that this regression only occurred because **Not(Dorsal)** was demoted so much; had it been demoted by only one position, the regression would not have occurred. If the child later reranks **Not(Dorsal)** higher, or **Not(Coronal)** lower, the correct (adult) output will be achieved.[32]

[31] Either the segment is underspecified for [Coronal] (so that **Survived** is irrelevant) or **Survived(Coronal)** is ranked below **Not(Coronal)** (since the ranking of **Survived** is irrelevant to the default: the default is present in the output for phonological, not lexical reasons).

[32] Macken (1980) assumes that such regressions only occur when the child has misperceived the adult forms. For example, the child may misperceive all velars as dentals, incorrectly hearing *cup* [tʰʌp]. When the child eventually realizes that the word actually begins with a velar, the child must correct the incorrect lexical entry. If the correction is done on a word-by-word basis, no errors result. However, if the child incorrectly decides that every [tʰ] that s/he has heard is in fact [kʰ], errors result: the child replaces the /t/ of words like *top* with /k/, leading to the regression [kʰɑp]. It should be noted

Finally, regressions may arise as a by-product of reranking for unrelated purposes. Consider a possible interaction between the deletion of initial unstressed syllables and the simplification of initial consonant clusters:

Prominent(Foot,Left) ||| **NotComplex(Onset)** ||| **Survived(C-Root)** ||| **Not(V-Root)**
NotComplex(PrWd) |||

The two highest-ranked constraints cause a word like *balloon* /bəluːn/ to reduce to a single left-prominent foot: [buːn]. **NotComplex(Onset)** prohibits initial clusters in words like *black* /blæk/. The low ranking of **Not(V-Root)** might suggest that a vowel would be epenthesized between the two consonants in the cluster: *[bəlæk]. However, the two high-ranked constraints prevent that from occurring, and so one consonant deletes instead: [bæk]. Now, suppose that the child reranks **Prominent(Foot,Left)** lower, so that outputs like *balloon* [bə'luːn] become possible; the reranking would occur in order to correct mispronunciations of words with initial unstressed syllables in the adult targets. However, because initial unstressed syllables are now possible, the relative ranking of **Survived(C-Root)** and **Not(V-Root)** becomes relevant; the child's pronunciation of *black* becomes [bə'læk]. Because of the earlier ranking, correcting the rankings for word-initial unstressed syllables leads to what looks like a trade-off regression for /bl/: increased faithfulness relative to the consonants, at the cost of decreased faithfulness relative to the foot structure of the word. Any approach to learning within OT predicts that such overgeneralization of newly mastered patterns should occur.

It is clear that the reranking of constraints will not necessarily lead to a change that is entirely in the direction of the adult pronunciation. In some cases, regressions may occur. However, changes usually do lead to improvements in pronunciation. Eventually, the child's constraint rankings converge on the adult constraint rankings, and the child's pronunciation becomes adult-like. Our approach to learning is a bit vague, and we cannot prove that it would allow a learner to find the ranking needed for the adult language, but it does allow for all the types of regression discussed here. Tesar and Smolensky's (in press) approach can probably allow a learner to find the ranking needed for the adult language, but cannot account for most trade-off regressions. Consequently, we will follow our proposals in this book.

4.12.3. DEVELOPMENT OF UNDERSPECIFICATION

We have often addressed the issue of underspecification. In this section, we discuss how feature specification in underlying representations might arise during phonological development. One particular problem relates to the input to the child. We have been assuming that output is fully specified. Thus, adult input to the child is fully specified. Taking that assumption, the child needs to derive un-

---

that there is as yet no study that has provided perceptual evidence that misperceptions underlie regressions of this sort. We are skeptical that regressions very often have such an etiology.

derspecification in some way. We outline several possibilities, and then give our perspective.

4.12.3.1. Full Specification Changing to Underspecification

Children might initially begin with fully specified feature matrices, taking the adult input at face value (Ingram, 1989c; 1992). During the course of development, predictable features would then be removed from the underlying representations (one feature at a time), until the adult state is reached. Presumably, patterns in the adult phonological system might be used to determine which feature values should be underspecified. For example, if a vowel is epenthetic, or prone to assimilate features from neighboring vowels, or transparent to assimilations, then that vowel could be recognized as the maximally underspecified vowel. All children acquiring a given dialect of a language would be exposed to the same set of adult phenomena, and thus would converge on the same system.

Ingram (1989c, 1992) takes this approach. His arguments against radical underspecification are based on the early two-lexicon approach. He posits underlying representations that are sufficient to account for the phonetic distinctions in the child's own speech, but that fail to make all the distinctions present in the adult input. For example, if all stops are voiced in the child's output, Ingram assumes that the feature [voiced] is not active in the child's representation. Thus, /p/ and /b/ have identical underlying representations, even though the child distinguishes them perceptually.

4.12.3.2. Universal System Changing to Language-Specific (Under)Specification

Children might start out with some universal set of underspecified values. Over the course of development, the errors that arise from using the universal default feature values would be corrected, and different (language-specific) default feature values would be set. In this approach, all children learning all languages would start out with the same underspecified values. However, learners of different languages would rapidly diverge. Learners of the same language, exposed to the same adult data, would end up with the same underspecified values. If the language being learned has no patterns that overtly signal underspecification, then the adult would retain the universal underspecified values (though there would be no surface evidence for those values).

4.12.3.3. Random Underspecified Values Changing to Language-Specific or Person-Specific Underspecification

Alternatively, children might start out with random underspecified values. Half of all children would underspecify [+Feature], and half would underspecify [-Feature]. If the target language includes patterns that signal underspecification, the children who start out with the correct (target) value of underspecification for a feature would simply retain that value. Children who started out with the incorrect value would observe the adult data and eventually change the underspecified value. If the language has no patterns that signal underspecification, then each child would retain the random values with which his/her system started out, and different adults would have different systems.

4.12.3.4. Early Learned Underspecification, Based on Adult Speech

A child could start out with underspecified values derived from some easily observable independent property within the *adult* input. All children would then begin with the same underspecified values as in the adult phonology. The difference in learning between this position and 4.12.3.1 above would be in the nature of the properties that signal underspecification. In the first approach, the child must learn large numbers of words before discovering the adult values. In this approach, in contrast, the information must be observable very early in development, before the onset of meaningful speech production, and possibly even before the onset of speech comprehension. We know that much phonological (perceptual) learning takes place at an early stage (Werker & Lalonde,1988; Kuhl et al., 1992). Underspecification would have a perceptual basis. Default features would be those of the most frequently heard phones in adult speech (Stemberger, 1991a, 1993c).

4.12.3.5. Automatically Derived Underspecification, Based on Child Speech, Changing to Be Based on Adult Speech

All children could begin with underspecification, which derives automatically from some independent property of the *child's* speech, either because of words in the child's lexicon, or because of the child's articulatory or perceptual capacities. In this case, facts about adult speech do not impact on the development of underspecification. In certain cases, the child's underspecified values will match the adults', whether because of chance, or because of universal properties of the vocal tract and perceptual limitations of the speech and hearing mechanism. If the child's underspecified values differ from those of adults, the changes needed to reach adulthood might derive from developmental changes in the child's articulatory, cognitive, and perceptual capacities and in the phonological system. Since the underlying foundation for underspecification is within the child's own speech, the child does not need to spot signals for underspecification in the adult speech. Because different children have different vocal tracts and different phonological systems, underspecified values could vary somewhat from child to child. Maturation of the speech and hearing mechanisms and convergence on the adult phonology may result in convergence on the same underspecified values by adulthood. Since all adults have similar systems, we might expect that all adults would have similar underspecified values, although there may be some variation.

4.12.3.6. A Hybrid Possibility

There may be a hybrid between the positions in §4.12.3.3 and §4.12.3.5. A certain randomness may be prevalent in the babbling and early-words period, with gradual self-organization taking place as a response to both the adult input and the child's own productions. This could account for antifrequency effects in default assignment. Certain phones might be frequent in adult speech, but beyond the child's articulatory capacity in early stages of word production. Where conflicts exist, a child might set up an alternative default, based on his or her own production capacity. Where the production capacity and perceptual basis match, the defaults would be similar to the adult system (see Beers, 1995; Bernhardt & Stoel-Gammon, in press).

4.12.3.7. Development of Underspecification: Our Perspective

In this book, we operate primarily with the perspective in §4.12.3.5, that underspecification derives automatically from an independent principle in the child's speech: phone frequency (see also Stemberger, 1991a, 1992a, 1996c). In order to construct the pronunciation of a word in language production, a speaker must select phonological elements from the full set of elements available to the language. Two important assumptions about the language processing model concern (a) the detailed processes that lead to the selection of the appropriate elements, and (b) the ways in which a speaker learns to select a given set of elements for a particular word. We present first a connectionist and then an OT perspective on the development of underspecification and the effects of phone frequency,

According to a connectionist model, the selection process is made on the basis of activation: the target word activates those elements that are appropriate for that particular word. But noise in the system arises because of activation of other words, either similar words or neighboring ones. If the noise can be inhibited, the target element can become sufficiently highly activated to be produced. The activation levels for the elements of the target word increase with each successful production while activation levels decrease for the competitive elements.

How the speaker learns which elements are appropriate is a different matter. The system just described has built-in biases. Given any input, there will always be an output. The trick is to make sure that the output is the desired pronunciation. On a first attempt at producing a word, the wrong output may result. The speaker then alters the connections between the word and the output units so that next time it will be more likely that the right elements will be selected. Learning is driven by errors: when errors occur, they are corrected. But in a complex system, it is dangerous to make changes in the system when the output is correct. Thus, when the correct output results, no changes are made.

All other things being equal, the system is biased towards the most frequent outputs. Frequent elements have the highest intrinsic activation levels, and so should be selected for output. If they are the correct output, no learning takes place. If a frequent element is erroneously accessed, however, because a low-frequency element should have been selected, then connections between the word and the correct (low-frequency) elements are strengthened. The next time, the correct element will have slightly more activation and will consequently be more likely to win the competition for selection. Over time, the system develops strong connections between words and lower-frequency elements, in order to inhibit the high-frequency ones. In contrast, only weak connections develop between words and high-frequency elements.

This is a psychological instantiation of underspecification. Strong connections between the input word and lower-frequency phonological elements are the implementation of nondefault features. The lack of a strong connection between the input word and the high-frequency output elements is the implementation of underspecification. Underspecification can be viewed, then, as an automatic consequence of the interaction of error-driven learning algorithms and mechanisms which select high-frequency elements by default through *automatic processing principles*, unless lower-frequency competitors are sufficiently activated. Underspecification is intrinsic to the child's system, based on statistical patterns in the child's output. The child does not need to "discover" complex patterns in adult words as is the case with most other hypotheses presented above.

When does underspecification arise, given the frequency effect hypothesis? We know that phone frequencies are established before the first words are produced, during the babbling period. Locke (1983) and Vihman (1992), among many others, have argued for a basic continuity between babbling and early words. Phone frequencies carry over with some modifications between babbling and early words (see §5.2). For most children with typical development, the most frequent consonant during babbling is an anterior coronal stop; thus [Coronal] and [-continuant] should become the underspecified features. These are in fact held to be underspecified values not just for adult English but for many languages (e.g., Paradis & Prunet, 1991b).

Stemberger (1993c), however, points out that vowels may be different from consonants in underspecification development (at least for English). Stemberger (1993c) shows that the maximally underspecified vowel of adult English is /ɛ/, but this is one of the last vowels to be acquired for English-learning children (see §5.6.2). Given that the most frequent vowels in babbling are [a] and [ɑ], the learning process adopted here suggests that low front or central vowels should be the maximally underspecified vowels for very young English-learning children. Loring (1995), reviewing the data on the acquisition of English vowels, argues that this is indeed the case. We then have a change between child and adult phonology for vowel underspecification. How can this change arise? Stemberger (1993c) points out that /ɛ/ is the most frequent stressed vowel in adult English. Once the child masters the entire vowel system, the phone frequencies will change to reflect the frequencies of adult speech. As the frequencies change, the element that wins out by default also changes (because the most frequent feature tends to be selected). The system converges on the adult pattern of (under)specification, because the phone frequencies converge on the adult pattern. The development of vowel underspecification suggests that underspecification may be different at different points in development and for different children. A hybrid position as in §4.12.3.6 (reflecting both child and adult speech influences) may be a more accurate reflection of how underspecification develops for vowels.

This hypothesis about the effects of frequency on the development of defaults

and nondefaults can also be framed within an OT approach, whether full specification or underspecification is assumed. Relative rankings of **Not** and **Survived**
constraints affect assignment of defaults and nondefaults for a phonological system. The higher the frequency, the lower the ranking for **Not(X).** The most frequent output is the default. In §4.6.1, we noted that the **Not** and **Survived** constraints for articulator nodes are ranked in the following way:

Not(Dorsal) ||| **Not(Labial)** ||| **Not(Coronal)**

Survived(Dorsal) ||| **Survived(Labial)** ||| **Survived(Coronal)**

Whether or not [Coronal] is underlying is unimportant, considering the relative
position of constraints affecting that feature. The ranking of the **Not** constraints
leads to [Coronal] being the default, replacing the other articulator nodes when
they are deleted. The ranking of the **Survived** constraints leads to a situation
where dorsal and labial consonants tend not to be involved in place assimilation
(thus violating **Survived**). If full specification is assumed, **Survived** is lowest-
ranked for [Coronal] and hence it is less important for [Coronal] to survive. If we
assume underspecification, the fact that [Coronal] does not have a relevant **Survived** constraint means that the **Survived** constraints for the other features also
result in [Coronal] being the target of assimilation.

Stemberger (1991a) argued that error-driven learning algorithms (as in connectionist models, and many other approaches to learning) lead to the situation where
default features do not require much of a lexical component. According to an OT
perspective, we can derive the rankings of the **Survived** constraints above from
the rankings of the **Not** constraints. Given the ranking of the **Not** constraints, *plus*
the assumption that all the **Survived** constraints are initially ranked lower than
all the **Not** constraints, we would derive a situation in which all nondefault features would be absent from the output, but the default features would be present.
To derive the nondefault features in the output, the **Survived** constraints for the
nondefault features would have to become higher-ranked than those for the default. Since the default features are already correctly produced, the **Survived** constraints for the default features are allowed to remain low-ranked. For the different
nondefault features, the **Survived** constraints must be reranked only as high as is
necessary to be ranked above the relevant **Not** constraint. The rankings given
above arise through the effects of an error-driven learning algorithm.

We suggest that it is possible to empirically test the hypothesis in §4.12.3.5,
which assumes that the child's phone frequencies affect the development of underspecification. To disprove the hypothesis, one needs to show a dissociation
between phone frequency and defaults/nondefaults. Of course we are not sure
whether type frequency or token frequency may be more relevant, or whether frequency in adult speech is more relevant than frequency in child speech/babbling.
One might look at unusual consonant frequency distributions and assimilation
patterns. Stoel-Gammon (1988) reported that hearing-impaired children produce
mostly labial consonants in babbling (rather than the more expected anterior coro-

nal consonants). According to the hypothesis proposed here, [Labial] should then be the underspecified place of articulation. Do hearing-impaired toddlers have unusual assimilation patterns, such as labials consistently assimilating to coronals, or /sp/ rarely being pronounced as [f]? If not, the hypothesis would be weakened. Vowel data may also be revealing. If a child's least frequent vowel behaves like the maximally underspecified vowel, the hypothesis would be disproved. In Chapters 5 and 8, we examine the development of underspecification further with available data.

Throughout this book, we will assume that underspecification derives automatically during development on the basis of phone frequency, and that children may have default values that differ from those of adults.

4.13. CHAIN SHIFTS

OT has inherent difficulties accounting for one very uncommon phenomenon: chain shifts (also known as counterfeeding orders). Hale and Reiss (1995) use chain shifts in child phonology as part of their argument that phonology should not be responsible for the phenomena of child phonology, implying that chain shifts are a dominant characteristic of child phonology. In fact, chain shifts are rare in child phonology—as rare as they are in adult phonology. Given the comprehensive nature of a book such as this, we do report a large proportion of known cases of chain shifts, but we want to emphasize here how uncommon they are.

In a chain shift, underlying A surfaces as B, but underlying B surfaces as C. This is a problem for any theory that motivates alternations via constraints on output. B is clearly possible in the output, since it appears (as the surface realization of A). Why, then, is B impossible as the surface realization of B? What constraints on output could sometimes create B and sometimes destroy B?

Consider the following example from §6.1.6.4.4:

twenty /twʌni/ [sʌni]
swing /swɪŋ/ [fɪn]

Underlying /sw/ fuses into [f] (with the [Labial] of /w/ surviving), but underlying /tw/ fuses into [s] (with the [Labial] deleting). If [Labial] survives (in preference to [Coronal]) in /sw/, why does it not do so in /tw/, especially given that /tw/ surfaces as a fricative [s]? This is a classic chain shift.

One possible way to account for this is to assume complex constraints (Kirchner, 1995; Reiss, 1995). Suppose that it is the /t/ and the /s/ that survive in the output, which pick up [Labial] or [+continuant] from the /w/. Then, the following compound constraint would account for these data:

Survived(continuant-OR-Coronal): Given an underlying coronal, the output must be faithful to either place or manner of articulation.

The cluster /sw/ may surface as [f] because the output is [+continuant] just like the input; this constraint allows unfaithfulness relative to place of articulation. The cluster /tw/, however, cannot change both place and manner of articulation; it could be faithful to manner but not to place ([p]), or it could be faithful to place but not manner ([s]), but it many not be unfaithful to both ([f]).

There are two things that are undesirable about such an analysis. (a) Complex input-to-output correspondence constraints of this sort make the theory so powerful that there is in principle no way to falsify it. It can handle any random pattern that we give to it, whether it is possible within human languages or not. This is a drawback. (b) It may not be able to handle all cases of chain shifts. We return to this topic in §10.2.1.

4.14. SUMMARY AND CONCLUSIONS

Over the past decade, constraints have come to play a larger and larger role in phonological theory, to the point where approaches such as OT use no processes at all. In this chapter, we have presented a set of constraints within OT that can be used to account for most of the phenomena that are encountered in phonology, both in adult languages and in early phonological development in children. The constraint system that we have presented differs somewhat from other proposals in the literature. The differences partly stem from differences of opinion about whether each constraint should be simple and have a single function (our position) or whether constraints should be complex and have multiple functions, with many similar constraints combining functions in slightly different ways (a common position in the literature). In addition, we have attempted to lay out the constraints in a systematic fashion by function, have aimed at completeness, and have given the constraints relatively transparent names that we hope will be easier to remember.

In later chapters, we apply these constraints to phonological development in children. We show how the phenomena of phonological development can be derived using these constraints. In many cases, child phonological patterns that would not be possible in an adult language can nonetheless be analyzed in a straightforward fashion using the same constraints that are needed for adult languages. We believe that this framework provides a more interesting and insightful story of what is going on in language acquisition than previous, process-based, frameworks.

One drawback of OT, however, is that constraint interactions can be complex. There are a large number of constraints, which can interact in many ways. Further, there are a large number of constraints that can be important in leading to a particular characteristic in the output. For example, deletion of a coda segment is accomplished via a violation of **LinkedUpwards(Root)** or **Survived(Root)**, but that violation may be forced by any number of higher-ranked constraints, including **Not(Coda)**, **NotTwice**, **Not**, **NoSequence**, and others. This ambiguity is not a problem for the theory, but in practical terms can cause the researcher problems. The researcher can have difficulty figuring out which constraints are relevant to a given set of data. To make this task easier, Appendix D provides some practical guidelines to use in determining which constraints are involved. These guidelines focus on particular surface phenomena, and list which constraints are certainly involved and which constraints are possibly involved. For the constraints that are possibly involved, we describe the evidence needed to decide which constraints are relevant. Used in conjunction with the detailed descriptions of phonological development in the remaining chapters of this book, we hope that Appendix D will make OT, and the constraint system presented in this chapter, of practical use even for the nonlinguist.

5

SEGMENTAL DEVELOPMENT

5.1. CHAPTER OVERVIEW

Chapter 5 focuses on feature and segmental development, independent of word position or sequence influences. (Word position influences are discussed in Chapter 6, and sequence effects in Chapter 7.) The introductory sections of the chapter present an overview of general developmental trends and research approaches, and a review of relevant constraints and repairs. Consonant and vowel acquisition are then discussed in detail from the perspectives of current theories.

5.2. TRENDS IN SEGMENTAL ACQUISITION

Although variability within and across children is the "norm" for segmental acquisition, there are some general trends. This section gives an overview of those trends as a background for the two major sections that follow, on theoretical approaches and acquisition of specific features.

Frequent phones within a language may be early developing. For example, coronals and stops are frequent in most languages, and they are also common in early inventories. When some phones are not yet produced, substitutions for those phones tend to be from within the child's inventory and the input language inventory (Leonard, 1992; Locke, 1983). For example, when glides are frequent in a language (such as in English), they are common substitutions for liquids, but when glides are infrequent or absent, other substitutions may appear for liquids, such as nasals (in Cantonese), or [ð] (in Spanish). Phones that substitute for other phones also tend to appear as matches to adult targets within a child's system (nasals for nasals, [ð] for /ð/). However, sometimes phones may appear as substitutions even when they do not appear as matches (chain shifts). For example, [θ] may appear for sibilants, at the same time as [f] appears for /θ/. Prosodic constituency is generally respected in substitution patterns: syllabic segments do not tend to replace nonsyllabic ones, or vice versa. Subsections §5.2.1–§5.2.5 outline more specific trends for the various features.

5.2.1. CONSONANT PLACE FEATURES

Major trends for consonant place of articulation are as follows:

1. Early words generally have either labial or coronal consonants or both, across children and language groups. In the first few months of life, velar articulations tend to predominate (due to the effect of the child's supine position on tongue position). As children become more upright, alveolar stops begin to predominate in babbling. At the intersection between babbling and speech, both labials and alveolars are frequent (with variation across children and language groups). (See De Boysson-Bardies et al., 1992; Vihman, 1992, 1996.)

Early features: [Coronal, +anterior]] and/or [Labial]; variability in mastery of [Dorsal].

2. The contrast between (flat) interdental and (grooved) alveolar fricatives is usually established later, as is the contrast between palatoalveolars and alveolars (as late as age 8 or 9).

Later features: [-anterior]; distinction for [grooved]

Again, trends in substitution patterns provide insight into underspecification and constraint rankings, as the following statements about place of articulation demonstrate.

3. Coronals often replace velars, and, less often, labials (except in assimilation patterns, as discussed in §7.4.2).

| /k/ > [t] | Default: Coronal | Fronting |
| /f/ > [s]/[t] | Default: Coronal | Backing; Apicalization |

4. Velars and labials infrequently replace coronals, except in assimilation patterns (see §7.4.2).

| /t/ > [k] | Default: Dorsal | Backing |

The only relatively common labial replacement of a coronal in English is [f] for /θ/.

| /θ/ > [f] | | Labialization |

5. Dorsals and labials seldom substitute for each other (*/k/ > [p], or */p/ > [k]). Nondefaults tend not to replace other nondefaults.

6. Alveolars may replace palatoalveolars or vice versa. Sibilants may vary between the two coronal places of articulation in early development, although alveo-

lars tend to replace palatoalveolars more often than the reverse (Ingram et al., 1980; Stoel-Gammon & Dunn, 1985; Bernhardt, 1990).

| /ʃ/ > [s] | Default: [+anterior] | Depalatalization |
| /s/ > [ʃ] | Default: [-anterior] | Palatalization |

7. Grooved coronal fricatives may replace ungrooved coronal fricatives or vice versa.

| /s/ > [θ] | Default: [-grooved] | Dentalization; Stridency Deletion |
| /θ/ > [s] | Default: [+grooved] | Apicalization |

5.2.2. CONSONANT LARYNGEAL FEATURES

The development of voicing features varies across language groups, word positions, and children (Stoel-Gammon & Dunn, 1985). Voicing substitution patterns often appear to reflect word position and language Voice Onset Time (VOT) differences.

Glottal stops and [h] appear in the babbling and early words of many children, even if they are not in the target language (De Boysson-Bardies et al., 1992; Lleó et al., 1996).

Early features: [+c.g.] and [+s.g.]

5.2.3. CONSONANT MANNER FEATURES

Major trends in manner are as follows:

1. Early inventories have a high frequency of stops, nasals and glides.

Early features: [-continuant], [+nasal]; both values of [consonantal] & [sonorant]

2. Fricatives and liquids tend to be mastered later (up to age 8 or 9), although particular members of those classes may appear in early inventories.

Later features or combinations:	[+lateral];
	[-son,+cont] (for fricatives);
	[Labial,Coronal,-consonantal] (for /ɹ/)

Trends in substitution patterns provide insight into status of features as defaults or nondefaults, and relative rankings of constraints, as the following statements show.

3. Stops may replace all other sound classes, although they are most likely to replace other obstruents (fricatives and affricates).

/z/ > [d]	Default: [-continuant]
/l/ > [d]	Defaults: [-continuant], [-sonorant]
	Stopping; Stridency Deletion; Delateralization

The fact that stops more commonly replace obstruents than sonorants shows faithfulness to values of [sonorant].

4. Oral stops are more likely to replace nasals than the reverse (given normal hearing and a normal oral mechanisms).

/m/ > [b]   *Default*: [-nasal]   Denasalization

The higher frequency of oral segments suggests that [+nasal] is a nondefault feature. Defaults tend to replace nondefaults. When children are unable to distinguish nasals and nonnasals perceptually, or in production, the default may be [+nasal]. (See §8.5.2.1.)

5. Glides and nasals are more likely to replace liquids than obstruents. Again, the sonority distinction is often respected in substitution patterns, with some exceptions. Glottal stops and glides sometimes serve as default onsets or codas, replacing a variety of segments. The glottal (glide?) [h] replaces fricatives more often than liquids or nasals, suggesting stronger ties between [+s.g.] and [+continuant] than between [+s.g.] and [+sonorant].

/l/ > [n]	Default: [+sonorant] (or [+nasal]?)	Nasalization, Delateralization
/l/ > [j], [w]	Default: V-Place	Gliding
/s/ > [h]	Default: [+spread-glottis]	Backing

5.2.4. FEATURE CO-OCCURRENCE IN CONSONANTS

In the previous sections, we focused on individual features. But segments are composed of varying numbers of manner, place, and laryngeal features. During the developmental process, a new feature may combine with all previously established features in the same time period (in an across-the-board fashion), or with only a subset of currently available features. For example, if a child produces labial and coronal voiced and voiceless stops, and then begins to combine [+continuant] with place and voicing features, all fricatives may appear within a very short time period, or they may appear one by one (i.e., first [s], then [f], then [z], etc.).

If two or more features cannot co-occur, elimination of one resolves the constraint (minimally). For example, if a child cannot produce a voiced labiodental fricative [v], eliminating one feature ([+continuant], or [+voice], or [Labial]) solves the problem. Sometimes, however, more than one of the features is eliminated (a nonminimal repair). Segments with multiple nondefault features may be more vulnerable in this regard. For example,

1. The most common stop replacements for coronal fricatives are coronal stops, but labial *or* coronal stops may replace /f/ and /v/, even if labial stops are

in the system. (Ingram, 1989b, labels the process "tetism.") Both nondefault features [Labial] and [+continuant] are lost, even though loss of [+continuant] alone would resolve the violation of **NotCo-occurring(-son, +cont)**. This nonminimal repair is a type of "parasitic" delinking (i.e., if one nondefault feature cannot be produced, the other is eliminated also).

2. Coronal and labial stops and nasals appear to be less likely than /k/ to lose both place and manner features.

e.g.,	/b/ > [p], [v], [w], [m], [d]
	/n/ > [d], [t], [j], [l], [m]
BUT:	/k/ > [g], [t], [s], [h]

Thus, /b/ is not likely to surface as [z], nor /n/ as [p]. Either the place or manner feature changes, but not both. For /k/, the later acquired place feature may change on its own ([t] for /k/) but a multiple feature change may occur, given the effects of **Not(Dorsal)**.

3. Liquids appear to replace fricatives more often than the reverse (although both patterns occur).

Because [+sonorant] is redundantly [+continuant], faithfulness constraints for [+continuant] can be obeyed by changing [-sonorant] to [+sonorant]. (Note: [l] appears more often than [ɹ] as a fricative substitution, possibly because [ɹ] has multiple place features or because both /l/ and fricatives are [+consonantal].)

5.2.5. VOWELS

Vowels tend to develop early, although some mid vowels and diphthongs (and, for some children, round vowels) may be acquired later (Otomo & Stoel-Gammon, 1992). Vowel substitutions are fairly variable, although centralization and lowering of vowels are possibly most common. Data are insufficient to comment further on general trends.

Acquisition of tone depends somewhat on the language type. In a combined cross-sectional, longitudinal study of Cantonese acquisition, So and Dodd (1995) noted accurate use of tone by age 2. This accords with previous research on tone in languages which have primarily lexical tone (see Clumeck, 1980, for a review). However, Demuth (1993) suggests that tone may be slower to develop in languages where tone is grammatical, in which surface and underlying tones are different (as in Bantu languages).

The asymmetries in substitution patterns and the trends in feature development support the concept of feature dependencies, similarities, and differences. There is usually some systematic way to account for differences between the adult target and the child substitution that respects the feature's status in the hierarchy, and its default or nondefault value. We return to this discussion throughout the chapter. With this overview of trends as a background, we turn now to research perspectives on segmental acquisition.

5.3. RESEARCH PERSPECTIVES

Linguistic theories have provided a rich basis for interpretation of developmental data in the past three decades. Many authors have proposed accounts of feature and segmental development. Here we provide an overview of those perspectives, finishing with a description of our own views and assumptions for the data sections that follow.

5.3.1. THEORETICAL PERSPECTIVES

One major enterprise has been the prediction of the order in which features and segments are acquired, based on the implications of various theories. This approach began with Jakobson's deterministic proposals (1968/1941) and continues with Ingram (1988a), Dinnsen (1992), Levelt (1994), and Beers (1995), among others. Jakobson hypothesized that acquisition should proceed in a consistent predictable order motivated by a principle of developing contrasts and "laws of irreversible solidarity" based on the distribution of features crosslinguistically (implicational universals). Phonemes that are rare across adult languages should appear late in acquisition. The child should begin the acquisition process with maximal feature/segment contrasts (C versus V), moving gradually to more and more refined oppositions. Although more recent researchers have deviated somewhat from Jakobson's views, this general approach continues. This perspective minimizes the importance of individual variation, a problem identified and discussed by many (e.g., Ferguson & Farwell, 1975; Macken & Ferguson, 1983; Menn, 1978, 1983; Stemberger, 1992a). The problem of individual variation is one caveat for the deterministic perspective. We focus here on other aspects of that approach.

Feature classification systems and assumptions about organizational relationships among features influence types of predictions made, as we discuss below.

5.3.1.1. Feature Classification

Features have been classified in various ways, as acoustic versus articulatory, binary versus privative, default versus nondefault, contrasting versus noncontrasting, distinctive versus nondistinctive, marked versus unmarked, ordered versus unordered, and so on. (See Chapter 3.) Different predictions are made for developmental sequence, depending on which of these classifications or combination of classifications are adopted. We discuss issues with respect to current feature systems in §5.3.1.2, and concentrate here on general issues in classification regarding specification, contrast, and markedness.

Different approaches to the representation of features and segments have been taken, from full specification to some version of underspecification, which may be more or less universal in scope. Underspecification and segmental complexity differences could imply (a) earlier acquisition of segments with fewer (nondefault) features, because they are less complex, and/or (b) later acquisition of segments with nondefault features (particularly multiple nondefault features), because of the early low ranking of faithfulness constraints for nondefault features. This appears to be generally true: segments with multiple default features (such as /t/) are generally established earlier than segments with multiple nondefault features (such as /ɹ/ or /v/). But to what degree are these predictions true? Bernhardt (1990, 1994c) and Gierut (1996) tested predictions relative to feature co-occurrence with children receiving phonological intervention. In Gierut's study, children acquired voiceless and voiced cognates in sequence rather than simultaneously (i.e., [f] before [v], or [s] before [z]). However, in the Bernhardt studies, some children acquired a new place or manner distinction across both voiced and voiceless cognates simultaneously, even when only one of the cognate pair was an intervention target. Thus, additive complexity is not always predictive of acquisition order.

Tied to the concept of specification is the issue of contrast. Is a feature established when a child uses segments with that feature, or is a feature established only when a child produces segments with contrasting features or feature values? Jakobson (1968/1941) initiated this discussion, stating predictions for order of acquisition in terms of oppositions or contrasts:

First contrast:	Consonant/vowel
	"Narrow" front consonants vs. "wide" back vowels: /pɑ/
Consonant contrasts:	(1st) Oral vs. nasal,
	(2nd) Labial vs. dental.
Vowel contrasts:	(1st) "Narrow" vs. "wide vowels": /i/ vs. /ɑ/,
	(2nd) front versus back; or, alternatively, mid vs. narrow-wide.

A number of developmental phonologists take a similar perspective regarding contrast (e.g., Dinnsen, 1992; Ingram, 1992; Dresher, Piggott & Rice, 1994; Beers, 1995; Rice, 1996). To illustrate, if nasals are acquired before other sonorant consonants, nasals are then classified as [+sonorant] rather than as [+nasal]; the relevant contrast at that point in development is between sonorants ([+sonorant]) and obstruents ([-sonorant]). Only when other sonorant consonants appear are nasals classified as [+nasal]. Rice (1996:12) asserts that this perspective minimizes the relevance of individual variation in order of acquisition:

> The global uniformity in the acquisition sequence across languages is met phonologically by hierarchies and a learning path that depends on the elaboration of structure under the pressure of contrasts. The local variability is met both phonologically and phonetically. Phonologically, an identical phonetic sound may have different representations depending on what it contrasts with. . . . Phonetically, local variability arises because of choices in enhancement. [Enhancement increases the salience of a phone through the addition of redundant phonetic features. See Stevens & Keyser, 1989.]

Such claims depend critically on a strong distinction between (lower level) phonetics and (higher level) abstract phonology. But the more abstract the concept, the more difficult it is to test empirically.

Not all researchers assume that the notion of feature *contrast* is integral to feature specification (e.g., Bernhardt, 1990; Chin, 1993; Stemberger, 1993a; Stoel-Gammon, 1993). Defaults are assumed to be present from early phases of development. When nondefaults become established, they are added to the pool of available features. Eventually, two values of a feature can be considered contrastive, but the contrast does not have to be present for one value of the feature to be considered active in the system. Taking the example of [nasal], if nasals are produced, they are considered to be [+nasal]. If nasals *replace* other sonorants, the feature [+nasal] may be considered a *predictable feature* until such time as other sonorants appear, but it is nonetheless present in the output. Its substantive properties do not change, although its default or nondefault status may. (See §4.12.3, regarding development of underspecification.)

The radical or default underspecification perspectives need not crucially include a notion of contrast, although a notion of feature distinctiveness may be assumed. Two sound classes may have the same value for a feature, but the feature may be contrastive for only one of those sounds classes. For example, fricatives and vowels are both [+continuant], but the feature [+continuant] is *contrastive* only for consonants. Similarly, a feature may be contrastive word finally but not word initially. Rime or margin constraints may affect feature specification status; see §6.1.12.4. (See also Dinnsen, 1996.)

Often allied with the theories of specification and feature contrast is the theory of markedness. Markedness is variably defined, in terms of frequency across adult languages, or acquisition patterns, or relative structural complexity of compared units. Jakobson (1968/1941) used adult languages as a basis for making markedness predictions about developmental sequence. He predicted that universally unmarked segments should appear developmentally earlier than marked segments, should substitute for them, and should be more frequent triggers of assimilation. He also proposed a number of implicational universals based on markedness.

1. Fricatives imply earlier acquisition of stops.
2. If only one fricative is present, it will be /s/.
3. Affricates imply an earlier fricative-stop contrast at the same place of articulation.
4. Back sounds imply earlier acquisition of front sounds.
5. Voiced obstruents imply earlier acquisition of voiceless obstruents.
6. Rounded front vowels imply earlier acquisition of unrounded front vowels.

Developmental data show trends in these directions, but *not* invariant patterns. For example, Mowrer and Burger (1991) note early acquisition of supposedly marked clicks and ejectives in Xhosa. "Unmarked" segments may be relatively more frequent (as matches and substitutions) in early inventories, but marked segments tend to have greater assimilatory power when they enter the system (Stemberger & Stoel-Gammon, 1991). Frequency in a language may be more relevant than a theory of universal markedness for at least some predictions regarding developmental sequence (see Pye et al., 1987; Ingram, 1988b).

The variety of perspectives on specification, contrast, and markedness provides an opportunity to test different predictions for order of acquisition. Most comparisons remain to be done systematically, however. This is also true for classification of features in terms of current geometric models.

5.3.1.2. Feature Organization and Position in the Feature Geometry

Current feature descriptions suggest that features are both autonomous and hierarchically organized. Various researchers have tested or adopted one or more of these aspects of current theory in the attempt to predict order of acquisition, with mixed results (e.g., Bernhardt, 1990; Dinnsen, 1992; Chin, 1993; Beers, 1995; Gierut, 1995; Rice, 1996).

One of the principles of multilinear theory is the autosegmental (independent) natures of features (feature autonomy). Feature autonomy could imply any number of random possibilities for developmental order of features. The noted variability in development does suggest that autonomy is a strong characteristic of features. However, the observable trends in acquisition suggest equally that unrestricted feature autonomy is unlikely.

Hierarchical organization of features could imply earlier acquisition of higher level (less embedded) features, because of their more general application (higher frequency) across phonological systems. For example, a high-level Root node feature such as [+continuant] refers to vowels, liquids, glides, and fricatives, whereas terminal place features such as [-anterior] or [+round] refer to a more restricted set of segments.

Determination of feature height is not straightforward, however. Different types of geometries may imply different heights. For example, if a Supralaryngeal (SL) node mediates Root and Place, and [+continuant] is considered a Root node feature, then [+continuant] is closer to the Root (higher) than C-Place. But if there is no SL node, can we say that [+continuant] is higher than Place (closer to the Root)? Both [+continuant] and Place link directly to the Root in the geometry we use here, yet they are different *types* of elements in the geometry. Place is an organizing node, and [+continuant] is a feature with phonetic content. Does type of element (organizing node or content feature) matter in addition to height? Does it matter whether the feature is binary or privative? Does it matter whether a feature is a default or a nondefault? To give another example with place features, the standard geometry assumes that all articulator features are at the same level (see §3.4). Place features are distinguished in terms of their default/nondefault status ([Coronal] being the default), but this distinction is not built into the geometry itself. Rice and Avery (1995), on the other hand, do build the default/nondefault distinction into the geometry. (See Figure 5.1.)

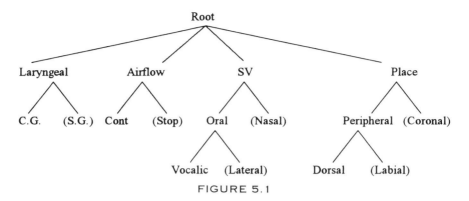

FIGURE 5.1

Coronal is considered the highest place feature (as the default feature of Place). Coronal contrasts with Peripheral, a node which dominates both Labial (the default peripheral feature) and Dorsal (the nondefault peripheral feature).

If one's theory of feature acquisition assumes that position in the geometry is the only relevant predictor for order of acquisition, one might expect an order of (highest-level) Coronal before Labial before (lowest-level) Dorsal based on this geometry. Velars often become established after labials and coronals, which gives some credence to the general height prediction based on the structure of this geometry. But some children acquire dorsals and labials before coronals (see Colin, §8.3), and hence a structure-based prediction is not borne out universally. (Note that Rice and Avery, 1995, build a notion of contrast into the geometry. Coronal is established only when it contrasts with Labial, etc. Hence, actual predictions about feature order based on their conceptualization of the geometry would crucially need to include the notion of contrast. Here we merely illustrate a structure-based prediction approach.)

Studies based on structure of the geometry have had mixed results. Bernhardt (1990) and Beers (1995) hypothesized that higher-level features might be established earlier, because they are less embedded in the geometry. Some children in their studies did master higher-level features first, but this was not the case for all subjects. Stoel-Gammon's (1993) study of the first 10 words of 55 English-speaking children had a similar outcome. Only six children had more higher (manner) features than lower (place) features in their words. Thus, for some children, lower-level features appear to be established first. This might follow from a prediction that higher-level nodes (i.e., Root) take longer to elaborate than lower ones, because most higher-level features have to combine with a number of features at lower levels. In other words, *both* height *and* feature co-occurrence might be relevant for order of acquisition. Chin (1993) comments in this vein that simple inventories have more place (lower-level features) than manner features. The Stoel-Gammon (1993) results show that some children (6/55) have more manner than place features at first, however, disconfirming the alternate prediction as universal.

Combining concepts from current theory, it might also be predicted that hierarchical organization, feature co-occurrence, and default status could be mutually influential in determining order of acquisition. For example, nondefaults at higher levels might combine with lower-level defaults before they combine with lower-level nondefaults. We might predict the acquisition of /s/ before /f/: the higher-level nondefault feature [+continuant] might combine earlier with the lower-level default feature, [Coronal], than with the lower-level nondefault feature, [Labial]. However, [f] sometimes precedes [s] in development, and thus this prediction is not upheld universally.

5.3.2. EMPIRICAL TESTING
OF DEVELOPMENTAL PREDICTIONS

As we have seen, a number of theoretical issues have to be considered before predicting developmental sequence or explaining trends in accordance with existing theories. Even if one adopts a particular and well-defined stance towards the theories, and makes all of one's assumptions explicit, testing of the theories is not a straightforward task.

Methodology in the behavioral sciences requires careful sampling procedures that pay attention to sample size and representativeness (in terms of socioeconomic status, cultural groups, age and gender, etc.), and replicability of results. Phonological acquisition studies tend to have large-sample cross-sectional designs, or very-small-sample longitudinal designs. The first gives large numbers, but limited information on individual patterns. Longitudinal designs may give details of individual development, but replicability is compromised. Even with larger samples, subgroupings may result in extremely limited numbers in one or more groups. For example, Dinnsen's (1992) study used data from 40 subjects (a large sample for phonological acquisition research). He argues for five levels of complexity (developmental "stages") for feature systems. However, the first and second levels are based on data from one subject each, reducing the reliability and validity of those levels in comparison to the others. Phonological acquisition research needs more longitudinal data from many more subjects.

Beyond subject number and type, other methodological factors can affect our interpretation of developmental trends. Data collection methods (e.g., single words versus conversational samples) and data analysis techniques (narrowness and reliability of phonetic transcription, phonological analysis, and instrumental measurement) can produce different outcomes (Shriberg & Lof, 1991; Morrison & Shriberg, 1992). How selective can we be about data collection and analysis methods? What is the best indicator that something is "acquired": emergence, partial mastery (75%–90%), mastery in one word position, or all of these?

Research methods vary significantly across studies, making comparability difficult. Even when similar investigations are conducted, different interpretations may be made of the same framework. For example, Beers (1995) followed Dinnsen's (1992) five-level model (of degree of complexity) for a study of Dutch acquisition. She included all features in assigning levels, including [Dorsal]. However, Dinnsen (1992) used only manner and voicing features, because he found the feature [Dorsal] too variable. (Some children acquired dorsals early, and some acquired it late.) This difference makes it difficult to compare Dinnsen's and Beers's studies.

In sum, before we can draw any inferences from data, we need to know how the data were collected and analyzed, and what data were considered relevant. (For a detailed review of methodological considerations in acquisition research, see Ingram, 1989a.) Assuming that theoretical assumptions are made explicit at the outset, and the data collected and analyzed in a well-motivated, systematic way, what conclusions can be reached at the end? We have little data beyond what the child can produce (and, within certain experimental bounds, perceive). What do we do with equivocal results? In Beers (1995), 80% of the subjects followed an order of feature acquisition predicted on the basis of feature geometry, acquisition factors, and Dutch phonology. But 20% of the children showed a different order. If a set of predictions is upheld probabilistically, what do we do with the data that do not fit: abandon one or more of the theories which led to the assumptions, redesign the experimental methods, alter the theory to account for the data, or abandon the notion of developmental prediction and explanation?

We promote the enterprise of theory application but caution that there is a difference between necessary predictions and mere possibilities. Many of the possibilities have not worked out across children. Feature hierarchies and feature co-occurrence are less predictive for developmental order than feature autonomy and underspecification. That is not to say that they are not relevant and useful in the study of phonological acquisition. We suggest that their relevance is more in the description and explanation of developmental phenomena that concern segments rather than in the prediction of acquisition order. In the next section, we review other key assumptions for this chapter.

5.3.3. ASSUMPTIONS REGARDING FEATURE ACQUISITION

The following key views serve as a foundation for this chapter:

1. Segments are composed of combinations of hierarchically organized autonomous features (see §3.4).

2. Features can be specified in underlying representations (nondefault) or unspecified (default). Default underspecification is assumed. Default values within a given child's phonological system may be different from those of the target language. (See §4.12.3 for a discussion of developmental predictions about underspecification.)

3. Learning is both error-driven and additive (see §4.12.1).

4. Phenomena reflect constraints on output, and developmental changes reflect changes in the rankings of constraints (see §4.12.1).

5. Repair strategies are useful descriptions of accommodations to constraints, but we do not attribute psychological reality to them; rather, they are an emergent property of the constraint rankings (see §4.2).

5.4. REVIEW OF FEATURE CONSTRAINTS

Primary constraints that directly concern feature and segmental development (independent of environment) are:

Not(Feature)
NotCo-occurring(FeatureA,FeatureB)
Survived(Feature)
LinkedUpwards(Feature)

If constraints are high ranked, feature production is restricted. Low-ranked constraints allow production of features or feature combinations (and often refer to default features). High ranking of faithfulness (**Survived**) constraints promote realization of the nondefault features. In early development, constraints are often high ranked; only default features are possible. Over time, the child's production capacity becomes refined, and more individual features and feature combinations can be realized. Faithfulness constraints for nondefault features are promoted, and the **Not(Nondefault)** and **NotCo-occurring(Nondefault, Nondefault)** constraints are demoted (ranked lower than faithfulness constraints). (See §4.12.1.)

Repairs involve: (a) deletion of features or feature links, and (b) insertion of default features, or links between features (assimilation or spreading). Repairs can be minimal (at the level of the feature) or nonminimal (at the level of C-Place, Root, or Timing Unit). (See §3.4.) During feature development, the majority of repairs appear to be feature-changing (minimal repairs).

The following constraint ranking describes Velar Fronting:

Survived/LinkedUpwards(C-TimingUnit)	**Survived/LinkedUpwards(C-Dorsal)**
Survived/LinkedUpwards(C-Root)	**Not(C-Coronal)**
Survived/LinkedUpwards(C-Place)	
Not(C-Dorsal)	

A true consonant must be produced (high ranking of the faithfulness constraints for C-Place, C-Root, and C-Timing Unit). However, dorsal consonants are not allowed (high ranking of **Not(C-Dorsal)**). The nondefault feature [C-Dorsal] deletes, and the default place feature [C-Coronal] is inserted and links up. (See §3.4.2 for a formal description of the repair process.)

The remainder of the chapter describes feature and segmental development. For consonants, the feature hierarchy (see §3.4) serves as an organizing framework for discussion. Vowel development is examined from the perspectives of different theories for vowel features. In each of the data subsections, we first present general trends in inventory development, and then compare adult targets and children's accommodations to those targets. We have not listed and discussed every possible developmental pattern, but have attempted to include the common patterns and several uncommon ones, based on available data. Data are drawn from a number of different children's corpora in order to provide information about a wide range of phenomena.

5.5. CONSONANT DEVELOPMENT

Our discussion of consonants is organized in terms of feature geometry. We examine developmental trends, constraints and repairs in turn for individual place, laryngeal and manner features, and for various feature combinations (co-occurrences). (Note: Nonminimal repairs involving deletion of prosodic constituents are not described here, but rather in Chapters 6 and 7.)

5.5.1. PLACE OF ARTICULATION

Segments containing major articulator features ([Labial], [Coronal], [Dorsal]) can be found in very early development. In Stoel-Gammon's (1993) study of children's first ten words, 48/55 children showed evidence of two or more places of articulation, with 24 children having all three places of articulation. On the other hand, contrasts for terminal place features ([anterior], [grooved], [distributed]) tend to be established later (Smit et al., 1990; Dinnsen, 1992).

Table 5.1 summarizes recent longitudinal studies of babbling and early words. Labials and coronals are generally established earlier than velars. If both labials

TABLE 5.1.   Place Features in Babbling and Early Words

Studies	Language, *n*	Labial	Coronal	Dorsal
De Boysson-Bardies et al., 1992; Vihman, 1992	American English: 10 French: 5 Japanese: 5 Swedish: 5	Lab highest (%): French: 5 English: 5 10% increase: Early words[b]	[da] most frequent σ: For all but 5 Eng. Ss.[a] Highest %: Swed., Jap.[b]	Velars low overall (%) Highest (%): Sweden, Japan (Dors = Lab)
Lleó et al., 1996	Spanish: 4 German: 5	Lab most: Spanish: 4 German: 1	Cor most: German: 4	Lowest % in both Spanish: Higher %[b]
Stoel-Gammon, 1993	American English: 55	Lab only: 5 Labials: 53	Cor only: 2 Coronals: 50	Dors only: 0 Dors, Cor only: 2 Dors, Lab only: 2 Dors used:

Note: Numbers = number of subjects

[a] Vihman comments: "Within-language differences seem to be as great as across-language differences . . . [in terms of] practised syllables" (1992:398).

[b] Reflects frequency in the target words of the language

and coronals are produced, their relative frequencies appear to vary across children and languages. For example, Lleó et al. (1996) report a higher proportion of labials in the speech of one of five German-learning subjects and all four Spanish-learning subjects. De Boysson-Bardies et al. (1992) note that 10 English-learning and five French-learning infants produced more labials than coronals. The target words in those languages also contained more labials. The Japanese infants, on the other hand, produced more dentals, also more frequent in target words. Neither [Labial] nor [Coronal] are strongly confirmed, therefore, as universal default places of articulation. [Dorsal] is the least likely default place feature in babbling and early words. (Velars are usually frequent during cooing in the first 3–6 months of life, but diminish or disappear in babbling after children become capable of sitting [Vihman, 1996].) Some children do use velars, but rarely exclusively, and velars may be particularly late for at least a portion of children with phonological disorders (Dinnsen, 1992; Bernhardt, 1990).

The data from the various studies demonstrate early emergence of more than one place and manner feature, and leave us uncertain as to whether there is a single (universal) default (as we discussed earlier).

Constraints on place of articulation can affect one or more sound classes. The comments on order of place acquisition made above apply primarily to stops and nasals. For fricatives, order of acquisition of place features may differ from that of stops, as we see when we discuss feature co-occurrence constraints. We now proceed to a detailed discussion of C-Place constraints and repairs, first for major articulator nodes, then for terminal features of [Coronal] and [Labial], and finally, for segments with two places of articulation (such as glides and clicks). In the following examples, constraints primarily concern individual features. Occasionally, for clarity and completeness, we refer to co-occurrence constraints on syllable position or between features. However, the major discussion of feature co-occurrence constraints is presented at the end of the consonant section §5.5.4. (See §6.1.12 regarding positional co-occurrence constraints.)

5.5.1.1. Major Articulator Constraints and Repairs

In §5.4, we gave a constraint ranking for the most typical constraint regarding place of articulation: Velar Fronting, which is the prohibition of a nondefault feature ([Dorsal]) and insertion of a default feature ([Coronal]). The example given was for a velar stop, but velar nasals and fricatives may show similar constraints and repairs. In Dutch, /x/ can be replaced with other more common "front" fricatives such as [f] or [s], as Beers (1991) shows:

/xat/   [fat]/[sat]   'goes'

(Replacement of /x/ with [f] is interesting, in that velars and labials usually do not replace each other. We do not know how common this exchange is in Dutch, or whether it just applies to fricatives, but note that it is a possible example of nondefault feature insertion. See the discussion of [f] for /θ/ in §5.5.1.2.)

A similar, but less common, pattern involves insertion of Coronal for Labial, most often seen for labiodental fricatives (/f/ > [s], or /f/ > [t]). Co-occurrence constraints are often operative in such cases, and hence, we return to this in §5.5.4.3.

Children do not always have the expected defaults. [Labial] or [Dorsal] may be the most common place feature, both in inventory and substitutions. We noted earlier the prevalence of labial substitutions in the speech of a deaf child, Dora (see also §8.5.3). Colin (§8.3) had a [Dorsal] default. In these cases, **Not(Coronal)** is higher-ranked than **Not(Dorsal)** or **Not(Labial)**, depending on which is the default. The following ranking creates a velar default:

Not(Labial)
Not(Coronal)   ⫾⫾⫾   **Not(Dorsal)**

Repairs involving place feature constraints are not always minimal. C-Place or the Root node can be delinked, with a default segment such as a glottal or a coronal stop arising. (Examples are discussed in §5.5.4.)

5.5.1.2. Terminal Features of [Coronal]: Overview

Coronal segments are produced from the alveolar ridge forward ([+anterior]) or between the alveolar ridge and midpalate region ([−anterior]). They may be grooved or ungrooved, and distributed or nondistributed. Generally, the features [+anterior], [−grooved], and [−distributed] are the system default values. However, [s] is the least marked coronal fricative, and it is [+grooved]. The constraint **Co-occurring(Coronal, + cont,-son→ + grooved)** is high-ranked, and so coronal fricatives are generally [+grooved].

Most children produce coronals as dentals ([+distributed]) rather than alveolars ([-distributed]). This may have an anatomical or functional basis. A child's tongue is large in comparison to the size of the oral cavity. Children (and some adults) also can have a forward resting tongue position and tongue-thrusting swallowing pattern (Laver, 1994), predisposing them to dental articulation of coronals. The dental fricative articulations may be grooved (as in adult Swedish) or ungrooved (as in adult English). The following section focuses on the terminal place features of coronal fricatives, because they contrast on all features of [Coronal] in adult English. However, we reiterate that all coronals may be produced farther forward than in adult speech. (Note also that because this section concerns place, we assume that fricatives are produced as fricatives.)

In this book we assume an articulatory feature [grooved] rather than the acoustic feature [+strident] of Chomsky and Halle (1968). In this section we address phenomena that could be viewed as evidence for [strident] rather than [grooved] (for some children).

5.5.1.2.1. [grooved] and [strident]

Two general issues arise in the treatment of sibilant fricatives in child phonology: whether children can vary in terms of what the defaults are, and whether features can be defined differently for different children (or, indeed, for different adult languages). English provides interesting data of relevance, because there is a place contrast between anterior coronal fricatives: strident /s/ (and /z/) versus nonstrident /θ/ (and /ð/). Examining the substitution patterns for these fricatives allows us to address these two issues. (Children may also neutralize the contrast between palatoalveolars and the other sibilants or between /f/ and /s/, and/or may show different substitution patterns for /θ/ versus /ð/. We assume in this section that /f/ surfaces as [f], and examine additional patterns in subsequent sections.)

Four common patterns of acquisition for the features [grooved] (or [strident]) are examined below, for the period in which fricatives are realized as fricatives. (The literature does not allow us to determine which of the patterns are the most prevalent.) For purposes of illustration, the patterns are addressed only in terms of the voiceless fricatives /s/, /θ/, and /f/. Voiced fricatives and palatoalveolars can also surface as ungrooved, and similar constraint rankings would apply. (Voiced fricatives often show in addition the effects of co-occurrence constraints concerning [+voiced] and [+continuant], as we discuss in §5.5.4.2. Palatoalveolars often surface as ungrooved [θ] or [ð].)

Pattern 1:	/s/ [s]	
	/θ/ [s]	Apicalization of /θ/
	/f/ [f]	
Pattern 2:	/s/ [θ]	Dentalization of /s/
	/θ/ [θ]	
	/f/ [f]	
Pattern 3:	/s/ [s]	
	/θ/ [f]	Labialization of /θ/
	/f/ [f]	
Pattern 4:	/s/ [θ]	Dentalization of /s/
	/θ/ [f]	Labialization of /θ/
	/f/ [f]	

(For data relevant to Pattern 4 which concerns alveolars and palatoalveolars, see §8.5.1.1.)

Analyses of the four patterns differ, depending on whether we assume radical underspecification or full specification. Full specification of course assumes that all the segments are specified for their major and terminal place features. Radical underspecification might assume the following:

/s/:	No underlying place features
/θ/:	[Coronal,-grooved] underlying
/f/:	[Labial] underlying

Constraint rankings needed to derive these patterns are the same regardless of specification. The analyses differ only in terms of whether the default features are underlying or inserted.

Patterns 1 and 2 are perhaps more straightforward because all of the fricatives are faithful to the underlying articulator node: [Coronal] or [Labial]. Coronal fricatives must be [+grooved] in the output.

Pattern 1: /s/ and /θ/ as [s]   As we noted above, the default value of [grooved] is assumed to be [-grooved], because coronal stops, nasals, and /l/ are ungrooved (Laver, 1994). Thus, **Not(-grooved)** is low-ranked. However, /s/ is [+grooved] because a high-ranked co-occurrence constraint requires coronal fricatives to be grooved. **Not** constraints for [+anterior] and [Coronal] are low-ranked, allowing insertion of default place for [s]. /θ/ surfaces as an anterior coronal (either because it is underlyingly [+anterior] or because [+anterior] is the default), but it cannot surface as [-grooved], because of the high ranking of the co-occurrence constraint. As a result, [+grooved] is inserted, and /θ/ surfaces as [s]. Additionally, **Survived(Labial)** is high-ranked, and /f/ surfaces as [f].

Co-occurring(Coronal, + cont,-son→ + grooved)
Survived(Labial)

Not(+ grooved)

Not(-grooved)
Not(Coronal)
Not(+ anterior)

Pattern 2: /s/ and /θ/ as [θ].   The ranking for Pattern 2 differs only in that the co-occurrence constraint is not high ranked. As a result, /s/ surfaces with the default value [-grooved], as does /θ/: [θ]. /f/ surfaces as [f].

Survived(Labial)
Not(+ grooved)

Co-occurring(Coronal, + cont,-son→-grooved)

Not(-grooved)
Not(Coronal)
Not(+ anterior)

Patterns 3 and 4 cannot be derived the same way as Patterns 1 and 2. We have to differentiate between /s/ and /θ/, because /s/ surfaces as a coronal, and /θ/ surfaces as a labial. Here the data raise the issues of what the features are and how they are specified. We first present alternative analyses for Pattern 3, then show how the second solution is problematical for Pattern 4, finally explaining how the third analysis accounts for both patterns.

Pattern 3: /s/ as /s/; [θ] as [f].

ANALYSIS 1   If /θ/ does not surface as a coronal, but /s/ is [s], one assumption is that there is a nonminimal repair involving a problem with an *underlying* [-grooved] feature. High ranking of **Survived(-grooved)** requires [-grooved] to survive and link upwards. However, the high ranking of the co-occurrence constraint makes this faithfulness a problem. Both constraints can be satisfied if [Coronal] delinks. This leaves the consonant with no articulator node, and thus one must be supplied: [Labial].

LinkedDownwards(C-Place)
Survived/LinkedUpwards(-grooved)
Co-occurring(Coronal, + cont,-son→ + grooved)

LinkedUpwards(Coronal)

Not(Labial)

Not(Coronal)

Inserting [Labial] as a default is problematical, however, if [Coronal, +anterior] is supposed to be the default place. We cannot account for this with full specification and the features that we are using here.

ANALYSIS 2   A more adequate solution is one that questions the motivation behind the substitution of [f] for /θ/. The segments [f] and [θ] are perceptually very similar and easily confused. Vellemann (1988) argues that children who make this substitution often do not perceive the difference. In some instances, we know that they do perceive the differences, but we could still argue that the substitution is not *phonologically* motivated but rather *perceptually* motivated: the child is attempting to match some aspect of the acoustic signal. Although this issue can be couched in terms of perception, it can equally well be couched in terms of the definitions of features. We assumed in the first analysis that the contrast was between [+grooved] and [-grooved], and that it was relevant only for coronals. Suppose instead that we use the following feature:

[+strident]:   segments with high-amplitude noise
[-strident]:   segments with no high-amplitude noise

Given this definition of [strident] (which is similar to that of Chomsky and Halle, 1968), stridency has no relation to coronality. Because both [f] and [θ] are low-amplitude fricatives, both should be [-strident]. This follows from a less complex definition of the feature than in Chomsky and Halle (1968), where the feature was relativized to high versus low amplitude *within labials* versus *within coronals*, and so on. Thus, even though [f] and [θ] are of comparable amplitude, [f] was [+strident] because it has (marginally) higher amplitude than bilabial [ɸ], but [θ] was [-strident] because it has much lower amplitude than [s]. According to the definition here, both are [-strident].

Substituting [-strident] for [-grooved] in the constraint ranking given above, we can derive Pattern 3 even with full specification. Since [-strident] must survive and link up, but coronal fricatives must be [+strident], the only option is to delete [Coronal]. The only other articulator node allowed with [-strident] fricatives in

English is [Labial]. Thus, [Labial] is inserted, and [f] results. These data could therefore be used to argue for the feature [strident], rather than [grooved]; or perhaps that [strident] is relevant for some speakers, and [grooved] for others.

ANALYSIS 3   With default underspecification, we can derive both Patterns 3 and 4 while still using the feature [grooved]. However, we must assume that the underlying specifications are different from those given above:

/s/:   [Coronal, +grooved] underlying
/θ/:   No underlying place features
/f/:   [Labial] underlying

It is reasonable to assume that /θ/ as [-grooved] would have no underlying specification for [grooved]. In adult English, /θ/ surfaces with the same [-grooved] feature as the nonfricative anterior coronals such as /t/. Using these assumptions, Pattern 3 can be derived as follows:

Survived(Coronal)
Survived(+ grooved)
Survived(Labial)

Not(+ grooved)

Co-occurring(Coronal, + cont,-son→-grooved)

Not(Labial)

Not(Coronal)
Not(-grooved)

Given this ranking, all the underlying nondefault features in /s/ and /f/ surface faithfully as is the case for Pattern 3. However, the high ranking of **Not (+ grooved)** prevents any token of [+grooved] in the output *unless it is underlying*, and the high ranking of the co-occurrence constraint requires that coronal fricatives be [+grooved]. The only resolution is to insert [Labial] in the output for /θ/, yielding [f], rather than inserting the general default [Coronal].

Pattern 4: /s/ as [θ]; /θ/ as /f/.   Analysis 2 above (with [strident]) runs into difficulties with Pattern 4. If there is something inherently wrong with the output [θ], so that the input /θ/ yields [f], how can the input /s/ lead to the output [θ]? With full specification, there is no obvious explanation for this chain shift. One would need a constraint such as

Co-occurring(INPUT[+ strident]→OUTPUT[Coronal])

If ranked high enough, this means that all underlyingly strident fricatives would surface as coronals, even if [+strident] is deleted on the surface. As noted in §4.7.1.8, we do not believe that such complex constraints are reasonable. Consequently, we view Analysis 2 as inadequate.

However, Analysis 3 can account for both patterns with alterations in constraint rankings. If we modify the constraint list above so that **Survived(+ grooved)** is low-ranked, the results will be the same, except that /s/ will not surface as [+grooved]. Because **Survived(Coronal)** is still high-ranked, /s/ surfaces as a coronal, but with default [-grooved] (even though that violates the lower-ranked co-occurrence constraint that coronal fricatives should be [+grooved]). Because /θ/ is underlyingly *underspecified* for [Coronal], however, *Survived*(**Coronal**) does not help. The only other option for fricatives in English is [Labial], and thus [Labial] is inserted instead of [Coronal] (or [Dorsal]). Thus, because of under-specification, the default fricative (/θ/) is more likely to show up with a nondefault articulator node ([Labial]) than is the nondefault fricative (/s/).

If we assume that children's underlying representations can differ in terms of which fricative has the underspecified value of [grooved], all four patterns can easily be derived. Full specification is incapable of accounting for the four patterns without using constraints of an undesirable type. If full specification is assumed, the substitution of [f] for /θ/ cannot be derived phonologically. We would have to consider it a perceptually based substitution. In contrast, default underspecifica-tion allows a cohesive *phonological* analysis of the data.

Before leaving this discussion, we consider a dental click substitution for sibi-lants reported by Bedore et al. (1994). This child substituted dental clicks for all coronal fricatives and affricates except interdentals, across word positions and of-ten in place of /s/-clusters.

some	/səm/	[ǀəm]
shark	/ʃaɹk/	[ǀaɹk]
was	/wəz/	[wəǀ]
judge	/dʒədʒ/	[ǀəǀ]
star	/staɹ/	[ǀaɹ]

The feature [strident] may also be relevant in explaining this substitution pattern. There is another aspect of the feature [+strident] that we did not mention above. The high-amplitude noise must be of sufficient duration for the segment to be considered [+strident]. Although no one has defined a minimum duration, it should be long enough for the segment to be realized as an affricate or fricative. Suppose, however, that the minimum duration needed to make a segment [+stri-dent] varies from child to child. Clicks also have high-amplitude noise (from their bursts), but with a much shorter duration. Clicks would then be [+strident] (re-gardless of place of articulation). Consider the following ranking:

Survived(+ strident)
LinkedUpwards(+ strident)
NotCo-occurring(-sonorant, + continuant)

Survived(+ continuant)

Not(-continuant)

This ranking results in stop substitutions for fricatives. In addition, high ranking of **Survived(+ strident)** means that those stops are strident: an affricate (strident stop) or a click. This could be viewed as a perceptually driven substitution that has nothing to do with phonological representations. However, if we assume that features can be defined differently for different children (and different adult languages), then we can make use of features that derive the substitution phonologically.

The data in this section raise many issues, but provide no final solutions. If we wish to account for all the substitutions phonologically, default underspecification provides the best analysis, since it allows us to assume that different children make different choices as to whether /s/ or /θ/ is specified for place features underlyingly. With full specification, we must assume that some children use a feature [strident] (while others may use [grooved]), and either that some substitutions are not phonologically based or that there are constraints of a more complex type than we use in this book.

5.5.1.2.2. [distributed]

The previous discussion concerned tongue grooving. Often, however, the lack of tongue grooving co-occurs with dental placement for at least the [+ anterior] targets (and sometimes for the palatoalveolar targets, as in Charles's data, §8.5.1.1). Even if children do produce grooved sibilants, however, anterior coronals often surface as dentals (not the least because of their tongue size relative to their oral cavity), in other words, as [+distributed]. **Co-occurring (Coronal→[+ distributed])** is high-ranked for phonetic reasons. Ironically, in spite of the dental placement of anterior coronals, and the tendency for ungrooved sibilants in the speech of many children, the interdentals /θ/ and /ð/ are often among the latest acquired segments in English (Smit et al., 1990; Edwards & Shriberg, 1983a).

It is assumed that as children's mouths grow, coronal anteriors will become produced at the alveolar ridge, as they are in adult speech (although some adults continue to have a dental setting [Laver, 1994]). We have little data on this developmental process, although Stoel-Gammon, Williams, and Buder (1994) have some data comparing productions of /t/ in English and Swedish toddlers and adults using perceptual and acoustic measures. They found that judges were able to use burst stimuli to distinguish between the English [t] and Swedish [t̪] for 14 out of 20 30-month-old children (10 American English, 10 Swedish) and for most of the adults. Furthermore, acoustic measures (particularly VOT, relative intensity, and burst standard deviation) confirmed the perceived distinction. The children's profiles were similar to those of adults' profiles in the study, although the difference between alveolars and dentals was less for most of the children. The fact that it is possible to detect a difference for some 30-month-olds suggests that children may be able to compensate articulatorily in such a way as to match aspects of the acoustic signal (even if they have advanced tongue placement).

5.5.1.2.3. *[anterior]*

In this section we focus on the feature [anterior]. (Again, we are only concerned here with *place* of articulation, and illustrate the patterns with voiceless segments.) The three major patterns are depalatalization (Pattern 1), backing of alveolars (Pattern 2), and palatalization (Pattern 3, in which neither palatoalveolars nor alveolars are possible).

Pattern 1:	/s/	[s]	
	/ʃ/	[s]	Depalatalization
Pattern 2:	/s/	[ʃ]	Backing of alveolars
	/ʃ/	[ʃ]	
Pattern 3:	/ʃ/	[ç]	Palatalization
	/s/	[ç]	
	/t/	[c]	(Palatal stop)

(Palatoalveolars or alveolars can also surface as velars, glottals, labials, etc., but in these cases, constraints other than those on the feature [anterior] are generally involved).[1]

Pattern 1 (*ship* as [sɪp], *chip* as [ʦɪp]) is the most common in English, and may persist in typically developing children until 8 or 9 years of age (Smit et al., 1990; Edwards & Shriberg, 1983a). In such cases **Not(-anterior)** is higher-ranked than **Not(+anterior)** and **Survived(-anterior)** and [Coronal,+anterior] is the system default. There may be some initial inconsistency in fricative placement (lack of contrast for [anterior]). Jeremy (Bernhardt & Gilbert, 1992; §8.4), had a default sibilant coda at age 3;3 which surfaced most of the time as [s], but also as [ʃ]. By 3;5, however, alveolar placement was consistent (with palatoalveolars surfacing as alveolars), and he did not acquire palatoalveolars until after age 4;6.

Pattern 1 is not universal, since palatoalveolars may be acquired before alveolar fricatives. Pye et al. (1987) reported early acquisition of [ʧ] in Quiche; Anderson and Smith (1987) reported early acquisition of [ʤ] in Puerto Rican Spanish. Pye et al. also noted that four of their five subjects substituted [ʃ] for /s/ (although the fifth child showed the opposite pattern). If a child produces all coronals as [-anterior], we might posit [-anterior] as the default value. However, because only fricatives tend to be subject to this substitution pattern, a co-occurrence constraint concerning [+grooved] or [+continuant] is probably relevant: **Co-occurring(Coronal, +continuant→-anterior)**. Note that the latter constraint could also account for front vowels (and /j/) being [-anterior]. The co-occurrence constraint for vowels potentially may influence consonant production for some children.

In English, Pattern 2 is less common. However, even if palatoalveolars do not

---

[1] If palatoalveolars are the only sibilants that surface as velars, a more general definition of [-anterior] may be appropriate for that child. In Chomsky and Halle (1968), velars were defined as [-anterior]. Such children may be treating all postalveolar consonants are [-anterior], with velars as the "default" [-anterior] segments. This kind of realignment of defaults is similar to what we saw for the feature [grooved] in §5.5.1.2.1.

consistently substitute for alveolars, English-learning children may use palatoalveolars before they use alveolar fricatives (high ranking of **Survived(-anterior)**).
Alveolar fricatives may show other patterns (dentalization, deletion, or debuccalization), as shown in the examples from Rockman (1983: *S3*). (See also §8.5.1.1.)

	push	/pʊʃ/	[pʊʃ]~[pʊ]~[pʊʰ]
	shine	/ʃaɪn/	[haɪn]
	charge	/tʃaɹdʒ/	[tʃadʒ]
	chip	/tʃɪp/	[tʃɪp]~[kɪp]~[tɪp]
BUT:	sing	/sɪŋ/	[hɪŋ]
	zoo	/zu/	[u]
	buzz	/bʌz/	[bʌdʒ]~[bʌd]~[bʌð]

In English, Pattern 3 (the substitution of true palatals for alveolars and palatoalveolars) typically occurs only for speakers with oral mechanism differences,
primarily cleft palate. (See §8.5.2.)

For the feature [anterior], the same issues arise as were discussed for [grooved]
in the previous section. If children have different surface patterns, we can either
assume alternate constraint rankings, or different underlying representations and
defaults, in which not only the constraint rankings, but also the relevant constraints, are different.

5.5.1.3. Terminal features of [Labial]: [round] and [labiodental]

The Labial node dominates the features [round] and [labiodental]. Within
the consonant and glide system, constraints on these features can affect /w/
([+round],[-labiodental]), /f/, /v/, and the labiodental glide [ʋ] ([+labiodental]),
or /ɸ/ and /β/ ([-labiodental]). Reports of substitution patterns that specifically
concern these terminal features are rare. In this section we focus only on the [la-
biodental] feature, with discussion on the feature [round] (V-Labial) in the next
section.

Lleó et al. (1996) note that both [β] and [v] appear in late babbling and early
words in Spanish. Stops often spirantize in Spanish and thus children might be
predisposed to earlier emergence of fricatives. (See Macken & Barton, 1980b.)
However, not all Spanish-learning children use labial or other fricatives at an early
age. In Anderson and Smith's (1987) study of six 2-year-olds learning Puerto
Rican Spanish, some children used bilabial stops in place of /f/ and /β/.

In English, /f/ and /v/ are [+labiodental]. **Co-occurring(Labial, + cont,-son
→ + labiodental)** is higher-ranked than **Not(-labiodental)**. Thus, [+labiodental]
is not distinctive for English, but is a redundant nondefault in the adult system (per
default underspecification). The status of [labiodental] in children's early English
development has not been well investigated. Both substitution of [+labiodental]
for [-labiodental] and the opposite have been observed. Sometimes bilabial fricatives substitute for the labiodental fricatives. Accounts of this phenomenon are
few, although it may be more common than reported. Stemberger (1988a) noted

that Gwendolyn initially produced bilabial ([−labiodental]) fricatives before learning the labiodentals. Bernhardt (p.c.) observed one 16-month-old child using bilabial fricatives in place of labiodentals when he first began to use fricatives. The co-occurrence constraint was low-ranked, allowing the system default [−labiodental] to be inserted.

This pattern can be phonetically grounded in some cases. Children with weakness in the oral mechanism may produce bilabials rather than labiodentals (e.g., as in Carolyn's production of *glove* as [gɑːβ], in Edwards & Bernhardt, 1973a).

The opposite pattern can also occur. Bilabials (stops, glides, and nasals) may be produced with labiodental articulation. This can be general, or specific to certain words. Laver (1994) describes a general labiodental "phonetic setting" in which individuals produce all labials with labiodental place. This may be stylistic (and normal), or a result of a pronounced overbite (in which case bilabial occlusion is difficult). In this case, **Not(+ labiodental)** is lowest-ranked, and so [+labiodental] is inserted as the system default for labials.

In a more specific case, Stemberger's daughter, Morgan, for a time produced a labiodental stop ([pʳ]) in coda for /f/ (e.g., *laugh* as [læːpʳ]); this occurred during the transition from [p] to [f], and covaried with those two pronunciations. This suggests that the [+labiodental] feature was underlying for fricatives (since underlying labial stops surfaced as bilabial stops), and not inserted via the co-occurrence constraint for fricatives discussed above. **Survived(+ labiodental)** allowed /f/ to surface as a labiodental, even when it became a stop.

In another case applying only to labial continuants, Rockman (1983) notes a lack of consistent contrast between /f/, /v/, and /w/ for one child with a phonological disorder.

fight	/faɪt/	[faɪt]
fast	/fæst/	[væt]
van	/væn/	[bæn]~[væn]
wash	/wɑʃ/	[wɑt][vɑt]
ring	/ɹɪŋ/	[wɪŋ][vɪŋ]
watch	/wɑʧ/	[wᵛɑt]
watching	/wɑʧɪŋ/	[wɑdɪŋ]

Co-occurrence constraints are overgeneralized among the continuants to include the glide /w/: **Co-occurring(Labial, + cont→ + labiodental)** rather than the more specific **Co-occurring(Labial, + cont,-son→ + labiodental)**. This can result in production of a fricative for the glide (loss of [-sonorant]) or a labiodental glide [ʋ].

Dutch has a labiodental glide [ʋ] in word onset as an allophone of /w/. Beers (1995) notes that [ʋ] appeared about the same time as /f/ across her group of subjects (age group 2;3−25), although the fricative was more consistently produced across subjects at that age. Substitution patterns are only briefly noted for one subject, who used [h] for the glide. Fikkert (1994) gives examples of both [h] and [c] substitutions for the labiodental glide (Jarmo, age 1;10 to 2;0). Note that [f] is produced, although [ʊ] is not.

Willy	/ʊɪliː/	[hiːliː]	'Willy'	1;10.9
water	/ʋaːtər/	[caːtə]	'water'	2;0.4
vogel	/voːχəl/	[foːχɔ]~[χoːχɔ]	'bird'	2;0.4

If labiodental fricatives are developmentally earlier than labiodental glides, co-occurrence constraints are probably implicated. **Co-occurring(σ-Margin→ +consonantal)** may prohibit glide onsets (probably the case for Jarmo). In addition, specific co-occurrence constraints may affect the labiodental glide. Segments with C-Place can be [+labiodental], but segments with V-Place cannot. This makes sense in terms of general redundancies of the system: vowels are always [−labiodental]. Therefore, high ranking of **NotCo-occurring(V-Labial, +labiodental)** is not unexpected (and in fact, labiodental glides are not as common as bilabial glides crosslinguistically).

5.5.1.4. Terminal Features of [Dorsal]: [high], [low]

The most common dorsals are [+high] velars, and we discussed them in §5.5.1.1. However [−high] dorsals occur, both in adult languages (uvulars and pharyngeals) and in disordered speech (particularly in cleft palate or deaf speech). (We discuss the disordered speech examples in §8.5.2 and §8.5.3.) As far as we know, typically developing children do not substitute nonhigh velars for other consonants in languages that do not have them as target segments.

Arabic has pharyngeals and uvulars. Although there are few data available, Shahin (1995) gives some data for development of Arabic pharyngeals (voiced and voiceless) for her son, Hosan.[2] The voiceless pharyngeal [ħ] was produced from age 1;11, first in word-medial and word-final positions, and then word initially, at age 2;2. It was more frequent word finally and medially, and in all positions surfaced as a glottal [h] when it did not surface as a match. (It also deleted once word finally.)

/ʔɪftəħ/	[ʔɪftəħ]	'open (it)' (2nd masc. sg.)	1;11
/ħæːmi/	[hæmi]	'difficult'	2;2
/ħæliːb/	[ħæliːb]	'milk'	2;2
/rˣuːħ/	[lʊh]	'to go' (ˣ=uvularized, pharyngealized; i.e., emphatics)	2;4

The voiced pharyngeal [ʕ] was also attempted from age 1;11 in initial and medial positions, but only matched the target twice word initially at 2;1 (for the word

---

[2] At home, Hosan was addressed almost exclusively in Arabic until about 3;0, and was in a monolingual Arabic environment from 0;4 -0;6. He heard English around the house between his brothers and parents, and was addressed in English at a childcare center from age 1;4.

eye). Otherwise, glottal stop surfaced word initially. In other word positions, the pharyngeal deleted or the vowel was lengthened.

/ʕˣʊsˣsˣ/	[ʔɑs]	'to press, squeeze'	1;11
/ʔʊkʊʕd/	[ʔʊkɑːd]	'Sit!' (2nd masc. sg.)	2;0
/mæʕ/	[mɑ]	'with'	2;0
/ʕain/	[ʕain]	'eye'	2;1

Note that the voiceless pharyngeal survived better in coda. High-ranked **Co-occurring(Rime→ + continuant)** possibly supported voiceless pharyngeals in coda position (see §6.1.12.2.2). The differences between the voiced and voiceless pharyngeals show effects of feature co-occurrence constraints and are discussed again in §5.5.4.2.[3] In terms of place features per se, Hosan produced [Dorsal, +high], [Dorsal,-high] (uvularized), and [Dorsal, +low] segments. Thus, all of the target feature combinations with [Dorsal] were possible early on, although nonhigh dorsals did not always survive (high-ranked **NotCo-occurring(Dorsal, -high)**). Glottals, rather than velars ([+high] Dorsals), surfaced as substitutions. The feature geometry we use in this book suggests that glottals have no place of articulation. Thus, when glottals replace pharyngeals, Place delinks (debuccalization). This is a possible analysis, but we might assume alternatively (for languages such as Arabic) that pharyngeals and glottals are subsumed under a node of their own (Pharyngeal, Radical). (Rose, 1994, makes a similar proposal for languages that have pharyngeals or uvulars in addition to laryngeals.) When one type of guttural is not possible, the other might replace it.

5.5.1.5. Segments with Two Articulator Features

Most segments have only one articulator feature. Some have more than one articulator: glides, clicks, palatals, doubly articulated segments (/kp/), and segments with secondary articulation such as labialization (/kʷ/), pharyngealization, etc. In typically developing English, the only segments with two articulators are the glides and velarized [ɫ], although disordered speech (particularly cleft palate speech) may show evidence of palatal stops or fricatives, or secondary articulations. (See §5.5.1.2.1 regarding click substitutions for sibilants.)

Segments with two articulator features may show effects of high-ranked co-occurrence constraints for the two place features. Typically, one of the place features fails to survive (a minimal repair). Nonminimal deletion or default insertion repairs also occur, but it can be difficult to determine whether those nonminimal repairs are a response to place feature constraints or some other type of constraints. This section addresses place feature constraints and repairs for /j/ and /w/, /ɹ/, clicks and palatals in turn. (Note: The only patterns that have been well documented are for English /ɹ/. See also §5.5.2.3.)

---

[3] Additionally, note that faithfulness to [s.g.] and [voiced] was high-ranked. The feature [+s.g.] surfaced in the voiceless pharyngeal or the [h] substitution. Similarly, the voiced pharyngeal surfaced as [ʔ], which is [-s.g.], and an expected substitution if [+s.g.] could not be inserted.

5.5.1.5.1. *Glides /j/ and /w/*

Both /j/ and /w/ have a [V-Dorsal] place feature which co-occurs with either [V-Coronal] (/j/) or [V-Labial] (/w/). In English, /w/ is redundantly [+round] and [−labiodental].

Interchanges of these two glides (involving minimal repairs) appear to be uncommon. If we assume that [V-Coronal] (/j/) is a default feature, and [V-Labial] a nondefault, then replacement of /w/ with [j] might be expected more often than the reverse, and the few examples we have found appear to support this hypothesis.

wave	/weɪv/	[jeɪv]	(Sally: Bernhardt, 1994b, p.u.d.)
watch	/wɑtʃ/	[jʌtn̥]	(Carolyn: Edwards & Bernhardt, 1973a)

(We found one example of [w] for /j/, but this appeared to be an assimilation: [wu] for /ju/. Robin: Bernhardt, 1994a.).

When [j] appears for /w/, and round vowels are also absent from the inventory, a high-ranked **Not(V-Labial)** constraint is probably implicated. However, if round vowels *are* in the inventory, and [j] replaces /w/, the relevant constraint is probably a co-occurrence constraint concerning the place features and the onset position: **NotCo-occurring(σ-Margin,V-Dorsal,V-Labial)**. Both examples above were of this type. An oral glide surfaced because of high-ranked **LinkedDownwards (V-Place)**(and σ▸**Onset**), but the co-occurrence constraint ruled out [w]. [V-Labial] could be sacrificed (low ranking of **Survived(V-Labial)**) and thus [j] appeared, with the default feature V-Coronal ([-round]).

σ▸**Onset**
LinkedDownwards(V-Place)
Survived/LinkedUpwards(V-Place)
NotCo-occurring(σ-Margin,V-Dorsal,V-Labial)
Survived/LinkedUpwards(V-Dorsal)

Not(V-Coronal)
Survived/LinkedUpwards(V-Labial)

In reviewing our own data and the literature, it appears that more frequent phonological patterns involving /w/ and /j/ include deletion, replacement by a glottal ([ʔ] or [h]), another sonorant, or even a stop. When a difference in manner is evident in the replacement pattern, place feature constraints are less likely to be relevant than manner feature constraints. However, if only one of the glides is replaced or deleted, place feature constraints may be implicated.

5.5.1.5.2. *English /ɹ/*

This subsection primarily addresses English /ɹ/, although we mention patterns for rhotics in other languages. The following substitution patterns are most likely, given place co-occurrence constraints:

Pattern 1: /ɹ/ > [w]	Labialization, gliding
Pattern 2: /ɹ/ > [j]	Gliding

The following pattern also can reflect place co-occurrence constraints:

Pattern 3: /ɹ/ > [l]   Lateralization

English /ɹ/ has two articulator features in onset: [V-Labial,+round] and [V-Coronal,-anterior]. If the two place features may not co-occur, eliminating one is a simple solution to the problem. Substitutions of [w] or [j] result, as in Patterns 1 and 2.

Pattern 1:   /ɹ/ > [w]

The most common substitution for /ɹ/ in English is [w]. [V-Labial] survives, and [V-Coronal] delinks. High ranking of **Survived(-consonantal)** ensures that [w] will replace /ɹ/ rather than some other labial.

Survived(V-Labial)	‖	**Survived(V-Coronal)**
NotCo-occurring(V-Labial,V-Coronal)	‖	**Not(+ back)**
Survived(-consonantal)	‖	
Survived(V-Labial)	‖	

Since [V-Coronal] is the default in adult English (/j/ as the default glide), **Survived(V-Labial)** is generally ranked higher than **Survived(V-Coronal)** in child systems. Faithfulness to the [Labial] nondefault results in substitution of the labial glide [w] more often than the coronal glide [j].

In coda position, /ɹ/ does not have a labial feature in English, but a round vowel is not an uncommon substitution for postvocalic /ɹ/ or rhotic vowels. In this case, we might assume that the child has categorized all allophones of /ɹ/ as labial underlyingly, and generalized the substitution pattern across word positions.

Pattern 2:   /ɹ/ > [j]

When /ɹ/ surfaces as [j], [V-Labial] is delinked and [V-Coronal] survives.

Survived(-consonantal)	‖	**Survived(V-Labial)**
NotCo-occurring(V-Labial,V-Coronal)	‖	**Not(V-Coronal)**
Survived(V-Coronal)	‖	

In such cases, we might expect a [-round] vowel as a substitution for postvocalic /ɹ/, but no one has systematically investigated this.

Pattern 3:   /ɹ/ > [l]

Sometimes [l] surfaces for English /ɹ/. This appears to be relatively uncommon, and it is not clear that place constraints are responsible for the pattern. It generally occurs when glides are impossible, and /j/ also becomes [l]. (See §5.5.3.1.)

5.5.1.5.3. Velarized Segments

The lateral /l/ in English has both plain and velarized allophones (the latter appearing in codas and before back vowels). During development, velarized coda or syllabic [ɫ] may surface as a vowel, while nonvelarized onset /l/ surfaces as a coronal ([j]). (See also §5.5.3.6.) Consistent documentation of the developmental process for the allophones is not available. Stemberger (p.u.d.) reports that when Morgan first used /l/ in a coda, it was nonvelarized [l] (just as in onsets). German has an alveolar /l/ in codas and onsets, and Lleó (p.c.) indicated that alveolar [l] can be found in codas among the first words (e.g., *Ball*, [bal]). Thus, the least complex [l] appears to be earlier. Additional articulator features complicate the learning process, and tend to delete.

5.5.1.5.4. Clicks and Palatals

Palatals and clicks are considered to have dorsal features in addition to their coronal (or in the case of labial clicks/), labial features. The glide /j/ has been discussed briefly above. Here we focus on other palatals and clicks.

PALATALS OTHER THAN /j/.　Palatal obstruents and laterals are infrequent crosslinguistically, and as such, might be acquired later. Palatal nasals occur about as frequently as alveolar nasals crosslinguistically (Laver, 1994), and might be acquired earlier than palatal obstruents, depending on their frequency within a particular language.

Developmental information on palatals other than /j/ is limited. Mowrer and Burger (1991) give some information on palatal affricates in their report on acquisition of Xhosa by 70 children. Xhosa has several types of affricates at different places of articulation (alveolars, palatoalveolars, palatals, and velars). Possibly because the palatal affricates are often produced as palatoalveolars in the adult dialect, these affricates were slowest to develop. They also showed the most variable substitution patterns. Ignoring the palatoalveolar substitutions (dialectally influenced), voiceless palatal affricates surfaced equally frequently as [k] or coronals, and the voiced affricate surfaced as [d(j)]. This variability supports the analysis of palatals as [Coronal] *and* [Dorsal], with options across children as to which feature survives.[4]

Palatal fricatives appear to have different acquisition points across languages. Sumio (1978) notes late acquisition of the palatal fricative in Japanese. However, Geilmann (1993) reports use of the voiceless palatal fricative by a German child as early as 1;7 (the earliest data set in his report). In German, the palatal fricative occurs in frequent words such as *ich* ('I'), *mich* ('me'), and *Milch* ('milk'). This frequency, plus the sharing of features with the front vowel, may predispose early acquisition of [ç] in German.

Palatal nasals appear to be acquired early in Spanish. Anderson and Smith (1987) found high accuracy rates for palatal nasals among their 2-year-old subjects (although the nasals were not particularly frequent). Goldstein (1996) found a high degree of accuracy for palatal nasals at age 3, even for children with phonological disorders.

---

[4]The voiced palatal affricate was fairly consistently realized as [d(j)], an alveolar stop with or without a following palatal glide. Because [g] has two nondefault features, high-ranked co-occurrence constraints possibly prohibited simultaneous production of [+voiced] and [Dorsal].

Overall, palatal consonants do not appear to be particularly difficult, and may even be a preferred place of articulation in some cases, because they share place of articulation with front vowels. For two English-learning children, Vihman (1992) and Waterson (1971) note use of palatals (which did not occur in the target language) in the transition from babbling to speech, but only when vowel features spread to consonants. (See §7.3.4.) S. Edwards (1995) reports use of palatal fricatives and stops for alveolar targets for a child with a phonological disorder (who had tongue tip weakness). Palatal substitutions for coronal consonants are common in cleft palate speech. (See §8.5.2.) In these cases, a high-ranked co-occurrence constraint results in all coronals being produced with a [C-Dorsal] component: **Co-occurring(C-Coronal→C-Dorsal)**.

CLICKS. Mowrer and Burger (1991) also report on clicks. Xhosa has dental, palatoalveolar, and lateral clicks, and children were using them proficiently by 2;6–3;0. Before using clicks, subjects in the Mowrer and Burger (1991) study generally replaced them with stops. In such cases, **NotCo-occurring(Dorsal, Coronal)** is high-ranked. A minimal repair results in delinking of one place feature for the clicks, resulting in a plain stop. A coronal stop most often replaced the dental click; [Dorsal] deleted. The velar [k] replaced the palatoalveolar and lateral clicks; [Coronal] deleted. It is unclear what determined which articulator feature deleted. The replacement patterns support the dual place feature analysis of clicks.

5.5.2. LARYNGEAL FEATURES

The laryngeal features discussed in this section are [voiced], [s.g.] and [c.g.]. The feature [voiced] is influenced partially by word position and sequence constraints and is also discussed in §6.1.12.1 and §7.3.4. In this section, we refer only to word onset position for [voiced].

5.5.2.1. [voiced]

VOT is defined as the time between the onset of glottal pulsing and the release of the initial stop consonants (Lisker & Abramson, 1964). Descriptions such as long lead (prevoiced), short lag, and long lag refer to the degree of VOT. Crosslinguistic differences in VOT for voiced and voiceless stops make it difficult to generalize about the acquisition of the feature [voiced]. For example, the VOT value for English voiced stops is similar to the VOT value for unaspirated stops in Romance languages. The English distinction between voiceless and voiced stops is primarily a distinction between short-lag and long-lag stops, although some English speakers prevoice stops (Lisker & Abramson, 1964). For English, then, the difference often entails a [s.g.] contrast rather than a [voiced] contrast. Voiced stops in the Romance languages do have consistently prevoiced VOT. Thus, for such languages, the feature [voiced] is relevant in the contrast (short-lag voiceless unaspirated versus long-lead prevoiced stops). Some languages have more than two-way contrasts, complicating the acquisition process. Thai, for example, has long-lead (prevoiced), short-lag, and long-lag stops. Hindi has long-lead, short-lag, long-lag, and murmured (breathy) voiced stops ([+voiced,+s.g.]). Acquisition studies for the various types of languages converge on some general patterns, although age of acquisition for various features and languages vary (because of study methodology, language, individual differences, or a combination of those factors).

Perceptual studies of infants show early abilities to distinguish speech sounds on the basis of VOT (Eimas et al., 1971), with refinement over time in the direction of the target language (Eilers, Gavin, & Wilson, 1979; Werker & Tees, 1984). Similarly, although short-lag stops tend to predominate in babbling (Preston, Yeni-Komshian, & Stark, 1967), distinctions in terms of VOT are also possible in production. Eilers, Oller, and Benito-Garcia (1984) report that short-lag stops were most frequent in the babbling of the 1-year-olds in their study (seven Cuban Spanish, seven American English), but a proportion of babbling utterances also had long-lag or long-lead VOT. By place of articulation, labial stops were the most likely to show long-lead VOT (40% of the labials in the Spanish-learning group, and 33% in the English-learning group), and velars to show long-lag (30% and 23% respectively). However, presence of such voicing distinctions in babbling does not necessarily predict presence of voicing contrasts in speech at age 2, according to the Eilers et al. (1984) study.

In general, phonemically contrastive values for the feature [voiced] are not commonly reported for most languages until at least age 2. Most studies report frequent use of short-lag stops (high ranking of **Not(+ voiced)**, and low ranking of **Not(-voiced)**). For Dutch, Beers (1995) notes that voicing contrasts appeared only after age 3 for her 45 subjects, following establishment of manner and place contrasts. For English, voicing distinctions do not appear to be customary until after age 2, although they can occur earlier (Macken & Barton, 1980a; Stoel-Gammon & Dunn, 1985; Tyler & Edwards, 1993). In early development, stops tend to have predominantly short-lag VOT. Long-lag (aspirated) stops emerge later (age 2 or older). In such cases, constraints possibly concern [+s.g.] more than [voiced]. Some children do show use of long-lead stops, however, showing that contrasts for [voiced] can be relevant for English. K. Davis (1995) notes that about the same proportion of 2-year-olds as adults used prevoiced stops in her study (14% and 17% respectively). Stemberger (p.u.d.) reports that Morgan produced prevoiced stops in babbling and in early words for voiceless and voiced targets (with equivalent amounts of prevoicing from -30 to -60 msec). The child visibly expanded the buccal cavities, apparently in order to maintain low enough oral pressure for voicing to occur. For example, both /p/ and /b/ were [b]: *pig* as [bɪʔ], and *ball* as [baʔ]. In such cases, [+voiced] is the default (low ranking of **Not(+ voiced)**). A developing contrast may shift VOT for both [+voiced] and [−voiced] stops, so that they are more like adult values. Similarly, in languages with a contrast between short-lag and long-lead (prevoiced) stops, audible and adult-like contrasts in VOT may be established anywhere from 2 to 5+ years of age. Again, most children first use voiceless unaspirated (short-lag) stops. In these cases, **Not(-voiced)** is low-ranked, and [−voiced] is the default. (For Spanish, see Macken & Barton, 1980a, b, Eilers, Oller, & Benito-Garcia, 1984, and Anderson & Smith, 1987. For Italian, see Bortolini et al., 1995. For French, see Allen, 1985.)

Languages with multiple contrasts such as Thai and Hindi appear to have a protracted acquisition period for voicing contrasts. In a cross-sectional study (seven subjects each at age 3, 5, 7, and 20+), Gandour et al. (1986) noted that voicing contrasts were all present only by age 7, with most difficulty found for the prevoiced stops /b/ and /d/. Developmentally, voiceless unaspirated stops preceded voiceless aspirated stops, which in turn preceded prevoiced stops. They suggest that there is something inherently difficult about prevoicing, but since it can be present in babbling and early words, this is not likely the (sole) motivation for the late development of the prevoiced stops. For Hindi, K. Davis (1995) reported use of prevoiced stops by 2-year-olds, but low proportions of them until after age 6. Murmured voiced stops, the most marked group, were used contrastively by only the 4-year-olds and adults in her study (and not by the 2-year-olds or 6-year-olds). She claims that children produce contrasts in minimal pairs with large VOT differences before producing contrasts in minimal pairs with small VOT differences, whatever the language being learned. While this may be generally true, the data for her 6-year-olds do not fully support this acoustic hypothesis. They showed a contrast between the pair /k/-/g/ before /k/-/gʰ/, even though the 4-year-olds showed the opposite pattern. Segmental complexity and markedness predict the late acquisition of murmured stops (as for the 6-year-olds). **NotCo-occurring(+s.g.,+voiced)** is generally high-ranked.

The data for voicing are complex and difficult to interpret. The definition of the feature [voiced] is more relative than absolute in this case, which confounds interpretation. We continue the discussion below and in §5.5.4.1 for languages in which [+s.g.] is relevant to the voicing distinction.

5.5.2.2. [+spread-glottis] in Fricatives and Stops

The feature [+s.g.] refers to stops, voiceless fricatives, and [h]. For voiceless fricatives, the feature is a redundant nondefault. **Co-occurring(+cont,-son, -voiced→+s.g.)** is high-ranked. If oral fricatives are not possible, but faithfulness constraints for this nondefault are high-ranked, a variety of (sometimes unusual) patterns can result, as is shown in §5.5.4.4. In the previous section, we noted that [+s.g.] is often the relevant feature for establishment of a word-initial "voicing" contrast in languages such as English. Since most phones in English are [-s.g.], it is reasonable to assume that [-s.g.] is the system default: **Not(-s.g.)** is ranked lower than **Not(+s.g.)**. If **Not(+s.g.)** is initially ranked too high, then only the default [-s.g.] can be present in the output (at least for stops, which are not helped by the co-occurrence constraint for fricatives). Aspiration will be impossible; English-learning children will show initial "voicing" (deaspiration). The aspiration of initial stops may arise in two ways. First, the nondefault feature (even though it is redundant) may be placed in the underlying representation, and **Survived(+s.g.)** may be ranked high enough to allow it to survive in the output.

Second, as proposed in §4.7.1.5, there may be a high-ranked constraint **Co-occurring(-voiced→ + s.g.)** that makes all voiceless segments (except [+c.g.] ones) [+s.g.]. By ranking this co-occurrence constraint high, the initial stop can be aspirated even if there is no specification for [s.g.] in the underlying representation. (See §4.7.1.5 for discussion of why aspiration is restricted to word-initial and foot-initial position in adult English.) Additionally, co-occurrence constraints concerning place of articulation can interact with [+s.g.] (see §5.5.4.1).

5.5.2.3. Glottal Segments

Glottal segments can be found in babbling and early words (Vihman, 1992; Lleó et al., 1996). (See Table 5.1 and §5.5.1.) Lleó et al. (1996) found [h] and [ʔ] onsets in the babbling data of both Spanish and German infants, even though European Spanish does not have such onsets. (Anderson and Smith, 1987, note use of [h] by their 2-year-old Puerto Rican Spanish subjects as both a match and substitution. This might be more expected for Puerto Rican Spanish since [h] alternates with [s] in codas.) In Lleó et al.'s (1996) study, glottals dropped in frequency when words first appeared, and then increased in frequency in both babbling and speech. Vihman (1992) also notes frequent use of [h] as a syllable-initial consonant (second in frequency to [d]). This was true even for the French-learning children, where the adult language lacks [h]. The [h] decreased quickly in use during word acquisition in French, but did not disappear immediately. (Thus, although the adult phonology is discontinuous with babbling and early words, there was no abrupt discontinuity between babbling and early words.)

Both of these studies show a possible universal predisposition for glottals without influence of the target language. The presence of glottal stops and [h] in babbling and early words, and the subsequent decrease in use in the languages where there are no adult targets of those types, suggests that the laryngeals have a universal default status. Some children continue to use them in words, even when they are not present in the adult language. Stemberger (1993a), Bernhardt (1990), and Fikkert (1994) give examples of later use of glottals as default consonants (nonminimal repairs). (See also §7.4.4.3 for a discussion of [h] as a default onset word medially, and §8.3.3, and §8.6.1 for a discussion of default glottal use in disordered speech. As we noted in §5.5.1.4, glottals may also replace pharyngeals, in what appears to be a minimal repair.)

Not all children use glottals in early development. Relevant constraints are: **Not(+s.g.)**, **Not(+c.g.)**, and **Co-occurring(σ – Margin→C-Place)**. The **Not** constraints prohibit the features themselves, and the margin co-occurrence constraint prohibit placeless segments in onset or coda positions. (See §8.3.4.) Although we suspect that [h] is more commonly prohibited than glottal stop, we have found no comparative data on this topic.

5.5.2.3.1. [+ spread-glottis]

If **Not(+s.g.)** is high-ranked, [h] and aspiration may be prohibited. Glottal stops, glides, or consonants may replace [h], or the segment may delete altogether.

(Stops will be produced as short-lag stops in most cases.) Consonant replacement usually indicates some other co-occurrence constraints and thus we concentrate in this section on glottal stop, and on glide replacements and deletion (but see §5.5.4.2).

If **Not(+ s.g.)** prohibits [h], but **Survived(-consonantal)** is high-ranked, either a glottal stop or a glide may substitute for [h]. The glottal stop possibly most commonly replaces /h/ (at least in English), but again, we have insufficient data to confirm this. (Fikkert, 1994, indicates that there were no stop substitutions for [h] in her Dutch data, but does not comment on possible *glottal* stop replacement.) Sometimes aspirated stops are prohibited along with [h]. If the repair is minimal, /h/ may be realized as [ʔ], and stops may surface as unaspirated (delinking of [+s.g.]). For example, Charles (Bernhardt, 1992b) used neither [h] nor aspirated stops word initially at age 5;11:

paper	/p(ʰ)eɪpɹ̩/	[peɪbɔᵊ]
tub	/t(ʰ)ʌb/	[t̪ʌbᵊ]
candle	/k(ʰ)ændl̩/	[kæ̃ndɔːᵊ]
hi	/haɪ/	[ʔaɪ]

Not(+ s.g.) was high-ranked, and constraints for the glottal stop were low-ranked. With no place features, the only other possible laryngeal feature is [+c.g.], which was consequently inserted in place of [+s.g.] for /h/.

Survived(-consonantal) ‖‖‖	
Not(Place)	**Not(+ c.g.)**
Not(+ s.g.)	**Survived(+ s.g.)**

Nonminimal repairs (oral glide substitutions or deletion) may also occur. When Morgan (Stemberger, p.u.d.) did not use [h] or aspirated word-initial stops, [h] deleted, in spite of the fact that glottal stops appeared word initially at the beginning of vowel-initial words. (Note also that stops could be aspirated word finally. Thus, the constraint against [+s.g.] was positional.)

| hop | /hɑp/ | [apʰ] |
| up | /(ʔ)ʌp/ | [ʔapʰ] |

In this case, it appears that [+c.g.] was underlying. Highest ranking of **Survived(+ c.g.)** ensured that glottal stops appeared at the beginning of vowel-initial words, but higher ranking of **Not(+ c.g.)** also prevented insertion of glottal stops when [h] was not possible.

| **Survived(+ c.g.)** ‖‖‖ | **Not(+ c.g.)** ‖‖‖ | **Not(+ s.g.)ₒₙₛₑₜ** ‖‖‖ | **Survived(+ s.g.)ₒₙₛₑₜ** |
| | | | **Survived(TimingUnit)** |

Another nonminimal repair is insertion of V-Place. Von Bremen (1990) gives an example of consistent use of [j] for /h/ by a pair of identical twins (e.g., *hops* as [jɑps]). When [j] replaces /h/, [+s.g.] deletes. As in Morgan's case above, [+c.g.] could not be inserted. However, **Survived(Root)** and **Survived(-conso-**

nantal) were high-ranked. Consequently, a V-Place node was inserted, with subsequent insertion of default [Coronal] for [j]. (Additional constraints ensured that the correct features for [j] were inserted.) The following constraint list and other complex ones in this and following chapters align the competing constraints as in previous tables, and also add a column for results of each major "competition," in order to clarify the individual interactions.

		RESULTS
Survived/LinkedUpwards(Root)		Root needed
Survived/LinkedUpwards(-cons)	Not(V-Place)	Glide insertion
Not(+ s.g.)	Survived/LinkedUpwards(+ s.g.)	No [h]
Not(+ c.g.)		No [ʔ]
	Not(Coronal)	/h/ > [j]

5.5.2.3.2. Obligatory Onsets?

Given high ranking of **Not(+ c.g.)**, there may be no glottal stop onset to vowel-initial words, or no insertion of [ʔ] as we noted in the previous two examples. Some adult languages do not have an obligatory glottal stop before word-initial vowels. Freitas (1996) noted that her three Portuguese-learning subjects often produced onsetless syllables early in development. For Spanish, Lleó et al. (1996) noted inconsistent use of glottal stops and [h] when words appeared, even though those segments do not occur in the target language. When children produce segments that are *not* in the target language, this may reflect universal (or at least individual) predisposition for such segments. However, when they do not use segments that are optional in the adult language, it is not clear whether the data reflect universal or language-specific tendencies. Gwendolyn did not use glottal stop onsets until 1;9, suggesting that there are options regarding development of onsets and glottal insertion even in languages which require them in many contexts.

5.5.2.4. Ejectives and Implosives

Very little is known about development of speech sounds in which the larynx is raised or lowered to control air pressure, although there is some preliminary information on ejectives. Mowrer and Burger (1991) comment that none of their Xhosa-learning subjects made errors on the ejective stops or implosive /ɓ/ (ages 2;6–6;0). Similarly, Cook (1995) reported use of ejectives by age 2;5 for a child learning Chipewyan (Joe). Pye et al.'s (1987) report on five Quiche Mayan toddlers from age 1;7–3;0 shows appearance of ejectives and implosives by age 2 at least, although not frequently, and not for all places of articulation. The implosive [ɓ] was most frequent, and in addition, one child had an ejective [k'].

More commonly, raising or lowering of the larynx is absent. If constraints for the relevant features are high-ranked (and one must ask whether those features include [+raised-glottis] and [+lowered-glottis]), this can be resolved by eliminating the glottal component of the segment. In the Chipewyan examples below from Joe at age 2;3 (Cook, 1995), the segment surfaces with voicing also (although other obstruents often surfaced as [+voiced] also).

/ʦ'ah/	[ʤa]	'hat'
/k'oθʧəðe/	[goʧele]	'scarf'
/tabés/	[debés]	'scissors'

5.5.3. MANNER FEATURE DEVELOPMENT

Manner classes are not represented equally in babbling and early words: stops, glides, and nasals are the most frequent sound classes, although oral glides may not always be in the early inventories. Some fricatives or liquids may occur in early development, but much less commonly across children. In even a small group of children, variability in order of acquisition is apparent for all sound classes but stops and nasals. We examine developmental trends and constraints/repairs for each of the following in turn: glides and glottals, true consonants, stops and nasals, fricatives, and liquids (/l/ and rhotics).

5.5.3.1. Glides and Glottals: [-consonantal]

Data about glide development are scarce. Vihman (1992) is the only researcher to discuss the set of glides in any detail in early words and babbling. (See also the notes from Lleó et al., 1996, above for glottals.) In her crosslinguistic data, [h] was second in frequency to [d], and [w] was fifth-ranked among consonant-like segments. Perhaps one simple way to adhere to the high-ranked σ▸**Onset** constraint is to use a glide, which is a "vowel" in a consonantal syllable position. Vihman does emphasize within- and across-language variability, however, particularly within her early samples. For example, English-speaking subjects used [wa] infrequently in comparison with the French, Japanese, and Swedish infants, but used [hʌ] syllables about twice as often as the other children (21% compared with 10–12%). As words became more frequent, within-language variability decreased, and proceeded in the direction of the adult language. Thus, [h] became less frequent in French and Swedish (reflecting language-specific inventory constraints for French, although not for Swedish).

Note that glides were not *the* most frequent consonant-like elements in the early syllables in Vihman's study. ([d] was most frequent as a syllable onset.) Because they contrast much less in sonority than stops with the following vowels, glides are less optimal onsets (see §4.7.1.3 and §6.1.12 on margin co-occurrence constraints). Furthermore, not all glides necessarily appear in early inventories. Although [w] and [h] were frequent, the glide [j] was not among the sixteen most frequent syllable onsets in Vihman (1992).

We concentrate here on phenomena affecting /w/ and /j/ that concern the feature [-consonantal]. (See also §5.5.1.5.) If **Not(-consonantal)** is high-ranked, glides are prohibited. **Co-occurring(σ-Margin→ + consonantal)**, which restricts syllable margins to true consonants, may also be involved. The following patterns are attested:

Pattern 1:	/w/	[b]	Stopping
	/j/	[d]	
Pattern 2:	/w/	[β] or [v]	Spirantization
	/j/	[ʝ]or [ʒ]	
Pattern 3:	/w/	[ɹ]	Liquid replacement
	/j/	[l]	
Pattern 4:	/w/	[m]	Nasalization
	/j/	[n]	

The literature does not give enough data to comment on the relative or absolute frequency of these patterns, or their differences across the developmental period. Ingram (1989b) suggests that patterns affecting glides are infrequent. Fikkert (1994) gives longitudinal examples for one subject, Jarmo. Stops (in reduplicative patterns) or [h] first replaced glides in Jarmo's system.

wipwap	/ʋipʋɑp/	[pi:pɑ]	'seesaw'	1;8.12
Willy	/ʋɪli:/	[hi:li:]	'Willy'	1;10.9
water	/ʋa:tər/	[ca:tɔ]	'water'	2;0.4

When [l] became possible, [l] then substituted for glides.

| wipwap | /ʋipʋɑp/ | [li:pa:] | 'seesaw' | 2;1.8 |
| Willy | /ʋɪli:/ | [li:li:] | 'Willy' | 2;1.8 |

Finally, they were mastered.

| water | /ʋa:tər/ | [ʋa:tə] | 'water' | 2;4.1 |

Fricatives, although acquired before [l], never replaced glides.

The same pattern does not necessarily apply to all oral glides. Co-occurrence constraints concerning the place features can result in different outputs. The following discussion presents further data and analyses for the above patterns. The first two patterns involve obstruent substitutions, and the last two involve sonorant substitutions.

Pattern 1: Stop Substitutions for Glides. Few examples of stop substitutions for glides are given in the literature. We gave Jarmo's examples above, but the particular tokens also show consonant harmony (reduplication of [p], [+sonorant] harmony for [h]), suggesting that sequence constraints may also have been implicated. Amahl (N. Smith, 1973) substituted [d] for /j/ at a point when fricatives were not in the system (e.g., *you* as [du]). Similarly, Colin (§8.3) substituted [b] for /w/ when fricatives were not available word initially. However, Colin did produce /j/ accurately in the word *yeah*, indicating that constraints concerning [Labial] and [-consonantal] were relevant for prohibition of /w/ production rather than general feature constraints on [-consonantal]:

why	/waɪ/	[bam]
wagon	/wægən/	[bæhæː]
yeah	/jɛː/	[jæː]

In repairs such as these, the underlying articulator node may remain ([Labial] or [Coronal]). However, it is necessarily realized as a consonantal articulation.

When **Not(-consonantal)** is high-ranked, and [-consonantal] deletes, all the other manner features ([+sonorant], [+continuant]) may delete also. In the above examples, **Co-occurring(σ-Margin→ +consonantal)** is high-ranked; glide onsets are prohibited. Other margin constraints may also be high-ranked. Thus, fricatives may also be prohibited in onset: **Co-occurring(σ-Margin→-continuant)**. Sonorants may also be prohibited: **Co-occurring(σ-Margin→-sonorant)**. (In the cases above, fricatives and liquids were not possible in any position in the word, due to independent constraints on features.) (As we will see for Colin in §8.3.4, additional constraints relating to feature co-occurrence for [+nasal] were also implicated.) Interestingly, for both boys, voiced stops replaced the glides, showing some faithfulness to the target. The theory of default underspecification provides an explanation for the faithfulness to voicing. The redundant nondefault feature [+voiced] can be present underlyingly, and thus subject to faithfulness constraints (high ranking of **Survived(+voiced)**). The following constraint ranking applies:

		RESULTS
Co-occurring(σ-Margin→ +cons)	**Not(+cons)**	**Consonant margin**
	Survived(-cons)	
Co-occurring(σ-Margin→-son)	**Not(-sonorant)**	**Obstruent margin**
Co-occurring(σ-Margin→-cont)	**Not(-cont)**	**Stop margin**
	Survived(+cont)	
Survived(+voiced)	**Not(+voiced)**	**Glide > Voiced stop**

Pattern 2: Fricative Substitutions for Glides. Reports of fricative substitutions for glides are few. We gave some examples of [v] substitutions for /w/ in the discussion of [+labiodental] (§5.5.1.3). Ingram (1989b) gives other examples of [v] substitution for /w/, and notes that Joan (Velten, 1943) used the alveolar [z] for the palatal glide. (See also §5.5.3.6.)

yellow	/jɛloʊ/	[zɑːwa]	1;11
yard	/jɑɹd/	[zɑːd]	2;0

Stemberger (1992a) reports that Morgan used an alveopalatal (ungrooved) fricative [ʐ] for /j/, and [v] or [β] for /v/ at different times.

When a glide is replaced by a fricative, [+continuant] survives, but [-consonantal] and [+sonorant] delete. Following default underspecification, the redundant nondefault feature [+continuant] of the glide is present in the underlying representation. Constraint rankings are similar to those above for stop substitutions with the exception of constraints regarding [+continuant]. **Survived/**

LinkedUpwards(+ continuant) promotes a continuant substitution: a redundant nondefault feature survives. However, redundant nondefault [+sonorant] is eliminated because of a co-occurrence constraint prohibiting sonorant continuants. (Full specification would also account for this.)

RESULTS

Co-occurring(σ-Margin→ + cons)		Survived(-consonantal)	Consonant margin
		Not(+ consonantal)	
Survived(+ continuant)		Not(+ continuant)	Continuant
Not(+ sonorant)		Survived(+ sonorant)	Obstruent margin
Survived(+ voiced)		Not(+ voiced)	Glide > Voiced
			fricative

Note that if glides surface as stops when fricatives are in the system, as Fikkert (1994) noted for Jarmo, we would then have to assume that [+continuant] is not specified underlyingly for glides, but only for fricatives (as would be predicted by radical underspecification and contrastive specification). If the glide was not possible, [continuant] would be realized with the system default value [-continuant]. Fricatives would surface as fricatives, because of high ranking of faithfulness constraints for the *underlying* feature [+continuant]. Other than this note for Jarmo, we have found no other examples of glides surfacing as stops when fricatives are possible in onset. This suggests that the feature [+continuant] is specified for glides for the majority of children. The evidence also points to maintenance of [+voiced] for most children (and see our comments on [l] substitutions below), suggesting that redundant nondefault [+voiced] is in the underlying representation. Default underspecification has relatively strong support. In learning, redundant nondefault features are often achieved via lexical specification rather than via constraint ranking.

Pattern 3: [l] Substitution for Glides (and Rhotics).   If [-consonantal] delinks, but [+sonorant] is maintained, a nasal or /l/ can replace a glide. (See Jarmo's examples above.) Stemberger (1992a) reports that Morgan substituted [l] for /j/ (and coronal fricatives):

yeah   /jɛː/   [laː]

If [l] is the only nonnasal [+consonantal] sonorant in the child's system, it substitutes for the glide. (It is not an accident that both /j/ and [l] are [Coronal]; [Coronal] survives.) However, [l] is more likely as a substitute for rhotics that are [+consonantal]. The replacement of trilled alveolar /r/ with [l] is fairly common (See Beers, 1991, for Dutch; Bortolini & Leonard, 1991, for Italian; and Yavaş & Lamprecht, 1988, for Brazilian Portuguese.) In these cases /r/ is coronal only, and the pattern is therefore not place-related, as it often is in English. The interchange probably involves margin co-occurrence constraints, with high ranking for **Sur-**

vived(+sonorant) and **Not(+nasal)**. In this case the redundant nondefault [+sonorant] must survive, and the constraint prohibiting insertion of [+lateral] is low-ranked.

Co-occurring(σ-Margin→ +consonantal)	‖‖	**Survived(-consonantal)**	
Survived(+sonorant)		**Not(+consonantal)**	
Not(+nasal)		**Not(+lateral)**	
		Not(+sonorant)	

Pattern 4: Nasal Substitutions for Glides. Nasal substitutions for glides are rare. Marcy (Bernhardt, 1994b, p.u.d.), a child with a phonological disorder, used nasals for glides before intervention at 3;3:

read	/ɹiːd/	[nːiə]
laugh	/læf/	[ɲæ̃]
yellow	/jɛloʊ/	[nːːiæ]
watch	/wɑtʃ/	[nɑ]

(See Lohuis-Weber and Zonneveld, 1997, for an additional report.) Constraint rankings are similar to those for the [l] substitution above. However, **Not(+nasal)** is lowest-ranked. The only sonorant consonant in her inventory was a nasal, and hence [+nasal] was inserted.

Co-occurring(σ-Margin→ +consonantal)	‖‖	**Not(+nasal)**
Survived(+sonorant)		
Not(+lateral)		

For Marcy, /l/ also surfaced as a nasal. Rice and Avery's (1995) feature geometry includes a Spontaneous Voicing (SV) node, in which [Nasal] is the default sonorant, and glides and laterals are specified in comparison with nasals. (See Figure 5.1 above.) Based on the Rice and Avery (1995) geometry, the constraint ranking would be:

Survived/LinkedUpwards(SV)	‖‖	**Not(Nasal)**
Not(Vocalic)		

The Rice and Avery geometry accounts well for the substitution pattern in which nasals replace other sonorants. It can also account for substitution of laterals for glides as in the previous example above (default [Lateral] inserted for the other Oral feature, [Vocalic]). However, their geometry does not account well for patterns in which obstruents and glides (or laterals) replace each other. In the Rice and Avery (1995) geometry, glides are (specified) dependents of the SV node while obstruents are dependents of the Airflow node, that is, they have no built-in connections within the geometry. Geometry which builds in the possibility of connections between the feature [continuant] and [sonorant] (as through the Root node, in the standard versions of feature geometry) accounts better for glide-obstruent replacement patterns.

5.5.3.2. True Consonants: [+consonantal]

True consonants tend to be present from the earliest stages of babbling. However, glides may replace one or more consonant classes. Depending on co-occurrence restrictions, either oral glides or glottals may replace consonants. If the constraint concerns [+consonantal] only, then replacement of true consonants by oral glides is only a minimal repair: [+consonantal] is delinked, and [-consonantal] is inserted. Other aspects of the geometry reflect that change: delinking of [+consonantal] implies delinking of C-Place (and possibly insertion of V-Place).

When a glottal replaces a true consonant, constraints beyond **Not(+consonantal)** are implicated, such as **Not(Place)** or **NotCo-occurring(Place,-consonantal)**. If either of these particular constraints is involved, glottal substitutions represent a minimal repair: the only possible replacement of a segment with no oral Place is a glottal. Other features of the target (C-Place, Labial, etc.) will automatically delink once [+consonantal] and Place are prohibited (because they are dependent on those other features for realization). If the relevant constraints concern *co-occurrence* of C-Place and other features, glottal substitutions may be nonminimal repairs, because elimination of C-Place or one of the other co-occurring features should solve the problem. In the following example, we assume that glottal substitution is a minimal repair, since we have no evidence for co-occurrence constraints.

Bernhardt (p.u.d.) has observed children clinically who do not use any consonants but glottals. (*S6* from Bernhardt, 1990, used glottal stops or [h] for most consonants, but only prior to the formal collection of data.) σ▸**Onset** and **Linked Downwards(TimingUnit)** ensured that some segment appeared in the onset. **Not(Place)** and **Not** constraints for all other nondefault features were higher-ranked than **Survived/LinkedUpwards** constraints for those features, prohibiting oral glides and consonants. Pruning of all features leaves a floating Root Node and Timing Unit. **Not(-continuant)** and **Not(+c.g.)** were sufficiently low-ranked that a glottal stop could be inserted to fill the empty slot.

			RESULTS
σ▸**Onset**	**Not(+cons)**	**Survived(+cons)**	**[-cons] onset**
LinkedDownwards		**Not(-cons)**	
(**TimingUnit**)	**Not(Place)**	**Survived(Place)**	**Glottal**
Survived(Root)	**Not(Nondefault)**	**Survived(⟨Nondef⟩)**	**No nondefaults**
LinkedUpwards(Root)		**Not(-cont)**	**Stop**
		Not(+c.g.)	**[?] default**

Fikkert (1994) comments that [h] often was a substitution if consonants did not delete outright. This was particularly true for other continuants. A similar ranking to the above is implicated, with low ranking for features of [h], and high ranking of **Survived(+continuant)**.

5.5.3.3. Stops and Nasals: ([-continuant]; [+nasal])

We include both stops and nasals in this section, in a general discussion of the feature [-continuant]. We assume that [-continuant] is the default value of [continuant] in the adult language, and that [+nasal] is a nondefault feature.

Both babbling and early words contain a high proportion of stops, both as matches for adult targets, and as substitutions for other sound classes. Stops were the only sound class used by all 55 subjects in Stoel-Gammon's (1993) study of infants (although some children additionally used nasals and/or fricatives). Vihman (1992) noted that [da] was the most frequent syllable in babbling and early words in her study of English, Swedish, Japanese, and French subjects. In that same subject group, Swedish-learning and English-learning children showed a higher proportion of stops than the French and Japanese infants, possibly reflecting the phonological properties of the target words attempted in the different languages (de Boysson-Bardies et al., 1992). The high frequency of stops strongly suggests that [-continuant] is the default value for child phonology.

Nasals, although present in the babbling and speech of many children, are not universally present, nor are they as frequent as stops. For example, in her study of 12 Dutch-learning subjects, Fikkert (1994) noted that nasals followed stops and glides in the developmental sequence. However, in the de Boysson-Bardies et al. (1992) study, a higher proportion of nasals was noted in the French and Japanese samples, reflecting frequency in the targets attempted. Nasals were more frequent word finally in French and Japanese, another fact congruent with input language frequency.

The following substitution patterns have been observed:

	Target	*Substitution*	
Pattern 1:	Nasal	Stop	Denasalization
Pattern 2:	Stop	Nasal	Nasalization
Pattern 3:	Stop	Fricative	Lenition
Pattern 4:	Nasal	Other sonorant	Denasalization
Pattern 5:	Stop	Nonnasal sonorant	Gliding; Lateralization

The first two patterns (nasal-stop interchanges) are the most common, although stops tend to replace nasals more often than the reverse. Fricatives may replace stops in intervocalic or coda positions because of sequence or rime co-occurrence constraints, but they are less likely to replace stops word-initially. (In a study of Mexican Spanish, Macken and Barton, 1980b, noted that fricatives commonly substituted for word-initial "stops" in the speech of the children, but spirantization is a common process in the adult language as well.) Fricatives may replace /k/ more often than other segments (suggesting relevance of co-occurrence constraints). For example, John (Edwards & Bernhardt, 1973b) and Darryl (§8.5.1.2) had lateral fricative substitutions for /k/ (but not for other voiceless stops). DE (§7.4.1.3) used [s] for word-initial /k/, as did Larissa for some words (Stemberger, 1993a). Aspiration is phonetically longer in /k/, and thus /k/ may be treated more like a fricative (?high ranking of **Survived(+s.g.)**). Generally, however, high ranking of margin constraints predisposes noncontinuants in onset. Fricatives and liquids develop later than nasals and stops, and thus are less likely to replace them. (We have found no examples of fricatives replacing nasals except where fricatives are general defaults, as in the case of Jeremy, §8.4.) Burton (1980) reports substitution of the glide [ɹ] for /n/ for one subject with a phonological disorder, but such reports are rare.

Pattern 1: Stop Substitutions for Nasals. A high-ranked **Not(+nasal)** constraint can prohibit production of nasals. This can result from phonological constraints or from structural impediments (nasal blockage). In a minimal repair, [+nasal] deletes, and the default feature [-nasal] is inserted. Typically, a homorganic oral stop results (e.g., /m/ > [b]). In some cases, the place of articulation also changes; all nondefault features may delete, as the result of additional co-occurrence constraints involving [+nasal].

Sally (Bernhardt, 1994b, p.u.d.) had examples of both homorganic stop substitutions for nasals, and default coronal stop substitutions. (The coronal stops appeared for a number of other segments, particularly in running speech, and/or if there were other coronals in the word.)

mask	/mæsk/	[pæks]	
mouthy	/mʌʊθiː/	[bʌʊθiː]	
music	/mjuːzɪk/	[tusɪk]	
noise	/nɔɪz/	[towəs]	(also [sɔɪts] 3 times)
plum	/plʌm/	[bapʰ]	

LinkedDownwards(Root) ‖	**Survived(+nasal)**
Not(+nasal) ‖	**Not(-nasal)**
‖	**Not(-continuant)**

Note that the resulting stops varied between [-voiced] and [+voiced]. She did not yet have a voicing contrast, and hence the feature [+voiced] for the nasal did not necessarily survive (except for reasons independent of the nasal itself). For other children (such as Colin, §8.3), stop substitutions for nasals surface consistently as [+voiced]. In such cases, the redundant feature [+voiced] is probably specified underlyingly as per default underspecification.

Pattern 2: Nasal Substitutions for Stops. If the velum does not shut off the nasal cavity, a stop may be nasalized completely (/b/ > [m]) or partially (/b/ > [b̃]). This is usually only the case when the oral mechanism is not structurally or functionally normal, as in cleft palate or neurogenically based disorders. The different vocal tract might lead to [+nasal] as a default feature. (Note: In such cases, sound classes other than stops also tend to be realized as nasals.)

LinkedDownwards(Root) ‖	**Not(+nasal)**
Not(-nasal) ‖	**Survived(-nasal)**
Co-occurring(-continuant→ +nasal) ‖	

(Deaf speakers also may produce nasals for stops because of perceptual difficulty. Again, [+nasal] might be the default, and [-nasal] might be the underlying feature.)

Pattern 3: Fricative Substitutions for Stops. If **Not(-continuant)** is high-ranked, stops and nasals can be prohibited. The feature [-continuant] fails to link up, and [+continuant] is inserted, resulting in production of a fricative. Fricatives tend not to replace nasals, unless a general default pattern is implicated (as for Jeremy, §8.4), or there is assimilation (as in Sally's example [sɔɪts] for *noise* above). Nasals and fricatives have no articulatory features in common. If a nasal is not possible, stops or sonorants are closer substitutes. (Of course if noncontinuants and sonorants are not possible in the child's speech, a fricative *could* conceivably replace a nasal.)

If fricatives generally replace stops, the following constraint ranking would apply.

Not(-continuant])	‖‖	**Not(+ continuant)**
		Survived(-continuant)

Spirantization is not uncommon for Spanish-learning children, probably because spirantization is a productive process in the target language (Macken & Barton, 1980b). However, it may be limited to intervocalic or initial position, just as in the adult phonology. Similarly, in the examples we have found for English, spirantization has been limited to specific stops or word positions (Jeremy, §8.4; DE, §7.4.1.3). In such cases, co-occurrence constraints are implicated.

Patterns 4 and 5: Nonnasal Sonorants for Nasals and Stops. Glides are more likely to replace nasals than stops, probably because both nasals and glides are [+sonorant] (but see Terry's data, §7.3.4.5).

In §5.5.3.1, we gave examples of Marcy's nasal substitutions for approximants at age 3;3. During the phonological intervention process, she began to use glides. At age 3;6, some temporary overgeneralization occurred (i.e., /n/ > [j]).

	nine	/naɪn/	[jaɪ]
	noisy	/nɔɪziː/	[juju]
BUT:	no	/noʊ/	[noʊ]

Replacement of nasals with glides shows maintenance of the redundant non-default feature, [+sonorant]. If consonantal sonorants are not possible in the child's system (high-ranked **NotCo-occurring(+ sonorant, + consonantal)**) the only possible sonorant consonant is a glide.

RESULTS

Not(+ nasal)	‖‖	**Survived(+ nasal)**	**No nasals**
NotCo-occurring(+ sonorant, + cons)		**Survived(+ cons)**	**No consonants**
Survived/LinkedUpwards(+ sonorant)		**Not(+ sonorant)**	**Sonorant**
		Not(-cons)	**Nasal > Glide**

5.5.3.4. Fricatives: [+ continuant],[-sonorant]

Fricatives, liquids, and glides (vowels) are all [+continuant], but [+continuant] is only distinctive for fricatives. Although we have defined the major constraint concerning fricative production to be a co-occurrence constraint (**Not Co-occurring(+ continuant,-sonorant)**), we discuss fricatives here as one of the sound classes rather than below in the co-occurrence section §5.5.4. (There is no single defining feature for fricatives that is equivalent to [+nasal] or [-consonantal], yet fricatives are considered to be a sound class on a par with the other sound classes.) The combination of [+continuant] and [-sonorant] appears to be difficult, since fricatives are relatively infrequent in babbling and early words, and fricative development may not be complete until age 8 or 9. Several researchers have noted language-specific influences on frequency of fricative use and order of acquisition. Lleó et al. (1996) observed a significantly higher proportion of fricatives in Spanish babbling and early word samples than in German babbling; they attributed this to the influence of the contextually conditioned spirantization process in adult Spanish. Japanese infants in de Boysson-Bardies et al. (1992) had a higher proportion of fricative productions in their early words than in their babbling repertoire, reflecting the target words attempted (although fricative codas were less frequent than nasal codas, also because of target word properties). Ingram (1988b) noted earlier acquisition of [v] in Bulgarian, Estonian, and Swedish than in English, and suggests that frequency in the input affects acquisition order. Although the velar fricative [x] is crosslinguistically marked, it appears to develop early in languages in which it is frequent: Polish (Ingram, 1988a), Quiche (Pye et al., 1987), Dutch (Beers, 1991), and German (Ornelas-Hesse, 1989).

Within English, various orders have been found both within and across studies. Some researchers have found that affricates appear *after* fricatives in English acquisition (e.g., Dinnsen, 1992) while others have found the opposite order (e.g., Ingram et al., 1980; Bernhardt, 1990, 1994b). Word length, familiarity, and word position studied are among the many variables that can influence results. M. Edwards (1979) found no uniform order of fricative acquisition for a small sample of six English-speaking children (from ages 1;6 to 2;6) when using a detailed longitudinal design that took all word positions into account.

The following fricative substitution patterns are found:

	Target	*Substitution*	
Pattern 1:	Fricative	Stop	Stopping
Pattern 2:	Fricative	Affricate	Affrication
Pattern 3:	Fricative	Nasal	Nasalization
Pattern 4:	Fricative	[l] or [ɹ]	Liquid replacement
Pattern 5:	Fricative	Glide	Gliding

The most common pattern in early phonology is Stopping. Affrication may also be relatively common. Liquids and glides are infrequent but attested substitutions. Nasals are infrequent substitutions (and usually indicate some kind of velopharyngeal insufficiency).

Not(+ continuant) or **NotCo-occurring(+ continuant,-sonorant)** prevent fricatives from being produced. In a minimal repair, only the feature [+continuant] or [-sonorant] delinks, with default values [-continuant] or [+sonorant] being inserted. If nasals or liquids replace fricatives, a more complex constraint ranking is indicated, as we will see below.

Pattern 1: Stop Substitutions for Fricatives.   Stops may appear only for oral fricatives, as for Dylan (§8.6), or for both /h/ and oral fricatives, as for Stuart's sample below (Bernhardt, 1994b). Relative ranking of **Not(+ s.g.)** can prohibit or promote [h] (for itself or for voiceless fricatives).

see	/siː/	[diː]
fish	/fɪʃ/	[bɪ]
horsie	/hɔɹsi/	[ʔɔʔi]

In Stuart's case, word-initial voiceless stops were unaspirated or voiced (short lag). Both **Not(+ s.g.)** and **NotCo-occurring(+ continuant,-sonorant)** were high-ranked.

RESULTS

Not(+ s.g.)	Survived(+ s.g.)	No aspiration or
NotCo-occurring(+ cont,-son)	Survived(+ cont)	fricatives
Not(+ sonorant)	Not(-sonorant)	No sonorant
		substitutions
	Not(-continuant)	Fricative > Stop

Pattern 2: Affricate Substitutions for Fricatives.   Some children produce affricates before producing fricatives. So and Dodd (1995) noted relatively frequent use of [ts] for /s/ in their 2-year-old Cantonese-learning subjects. This pattern occurred even though they used [t] for the Cantonese phoneme /ts/ (a chain shift).

A child learning Chipewyan (Joe) had similar patterns at age 2;3 (Cook, 1995). Chipewyan has a rich inventory, including a variety of coronal affricates and fricatives (/tɬ/, /tθ/, /ts/, /tʃ/, plus voiced and ejective counterparts, and homorganic fricatives). Joe inconsistently produced affricates for fricatives and target affricates. Stops often replaced affricates, however (another example of chain shifts, showing lack of contrast between stops, fricatives, and affricates).

/seðá/	[dzedzá]	'my mouth'
/ʃét/	[tʃétɪ̯]	's/he is eating'
/tsʼeré/	[dará]	'blanket'
/tsʼah/	[dza]	'hat'

Affricate substitutions for fricatives are perhaps less common in English, but do occur (e.g., Roger: Bernhardt, 1994b, p.u.d.).

fish	/fɪʃ/	[pʰɪtʃ]
six	/sɪks/	[tsɪʔ]
shoe	/ʃu/	[tʰu]~[tʃu]

All of these children produced stops as stops during this period.

Deciding how to account for affricate substitution for stops is difficult, because classification of affricates is problematical in general. Assuming a branching [continuant] feature for affricates, we might assume a high-ranked co-occurrence constraint: **Co-occurring(σ-Margin→-continuant)**, requiring a consonant to be [-continuant] *even if* [+continuant] survives:

Co-occurring(σ-Margin→-continuant)	**Not(-continuant)**
Survived/LinkedUpwards(+ continuant)	**Not(+ continuant)**
NoSequence(+ continuant...-continuant)	

(The ranking of the two **Not** constraints does not matter here, though **Not(+ continuant)** is likely to be ranked higher.) The feature [+continuant] survives, and [-continuant] is inserted in front of it (due to sequence constraints within the segment).

An analysis of affricates as strident stops also may presuppose a margin co-occurrence constraint, but additionally, **Survived(+ grooved)** is high-ranked, ensuring that [+grooved] will be realized. However, margin co-occurrence constraints require a [-continuant] segment, and hence, a strident stop is produced.

Co-occurring(σ-Margin→-continuant)
Survived/LinkedUpwards(+ grooved)

Survived(+ continuant)

Not(-continuant)
Not(+ grooved)

This works well for the Cantonese data and for Roger's data, because only grooved sibilants were affected. However, it does not work well for Joe's data, because it cannot represent the lateral and interdental affricates in *adult* Chipewyan. If we ignore that, there is an interesting additional fact. Joe produced underlying interdental fricatives as grooved fricatives. We would have to assume that [+grooved] was a redundant nondefault feature for sibilants as per **Co-occurring(Coronal, + continuant→ + grooved)**. (See §5.5.1.2.1.) Nonetheless, as per default underspecification, this analysis requires that [+ grooved] be underlying.

Pattern 3: Nasal Substitutions for Fricatives.   Nasals are rare substitutions for fricatives, just as fricatives are rare substitutions for nasals. Lohuis-Weber and Zonneveld (1997) report this substitution for a normally developing child. More commonly, inability to close off the nasal cavity can result in nasal substitutions for fricatives, as in cleft palate speech. These nasals may be voiced or voiceless. (See §8.5.2.)

VOICED NASAL SUBSTITUTION.   Voiced nasals have been observed as substitutions for fricatives (Norris & Harden, 1981). As noted above, Marcy used nasals for approximants. Although stops were generally stops, and [h] appeared for most word-initial fricatives, [n] appeared for /z/ in the word *zoo* (age 3;3).

	zoo	/zuː/	[nuː]	(twice)
BUT:	zipper	/zɪpɹ̩/	[hɪha]	

Her use of [n] for the fricative calls into question a Spontaneous Voicing node analysis as we suggested for her nasal substitutions for glides. Exchanges between the SV node and Airflow node appear unlikely, given the Rice and Avery (1995) geometry. Her data show lack of distinctiveness between [+continuant] and [+sonorant], suggesting the two features might be better considered terminal features of the same node (i.e., the Root), as they are in standard feature geometry. However, beyond the fact that [continuant] and [nasal] are dominated by Root, standard geometry also does not predict interaction of the two features.

Velopharyngeal incompetence often results in nasal substitutions for obstruents. (See §8.5.3.) Since nasal fricatives are highly marked, [+continuant] deletes, and [-continuant] is inserted:

NotCo-occurring(-sonorant, +continuant, +nasal)	‖‖	Survived(-nasal)
Not(-nasal)	‖‖	Not(+nasal)
		Survived(+continuant)
		Not(-continuant)

VOICELESS NASAL SUBSTITUTION FOR SIBILANTS.   Voiceless nasals may be more frequent as substitutions for fricatives than voiced nasals. Some typically developing children use voiceless nasals as onset replacements for /sn/ or /sm/ clusters. M. Edwards and Bernhardt (1973a) give examples from Carolyn, a child with no obvious functional or structural abnormalities of the velum who used nasal "snorts" (voiceless nasals with turbulent airflow at the nostrils) frequently for word-final sibilants (regardless of underlying voicing):

	juice	/ʤuːs/	[duːn̥]
	eyes	/(ʔ)aɪz/	[jan̥]
	watch	/wɑʧ/	[jʌtn̥]
	bridge	/brɪʤ/	[bɛʔn̥]
	six	/sɪks/	[sɛkn̥]
BUT:	mouth	/maʊθ/	[mʌtf]

The voiceless nasal is turbulent, but is [-continuant] by definition, since there is no airflow through the oral cavity. The features we have been using in this book do not work well for this unusual substitution, but there is a sense of some acoustic faithfulness to the underlying fricative target. (A feature [+fricative] might be useful here.) We note that the child used nasal snorts only for underlying grooved fricatives. If we were instead to use the feature [strident] for high-amplitude turbulence (§5.5.1.2.1), both /s/ and [n̥] would be [+strident]. If **Survived (+strident)** is ranked high, but **Survived(+continuant)** is ranked low, a strident nasal stop (the snort) would result. Co-occurrence constraints would preclude turbulent voiced nasal fricatives. It is unclear to us what negative constraint was driving this substitution, since it affected only grooved consonants in word-final position. We tentatively posit **NotCo-occurring(+ continuant, + strident)**, under the assumption that affricates are both [+continuant] and [-continuant], and that there is no other way for oral stops to be [+strident].

RESULTS

NotCo-occurring(+ continuant, + strident)	Not(-continuant)	No fricatives or
	Not(-strident)	affricates
NotCo-occurring(+ strident, + voiced)	Survived(+ cont)	
	Survived(+ voiced)	
Survived/LinkedUpwards(+ strident)	Not(+ nasal)	Nasal
		"fricative"

According to our definition of [strident], labiodentals and interdentals are [-strident]. This predicts that they would not be produced as nasals and they were not in her speech (although some children with velopharyngeal incompetence might do so, due to general inability to produce oral obstruents).

Pattern 4: Liquid Substitutions for Fricatives. The substitution of liquids for fricatives reflects co-occurrence constraint interactions at the Root node for [+continuant] and [-sonorant]. Survival of the [+continuant] feature can result in a glide or liquid substitution, but such substitutions are infrequent. (Note: This is contrary to the liquid > fricative acquisition sequence suggested by Dinnsen, 1992.) This is an interesting repair, in that the status of the feature [+continuant] changes from contrastive nondefault to redundant nondefault. Examples of this pattern can be found in early phonology. Beginning at age 16 months, Morgan showed use of [l] for /s/ (and later, for [θ]): for example, *sock* [lɑtʰ].[5]

NotCo-occurring(+ cont,-son)	Not(+ sonorant)
Survived/LinkedUpwards(+ cont)	NotCo-occurring(+ cont, + son)
	Not(+ lateral)

Pattern 5: Glide or Glottal Substitutions for Fricatives.

[w] OR [j] SUBSTITUTIONS. Sometimes the feature [+continuant] can only co-occur with [+sonorant] and V-Place (vowels, glides). When a glide replaces a

---

[5] At age 26 months, Morgan showed a regression in which word-initial /l/ became the voiced lateral fricative [ɮ], suggesting some indefiniteness in the boundaries between fricatives and laterals in her system in early phases.

fricative, **Survived(+continuant)** is high-ranked, but survival of C-Place is not a priority. High-ranked **Co-occurring(+continuant→V-Place)** ensures that continuants will be vowels or glides. Insertion of V-Place requires changes in the values of [consonantal] and [sonorant] also.

For Larry (Bernhardt, 1994b, p.u.d.), stops surfaced as stops, affricates as affricates (except once in an assimilative context, *jumping*), and glides as glides:

teeth	/tiːθ/	[tʰit]
dive	/daɪv/	[daɪd]
chair	/ʧɛɹ/	[ʧɛ]
gum	/gʌm/	[gʌm]
gummy	/gʌmi/	[dʌmi]
jumping	/ʤʌmpɪŋ]	[ʤʌmpi] (E), [wʌʔmi] (S)
hang	/hæŋ/	[hæŋ]

However, fricatives and liquids surfaced as [w] in word-initial position. (Elsewhere, fricatives were fricatives or stops.)

leaf	/liːf/	[witʰ]
waving	/weɪvɪŋ/	[weɪvĩŋ]
you	/ju/	[ju]
feather	/fɛðɹ̩/	[wɛðə]
van	/væn/	[wæn]
thumb	/θʌm/	[wʌm]
sauce	/sɑs/	[wɑs]
sun	/sʌn/	[wʌn]
zoo	/zu/	[wu]

Exceptions were /ð/ (realized as [d]), and the word *see*.

that	/ðæt/	[dæt]
see	/siː/	[hi]

We could assume that low-amplitude /ð/ was misperceived as a stop, and that the affricates were (strident) stops. **NotCo-occurring(+cont,-son)** was higher-ranked in onsets. **Survived(+continuant)** was also high-ranked, so that a sonorant continuant surfaced. Since the child had no liquids in the system, a glide was the only possible output. But glides do not have C-Place. Consequently, C-Place was deleted, and V-Place was inserted. Thus, the glide [w] appeared for fricatives in onsets. The insertion of [Labial] is somewhat unexpected in his system. Velar consonants surfaced sometimes as coronals, as did /v/ and /f/, suggesting that [C-Coronal] was the default articulator feature for consonants. However, for vowels, default place was presumably [V-Dorsal,+back] (as in [ə]). Since a back glide must also be [+high] and [V-Labial], those features were also inserted.

RESULTS

NotCo-occurring(+continuant,-sonorant)	Survived(-son)	No fricatives
Survived/LinkedUpwards(+continuant)	Not(+continuant)	Continuant
Co-occurring(+continuant→V-Place)	Not(V-Place)	=
NotCo-occurring(-consonantal,C-Place)	Survived(C-Place)	Glide
	Not(-consonantal)	
	Not(+sonorant)	
Co-occurring(C-TimingUnit,V-Place→+high)		Glide = [+high]
Co-occurring(+back,+high→Labial)	Not(+back)	[w]
	Not(V-Labial)	

GLOTTAL [h] SUBSTITUTIONS. The glottal [h] may be a more frequent substitution than oral glides for (at least onset) fricatives (Stemberger, 1993a; Bernhardt, 1990, Blair [S2], Sean [S4], Chrissie [S6]). Again, **Survived(+continuant)** and **NotCo-occurring(+continuant,-sonorant)** are high-ranked. But V-Place and [+lateral] cannot be inserted (though underlying glides and laterals survive): **Not(V-Place)** and **Not(+lateral)** are higher-ranked than **Not(+s.g.)**, preventing default insertion of glides.

RESULTS

NotCo-occurring(+cont,-son)	No oral fricatives
Survived/LinkedUpwards(+cont)	Must be [+continuant]
Survived/LinkedUpwards(V-Place)	Lower level features must
Survived(+lateral)	survive
NotCo-occurring(-cons,C-Place)	

| Not(+lateral) | No /l/ |
| Not(V-Place) | No oral glides |

Survived(Place)	Place delinks
Not(+s.g.)	[h] insertion
Not(-consonantal)	
Not(+sonorant)	

The only way to rescue the [+continuant] feature in such cases is to sacrifice Place. The value of [consonantal] and [sonorant] change to accommodate [h], the generic fricative-like continuant. We have not yet dealt with the [voiced] feature. Since [h] is [-voiced], it may be assumed that [h] will only replace voiceless fricatives. If **Survived(+s.g.)** is the relevant constraint, that may well be true. However, Blair (S2), Sean (S4), and Chrissie (S6), in Bernhardt (1990) and others, such as Hugh, Bernhardt et al. (1993), replaced voiceless and voiced fricatives with [h]. In such cases, the repair appears to be driven by two major constraint types: a positive one promoting faithfulness to [+continuant], and negative ones, prohibiting insertion of oral sonorant defaults. Survival of [voiced] is less important than faithfulness to [continuant]. Since [+voiced] is only possible if there is a place of articulation (**Co-occurring(+ voiced→Place**)), [+voiced] deletes.

In the examples that follow from Blair (Bernhardt, 1990, *S2*), note that the only variability was with /ð/ (as it was for Larry in the example above). Blair produced glides and [l], but with the exception of the word *that*, [w] replaced only /ɹ/ in his system. Coronal fricatives were possible in coda and intervocalic position. Thus, the [h] was a default word initially only, again showing a similarity with Larry's data above. The constraint ranking above applies to his system, with the addition that **Survived(+ voiced)** was low-ranked.

feather	/fɛðɹ̩/	[hadɛᵊ]
van	/væn/	[hæn]
thumb	/θʌm/	[h̃ʌ̃m]
that	/ðæt/	[wæʔ]~[dæ]
the	/ðə/	[ðə]
this	/ðɪs/	[hɪs]
those	/ðoʊz/	[hoç]
soap	/soʊp/	[hoʊp]
shoe	/ʃu/	[hju]
zoo	/zu/	[hju]

5.5.3.5. Affricates

Affricates are acquired at different times for different children, both within and across languages (Ingram et al., 1980; Anderson & Smith, 1987; Pye et al., 1987). The most common substitution patterns are as follows:

Pattern 1: Affricate > Stop
Pattern 2: Affricate > Fricative

Nasals or liquids sometimes surface for affricates, but usually only when nasals or liquids are general default segments or there is some structural abnormality of the oral mechanism. They appear never to substitute just for affricates.

Pattern 1 is the most frequent (e.g., Marcy: Bernhardt, 1994b, p.u.d.):

chair	/tʃɛɹ/	[tʰɛə]
jump	/dʒʌmp/	[dʌm]

Pattern 2 is also fairly frequent (e.g., Miles: Bernhardt, 1994b, p.u.d.):

church	/tʃɹ̩tʃ/	[ʃɹ̩ʃ]
jumping	/dʒʌmpɪŋ/	[ʃʌmpĩŋ]

Voicing and place may or may not be maintained (compare Marcy's examples with those of Miles). Place changes can result in a [ts]/[dz] or [s]/[z] substitution (see the discussion of [-anterior]). Patterns may be the same or different for the voiced and voiceless affricates, depending on co-occurrence constraints. Gerry (Bernhardt, 1994b, p.u.d.) used fricatives or affricates for /tʃ/, but stops for /dʒ/.

	chair	/tʃɛɹ/	[sijə]
	cherries	/tʃɛɹiz/	[tsɛwiːs]
	chicken	/tʃɪkn̩/	[sɪːʔɪn]
	church	/tʃɹtʃ/	[θəʔts]
BUT:	jump	/dʒʌmp/	[dʌmp] (twice)
	jumping	/dʒʌmpɪŋ/	[dæ̃mʔĩːŋː]
	"G"	/dʒiː/	[di]
	"J"	/dʒeɪ/	[tʰeːə]
	van	/væn/	[bæ̃n]

(We will show other examples of such patterns in our discussion of co-occurrence constraints in §5.5.4.2.)

We discussed feature designation of affricates in §3.1.1. We can account for patterns like Gerry's above if we consider affricates to be strident stops, and [-continuant] to be the nondefault value for [continuant] (as does LaCharité, 1993). Whether a stop or fricative surfaces, we can posit a high-ranked **Not Co-occurring(-cont, +grooved)** constraint. If an affricate appears as a stop, [+grooved] has deleted:

NotCo-occurring(-continuant, +grooved)	‖	**Not(-continuant)**
Not(+continuant)	‖	**Survived(+grooved)**
	‖	**Not(-grooved)**

If the affricate surfaces as a fricative, [+grooved] must survive. The co-occurrence constraint blocks the insertion of [-continuant], and thus [+continuant] is inserted instead:

Survived/LinkedUp(+grooved)
NotCo-occurring(-continuant, +grooved)

═══════════════════════════════════════

Not(+continuant)

═══════════════════════════════════════

Not(-continuant)

Problems for the strident stop analysis of affricates arise if the child substitutes ungrooved dental affricates (tθ] and [dð]) for palatoalveolar affricates (see Charles's data in §8.5.1.1). Both the [-anterior] feature and the [+grooved] feature are deleted. If affricates are defined as strident stops, loss of [+grooved] automatically makes them stops, not affricates. It does not appear that affricates can always be treated as strident stops.

The branching [continuant] analysis of affricates may be more useful. When ungrooved interdental affricates arise, the branching specification for [continuant] survives, (high ranking of **Survived(+continuant)**) but [+grooved] and [-anterior] do not. Note that in such cases, [-continuant] would have to be underlying (as part of the branching feature); otherwise it would not be inserted (once the nondefault feature [+continuant] was linked up).

Survived/LinkedUpwards(+continuant)					Survived(-anterior)
Survived/LinkedUpwards(-continuant)		Not(-grooved)
Not(+grooved)		Not(+distributed)
Not(-anterior)		NotComplex(Root)

When affricates surface as stops, the nondefault [+continuant] is disallowed, but [-continuant] is possible. Branching segments are also disallowed.

| NotComplex(Root) | ||| | Survived(+continuant) |
| Survived/LinkedUpwards(-continuant) | | |

When [-continuant] fails to surface, the ranking of the **Survived** constraints is the reverse. The ranking in this constraint list goes against our basic assumptions, however, because the **Survived** constraint for the default [-continuant] is ranked higher than that for nondefault [+continuant], the opposite of the usual ordering. The analysis also requires the default [-continuant] to be specified in underlying representations, but that cannot be avoided with this analysis, since underlying [-continuant] is the only feature that can distinguish affricates from fricatives.

Neither analysis given here works well.[6] It is possible that children's systems differ in the classification of affricates: some children may treat them as strident stops, while others may treat them as both [-continuant] and [+continuant]. Variability in underlying representation could result in the variety of patterns found.

5.5.3.6. /l/ and Rhotics

Rhotics and /l/ are rare in early development, though they can occur. De Boysson-Bardies et. al. (1992) report a low proportion of liquids in all samples, with the lowest proportion for Japanese. The general lack of these segments is predictable from universal markedness. The specific lack in Japanese suggests a negative influence of input. Like fricatives, development of the liquids may occur over an extended period of time. However, both Elsen (1991) and Geilmann (1993) report acquisition of the uvular [ʀ] early in the second year. Dutch-learning children in Beers (1995) were either learning apical or uvular trilled rhotics and these were present for many children (syllable-initially at least) by age 3. The uvular variant is perhaps phonetically "easier" than the palatoalveolar "bunched" /ɹ/ of English or the trilled alveolar /r/. Typically, children acquire /l/ before rhotic consonants, but both orders have been observed for English by Bernhardt (1990) and Dinnsen (1992), and for Dutch by Beers (1995). Furthermore, rhotics are not a uniform category crosslinguistically.

Like nasals, rhotics and [l] serve relatively infrequently as substitutions or defaults. If they do, they more typically replace other sonorants (as we noted in the

---

[6] Salish also has interdental affricates, and other languages have dorsal affricates (e.g., Xhosa), or labial affricates (German) and they also must be considered nonstrident. Hence, the problem of affricate designation is difficult for adult phonology also.

glide section §5.5.3.1 above). They occasionally replace fricatives or stops, although this may be more common in Spanish and Greek than in English (at least for interdentals, according to Macken, 1993).

Glides typically surface for /l/ and rhotics in onsets, whereas in codas, either vowels or offglides may replace them. Syllabic vowels may replace them in codas whether or not the liquid is syllabic in the target form (§6.1.4.3). Consequently, prosodic structure sometimes changes to accommodate the loss of liquid features. Nasals, stops, and fricatives are probably more frequent substitutes in onsets, in keeping with margin constraints favoring consonant-like onsets.

Very few studies have focused specifically on development of /l/ and rhotics, except to note that vocalic substitutions are common, and that there may be differences across word positions for liquid development reflecting allophonic differences (Edwards, 1973; Greenlee, 1974). For example, the English /ɹ/ is not rounded in codas after unrounded vowels, whereas prevocalic /ɹ/ has a [Labial] feature, and order of acquisition and substitution patterns may reflect those differences. Similarly, the velarized production of /l/ in codas and in onsets before back vowels may result in different acquisition patterns for /l/ in those contexts compared with acquisition of nonvelarized /l/. Some children appear to acquire /l/ or rhotics first in clusters, where coarticulation may facilitate production (Greenlee, 1974; Bernhardt, 1990: *S3* and *S4*).

5.5.3.6.1 /l/

If **Not(+ lateral)** is high-ranked, a variety of substitution patterns for /l/ are possible:

	Target	Substitution	
Pattern 1:	/l/	Glide	Gliding
Pattern 2:	/l/	Stop	Stopping
Pattern 3:	/l/	Nasal	Nasalization
Pattern 4:	/l/	Fricative	Spirantization

In §5.5.3.1 we gave one example of a nasal substitution for /l/ (in Marcy's glide and /l/ data). Nasals are infrequent substitutions for /l/ in typical English development, but they can occur when there is velopharyngeal insufficiency, or in languages in which they interchange in the adult form (e.g., in certain Chinese dialects). Here, focus is on the more common glide and obstruent substitutions.

Pattern 1: Glide Substitutions for /l/. The glides [w], [j], or [ɹ] may surface for (onset) /l/. We focus here on the [w] and [j] substitutions, which are the most common. If [+lateral] deletes, but [+sonorant] remains, a glide or nasal may surface for /l/. If [j] substitutes for /l/, the articulator feature remains the same, but the value of [consonantal] changes from [+] to [-]; this reflects the survival of both [+sonorant] and [+continuant]:

RESULTS

Not(+ lateral)			No [l]
Survived(+ sonorant)	Not(+ sonorant)		Must be [+ son]
Survived(+ continuant)			Must be [+ cont]
NotCo-occurring(+ continuant, + nasal)	Not(-nasal)		Cannot be [+ nas]
	Not(-consonantal)		Can be glide
	Not(V-Place)		/l/ > [j]
	Not(Coronal)		

The feature [+continuant] may be underlying even though it is predictable for laterals, as per default underspecification. When [w] appears for /l/, [V-Labial] is inserted rather than [V-Coronal]. This results from high-ranked faithfulness constraints for [Dorsal] if /l/ is represented underlyingly as velarized /ɫ/ by the child. (Our feature classification does not predict that alveolar /l/ will become [w].)

Pattern 2: Stop Substitutions for /l/. Stop substitutions for /l/ are relatively infrequent. Ingram (1989b) suggests they may occur only in early development. Sally (Bernhardt, 1994b, p.u.d.) used stops sometimes for /l/ (not exclusively, since they appeared for all other sound classes at least some of the time).

laughing	/læfɪŋ/	[dafiʔ]
leaf	/liːf/	[tɪˆf]

Carolyn (Edwards & Bernhardt, 1973a) sometimes produced epenthetic syllables with stops for word-final /l/, even though onset /l/ was produced as [j] (as was /w/).

	pail	/peɪl/	[pʊwədə]
	tail	/teɪl/	[tʰɔˤdɪⁿ]
BUT:	ball	/bɑl/	[bɑʊwə]

(Words with word-final voiced stops and sonorants often had syllable additions. Thus, the epenthesis is unrelated to the /l/.)

When /l/ surfaces as [d], this does not constitute evidence that /l/ is [-continuant] (Chomsky & Halle, 1968). Rather, [+continuant] is not specified underlyingly, nor is [+sonorant]; they are redundant nondefault features. When [+lateral] deletes, there is no reason to insert [+continuant], and the default features [-continuant] and [-sonorant] are inserted. A stop results.

Not(+ lateral)	Survived(+ lateral)
	Not(-continuant)
	Not(-sonorant)

For Sally above, voicing was not necessarily maintained in the substitutions. Generally, if [+voiced] survives, the feature [+voiced] has to be underlying (either because of full specification or as a redundant nondefault feature, as per default underspecification). In Sally's case, a voicing contrast was not present for target stops either, however. Thus, the status of [+voiced] for /l/ is not clear.

Pattern 3: Fricative Substitutions for /l/. Sometimes, the [+continuant] aspect of the liquid remains, but [+sonorant] does not, and fricatives replace /l/. Either voiced or voiceless fricatives may appear, and these are typically coronal. DE (Stoel-Gammon & Dunn, 1985) showed this pattern some of the time.

	leaf	/liːf/	[sif]
	Luke	/luːk/	[zʌt]
BUT:	like	/laɪk/	[let]

DE's patterns were somewhat unusual, in that coronal fricatives and affricates were frequent word-initial substitutions. The [+continuant] feature for him appeared to have a default status word initially, and thus fricatives surfaced for word-initial /l/, as they did frequently for word-initial stops. (Voicing often matched the adult target, but not consistently, showing that [+voiced] was not necessarily underlying for /l/ targets.)

Fricative substitutions for /l/ can also occur when both stops and fricatives occur in onset. For example, Joan (Velten, 1943) produced *lady* as [zudu] at a time when [d] was a possible onset (*table* as [dubu]). (Recall that she additionally produced /j/ as [d] at that time, as in [zɑːd] for *yard*.) In such cases, survival of [+continuant] is high-ranked, and survival of [+sonorant] is low-ranked, resulting in a fricative substitution.

Not(+ lateral)	Survived(+ lateral)
Survived/LinkedUpwards(+ consonantal)	Survived(+ sonorant)
Survived/LinkedUpwards(+ continuant)	Not(+ continuant)

5.5.3.6.2. Rhotics Other Than English /ɹ/

Crosslinguistically, the trilled alveolar /r/ is much more frequent than other rhotics (43% of the variants, according to Maddieson, 1984), although not much developmental information is available for any of the variants other than English /ɹ/. Patterns reported include:

Pattern 1:	/r/	[l]	Lateralization
Pattern 2:	/r/	[h]	Debuccalization
Pattern 3:	/r/	[ʀ]/[r]	Rhotic exchange
Pattern 4:	/r/~/ʀ/	[j]/[ʋ]	Gliding

When alveolar [l] replaces alveolar /r/ as in Pattern 1 (or vice versa), only manner of articulation changes, not place (§5.5.3.1). In the second pattern, reported for Puerto Rican Spanish (Anderson & Smith, 1987), the [h] is perhaps similar to [x], which alternates with [r] in that adult dialect. In either case, [+continuant] survives, and Place deletes. The [-voiced] and [+s.g.] features of [h] may have more to do with survival of those features for /x/ than loss of [+voiced] for /r/. Lleó (p.c.) noted that other rhotics (uvulars or English [ɹ]) can surface for the trilled /r/ of European Spanish. This suggests that it might be useful to include a feature [+rhotic] in the description of /r/ (as Beers, 1995, does). The feature [+rhotic] survives when uvular [ʀ] or palatoalveolar [ɹ] replace the alveolar /r/, even though place and manner change (high ranking of **Survived(+rhotic)**). The final pattern (for apical or uvular rhotics in Dutch) is consistent with glide replacement of rhotics in English (discussed in §5.5.1.5.2) but the labial glide that surfaces is labiodental in keeping with Dutch phonology. Patterns thus appear to be somewhat different, depending on the type of rhotic, although much remains to be discovered about the range of patterns.

5.5.4. CO-OCCURRENCE CONSTRAINTS ON CONSONANTS

Throughout the previous sections, we have referred to various feature co-occurrence constraints in accounting for observed phonological patterns. We noted on occasion that voiced and voiceless cognates sometimes differ in output patterns, and that members of a sound class (e.g., fricatives) may show different patterns that reflect co-occurrence constraints. In this section we focus specifically on co-occurrence constraints affecting Place-Laryngeal combinations and Manner-Place or Manner-Place-Laryngeal combinations. The discussion draws on the concept of combinatorial specification (Archangeli & Pulleyblank, 1994), which suggests that certain types of feature combinations are possible, and others are not, because of formal or phonetic grounding conditions. Just as languages show inventory gaps demonstrating co-occurrence constraints, so may children.

Because of the multiplicity of feature combinations, we will not give an exhaustive list from all the languages on which we find data, but give some examples as a means of outlining the phenomena. Some combinations are more likely to be prohibited than others, particularly those with more than one nondefault feature. In general, not all features of a combination change during a repair, although they may: repairs may be minimal or nonminimal. We proceed from Place-Laryngeal combinations through Manner-Laryngeal combinations to Manner-Place combinations, ending with Manner-Place-Laryngeal combinations.

5.5.4.1. Place-Laryngeal Feature Co-Occurrence Constraints

Children may be able to produce only certain combinations of place and laryngeal features: for example, [p], [b], [t], [d], and [k], but not [g] (as we exemplify below). Macken and Barton (1980a) note that two of their four subjects acquired a voicing contrast first for coronals, then for labials, and finally for velars, whereas one child produced a contrast in coronals and velars, but not in labials. Three out of four children had most difficulty with voiced velars.

Here we give examples of **NotCo-occurring(Artic, +voiced)**, and **NotCo-occurring(Artic, +s.g.)** constraints. We are unsure how common these co-occurrence constraints are, or what the most frequent substitution patterns may be.

5.5.4.1.1. *Voicing and Place*

Sally (Bernhardt, 1994b, p.u.d.) had different realizations of velars. The voiceless /k/ usually matched the adult target, but /g/ was often [d]. **NotCo-occurring(Dorsal, + voiced)** was high-ranked, prohibiting [g]. **Survived(C-Place)** was also high-ranked, ensuring that a consonant appeared. Low ranking of **Not(Coronal)** allowed realization of [d]. (Coronal stops were frequent substitutions in her system as we have shown previously in §5.5.3.3 and §5.5.3.6.1.). Because [k] appeared, **Survived(Dorsal)** was higher-ranked than **Not(Dorsal)**. (Voicing contrasts were not yet established, and thus the ranking for **Survived(+ voiced)** was unstable; it was variably ranked lower than **Not(+ voiced)**.)

RESULTS

NotCo-occurring(Dorsal, + voiced)	No [g]
Survived/LinkedUpwards(+ voiced)	**Must be [+ voiced]**
Survived/LinkedUpwards(C-Place)	**Must have C-Place**
Survived(Dorsal)	/k/ > [k]
Not(Dorsal)	
Not(+ voiced)	
Not(Coronal)	/g/ > [d]

5.5.4.1.2. *Aspiration*

Children may show differences between places of articulation and development of aspiration in word-initial stops (Macken & Barton, 1980a; Tyler & Edwards, 1993). They may also master [h] before they master aspirated stops, showing a general **NotCo-occurring(Artic, + s.g.)** constraint. (See the Manner-Laryngeal section, §5.5.4.2, for co-occurrence constraints that affect /h/ itself.) Shawn (a child with a phonological disorder) first developed aspiration on /t/, then on /k/ and finally on /p/, without specific intervention that targeted aspiration (S. Edwards, 1995). The constraint rankings were the following; developmentally, **Survived(+ s.g.)** was reranked above the **NotCo-occurring** constraints, one by one.

NotCo-occurring(Labial, + s.g.)

NotCo-occurring(Dorsal, + s.g.)

NotCo-occurring(Coronal, + s.g.)

Survived/LinkedUpwards(+ s.g.)

The first segment which became aspirated was /t/, with its default place feature [Coronal]. Note that the child's developmental progression respects segment complexity: nondefault [+s.g.] combined with a default place feature before combining with other nondefault features.[7] Common developmental progressions across children are not known for this feature combination.

Co-occurrence constraints concerning [+s.g.] can have widespread effects in the system. In §7.3.4.5, we exemplify this type of interaction with data from Terry, a 4-year-old with a severe phonological disorder (Bernhardt, 1994b, p.u.d.); it cannot be addressed here, because CV interactions were also involved.

5.5.4.2. Manner-Laryngeal Feature Co-Occurrence

Co-occurrence constraints can also affect combinations of voice and manner features. Voiceless fricatives may occur, but voiced fricatives may be prohibited (with a variety of other phones replacing them). Other Manner-Laryngeal co-occurrence restrictions can affect [h] or glottal stop, while oral glides remain unaffected. We do not know how common any of these patterns are.

5.5.4.2.1. Constraints on Fricatives Involving Voicing

High ranking of **NotCo-occurring(+ continuant,-sonorant, + voiced)** prohibits voiced fricatives, even though voiceless fricatives, and voiced and voiceless stops may be present.[8] In English acquisition, one of a voiced-voiceless cognate pair may appear before the other (Gierut, 1996). Different substitution patterns may affect the members of the pair. Interdentals in particular often have different realizations, /ð/ appearing as [d] and /θ/ as [f] or [s] (Smit et al., 1990). Data from Charles (Bernhardt, 1992b) are as follows:

thin	/θɪn/	[fɪn]
this	/ðɪs/	[dɪs]

Gerry's example in §5.5.3.5 showed different patterns for /tʃ/ and /dʒ/. Similarly, DE (Stoel-Gammon & Dunn, 1985) produced [b] for /v/ (rather than [z], [v] or [dʒ]) but [s], [f], or [ts] for /f/ (rather than [p]).

vase	/veɪs/	[bes]
fork	/fɔɹk/	[sɔɪt]
feather	/fɛðɹ̩/	[tsɛdə]
finger	/fɪŋgɹ̩/	[fɪndə]

In these cases (which are not atypical), it seems that frication is more likely to co-occur with [-voiced] than [+voiced]. With multiple nondefaults in the target, [+continuant] can only survive if no other nondefaults do.

Serena (Bernhardt, 1994b, p.u.d.) had particular difficulty with voiced fricatives. She was able to produce voiceless fricatives, voiceless affricates, and voiced stops. However, most voiced fricatives and affricates surfaced as glottal stops

---

[7] The /k/ was an intervention target for place of articulation. Hence, he may have learned [kʰ] earlier than [pʰ] because of imitative practice in the intervention context.

[8] Voiced fricatives are less frequent in world languages also (Maddieson, 1984). It is phonetically difficult to maintain sufficient airflow for turbulence of fricatives while voicing. Approximants are generally unaffected by voicing constraints on continuants, because they are spontaneously voiced.

word-initially. (Coda constraints often prohibited consonant production elsewhere in the word.)

zoo	/zuː/	[ʔɪʊː]	Glottal default insertion
zipper	/zɪpɹ̩/	[ʔɛpɛ]	Glottal default insertion
jumping	/dʒʌmpɪŋ/	[ʔʌːpĩⁿ]	Glottal default insertion

High ranking of faithfulness constraints for lower-level features in conjunction with the co-occurrence constraint was only resolvable by a nonminimal repair: C-Root and Place delinked, with insertion of a default glottal stop. (For further details on such constraint rankings, see §5.5.3.4 regarding glottal substitutions.)

σ▸Onset	
LinkedDownwards(TimingUnit)	**LinkedUpwards(Root)**
Survived(Root)	**Not(Root)**
NotCo-occurring(+ continuant, + voiced)	
Survived/LinkedUpwards(+ voiced)	
Survived/LinkedUpwards(+ continuant)	**Not(-continuant)**
	Not(+ c.g.)

5.5.4.2.2. NotCo-occurring(-consonantal, + s.g.): [h] Prohibited

Co-occurrence constraints may prohibit combinations of [+s.g.] and particular manner features. In §7.4.1.3 we present data from DE (Stoel-Gammon & Dunn, 1985), for whom **NotCo-occurring(-continuant, + s.g.)** (prohibiting aspirated stops) was high-ranked along with **Survived(+ s.g.)**. This resulted in fricative substitutions for aspirated stops word initially (insertion of nondefault [+continuant]). When **Survived(+ s.g.)** is high-ranked, and **NotCo-occurring(-consonantal, + s.g.)** (prohibiting voiceless vowels and glides) is also high-ranked, voiceless fricatives may replace /h/ (typically, [s]; insertion of C-Place).

Carolyn (Edwards & Bernhardt, 1973a) used [s] for initial /h/ (as in *hanger* as [sænʊɛk]). She was able to produce the glide [j] and glottal stops, but did not use them to replace /h/. In word-initial position, faithfulness constraints for the features [+s.g.] and [+continuant] were high-ranked. But these features could not co-occur with [-consonantal], and hence, the value of [consonantal] changed. The feature [+consonantal] implies C-Place; default [C-Coronal] was inserted, and [s] resulted.

RESULTS

NotCo-occurring(-consonantal, + s.g.)		No [h]
Survived/LinkedUpwards(+ s.g.)	**Not(+ s.g.)**	Must be [+ s.g.]
Co-occurring(+ consonantal→C-Place)	**Survived(-consonantal)**	Can be [+ cons]
	Not(C-Place)	
	Not(+ consonantal)	
Survived/LinkedUpwards(+ continuant)	**Not(+ continuant)**	Must be [+ cont]
	Not(C-Coronal)	/h/ > [s]

5.5.4.3. Place–Manner Co-Occurrence

Interactions involving manner and place features have been mentioned in previous sections. Typical Manner-Place co-occurrence constraints are as follows. Common ones are checked (✔).

NotCo-occurring(-consonantal,Place): Segments that are [-consonantal] can occur, but not if they have oral place features: glottals may occur, but not glides. True consonants may have place.

NotCo-occurring(-consonantal,Labial): Glides may occur, but not labial ones (*[w], *[ɹ]). True consonants may be labial.

NotCo-occurring(+ continuant,Place): The only possible [+continuant] consonant is [h]. Stops and nasals with C-Place can occur because they are [-continuant]. If [l] can occur in this context, then either (a) [+continuant] is supported independently by **Co-occurring(+ lateral→ + continuant)**, or (b) laterals are [-continuant] in the child's system.

✔**NotCo-occurring(+ continuant,C-Place):** Continuants can occur, but only if they have V-Place (oral glides) or have no Place ([h]). A not infrequent substitution for word-initial fricatives is [h] (e.g., Bernhardt, 1990: *S2*, *S4*; Stemberger, 1993: Larissa). Stops and nasals can occur, because they are [-continuant]. If [l] can occur, then either (a) [+continuant] is supported independently by **Co-occurring(+ lateral→ + continuant)**, or (b) laterals are [-continuant] in the child's system.

NotCo-occurring(+ continuant,Labial): Coronal fricatives, laterals, and glides can occur, as can glottals and labial stops. But labial fricatives and glides (including [ɹ]) are absent.

✔**NotCo-occurring(+ nasal,C-Dorsal):** Nasals and velar consonants are present, but not /ŋ/.

To exemplify these types of co-occurrence constraints, we focus on fricatives, a category which often shows evidence of such constraints.

5.5.4.3.1. Manner–Place Feature Co-Occurrence: Fricatives

Fricatives tend to be acquired one by one, rather than simultaneously as a sound class. Constraints on both individual features and combinations of features result in this protracted learning period. If segmental complexity is relevant for acquisition we might first expect combinations of defaults, then combinations of defaults and nondefaults, and then finally combinations of nondefaults. This would suggest the acquisition of /s/ before /f/ in English, an order of acquisition which is observable for some children. However, many English-speaking children show the opposite pattern: they acquire /f/ before /s/ (Templin, 1957; Moskowitz, 1975). If [Coronal] is the default for place, then the nondefault [+continuant] does not necessarily combine first with default place. Orders of acquisition that do not necessarily reflect segmental complexity have also been observed for other languages. A Brazilian Portuguese child (Yavą and Hernandorena, 1991) used [x] and affricates before using labiodental and coronal fricatives, even though labial and coronal stops were in the inventory. Beers's (1991) Dutch subjects acquired dorsal and coronal fricatives before labial and palatoalveolar fricatives, even though labial stops were present from early samples.

The following exemplify restrictions on coronal fricatives with stop substitutions. Similar restrictions can result in stop substitutions only for labiodentals (Bernhardt, 1994b: Roger, Colin, and Stuart), or [h] substitutions only for coronal fricatives (Bernhardt, 1990: S6), or [w] substitutions for all fricatives but /ð/ (see Larry, §5.5.3.4), etc.

If some fricatives surface as fricatives, but others surface as stops, glides, or glottals, the feature [+continuant] may co-occur with some C-Place features, but not others. Faithfulness to [+continuant] thus depends on the ranking of the co-occurrence constraints. In the example here from Mandy at age 4;2, a child with a phonological disorder (Bernhardt, 1994b, p.u.d.), labiodentals were possible, but coronal fricatives surfaced as stops. A co-occurrence constraint concerning [+continuant] and [Coronal] was operative.

	feather	/fɛdɹ/	[fɛɪɹ]
	five	/faɪv/	[faɪ]
	flower	/flauwɹ/	[bɑːˈjɹ]
	van	/væn/	[væ̃ː]
BUT:	soap	/soʊp/	[dɔʊpʰ]~[boʊpʰ]
	sister	/sɪstɹ/	[dɪɹ]
	zoo	/zuː/	[duː]
	thumb	/θʌm/	[dʌm]

NotCo-occurring(+ continuant,-sonorant,Coronal) was higher-ranked than **NotCo-occurring(+ continuant,-sonorant,Labial)** and faithfulness constraints for [+continuant]. Place survived, rather than manner, with default [-continuant] being inserted for target coronal fricatives.

NotCo-occurring(+ cont,-son,Coronal) ‖	**NotCo-occurring(+ cont,-son,Labial)**
Survived/LinkedUpwards(Coronal) ‖	**Survived(+ continuant)**
‖	**Not(-continuant)**
‖	**Not(-sonorant)**

This ranking assumes that [Coronal] was specified in her system. It is possible that [Labial] was the default (underspecified) articulator. Or it may be that default underspecification is wrong, and default features may be specified underlyingly. Data are insufficient to choose between these analyses. The co-occurrence constraint involving [Labial] may be ranked low due to the role of visual information. The child can observe the articulation of labiodental fricatives, but not coronal fricatives, and this may accelerate acquisition of labiodental fricatives.

5.5.4.4. Manner–Place-Laryngeal Co-Occurrence Constraints

In some cases, all of the major nodes are involved in co-occurrence constraints. A place feature may be possible, but only in combination with certain manner features and one value of a voiced feature. For example, /k/ might be possible but not /g/ or /ŋ/. Blair (Bernhardt, 1990: S2) had particular difficulty acquiring velars. After two intervention cycles (12 weeks), he began to be able to produce [k] spontaneously in words. However, at the end of three cycle (18 weeks), he was only beginning to use [g] spontaneously, and still had not acquired [ŋ]. The constraint rankings were the following; developmentally, **Survived(Dorsal)** was reranked above the **NotCo-occurring** constraints one by one.

NotCo-occurring(C-Dorsal, + nasal)

NotCo-occurring(C-Dorsal, + voiced,-continuant)

NotCo-occurring(C-Dorsal,-voiced,-continuant)

Survived(C-Dorsal)

This sort of constraint involves velars more often than labials or coronals, probably because labial and coronal stops and nasals are often early acquired segments.

5.5.5. CO-OCCURRENCE CONSTRAINTS: CYCLICITY PRINCIPLE?

Gierut (1995) proposed a principle of cyclicity in development between supralaryngeal and laryngeal features which is related to the notion of co-occurrence constraints. She claims that new voiceless members of a voiced-voiceless cognate pair are mastered before the voiced members. Some children do acquire voiced and voiceless cognates in sequence, exemplifying particular co-occurrence constraints (as we noted for Blair above). However, many do not. Beers (1991) notes that voice contrasts appeared after *all* place and manner contrasts in Dutch children with and without phonological disorders. In Bernhardt's (1990, 1994b) intervention studies, some children acquired both voiced and voiceless cognates simultaneously (e.g., /f/ and /v/, or /k/ and /g/); others had lags in appearance of cognates (one-by-one development as shown for Blair above). There does not appear to be a necessary developmental principle of cyclicity. However, combinatorial specification and OT are useful in explaining the variable patterns that occur. Combinatorial specification predicts that feature combinations may become incrementally more complex, which explains the cyclic patterns described by Gierut (1996). Constraint-based theory suggests that some children will have greater difficulty with the more complex combinations than others; the co-occurrence constraints may begin high-ranked or low-ranked, as part of the initially partially random ranking of constraints that we posit in this book. (A further confound in the discussion is the issue of segment frequency. Before we can be assured that additive complexity is the driving factor for developmental sequence, we need to know the relative input frequency of the various segments.)

5.5.6. CONSONANT HARMONY AS A RESPONSE
TO UNDERSPECIFICATION

A discussion of consonant features would not be complete without a discussion of consonant harmony. Consonant harmony is probably most often a response to sequence constraints, and is discussed in detail in §7.4.2. But underspecification can also motivate harmony. If a certain feature or combination is impossible, a nondefault feature or features may spread from elsewhere in the word to accommodate a high-ranked **Survived(TimingUnit)** constraint (in any direction). Harmony indicates low ranking of **SinglyLinked** for the spreading nondefault feature(s), and high ranking of negative constraints for the features that do not appear.

Harry (a 4-year-old child with a phonological disorder) had severe constraints on feature production (Stemberger & Bernhardt, in press). Labial harmony, nasal harmony, and default insertion of coronal stops were pervasive repairs. Underspecification and sequence constraints motivated the repair. Nasal harmony was only from right to left, indicating **NoSequence(− nasal... + nasal)** (as also in adult English for vowel-consonant sequences). Labial harmony was bidirectional, and occurred whenever a labial was in the word; this probably reflects spreading as an alternative to filling in default features.

Nasal harmony: R-to-L

	kwin	/kwiːn/	[nin]
	string	/strɪŋ/	[nin]
BUT:	snake	/sneɪk/	[neɪt]
	mouth	/maʊθ/	[maʊ]

Labial harmony:

R-to-L:

	soap	/soʊp/	[bop]
	cowboy	/kaʊbɔɪ/	[pʌbɔɪ]

L-to-R:

	page	/peɪdʒ/	[peɪb]
	boat	/boʊp/	[bop]

Such pervasive harmony is fairly rare even in children with phonological disorders, and is usually found only very early in normal development. Jose, a typically developing child (Lleó, 1996), had feature constraints and repairs similar to those for Harry above, but prior to age 2. **Not** constraints were high-ranked for nondefault features; Jose used few fricatives, liquids, or velars. Either a default feature was inserted (e.g., [-continuant], [Coronal]), or an established nondefault feature spread to the target positions containing the impossible features or segments ([Labial] or [+nasal]):

sombrero	/som'brero/	[ba'bɛlo]~[ba'βɛjo]	'hat'
lengua	/'lengwa/	['peɪba]	'language'
nariz	/na'ris/	[na'ni]	'nose'

globo	/'globo/	['boɤ]	'balloon'
caramelos	/ˌkara'melos/	[ma'mɛno]	'candy'
paloma	/pa'loma/	[pa'bɔpa]	'bird'

For more detailed discussion of this phenomenon, see Stemberger and Bernhardt (in press).

5.5.7. SUMMARY STATEMENT ABOUT CONSONANT DEVELOPMENT

We have presented many examples of phenomena for consonant acquisition and paid attention to trends in development. Throughout, it is clear that the concepts of default versus nondefault, and of constraint ranking can give us insights into those phenomena. Whereas prediction of developmental order is subject to a vast array of difficulties, the analysis of phenomena is enhanced by the new concepts. Overall, the features appear to have autonomy, in accordance with autosegmental theory. Yet at times, more than one feature may be inextricably bound with another in such a way as to result in a nonminimal repair eliminating both. Similarly, features can be individually prohibited or allowed, or may be subject to particular co-occurrence constraints, affecting two or more of the major nodes. There is tremendous individual variation in patterns of development, yet there are some patterns that are more typical, and some that appear not to occur. The concepts of feature hierarchy, underspecification, and constraint ranking were useful in describing patterns, although it was not always clear what the best features might be, or what the defaults were in a particular child's system. We further explore these concepts in the next section, on vowels.

5.6. VOWEL DEVELOPMENT

Vowel development has been much less studied than consonant development. Vowels tend to be acquired earlier than consonants, and perhaps have been considered less interesting for that reason. Furthermore, phonetic transcription and acoustic analysis are very difficult for children's vowels. Small vocal tracts result in different and higher formants for vowels. Assignment of phonetic symbols is based on the adult's system and perceptions, but that may or may not be a valid means of describing children's vowels. Given these caveats about the data, we will summarize what is known about vowel development. At the end of the discussion, we also include a note on acquisition of tone. Studies have examined both phonetic (articulatory and/or acoustic) and phonemic trends in vowel development. Some of the results converge, but others diverge, both because of variability in acquisition and because of differences in data collection and analysis methods. Conclusions are tentative, because much remains to be discovered.

5.6.1. VOWEL INVENTORY DEVELOPMENT
IN THE TRANSITION FROM PRELINGUISTIC
VOCALIZATION TO EARLY WORDS

Children phonate from birth and can therefore produce vowel-like sounds from day 1. These reflexive sounds form the basis for vowel productions, which become more refined over the first year. Examining the transition from prelinguistic vocalizations to early words can provide insights into the learning process and into the organization of the phonological system in terms of defaults and nondefaults.

Infants as young as 6 months can *articulate* a variety of vowels, although frequency of vowel types varies over time. Back vowels are frequent in the first 3 months, become rarer after 6 months, and then increase again in frequency in the second year (Irwin, 1948; Stoel-Gammon & Dunn, 1985). Davis and Mac-Neilage (1990) note that studies of babbling show a preponderance of vowels concentrated in the lower left quadrant of the vowel triangle: front and central mid and low vowels (Leopold, 1947; Irwin, 1948; Smith & Oller, 1981).

0–0;3:   Back vowels most frequent during cooing
0;3–1;0: Front and mid vowels most frequent in babbling phase
1;0–2;0: Back vowels increasing in relative frequency
   2;6:   Distribution similar to adult frequency

Changes in physical constraints through maturation probably affect the change in the frequency distribution. In the cooing phase, children tend to vocalize while supine. The tendency to back vowels and consonants perhaps results from a backed resting tongue position while supine. Physical maturation gives the child the capacity to sit or crawl while vocalizing in the babbling phase. The resting tongue position then tends to be more forward, with vocalizations reflecting that more forward tongue position. As the child's vocal tract expands at the end of the first year, the resting tongue position may be more central. Since tongue movements are less restricted by the physical space, back vowels and high vowels are then more easily produced independent of body position (Kent, 1981).

Focusing on the transition from babbling to early words provides insight into the development of defaults. Vihman (1992) examined the early syllable productions of 20 children: four Japanese, four Swedish, five French, and ten American English-learning children. Although the study primarily concerned syllable production, general conclusions about vowels were as follows:

[a/æ]: Low front vowels most frequent across languages
[ʌ/ə]: Mid central vowels second in frequency in English (Stanford) samples and Swedish samples, and third in frequency for the other samples
[e/ɛ]: Mid front vowels second in frequency in English (Rutgers) and French samples
[o/ɔ]: Mid back vowels second in frequency in Japanese samples

Note that mid back vowels were frequent only in the Japanese data, perhaps reflecting input frequency.

What do these frequency distributions imply for defaults? The distribution of vowel types does not reflect adult frequency in early phases. In §4.12.3.7, we suggested that underspecification may arise from the child's production frequency rather than input frequency. In a small vocal tract with a proportionally large tongue, the most comfortable position is possibly forward and low, resulting in default vowel production in the low-to-mid front-to-central range, independent of target language.

Input does begin to affect vowel frequency in the late babbling phase, and subsequently affects default and nondefault values. Lieberman (1980), in a small *n* transcription and acoustic study of English vowels, noted that most vowels produced in late babbling were identifiably English vowels, supporting the hypothesis of continuity between babbling and speech. Acoustic analysis also supported that hypothesis: the decrease in vowel formant values over time was gradual, reflecting the gradual process of physical maturation. Although Vihman (1992) does not specifically comment on vowels, she does report that 15/23 subjects used the same type of syllables in early words as they used in babbling; continuity in syllable production was noted for 65% of the subjects. She further notes that "the syllable may not be the most appropriate unit to consider [for examining the continuity hypothesis] for some children" (1992:409), meaning that vowel production may have been more continuous than the numbers show. B. Davis and MacNeilage (1990) caution, however, that vowels may show less continuity in the transition from babbling to speech than consonants. They note that early words often contain high vowels, phones which are not typically frequent in babbling. If continuity needs to reflect frequency *in addition to* occurrence, then there is some discontinuity between babbling and speech for vowels. In general, however, the process appears continuous, but the relative frequency of vowel types changes over time, with defaults gradually moving in the direction of the adult system.

In terms of the learning process itself, Lieberman (1980) suggests that a "perceptual normalization mechanism" may be involved for vowel acquisition. He bases this suggestion on the fact that in his study, children's vowels [ɪ], [ɛ], and [æ] had high formants, even though those particular vowels do not require larger vocal tracts to be produced with (the more appropriate) lower formants. The children's vowel triangles remain relatively proportional to those of adults, even though absolute values are not identical. This suggests that auditory feedback is primary in vowel acquisition. The normalization mechanism concept suggests that faithfulness constraints may have an acoustic basis for vowels.

5.6.2. VOWEL INVENTORY DEVELOPMENT AFTER THE FIRST YEAR

Mastery of the vowel system (at least in articulatory terms) usually occurs by the end of the third year (with the exception of syllabic /ɹ/). In the next section, we present general trends for inventory development, focusing primarily on English and other Germanic languages (on which most studies have been done), but also including sections on languages with small vowel inventories, and on languages with nasalized vowels.

5.6.2.1. Vowel Inventory Development in Germanic Languages

Most of the small amount of data collected is for English. Summarizing English phonemic studies of vowel development, Stoel-Gammon and Herrington (1990) and Otomo and Stoel-Gammon (1992) divide acquisition into three developmental periods:

1. Early mastery: The basic vowel triangle /i/, /ɑ/, /u/
                   Mid back tense /oʊ/
                   Mid central /ʌ/
2. Mid mastery: Back and central lax vowels /ʊ/, /ɔ/, /ə/
                   Low front /æ/
3. Late mastery: Front nonlow vowels /eɪ/, /ɛ/, /ɪ/
                   Rhotic vowels

Individual studies give more detailed perspectives on the process of acquisition. The diary studies of Velten (1943) and Leopold (1947) include discussion of vowel development. (In both those cases, it is important to note that the children had more than one language input: Velten's daughter Joan heard English, Norwegian, and French in the home, and Leopold's daughter Hildegard was bilingual in English and German.) Menn (1976) discusses vowel development for English for her son Jacob, although that was not the focus of her study. To supplement data from those studies, we provide inventory development charts from Stemberger's daughters, Gwendolyn and Morgan (Tables 5.2–5.6), based on diary studies beginning at the onset of word use.

The following general developmental progressions were noted for the aforementioned individual children.

1. First vowels:
      Low vowels: All subjects (one or more of [ɑ], [a], [æ])
      Mid vowels: [ʌ]—Jacob, Morgan ([ʌ]~[a])
                     [ɛ]—Hildegard ([ɛ]~low V's)
2. Height split: High vowels appear, contrasting with low or mid vowels of
      first phase.
      High back rounded vowel [u]   (Gwendolyn, Joan, Jacob)
      High back tense unrounded vowel [ɯ]   (Morgan)
      High front vowel [i]   (Hildegard)

Gwendolyn used [u] only in the word *moo*. The high front vowel /i/, although emerging later, was mastered first.

3. Multiple possibilities: Place split, or further height split, or tenseness split,
      or a combination of the three:
      Joan, Jacob: Front/back for high
      Hildegard: Tense/lax for mid front ([e] vs. [ɛ])

TABLE 5.2. Gwendolyn's Stressed Vowel Inventory: 1;0 to 2;0

Age	Vowels			Place[a]	Height	[tense]
1;0	aː			[-back](?)	[+low]	?
1;1		uː		[+back] [+round]	[+high]	[+tense]
1;5	iː ɪ			[-back]	[-low]	[-tense]
			o		[-high]	
	aɪ			VV: [-back]	VV: [+low]– [+high]	
1;8			ou		VV: [+back]	VV: [-low]
			ɒː			
1;9						
	ʌ			Central		
			ɒʊ	VV: [+back]	VV: [+low]– [+high]	
1;10	iːə					
	eɪ					
	ɛ	əː				
	ɔː				VV: [-high]– [+high]	
	ɛʊ	ʌʊ	ɔːə			
	aʊ		ɑːə	VV: [-back]– [+back]	VV: [+low]– [-low]	
1;11		əʊ				
2;0[b]			uo		VV: [+high]– [-high]	
	ɛə					

Note: Redundant features are not included.

[a] Within columns, segments and features are cumulative and independent of syllable type, as open or closed.

[b] [æɪ] at 2;4; [æː] at 2;10; [ɔɪ] at 2;11; [ʊ] at 5;7.

	Morgan:	Front/back for high
		Tense/lax for high front
		High/mid for front
	Gwendolyn:	Front/back for high
		Tense/lax for front high
		High/mid for back

4. Other splits not occurring in previous period (c).

	Joan:	Mid front > mid back > low vowel split
	Jacob:	Mid back (data end there)
	Hildegard:	High back > mid back
	Morgan:	Tense/lax for other vowels > front/back for low vowels > [+round] vowels
	Gwendolyn:	Front/back for low vowels > tense/lax for mid vowels > high back lax [ʊ]

TABLE 5.3.   Gwendolyn's High Vowels[a]

| Target Vowel | Age | Child form | Relevant feature substitutions | | | Mastery σ-Type |
			Place	Height	[tense]	
iː	**1;5**	iː				**Mastery**
ɪ	1;10	iː			[+tense]	Match:
		ɪ			(open σ)	Closed σ
	2;2	ɪ				**Mastery**
uː	1;9	(uː)				Marginal
	1;10	uː				
		ʌː	[-round]	[-high]	[-tense]	ʌː
		ʌʊ		[-high]– [+high]		Closed σ
	1;11	uː		[-high]		uː
		oʊ				Open σ
		ɒː		[+low]–		
		ɒʊ		[+high]		
	2;2	Same, no ɒʊ				
	2;5	uː				**Mastery**
ʊ	1;10	a	[-back] [-round]	[+low]		
	2;7	ə	[-round]	[-high]		
	5;7	ʊ				**Mastery**

Notes: Redundant features are not included. Master = 100% accuracy

[a] Other vowel substitutions: /æ/ > [a]; /æ/ > [i]/_[+nas]; /ɛ/ > [a]; /ɛ/ > [ai]/_[Dorsal] (Stemberger, 1992a)

Note in Table 5.2 Gwendolyn's rapid development in vowels at 1;10. All vowels except [ʊ] were used at least some of the time. She also had a rapid vocabulary increase in that month (from 57 words to more than 200 words), an interesting simultaneous development.

The data from individual English-learning children are generally consistent with the summaries presented at the beginning of this section. In general, low vowels emerge early on, height contrasts are among the first to develop, and after that, many possible developmental paths are open. Even the height split might be considered from another perspective for at least some of the subjects: as a contrast in rounding ([ɑ]-[u]), or place (front-back, [ɑ]-[i]). The variability in order of acquisition after the first height contrast is not surprising, given that the child has to learn combinations of four vowel feature types: height, place, rounding, and tenseness.

For languages other than English, there are even fewer studies of vowel acquisition. We present here some information on German and Dutch, which have complex vowel systems similar to that of English (but also including a front rounded

TABLE 5.4. Morgan's Stressed Vowel Inventory: 0;11 to 2;6

Age	Vowels	Place[a]	Height	[tense]
0;11	ʌ	[+back]	[-low]–[-high]	[-tense]
	a[a]	[-back]	[+low]	
1;2	ɯ(:)(u:)[b]	[+round]/_Lab C	[+high]	[+tense]
1;3	ɤ(:) (o)[b]	([+round])		
1;4	i ɪ			
	eɪ	VV: [-back]	VV: [-high]	
	aɯ	VV: [-back]–	VV: [+low]–	
		[+back]	[+high]	
1;5	i:	Regression:		
	aɪ	No [+round] V		
1;6	æɪ (for /æ/ in some contexts			
1;8	(ʊ) ω	VV: [+back]–		
	ɛ ɤi(:)	[-back]		
2;2	ɑ:			
2;5	æ			
	æɯ[c]			
2;6	ʊ u:	[+round]		
	o:/oʊ	VV: [+back]		
	oɪ:			

Notes: Redundant features are not included. Features and segments are cumulative and independent of syllable type (i.e., open or closed).

[a] [a] and [ʌ] alternate until 1;8.

[b] From 1;2, round vowels sometimes surfaced in the context of labial consonants. From 1;3–1;4, there was temporary use of the mid round vowel in the lexical items *no* and *don't*. A regression followed, with loss of the round vowel, and realization of the labial feature in an [m] coda.

vowel series) and on Hungarian and Spanish (Fee, 1991) and Japanese (Ueda, 1996), which have smaller vowel inventories.

Levelt's (1994) 12-subject study of Dutch shows developmental patterns similar to those observed for English:

> Early mastery: The basic vowel triangle [i], [ɑ], and [u]
> Mid mastery: Lax high front vowel [ɪ]
> Mid vowels [e], [o], [ɔ]
> Late mastery: Lax mid front vowel [ɛ]

Levelt does not include the front round vowels in her summaries, but her data show that they were sometimes produced accurately in early words, and sometimes as front unrounded vowels. Furthermore, sometimes back rounded vowels were produced as front rounded vowels.

TABLE 5.5.   Morgan's Round Vowels and Dipthongs: 1;2–2;6

Target vowel	Age	Child form	Relevant feature substitutions			Mastery σ-Type
			Place	Height	[tense]	
uː	1;2–1;6	ɯ	[-round]			Closed
	1;2	ɯː	[-round]			Open
		(uː/ Lab C)				
	1;6	ɯː	[-round]			All σ
	2;6	uː				**Mastery**
ʊ	0;11–1;4	a∼ʌ	[-round]	[-high] [+low]		
	1;4–1;9	ɯ	[-round]		[+tense]	
	1;6–1;;9	ɯː	[-round]		[+tense]	
	1;8	ω	[-round]			
		(ʊ/(u)_ Lab C (rare)			[+tense]	
	2;6	ʊ				**Mastery**
oː	1;0–1;6	a∼ʌ	[-round]	([+low])		Mostly in open σ
	1;3–1;4	oᵃ,u		([+high])		
	1;3	ɤ	[-round]			
	2;6	oː∼oʊ				**Mastery**
ɔɪ	1;4	ɤ/a	[-round]	[-high] /[+low]		
	1;6	eɪ	V1: [-round], [-back]			
	1;8	ɤɪ	[-round]			
	2;6	ɔɪ				**Mastery**
aʊ	1;0–1;6	a	[-round]			
	1;6–2;5	aɯ	[-round]			
	2;5	æʊ				

Note: Redundant features are not included. Mastery = 100% accuracy.

ᵃ Only in the words *no* and *don't* for one month

ᵇ The diphthong /oʊ/ was produced as [oː] except in open syllables, where it was often [oʊ] (consistent with the Minnesota dialect).

	uit	/œyt/	[œyɸ]	'out'	Tom	1;0;10
	bruin	/bʀœyn/	[dɛin]	'brown'	Tom	1;11;26
	neus	/nøs/	[nɛs]	'nose'	Eva	1;4
BUT:	stoel	/stul/	[dy]	'chair'	Robin	1;7;13

TABLE 5.6. Morgan's Unrounded High and Mid Vowels[a]

Target vowel	Age	Child form	Relevant feature substitutions Place	Height	[tense]	Mastery σ-Type
iː	1;0–1;4	ɯ	[+back]			
	1;3–1;4	a		[+low] [-high]	[+tense]	
	1;4–1;6	i				Closed
	1;5	iː				Open
	1;6	**iː**				**Mastery**
ɪ	1;2–1;6	iː (rare)			[+tense]	
	1;3–1;4	a		[+low] [-high]		
	1;4	**ɪ**				**Mastery**[b]
eɪ	1;0–1;5	a		[+low]		
	1;4–1;5	ɛ/e (rare)			([-tense])	
	1;6	eɪ				**Mastery**[c]
ɛ	0;11–1;1	ɪ(ː)		[+high]		
	1;4–1;9	a~ʌ	([+back])	([+low])		
	1;5–1;10	e(ɪ) (eː)			[+tense]	
	1;7	ɪ		[+high]		
	1;9	**ɛ**				**Mastery**
ʌ/ə	0;11–1;8	a	([-back])	([+low])		
	1;8	ʌ				**Mastery**

Note: Redundant features are not included. Mastery = 100% accuracy.
[a] Low vowels: [a]~[ʌ] until 1;6; [a] until after age 2. /æ/ often a nonlow front vowel before nasals until 1;5.
[b] Rare use of [ʌ] and [eɪ] for single lexical items.
[c] Rare use of [aɪ] or [iː] till 1;8; [i] in unstressed syllables until 2;1.

Beers (1995) collected data from 45 Dutch-learning subjects in cross-sectional groups from age 1;3 to 3;2. Her data generally agree with Levelt's (1994) results and those of English studies, with the exception of earlier mastery of the lax mid vowels. (She notes that most vowels were acquired by the early part of the third year.)

Early mastery: The corner vowels [i], [a], [u]
Lax front vowels [ɪ] and [ɛ]
Mid mastery: Tense mid central vowel [ʌ]
Lax mid back vowel [ɔ]

Later mastery: Tense mid vowels [e], [o]
                Lax mid unrounded vowel [ɤ]
                Front rounded vowels

Beers (1995) interprets the later mastery of the tense mid vowels as supportive of predictions of feature geometry, that vowels with more nondefault features will be acquired later. (She considers [+tense] to be the nondefault value.) This was true for the mid vowels [e] and [o] versus [ɛ] and [ɔ] in her study but not of the high vowels nor of the central vowels. Furthermore, it was not true of Levelt's (1994) data or most English data. Hence, that prediction is not upheld. Because the length of vowels is generally correlated with tenseness in Germanic languages, predictions based on the feature [tense] may be irrelevant, in any event.

Data from individual children are available for German (Stern & Stern, 1907; Elsen, 1991; Geilmann, 1993). All report the early frequent use of low vowels: front [a] or central [ɑ] (or [ɐ]). The German data also show early use of the vowel [ɛ]. Elsen states that /ɛ/ was the third vowel to become stable, after [a/aɪ] and [ɪ/ə]. Front rounded vowels were often produced as front unrounded vowels. Occasionally, front unrounded vowels surfaced as round vowels (Geilmann, 1993):

	möchte	/mœçtə/	[bœçtə]	'might'
	frühstücken	/fʁyːʃtykən/	[fryːʃtim]	'to have breakfast'
BUT:	Trecker	/tʁɛkɐ/	[dʁœkɐ]~[dʁɛkɐ]	'tractor'

The German data are similar to the English and Dutch data, with divergent results noted for the lax mid vowel /ɛ/. In Dutch and German, the presence of a large number of front vowel types may promote earlier production of front vowels. Regarding this point, Dutch and German children often substitute front unrounded vowels for front rounded vowels, suggesting robustness for the [-back] feature, whether it is treated as a default or nondefault.

5.6.2.2. Development in Languages with Small Vowel Inventories

Japanese has five basic vowels (/i/, /e/, /a/, /o/, /ɯ/), as does Spanish (/i/, /e/, /a/, /o/, /u/), the difference between the two concerning rounding of the high back vowel. Hungarian has these same vowels, but in addition, has /ø/ and /y/, (phonetic) [ɛ] and [ɔ], a length distinction, and Vowel Harmony (see §9.2.1).

A summary of Japanese vowel acquisition is provided in Ueda (1996). According to reports (Murai, 1961; Ito, 1990), the most frequent vowel in babbling is a mid central vowel (not unlike what is found in other language groups). The vowels [a], [e], and [o] appear to precede the high vowels [i] and [ɯ]. Fee (1991) examined data at two acquisition points from four Hungarian-learning children (ages 1;2–1;11), and three Spanish-learning children (1;0–2;11). As in Japanese, the vowels /a/, /e/, and /o/ were the first to be used productively by the seven children, and /u/ was the last of the five core vowels to be used productively. (Short vowels were acquired prior to long vowels or diphthongs.) The frequency of vowels in the lower left part of the vowel quadrangle accords well with data from English, and the later acquisition of /u/ is also not unattested in English. The early presence of [o] is interesting in terms of crosslinguistic frequency of vowels, since /o/ is more frequent than /u/ in languages of the world (Maddieson, 1984). The data do diverge somewhat, however, from the general trends reported above, particularly in terms of the lack of *any* high vowels. A front-back contrast was present, a [round] contrast was present, but a height contrast was present only involving the feature [low]. The clue to the difference between Fee's (1991) study and those for English, Dutch, and German may reflect a difference in the methodology used to determine productivity. An examination of the vowel inventories for each child presented in Fee (1991) shows that all children did in fact use the five core vowels in the early samples, but that [a], [e], and [o] were used more frequently (including in substitutions). In the studies reported for English, Dutch, and German, a criterion of frequency may not have been used to determine mastery, as it was in Fee (1991). However, it remains interesting that the smaller vowel inventories appear to show similar patterns of acquisition overall, with mid vowels earlier than high vowels. We have insufficient information on relative vowel frequency in the input to children to know whether that factor may have an impact. Certainly, in English, high front vowels are frequent in language to children because of the morpheme "-y" (as in *doggy*), which is also used frequently in German (Elsen, p.c.). The Spanish epenthetic vowel is /e/, and /o/ and /a/ are very frequent word endings, as they are in Japanese. Clearly, more comparative work needs to be done crosslinguistically to determine (a) if there are notable differences in acquisition paths and what they are, and (b) what the effects of input are on the development of vowel systems.

5.6.2.3. Nasalized Vowels

Very little is known about the development of nasalized vowels in languages such as French and Portuguese. Vihman (1996) includes examples from Laurent (a French-learning infant), showing that vowels are oral at first, but that nasalized vowels appear within the early word period:

tiens	/tiẽ/	[da]	'Here.'	0;10
non	/nõ/	[nɛ]	'No.'	1;2
non	/nõ/	[noc]~[nã]	'No.'	1;3
ballon	/balõ/	[palõ]	'balloon'	1;3

Although there are very few examples in Freitas (1996: Inez), the same pattern appears for early words in Portuguese (i.e., without nasalization):

| cão | /kãõ/ | [ka] | 'dog' | 1;1 |
| João | /ʒuãũ/ | [eɑ] | 'Joao' | 1;5 |

Similarly, very little is known about the development of context-sensitive vowel nasalization in English. We return to that discussion in §7.3.4.4.

5.6.2.4. Vowel Constraints and Repairs

How accurate are the productions of vowels in real word attempts, and what kind of repair patterns are seen? B. Davis and MacNeilage (1990) comment that vowel production was relatively inaccurate in early words for their subject: only 60% of the vowels matched adult targets in identifiable words. This was comparable with match data from Paschall's (1983) group of 16-18-month-olds. Particularly susceptible in both studies were the mid front vowels and rhotic vowels.

All varieties of repairs have been attested for vowels (Otomo & Stoel-Gammon, 1992; Pollock & Keiser, 1990): raising or lowering (with the latter becoming more frequent over time), backness changes (backing, fronting, or centralization), rounding/unrounding, and vowel timing unit changes (diphthongization, monophthongization, shortening, lengthening). (We ignore the latter structural changes in this section.) Default front/central or low/mid vowels often replace other vowels (Paschall, 1983; Vihman, 1992; Gwendolyn's substitution for /ʊ/ below). The following general statements can be made:

1. As was the case for consonants, constraints can affect individual features or feature combinations. Examples of Not constraints are:

Not(V-Labial):   *{[oʊ],[u],[ʊ],[ɔ]}
Not(-back):   *{[i],[ɪ],[eɪ],[ɛ],[æ]}
Not(+high):   *{[i],[ɪ],[ʊ],[u]}

Not(<Feature>) may be high-ranked initially. For example, **Not(V-Labial)** prohibits all round vowels. However, as the feature becomes possible, more specific co-occurrence constraints may limit particular vowels within the round series. For example, **NotCo-occurring(V-Labial,+high)** may prohibit only [u] and [ʊ], but not [o]. Some other examples are:

NotCo-occurring(-back,-low):   *[ɛ], *[eɪ], *[ɪ], *[i]; but [æ], [a]
NotCo-occurring(V-Place,+nasal):   *Nasal vowels
NotCo-occurring(V-Labial,-back):   *Front rounded vowels

Positive (implicational) constraints may also be high-ranked. **Co-occurring (+back,-low→V-Labial)** (leading to rounded /u/ and /o/ rather than unrounded /ɯ/ and /ɤ/) is high-ranked in adult English (and most adult languages), and children may abide by that constraint from the outset. On the other hand, a child may have his or her own particular high-ranked co-occurrence constraints (e.g., **Co-occurring(-back→+high)**), ensuring that all front vowels are high.

2. Vowel repair processes are similar to consonantal repairs, in that nondefault features delete; defaults then replace either one of the features (minimal repair), or more than one (nonminimal repair). In nonminimal repairs, more than one feature value (or all features) may change to accommodate a constraint. When high-ranked **NotCo-occurring(-high,-back)** prohibits /ɛ/, only the value for the feature [high] or [back] needs to change to circumvent the constraint; the output should be [ɪ] or [ʌ]. If, however, the vowel [ɑ] replaces /ɛ/ [low] and [back] have both changed: a nonminimal repair.

If all features of a particular vowel delete, the vowel nucleus itself could delete, or a default vowel could be inserted. Because we are concerned in this chapter with feature changes rather than prosodic structure changes, we focus here on default vowel insertion. Patterns of centralization, lowering, or unrounding appear to be more common than raising or rounding. These common types of repairs result in production of the front/mid or low/central vowels, which we noted to be frequent in early inventories.

3. Tenseness changes in English may reflect changes in vowel length, and the status of a syllable as open or closed, although they are not always associated with length changes. (See Gwendolyn's substitution data in Table 5.3, showing differences in vowel substitutions in closed and open syllables.)

4. Identification of default and nondefault values is generally much more difficult for vowels than consonants. This difficulty stems from several factors. At the outset, it is difficult to characterize children's inventories because of uncertainty regarding transcription of the vowels, and uncertainty as to the optimal feature designation. Furthermore, substitution patterns are often short-lived and few in number, since vowels are acquired reasonably quickly. Strong and pervasive substitution patterns help make clearer what the defaults are. It appears that, at least for some languages and children, default values may change over time, making characterization at any given point difficult.

In the next section, we give examples of constraints and repairs for vowels. We focus on two types of vowels: the mid front lax vowel /ɛ/, and back round vowels. The alternate patterns presented for /ɛ/ and the round vowels illustrate the variety of constraints and repairs that affect vowels. These vowel types contrast in place, height, roundness and tenseness, thus covering the range of vowel features. As we noted earlier, the mid front lax vowel is often late in English development, and hence it is subject to a variety of repairs, with all features subject to change (except that [V-Labial] is never inserted to create a rounded vowel). Many children produce back rounded vowels early on, but some children do not, with different resolutions of the constraints on [V-Labial]. The feature [V-Labial] itself may delete, or changes in height, tenseness, or place may accommodate co-occurrence constraints involving [V-Labial].

5.6.2.4.1. Constraints and Repairs for /ɛ/

The vowel /ɛ/ is often late to emerge in English. A variety of repairs have been noted in the literature (Otomo & Stoel-Gammon, 1992; Pollock & Keiser, 1990): lowering, backing, raising, and tensing. (In other words, any feature may change.) The subject of our discussion in this section (Gordon: Bernhardt, 1990: S5) primarily showed lowering of /ɛ/, but backing, raising, and tensing also occurred. (Lowering is a frequent pattern for /ɛ/, according to Otomo & Stoel-Gammon, 1992.) We can thus demonstrate the range of repairs for /ɛ/ with Gordon's data.

Gordon was a 6-year-old with a severe phonological and morphosyntactic production disorder who had difficulty with both consonants (liquids and sibilants) and vowels. Although the focus of this section is on the vowel /ɛ/, we first present an overview of his whole vowel system to provide a context for the discussion of /ɛ/. The vowels /i/, /ɔ/, and /ʌ/, and the diphthongs were established. (The diphthong /eɪ/ did sometimes surface as [i], e.g., *baby* [pʰeɪbeɪ]~[biˇbi]~[bibeɪ].) The following vowels presented the most difficulty: /ʊ/ (40% match), /ɛ/ (32% match), /ɪ/ (20% match), and especially /u/ (8% match). There was also some random variation among the low vowels [a], [ɑ], and [æ], with [a] being the most frequent variant. If we include just the established vowels, Gordon's vowel (and diphthong) quadrilateral was as follows:

```
i
eɪ       ʌ      oʊ
                 ɔ
a/aʊ/aɪ
```

All vowel features of English were in the system:

[+back]:	[ɔ], [oʊ], [ʌ], ([u], [ʊ])
[-back]:	[i], [eɪ], ([ɪ], [ɛ], [æ])
[+high]:	[i], ([ʊ], [u])
[-high]:	[eɪ], [ɔ], [oʊ], [ʌ], ([ɛ], [ə])
[+low]:	[a], ([æ], [ɑ])
[-low]:	[eɪ], [ɔ], [oʊ], [ʌ], ([ə], [ɛ])
[Labial]:	[ɔ], [oʊ], ([ʊ], [u])
no [Labial]:	[i], [eɪ], [a], [ʌ], ([ɛ], [ɪ], [æ], [ɑ], [ə])
[+tense]:	[i], ([u])
[-tense]:	[ʌ], [a], [ɔ], ([ə], [ɛ], [ɪ])

Not constraints for the individual features were thus generally low-ranked. On the other hand, high-ranked co-occurrence constraints prohibited particular round vowels ([u], [ʊ]), nonlow vowels ([ɪ], [ɛ], [ə]), and low vowels ([æ] and [ɑ]). Major high-ranked co-occurrence constraints were:

NotCo-occurring(V-Labial, + high):	*[u], *[ʊ]
NotCo-occurring(-back,-low,-tense):	*[ɪ], *[ɛ]

Minimal one-step place or height changes generally accommodated the constraint. The typical height change was from mid to low vowels (i.e., a change from [-low] to [+low] as in [1] below). A single place change was also relatively common: [-back] to [+back] (as in [2] below).

1. Frequent minimal repair: Lowering of /ɛ/ to [a]/[æ]

bed   /bɛd/   [baᵊd]

NotCo-occurring(-back,-low,-tense)	‖‖	**NotCo-occurring(-back, + low)**
	‖‖	**Survived(-low)**
	‖‖	**Not(+ low)**
Survived(-back)	‖‖	**Not(-back)**
Survived(-tense)	‖‖	**Not(-tense)**

In this case, [-low] deleted. Default [+low] (reflecting the high frequency of [a] in Gordon's system) could be inserted because of the low ranking of **Not (+low)**. Replacing [-low] with [+low] accommodated the co-occurrence constraint with only one feature change.

    2. Alternate minimal repair: Backing of /ɛ/ > [ʌ]

present   /pɹɛznt̩/   [pʰʌ̃ntθĩn]

NotCo-occurring(-back,-low,-tense) ‖‖	**NotCo-occurring(+back,-low,-tense)**
‖‖	**Survived(-back)**
‖‖	**Not(+back)**
Survived(-tense) ‖‖	**Not(-tense)**
Survived(-low) ‖‖	**Not(-low)**

In this alternate repair, **Survived(-back)** was low-ranked, and [-back] deleted. **Not(+back)** was also low-ranked, and therefore (default) [+back] was inserted. The [ʌ] is not uncommonly a default vowel (see, e.g., Morgan's alternation above between [a] and [ʌ]). Centralization also resolves the co-occurrence constraint. Changing [-back] to [+back] accommodated the co-occurrence constraint with only one feature change.

    3. Nonminimal repair: Lowering and backing of /ɛ/ > [ɑ]. An infrequent non-minimal change for Gordon involved changes in both height and place. He *occasionally* produced an [ɑ] for /ɛ/:

dress   /dɹɛs/   [t̪θwɑˀt̪] (varying with [ᵈðæd₀] and [ᵈðwæ ˀtθ])

The vowels [a] and [ɑ] also alternated occasionally in words with /ɑ/ targets, for example, *on* [ãn] (2 tokens) or [ãn]. This substitution for /ɛ/, then, may reflect instability for [back] in low vowels, rather than particular constraints involving /ɛ/.

    If a child *did* show consistent replacement of /ɛ/ by [ɑ], even though [ʌ] was in the system, the constraint ranking would involve high ranking of **Survived/ LinkedUpwards** constraints for the individual features and the Root node, except for low ranking of **LinkedUpwards(Root)**. The /ɛ/ would be floating (and so not pronounced), and the default vowel [ɑ] would be inserted to replace it (since *some* vowel would be required).

		RESULTS
Survived/LinkedUpwards(μ) ‖‖		**Vowel required**
LinkedDownwards(μ) ‖‖		
NotCo-occurring(-back,-low,-tense) ‖‖		**No [ɛ]**
Survived(Root) ‖‖	**LinkedUpwards(Root)**	**/ɛ/ floating**
Survived/LinkedUpwards(-back) ‖‖		
Survived/LinkedUpwards(-low) ‖‖		
Survived/LinkedUpwards(-tense) ‖‖		
‖‖	**Not(+back)**	**Default [ɑ]**
‖‖	**Not(+low)**	
‖‖	**Not(+tense)**	

This ranking assumes that features in floating segments do not violate co-occurrence constraints; see discussion in §4.7.1.2.)

4. Nonminimal repair: Raising and tensing of /ɛ/ > [i]. Occasionally, /ɛ/ surfaced as [i] (e.g., *bear* as [bijo]). The particular context may have influenced the repair (although /ɛ/ matched in *chair* /tʃɛɹ/ [ˈθɛɹjo(ʊ)]). However, for purposes of illustration, we concentrate on the substitution itself. Recall that [ɪ] was often problematical (surfacing as [ɛ] or [i]). **NotCo-occurring(-back,-low,-tense)** prohibited [ɛ] and [ɪ]. If [ɛ] raised (deletion of [-high] and insertion of [+high]), it was more likely to surface as [i] than [ɪ] (deletion of [-tense]).

		RESULTS
Survived(V-Root)		**[eɪ] only if in UR**
NotComplex(Nucleus)		
NotCo-occurring(-back,-low,-tense)	**Survived(-tense)**	**No /ɛ/**
	Survived(-high)	
NotCo-occurring(-back,+tense)		**No [e]**
NotCo-occurring(+high,-tense)		**No /ɪ/**
Survived(-back)	**Not(-back)**	**Must be front V**
Survived(-low)	**Not(-low)**	**Must be nonlow**
Co-occurring(-low→ +high)	**Not(+high)**	**Can be high**
	Not(+tense)	**Can be [i]**

The vowel raised to [i] (changing both tenseness and height) rather than just tensing to [e]. This is probably because tense [e] occurs in adult English only as part of a diphthong (never as a tense nonhigh monophthong), and other high-ranked constraints prevented diphthongization unless it was underlying.

For Gordon, the majority of substitutions involved minimal repairs with one feature change. Even when default vowels appeared as substitutions, this could be accounted for in terms of single feature changes or as a response to other general constraints. In the next section, we examine both minimal and nonminimal repairs for round vowels; there may be more opportunities for nonminimal repairs for round vowels.

5.6.2.4.2. Constraints and Repairs for Round Vowels

In our discussion of consonants, we noted that segments which have only non-default features are sometimes mastered later than segments which have default features. Because we consider [Labial] to be a nondefault feature for vowels, it is expected that some children may have delayed acquisition of rounded vowels. Beers (1995:84) makes the same prediction for Dutch, based on segmental complexity. Constraints on rounded vowels may affect all or some of the rounded vowels in a system. If all rounded vowels are prohibited, **Not(Labial)** is high-ranked. Morgan (see Table 5.3) used rounded vowels only sporadically (and primarily in the context of labial consonants) until 2;6. Alternatively, high-ranked co-occurrence constraints may prohibit particular rounded vowels. Examples of such co-occurrence constraints are the following:

NotCo-occurring(Labial, + high): *[u], *[ʊ], but [o], [ɔ]
   (Bernhardt, 1990: Gordon; Bernhardt, Rempel, & Pegg, 1994: Lori)
NotCo-occurring(Labial, + tense):: *[u], *[o], but [ʊ], [ɔ]
   (Fee, 1994)
NotCo-occurring(Labial,-tense, + high): No /ʊ/
   (see Table 5.2: Gwendolyn)

Not(+ round). Morgan used rounded vowels only occasionally before 2;6, and then only variably and only in the context of labial consonants (see §7.3.4.2). In place of the rounded vowels, an unrounded back vowel of the same height was usually produced (early [a] or [ʌ]; later [ɯ], [ɤ], [ɯ]).

food	/fuːd/	[bɯʔ];	later [fɯːd]
book	/bʊk/	[baʔ];	later [bɯʔ]
open	/oʊpən/	[ʔʌbə];	later [ʔɤːpən]

Children tend not to use substitutions that are not in the target language. In using nonlow back unrounded vowels, Morgan achieved faithfulness to the other features in the target vowel but only by using non-English vowels. (Note, however, that [ɯ] and [ɤ] are perceived by adult English listeners as their rounded counterparts, because there is no contrast in English between the rounded and unrounded vowels. They are a minimal deviation from English.) A straightforward constraint ranking derives the prohibition against rounded vowels:

| **Not(V-Labial)** | ‖‖ | **Survived(V-Labial)** |
| **Survived(Other V features)** | ‖‖ | **Not(Other V features)** |

At 2;6, **Survived(V-Labial)** was reranked higher than **Not(V-Labial)**. All the rounded vowels of adult English appeared at the same time. (Rather than **Not (V-Labial)**, the data could reflect high-ranking for **NotComplex(V-Place)**; [V-Labial] might survive, but not in the vowel. See §7.3.4.2 for discussion.)

Between 1;3 and 1;4, the words *no* and *don't* appeared with [o]. However, [o] appeared in no other words, and was short-lived even in these lexical exceptions. It is interesting that two high frequency words with social-pragmatic power were temporarily more faithful to the adult targets.

NotCo-Occurring(Labial, + high). Gordon and Gwendolyn had longstanding co-occurrence constraints on particular rounded vowels (after age 6 and 5, respectively). (Furthermore, Gordon's acquisition of rounded vowels occurred at least partially as a result of phonological intervention. See Bernhardt, 1990.)

Gordon typically produced /u/ and /ʊ/ as a mid back vowel [o] (with or without short offglides). (Fee's, 1991, Hungarian data showed occasional similar patterns of /u/ > [o]). Occasionally, /u/ was produced as a lax vowel [ʊ]. There were occasional matches of /ʊ/ and /u/ to the target, but mostly in imitation. This pattern is interesting in terms of crosslinguistic frequency of vowels, since /o/ is more frequent than /u/ in languages of the world (Maddieson, 1984).

boot	/buːt/	[boʊt] (S); [bʊt] (E)
smooth	/smuːð/	[θmov] (E)
zoo	/zuː/	[θoᵁʔ] (S)
to	/tuː/	[to]~[tʊ] (S); [tu] (E)
cook	/kʊk/	[kʰok] (S)
cookies	/kʊkiz/	[kʰoˆkɛɪð] (S); [kʰoᵘkʰið]~[kʊkɛˆɪð] (E)
good	/gʊd/	[goᵈd] (S)
snowman	/snoʊmæn/	[θnõmãn] (S)
story	/stɔɹi/	[θɔwi] (S)
cow	/kaʊ/	[kʰaʊ] (S)
cowboy	/kaʊbɔɪ/	[kaᵘbɔˇɪ] (S)

We focus here on the typical output [o] for the sake of simplicity and brevity. Given a co-occurrence constraint on [Labial] and [+high], either feature could delete, with insertion of a default feature. The [Labial] feature is not likely to delete, since the result would be a non-English high back vowel [ɯ], which most children avoid (though see Morgan above). **Survived(V-Labial)** was high-ranked. The only alternative minimal repair was delinking of [+high], with insertion of the [-high]: [o].

TABLE 5.7

/smuːð/	θmuːv	θmɯv	θmov
NotCo-occurring(Labial,+high)	*!		
Survived(Labial)		*!	
Survived(+high)			*
Not(-high)			*

NotCo-Occurring(Labial,+high,-tense). Initially, Gwendolyn typically substituted [a] for /ʊ/. After she was able to produce mid central vowels, the latter occasionally appeared in place of [ʊ].

| cookie | /kʊki/ | [tʰaːdi] |
| good | /gʊd/ | [daː] |

Why was /ʊ/ late, even though other round vowels were possible? First, /ʊ/ is of low frequency in English. Second, /ʊ/ has three nondefault features: [+high], [Labial], [-tense]. Third, /ʊ/ is the only short rounded vowel in the dialect of English that Gwendolyn was learning. Nondefault [V-Labial] more commonly occurs in tense (long or diphthongal) vowels in English; this suggests a constraint (**Co-occurring(V-Labial→μμ)**, requiring rounded vowels to be long.

Given that other round vowels and central vowels were possible substitutions, why did [a] appear as a frequent substitution for /ʊ/? For Gwendolyn (as for many children; see above), [a] was an early and frequent vowel, and possibly a default from the outset. This implies default features [-back], [-high], [+low], and [-tense]. The [a] and the /ʊ/ differ in place, height, and rounding, but both are short ([-tense]). If **Not(μ)** was ranked higher than **Co-occurring(V-Labial→μμ)**, the vowel had to remain short; the co-occurrence constraint could not force the insertion of a mora, to yield tense [uː] (which was possible in the child's system). Avoidance of non-English vowels prevented simple deletion of [V-Labial] (*[ɯ]), or simple changes of [high] (no mid *[ɔ]) or [tense] (no short [u]). The mid vowels [ʌ] and [ə] were possible and reasonable outputs, because they are the closest English ([+back]) vowels to /ʊ/. However, *all* nondefault features were lost. According to our analysis of nonminimal repairs, *individual features* must remain linked to higher structure via high-ranking of the **Survived/LinkedUpwards** constraints. If prosodic structure must be maintained, and the particular features cannot co-occur in the output, the only solution is to delink an intermediate-level node, in this case the Root node (via low ranking of **LinkedUpwards(Root)**). The higher structure must be linked downwards, and hence a default vowel with all default features is inserted. (This assumes that floating segments do not violate co-occurrence constraints.)

RESULTS

Not(μ)	Co-occurring(V-Labial→μμ)	No insertion of μ
LinkedDownwards(μ)		
Survived(V-Root)	LinkedUpwards(V-Root)	Floating V-Root
	Not(V-Root)	
NotCo-occurring(V-Labial, + high,-tense)		No [ʊ]
Co-occurring(+ tense→μμ)		No short [u]
Survived/LinkedUp(<Features of /ʊ/>)	Not(+ low)	
	Not(-back)	
	Not(-tense)	/ʊ/ > [a]

5.6.3. VOWEL HARMONY AS A RESPONSE TO UNDERSPECIFICATION

In §5.5.5, the final section on consonant repairs, we noted that deletion and default insertion are not the only repairs that can accommodate constraints on features. Like consonant harmony, double linking of established features can accommodate high-ranked **Not(<Feature>)** constraints. Fee (1991:459) comments about her Spanish and Hungarian samples:

> Directionality [of harmony] is determined solely by which vowel or syllable slot is left unspecified.

Although Fee provides few examples, two children do appear to show double linking of different (frequent) vowel features in a way that suggests that underspecification may be motivating the repair. Consider the following data from Claudio (a Spanish-learning child):

dulce	/dulse/	[eβle]	'sweet'	*[u]	R-L
meti	/meti/	[pete]	'?'	*[i]	L-R
lado	/lado/	[jaja]	'side'	*[o]	L-R

Both [e] and [a] were frequent vowels, appearing as both matches and substitutions. The [u] and [i] were infrequent, and prone to substitutions. The [o] was fairly frequent, but when it was in a weak domain (an unstressed syllable) it was less likely to survive than frequent [a]. Whether one or both vowels was spreading, or one was being inserted as a default, we cannot determine from the data given. The child forms merely show double linking of features in the two syllables.

Fee also provides data from T.A. (a Hungarian-learning child):

magnó	[magna]	*[o]	'tape recorder'	L-R
cipo	[popo]	*[i]	'shoes' or 'bread'	R-L

The more frequent vowel in each case was the one that became doubly linked: [a] was more frequent than [o] and [o] was more frequent than [i]. Again, insufficient data are given to determine conclusively what the default and spreading features may have been.

Vowel harmony appears to be relatively infrequent (except in early reduplication), but the insufficient treatment of this subject in the literature does not allow us to draw firm conclusions about harmony and underspecification in vowels.

5.6.4. ACQUISITION OF TONE

Although tonal features are not vowel features, tones are realized on vowels, and hence we include this discussion here. Studies of tone are even fewer than studies of vowels, with more work done on Asian languages than on African languages. Some aspects of tone are acquired by age 2 in both language groups.

In Asian languages, tone is primarily lexical and there are few differences between underlying and surface tones. There is early acquisition of lexical tone (before 3), and later acquisition of tone sandhi (Chao, 1971; Li & Thompson, 1977; K.-P. Tse, 1978; A.C.-Y. Tse, 1991; S.-M. Tse, 1982; So & Dodd, 1995).

Cantonese has six tones: high level, mid level, low level, high rising, low rising, and low falling. It also has "entering" allotones (high, mid, and low). In the largest cross-sectional study, So and Dodd (1995) reported that only two of 268 Cantonese-learning subjects (ages 2;0–5;11) made any tone errors (two and three errors respectively). For four subjects followed longitudinally, they noted the following commonalities:

        1;4: High level, mid level tones
        1;6: High rising
    1;6–1;7: Allotones

The low tones appeared after the higher tones, although order of acquisition differed across subjects.

    1;8: Low level (Subjects A and B)
          Low rising (Subject C)
    1;10: Both (Subject D)
    1;11: Low rising (Subjects A and B)
    2;0: Low level (Subject D)

These data were both similar to and different from Tse (1978). Reporting on both Cantonese and Mandarin, he noted that children seem to learn the highest level tone first, and then either the lowest level tone (if there are several level tones in the language) or the falling tone, with other contour tones generally being learned later. Li and Thompson (1977) also noted later acquisition of contour tones, particularly rising tones. Most results suggest that children may begin with the highest level tone, but that there are options after that. However, there may even be some variation with respect to relative ease of the high-level tone. Tse (1982) commented that substitutions were infrequent overall for his three subjects, but the most frequent of those that did occur were "upper going" for the high-level tone, and lower rising for the upper rising tone. Thus, it is difficult to make any strong claims about order of acquisition of lexical tones in Cantonese and Mandarin, except that they are acquired early but not simultaneously, and that high-level tones are often acquired first. This suggests that tones (like vowels) are fairly easy for the child to master.

Studies of tone in African languages are even rarer. Demuth (1993) presents information for Sesotho, and refers to studies of Chichewa (Chimombo & Mtenje, 1989) and Zulu (Suzman, 1991). In Bantu languages, tone is primarily grammatical, and there is more tone sandhi; there are many alternations between underlying and surface forms and consequently, surface inconsistency for particular morphemes. Earlier acquisition of tone sandhi may occur in African languages than Asian languages. Demuth hypothesizes that, in a language which has differences between surface and underlying tone (such as Sesotho), learning patterns of tone sandhi may help a child derive the underlying representation of tones in verb roots. Learning the correct underlying representations for the tones in a morpheme can then in turn assist learning about alternations (tone sandhi), resulting in mastery of many aspects of both around the same age. (On the other hand, in languages in which tone is more lexical than grammatical such as Mandarin, tone sandhi may be learned as late as 5 or 6, because the alternations are independent of lexical tones.)

Demuth (1993) noted accurate tone marking of some morphemes (in particular, subject markers) in a Sesotho-learning subject by age 2;0. Tone marking for verb roots was not consistently correct till after age 3;0, however. This was similar to results for Zulu (Suzman, 1991). Demuth (1993) suggests that there are different timelines and patterns in tone acquisition in the two language groups, because of differences in tone function. Interestingly, Demuth (1993) and Suzman (1991) found earlier acquisition of high tone than low tone in the verb systems for their

Sesotho-learning and Zulu-learning subjects, with overgeneralization of high tone in error patterns. This is similar to the observations made for Cantonese in at least some of the studies. Demuth (1993) hypothesizes that the child she studied had a default high tone until about age 3;0, even though low tone is the default in the adult language.[9]

Without more information and examples from the languages in question, we cannot make definitive claims about the acquisition of tone. It is interesting that high tones generally appear to be acquired earlier than low tones in both Asian and African languages, though we do not know why that should be the case. The different patterns and timelines for development of the high and low(er) tones suggest a pattern of defaults and nondefaults similar to what has been discussed for segmental features, with **Not(Low)** higher-ranked than **Not(High)** for a longer period. This is consistent with our perspective on underspecification, that defaults arise from frequency in the child's system. Like many other aspects of phonological development, however, the topic of tone acquisition is waiting for more in-depth investigations.

5.6.5. VOWEL DEVELOPMENT: MARKEDNESS, UNDERSPECIFICATION, AND FEATURE GEOMETRY

What kind of conclusions can be drawn about vowel feature geometry, markedness, and underspecification in development?

Throughout the vowel discussion, we referred to traditional (binary) vowel features. They appeared to account for the data reasonably well in most cases. In terms of place and height features ([back], [high], [low]), other vowel geometries have been proposed with separate place and height nodes (e.g., Lahiri & Evers, 1991, or Rice & Avery, 1995). Such geometries may have some support, since place and height can act independently. Children vary in terms of the place dimension in which the first height split occurs (i.e., either back or front high vowels may appear after the first low or central vowels). However, current theory also suggests that the traditional features [high], [low], and [back] are autonomous (even if they are all dominated by the same node). Thus, separate nodes may not be necessary to account for different patterns relative to height and place.

Whether features are binary or privative is another issue for debate. We have seen that some children neutralize contrasts for certain vowels. Random interchange of a (minimal) pair of vowels that contrast on one feature (e.g., [i]/[ɪ]) may indicate lack of contrasting (binary) values for that feature that distinguishes them (variable ranking of **Not(+tense)** vs. **Not(-tense)**). On the other hand, consistent production of each vowel of a minimal pair does not necessarily mean that the distinguishing feature has binary [+] and [-] features. One feature may be specified (as [+] or [-]) and the other may have no specification ([]). Clearly, much work remains to be done on vowel feature classifications.

How does the theory of underspecification fare in describing patterns of vowel development? Children's frequent use of one or two vowels in early development suggests that those vowels (and their features) act as defaults. As early as 1907, the Sterns commented on the use of frequent default vowels ("Urvokale") in their children's speech. Children's default vowel features are not necessarily those of the adult system, however, just as children's default consonant features may not necessarily be the same as those of adults. This possible difference and the particular substitution patterns can make it difficult to determine what the defaults are for a child. If two frequent (and substituting) vowels are in random variation with each other (such as Morgan's [ʌ]~[a] alternation), which vowels and features are the defaults? If two vowels do not alternate with each other, but are both frequent substituting vowels, which is the default? Fee (1991) noted that both [e] and [a] were frequent matches and substitutions in the Hungarian and Spanish samples. The vowel [a] sometimes replaced /e/, however, suggesting that [a] ([+low], [-high], and [-back]) was the default. If **Not(-high)** and **Not(-back)** were always low-ranked, and **Not(+low)** was sometimes high-ranked, [e] could sometimes substitute for other vowels. The theory of underspecification (or at least, the theory of defaults) does appear useful for describing vowel patterns, if supplemented with a theory of variable constraint rankings.

In the introduction to this chapter, we outlined problems with predictions based on markedness and feature geometry. We will not repeat the arguments here, but add that, because feature geometry is even less well confirmed or agreed upon for vowels (as discussed briefly above), the problems are even greater for prediction of order.

Jakobson (1968/1941) was the first to make strong predictions for vowel development based on markedness and maximal contrast. He predicted that the first vowel contrast should reflect distinctions in terms of openness: narrow /i/ versus wide /ɑ/. After that, either place or height contrasts were predicted. Marked vowels, such as front rounded vowels, were predicted to emerge later.

1. first vowel: a low "wide" vowel /ɑ/
2. a narrow–wide contrast: /i/ versus /ɑ/
3. a front–back contrast(/i/-/u/) or a further height contrast, giving mid vowels
4. later acquisition of marked vowels, such as front rounded vowels

Vowel development is partly consistent with Jakobson's predictions, in that low/mid front/central ("wide") vowels are often the first vowels. The particular low vowel that appears may be different across children, but it is usually not a back vowel. As we noted previously, the first predicted vowel contrast (narrow-wide) could alternatively be called a front-back contrast, or a round-nonround contrast, depending on which contrasting vowels are produced. Subdivision within the vowel system is perhaps defined generally enough that it can be confirmed without too much divergence.

Continuing in the Jakobsonian tradition, Beers (1995) evaluated predictions of developmental order, but she states at the outset that, "since vowels are by definition always represented with lower level place features, predictions cannot be made on the basis of position in the feature hierarchy, that is, that 'higher-level' features appear before 'lower-level' features" (1995:80). She based predictions instead on segmental complexity and markedness, suggesting that /ʌ/ and /ɪ/ would be the earliest vowels, /ʌ/ being [low] according to her description of Dutch, and /ɪ/ being [front]. Because her youngest group of subjects (1;3–1;8) already showed evidence of a number of vowels (/i/, /ɪ/, /u/, /ɛ/, /a/), the predictions could not be fully evaluated. The vowel /ʌ/ was acquired after five other vowels, including [a], which had been predicted to be later because it had more features ([+tense] and [+low]). Furthermore, she predicted that /u/ would be acquired with other round vowels, but it preceded them. In general, the tense-lax distinction was predicted to be late, but the contrast appeared early for some vowel pairs, and later for others. As we noted for consonants, predictions of developmental order are rarely fully confirmed.

5.7. FINAL COMMENTS

In this chapter we have presented a large number of examples of constraints and repairs that affect consonant features, and many (but far fewer) that affect vowels and tones. The development of consonants is the most studied aspect of phonological development. We have drawn substantially on the work of predecessors and contemporaries, bringing new data to bear from our own research. The most useful of the current concepts for explaining the data are underspecification and defaults (which show relationships and asymmetrical patterns among features and feature combinations) and constraint ranking (which show the interplay of nondefault and default features in patterns that arise). A number of issues arose about feature designation, underspecification, and order of acquisition throughout the chapter, and we return to that discussion in Chapter 10.

6

PROSODIC DEVELOPMENT

The focus of most of the research within phonological development has been on segmental development. It has been long been clear, however, that young children also begin with reduced prosodic structure (e.g., Jakobson, 1968/1941): children do not show the same richness of syllable structure, foot structure, and prosodic word structure that is found in most adult languages. Most of the details of young children's restrictions on prosodic structure are still unknown. Some specific topics have received much attention (such as the development of word-final codas, word-initial consonant clusters, and word-initial unstressed syllables), but many other topics are relatively unexplored.

In this chapter, we explore what is known about prosodic development. We begin with the smallest groupings (that of segments into syllables), proceeding to the next larger grouping (that of syllables into feet), and then to the largest grouping (that of feet into prosodic words). Finally, we turn to the effects of prosodic structure on morphology and syntax. We do not address sentence intonation, which is notoriously difficult to transcribe reliably and which phonological theories have little to say about.

We also return to a topic deferred from Chapter 5: the interaction of segmental development and prosodic development. This includes discussion of the effects of position in the word on different features, in terms of (a) mastery of target features in those word positions, and (b) insertion of nontarget features in those word positions. This chapter is concerned only with those instances in which constraints on prosodic structure, and not conflicts between the particular features of the segments involved in a sequence, are responsible for the patterns observed; see Chapter 7 for discussion of constraints on sequences of consonants.

We stress that different children show different patterns and the effects of different constraints. Although prosodic structure is reduced for all children at the outset, not all aspects of prosodic structure are equally reduced in all children. We address the full range of known phenomena (and provide speculation about other patterns that we expect to occur).

6.1. THE DEVELOPMENT
OF SYLLABLE STRUCTURE

In this section, we discuss the development of syllable structure. At the beginning of our discussion, we focus on words with a single syllable. Words with two or more syllables have additional complexities that can lead to special properties. The syllable structure properties of monosyllables also generally hold for polysyllables, and we include such data where appropriate. We take it for granted that syllables exist, and that every segment of every utterance produced by a child or by an adult is a part of a syllable. We also assume that syllables obligatorily have a nucleus; although this has been questioned recently for some languages (Shaw, 1996), it seems to hold for most languages and for phonological development.

6.1.1. PREDICTIONS AND CONSTRAINTS

Syllables are a required part of the output. Even if the input does not contain syllable structure, it will appear in the output. This is required by the **Linked-Upwards** constraint family:

LinkedUpwards(Root):	Every Root node must be linked upwards.
Root◂TimingUnit:	Root nodes link upwards to timing units.

These two constraints force a Root node in the lexical representation to link upwards to a timing unit. Similar constraints lead to syllable structure:

LinkedUpwards(V):	Every V timing unit must be linked upwards.
V◂Nucleus:	V timing units link upwards to nucleus nodes.
LinkedUpwards(C):	Every C timing unit must be linked upwards.
C◂Onset OR C◂Coda:	C timing units link upwards to onset or coda nodes.
LinkedUpwards(Nucleus):	Every nucleus must be linked upwards.
Nucleus◂Rime:	The nucleus node links upwards to a Rime node.
LinkedUpwards(Coda):	Every coda node must be linked upwards.
Coda◂Rime:	The coda node links upwards to a Rime node.
LinkedUpwards(Rime):	Every Rime node must be linked upwards.
Rime◂σ:	The Rime node links upwards to a syllable node.
LinkedUpwards(Onset):	Every onset node must be linked upwards.
Onset◂σ:	The onset node links upwards to a syllable node.

These are the basic constraints that lead to the presence of syllable structure in the output. Given faithfulness with underlying segments and timing units (which can be violated, of course), these constraints generally (but not always) result in syllable structure.

There are also constraints that require downwards structure: a given element must link downwards to the required element in order for these constraints to be unviolated. Our assumptions that a nucleus must always be present in a syllable is guaranteed by the following set of constraints, which are very high-ranked in (almost) all human languages, regardless of the age of the person:

σ►**Rime**: Syllables must dominate a rime.
Rime►Nucleus: Rimes must dominate a nucleus.

No other part of the syllable is absolutely obligatory, but there is a strong tendency for syllables to have onsets. This is governed by the following constraint:

σ►**Onset**: Syllables must dominate an onset.

If this constraint is very low-ranked, then syllables can freely lack onsets. If it is very high-ranked, then every syllable must have an onset. At an intermediate ranking, it is possible for syllables to lack onsets, but there will be a tendency for an onset to be present. A child acquiring English may rank this constraint too high, so that every syllable must have an onset.

In no language is a coda required in every syllable. In §4.5.1.2, we suggested that no downwards structure constraint requires a coda to be present. However, there can be particular environments in which a coda might be obligatory, if its presence is required by some other constraint (see §6.1.5).

In addition to these constraints on structure and linkage, there are the general constraints that prevent the presence of elements:

Not(σ): Syllables are not allowed.
Not(Rime): Rimes are not allowed.
Not(Nucleus): Nuclei are not allowed.
Not(Onset): Onsets are not allowed.
Not(Coda): Codas are not allowed.

The first constraint ensures that there will be as few syllables as possible in a word, a phenomenon that is known as Zipf's Law (see Zipf, 1935); it helps to prevent the epenthesis of vowels. The last constraint (**Not(Coda)**) is the most important. Rimes and nuclei are obligatory if there is a syllable, and onsets are frequently required by the downwards structure constraints. Codas, however, are not protected by any downwards structure constraint; consequently, a high ranking for **Not(Coda)** can prevent codas from appearing in the output. A young child who misranks **Not(Coda)** in this way has repair strategies that prevent codas in the output.

The last relevant set of constraints deals with complexity within the syllable:

NotComplex(Onset): An onset may have only one segment (Root node).
NotComplex(Coda): A coda may have only one segment (Root node).

These two constraints limit onsets and codas to a single segment. Note that *two* constraints are involved: one for onsets, one for codas. This implies that consonant clusters may be allowed only within onsets, or may be allowed only within codas. A high ranking of these two constraints in a child's system would lead to the absence of consonant clusters within a single syllable.

NotComplex(Nucleus):   A nucleus may have only one segment
                                       (Root node).

This constraint prevents diphthongs. An incorrectly high ranking might lead to the monophthongization of diphthongs.

Although most of the phenomena of child phonology involve reduction, our theory predicts that some children may have more elaborated phonological abilities than adults, in some respects. An adult language might prohibit codas, but a child acquiring that language might produce codas. There is some (very limited) evidence for this.

6.1.2. SIMPLE ONSETS

All children produce onset consonants (e.g., Jakobson, 1968/1941; Stoel-Gammon, 1985; Hodson & Paden, 1981). We are unaware of even a single report, from any language, of a child who completely lacked onsets, at any age. This is because of the high ranking of the downwards structure constraint σ▸**Onset**, which requires a syllable to have an onset. As a result, onset consonants tend to survive. To the extent that onset consonants are deleted, it is often because they contain specific features or feature combinations that are impossible in the child's system. (Because onsets are a strong prosodic domain, there are fewer problems with features than in codas.) In those instances in which an onset consonant is deleted, there is no effect on the length of the following vowel (no compensatory lengthening).

6.1.3. ?OBLIGATORY ONSETS?

Are onsets ever obligatory in the speech of a child? When the adult pronunciation of a word has no onset, does this cause difficulties for the child? If σ▸**Onset** is ranked too high, an onset might be required. This could be resolved either by inserting an onset (thereby violating **Not(Root)** and **Not(C)**, which consequently must be ranked lower) or by deleting the vowel in the onsetless syllable (violating **Survived(Root)**, **Survived(V)**, etc.), which must consequently be low-ranked). This can be the case, but we have no evidence bearing on how common it is across children. As long as σ▸**Onset** is ranked below all of these constraints, onsets will survive when they are present underlyingly, but no onset will be inserted if one is not already present.

It is clear that onsets are not necessarily obligatory. In some instances, English-learning children do not yet use a glottal stop with "vowel-initial" words, or do not insert one when an onset consonant is deleted. Stemberger (1988a) notes that Gwendolyn deleted word-initial glottal stop until 1;9:

apple   [aː]   (narrow transcription: no [ʔ])

Morgan produced [ʔ] where it was found in adult speech, but produced an onset-less syllable (with no [ʔ]) in place of word-initial /h/, through 1;4 (though she later had obligatory onsets in both initial and medial position; see below):

hop   [apʰ]

Larissa, although she had obligatory onsets at an earlier stage, eventually deleted some word-medial consonants, rather than substituting something else for them (Stemberger, 1993a):

Peter   [pʰiːə]

Freitas (1996) demonstrates that Portuguese-learning children do not always have obligatory onsets:

/agwa/   [aβa]   'water'
/ãda/   [ana]   'come'

However, there is no information available about whether such data are common or uncommon in child phonological development. Fikkert (1994) claimed that Dutch-learning children pass through a stage at which onsets are obligatory, at least in word-initial position, but this does not seem to be universal. Fikkert, how-ever, takes a weak version of stage theory, in which some children "skip" stages and so never show the predicted patterns. Some of her children began with her final stage for the acquisition of simple onsets (Stage 3), in which onsetless syl-lables are possible.[1] There is no reason to believe that all children initially require all syllables to have onsets.

Before reviewing further evidence, we must address the issue of whether adult English and adult Dutch have words without word-initial consonants. In English, there are words that are spelled without initial consonants, such as *up* and *eat*. However, when these words are pronounced in isolation, or after a pause, they are pronounced with a glottal stop [ʔ] at the beginning. In fluent speech after another word, however, these words usually lack an initial consonant: *John eats* [dʒɑn iːts], not (usually) [dʒɑn ʔiːts]. Given this variation, we must ask how young English-learning children deal with these words. There are three possibilities. (a) They learn the words in isolation or after pauses, and think that they begin with a glottal stop. The children assume that the glottal stop is a part of the underlying representation, much like any other consonant. There are thus no vowel-initial

---

[1] Levelt (discussion section at the UBC International Conference on Phonological Acquisition, June 1995) reported that the symbol [ʔ] was used as a code to flag word-initial position to facilitate computer-based searches of the data. Whether glottal stops were actually present was not coded (or transcribed). Thus, it is unknown to what extent word-initial onsets were actually obligatory in Fikkert's data.

words, *as far as the child knows*. (b) They learn the words in contexts in which no glottal stop is present, and so assume that the words begin with a vowel. They later learn to insert glottal stop after pauses. (c) They learn the words from both contexts, and note the variation in the presence vs. absence of the glottal stop; it is unclear whether their underlying forms contain a glottal stop or not. We do not know which of these possibilities is correct, and it is possible that all may be correct, for different children. For English and other Germanic languages, we must view word-initial position with suspicion relative to this hypothesis; we cannot be sure that a consonant is inserted, because it is possible that the glottal stop is present underlyingly.

Stemberger (1988a, 1993a) notes that the three children in his studies all produced word-initial glottal stop obligatorily (though not in the earliest periods of acquisition, only later), even when the word was postpausal. For one child (Larissa), who had a process that epenthesized a schwa to break up a sequence of consonants at word boundaries, the glottal stop clearly counted as a consonant (at one period) and triggered Schwa Insertion when the previous word ended with a consonant. These three children appeared to treat [ʔ] as a consonant like any other consonant.

Stemberger (1988a) reported an interesting phenomenon when the glottal stop finally became optional in Gwendolyn's speech. For the first time, sequences of vowels arose at word boundaries. Although this was often tolerated, one of the vowels was often deleted:

This on! Me want *this on*! Me want *this on*! (2;6.19)
[dan]   [dan]   [.diː.an.]

Hold up tent, papa! Mama, *hold up* tent, too. (2;6.26)
[hap   tʰɛt]   [.haː.ʌp. tʰɛt]

Such vowel deletion at word boundaries (and morpheme boundaries) is common across adult languages. Prince and Smolensky (1993) propose that one of the vowels is deleted in order to avoid a second syllable that has no onset. In [.diː.an.], there is one syllable without an onset, but in [.dan.], the (only) syllable has an onset. This suggests that syllables with onsets are more optimal.

This is not completely convincing, since there is another possibility. The traditional explanation of deletion in this context is that two vowels are not allowed in sequence: **NotTwice(Nucleus)**. Prince and Smolensky (1993) state that there is no reason to prefer this alternative explanation. However, they provide no compelling reason to prefer their explanation.

Cruttenden (1978) suggests that some English-learning children may assume that words with glottal stops are vowel-initial, and furthermore, that consonantal onsets are obligatory. In order to give these words a "proper" onset, a consonant may be epenthesized that takes on the place of articulation of a later consonant (low ranking of constraints allowing double linking of C-Roots).

apple	/æpəl/	[pʰapa]
about	/əbaʊt/	[bəbaʊ]
all-gone	/ɑlgɑn/	[gʊgʊn]

σ▸Onset ‖‖ **Not(Link)**
        SinglyLinked(Root)
        Not(C-TimingUnit)

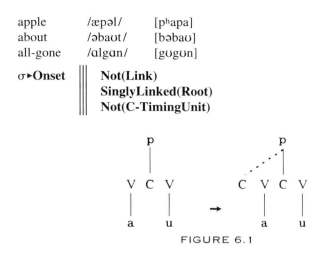

FIGURE 6.1

Fikkert (1994) reports similar data for Dutch-learning children. (Alternatively, there might be two separate tokens of /p/ in the output, a violation of **Singly-Expressed(C-Root)**. If the two tokens of /p/ have different laryngeal features, such as [+s.g.] in the first /p/ and [-s.g.] in the second /p/, it is problematical to have a single doubly linked token of /p/. We assume that double linkage is more common, however.)

However, it is possible that this is actually the assimilation of [ʔ] (present in the adult pronunciation but not transcribed) to a later stop. Similarly, Bernhardt (previously unpublished data, i.e., p.u.d.) notes that three of the children with phonological disorders in her studies inserted nasals or glides in word-initial onsets that were clearly not instances of assimilation, but reflected feature constraints of the child's system (Colin, §8.3, and Marcy, §5.5.3.1 substituted [n], and Kendra, §7.3.1.9, substituted [j]). In combination with a high-ranked constraint such as **Root▸Place**, which requires that all segments have a place of articulation, glottals are prevented from surfacing as glottals.

To be more certain about whether onsets can be required, we must seek data elsewhere. In English and other Germanic languages, this means examining onsets in word-medial position. Alternatively, we can examine data on the acquisition of languages that truly have vowel-initial words, such as the Romance languages.

English does have instances in which noninitial syllables lack an onset (e.g., *eon* /.i.ɑn./). Further, in some cases, children take words like *fire* /faɪɹ/ that are (arguably) only a single syllable in the adult pronunciation and make the /ɹ/ or /l/ into a vowel like [o], [oʊ], [u], or [ə] (see §6.1.4), creating a second syllable. Regardless of whether the second syllable is in the adult pronunciation or not, there are two possibilities, which are both commonly found in child speech: either there is no onset, or one is epenthesized. The lack of epenthesis is not interesting, as it reflects the adult state of affairs. Although we have reports of particular children who create a medial onset, no large study has addressed the issue; we do not know how common it is across children.

Gwendolyn (Stemberger, 1988b) obtained an onset for a noninitial syllable by lengthening any preceding glide:

higher	/.haɪ.ɹ./	[hajːoʊ]
flower	/.flaʊ.ɹ./	[fawːoʊ]

FIGURE 6.2

The resulting double linking makes the glide long. This arises through the following constraint ranking:

σ▸Onset   ‖‖   **SinglyLinked(Root)**

Similar data have been reported for normally developing children by Bleile (1987), and for children with speech disorders by Bernhardt (1990). We suspect that this is very common. Onsets can be closer to being obligatory than they are in adult English.

Priestly (1977), in his discussion of Christopher, implies the following syllabification:

fire	/.faɪ.ə./	[.fa.jə.])
flower	/.flaʊ.ə./	[.fa.wə.]

Although English treats the second part of the diphthong as part of the nucleus of the first syllable, universal syllabification algorithms actually predict that it should be in the onset of the second syllable. Christopher apparently followed a pattern that is more common crosslinguistically than the adult English pattern: the glide is an onset in order to provide the second syllable with an onset. See §6.1.13 for discussion of the adult English pattern.

Default onsets have also been reported for young children. Insertion can occur when the adult form lacks an onset, as for Morgan (Stemberger, 1992a):

higher	/.haɪ.ɹ./	[.haɪ.dɤ]
flower	/.flaʊɹ./	[.faʊ.dɤ.]
lion	/.laɪ.n̩./	[.laɪ.dən.]

In Morgan's case, [d] was not used as a substitute for other onsets, but was inserted only when the second syllable had no onset. Such insertion arises through the following constraint ranking:

σ▸Onset	‖‖	Not(Root)
Survived(Root)	‖‖	
SinglyLinked(Root)	‖‖	

The high ranking on σ▸**Onset** requires that an onset be present. The high ranking of **SinglyLinked(Root)** prevents the lengthening of the glide at the end of the first syllable. The high ranking of **Survived(Root)** prevents the deletion of the second syllable. The low ranking of **Not(Root)** allows the avoidance of a violation of σ▸**Onset** via the insertion of a consonant, with default features.[2] Medial onsets can be obligatory, and constraint rankings can be such that a consonant is inserted. The segmental content of the default onset in medial position is unpredictable; in addition to [j] and [d], attested default onsets include [h] (Stemberger, 1993a), [l] (Vihman & de Boysson-Bardies, 1994), [ð] (Eric, §7.3.4.4, Bernhardt et al., 1993), [z]~[ʒ] (Bernhardt, 1990: *S4*), [p]~[b]~[m] (Robin, §7.3.1.6, Bernhardt, 1994a), [n] (Bernhardt, 1994b: Brad), and [ʔ] (Dylan, §8.6).

There is evidence from Romance languages that word-initial onsets can be obligatory, leading to epenthesis. In adult Romance languages, words can truly begin with a vowel (and never with a glottal stop). Lleó (1996) reports instances where a word-initial consonant is inserted. The inserted stop can be a default (such as glottal stop), or can assimilate to a following consonant:

Alberto   /alβerto/   [ʔɐbɛto]~[babeto]

Onsets are a part of the optimal syllable in the speech of young children. No child deletes onset consonants just because they are in the onset. For some children, onsets are an obligatory part of the syllable.

6.1.4. SIMPLE CODAS

Some children begin language acquisition with a ranking for **Not(Coda)** that is fairly adult-like (Stemberger, 1996b, 1996d). It is low-ranked enough that codas are permitted. Morgan had codas from 0;11, even in her very first word (*up*):

up   /(ʔ)ʌp/   [ʔapʰ]
out   /(ʔ)aʊt/   [ʔatʰ]~[ʔaʔ]

At no stage of development did she ever delete a word-final coda; even if a given segment was not possible, a default consonant (such as [ʔ]) was always present. There have been no studies designed to see how common this might be across children.[3] Fikkert (1994) and Fee (1995a) posit a developmental stage at which

---

[2] The [+voiced] of Morgan's [d] is a reflection of the plateauing of [+voiced] in intervocalic position: a single [+voiced] feature linked to both vowels and to the epenthetic consonant. Larissa's [h] default reflects plateauing of [+continuant]; see §7.4.4.3 for extended discussion.

[3] Stoel-Gammon (1985) is one of the few studies that is relevant, since it investigates which consonants develop first in codas. However, we are not told whether the child attempted words with codas in the adult targets because it is a study of phonetic development. Further, the study presents data only

codas are absent. However, they use a weak form of stage theory that allows stages to be skipped. Some children allow codas even in the earliest words.

Further, there is nothing odd or difficult about a word such as *me* [miː] that has no coda. Such words are almost universally produced without a coda. This suggests that there is no constraint that would generally require that a coda be present (but see §6.1.5). This has been the standard viewpoint since Jakobson (1968/1941).

Codas most often are not possible at the earliest periods of acquisition. The child's pronunciation of words with codas in the adult form must accommodate to the lack of codas in the child's speech. Consider the child's syllabification of a word like *bed*, if the child's system does not permit codas in the output:

FIGURE 6.3

Both the vowel /ɛ/ and the initial /b/ can be integrated into the syllable. The final /d/ cannot be added to the syllable, because codas are not permitted. Floating consonants are, however, not generally allowed in the output (due to **Linked-Upwards**).[4] This constraint violation can be resolved in more than one way. In adult languages, unsyllabifiable consonants can be deleted (either outright, violating **Survived**; or because floating segments are not phonetically realized), vowels can be epenthesized after them (violating constraints that prevent epenthesis, such as **Not(Root)**, **Not(V)**, **Not(σ)**, etc.), or they are made syllabic. All three repair strategies have been observed in phonological development. Constraint tables illustrating these strategies were given in §4.2.1.

6.1.4.1. Deletion Repairs

The most common resolution of the floating consonant in child phonology is probably deletion: [bɛ]. This is derived through the following constraint ranking:

Not(Coda)	⫴	Survived(Root)
	⫴	LinkedUpwards(Root)

As noted, the absence of the coda consonant in the pronunciation is ambiguous. It may be deleted outright and not be a part of the output (violating **Survived**), or it may be present but floating in the output, so that it has no phonetic realization (violating **LinkedUpwards**).

---

from when the child was using 10 or more different words. Children who had final [t] by the end of the first ten words may not have had any codas earlier. As a result, we cannot tell whether the children allowed codas from the beginning.

[4]Fee (1995a) assumes that deleted consonants are floating at first, but are later deleted. In Optimality Theory (OT), unsyllabified consonants are deleted in one step.

6.1.4.2. Epenthesis (Addition) Repairs

Instead of being deleted, the final consonant can be rescued via the creation of another syllable following it. If a vowel is epenthesized after the consonant, then the consonant can become the onset of a second syllable, and so can be produced:

FIGURE 6.4

This repair strategy arises through the following constraint ranking:

Survived(Root) LinkedUpwards(Root)	‖	Not(Coda)	‖	Not(σ) Not(Root)

The high ranking of **Survived** and **LinkedUpwards**, relative to **Not(Coda)**, means that the final consonant must be produced. However, **Not(Coda)** is still high-ranked enough to prevent a coda from appearing in the output. Instead, the low ranking of the **Not** constraints allows a vowel to be epenthesized. Although there are no studies that overtly address this issue, our impression is that epenthesis is not a common repair strategy for rescuing codas, and that it appears mostly in the speech of very young children (before 1;6, as in Matthei, 1989).

The particular vowel that is epenthesized is not a matter of syllable structure, but is determined by other factors. For some children, the inserted vowel has the default features for unstressed vowels, such as [ə]; these are the features that correspond to the lowest-ranked **Not** constraints for vowel features. For some children (e.g., the one in Matthei, 1989), the epenthetic vowel is highly variable, being different in different words or even from token to token of the same word; this derives from variable ranking of the **Not** constraints for vowel features.

For other children, the vowel assimilates to the preceding vowel (Ross, 1937): *bed* [bɛdɛ], *big* [bɪdɪ], *hot* [hata], etc. In the most extreme cases, full reduplication is observed: *bed* [baba]. Schwartz et al. (1980) and Fee and Ingram (1982) report that reduplication, as a strategy to avoid the deletion of coda consonants, is present in only a minority of children, and even then only before 1;8 (or even 1;6). In our system, the assimilation of the /d/ in *bed* to the initial /b/ would be due to constraints that are independent of syllable structure; as discussed in Chapter 7, the second consonant is subject to severe constraints on the sequencing of consonant features, so that it often may not have any features that are independent of the first consonant. That such constraints are independent of the epenthesis of the vowel is suggested by two facts: a) children who reduplicate to rescue coda consonants also show reduplication for words with two syllables in the adult speech (such as *monkey* [mama]; Fee & Ingram 1982), and b) some children have epenthesis with the accurate pronunciation of the "coda" consonant. Reduplication suggests that epenthesis of the vowel may be occurring to rescue not the consonant per se, but rather the consonant's timing unit (through high ranking of **Survived(C)**):

FIGURE 6.5

Similarly, a vowel might be epenthesized to rescue the consonant timing unit, and a default consonant such as [ʔ] might be inserted to fill the C timing unit, if sequence constraints prevented the underlying consonant's features from surfacing (see §7.4.1.2). Epenthesis takes a consonant (or timing unit) that is in a coda in the adult target and places it in onset position, when codas are not possible in the child's speech.

Fee (1995a) suggests that the reduplication might be motivated not by the rescuing of a coda consonant, but rather to fit a minimal word that requires two syllables to be present (see §6.2.3.4). However, most children do not reduplicate monosyllabic vowel-final words such as *me* and *blue*, and so this suggestion seems to be incorrect, for most children.

It should be noted that the "epenthetic" vowel might sometimes be added for apparent morphological purposes (Stoel-Gammon & Dunn, 1985). In English, nouns can receive the suffix -*y*; this is often described as a diminutive form, but it appears to have little semantic effect. This is often used by young children in nouns like *doggy*, *piggy*, etc. Some parents also use the -*y* suffix on adjectives (*goody*), verbs (*walkie*, *jumpie*), and even particles (*uppy*). The -*y* suffix may have the function of rescuing unsyllabifiable final consonants. However, it is a part of speech to children by adults, and consequently is used even by children whose syllables allow codas. Further, it is added to words that end in vowels and diphthongs, which do not have unsyllabifiable consonants, as in *owie* (used to refer to hurts, based on the exclamation *ow*). The ultimate origin of -*y* in speech to children, however, may have been to provide a way to rescue final unsyllabifiable consonants in nouns. A child is exposed both to *doggy* and to *dog*, but may choose to use *doggy* exclusively, avoiding *dog* because of the difficulty of the coda.

Goad (1996a) argues that "epenthesis" may occur without any vowel actually being inserted. This still leads to a resyllabification of the coda consonant:

FIGURE 6.6

Goad argues that phonetically the final consonant in such structures is long:

bad	/bæd/	[bæ·dː]
cake	/keɪk/	[ke·kː]
book	/bʊk/	[bu·kː]~[buki]

Goad suggests that such syllabification can also be expressed phonetically as clear and audible release of voiced consonants (including nasals), and as aspiration of final voiceless consonants. Such syllabification would arise if **Survived(C-Root)** is ranked higher than **Not(σ)**; if **Not(V-Root)** is ranked high, or if **Linked-Downwards(σ)** is ranked low, then no vowel will be inserted. We are uncertain whether such an analysis is required here, but leave it as an open possibility.

6.1.4.3. Making Consonants Syllabic

A third possible resolution when consonants are unsyllabifiable is to make them syllabic. This is unlikely with an obstruent like /b/. Crosslinguistically, it is most frequent with glides. Because glides are merely nonsyllabic vowels, they become true vowels when they are made syllabic. Since vowels are possible in all languages and for all children, this is an easy change to effect. It is also common with sonorant consonants (liquids and nasals), as in adult English. In phonological development in English-learning children, this is most frequently observed with /ɹ/ and /l/, most often after diphthongs or (less commonly) long vowels.

smile	/smaɪl/	[.m̩aɪ.u.]
flower	/flaʊɹ/	[.faʊ.ə.]
fire	/faɪɹ/	[.faɪ.oʊ.]
feel	/fiːl/	[.fiː.ə.]

The /ɹ/ and /l/ tend to be realized as one consistent vowel by a particular child, but different children use different vowels; [oʊ], [u], [ə], [a], and [ɪ] have been observed.

In this repair strategy, a C timing unit is converted into a V timing unit.[5] Recall from §3.6 that timing units can be viewed as a basic unit of timing (X) plus the feature [syllabic]; the feature [syllabic] is part of the definition of C versus V timing units. We have been using the symbols "C" and "V" without explicitly mentioning [syllabic], but [syllabic] is part of the representation. When a consonant is made syllabic, [+syllabic] is inserted; if [-syllabic] is present underlyingly, it is deleted. We can effect this resolution via the following constraint ranking:

Survived(Root) ‖	Not(Coda) ‖	Not(+syllabic)
LinkedUpwards(Root)		Survived(-syllabic)
Survived(X)		

[5] Intuitions differ as to whether /ɹ/ and /l/ in words like *fire* and *feel* are syllabic in adult speech. In words like *car*, *here* and *fill*, which adult native speakers of English agree are monosyllabic, children rarely make the /ɹ/ or /l/ syllabic. It is our judgment that they are not syllabic in adult speech, and hence the discussion here. If they are syllabic in adult speech, then children rarely rescue a coda consonant by making it syllabic.

Once the consonant has been made syllabic, it may be subject to insertion of default vowel features, though it is common for the [Dorsal] feature of the (dark, velarized) /l/ to survive (making the vowel back) and for the [Labial] feature of /ɹ/ to survive (making the vowel rounded).

Codas are made possible when **Not(Coda)** is reranked so that it is the lowest-ranked of the relevant constraints. It thus becomes easier to produce a coda than to delete a consonant or to insert a vowel. Most English-learning children develop the ability to produce at least one coda consonant before 2;0 (Stoel-Gammon, 1985).

We would like to emphasize that not all coda consonants are created equal, however. Some features are tolerated in codas more than others. In such systems, a child might produce some coda consonants, but constraints on other coda consonants might lead to deletion, epenthesis, or changes in syllabic status for the consonant. This is not a matter of simple syllable structure, but derives from interactions between syllable structure and features. See §6.1.12 below.

6.1.4.4. Metathesis (Migration)

A rare way to avoid complex codas is to move the coda consonant elsewhere in the word. Chin (1996) reports examples such as the following:

| bath | /bæθ/ | [psæ] |
| badge | /bædʒ/ | [pʃæ] |

This violates **Contiguity** (and **Linearity**, if such a constraint exists), but allows all underlying consonants to survive. Children rarely shift whole segments in this way, for any reason.

6.1.4.5. Compensatory Lengthening

When a coda consonant is deleted, sometimes the length of the preceding vowel changes. Typical productions of the word *bib* are the following:

/bɪb/   [bɪ]   *or*   [biː]

The pronunciation with the short lax vowel seems to be taken as the expected output in research on phonological development. Stemberger (1992c) reports that Gwendolyn changed the vowel to a long tense vowel when the coda consonant was deleted. This derives from the loss of the Root node of the coda consonant, but the survival of its timing unit:

Not(Coda)	‖	**Survived(C-Root)**
Survived(TimingUnit)	‖	**SinglyLinked(V-Root)**
LinkedDownwards(TimingUnit)	‖	**Co-occurring(V-Root,μμ→ + tense)**

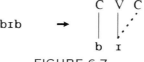

FIGURE 6.7

The above ranking causes the coda's timing unit to survive even though the consonant does not. Since the timing unit must be linked to a segment, it links instead to the vowel, making it long. In adult English, long vowels are tense, and so the vowel becomes tense. Compensatory lengthening has not often been addressed in studies of phonological development. We do not know how common it is across children.

6.1.4.6. When the Adult Language Allows No Codas

We have been illustrating our discussion here with data from English-learning children, but we note that there is an intriguing possibility regarding codas for children acquiring languages that do not allow codas. Some English-learning children have codas in their very first words, showing that **Not(Coda)** can be low-ranked from the beginning. That low ranking is appropriate for English, but would be inappropriate for a language that does not allow codas, such as Hawaiian or Sesotho. A child learning such a language might produce a coda under a particular circumstance: to rescue a consonant that would otherwise be deleted. Since children usually have an upper limit of two syllables in a word (see §6.2 below), such deletion is not uncommon in long words. Consonants within the deleted syllable are most often deleted along with the vowel. However, if **Not(Coda)** is ranked low enough, perhaps such a consonant could be rescued. For a hypothetical word such as /tulinako/, we might observe [tulin]:

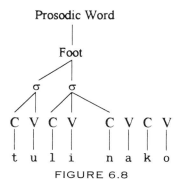

FIGURE 6.8

Only the first two syllables are linked upwards to a prosodic word (due to constraints on prosodic words and/or on feet), so that the last three segments (/ako/) are deleted. However, the /n/ at the beginning of the third syllable can be rescued from deletion by making it the coda of the second syllable. This would result from the following constraint ranking:

Binary(Foot,σ)	Survived(Root)	Not(Coda)
NotComplex(ProsodicWord)	LinkedUpwards(Root)	
Contiguity	Survived(C)	
	LinkedUpwards(C)	

The high ranking of the constraints on feet and prosodic words cause all but two syllables to be deleted. The high ranking of **Survived** and **LinkedUpwards** leads to the survival of one of the consonants in a deleted syllable, and **Contiguity** (to the vowel /i/) requires that it be the /n/ that survives. The low ranking of **Not(Coda)** allows the /n/ to be realized as a coda, even though no codas ever appear in the adult language.

We are unaware of any data of exactly this sort. However, Demuth (p.c.) reports something that is related. In Sesotho, there are no codas, but syllabic nasals do appear in the adult language. When prosodic constraints reduce the number of syllables in the word, these syllabic nasals can survive by becoming coda consonants:

/.na.si.m̩.ba./   [.sim.ba.]   'a brand of potato chips'

Faithfulness to segments can thus lead to the presence of codas even if the adult language does not permit codas. Smolensky (1996b) assumes that faithfulness in child speech can never be greater than in the target adult language, and thus his approach to learning predicts that data of this type should not be found; this assumption appears to be incorrect (and see also the introduction to Chapter 9). However, we do not expect such patterns to be common, since most English-learning children begin with systems that disallow codas; most Sesotho children probably also begin with systems that disallow codas.

6.1.5. ?OBLIGATORY CODAS?

No constraints force every syllable in a word to have a coda, and no such language (adult or child) has ever been observed. However, there is a way to require that word-final syllables end in a coda, and such adult languages have been observed. Stemberger (1996b, 1996d) argues that this might arise in child phonology for two separate reasons.

As we discuss later in this chapter, some children reduce all words to a single syllable. The constraint **Binary(Foot,μ)** requires syllables to have two timing units in the rime of that single syllable: a long vowel, a diphthong, or a short vowel plus a coda. If the child's system also lacks long vowels and diphthongs, so that the vowel is short, then the syllable must have a coda in order to satisfy foot binarity. We are unsure if this pattern has ever been observed in child phonology. If it does occur, it is not because a coda is required in every syllable. It is because words are so small that a coda is required to bring the word up to a minimal size. There is a coda in every syllable, but in a trivial sense.

It is also possible for a word-final syllable to end in a coda regardless of the size of the word or foot. To achieve this, McCarthy and Prince (1994) use a constraint called Final-C, but in §4.5.2.6 we introduced **WordFinalMassiveness**, requiring a word to end in extra nonprominent material (a coda, or an unstressed syllable, or possibly a larger-than-usual coda). Stemberger (1996d) reports that [?] could be inserted after vowel-final words in Morgan's speech. In both disyllabic and monosyllabic words through 1;4, this occurred optionally, including in reduplicated words (which disappeared at 1;4):

mama	/mɑmə/	[mama]~[mama?]
lizard	/lɪzɹd/	[lɪlɪ]~[lɪlɪ?]
me	/miː/	[miː]~[mi?]

Note that in general there was no requirement that all syllables had to end in a coda: the first syllables of *mama* and *lizard* lack a coda. The variability suggests an unstable ranking for epenthesizing a word-final coda. The constraint prevented deletion of underlying codas, however: from the first word on, Morgan never deleted word-final codas.

Leonard and Brown (1984) present a clear instance of an obligatory final coda in the speech of an older child with a phonological disorder. The inserted consonant was [s]:

blue	/bluː/	[bus]
candy	/kændi/	[kanəs]
go	/gow/	[gɔs]
doctor	/dɑktɹ/	[dadas]

This child also converted most word-final consonants to [s] (though labials surfaced as [p]). This reflects a preference for fricatives in codas (see §6.1.12.2.2), combined with the default [Coronal] place feature. Again, the [s] was epenthesized only in word-final syllables; codas were not possible elsewhere in the word.

Codas can thus be obligatory in word-final syllables (due to **WordFinal-Massiveness**). There is no way to require codas in all syllables, and no child has ever been reported to do so.

6.1.6. COMPLEX ONSETS

There are many adult languages (such as Arabic and Hawaiian) in which the onset is restricted to a single consonant. Jakobson (1968/1941) reported that the onset is also originally restricted to a single consonant in the speech of most children. Some children develop some clusters by 1;4 (Stoel-Gammon, 1993), but it is not uncommon for clusters to be absent even at 2;6. We cannot rule out the possibility that some children have consonant clusters in their first words, but this has never been reported, and consequently it must be either rare or nonexistent.

When the onset in the adult target word is more complex than a single consonant, not all of the consonants can be syllabified: only one consonant can be placed in the onset of the syllable that is based on the underlying vowel. The other consonant(s) are unsyllabifiable. As with unsyllabifiable coda consonants, the leftover consonant can be treated in three different ways: it can be deleted, or it can be rescued, either via the insertion of a vowel or by becoming syllabic. All three resolutions have been observed, though again it is unusual for a consonant to become syllabic.

Greenlee (1974) lays out the following "ideal" developmental progression of word-initial (and hence syllable-initial) clusters like /bl/ and /st/:

1. All consonants in the cluster are deleted.
2. One consonant is produced.
3. Two consonants are produced.

Ingram (1989a) and Chin and Dinnsen (1992) note, however, that deletion of both members of the cluster is rare and tends to be found only in very young children or older children with severe phonological disorders. Fikkert (1994) does not mention the possibility of deleting both consonants.

6.1.6.1. Deletion Repairs

When complex onsets are impossible in the child's speech, the most common resolution is deletion. Two degrees of deletion are observed: deletion of both consonants, or deletion of just one consonant.

6.1.6.1.1. Deletion of Both Consonants

Greenlee (1974), Ingram (1989b), and Chin and Dinnsen (1992) report that some children (mostly very young children or children with severely disordered phonology) delete both members of an onset consonant cluster:

| play | /pleɪ/ | [eɪ] |
| stop | /stɑp/ | [ap] |

This has not been reported often, and, when it has, comes from studies using fairly broad transcription. We are unsure whether a glottal stop may actually have been present. If the data are taken as accurate, however, it is not clear how to derive such data within Optimality Theory (OT). Deletion of both consonants cannot be motivated by syllable structure, since it is optimal to have an onset, and an onset can be obtained by linking up one of the two consonants.

One possibility derives from a possible conflict between different constraints. Reducing /pl/ to [p] violates **Contiguity**, but reducing it to [l] violates **Co-occurring(σ-Margin$\rightarrow$-sonorant)** and leads to a less optimal onset (see §6.1.6.1.2). Suppose that both constraints were ranked as equals and also ranked high. Then the outputs [p] and [l] would both violate an important constraint. We could avoid a violation of *both* constraints by having no onset at all; that would violate both **Survived(Root)** (twice) and σ▸**Onset** (violations that are permissible as long as the constraints are ranked low enough). Unfortunately, this same ranking predicts that sonorant consonants must always be deleted from onsets, even when they are singletons, because **Survived** is so low-ranked. That is probably not the case (though the data are very scanty). Further, this solution cannot account for the deletion of both consonants in clusters such as /st/, where contiguity and sonority considerations both favor [t].

Generalized alignment also provides no solution here. There could be a conflict between sonority considerations (favoring [t]) and alignment, if the left edge of the base morpheme must also be the left edge of the prosodic word: **Aligned (ProsodicWord,L,BaseMorpheme,L)**. If /st/ is reduced to [t], **Aligned** is violated once. Unfortunately, deleting both members of the cluster is even worse, since beginning the prosodic word with the vowel violates **Aligned** twice (since both the /s/ and the /t/ are skipped). Thus, alignment cannot motivate the deletion of both members of the cluster.

We could conceivably use a new type of complex constraint. If there is a constraint that prevents just one member of an onset cluster from being produced, and it is impossible to produce both, then both must be deleted. We view this type of constraint as unlikely and undesirable.

There are non-OT explanations. In a resource-based theory, attempting to produce two consonants can spread resources too thin, so that there are insufficient resources to access even one of the two consonants. This is analogous to a situation in which attempting to perform two tasks at once leads to poor performance on both tasks (e.g., doing complex math problems while driving in heavy traffic). In connectionist models, competition between the two competing consonants can be so strong that neither gains enough activation to be produced. As suggested above, this second explanation could be imported into a variant of OT. Extreme competition lowers activation levels; if the ranking of the **Survived** constraints is influenced by activation levels, then competition between Root nodes would lead to a lower ranking of **Survived(Root)**, possibly low enough (e.g., below **Not (Root)**) that both Root nodes are deleted. It does not matter whether the actual output has no onset or has the default onset [ʔ]. Other constraints would govern the insertion of glottal stop, and this would not interact much with the constraints that delete both members of the consonant cluster.

Another possible explanation is that there is no such thing as an consonant cluster in an onset. A. Moskowitz (1970) and Menyuk (1972) proposed that children treat clusters such as /st/ and /bɹ/ as single consonants. If they are single consonants, they can be deleted if the individual features must be linked up, but constraints on feature co-occurrences prevent all the features from being present in the same segment. (See §4.7.1 and §5.5.4 for discussion.) We are unconvinced that children treat clusters as single segments, although that would eliminate the problem of having to delete two segments of a cluster.

Deletion of both members of a cluster is unusual, but it is attested. Such data are challenging for most versions of OT, which predict that one segment or the other will always surface. However, variants of OT that are more realistic from the standpoint of cognitive processing (such as the one we are suggesting in this book) can more easily account for such phenomena.

6.1.6.1.2. Deletion of Just One Consonant

The most common resolution of initial consonant clusters is deletion: only one consonant links up to the syllable, and the other consonant is deleted. For most children, the consonant that links to the syllable is the consonant of lesser sonority: in *black* and *stamp*, the /b/ of /bl/ and the /t/ of /st/ (Jakobson, 1968/1941;

N. Smith, 1973; Greenlee, 1974; Chin & Dinnsen, 1992; Fikkert, 1994; Ohala, 1994; and many others).

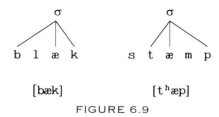

FIGURE 6.9

This follows the most common crosslinguistic pattern in adult languages, in which onset consonants are optimally low in sonority (see §4.7.1.3).

Sonority-based syllable construction is fairly unusual in adult phonology. Syllabification is usually achieved in peak-outwards fashion (Kahn, 1976; Clements & Keyser, 1983). The consonants contiguous to the vowel are first linked up to the onset and coda; then the consonants that are outside of those consonants become linked up, and so on. This matches the child's reduction of the /st/ in *stamp* to [tʰ], since the /t/ is the consonant that is immediately before the vowel. However, this yields the wrong result for the child's reduction of the /bl/ in *black* to [b]; because the [l] is immediately before the vowel, we expect (incorrectly) that /l/ should link up, and that /b/ should be deleted.

The constraint that is responsible for "peak-outwards" syllabification is **Contiguity**, which holds that segments that are adjacent in the underlying form should be adjacent on the surface. Since the consonant in front of the /æ/ in *black* in the input representation is /l/, the /l/ should precede the /æ/ in the output pronunciation. **Contiguity** is violated in the pronunciation of *black* as [bæk], since the /b/ and the /æ/ are not contiguous in the underlying form. It is unusual for **Contiguity** to be violated in basic syllabification in adult speech, except in reduplicative affixes (McCarthy & Prince, 1993a, 1994).

Other constraints might favor the /b/, however. One constraint that would do so is **Aligned(Root,L,PrWd,L)**: the left edge of a root morpheme should be the left edge of a prosodic word. **Aligned** is satisfied if the output starts with the first segment of the underlying representation: [bæk]. **Aligned** is violated if /st/ is reduced to [t], however, and so this does not work. It's far more likely that the sonority-based syllabification derives from constraints on the optimal syllable margin:

Co-occurring(σ-Margin→ + consonantal)
Co-occurring(σ-Margin→-sonorant)
Co-occurring(σ-Margin→-continuant)

As discussed in §4.7.1.3, these constraints reflect a general rhythm-based pattern, in which the optimal nonsyllabic segment has a closed vocal tract, and the optimal syllabic segment has an open vocal tract. By referring to such constraints, we can account for the difference between /bl/ and /st/: both reduce to the stop, which is a more optimal nonsyllabic segment than a liquid or a fricative. It does not appear that it matters which consonant is the leftmost in the word.

If **Contiguity** is ranked very high, then the consonant immediately before the vowel must link up to the syllable: /bl/ and /st/ are reduced to [l] and [tʰ], respectively. While this is the most common result for /st/, it is a minority option for /bl/. Clearly, **Contiguity** must be ranked lower than sonority for most children. As a faithfulness constraint, it is expected that **Contiguity** would initially be ranked low in child phonology.

If **Contiguity** is ranked lower than the **Co-occurring** constraints, then contiguity tends to be violated. Since the **Co-occurring** constraints reflect sonority, the least sonorous consonant is the more optimal onset. (See Tables 6.1a and 6.1b.) Since /b/ is a more optimal onset than /l/, contiguity is violated, and [bæk] results. However, since /t/ is a more optimal onset than /s/, contiguity is preserved.

TABLE 6.1A

/blæk/	blæk	bæk	læk
NotComplex(Onset)	*!		
Co-occurring(σ-Margin→-sonorant)			*!
Co-occurring(σ-Margin→-continuant)			*!
Contiguity		*	

TABLE 6.1B

/stæmp/	stæmp	sæp	tæp
NotComplex(Onset)	*!		
Co-occurring(σ-Margin→-sonorant)			
Co-occurring(σ-Margin→-continuant)		*!	
Contiguity		*	

Although it is the stop of /s/-stop clusters that survives in the speech of most children, the /s/ does survive for a minority of children. This is due to a high ranking of **Survived(+continuant)** (or, more generally, **Survived(NonDefault-Features)**). We return to this below.

In §4.7.1.3, we noted one major difference between our approach to sonority versus more "standard" approaches such as that of Prince and Smolensky (1993). Prince and Smolensky treat sonority as a concept that is defined over entire segments; segment A is always of lesser sonority than segment B. Given whole-segment sonority, we predict that only sonority will matter for deletion in child phonology. The degree of difference in sonority between the two segments should not matter. The element of least sonority should be in the output, for all children.

In contrast, we address individual properties that correlate with sonority: [+sonorant] versus [-sonorant], [+continuant] versus [-continuant], etc. We predict that there should be little variation between children for some consonant clusters, but greater variation for others. For obstruent-glide and obstruent-liquid clusters, the obstruent should survive. For fricative-stop clusters, the stop should survive. But for fricative-nasal clusters, things are less clear. Consider the following ranking:

Co-occurring(σ-Margin→-sonorant) ||| **Co-occurring(σ-Margin→-continuant)**

Since it is more important that an onset be an obstruent than a stop (oral or nasal), the /s/ of /sn/ should survive, rather than the sonorant /n/. But, with the opposite ranking, we expect the [-continuant] nasal to survive, rather than the (merely obstruent) fricative. The feature-based approach thus predicts that /sn/ and /sm/ clusters will be reduced in a more variable manner, across children, than either the /s/-stop or obstruent-approximant clusters. It is our impression that this is the case (Stemberger, Pollock, & Salck, 1990; Fikkert, 1994). Ohala (1994), in an experimental study of 16 English-learning children, reported that /s/-stop clusters were more often reduced to the stop, while the /s/-nasal clusters were more even (but slightly favored the fricatives). Since the whole-segment-sonority approach does not make this prediction, we conclude that a feature-based approach is preferable (such as ours; see also Clements, 1990; Rice & Avery, 1995), and has more to offer work on language acquisition.

A cluster can always be reduced to the more sonorous member in order to allow a particular feature to survive. Fikkert (1994) reported that one subject always reduced /kl/ and /kn/ clusters to [l], presumably because **Survived(+sonorant)** was high-ranked. Some children reduce /sp/ and /st/ to [s], so that **Survived (+continuant)** is not violated (e.g., Chin & Dinnsen, 1992; Fikkert, 1994).

We also make some crosslinguistic predictions. In English, "r" is a (high-sonority) glide [ɹ]. In many other languages, "r" is an alveolar [r] or uvular [ʀ] trill, and hence is lower in sonority. The more consonant-like the "r" is, the fewer features there are that can override contiguity, and the more likely it is that contiguity will be preserved. We predict that children learning languages in which "r" is a trill should be more likely than English-learning children to reduce clusters like /br/ to [r]. The limited data available on this issue do suggest that this may be the case (Greenlee, 1974; Bortolini & Leonard, 1991).

A small minority of children may reduce onset clusters to the first consonant, regardless of which segments are involved. Although **Aligned** could be invoked in such circumstances, there are two other possibilities. First, there is **Priority (Left,C-Root)**: when the system must choose between two consonants, it opts for the first one. A drawback to this analysis is that it implies that other children might rank **Priority(Right,C-Root)** higher, in which case all clusters would be reduced to the second member; this seems unlikely (though the same prediction is made via a high ranking for **Contiguity**). Second, it may fall out of the correlation between the ranking of **Survived** and activation levels. In §4.7.1.5, we noted that the second consonant of a cluster is a weak prosodic position, in which segments have lower activation levels; consonants in this position are more prone to error in adult speech and are more subject to **NotTwice** constraints. It follows that competition between the first and second members of a cluster could be resolved in favor of the (higher-activation-level) first consonant. We assume that this is the best analysis. We also note, however, that differences between particular consonants are often more important. We do not know how common it is for children to reduce all initial clusters to the first consonant.

6.1.6.2. Epenthesis (Addition) Repairs

Epenthesis is a possible way to resolve the unsyllabifiable consonant in clusters. For example, [ə] can be inserted between the consonants:

FIGURE 6.10

Epenthesis derives from the following constraint ranking:

NotComplex(Onset)	‖	**Not(V-Root)**
Survived(C-Root)	‖	
LinkedUpwards(C-Root)	‖	

The three high-ranked constraints prevent the deletion of a segment, but prevent both segments from being in the onset. This conflict is resolved by inserting a vowel, so that each consonant can occur in an onset as a single consonant.

Epenthesis is a minority strategy across children for rescuing consonants in complex onsets. Furthermore, for some older children with developmental disorders, epenthesis is sometimes a strategy taught by a speech-language pathologist rather than a spontaneous creation on the part of the child. However, it clearly occurs naturally in some children (e.g., Bernhardt, 1990; Fikkert, 1994). Its rarity derives partly from the fact that the child must be able to produce word-initial unstressed syllables, and many children cannot produce them. If a child reduces words like *balloon* /bəluːn/ to [buːn], that child is unlikely to create similar sequences ([bəlæk]) as a resolution of complex onsets. Only if a child can produce word-initial unstressed syllables is epenthesis an option. Although the presence of word-initial unstressed syllables makes epenthesis an option, it does not make it necessary. Epenthesis is uncommon even when the child can produce word-initial unstressed syllables.

6.1.6.3. Making the Consonant Syllabic

A second minority option is to make one of the consonants syllabic. This has never been observed with /s/-stop and /s/-nasal clusters.[6] It is rarely the case that the liquid or glide simply becomes syllabic, and there are reasons for that. If the word *black* were to be pronounced [.bu.ˈæk.], (a) the word would begin with an unstressed syllable, which English-learning children find difficult, and (b) the second syllable would lack an onset, and this is generally avoided in human languages. Observed instances in which the liquid or glide has become syllabic have involved the original vowel becoming a glide (or even being deleted). There were two instances of this repair strategy in Morgan's speech (Stemberger, p.u.d.). First, the glide /j/ (in the rising diphthong /juː/) was made syllabic, creating the diphthong [ɪɯ], which appeared independently in her speech as the realization of adult /ɪl/ and /ɪɹ/ in words like *fill* [fɪɯ] and *here* [hɪɯ].

| music | /mjuːzɪk/ | [mɪɯdɪkʰ] |
| computer | /km̩pjuːtɹ̩/ | [pʰɪɯdɤ] |

This change is driven by **Survived(Root)**. The glide /j/ would have to be deleted if it were nonsyllabic. However, by making it syllabic, both the /j/ and the /u/ survive:

FIGURE 6.11

Note that the /j/'s timing unit is deleted, just as the timing unit for most deleted consonants is deleted. But the /j/ spreads to the first vowel position, causing the first link of the /uː/ to be deleted; the remaining link of the /u/ makes it the second portion of a diphthong. This spreading depends on the following ranking:

Survived(Root) ||| **Survived(Link)** ||| **Not(Link)**

In other instances, the vowel that was originally present deletes, and the consonant replaces the vowel as the head of the syllable. Just before clusters first appeared in onsets in Morgan's speech, and when the vowel was the diphthong

---

[6] Some children do greatly lengthen segments in such clusters. Bernhardt (1990) reported that Blair (*S2*) pronounced words like *snake* /sneɪk/ with lengthened [s] ([sːːneɪk]) or [n] ([nːeɪk]), and words with /s/-stop clusters with very long lag Voice Onset Time (VOT) (and no [s], e.g., *spoon* as [bːun]). This was most likely an artifact of therapy, in which the therapist exaggerated the duration of the initial consonant to draw the child's attention to it.

Alderete et al. (1996) presented an analysis for an adult language in which /s/ reduplicates as [i]. They would predict that pronunciations such as *stop* ʔ[itʰap] should be possible for some children. We know of no such reports in the literature. If such data never occur in child language, it casts some doubt on their analyses of adult language.

/eɪ/, an /l/ or /ɹ/ in a cluster could be realized as syllabic [ɤ] (as also happened to adult syllabic /ɹ̩/ and /l̩/):

play   /pleɪ/   [pʰeɪ]   >   [pʰeɪ]~[pʰɤɪ]   >   [pʰɥeɪ]

Developmentally, the /l/ or /ɹ/ was originally deleted, and optionally showed up as the syllabic portion of a diphthong [ɤɪ] only when the adult vowel was [eɪ]. This depends on the following ranking:

Survived(C-Root)   ║║║   **Survived(V-Root)**
                                  Survived(Link)

Larissa also showed a few words where /ɹ/ became syllabic and replaced a schwa:

zebra   /ziːbɹə/   [ziːbɹ̩]
ostrich   /astɹɪtʃ/   [ʔastoʊtʃ]

Note that there were relatively few words of this sort.

Hoff (1995) and Matthei (1989) report that making an onset consonant syllabic can also occur when clusters are not involved, with deletion of the vowel (data from Hoff):

shoe   /ʃuː/   [ʃ̩]
cheese   /tʃiːz/   [t͡s̩]

This is highly unusual.

6.1.6.4 Fusion (Coalescence)

It is not always the case that one segment or the other is entirely deleted. In some instances, a single consonant is produced, but that consonant combines features from both of the segments that make up the cluster; we will refer to this as *fusion* (but the term *coalescence* is also common). In fact, it is often difficult to tell *which* of the two segments is really present. When /sp/ is pronounced as [f], does the /s/ survive, to which is added the [Labial] of /p/? Or does the /p/ survive, to which is added the [+continuant] of /s/? Or, indeed, is this an ill-formed question that makes no sense (see below)? The answer to these questions is unclear. Some typical examples are the following:

/sp/   [f]   [+continuant] from /s/
                 [Labial] from /p/
/sm/   [f]   [-sonorant,+continuant] from /s/
                 [Labial] from /m/
/sm/   [m̥]   most features from /m/
                 [-voiced,+s.g.] from /s/
/kɹ/   [p]   [-sonorant,-continuant] from /k/
                 [Labial] from /ɹ/
/bl/   [v]   [-sonorant,Labial] from /b/
                 [+continuant] from /l/

Fusion might derive from linking up one of the two segments to the syllable, and spreading one or more features from the other (deleted) segment (Chin & Dinnsen, 1992):

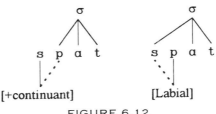

FIGURE 6.12

Since /s/ and /p/ differ only in terms of which nondefault feature is present, spreading the one feature yields [f], regardless of the analysis.

Recall that we are assuming that deletion is most often outright. We thus assume that the segment that cannot link up to the syllable is not a part of the output; it is not floating, as shown here. However, every feature does not have to delete. **Survived** can be ranked so high for some feature that it may not be deleted, even though every other feature of the segment is deleted. **LinkedUpwards** then forces that one stranded feature to link up to a different segment than it was linked to in the underlying representation:

Survived(+ continuant)		**Survived(Link)**		**Not(Link)**
LinkedUpwards(+ continuant)		**Survived(Root)**		
Contiguity				
NotComplex(Onset)				

The four high-ranked constraints limit the onset to a single segment, which must be /p/, because it is contiguous to the vowel. The feature [+continuant] from the /s/ must also survive and link upward. The three low-ranked constraints lead to the /s/ being deleted, except for the feature [+continuant]. But to satisfy **LinkedUpwards(+ continuant)**, [+continuant] links up to the /p/, yielding [f]. It is crucial that **Survived(Link)** be ranked low. If **Survived(Link)** was ranked very high, and [+continuant] survived, then the link to the Root node of the /s/ would also survive, which means that the Root node of the /s/ would survive: the /s/ would be floating, rather than deleted outright. If that were the case, the feature [+continuant] would be locally well formed, and there would be no reason for it to spread to the /p/. Our analysis crucially assumes that the Root node, and the link between the Root node and [+continuant], are deleted outright. Fusion occurs so that the surviving feature [+continuant] is not floating.

The stranded feature generally links to the other member of the consonant cluster. This derives from the high ranking of **Contiguity**. By linking to the segment either before or after its original location, there is a minimal violation of contiguity. For example, when /sp/ fuses to [f], [+continuant] is still in word-initial position, and [Labial] still precedes the vowel. If the feature were to link to a more distant segment, there would be a greater violation of contiguity. A consonant feature most often links to the other segment in the cluster (rather than to a vowel), since C-features preferentially link to C-elements, not to V-elements.

The stranded feature can, however, link to the vowel, violating **Contiguity** minimally, but also violating **UpwardsStructure** constraints on the linkage of C-elements. In some instances, different stranded features from the same deleted segment link to different segments in the output. A particularly good example was discussed by Lorentz (1976), with similar patterns reported more recently by Ringo (1985) and Stemberger (p.u.d.). The words *snow* and *smoke* were rendered as [sõũ] and [fõũk] (Lorentz, Ringo) or [sõː] and [fõːk] (Stemberger).[7] This would be represented as follows:

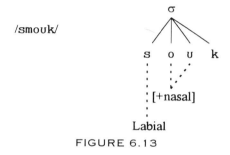

FIGURE 6.13

The feature [+nasal] cannot spread to the /s/, due to a constraint against nasal fricatives: **NotCo-occurring(-sonorant, + continuant, + nasal)**. But if [+nasal] must survive and link up, even though the /m/ is deleted, it links to the vowel instead. For the /sn/ cluster, this is all that happens. However, with /sm/, the feature [Labial] from the /m/ also spreads to the /s/, yielding [f] plus a nasalized vowel.

Notice that the realization of /sm/ as [f] looks like a fusion of the /s/ and the /m/. But [+nasal] is also spreading to the vowel here. Fusion (if such a mechanism exists) takes two segments and merges them into one. No provision is made for splitting a segment and fusing the parts with two different segments. The easiest analysis of these data is that the nasal is deleted, that some of the features of the nasal ([+nasal], [Labial]) must survive and link upwards, and that they link to some other segment in the word. If that is what is going on in this clear case, then that is also probably what is going on in unclear cases, where two contiguous consonants appear to be fused into one consonant.

Smith (1973) provides an example where **Contiguity** is violated more exten-

---

[7]The children reported by Lorentz and by Ringo were acquiring dialects of English with the standard diphthong [oʊ]. The child reported by Stemberger was acquiring a Minnesota dialect in which the vowel is more often a monophthong [oː].

sively. [Labial] spread from a deleted /w/ in a word-initial cluster onto a final coronal, as in *queen* /kwiːn/ [kiːm] and *quit* /kwɪt/ [kɪp]:

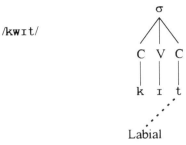

FIGURE 6.14

Survived(Labial) prevented the [Labial] element of the /w/ from being deleted along with the rest of the segment. **LinkedUpwards(Labial)** required [Labial] to link up somewhere. [Labial] consequently linked to the final consonant when the final consonant was an anterior coronal, which has default place of articulation. In our analysis, the final coronal has no underlying place of articulation, and it obtains a surface place of articulation through the independently available [Labial], rather than through the insertion of default [Coronal]. However, this occurred only if the [Labial] was not otherwise linked to any segment.[8] Further, it is possible only with the following constraint ranking:

> **Not(Coronal)**   ‖‖‖   **Not(Link)**

It must be easier to add a link to the output than to add [Coronal]. Note that [Labial] could not simply attach to the /k/, since (a) [kp] was not a possible output segment, due to the high ranking of **NotComplex(C-Place)** in consonants in English (so that true consonants can have only one articulator node), and (b) the feature [Dorsal] in the /k/ had to survive. In order to survive, the feature [Labial] had to link to a more distant segment. Presumably, such distant spreading is unlikely to be due to any special mechanism like fusion. We are dealing with the survival of features from a deleted segment, which attach where they can: often to the other member of the onset cluster, but sometimes to the vowel or a coda consonant. (See also §7.4.3.1.)

There have been no general studies of fusion, but there seem to be four patterns attested.

Pattern 1: All nondefault features survive.
Pattern 2: One of two nondefault features survives.
Pattern 3: Both nondefault features fail to survive.

---

[8] Double linkage violates **SinglyLinked(Labial)**, which was ranked high enough to prevent left-to-right labial harmony in Amahl's speech at the time.

Pattern 4: A redundant nondefault feature survives, usually [+s.g.] or [+continuant].

We address each pattern in turn, then turn to an alternative analysis of fusion (McCarthy, 1995; Gnanadesikan, 1995).

6.1.6.4.1. All Nonredundant Nondefault Features Survive

The most common fusions involve the unexpected survival of a nondefault feature. This happens when the nondefault feature can be combined with the nondefault features of the other segment. The prototypical example is /sp/ as [f], combining the nondefault place feature [Labial] of /p/ with the nondefault feature [+continuant] of /s/. Stemberger and Stoel-Gammon (1991) and Chin and Dinnsen (1992) note that there are many reported instances of /sp/ as [f], but none as [t], in which the default features are present in the output. Both papers attribute this to underspecification: only nondefault features are present underlyingly, and these are combined in the output; children do not delete the nondefault features and insert the defaults instead. An additional alternative within OT holds that both default and nondefault features are present underlyingly, but that **Survived(Non-Default)** is always ranked higher than **Survived(Default)**. As a result, if the system must choose between an output in which an underlying nondefault feature survives, versus an output in which an underlying default feature survives, the output with the nondefault feature is optimal. Either approach can account for this fusion pattern.

6.1.6.4.2. One of Two Nonredundant Nondefault Features Survives

Another common fusion pattern is one in which there are two nondefault features, and only one of the two features survives. This happens when the two features are incompatible within the same segment. This was noted above for manner features in /sm/: both [+nasal] and [+continuant] are nondefault manner features, but no consonant can be both [+nasal] and [+continuant]. As a result, the system must choose between the two features. The choice is governed by **Survived (+continuant)** and **Survived(+nasal)**; whichever constraint is ranked higher, that determines whether the output is the fricative [f] (a fusion) or the nasal [m] (simple deletion of /s/). Such feature incompatibilities also arise with place of articulation. A cluster such as /kw/ can be realized as [p], if **Survived(Labial)** is ranked higher than **Survived(Dorsal)** (since high-ranked **NotComplex(C-Place)** prevents more than one place feature). This pattern is easy to explain within OT.

6.1.6.4.3. Neither Nonredundant Nondefault Feature Survives

A third type of fusion is more problematic. There are two competing nondefault features, and neither feature survives. Instead, the default feature is inserted. We do not know how common this pattern is, but suspect that it is rare. Larissa (Stemberger, p.u.d.) optionally showed this pattern for /sm/ and /sn/ clusters. At one period, in addition to fusion as a fricative, she produced forms with a voiceless stop:

| smoke | /smoːk/ | [fõːk]~[pʰoːk] |
| snow | /snoː/ | [sõː] ~[tʰoː] |

[+nasal] and [+continuant] are not compatible within a single segment, and so a fricative was produced, with [+nasal] spreading to the vowel. The variability of output suggests that the constraints were ranked unstably. When [+nasal] did not link to the vowel, the incompatibility between [+nasal] and [+continuant] was still unresolved. The conflict was resolved by deleting both features, and inserting default [-continuant,-nasal]. In a full-specification analysis, /s/ would be underlyingly [-nasal] and /m/ would be underlyingly [-continuant], and we could argue that [pʰ] merely preserves both (redundant, default) features. However, we noted above that /sp/ never seems to yield [t], with the default features preserved. There is a strong bias to preserve only nondefault features. Given the feature conflict here, OT predicts that one of the nondefault features will survive. It is not obvious how to account for deletion of both features.

We assume that we would not want to create complex conjoined constraints such as:

Given A & B in the input, it cannot be the case that exactly one of them (only A or only B) is present in the output.

Such a constraint would be violated if only A (a nasal) or only B (a fricative) was present in the output. It would not be violated if both A and B (a nasalized fricative) were present in the output. And it would not be violated if neither A nor B (an oral stop) were present in the output. In essence, if the system cannot have it all, it opts for nothing. We view this type of constraint as both undesirable and unlikely.

In a resource-based theory such as ours, an explanation is available. Attempting to access two nondefault features (which require more resources) in a single segment (thus requiring even more resources) overtaxes the system, and both nondefault elements are lost. Enough resources remain to fill in the default features. In a connectionist system, competing elements inhibit each other, lowering each other's activation levels. It is possible for equally strong competitors to inhibit each other to such a degree that neither is sufficiently activated, and the default feature (the highest-frequency output) replaces both. In §4.7.1.5, we discussed a possible variant of OT in which the ranking of the **Survived** constraints is derived from the activation levels of the elements involved. The activation levels are affected by inhibition from close competitors. Strong competition between [+nasal] and [+continuant] would lead to lower ranking of **Survived(+nasal)** and **Survived(+continuant)**. If the **Survived** constraints come to be ranked lower than **Not(+nasal)** and **Not(+continuant)**, then the default features would be inserted in place of both nondefault features. We caution that this explanation is speculative. However, we know of no other explanation that can explain this type of fusion, while still accounting for the statistical patterns of other types of fusion.

6.1.6.4.4. A Redundant Nondefault Feature Survives

Some common fusions involve the survival of a redundant nondefault feature from the deleted segment. The most common example is the reduction of /sm/ and /sn/ to voiceless nasals: *smile* /smaɪl/ [aɪo], *snow* /snoʊ/ [n̥oʊ]. The fusion combines the feature [+s.g.], which is redundant in /s/, with the nasal. Recall that our approach to underspecification, default underspecification, predicts that redundant nondefault features can be present in the underlying representation. As a result, these features can survive (high ranking of **Survived(+s.g.)** and **LinkedUpwards(+s.g.)**) even when the /s/ is deleted. In order for [+s.g.] to link to the /n/ (and thus violate **Contiguity** minimally), the constraint that requires nasals to be voiced (**Co-occurring(+sonorant→+voiced)**) must be relatively low-ranked, allowing for voiceless nasals under this special circumstance.

Redundant manner features may also be involved in this third type of fusion. Larissa (Stemberger, p.u.d.) fused stop-approximant clusters into fricatives:

play	/pleɪ/	[feɪ]
branch	/bɹæntʃ/	[væns]
twenty	/twʌni/	[sʌni]
swing	/swɪŋ/	[fɪn]

The redundant feature [+continuant] from the deleted approximant linked up to the surviving segment, producing a fricative. Again, this makes sense if the redundant nondefault feature is underlying, as is allowed by default underspecification. (Darryl [see §8.5.1.2] also fused /bl/ to [v].) Note the chain shift here. The cluster /sw/ fuses into [f], with manner from /s/ but place from /w/. The cluster /tw/ fuses into [s], with place from /t/ and manner from both /t/ and /w/. We would have expected /tw/ to fuse into [f]. OT does not do a good job with chain shifts; but they are uncommon.

At an earlier stage, Larissa's pronunciations of these clusters was slightly different. The later development of the clusters to fricatives provides some evidence about how to analyze the earlier pronunciations. All clusters had earlier been reduced to affricates:

play	/pleɪ/	[pfeɪ]
branch	/bræntʃ/	[bvæns]
twist	/twɪst/	[tsɪs]
spider	/spaɪdɹ̩/	[pfaɪdə]

Affricates are perceptually difficult to distinguish from clusters; thus, such pronunciations could have been interpreted as the child's first clusters. However, since they were later replaced by fricatives, and there were no clusters at the later stage, it is probable that these were affricates rather than clusters. In §3.1.1, we noted that the representation of affricates is controversial. They may be grooved (strident) fricatives, or both [+continuant] and [-continuant]. The fusion of /pl/ and /tw/ to [pf] and [ts] implies the latter analysis. Since neither input segment is [+grooved] or [+strident], no fusion could lead to a [+grooved] or [+strident] output. The [+continuant] feature of the approximants and fricatives appears to survive, leading to a complex segment:

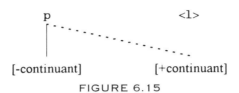

FIGURE 6.15

This analysis implies (counter to our assumptions) that the default feature [-continuant] of /p/ is specified lexically. If [-continuant] were inserted in the output due to a high ranking for **LinkedDownward(Root)**, the linkage of [+continuant] from the approximant would satisfy that constraint; there would be no need to fill in [-continuant], and a simple fricative would result (as it did, at a later point in development). It is not possible to invoke a high ranking for **Co-occurring(σ-Margin→-continuant)**, which would require the insertion of [-continuant], because that would convert input fricatives to affricates, which never occurred: *fall* [fɑʊ], *[pfɑʊ]. These fusion data thus constitute some (rare) evidence for the underlying specification of default features.

Some apparent fusions are more problematical. Dyson (1986) and Bleile (1991) report that /kl/ and /gl/ can surface as [p] and [b], if the child tends to substitute [w] for /l/ in singleton onsets (*like* [waɪk]; §5.5.3.6.1): *glasses* /glæsəz/ [bæsəz]. In this case, a feature that is not a part of the /l/ in the adult pronunciation ([Labial]), appears in the output and links up to the velar, producing the fusion [p] or [b]. No approach to specification predicts this. We believe that the child has an inaccurate underlying representation in which /l/ is represented as labial (/lʷ/). In order to account for historical sound changes, Ohala (1974) and Greenlee and Ohala (1978) argue that children may misinterpret ambiguous aspects of the acoustic signal. A dark [ɫ] is associated with a low F2, in a way that is strikingly similar to the F2 of labial [w]. Velarization and rounding have similar effects on F2. If the child attends to visual information, it is clear that /l/ is not rounded. However, if the child does not attend to visual information, the child may misattribute the low F2 of velarized [ɫ] to rounding. We are not suggesting that the child misperceives [ɫ] as [w]; the child may perceive [ɫ] as a labialized lateral [lʷ] or [ɫʷ]. Ohala's theory of sound change assumes that children occasionally make such errors of interpretation. We believe that this underlies fusions of /gl/ to [b]. We return to this learning error in §10.1.2.

6.1.6.4.5. Fusion as Multiple Correspondence

McCarthy (1995) presents an alternative approach to fusion, based on an expanded notion of correspondence between input and output. He suggests that two

segments in the input can correspond to a single segment in the output. Gnanadesikan (1995) and Barlow (1995) apply this to fusions in initial consonant clusters in child phonology. When /sp/ is realized as [f], the [f] reflects both the /s/ and
the /p/. Gnanadesikan is clear about the motivation for this. Instead of using **Sur-
vived(Feature)**, this alternative approach makes use of **Ident(Feature)**, in which
a feature is constrained to survive only if the segment that contains it survives; if
a segment deletes, all its features also delete. It follows that fusion does not involve deletion of any segment, since that would entail loss of every feature in the
segment, and at least one feature of each segment survives in fusions. If a single
output segment corresponds to two input segments, this would be a violation of
NoMultipleCorrespondence, or, in our system, **Distinct(Root)**. If **Distinct** is
ranked high enough, fusions are impossible. If **Distinct** is low-ranked, fusions
result when **NotComplex(Onset)** prevents the distinct realization on both
segments.

This alternative has the advantage of not requiring us to decide which segment
is the one that survives: both survive. Further, it makes some predictions about
which features should survive. If a single output segment corresponds to two input
segments, then there must by definition be conflicts between the features involved. Given /s/ and /p/ in the input, the output cannot be *both* [Labial] *and*
[Coronal], or *both* [+continuant] *and* [-continuant]. But independently needed
constraint rankings predict which of the conflicting features will survive (see also
Gnanadesikan, 1995):

| **Survived(Labial)** | ‖ | **Survived(Coronal)** |
| **Survived(+ continuant)** | ‖ | **Survived(-continuant)** |

This ranking, which we deal with extensively in Chapter 7, correctly predicts that
the result will be a labial fricative ([f]). Note that this analysis requires variation
between children in terms of the specification of redundant nondefault features. If
the approximants /l, ɹ, w, j/ are specified as [+continuant], and /sp/→[f], then /pl/
must also yield [f] (which is correct for some children). In order to derive /pl/→[p]
(correct for other children), then /l/ cannot be specified for [+continuant]. Thus,
this approach requires assumptions about feature specification that are similar to
those of our approach.

One drawback to this analysis, noted by both Gnanadesikan and Barlow
(though neither suggest that it is a drawback), is that it requires a fusion analysis
of *all* clusters in the child's speech, even ones that do not look like fusion. If
/sp/→[f] is a fusion, then /sk/→[k] and /pl/→[p] are also fusions. Gnanadesikan
argues that the survival of all the features of one segment is predicted by the constraint rankings. [Labial] and [Dorsal] win out over [Coronal], yielding the nondefault place features of /k/ and /p/ rather than the default place of /s/ and /l/.
Since *[x] is not a possible output in English, the stop [k] results instead, if
Survived(Dorsal) ≫ **Survived(+ continuant)**;[9] had these two constraints been

---

[9][x] is ruled out if **NotCo-occurring(Dorsal, − sonorant, + continuant)** is ranked high. If that
constraint is ranked low, then [x] results. Rockman (1983) reported a child who produced [x]: *scrape*
/skɹeɪp/ [xeɪp], *school* /skuːl/ [xu]. Because adult English lacks [x], this is uncommon.

ranked in the opposite order, [s] would have resulted. We do not find it plausible
that in /kl/→[k], the [k] corresponds to both the /k/ and the /l/; and there is no
evidence for such correspondence.

There is another drawback to this analysis. In any fusion, there must be multiple correspondence. In the example above from N. Smith (1973), in which /kwiːn/
is realized as [kiːm], the output final [m] must correspond to both input final /n/
and input nonfinal /w/; contiguity and linearity are not respected. In /smoːk/ as
[fõːk], the input /m/ corresponds to both output [f] and output [õ]; although naively one would have thought that the /m/ was deleted, in fact it appears twice in
the output. In order for this analysis to work, it must be assumed that, potentially,
every segment in the input can correspond to every segment in the output (Mc-
Carthy & Prince, 1995). This leads to an immense amount of power and to coun-
terintuitive analyses.

There is one point where the predictions between the two approaches differ: in
Larissa's variation in the realization of /sm/ and /sn/ clusters. If [+nasal] was
realized on the vowel, the onset was a fricative: *smoke* /smoːk/ [fõːk], *snake*
/sneɪk/ [sẽɪ̃k]. If the vowel was realized as oral, then an oral stop appeared:
[pʰoːk], [tʰeɪk]. In our analysis, this reflects variability in whether the feature
[+nasal] can link to the vowel; if it can, that resolves the conflict between
[+nasal] and [+continuant], allowing [+continuant] to survive in the onset; if it
cannot link to the vowel, then competition between the two features leads to the
deletion of both features. The deletion of both features is as awkward in Gnanadesikan's analysis as in ours. But her analysis predicts two additional variants: an
oral stop plus a nasalized vowel (*[pʰõːk], *[tʰẽɪ̃k]), and a fricative plus an oral
vowel (*[foːk], *[seɪk]). In her approach, the resolution of the competition between features in the onset consonant is entirely independent of whether the input
nasal also corresponds to the vowel. The fact that these two variants never occurred, while the other two variants were common, suggests that our approach is
preferable. We predict a correlation between the survival of the feature [+nasal]
in the vowel and in the onset. Since our analysis is more adequate in this instance,
we follow it throughout this book.

6.1.6.4.6. Fusion as Regression

Macken (1987, 1992) notes that fusion can arise as a type of regression. She
discusses a child who initially reduced the clusters /pɹ/, /tɹ/, and /kɹ/ to stops
through the deletion of the approximant, but who later fused the two consonants
into [f], preserving the [+continuant] and [Labial] of the /ɹ/, at the expense of loss
of the place features and [-continuant] of the stops. Similarly, in the discussion
above, we saw that Larissa fused /pl/ into [f] (late) or [pf] (earlier), but she had
simply produced the stop at an even earlier stage ([pʰ]). Such regressions come
about through the reranking of faithfulness constraints. By reranking **Survived**
(**+continuant**) higher, the approximant can survive. However, as long as clusters
are impossible, reranking **Survived** higher does not lead to a consonant cluster,
but simply makes fusion likely. The result is a partial advance (since features

survive that earlier had not) and a partial regression (since features that had earlier survived are now deleted). Such trade-off regressions are an expected part of constraint reranking in our system, but are not possible for Tesar and Smolensky's (in press) approach to learning. (See §4.12.2.)

6.1.6.5. Metathesis (Migration)

A rare way to resolve complex onsets is to move one of the consonants elsewhere in the word. Menn (1976) and several others report the following example:

snow   /snoʊ/   [noʊs]

This violates **Contiguity** (and **Linearity**, if such a constraint exists), but allows all underlying consonants to survive. Children rarely shift whole segments in this way, for any reason (but see Colin's data, §7.4.3.2.)

6.1.6.6. Three-Member Clusters in Onsets

Clements and Keyser (1983) raise an issue for consonant clusters with three members: /spɹ/, /spl/, /spj/, /stɹ/, /skɹ/, /skl/, /skw/, and /skj/. They posit two possible developmental scenarios. (a) The reduction of these clusters might be related to the exact number of segments the child can produce in onsets. (b) The reduction of the clusters does not depend on the exact number of consonants, but on the possibility of the "local" sequences within the cluster. By "local" sequences, we mean the pairs of contiguous consonants, such as /sp/ and /pl/ in /spl/. Consider the two scenarios:

	Point I	Point II	Point III
(a) /pleɪ/:	[p]	[pl]	
/spɑt/:	[p]	[sp]	
/splæʃ/:	[p]	[pl]	[spl]

In this scenario, at Point I, there are a maximum of two consonants in the onset. Deletion occurs only in three-consonant clusters.

	Point I	Point II
(b) /pleɪ/:	[p]	[pl]
/spɑt/:	[p]	[sp]
/splæʃ/:	[p]	[spl]

In this scenario, what matters is only the consonant-to-consonant sequences, not the absolute number of consonants. As soon as both [sp] and [pl] are possible in the child's speech, then [spl] is also possible. Although we have phrased this issue in terms of deletion, a similar issue arises if epenthesis is used to resolve complex onsets: when [sp] and [pl] are possible outputs, is [spl] a possible output, or must it be realized with epenthesis ([səpl] or [spəl])?

Clements and Keyser (1983) examine Amahl's data (N. Smith, 1973) and report that scenario (b) is true there. Fikkert (1994) reports that this was the case for her subjects. We have also observed this for several children (including Gwendolyn and Morgan). But scenario (a) also appears to be true for some children with phonological disorders (and perhaps typical development). (See Bernhardt, 1990: Charles, *S1*; Blair, *S2*; Gordon, *S5*).

Cluster development in some children is tied to the absolute number of consonants that are produced. Since each consonant adds one more violation to the constraint **NotComplex(Onset)**, two-member consonant clusters (one violation) develop before three-member consonant clusters (two violations). Eventually, the child's system develops to the point where two violations of **NotComplex(Onset)** are permitted.

The reasonableness of this proposition is not obvious within standard OT. In a system that is based on resources and their allocation, however, it is reasonable. If there is a limit to the amount of resources that can be allocated to an onset, that sets an upper limit on how many consonants can appear in the onset, whether one, two, three, or more. However, many versions of OT are not resource-based, but rely on strict dominance of the constraints. Prince and Smolensky (1993) would hold that a cluster should be reduced to a single segment as long as maintaining a simple onset is more important than linking all the segments into the syllable. However, if it is more important to link up the segments into the syllable than to maintain simple onsets, then all the segments of the cluster should surface. In order to limit the onset to just two segments, the following would need to be true:

> One violation of **NotComplex(Onset)** is *less* important than a violation of **Survived(Root)/LinkedUpwards(Root)**.
>
> Two violations of **NotComplex(Onset)** are *more* important than a violation of **Survived(Root)/LinkedUpwards(Root)**.

This would appear to be a situation in which two constraints are ranked in one way if the constraints are violated only once, but are ranked in the opposite order if the constraints are violated twice. Prince and Smolensky presuppose (without any empirical evidence) that this is not possible. To maintain their point of view, it must be the case that no child (or adult language) has an upper bound of two segments in an onset. If a child has [sp], [pl], and [sl] clusters in outputs, but nonetheless reduces /spl/ to [sp], this would appear to falsify their position.

There is a possible solution, however. The data would probably allow us to claim that two-member consonant clusters are limited to word-initial position. If so, we could maintain that the onset never has more than one segment. The other member in the cluster might be part of an appendix. Thus, [stɑp] might be made up of [s] in an initial appendix that is limited to one segment, plus [t] in an onset that is limited to one segment. In this way, the maximal initial consonant cluster has two segments. As noted in §3.7, we are not convinced that syllable appendices exist. However, we cannot rule out this possibility at the present time.

For some children, however, it is not the absolute number of consonants that is important, but rather the ability to produce particular segments contiguously within an onset. The role of sequence constraints within clusters will be examined extensively in §7.3.

6.1.6.7. ?Requiring Complex Onsets?

According to OT, complex onsets may be simplified, but simple onsets should never be made complex simply for the sake of having a complex onset. An onset may become complex in order to preserve features or segments (see §7.3.1.9, Robin: Bernhardt, 1994a; Chin, 1996), but there is no constraint that would lead to the creation of a complex onset for its own sake. We know of at least one instance in which this occurred.

Stemberger (1992a) reported the following regression in Gwendolyn's speech. At 3;3, the first word-initial cluster appeared: a [w] after the initial consonant:

	Point 1	Point 2	Point 3
tree	[tʰiː]	[tʰiː]~[tʰwiː]	[tʰwiː]
top	[tʰɑːp]	[tʰɑːp]~[tʰwɑːp]	[tʰɑːp]

Initially, consonant clusters were simplified to a single consonant (the consonant of lowest sonority). Gwendolyn neutralized such adult contrasts as /t/-/tɹ/-/tw/ and /k/-/kw/-/kɹ/-/kl/ as [tʰ]. At Point 2, a [w] was added to these clusters to realize adult /w/, /ɹ/, and /l/. The glide was optional, so that the old and new pronunciations vacillated freely. The glide became common on the third day of the change. On that day, a regression occurred: the [w] was variably added to a large number of words, such as *top*, *stop*, *book*, and *cookie*, that do not have approximant-clusters in adult speech. This incorrect pronunciation lasted 9 days for most words, but 24 days for words with the vowels /ʊ/ and /ɔɪ/.

The regression before the vowels /ʊ/ and /ɔɪ/ can be motivated. These were the only two vowels that are rounded in adult speech that were unrounded in Gwendolyn's speech at the time: /ʊ/ was realized as [ə], and /ɔɪ/ was realized as [eɪ]. The feature [Labial] in these vowels had been deleted. When the regression occurred, a consonant was created in the onset to which the formerly deleted [Labial] attached: *toy* [tʰweɪ], *book* [bwət]. A high ranking for **Survived(Labial)** and **LinkedUpwards(Labial)** caused the creation of a glide in the onset to which the feature could link (thus violating **NotComplex(Onset)** and **Not(Root)**). Because this pronunciation has a cluster where none is present in the adult pronunciation, Gwendolyn quickly (within 24 days) reranked constraints so that these words began with a singleton consonant rather than a cluster.

It is also possible to justify pronunciations like *stop* [tʰwap]. Although the adult pronunciation (/stɑp/) does not contain a glide in the onset, the child's pronunciation is faithful to the number of timing units: CC (not just C). If the only clusters allowed in the child's system contain [w] as the second member, /st/ could be realized as [tʰw] if **Survived(TimingUnit)** is ranked higher than the **Not** constraints that should prevent the insertion of the [w]. Again, this pronunciation did not last long. Because it was so unfaithful segmentally, the child quickly (within 9 days) reranked constraints so that the [w] would not be epenthesized.

However, the regression in other lexical items is difficult to explain. Since there is only a single timing unit in the adult pronunciation, the cluster is unfaithful to the number of timing units. Since there is no source in the word for the feature

[Labial] of the [w], the pronunciation with a cluster is also unfaithful segmentally. To derive the cluster, there must be a constraint that requires a consonant cluster to be present. We know of no such constraint. These data are problematical, and we have no explanation for this regression (in terms of phonological theory, at any rate).

6.1.7. COMPLEX CODAS

There is much less information available about the development of clusters in codas. It appears that the phenomena associated with complex codas are more restricted than those associated with complex onsets.

6.1.7.1. Deletion Repairs

For most children, once codas are allowed, at first only one consonant is possible within any particular coda. Extra consonants are deleted, due to an initial high ranking for **NotComplex(Coda)**. Two degrees of deletion are observed: deletion of both consonants, or deletion of just one consonant.

6.1.7.1.1. Deletion of Both Consonants

Just as with onsets, it can happen that both members of a coda cluster are deleted. Gwendolyn (p.u.d.) deleted both members of coda fricative-stop clusters until 2;10:

| fast | /fæst/ | [faː] |
| lift | /lɪft/ | [jiː] |

However, this was not a general treatment for consonant clusters, since it did not occur for other cluster types: stop-stop, stop-fricative, or nasal-stop. Thus, there were interactions with segmental features. Deletion of both members of the cluster occurred only at a point in development when all fricatives in codas were deleted; and ended at 2;10 when fricatives became possible in codas. It appears that the /s/ in *fast* could not link to the coda because it was a fricative, but **Contiguity** prevented the child from linking up the /t/. However, **Contiguity** did not prevent /t/ from linking up in a final /nt/ cluster: *tent* [tʰat]. Thus, the story is more complex than this. Resolution will be along the lines suggested for onsets in §6.1.6.1.1; it is currently something of a problem for standard versions of OT.

6.1.7.1.2. Deletion of Just One Consonant

More commonly, complex codas are reduced to a single consonant:

fix	/fɪks/	[fɪs]
fast	/fæst/	[fas]
hand	/hænd/	[han]

We know relatively little about which consonant is preserved when the cluster is reduced. There is often a preference for low-sonority segments, but there is also often a preference for high-sonority segments; see discussion in §6.1.12, and §7.3.2.

There are no large detailed cross-sectional studies of clusters in codas. The largest sample that we know of is Fikkert (1994), who reports on 12 Dutch-learning children. Fikkert argues that final clusters tend to be reduced to an obstruent, but does not address clusters made up of two obstruents; she does not address coda clusters in the same detail that she addresses onset clusters or simple clusters. Ohala (1994), in an experimental study with 16 English-learning children, reported that final fricative-stop clusters tended to be reduced to the fricative. Overall, however, there is insufficient information in the literature about coda clusters. We say here what we believe to be the general patterns. We focus only on reductions of complex codas that are purely based on complexity, when the child's system allows only a single coda consonant. When a child allows certain clusters but not other clusters, the restrictions are not on codas so much as on sequences of segments containing particular features; see §7.3.

Clusters made up of a nasal followed by a stop are fairly consistent across children (Braine, 1976). Clusters with voiceless stops (/mp, nt, ŋk/) tend to be reduced to the stop: [p, t, k]; but reduction to the nasal has also been reported (Bleile, 1987). The English cluster with a voiced stop (/nd/) tends to be reduced to the nasal: [n].[10] Braine (1976) argues that the difference between these two types of clusters derives from perceptual factors: the nasal is very short before voiceless stops in English, and children may not even be perceiving the nasal. Alternatively, it may reflect a preference for voiceless stops in codas versus a preference for sonorant elements in codas, with a general avoidance of marked voicing and manner features in obstruents in codas. See §6.1.12.1 (and §7.3.2) for discussion.

Little is known about nasal-fricative clusters. Morgan (p.u.d.) initially reduced such clusters to the nasal, at a time when coda fricatives were reduced to [ʔ]. When coda fricatives were later reduced to [tʰ], the clusters (immediately) came to be reduced to the "fricative":

		Point I	Point II
mouse	/maʊs/	[maɯʔ]	[maɯtʰ]
bounce	/baʊns/	[baɯn]	[baɯtʰ]

We do not know what is common or uncommon across children.

With clusters involving a stop plus a fricative, or involving two stops, very little is known. There is clearly variability. For example, both /sk/ and /ks/ (as in *ask* /æsk/ and *ax* /æks/) can be reduced to either the /k/ ([æk]; Morgan) or the /s/ ([æs]; Gwendolyn). It is unknown what is common or uncommon across children. We also know very little about the development of larger clusters, as with the /mpt/ of *prompt* or the /ŋks/ of *lynx*. Further data are needed.

---

[10]The clusters /mb/ and /ŋg/ do not occur word-finally (or syllable-finally) in English. In medial position, however, they do occur, and they tend to be reduced to the nasal in child phonology: *number* [nʌmo].

In adult English, there are "clusters" in which a glide (as the second part of a diphthong) or a liquid is followed by an obstruent or a nasal. The glide seems to present little difficulty for most children: diphthongs occur within both open and closed syllables (but see §6.1.10); this probably reflects the fact that the glide portion of a diphthong is in the nucleus, and there is no complex coda. For clusters like /ɹt/ (as in *heart*) and /lp/ (as in *help*), it appears that the final obstruent or nasal generally survives. When the liquid is deleted, the resolution of coda clusters resembles the resolution of initial clusters, in which the lower-sonority segment links to the syllable.

6.1.7.2. Epenthesis (Addition) Repairs

In theory, an impossible coda cluster could be rescued via epenthesis. For English, hypothetical data would be:

ask	/æsk/	?[æsək]
hand	/hænd/	?[hænəd]
help	/hɛlp/	?[hɛləp]

We are not aware of a single report of such epenthesis for English-learning children. Fee (1996) suggests that Dutch-learning children have been reported to epenthesize for some of these clusters:

melk	/mɛlk/	[mɛlək]	'milk'

However, such epenthesis is actually a common feature of adult Dutch. The actual input to Dutch-learning children is more commonly /mɛlək/. We do not know whether Dutch-learning children utilize epenthesis to rescue consonants in coda clusters when there is no epenthesis in the adult pronunciation.

Epenthesis is a minority option in onset clusters, but it appears to be even rarer in codas. We report some data (involving constraints on sequences of consonants) from Elsen (1991) for German in §7.3.2.2. This is probably because **Survived** constraints are ranked lower in codas (see §4.7.1.4). Epenthesis occurs when **Survived(Root)** is ranked so high that deletion is impossible under all circumstances. The lower ranking of faithfulness constraints in codas leads to the rarity of epenthesis to rescue consonants in complex codas. Because faithfulness constraints are ranked higher in onsets, epenthesis is more likely (but still not common). Our theory does, however, predict that an occasional child will use epenthesis to resolve complex codas; if such children are never found, it will represent a failure of our approach.

6.1.7.3. Making the Consonant Syllabic

We are unsure whether consonants ever become syllabic (or even a part of a complex vowel) specifically to avoid a complex coda. Liquids do show up as the glide portion of diphthongs:

help	/hɛlp/	[hɛʊp]
heart	/hɑɹt/	[hɑʊt]

However, liquids often become glides postvocalically in words like *fall* ([faʊ]) that do not have a complex coda. To be a resolution of complex codas, the liquids must appear as liquids in simple codas but as glides in complex codas; we are not aware of any report of such a pattern.

In some cases, the liquid can become syllabic, with the original vowel deleting, as with this example from Morgan:

milk   /mɪlk/   [mɤːkʰ]

The underlying /ɪ/ does not survive, and the "syllabic /l/" shows up as [ɤː] (as underlying syllabic /l/ always did at the time). However, this was idiosyncratic to this one word, rather than being a general property of /l/ in complex codas; and [l] was not possible in codas at the time. It is unclear whether a coda consonant ever becomes syllabic specifically to avoid having a complex coda.

6.1.7.4. Fusion

We know nothing about fusions involving complex codas. While many children have been reported to fuse /sp/ to [f] in onsets, we know of no child who has been reported to fuse /sp/ or /ps/ to [f] in codas, in words like *wasp* and *glimpse*. Fusions appear to be less common in codas than in onsets. This suggests that nondefault features are less likely to survive in codas. We noted in §4.7.1.4 that codas are a weak domain, and that faithfulness constraints are ranked lower in codas. The rarity of fusions in codas is probably due to this low ranking of **Survived** constraints. See also §6.1.12.1.

Larissa (p.u.d.) presented one instance that might be a fusion in a coda. After a period in which affricates were reduced to stops in codas, they emerged as (dental) affricates. Simultaneously, final [ts] and [dz] "clusters" appeared:

catch	/kætʃ/	[tʰæts]		
bridge	/bɹɪdʒ/	[bɪdz]		
cats	/kæts/	[tʰæts]	?or?	[tʰæts]
dogs	/dɑgz/	[dɑdz]	?or?	[dɑdz]

It is suspicious that affricates and the child's first clusters emerged at the same time. It is possible that /t/ and /s/ fused into an affricate (just as /b/ and /l/ fused into an affricate in onsets; see §6.1.6.4.4). This is not entirely convincing, however, since it is possible that the affricate /tʃ/ was being split apart into a cluster. But this is the only possible example of fusion in a coda that we have come across.

6.1.7.5. ?Requiring Complex Codas?

Just as it is impossible to require all syllables to have codas, it is impossible to require that all codas be complex. However, it might be possible for a coda to be more complex in the child's speech than in adult speech. This may be what underlies the following puzzling phenomenon (from Larissa's speech at 1;11–2;1, lasting for about a month and a half), limited to utterance-final position:

up	/ʌp/	[ʔʌpʰpʰ]	(nonfinal [ʔʌpʰ])
sick	/sɪk/	[hiːkʰkʰ]	(nonfinal [hiːkʰ])
put	/pʊt/	[pʰʊtʰtʰ]	(nonfinal [pʰʊtʰ])
rub	/ɹʌb/	[wʌp]	
bed	/bɛd/	[bɛt]	

A final voiceless (aspirated) stop was articulated twice in utterance-final position; this did not occur when another word followed in the utterance, or with (devoiced) voiced stops. Other children with this pattern have been reported (Camarata, 1989, and references therein).

Bernstein Ratner (1993) has suggested that such pronunciations were probably artifactual. The child may earlier have lacked final codas. Adults may have emphasized the codas to the child. The child may have responded by emphasizing the codas once they were pronounceable, sometimes by doing the coda twice. However, Larissa's family did not engage in such behavior. Even if they had, it does not account for Larissa's data. She had been using codas for a number of months (Stemberger, 1993a), so why did such pronunciations suddenly arise? At the time in question, the child did devoice final voiced stops, and, had the family overemphasized the final voiced stop (which they did not), perhaps words ending in final voiced stops would be doubled by the child—but they were not, only the voiceless stops, which the child had been producing correctly for months. Some other explanation must be sought.

We have only one suggestion to offer. Perhaps **WordFinalMassiveness** was ranked high enough in the child's speech to lead to the epenthesis of extra non-prominent elements in utterance-final position. However, the child had severe constraints on consonant sequences at the time (see Stemberger, 1993a), and also did not allow voiced obstruents in codas (preferring to devoice them). Sequence constraints may have limited the epenthetic consonant to the default manner of articulation and voicing (a voiceless aspirated stop), and required that place of articulation not be different from that of the preceding consonant (see Stemberger, 1993a). Thus, the epenthetic consonant was a voiceless aspirated stop that had the same place of articulation as the preceding stop: the final voiceless aspirated stop was articulated twice. We are unsure about this explanation, but note that the phenomenon is extremely uncommon across children.

Another possibly relevant constraint is the following:

SinglyExpressed(Root):   An input segment appears only once in the output.

In [ʔʌpʰpʰ], this constraint might be violated in order to satisfy **WordFinalMassiveness**. **SinglyExpressed** is ordinarily very high-ranked, however. It is rarely violated.

6.1.7.6. Complex Codas in Unstressed Syllables

It appears that (word-final) codas can sometimes be allowed if the syllable is stressed, but not if it is unstressed. Bernhardt (1990; p.u.d.) found this to be true of three children in her studies (Blair at 4;2, whose data are shown; Faith at 3;7; Kendra at 3;9):

front   /fɹʌnt/   [hʌ̃nt]   present   /pɹɛznt̩/   [pʌʔə̃n]

Unstressed syllables are a weak prosodic domain, in which faithfulness is ranked lower than in stressed syllables (§4.7.1.5). The following ranking allows consonant clusters in codas only in stressed syllables:

Survived$_{\text{Stressed}}$(C-Root) ||| **NotComplex(Coda)** ||| **Survived$_{\text{Unstressed}}$(C-Root)**

It is unknown how common it is for children to show this sort of difference between stressed and unstressed syllables. See also §6.2.5.3.

6.1.8. SIMPLE NUCLEI: SHORT MONOPHTHONGS

Short monophthongal vowels are present in babbling and in the earliest words, for all children. The nucleus is treated as an obligatory part of the syllable (via high ranking of σ▸**Nucleus**). Shaw (1996) argues that nuclei are not obligatory in all adult languages. Nuclei may be obligatory for all children; however, we lack developmental data for languages in which the nucleus in not obligatory, and we regard such languages as the most likely place for children to treat nuclei as nonobligatory.

As long as faithfulness preserves the vowel in the output, there will be a syllable:

Survived(V-Root) ||| **Not(σ)**

As long as a syllable is allowed at all, the vowel will tend to survive.

6.1.9. COMPLEX NUCLEI: DIPHTHONGS

Complexity can cause difficulties for nuclei just as it does for onsets and codas. A vowel can be complex in two ways. (a) Most obviously, a vowel is complex if it is a diphthong, since the vowel is actually a sequence of two vowels within the nucleus, of which one is more prominent and is thus the peak of the syllable. (b) Less obviously, long vowels are complex because they have two timing units. Long vowels are less complex than diphthongs, however, because they have only a single Root node. Note that diphthongs share this complexity (two timing units) with long vowels.

Complexity within the nucleus is governed by the following constraint:

NotComplex(Nucleus):   A nucleus may have only a single segment.

In adult English, which allows diphthongs, this constraint is ranked low enough that diphthongs can surface:

Survived(Root) ||| **NotComplex(Nucleus)**
LinkedUpwards(Root)
Not(σ)

This ranking means that neither part of the diphthong can be deleted. Nor can the two parts be split into two syllables (e.g., *cow* *[.kʰɑ.u.]). It is preferable to have a complex nucleus with a diphthong. If the complexity constraint is ranked higher, other outputs are possible.

We focus almost completely on diphthongs here, though long vowels also add complexity. A child might not tolerate such complexity, and might shorten all long vowels: *sleep* /sliːp/ [sip], *bee* /biː/ [bi]. It is difficult, however, to bring any data to bear on this issue, for two reasons. (a) It is a common practice in research on phonological development to transcribe the English long vowels simply as tense [i] and [u], without recording whether they were long or short. (b) There are interactions between vowel length and constraints on the minimal size of feet that lead us to expect that long vowels often must remain long. Fikkert (1994) maintains that Dutch children do not at first use vowel length contrastively. However, the transcriptions show both long and short vowels from the beginning, with length occurring on the same vowels as in adult speech: short [ɪ] versus long [iː], for example. The children did show interchanges in length (e.g., /ɪ/ surfacing as [iː], or /iː/ as [ɪ]), but this might have reflected a problem with vowel tenseness, rather than with length.[11] We return to this issue in §6.2.3 in our discussion of feet.

6.1.9.1. Deletion Repairs

It appears to be common for the glide portion of a diphthong to delete. This derives from the following ranking:

NotComplex(Nucleus) ‖ **Survived(Root)**
Not(σ) ‖ **LinkedUpwards(Root)**

This ranking allows neither a complex nucleus nor the splitting of the two parts of the diphthong into two syllables. One part of the diphthong is deleted. In theory, either part of the diphthong could be deleted: /aɪ/ could surface as either [a] or [ɪ], /eɪ/ as either [ɛ] or [ɪ], /aʊ/ as either [a] or [ʊ], etc. In practice, however, children seem to preserve the first (syllabic) portion of the diphthong:

cow	/kaʊ/	[tʰaː]	(Gwendolyn, 1;10; Stemberger, 1992b)
bite	/baɪt/	[bat]	

This is predictable given the constraints on syllable nuclei discussed in §4.7.1.3. The optimal syllable peak has a maximally open vocal tract: a low vowel:

Co-occurring(Rime→-high)
Co-occurring(Rime→ + low)

These two constraints mean that, if the system has a choice between two vowel-like segments as the head of the syllable, there will be a tendency to link up a low vowel, if one is present. If no low vowel is present, then a mid vowel (still [-high]) will be linked up. If neither a low vowel nor a mid vowel is present, then a high

---

[11]The fact that many errors occurred in which vowels lengthened in closed syllables suggests that the error may have been driven by tenseness, not by length.

vowel may be linked up. In English (as in most languages), diphthongs begin with a low or mid vowel as the syllabic portion, and end with a high vowel as the nonsyllabic portion. Constraints on rimes thus predict that the syllabic portion of the diphthong should, in general, link up. This does appear to be the most common way that children reduce diphthongs. We caution, however, that there have been no studies that address the acquisition of diphthongs in large numbers of children. We do not know whether diphthongs are in general a problem for young children.

For complex onsets and codas, sometimes both consonants delete. We do not believe that this will happen to complex nuclei. Because the nucleus is a required part of the syllable, both parts of the nucleus cannot be deleted; one part of the diphthong always survives.

6.1.9.2. Epenthesis (Addition) Repairs

Epenthesis cannot be used to break up a complex nucleus. Breaking up the parts of the nucleus would presumably make the second part syllabic: *cow* /kaʊ/ ?[kadʊ]?. We are unaware of such a thing in child phonology. See the next subsection.

6.1.9.3. Making the Glide Syllabic

A complex nucleus can be eliminated by making the glide portion of the diphthong syllabic. There are two ways that this can happen: (a) by splitting the single complex nucleus into a sequence of two simple nuclei, and (b) by deleting the underlyingly syllabic element and replacing it with the glide portion of the diphthong. We address each in turn.

A complex nucleus could be split into two simple nuclei, via the following ranking:

| Survived(Root) | | NotComplex(Nucleus) | | Not(σ) |
| LinkedUpwards(Root) | | | | Not(+syllabic) |

Both portions of the diphthong must survive, but it is better to make the second part syllabic and create a new syllable, than to have a diphthong. We know of no reported instance of this in child phonology.[12] At the young ages at which the complexity of the nucleus might be a problem for the child, constraints on the number of syllables in a word tend to be even stronger (§6.2.3.2). It is thus unlikely that a child would increase the number of syllables in a word in order to preserve both members of a diphthong. But we note that this is a possibility, and predict that some small proportion of children show this pattern.

The second portion of the diphthong can become syllabic, but the vowel portion of the diphthong deletes; there is a single nucleus in the output. This would derive from the following ranking:

| Survived(+high) | | Co-occurring(Rime→-high) |
| Survived(Labial) | | |

[12] Some adults might provide input to support such an analysis, pronouncing the words *hi* and *bye* as [.hɑː.iː.] and [.bɑː.iː.].

This ranking requires that the features [+high] and [Labial] must survive in the output, if they are present in the underlying representation. Since the second portion of the diphthong is always [+high], and is [Labial] in /aʊ/ and /oʊ/, this ranking could lead to outputs such as *couch* /kaʊtʃ/ [kʰʊtʃ], *bite* /baɪt/ [bɪt]. We are uncertain whether such pronunciations ever occur in child phonology.

The second portion of the diphthong may survive for another reason. In the speech of some children (such as Gwendolyn and Morgan), the vowel [a] was always short in a closed syllable. If /aɪ/ is reduced to [a] in *bite*, then the output has only one timing unit, even though there are two timing units in the underlying representation; **Survived(TimingUnit)** is violated. The child's system must choose between the following:

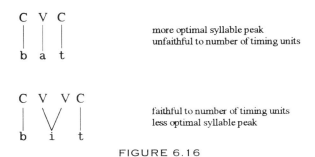

FIGURE 6.16

Which pronunciation is more optimal depends on which one of these two factors is more important in the child's system. Stemberger (1992c) reports that Gwendolyn varied between these two pronunciations at one point.[13] We suspect that it is more common for children to reduce diphthongs to the more optimal syllable peak, at the expense of the number of timing units. However, there are few data available. Unfortunately, vowel length is rarely transcribed for low vowels (since they do not contrast for length in adult English), and so we do not even know how often the vowels [æ], [ɑ], [ɔ], and [a] are phonetically short versus long in closed syllables in child language; they are phonetically long in adult English (e.g., Peterson & Lehiste, 1960). More research, using narrower transcription, is needed.

6.1.9.4. Fusion

In adult languages, diphthongs can fuse. The diphthong /aʊ/ can fuse to [ɔ] (combining the [+round] of /ʊ/ with the /a/), and /aɪ/ can fuse to [e] (combining the [-high] of /a/ with the /ɪ/). We are unaware of any report of such fusions in child phonology. Fee (1991) gives one example from Spanish (for unrelated purposes) that could be viewed as a fusion of the diphthong /we/ to [o]:

huevo   /webo/   [oβo]   'egg'

[13]Only in closed syllables, however, and only for diphthongs ending in [ɪ], never for diphthongs ending in [ʊ].

However, this could also just be deletion of the /w/, along with vowel harmony (/e/ assimilates to the following /o/). Charles (Bernhardt, 1990: *S1*) produced the /ju/ of *music* once as [y] (front rounded vowel). We know of no report of a child who used fusion commonly within diphthongs. The theory predicts that some small proportion of children should show such fusions.

6.1.9.5. ?Requiring Complex Nuclei?

There are no constraints that could cause all nuclei to be complex. However, feet must have at least two moras (see §6.2). If a child lacked codas, any monosyllabic word (or foot) would have to have a long vowel or diphthong, in order for the foot to have two moras. If that child also reduced all words to a single syllable, then only long vowels and diphthongs would be possible; short monophthongs (simple nuclei) would not occur. We suspect that it is common for such children to produce long vowels, but, since vowel length is rarely transcribed, we cannot know for certain. We know of no child who regularly produced diphthongs (e.g., *saw* (/sɑ:/) as [saj]), however.

6.1.10. COMPLEX RIMES

Some children seem to show an effect of complexity within the rime. Commonly, a rime may be maximally binary: it may contain only two timing units. This means that a rime may consist of a long vowel, or a diphthong, or a short vowel followed by a single consonant. This is a common pattern in many adult languages (e.g., Choctaw, Arabic, etc.); see Goldsmith (1990) and Kenstowicz (1994) for an overview and discussion.

A child that shows such a pattern will have long vowels and diphthongs in open syllables, but only short vowels in closed syllables. Morgan (see Table 5.6 in Chapter 5) showed such a pattern at 1;2:

| see | /siː/ | [siː] |
| beat | /biːt/ | [bit] |

Adult long vowels always surfaced as tense. However, they were long only in open syllables, and were shortened in closed syllables. Gwendolyn (Stemberger, 1992c) showed a similar pattern with the vowel [a]:

cow	/kaʊ/	[tʰaː]
cat	/kæt/	[tʰat]
Papa	/papa/	[pʰaːpa]

The vowel [a] was long in open syllables (whether it was word-final or not) but was short in closed syllables. Demuth and Fee (1995) state that children develop codas before they use vowel length contrastively, suggesting that this may be a common pattern; however, their data (and also, Fee's, 1996, data) appear to show that codas do not appear before children use vowel length *noncontrastively*.

The pattern shown for Gwendolyn does not derive from the constraint **Not-Complex(Rime)**. **NotComplex(Rime)** merely prevents the Rime node from dominating more than one element, thus permitting only a Nucleus node, and preventing a Coda node. Instead, it derives from a set of constraints:

Co-occurring(Rime→μ):   All segments within the rime must be moraic.
Binary(σ,μ):   A syllable may have at most two moras.
NotComplex(M):   A mora may link to only a single Root node.

Together, these constraints limit a rime to either one long segment (the vowel or a syllabic consonant) or to two short segments.

If an input form violates this constraint by having a long vowel in a closed syllable, it can be resolved in three ways. First, the long vowel can be shortened (as in Morgan's data above). Second, the coda consonant can be deleted. This appears to be uncommon, but see §6.1.10.1 (Gwendolyn and Jarmo) and §8.6 (Dylan). Bernhardt (1994c) recommends that short vowels be used when clinically targeting codas in CVC words; she suggests that children may show faster success with codas if short vowels are used (as in *slip* /slɪp/) than when long vowels are used (as in *sleep* /sliːp/), but there is no systematic study that proves that this is the case. Finally, a child might epenthesize a vowel when a coda follows a long vowel, so that the consonant can appear in the onset of the next syllable (as in *sleep* /sliːp/ [siːpə]); but no epenthesis would occur if the coda followed a short vowel (as in *slip* /slɪp/ [sɪp]). We suspect that these last two repair strategies are uncommon. However, since there are almost no data available concerning the first strategy (vowel shortening), we cannot even be certain how often children have difficulty with such sequences.

It is much clearer that sequences of a diphthong followed by a coda can be difficult. Stemberger (1992c) reports that Gwendolyn disallowed diphthongs in closed syllables until about 2;6. (See also Sean's data in Bernhardt, 1994d). With the diphthongs /oʊ/ and /aʊ/, the second portion was simply deleted in closed syllables, but was produced in open syllables:

cow	/kaʊ/	[tʰaʊ]
clown	/klaʊn/	[tʰan]
go	/goʊ/	[doʊ]
home	/hoʊm/	[hʌm]

There was only one variant with /oʊ/ and /aʊ/ in closed syllables; it was never the case that the coda consonant was deleted, or that the first portion of the diphthong deleted. However, the diphthongs /eɪ/, /aɪ/, and /oɪ/ could optionally surface with a long [iː] or with the coda deleted:

day	/deɪ/	[daɪ]
grape	/gɹeɪp/	[dap]~[diːp]~[daɪ]
dry	/dɹaɪ/	[daɪ]
bite	/baɪt/	[bat]~[biːt]~[baɪ]

There was a greater tendency for the high front glide in /aɪ/, /eɪ/, and /oɪ/ to survive, than for the high back glide in /oʊ/ and /aʊ/ to survive. Rounded vowels were in general difficult for this child (see §5.6.2.2). They were acquired later than similar unrounded vowels in almost every instance; **Survived(V-Labial)** was ranked low enough that other constraints often prevented [Labial] from surviving. It was more optimal to delete the [+round] second portion of /aʊ/ and /oʊ/, than to delete the coda.[14]

The variation between [bat] and [baɪ] for /baɪt/ shows that the front glide was not subject to this difficulty. It was equally optimal to retain the glide or the coda, and so the child varied between the two pronunciations. But it is the variant [biːt] that is most interesting here, because there is a long vowel followed by a coda. Stemberger (1992c) notes that the child had no problem producing length in closed syllables. This suggests that the constraints limiting the rime to two short elements were not very constraining at this period. They did prevent the predictable allophonic lengthening of low vowels in short syllables (*bat* [bat] rather than *[baːt]; cf. adult English [bæːt]). However, they did not cause underlyingly long vowels to shorten. These constraints thus were not responsible for the simplification of diphthongs before codas, or the deletion of codas after diphthongs.

It would appear that there was a constraint on the number of *segments* present. A rime like [iːt] has only two Root nodes, whereas [aɪt] has three. It is undesirable to have a constraint like ⊗**Binary(Rime,Root)**, limiting a rime to two segments. There are two reasonable possibilities. First, it could be that the child was treating the glide portion of the diphthong as a coda rather than as a part of a complex nucleus (due to a high ranking for **NotComplex(Nucleus)**). If so, then **NotComplex(Coda)** would prevent a rime in which there was both a diphthong and an additional consonant; in /baɪt/, the coda would then have to contain two segments (/ɪt/). Analyzing the glide portion as part of the coda would be entirely parallel to the analysis of glides before the vowel in English; in *wet* /wɛt/ and *twice* /twaɪs/, the /w/'s are viewed as part of the onset, not as part of the nucleus. Perhaps the child disallowed complex nuclei, and treated all glides as structurally equivalent to true consonants, placing them in onsets and in codas, never in the nucleus. Second, **NotTwice(σ-Margin)** might have prevented a sequence of two nonsyllabic segments. Such a constraint would not be violated in /biːt/, since the long vowel does not contain a nonsyllabic segment, but would be violated in /baɪt/. We are uncertain which of these alternatives is correct.

In summary, there are patterns in which the number of elements in the rime is limited. **Binary(σ,μ)** can limit a rime to a long vowel or diphthong, or a short vowel plus a single coda consonant; codas may not follow long vowels or diphthongs. Other constraints may prevent diphthongs in closed syllables, but allow long vowels in closed syllables. None of these constraints is a constraint on complexity per se.

---

[14] The labial segment was deleted here only because the system had the option of linking up the unrounded vowel; something had to be deleted, and that was the rounded vowel. When only a single rounded vowel was present, as in *boot* /buːt/, the system did not have the option of linking up some other vowel, and so the rounded vowel linked: [buːt]. This is a common phenomenon in OT: something is avoided only when there is a choice.

6.1.10.1. Complex Rimes and Coda Features

There have been at least two reports of data that seem to involve the complexity of the rime, but where only some coda consonants cause a problem. The interaction is challenging for our approach, and may bear on the issue of syllable appendices.

Stemberger (p.u.d.) observed a change in Gwendolyn's speech that at first appeared to involve lexical variability. When Gwendolyn began producing word-final voiced stops at 2;7, the change began abruptly. The child had always deleted word-final voiced stops; e.g., *bed* [baː], *rub* [ʋaː]. In the last hour before bedtime on 2;7.14, the child used only two words with target word-final voiced stops, but consistently used voiced stops, without devoicing. The next morning, final voiced stops were produced in all appropriate words: obligatorily in most words, but optionally in others, giving the impression of lexical idiosyncrasy. However, on examination, an effect of vowel length was found: short versus long/diphthongal (including postvocalic /ɹ/ or /l/, which always led to surface diphthongs at the time). The following table lists the number of word types that were variable or nonvariable, as a function of vowel length:

	Nonvariable	*Variable*
Short V	29	5
Long V	8	12

More than half of the words with long vowels were variable, for a period of about 25 days. There was some lexical variability, since some common words were not variable (*hide*, *ride*), while others with the same vowel were variable (*side*, *slide*). Most words with short vowels (85.3%) were not variable, with the following exceptions: words ending in /ɪɡ/[15] ([ɪd]), the minimally variable word *hug* (observed many times with the stop, and only once without), and the words *did* and *should*. The words *should* and *did* may have been variable because they are closed class lexical items; in §4.7.1.5, we suggested that closed class lexical items constitute a weak prosodic domain, and faithfulness is more often violated there. The major effect, however, was that voiced stops were consistently produced after short vowels, but inconsistently produced after long vowels and diphthongs. This difference between words with short vowels and words with long vowels is significant ($\chi^2(1)$ = 9.96, $p < .005$). In contrast, voiceless stops were not deleted, after either short or long vowels.[16]

Fikkert (1994) presents similar data from Jarmo, a Dutch-learning child. The child acquired obstruents in codas before sonorants. When nasals first began to

[15] These two words varied much longer than all other words except *egg* and *leg*; *leg* varied between [jeɪ] and [jeɪd] for 1 additional week; *pig* varied between [pʰɪd] and [pʰiː] for an additional 5 weeks; *egg* varied for 8 additional weeks; *big* varied for an additional 14 weeks. The fact that these laggards all ended with a velar in adult speech is interesting. Deletion of velars in a coda was an option that was not available for alveolars. Despite Velar Fronting, the child did not treat velars and alveolars in a fully comparable fashion.

[16] Except in a few idiosyncratic words ending in velar /k/, such as *make* and *take*.

appear in the coda (at 1;7.29), obstruents were still occasionally deleted, at equal rates after short vowels (12.5% of tokens) and after long vowels (10.9% of tokens). Sonorants were still deleted more often than obstruents, both after short vowels (52.6% of tokens) and after long vowels (83.5% of tokens). Deletion of sonorants was significantly more frequent after long vowels and diphthongs than after short vowels ($\chi^2(1) = 6.89$, $p < .01$).[17] The complexity of the vowel had no effect on the deletion of obstruents, but influenced the deletion of sonorants.

Fikkert's explanation of these facts relies on another pattern regarding vowel complexity that she found in the data. When Jarmo produced a coda, target long vowels were often shortened, whether the coda was an obstruent (15.5% of tokens) or a sonorant (57.1% of tokens); and target short vowels were often lengthened, whether the coda was an obstruent (22.2% of tokens) or a sonorant (11.1% of tokens). She noted that these interchanges were equally common before obstruents, but that shortening was more common than lengthening before sonorants. She suggested that the child was dealing with a restriction of two timing units on a rime containing a sonorant consonant. This most often led to the deletion of the sonorant consonant after a long vowel or diphthong, but occasionally led instead to the shortening of the vowel. However, there was no such restriction on rimes containing an obstruent. Further, this restriction on rimes has no known parallel in adult languages. Fikkert consequently went on to propose the following (p.141):

> Since vowel length errors before obstruents mainly occur in closed syllables, and involve both shortening and lengthening, we may conclude that vowel length is nondistinctive before obstruents; all vowels are monopositional in this position.

Thus, [iːt] and [ɪt] should be treated as /it/, with no contrastive vowel length; long vowels are long only phonetically, not phonologically. This proposal cannot be true. If there had been no phonological/lexical distinction between long and short vowels, then the adult contrast between long and short vowels should have been completely neutralized. Underlying long and short vowels should have been phonetically long in an equal proportion of tokens. However, vowel length was accurate most of the time before an obstruent: 77.8% of tokens for short vowels, 84.5% of tokens for long vowels. This difference (short vowels produced short; long vowels produced long) is significant ($\chi^2(1) = 37.37$, $p < .005$). Thus, the underlying complexity of the vowel was generally maintained. The child produced long vowels with two timing units, and short vowels with one timing unit. It is not the case that all rimes were restricted to two timing units. Rimes with obstruent codas could have three timing units, but rimes with sonorant codas could have only two timing units.

These data appear to be problematical for OT. A coda consonant with a certain feature might not be possible, or the syllable structure might prohibit a coda after a diphthong. But the constraints do not predict any interactions: the restriction on

---

[17] We report the statistics here to establish that the pattern is reliable, because Fikkert gives no statistics in her book.

syllable structure is unrelated to the restriction on features in the coda. There is no reason for a feature ([+voiced] for Gwendolyn, [+sonorant] for Jarmo) to be possible in a coda after a short vowel, but not after a long vowel.

Within a resource-based model, such interactions are expected. It is relatively difficult to have a coda after a long vowel. It is relatively difficult to have particular features in the coda. Separately, the relative difficulties might not have much effect. But if the difficulties are summed, the overall level of difficulty is too great, and the coda consonant is deleted. Put in connectionist terms, voiced stops in Gwendolyn's speech had a marginal level of activation that barely allowed the segments to be accessed. More activation was needed to access a coda after a long vowel than after a short vowel, due to inhibition between the coda consonant and the second part of the vowel. That inhibition was enough to lower the activation of the voiced stop below a critical threshold, and the consonant tended to be deleted. We have suggested at several points that the **Survived** constraints are ranked according to level of activation. We thus predict that **Survived** constraints should be ranked lower for coda consonants after a long vowel or diphthong than for coda consonants after a short vowel. Our borrowing of this connectionist principle allows us to predict and account for such data.

If this analysis is rejected, we can think of only one other analysis. It is possible that Gwendolyn and Jarmo allowed a maximum of two timing units in the rime. When consonants required an additional timing unit, it was possible to place the consonant in a word-final appendix:

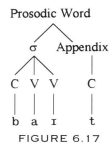

FIGURE 6.17

Goldsmith (1990) argued that appendices often prohibit nondefault features. For Gwendolyn, [+voiced] was prohibited in the appendix, except in a nasal consonant (where it was supported by **Co-occurring(+sonorant→+voiced)**). For Jarmo, [+sonorant] was prohibited in the appendix. For both children, the coda allowed a fuller set of features. Thus, after a short vowel, a voiced stop (Gwendolyn) or a nasal (Jarmo) could appear in the coda, and was consequently not deleted. When the vowel was long, there could be no coda, and a consonant that was prohibited in the appendix was deleted.

We are not happy with the concept of the appendix. We prefer to believe that all segments must be integrated into the syllable. However, within standard OT, these data seem to require a word-final appendix. The only alternative is to assume that the relative ranking of the **Survived** constraints is dependent on the amount of activation, and that activation levels are lower in coda consonants after long vowels than after short vowels. We prefer the activation-based explanation.

These data may also reflect other factors that were not initially noted. Upon reexamining Gwendolyn's data, we found an additional pattern. With respect to the vowels, the following was observed (where diphthongs are considered front if they end in a front glide /eɪ/, /aɪ/, or /ɔɪ/, because the glide is the portion of the vowel that is contiguous to the coda):

	Nonvariable	Variable
High front short V	1	3
High front long V	2	10
Other short V	28	2
Other long V	6	2

Almost all words with vowels that end in a high front position (81.3%) were variable; few other words were variable (10.5%). This difference is significant ($\chi^2(1)$ = 22.932, $p < .005$). What could lead to this? Almost all of the words ending in voiced stops ended in [d] (50/54 words), and all of the variable words ended in [d]. This suggests a dissimilatory effect, wherein a coronal consonant could not follow a coronal vowel: **NotTwice(Coronal)**. However, the effect was only on voiced stops, not on voiceless stops or nasals. We might need to assume additionally that stops were in an appendix, and that **NotTwice** was ranked higher than **Survived** in the appendix (but lower than **Survived** in the coda, where voiceless stops reside; such interactions between **Survived** and negative constraints are often observed in domains that differ in strength). An activation-based account would also work. A third analysis might also work: that dissimilation had a greater effect if both segments were [+voiced] (see §7.4.4.3). Thus, voiced stops were subject to dissimilation but nasals and voiceless stops were not. This last possibility cannot be ruled out. These data cannot be taken as strong evidence for the existence of the appendix.

Since Fikkert breaks down Jarmo's data only by vowel length, and not by vowel quality, we have no way of knowing whether similar patterns were in his data. Thus, his data may or may not constitute evidence for an appendix.

6.1.11. DIFFERENT POSITIONS IN WORD AND SYLLABLE

To this point, we have addressed issues of development within the three major parts of the syllable: onset, nucleus, and coda. What is known about the rates of development of the different parts of the syllable relative to each other? We have already addressed this to some extent, when we noted that codas tend to develop later than onsets and nuclei. But there are additional questions that can be raised.

One might ask to what extent onsets and nuclei are developmentally ahead of codas. Do complex nuclei (diphthongs) and complex onsets (initial consonant clusters) develop before codas develop? Bernhardt and Stoel-Gammon (1996) report that most normally developing children acquire codas before they develop complex onsets. A number of older children with phonological disorders have been reported to develop complex onsets before they develop codas (Bernhardt, 1990; Chin, 1996). Nothing general is known about the relative appearance of codas versus diphthongs.

A related issue concerns predictions about complexity, and whether it develops first in onsets, nuclei, or codas, but little is known about this for certain. We suspect that diphthongs develop before complex onsets and complex codas, because vowels are in general ahead of consonants in development. This was the case for Gwendolyn, Morgan, and Larissa (Stemberger, p.u.d.). Also, we have seen many papers with examples in which diphthongs were present but not consonant clusters. However, we are reluctant to hazard a guess regarding mastery points for complex onsets versus complex codas. We *suspect* that either may develop first, and that it is very much dependent on particular types of clusters; final [nt] clusters may often appear before initial [st] clusters, for example. We do not know whether the first consonant clusters are consistently in onsets or in codas, across children.

Finally, one may ask about the development of onsets and codas in different parts of the word. Do clusters in medial onsets appear at the same time as clusters in word-initial position? No information is available. Do medial codas appear at the same time as final codas? Here, we have reason to expect two different patterns.

6.1.11.1. Final Codas before Medial Codas

We might expect to find word-final codas in both monosyllabic and multisyllabic words. Such codas are governed by **Not(Coda)** alone (but see §6.2.4.1 on codas in unstressed syllables). Medial codas, in contrast, have additional constraints on them. To have a medial coda, there must also be a medial onset, because a single medial consonant tends to be an onset. (But see §6.1.13.) Thus, a medial coda tends to involve a consonant cluster, as in /ŋk/ in *donkey* /dɑŋki/ or /st/ in *sister* /sɪstɹ̩/. Medial codas may be subject to constraints on sequences far more than word-final codas are (§7.3.2). Medial codas may develop later than final codas. This is clearly sometimes the case. Gwendolyn, for example, went through a period where medial codas were not possible, even though final codas were common.

kiss	/kɪs/	[tʰɪs]	
sister	/sɪstɹ̩/	[sɪtoʊ]	*[sɪstoʊ]

There is no information available about the frequency of this pattern across children, however.

6.1.11.2. Medial Clusters before Initial or Final Clusters

Sometimes children can produce CVCCV(C) words, with a medial cluster, before they can produce CCV or VCC words. This is a common pattern in adult languages (e.g., in Arabic or Choctaw). If V, CV, VC, and CVC are the only possible syllable types, and they can be freely combined into two-syllable words, then VCCV, CVCCV, VCCVC, and CVCCVC words should arise. Thus, medial consonant clusters arise because one consonant is in a coda and the second consonant is in an onset, even when the prohibition against complex onsets and complex codas prevent word-initial and word-final consonant clusters. Such patterns are found. Morgan had medial [ŋk] in words like *donkey* when word-initial and word-final clusters were prohibited. However, we have no information about how general such a pattern might be.

6.1.11.3. Medial Codas before Final Codas

In some adult languages, word-final codas are prohibited, but word-medial clusters are possible (Prince, 1984). The general explanation is that coda consonants in such languages may not have an independent place of articulation (Itô, 1986). A final consonant, which must have an independent place feature, is thus impossible. However, a medial coda is possible if it shares place with a following onset consonant, as in word-forms such as [ampi] or [apːi]. To our knowledge, this pattern has never been reported for young children learning English. In every instance that we are aware of, children with medial clusters such as [mp] also have word-final codas in monosyllabic words like *up*. Bernhardt (p.u.d.) found no examples of this in her database of children with phonological disorders, and we know of no relevant reports in the literature.

6.1.12. ONSET-CODA ASYMMETRIES

Codas present special problems because, as noted in §4.7.1.4, it is often the case that fewer elements are allowed in codas. In this section, we examine constraints on the features that may appear in codas. There are two conflicting sets of constraints: constraints against nondefault features which have their strongest effects in codas, and constraints requiring onsets to be consonant-like and codas to be vowel-like.

When nondefault features are marginal in a child's system, negative constraints are ranked higher than the corresponding **Survived** and **LinkedUpwards** constraints. If the high-ranked negative constraint is **Not**, the nondefault feature may be entirely absent from the child's speech (§5.4). If other negative constraints are high-ranked, the nondefault feature is prohibited only in restricted environments. The coda is one of those restricted environments. It is often more optimal to have no coda than to have a nondefault feature in the coda. Children resolve violations either by deleting the offending feature (a minimal repair) or by deleting the whole segment or the Place node (a nonminimal repair).

As discussed in §4.7.1.3, the optimal syllable margin has a closed vocal tract, but the optimal rime has an open vocal tract:

Optimal syllable-margin	*Optimal rime*
-sonorant	+sonorant
+consonantal	-consonantal
-continuant	+continuant
C-Place	no C-Place
no V-Place	V-Place
	Dorsal
	-high
	+low

There should be asymmetries between onsets and codas. Onset consonants should optimally have consonant-like manner features. However, underlying non-default features may be tolerated in onsets, if faithfulness constraints are ranked high in onsets. Coda consonants, in contrast, are pulled in two different directions. On the one hand, they should have consonant-like (default) manner features just like onsets. Further, since faithfulness constraints are low-ranked in codas, it is often the case that nondefault features are not tolerated in codas. On the other hand, codas should be as vowel-like as possible, and contain features such as [+sonorant] and [+continuant] that are nondefault consonant features. We expect codas sometimes to show the same patterns as onsets, sometimes to allow only a subset of the segments allowed in onsets, and sometimes to show preferences for vowel-like manner and place features. All of these predictions are borne out for phonological development.

6.1.12.1. Prohibiting Nondefault Features in Codas

Fewer nondefault features (and thus fewer consonant phonemes) are allowed in codas than in onsets. There is one consonant with no nondefault features: /t/. As a result, we predict that [t] should be a possible coda, provided that codas are allowed at all.[18] Stoel-Gammon (1985) reports that /t/ was the first coda consonant to appear in the speech of more than half of the (34) children in her study.

In adult English, almost all consonant features appear in codas, and children attempt such words eventually. Recall that the nondefault consonant features are (in adult English and for most children):

[+voiced]   (voiced obstruents)
[+continuant] (fricatives)
[+sonorant]   (nasals and liquids)
[+nasal]   (nasals)
[Labial]   (bilabials and labiodentals)
[Dorsal]   (velars)

[18] If we assume underspecification of [Coronal], a second pattern is also possible. If the constraints prevent the insertion of default features, then [t] is not a possible output, even though [p] and [k] occur. Bernhardt (p.u.d.) followed up Sean (*S4*) from her 1990 study until he was 12 years of age. [Coronal] was marginal in codas, being found only in [n] and [t]. [Labial] and [Dorsal] were allowed in a full range of segments.

[-anterior]   (palatoalveolars, including affricates)
[+distributed] (interdentals)

What happens when one of these features is specified for a word-final consonant? There are several possibilities. We caution that little is known about how frequent the different options are across children; studies of large numbers of children have tended to report only whether a sound was mastered, not what happened to it before it was mastered. We have intuitions about commonness, but it would be desirable to have empirical confirmation of the intuitions.

The mechanism that underlies the restrictions on nondefault features in codas is unclear. In theory, the restrictions could be specific to codas, such as

NotCo-occurring(Coda, + voiced):   Coda consonants may not be voiced.

As discussed in §4.7.1.3, this constraint is phonetically grounded in the interaction of speech perception and articulation. Thus, this particular constraint is plausible. However, we do not believe that such specific constraints are plausible for most nondefault features. We know of no articulatory or perceptual reason why fricatives would be more difficult in codas than in onsets. Positing constraints against the occurrence of [+continuant] in a coda seems difficult to justify (and is difficult for empirical reasons; see §6.1.12.2.2).

Restrictions on features in codas probably derive from the fact that codas are a weak prosodic position. Faithfulness constraints are ranked lower for codas than for onsets:

$$\text{Survived}_{\text{Onset}}(+\text{voiced}) \quad ||| \quad \text{Not}(+\text{voiced}) \quad ||| \quad \text{Survived}_{\text{Coda}}(+\text{voiced})$$

If a negative constraint is ranked lower than faithfulness for onsets but higher than faithfulness for codas, the feature is possible in an onset but not in a coda. No special constraint is needed to prevent a nondefault feature from occurring in a coda.

Note that default features should not be affected in the same way. Default features are unaffected by survival: they occur because some feature must be present, and it rarely makes a difference whether default features are underlying or inserted. Since **Survived** constraints are irrelevant to default features, the lower ranking of **Survived** in codas is irrelevant. Thus, default features tend to be possible in codas, to the same degree that they are possible in onsets.

Additionally, default manner features are supported by **Co-occurring(σ-Margin)** constraints. If one of these constraints is ranked above faithfulness for nondefault features in coda consonants, the nondefault feature cannot be included in the coda.

If a given nondefault feature is impossible in a coda, it can be dealt with in three ways.

Pattern 1: The nondefault feature may be deleted, and a default feature may be inserted (a minimal repair).

Pattern 2:   Some other feature may be changed, so that the nondefault feature becomes redundant; the nondefault feature is supported by another feature (via **Co-occurring**), enough to allow it to survive.

Pattern 3:   An element higher than the feature may be deleted (a nonminimal repair).

Pattern 4:   The offending element can be made part of an onset (a nonminimal repair).

6.1.12.1.1. Minimal Repair I: Deletion of Features

The most common resolution is for the offending nondefault feature to be deleted in the coda. Recall that deletion of nondefault features usually leads to the insertion of default features; **LinkedDownwards** constraints require a feature to be present, and the feature corresponding to the lowest-ranked **Not** constraint is inserted. The following "processes" arise through the deletion of the nondefault feature, followed by the filling in of the default feature:

[+voiced]	Final Devoicing
[+continuant]	Stopping (of fricatives)
[+nasal]	Stopping (of nasals)
[Labial]	Labial Backing (labial becomes alveolar)
[Dorsal]	Velar Fronting (velar becomes alveolar)
[-anterior]	Fronting or Depalatalization (palatoalveolar becomes alveolar)
[+distributed]	Backing (interdental becomes alveolar)

Morgan (Stemberger, 1992a) provided typical examples of this type of repair strategy. At 1;10, neither [+voiced] nor [+continuant] was allowed within a coda (and [Labial] was often impossible, but due to **NoSequence** constraints, not to syllable structure; see §7.4.1.3). The child showed Devoicing and Stopping:

buzz	/bʌz/	[bʌt]
give	/gɪv/	[dɪt]
rub	/ɹʌb/	[wʌp]

6.1.12.1.2. Minimal Repair II: Making the Feature Redundant

A less commonly observed way to preserve the offending feature is to make it redundant. Some features, such as [+voiced], are allowed in codas as long as they are redundant because they are required by other nondefault features in the segment. The high ranking of **Co-occurring(+ sonorant→ + voiced)** leads to nasals and liquids being voiced even when they are in codas. [+voiced] in an obstruent can survive if features are introduced to make the segment a sonorant. A stop could become a (full or partial) nasal:

Clark and Bowerman, 1986:

bed	/bɛd/	[bɛn]	big	/bɪg/	[bɪŋ]

Fey and Gandour, 1982:

bed   /bɛd/   [bɛdⁿ]   big   /bɪg/   [bɪgⁿ]

Clark and Bowerman, 1986:

bed   /bɛd/   [bɛnt]   big   /bɪg/   [bɪŋk]

These researchers make it clear that voiceless stops surfaced faithfully as voiceless stops; this was a problem with voiced stops only. If the stop does not become a full nasal, the partial nasality of a postnasalized stop is sufficient to facilitate voicing; Maddieson (1984) notes that prenasalized and postnasalized stops in adult languages are generally voiced. Alternatively, [+voiced] can be flopped out of the stop (which becomes voiceless) and a nasal segment can be inserted to take the feature.

6.1.12.1.3. Nonminimal Repair I: Deletion

The feature violation can be repaired in a nonminimal fashion by deleting at a higher level than the feature itself. There are several variations on this theme, depending on what is deleted.

Deletion of Coda Consonant.   An uncommon way to avoid a nondefault feature in a coda is to delete the entire segment containing the nondefault feature. Prince and Smolensky (1993) note this in (adult) Lardil. Gwendolyn (Stemberger, 1988a) used deletion to resolve impossible coda features. The system was as follows. There are no changes other than those given; thus, when we say that at 2;3 "all other segments are deleted," this generalization excludes all segments that were pronounced at 1;10; and so on for later points in development.

1;10: [t] appeared in codas.
       [p] appeared after a lag of (ca.) 10 days.
       /k/ underwent Velar Fronting to [t].
       /ɹ/ and /l/ became the second part of a diphthong.
       All other segments were deleted.
2;3:   [n] appeared.
       [m] appeared after a lag of 4 days.
       /ŋ/ underwent Velar Fronting to [n].
       All other segments were deleted.
2;7:   [d] appeared.
       [b] appeared at the same time.
       /g/ underwent Velar Fronting to [d].
       All other segments were deleted.
2;10: [s] appeared (after undergoing Stopping for two weeks).
       All other segments were deleted.
2;11: [f] appeared.
       [v] appeared (after undergoing Gliding for a few days).
       [z] appeared (after undergoing Gliding for a few days).

In general, the child simply deleted the segments that contained impossible coda features (though there was sometimes a short period of substitution just prior to correct production).

The deletion of the entire segment that contains the impossible feature is a nonminimal repair, since deleting just the offending feature would have resolved the constraint violation. We suspect that full deletion of the segment containing the impossible feature(s) is a minority option across children, and that most children use minimal repairs. In our system, nonminimal repairs arise when the nondefault features must survive and link up in the output: all the features in the segment must be linked up, and a Root node must be present. However, the negative constraint that prevents the nondefault features from being in a coda are strong enough to prevent the Root node from linking to a syllable node. The consonant remains floating and hence is not overtly pronounced:

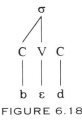

FIGURE 6.18

This is one of the few instances where we need to assume that an element is present in the output but floating.

Deletion of Place (Glottal Replacement).   A second option for dealing with nondefault place features is to delete the Place node. This leads to a glottal: [ʔ] or [h]. For example, if [Labial] is not allowed in a coda, /f/ can be realized as [h] and /p/ can be realized as [ʔ]. This results from deleting the Place node (due to ranking **Not(Coronal)** higher than **Survived(Place)**): it is more optimal to delete the underlying Place node than to insert a default [Coronal] feature to replace the deleted nondefault place feature. If manner is preserved, (fricatives as [h], stops as [ʔ]), the deletion may be at this level. Bernhardt (1994b) reports a developmental progression for coda consonants in the speech of some children with phonological disorders: (a) deletion (an extreme nonminimal repair), (b) reduction to [ʔ] (survival of Root but not of Place; a less extreme nonminimal repair), and (c) reduction to default coronal place of articulation (a nonminimal repair). Morgan (p.u.d.) showed a similar progression (1;0–1;9).

However, glottal replacement can also reflect a nonminimal repair in which the Root node is deleted. If [ʔ] is used to replace many consonants, regardless of manner, it is possible that the underlying Root node has been deleted, but not the consonant's timing unit. Since the timing unit must be linked downwards to a Root node, a Root node can be inserted and filled with default features; this default consonant is often a glottal, since it is not necessary to insert a Place node. Glottals do not violate **NotCo-occurring(Rime,C-Place)** (see §4.5.1.2, and the next sub-section of this chapter); if that constraint is high-ranked, [ʔ] is an optimal conso-nant to insert in a coda.

Deletion of C-Place (Gliding).   Another possible output when C-Place is de-leted from a coda consonant is V-Place (through insertion). This would convert any final consonant into a glide. A coronal consonant would become a front glide [ɪ], while a labial or velar consonant would become a back glide [ʊ]. Hypothetical data would be:

pot	/pɑt/	?[paɪ]
off	/ɑf/	?[ʔaʊ]

We know of no reports of this for child phonology, but note that it is in theory possible. The only gliding that is common is of liquids. Since English /l/ is velar-ized [ɫ] in codas, it already has V-Place. The gliding of /l/ is not an example of this sort of repair. Since /ɹ/ is a glide, it already has V-Place, and is also not an example of this.

6.1.12.1.4. Nonminimal Repair II: Epenthesis and Syllable Division

An alternative way to deal with a feature that is impossible in a coda is to shift the consonant into an onset, where the feature is possible. This can be achieved via the insertion of a vowel, but can also be achieved by making use of an existing vowel.

Epenthesis.   One option would be to create a new syllable for the offending segment. If a vowel is epenthesized after this consonant, the consonant can be in the onset of the new syllable, where its features might be possible. Carolyn (Edwards & Bernhardt, 1973a) showed this type of pattern some of the time for word-final nasals and always for word-final voiced stops.

thumb	/θʌm/	[ˈʃɑnʊʔ]
comb	/koʊm/	[kˣɔmə]
pig	/pɪg/	[pʰɛɪˈdˀ]
pail	/peɪl/	[pʰɛʊdə]
chair	/tʃɛɹ/	[tʰœɔdʊ]

Producing voiced segments, especially stops, was apparently difficult in coda, and thus, a vowel was epenthesized to rescue [+voiced]. Coda was evidently a weak position for her. She also heavily aspirated voiceless stops (to the point where voiceless vowels were sometimes perceived), and produced nasal snorts for sibi-lants in word-final position (§5.5.3.4). Thus, to rescue codas generally, the final consonant was often produced with extra effort of some kind (**WordFinal-Massiveness** saving codas?).

kick	/kɪk/	[kʰɑtʰ]
book	/bʊk/	[bʌtʰˀ]
jamas	/dʒæməz/	[tʰɑ.ə.mʊN̥]

Alternatively, the impossible consonant might trigger reduplication. Morgan showed such a pattern in her early words (1;1 – 1;3). Word-final voiceless stops were present in codas on first attempt, but other word-final consonants, including /l/, triggered reduplication:

up	/ʌp/	[ʔapʰ]
out	/aʊt/	[ʔatʰ]
bird	/bɹ̩d/	[baba]
ball	/bɑl/	[baba]

After 1;8, reduplication to rescue unsyllabifiable word-final consonants is rare according to studies by Schwartz et al. (1980), Fee and Ingram (1982) and Ferguson (1983). However, those studies do not report whether children were able to produce codas in some words, if the right set of features was present. Epenthesis may be uncommon as a way to rescue impossible features in a coda, but we know of no study that specifically addresses this issue.

Syllable Division.   Rather than creating a new syllable for the segment with the offending feature, the segment can be moved into a preexisting following syllable. This is only possible when the next word starts with a vowel. Stemberger (1988a) reports that Gwendolyn did this sporadically with final voiced stops:

head	/hɛd/	[haː]
(Put your) head over (here).		[.haː.doʊ.]

The final /d/ in *head* was normally deleted at this time (2;6), but not when the next word started with a vowel. Normally, the domain of syllabification is the word, but resyllabification across word boundaries occurred if it would allow a consonant to survive. It is unknown how common this phenomenon is across children.

6.1.12.2. Tolerating or Requiring Nondefaults in Codas

In child phonology, (certain) nondefault features tend to be tolerated or even required in codas. Codas sometimes allow fricatives when fricatives are as yet impossible in onsets. Codas can be restricted to fricatives, or to nasals. Even when voiceless stops are possible in codas (the dominant pattern), there can be a preference for fricatives and nasals in codas (seen in the way that clusters are reduced, or through assimilations). Prince and Smolensky (1993) note that many adult languages show a preference for sonorants in codas. There are languages that allow only liquids in codas, and others that allow liquids and nasals but exclude obstruents. The child language data are somewhat different, in that codas also show a preference for fricatives.

Similarly, some sonorant consonants appear quite early in codas. Stoel-Gammon (1985) reports that both nasals and /ɹ/ are among the earliest consonants to appear in codas in English-learning children. While some children develop voiceless stops first in codas, others develop nasals first. Even when voiceless stops are first in codas, nasals are usually next, before fricatives or voiced stops (as with Gwendolyn's data above in §6.1.12.1.3).

As discussed in §4.7.1.3 and above, constraints on rimes lead to a vocal tract that is as wide-open (and hence vowel-like) as possible. However, since the effects are on individual features, codas need not be very vowel-like: fricatives are like vowels in being [+continuant], but differ on most other features.

In some instances, these constraints can lead to a feature being possible only in a coda. There are two features for which this has been commonly noted for child phonology: [+continuant], and [C-Dorsal]. First, fricatives often appear first in codas (Ferguson, 1975; Farwell, 1977; M. Edwards, 1979, 1996; Stoel-Gammon & Cooper, 1984; Leonard & MacGregor, 1991; Fikkert, 1994; Dinnsen, 1996; Lohuis-Weber & Zonneveld, 1997). In her sample of 34 children, Stoel-Gammon (1985) noted that this was a common pattern, but that fricatives often appeared first in onsets also (and see §6.1.12.1.3.: Gwendolyn). Children who do produce fricatives first in codas may even replace stops with fricatives in codas. Second, velars often appear first in codas (Stoel-Gammon, 1985, 1996), although Stoel-Gammon also reports that some children produce velars first in onsets. When children do produce velars first in codas, it can often be quite noticeable. Morgan (Stemberger, p.u.d.) first showed velars in codas at 1;5, but did not produce velars in (word-initial) onsets until 2;2, seven months later. This pattern of development is so pervasive with velars that speech-language pathologists often introduce velars in coda position when trying to establish velar consonants in the speech of an older child with phonological disorders.

6.1.12.2.1. Velars in Codas

Trigo (1988) observed that codas have an affinity for velar consonants in adult languages also. For example, in many adult languages (including English), the velar nasal [ŋ] is restricted to codas:

*[ŋɑg] versus [gɑŋ]

Further, in many languages, when nasals are restricted to a single place of articulation in codas, that place of articulation is often velar. This is true of many dialects of Spanish and Chinese, and is a common historical change. In Seri (Marlett, 1981), the default place of articulation for nasals can optionally be replaced with velar, but only in codas. The lateral /l/ also often has allophones that reflect the affinity of coda consonants for [Dorsal]. In English and Classical Latin, /l/ within a coda is always velarized "dark" [ɫ], but is often nonvelarized "light" [l] in onsets: *pill* [pʰɪɫ] versus *lip* [lɪp] (e.g., Schein & Steriade, 1986; Ladefoged, 1993). Trigo proposed that [Dorsal] is the default place feature in codas, but Paradis and Prunet (1994) argue against this.

Codas often prefer velar consonants because of the constraint **Co-occurring (Rime→Dorsal)**. We have posited this constraint as part of the general optimal nature of an open vocal tract in rimes; in order to have the widest possible vocal tract, there must be a dorsal gesture, where the back of the tongue is moved downwards in order to widen out the vocal tract. However, [Dorsal] does not become the default in codas. Velar consonants tend to develop later than coronals (and usually later than labials) even in codas (Stoel-Gammon, 1985), because of the nondefault nature of the feature [Dorsal].

However, the presence of this **Co-occurring** constraint does give [Dorsal] an advantage in codas, leading to a situation in which velar consonants can occur in codas but not in onsets. It is not so much that velars are more optimal in codas as that no particular constraint helps velars in onsets. In order for the feature [Dorsal] to be produced, there must be a positive constraint requiring [Dorsal] in the output that is ranked higher than **Not(Dorsal)**. If that positive constraint is **Survived (Dorsal)**, then velars are possible in all positions in the word. However, velar consonants are in general impossible given the following ranking:

Not(Dorsal) ||| **Survived(Dorsal)**

A velar consonant can then surface only if some other positive constraint requires [Dorsal] in the output (see Table 6.2):

TABLE 6.2

/pɪk/	pɪk	pɪt
Co-occurring(Rime→Dorsal)		*!
Not(Dorsal)	*	
LinkedUpwards(Dorsal) Survived(Dorsal)		*

Velar Fronting is ruled out for the final velar, because that would violate **Co-occurring(Rime→Dorsal)**. However, the velar cannot surface in an onset (see Table 6.3):

TABLE 6.3

/kaʊ/	kʰaʊ	tʰaʊ
Co-occurring(Rime→Dorsal)		
Not(Dorsal)	*!	
LinkedUpwards(Dorsal) Survived(Dorsal)		*

Because no special constraint requires [Dorsal] to be in an onset, [Dorsal] is impossible in onsets, and Velar Fronting occurs.

The constraint rankings presented here cause some difficulties for underspecification. The high ranking of **Co-occurring(Rime→Dorsal)** is violated whenever labials or alveolars appear in the coda, and we need to prevent labials and alveolars from becoming velars. For labials, ranking **Survived(Labial)** high will accomplish this. For coronals, underspecification causes a problem. Since [Coronal] is not present underlyingly, how do we prevent [Dorsal] from being inserted, so that /t, d, n/ do not become [k, g, ŋ]? We could hold that [Coronal] is specified underlyingly for coda consonants; thus, **Survived(Coronal)** could prevent [Dorsal] from being inserted. However, Morgan (Stemberger, 1992a) showed a pattern of data that still could not be accounted for:

flip	/flɪp/	[fɪtʰ]
pot	/pɑt/	[pʰatʰ]
talk	/tɑk/	[tʰakʰ]

Velars survived only in codas. Alveolars did not become [Dorsal] in codas. Labials often did not survive in codas, but they did not become [Dorsal]; they became [Coronal]. The backing of labials to [Coronal] implies that [Coronal] was the default and was actively inserted in codas when it was not underlying. These data suggest that underlying [Dorsal] could survive, but that there was no tendency for [Dorsal] to be inserted. In order to derive that pattern, it would be useful to have the constraint **Lexical(Dorsal)**: [Dorsal] may not be inserted. In §4.4.2 we noted that **Not** does the same job that **Lexical** does, plus additional functions. This is the one instance we know of (in child or adult phonology) in which **Lexical** is independently useful. The rankings needed here are the same as given above, with **Lexical(Dorsal)** also ranked high.

It should be noted that there is also an activation-based account of why [Coronal] is still inserted in codas. Suppose that the [Dorsal] element requires 1.0 units of activation in order to be present in the output. If underlying [Dorsal] supplies the output element with (an insufficient) 0.5 units of activation, there is deletion of [Dorsal] in the output. If **Co-occurring(Rime→Dorsal)** supplies the output [Dorsal] element with 0.5 units of activation, this also is insufficient, and [Dorsal] cannot be inserted in the output (to replace coronal consonants). However, when the activation from **Co-occurring** sums with the activation supplied by underlying [Dorsal], the output [Dorsal] element reaches 1.0 units of activation; this is sufficient, and [Dorsal] is present in the output. If our constraints were implemented in this fashion, the **Co-occurring** constraints would not present any difficulty in handling the patterns under discussion.

Note also that we do not *require* this interaction between velars and syllable structure to be present. If **Co-occurring(Rime→Dorsal)** is low-ranked, it provides no help to [Dorsal] and is irrelevant. If that is the case, then there are two other patterns that could arise in the acquisition of velar consonants. First, velars could be acquired simultaneously in onsets and codas; this would occur if the only two relevant constraints were **Survived(Dorsal)** and **Not(Dorsal)**. As soon as **Survived(Dorsal)** is ranked higher than **Not(Dorsal)**, velars appear in all positions in the word and syllable. Second, velars could appear first just in onsets, and undergo Velar Fronting in codas. This would be the case if the nondefault status of [Dorsal] prevented it from appearing in codas (as discussed in §6.1.12.1). Thus, we predict three possible patterns in the acquisition of velar consonants. There are no data revealing which is the most common pattern across children. We suspect that velars generally appear in codas before they appear in onsets (unless the child allows no codas at all), but this is speculative at the present time.

6.1.12.2.2. Fricatives in Codas

Fricatives often appear first in codas for a similar reason. Children often have difficulty with fricatives, converting them into stops (due to high ranking for the constraints **NotCo-occurring(-sonorant, + continuant)** and **Co-occurring (σ-Margin⟶-continuant)**). There is no constraint that can provide extra help to [+continuant] in onsets, but in codas there is **Co-occurring(Rime⟶ + continuant)**, grounded in the fact that vowels must be made with an open vocal tract. The extra help from this constraint can lead to the presence of fricatives in codas but not in onsets. If this **Co-occurring** constraint is low-ranked, however, fricatives might appear in onsets before they appear in codas (see §6.1.12.1.1 and §6.1.12.1.3) or simultaneously in onsets and codas. All three patterns have been observed in child phonological development, and we do not have good information about which pattern is more common across children.

Some children develop fricatives in codas before oral stops are allowed in codas (Stoel-Gammon, 1985). Dinnsen (1996) proposed that some children treat [+continuant] as the default manner feature for obstruents in codas (arguing that [+continuant] should be underspecified in codas in underlying representations). We prefer to say that [-continuant] is the default feature: it reflects the lowest-ranked **Not** constraint (irrespective of position in the syllable). However, if **Co-occurring(Rime⟶ + continuant)** is ranked higher than **Not(+ continuant)**, the constraint imposes a requirement on rimes that in effect makes [+continuant] the default feature in rimes, in that it will be inserted, rather than [-continuant].

A preference for fricatives in codas has commonly been reported in the speech-language pathology literature. Leonard and Brown (1984) report on a child with only two coda consonants: [p] and [s]. The [s] was the general default, and was even inserted if the adult pronunciation ended in a vowel; note that [s] has the default place feature [Coronal]. The [s] was an optimal coda because of **Co-occurring(Rime⟶ + continuant)**. However, [p] was tolerated in codas because of a high ranking for **Survived(Labial)** and **LinkedUpwards(Labial)**. No other labial consonants appeared in codas because of **NotCo-occurring(Labial, + continuant)** and **NotCo-occurring(Labial, + nasal)**; the nondefault place feature [Labial] could not co-occur with nondefault manner or voicing features (see §5.5.4). Leonard and MacGregor (1991) report on a child showing metathesis of fricatives from onset to coda, in order to have the fricative in the most optimal position in the syllable. (See also Jeremy in §7.4.3.2 and §8.4):

| fine | /faɪn/ | [aɪnf] |
| zoo | /zuː/ | [uːz] |

The affinity of fricatives for codas often is observable in a more subtle fashion. Consider the way that the cluster /st/ was reduced to a single consonant by Gwendolyn at 2;11 (Stemberger, p.u.d.):

/st/	initial:	[tʰ]	stop	/stɑp/	[tʰɑp]
			stand	/stænd/	[tʰiːn]
	medial:	[t]	sister	/sɪstɹ̩/	[sɪtoʊ]
			mustard	/mʌstɹ̩d/	[mʌtoʊd]
	final:	[s]	twist	/twɪst/	[tʰɪs]
			first	/fɹ̩st/	[foʊs]

In initial and medial position, in which we would expect a single consonant to be an onset, the cluster was reduced to a stop; this is a more optimal onset than a fricative, because it has a more closed vocal tract. In final position, where the single consonant is unarguably a coda, the cluster was reduced to a fricative, because that is a more optimal rime consonant. Of course, this is only one possible pattern; there is a conflict between constraints on nondefault features in codas and this rime co-occurrence constraint. If those two constraints are ranked so that it is more optimal to avoid nondefault features in codas, then /st/ will be reduced to [t] everywhere. Morgan (Stemberger, p.u.d.) showed this second pattern, even after fricatives first appeared in codas:

kiss	/kɪs/	[tʰɪs]				
stop	/stɑp/	[tʰɑp]	*and*	fast	/fæst/	[fætʰ]

No information is available concerning which of these patterns is more common across children.

6.1.12.2.3. Nasals in Codas

Nasal consonants, as sonorants, also show an affinity for codas. However, unlike fricatives and velars, nasals are rarely restricted to codas and absent from onsets. Nasals are acquired early in onsets (Stoel-Gammon, 1985), usually in the first few words, before there are any codas. However, children may allow nasals as their only coda consonants (Stoel-Gammon, 1985), due to a general preference for sonorant consonants in codas: **Co-occurring(Rime→ + sonorant)**; see the next section, on liquids. Nasals also show their affinity for codas in a more subtle way. It is not uncommon for nasals to develop as the second manner of articulation in codas, after oral stops (Stoel-Gammon, 1985; and see §6.1.12.1.3: Gwendolyn), and well before fricatives and affricates.

The treatment of nasal-stop clusters (which appear only medially and finally in adult English) may also reflect the affinity of nasals for codas.[19] Braine (1976)

---

[19] This will be addressed further in Chapter 7, in terms of sequence constraints.

noted that final /nd/ is most often reduced to [n] (as in Gwendolyn's data, Stemberger, p.u.d.):

| hand | /hænd/ | [hiːn] |
| find | /faɪnd/ | [faɪn] |

The cluster may reduce to [n] because nasals make a better coda than a voiced stop. Braine also noted that final /nt/, /mp/, and /ŋk/ generally reduce to the voiceless stop (again using Gwendolyn's data):

| hunt | /hʌnt/ | [hʌt] |
| ramp | /ɹæmp/ | [βiːp] |

Braine proposes that this might have a perceptual component, because the nasal is so short before the voiceless stop that the child chooses to delete it (and Macken, 1979, goes further in suggesting that the child might not even perceive the nasal). However, children often develop voiceless stops in codas before they develop nasals, because voiceless stops have only default manner and voicing features. The reduction of /nt/ to [t] may reflect the optimality of having only default features in the coda, while the reduction of /nd/ to [n] may reflect the preference for sonorants in codas and the prohibition against voiced obstruents in codas. Even if /t/, /n/, and /d/ are all possible in codas, these interactions between segments and syllable structure can influence how clusters are reduced. Perceptual factors are not needed to account for reduction such as this (though it is possible that perceptual factors may also be relevant). Of course, if **Co-occurring(Rime→ + sonorant)** is ranked even higher, it might be more optimal to reduce /nt/ to [n] (as reported in Bleile, 1987), because a nasal is an even more optimal coda than a consonant with only default features.

In medial position, nasal clusters are often reduced to a single long consonant, and the same preferences are probably present (though there is less information available concerning this). Consider the following data from Morgan:

number	/nʌmbɹ/	[nʌmːɤ]
window	/wɪndoʊ/	[ʊɪnːɤ]
finger	/fɪŋgɹ/	[fɪnːɤ]
pumper	/pʌmpɹ/	[pʰʌpːɤ]
donkey	/dɑŋki/	[dɑkːi]

Since the first half of the long consonant is in the coda, the clusters are reduced so as to prefer a nasal over a voiced stop, but to prefer a voiceless stop over a nasal.

Sometimes these clusters are reduced to a single short consonant, which might be in an onset and therefore *not* preferentially a nasal. Our impression is that /mp/, /nt/, and /ŋk/ are usually reduced to the voiceless stop (e.g., *donkey* [daki]), though they can be reduced to the nasal (Elsen, 1991); but that /mb/, /nd/, and /ŋg/ can be reduced either to the stop or the nasal (e.g., *finger* as [fɪŋo] or [fɪgo]). We are unsure which is more frequent. If the single consonant is in the onset, we would expect the voiced stop to be more optimal than the nasal. This accounts for the reduction of /mp/, etc., to the voiceless stop, but not for the reduction of /mb/, etc., to the nasal; it may be that the medial consonant is a coda in some instances (see §6.1.13).

Stemberger (1988a) reports an instance of assimilation that may reflect this affinity of nasals for coda position. In Gwendolyn's speech, only oral stops were allowed in codas until late 2;3, when nasals first appeared. At that point, a nasalization assimilation process appeared for the first time, in which [+nasal] optionally spread from an onset nasal onto a coda oral stop, even across word boundaries:

help me	/hɛlp miː/	[hʌm miː]
want more	/wʌnt mɔɹ/	[ʊʌn moʊ]
oatmeal	/oʊtmiːl/	[ʔʌnmiː]

As soon as the child's system was altered to allow [+nasal] in codas at all, [+nasal] spread onto the coda from a following consonant. This probably reflects the affinity of codas for sonorant consonants. There is no information on the frequency of such assimilations across children.

6.1.12.2.4. Liquids in Codas

We also predict that liquids should show an affinity for codas. There are few data bearing on this. Stoel-Gammon (1985) reports that the English /ɹ/ tends to be acquired in coda position early, long before it is acquired in onsets. However, the English /ɹ/ is actually a glide. The only liquid in English is /l/, and even it has a nonapical variant in codas (especially before noncoronal consonants in words such as *milk*); we suspect this (adult) nonapical allophone may actually be a glide. Lleó et al. (1996) report that /l/ is acquired early in codas in German (*Ball* [bal]), where the adult target is always light (nonvelarized) [l]. We suspect that the velarization of the /l/ in codas in English and the tendency for /l/ to be nonapical make it unlikely that /l/ will be acquired early in codas in English. However, the co-occurrence constraints make the light /l/ of other languages a reasonable candidate for early acquisition. Of course, both /ɹ/ and /l/ are sometimes acquired first in onsets, since any consonant with nondefault features may be acquired late in codas.

Onset-coda asymmetries are not uncommon in child phonology. They often reflect an affinity of vowel-like features (reflecting an open vocal tract) for rimes, so that nondefault features are more optimal in coda consonants. In more extreme instances, velars and fricatives are acquired in codas before they are acquired in onsets. However, the affinity is often observable in a more subtle form, with clusters being reduced to the fricative or sonorant in codas (but not in onsets), or with fricatives or nasals being created in codas through assimilation.

6.1.12.3. ?Prohibiting Features in Onsets?

Codas are usually the weak prosodic position in the syllable; consequently, there are greater constraints on features in codas than in onsets. Rime co-occurrence

constraints can promote certain features in codas (such as [Dorsal] or [+continu-
ant]), but onset consonants generally show a richer abundance of features. In rare
instances, a child has more difficulty producing features in onsets than in codas;
default features appear in place of nondefaults. We are not sure how often this
occurs in typical development, but it is infrequent in disordered development.
Among the 35 children followed in the nonlinear intervention studies (Bernhardt,
p.u.d.), only two children had pervasive word-initial defaults: John used [k] or [h],
and Dan used [h] or [ʔ]. For Dan, the glottals appeared (randomly) for all initial
consonants (with occasional productions of other sonorants: [m], [n] or [w]).
However, codas allowed all voiceless stops, [d], the fricatives [s] and [ʃ], and the
affricate [ʦ]. For John, there was a breakdown according to sonority: [h] appeared
for other glides and /l/, and [k] appeared for coronal and velar stops, and for all
fricatives. (Labials and nasals were exempt.) However, in medial and final positions, all consonants but the palatoalveolars and /v/ were established (and there
was some use even of those).

It appears that some children may have severe restrictions on features in onsets,
but allow a wide variety of features (both defaults and nondefaults) in codas and
intervocalically. For these children, we suggest that word-initial position and onset
position are not strong prosodic positions, as they are for most children and adults.
They constitute the weakest domains in the word, and consequently there are few
features allowable in initial position.

It is more common for individual features to be impossible in onsets. In
some instances, the impossible features are filled in via assimilation to the following vowel. Initial consonants might become fricatives, or sonorant, or voiced
(§6.2.5.3.1 and §7.3.4).

6.1.12.4. ?Context-Sensitive Underspecification?

Dinnsen (1996) has discussed some of the consequences of onset-coda asymmetries for feature specification. He especially addresses the fact that for some
children obstruents are preferentially [+voiced] in word-initial position but
[-voiced] in word-final position; initial obstruents voice, and final obstruents devoice. He argues for two different defaults: [+voiced] in initial position, [-voiced]
in final position. If the default is underspecified, this would mean that obstruents
are specified for [+voiced] in final position (as we have been assuming), but that
obstruents are specified for [-voiced] in initial position (contra our assumptions).

The facts do not require this solution. It works well to assume that [+voiced]
is specified everywhere, but that constraints force the deletion of [+voiced] in
some environments and the insertion of [+voiced] in other environments. There
is one system default ([-voiced]) that is never specified in lexical representations.
The default is determined by constraint ranking: **Not(-voiced)** is ranked lower
than **Not(+voiced)**. The underlying representation of a segment like /b/ need not
be different in different parts of the word.

However, we cannot rule out Dinnsen's proposal for some children. Suppose
that the system default is [-voiced], but another constraint causes the insertion of

[+voiced] in word-initial position. One candidate is **NoSequence(-voiced...+voiced)**, ruling out a voiceless obstruent before a vowel. If the constraint is ranked high enough to prevent violations, the only options are to devoice the vowel, voice the obstruent, or delete the obstruent (§7.3.4.3). If **Survived(-voiced)** is ranked high enough, specifying an initial voiceless obstruent as [-voiced] would improve faithfulness, but another option would be to rerank constraints. Our view of specification assumes that different children choose different strategies: some specify features while others rerank. However, since **Survived(-voiced)** is initially low-ranked for most children, specifying the default feature would generally not improve faithfulness. In a small minority of children, **Survived(-voiced)** starts out high-ranked by chance. A subset of those children might specify [-voiced] in some environments. We thus do not believe that most children have context-sensitive underspecification. However, a small minority of children might have.

6.1.13. INTERVOCALIC CONSONANTS: ONSETS OR CODAS?

Intervocalic consonants are generally assumed to be onsets (e.g., Clements & Keyser, 1983; Prince & Smolensky, 1993). However, as noted in §3.7, many researchers have argued that intervocalic consonants in adult English are not (pure) onsets if they are in an unstressed syllable. It is often suggested that intervocalic consonants such as the /k/ in *bucket* /bʌkət/ are ambisyllabic, constituting both the coda of the first syllable and the onset of the second syllable. While this is controversial for adult English, it does raise the issue of whether constraints might force a medial consonant to be in a coda rather than in an onset; this is entirely separate from the issue of whether the consonant is in *both* the coda and the onset. Within OT, this must in fact be the case. Bernhardt and Stemberger (in preparation) report that some evidence favors a coda analysis of at least some intervocalic consonants, but that most of the data suggest that intervocalic consonants are onsets.

More than one constraint affects the syllabification of a medial consonant. Prince and Smolensky (1993) emphasize the role of σ►Onset and **Not(Coda)**. Syllabifying a medial consonant as a coda violates both constraints, but syllabifying it as an onset violates neither (see Table 6.4):

TABLE 6.4

/bʌkət/	.bʌ.kət.	.bʌk.ət.
σ►Onset		*!
Not(Coda)		*!

However, other constraints affect the feature content in onsets and codas differently. Features such as [Dorsal] and [+continuant] might be allowed only in codas and never in onsets (§6.1.12.2). Such constraints can lead to a medial consonant being syllabified as a coda rather than as an onset, even at the cost of the second syllable having no onset.

This may often be the case with intervocalic velars in child speech. Velars often occur in codas but not in onsets. This leads to a potential problem with syllabification. If the medial /k/ in *bucket* /bʌkət/ is syllabified as an onset, then the velar is not possible; [Dorsal] must be deleted in the output: [.bʌ.tət.]. Such an output is unfaithful to the underlying features. In order to be faithful to the underlying feature [Dorsal], the /k/ must be in a coda: *bucket* [.bʌk.ət.]. Such an output syllabifies the medial consonant as a coda, however, violating both σ▸Onset and Not(Coda). Consider the following constraint ranking:

Co-occurring(Rime→Dorsal) ‖	Not(Dorsal) ‖	Survived(Dorsal) ‖	σ▸Onset
			Not(Coda)

The first three constraints are ranked in such a way that [Dorsal] is possible in codas but not in onsets. The low ranking of the syllable-structure constraints subordinates the drive to have onsets and avoid codas to the drive for faithfulness with regard to the feature [Dorsal]. Thus, the medial consonant becomes a coda, so that it can surface correctly as a velar. Within OT, it is impossible to prevent systems with such unusual syllabification from occurring (without also losing the ability to account for the fact that onsets are not obligatory in most languages).

We would like to remind the reader that we are predicting that such odd syllabification will mostly affect consonants that otherwise would be in the onset of an unstressed syllable. We believe that stressed syllables are more likely to retain their onsets.

Chiat (1989), M. Edwards (1996), Stoel-Gammon (1996), and Lohuis-Weber and Zonneveld (1997) report that stress sometimes matters. Chiat's (1989) subject changed fricatives into stops in onsets, but allowed them to surface as fricatives in codas. An intervocalic fricative that followed a stressed vowel (as with the /s/ of *person*) was also correctly produced as a fricative. However, a fricative before a stressed vowel (as with the /s/ in *decide*) or between two unstressed vowels (as with the /s/ in *opposite*) were stops. Chiat argues that a stressed syllable attracts a coda, allowing the fricative to be produced as a fricative. An unstressed syllable tends not to allow a coda (see §6.2.4.1), and so this option was not possible when the fricative followed an unstressed syllable. M. Edwards (1996) and Lohuis-Weber and Zonneveld (1997) reported a similar pattern for fricative realization. Stoel-Gammon (1996) discussed a similar pattern of realization for velars: velars in codas and intervocalically after a stressed syllable, but dentals in onsets and intervocalically before a stressed syllable.[20] Stemberger (1993a) noted this realization pattern for velars for Morgan and Larissa, but also noted that Larissa treated the /k/ in *raccoon* in an unusual fashion:

raccoon   /ɹæˈkuːn/   [ˌwakəˈhuːn]

---

[20] Stoel-Gammon does not address intervocalic consonants between two unstressed vowels.

The adult aspirated [kʰ] was split into two segments, allowing the velar to survive, but also allowing the final syllable to have an onset.[21]

Such syllabification might occur with consonants that are allowed in both onsets and codas. Medial nasals, for example, would be acceptable onsets or codas for most children, from the point at which codas are possible in the child's speech. However, they may be nonoptimal onset consonants. If the relevant **Co-occurring** and **NotCo-occurring** constraints are ranked higher than **Not(Coda)** and σ▸**Onset** constraints, the medial consonant may be syllabified as a coda rather than as an onset. We believe that this occurs with glides even in adult English. Consider the following words:

lion	/laɪn̩/	[.laɪ.n̩.]	*[.la.jn̩]
flower	/flaʊɹ̩/	[.faʊ.ɹ̩.]	*[.fla.wɹ̩]

Our intuitions are that these words have diphthongs, and that the glide portion of the diphthong is part of a complex nucleus which is entirely within the first syllable. The glide is not the onset to the second syllable, even though the syllable algorithms assumed by Prince and Smolensky (1993) would require it to be in the onset. A glide is a poor onset, but is an excellent rime segment. As a result, the glide is in the rime in English if it can be, not in the onset. We believe that similar syllabification is possible in child phonology for any of the features that are more optimal in rimes.

Young children also tend to syllabify the medial glide as a part of the rime of the first syllable. Unlike adults, however, children often do supply the second syllable with an onset, by spreading the glide to onset position (Stemberger, 1988a; Bleile, 1987), although this violates **SinglyLinked(Root)**. The resulting double linkage of the glide leads to phonetic gemination:

/.flaʊ.ɹ̩./	[.faʊ.woʊ]
/.laɪ.ən./	[.jaɪ.jən.]

Our general prediction is that medial consonants will tend to "act like" coda consonants. In particular, the phonetic realization will often be like that of coda consonants rather than like onset consonants. We do not know how often this is true. Medial consonants sometimes show the same substitution patterns (or lack thereof) as word-initial (and hence syllable-initial) consonants. Children usually have medial consonants at a time when codas are not possible, suggesting that those children at least are syllabifying the medial consonants as onsets. Indeed, the children who epenthesize a word-final vowel to rescue a coda consonant (§6.1.4.2) appear to be treating the (now-medial) consonant as an onset, after epenthesis. Bernhardt and Stemberger (in preparation) show that medial consonants often are realized in the same way as onsets, rather than as codas. Stemberger (1992a) reports this for Morgan. The lateral /l/ was correctly produced as (light) [l] in word-initial onsets from the first attempt at 1;4. In codas, /l/ was produced

---

[21] The schwa between the [k] and [h] was inserted to avoid the sequence of consonants. See Stemberger (1993a), as well as §7.4.4.3 and §9.1.6.

as the glide portion of a diphthong ([ʊ]). Medial /l/ varied between [l] and [ʊ], apparently unpredictably. We conclude that medial consonants are often onsets but can be codas, and that children vary on the extent to which medial consonants can be codas.

We do caution that medial consonants can show substitution patterns that are distinct from the patterns of both initial and final consonants. At one point, Morgan showed the following patterns with adult /ð/:

initial:	[d]	then	/ðɛn/	[dɛn]
medial:	[l]	mother	/mʌðɹ̩/	[mʌlɤ]
final:	[z]	breathe	/bɹiːð/	[biːz]

The special patterns affecting medial consonants generally involve plateauing: the medial consonant takes on some feature ([+sonorant] in this case) from the preceding and following vowel, so that the feature needs to be specified once for the entire sequence. See §7.4.4.3.

Medial consonants are not necessarily syllabified as onsets to the second syllable, as is often assumed. Other constraints can force the medial consonant to be syllabified as the coda of the first syllable, but only when those constraints are high-ranked. After our discussion of constraints on feet, we return to further constraints that can force such unusual syllabification (§6.2.4.2).

6.1.14. HIERARCHICAL SYLLABLE STRUCTURE

In §3.7, we noted that there is some argument about the existence of internal syllable structure. Are there onsets, nuclei, and codas? Or is syllable structure flat? Is there any evidence from phonological development that bears on this issue? We have been using such structure, but is it absolutely required to account for the data?

There is relatively little clear evidence. Although we need to refer to "onsets" and "codas," these terms could just designate the consonants that either precede or follow the vowel within the syllable. There is very little evidence that can (even in principle) tell us about groupings of segments within the syllable. One asymmetry would have been taken as evidence for the onset-rime distinction until recently. We noted above that there can be interactions between diphthongs and codas, such that one or the other can be present, but not both:

bite   /baɪt/   [bat]~[baɪ]

However, diphthongs never interact with onsets in that way: a diphthong is possible whether or not there is an onset. Since the complexity of the vowel can affect whether a coda can be present, but cannot affect whether an onset can be present, this could reflect a division of the syllable into onset versus rime. However, as discussed above, it might also simply reflect a representation in which the glide portion of a diphthong is structurally parallel to a coda consonant; if a diphthong is present, a coda would not be possible, but an onset, of course, would be unaffected. A second piece of evidence that could be used to argue for such a division of the syllable would be that the onset makes up a unit in phonological phenomena. One could argue that the deletion of entire onsets could be evidence for onsets. In general, we have a difficult time accounting for such patterns in OT. While this might be a possible interpretation, we suspect that it could arise simply from competition between two consonants (in an activation-based competition system, such as connectionist models).

Some evidence from studies of the metalinguistic skills of older children suggests that the division between the onset and the rime is a real one. When children first develop the ability to split a word into parts, they tend to be able to strip off the onset of the first syllable. They can then generate other words that start with the same onset, etc. At first, they tend to be unable to further split the onset into segments, and they tend to be unable to split the rime into segments. This has been used as evidence for hierarchical syllable structure. (See Treiman, 1988, for a review.)

Fikkert (1994) makes a number of claims about hierarchical syllable structure. She argues that the /s/ of /s/-stop clusters is not part of the onset. Her analysis does not allow any violations of sonority sequencing (higher-sonority /s/ before a lower-sonority stop) within onsets. If we assume, however, that sonority can be violated, her arguments (that children treat such clusters differently from other clusters) lose their force. For rimes, Fikkert argues that there is a special position for sonorants within the nucleus, followed by a coda, followed by an "extrarhymal position." Evidence for the sonorant position within the nucleus comes from Jarmo, who did not allow sonorants after long vowels. However, Gwendolyn did not allow voiced stops after long vowels. Therefore, such patterns are feature-based, not structure-based. Fikkert also posits an Appendix that is limited to coronal obstruents, but again bases it on the fact that coronal obstruents can appear at the end of especially large clusters; in §7.3.2, we attribute such effects to constraints on sequences of features. Data showing that certain features may appear in word-final position only after short vowels may provide some evidence for an appendix (albeit one not restricted as to place or manner). However, it is unclear whether child phonological development provides clear evidence regarding hierarchical syllable structure.

6.2. THE DEVELOPMENT OF FOOT STRUCTURE

Syllables are combined into groupings called feet. We assume that all syllables must link to a foot, due to the following upwards structure constraint:

σ◂Foot

We assume (contra the "standard" analysis; §3.8) that syllables may never link directly to prosodic words. As long as the child is producing speech, syllables are grouped into feet.

In English and many other languages, feet also determine which syllables are stressed: the head of a foot is stressed, and all non-head syllables are unstressed. In some languages (such as Sesotho), the head of the foot is prominent in some other fashion, such as increased length (see summaries in Goldsmith, 1990; Kenstowicz, 1994). In this section, we consider the following basic aspects of foot structure: the minimal foot, the maximal foot, headedness (left-prominent versus right-prominent), and the heaviness of both stressed and unstressed syllables. We also need to address what happens when the child's system differs from the adult pronunciation.

Phonological theory is designed to account for very complex stress systems, with properties that allow for a wide range of stress types. Since all young English-learning children are learning English, many of the properties of the system go unused. Only a crosslinguistic investigation of stress, examining children learning many disparate stress systems, would inform us on all aspects of the phonological theories of stress. We know too little about the acquisition of stress even within English, less about Dutch and Spanish, and next to nothing about non-Indo-European languages. As a result, acquisition data as of yet do not inform us on many aspects of theories of stress.

Psycholinguistic studies of adult speech have led to the conclusion that stress is stored in lexical representations in English and Dutch (see Levelt,1989, for an overview). In all probability, stress is also stored lexically for young children. The following constraint should be important:

Survived(FootHead):   An underlyingly prominent syllable should also be prominent in the output.

This constraint leads to a tendency for children to place stress on the same syllables that are stressed in the adult target word. All the developmental studies of stress that are discussed here have concluded that this is the case for most children. Some note, however, that individual children can violate faithfulness to prominence within the foot.

There have been several recent studies of foot structure within nonlinear phonology. Fikkert (1994), Gerken (1991, 1994), Fee (1995), Archibald (1995), and Kehoe (1995) take a process-oriented approach. Demuth (1993, 1996c) and Demuth and Fee (1995) take an OT approach. This work has focused on the types of phenomena that occur, how they are to be accounted for, and whether there are predictable stages in development. Our proposals differ from theirs in a number of ways.

Foot structure must be addressed in two ways. First, it must be addressed in its own right. It is necessary to discuss basic constraints on feet and how children acquire feet. This is especially the case in the majority of words in English (and Dutch and Spanish), which have only a single foot. Second, it is necessary to address interactions between foot structure and the structure of prosodic words, especially in words with more than one foot (and hence with two or more stressed syllables). A few recent studies have addressed the effects of word structure. In this section of the chapter, we will address issues relating to feet, and turn to word structure in the next section. Most of the generalizations that we make in this section are based on data from words that contain a single foot (and hence a single stressed syllable), where the adult target word had two or three syllables in total; few English words with a single foot have four syllables, and five syllables is (almost) impossible. The constraints also hold for words with two or more feet, however (§6.3).

6.2.1. ACOUSTIC CUES FOR STRESS

Before beginning, we should address the issue of how reliably stress can be heard and transcribed in child speech. The acoustic cues for stress are complex, and there are indications that young children may not be able to control them very well. Pollock and Brammer (1993) and Vihman and de Boysson-Bardies (1994) also report that the acoustic cues for stress are not well established in the speech of many children younger than 24 months. When transcribing the speech of very young children, it is often difficult to transcribe stress consistently; a given word may seem variable. In Morgan's diary study at 1;3, Stemberger (p.u.d.) transcribed words like *Mama* as varying between [.'ma.ma] (greater stress on first syllable), [.ma.'ma] (greater stress on second syllable), and [.'ma.'ma] (equally stressed). There may not have been any variation, but simply an ambiguous acoustic signal that was being shoe-horned into a perception of stress, a resolution that led to the perception of stress on different syllables in different tokens. This is a separate issue from the nature of the foot structure of children's speech. We assume that young English-learning children have some sort of foot structure from the beginning of speech, but that some children may not yet have acquired the articulatory abilities to consistently realize the stressed syllable as louder, longer, and higher-pitched than the unstressed syllable.

Our justification for assuming that the young child has phonological foot structure comes from syllable deletion. As noted below, even when children cannot accurately control stress cues, the syllables that are stressed in the adult target tend to survive in the child's pronunciation. We thus assume that foot structure is present and can that stressed syllables can be identified, but that the child's articulatory system is unable to accurately reflect the difference between stressed and unstressed syllables.

6.2.2. LEFT-PROMINENT VERSUS RIGHT-PROMINENT FEET

Some syllables are more prominent than others. In a two-syllable word, either syllable can be the prominent one; but for a given language, the default stressed vowel is fairly consistent. Prominence is determined by the following two constraints:

Prominent(Foot,Left):   The syllable on the left is prominent.
Prominent(Foot,Right):   The syllable on the right is prominent.

Depending on which constraint is ranked higher, the stress is on the left syllable (a trochaic foot) or on the right syllable (an iambic foot).

Most feet in adult English are left-prominent, especially in the native Germanic vocabulary which tends to predominate in speech to and by children. We expect that English-learning children should be sensitive to the high frequency of left-prominent feet. Children should use left-prominent feet early in development, but might not develop right-prominent feet until later. We stress that this prediction can be based on the idea that children quickly learn the headedness of the foot system in the adult language. If the language has right-prominent stress (as in French), we would predict that right-prominent feet would develop first.

6.2.2.1. Deletion

Almost all English-learning children pass through a period where a bisyllabic foot must be left-prominent (Allen & Hawkins, 1978; Klein, 1981, 1984; Carter Young, 1991; Gerken, 1991, 1994; Kehoe, 1995; Demuth, 1996c; Devers & Broen, 1996). Thus, words like *bucket* and *lizard* can be reproduced faithfully (in terms of number of syllables and location of stress), but words like *balloon* and *giraffe*, with stress on the second syllable, cannot be. This leads to patterns such as the following (using hypothetical data):

Left-prominent:	bucket	[.'bʌ.kə.]
	lizard	[.'wɪ.jə]
Right-prominent:	balloon	[.buːn]
	giraffe	[.dæf.]

Because the head of the foot is located on the left syllable in *bucket*, a left-prominent foot can be created that includes both syllables.

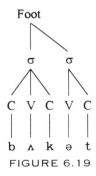

FIGURE 6.19

However, in *balloon*, there is a problem. The initial syllable is unstressed in the adult target, and so it should not be the head of a left-prominent foot; the output should not be *[.'bə.luːn], with stress on the initial syllable. This is also ruled out because (a) schwa should never be stressed, and (b) the long vowel [uː] cannot be unstressed (§6.2.4). Further, both syllables cannot be stressed (§6.3.2). The child must create a single left-prominent foot, and the head must be the syllable that contains the long vowel [uː]; the initial syllable cannot be a part of the foot that is created, because that would mean that the foot would be right-prominent. The result is the following structure:

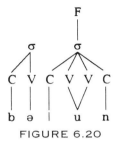

FIGURE 6.20

Since no foot can be erected on the schwa in /bə/, the first syllable is deleted.[22] We assume that the unstressed syllable is usually deleted outright, so that it is not a part of the output at all. However, in some instances, it may be present in the output, but remain floating.

To produce right-prominent feet in words like *balloon* accurately, the following ranking is needed:

LinkedUpwards(σ) ‖‖	**Prominent(Foot,Left)** ‖‖	**Prominent(Foot,Right)**
Survived(Root)	[or: σ◄Foot]	[or: σ◄PrWd]

No segments may be deleted (high ranking of **Survived(Root)**), and all syllables must link upwards, even if that requires a right-prominent foot (lowest-ranked). We also assume the upwards structure constraint σ◄**Foot**, which requires syllables to link to feet. We remind the reader that others assume a different (lower-ranked) upwards structure constraint: σ◄**PrWd**; a syllable links to a foot if possible, but otherwise links to a prosodic word. Such researchers assume that there is no right-prominent foot in *balloon*; there is a left-prominent foot with one syllable (/luːn/) plus a syllable that links to the prosodic word (/bə/). This alternative analysis requires the alternative ranking on the second line of the above constraint list. Demuth (1996b) takes this approach. In contrast, if faithfulness is ranked lower than the constraints in the middle cell above, then the initial unstressed syllable is deleted.

Deletion of the unstressed syllable of the adult target is a very common phenomenon in early child speech. It holds true for the majority of young English-learning children.

6.2.2.2. Stress Reversal

Klein (1984), Carter Young (1991), Fikkert (1994), Archibald (1995), and Kehoe (1995) report that young children on occasion do construct left-prominent

---

[22] We address below the question of which consonant associates with the stressed syllable when an initial unstressed syllable deletes. It is not always the consonant that begins the stressed syllable in the adult pronunciation.

feet on words such as *balloon* and *giraffe*. When they do so, the first syllable tends to contain something other than schwa, and the second syllable tends to be reduced to schwa (or at least a short vowel): ['bʌlən], ['ʤ ræf]. Comparing stress reversal to syllable deletion, the child is more faithful to the consonants and to the number of vowels, but is less faithful to the segmental content of the vowels and to the number of timing units in the underlyingly long vowels. However, two syllables are present in the output. Fikkert (1994) posits this as a basic "stage" in development, but notes that not all children show such pronunciations. Kehoe (1995) stresses that this is a minority option; few children produce left-prominent feet when the foot is right-prominent in the adult pronunciation. (In this section, we refer to Kehoe, 1995, which is the most complete presentation of her work; smaller but more accessible presentations of her work appear in Kehoe & Stoel-Gammon, 1997, and Kehoe, in press.)

6.2.2.3. ?Trochaic Bias?

Early development of left-prominent feet has been reported for other languages. This is clearly the case for languages in which left-prominent feet are more frequent than right-prominent feet: Dutch (Fikkert, 1994; Wijnen, Krikhaar, & Den Os, 1994; Lohuis-Weber & Zonneveld, 1997), Spanish (Hochberg, 1988), and Sesotho (Demuth, 1996a). Allen and Hawkins (1978) also claimed that left-prominent feet develop early in Quiche Mayan, even though feet in the adult language are right-prominent. This claim was based on the fact that young Quiche Mayan children often reduce words to a single stressed syllable (in the same way that young English-learning children reduce right-prominent words like *balloon* to a single syllable). This implies a "trochaic bias" towards left-prominent feet, regardless of the foot patterns of the target language.

Several researchers have more recently argued that there is no universal bias towards left-prominent syllables. Hochberg (1988) argued against such a bias for Spanish-learning children, on the grounds that stress does not shift onto initial unstressed syllables. Archibald (1995) cautions that this fact is ambiguous, unless it is known whether initial unstressed syllables are more likely to be deleted in Spanish. Perhaps children just deleted those syllables, rather than shifting stress. Gennari and Demuth (1997) show (for one Spanish-learning child) that initial unstressed syllables are more likely to be deleted than other unstressed syllables, and argue for a trochaic bias for Spanish-learning children. Demuth (1996a) argues that the Quiche Mayan data are not compatible with left-prominent feet, since there is only a single syllable; there is no tendency to insert a syllable after the final stressed syllable, as might be expected if it were a left-prominent foot (see §6.2.3.4).

French is the only other language requiring right-prominent feet for which there are acquisition data. Paradis, Petitclerc, and Genesee (1997) report that children use right-prominent feet, with initial unstressed syllables; they argue against a universal bias towards left-prominent feet. Vihman (1992) presents the first words for several French-learning children. Bisyllabic words were produced accurately with two syllables, without deletion of initial unstressed syllables, suggesting that right-prominent feet were present from the beginning. Chevrie and Le Breton (1973) report that children often delete the first weak syllable in early words, a finding different from Vihman's, but one that is consistent with the bias towards right-prominent feet in French.

Kehoe (1995) reports that one English-learning child in her study consistently used right-prominent feet for all words:

apple	/ˈæpl̩/	[.æ.ˈpʊː.]
monkey	/ˈmʌŋki/	[.mʌ̃ŋ.ˈkiː]
open	/ˈowpn̩/	[.o.ˈpɹ̩n]

This exceptional child constitutes proof that a bias towards left-prominent feet is not universal, even among English-learning children.

The bias towards left-prominent feet for children learning English, Dutch, and Spanish is probably based on exposure to adult data, in which left-prominent feet predominate statistically. Children are sensitive to the statistics of the adult language, and consequently produce left-prominent feet from the beginning. In French, in contrast, where all feet are right-prominent, right-prominent feet are developmentally early.

6.2.3. SIZE OF THE FOOT: MINIMAL AND MAXIMAL

Crosslinguistically, the optimal foot is binary:

Binary(Foot,μ): A foot has exactly two moras (regardless of number of syllables).

Binary(Foot,σ): A foot has exactly two syllables (regardless of number of moras).

A foot violates the first constraint if it has one mora or three (or more) moras. A foot violates the second constraint if it has one syllable or three (or more) syllables. For a foot to violate neither constraint, it must have two syllables that have only one mora each. Generally, one of the two constraints is ranked higher, and that ranking determines whether feet must have two moras (so that monosyllabic feet are tolerated) or two syllables (so that feet with three moras are tolerated). In adult English, monosyllabic feet are common; the mora-based constraint is ranked higher.

The "minimal foot" in any language thus has two moras. However, this constraint is in principle violable: it is possible for a foot to have a single light (monomoraic) syllable, under some conditions.[23] There are no words in adult English that are made up of a single light syllable, except for clitics; a few function words such as *the* and *a* occur as a single light syllable, but they are usually not stressed

---

[23] Demuth and Fee (1995) refer to light monomoraic feet as "subminimal" feet. Since "subminimal" is an oxymoron, we avoid the term here.

and are phonologically part of a nearby word (so that the phrase *the dog* is produced with a single right-prominent foot). If these clitics are produced as independent words, they often have two moras: [ðiː] (with a long vowel) and [eɪ] (with a diphthong). However, many speakers stress these clitics while maintaining a monomoraic foot: ['ðʌ] and ['ʔʌ]. Further, it is common for English speakers (from kindergarten on) to name consonant sounds using a stressed schwa: ['bə], ['sə], etc. Monomoraic feet thus have a marginal toehold in adult English.

Complexity constraints can limit the maximal size of a foot:

> **NotComplex(Foot)**:   A foot may contain only one syllable.[24]
> **NotComplex(Rime)**:   A rime may not contain a coda.
> **NotComplex(Nucleus)**: A nucleus may contain only a short vowel.

The first constraint limits a foot to a single syllable. The second and third constraints together limit a syllable to a single mora. All three together would limit the foot to a single syllable with a single mora; but that violates the **Binary** constraints.

6.2.3.1. Tolerating a Monosyllabic Foot

Monosyllabic feet are tolerated if **Binary(Foot,σ)** is ranked lower than negative constraints such as **Not(σ)**. More than one syllable can be present, if underlying segments require it, but a syllable cannot be inserted just to make the foot binary. If **Binary(Foot,μ)** is additionally ranked low, even monomoraic feet are tolerated. Since monosyllabic feet are common in adult English (and Dutch), we expect that monosyllabic feet will be tolerated by most children from the beginning. This appears to be the case. Ingram (1996) reported that it also held true for a Japanese child.

It is less clear whether monomoraic feet are tolerated. The main source of monomoraic feet is the reduction of larger words, through the deletion of final consonants or unstressed syllables. Transcriptions often seem to contain feet of this sort:

| bed | /bɛd/ | [bɛ] |
| sit | /sɪt/ | [sɪ] |

However, it is likely that the vowels are phonetically long, if for no other reason than that word-final vowels are lengthened phonetically in all languages (Fowler, 1980): [bɛː], [sɪː]. They are not transcribed as long because (a) listeners expect vowels to be long in this environment, and (b) English speakers do not tend to notice length on these vowels, which are always short in adult English. Thus, these vowels may be phonologically long (?[bɛː], ?[sɪː]), with the result that most children produce a bimoraic foot. Fikkert (1994) (often cited by Demuth & Fee, 1995,

---

[24]This can also be accomplished via alignment (McCarthy & Prince, 1993b). **Aligned(σ,L,Foot,L)** requires every syllable to begin a foot; obviously, only one syllable in a foot can actually do so. If ranked higher than **Survived(Root)**, only one syllable is possible, and every segment that cannot fit into that syllable is deleted.

Demuth, 1996a, and Fee, 1996) argues that such reduction can lead to monomoraic feet in the speech of very young Dutch-learning children; their transcriptions show that children can be variable between producing the syllables as long or as short. However, the transcriptions show length associated with the same vowel quality as in adult Dutch (such as short lax [ɪ] versus long tense [iː]). Length may have been transcribed following the biases of adult Dutch, rather than faithfully recording the length of the vowel in the child's speech; Fikkert's (1994:28) statements that the length mark "does not necessarily mean phonetically long" but rather reflects "a phonologically long vowel" may indicate such a transcription bias. We suspect that short monosyllabic words without codas are quite rare, and that young children generally pronounce vowels long when they delete codas. We suspect that the speech of almost all children, from the beginning, is constrained in such a way that feet are usually bimoraic or larger, although Fikkert's data have been interpreted as showing that some children produce monomoraic feet.

6.2.3.2. Requiring a Monosyllabic Foot

A child might have a maximal foot of only one syllable. If **NotComplex(Foot)** is ranked higher than **Binary(Foot,σ)**, feet must be monosyllabic. Matthei (1989) discusses a child who initially (and briefly) truncated all bisyllabic (and larger) words to a single syllable. We suspect that situations like this may not be limitations on the size of feet so much as limitations on sequences of consonants. Matthei remarks that this particular child had strong constraints on the consonant at the beginning of the second (unstressed) syllable. If the underlying consonant and vowel of the second syllable are ruled out by constraints, there are only two options. (a) The second syllable could be produced as identical to the first syllable (§7.4.2). (b) The second syllable can be deleted. Although this impacts on feet by preventing the second syllable from having any phonetic content of its own, it is not due to constraints on feet per se.

A possible combination of constraints could force all feet to be made up of a single light syllable. First, **NotComplex(Foot)** could lead to the deletion of all syllables except one. Second, **Not(Coda)** could lead to the deletion of all codas. Third, **NotComplex(Nucleus)** could prevent diphthongs and long vowels (as would **SinglyLinked(Root)**). If all four constraints are ranked higher than **Binary(Foot,σ/μ)**, then all feet would be reduced to a single monomoraic syllable. Demuth and Fee (1995) and Goad (1996a) assume that such "subminimal words" must reflect a stage at which the child does not include feet in phonological representations. Feet can be present, but reduced below the usual foot-size of adult languages by the high-ranking of negative constraints. It appears that the high-ranking of all four constraints is unusual, and present only in very early speech (if ever).

Monosyllabic feet are more likely to have two moras, because they contain a long vowel (or diphthong) or a coda. Given a specific constraint ranking, **Binary(Foot,μ)** could cause the insertion of word-final codas in monosyllables. If **SinglyLinked(Root)** causes a long vowel in monosyllabic words like *see* to shorten, there would be a violation of **Binary(Foot,μ)**. If **Not(Root)** is ranked lower than both these constraints, however, a bimoraic foot will be maintained through the insertion of a default coda consonant:

no	/noː/	[nɤʔ]
me	/miː/	[miʔ]

Morgan (Stemberger, p.u.d.) optionally produced such forms. At a time when long vowels were obligatorily shortened in closed syllables (in words like *sheep* [ʔiʔ]), word-final long vowels in monosyllabic words were pronounced either long, or optionally shortened with a final glottal stop inserted. (But see §6.1.5 for discussion of whether some other constraint forced the insertion of the [ʔ], with concomitant shortening of the vowel.) We know of no child who *obligatorily* shortened all word-final vowels and who then obligatorily inserted a default coda. However, we predict that such children exist. We do not expect them to be common, however, because most English-learning children learn to produce long vowels (especially in open syllables) at a very early stage of development. Demuth and Fee (1995) posit that at the earliest stage of development, children do not have vowel length contrasts. However, many clearly do have vowel length (or at least, vowels of long duration) in open monosyllables, and we assume that it is more important to account for the child's pronunciation than just for the apparent contrasts (see §5.3); children may have long vowels even if length is predictable from other aspects of the word in the child's output. (Ingram, 1996, reported that all words were initially monosyllabic with a long vowel in the speech of a Japanese child.)

6.2.3.3. Tolerating a Bisyllabic Foot

Most children learning English (and Dutch, Spanish, and Sesotho) begin with a maximal foot of two syllables. Words with two syllables in the adult pronunciation are produced with two syllables. Because bisyllabic feet are so common in the adult language, constraint rankings that allow them are acquired early. Most children do not reduce bisyllabic feet to a single syllable.

Longer words, however, are truncated to two syllables. For example, *rhinoceros* might be reduced to [.'nɑ.sə], and *hippopotamus* might be reduced to [pʰɑmə].

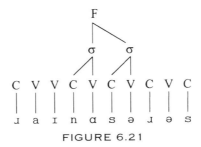

FIGURE 6.21

This would derive from the following constraint ranking, given additional constraints (§6.3.2) that limit the prosodic word to a single foot:

Binary(Foot,σ)   ‖‖   **Survived(Root)**

It is better to delete segments than to create a foot such as [nɑsəɹəs] with three syllables. Ranking **Survived(Root)** highest, in contrast, leads to the full complexity of English foot and word structure: feet with three syllables are tolerated if (a) an additional foot with one syllable is prohibited (§6.4.3), and (b) underlying segments may not be deleted.

When one of two adjacent unstressed syllables is deleted, it could in principle be either the first or the second syllable. *(hippo)potamus* could be reduced to either [pʰɑdə] or [pʰɑmə]. Echols and Newport (1992), Echols (1993), Kehoe (1995) and Devers and Broen (1996) reported that the word-final unstressed syllable is more likely to survive than the medial unstressed syllable. However, Kehoe emphasized that both outputs are possible. Wijnen et al. (1994), Gerken (1994), and Demuth (1996c) maintained that it is equally likely for either syllable to survive. Kehoe suggested that the final syllable of words such as *elephant* and *animal* may survive because they have a labial in the final syllable; if [Labial] tends to survive (see §6.1.6.4 and §7.4.1.3), then the labial consonant survives, and segments following the labial also survive (in order not to violate **Contiguity**). Kehoe (1995) and Carter Young (1991) also suggest that medial CV syllables that start with a sonorant as in *eLEphant* may be prone to deletion (as in [ɛʊfət]) the sonorant can be syllabified as a fairly optimal coda (§6.1.12.2.4), leaving the vowel by itself and making it more likely to be deleted (with σ▸**Onset** ranked above **Survived(V-Root)**). Thus, it may not be position in the word (**Priority(Left)** or **Priority(Right)**) that determines which syllable survives. Rather, low-level interactions with the particular segments present may at least partially affect which syllable survives in the output. Devers and Broen (1996), however, reported that it did not matter whether the first consonant was a sonorant or an obstruent, or whether the second consonant was a labial or not. Devers and Broen suggested, however, that the second syllable was especially likely to delete if there was a single consonant (as in *elephant*) rather than a cluster (as in *obvious*), because that consonant could be syllabified as a coda, leaving the vowel without an onset and free to delete. The data currently do not allow us to state any firm conclusions. To demonstrate a tendency for the first or second syllable to survive, one must control for other factors; optimally, one might do an experiment using repetition of nonce words: /.'bɛ.pə.kə.] versus /'bɛ.kə.pə/.

One might expect **Contiguity** to play a role in which syllable survives. We predict that there might be a tendency for the syllable that is adjacent to the stressed syllable to survive. As noted, the evidence for English is mixed, and a careful study controlling for relevant factors remains to be done. There is some evidence from French and Spanish, however. Paradis, Petitclerc, and Genesee (1997) studied French-learning children's imitation of four-syllable words with stress on the final syllable. They reported that the stressed syllable almost always survives, and that the third syllable (the one before the stressed syllable) was the unstressed syllable that usually survives. Gennari and Demuth (1997) showed that one Spanish-learning child generally deleted the first (initial) unstressed syllable in a WWS sequence. This might reflect contiguity: the syllable contiguous to the stressed syllable survives. However, in all the examples that they provided, the initial syllable had no onset. Thus, it could be that the second syllable survived because it had an onset. Gerken (1994) reports that in SWWS words (two un-stressed syllables between two stressed syllables), the word may be reduced to the first stressed syllable and the one immediately following the unstressed vowel; this would appear to be the effect of contiguity in terms of which syllable survives. More research on the role of contiguity is needed.

6.2.3.4. Requiring a Bisyllabic Foot

The child's minimal foot might be required to have two syllables, given the following ranking:

Binary(Foot,σ) ||| **Not(σ)**
||| **Not(Root)**
||| **SinglyLinked(Root)**

If this were the case, any word that is monosyllabic in the adult pronunciation would be made bisyllabic in one of the following ways:

1. addition of a "dummy" syllable of fixed shape

    straw   /stɹɑ/   [fowə]   (Fee, 1996)
    tee   /teː/   [teijə]   (Fikkert, 1994)

2. reduplication

    see   /siː/   ?[sisi]
    high   /haɪ/   ?[haha]

We have not encountered any reports of reduplication for such words. Fikkert (1994), Demuth and Fee (1995), Demuth (1996a), and Fee (1996) argue that the epenthesis of a final vowel is common, and that it is one stage in the development of feet in English and Dutch. Fikkert notes that not all children pass through such a stage, however. Kehoe (1995) reports that such pronunciations are rare for En-glish-learning children. Although epenthesis to create a bisyllabic foot is possible, it does not seem to be the dominant pattern in child phonology. Children tend to delete syllables more than they tend to insert them (just as epenthesis is not a dominant repair strategy within consonant clusters).

We caution here also that schwas may be inserted after vowels for reasons that are unrelated to foot structure. At 1;5, Morgan (Stemberger, p.u.d.) optionally epenthesized a final schwa after all final high vowels, regardless of the number of syllables in the word. One of Bleile's (1987) subjects showed a similar pattern. Why epenthesis occurred is unknown. Before interpreting examples of schwa insertion as foot-related, the child's whole corpus must be systematically examined to make sure that all instances of epenthesis can be explained in that way. To our knowledge, this has never been done.

A high ranking of **Binary(Foot,σ)** can prevent feet from being larger than two syllables: SWW. For most children, one of the unstressed syllables is deleted. A rarely observed alternative is to alter the stress placement, so that the single left-dominant foot is binary. Archibald (1995) emphasizes such data for one Spanish-learning child (from Hochberg, 1988):

| cascara | /'kaskara/ | [kas'kala] |
| hipopotamo | /hipo'potamo/ | [popo'tamo] |

The child had a single foot at the right edge of the word, with two syllables. In order to prevent the deletion of word-final segments, the child shifted the stress to the penultimate syllable. As noted above, stress rarely shifts off stressed syllables in this way (due to a high ranking for **Survived(FootHead)**). Note that this explanation implies that the initial unstressed syllables are not part of the foot; if they were, the feet in these examples would not be binary. See the next subsection. We are unaware of data like this from English-learning children. This may reflect different statistics for unusual stress patterns in the two languages (with more irregular forms in English), or it may just be that the pattern is rare and by chance has yet to be observed for English.

6.2.3.5. Tolerating Larger Feet

No child requires a foot to have three or more syllables, and initially all children seem to reduce feet to two syllables (or even to one syllable). Eventually, larger feet emerge, as the faithfulness constraints come to be ranked higher than the **Binary** constraints.

The discussion to this point implies that any foot with three or more syllables is equally nonoptimal. The following words are not necessarily comparable; we list the constraints that they violate:

banana	three syllables (**Binary(Foot,σ)**)
	initial unstressed syllable (**Prominent(Foot,Left)**)
battery	three syllables (**Binary(Foot,σ)**)

Since *banana* has the extra unstressed syllable in a location that violates left-prominence, we might predict that it would develop later than words like *battery* (and the final foot of *hippopotamus*). However, it seems that children often master word-initial unstressed syllables even in words like *banana* before they master words with two contiguous unstressed syllables (Gerken, 1994; Fikkert, 1994). We suspect that the following constraint exists:

NotTwice(Unstressed)):   Two unstressed syllables may not be adjacent.

Such a constraint would be grounded in rhythms, since two contiguous unstressed syllables disturb a regular rhythm. Depending on the relative ranking of left prominence with this **NotTwice** constraint, a child might match the number of syllables first in *battery* (left prominence more important) or in *banana* (regular rhythm more important). Kehoe (1995) found that words with two contiguous unstressed syllables tended to be mastered first, however. It appears that different children may show different orders of acquisition.

The approach to stress that we take here has an additional consequence for word-initial unstressed syllables. The word *banana* has a foot with three syllables, whereas *balloon* and *giraffe* have only two syllables. Since **Binary(Foot,σ)** limits a foot to two syllables, it should be the case that *balloon* and *giraffe* are mastered (with two syllables) before *banana* is mastered (with three syllables). If this prediction is *never* true, that fact might constitute evidence that initial unstressed syllables attach directly to the Prosodic Word node, and are not a part of the foot that contains the stressed syllable. Kehoe (1995) did present some data that are relevant, from children at 2;3. However, there was so much variability between words (from 69% syllable deletion in *giraffe* to 31% in *caboose*) that it is impossible to determine whether the number of syllables in the word affected output. Further research is needed.

Gennari and Demuth (1997) report an unusual chain shift pattern for one Spanish-learning child. Although an initial unstressed syllable was deleted from WSW words, WWSW words were reduced to WSW:

muñeca	/mu'ɲeka/	[meka]
arbolito	/arbo'lito/	[bo'lito]

In our system, it is difficult to account for chain shift patterns. If WSW was a tolerable output pattern (so that it could serve as the output of WWSW words), why was it not tolerated for WSW words? This is not the only chain shift pattern discussed in this book; we could simply add it to the others, and return to it in §10.2.1. If we wished to account for it here, we can see two possibilities. (a) We could create a constraint that required the deletion of exactly one word-initial unstressed syllable. This would have to be an "unfaithfulness" constraint: a word-initial unstressed syllable in the input must correspond to nothing in the output. In §4.2.2, we rejected such constraints in principle. (b) We could assume a different EVAL function than usual: one violation of **Survived** is tolerated, but two violations are impossible. Either alternative would involve a major change in the theory, with rejection of a basic principle. We believe that the second alternative is plausible, however.

6.2.4. HEAVINESS

There are two constraints that deal with the number of moras in each of the syllables of a foot:

Heavy(Stressed):   A stressed syllable optimally has two moras.
Light(Unstressed):   An unstressed syllable optimally has one mora.

These constraints can determine which syllables in the word are stressed and how the syllables are realized phonetically. The first constraint tends to cause stress to be placed on syllables that have two underlying moras. If there is only one underlying mora, a second mora may be inserted, or a segment from the onset of the next syllable may move into the coda. The second constraint tends to allow only a light syllable to be unstressed. If a heavy syllable is forced to be unstressed, the constraint may cause the syllable to become light, generally via shortening of the vowel or deletion of a coda consonant.

6.2.4.1. Avoiding Heavy Unstressed Syllables

The second syllable of a word like *balloon* /bəluːn/ must be stressed. **Light (Unstressed)** and **Heavy(Stressed)** make /luːn/ an optimal stressed syllable and a nonoptimal unstressed syllable. When stress reversal (to achieve a left-prominent foot) leads to /luːn/ being unstressed, the constraints cause the syllable to lighten: ['bʌlən] (Carter Young, 1991). Kehoe (1995) also reports that, if stress shifts onto a syllable, it is most likely that the syllable receiving stress is heavy.

The constraint that unstressed syllables must be light can lead to additional repairs, if the target unstressed syllable is heavy. In English, this possibility arises when the second syllable of a bisyllabic word has a coda, as in *bucket* /bʌkət/. In order to have a left-prominent foot, the first syllable must be stressed, but in a word like *bucket*, that entails an unstressed syllable that is heavy because it contains a coda: /kət/. If faithfulness is strong enough, the final consonant will be produced despite this. We predict three patterns, for different children or at different points in development for a single child.

6.2.4.1.1. Pattern 1: Codas Allowed in Both Stressed and Unstressed Syllables

Most researchers have taken the following pattern to be the most common. Morgan (Stemberger, p.u.d.) had codas in both stressed and unstressed syllables from the beginning.

| hit | /hɪt/ | [hɪtʰ] | bucket | /bʌkət/ | [bʌkətʰ] |
| up | /ʌp/ | [ʔʌpʰ] | ketchup | /kɛtʃəp/ | [tʰɛtəpʰ] |

6.2.4.1.2. Pattern 2: Codas Allowed Only in Stressed Syllables (Minimal Repair)

If **Light(Unstressed)** is ranked higher than **Survived(Root)**, the word-final consonant is deleted in order to ensure that the final unstressed syllable is light.

| hit | [hɪtʰ] | bucket | [bʌkə] |
| up | [ʔʌpʰ] | ketchup | [tʰɛtʃə] |

Larissa (Stemberger, p.u.d.) originally showed this pattern (e.g., 2;0).

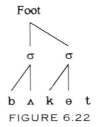

FIGURE 6.22

Deleting just the offending consonant is a minimal repair. Note that it is unlikely that the child would instead epenthesize a vowel to put the offending consonant in a syllable of its own. That would create a foot with three syllables, thus violating **Binary(Foot,σ)**, which apparently is generally higher-ranked in child speech than **Light(Unstressed)**. The deletion of the final coda made these words fit a common pattern in Larissa's output, in which final unstressed syllable were open and light:

| happy | /hæpi/ | [hæpi] |
| zebra | /ziːbɹə/ | [ziːbɹ̩] |

Deletion in the final syllable was determined by stress rather than the fact that it was the second syllable of the word; final consonants were unaffected in words with right-prominent feet (in adult speech), such as *balloon*.

6.2.4.1.3. Pattern 3: Codas Allowed Only in Stressed Syllables (Nonminimal Repair)

A nonminimal repair is also possible, although, we suspect, very unusual. A nonminimal repair would involve the deletion of some higher element other than just the offending coda consonant; the only relevant higher element here would be the syllable. Stemberger (1994b) reported that Gwendolyn had a nonminimal repair for unstressed heavy syllables:

bucket	/bʌkət/	[bʌː]
bottom	/batm̩/	[baː]
yellow	/jɛloʊ/	[jaː]

In contrast, when the final unstressed syllable was light, in words such as *happy* [haːpi] and *zebra* [jiːba], the unstressed syllable was never deleted. Nor were similar coda consonants in monosyllabic words deleted.

This nonminimal repair is handled in OT in a way parallel to all such repairs. **Survived(Root)**, **LinkedUpwards(Root)**, **Survived(TimingUnit)**, and **Linked-Upwards(TimingUnit)** are high-ranked, and so the word-final coda consonant cannot be deleted. The coda consonant must link up to a syllable. However, if the syllable links up to the Foot, this violates **Light(Unstressed)**. Apparently, **LinkedUpwards(σ)** was the lowest-ranked of all these constraints: the syllable containing the heavy unstressed syllable was floating (and hence unpronounced):

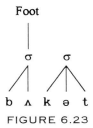

FIGURE 6.23

The constraint interactions are illustrated in Table 6.5 (where the bracketed material is present in the output but floating):

TABLE 6.5

/bʌkət/	bʌkət	bʌkə	bʌ <kət>
Survived(Root) LinkedUpwards(Root)		*!	
Light(Unstressed)	*!		
LinkedUpwards(σ)			*

If the constraints in this table are reranked, so that **Survived(Root)** is lowest-ranked, then a minimal deletion of just the final consonant is the optimal candidate ([bʌkə]). And if **Light(Unstressed)** is the lowest-ranked constraint, then the optimal candidate is the most faithful one, with no segments deleted but with a heavy unstressed syllable (the adult [bʌkət]).

J. Paradis et al. (1997) addressed the deletion of heavy unstressed syllables for French-learning children. They were working from a prediction that heavy syllables might be less prone to deletion, but felt that, since adult French is not quantity-sensitive, child French should also not be quantity-sensitive. They found no significant difference between heavy and light syllables. However, there was a trend that just missed significance ($p < .095$) for heavy syllables to delete more often than light syllables. This trend was most likely due to unstressed syllables, since almost no stressed syllables were deleted; by including stressed syllables in the statistics, it is likely that the effect was watered down. We predict that heavy syllables are preferred for stressed syllables, but that light syllables are preferred for unstressed syllables. Paradis et al.'s data suggest that French children are more likely to delete unstressed heavy syllables (in words beginning with three unstressed syllables). This implies that children may treat syllable weight as relevant to stress even when the adult target language does not. More research is clearly needed.

6.2.4.2. Avoiding Light Stressed Syllables

There may also be effects from a very high ranking of **Heavy(Stressed)**. Every stressed syllable would have to be heavy: either with a long vowel or diphthong, or with a coda. The word *bucket* would be a problem, if the syllabification were [.bʌ.kət.], because the stressed syllable [bʌ] would be light. There are two possible resolutions here. First, if **Not(μ)** is ranked low enough, the vowel of the first syllable can be made long: [.bʌː.kət.]. This seems unlikely, since in adult English [ʌ] is always short. Second, if σ▸**Onset** and **Not(Coda)** are ranked low enough, the medial /k/ can be a coda in the first syllable rather than an onset in the second syllable: [.bʌk.ət.]. Providing the stressed syllable with a coda makes the syllable heavy, as required. Dylan (§8.6) may have had a tendency in this direction. Medial consonants were relatively unlikely to be deleted after short vowels in his speech (and quite likely to be deleted after long vowels and diphthongs), suggesting that they were being syllabified as codas after short stressed vowels.

Heaviness for a stressed syllable could also be achieved by geminating the medial consonant, but we are unsure whether this ever occurs. Morgan (Stemberger, p.u.d.) may have shown such pronunciations as an optional variant at 1;8–1;10:

bunny	/bʌni/	[bʌni]~[bʌnːi]
tunnel	/tʌnl̩/	[tʰʌnɤ]~[tʰʌnːɤ]

A medial nasal after a short vowel was optionally geminated. This was restricted to nasals; medial oral stops and [l] never geminated, and there were no other medial consonants at the time. The restriction to nasals may have reflected the constraint **Co-occurring(Rime→ + sonorant)**, which leads to nasals being more optimal codas than oral stops; since [l] never occurred in a coda at the time, /l/ did not geminate. This would result from the following constraint rankings:

Co-occurring(Rime→ + sonorant)	**SinglyLinked(Root)**
Heavy(Stressed)	**Not(Coda)**
σ▸**Onset**	

The three highest-ranked constraints require that a stressed syllable be heavy, that the unstressed syllable must still have an onset, and that a consonant spreading into the coda must be a sonorant. The two lowest-ranked constraints are violated, allowing a coda to exist, and allowing a consonant to geminate in order to provide a coda to make the stressed syllable heavy. Since the gemination was optional, the relative ranking of **Heavy(Stressed)** and **SinglyLinked(Root)** must have been unstable; when **SinglyLinked** was ranked higher, gemination was prohibited. We do not know how often gemination occurs in order to make a stressed syllable heavy.

Constraints on the heaviness of stressed vowels can lead to unusual syllabification, with medial consonants making up a coda after a short stressed vowel, where we would expect the consonant to be in the onset of the following syllable.

If this leads to gemination, it is fairly obvious. If it leads to a medial consonant being syllabified as a coda, however, it may be difficult to detect (and rarely transcribed). See §6.1.13 for discussion.

6.2.5. CONSONANTS AND INITIAL UNSTRESSED SYLLABLES

There are several interesting patterns relating to the consonants in words with an initial unstressed syllable. The initial consonant may survive even when the initial syllable is deleted. The consonant at the beginning of the stressed syllable may fail to survive even when no syllable is deleted. The initial unstressed syllable may be produced, but be subject to reduplication or may contain a default (dummy) syllable. We address each of these in turn.

6.2.5.1. Consonants in Deleted Initial Unstressed Syllables

When an unstressed initial syllable is deleted, there is variation in terms of which consonant survives in the child's pronunciation: the word-initial consonant, or the consonant from the onset of the stressed syllable. For words like *pajamas*, two pronunciations are common.[25]

/pədʒæməz/:   [dʒæmə]   *or*   [pʰæmə]

What determines which consonant survives?

Ingram (1989a) and Demuth (1996c) note that these data provide important information about what is going on in syllable deletion. It might in theory be possible that children do not attend to the initial unstressed syllable, or perceive the segments within the unstressed syllable only poorly. The fact that a consonant from within the unstressed syllable can survive and link up to one of the surviving syllables is evidence that the unstressed syllable is perceived well. Further, such data show that the child is not simply picking out syllables from the word for deletion or production, but is actively constructing the syllables and feet.

We can identify four likely factors that could influence the choice. Consider the /b/ and /l/ of the word *balloon*:

[b]: low sonority
    left edge of word
    noncontiguous to the stressed vowel /uː/
    [b] is a possible output in the child's system
[l]: high sonority
    word-medial
    contiguous to the stressed vowel /uː/
    [l] is not a possible output in the child's system

---

[25] We abstract away from the fact that the adult pronunciation may be /pədʒɑməz/, and that the child may make substitutions for the vowels and consonants.

We have already noted that children almost invariably reduce the cluster /bl/ to [b], because it is preferable to have an onset of low sonority; this factor would favor /b/. If position in the word matters, it would presumably favor the word-initial consonant, which is again /b/; this might involve the constraint **Aligned**, requiring the alignment of the left-most consonant of the base morpheme with the left edge of the prosodic word (Demuth, 1996a). **Contiguity**, in contrast, would favor the consonant that is contiguous to the stressed vowel; in this case, the /l/ is favored. If sonority or alignment is more important than contiguity, then we expect the pronunciation [buːn]. If contiguity is more important, than we expect [luːn]. Most English-learning children say [buːn] at first. Since the word-initial consonant is favored more if it is low in sonority, it appears that sonority is the important factor, not alignment.

The fourth factor (whether the child can faithfully pronounce the consonants) is perhaps the least important factor. According to the theory that we are assuming, reduction of sequences of consonants should follow the same patterns, whether they are in a cluster in the adult pronunciation or not. We expect to find the same reduction patterns in consonant clusters and in syllable deletion. Whether the consonant can be pronounced does not seem to be the most important factor in the reduction of consonant clusters. For example, children often acquire [w] early but velars late. Gwendolyn produced the following data (Stemberger, p.u.d.):

win	/wɪn/	[wɪn]	
kiss	/kɪs/	[tʰɪs]	
quit	/kwɪt/	[tʰɪt]	*[wɪt]

Even though the child could pronounce [w] but not *[kʰ], the child reduced the cluster to /k/, which underwent Velar Fronting to [tʰ]. Factors other than segmental faithfulness may also be more important in determining which consonant survives in this case.

Stemberger, Pollock, and Salck (1990) tested whether word position or sonority were more relevant. Stimuli were CV'CV nonsense words: for example, /.lə.ˈbɑ./ versus /.bə.ˈlɑ./. Children who reduced the words to single syllables pronounced both words as [bɑ], suggesting that sonority is more important than word-initial position or contiguity. Fikkert (1994), and Gnanadesikan (1995) reached a similar conclusion. Stemberger, Pollock, and Salck (1990), Kehoe (1995), and Lohuis-Weber and Zonneveld (1997) also suggested that there is a tendency for nondefault features (such as [Labial] and [Dorsal]) to survive rather than default features.

If sonority is more important than contiguity or position in the word, then we predict an interesting possibility with /s/ and /p/: the result should tend to be [p] regardless of order; /.sə.ˈpʌk/ and /.pə.ˈsʌk/ should both come out [pʰʌk]. Again, this was the case.

Stemberger et al. (1990) also took one instance where the predictions were less clear. In /sn/ clusters, it is common for children to reduce the cluster to [s] or to [n]/[n̥], depending on whether the child favors onsets that are [-sonorant] ([s]) or

that are [-continuant] ([n]/[n̩]). Sonority thus should not lead to a consistent resolution of /.sə.'næt/ versus /.nə.'sæt/. It was found that the order of the two consonants did matter here: there was a tendency to produce the consonant that was
contiguous to the stressed vowel. Contiguity matters, but only when sonority does
not decide the issue. As far as is known, position in the word and **Aligned** play no
role in determining which consonant survives.

For many words, such as *pajamas*, the relative preference for [pʰ] versus [ʤ]
in onsets in a given child's speech is unclear, because adult English has no word-
initial clusters like /ʤp/ or /pʤ/. Across children, it looks like sometimes one is
more optimal, sometimes the other, on the basis of the way that words like *pajamas* are pronounced ([bæmə] or [dæmə]). However, on the basis of reduction
patterns in clusters and of consonant harmony patterns (§7.3 and §7.4.2), we
would predict a general preference for nondefault features over default features,
and no clear prediction when two nondefault features are involved. No systematic
research has been done on this issue.

Additionally, a child may produce a fusion of the two consonants, just as with
simple consonant clusters. Gwendolyn produced words like *tomato* and *Pinocchio*
with voiceless nasals ([m̥eɪ] and [m̥oʊm̥oʊ]), just as with /sm/ clusters (*smile*
[m̥aɪ]). A few children in the Stemberger et al. (1990) study pronounced /pəsʌk/
or /səpʌk/ as [fʌk], and also reduced /sp/ to [f]. Fikkert (1994) reports fusions for
Dutch-learning children: **banaan** /baː'naːn/ as [maːn]. Fusions are reasonable,
since the features of deleted elements may survive and link up to a surviving segment. The constraint rankings that predict this are the same as those that lead to
fusion in clusters. We predict that fusions should tend to favor nondefault features;
Fikkert remarks that nondefault [Labial] and [Dorsal] are favored, just as with
cluster fusions. We predict that if fusion occurs in clusters, it will probably also
occur when initial unstressed syllables are deleted.

6.2.5.2. Consonants at the Beginning of the Stressed Syllable

We know of one unusual treatment of initial unstressed syllables for which we
have only a speculative account. Morgan briefly showed a transitional form for
the words *balloon*, *barrette*, and *giraffe* (the three relevant words in her system
with intervocalic /l/ or /ɹ/):

	balloon	*barrette*	*giraffe*
	/bə'luːn/	/bə'ɹɛt/	/ʤə'ɹæf/
Early monosyllables:	[buːn]	[bɛtʰ]	[daːtʰ]
Transitional:	[ˌbuːˈuːn]	[ˌbɛːˈɛtʰ]	[ˌdaːˈaːtʰ]
Late bisyllables:	[bə'luːn]	[bə'vɛtʰ]	[də'vaːtʰ]

The early monosyllabic forms include the initial stop in the output, as expected,
and the later bisyllabic forms were adult-like, with the substitutions for /ɹ/ and
/ʤ/ expected in her system at the time. The first bisyllabic forms that Morgan
produced, however, had secondary stress on the first syllable, which had a full
vowel, the features of which were obtained via spreading from the vowel of the

second syllable. The second (stressed) syllable had no onset (except in one unusual token of *ballon*: [ˌbɯːˈɯːn]). Such transitional forms were found with only these three words (the only three words with /l/ and /ɹ/ at the beginning of the stressed syllable); words like *pajamas* and *machine* stayed monosyllabic until they were correctly bisyllabic.

There are two possible explanations for such forms. First, it is possible that the medial consonants were deleted because of sequence constraints on medial consonants; but this seems unlikely, since medial [l] was not subject to sequence constraints at the time. Further, we need to explain the absence of the child's default onset, which was usually [d] (in words like *lion* [laɪdən]); the pronunciation *[bɯːdɯːn] never occurred. Finally, this first explanation does not account for secondary stress on the first syllable. The second possibility is more likely. A foot with secondary stress was constructed on the first syllable, which consequently had to be made heavy. To achieve heaviness, the first syllable borrowed the timing unit from the medial consonant, which was consequently deleted. Since a long schwa was not possible (just as in adult English), segmental information for the first syllable was obtained via assimilation:

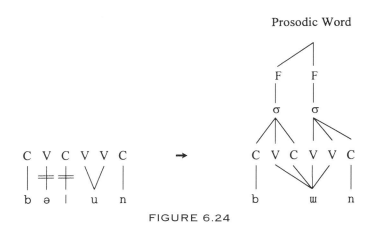

FIGURE 6.24

This transitional form did not improve faithfulness to the segments (though it was no less faithful than the earlier monosyllabic pronunciation), but did increase faithfulness to the timing units.

This analysis does not capture the fact that this treatment of words with right-prominent feet was restricted to the words with intervocalic /ɹ/ and /l/. It is possible that /ɹ/ and /l/ were realized as syllabic in this case. This should have led to their being realized as [ɤː]: *balloon* "/blˌuːn/" *[bɤːɯːn] (*cf. apple* /æpl̩/ [ʔapɤ]) and *barrette* "/bˌɹɛt/" *[bɤːɛt] (*cf. bird* /bˌɹd/ [bɤːt]). If this were combined with Vowel Harmony (spreading of the entire V-Place node) from the stressed vowel to the unstressed vowel (in a weak prosodic position), the observed pronunciations would be derived. In this way, we account for why such forms were not observed with other intervocalic segments like the /ʃ/ in *machine*, which could never be syllabic (in Morgan's speech or in adult English). Because sequences of vowels were otherwise separated by epenthetic [d], these three words were the only three with vowel sequences at this time. We can assume that total vowel harmony occurred whenever the vowels were adjacent (unseparated by a consonant). (See also §7.3.3.)

6.2.5.3. Initial Unstressed Syllables as Weak Prosodic Domains

In §4.7.1.5, we discussed the idea that unstressed syllables constitute a weak prosodic domain, with the consequence that faithfulness constraints are ranked lower than in stressed syllables. Available evidence supports such an analysis of word-initial unstressed syllables. When such syllables are finally present in the child's speech, there may be deviations from faithfulness that are never observed in initial stressed syllables. Three phenomena have been reported. (a) The initial unstressed syllable has a set form, regardless of the segments present in the adult target word. (b) The initial unstressed syllable reduplicates one or more segments from the following stressed syllable. (c) Substitutions are observed only in unstressed syllables.

6.2.5.3.1. *"Default" Unstressed Syllables*

Smith (1973:172) reported that Amahl at one stage tended to replace all initial unstressed syllables with the dummy syllable [ɹi] (though some variability was observed, in which the segments were more faithful to the adult target):

guitar	/giˈta/	[ɹiˈtʰaː]
disturb	/dɪˈstəːb/	[ɹiˈstəːv]
enjoy	/ɛnˈʤɔɪ/	[ɹiˈʤɔɪ]

Note that an initial [ɹ] was inserted if the word did not begin with a consonant, and that any coda in the unstressed syllable was deleted. Smith suggests that the child may have been substituting the prefix *re-*, but there is nothing to suggest this. We would assume that there were severe constraints on the content of the unstressed syllable, which were resolved through the use of a default consonant and a default vowel. The vowel [i] is not an unreasonable default. The glide [ɹ] seems quite odd; one would not expect this to be the default consonant. However, it may derive from the following constraint ranking:

Co-occurring(Root→Place)	‖	Not(C-Place)	‖	Not(V-Place)
NotTwice$_{Dependents}$(Root)	‖	Not(V-Labial)	‖	Survived(C-Place)
Co-occurring(V-Coronal→-ant])	‖		‖	Not(V-Coronal)

A high-ranked **Co-occurring** constraint requires the initial consonant to have place (ruling out [ʔ] and [h]). The ranking of the two **Not(Place)** constraints defines V-Place as the system default; thus, the initial consonant must be a glide. The low ranking of **Survived** leads to deletion of any underlying C-Place. We would expect underlying V-Place to survive. Indeed, in the few words that begin with segments that always surface as glides in Amahl's speech (including the realization of /v/ as [w] that was common at the time), there is no [ɹ]:

vanilla	/və'nɪlə/	[wə'nɪlə]
Veronica	/və'rɔnikə/	[wə'rɔŋikə]
yourself	/jɔː'sɛlf/	[jɔː'slɛf]

Let us also suppose that the default glide was [Coronal,-anterior] ([j]), through the low ranking of **Not(Coronal)** and the high ranking of a **Co-occurring** constraint that requires coronal vowels to be [-anterior] (see constraint list above). However, since the vowel of this syllable was usually [i] or [iː], this would create a sequence [ji], with two identical Root nodes; this would be ruled out by **NotTwice(Root)** (see discussion of data from Priestly, 1977, in Stemberger, 1993a, and in §7.4.4.3). The sequence of identical Root nodes is avoided if [V-Labial] is inserted in the consonant. The result is the other coronal glide of English: [ɹ]. Though it at first appears odd, there is a reasonable constraint ranking that can derive [ɹ] in initial unstressed syllables before the vowel [i], if we presuppose that faithfulness constraints are low-ranked.

Gnanadesikan (1995) also reports on a child who used a default consonant in the initial unstressed syllable. This child used [fi]:

Christina	/kɹɪs'tiːnə/	[fi'dinʌ]
mosquito	/mə'skiːtoʊ/	[fi'giro]
advisor	/ædvaɪzɹ̩/	[fi'vaɪzʌ]
balloon	/bə'luːn/	[fi'bun]
koala	/ko'ala/	[fi'kala]

As with Amahl's data, [f] was inserted if the word had no initial consonant, and any coda in the unstressed syllable was deleted. Gnanadesikan assumes that the child had a set syllable [fi] that was imposed on the word. It did not replace all initial consonants; some were shifted to the beginning of the stressed syllable (as in *balloon*), if they were lower in sonority than the consonant that would normally appear there. Gnanadesikan argues that this is because they make a better onset than the underlying medial consonant (as also in our system). We noted above that when the initial syllable is deleted, this is the usual result; like deletion, only one of the two consonants can survive here, and so the same results obtain in terms of which survives. A drawback to this analysis is that the source of the /fi/ syllable is unexplained.

Let us instead pursue an analysis in which consonants are changed into [f]. The manner of articulation can be derived through the following ranking:

| **Co-occurring(σ-Margin→-sonorant)** | ‖ | **SinglyLinked(+ continuant)** |
| **Not(-continuant)** | ‖ | **Survived** |

The initial consonant is an obstruent due to a high ranking of **Co-occurring**. Since the unmarked obstruent is a stop, we might expect the consonant here to be a stop. However, it is a fricative because it assimilates [+continuant] from the following vowel (ranking of **SinglyLinked(+ continuant)** below **Not(-continuant)**), so that it is better to spread than to insert). (See §7.3.4.3 regarding voicing assimilation as a similar case.) The consonant is voiceless, because that is the unmarked value for [voiced] in obstruents. There are three possible explanations for why it is [Labial], rather than [Coronal]. (a) It might be that [Labial] is the child's default place of articulation. However, Gnanadesikan shows that [Labial] behaves more like a nondefault feature in fusions (since it survives rather than [Coronal]). Further, we are assuming that the **Not** constraints are ranked in the same way in different prosodic domains; if [Coronal] is the default in stressed syllables, it must also be the default in unstressed syllables. (b) It might actually be that [Labial] survives from the unstressed syllable in the adult form (the /m/ of *mosquito*, the /o/ of *koala*) or spreads from a following consonant (as in [fi'bun]). This works for every example that Gnanadesikan gives except for one: *container* has no rounded consonants or vowels in the adult pronunciation. Even here, we might argue that the final syllabic /ɹ/ is underlyingly [Labial,+round], and that this is shifted to the initial unstressed syllable. (c) **NotTwice(Coronal)** prevents a sequence of a (default) coronal consonant and a coronal vowel: *[si]. Since default [Coronal] cannot be inserted, and the next-lowest-ranked **Not** constraint is **Not(Labial)**, [Labial] is inserted, and [f] results. Thus, this unusual-looking default syllable can be accounted for via constraint rankings.

These are the only two reports of default initial unstressed syllables of which we are aware. Both show a reasonable default vowel ([i]) and an odd default consonant. In both instances, the odd features are due to interactions between the consonants and the vowel, including assimilation and dissimilation. We would like to emphasize that the only source of nondefault consonants features in our system involves interactions with the vowel. Had the default vowel in N. Smith (1973) been [ə], **NotTwice(Root)** would have been irrelevant, and we would not have been able to derive the [ɹ] of the default syllable. Although our approach can lead to many different consonants in these default syllables, there are also many consonants that would be impossible. These data also illustrate the complexity of constraint interactions.

6.2.5.3.2. Reduplication of the Following Stressed Syllable

Several researchers have reported instances where an unstressed syllable in a prefix or a clitic reduplicates the following stressed syllable or initial consonant:

Munson and Ingram (1986):	more cookie	[kʰʌkʰʊki]	
	more swing	[swʌswɪŋ]	
Stemberger (1988a):	the Mall	[məmɒʊ]	
	a bee	[bəbiː]	
	it root	[βɪʔβɒː]	
Smoczyńska (1985):	do mamy	ma-mamy [26]	'to Mom'
	na stole	to-tote	'on table'
	po kupkach	kup-kupkach	'on cow poop'

---

[26] Smoczyńska reports the forms using orthography rather than phonetic transcriptions.

If faithfulness is ranked low in an unstressed syllable, but the timing units of the syllable must survive, the positions can be filled by spreading the segments of the following syllable. This is similar to reduplication involving unstressed syllables following the stressed syllable (§6.1.4.2). For the children in Munson and Ingram (1986) and Stemberger (1988a), unstressed syllables were usually deleted unless they were a separate morpheme; see §6.4.1.2 for further discussion. Thus, there was no reduplication in words such as *balloon* and *machine*.

Lleó (1996) shows that such assimilation can also occur when the initial unstressed syllable is not a separate morpheme, using data from a Spanish-learning child:

caballo	/ka'baʎo/	[ba'bajɔ]	'horse'
zapato	/θa'pato/	[pa'pato]	'shoe'
sombrero	/som'brero/	[ba'bɛlo]	'hut'

Low-ranking of faithfulness in the initial unstressed syllable led to assimilations.

6.2.5.3.3. Substitution of Default Features

Substitutions that would not occur in stressed syllables might occur in unstressed syllables, because faithfulness is low-ranked. This is somewhat like the default syllables in §6.2.5.3.1, but without assimilations, and with a greater degree of faithfulness. For example, place of articulation and voicing might be faithful, but manner of articulation may be subject to change. We are uncertain how often this occurs. One example may be Denasalization in the French-learning child reported by Vinson (1915):

mouton	/mu'tõ/	[po'tɔ̃]	'sheep'
morceau	/moʀ'so/	[ba'ʃo]	'piece'

Klein and Spector (1985) report that voiceless stops in initial unstressed syllables may surface as voiced, even when voiceless stops in stressed syllables are aspirated: *potato* /pəteɪtow/ [botʰeɾo]. They also note that codas within initial unstressed syllables may delete even when nonfinal codas in stressed syllables do not delete. Carter Young (1991) reports that /ʤ/ may be accurately produced in stressed syllables, but stopped to [d] in initial unstressed syllables: *giraffe* /ʤə'ɹæf/ [də'wæf].

Children frequently delete word-initial unstressed syllables. When they do produce such syllables, they are often less faithful to the segments in them than they are to those in initial stressed syllables. This is expected, since unstressed syllables are a weak prosodic domain.

6.3. THE DEVELOPMENT
OF PROSODIC WORDS

Feet are grouped into prosodic words, via the upwards structure constraint **Foot◄ProsodicWord**. Prosodic words have heads, determined by the following constraints:

Prominent(PrWd,Left):   The foot on the left is prominent.
Prominent(PrWd,Right):   The foot on the right is prominent.

Depending on which constraint is ranked higher, the primary stress in the word is on either the left-most or right-most foot. Like lower prosodic units, the complexity of prosodic words can be constrained, and there are possible constraints on the foot that is the head of the prosodic word. The basic concerns for development are minimal prosodic words, maximal prosodic words, and headedness. A number of recent studies have addressed development of the prosodic word in English (Shriberg & Kwiatkowski, 1980; M. Edwards & Shriberg, 1983; Klein, 1984; Carter Young, 1991; Gerken, 1994; Archibald, 1995; Demuth & Fee, 1995; Kehoe, 1995; Demuth, 1996c), Dutch (Fikkert, 1994; Wijnen et al., 1994; Lohuis-Weber & Zonneveld, 1997; Demuth & Fee, 1995; Demuth, 1996a), Spanish (Gennari & Demuth, 1997), and Sesotho (Demuth, 1996c).

In English, words are allowed to have two or more feet. When two feet are present, there is some variation as to which foot is more prominent. The dominant pattern (see discussion in Goldsmith, 1990) is a complex one. Right-prominent feet are the dominant pattern if the right-most foot has two or more syllables:

> right-prominent (two syllables):   demonstration
>   avocado
>   Mississippi

However, if the right-most foot has only a single syllable, then the prosodic word tends to be left-prominent:

> left-prominent (one syllable):   demonstrate
>   hurricane
>   octopus

Note the alternation in stress in the morpheme *demonstrate* (base) versus derived *demonstration*. There are, however, exceptions to both these generalizations:

> right-prominent (one syllable):   Tennessee
>   mandolin
> left-prominent (two syllables)   helicopter
>   alligator

The word-level prominence is not completely predictable.

The standard assumption among psycholinguists working on adult English (and Dutch) is that stress must be stored lexically, even for "regular" words. See Levelt (1989) for a review of data from slips of the tongue and the tip-of-the-tongue phenomenon. For adults, it is probably the case that feet and prosodic words are stored lexically rather than computed by rule. It is reasonable to assume that children would also store them lexically.

When considering the development of word structure in English-learning children, we need to address the effect of different foot structures in the adult targets. Minimally, we need to address:

left-prominent SWS   (octopus)
left-prominent SWSW   (helicopter)
left-prominent SS   (toucan)
left-prominent SSW   (raspberry)
left-prominent SWWS   (stereotype)
right-prominent SWS   (Tennessee)
right-prominent SWSW   (stegosaurus)
right-prominent SS   (raccoon)
right-prominent SSW   (rambunctious)
right-prominent SWWS   (Kalamazoo)

Additionally, the presence or absence of an initial unstressed syllable might matter.

Although some English words have three or more feet, we can say nothing about them in terms of acquisition. The sorts of words that have three or more feet are quite rare in speech to and by children.

6.3.1. MINIMAL PROSODIC WORDS

The minimal prosodic word in all human languages is a single foot. No adult language requires all words to contain two feet (and thus two stressed syllables). Young children are no different.

Demuth and Fee (1995) assume that this is not true for the youngest children. They suggest that, at first, young children might have only syllables, without feet or prosodic words, which develop later on. Their evidence is that some very young children produce monosyllabic monomoraic utterances (see §6.2.3.1), which is smaller than the smallest allowable foot or prosodic word in most adult languages. However, this does not constitute evidence that feet and prosodic words are absent, since constraints are violable; the child's minimal foot could be smaller than in adult languages. We assume that prosodic words are an important part of the temporal organization of words, and that they are present from the beginning of meaningful speech (and possibly before).

6.3.2. MAXIMAL PROSODIC WORDS

In some languages, prosodic words are limited to a single foot, enforced by the following constraint: [27]

NotComplex(ProsodicWord):   A prosodic word may contain only one foot.

This is generally the case with the youngest children learning English (Gerken, 1994; Archibald, 1995; Kehoe, 1995), Dutch (Fikkert, 1994; Wijnen et al., 1994;

---

[27] Alternatively, **Aligned(Foot,L,PrWd,L)** requires that all feet begin the word. If high-ranked, this causes the word to reduce to a single foot (Demuth, 1996a; Pater & Paradis, 1996).

Demuth & Fee, 1995; Lohuis-Weber & Zonneveld, 1997), and Spanish (Gennari & Demuth, 1997). Words are allowed to have only one stressed syllable. Larger words (like *hippopotamus*) are initially truncated to a single foot (e.g., [pʰɑmə]). Fikkert (1994) has proposed this as one early stage in the development of prosodic words. Kehoe (1995) reports that children at 1;10 reduce words in this way, but that by 2;4 children tend to match the number of feet in the adult target. Words with two feet can be reduced to one foot, regardless of the complexity of the feet involved: SS, SWS, SSW, SWSW, or SWWS.

It is not always possible to predict which foot survives. Fikkert (1994) and Archibald (1995) proposed that the right-most foot survives. Gennari and Demuth (1997) also reported this for their Spanish-learning child. Lohuis-Weber and Zonneveld (1997) reported it for their Dutch-learning child. Gerken (1994) reported that either foot could survive, with about equal probability. Kehoe (1995) reported a statistical tendency for the right-most foot to survive, but noted that there was a great deal of variability. Which foot survives is not entirely predictable.

Generally, if two syllables are present in the single foot that is produced, they are the two syllables of that foot in the adult speech. Kehoe (1995) reported several deviations from this.

1. Sometimes the first stressed syllable is combined with the word-final un-stressed syllable, with the syllables in between deleted.
2. Sometimes both stressed syllables survive, but the second one is un-stressed (yielding a left-prominent foot). Fikkert (1994) also reported this for Dutch: *telefon* /ˌteːləˈfoːn/ [ˈtɛfoː]. Fikkert suggests that such forms are developmentally later than reduction to the rightmost foot, but there are insufficient data to support that claim.
3. Two different syllables may fuse (see §6.2.5.1 on word-initial unstressed syllables).

In general, the choice between these three patterns is made on the basis of segmental reasons. For example, in a particular word, the segments in the final syllable might make a more optimal nucleus, onset, or coda than the segments in the other syllable. Since segmental interactions are specific to the particular segments that are present, we expect that some words will follow one pattern (such as the output containing the two syllables from the adult foot) and other words will follow a different pattern (such as retaining a word-final syllable).

6.3.2.1. Size of Feet in Two-Foot Prosodic Words

At some point (before 2;4), prosodic words are expanded to allow two or more feet. For the first time, there can be two or more stressed syllables in a word. At that point, pronunciations such as [ˌhɪpəˈpʰɑmə] (or [ˌhɪːˈpʰɑː], if feet are more restricted) appear. Feet in such words are not necessarily as elaborated as they are in words with a single foot, however.

Matthei (1989) discussed a child whose words at the one-word stage were limited to two syllables. When the child began to produce two-word sentences, those sentences were limited to two syllables:

one-word sentences:	baby	/beɪbi/	[beɪbi]
	book	/bʊk/	[bʊkɔ]
two-word sentence:	baby's book	/beɪbiz bʊk/	[beɪ bʊ]

There was an absolute upper limit of two syllables in an utterance. This is not predicted. The limitation of words to two syllables is done via the maximal foot: a foot may have no more than two syllables (**Binary(Foot,σ)**). When two feet are finally allowed to be put together, however, we predict that utterances with two feet can be up to four syllables in length (two syllables per foot). We also expect that each word in a two-word sentence will have a foot of its own (and thus a stressed syllable of its own). We thus incorrectly predict that the maximal sentence in Matthei's study would be four syllables in length. Unfortunately, Matthei does not discuss stress. The two-word sentences may have had only one stressed syllable, so that only one foot was present. In that case, the maximal prosodic word was only one foot, which was limited to two syllables (only one of which was stressed). However, we suspect that both syllables were stressed, and that these data must be accounted for in some other fashion.

Although we have been using **Binary** for syllables and feet, this constraint family should possibly be extended to the prosodic word level, as follows:

Binary(ProsodicWord,Foot):	A prosodic word should have no more than two feet.
Binary(ProsodicWord,σ):	A prosodic word should have no more than two syllables.
Binary(ProsodicWord,μ):	A prosodic word should have no more than two moras.

These constraints would give an upper bound on the size of prosodic words: at most two feet, two syllables, or two moras. There is no evidence that the constraints also establish a lower bound on the size: never a single foot, a single syllable, or a single mora; **Binary(σ,μ)** also establishes only an upper bound (at most two moras in a syllable) without establishing a lower bound (so that syllables with a single mora are also well formed). The middle constraint here, restricting a prosodic word to two syllables, gives the results reported by Matthei. These constraints are less well-attested than the other **Binary** constraints, but they are a possible explanation for Matthei's data.[28]

Matthei's study is unusual because two-word utterances were involved, but we find similar restrictions within two-foot words. A medial unstressed syllable is more likely to delete than a final unstressed syllable (Shriberg & Kwiatkowski,

---

[28] Note that one of these constraints refers to the level that is immediately under the prosodic word: feet. The other two constraints refer to more deeply embedded levels: syllables (under feet) and moras (under syllables). This is parallel to the way that **Binary** works with feet. One constraint refers to the level immediately under feet (syllables), and the other to the level below that (moras).

1980; M. Edwards & Shriberg, 1983; Klein, 1984; Fikkert, 1994; Kehoe, 1995; Lohuis-Weber & Zonneveld, 1997). The following reductions are common (using data from Kehoe's study):

SWS: the unstressed syllable is deleted
   dinosaur ['daɪˌsɔː]
   telephone ['tʰɛlˌfo]

Given that two feet are produced (which is not always the case, especially for the youngest children), it may still happen that the unstressed syllable is deleted. Kehoe reported that the unstressed syllable is more likely to be deleted in words with final primary stress, like *kangaroo*, than in words with initial primary stress, like *dinosaur*. She notes that metrical theory does not predict such a difference. We suggest that a foot with secondary stress is a weaker prosodic domain than a foot with primary stress. Consequently, faithfulness is ranked lower in feet with secondary stress than in feet with primary stress; deletion of unstressed syllables is thus more likely if the foot has secondary stress.

A similar effect on medial unstressed syllables occurs with larger words (again using data from Kehoe's study):

SWSW: the FIRST unstressed syllable is deleted
     the SECOND unstressed syllable survives
     alligator ['ʔælˌgeɪɾɪ]
     avocado [ˌʔeɪ'kʰɑdʌ]

Except in the youngest children (who may delete both of the unstressed syllables), the final unstressed syllable is not deleted; it is unusual for the final unstressed syllable to be deleted if the nonfinal unstressed syllable survives (though Kehoe, 1995, reported that this does happen occasionally).

None of the constraints discussed thus far account for the survival of only the word-final unstressed syllable; all feet should have the same possible maximum size. However, we have seen something similar earlier in this chapter. We noted in §6.1.11 that some children first develop codas in word-final position, at a time when codas may not appear in nonfinal syllables. Both codas and unstressed syllables are weak prosodic positions, and some children allow those weak positions only in word-final position. For codas, we argued that it was not position in the word that was relevant, but rather the segmental environment: word-final codas are not followed by an onset, whereas nonfinal codas usually *are* followed by an onset consonant. We suggested that a constraint such as **NotTwice(C-Root)** or **NotTwice(σ-Margin)** prohibited codas in nonfinal position. It may well be that a similar constraint prevents a nonfinal unstressed syllable.

This effect might also reflect the following constraint:

WordFinalMassiveness: Extra material is tolerated word-finally.

In §4.5.2.6, this was proposed as a phonological version of Word-Final Lengthening. If ranked higher than **NotComplex(Foot)**, it leads to a modification whereby the final foot is allowed to have an additional syllable. We provisionally suggest that this may underlie the loss of medial unstressed syllables.

WordFinalMassiveness ‖ **NotComplex(Foot)** ‖ **Survived**

The basic foot size is a single syllable. In word final position, however, one extra syllable is allowed. Thus, SWSW syllables should reduce to SSW. (An alternative would be to assume that the child allows one "extrametrical" syllable in word-final position that attaches to the prosodic word rather than to a Foot node.)

In opposition to such reductions, Fikkert (1994) argues that children can insert a medial epenthetic syllable in order to make the first syllable binary:

garage   /χaːˈraːʃə/   [ˈχɑndəˈʀaːjə]

Kehoe (1995), however, reports that medial epenthesis is very rare, and often is not motivated by foot binarity, as in the following example:

octopus   /ˈɑktəˌpʊs/   [əˈgʌtətəˈpɪs]

Since there is already an unstressed medial syllable, the extra medial unstressed syllable serves no metrical purpose. Although there can be epenthesis in the first foot, most children follow the opposite pattern, in which binary feet are limited to word-final position.

6.3.2.2. Stress Clash

Kehoe (1995) points out that the loss of nonfinal unstressed syllables in SWS(W) words should be nonoptimal, according to linguistic theories of stress. Adult languages often show the effect of *stress clash*: two stressed syllables may not be adjacent (see Goldsmith, 1990, Kenstowicz, 1994, and Hayes, 1995, for extensive discussion and illustration). In our system, this would derive from the constraint **NotTwice(Stressed)**: two prominent syllables may not be adjacent. It seems that this constraint, although it may play a role in many adult languages, does not play a strong role in the early phonological development of English-learning and Dutch-learning children. Stress clash routinely arises when nonfinal unstressed syllables are deleted. Interestingly, the theory predicts that some children may have stress clash ranked high, in which case they would not show reductions in SWS words, but might reduce SWSW words to SWS (if **WordFinalMassiveness** is ranked low), or might epenthesize a medial syllable in SS and SSW words. It is unclear whether such data exist.

The issue of stress clash also arises in two-syllable words that have two feet, such as *cartoon* and *raccoon* (right-prominent prosodic word) and *toucan* and *crouton* (left-prominent prosodic word). Carter Young (1991) and Kehoe (1995) report that such words are produced with two feet early, generally at the same time that three-syllable words like *dinosaur* are produced with two feet. The heads of the two feet are adjacent in such words, causing stress clash, but this does not delay acquisition. The initial syllable of *raccoon*, with secondary stress, is generally mastered before the fully unstressed initial syllable of words like *balloon*.

Yip (1988) discussed a phenomenon associated with stress clash in (adult) Italian. When a word-final stressed syllable ending in a vowel precedes a word-initial stressed syllable beginning with a consonant, the word-initial consonant geminates. Yip argued that this is a way of separating the two stressed syllables in time. We agree that the extra duration of the consonant would have the effect of separating the stresses, but the linguistic theory that we are using does not actually acknowledge that fact. In fact, standard metrical theory (even the variant that Yip was using) fails to capture that separation (for technical reasons). Whatever the cause, we accept that stress clash can lead to gemination of an intervocalic consonant in order to further separate the stressed vowels.

Gwendolyn (Stemberger, p.u.d.) showed exactly this phenomenon in words with two monosyllabic feet. The intervocalic consonant was geminated:

raccoon	/ˌɹæːˈkuːn/	[ˌʊaˈtːʰuːn]
crouton	/ˈkɹuːˌtɑːn/	[ˈtʰuːˌtːʰɑːn]
toucan	/ˈtuːˌkæːn/	[ˈtʰuːˌtːʰiːn]
protein	/ˈpɹoʊˌtiːn/	[ˈpʰaˌtːʰiːn]

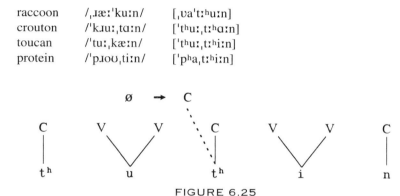

FIGURE 6.25

This has never been reported before, to our knowledge, possibly because most studies use an overly broad transcription in which consonant length and vowel length are not transcribed. However, we suspect that it is an uncommon phenomenon.

6.3.2.3. Adding Feet

In some instances, children produce a word with two feet, when the adult target has only one foot. We know of no instances of epenthesis. In every case, a foot is built on a syllable that is unstressed in the target word (Carter Young, 1991; Fikkert, 1994; Archibald, 1995; Kehoe, 1995). Kehoe reports data such as the following:

| banana | /bəˈnænə/ | [ˌbʌˈbænɑ] |
| elephant | /ˈɛləfn̩t/ | [ˈɛləˌfɪnt] |

Fikkert suggested that children do this systematically at one stage (after the stage at which the unstressed syllable is deleted, but before it can be produced as unstressed), but noted that not all children show such data. Kehoe reported that it is very uncommon. This pattern emerges when **Survived(Root)** is ranked high enough that deletion of segments is no longer tolerated, but feet must still be left-prominent and maximally binary. If the prosodic word is limited to one foot, the excess syllables must be deleted; but if words with two feet are possible, then the syllable can be rescued by making it into a foot of its own.

6.3.3. HEADEDNESS

In adult English, prosodic words are usually right-prominent if the second foot is bisyllabic or if both feet are monosyllabic, as in words like *cooperation, hippopotamus, raccoon,* and *cartoon*.[29] However, if the right-most foot has only a single syllable, and the preceding foot has two or more syllables, primary stress falls on the earlier foot: *cooperate*.[30]

Kehoe (1995) reported instances in which the wrong foot was made the head of the prosodic word. The pattern that she reported is difficult to interpret. Words that are left-prominent in the adult pronunciation can be produced as right-prominent by the child. Words that are right-prominent in the adult pronunciation can be produced as left-prominent by the child. We might conclude from this that children have a difficult time setting constraints to derive the adult pattern, which is sometimes right-prominent (if the final foot has two or more syllables, or if both feet are monosyllabic) and sometimes left-prominent (if the final foot is monosyllabic but the first foot has two syllables). To derive this pattern, the constraints must be set fairly finely.

Fikkert (1994) and Archibald (1995) proposed that initially both feet are equally prominent; in our terms, neither (or both) are heads. However, Fikkert notes that not all children show such data, and suggested that the equal-stress "stage" can be skipped. It is not clear to us that children ever consistently have equal prominence on both feet; Kehoe (1995) found that children who produce words with equally prominent feet also produce words in which the left foot is prominent and words in which the right foot is prominent. It is unclear whether a "stage" is involved.

In adult English, stress tends to fall on a branching foot. Fikkert (1994) proposed that Dutch-learning children pass through such a stage. In words such as *telefon* /ˌteːləˈfoːn/, this may lead to stress shift, with primary stress inaccurately falling on the first foot. Kehoe (1995) found such a tendency at 2;10 (but not at 1;10), with words such as *kangaroo* /ˌkæŋɡəˈɹuː/ [ˈtʰendʒəˌɹu]. It appears that children are learning that primary stress in the adult languages is sensitive to whether the foot branches children may "regularize" exceptions.

The available data are intriguing, but this issue has not been extensively studied. Further studies investigating the stability of prominence in prosodic words are clearly needed.

---

[29] Again, there are lexical exceptions, in words like *toucan* and *protein*.

[30] There are exceptions with a right-prominent prosodic word, as in *Tennessee* and *Brigadoon*.

6.4. INTERACTION BETWEEN PROSODIC DEVELOPMENT AND MORPHOLOGY

Our focus in this book is on phonological development. However, morphology and phonology interact in adult phonology (e.g., McCarthy & Prince, 1993a), and the same is true of phonological development. In order to produce plural forms such as *cats* and *horses*, it is necessary to produce a coda that contains a consonant cluster (/ts/ in *cats*) or a foot with two syllables (*horses*). Children do not always have the ability to produce codas, clusters within codas, or final unstressed syllables (containing a coda). In this section, we address the impact of the child's prosodic constraints on the expression of morphology.

The inflectional suffixes of adult English all involve coda consonants, and some also involve final unstressed heavy syllables. The suffixes that may be realized as a coda consonant are:

-s:	plural, possessive, present-tense	
	simple codas:	/z/ (sole member of coda)
	complex codas:	/s/ (after voiceless segments)
		/z/ (after voiced segments)
-ed:	past, perfect, passive	
	simple codas:	/d/ (sole member of coda)
	complex codas:	/t/ (after voiceless segments)
		/d/ (after voiced segments)

The suffixes that may be realized as heavy unstressed syllables are:

-ing:	progressive:	/ɪŋ/
-s:	after strident consonants:	/əz/
-ed:	after /t/ or /d/:	/əd/

Every allomorph of every affix involves phonological elements that may be absent from the child's phonological system.

Kelly (1989, 1992) reports that the adult English lexicon reflects avoidance of words that violate some constraints. Monomorphemic English words commonly end in two unstressed syllables (SWW), but few end in three (SWWW). Kelly notes that SWW verbs are rare, and argues that this is because the *-ing* suffix would create SWWW words. Adjectives that take comparatives and superlatives in *-er* and *-est* similarly are rarely SWW, because SWWW words would result. Nouns that end in grooved fricatives and affricates are rarely SWW, because the plural allomorph is [əz], and SWWW forms result. Kelly notes that the prohibition is not absolute. Nouns such as *hippopotamus* are possible, as is the plural *hippopotamuses*, even though a SWWW foot results. Kelly suggests that adults avoid such words; historically, such words are more likely to be lost from English and less likely to be coined or borrowed from other languages.

In OT, inflected forms are subject to the same set of constraints as morphologically simple words. If no codas are allowed in morphologically simple words, it is reasonable to expect that they will not be allowed in inflected forms. If codas are restricted to a single consonant, then -*s* and -*ed* might cause problems when they create clusters. The researcher might misinterpret the child's phonological difficulties as morphological (or syntactic) difficulties.

In addition to constraints on phonology, we must deal with constraints on morphology (illustrated here with past tense):

Expressed(Past):	When encoding of past tense is appropriate, past tense must be encoded.
Past(/d/,R):	Past tense forms must end in /d/.
Distinct:	Inflected forms must be phonologically different from the input form.
	(Lack of faithfulness for communicative reasons)
SinglyExpressed(Past):	Past tense should be marked only once.

Together, these constraints require the inflectional category to be expressed via a phonological modification of the base word, supply a specific modification, and allow that modification to appear only once in the output. If any morphological constraint is ranked below phonological constraints, the expression of morphology is affected. We address such effects relative to the type of repair (deletion versus epenthesis).

6.4.1. DELETION

Affixes often involve codas, complex codas, and unstressed syllables, where deletion is common in child phonology. The deletion that occurs may be the same as with base-internal segments. The deletion may be different. Deletion may be present only base-internally or only for the affix.

6.4.1.1. Deletion of Segments (Same for Both)

If the morphological constraints are ranked lower than phonological constraints, we expect that final consonant clusters should be reduced in the same fashion, whether they are base-final or include an affix. All the factors that can affect the reduction of clusters in codas (§6.1.7.1) should be relevant for determining whether it is the first or second member of the cluster that survives.

Stemberger (1995) and Stemberger and Bernhardt (1996) report that this expectation is correct. For Gwendolyn at 3;0, codas were limited to a single segment; plural and past tense forms were expressed only if the base morpheme ended in a vowel:

Base-final:	seed	[siːd]
	hide	[haɪd]
Past after V:	peed	[pʰiːd]
	cried	[tʰaɪd]
Past after C:	kissed	[tʰɪs]
	rained	[weɪn]

Although the last set of words were identical to the simple forms of the verbs, we know that they were past tense because they were used to refer to past events. However, the affix was deleted, for phonological reasons. **NotComplex(Coda)** was ranked higher than the morphological constraints.

Base-final consonant clusters and clusters in inflected forms can be treated in the same fashion. For Morgan at 1;10–2;3 (Stemberger, p.u.d.), final /s/ was deleted from a /ks/ cluster:

monomorphemic:	fox	[fakʰ]
	fix	[fɪkʰ]
plural:	rocks	[wakʰ]
	sticks	[tʰɪkʰ]

For Morgan, not all clusters were reduced to the first consonant. /ks/ was reduced to [kʰ] because of a higher ranking for **Survived(Dorsal)** than for **Survived(+ continuant)**.

Both types of cluster may also be reduced to the second consonant. Morgan (2;9–2;10, just after final fricatives emerged in her system), reduced all /ft/ and /st/ clusters to the /t/:

first	/fɹ̩st/	[foːtʰ]			
soft	/sɑft/	[saːtʰ]			
guessed	/gɛst/	[gɛtʰ]	*cf.* guess	[gɛs]
laughed	/læft/	[læːtʰ]	*cf.* laugh	[læːf]

The nondefault feature [+continuant] was marginal in codas (having just recently become possible at all). It was more important to express past tense than for [+continuant] to survive in codas, and so the fricative deleted:

NoSequence(+ continuant...-continuant)	‖‖‖	**Survived(Root)**
Expressed(Past)		**Survived(+ continuant)**

In Polish, several nonsyllabic prepositions are clitics on the following word; if the following word begins with a consonant, a cluster is created. Smoczyńska (1985:622) reported that such prepositions are deleted at a time when syllabic prepositions are not:

/z mamã/   [mamã]   'with Mommy'

She attributes this to "phonetic reduction of an initial consonant cluster," but provides no baseline data on cluster simplification in monomorphemic words.

6.4.1.2. Deletion of Syllables (Same for Both)

Gwendolyn (Stemberger, p.u.d.) also showed a relationship between unstressed syllables and the affixes -*ing*, -*ed*, and -*s*. Heavy unstressed syllables were deleted through 2;10 (e.g., *carton* as [tʰaʊt], *pocket* as [pʰaː]) but appeared at 2;10 (e.g., *carton* as [tʰaʊtən], *pocket* as [pʰaːtət]). (See §6.2.4.1.) Also at 2;10, the suffix -*ing* and the syllabic allomorphs /əd/ and /əz/ of -*ed* and -*s* appeared and became obligatory. Deletion of the unstressed syllable disappeared simultaneously in morphologically simple words and in inflected forms. When the foot is elaborated enough to allow a heavy unstressed syllable in simple words, suffixes like *-ing* and *-ed* become possible.

Within the field of speech-language pathology, the role of phonological factors in apparent morphological problems has been addressed with respect to children with Specific Language Impairment (SLI). SLI children are often described as having problems with inflectional morphology (e.g., Gopnik, 1990; Gopnik & Crago, 1991). Leonard, McGregor, and Allen (1992), however, pointed out that SLI children also have phonological difficulties, and suggests that the morphological difficulties may derive from the phonological ones. Stemberger (1995) argued in more detail that this might be the case, taking into account psychological characteristics of lexical access in speech production.

Gerken (1991, 1994) argued that constraints on feet may underlie a similar difficulty that most young children have with the closed-class lexical items of English, such as articles, auxiliaries, prepositions, pronouns, etc. Children often delete such words. Gerken pointed out that these words are most often unstressed, and wind up being produced as an initial unstressed syllable in a right-prominent foot, as in *the dog*. Children often have trouble with the unstressed syllable in a right-prominent foot (§6.2.2). Gerken demonstrated experimentally that stress is the most important factor. She reported that articles like *the* are deleted much more often in sentence-initial position, where they must be foot-initial, then in sentence-medial position, where they can in principle be foot-final. In a sentence like *I saw the dog*, the feet could be:

> (foot 1)   I
> (foot 2)   saw the
> (foot 3)   dog

If the child can produce unstressed syllables in a left-prominent foot (as most children can), this would allow the child to produce the word *the* in sentence-medial position.[31] Since deletion is far less common in sentence-medial position, Gerken argued that this is the case. Gerken (1994) reported that children's MLU (mean length of utterance, in words) was correlated with the proportion of deleted stressed syllables. Children who deleted many unstressed syllables also deleted closed-class lexical items and had a low MLU; children who deleted few unstressed syllables did not delete many closed-class lexical items, and had a high MLU.

The correlation is not perfect, however (Demuth, 1996b; Stemberger, p.u.d.). Stemberger addressed the issue using data on the articles *a* and *the* in Gwendolyn's speech from 1;11 to 2;9. Gwendolyn first used these clitics at 1;11, but only optionally; they appeared in 5–10% of the phrases in which they appear in adult

---

[31] The cliticization of *the* to the preceding word can be viewed as parallel to the cliticization of the auxiliary *is* on preceding word, as in *John's going*. The clitic *is* becomes part of the phonological word of *John*, even though syntactically *is* groups with *going*.

speech. However, word-initial unstressed syllables were otherwise *always* deleted at that age.

adult	[daʊt]
tomato	[m̥eɪdo]
a bee	[ʔəbiː]~[biː]
the Mall	[dəmɑʊ]~[mɑʊ]

Although the articles were usually not present, their optionality means that they were treated differently from morphologically simple words, which never had an initial unstressed syllable. Use of the articles remained low until 2;9, when word-initial unstressed syllables were no longer deleted from words like *balloon* and *giraffe*. Simultaneously, use of the articles *a* and *the* became obligatory. Articles were thus treated like morpheme-initial unstressed syllables in that they were first sometimes deleted and in then later became obligatory at the same time as unstressed syllables within morphemes. However, they were different in that they were deleted less often. Demuth (1996b) reports the following development for one Spanish-learning child. At first (1;8 – 1;11), clitics and word-initial unstressed syllables were almost always deleted. For a brief period (2;0 – 2;1), word-initial unstressed syllables were still usually deleted, but clitics were much less commonly deleted. After that (2;2 on), any deletion was rare. Demuth (1996b) posits a special position in phonological structure to which only clitics can link; when that finally develops, clitics are no longer deleted, but word-initial syllables are. However, this does not capture Stemberger's observation that for Gwendolyn clitics did not become obligatory until word-initial unstressed syllables always survived, even though they had been optional for 10 months. We suggest that the independent lexical status of clitics and their high frequency in English makes it easier for the child to maintain the syllable and add it to the following foot. The constraint **Distinct** requires the clitic to be present phonetically, to encode the differences in meaning overtly. If **Distinct** is ranked high enough, it can overcome constraints on foot structure, and clitics are deleted less often than word-initial unstressed syllables (for which this constraint is not relevant).

Mills (1985 : 154) noted that the German perfect prefix *ge-* is frequently missing in the speech of young children: *genommen* [nomən], *gemacht* [maxt]. She suggested that the prefix is deleted because it is an unstressed syllable. However, no baseline data on initial unstressed syllables in monomorphemic words were provided.

6.4.1.3. Deletion of Segments (Different for Each)

Inflections are not always subject to the same repairs as morphologically simple words, however. Inflections may show different repairs, even though they may be motivated by the same constraints.

An example of different treatment comes from Gwendolyn at 2;11 – 3;1 (Stemberger & Bernhardt, 1997). The word-final cluster /ks/ was simplified to a single consonant, because codas were restricted to a single consonant. However, /ks/ was simplified differently for inflected versus uninflected words.

fox	/faks/	[faːs]			
fix	/fɪks/	[fɪs]			
rocks	/ɹaks/	[waːt]	*cf.*	rock	[waːt]
sticks	/stɪks/	[tʰɪt]	*cf.*	stick	[tʰɪt]

In morphologically simple words, the /k/ deleted, yielding the single coda consonant [s]. In inflected forms, whether plurals, possessives, or present tense forms, the /s/ of the suffix deleted.[32] We suspect that this sort of difference may be common across children.

Base-final /ks/ clusters were reduced to [s] because of high ranking for **Survived(+continuant)** or **Co-occurring(Rime→+continuant)**; /st/ was also reduced to [s]. However, plural /s/ did not survive, due to the following ranking:

   NotComplex(Coda) ||| **Survived(Root)** ||| **Expressed(Plural)**

It was more optimal for a base-final consonant to survive than to express past tense; the base-final /k/ survived (as [t]), and not the [s] of the suffix. Since **Expressed(Plural)** is not relevant for the singular form *box*, other factors can determine whether the /k/ or the /s/ survives.

If **Expressed(Plural)** is ranked higher than **Survived(Root)**, we predict that hypothetical data like the following are possible:

fox	/faks/	[fak]			
rocks	/ɹaks/	[was]	*cf.*	rock	[wak]

Since the plural must be expressed, the base-final /k/ is lost, even though /ks/ is normally reduced to [k]. We have not come across clear data of this sort from child phonology. It appears that **Expressed(Past)** is most often lower-ranked. This may be related to the proposal in §4.7.1.5 that affixes are weak prosodic domains. When the system must choose between a base-final consonant in a strong domain versus an affixal consonant in a weak domain, the system chooses the segment in the strong domain. **Expressed(Plural)** must be very high-ranked to overcome this inherent bias in the system. Consequently, it is relatively rare to encounter such data.

A complex example of different treatment of intervocalic /st/ was observed for Gwendolyn at 2;11–3;1. Base-internal medial /st/ was reduced to [t], but it was reduced to [s] in inflected forms:

sister	[sɪtoʊ]			
twisted	[tʰɪsəd]	*cf.*	twist	[tʰɪs]

Note that both consonants of the medial /st/ in *twisted* belong to the base. Thus, unlike the previous examples, this is not a matter of priority between base and affix consonants. The child deleted the same phoneme in *twisted* that she deleted

---

[32] Note that the /k/ surfaced as [t]. All velars were produced as coronals in her speech at the time.

in *twist*. McCarthy and Prince (1994, 1995) might attribute this to output-to-output correspondence: [s] survives in *twisted* because it survives in *twist*. We prefer to avoid such complex constraints; we argued in §4.7.1.5 that the theory has too much power if there are too many correspondence constraints. We suggest that the base-final [s] in *twisted* was syllabified as a coda, and /st/ was reduced to [s] in a coda; but morpheme-medial /st/ in *sister* was syllabified as an onset and so was reduced to [t]. It may be that the domain of syllabification was the base morpheme (rather than the entire word, as in adult English), so that base-final /st/ did not go into the onset of the affix's syllable. This may also be achieved via **Aligned(Base,R,σ,R)** (a base-final segment must appear at the end of a syllable).

Note an additional aspect of the word *twisted* here. Although the word has the same allomorph of *-ed* as in adult speech ([əd]), it does not have the same phonetic environment *on the surface*: it follows [s] here, but follows only [t] or [d] (or [r]) in Adult English. This is expected if /t/ is not deleted outright. If /t/ is floating, it can still condition the insertion of the schwa. The floating /t/ cannot be a part of the second syllable because that would create a cluster ([st] in *[tʰɪstəd]), which was prevented by **NotTwice(+ consonantal)**.

6.4.1.4. Deletion in Base-Internal Clusters Only

Rankings may also lead to clusters being tolerated only when an affix is present:

Expressed(Plural) Priority(Base)	|||	NotComplex(Coda)	|||	Survived(C-Root)

The highest-ranked constraints require the base-final consonant to survive and plurality to be expressed. In plurals, only a cluster satisfies both constraints. Since **Expressed(Plural)** is not relevant to a base-final cluster, the cluster is reduced to a single consonant. After the period above, from 3;1 to 3;7, Gwendolyn continued to simplify tautomorphemic /ks/ to [s], but realized heteromorphemic /ks/ as a cluster.

fox	[faːs]	rocks	[waːts]
fix	[fɪs]	sticks	[tʰɪts]

Morgan showed a similar pattern for /ft/ at 2;11: base-final [tʰ] versus past tense [ptʰ].

6.4.1.5. Deletion of Affix Only

The base-final consonant cluster may be produced, but the affix is deleted if it appears in a cluster. The only report that we know of for a normally-developing child is N. Smith (1973) for Amahl:

six	/sɪks/	[sɪkt]
box	/bɑks/	[bɔkt]~[bɔk]
cheeks	/tʃiːks/	[tʰiːk]
socks	/sɑks/	[gɔk]

The final /s/ was optionally realized as [t] in simple words, but was always deleted in inflected forms.

A similar pattern of data has been observed for regular inflectional morphology in the speech of children with SLI. Gopnik (1990), Gopnik and Crago (1991), and Pinker (1991) claimed that such problems are specific to morphology and (given the fact that the impairment has a genetic component) show that morphological abilities are innate. These researchers have paid minimal attention to the possible role of phonological factors. Gopnik and Crago noted that their subjects had phonological problems, including some difficulty with consonant clusters in codas and with unstressed syllables. They discounted the role of phonology in the impairment because the morphological impairment was, they claim, more severe than the phonological impairment (though Fee, 1995b, showed that for these same subjects, more than half of the tokens with word-final cluster targets were simplified via deletion of one of the consonants). Stemberger (1995) and Hoeffner and McClelland (1993) presented connectionist analyses to show that the greater severity of the morphological impairment is predictable. OT provides a similar analysis. It is not necessary to assume that the impairment is specific to morphology.

Consider Table 6.6. The lowest-ranked constraints are the ones for the expression of morphology, whether for regular or irregular forms. The details for handling morphologically irregular forms are beyond the scope of this book; we assume here a lexically specific constraint that determines the irregularity of each word. The following ranking leads to marking of irregular past but not of regular past:

TABLE 6.6

	sɪŋ		pɪk		ækt	
	sæn	sɪŋ	pɪkt	pɪk	ækt	æk
Survived(Root) LinkedUpwards(Root)						*!
NotComplex(Coda)			*!		*	
\<PastTenseConstraints\>		*!		*		

The highest-ranked constraint (**Survived(Root)**) prevents the deletion of any segment from the base morpheme. Thus, a word such as *act* /ækt/ must be pronounced with a final consonant cluster. If the past tense form is irregular, there is no final consonant cluster in either the base form or the irregular past tense form, and so the irregular form is phonologically well formed; *sang* is more optimal than the base form *sing*, because it expresses past tense. For a regular form like *picked*, however, the inflectional constraint **PastTense(/d/,R)** would create a word-final consonant cluster. Since **NotComplex(Coda)** is ranked higher than the inflectional constraints, it is more optimal if the word is not inflected for past tense. The child is faithful to the phonology, not the morphology. If stable, this ranking would lead to a situation where the child would never delete in *base*-final consonant clusters, but would always delete *affixal* consonants. If additional phonological constraints are ranked higher than the morphological constraints (such as **Not(V-Root)**, which prevents epenthesis) and **Not(Coda)** (which prevents codas altogether), then the regular *-ed* suffix could never appear in the output. The absence of the suffix in the output is motivated by phonological constraints, not morphological ones, even though the constraints have an effect only on affixes. SLI children have a problem in which negative phonological constraints are (variably) ranked too high. They do not have an impairment of inflectional morphology. Insofar as there is a genetic component to the SLI impairment, it is that they are less skilled at articulation than normals.[33]

6.4.2. EPENTHESIS

We noted in §6.7.1.2 that epenthesis is uncommon in child phonology as a resolution of complex codas. We know of no instances in which a child epenthesized within or after a base-internal coda cluster, and also did so (or failed to do so) within similar clusters that include an affix. There are instances in which a child epenthesized only before an affix, however.

6.4.2.1. Epenthesis Only for Affixes: Phonological Resolution

For a brief period at 2;10, Morgan epenthesized schwa in /st/ (and /zd/) clusters if the stop was an affix, but deleted the /s/ in base-internal clusters (Stemberger & Bernhardt, 1997):

| first | /fɹst/ | [foːtʰ] |
| kissed | /kɪst/ | [tʰɪtʰ]~[tʰɪsəd] |

This derived from the following ranking:

Expressed(Past)	‖‖	NotComplex(Coda)	‖‖	Survived(C-Root)
Priority(Base)	‖‖	**Not(σ)**	‖‖	
	‖‖	**Not(V-Root)**	‖‖	

In base-final /st/ clusters, the /s/ deleted (see above). However, a base-final segment had to survive, and so two consonants were present in an affixed form. The constraints make it more optimal to insert a schwa than to produce a cluster, however. Bleile (1987) reported similar data for Jake: base-final /nd/ was reduced to [n], but a vowel was epenthesized before *-ed* (in *burned* [bɔnɪd]).

---

[33] Children with Specific Language Impairment (SLI) are actually more variable than this. For the particular subjects Fee (1995b) describes, final consonant clusters are reduced half the time even in simple words. There are some errors even with irregular morphology. Regular inflected forms are sometimes produced. The rankings given here must be unstable, so that variability arises.

6.4.2.2. Epenthesis Only for Affixes: Morphological Resolution

The epenthesis can be achieved morphologically, by adding two tokens of the
-*s* or -*ed* affixes. Stemberger (1995) reported a pattern of *double marking* for
Larissa's past tense forms that interacted with her development of word-final consonant clusters. At the time, the child could produce any consonant after a vowel
or approximant, but consonant clusters were limited to those ending in /s/ or /z/,
or those with a nasal[34] followed by a voiceless stop, including /nt/ (left column):

seed	[siːd]	round	[wawn]
beard	[biɹd]	act	[ʔæːk]
jump	[zʌmp]	lift	[lɪf]

All other clusters (right column) were simplified by retaining the first consonant
and deleting all that followed (via a high ranking for **Contiguity**, guaranteeing
that the consonant contiguous to the vowel survived). The distribution of doubled
-*ed* follows these two categories exactly. There was no doubling if the -*ed* followed a vowel or approximant or could create a cluster made up of a nasal plus
voiceless stop (left column). There was doubling if any other cluster resulted
(right column).

peed	[pʰiːd]	turned	[tʰɹndəd]
scared	[sɛɹd]	keeped	[tʰiːptəd]
jumped	[zʌmt]	kissed	[tʰɪstəd]
smelled	[fɛʊd]	jumped	[zʌmptəd]

One form in the left column had an unpronounceable cluster: the /mpt/ in *jumped*.
The child sometimes doubled the affix here, but sometimes resolved constraints
on the cluster by deleting the /p/. This created a new cluster [mt] that fit the nasal/
voiceless-stop pattern of the existing clusters [mp], [nt], [ŋk]. The same patterns
were observed for regularizations, showing the productivity of the pattern:

see-ed	[siːd]	winned	[wɪndəd]
heared	[hiɹd]	losed	[luːzdəd]
drinked	[ziŋt]	drinked	[ziŋktəd]

The child's syllable development allowed the forms in the left column to be produced (almost) correctly, but not the forms in the right column. Particular sequences within codas were ruled out by **NoSequence** constraints (see §7.3.2):

| **Expressed(Past)** ‖ **SinglyExpressed(Past)** |
| **NoSequence**   ‖ |

Survived(Root) and **Expressed(Past)** were both ranked high, so that two consonants had to be produced. **SinglyExpressed(Past)** was low-ranked, allowing the

---

[34] The nasal was pronounced fairly long, as in Italian, not as in adult English.

suffix to appear twice. Since the second token of the suffix followed [d] or [t] (in the first token), a schwa was epenthesized, as it always is in that environment in English. This created a syllable for the first token of -*ed* to link to as an onset, thereby eliminating the ill-formed complex coda. The doubling of the -*ed* suffix was not entirely a morphological phenomenon.[35]

Although the nasal-voiceless stop clusters were treated in a similar fashion in both monomorphemic and past-tense forms, it should be noted that nasal-voiced stop clusters were treated in different fashions. In monomorphemic words, constraints on final /nd/ were resolved via deletion of the voiced stop: *round* [waʊn], never *[waʊndəd]. The high ranking of **Expressed(Past)** prevented the /d/ of the suffix from being deleted; thus, constraints for the /nd/ cluster in *turned* could not be resolved in the same way as for the /nd/ cluster in *round*. The doubling of the -*ed* suffix was not entirely a phonological phenomenon.

6.4.3. SYLLABIFICATION
AND MORPHOLOGICAL BOUNDARIES

Prosodic factors can influence the effects of morphological structure on syllabification. In general, word boundaries tend to coincide with syllable boundaries, so that word-initial consonants tend to be syllable-initial. This can derive from stipulating that the primary domain of syllabification is the morphological word, or from the use of generalized alignment (**Aligned(MorphologicalWord,L,σ,L)**). Faithfulness to segmental content may sometimes override this.

We noted above an instance where Gwendolyn syllabified /st/ as a coda when it was base-final. Gwendolyn (Stemberger, p.u.d.; 3;10–4;6) presented a similar pattern with /l/, except that deletion was not involved. A syllable-initial /l/ was always realized as the glide [j], while a syllable-final /l/ was realized as the post-vocalic glide [ʊ].

less	[jɛs]	fall	[faʊ]
live	[jɪv]	spill	[pʰɪʊ]

An intervocalic /l/ was realized as [j] in morphologically simple words, but as both alternatives, [ʊj], in morphologically complex words.

millet	[mɪjət]	falling	[faʊjɪn]
wallet	[wɑːjət]	spill it	[pʰɪʊjɪt]

This phenomenon is treated as the doubling of the /l/ in Stemberger (1988a, 1988b), restricted to morpheme-final /l/. It appears that base-final /l/ was made into a coda, leaving the suffix or clitic without an onset consonant; the /l/ spread

---

[35] Rumelhart and McClelland (1986) predicted that suffix doubling could occur for phonological reasons, though the particular conditioning that they reported for their simulation was different from the conditioning here. Pinker and Prince (1988) expressed skepticism that phonological factors could lead to affix doubling. Phonology clearly can underlie affix doubling.

into the second syllable to provide it with an onset. The /l/ could be forced into the coda via alignment: **Aligned(BaseMorpheme,R,σ,R)**. Alternatively, if the preferred domain of syllabification is the base morpheme, then base-final consonants should tend to be treated as if no segments follow, and thus should be syllabified as a coda. The medial /l/ of *wallet*, because it is not base-final, is not subject to this constraint and is free to be syllabified as an onset.

Between 1;9 and 2;1, Morgan (Stemberger, p.u.d.) occasionally produced compound nouns with a different syllabification (and segmental content) than expected:

seagull	/siːgʌl/	[.çiːk.ʔɑɯ.]	*expected*: *[.çiː.dɑɯ.]
ski trail	/skiːtɹeɪl/	[.tʰiːt.ʋeɪ.ɤ.]	*expected*: *[.tʰiː.tʰeɪ.ɤ.]
flyswatter	/flaɪswɑtɹ̩ /	[.faɪt.ʋɑː.dɤ.]	*expected*: *[.faɪ.sɑː.dɤ.]

Only a few words showed this pattern, though the pronunciation was consistent for those words. At the time, onset velars surfaced as anterior coronals, but coda velars were realized accurately as velars. In *seagull*, the /g/ was syllabified as a coda (rather than as an onset, as expected), and a default onset [ʔ] was inserted in the second syllable. This odd syllabification allowed the feature [Dorsal] to survive, whereas standard syllabification would not have done so. In the other two words, the cluster should have been simplified to a single consonant. The child was able to produce both members of the cluster by splitting it between two syllables, but only at the cost of violating the usual domain of syllabification. Thus, segmental faithfulness can lead to unusual syllabification, in which word boundaries are ignored.

Stemberger (1988a) reports a related phenomenon in Gwendolyn's speech (see §6.1.12.4). He notes that some word-final consonants that were prohibited from codas (such as voiced stops) were occasionally rescued when the next word began with a vowel. Rather than being deleted, the unsyllabifiable word-final consonant was placed in the onset of the syllable at the beginning of the next word. This was possible only when the syllable beginning the next word did not have an onset of its own. Faithfulness to segments was achieved, but only at the cost of an unusual syllabification, in which word boundaries and syllable boundaries did not coincide.

6.5. SUMMARY AND CONCLUSIONS

We have reviewed what is known about prosodic development in young children. There is reduction at all levels. Children tend to have reduced syllable structure, foot structure, and word structure. When segments are in a disallowed coda, syllable, or foot, there are a variety of ways in which the ill-formedness can be resolved, just as there are in adult phonology. Also as in adult phonology, there are asymmetries between onsets and codas, with different restrictions on features in codas versus onsets. There are also interactions between syllable structure and foot structure: stressed syllables tend to be heavy and unstressed syllables tend to be light. We have also shown that phonological constraints can be ranked higher than morphological constraints, so that affixes are possible in some phonological environments but not in others.

7

SEQUENCES OF ELEMENTS

The previous two data chapters examined phenomena which reflect the autonomy and hierarchical organization of phonological elements. In this chapter, we focus on contiguous and noncontiguous sequences of elements (the major subdivisions within the chapter). Most of the discussion concentrates on the effects of **NoSequence** and **NotTwice** constraints. In some cases, changes in sequence accommodate other types of constraints and these are also examined briefly. As in previous chapters, we utilize examples from a number of different children, in order to cover the full range of phenomena. Order of repair strategies within each data section is generally deletion, addition, default insertion, harmony, and flop. As a summary of constraints and repair types, one child's alternate and variable productions of clusters concludes the chapter.

Key to the discussion of sequence constraints are the definitions of (a) sequences and adjacency, (b) sequence constraint types, and (c) repair types. An overview of sequence constraints and developmental trends for sequence phenomena follows. For more detail, see §4.7.2 and §4.7.3.

7.1. SEQUENCE CONSTRAINTS IN REVIEW

A variety of sequence constraints are found in developing phonologies. Failure to note sequence constraints may make a systematic pattern look variable, and/or give the impression that a child has many "lexical exceptions." Depending on whether tier, syllable, timing unit, or Root adjacency is relevant, contiguous and/or noncontiguous elements may be affected (see §3.5). We assume throughout that consonants and vowels are on separate planes (see §3.4.3).

Constraints that specifically concern sequences are as follows:

NoSequence(A . . . B): Given two segments, A cannot be in the first
segment if B is in the second segment.

NotTwice: An element may not appear twice if the two tokens
are adjacent.

Both types of constraints can be operative at a variety of levels, although **Not-Twice** is more likely to affect prosodic constituents than **NoSequence**.[1] These two constraint families are not always involved when there are changes in sequences of elements; changes in sequences can accommodate other high-ranked constraints. For example, when /snoʊ/ surfaces as [nos], and other clusters are also impossible, **NotComplex(Onset)** probably motivated the flop, rather than **NoSequence(+ continuant...-continuant)**. Identification of sequence constraints as compared with other constraints requires sufficient exemplars to detect patterns.

Other more general (and usually high-ranked) constraints also concern position of elements and can be implicated in sequence effects: **Uninterrupted, Contiguity,** and margin and rime co-occurrence constraints. **Aligned** and **Ordering** could also be involved, but, as noted in §4.4.4 and §4.6, we have found that these two constraints are not generally needed.

Sequence constraints may be defined at the level of the feature (in place, manner, or voicing), or at the level of a prosodic unit such as a timing unit, syllable, or foot.[2] Typically, **NoSequence** constraints affect similar features (e.g., two place features, or two tokens of [continuant]). The element affected by a given sequence constraint or repair is not necessarily predictable in terms of right or left position (but see §7.2).

Patterns such as the following can be informative in trying to determine whether sequence constraints are operative in a child's system, and what they are (see also Appendix D):

1. If one member of a category is realized correctly but others are not, a sequence constraint may be implicated. Determination of the relevant constraint means looking across a variety of constituents and structures. For example, if /sp/ surfaces as [p], and we just look at that example, we do not know whether the constraint is **NotComplex(Onset)**, **NoSequence(Coronal...Labial)**, **NotTwice(+ consonantal)**, or **NoSequence(+ continuant...-continuant)**. However,

---

[1] However, recall that **NotTwice** may be a special type of **NoSequence** constraint, where identity of segments is involved: two elements cannot occur in a sequence if they are identical.

[2] Sequence constraints on prosodic elements can be described alternatively as structural complexity constraints. For example, in §6.1.6, we showed how **Not(Complex)** can prevent the realization of clusters. In such cases, feature content of the consonants is irrelevant. In this chapter we concentrate on examples that implicate feature content. For example, the child may be able to produce clusters but only with certain feature sequences. The limitation does not concern onset complexity, but sequences of particular consonant features.

if we also observe that /st/ surfaces as [t], but /tw/ and /pl/ surface as [tw] and [pl], then we can assume that **NotComplex(Onset)**, **NoSequence (Coronal...Labial)**, and **NotTwice(+ consonantal)** are not relevant, and that the operative constraint is **NoSequence(+ continuant...-continuant)**.

2. Longitudinal data may help elucidate the relevant constraints at a given point in time. A general constraint may initially inhibit all members of a category, but later a more specific and limited constraint may affect only one member of a category. For example, all /s/-stop clusters may initially be prohibited due to high ranking of **NoSequence(+ continuant . . . -continuant)**. Later on, the child may overcome this constraint, but high ranking of **NotTwice(Coronal)** might still result in prohibition of /st/-clusters. The latter constraint may have always been present, but have become visible only when the general manner constraint has lost its "grip."

Before proceeding to examination of specific data, we review general developmental trends with respect to sequences.

7.2. SEQUENCE CONSTRAINTS AND REPAIRS: OVERVIEW

In this section, we summarize a variety of statistical properties of phenomena as a further background for the data sections. Frequency differences occur for repair types, elements affected, and position of affected elements, and these are outlined below.

7.2.1. REPAIR TYPE FREQUENCY

Frequency of repair types across children generally appears to be (in descending order): deletion > insertion of defaults > spreading > epenthesis > flop. The frequency of repair types tends to change over time. In early development, the simplification repairs (deletion, insertion of defaults, spreading) are more common. Epenthesis tends to occur later (Bernhardt, 1992a; Kehoe, 1995). Sequence constraint type, constituent type, and ranking of other constraints affect repair type frequency, as discussed below.

1. Sequence constraints and repair types. **NoSequence** can lead to any type of repair, but **NotTwice** generally leads only to deletion, epenthesis (addition), and spreading. Flopping two identical elements clearly cannot repair a **NotTwice** sequence. Insertion of defaults is possibly less viable as a repair of **NotTwice** constraints, because new *dissimilatory* sequences would result.[3] For example, if

---

[3] **NotTwice** violations are more likely to be resolved via the merging of adjacent identical elements (violating **Distinct**) than by the changing of one of those elements into something else, even in adult phonology (McCarthy, 1986).

[-voiced] were to be inserted for one segment in the sequence /dd/, [dt] or [td] would result, a possibly even more difficult articulatory sequence than [dd]. Deletion of one [d] or double linking would be more likely: [d] or [dː].

2. Constituent types and repair types. Deletion has the widest distribution by constituent type, occurring for all constituent types except perhaps as a nonminimal repair of CV sequence constraints. Spreading and flop also occur across constituent types.

Deletion plus insertion of defaults occurs for both noncontiguous and, to a lesser extent, contiguous sequences. Other constraints are relevant in the latter case. For example, if **NoSequence(+ continuant...-continuant)** prohibited /sp/, default [-continuant] could be inserted for the /s/ of /sp/. However, this would result in the non-English onset *[tp], which is prohibited also by **NoSequence (Coronal...Labial)**. Thus, default insertion would be unlikely. Alternatively, if **NoSequence(Coronal...Labial)** prohibited /sp/, *and* default Coronal place surfaced for the /p/, [st] would result, a permissible English onset. In this case, default insertion would be a viable repair (unless **NotTwice(Coronal)** were also highranked).

Addition (epenthesis) is most limited, repairing primarily onset clusters.

3. Other constraints and effect on repair type frequency. Other high-ranked constraints can also influence which repairs are the most viable options for sequence constraints. Content faithfulness constraints are generally low-ranked in early phonology. Deletion eliminates content, and is thus compatible with this ranking. In contrast, content faithfulness constraints are higher-ranked in later development. Epenthesis possibly occurs more frequently in later development because it allows content to survive.

Epenthesis and flop result in contiguity violations, and more complex word structure or sequences. **Contiguity** is generally a high-ranked faithfulness constraint, and less likely to be violated. Word structures with extra syllables or unusual sequences are less likely to be allowed. For example, epenthesis of a vowel in onset clusters creates an initial unstressed syllable. Epenthesis is only a viable repair if a child can produce a right-prominent foot. The lower frequency of epenthesis as a repair strategy may be attributable to constraints on word stress in English.

Further frequency effects can be found with respect to particular features, as we see in the next section.

7.2.2. FEATURES AFFECTED

Sequence constraints generally affect place features more than other types of features. In some contexts, however, constraints and/or repairs may affect multiple features. For example, place assimilation frequently appears in conjunction with manner assimilation in onset clusters ([fw] for /kw/). Two features may flop to repair a constraint on one feature.

1. Place sequence constraints. Place is implicated across constraint, constituent, sequence, and repair types. Constraints on places of articulation (on two different features, or on two identical features) are commonly observed. Dissimilation is least common, possibly because it would create sequences that are ruled out by other constraints.

2. Manner sequence constraints. Manner sequence constraints are less frequent, but are still common in onset clusters and in intervocalic position (especially in early development). The feature [continuant] is most often involved, with spreading of [+continuant] (and intervocalically, sometimes [+sonorant]). In intervocalic position, **Uninterrupted(+continuant)** appears to motivate the spreading. In clusters, however, **NoSequence(-continuant...+continuant)** appears relevant. Noncontiguous manner harmony is relatively rare, although nasal harmony (and less frequently, fricative harmony) does occur (Elsen, 1991; Stoel-Gammon & Stemberger, 1994).

Several factors may lead to the lower frequency of manner sequence constraints: order of acquisition for sound classes, effects of other higher-ranked constraints, and phonetic grounding. In early development, children tend to use only stops and nasals. The nondefault feature [+nasal] spreads, which is not unexpected given the asymmetry in spreading between default and nondefault features. By the time children acquire fricatives and liquids, simplification repairs are generally less frequent, only showing up in complex constituents such as clusters. Furthermore, in early phases, rime and margin constraints may be higher-ranked than sequence constraints. For example, [+continuant] may be favored in rimes, and [-continuant] may be favored in onsets, independent of manner sequence.

3. Voicing sequence constraints. Sequence constraints on voicing resulting in voicing assimilation or dissimilation may occur in both intervocalic and syllable-initial contexts. Intervocalically, a voiceless consonant may be voiced if there is high ranking of **Uninterrupted(+voiced)** for the surrounding vowels. Alternately, **NotTwice(+voiced)** may motivate dissimilation of voicing intervocalically. Word-initial consonants may be voiced if **NoSequence(-voiced...+voiced)** is high-ranked. Noncontiguous voicing harmony or flop is rare; Matthei (1989) reports voicing harmony for one child, but gives few details.

7.2.3. WORD POSITION AND AFFECTED ELEMENTS

Sometimes high-ranked rime and margin constraints can affect outcomes with respect to sequence constraints. The **NoSequence** constraint may in fact be a derivative of one of those general syllable position constraints.

In addition, general constraints of the language can affect outcomes. The sequences *[tp] and *[tk] are not permissible English clusters except in proper names across syllable boundaries. Some children appear to have sequence constraints prohibiting default features before nondefault features, which perhaps reflects constraints of the adult English system.

Although the description of a **NoSequence** constraint appears to treat both elements equally, one of the elements may be more problematical. In noncontiguous sequences, the second element is relatively less prominent and appears later developmentally. Codas and medial consonants are later acquired, more marked, and less prominent acoustically than word onsets. Thus they are more likely to be problematical. In clusters, the sonority hierarchy may be relevant, affecting /s/-clusters differently from stop-approximant clusters. Furthermore, later-acquired segments such as /s/ or liquids may result in different constraints and repairs for cluster types.

Usually the offending element or both elements are the targets for repair. Ironically, in consonant harmony in monosyllabic words, the repair often targets the first consonant, particularly if that consonant has default features.

7.2.4. FREQUENCY DIFFERENCES IN SEQUENCE CONSTRAINTS AND REPAIRS

In the previous discussion, we offered hypothetical explanations for the frequency differences found. In summary, these were:

1. Developmental asynchrony among sound classes. General order of feature acquisition can also affect sequence constraints and repair types.

2. Phonetic grounding. Some kinds of articulatory gestures appear to be phonetically more difficult, particularly gestures involving changes of place.

3. Defaults and nondefaults. Feature asymmetries in repairs suggest relevance for theories which classify features as defaults and nondefaults. Nondefaults tend to be more subject to constraints, but also may survive more often than defaults.

4. General phonotactics of the language. Phonotactic constraints in the adult phonology may influence developmental patterns. Although a constraint against */tp/ is part of the English adult phonology, children may extend such a constraint to noncontiguous sequences. Frequency differences between onsets and codas in the adult language may also affect which features or elements are more problematic in sequences (low-frequency elements being more problematic).

5. Resource limitations. Children appear to have trade-offs in development (Crystal, 1987). As complexity increases in one domain, another domain may lose complexity. In resolving violations of sequence constraints, types of repairs change over time. Different types of complexity are allowed at different phases of development, and constraint rankings reflect that. (The individual profile on onset cluster development at the end of the chapter in §7.5 demonstrates this.)

We return to these issues throughout the chapter, pointing out where data support or call into question the assumptions made and the explanations given.

7.3. CONTIGUOUS SEQUENCES

This section discusses consonant clusters, diphthongs, and CV sequences. The major focus is on word-initial consonant clusters, because most of the data avail-

able concern this type of sequence. At the end of the chapter (§7.5), a profile of
Charles's various repairs for clusters exemplifies variability in repair types.

7.3.1. WORD-INITIAL CLUSTERS

Determining cluster sequence constraints in developmental phonology is not a
straightforward task. Clusters are often subject to very high-ranked **NotCom-
plex(Onset)** constraints. Sequence constraints may also be present, but they are
less relevant than constraints on onset complexity in early development. As children become capable of producing diconsonantal onsets, particular sequences of
consonants remain difficult. At this point, the sequence constraints become
relevant.

In order to examine the possible types of sequence constraints, we review the
types of onset clusters found in English, Dutch, and German, concentrating on
English (see Tables 7.1–7.4). Tables 7.2 and 7.3 list the sequences in order of
descending frequency by place or manner type. Individual clusters are listed hori-
zontally within each type by token frequency based on a count of the Brown corpus of adult written English (Stemberger, 1990). It is not known whether type or
token frequency may be more relevant in acquisition. Table 7.1 lists the overall
order of frequency for the English clusters based on Stemberger (1990). Frequency in the adult written corpus does not necessarily mirror frequency in oral
input to children. Note that /sn/ is low frequency in the written corpus, but children often hear the words *snack, snow,* and *snake.* Although /pɹ/ is high in text
frequency, children probably hear [pl] and [bɹ] more frequently than /pɹ/ (*'Say*

TABLE 7.1   Order of Frequency of English Clusters[a]

pɹ	.01190	sk	.00221	sn	.00037
st	.00952	kw	.00182	kj	.00032
fɹ	.00731	bl	.00158	vj	.00031
tɹ	.00496	fl	.00157	pj	.00021
gɹ	.00450	sl	.00125	ʃɹ	.00012
pl	.00358	sm	.00121	bj	.00009
bɹ	.00334	sw	.00087	dw	.00007
kl	.00332	gl	.00073	sf	.00004
sp	.00311	mj	.00058	ʃw	.00003
kɹ	.00287	hj	.00048	ʃn	.00002
dɹ	.00242	tw	.00047	gw	.00002
θɹ	.00230	fj	.00039	θw	.00001[b]

[a] Based on Stemberger's (1990) analysis of the Brown written corpus
(Francis & Kučera, 1982, n = 1,014,000 words). Number = % words starting
with that cluster.
[b] ʃl,ʃm: Less than .00001.

TABLE 7.2   English Diconsonantal Onset Clusters: Place Sequences[a]

Sequence	Cluster
Coronal-Labial	tɹ, sp, dɹ, θɹ, sm, sw, tw, ʃɹ, dw, sf, ʃw, θw, ʃm
Labial-Coronal	pɹ, fɹ, pl, bɹ, bl, fl, mj, fj, vj, pj, bj
Coronal-Coronal	st, tɹ, dɹ, θɹ, sl, sn, ʃɹ, ʃn, ʃl
Dorsal-Coronal	gɹ, kl, kɹ, gl, kj
Dorsal-Labial	gɹ, kɹ, kw, gw
Labial-Labial	pɹ, fɹ, bɹ
Coronal-Dorsal	sk
Glottal-Coronal	hj
Glottal-Labial	hw

[a] Within each category, order of descending token frequency is left to right (based on Stemberger, 1990).

TABLE 7.3   English Disconsonantal Onset Clusters: Manner sequences[a]

Sequence	Cluster
[-son][+son]	pɹ, fɹ, tɹ, gɹ, pl, bɹ, kl, kɹ, dɹ, θɹ, kw, bl, fl, sl, sm, sw, gl, mj, tw, fj, sn, kj, vj, pj, ʃɹ, bj, dw, ʃw, ʃn, gw, θw, ʃl, ʃm
[+cons][-cons]	pɹ, fɹ, tɹ, gɹ, bɹ, kɹ, dɹ, θɹ, kw, sw, mj, tw, fj, kj, vj, pj, ʃɹ, bj, dw, ʃw, gw, θw
[-cont][+cont]	pɹ, tɹ, gɹ, pl, bɹ, kl, kɹ, dɹ, kw, bl, gl, mj, tw, kj, pj, bj, dw, gw
[+cont][+cont]	fɹ, θɹ, fl, sl, sw, hj, fj, vj, ʃɹ, sf, ʃw, θw, ʃl
[+cont][-cont]	st, sp, sk, sm, sn, ʃn, ʃm
[+son][+son]	mj, hj, hw
[-son][-son]	sf

[a] Within each category, order of descending token frequency is left to right (based on Stemberger, 1990).

please,' play, playdough, breakfast, break, broken). Because frequency counts in adult speech to children are not available, adult-based counts must be used in order to have *some* idea of frequencies.

In English, obstruent-approximant clusters predominate: ([-sonorant]...[+sonorant]). Stop-approximant clusters ([-continuant]...[+continuant]) are especially common. Least frequent are /s/-stop ([+continuant]...[-continuant], [-sonorant]...[-sonorant]) sequences. Many specific [-sonorant]...[+sonorant] clusters are also high in token frequency. However, /st/ and /sp/ are also high in token frequency, changing the status of /s/-stop sequences in the overall picture. Some sequences are missing: [+sonorant]...[+sonorant] (except in /j/-clusters like /mj/ in *music*), and [+sonorant]...[-sonorant]. This pattern follows from sonority principles and margin constraints, favoring obstruents in leftmost position.

TABLE 7.4   Word-Initial Clusters in Dutch (D) and German (G)
Not Found in English[a]

Sequence	Cluster
Labial-Coronal	vl (D); vr, pfl (G)
Coronal-Labial	ʃp, ʃm, tsv, ʃv (G); zv (D)
Coronal-Coronal	ʃl, ʃn, ʃt
Dorsal-Coronal	kn (D, G); χ, xl, χɹ(D); gn (G)
Coronal-Dorsal	sχ (D); ʃʁ (G)
Dorsal-Labial	χr, kʊ, tʊ (D); kv (G)
[-son][+son]	kn (D,G); gn (G); xl, χl, vl, χr (D); ʃm, ʃn (G); kʊ, tʊ (D); pfl (G)
[+cont][+cont]	vr, sχ, χl, xl, vl, χr, zv (D); ʃʁ, tsv, ʃl, ʃv (G)
[+cont][-cont]	ʃt, ʃp, ʃm, ʃn (G)
[+cont][+son]	xl, χl, vl, χr (D)
[-cont][-cont]	kn (D, G); gn (G)
[-cont][+cont]	kv, (tsv, pfl) (G)

[a] /r/ may be the alveolar trill /r/, the uvular trill /ʁ/ or fricative /ʁ/, depending on the dialect. Clusters with /w/, /j/, and /θ/ are not found in Dutch or German. German has /s/ in onset only rarely in borrowings. Dutch has no /sk/.

In terms of place, the most common English clusters are Labial...Coronal (due to the fact that /l/, /ɹ/, and /j/ are often second in the cluster). The next most frequent are Coronal...Labial, with /s/ onsets and the /ɹ/ and /w/ approximants affecting that frequency. Less common are Labial...Labial, and sequences with [Dorsal]; the least frequent is Coronal...Dorsal (/sk/ and /Cw/; assuming that /ɹ/ does not have a dorsal component). Token frequency for individual clusters shows some differences here. Particular homorganic clusters are more frequent than they are in type frequency (/pɹ/, /st/, /fɹ/). The Labial...Coronal sequences /pɹ/, /pl/, and /bɹ/ are of high frequency in both type and place sequence, however.

In terms of voicing, [-voiced]...[+voiced] clusters are of high type and token frequency.

Constraints can be defined over any of those sequences. Note that more opportunities exist for **NoSequence** constraints than **NotTwice** constraints in terms of type frequency, since there are fewer clusters with the same features in the two consonant slots.

Assuming that some type of frequency is relevant, the most frequent sequences would probably be acquired earlier. Thus, we could predict for English:

1. Earliest acquisition of obstruent-approximant clusters (because of type and token frequency, and additionally, sonority order);

2. Later acquisition of the less common fricative-stop sequences (by type, although according to token frequency, /st/ and /sp/ could be acquired early);

3. Order of /s/-cluster acquisition as follows:
   /st/ > /sp/ > /sk/ > /sl/ > /sm/ > /sw/ > /sn/;

4. Appearance of Labial...Coronal (combining type and token frequency) and homorganic sequences (token frequency) before other sequences.

Target segment type and substitution type for that adult target, might result in additional or different predictions.

1. Effects of segment type. If a feature, such as [Dorsal], is rare in clusters, *and* it is generally later in consonant acquisition (as noted in §5.5.1.1), both of those factors will delay production of clusters with that feature. Liquids and /s/ are later developing segments, and thus clusters containing them should match the adult targets only when [s] and liquids are in the system, even if they are frequent in the adult input.

In Dutch and German, sequences with [Dorsal] might be earlier than in English, because the velar fricative is an early developing segment, according to Beers (1995).

2. Effects of substitution type. If a substitution for a segment is not affected by any other constraints, a cluster with two elements may appear. The stop-liquid clusters may surface with *two consonantal elements* in early development, even if they do not match the adult targets segmentally, because glides such as [w] or [j] can appear in place of the liquids. However, the typical substitution for a fricative is a stop. The /s/-stop clusters cannot be realized as stop-stop clusters, because of the very high ranking in onsets for **NotTwice(-continuant)**: *[tp], *[tk], *[tt], *[tm], *[tn].

How do the general trends compare to these predictions? In the next sections, we first review the data available, and then give examples of repairs for clusters. Stoel-Gammon and Dunn comment that it is "difficult to identify developmental stages for consonant clusters" in English (1985:33) or any other language, because of the lack of comparability in methods of data collection and the limited number of studies. Data from Templin (1957), Ingram (1989b), Bernhardt (1990), Elsen (1991), Chin (1993), and Fikkert (1994) are utilized to test predictions made above about order of cluster acquisition in general and for fricatives, and the effects of segment and substitution type on child productions.

7.3.1.1. General Order of Acquisition

Obstruent-approximant ([-sonorant]...[+sonorant], and/or [+consonantal]... [-consonantal]) clusters were predicted to be the earliest based on frequency and the sonority hierarchy. Many studies of English, Dutch, and German show stop-approximant ([-continuant]...[+continuant]) clusters to be the earliest clusters (Templin, 1957; Ingram, 1989b; Chin, 1993; Fikkert, 1994; Beers, 1995).

In Elsen's (1991) diary study of German, she notes that Annalena actually produced occasional fricative clusters in the same time period as stop-approximant clusters, but that the latter were more frequent and robust. Fikkert (1994) summarizes the order of manner type acquisition for Dutch as in Table 7.5. Seven of nine individual subjects adhered to the predicted order. Two, however, acquired /s/-stop clusters first (Robin and Noortje).[4] As we have remarked previously, there is always variability across children.

TABLE 7.5   Order of Cluster Acquisition by Manner Category in Fikkert's (1994) Study of Dutch[a]

Cluster Type	#-Ss $n = 12$
/s/-Stop	2
Stop-Liq $>$[b] Fric-Liq	1
Stop-Liq $>$ /s/-Stop	1
Stop-Liq $>$ Fric-Liq	1
Stop-Liq $>$ Fric-Liq $>$ /s/-Stop	1
Stop-Liq $>$ Fric-Liq $>$ Stop-Glide $>$ Stop-Nas $>$ Fric-Nas	1
Stop-Liq $>$ Fric-Liq $>$ Stop-Glide $>$ /s/-Stop $>$ /s/-Fric	1
Stop-Liq $>$ Fric-Liq $>$ Stop-Glide $>$ /s/-Fric $>$ /s/-Stop $>$ Fric-Glide, Stop-Nas	1
No data provided	3

[a] Fikkert, 1994: 106
[b] $>$ = Before.

The following constraints and rankings account for the early emergence of stop-approximant clusters:

1. If no fricatives are in the system, high-ranked **NotCo-occurring (+continuant,-sonorant)** prohibits fricatives without reference to sequence.
2. If fricatives do appear as singletons, but only stop-approximant clusters are produced (as in Bernhardt, 1990: *S2*, *S3*, and *S4*), the following ranking of sequence constraints is in effect:

NotTwice(+continuant)	‖‖	**NoSequence(-cont...+cont)**
NoSequence(+cont...-cont)	‖‖	

[4] Fikkert also reported in this regard that in triconsonantal cluster acquisition, the children who started with stop-liquid clusters reduced triconsonantal clusters to stop-liquid clusters, whereas the two children who started with /s/-clusters reduced triconsonantal clusters to /s/-stop clusters. Early patterns therefore persisted.

If the first clusters are /s/-stop sequences, an alternate ranking is in effect:

NoSequence(-cont...+cont) ||| **NoSequence(+cont...-cont)**

Eventually, the **Survived** constraints for timing units and features outrank the sequence constraints, and the clusters become possible.

Few details are available as to *which* stop-approximant clusters are earliest. Elsen's (1991) German diary study shows [bʁ] to be earliest, appearing at 1;6, but other stop-approximant clusters appeared within a month or two. In intervention, Charles (Bernhardt, 1992b) learned to produce the infrequent /tw/, /kw/, and /Cj/ clusters first (as therapy targets), after which a variety of stop-approximant and /s/-clusters emerged spontaneously. Thus, type frequency of adult targets is not necessarily a condition for early acquisition, at least in the intervention situation. (However, because of Charles's substitution of [w] for /ɹ/ and [j] for /l/, [tw], [kw], and [Cj] were potentially frequent outputs for him.)

7.3.1.2. Order of Fricative Clusters

Fricative cluster order appears to differ across children. If the cluster elements have identical place features, this can affect output. **NotTwice(C-Place)** (along with **Distinct** and **SinglyLinked**) is relevant in those cases. The sonority hierarchy also appears relevant for some children.

For individual English-learning children, various fricative clusters have been reported to be the first: [sl] (Smith, 1973: Amahl); [st] (Ringo, 1985: Megan); [sn] (Bernhardt, 1990: 3/6 *S*s, although two of those subjects showed use of [fw] at the same time). In all of these cases, double linking of C-Place (whether Coronal or Labial) appeared to facilitate cluster production, as predicted. If place is doubly linked, fewer resources are required for place, and more are available for manner and timing unit realization. Double linking for manner ([+continuant]) only appeared to be relevant for [fw] (see §7.3.1.5).

Note that [sn] was the earliest /s/-cluster for three subjects in Bernhardt (1990), even though it is a low-frequency English cluster. The word *snake* perhaps facilitates this production, since the [s] sound of the snake is part of the word. Bernhardt observed that parents tended to extend the [s::] in that context. Ringo's (1985) subject acquired [sn] later than [st] but earlier than [sm], again showing that double linking of place may be generally facilitative.

For German, Elsen (1991) notes that her daughter used a variety of fricative clusters early in development. The most frequent early cluster was [ʃm], with [ʃt] and [ʃn] close behind. In two of those cases, Coronal...Coronal sequences are present, according with the data above from English, although in the case of German, the value of the terminal feature [anterior] was not the same ([-anterior]... [+anterior]).

Fikkert's (1994) and Beers's (1995) Dutch data are not organized in a way to show a specific order for fricative clusters. However, Fikkert (1994) notes that double linking of place appeared facilitative. Non-Dutch sequences such as [fm] appeared, promoting realization of two cluster elements with doubly linked Place.

Double linking of features thus can facilitate cluster production, a fact that is not predictable from type or token frequency, but from the phonology itself. In such cases, **NotTwice(C-Place)** is high-ranked, but **Survived(TimingUnit)** is also high-ranked. Those are both accommodated if **SinglyLinked** and **Distinct(C-Place)** are low-ranked, allowing fusion of the place features. But shared features are not necessarily facilitative for all clusters. For some children, the most frequent English /s/-cluster (/st/) is last to be acquired (N. Smith, 1973; Bernhardt, 1990: Charles, Gordon); the cluster /st/ appears as a singleton [t], [θ], or [s] (depending on the child).

The sonority hierarchy promotes earlier acquisition of stop-approximant clusters over fricative clusters. It *can* also affect the order of fricative acquisition, hence the earlier acquisition of /sn/ or /sl/ in comparison with /st/. (The late emergence of /sw/ may be a reflection of its low frequency in English.) The /st/-cluster can be later than /sp/ or /sk/ if the following ranking is relevant for the child:

NotTwice(Coronal) ‖‖ **Survived(Root)** ‖‖ **NoSequence**
SinglyLinked(Coronal) ‖‖

The child cannot have two coronals in a row, nor can they be doubly linked (high ranking of **SinglyLinked**). These are more highly ranked than **Survived (Root)**, and hence one of the coronals deletes. The **NoSequence** constraints are low-ranked and hence the other clusters are possible. They contain nondefault features, and **Survived** constraints are high-ranked for those features. The system avoids insertion of two adjacent identical default features.

7.3.1.3. Consonants as Singletons versus Cluster Elements

In general, if a segment appears late as a singleton, it appears even later in clusters. This could be predictable from frequency data, since singletons are more frequent in adult speech.

Both Bernhardt (1990) and Fikkert (1994) note that, if liquids are later acquired segments, they tend to appear as singletons before appearing in clusters. The same is generally true of fricatives (Edwards & Shriberg, 1983). **NoSequence** constraints can prohibit features, even if **Survived(Feature)** is generally high-ranked.

NoSequence(A...B) ‖‖ **Survived(Feature)** ‖‖ **Not(Feature)**

The failure of certain units to be realized in complex contexts is not an uncommon phenomenon in child phonology. It suggests the relevance of resource limitations in an information-processing model. As demands increase in prosodic complexity (here, from singleton to cluster onset), the capacity to produce the lower-level distinctions is exceeded, because of cumulative complexity for the output as a whole.

Not all trends are absolute, however. Segments can appear in clusters first. Fikkert (1994) notes this to be true for Jarmo, who acquired liquids and glides in clusters earlier than in singleton onsets (or at least at the same moment, as the example with *Willy* and *train* show). (Word-initial /l/ did not appear until 2;1.8, however.) When word-initial liquids were first attempted, they were produced as stops. Glides appeared as stops or [h].

	Willy	/ʋɪːliː/	[hɪːliː]	'Willy'	1;10.9
	regen	/reːχə(n)/	[teːχə]	'rain'	1;11.20
	water	/ʋaːtər/	[caːtə]	'water'	2;0.4
	lekker	/lɛkər/	[lɛʒkə]	'good'	2;1.8
	weg	/ʋɛχ/	[ʋɛχ]	'gone'	2;3.9
BUT:	klaar	/klaːr/	[kʀaː]	'clear'	1;8.12
			[kʁaː]~[klaː]		1;11.6
	train	/trɛin/	[tlɛɪ]	'train'	1;10.9
	twee	/tʋeː/	[tʋeː]	'two'	

7.3.1.3.1. Analysis 1

If a segment does not appear as a singleton, we generally assume high ranking of **Not(Feature)** compared with **Survived(Feature)**. Taking /l/ as an example:

Not(+lateral)   ⫴   **Survived(+lateral)**

If a segment appears in clusters, we could posit the following very specific context-conditioned ranking:

Survived$_{\text{Onset-cluster}}$(+lateral)
═══════════════════════
Not(+lateral)
═══════════════════════
Survived$_{\text{Elsewhere}}$(+lateral)
═══════════════════════

Although this describes the results for Jarmo's data (in a way reminiscent of rule-based phonology), it does not accord with a basic principle of Optimality Theory (OT): that constraints should be general rather than highly specific. It was necessary to build the environment into the constraint (as in previous rule-based theories). It is best to handle such specificity through the interactions of constraints.

7.3.1.3.2. Analysis 2

Fikkert (1994) suggests that the sonority hierarchy is relevant in Jarmo's case, although she does not develop the argument. In the clusters, the word-initial consonant is a stop. Faithful production of the cluster preserves the sonority hierarchy, and provides a maximal sonority contrast between onset and nucleus. The liquid or glide can be produced accurately, and not impinge on that sonority contrast. Constraints are as follows:

1. The optimal onset is an obstruent: **Co-occurring(σ-Margin→-sonorant)**. This results in deletion of sonorant features for the singleton liquid (by lower ranking of **Survived(+lateral)**).

2. **LinkedDownwards(TimingUnit)** is high-ranked, prohibiting simplification of the cluster to a singleton.

3. **NotTwice(-sonorant)** prohibits onsets with two obstruents, such as would arise if /l/ surfaced as a stop or fricative.

4. Obstruents cannot be [+lateral] (**NotCo-occurring(+lateral,-sonorant)**). Thus, the best solution is to produce the cluster with the stop and liquid as in the target. High ranking of **Survived(+lateral)** in contrast with **Not(+lateral)** allows production of the cluster.

LinkedDownwards(TimingUnit)			
Co-occurring(σ-Margin→-son)			
NotCo-occurring(+lat,-son)	Survived(+lateral)		Not(+lateral)
NotTwice(-son)			

This ranking means that [+lateral] could survive (as it does in clusters), but was prevented from doing so in specific environments (a syllable margin containing just [l]). At the later point where liquids and glides appear as singleton onsets, the margin constraint has become low-ranked, and the feature faithfulness constraints become high-ranked overall.

These data are useful because they remind us of the importance of considering the system as a whole. Feature constraints, margin constraints, sequence constraints, and syllable structure constraints all interact. We cannot discuss one part of the system without discussing other parts of the system. In this case, sequence constraints were not relevant (except insofar as they *prevented* changes) even though we were dealing with clusters (where sequence constraints often force changes). Margin and feature constraints affected the outcomes. But the example is similar to the generic case, in which sequence constraints can outrank feature constraints.

7.3.1.4. Summary of Trends for Word-Initial Clusters

The data show that sequence constraints play a role in cluster acquisition. If children simultaneously acquired *all* clusters, the only relevant constraint in cluster acquisition would be **NotComplex(Onset)**. However, both **NoSequence** and **NotTwice** are operative at some point in development, in different ways for different children. In general, the sonority hierarchy and double linking of C-Place are relevant factors in order of acquisition. If clusters are not possible because of sequence constraints, a variety of repairs can occur, as we show in the following sections. Order of frequency of repairs (most to least) across children appears to be deletion (with or without default insertion) > assimilation > epenthesis (addition) and flop (metathesis or migration). Repairs are discussed in that order. Separate subsections address repairs for **NoSequence** and **NotTwice** constraints, for obstruent-sonorant clusters, and /s/-clusters.

7.3.1.5. NoSequence Constraints for Word-Initial Clusters: Deletion and Default Insertion Repairs

This section provides examples of minimal and nonminimal deletion repair for clusters with obstruents and sonorants that are a response to **NoSequence** constraints. We first examine general patterns, then specific repairs affecting first stop-sonorant clusters, including stop-nasal clusters. A short section on fricative-sonorant clusters concludes the subsection. (**NotTwice** constraints appear to affect fricative-sonorant clusters more often than **NoSequence constraints**.) Because minimal deletion repairs also involve default insertion, that discussion is included here.

In English, stop-glide clusters are often the first clusters (Ingram, 1989b), and in Dutch stop-liquid clusters (Fikkert, 1994) are often first. In early phases, **Not** constraints for the particular features affect production of cluster segments, but even when the system permits the particular segments, a **NoSequence** constraint can inhibit production of the segment in the cluster. For example, just because a child begins to produce [l], the [l] does not necessarily appear in the clusters, because of sequence constraints relative to the feature [+lateral] or [+sonorant].[5] The sequence constraint is ranked higher than **Survived** for the relevant features in the prosodically weaker second-consonant position (§4.7.1.5) in the typical case. **Co-occurring(σ-Margin→-sonorant)** may also be relevant (promoting obstruents in margins).

NoSequence(-sonorant...+sonorant)
Survived(TimingUnit)
Co-occurring(σ-Margin→-sonorant)
Survived$_{Strong}$(Features) ||| **Survived$_{Weak}$(Features)**

Typically, the developmentally later feature or its segment deletes, but not always. We give examples from English, Dutch, and German, showing similarities and differences in deletion patterns within and across languages.

7.3.1.5.1. Deletion and Sonorant Consonants

Clusters made up of an obstruent followed by a sonorant consonant are difficult. We treat the relevant constraint as **NoSequence(-sonorant...{+consonantal,+sonorant})**, though **NotTwice(+consonantal)** may also be relevant. Features from either the sonorant or the stop can delete, and default features potentially replace them. Typically, the sonorant consonant is affected, either minimally or maximally (through Root level replacement, or full deletion). We

---

[5] Gwendolyn used [j] as a singleton for /j/ and /l/, but only used it in clusters *much* later. [Cw] was her only cluster for some time, beginning at 3;3: *cute* /kjuːt/ [tʰwuːt]. The /j/-clusters are low frequency in English, and although /w/-clusters are also low frequency, many children use [w] for /ɹ/ (and /l/); hence, [w]-clusters are frequent in child phonology, accounting for the later appearance of coronal-approximant clusters.

first consider examples where substitutions appear for /l/ and /ɹ/, i.e., minimal repairs. (Note that normally we do not classify /ɹ/ as [+consonantal] but some children appear to treat /ɹ/ and /l/ the same way. Hence, for simplicity, we treat /ɹ/ as [+consonantal] in this section.)

In English, glides often replace /l/ and /ɹ/, and this is true in clusters also, whether the repair is motivated by complexity or sequence constraints. At 4;6, Dylan, a child with a phonological disorder, used [w] for /ɹ/ and /l/ as singletons and cluster elements. However, singleton /l/ surfaced some of the time as [l] in onsets (see §8.6). When [l] and [ɹ] were produced more consistently as singletons, they still failed to surface some of the time in clusters. This was true as late as age 7, 2 years after phonological intervention was discontinued.

	black	/blæk/	[bwæɪ]
	flower	/flaʊwɹ̩/	[ɸwawɪʔ]
	glasses	/glæsəz/	[gwæʔɪ]
BUT:	leaf	/lif/	[wiː]
	look	/lʊk/	[lʊ]

Not(Liquid-Features) and **Survived(Liquid-Features)** were unstably ranked. Sometimes the **Survived** constraint outranked the **Not** constraints. Sometimes the **Not** constraints were ranked higher, resulting in substitution of the glide [w]. In clusters, **NoSequence** always induced glide substitutions. Thus, the generic constraint ranking given above applied absolutely, with additions allowing the glide substitution:

NoSequence(-son... + cons) Survived/LinkedUpwards(Root) ‖‖‖	Survived(Liquid-F) ‖‖‖	Not(-cons) Not(Labial) Not(Liquid-F)

As shown in §5.5.1.5.2 and §5.5.3.6, English-learning children may alternatively use [j] glides for /l/ and /ɹ/. A minimal delinking of [Labial] can result in [j] for /ɹ/. Delinking of [+lateral], and maintenance of [+sonorant] and [Coronal] can result in [j] for /l/, if **Not(+ nasal)** is high-ranked.

A more drastic type of nonminimal repair often occurs, especially in early samples: segment deletion. This is only the result of a sequence constraint when other clusters with different features are possible. Charles, another subject with a phonological disorder, had such repairs all the time for /l/-clusters at the onset of intervention, although clusters with [w] and [n] as C_2 were possible (Bernhardt, 1992a; see also §7.5). Charles used [j] for /l/ most of the time, and [w] for /ɹ/, in singletons. (We ignore epenthesis for our purposes here.)

		5;10	6;0
black	/blæk/	[bæk]	[bᵊwæk]
blue	/bluː/		[bjuː]~[bᵊjuː]~[bwuː]
laugh	/læf/	[jæf]	[læːᵊf]
like	/lʌɪk/	[jʌɪk]	[lʌɪk]

snake	/sneɪk/	[θneɪk]
bread	/bɹɛd/	[bwʌd]
crayons	/kɹeɪ(j)ɑnz/	[fwɛɪjɔ̃nð]~[kəwɛɪjɔ³n]

The variability between the /l/-clusters and other clusters suggests a sequence constraint for the /l/-clusters, rather than a general complexity constraint. The /ɹ/ -clusters (and some /s/-clusters) often surfaced with two elements ([fw] or [θn]) or with epenthesis ([dəw]); see §7.5. Thus, **NotComplex(Onset)** was not operative at this point in development, nor was there a constraint against realization of glides in onsets. The sequence constraint targeted [l] and [j], whether [j] was a target or a substitution for /l/; both are coronal. **Survived** constraints for Root nodes and higher structure were low-ranked for segments that had default [Coronal] place and that were in a prosodically weak position. In connectionist terms, such segments did not have sufficient activation to overcome powerful sequence constraints. In OT terms, insertion of default place was prohibited if sequence constraints and **Not(Coronal)** were high-ranked, and **Survived(+ sonorant)** was low-ranked.

NoSequence_{Onset}(Artic...Coronal)	**Survived(+ sonorant)**
Survived(Labial)	**Survived(Root)**
Survived(Dorsal)	**Survived(TimingUnit)**
Not(Coronal)	**Survived(+ lateral)**

Over time, minimal repairs became more common in Charles's clusters, until both cluster elements surfaced as matches (although with epenthetic vowels separating them).

Fikkert (1994) observed similar patterns for Dutch. Some children produced stop-liquid clusters as stop-glide clusters even though they had singleton liquids (although she does not give specific examples for the singletons).

Thus, features of the liquid can delete, given sequence-based limitations on segmental realization. Such examples may reflect developmental precedence: the segment that was acquired earliest is retained. Alternatively, they may suggest some relevance to the sonority hierarchy in syllabification. An optimal onset (the obstruent) is maintained (§6.1.6.1.2).

Our examples to this point have been of clusters with /l/ and /ɹ/. A less usual stop-sonorant cluster is /kn/, found in Dutch and German. Diachronically, English lost the /k/ of that sequence (though the <k> has been retained orthographically). However, the /n/ is often the affected element in acquisition (Beers, 1993; Elsen, 1991; Fikkert, 1994), just as with /l/ and /ɹ/. Nasals are less optimal onsets than stops, because of their sonority (§4.7.1.3, §6.1.4, and §6.1.12). Hence, the trend towards nasal deletion in /kn/ clusters is not unexpected. Fikkert also notes that nasals emerged later than stops in onsets for all of the children (1994:64). Hence, in keeping with the patterns observed for most of the children in her study, the later-acquired manner feature was subject to deletion.

However, another developmental factor might predict loss of the /k/. Dorsal consonants often are acquired later than other place consonants (§5.5.1.1). Thus, if developmental precedence were the most relevant factor, one might expect retention of the early acquired nasal /n/ rather than the later acquired Dorsal stop. This did happen some of the time in Fikkert's study, suggesting that, for some children, developmental precedence with respect to place may have been a relevant factor. (For those children, **Contiguity** may also have been a high-ranked constraint, prohibiting contiguous appearance of the stop and the vowel in the output.) Deletion of /n/ (nonminimal repair), delinking of [+nasal] with default insertion (minimal repair), or partial reduplication were the most common types of repairs.

	knoop	/knoːp/ [koːp]	'button'	/n/ deletes	(Jarmo, 2;2.6)
	knuf	/knuf/ [kluf]	'cuddle'?	[+nasal] delinked; [+lateral] inserted	(Tom,1;10.8)
BUT:	knoeien	/knuːjə[n]/	[nuːjə]	'make a mess'	Deletion of /k/
	knopje	/knopjə/	[mɔpjə]	'little button'	Deletion of /k/, Labial harmony (Robin, 2;0.4, 2;1.7)

(Note: Robin had use of /k/ at that time in singletons.)

Note that in the second example above, the /n/ surfaced as another coronal sonorant, an [l]; this possibly reflected high ranking of **NotTwice(-continuant)**. Fikkert (1994) comments that /l/ never surfaced as [n] in clusters in her data. Thus, even though nasals are generally earlier than /l/ in acquisition, and presumably less marked in general, the higher frequency of /l/-clusters (and the relative markedness of /kn/) possibly resulted in substitution patterns in the direction of [l] rather than [n]. The [l] replaced the labiodental glide also in Dutch, a marked and less frequent segment. The default coronal sonorant appeared to be [l]. Overall, in constraints and repairs, the nasal cluster behaves like clusters with other sonorant consonants.

7.3.1.5.2. Deletions and Stops in Clusters with Sonorant Consonants

Sometimes, the stop may be the affected element. Nondefault place features or the stop itself may delink. We illustrate with examples from Dutch and English.

Tom (a Dutch-learning subject in Fikkert, 1994:77) had this pattern at one point in stop-/l/ cluster development. Although he had produced the stops accurately in the previous stage, and did again in the subsequent one, during this period, the place features for the stop delinked and default Coronal Place appeared. (Fikkert does not give actual examples for Point 1 and Point 3; hence, examples are only from the intermediate point.)

clown	/klɑʊn/	[tlaun]	'clown'
bloemen	/bluːmə[n]/	[tluːmə]	'flower'

Note that sequence constraints of the adult language were not relevant for the child, since [tl] is not a permitted onset in adult Dutch. Deletion was not permitted because of high ranking for **Survived(TimingUnit)** and **Survived(+ lateral)** but sequences with different place of articulation were disallowed. Hence, [Coronal] was inserted for both elements.

Survived(TimingUnit) NoSequence(Labial...Coronal) NoSequence(Dorsal...Coronal) Co-occurring(+lateral→Coronal) Survived(+lateral)	Survived(Labial) Survived(Dorsal)	Not(Coronal)

Blair (Bernhardt, 1990: *S2*) showed a similar pattern in dorsal stop production. Development of dorsals was delayed in general. When he began to produce dorsals, **Survived(Dorsal)** was unstably ranked. In clusters, [Coronal] was inserted, just as it had been for singletons. Note that spreading of [Labial] was prohibited by high ranking of **SinglyLinked(Labial)**. Epenthesis is ignored here as a separate issue. (See Dyson, 1986, for additional examples.)

cooking   /kʊkɪŋ/   [kʰʊʔĩn]
Christmas   /kɹɪsməs/   [təwɪˇθmʌᵊθ]

NoSequence(Dorsal...Labial) Survived(Labial) SinglyLinked(Labial)	Survived(Dorsal)	Not(Coronal)

Nonminimal repairs can also inhibit stop production. Above we showed how Charles (Bernhardt, 1992b) deleted the /l/ and /j/ frequently in early cluster development. Clusters with [w] tended to be realized with two elements, although some deletions occurred. At 5;10, /bɹ/ sometimes surfaced as [b], but /tw/ surfaced as [w] or [fw]. Just as coronal approximants failed to surface for /l/-clusters and /j/-clusters, so did the coronal stop in /tw/. **Survived** constraints for the nondefault place features were high-ranked, and **Not(Coronal)** was apparently sufficiently high-ranked that, given a sequence constraint involving default place, it would not be inserted when in competition with a segment with nondefault place. (We will see further constraints involving coronals for Charles in terms of **NotTwice** and /st/ realization, in §7.5.)

NoSequence(Coronal...Artic) Survived(Labial)	Not(Coronal) SinglyLinked(Labial)

7.3.1.5.3. Repairs in Fricative-Sonorant Consonant Clusters

Fricative-sonorant consonant clusters are less frequent than stop-sonorant consonant clusters, and hence are expected to develop later. Because both liquids and fricatives are later-acquired segments, and because they are relatively close on the sonority scale, either or both may be particularly vulnerable in a sequence. However, since both are [+continuant], double linking of [+continuant] may facilitate cluster production for a particular child. A cluster such as [sl] may appear early (N. Smith, 1973: Amahl). No detailed studies across children are available to inform us on the relative frequency of liquid or fricative deletion, but we present some examples from Dutch.

Fikkert (1994) notes that some Dutch-learning children in her study had substitutions for fricatives in fricative-sonorant clusters, even though they used the fricatives as singletons at that time or earlier. (She does not provide singleton examples.) Tom showed the effects of **NotTwice(+continuant)**:

vlinder   /vlɪndər/   [plɪn]

Violation of the constraint was avoided by deleting [+continuant] from the fricative, followed by insertion of default [-continuant]. (The change in voicing is independent.) The next section, on **NotTwice** constraints, contains further examples. **NotTwice** constraints appear to affect fricative-sonorant consonant clusters more than **NoSequence** constraints.

In summary, **NoSequence** constraints may restrict both place and manner sequences, with the most frequent restrictions on the features [-sonorant] and [+consonantal]. Deletion repairs can be minimal or nonminimal, often reflecting earlier patterns with singleton consonants, and changing over time from nonminimal to minimal. Sometimes feature deletion with default insertion results in sequences that are not in the adult phonology, for example [tl] or [hl], showing that the child's output sequence constraints are different from the adults'. Usually, singleton production is ahead of cluster production for a given segment. Most of the time, the obstruent surfaces in stop-sonorant clusters, but other patterns are attested. The sonority hierarchy and relative developmental lateness of a particular segment can determine which element may be subject to repair. Neither factor accounts for all patterns in all children, general system constraints often being implicated in the specific cluster repairs. As we have often noted, it is difficult to discuss one part of a child's system without considering the rest of it. The next section provides further support for several of these comments.

7.3.1.6. NotTwice Constraints for Word-Initial Clusters: Deletion Repairs

Constraints on repetition of identical elements most often result in double linking repairs at the feature level and facilitation of cluster production, rather than deletion of a feature (dissimilation) or segment deletion. This is usually facilitative for cluster production. Sometimes these constraints do result in deletion, however. We include examples for obstruent-sonorant clusters, and /s/-clusters, examining various **NotTwice** effects.

7.3.1.6.1. NotTwice(+continuant): Nonminimal Repairs for Fricative-Sonorant Clusters

Since fricatives, glides, and /l/ are [+continuant], a high-ranked **NotTwice(+continuant)** constraint can affect such clusters. Jeremy and Blair (Bernhardt, 1990: *S3* and *S2*) had nonminimal segmental deletion patterns for fricative-sonorant clusters that reflected both their general segmental acquisition patterns and **NotTwice(+ continuant)**. Jeremy deleted the approximant, whereas Blair deleted the fricative.

At age 3;4, Jeremy used [s] and [f] earlier than [l], though [s] was only in codas (see §8.4). (Initially, [ʔ] surfaced in place of /l/ in onset.) Both [s] and [l] appeared in onsets as singletons at about the same time (3;8). However, fricative-sonorant clusters were late to emerge in comparison with other /s/-clusters with stops or nasals. The /l/ failed to surface, even though [l] was established as a singleton onset at that time.

	leaf	/liːf/	[lif]
	flower	/flaʊwɹ/	[faʊwʊˤʔ]
	slipper	/slɪpɹ/	[sɪpʊ]
	sweater	/swɛtɹ/	[sɑtɛˤ]
	wagon	/wægn̩/	[wægən]
BUT:	snap	/snæp/	[snæp]
	small	/smɑl/	[sːmɑ ə]
	spoon	/spuːn/	[spūn]

A combination of high-ranked **NotTwice(+ continuant)** and high-ranked **Survived(Features)** inhibited cluster production, outranking **LinkedUpwards(Root)** and **Survived(TimingUnit)** for one of the elements:

		RESULTS
NotTwice(+ continuant)	LinkedUpwards(Root)	**Floating sonorant**
Co-occurring(σ-Margin→-sonorant)	Survived(TimingUnit)	
Survived(Features)		**Fricative**
LinkedUpwards(Features)		

Thus, both developmental precedence and sequence constraints affected acquisition of onset fricative clusters. (The nonminimal /l/ deletion repair was consistent with his original deletion of /l/ as a singleton onset. The /w/ also deleted some of the time in onset in early samples.)

Blair, at 4;2, had the opposite deletion pattern. He retained /l/ rather than fricatives in early production of /fl/ and /sl/ (Bernhardt, 1990: *S2*). Although /l/ appeared as a singleton onset, /s/ appeared only in codas, surfacing as [h] word-initially (**NotCo-occurring(+ continuant,Coronal)**). (See §5.5.3.4.) The /fl/ and /sl/ clusters behaved like other /s/-clusters: the fricative deleted, even though stop-/l/ clusters surfaced with both elements plus an epenthetic vowel.

	fly	/flaɪ/	[laɪ]	Deletion of /f/
	sleeping	/sliːpɪŋ/	[lipʔɪn]	Deletion of /s/
	starry	/stɑɹi/	[tɑwi]	Deletion of /s/
BUT:	black	/blæk/	[bəlæʔ]	Retention of stop and /l/, epenthesis
	dress	/dɹɛs/	[das]	Deletion of /ɹ/, /s/-coda
	sit	/sɪt/	[hɪt]	Deletion of C-Place

If he had maintained his onset fricative substitution pattern in clusters, [hl] would have been produced. (He did use [hl] once in the second sample probe at age 4;4: *sleeping* [hlipɪn].) However, generally, /l/ survived and the fricative deleted. Most likely, **NotTwice(+ continuant)** was operative at Point 1, as it was for Jeremy. However, the segment that survived was the better established segment in his inventory, the [l]. [l] is, furthermore, a better onset than [h]. High-ranked co-occurrence constraints in competition with low-ranked **Survived(Root)** and **Survived(TimingUnit)** prohibited the fricative.

NotTwice(+ continuant)	**LinkedUpwards(Root)**
Co-occurring(σ-Margin→ + cons)	**Survived(TimingUnit)**
NotCo-occurring(+ continuant,-sonorant)	
Survived/LinkedUpwards(Fricative Features)	

At Time 2, nonminimal repairs continued to accommodate the constraints, but these involved delinking of C-Place and insertion of Laryngeal features ([hl]) or double linking of /l/ features.

slipper   /slɪpɹ̩/   [lːɪ˘pᶲʊᵊ]   Timing unit for both elements, double linking of /l/

Previously high-ranked **NotTwice(+ continuant)** was low-ranked in comparison to **Survived(TimingUnit)**. Some kind of sequence constraint continued to be relevant, however, perhaps at the level of place.

7.3.1.6.2. NotTwice(+ voiced): Minimal Repairs for Fricative-Sonorant Clusters

In the previous section, we gave examples from Fikkert (1994) for fricative-sonorant clusters, which showed possible voicing dissimilation. Sometimes [+voiced] delinked in conjunction with other features, and sometimes alone, as in the following (from Tirza):

vlinders   /vlɪndərs/   [flĩdəs]   Delinking of [+voiced]
vlecht   /vlɛχt/   [slɛχt]   Delinking of [+voiced] & [Labial]

NotTwice(+ voiced) may be responsible. Voiceless obstruents are more frequent as first consonants in clusters overall in English. Perhaps similar frequency effects can influence dissimilation patterns in Dutch.

In such cases, **NotTwice(+ voiced)** is ranked higher than **Survived(+ voiced)**. The feature [+voiced] deletes in the segment in which it is a contrastive feature. Deletion in the sonorant would lead to a voiceless sonorant, which is prohibited by **Co-occurring(+ sonorant→ + voiced)**. A [+voiced] feature that is not supported by co-occurrence constraints has a greater probability of being deleted.

7.3.1.6.3. NotTwice(Artic): Obstruent-Sonorant Clusters

Minimal repair deletions appear to be unlikely responses to place identity constraints. We have found no examples where /pɹ/ and /bɹ/ become [pj] and [bj], or

[tw] and [dw] to avoid **NotTwice(Labial)**. Nonminimal repairs may be possible (with segment deletion), but we have found no convincing examples of deletion that appear to reflect sequence constraints. Such examples would look like:

	/dw/, /dɹ/	>	[dw]
	/tw/, /tɹ/	>	[tw]
	/gw/, /gɹ/	>	[gw]
	/kw/, /kɹ/	>	[kw]
BUT:	/bɹ/	>	[b] rather than [bw]
	/pɹ/	>	[p] rather than [pw]
	/fɹ/	>	[f] rather than [fw]

Charles (Bernhardt, 1992b; §7.5) had a tendency in that direction. However, even though he sometimes deleted /ɹ/ from /bɹ/, /pɹ/, and /fɹ/, he also used a large number of [fw] clusters as substitutions for stop-liquid clusters. (The /fɹ/ was the last sonorant cluster to be realized with two elements.)

7.3.1.6.4. NotTwice(Artic): Nonminimal and Minimal Repairs for /s/-Clusters

Minimal repairs of **NotTwice** constraints for /s/-clusters are unattested other than double linking of [Coronal], which leads to adult-like clusters. Examples of such repairs would be the use of [sp] for /st/ to accommodate **Not-Twice(Coronal)**, alongside correct production of /sk/ and /sw/.

Nonminimal repairs are attested, however. For Charles and Gordon in Bernhardt (1990), /st/ was produced as a singleton [θ] long after *all* other diconsonantal clusters were produced with two elements. Examples from Charles at age 6;4 follow.

star	/stɑɹ/	[θaːʊ]
smooth	/smuːð/	[s̩muːv]
snowing	/snoʊɪŋ]	[s̩nowɛ̃n]
spoon	/spuːn/	[θpūn]
sweater	/swɛtɹ̩/	[θʊwɛɾɔ]
sleep	/sliːp/	[θəlip]

Comparing Charles's obstruent-sonorant and /s/-clusters, we see the relevance of feature specification status in determining which elements deleted. This was independent of the type of sequence constraint. In Charles's /st/, /f/-cluster, and /tw/ clusters, the least specified segment deleted: either the stop /t/ (in /st/ and /tw/), or the default glide [w] from /f/-clusters. We noted earlier that default features may be the target of assimilation or deletion, with nondefault values surviving at the expense of default insertion. For /st/ and /tw/, the nondefault [+continuant] feature of /s/ and /w/ survived.

Deletion is not a common resolution of **NotTwice** constraints. Double linking of the "repeated" feature can actually be used to avoid sequence constraints and thus facilitate production of two segments.

7.3.1.7. NoSequence Constraints for Word-Initial Clusters:
Epenthesis (Addition) Repairs

Vowel epenthesis can be either a minimal or nonminimal repair. Other types of (segmental) addition repairs are either nonexistent or unattested.

Epenthesis is infrequent in cluster development (Ingram, 1989b; Chin & Dinnsen, 1992). Chin (1993) states that, in a subject pool of 48 children with phonological disorders, epenthesis accounted for only 0.9% of the cluster errors, and only 12 of the children used epenthesis at all. Fikkert comments that, in her study of 12 Dutch-learning subjects, epenthesis occurred only "during a short period in the [children]'s production of target plosive-liquid clusters" (1994:78), and that it never occurred for fricative-sonorant clusters. In Bernhardt (1990), however, all six children with phonological disorders used epenthesis in obstruent-sonorant clusters, variably, but frequently enough to be noticeable (including a few examples with fricative-sonorant clusters). Intervention strategies which used prolongation of a vowel to anticipate the sonorant consonant of the cluster (e.g., [tuːːwɪn] for *twin*) possibly promoted this for two subjects (Sean and Jeremy), but the other four used epenthesis before intervention. Epenthesis in clusters is not common across children for prosodic reasons. Children need to be able to produce initial unstressed syllables if they epenthesize within an onset cluster. The developmental lateness of initial unstressed syllables (§6.2.2) makes epenthesis in word-initial clusters less likely.

We discuss epenthesis only as it repairs **NoSequence** constraints. We have found no examples of such repairs for **NotTwice** constraints. An example would be production of /st/ and /sn/ as [sət] and [sən] in response to **NotTwice (Coronal)**, with no epenthesis for [sp] and [sm]. We discuss general patterns for obstruent-approximant clusters, with specific examination of C_2 and C_1 effects within the sequences.

7.3.1.7.1. Epenthesis in Obstruent-Sonorant Clusters

Whether sequence or complexity constraints give rise to epenthesis, certain characteristics are present. We review those characteristics first, and then present some **NoSequence** examples. Epenthesis separates two elements by insertion of a timing unit, and in so doing, creates a right-prominent foot (with an initial unstressed syllable). Features for the empty slot arise in these two ways.

1. by default feature insertion (e.g., schwa epenthesis)
2. by spreading from the following approximant (i.e., [ʊ] or [oʊ] from a [w], [l], or [ɹ], or [ɪ] or [i] from [j]).

Children may use one type of epenthetic vowel (of a fairly consistent length), or may use different vowel types and lengths. In Bernhardt (1990), four out of six children showed variability in vowel types and lengths. Blair (*S2*) consistently used schwa, and Jeremy (*S3*) consistently used round vowels which anticipated the liquid or [w] (e.g., *glove* was [gᵘlʌ̥ɣ]). Examples of differences (for Charles, *S1*, at Time 2) are shown here:

| twins | /twɪnz/ | [dəwĩn]~[tᵊwɛ̃nð]~[tᵘwĩndð] |
| glove | /glʌv/ | [gʲjʌv]~[gʌv] |

(The superscripts indicate a very reduced epenthetic vowel. See Eveson, 1996.)

Considering the actual consonant sequences, we noted above that epenthesis tends to occur mostly in stop-sonorant consonant clusters (Fikkert, 1994; Bernhardt, 1990), but epenthesis with /s/-nasal clusters also occurs (Chrissie at 3;5; Bernhardt, 1990: *S6*):

| snow | /snoʊ/ | [θᵊnoʊ] |

The highest-ranked constraint in the case of stop-sonorant consonant clusters is **Nosequence(-sonorant...{ + consonantal, + sonorant})**. **Not(σ)** (creation of a new syllable) and **Contiguity** (separating the two consonants) are ranked low. High ranking of **Survived(Root)** guarantees survival of both consonants.

NoSequence(-sonorant...{ + consonantal, + sonorant}) ‖‖	**Not(σ)**
Survived(Root)	**Not(V-Root)**
	Contiguity

Epenthetic vowels may appear only after certain initial consonants for some children. Charles (Bernhardt, 1992b) used epenthesis at assessment only with coronal and dorsal stop onsets, and not with labials (when [w] appeared for the liquid, as we show in §7.3.1.8.1).

train	/tɹeɪn/	[dəweĩnᵊ]	
grey	/gɹeɪ/	[gəwɛɪʲᵊ]	
crayon	/kɹeɪ(j)ɑn/	[kəwɛɪjɔˢn]	(Charles, age 5;10)

The absence of epenthetic vowels in labial stop-approximant clusters probably reflects the fact that [Labial] can be doubly linked between the stop and glide [w], reducing onset complexity. This option was available for the lingual consonants, but only at the cost of unfaithfulness to the adult target ([fw] substitution). The difference between the labial sequences and the others suggests that the two tokens of [Labial] were being merged (violation of **Distinct(Labial)**) into one doubly linked token of [Labial]. Thus, there is no longer a sequence of articulator nodes, and epenthesis is not necessary (as it is in other clusters):

NotTwice(Labial) ‖‖	**Distinct(Labial)**
NoSequence(ArticA . . . ArticB) ‖‖	**SinglyLinked(Labial)**

7.3.1.7.2. Epenthesis in /s/-Stop Clusters

Epenthesis is less common for /s/-stop clusters than for other clusters in phonological development. Epenthesis of a default vowel is the only possible type of epenthesis in this case, since no features are likely to spread from the stop. The vowel may be added before the first consonant (as in adult Spanish historically), rather than between the two. None of the subjects in Bernhardt (1990) had epenthesis in /s/-stop clusters. Two examples from Elsen's (1991) daughter are:

| Stift | /ʃtift/ | [əs-dif-d] | 'pencil' |
| gespielt | /gəʃpiːlt/ | [səpilt] | 'played' |

The second example can also be analyzed as flop of the /s/ to replace the /g/. However, the point remains that a vowel ended up between the cluster elements. Survival of the two consonants depended on their being separated by a vowel.

In this and previous sections, we have given examples several times of the relevance of double linking for cluster sequence repairs. The next section examines assimilation repairs in clusters in more detail.

7.3.1.8. Sequence Constraints for Word-Initial Clusters: Assimilation Repairs

Assimilation is fairly common in the early development of clusters (Ingram, 1989b; Chin & Dinnsen, 1992). It can facilitate production of two consonants by simplifying sequences on various feature tiers. Single or multiple features may be doubly linked. We give examples for both obstruent-sonorant and /s/-stop clusters. We focus here on assimilations motivated by **NoSequence** constraints. However, double linking also can repair **NotTwice** constraints; when two adjacent identical elements are merged (violating **Distinct**), there is no longer a violation of **NotTwice**; see §7.3.1.7.1.

7.3.1.8.1. NoSequence Constraints: Sonorant Clusters and Assimilation Repairs

Obstruent-sonorant target clusters are often produced as [fw] in early development (Ingram, 1989b). [Labial] and [+continuant] from [w] become doubly linked to the C_1 slot. The problematic element in the sequence is the sonorant, usually [w] (appearing as a substitution for /ɹ/ and/or /l/). The repair usually involves leftward spread from this problematic element to the first consonant. Nonlabial and stop features in C_1 delete (or are never inserted), with double linking of [+continuant] and [Labial] resulting in [fw]. Frequency and economy possibly also play a role in this situation. Since [w] occurs across a variety of clusters, a single solution solves the problem for all clusters (link to the [w], no matter what the C_1). If the features of C_1 were to spread instead, geminate onsets could result (e.g., /kɹ/ > [kː]); all the features would have to spread, since dorsal liquids are unusual. Since geminate onsets are rare crosslinguistically, that type of repair is also rare. A [fw] cluster, although not allowable in adult English, is nonetheless less marked than [pː] in onset, and is more faithful to the underlying forms, since at least some features of both elements appear.

If labial or [+continuant] features are already present in C_1, of course, 'invisible' double linking resolves the **NotTwice** constraint. Charles's use of labial clusters at assessment (age 5;10) was mentioned in previous sections, and we continue with his example here.

bread	/bɹɛd/	[bwʌdᵊ]
brushing	/bɹʌʃɪŋ/	[bwʌθĩn]
brush	/bɹʌʃ/	[vwʌθ]
dressed	/dɹɛst/	[vwʌθt̪]
twenty	/twɛnti/	[fwɛntiˈ]
glove	/glʌv/	[vwʌbᵊ]
sleep	/sliːp/	[fwip]
sweater	/swɛtɹ̩/	[fwʌdɔ]
quiet	/kwaɪ(j)ət/	[fwɑɪjɛt]

Labial stops generally resisted [+continuant] spread. Out of four /bɹ/-cluster tokens, three surfaced as [bw]; only *brush* surfaced with [vw]. If [Labial] was doubly linked, then double linking of [+continuant] was less necessary (prohibited?). It is difficult to explain interdependencies of place and manner features, since they are generally considered to be separate in the geometry.

Parasitic alignment (Cole & Kisseberth, 1994) could be involved. (There was no independent reason to suspect any high-ranked constraints on the alignment of [Labial], since there was no metathesis or labial harmony across vowels.) If [Labial] spreads from [w], then [+continuant] must also spread, so that the edges of the two features are perfectly aligned in the output:

Survived/LinkedUpwards(Labial)	**Survived(Dorsal)**
Distinct(Labial)	**SinglyLinked(Labial)**
Aligned(Labial,L,+continuant,L)	**SinglyLinked(+continuant)**
NoSequence(Coronal...Labial)	
NoSequence(Dorsal...Labial)	

Two underlying tokens of [Labial] could not merge on the surface, and both had to survive in the output. Since the second token of [Labial] did not spread to /p/ or /b/, neither did [+continuant]; /p/ and /b/ surfaced as stops. However, [Labial] spread in other clusters, and so [+continuant] spread with it.

An alternative explanation involving full specification might be that survival of underlying place (high ranking of **Survived(Labial)**) results in survival of underlying [continuant]. This would imply that [-continuant] was specified for stops. Charles did show occasional substitution of [θ] for /t/ in onset (see §8.5.1.1); thus, [-continuant] may have been underlying, and [+continuant] might have been the default. However, further explanation is needed. There could be compound constraints such as **Survived(Labial&continuant)** (both features must survive, not just one); we feel that this type of constraint is too complex. Alternatively, activation levels could be considered (see §4.7.1.5). If one element in a segment deletes, that decreases activation to other elements in the segment, which also may delete. The activation-based explanation does not need to assume that [-continuant] is underlying. As a default, [-continuant] might fail to be inserted if activation of co-occurring features was too low; it might be preferable to spread a nondefault feature from elsewhere. Data do not allow us to choose between explanations here, but all theories need to be able to account for such patterns. See §10.2.2 for further discussion.

At Time 2 (age 6;0), Charles showed a decrease in cluster assimilations, particularly for clusters with dorsal and labial stops, and /s/. However, the coronal stops were still subject to double linking.

| try | /tɹaɪ/ | [fwaɪ] |
| dropped | /dɹɑpt/ | [fwapt] |

Specification status was more relevant for the repair at Time 2. Nondefault features (Dorsal, Labial) surfaced without alteration (sometimes facilitated by epenthesis, as discussed above). The default coronal feature, however, was subject to 'takeover' by the features from the [w]. Default features are often at a disadvantage in assimilations.

7.3.1.8.2. *NotTwice Constraints: Double Linking and /s/-Clusters*

We have previously noted that sequences of identical elements can facilitate cluster production or inhibit them, depending on the relative ranking of **NotTwice, SinglyLinked,** and **Distinct**. If **SinglyLinked** and **Distinct** are low-ranked, then fusion of the two elements may occur. If **SinglyLinked** is high-ranked, two elements may be produced (but possibly with dissimilation).

Double linking usually affects /s/-clusters that have the same *place* of articulation, such as /st/, /sn/, /sl/, or that have two [+continuant] elements, such as /sl/ or /sw/. Double linking of [+continuant] in /sw/ can *promote* double linking of place, with [fw] appearing after leftwards spread of [Labial]. Similarly, double linking of [+continuant] in /sl/ can result in leftwards spread of the [+lateral] and production of [ɬ]. Sharing of [+continuant] and Coronal place can promote sharing of [-voiced], resulting in [sɬ].

Overall, opportunities for simplification arise from assimilation. Sometimes a feature can be the target of assimilation independent of its relative specification status. Other times, only the default features are subject to assimilation. Assimilation does not necessarily result in more intelligible speech, because of the homonymy created.

7.3.1.9. NoSequence Constraints in Word-Initial Clusters: Flop Repairs

Flop repairs are rare but do occur, either locally or at a distance in words. Single or multiple features may flop. Local flop occurs only for /s/-stop clusters, since stop-/s/ clusters are possible onsets (at least in some languages), but sonorant-obstruent clusters are rarely if ever possible in word-initial position (*[wt], *[lp], *[nk]). Flop does occur for obstruent-sonorant clusters, but not locally (see §7.5 for long-distance flop).

Word-initial /s/-stop clusters appear to present a particular sequence problem for some children, because they violate the sonority hierarchy. The more-sonorous /s/ is further away from the vowel than the less-sonorous stop. A **NoSequence**$_{\text{Onset}}$(**+continuant...-continuant**) constraint is typically operative in young children. Moving the [+continuant] feature closer to the vowel can resolve the constraint. We give examples for all of the two-element /s/-clusters.

Lorentz (1976) describes the appearance of [ks] for /sk/ in the speech of one child (Joe) with a phonological disorder:

scout   /skaʊt/   [ksaʊt]

Other /s/-clusters appeared as singletons: /sp/ > [f] and /sm/ > [f] (with nasality on the vowel; see §6.1.6.4.). Faithfulness to features and to the /sonority hierarchy was high; **Survived(Nondefault)** and **NoSequence_Onset(+ continuant...-continuant])** were high-ranked.

Lorentz suggested that the child could resolve those high-ranked constraints for /sp/ and /sm/ by fusion of [+continuant] and [Labial], because [f] is a segment of English (because of low ranking of **NotCo-occurring(-sonorant, + continuant,Labial)**). In contrast, **NotCo-occurring(-sonorant, + continuant,Dorsal)** prohibits non-English *[x], the segment which would result from fusion in /sk/. Low ranking of **NoSequence_Onset(-continuant... + continuant)** (as in stop-approximant sequences) allowed [ks] to appear. Even though [ks] is not an English onset, the sequence does occur in codas, making it less unusual than *[x]. Table 7.6 shows a constraint ranking for the flop repair. This ranking assumes feature flop, rather than segment exchange. High ranking of **NoSequence(+ continuant . . . -continuant)** prohibited /s/-stop clusters. However, nondefault features [C-Dorsal] and [+continuant] had to survive (high ranking of **Survived (C-Dorsal)** and **Survived(+ continuant)**). Where the features linked up did not matter as long as they linked up in the onset (low ranking of **Survived(Link)**). Faithfulness to nondefault features was more important than faithfulness to individual roots, to contiguity, or to association lines. Ironically, the constraints avoided a non-English segment (*[x]) by creating a non-English word-initial cluster (*[ks]). Because Joe could pronounce [f], a cluster was not necessary for feature realization of /sp/.

TABLE 7.6

/sk/	sk	x	k	s	ks
NotCo-occurring(-son,+cont,Dorsal)		*!			
NoSequence_Onset(+cont...-cont)	*!				
Survived(C-Dorsal)				*!	
Survived(+continuant)			*!		
Survived(Root)		*	*	*	
Contiguity				*	*
NoSequence_Onset(-cont...+cont)					*
Survived(Link)		*	*	*	*

While flop in /sk/ is relatively unique, transposition of /st/ to [ts] or /sp/ to [ps] may be slightly more common (possibly because velars are often later-acquired segments). Bernhardt (1994a), Chin (1996), and Edwards (1995) report instances of /sp/ flop. Bernhardt's (1994a) subjects, Kendra and Robin, also used [ts] occasionally for /st/ and /sk/ (with Velar Fronting in /sk/ as in all velars in the children's speech). Onset maximization in accordance with rising sonority towards the nucleus can generally account for this type of flop. However, Bernhardt (1994a) suggests that other constraints may also be implicated. We give some examples from their assessment samples and after one block of treatment (for Kendra, after 8 weekly sessions, and for Robin, after 12 biweekly sessions), and discuss constraints involved. First, Kendra:

		3;9	3;11 (End of Block 1)
spoon	/spuːn/		[psūn]
story	/stɔɹi/	[tɔwi]	
starry	/stɑɹi/		[tsaʊi]
squirrel	/skwɹl̩/	[tsʊəo]	[tsɹwə]
snow	/snoʊ/	[hoʊ]	[soʊ]
snake	/sneɪk/	[sːeɪt]	[set]
sleep	/sliːp/	[tsip]	[sip]
sleeping	/sliːpɪŋ/	[sipĩ]	[sipɪŋ]
sweater	/swɛtɹ̩/	[hɔdə]	[sɛdʊ]

Kendra was in the process of developing /s/ as a singleton, with [h], [t], and [ts] replacements for /s/ in onset.[6] Second, Robin:

		3;3	3;5 (End of Block 1)
spoon	/spuːn/	[sūn]	[psūn]~[spsūn]
spear	/spiɹ/		[psiə]
star	/stɑɹ/		[tsaʊ]
starry	/stɑɹi/	[sːawi]	[saʊwi]
scarf	/skɑɹf/	[tʰaʊʃ]	
sleep	/sliːp/	[sip]	[sip]
smooth	/smuːð/		[smus]~[psus]
Smurf	/smɹ̩f/		[sʊs]
snake	/sneɪk/	[seɪʔ]~[tseɪʔ]	[sik]
sweater	/swɛtɹ̩/	[soə]	[sæwə]

In Robin's pretreatment data, [ts] varied with [s] (and occasionally [t]) as a realization of /st/.

The [ps] cluster arose in spontaneous productions during the intervention process for both children. (They used no other onset clusters.) Mastery of the clusters in spontaneous speech took several months for both children, although they were

___

[6]Kendra did produce *mask* as [mæst] once each in Sample 1 and Sample 2, showing that [+cont]...[-cont] could appear in a coda (though it was absent from onsets). Robin used no [+cont]... [-cont] codas (*mask* was [mæs]), but did have many [-cont]...[+cont] codas, either as matches or as substitutions for singletons.

able to imitate the correct sequence in single words in structured drill situations. Note that even /sm/ appeared once as [ps] for Robin, underlining the strength of the **NoSequence(+continuant...-continuant)** constraint.

To account for the flop patterns, we also need to look at deletion repairs (the major repair). **NotComplex(Onset)** was a high-ranked constraint in general, and the simplest solution in that case is to delete. Kendra's deletions followed sonority principles: the least sonorous element tended to be retained in the onset (see §6.1.6.1.2). (Interacting with this was her general difficulty with producing onset [s], however.) Robin usually produced [s] rather than the other segment, especially at Point 1 (although /sk/ surfaced as [t]); the survival of the nondefault feature [+continuant] was more important than having a low-sonority onset. However, when he produced /s/-stop clusters with both elements, the /s/ remained next to the vowel in accordance with sonority sequencing principles. For both repairs, **Contiguity** was low-ranked.

Feature co-occurrence and segment (de)composition may also have been relevant for Robin's [ps] and [ts] clusters. We have been assuming that cluster elements have two timing units and two Root nodes. One might propose alternatively that clusters have only one timing unit and one Root node.[7] The [ps] and [ts] would then be complex segments with ordering predicted from sonority. Robin had a number of what appeared to be complex segments in his coda inventory, particularly stop-fricative segments (often Labial-Coronal). (One or two word-initial segments of this type were also noted.) Examples follow.

noise	/nɔɪz/	[nɔɪb̥s]
chicken	/tʃɪkn̩/	[tʃɪpʃən]
one	/wʌn/	[bwʌ̃n]~[wʌ̃n]~[vʌ̃n]
see	/siː/	[tsi]~[si]
glove	/glʌv/	[dʌys̥]

These complex segments show a splitting apart of nondefault place and manner features into what looks like two segments. This suggests high-ranked **NotCo-occurring(Nondefault,Nondefault)**.

Of course, even if [ps] and [ts] were two segments (as we believe), they are not completely unusual for English. Since these sequences occur elsewhere in English (such as in plurals), all feature sequences are acceptable in adult English in general, just not in onsets. The data could be viewed as the result of generalizing clusters from elsewhere in the word to word-initial position.

7.3.1.10. Word-Initial Clusters: Summary

The introductory sections §7.1 and §7.2 summarized repair types and discuss general trends and issues in cluster sequence constraints and repairs. Other general comments are:

---

[7] It has often been argued that a cluster is one unit in child phonology. (See Barton, Miller, & Macken, 1980; Kornfeld, 1971; Menyuk & Klatt, 1968.) Furthermore, complex segments in other languages have been described similarly both in feature composition (Margi, /ps/) and processes (Ewe reduplication of /ps/ and /ts/) by Sagey (1986) and Dunlap and Padgett (1990).

1. Sequence constraints interact in complex ways with the other constraints in the system. The flop repair section demonstrates that interaction strongly.

2. Status of features as defaults or nondefaults is often relevant for repair phenomena. Default features either appear in repairs, or are the target of repairs (particularly in assimilation).

3. The sonority sequencing principle is relevant in many cases, and for deletion and flop repairs, in particular. However, not all repairs reflect sonority.

4. Phonotactic constraints of the adult phonology are not always constraints for the child. Similarly, children can have constraints that are not observable in the ambient language. This was observed for deletion and flop repairs.

5. Repairs do not always result in greater intelligibility or "simplicity," but sometimes can result in more complex word structures or sequences than the adult targets, or in greater homonymy. The motivation to approximate the adult target more closely does not immediately result in the desired change. As constraints are reranked bit by bit, and repairs altered, progress may seem regressive at times.

These conclusions also hold true of consonant clusters elsewhere in the word. We now turn to such clusters.

7.3.2. MEDIAL AND FINAL CLUSTERS: PREDICTIONS AND GENERAL DEVELOPMENTAL PATTERNS

Children often have differences in development between word-initial clusters and clusters elsewhere in the word. Bernhardt and Stoel-Gammon (1996) report that children receiving phonological intervention in Bernhardt's (1994) study differed in whether word-initial or word-final clusters appeared first. Two children produced word-initial clusters before word-final clusters, and seven produced final clusters before initial clusters. However, few studies have addressed the acquisition of final and medial clusters. In this section, we follow the same general format as for word-initial clusters, although subsections are organized in terms of constituent types and repairs rather than in terms of sequence constraints. It is not always possible to determine whether complexity or sequence constraints motivate the repairs, partly because of a paucity of data.

We cannot directly compare word-initial clusters with clusters in other positions, because there are many opposite sequences. General issues such as the relevance of sonority, feature status, adult versus child phonotactics, and so on, can be addressed for all clusters, however. Furthermore, comparisons can be made between intervocalic and word-final sequences. Falling sonority from the nucleus to the coda can result in different types of deletion patterns than we saw for onsets; rime co-occurrence constraints can result in retention of different segments than are retained in word-initial clusters: fricatives, nasals, or dorsals.

In §7.3.1, we outlined cluster sequences for word onset in order to assess possible influences of sequence frequency on output. Final clusters of English are listed in Tables 7.7 and 7.8 in order to evaluate type frequency. We do not have

TABLE 7.7 Place Sequences in English Coda Clusters[a]

Sequence	Cluster
Cor–Cor	ts, st(s), dz, zd, lt, l(t)s, lz, ld(z), lθ(s), lʃ(t), ltʃ(t), ldʒ(d), θs, θt(s), nt(s), nd(z), ntʃ(t), nz, ndʒ(d), ntθ(s), ɹ(n)t(s), ɹ(n)d(z), ɹs, ɹz, ɹst, ɹn(z), ɹʃ(t), ɹtʃ(t), ɹdʒ(d), ɹθ, ɹð, ðz, ðd, tθ(s), dð(z), dʒd, tʃt, ʃt, ʒd
Lab–Cor[b]	pt, ps, pts, bd, bz, mpt, mps, mpθ, mz, fs, vz, vd, ft(s), fθ(s)
Dors–Cor	kt(s), ks(t), ksθ(s), gd, gz(d), ŋkt, ŋks, ŋkθ(s), ŋz
Cor–Lab	sp, lp, (lm), lv, lf, ɹp, ɹb, ɹf, ɹv, ɹm, ɹsp
Cor–Lab–Cor	spt, sps, lpt, lps, lmd, lms, lft, lfθs, lvd, ɹpt, ɹps, ɹbd, ɹbz, ɹft, ɹfs, ɹvd, ɹvz, ɹmd, ɹmz, ɹspt, ɹsps
Cor–Dors	sk, lk, ɹk, ɹg
Cor–Dors–Cor	skt, lkt, lks, sks, ɹkt, ɹks, ɹgd
Dors–Dors	ŋk
Lab–Lab	mp

[a] Not organized in terms of frequency. Cor = Coronal; Lab = Labial; Dors = Dorsal.
[b] English /ɹ/ is not labial postvocalically.

TABLE 7.8 Manner Sequences in English Coda Clusters

Sequence	Cluster[a]
[+son][-son]	mp(t), mp(s), mpθ, mz, nt(s(t)), ntθ(s), nz, ntʃ(t), ndʒ, ŋk((t)(s)), ŋk(θ(s)), ŋz, l(t)s, lz, lp(s), lt(s), ld(z), lf(s), lv(z), ltʃ, ldʒ, lθ(s), ɹt(s), ɹ(d)z, ɹp(s), ɹb(z), ɹk(s), ɹg(z), ɹs, ɹz, ɹʃ, ɹtʃ, ɹdʒ, ɹf(s), ɹv(z), ɹθ(s), ɹð(z)
[-son][-son]	pt(s), kt(s), bd, gd, tʃt, dʒd, ft, fs, vd, vz, (k)θs, ðz, ks(t), sp(t), ps(t), st, ts, bz, dz, gz(d), zd, skt, sps, sts, tst, sks, fts, θt, ðd, θs, ðz, fθ(s), dð, ʃt, ʒd, dzd
[+son][+son]	lm, ɹl, ɹn, ɹm
[-cont][+cont]	ps, ts, ks, bz, dz, gz, mps, nts, ŋks, kθ(s), ksθ, mpθ(s), mz, nz, ndz, ŋz, ntʃ, ndʒ, ntθ, pts, kts
[+cont][-cont]	sp, st, sk, lp, lt, ld, lk, lm, ltʃ, ldʒ, l(t)st, ɹp, ɹb, ɹt, ɹd, ɹk, ɹg, ɹm, ɹn, ɹtʃ, ɹdʒ, ft, vd, ɹst
[+cont][+cont]	ls, lz, lf(s), lv(z), l(f)θ(s), ðz, ɹs, ɹz, ɹf(s), ɹv(s), ɹθ(s), ɹð(z), fs, vz, θs, ðz, fθ(s)
[-cont][-cont]	pt, kt, bd, gd, mp, mpt, nt, nd, ŋk, ŋkt, gd(tʃt, dʒd)
[-cont][+cont][-cont]	pst, kst, bzd, gzd, ndzd, ndʒd, (n)tθt, ntst, ntʃt, ŋkst
[+cont][-cont][+cont]	sps, sts, sks, lps, lts, lms, ɹps, ɹbz, ɹmz, ɹsps, fts
[-son][+son]	None, unless syllabic C's counted
[+cons][-cons]	None, unless syllabic /ɹ/ included

[a] Not organized in terms of frequency

token frequency information. Clusters which arise only because of morphological endings are included. Postvocalic /ɹ/ is included but syllabic consonants are omitted. Inclusion of postvocalic /ɹ/ is possibly misleading because it *can* be interpreted as part of the nucleus rather than as part of a consonant cluster in this context.

Labial-Coronal and Coronal-Labial sequences are again frequent. Unlike in word-initial position, Dorsal-Dorsal sequences are found. Furthermore, Coronal-Coronal sequences are far more frequent in codas, partly because of morphological endings. Nasal-stop sequences are all homorganic for place. In terms of manner, [-sonorant]...[+sonorant] and [+consonantal]...[-consonantal] sequences are missing (unless syllabic consonants are included), which follows from the sonority sequencing principle: the most sonorous elements are closest to the nucleus. Frequency of [+continuant]...[-continuant] sequences and [+continuant]...[+continuant] sequences is far greater than in onset, which again follows from sonority and margin constraints. Other sequences not found in onset (in English) are [-continuant]...[-continuant], [+sonorant]...[-sonorant], and [-continuant]...[+continuant]...[-continuant].

Based on type frequency and patterns for word-initial clusters, we predict the following variable patterns for order of coda cluster acquisition:

1. Very early or very late acquisition of clusters with one or more identical features in the two elements (particularly place features), depending on whether a doubly linked token of the feature is possible (early) or impossible (late).

2. Earlier development of tautomorphemic clusters than clusters which arise following addition of morphological endings, because of a negative influence of interactive constraints between phonology and morphology, or earlier development of heteromorphemic clusters in response to high frequency of the coronal affixes /t/, /d/, /s/, and /z/. See §6.4.

3. Earlier or later establishment of clusters with stops and nasals. The generally early emergence of stops and nasals could favor them. However, rime constraints favoring [+continuant] segments may result in earlier emergence of clusters with continuants, at least when compared with their development in onset.

4. Earlier establishment of coda clusters with voiceless obstruents, because of co-occurrence constraints against voiced obstruents in codas.

5. Unpredictable and variable order of /sC/-clusters and /Cs/-clusters. The /sC/-clusters may develop before the /Cs/-clusters, because they conform to falling sonority. On the other hand, rime co-occurrence constraints and morphological frequency may facilitate earlier emergence of clusters that end in /s/ and /z/.

6. Late development of stop-stop sequences, since these do not occur in onset, are reasonably uncommon in the adult language, and do not follow the usual pattern of falling sonority within the coda.

Word internally, most of the same sequences are possible. Additional sequences arise across syllable boundaries (for example, /tp/, /kp/, and /tk/ in proper names or compounds, such as *Atkinson* or *crockpot*, or stop-approximant sequences such as *Kitwell*). Similar order of acquisition might be expected for sequences identical to coda sequences with some variation to account for the additional permissible sequences.

In English, it is difficult to determine whether word-internal sequences are tautosyllabic or heterosyllabic. In words like *candle*, there are three possibilities: (a) /n/ and /d/ may form a coda, with the syllabic /l/ in a syllable by itself, (b) /d/ might be an onset to the second syllable, or (c) the /d/ may be ambisyllabic. Children's patterns might reflect one or the other of these hypotheses about English syllable structure, leading to different developmental phenomena with respect to repairs. (See §7.4.3.)

In Templin's (1957) study, results agree with some of the predictions made above based on cluster type-frequency and relevance of shared place of articulation between the two consonants. This cross-sectional study has severe limitations as a normative study because each cluster was elicited only once, and because words differ in terms of word length and frequency. In any event, by 3;0, only /ŋk/ had reached criterion. By age 4;0, 75% of the subjects had acquired half of the clusters tested: nasal-stop clusters except for /nt/, /ks/, /ft/, /pt/, and liquid-stop clusters /lp/, /lt/, /ɹm/, /ɹt/, and /ɹk/. Voiced obstruents did not reach criterion until 5;0 in clusters. The majority of liquid-stop clusters were acquired by 6;0 and the liquid-fricative clusters by 7;0. The last clusters in her study to be acquired were /kt/ and /sp/.

Predictions upheld by her study are the following:

1. The later acquisition of clusters with voiced obstruents as predicted in (4) above.

2. The later development of liquid-fricative sequences as per prediction (5), since liquids and fricatives are both late-acquired manner classes.

3. The earlier emergence of /pt/ than /kt/ concords with the higher general frequency of Labial-Coronal sequences and the earlier emergence of labials in comparison with dorsals. Word choice for the comparison may have influenced the outcome however, considering the familiarity and frequency of the word *jumped* (which actually has a [mpt] cluster), compared with the infrequent unfamiliar word *conduct*.

4. The earlier acquisition of /ks/ compared with /sp/ may reflect general frequency effects for the cluster (morphological frequency of /ks/). However, the word *grasp* is far less frequent and familiar than the word *books*, the two elicitation items used, and thus experimental artifact may have produced the results, as in (3).

Other differences may also reflect experimental artifacts deriving from differences in word familiarity, frequency, and word length. For example, the late acquisition of /nt/ possibly reflects the elicitation item *elephant*, in which the /nt/ is in the third syllable of the word, which is the second of two unstressed syllables; see §6.2.3.4 and §6.2.4.2. It might in addition reflect one of the conundrums of cluster acquisition: that shared place can be inhibitory for timing unit realization as per prediction (1), but we would need to compare productions in monosyllabic words (in a word such as *ant*).

7.3.2.1. Medial and Final Clusters: Individual Developmental Patterns

Longitudinal individual data are even rarer in the literature than group data, particularly for word-medial cluster acquisition. We report here data for English from two children with phonological disorders (Jeremy and Sean; Bernhardt, 1990: *S3* and *S4*), and data for German from a typically developing child (Annalena: Elsen, 1991), noting similarities with other data when relevant.

Sean and Jeremy were between 3;3 and 4;0 when data were collected (during an intervention study), and at the very beginning stages of cluster acquisition. Intervention did not focus on word-final or medial clusters for either boy during the study. One year posttreatment, Sean still had not acquired nasal clusters, and thus they became therapy targets briefly (see Bernhardt, 1994d). Table 7.9 shows developmental patterns for a number of words. We introduce this table here to show the patterns, and address particular examples further in the repairs section.

TABLE 7.9   Sean's Development of Nasal Clusters: 3;7–4;0

Target		3;7[a]	3;9	4;0
jump	/dʒʌmp/	dʌpʰ	dɑpʰ	dᵓɑp
camping	/kæmpɪŋ/		kʰæpĩn	
jumping	/dʒʌmpɪŋ/	dʌpintʰ	dapĩn	dᵌᵘapĩn
tent	/tɛnt/		tʰɛtʰ	tʰɛtʰ
present	/pɹɛznt/	pʊʷɛⁱ	pʰɛsæᵌn	pʰɛʲɪʔ
		pazɛˆᵓʔ	pʰɛzæᵓ	pʰɛzitʰ
elephant	/ɛləfn̩t/	ʔɑᵓʃ<	ʔafɪ(ɛ)ᵌn	
				ʔɑᵓfətʰ
hand	/hænd/		ʔæ̃nᵓ	ʔæn
Brandy	/bɹændi/	bædiː		
candle	/kændl̩/	gɑdoʊʔ	kʰæᵌndoˇʔ	kʰænɔʊ
		kʰædʌᵓ	kʰæ̃ᵌdoʔ	kʰæ̃ndɔʊ
orange	/ɔɹɪndʒ/	ʔɔs		ʔɔ̃ndz̥
pink	/pɪŋk/	pʰik		
donkey	/dɑŋki/	dɑᵓkʰi		
finger	/fɪŋgɹ/	ʔægʊᵓ	fɛgʊᵓʔ	fɪgə
longer	/lɑŋgɹ/			lʊgʊᵓ
hungry	/hʌŋgɹi/	hʌgɹⁱ		hʌŋkwⁱ

[a] After one 6-week block (18 sessions) of intervention. Two subsequent 6-week blocks followed until age 4;0. Final clusters were not intervention targets.

The order of word-final cluster acquisition for Sean, Jeremy, and Annalena was not completely consistent with the Templin (1957) study. Annalena's clusters developed early, with two-element clusters appearing at about 15 months, and three-element clusters at about 18 months. Sean and Jeremy were delayed, partly because they had phonological disorders, including difficulty with singleton codas. The following observations can be made about final cluster acquisition for the three children.

1. Nasal clusters. For Jeremy and Annalena, [nt] was the earliest sequence, not one of the latest (as found in the Templin study). This follows from prediction (1) and (4) above, that clusters with shared place and with early-developing features might appear early. Annalena used [nt] first at 1;2, and in "complex words" (Elsen's, 1991, term) at 2;5. Jeremy (at 3;5) sometimes even used [nt] as a substitution for a singleton voiced stop:

mad   /mæd/   [mæ̃ntʰ]

For Jeremy, the /mp/ sequence, on the other hand, varied between [p] and [mp] for some time. Thus, nasal-stop sequences varied in their point of establishment for Jeremy, just as they did for children in the Templin study, but in the opposite direction.

Sean appeared to have particular difficulty with nasal-stop clusters, acquiring them after the supposedly more 'difficult' stop-fricative and fricative-stop clusters. (Colin, §8.3, continued to have difficulty with nasal clusters at age 9, varying between [n] and [d] for /nd/ targets.)

Lack of data makes it difficult to make more than a few comments about the order of acquisition for word-medial clusters independently or in relation to onset and word-final clusters. Jeremy acquired heterosyllabic nasal-stop sequences ([ŋ.d] or [n.d]) before acquiring final clusters. Sean had delayed development of both word-medial and word-final nasal clusters with many similar deletion patterns. Heteromorphemic and tautomorphemic clusters appeared to have equivalent patterns. (Compare *longer* and *finger* in Table 7.9.) Chervela (1981), for Telugu, and Macken (1979), for Mexican Spanish, also found early acquisition of medial nasal-stop clusters, particularly /nt/.

2. Liquid-stop clusters. For Sean and Jeremy, liquid-stop clusters were acquired later than in the Templin (1957) study because both boys acquired liquids late. (Sean required intervention at age 9 to acquire these clusters.) Annalena started using liquid-stop clusters consistently at 1;6. In Chervela's (1981) study of four children learning Telugu, [lt] clusters appeared word medially around age 3;0, but in general liquid-stop clusters were absent.

3. Stop-stop clusters. Sean and Jeremy did not use stop-stop clusters during the course of the intervention study (by age 4), which was consistent with the Templin norms. Annalena, on the other hand, started using [kt] and [pt] before 18 months. Chervela (1981) gives examples of word-medial geminates [dː], [tː], and [cː] (all

as substitutions for a variety of clusters) and additionally, [dt], [dg] (also substitutions, for /ḍt/ and /ḍg/) for her four Telugu-learning subjects (ages 1;7–3;6).
Thus, they can appear at early stages.

4. Stop-fricative and fricative-stop clusters. Annalena first used stop-fricative
clusters at 1;3 ([ts] and [ps]), and they were established before age 2. A variety
of fricative-stop clusters appeared at about 1;6, slightly after the stop-fricative
clusters.

For Sean, final /Cs/-clusters matched the adult targets in advance of /sC/-clus-
ters (as was the case for Annalena). There was some hint that heteromorphemic
forms were in advance of tautomorphemic forms, although particular sequences
may have influenced those patterns more than the morphological status. For example, [ts], with repetition of [Coronal], was earlier than [ks]. (See Table 7.10.)

In terms of /s/-clusters, Sean's final and initial /s/-clusters appeared to develop
earlier than medial /s/-clusters for at least some words. At 4;0, *mask* was produced
as [mæks], but *basket* was produced as [bægɛt]. The compounds *ice cubes* and
toothbrush did appear with a heterosyllabic sequence with [s]. Thus, for medial
/s/-clusters, it appears that heteromorphemic forms were slightly advanced over
tautomorphemic forms (as was the case for final /s/-clusters). Note that /s/-loss
was the common repair, no matter what the cluster or context, except at 3;5, a time
when default [s] codas were relatively frequent. More examples of developmental
patterns are presented below. Again, comparison data are few, but Chervela (1981)
for Telugu gives examples of medial [ks] (Madhavi) and [st] (Kalyani). Thus,
either order of stop-fricative acquisition appears possible word-medially.

All varieties of repairs are possible to accommodate sequence constraints for

TABLE 7.10   Sean's Word-Medial and Final /s/-Clusters: 3;5–4;0

Target		3;5	3;7	3;9	4;0
boots	/buːts/	bup	butʃ	buts	buts
lots	/lɑts/			lɑts	
fits	/fɪts/			ᵖfɪs	fɪts
starry	/stɑɹi/	tɔˆwɛᵊ	tʰɑᵊ	dɑɪ	stɔi
fix	/fɪks/				fɪk
mask	/mæsk/	mæs	mæk	mæk	mæks
basket	/bæskət/	bægi	bækʰi	bægɛt	
scarf	/skɑɹf/	kɑs	kɑf	kʰɑf	kʰɑf
Christmas	/kɹɪsməs/			kʰɪmɪs	
ice cubes	/ʌɪskjuːbz/		ʔaˈkʰʊᵊs	ʔæˈskʰjubᵊ	
toothbrush	/tuːθbɹʌʃ/		tˠubʷʌsʔ	tʰusbɛˠᵊs	tʰusbɑᵊf

non-word-initial clusters. As with word-initial clusters, the most frequent repair is segment deletion. Deletions may occur with or without compensatory lengthening (either of vowels, or of consonants). As for word-initial clusters, repetition of C-Place may facilitate or impede cluster production. Flop and addition repairs are less frequent, although they do facilitate production of two elements. Most data available concern /s/-clusters and nasal-stop clusters, and thus we focus on those, examining both **NoSequence** and **NotTwice** constraints where they apply.

7.3.2.2. Medial and Final Clusters: Deletion Repairs

Deletion resolutions of the sequence constraints could occur at a number of levels: at the feature level (resulting in a different sequence of segments), or at a higher prosodic level (eliminating segments). As with word-initial clusters, deletion sometimes reflects a complexity constraint rather than a sequence constraint, and the examples given are often ambiguous on that point. Nasal-stop clusters and /s/-clusters are discussed (the most frequent types of clusters for which data are available), including both minimal and nonminimal repairs.

7.3.2.2.1. Nasal-Stop Clusters: Deletion Repairs

The different nasal clusters can appear at different times, depending on the voicing status of the stop, length of the word, word position, or even lexical item. Both **NotTwice** and **NoSequence** constraints are involved: **NotTwice (+ voiced)**, **NotTwice(Artic)**, **NoSequence(+ voiced...-voiced)**, and **NoSequence(+ nasal...-nasal)** are the most common. Patterns can be identical for medial and final clusters, or divergent. Minimal deletion and default insertion repairs do occur, but nonminimal repairs appear to be more common, with deletion of either the stop or the nasal. We examine, in the following order, patterns from three individuals: Sean (Bernhardt, 1990), Annalena (Elsen, 1991), and Morgan (Stemberger, 1990).

Beginning with the few two-element nasal clusters that Sean did produce, we observe interactions between sequence, linking, and faithfulness constraints. Clusters were realized both word-medially in *hungry* and *candle*, and word-finally in *orange* (see Table 7.10). For *candle*, double linking of [+ voiced] facilitated production of [nd] in two tokens, a phenomenon seen previously for word-initial clusters. But *hungry* and *orange* showed voicing *dissimilation* ([hʌŋkwɪⁱ], [ʔɔ͡ʊnd̥ᶻː]); the affricate was only partially devoiced, suggesting that the phonetic implementation of a repair can be somewhat less than total. Double linking of [+ voiced] facilitated cluster production. They also show that **NotTwice(+ voiced)** was a high-ranked constraint. Other high-ranked constraints were **Survived(Root), Survived(TimingUnit)**, and **Survived(+ nasal)**. **Survived(+ voiced)** and **Distinct (+ voiced)**were unstably ranked with respect to **SinglyLinked(+ voiced)**; when **SinglyLinked(+ voiced)** was higher-ranked, one token of [+ voiced] deleted (dissimilation, devoicing); when **SinglyLinked(+ voiced)** was lower-ranked, the two tokens of [+ voiced] were merged, and the obstruent surfaced as voiced.

NotTwice(+ voiced) Survived(Root) Survived(TimingUnit) Survived(+ nasal)	‖‖‖	Survived(+ voiced)	‖‖‖	SinglyLinked(+ voiced) Distinct(+ voiced)
		*UNSTABLE RANKING /ŋg/		*UNSTABLE RANKING /ŋk/

Most of the time, however, Sean's nasal clusters were subject to reduction. There were alternate patterns depending on voicing of the stop, and on word position. Word finally, voiced stops deleted. Word medially, either the nasal or voiced stop deleted (*candle, finger, longer*). A general constraint prohibiting voiced obstruent codas (observed in his earlier samples) may have resulted in deletion of the stop word finally. The variability for medial consonants may reflect the ambiguous status of the stop word medially. If treated as an onset, the stop would be maintained, via margin constraints promoting stops in onsets (**Co-occurring(σ-Margin→-cont)**). If treated as a coda, it would delete, as in *hand*. Voiceless stop clusters showed deletion of the nasal (even though devoiced stops occurred following medial nasals in the words *hungry* and *orange*, a chain shift phenomenon). These voicing-related outcomes for nasal clusters are all common patterns (see §6.1.7.1.2).

What kind of constraint ranking accounts for these phenomena? **NoSequence** constraints are implicated: **NotTwice(+ voiced)** as we have seen above, and either **NoSequence(+ nasal...-nasal)** or **NoSequence(+ voiced...-voiced).** These are among the highest-ranked constraints. In nonminimal repairs involving full segment deletion, **Survived/LinkedUpwards(Feature)** is high-ranked, and **LinkedUpwards(Root)** is low-ranked; all segments survive, but only in a floating segment which is not realized phonetically. The constraint ranking we showed above for the words in which clusters *were* produced needs only slight modification to account for the nonminimal repairs: low ranking of **LinkedUpwards(Root)**.

The opposite patterns for voiced and voiceless nasal stop clusters may reflect underspecification/markedness or perceptual factors. In terms of underspecification, note that nondefault features ([+voiced] or [+nasal]) delete, or the segment containing them deletes. Given a nasal and a voiced stop, the more marked element in the coda is a voiced stop. (Nondefaults are less likely to survive in weak prosodic positions. Thus, **Survived(+ voiced)** is low-ranked in codas.) Given a nasal and a voiceless stop, the more marked (nondefault) element is the nasal. In some cases, [+nasal] may also survive in the voiceless nasal-stop clusters, by being realized on the vowel. Given these possibilities for feature survival elsewhere in the word, Root nodes can perhaps be sacrificed.

We cannot rule out input and perceptual explanations for the cluster realization patterns, in terms of lexical representation for these clusters. Nasals are shorter before voiceless stops than before voiced stops, and vowels are nasalized before nasals. Thus, nasals may not be perceived as full segments before voiceless stops, but as extensions of the nucleus. By comparison, nasals preceding voiced stops are long, and possibly more perceptible than nasals preceding short voiced stops.

Further regarding the issue of variability, we noted above, in our discussion of the Templin (1957) findings, that word length and lexical variability may affect cluster realization. We suggested that the late appearance of [nt] in Templin (1957) may have resulted from difficulty with production of the multisyllabic word *elephant*. Sean had alternate realizations of this particular item, supporting that conjecture. The nasal deleted in one token of *elephant*. In another, however, the voiceless stop disappeared word finally (i.e., a pattern opposite to his typical pattern). Kehoe (1995) noted that different segments may appear in different productions of the same multisyllabic word in her study of children's development of stress. Perhaps stability of patterns is particularly compromised in weak syllables of multisyllabic words, because of competition between prosodic faithfulness and segmental faithfulness.

| elefant | /ɛəfənt/ | [ʔɑfĩ̃n] | (S) | Stop deletion |
| | | [ʔaəfətʰ] | (E) | Nasal deletion |

Regressions have also been observed. Annalena (Elsen, 1991) generally retained the nasal (word finally and word medially), showing a high ranking for **Survived(+ nasal)**. However, a few words showed deletion of [+nasal]. The progression with the word 'Ente' *(duck)* is interesting. In the early attempts, two elements were produced, but with double linking of [+voiced] (/t/ > [d]). This probably reflected plateauing of voicing between vowels, due to high-ranked **Uninterrupted(+ voiced)**, as is common for medial obstruents. The double linking of [+voiced] possibly promoted production of the cluster. However, when she began to produce the word with a voiceless stop, the nasal deleted. Both the double linking and nonminimal deletion repairs suggest high-ranked **No-Sequence(+ voiced...-voiced)**. Adjacent consonants with different values of [voiced] could not be in a sequence, unless morpheme-final: /-nt-/ > [-nd-] or [-t(ː)-], but /nt#/ > [nt] or [nθ].

	anders	/andɐs/	[ʔanːas]	'other'
	Hemd	/hɛm(p)t/	[ʔɛm]	'shirt'
	Computer	/kɔmpjʊtɐ/	[kɔmjɯtə]	'computer'
	Pampers	/pæmpɐs/	[pɛmːəs]	'Pampers'
BUT:	Lampe	/læmpə/	[lapːa]	'lamp'
	Mond	/mɔnt/	[mɔn]~[mɔns]	'moon'
	Mund	/mʊnt/	[manθ]~[mant]~[mən-t]	'mouth'
BUT:	Ente	/ɛntə/	[nɛndə] > [ɛndə] > [ɛt(ː)ə] > [ɛntɛ]	'duck'

Note that Annalena's forms often preserved the timing units of the word-internal cluster (in the form of a geminate consonant), even though the features for one of the elements deleted. (See §7.3.2.3.)

7.3.2.2.2. Medial and Final /s/-Clusters: Deletion Repairs

Non-word-initial clusters with /s/ also appear to have variable deletion patterns, depending on sequence type, lexical item, word position, and word length. Generally, the repairs are nonminimal, with segment deletion. In some cases, the patterns are the same as in word-initial /s/-clusters (see Megan's examples below and Sean's examples in §7.4), and sometimes they differ, because of general rime and margin constraints promoting fricatives in coda and stops in onsets (see Gwendolyn's examples below). Sometimes the /s/ deletes, as Sean's example with *fix* shows, and sometimes the stop deletes, as Gwendolyn's example with *box* shows.

In the following example from Gwendolyn, the reduction pattern for /s/-clusters differed depending on word position. (D. Ohala, 1994, suggests that this difference between word-initial and word-final position may be common for clusters.) Sequence constraints inhibited cluster production. Rime co-occurrence constraints promoted retention of the /s/ in coda, and margin co-occurrence constraints promoted retention of the stop in onset. Word initially and medially, all /s/-stop clusters were realized as stops, even though singleton /s/ was realized correctly (see *sit* below). Word finally, the /s/ surfaced, rather than the /t/.

	stop	/stɑp/	[tʰap]
	sister	/sɪstɹ/	[sɪtoʊ]
BUT:	box	/bɑks/	[bas]
	kiss	/kɪs/	[tʰɪs]
	sit	/sɪt/	[sɪt]

The following constraint ranking accounted for the patterns observed.

1. σ▸**Onset** was highest-ranked, and **Not(Coda)** was lowest-ranked, resulting in at least one consonant being produced in onset and coda.

2. **NotTwice(C-TimingUnit)** was high-ranked, prohibiting all clusters. We know that complexity constraints are not to blame here, because they are not relevant to a cluster that is split by a syllable boundary: in medial position, there can in theory be a singleton coda consonant followed by a singleton onset consonant. Thus, in medial position, it is sequence constraints that prohibit clusters, as with the word *sister*.

3. **Survived(Root)** and **Survived(TimingUnit)** were low-ranked, allowing one segment to delete.

4. **Co-occurring(Rime→ + continuant)** and **Co-occurring(σ-Margin→-continuant)** were high-ranked, but they had an effect only when the system had to choose between two competing segments. They could not motivate the deletion of singleton consonants, nor the insertion or deletion of features. In the coda, the rime constraint reduced /st/ to [s]. In the onset, the margin constraint reduced /st/ to [t]. In medial position, only one consonant was possible, and that had to be an onset. Consequently, /st/ was reduced to [t] there also.

σ►**Onset**

NotTwice(C-TimingUnit)

Co-occurring(Rime→ + continuant)

Co-occurring(σ-Margin→-continuant)

Survived(Root)
Survived(C-TimingUnit)
Not(Coda)

Some children have similar deletion patterns across syllable positions; rime or margin constraints are not implicated in the rankings for the clusters. Ringo's (1985) subject, Megan, deleted the /t/ of /st/ in all contexts, suggesting high ranking of **Survived(+ continuant)**. (See also Sean's /sk/-clusters in Table 7.10.)[8]

sister	/sɪstɹ̩/	[sɪsə]
monster	/mɑnstɹ̩/	[mansə]
rest	/ɹɛst/	[ɹɛs]
stool	/stuːl/	[suʊ]

7.3.2.3. Medial and Final Clusters: Epenthesis (Addition) Repairs

Epenthesis is even rarer in non-word-initial clusters than in word-initial clusters (§6.1.7.2). However, Elsen (1991) does report a few instances of this in Annalena's speech, mostly with /l/-clusters. Epenthesis and pauses were types of additions. (See §10.1.6 for further discussion of nonphonological strategies.)

elf	/ɛlf/	[ɛləf]	'eleven'
malt	/mɑlt/	[mɑlət]	'paints'
gelb	/gɛlp/	[gɛl—pʰ]	'yellow'
Hans	/hans/	[hɑn—θ]	'Hans'
Kopf	/kɔpf/	[kɔp—f]	'head'[9]

Epenthesis was used for homorganic clusters, and for clusters with /l/. In the case of /l/-clusters **NoSequence(+ lateral... + consonantal)** is implicated. In the case of the clusters with shared C-Place, **SinglyLinked** and **NotTwice** constraints are circumvented by pausing between the elements.

---

[8]**LinkedUpwards(+ cont)** is satisfied even in a floating segment. If **LinkedUpwards(Root)** is ranked high enough, no floating segment is tolerated. The ranking here assures phonetic realization of [+cont].

[9]The separation of [p—f] implies that Annalena interpreted /pf/ as a cluster rather than as an affricate.

7.3.2.4. Medial and Final Clusters: Double-Linking Repairs

In the deletion repairs section, we referred to double linking on occasion, either at the Root level (gemination), or for [+voiced]. We elaborate briefly on these repairs here, although data are few in comparison to the deletion data.

In adult English and German, nasal-stop clusters are homorganic. Double linking of C-Place possibly promotes the typically early acquisition of those clusters (as double linking does for some children's word-initial clusters). We showed examples in the deletion section above from Annalena (see *Ente*), and noted that a high-ranked **Uninterrupted(+voiced)** constraint probably resulted in the multiple linking of [+voiced] across the word. Another example is *Pampers*. At Point 1, **NoSequence(+nasal...-nasal)** prohibited the cluster; constraint rankings are similar to those of Morgan in Table 7.11, but **Not(+voiced)** and **Singly-Linked(+voiced)** are lower-ranked, allowing spread of nasality and voicing onto the voiceless stop. At Point 2, we observe double linking of C-Place and [+voiced], with [+nasal] singly linked.

Pampers	/pampɐs/	[pɛmːəs]	'Pampers'	Point 1
		[pɛmbəs]		Point 2

Low ranking of **SinglyLinked(+voiced)** and **SinglyLinked(C-Place)** and high ranking of **NoSequence(+nasal...-voiced)** promoted the spreading of [+voiced] and the double linking of C-Place.

Gemination repairs (the first rendition of *Pampers* above), are nonminimal, but do not result in deletion of structure above the Root. The Root node and timing units remain doubly linked. Chervela (1981) gives a number of repair examples from four children learning Telugu, a language which has geminates:

/saːnd̪ilsu/	[taːnditːu]	Swati (1;8)
/nidra/	[nidːay]	Swati (1;9)
/rikʃa/	[ricːa]~[riʃa]	Madhavi (3;1)

Chervela comments that more well-established ("less complex") segments substituted for others in the cluster gemination, even if the child could produce the "more complex" segment as a singleton (e.g., /kt/ > [tː] as in [latːam] for /raktam/). Often, nondefault features deleted and default features were inserted and doubly linked as in [nidːay] and [taːnditːu] above. This indicates high ranking of **NoSequence(Nondefault...Default)**. In other cases, fusion of features from both segments occurs, with maintenance of the timing units (/kʃ/ > [cː], giving a [-anterior] stop). **NoSequence(-continuant...+continuant)** results in a [-continuant]...[-continuant] sequence. A further **NoSequence(Dorsal...Coronal,-anterior)** sequence constraint results in deletion of [Dorsal] and creation of a palatal stop (closest place of articulation to the [-anterior] fricative.)

Chervela notes additionally that geminates may degeminate if a triconsonantal sequence would be formed as a result of vowel deletion.

/konukːunːa/	[konkunːa]	Kalyani (2;2)
/gucːukunt̪ay/	[guckuntay]	

Thus, geminates, although one strategy to rescue timing units when sequences of consonants were not possible, were vulnerable when new sequences were created through vowel deletion. Chain shifts are challenging for us to deal with; see §10.2.1.

As we saw for Annalena above, consonant gemination also occurs in languages without geminates as a way to preserve timing units when particular sequences are not possible. This was also true for Morgan for English (Stemberger, 1990):

finger	/fɪŋgɹ/	[fɪŋːɤ]
only	/oːnli/	[ʔɤkːnːi]
monkey	/mʌŋki/	[mʌkːi]

In Morgan's case, voicing status of the stop affected outcomes. The nasal was maintained rather than a voiced stop (as it was some of the time for Sean). In *monkey*, however, the nasal deleted. The following rankings are suggested, similar to what we have shown above for Sean, but with high ranking of **Survived (TimingUnit)**. **NoSequence(+ nasal...-nasal)** prohibited the cluster. **Singly-Linked(+ voiced)** prevented [ŋ]. Nasals cannot be voiceless, and hence spreading of nasal onto the voiceless stop is impossible (high ranking of **Co-occurring(+ nasal→ + voiced)**. To maintain the timing units, gemination of the /k/ solves the problem; **Survived(+ nasal)** was low-ranked.

TABLE 7.11

/mʌŋki/	mʌŋki	mʌŋŋi	mʌŋːi	mʌkːi
Survived(TimingUnit)				
SinglyLinked(+voiced)			*!	
NoSequence(+nasal...-nasal)	*!			
Co-occurring(+nasal→+voiced)		*!		
Survived/LinkedUpwards(+nas)				*
Not(+nasal)	*	*	*	
SinglyLinked(+nasal)		*	*	
Not(-nasal)	*			*

We also observed in the deletion repairs section that double linking did not facilitate nasal cluster production for Sean most of the time. Double linking of C-Place and [+voiced] did promote cluster realization in *candle* twice, but the other clusters that did appear had voicing *dissimilation* (i.e., the opposite repair). In Sean's /s/-clusters, the /ts/ cluster appeared in advance of the /ks/ cluster, one indication of the facilitative effect of shared C-Place in cluster production. For Annalena, a variety of final clusters with fricatives were early; hence double linking was not a major factor in their development.

Similarly to what we observed for onset clusters, double linking at the feature level can facilitate production of complex structure, or result in collapse of it through fusion up to the level of the timing unit.

7.3.2.5. Medial and Final Clusters: Flop Repairs

Flop is a rare phenomenon for non-word-initial clusters. Local flop is observed primarily for the /s/-clusters. Other clusters often require additional repairs. For example, when flop occurs rightward in liquid clusters, the liquid necessarily becomes syllabic (see *Helm* below). Other liquid cluster and /s/-cluster examples follow. We discuss long distance migration or flop in §7.4.4.3, in the section on noncontiguous sequences.

7.3.2.5.1. Liquid Clusters

Elsen (1991) and Smith (1973) give a few examples of liquid flop.

Helm   /hɛlm/   [hɛml̩]   'helmet'   (Elsen, 1991)

Smith (1973) gives a few examples from Amahl's speech of rightward liquid exchanges with fricatives or stops, but because he does not indicate whether the coda liquids become syllabic, we do not include those examples here. One word-medial example was:

helping   /hɛlpɪŋ/   [ɛplin]

Two leftwards flops resulting in onset clusters were:

film   /fɪlm/   [flɪm]
milk   /mɪlk/   [mlɪk]

Although [fl] and [pl] are more frequent clusters than /lm/, [ml] is not a permissible onset in adult English. It appears that **NoSequence(+ continuant...-continuant)** was high-ranked (even for those examples that we are unclear about), and that **Survived(Link)** and **Not(Link)** were low-ranked. Leftward flop in the word *film* is somewhat surprising, since other liquid clusters had rightward flop of [+lateral], and [ml] sequences were allowed (see *milk*). But nasal-lateral sequences are rare in English compared with [fl], and thus, were of low probability if something else was possible.

Whether it is more plausible to describe these data as the flop of segments or the flop of features is debatable. Where /l/ and /m/ interchange, the flop of multiple features does account for the data: [Coronal]-[Labial], and [+nasal]-[+lateral]. But where /l/ and stops exchange places, [+continuant] and [-continuant] change places, [+lateral] moves, and additionally, [Coronal] and [Labial] or [Coronal] and [Dorsal] flop. This seems contrived and complex compared with the simplicity of Root metathesis (a nonminimal repair). Furthermore, when the lateral metathesizes with a vowel, as in *film* and *milk*, several features would have to move between the C-plane and the V-plane, with additional feature insertion to ensure faithfulness to the target segments. Although trans-planar feature spreading does occur (see §7.3.4), this is not common. In spite of our previous claims that features flop, rather than Root nodes, the simpler description for at least Smith's data is exchange of Root nodes (violation of **Contiguity**).

7.3.2.5.2. /s/-Stop Clusters

The most common word-initial flop patterns are for /sp/. Word-finally, there are few words with /sp/. Consequently, we cannot compare the frequency of word-initial and word-final flop for that cluster. It appears that more flop examples have /sC/ > [Cs] patterns than /Cs/ to [sC] patterns, but this is only an impression.

Examples of /st/ and /sk/ local flop follow. When /st/ flops, only the feature [+continuant] migrates rightwards. When /sk/ flops, [+continuant] flops rightwards, and [Dorsal] flops leftwards.

Annalena: Elsen (1991)

| Biest | /biːst/ | [bits]~[bis] | 'beast' | [+cont] flop |
| Kiosk | /kiɔsk/ | [kiːjɔks] | 'kiosk' | Dorsal & [+cont] flop |

Sean: Bernhardt (1990), Time 4

| mask | /mæsk/ | [maks] | | Dorsal & [+cont] flop |

There appears to be a **NoSequence(+continuant...-continuant)** constraint. For Annalena, this constraint applied some of the time to liquid clusters and /s/-clusters. A similar constraint was observed for Robin's and Kendra's word-initial clusters. It is clear that sequences can be prohibited anywhere in the word, and across a variety of cluster types, with similar repairs accommodating them.

7.3.2.6. Medial and Final Clusters: Summary

The earliest medial and final clusters for most children are nasal-stop clusters, either intervocalically or word finally. Double linking of C-Place does not always facilitate cluster production, however, as Sean's data show. As is true for word-initial clusters, nondefault features often have priority over default features. Rime and margin constraints have an impact on final cluster production some of the time, just as they do on singleton coda development. They in fact may reappear when clusters are the targets, even though they no longer apply in singleton production (Gwendolyn's data).

As far as we know, many constraints that hold true of the adult target language are never overcome. For English-learning children, clusters like /kt/ and /nd/ eventually emerge, but /tk/ and /dn/ remain unusual throughout life (even though they are eventually mastered in names like *Atkinson* and *Sydney*).

Sometimes the patterns for non-word-initial clusters are similar to the ones for word-initial clusters, and sometimes they are different. The same types of repairs are noted, with deletion again being frequent, and addition and flop being infrequent. Double linking repairs are less frequent for non-word-initial clusters, possibly because of the lack of obstruent-sonorant clusters word finally (the context for assimilation in word-initial clusters).

7.3.3. CONTIGUOUS VOWEL SEQUENCES

Vowel sequences (diphthongs) may be subject to sequence constraints. However, there is very little information on vowels, and virtually none that allow us to make comments on diphthong sequence constraints.

Sequence constraints would imply differences between diphthongs such as /aɪ/ and /ɔɪ/, or /aɪ/ and /aʊ/. We would need to show low ranking for feature constraints, such as **Not(Labial)** or prosodic structure constraints, such as **Not-Complex(Nucleus)**, and be able to account for the differences only in terms of sequence constraints, for example, **NoSequence(Labial...+high)** or **No-Sequence(+low...Labial)**.

English /ɹ/ is also a glide, and [ɫ] is often glide-like postvocalically. More examples demonstrating sequence constraints for vowel-/ɹ/ and vowel-/l/ sequences may be available, because /ɹ/ and /l/ are more studied and their acquisition is sufficiently protracted that some sequences may appear before others. One-by-one learning for vowel-/ɹ/ sequences is commonly found in phonological intervention, although different children may find different sequences easier at first. For example, Gordon (Bernhardt, 1990:S5) first pronounced /ɹ/ after low back vowels: [ɑɹ] and [ɔɹ]. His facility with the back vowel context (except for /u/ which he could not pronounce in any case; see §5.6.2.2.1) suggests that high ranking of **NotTwice(Coronal)** and **SinglyLinked(Coronal)** prohibited /ɹ/ after front vowels. Sean (Bernhardt, 1990:S4), on the other hand, learned to pronounce /ɛɹ/ and /iɹ/ first, and took much longer to produce the back vowels with /ɹ/, suggesting a high-ranked **NoSequence(Dorsal...Coronal)** constraint and low ranking of **SinglyLinked(Coronal)**.

Larissa (Stemberger, p.u.d.) had two patterns involving sequence constraints on vowels and postvocalic /ɹ/ and /l/. She reduced postvocalic /ɹ/ to the glide [ɪ] after back vowels, but to schwa after front vowels.

	/oɹ/	[ʌɪ]	
	/ɑɹ/	[ɑɪ]	(cf. /aɪ/ [aɪ])
	/ɹ̩/	[əɪ]	
BUT:	/iɹ/	[iə]	
	/ɛɹ/	[eə]	

This also suggests **NotTwice(Coronal)**. The [Coronal] feature of the /ɹ/ deleted after front vowels, but V-Place remained. Default vowel features for schwa were inserted.

NotTwice(Coronal)	‖‖	Survived(Coronal)
Survived(V-Place)		**Not(Dorsal)**
Priority(Left)		**Not(-high)**

A nonminimal repair occurred for the same child in response to **NotTwice(V-Labial)**. Typically, postvocalic /l/ was realized as [ʊ] in a diphthong:

fall	/fɑl/	[faʊ]	
yell	/jɛl/	[jɛʊ]	
follow	/fɑloː/	[faʊ]	*[faʊo]
yellow	/jɛloʊ/	[jɛʊ]	*[jɛʊo]

Words ending in the sequence /loː/ should have been produced as *[ʊo]. However, the /oː/ failed to surface following the [ʊ] substitution. This is a nonminimal repair, in which the /o/ was deleted (left floating) in order to avoid a violation of **NotTwice(Labial)**. The leftmost vowel was retained.

NotTwice(V-Labial)	**Survived(TimingUnit)**
Priority(Left)	**Survived(Root)**
SinglyLinked(V-Labial)	
Survived/LinkedUpwards(Labial)	

As stated at the outset of this short section, we need much more information on vowel acquisition in general, and on sequences of vowels and glides in particular. (See also §6.2.5.2.)

7.3.4. CONTIGUOUS SEQUENCES OF CONSONANTS AND VOWELS

The most common contiguous sequences are sequences of consonants and vowels. Most words contain at least one consonant and one vowel. Since CV is the most common sequence, is CV the most likely to be involved in sequence constraints? Consonants and vowels might be expected to interact in major ways, because of coarticulatory effects in speech production. On the other hand, the high frequency of CV sequences might make them more resistant to sequence constraints.

In spite of coarticulatory effects (phonetic nasalization of vowels before nasal consonants; rounding of consonants before rounded vowels), consonants and vowels usually act independently of one another in phonological patterns. This follows from the concept of planar segregation for consonants and vowels (§3.4.3). Even though consonants and vowels can be contiguous, they are adjacent only at the level of the timing unit. Timing units are relatively neutral with respect to segmental content. Thus, timing unit adjacency may be less relevant for sequence interactions than tier adjacency, which directly concerns segmental content: C-Place, [voiced], [sonorant], [continuant], and so on. Thus, the lack of interaction between consonants and vowels may be explicable in terms of adjacency level.

Although CV interactions are infrequent, they are attested in the literature. Those few examples typically concern place interactions (e.g., Fudge, 1969; Waterson, 1971; Braine, 1974; Stoel-Gammon, 1983, 1996; Williams & Dinnsen, 1987; B. Davis & MacNeilage, 1990; Levelt, 1994). However, height interactions have also been noted (Camarata & Gandour, 1984; Levelt, 1994; S. Edwards, 1995). We report here on this type of interaction, and additionally, on an interaction involving the feature [tense]. The most common repair of **NoSequence** constraints between consonants and vowels is assimilation of vowel features, as we show for place, manner, and voicing features. Double linking of place or height can also positively resolve a **NotTwice** constraint. Deletion and default insertion occur as repairs, but less commonly. We have found no examples of epenthesis repairs (to separate the consonant and the vowel), or flop repairs to resolve a sequence constraint between consonants and vowels. (Flop of [+nasal] from a consonant to a vowel, or vice versa, is usually not a result of sequence constraints, but of other constraints, as in §7.3.4.3.)

7.3.4.1. CV or VC Sequences and Constraints

Sequence constraints between consonants and vowels can reflect place, height, tenseness, voicing, and manner. All of these interactions have been attested.

1. Consonants and vowels which are produced in the same articulatory area may dissimilate, because of, for example, **NotTwice(Artic)**, or **NotTwice(+high)** (Bernhardt, 1994b; Edwards, 1995).
2. Consonants and vowels produced in different articulatory areas may assimilate, because of **NoSequence(ArticA...ArticB)** (Fudge, 1969; Stoel-Gammon, 1983, 1994; Levelt, 1994). Consonants may develop in contexts that share place or height with a vowel (S. Edwards, 1995).
3. Consonants may assimilate to vowels in terms of voicing or manner when between vowels: **Uninterrupted(+voiced)** (intervocalic voicing), or **Uninterrupted(+continuant)** (intervocalic spirantization). The feature [+nasal] may migrate or spread from consonants to vowels.
4. Glides and vowels may show **NotTwice** or **NoSequence** constraints, because both have vowel features.
5. The majority of reported interactions show anticipatory effects from the vowel to the preceding consonant. This is true also of many consonant sequence effects (especially for assimilation and harmony).

The difficult task for the phonologist is to find a feature geometry which can account both for these interactions and their rarity (see §3.3). Theories which propose similar features for the two types of segment classes predict a higher frequency of CV interactions than those that propose different features. The following subsections outline place and height sequences, voicing sequences, and manner sequences, with a primary focus on the challenges for description.

7.3.4.2. CV or VC Place and Height Sequences

Vowel feature descriptions of Chomsky and Halle (1968) predict minimal interaction between consonants and vowels because of lack of similarity in features (except for dorsal consonants and vowels). Yet there are some examples. We look first at coronal and labial features.

7.3.4.2.1. Coronals and Labials

Interactions between front vowels and coronal consonants are the most commonly reported CV interactions. Less frequent are interactions between labial consonants and round vowels (Fudge, 1969; Stoel-Gammon, 1983; B. Davis & MacNeilage, 1990; Levelt, 1994). Both Levelt (1996) and Stoel-Gammon (1996) comment that such phenomena are typical of very early phonologies only. How can we account for /bi/ > [di] and /du/ > [bu]?

Using vowel features ([back], [high], [low], and [round]), cumbersome sequence constraints need to be posited.

| /du/ | [bu] | **NoSequence(Coronal... + round, + high, + back)** |
| /bi/ | [di] | **NoSequence(Labial...-back, + high)** |

Given these features, it is not clear why such a constraint would exist.

The articulator features used in this book account better for such interactions. If [Labial] is used for labial consonants *and* round vowels, and [Coronal] for front vowels *and* coronal consonants, a more sensible description is possible:

| /du/ | [bu] | **NoSequence(Coronal...Labial)** |
| /bi/ | [di] | **NoSequence(Labial...Coronal)** |

Place sequence constraints may or may not be implicated, however. If the onset is a weaker domain in comparison to the syllable nucleus, production of any [C-Artic] may be difficult in an onset. If the [C-Artic] deletes, spreading the [V-Artic] provides the consonant with a place feature. It is possible, however, that a sequence constraint, **NoSequence(C-Artic...V-Artic)** could be involved.

> **Survived(C-Place)**
> **Survived(V-Artic)**
> **(NoSequence(C-Artic...V-Artic))**
> ========================
> **Not(C-Artic)**
> ========================
> **Survived(C-Artic)**
> **SinglyLinked(V-Artic)**
> **Not(V-Artic)**

In the case of /du/, [Coronal] would generally be inserted by default for [d]. If this cannot happen (whether because of sequence constraints or weak activation of C-Artic), [V-Labial] spreads and /d/ surfaces as [b]. (Although Ní Chiosáin and Padgett, 1993, suggest that the consonant does not become [+round] like the vowel, this seems unlikely. Lubker and Gay (1982) report that consonants before rounded vowels are always rounded in adult English, due to coarticulation.)

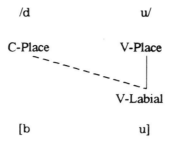

FIGURE 7.1   **NoSequence(C-Artic... V-Artic)** and transplanar spreading of V-Artic to C-Place

Where [bi] surfaces as [di], [C-Labial] does not survive. In such cases, the vowel features have precedence in coarticulation (anticipatory assimilation), or higher activation. Thus, the feature [C-Labial] deletes. There are two possible descriptions of that data. It is possible that [V-Coronal] spreads from the vowel. Alternatively, it is possible that default [C-Coronal] is inserted for the consonant. If the child also has [bu] for /du/, the assimilation analysis seems likely.

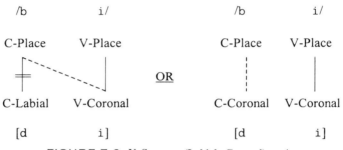

FIGURE 7.2   **NoSequence(Labial...Coronal)** repairs

This type of CV interaction assumes timing unit adjacency and trans-planar spreading. Even if the features are not *identical*, their similarity is captured by this type of feature system. [V-Artic] and [C-Artic] are both instances of [Artic] and so may interact, although [V-Artic] normally links to V-Place (high-ranked **V-Artic◄V-Place**), and thus interactions are not common. However, other high-ranked constraints can force V-Artic to link to C-Place. Thus, this solution seems plausible for interactions between round vowels and labial consonants, and front vowels and coronal consonants.

In the previous examples, the vowel influenced the consonant. Less commonly, consonant features can affect vowel production. Morgan (Stemberger, 1992a) originally had no rounded vowels or glides, substituting the equivalent unrounded back vowels and glides (see Table 5.6.). **Not(V-Labial)** was generally high-ranked. However, **Survived(C-Labial)** was high-ranked (at least in onset). In words with labials, such as *boo* and *moon*, spread of [C-Labial] to the vowel allowed a rounded vowel to be produced.

| boo | /buː/ | [bɯː~[buː] |
| moon | /muːn/ | [mɯːn]~[muːn] |

In the above examples, features spread, or were inserted (minimal repairs), but no higher level structures were affected. As we have shown throughout the book, nonminimal repairs can also occur (although they are rarer). Furthermore, sequences can sometimes be created to resolve other constraints. Continuing with Morgan's data (Stemberger, 1992a), she showed an additional way to save [V-Labial] that involved creation of a VC sequence, at 1;6–1;8. When any rounded vowel appeared in word-final position, she unrounded it as always, but optionally produced an [m] after it:

| no | /noː/ | [nɤː]~[nɤːm] |
| tiger | /taɪɡɹ/ | [tʰaɪɡɤː]~[tʰaɪɡɤːm] |

These data suggest that [V-Labial] was prohibited not by the high ranking of **Not(V-Labial)**, but by a complexity constraint such as **NotCo-occurring(V-Labial,V-Dorsal)**. Although [V-Labial] could not survive in the vowel, it could survive if it was shifted to a following consonant. It could not be added to any existing consonant (implying that final coronal consonants might have to be specified as [Coronal] underlyingly), so [V-Labial] simply deleted when there was a following consonant. In word-final position, a consonant was inserted for [V-Labial] to link to. The inserted consonant was a sonorant, since sonorants are often preferred in codas; the only sonorant true consonant in Morgan's system at the time were nasals.

RESULTS

NotCo-occurring(V-Labial,V-Dorsal)	**No round vowels**
NotCo-occurring(V-Labial,C-Artic)	**No rounded consonants**
Survived(V-Dorsal)	**Back vowels surface**
Co-occurring(Rime→ + sonorant)	**Coda C = [+ sonorant]**
Survived(V-Labial)	**V-Labial must survive**
V-Place◄V-Place	**V-Artic does not have to associate to V-Place**
Not(C-Root)	
Not(C-Place)	
Not(+ nasal)	
Not(+ sonorant)	
Not(Link)	

In this case, creation of a VC sequence resolved a feature-based constraint (whereas in this chapter, we have primarily addressed underlying sequences that are resolved by feature or other changes).

7.3.4.2.2. Dorsal Consonants and Vowel Features

Interactions have also been reported between dorsal consonants and back vowels (Fudge, 1969; Williams & Dinnsen, 1987; B. Davis & MacNeilage, 1990), or dorsal consonants and nonlow vowels (Camarata & Gandour, 1984; S. Edwards, 1995). When target dorsal consonants appear with back vowels only, **Not(C-Dorsal)** or **NotCo-occurring(+consonantal, +back)** may be high-ranked, with survival of [Dorsal] (or [+back]) dependent on spreading of [V-Dorsal]). (See also §7.4.2.3.) For target coronals, high ranking of **NoSequence(Coronal...Dorsal)** may inhibit insertion of default [C-Coronal]. To rescue [C-Place], [V-Dorsal] spreads to fill the consonant slot with a place feature.

For height interactions, S. Edwards (1995) discusses a speech therapy session in which a 4-year-old, Shawn, was just learning to pronounce /k/ and /g/. **Not(Dorsal)** was high-ranked. The first facilitative vowel context for velars was a preceding [+low] (back or front) vowel /ɑ/ or /æ/. This suggests a dissimilatory effect, with high ranking of **NotTwice(-low)** promoting a [-low] consonant after [+low] vowels. However, Camarata and Gandour (1984) account for similar patterns in their data with the feature [diffuse] (an acoustic feature of Jakobson, Fant, & Halle, 1951).[10] In that feature system, velars and low vowels are both [-diffuse] (and different from coronals and high vowels which are [+diffuse]). If [diffuse] is used, **NotTwice(-diffuse)** might be resolved by merging the two tokens of [-diffuse] (via low ranking of **SinglyLinked(-diffuse)** and **Distinct(-diffuse)**); the repair could be viewed as assimilatory, not dissimilatory. In any case, the child was next able to pronounce velars after the diphthong /oʊ/ (first using a [-low] voiced uvular fricative, then a [g]). This calls into question both the [diffuse] and [low] analyses, because of the [+high] component of the diphthong. If he could pronounce the diphthong before a velar, why could he not produce the high vowels in that context? If he could pronounce [oʊk], why was [ɛk] impossible at first? Perhaps, because [oʊ] is also [+back], a [-low] feature could be tolerated when it co-occurred with [+back]. Similarly, perhaps [æ] was only tolerated because it was [+low] or [-diffuse] (even if [-back]). Having both [-low] and [-back] features made sequences with the [+high] and [+back] velars too difficult (multiple simultaneous negative sequence constraints).

Tolerated sequences:	a.	[+bk]...[+bk]		
		[+lo]...[-lo]	[ɑk]	Dissimilatory?
	b.	[-bk]...[+bk]		
		[+lo]...[-lo]	[æk]	Dissimilatory?
	c.	[+bk]...[+bk]		
		[-lo]...[-lo]	[oʊk]	Assimilatory?

[10]Camarata and Gandour (1984) discuss a CV interaction for one child reflecting height. Coronal consonants were produced with high vowels, and dorsals with low vowels, with labials basically neutral in the interaction. The [-diffuse] vowels /æ/, /ə/, /ɑ/, and /o/ were produced with [-diffuse] /g/. The diffuse high vowels were produced with the [+diffuse] /d/. The labials, also [+diffuse], were subject to this effect only with the high vowel /i/, however. Thus, the analysis does not completely capture the data.

Prohibited sequences: d. [-bk]...[+bk]
                            [-lo]...[-lo]   [ɛk],[ik]   Dissimilatory?
                        e. [+bk]...[+bk]
                            [+hi]...[-hi]   Dissimilatory?

The data are not totally comprehensible with the feature systems available, but demonstrate in any event that some vowel contexts may be easier for some children than others.

The Chomsky and Halle (1968) feature designation might imply more frequent interactions between dorsal consonants and vowels than between coronal and labial consonants and vowels. The Jakobson et al. (1951) feature system might predict more interactions between nonhigh vowels and velars (and palatals) and between high vowels and coronals. The feature system used in this book (with Dorsal, Labial, and Coronal) might predict interactions for each of the three similar features. We do not have sufficient information to decide between feature systems, but it looks as though children may vary in the way they organize their feature systems.

7.3.4.3. CV and VC Voicing Sequence Constraints

Prevocalic and intervocalic voicing are long-reported phenomena for child (and adult) phonology (M. Edwards & Shriberg, 1983). Prevocalic voicing may or may not reflect sequence constraints. Some authors (M. Edwards & Shriberg, 1983; Stoel-Gammon & Dunn, 1985) do refer to "prevocalic voicing assimilation." This could come about for two different reasons. First, it might not be possible for any value of [voiced] to survive or be inserted in the onset; since there must be some value of voicing, [+voiced] spreads from the vowel (which is voiced because it is a sonorant):

LinkedDownwards(Laryngeal) Co-occurring(+ sonorant→ + voiced)	RESULTS Redundant voicing in sonorants
Not(+ voiced)	[+ vcd] is neither inserted nor survives in onset
Survived(+ voiced) Not(-voiced)	
SinglyLinked(+ voiced)	Spread [+ voiced] from vowel

Alternatively, voicelessness in the consonant might be prohibited by a sequence constraint such as **NoSequence(-voiced... + voiced)**; constraint rankings are otherwise similar.

This may be a motivation for prevocalic voicing, but problems inherent in analysis and interpretation of Voice Onset Time (VOT) make it difficult to ascertain what constraints are operative (see §5.5.2.1). Most children with "prevocalic voicing" are probably producing voiceless unaspirated stops (see §5.5.2.1). Some children (such as Morgan), do show prevoicing; [datʰ] for /kʰæt/, and [bapa] for /pʰapa/. Even when this is the case, however, we cannot rule out a nonassimilation analysis. If the system default is [+voiced], it may be filled in for consonants as well as vowels:

Not(-voiced)	‖‖	Survived(-voiced)
Not(+s.g.)	‖‖	Survived(+s.g.)
	‖‖	Not(+voiced)

Intervocalic voicing may also (and perhaps more clearly) result from sequence constraints. Plateauing of [+voiced] may occur:

> icy   /ʌɪsi/   [ʔæzˀɪːⁱ]   (Sean: Bernhardt, 1990, *S4*)

The two tokens of [+voiced] in the vowels are merged, and also link to the intervocalic consonant to avoid interrupted linkage:

Not(+voiced)	‖‖	SinglyLinked(+voiced)
Uninterrupted(+voiced)	‖‖	Distinct(+voiced)

Allen (1985) reports that French-learning children may use plateauing to maintain the voicing of word-initial stops. The six children in his study produced only three word-initial prevoiced stops in a sample of 193 tokens. However, voiced stops were produced in noninitial utterance positions in 43/51 cases. The voiced stops occurred after nasal consonants (the most frequent epenthesized segment, emanating perhaps from the articles 'un' or 'une'), neutral vowels, and nasalized vowels. (*S4* exclusively used nasals,, e.g., 'ballon' as [ʔm̩balo], and 18/20 were homorganic). Voicing was maintained throughout the stop closure for 33/43 (77%) of the voiced stops, suggesting that the epenthesized segment was there as a support for voicing in the stop. In contrast, only 99/142 voiceless stops were produced in noninitial utterance position, and only 3/99 (3%) had voicing throughout. There were additionally three instances of prefixed *voiceless* vowels, further showing a contrast between voiced and voiceless stops, although the spreading of [-voiced] is unexpected. (Without more individual examples or data it is difficult to evaluate the pattern.) In any case, epenthesis does occur, and in a way that suggests support for a problematic feature, plus a sequence constraint.

To the above ranking, add an intermediate ranking of **Survived(+voiced)** and a low ranking of **Not(V-Root)**; the system prefers to insert a vowel, with plateauing of [+voiced], than to devoice a consonant.

Whether dissimilation between voiced consonants and vowels occurs, we do not know.

7.3.4.4. CV and VC Manner Sequence Constraints

Manner features can spread from consonants to vowels, or vice versa. This generally involves [+continuant] spreading to intervocalic consonants.

In adult phonology, languages show evidence of stops becoming fricatives between vowels (diachronically, or synchronically as in Spanish). This lenition repair accommodates **Uninterrupted(+ continuant)**, with trans-planar spreading of [+continuant] from the vowel(s) to the intervening consonant. In child phonology, such minimal double-linking repairs can also occur.

radio   /ɹeɪdio/   [wɑzɛˀ]   (Sean: Bernhardt, 1990, *S4*)

Given a low ranking of **Distinct(+ continuant)**, the two tokens of [+continuant] in the vowels are merged, and the intervening consonant also links to that token of [+continuant], to avoid a violation of **Uninterrupted(+ continuant)**.

For Sean, the fricative replacement may have involved deletion of the underlying intervocalic consonant, with insertion of a default onset: a nonminimal repair. The default voiced sibilant replaced a wide range of consonants (nasals, liquids, and stops, of different places of articulation):

chicken	/tʃɪkn̩/	[gæːz˒ɪ˄ˀ]
zipper	/zɪpɹ̩/	[ʔæzi]
running	/ɹʌnɪŋ/	[bʌʒɛˀ]
bunny rabbit	/bʌniɹæbət/	[bawazɪː]
merry	/mɛɹi/	[mæzi]

The typical nonminimal rankings apply (i.e., high ranking of **Survived/Linked Upwards** for other features of the target, and **Survived(Root)**, but low ranking of **LinkedUpwards(Root)** and **Not** constraints for the default consonant):

Uninterrupted(+ continuant)	**LinkedUpwards(C-Root)**
Uninterrupted(+ voiced)	**Not(C-Root)**
Survived(Root)	
Survived/LinkedUpwards(Features)	**Not(Coronal)**
	Not(-sonorant)
	Distinct(+ continuant)
	Distinct(+ voiced)
	SinglyLinked(+ continuant)
	SinglyLinked(+ voiced)

Another example of default sibilant insertion is Eric's (Bernhardt, p.u.d.) use of the [+distributed] ([ð] or [θ]) defaults which usually respected the voicing status of the target.

mommy	/mʌmi/	[mʌði]
mockingbird	/mɑkɪŋbɹd/	[mɑðibou]
open	/(ʔ)oupn̩/	[ʔouˈθən]
yellow	/jɛlou/	[wɛðu]~[wɛlʊ]

We return to this discussion in §7.4.4.3 when we discuss constraints on noncontiguous vowel sequences and their effects on intervening consonants.

We noted in the section on place interactions that features can spread from consonants to vowels or vice versa to resolve other constraints. The feature [+nasal] is a manner feature which can be realized on both vowels and consonants.

When it cannot appear in a consonant slot, it can flop onto a neighboring vowel slot (Lorentz, 1976; Ringo, 1985; Stemberger, p.u.d.; see §6.1.6.4).

smoke	/smoũk/	[fõũk]
snow	/snoʊ/	[sõũ]

Freitas (1996) reports for Portuguese that [+nasal] may also flop from vowels to consonants. If nasalized vowels are impossible (high-ranked **NotCo-occurring (V-Root, +nasal)**), [+nasal] can be realized on a neighboring stop:

/ãda/   [ana]

These flops of [+nasal] are not due to sequence constraints, but rather are responses to constraints on the complexity of segments or onsets. We include them here to demonstrate one type of repair that involves sequences of consonants and vowels.

7.3.4.5. CV and VC Glide-Vowel Sequence Constraints

Oral glides have the same features as their vowel cognates (/w/-/u/, /j/-/i/), and thus **NotTwice** constraints can be relevant. For glottals, interaction with features is less straightforward. Glottals have no oral place features. We present examples of an interaction with glides here, involving height, place, and tenseness.

Li (1992) reported that Ho-jong, a Korean-learning child, did not allow glides before vowels of the same backness and rounding. Ho-jong showed Gliding for /l/, with subsequent deletion before any front vowel:

	/milə/	[mijə]	'push'
	/kalu/	[kaju]	'powder'
BUT:	/kæguli/	[kæguiː]	'frog'
	/kɨ læ/	[kɨæː]	'yes'

A similar phenomenon occurred when a labial glide was expected before a rounded vowel. This reflected high ranking of **NotTwice(-consonantal,Coronal)** and **NotTwice(-consonantal,Labial)**, leading to the deletion of the glide. (The vowel always became long, via compensatory lengthening. This suggests that the onset consonant had a timing unit (C or X) that linked to the vowel after deletion; the data are difficult to account for within moraic theory.) Adult Korean shows similar prohibitions, and so it is possible that the constraint was learned on the basis of adult input. However, adult Korean has no alternations showing the effects of this constraint; it must be inferred from the lack of words that violate it. Further, adult Korean allows sequences such as [je] and [jæ], which were prohibited in Ho-jong's speech.

Terry, a child with a phonological disorder and some oral-motor coordination difficulties (Bernhardt, 1994b, p.u.d.), produced nasals, voiced stops, unaspirated [p], and glides in word-initial onsets (but had limited use of codas and intervocalic onsets). He primarily used [w] (or sometimes [β]) for word-initial fricatives, voiceless stops, and *all* liquids. However, before high tense vowels, a (lightly articulated) palatal fricative [ç] (or occasionally, a velar fricative [x]) appeared. (The velar appeared before [u] only, showing a place interaction.) The fricative was barely audible (almost an [h] in many instances).

	tickle	/tɪkl̩/	[wɪʔoʊ]
	toe	/toʊ/	[woʊ]
	coffee	/kɑfi/	[wɑʔi]
	five	/faɪv/	[wʌɪ]
	sis	/sɪs/	[wɪʔ]
	read	/ɹiːd/	[wi]
	leaf	/liːf/	[wi]
BUT:	teeth	/tiːθ/	[çi]
	tooth	/tuːθ/	[çu]
	key	/kiː/	[çi]
	zoo	/zuː/	[çu]
	shoe	/ʃuː/	[xu]

We first address the non-English voiceless fricative substitutions (arguably simpler!). First, in terms of manner and laryngeal features, [+s.g.] (for the aspirated stop) and [+continuant] (for the fricatives) survived, although [+s.g.] was inserted as a default for target voiced fricatives. High-ranked constraints were **Survived(+s.g.)** and **Survived(+continuant)** promoting the fricative substitution, but **NotCo-occurring(+s.g.,-continuant)** and other **NotCo-occurring** constraints prohibited fricatives with the correct place of articulation. **Not(+voiced)** was ranked higher than **Not(-voiced)**; [-voiced] was the default.

Because a place of articulation had to be present (high ranking of **Linked Downwards(Root)**), but co-occurrence constraints prohibited realization of C-Place, the V-Place of the following vowel spread to the consonant (low ranking of **SinglyLinked(V-Place)**). The high vowel [i] has both coronal and dorsal features; the fricative equivalent is palatal [ç]. The high vowel [u] has [V-Dorsal] and [V-Labial]; the fricative equivalent is a (rounded) [x]. (The presence of [ç] before [u] in some words suggests that underlying [C-Coronal] could survive on occasion. [C-Coronal] was underlying because the child was unable to produce consonant articulator features. Lexical storage is one strategy for getting features into the output, because faithfulness can be used for that purpose.)

Note, however, that the lax vowels [ɪ] and [ʊ] did not trigger this repair. Fricatives are [+tense] consonants if voiceless. Thus, a lax vowel would only trigger a voiced fricative. Voiced fricatives were prohibited by high-ranked **NotCo-occurring(-sonorant,+continuant,+voiced)**. The relevance of [tense] for this constraint suggests that [tense] was dominated by V-Place in his geometry. Most phonologists have been silent about where [tense] goes in the feature geometry, and these data constitute evidence relevant to the issue.

How is it that [w] could arise in other contexts?[11] (We assume that [w] for /l/ and /ɹ/ arises as it usually does, and is irrelevant here. See §5.5.1.5.2 and §5.5.3.6.) Dorsal fricatives such as [ç] and [x] are [+high]. Spreading V-Place from a non-

---

[11] We unfortunately have no examples with /wi/ or /wu/.

high vowel would have led to a uvular or pharyngeal consonant. If we assume that the child had the same **NotCo-occurring** constraints against uvulars and pharyngeals that are found in adult English, these could have blocked the spread of V-Place to the consonant. Since place features had to be present, they were inserted. The feature [Labial] was a default in his system. If V-Place could not spread to give place features in the onset, then [V-Labial] was inserted, with [w] (or, since it was attached to C-Root, lightly fricated [β]) resulting.

Terry's system is unusual and complex. It shows a variety of independent consonant constraints, and CV interactions, with height, tenseness, and place relevant to the output.

7.3.4.6. CV Sequences: Final Comments

Although we gave several examples in this section of CV interactions, they are not common, as we have stated throughout. Some of the issues that arise are provocative:

1. A feature system is needed that makes CV interactions infrequent but possible. We have shown some of the problems with feature designations for vowels in particular.

2. Most of the interactions in child phonology are from vowels to consonants. Vowels develop earlier. Perhaps for some children survival is so low for some consonant features that it is more optimal to spread vowel features. However, not all interactions are from vowels to consonants. Thus, mutual interactions must be allowable in any theory of features for the two types of segments (contra Ní Chiosáin & Padgett, 1993).

Levelt (1994) interprets CV place interactions as word-based place assignment. Such an analysis runs into several problems (e.g., why place and not manner, why different types of feature systems over time [discontinuities], etc.) (See §2.2.1.)

3. Plateauing of vowel features in intervocalic position seems to occur in child phonology, with some of the same features ([+voiced], [+continuant], and [+sonorant]) for which it is observed in adult phonologies and in diachronic sound change.

We have considered a variety of contiguous sequences in this section of the chapter. We have focused most of our attention on word-initial consonant clusters, since we have the most data on those elements, and because sequence constraints and repairs are richest for that type of sequence. Many of the phenomena discussed here also appear in the next major section of this chapter, on noncontiguous sequences.

7.4. NONCONTIGUOUS SEQUENCES

Noncontiguous sequences can be subject to the same constraints and repairs as contiguous sequences, but with a different level of adjacency than strict contiguity. Common repairs for noncontiguous sequences are deletion (with concomitant insertion of defaults), harmony (including both assimilation and reduplication), and flop.[12]

Information on noncontiguous sequences is relatively limited. A few authors have reported that some children produce words with more than one place of articulation in a front to back order (e.g., labials before coronals before velars) (Ingram, 1974; Levelt, 1996; Velleman, 1996). Other researchers have observed some similar and some different patterns. In Stoel-Gammon's (1993) study of 55 children, Dorsal-Coronal and Coronal-Dorsal consonant sequences appeared to be equally probable in CVCV words. However, words containing labials tended to show labial reduplication, suggesting more constraints on sequences containing labials. Menn (1975) observed that some children's words have back to front orders in terms of place of articulation. This section brings additional individual data to the discussion, first for consonants and then for vowels, but we emphasize that more large-sample studies are needed.

7.4.1. DELETION TO REPAIR SEQUENCE CONSTRAINTS

Both minimal and nonminimal deletions may resolve noncontiguous violations of sequence constraints. We first examine data which might involve nonminimal repairs, which are uncommon. We then turn to the more common minimal repairs (deletion with concomitant insertion of defaults).

7.4.1.1. Nonminimal Deletion: Root Nodes

For monosyllabic words, we have found no clear-cut examples in which segment deletion is a response to sequence constraints, but they may exist. For example, a child might generally produce codas, but show deletion of /p/ in a coda when /k/ is in the onset. Multisyllabic words commonly show reductions because of complexity constraints, but in addition, particular sequences may be especially problematic. Jeremy (Bernhardt, 1990: S3; §8.4) showed some possible examples of such additional constraints, and we exemplify nonminimal repairs with his data.

At age 3;4, 60/115 bisyllabic target words in an assessment sample were reduced to monosyllables. The prevalence of syllable deletion suggests a general constraint on foot construction.

banana	/bənænə]	[nɑ̃ˀ]	(E)
lady	/leɪdi/	[wɪⁱ]	(E)
gummy	/gʌmi/	[bʌɪm]	(E)

---

[12] We have only found one example of epenthesis to break up a noncontiguous sequence. Roland, age 2;0, created a word-initial /l/-cluster ([bl] or [ml]) to allow production of onset labials in words with Labial-Coronal noncontiguous sequences. For example, *buzz* was [blʌs] or [ʌs] and *man* was [mlæn] (Bernhardt, p.u.d.). Initial labial consonants deleted when [l] was not inserted. At the point that labials became frequent in onset, [l] dropped out except in *vitamins* ([mlɛmlɛ]). This is an unusual pattern for which we have as yet no coherent explanation. Why was a *noncontiguous* [Labial... Coronal] sequence prohibited, but a *contiguous* [Labial...Coronal] sequence ([ml]) allowed? (Note: *ball* was [bɑ].)

For words in which two syllables surfaced, medial consonants generally appeared if (a) there was no initial consonant in the target, or (b) the initial consonant was a (placeless) glottal and the medial consonant was a labial, or (c) the medial and initial consonants were identical (see §7.4.2):

	apple	/æpl̩/	[æpʊ]	(S)	No onset consonant
	happy	/hæpi/	[ʔæpi]	(S)	Placeless onset consonant
	mommy	/mʌmi/	[mʌ̃mi]	(S)	Identical consonants
	daddy	/dædi/	[dædi]	(S)	Identical consonants
	TV	/tiːviː/	[tʰitʰi]	(S,E)	Total consonant harmony
	night-night	/nʌɪtnʌɪt/	[næ̃ni]	(S)	Identical consonants
BUT:	combing	/koʊm+ɪŋ/	[kʰomĩn]	(E)	Dorsal-Labial; Stop-Nasal
			[bowĩŋ]	(E)	Labial-Labial; Gliding

Some of those same medial consonants deleted some of the time (e.g., [n], [m], [v]). In these cases, the second vowel was usually incorporated into the first syllable as a glide. Medial nasals were more frequently deleted than other consonants, but this may have been an artifact of word-sampling frequency. (The words *funny* and *mommy* were very frequent.)

funny	/fʌni/	[fʌi]	(S)	(6/7 tokens)
mommy	/mʌmi/	[mʌɪ]	(S)	(1/6 tokens)
water	/wɑɹ̩/	[wɑɹ̩]	(S)	(1/2 tokens; [was])
running	/ɹʌnɪŋ/	[wʌĩn]	(E)	(1/1 token)
glovey	/glʌvi/	[gʌɪ]	(E)	(1/1 token)

When examples with medial consonants versus without are compared, the effect of sequence constraints on place features becomes apparent. The only two words containing sequences with two place features were *combing* (once) and *gummy*, both containing Dorsal-Labial sequences. It would appear that **Survived** was high-ranked for the two nondefault features, [Labial] and [Dorsal] (as is common). However, both *combing* and *gummy* were produced in imitation and were not typical of his productions (Horsley, 1995). Furthermore, [Dorsal] deleted in one token of *combing*, and [Labial] was doubly linked. The prevalence of reduction suggests a general constraint on place features: **NotTwice(C-Place)**. High ranking of **Priority(Left)** (or of **Survived** in the strong prosodic domain of word-initial position) forced deletion of features in the less prominent medial position (an effect of primacy or of the weaker prosodic domain of medial position). The medial consonant was at a disadvantage even when the second syllable was stressed and contained a segment used in other word position (e.g., [v], as in *TV*). (We include the rankings of **SinglyLinked** here to allow comparison with rankings for Jeremy's harmony repairs in §7.4.2.)

Segment deletion was also found elsewhere in Jeremy's system; this is not unexpected, given that a single constraint ranking is used for all words and repairs. Segment deletion occurred in response to complexity constraints, which were ranked higher than **LinkedUpwards(Root)**. As we noted, **Survived(Artic)** was high-ranked in words like *gummy*. This same high ranking for features applies in the nonminimal repair.

		RESULTS
Survived(Root)	LinkedUpwards(Root)	**Floating segment**
LinkedDownwards(TimingUnit)	Survived(TimingUnit)	**Timing Unit can delete; links if present.**
NotTwice(C-Place)		
Survived/LinkedUpwards(ArticA)		**Features must**
Survived/LinkedUpwards(ArticB)		**survive, and so**
Survived/LinkedUpwards(C-Place)		**segment deletes.**
SinglyLinked(C-Place)		**No reduplication**
SinglyLinked(Root)		**No reduplication**
Priority(Left)		**Left C survives.**

The constraints on place features required that all articulator and place nodes survive and link upwards with no double linking allowed, but also ruled out a sequence of two C-Place nodes. The Root node of the medial consonant was floating, and its timing unit deleted.

7.4.1.2. Nonminimal Deletion: C-Place

Nonminimal deletion may affect just C-Place rather than the whole segment, though this also appears to be infrequent. Applegate (1961) provided an example. When the initial consonant was identical to a later consonant, the later consonant was replaced with a glottal stop.[13]

daddy	/dædi/	[dæʔiy]
Bobby	/bɑbi/	[bɑʔiy]
toot	/tuːt/	[tuwʔ]

The constraint ranking differs from that in §7.4.1.1 in that **LinkedUpwards(C-Place)** is lowest-ranked. Consequently, C-Place of C_Z floats.

NotTwice(C-Place)	
Survived(C-Place)	LinkedUpwards(C-Place)
SinglyLinked(C-Place)	Survived(TimingUnit)
Survived/LinkedUpwards(Root)	
SinglyLinked(Root)	
Priority(Left)	
Survived/LinkedUpwards(ArticA)	
Survived/LinkedUpwards(ArticB)	Not[-continuant]
	Not[+c.g.]
LinkedDownwards(TimingUnit)	

[13] We preserve Applegate's transcription, which was standard at the time it was written. We suspect that we would transcribe the child's words [dæːʔi], [bɑʔi], and [tʰuːʔ].

7.4.1.3. Minimal Deletion Repairs and Default Insertion

If C-Place and higher level structure must survive, but there is a constraint on sequences of articulator features, a default articulator feature may be inserted. This subsection contains two examples of sequence constraints involving [Labial]. In the first case, labials were prohibited after other consonants, and in the second, labials were prohibited before other consonants.

7.4.1.3.1. Pattern 1: Labial Prohibited on the Right

In the introduction to §7.4, we noted some previous reports in the literature that proposed a constraint against [Labial] "on the right." Morgan had such a pattern which clearly indicated sequence constraints (Stemberger, 1992a). Labials appeared on the right only if the first consonant was a placeless glottal or another bilabial. (Only oral stops appeared after glottals. The nasal [m] surfaced in a coda only when [m] also appeared in the onset.) Otherwise, in monosyllables, a coronal substituted for the labial in codas.

	up	/ʌp/	[ʔapʰ]
	hop	/hɑp/	[hapʰ]
	bump	/bʌmp/	[bapʰ]
	mom	/mɑm/	[mam]
BUT:	dump	/dʌmp/	[datʰ]
	lip	/lɪp/	[lɪtʰ]
	flip	/flɪp/	[fɪtʰ]
	arm	/ɑɹm/	[ʔan]

Patterns for intervocalic consonants were similar, but with a different default articulator node ([Dorsal]). Medial [p] surfaced when there was a glottal onset; or when there was a word-initial /p/ and the final vowel was not [ɤ]. When the initial consonant was /p/ and the intervening vowel was long, the medial /p/ varied between correct [p] and incorrect [k]. When the initial consonant was a coronal, [k] surfaced for medial /p/.

papa	/pɑpa/	[pʰapa]
apple	/ʔæpl̩/	[ʔapɤ]
people	/piːpl̩/	[pʰiːpɤ]~[pʰiːkɤ]
paper	/peɪpɹ̩/	[pʰeːpɤ]~[pʰeːkɤ]
slipper	/slɪpɹ̩/	[siːkɤ]
nipple	/nɪpl̩/	[nɪkɤ]

Labials could occur after initial glottals or bilabials. This shows that no independent constraint limited labials to word-initial position; thus, **Aligned(Labial, L,PrWd,L)** was not implicated. Table 7.12 shows constraint rankings reflecting **Distinct** and **NoSequence** constraints as follows (and ignoring the deletion of /l/, which was unrelated):

1. All segments had to survive and link upwards (unless other high-ranked structural constraints prevented them). Only the place feature changed, from [Labial] to [Coronal] or [Dorsal], depending on word position (a minimal repair).

TABLE 7.12   Constraint Ranking for **NoSeque/nce(C-Artic . . . Labial)**

/flɪp/	fɪp	fɪʔ	fɪ	fɪt
Survived/LinkedUpwards(Root)			*!	
Survived/LinkedUpwards(C-Place)		*!	*	
NoSequence(Artic...Labial)	*!			
Survived/LinkedUpwards(Labial)		*	*	*
SinglyLinked(Labial)	*			
Not(Coronal)				*

2. Low ranking of **Distinct(Labial)** promoted bilabials in second position when they also occurred word initially. **Distinct** requires that elements that are distinct in the input must be distinct in the output. Because **Distinct** was low-ranked, two tokens of [Labial] in the input fused into a single token of [Labial] in the output (multiple correspondence). **SinglyLinked(Labial)** was also low-ranked, allowing double linking of [Labial]. Thus, both tokens of [Labial] in the input survived in the output (albeit as a single nondistinct token). (This double-linking was only variable for medial /p/ in some words. Perhaps the medial /p/ assimilated [Dorsal] from the following [ɤ]. This competing assimilation was sometimes preferable to having a doubly linked [Labial] node. There was no competing assimilation possible in word-final position, and consequently, final labials were always doubly linked to a preceding labial. This is not shown in the constraint table.)

Another limitation concerned the redundant feature [+labiodental]. When /f/ was in onset, a default [t] was inserted in coda. The **NotTwice_{Dependents}(Labial)** constraint allowed two identical tokens of [Labial] to fuse. When the two tokens of [Labial] had different dependents, however, fusion was not possible; insertion of default [Coronal] occurred, as in other environments.

3. Ranked below the identity constraint was the more general **NoSequence (C-Artic . . . Labial)** constraint, which ruled out labials after consonants with articulator features (including labiodentals), and allowed them after placeless consonants.

4. Also ranked below the identity constraint was **NotCo-occurring(Labial, +nasal)** which ruled out labial nasals in codas unless the Root node was doubly linked to onset position. **Survived(Labial)** was ranked lower than **NotCo-occurring** in codas (a weak prosodic position with low-ranked faithfulness constraints) but higher than **NotCo-occurring** in word-initial onsets (a strong prosodic domain with high-ranked faithfulness constraints). Via double linking between onset

and coda, the final consonant could be a labial nasal because faithfulness was ranked high enough in the onset to allow a labial nasal.

5. Lowest-ranked constraints were **Not(Coronal)** (allowing the insertion of default [Coronal] in final position) and **Survived/LinkedUpwards(Labial)** (allowing deletion of [Labial]).

7.4.1.3.2. Pattern 2: Labial Prohibited on the Left

In a counterexample to "fronting" (see also Menn, 1975), Stoel-Gammon and Dunn (1985) describe a child, DE, who showed a prohibition of voiceless labials on the left. His data are complex, with limitations on initial voiceless labials reflecting more than one type of constraint. We present here those aspects of the analysis most relevant to the discussion. (For a full analysis, see Bernhardt & Stoel-Gammon, 1997).

As the examples below show, labials with nondefault [+voiced] and [+nasal] features occurred in all word positions (with /v/ undergoing Stopping to [b] word-initially).

makeup	/meɪkʌp/	[metəp]
book	/bʊk/	[but]
vase	/veɪs/	[bes]
TV	/tiːviː/	[sivi]

In word onset, voiceless labials either failed to surface ([p]) or were infrequent ([f]), although they did occur elsewhere in the word.

	four	/fɔɹ/	[fɔə]
	finger	/fɪŋɡɹ/	[fĩndə]
	football	/fʊtbɑl/	[fʌtba]
	flower	/flaʊ(w)ɹ/	[flaʊə]
	paper	/peɪpɹ/	[fæfɹ]
BUT:	fork	/fɔɹk/	[sɔɪt]
	fish	/fɪʃ/	[sɪs]
	Fall Guy	/fɑlgaɪ/	[sʌdaɪ]
	open	/opn̩/	[otɛ̃n]
	page	/peɪdʒ/	[sets]

DE's primary difficulty regarding production of initial voiceless labials concerned aspiration rather than sequence constraints (although sequence constraints were also relevant, as we show below); **NotCo-occurring(-continuant, +s.g.)** was high-ranked. Only occasional aspirated stops were observed (as in *toothbrush*). The feature [+s.g.] was possible only in fricatives ([f], [s]), where it is redundant.

ten	/tɛn/	[zɛ̃n]
toothbrush	/tuːbɹʌʃ/	[tʰusɹəʃ]
cup	/kʌp/	[sʌp]
soap	/soʊp/	[sop]

Stops often became fricatives (/p/ > [f]; /k,t/ > [s]) in order to preserve underly-ing [+s.g.]. (See §5.5.4.2 for discussion of underlying [+s.g.] in word-initial as-pirated stops in English.)

In addition, there were constraints on sequences involving voiceless labials. Initial [Labial] was more frequent in words with other voiceless labials (double linking), no other consonants, or *after* coronals.

	four	/fɔɹ/	[foə]	No other consonants
	zipper	/zɪpɹ̩/	[zɪpə]	Coronal...Labial ✔
	paper	/peɪpɹ̩/	[fæfɹ̩]	Labial...Labial ✔
BUT:	fork	/fɔɹk/	[soɪt]	*Labial...Coronal
	open	/oʊpn̩/	[otẽn]	*Labial...Coronal
	page	/peɪdʒ/	[sets]	*Labial...Coronal

A constraint on Labial-Coronal sequences appears to have been present. How-ever, this constraint had an effect only on voiceless obstruents, especially on /p/. Segments that combined [Labial] and [+voiced] were never subject to this se-quence constraint, and [f] was sometimes possible (but most of the examples with [f] have another labial in the word, with double linking perhaps being facilitative).

At the beginning of this chapter we noted that sequence constraints generally target only one type of feature, usually place. In DE's case, the constraint appeared to involve both place and voicing features: **NoSequence(Labial,-voiced...Coro-nal)**. This type of description appears too specific and somewhat inelegant. In our version of OT, there is a possible alternative, since we link the ranking of **Sur-vived** constraints to activation levels. Dell (1986) argued that features within a segment reinforce each other's activation level through feedback. In this system, [Labial] and [+s.g.] were both weakly activated features. Activation for [Labial] increased when in combination with strongly activated features such as [+voiced]. On the other hand, a combination of weakly activated place and laryngeal features made production of [p] and even [f] difficult ([f] less so because of the high ac-tivation for [+continuant], which reinforced the activation level of [+s.g.]). **NoSequence(Labial...Coronal)** was ranked above **Survived(Labial)** in these marginal [+s.g.] segments, and so [Labial] did not survive. In stronger segments, **Survived(Labial)** was ranked higher; thus, the **NoSequence** constraint had no effect. This explanation of the interactions is more satisfying than the overly spe-cific constraint mentioned above.

7.4.2. HARMONY AS A RESPONSE
TO SEQUENCE CONSTRAINTS

In §5.5.5, we observed that consonant harmony may be a response to the status of features as defaults/nondefaults (underspecification). In this section, we focus on harmony in response to sequence constraints, giving specific examples, and discussing general trends. (See Stemberger & Bernhardt, 1997, for a description of a child who showed pervasive use of harmony resulting from both sequence constraints and underspecification, and Stoel-Gammon & Stemberger, 1994, for a general discussion of harmony.)

If two features cannot occur in a sequence, one way to avoid the sequence is to produce one of the segments twice (double linking). To illustrate this, we return to Jeremy's data (see §7.4.1.1). Medial consonants were often deleted, but not when they were identical to the initial consonant. Double linking was a repair strategy which allowed realization of two consonants, but only if they were identical.

mommy	/mʌmi/	[mami] (5/6 tokens)
daddy	/dædi/	[dædi]
Blueboy	/bluːbɔɪ/	[bubɔɪ]
night-night	/nʌɪtnʌɪt/	[nani]
TV	/tiːvi/	[tʰitʰi]
Fudgie	/fʌdʒi/	[fafa]

For those words in which there are two identical consonants in the underlying representation, the second consonant can be promoted via a low ranking of **Distinct(Root)**. When the two consonants are identical, they can correspond to a single consonant in the output, and both consonants can be said to survive. In order for timing units and underlying association lines to survive, the single token of the Root node must be doubly linked in the output. If **Distinct** is ranked high, the two identical consonants may not fuse into a single token. Ranking of **Distinct (Root)** and **SinglyLinked(Root)** below the relevant negative constraint (here **NotTwice(C-Place)**) allows fusion. See §7.4.1.1 for ranking of the other constraints involved.

This constraint ranking is fairly typical for harmony repairs. Some negative constraint (most often a **NoSequence** constraint, but sometimes a **NotTwice** constraint) is ranked high. A **SinglyLinked** constraint is low-ranked. A faithfulness constraint (generally a **Survived** constraint, but sometimes a **Distinct** constraint) is also low-ranked. We now explore the general trends observable with respect to harmony in child phonology. Harmony can be more or less frequent (across children) depending on the features involved and the direction of spreading.

7.4.2.1. Harmony and Feature Classes

In terms of features, place harmony is much more common than manner or voicing harmony (the latter being reported only by Matthei, 1989). Manner harmony most often involves [+nasal] or (less commonly) [+continuant], and may be combined with place harmony (Elsen, 1991; Stoel-Gammon & Stemberger, 1994; Stemberger & Bernhardt, 1997). Default features ([Coronal] and [-continuant,-sonorant]) are the most frequent targets of harmony, being replaced by nondefault features such as [Labial], [Dorsal], [+nasal], and [+continuant]. (See the analysis of Dylan's speech in §8.6.) Perhaps half of normal English-learning children show labial or dorsal harmony at early points in development (Stemberger & Stoel-Gammon, 1991). On the other hand, there is no clear trend across children for nondefault place features with respect to each other (i.e., as many children assimilate dorsals to labials as assimilate labials to dorsals).

Harmony may be more likely between consonants which share features. For example, place harmony can often be restricted to [-continuant] consonants (stops and nasals), with fricatives and glides being exempt. Stemberger (1992b) and Berg (1992) make this claim explicitly although no one has yet tested this claim systematically. In our system, some of these similarity effects (specifically some of those involving manner harmonies in which the target must be similar to the source) can be accounted for via feature co-occurrence constraints. Others (specifically those in which the source must be similar to the target) are more difficult to account for.

When the target must be similar to the source, only certain classes of sounds act as a target, while other classes do not. In some instances involving manner harmonies, it is possible to say that a feature may spread *unless* that would violate a co-occurrence constraint. Consider **NoSequence(-nasal... + nasal)**, which is active in adult English in the nasalization of vowels before nasal consonants. In child phonology, the sequence constraint may be ranked higher than **Not(-nasal)** and (even lower) **SinglyLinked(+ nasal)**, so that a nonnasal consonant may become a nasal when it precedes a nasal, even when separated by a vowel (e.g., *down* /daʊn/ [naʊn]). Given co-occurrence constraints on nasal consonants, the target segment must also become [+sonorant] and [-continuant]. These co-occurrence constraints can prevent the spread of [+nasal] to some targets. Consider the limitation of nasal harmony to stop targets:

NoSequence(-nasal... + nasal)	Not(-nasal)	SinglyLinked(+ nasal)
Co-occurring(+ nasal→-continuant)		Not(+ sonorant)
Co-occurring(+ nasal→ + sonorant)		
Survived(+ continuant)		

The high ranking of **Survived(+ continuant)** and co-occurrence constraints regarding [nasal] and [continuant] prevent a fricative, liquid, or glide from becoming [+nasal]. Only [-continuant] elements (i.e., oral stops) may become [+nasal], and even then only because **Not(+ sonorant)** is ranked low enough to allow that feature to be inserted after nasality spreads. If **Not(+ sonorant)** is ranked higher than **SinglyLinked**, then [+sonorant] cannot be inserted. In such a case, stops (and fricatives) may not undergo nasal harmony. If **Survived(+ continuant)** is also ranked low, then only sonorant consonants (liquids and glides) may undergo nasal harmony. Pater (in press) discusses a child (from Compton & Streeter, 1977) with this latter pattern (though he attributes the assimilation to constraints on features in onsets rather than to sequence constraints). With either pattern, only targets that share a certain feature with the source (either [-continuant] or [+sonorant]) may undergo nasal harmony. However, this similarity may be accidental. It is not that similarity promotes assimilation; if a nonsimilar feature is present in the input, feature co-occurrence constraints prevent [+nasal] feature from spreading onto a potential target segment. (This is parallel to place harmonies, where the use of privative features makes it less obvious. A coronal may assimilate to a labial, since both are nondorsal, but a dorsal does not assimilate to a labial.)

When similarity effects instead restrict the *source* segment, so that the same target undergoes assimilation near one potential source but not near another, it is clear that similarity underlies the restriction. Gwendolyn (3;1–3;4) (Stemberger, p.u.d.) showed some limited examples of manner and voicing interactions. Fricative harmony occurred between voiced segments only: /l/ (otherwise [j] in onsets) became [z] before [z] but not before [s].

Harmony:	lizard	/lɪzɹd/	[zɪzoʊd]
	Lizzie	/lɪzi/	[zɪzi]
	television	/tɛləvɪʒn/	[tʰɛzəvɪzən]
	lose	/luːz/	[zuːz]~[juːz]
No harmony:	Lucy	/luːsi/	[juːsi]
	listen	/lɪsn/	[jɪsən]
	molasses	/məlæsəz/	[jaːsəz]

Feature co-occurrence constraints are not relevant, since the same potential target (/l/) is subject to the same co-occurrence constraints in both environments. Manner harmony between fricatives and liquids/glides tended to be restricted to voiced fricatives, because they were more similar to the (redundantly) voiced liquids and glides. It is unclear how to account for such similarity effects within OT. Cole and Kisseberth (1994) posit parasitic alignment: the edges of two features must be aligned; if one feature spreads, so must the other. In this instance, perhaps **Distinct(+ voiced)** was low-ranked, so that /l/ and /z/ (both underlyingly [+voiced]) shared a single doubly linked token of [+voiced] in the output. If [sonorant] must be parasitically aligned with [voiced], then [-sonorant] must also be doubly linked to the /l/ and the /z/. Since we reject generalized alignment (because it makes too many incorrect predictions), this solution is not open to us. We return to this issue in §10.2.2.

7.4.2.2. Directionality of Harmony

Consonant harmony in child phonology is right-to-left (R-to-L) about two-thirds of the time (Vihman, 1978), and is exclusively R-to-L in the speech of some children. Thus, there is often velar harmony in *take* (/teɪk/ [kʰeɪk]) but not in *Kate* (/keɪt/ [kʰeɪt]). Direction of harmony appears to be sensitive to feature status (default/nondefault), general sequence constraints of the language, and stress patterns.

The order of nondefault and default place features is relevant in explaining the directionality of harmony. In contiguous English sequences, Coronal-Labial and Coronal-Dorsal sequences are generally not allowed: *[tp], *[tk] (see §7.2.3). In noncontiguous sequences, the same constraints can apply, if adjacency is defined on the C-plane: *[tʰap], *[tʰʌk]. Correct production of *pot* is possible, because the nondefault feature [Labial] precedes the default feature [Coronal]. In *top*, however, **NoSequence(Coronal...Labial)** prohibits production of *[tʰap]. Double linking of the nondefault feature [Labial] (R-to-L harmony) is one way to avoid a Coronal...Labial sequence.

The general sequence constraints of the language and the vulnerability of default consonants results in more R-to-L (anticipatory) or bidirectional harmony than perseveratory (L-to-R) harmony in monosyllabic words. Some children may have the opposite type of constraint, prohibiting a nondefault before a default: **NoSequence(Labial...Artic)**, in which case L-to-R harmony resolves the constraint violation for the same reasons (see DE, §7.4.1.3).

L-to-R spreading does occur in monosyllables, and seems to be more likely when two nondefault features (Dorsal and Labial) are involved. In *cup*, the final [Labial] element might be prohibited by a general **NoSequence(Artic...Labial)** constraint. If **Survived(Labial)** is ranked higher than **Survived(Dorsal)**, R-to-L harmony can occur: [pʰʌp]. However, if **Survived(Dorsal)** is ranked higher than **Survived(Labial)**, L-to-R harmony occurs: [kʰʌk]. The production of [kʰʌk] implies that insertion of default [Coronal] place is not an option when the Dorsal-Labial sequence is prohibited. Thus, *cut* [kʰʌt] should also be ill formed, with [kʰʌk] appearing also for *cut*. We predict generally that

> harmony between two nondefault place features implies the presence of harmony between one nondefault place feature and default place (whatever the child's default place might happen to be).

This prediction holds for both R-to-L harmony and L-to-R harmony. If the sequence constraint makes *cup* come out as [pʰʌp], then *top* should also come out as [pʰɑp], given that coronals are the default in the child's system. It should be noted that there has been no explicit study testing this prediction. Particular papers (such as Stemberger & Stoel-Gammon, 1991, and Berg, 1992) have noted this for particular children, but Dinnsen, Barlow, and Morrisette (in press) reported a child with the opposite pattern. Our system has some difficulty with the opposite pattern. We assume that [Coronal] is not underlying in /t/. If /k/ deletes [Dorsal], we must assume that the system would rather spread [Labial] than insert default [Coronal]. But if that is the case, then /t/ should also undergo Labial Harmony. One solution is to assume that /t/ is underlyingly specified for [Coronal], and that the presence of this feature prevents the spread of [Labial]; this entails that default features can be present in the underlying form (contra our approach). (See also §8.5.1.2.) There is also an activation-based solution. If [Dorsal] deletes, the activation level of the C-Place node is decreased, so that faithfulness constraints are low-ranked. If C-Place were to delete and then be replaced by the C-Place node of a labial, we would then expect that to occur also with word-initial glottal stops (so that /ʔʌp/ would be [pʌp]). However, **Distinct(C-Place)** is relevant in the distinction between labials and glottals. If low-ranked, the two C-Place nodes can merge into a single doubly linked token of C-Place, which dominates [Labial]. This cannot happen with glottal stop, since glottal stop has no C-Place to merge.

Stress patterns can also be a factor in directionality. L-to-R harmony is more likely in multisyllabic words with trochaic stress (Strong-Weak), and R-to-L harmony is more typical when the first syllable is weak. See §6.2.5.3.2 for discussion. Underlying features fail to survive in the weak prosodic domain of an initial un-stressed syllable (or even a final unstressed syllable), and nearby segments spread to replace them (as in these data from Jose at 1;7; Lleó, 1996):

trompeta   /trom'peta/   [bu'bɛta]   'trumpet'

7.4.2.3. Harmony and CV Interactions

In §7.3.4, we discussed feature interactions between contiguous consonants and vowels (assimilatory and dissimilatory). Noncontiguous consonant sequences can occasionally show interactions between each other *and* contiguous interven-ing vowels. Stoel-Gammon (1996) discusses a child who used coronals for dorsal consonants at the beginning of the word (in words like *key*, as [ti]). The child showed Velar Harmony only when the word contained certain vowels.

1. For words which ended in dorsal consonants, *and* had front vowels, there was no Velar Harmony (as in *stick, dig,* and *take*).
2. For words which had back vowels *and* dorsal codas, there *was* Dorsal Har-mony (as in *duck* and *dog*).

In consonant harmony, the intervening vowel is generally transparent, and does not take part in the harmony. For example, in *cup* /kʌp/ [pʌp], the intervening vowel does not become [Labial] (*[pop]), but also does not block the assimilation. In this instance, however, the intervening vowel can be opaque and block assimilation.

This appears to be harmony in which the intervening timing unit (that of the vowel) cannot be skipped. We have the following:

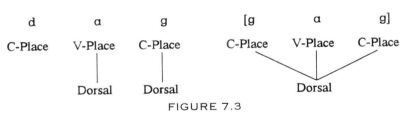

FIGURE 7.3

The two [Dorsal] nodes (of the final velar and the back vowel) merge, and the doubly linked Dorsal feature spreads to the (underspecified) onset consonant. For this child, velar consonant harmony occurred only if the intervening vowel took part in the assimilation; since dorsal consonants are [+back], only [+back] vow-els could participate in the spreading. This is an example of trans-planar spread-ing. The assimilation does not neutralize the back vowel, since underlying /ɑ/ surfaces as [ɑ].

There is a problem relative to this trans-planar spreading. Dorsal conso-nants are redundantly [+high]. This mismatch between the height of consonants ([+high]) and the height of the vowels ([-high]) plagues other studies also.

Archangeli and Pulleyblank (1994) provided an analysis of an Inuit language in which the [Dorsal] node of velar consonants spreads to an underspecified vowel, in which it is realized as [+low] [a]. Levelt (1994) assumed that [Dorsal] spreads from any back vowel ([+high], [+low], or [-high,-low]) to a consonant (which is [+high]).

One possible solution could involve splitting of the doubly linked Dorsal node into two parts. After this splitting (which might be called mitosis or cloning), the default feature [+high] can be filled in for the consonants. We are uncomfortable with this analysis, since it seems inimical to the basic insight of multilinear phonology, that assimilation is merely the realigning of the timing of one gesture relative to others. Cloning is a complication that goes beyond mere realignment.

There is another analysis which does not require the formalism of splitting. Trans-planar spreading involves the spreading of common features, but not all features become doubly linked. When the articulator feature spreads, the expression of that feature on the other plane will be with the terminal features relevant to that plane. Thus, the redundant feature [+high] for the velars is still inserted (due to high ranking for **Co-occurring(C-Dorsal→ +high)**):

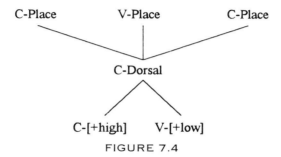

FIGURE 7.4

Dorsal is multiply linked, but its realization in terms of dependent features depends on the plane on which those features are found. Additionally, the V-[+low] of the /ɑ/ survives. The dependent C-features have phonetic priority for consonants. The dependent V-features have phonetic priority for vowels.

This is an unusual type of consonant harmony for child phonology. Consonant harmony ordinarily creates an interrupted gesture: the consonant feature begins in the first consonant, is interrupted by the vowel, then resumes in the second consonant; **Uninterrupted(Dorsal)** is ranked low. Here, **Uninterrupted** is ranked high:

NoSequence(Coronal...Dorsal)	Not(Coronal)	Distinct(Dorsal)
Uninterrupted(Dorsal)		SinglyLinked(Dorsal)
		C-Dorsal◄C-Place

Generally, **Uninterrupted** prevents consonant harmony when ranked higher than **NoSequence**, because the vowel does not participate in the assimilation. However, in this instance, the vowel can participate in the assimilation, because of the low ranking of the upwards structure constraint that requires C-Dorsal to link to C-Place. The [Dorsal] gesture is not interrupted by the vowel.

7.4.2.4. Harmony and Transparency

Most studies have reported harmony only between consonants that are adjacent on the consonant plane; ignoring the vowel, the two consonants are next to each other (such as the /d/ and /k/ in *duck*). We are aware of two studies that report assimilation between more distant consonants, with some consonants opaque and some transparent. Stemberger (1988a, 1993a) reported that Gwendolyn showed Labiodental Harmony, in which bilabial /m/ became labiodental [ɱ] near a labiodental (/f/ or /v/):

	small home	[fɱɑʊ hoʊɱ]
BUT:	small comb	[fɱɑʊ tʰoʊm]

The assimilation occurred if no segments separated the /m/ and the labiodental, or if a vowel, a glottal, or a glide intervened; it was blocked if any consonant with a C-Place node intervened. Li (1992) reported that Ho-jong showed Labial Harmony in which /l/ (normally realized as [j] via Gliding; see §7.3.4.5) became labial [w] before a labial consonant:

	/milə pwa/	[miwə pwa]	'push, please'	
	/iliwa/	[iwiwa]	'come here'	
BUT:	/ilicwə/	[iːcwə]	'give (it) to me'	*[iwicwə]
	/kalæcima/	[kaæːcima]	'don't let (him) go'	*[kawæcima]

An intervening vowel did not block the assimilation. However, an intervening consonant was opaque and blocked the assimilation. Again, any intervening segment with a C-Place node prevented assimilation. (If Labial Harmony would lead to [w] before a rounded vowel, **NotTwice(-consonantal,Labial)** would be violated; see §7.3.4.5. In that environment, the /l/ was simply deleted, stranding its timing unit, which linked to the vowel, causing it to become long: /milumjən/ [miuːmjən] 'if postponed'.)

Both Stemberger (1988a, 1993a) and Li (1993a) attribute the opacity of intervening true consonants to the constraint against crossing association lines. If, in these examples, C-Place spreads from one consonant to another, then the intervening vowel (lacking C-Place) does not cause a line-crossing violation. Nor do intervening glides (which have V-Place rather than C-Place) or glottals (which have no Place node at all). Only intervening true consonants have a C-Place node, and so only they cause a line-crossing violation and prevent the assimilation from occurring. One drawback to this analysis is that we must assume that it is the C-Place node that is spreading. If instead it is [C-Labial] that spreads, and the intervening consonant is nonlabial, then there is no line-crossing violation, and we cannot account for the opacity of the intervening consonant.

It is possible that these data reflect constraints on interrupted gestures. We have discussed only one possible definition of **Uninterrupted(Labial)**: if there is any interruption to the [Labial] gesture, the constraint is violated. If a vowel or consonant intervenes, **Uninterrupted** is violated and (if high-ranked) prevents assimilation. However, this cannot account for a situation in which vowels are transparent but a consonant is opaque. We suggest that there may be several variants of **Uninterrupted**:

Uninterrupted$_{\text{TimingUnit}}$(Labial):   [Labial] must be linked only to adjacent timing units.

Uninterrupted$_{\text{Root}}$(Labial):   [Labial] must be linked to adjacent Root nodes on the relevant plane, whether they occupy adjacent timing units or not.

Uninterrupted$_{\text{C-Place}}$(Labial):   [Labial] must be linked to adjacent C-Place nodes, whether they occur in adjacent Root nodes or not.

This establishes several grades of violation: any interrruption versus interruption with gestures of varying degrees of similarity. By definition, harmony involves low-ranking of **Uninterrupted$_{\text{TimingUnit}}$**. (As noted in §7. 4.2.3, however, "harmony" is also possible with high ranking of this constraint, as long as the intervening segment participates in the assimilation.) If the other constraints are also low-ranked, harmony occurs with greater and greater degrees of separation between the target and the source. It is unknown how common such distant harmonies are in child phonology.

7.4.3. FLOP IN RESPONSE TO NOSEQUENCE CONSTRAINTS

Flop is not common in child phonology, just as it is not common in adult phonology. There are few occurrences of this repair type. Furthermore, those few examples that are reported are difficult to analyze coherently, since little general information tends to be provided on the children's whole phonological system. Here we provide analyses of two types of flop repairs: one involving place, and one involving a combination of flop and other repairs. We note where data are insufficient to make claims.

7.4.3.1. "Fronting" in Child Phonology

Ingram (1974: Philip) gives examples of long-distance flop resulting from constraints on place sequences. (See also Velleman, 1996.) [Labial] is prohibited after [Coronal] or [Dorsal].

cup	/kʌp/	[pʌk]	Labial & Dorsal flop
coffee	/kɑfi/	[baki]	Labial & Dorsal flop
Gumby	/gʌmbi/	[baŋgi]	Labial & Dorsal flop
candle	/kændl̩/	[naŋu]	Dorsal flop; Coronal default

cream	/kɹiːm/	[miŋ]	Labial & Dorsal flop
			Nasal harmony
hammer	/hæmɹ̩/	[mænu]	Labial flop; Coronal default
			Nasal harmony
animal	/ænəml̩/	[mænu]	Labial flop: Coronal default

Several of the words show nontarget segments in the output form (e.g., [ŋ] in *Gumby*, [n] in *hammer*), demonstrating that features, not segments, were migrating. Features that flopped were [Dorsal] and/or [Labial]; in addition, [+nasal] spread. When a nondefault feature flopped into another segment, the original segment was left underspecified for that type of feature; this necessitated the insertion of default [Coronal] or [-continuant]. This is particularly evident for the medial [n] in *hammer*, where no feature [Coronal] was present in the target, but we assume the same operation for words like *candle* also.[14]

The outputs do appear to honor a front-back order. [Dorsal] could not occur before other articulator features. [Labial] could not occur after other articulator features. Expression of the constraints is not completely straightforward. We could posit two constraints: **NoSequence(Dorsal...Artic)** and **NoSequence(Artic...Labial)**. Yet [Labial] migrated to the left even when /h/ preceded it. The feature geometry we have adopted assumes that /h/ is placeless, and thus /h/ should be immune to the sequence constraint (as it was for Morgan's data discussed in §7.4.1.2). McCarthy (1991) assumes that /h/ does have place features: a Pharyngeal articulator node under Place. If this is the case, then **NoSequence (Artic...Labial)** would be violated when the first consonant is [h]. However, in that case, the features for /h/ should have been able to migrate to medial position, and they did not. Thus, a constraint such as **NoSequence(C...Labial)** may have been operative.

Velleman (1996) and Levelt (1996) suggest that alignment constraints may be involved in such cases. Presumably, the edges of articulators are aligned with the left or right edge of the word. A high ranking for **SinglyLinked** does not allow for harmony, and so flop occurs instead. More likely explanations concern other common child phonology constraints. The tendency for dorsals to be on the right reflects rime co-occurrence constraints promoting dorsals in the rime, **Co-occurring(Rime→Dorsal),** as discussed in §6.1.12.2.1. The tendency to flop the nondefault [Labial] feature in front of the default coronal feature probably relates to the tendency to put the nondefault (strong) feature in the strong (prominent) word position (i.e., the onset). It is true that in some of the examples, [Dorsal] is flopped to medial position, which has ambiguous status in terms of rime/onset. But [ŋ] is

---

[14] In this particular data set, there were additional constraints relating to [+nasal] and [+voiced]. In *cream, candle,* and *hammer,* there was nasal harmony (double linking of [+nasal]). However, [+nasal] was not doubly linked in *Gumby*. This possibly reflects specification issues, although we cannot determine that from the limited data. That is, [+nasal] could spread if the target had no [+voiced] feature, but not if it did. The presence of a nondefault [+voiced] feature prohibited the spread of a sonorant with a redundant [+voiced] feature (different relative strength of the nondefault and default?).

typically a coda consonant, in all parts of the word (*candle*); in *Gumby*, the [ŋ] is definitely a coda. In *coffee*, there is no coda consonant at the end of the word. The flop to the right is therefore limited in terms of how far it can go.

In any case, the data are very limited, making definitive statements about constraint rankings very difficult. However, the major constraint rankings are probably as follows:

1. The target place features had to survive (or be linked up, if default). Hence, **Survived/LinkedUpwards(Artic)** was high-ranked.

2. Features were allowed on the surface in a segment different from their lexical representation. **Survived(Link)** was low-ranked. **Not(Link)** was ranked low enough to allow features to link to a new location.

3. When the place feature [Labial] flopped onto an onset position in which /h/ was the target, no place feature could flop in turn onto medial position, since /h/ is placeless. Instead, [Coronal] was inserted in medial position, because of low-ranked **Not(Coronal)**.

Co-occurring(Rime→Dorsal)	
NoSequence(Dorsal...Artic)	
NoSequence(C...Labial)	**Not(Coronal)**
Survived/LinkedUpwards(Artic)	**Survived(Link)**
SinglyLinked(Artic)	**Not(Link)**

7.4.3.2. Flop and Other Repairs

Jeremy (Bernhardt & Gilbert, 1992) had a variety of repairs for sequence constraints and prosodic structure constraints, two of which we have already discussed in this chapter (deletion and harmony). Another repair involved default insertion of coda [s] *plus* flop (from coda to onset) in both monosyllabic and multisyllabic words. Generally, nondefault features were prohibited to the right of other features. This was usually true of place features, but also affected [+nasal] (see *Bandaid*).

milk	/mɪlk/	[ŋʌs]	Flop Dorsal; default [s]
jeep	/dʒiːp/	[bɪs]	Flop Labial; default [s]
truck	/tɹʌk/	[gʌs]	Flop Dorsal; default [s]
Bandaid	/bændeɪd/	[mɛ˞s] (E)	Flop [+nas]; default [s]; truncation
diving	/daɪvɪŋ/	[ᵇvɑ.'ɪs] (E)	Flop labial, [+cont]; default [s]
sleeping	/sliːpɪŋ/	[bɛ's˃] (E)	Flop labial; default [s]; truncation

Nondefault features of the coda flopped into the onset; a default [s] appeared in the coda. Both **NoSequence(Artic...NondefaultArtic)** and **Co-occurring (Rime→ +continuant)** were implicated for the [s] coda. High ranking of **Survived(Nondefault)** resulted in flop of the coda nondefault place feature. Nondefaults were not equivalent in strength: **Survived/LinkedUpwards(Dorsal)** outranked **Survived/LinkedUpwards(Labial)** as shown for the word *milk*, and **Survived(+nasal)** was also clearly high-ranked (so that the segment [ŋ] was permissible in onset, even though it is not permitted in English). Ignoring irrelevant effects on /l/ and /ɪ/, Table 7.13 shows how the child's output can be derived:

TABLE 7.13   Constraint Ranking for Flop Repair of **NoSequence** Constraint

/mɪlk/	mɪk	kɪm	mɪ	mɪs	ŋʌs
NoSequence(Artic...NondefaultArtic)	*!	*!			
Survived/LinkedUpwards(Root)			*!		
Survived/LinkedUpwards(Dorsal)			*	*!	
Survived/LinkedUpwards(+nasal)					
Cooccurring(Rime→+continuant)	*	*			
Survived/LinkedUpwards(Labial)					*
Survived(Link)		*	*		*

In most of the above cases, flop involved single features only. Simultaneous flop of multiple features also occurs. In Jeremy's sample, this was the case for the [+continuant] and [Labial] features of *diving* ([ᵇvɑ.ɪs]). Given one example, it is not possible to determine whether an entire segment migrates or whether several features migrate independently but simultaneously. In Jeremy's other examples, however, single nondefault features did migrate, with resultant insertion of default features to fill empty nodes (similar to Philip's data above).

Velleman (1996) gives examples of multiple flop, which in some cases even seem to show segment transposition.

sheep   /ʃiːp/   [pitʃ]   (Jaeger, in prep.: Alice)

In this case, [-anterior] and [+continuant] flop rightwards, and [Labial] flops leftwards. The palatoalveolar affricate in the output is not identical to the input fricative, and hence we can assume multiple feature migration, rather than segment transposition. Without knowing more about the child's system, we cannot posit a constraint ranking, but the familiar **NoSequence(Artic...Labial)** appears operative (forcing [Labial] flop), as does **Co-occurring(Rime→ + continuant)** (promoting [+continuant] flop).

Velleman suggests that the following is another example of possible segment metathesis.

monkey   /mʌŋki/   [kami]   (Berman, 1977: Shelli)

Even if medial /m/ resulted from flop of [Labial] onto a medial /n/, where has the initial nasal gone (i.e., why not [ŋ] instead of [k]?) And where is the medial consonant cluster? Looking more broadly, however, we could postulate a series of constraints that would cause the flop of individual (multiple) features: (a) **No**

Sequence(Labial...Dorsal), (b) a constraint against medial clusters, leaving one timing unit available, (c) a high-ranked faithfulness constraint for nondefault features such as [+nasal], leaving the [+nasal] feature present word medially, and unlike for Jeremy above, (d) a constraint prohibiting velar nasals in onset (as in adult English). In onset, [+nasal] delinked when co-occurring with [Dorsal], the higher-ranked constraint being **Survived/LinkedUpwards(Dorsal)**.

NoSequence(Labial...Dorsal)
Survived/LinkedUpwards(Dorsal)
Survived/LinkedUpwards(Labial)
NotTwice(C-Root)
NotCo-occurring(Dorsal, + nasal)$_{Onset}$

Survived/LinkedUpwards(+ nasal)

Survived/LinkedUpwards(C-Root)
Survived(Link)

The few examples available and the general lack of data about a given child's system make it difficult to determine categorically whether the Root nodes or individual features are transposing. But these examples suggest that multiple constraints on individual features and structure can result in multiple feature migration which has the *appearance* of segment metathesis.

7.4.3.3. Flop Resulting in Noncontiguous Sequences

Although our focus in this chapter is on sequence constraints, we noted in the introduction that sequence changes can help repair violations of other constraints. Long-distance flop is perhaps the most visible repair of this type. Contiguity can be violated to accommodate other constraints. We present here examples of flop from initial and medial clusters into codas. (See also §6.1.6.5 and §6.1.7.5.)

Colin (§8.3) showed migration of [+nasal] to coda position (whether or not there was a coda target) from initial /s/-nasal clusters (at age 5;6 and 5;10 sampling points).

snow	/snoʊ/	[don]
smooth	/smuð/	[ʃuen]

He generally did not produce clusters (high ranking of **NotComplex(Onset)**), with deletion of one consonant being the most common repair. However, the /s/-nasal clusters had a different solution. Apparently, **Survived(+ nasal)** was high-ranked. If there was another consonant in the coda, features of that consonant were sacrificed to allow survival of [+nasal]. If there was no coda, one was created (Node Generation). Deletion of the fricative could have accommodated the faithfulness constraint for [+nasal], ([n] was a possible onset, although [m] was not), but there was in addition some constraint favoring retention of the obstruent (as either a fricative or a stop). Onsets favored low-sonority default features, while codas favored high-sonority nondefault features (see §6.1.12). (In earlier samples, fricatives appeared only in noninitial positions, giving credence to a rime co-occurrence analysis.) The feature [+nasal] migrated to the coda, where it was supported by **NotCo-occurring(Rime→+sonorant)**. Note that the obstruent and nasal surfaced in the same order as in the input, but now separated by a vowel.

Sean (Bernhardt, 1990: *S4*, at 4;0) showed examples of rightward migration of [+nasal] with associated medial cluster reduction. Other clusters were possible at this time, but nasal clusters were particularly problematic contiguous sequences.

blanket   /blæŋkət/   [bᵊlæːgẽˢn]

When the cluster was reduced, [+nasal] survived and linked to the word-final coda, replacing the default [-nasal] of the underlying /t/. Faithfulness for nondefault features was high-ranked, as was **NoSequence(+nasal...-nasal)**. Flop of [+nasal] allowed violations of these constraints to be avoided.

7.4.4. NONCONTIGUOUS VOWEL SEQUENCES

There are few data available on vowel sequence phenomena. Based on adult phonology, the most likely repair for impossible vowel sequences is vowel harmony. This is common in adult languages, but is of relatively low frequency in child phonology. We present a few examples in this section. Deletion, with or without default insertion, is a possible repair, but we have found only one example (in Ingram, 1974). Epenthesis of a vowel (to separate the two vowels) is also a possibility, but we have found no certain examples of it. There are two examples of flop repairs reported in the literature (Ingram, 1974; Vihman, 1976).

Sequence constraints on noncontiguous vowels can also have an effect on the intervening consonant: default consonant or glide insertion. The major part of this section focuses on such CV interactions.

7.4.4.1. Vowel Harmony

Ingram (1974) proposed that children not only can have a front-to-back order for consonants, but also for vowels. Fernande (a French-learning child) variably did not produce back (round) vowels followed by front (unrounded) vowels. Epenthesis of [ə] was suggested to be an alternative repair for the sequence.

	poupée	/pupe/	[pəpɛt]	'doll'
	buchette	/buʃɛt/	[pəkɛkə]	'log'
	bouteille	/butejə/	[bəbɛtʃ]	'bottle'
BUT:	soulier	/sulie/	[bɔbədɛtʃ~[bobɛθ]	'shoe'

Data are too limited to determine exactly which sequence constraints were operative for the vowels. However, substitution patterns suggest that the most likely candidate was perhaps **NoSequence(+high...-high)** rather than a back-front constraint. The substitution for /u/ was also a [+back] vowel ([ə]). Round-nonround sequences were possible, as *soulier* shows. But all of the examples show height harmony (two mid vowels appearing in the word. Schwa is also a mid vowel). The nondefault feature [+high] delinked, and the [-high] default feature was doubly linked, to repair the constraint. The [+round] feature would sometimes delete, perhaps because of constraints against [+round] (or [V-Labial]) in general (see §5.6.2.2.2), and sometimes would remain.

Fernande's example of height harmony is one type of vowel harmony. Vowel harmony can affect individual features or the whole vowel. In order for harmony to occur, there must be ill-formedness in either the focus or source segments. As noted in Chapter 5, consonants develop slowly and are subject to a variety of constraints. Vowels, in contrast, tend to develop much earlier. In many children, the vowel system is complete by 24 or 30 months, when perhaps only half or two-thirds of English consonants have been mastered. This difference in mastery implies that negative constraints on vowels are overcome far more easily than negative constraints on consonants. As a result, we correctly predict that vowels should be less prone to harmony than consonants.

For English, it may also be that vowels are less prone to harmony because sequences of vowels in adult English are more restricted than sequences of consonants. When separated by vowels, virtually all possible combinations of consonants occur. But sequences of vowels generally involve one stressed vowel and one unstressed vowel, and there are heavy constraints on unstressed vowels. The most common unstressed vowels are [i] and [ə] (French et al., 1930; Denes, 1963), with [oʊ], [u], and syllabic [ɹ] being far less common. No other unstressed vowels occur with any frequency. For example, *['bækæt] or *['biːjeɪt], etc. This severely reduces the sequences of vowels that a child is exposed to, and it is possible that the nonoccurring sequences are the ones that would be most prone to harmony (but we will never know). In French and Spanish, in contrast, there is greater variety in what types of vowels appear in unstressed syllables. It is possible that vowel harmony might be more common in French and Spanish, though there are no studies that have addressed that hypothesis.

For German, Elsen (1991) reports some examples of vowel harmony from Annalena in early samples:

| Baby | /bebi/ | [baba] |
| Helikopter | /hɛlikɔptɐ/ | [hɔlɔkɔktə] |

In the first case, total reduplication of the first syllable also involves an early default vowel [a]. In the second case, the secondarily stressed vowel /ɔ/ is the one which dominates. A sequence of [-back]...[+round] or [-back]...[+back] is thus avoided. A dominance of roundness and/or backness is evident. Without more knowledge of her vowel system, we cannot comment further on these.

In these examples, the intervening consonant is transparent to the assimilation, implying a low ranking for **Uninterrupted**_{TimingUnit}: the vowel gesture could be interrupted. Stemberger (1993a) reported that Larissa showed vowel harmony only when there was an intervening [h]:

	Larissa	/ləɹɪsə/	[wɪhɪ]
	music	/mjuːzək/	[mʊhʊ]
BUT:	biscuit	/bɪskət/	[bɪkə]

However, an intervening true consonant (limited to [k] at the time) blocked the assimilation. The opacity of the /k/ suggests that **Uninterrupted**$_{Place}$ was high-ranked. The V-Place gesture could be interrupted by a placeless segment, but not by a segment with a Place node (whether V-Place or C-Place). Alternatively, the V-Place gesture could not be interrupted. V-Place perhaps linked to intervening [h], and then to the following vowel. However, other constraints (such as **Not-Complex(Root)**, or **NotCo-occurring(V-Place, + consonantal)**) prevented V-Place from linking to a [k], and so it could not spread to the following vowel. Vowel harmony may show different transparency effects for different children.

7.4.4.2. Vowel Flop Repair

Flop of vowel features is possibly even rarer than flop of consonant features. Ingram (1974) gives the example of [binta] for *Snoopy* /snuːpi/ (Philip), suggesting that the [-back] feature flopped to the first syllable (as did [C-Labial]) to avoid an *[u . . . i] (back-front) sequence.

Vihman (1976) reports the following for Virve in Estonian:

isa	'father'	/isa/	[asi]
ema	'mother'	/ema/	[ami]~[ani]

NoSequence(-low... + low) was possibly operative; [+low] and [-low] (and therefore [+high]) exchanged places. (Virve was learning both Estonian and English. Consequently, the Estonian words may have been influenced by the dominant English pattern, in which [i] is a common final vowel.)

7.4.4.3. Vowel Constraints Resolved via Consonant Insertion

Some CV interactions reflect **Uninterrupted(+ voiced)** and **Uninterrupted (+continuant)** (see §7.3.4.2.2). In such cases, vowel features become doubly linked to the C timing unit through trans-planar spreading. In this section, we extend the discussion to cases in which **NotTwice** constraints on vowel features are implicated, resulting in voicing or sonorance dissimilations between consonants and vowels. A voiceless stop may be inserted on the C-Plane to interrupt the [+voiced] or [+sonorant] sequence on the V-Plane. We give examples from Priestly's son Christopher (Priestly, 1977) and from Larissa (Stemberger, 1993a). In §8.3, we discuss similar data from a child with a phonological disorder (Colin).

Both Larissa and Christopher showed a variety of patterns for intervocalic consonants reflecting CV and vowel sequence constraints. Neither child showed sequence constraint effects for monosyllables of the same nature, suggesting that the strongest constraints arose from the vowel sequence and/or the vowel-consonant-vowel sequence, rather than from sequence constraints on consonants.

At the time, Larissa's words were limited to a single left-prominent foot. Her word-initial and word-final consonants were as follows:

1. There were no systematic default segments.
2. There were word-initial voiced and voiceless stops and nasals.
3. Word-initial voiceless fricatives surfaced as [h].

4. Word-initial /l/ and /z/ surfaced as [ʔ].
5. There were word-final voiceless aspirated stops (adult voiceless stops), voiceless unaspirated stops (adult voiced stops), and nasals.

Word medially, consonants were far more restricted.

1. The voiceless stop /k/ matched the adult target:

    bucket   /bʌkət/   [bʌkə]

2. When the initial and medial consonants were identical (in the input or as the result of spreading), the medial consonant survived (see §7.4.2):

    Mommy   /mɑmi/   [mami]
    Gwendolyn   /gwɛndəln̩/   [nanːa]
    Papa   /pɑpə/   [pʰapa]

3. Otherwise, a default onset [h] appeared in intervocalic position, even when no consonants with oral place features preceded it:

    rabbit   /ɹæbət/   [wahə]
    money   /mʌni/   [mʌhi]
    apple   /æpl̩/   [ʔahu]

The question for this discussion is why /k/ and consonants identical to onset consonants were permitted medially, but others were not. For this, we need to consider a number of high-ranked constraints as in Table 7.14:

TABLE 7.14   Vowel Sequence Constraints and Word-Medial [h] Insertion

/mʌni/	mʌni	mʌmi	mʌi	mʌʔi	mʌhi
Survived/LinkedUp(TimingUnit) Survived/LinkedUp(Root)			*!		
SinglyLinked(C-Place)		*!			
Not(+continuant)	**!	**	**	**	*
Uninterrupted(+continuant)	*!	*		*!	
NotTwice(+voiced)	*	*	*		
Survived(C-Place)			*	*	*
Distinct(C-Root)		*			
Distinct(+continuant)					*
Not(+s.g.)					*

1. The effect of identity between the onset and medial consonant suggests low ranking of **Distinct(C-Root)** (allowing the two input consonants to merge into a single output consonant) and of **SinglyLinked(C-Root)** (allowing the single consonant to be doubly linked). This is similar to what we saw for Jeremy in §7.4.2. **Survived(Root)** and **Survived(TimingUnit)** were high-ranked: No segments could be deleted. Since this consonant was both initial and medial, it was not subject to other constraints on medial consonants.

2. The [+continuant] nature of the medial [h] suggests that the medial consonant was assimilating [+continuant] from the surrounding vowels. Plateauing is driven by **Not(+continuant)** being ranked above **Distinct(+continuant)**; this allows the two tokens of [+continuant] in the vowels to fuse into one doubly linked token. It was more optimal to have *one* token of [+continuant] than two (hence the double asterisks in Table 7.14). **Uninterrupted(+continuant)** prevents the doubly linked token of [+continuant] from being interrupted by a consonant that is not also linked to [+continuant]. This limits medial consonants to fricatives and liquids; but these were impossible in Larissa's system at the time. Medial stops and nasals were prohibited. However, [+continuant] [h] was allowed. When [+continuant] linked to the medial consonant, C-Place could not survive (because fricatives were not possible; low ranking of **Survived(C-Place)**). Since a placeless continuant phone is [-nasal], [-voiced], and [+s.g.], all other features of the medial segment were also deleted.

3. A medial [k] was allowed. **Co-occurring(Rime→Dorsal)** was high-ranked for this child, allowing [Dorsal] to survive in word-final and medial position (and also allowing C-Place to survive). Since no fricatives were possible in the child's system, the velar consonant had to remain a stop. This violated **Uninterrupted (+continuant)**; consequently, **Uninterrupted** must have been lower-ranked. Voiced *[g] was not possible, however, because nondefault [+voiced] could not be combined with nondefault [C-Dorsal] at that time. (Possibly also the medial consonant had to be [-voiced] to separate the two tokens of [+voiced] in the vowels, if **NotTwice(+voiced)** was high ranked.)

Christopher (Priestly, 1977) had similar patterns for intervocalic consonants, but with a [j] default. (In Bernhardt's studies of disordered phonologies, [?] and [j] are more common medial defaults than [h].) Christopher's words were limited to a single left-prominent foot. He had no default onset in word-initial position. A wide range of consonants were allowed in initial and final position. In medial position, consonants were far more restricted:

1. Voiceless stops matched the target. Voiceless stops are often the first segments allowed in codas (§6.1.12.1), due to high ranking of **Co-occurring(σ-Margin→<ConsonantDefaults>)** combined with low ranking of faithfulness in a weak prosodic domain. We suggest that they were the only singly linked type of segment allowed medially in Christopher's speech, except in special environments. The only nondefault features that were freely possible were place features

([Dorsal] and [Labial]), as is also often the case in codas. If any nondefault manner or voicing features were present, it was more optimal for a default onset to appear.

hippo	/hɪpoʊ/	[hɪpoʊ]
butter	/bʌtə/	[bata]

2. Medial consonants that were identical to the initial consonant were allowed (low ranking of **Distinct(C-Root)** and **SinglyLinked(C-Root)**):

Mommy	/mʌmi/	[mami]
Nana	/nana/	[nanə]

3. The default onset [j] appeared in intervocalic position for other target consonants (discussed in detail below).

rabbit	/ɹæbət/	[ɹajat]
dragon	/dɹægən/	[dajan]
bison	/baɪsən/	[bajas]

4. When the vowel of the second syllable was /i/, the default onset did not surface, due to **NotTwice_{Dependents}(V-Root)**. The glide [j] and the vowel [i] have identical segmental representations, being distinguished solely by syllabic factors that are predictable from either the timing units (C versus V) or position in the syllable (nonhead versus head). The constraint against *[ji] made the child's default insertion repair strategy impossible, and segments that were usually ruled out by the sequence constraints were allowed to surface. (See Stemberger, 1993a, for greater details of this analysis. See §6.2.5.3.1 for discussion of this constraint in Amahl's speech.)

*[ji]:	money	/mʌni/	[mʌni]	(*[mʌji])

5. Additionally, the intervocalic consonant (or its features) flopped to coda, when no other [+consonantal] coda was present. **Survived(Feature)** for the intervocalic segment was ranked higher than **NotCoda**. However, since this violated **Contiguity**, it generally did not occur if a word-final coda consonant was already present. (Devoicing of /g/ to [k] in *tiger* was due to an independent constraint on final voicing.)

panda	/pændə/	[pʰajan]
tiger	/taɪgə/	[tʰajak]
pillow	/pɪloʊ/	[pʰijal]

Christopher's data are similar to Larissa's, but the differences suggest that the constraints involved were not identical.

1. **NotCo-occurring** and **Co-occurring** constraints prohibited most consonants from linking up, but σ►**Onset** was ranked high enough that an onset was required. **Not(Root)** was ranked low enough that an onset was inserted.

2. A glide presumably resulted from spreading of vowel features (plateauing, with [+sonorant] and [+continuant] being especially likely candidates); this results from low ranking of **Distinct** and **Uninterrupted**, as in Larissa's case.

3. Unlike in Larissa's case, the default place may have been V-Place (rather than C-Place); a glide resulted, with default (front vowel) features. The medial consonants were not deleted, but were rather floating, and so could link up to coda position, where a wider range of feature combinations was allowed; apparently, coda position was a stronger prosodic domain than medial position, for this child. However, **NotTwice(V-Root)** prevented the insertion of a default consonant when the following vowel was [i]. In that case, because an onset consonant was required, the underlying medial consonant linked up.

We do not know how common the above patterns are in children with normally developing speech.[15] For children with severe phonological disorders, it is not uncommon for glide or glottal stop substitutions to appear intervocalically (Bernhardt and Stemberger, in preparation). However, children with these patterns often have very simple word structure. Sometimes they do not even produce a medial consonant, CVCV words appearing as CVV words (see Jeremy's data in §7.4.2). Thus, at least some of the time their patterns probably reflect syllable structure and word complexity constraints rather than sequence constraints as described in this section.

7.4.5. REPAIRS ACROSS WORD BOUNDARIES

Throughout the chapter, we have focused on constraints and repairs within words. Between words, similar constraints and repairs are sometimes found.

Larissa (Stemberger, 1993a) showed such between-word relevance of **Not Twice(C-Place)**, which prohibits a sequence of two consonants with independent C-Place nodes. When two-word utterances began at 1;9, the most common repair was (nonminimal) deletion of the consonant that began the second word:

Watch, Papa.   /wɑtʃ pɑpə/   [wak apa]

After a week, a new (nonminimal) repair emerged, similar to what we have just discussed above: insertion of a default [h]. In this case, the [h] facilitated production of a C-Root, but without place features, suggesting that the major constraint in these contexts was **NotTwice(C-Place)**.

Gone moon.   /gɑn muːn/   [dan huːn]

---

[15] Matthei (1989) also reports on a subject with similar patterns: (a) use of identical consonants in medial position, (b) presence of medial voiceless stops, and (c) a range of medial consonants if there were no initial consonants. The first two patterns are reminiscent of the patterns for Christopher and Larissa, but the third suggests that constraints on consonant sequences were more relevant than constraints on vowel sequences.

A few weeks later, epenthesis of [ə] resolved the constraint by making the two consonants nonadjacent. Both consonants survived:

    Help me.   /hɛlp miː/   [hapə miː]

Assimilation repairs also can occur. Merging of identical adjacent elements can circumvent ill-formedness. Morgan showed replacement of [Labial] with [Coronal] in codas (§7.4.1.3), unless [Labial] could be doubly linked. When she began to use two-word utterances at 1;8, an optional assimilation occurred, in which [Labial] in a following word-initial stop spread left to yield a doubly linked [Labial] node.

    Jump, Papa.   /ʤʌmp pɑpə/   [dʌtʰpʰapa]~[dʌppʰapa]

Although [Labial] was not normally tolerated after a nonlabial consonant (high ranking of **NoSequence(Artic...Labial)**), merging of a coda [Labial] with the following word-initial [Labial] facilitated production of that feature. The feature in a prosodically weak position was strengthened by being merged with another token of the same feature in a prosodically strong position. Since the feature survived in the strong position, it survived in the weak position also. (This merger was made possible by low ranking for **Distinct(Labial)** and **SinglyLinked (Labial)**.) Elsen (1991) also gives a few such examples from Annalena's speech.

| kann man | /kan man/ | [kamːan] | 'can one' |
| Komm her | /kɔm hɛʀ/ | [kɔmːɛə] | 'come here' |

In the first case [Labial] is doubly linked, and default [Coronal] fails to be inserted for /n/. In the second case, the /h/ disappears, and the features of /m/ are doubly linked between words. Because /h/ has no place features, C-Place doubly links between the two Roots for /m/ and /h/, and a geminate [mː] results.

Between-word sequences can show patterns similar to those for single words. More data are needed in order to make a full comparison, however.

7.5. REVIEWING REPAIRS: VARIABILITY IN ONE CHILD'S SYSTEM

Throughout this chapter, we have used data from a variety of children in order to be able to illustrate as many of the constraints and repairs as possible. Charles's clusters showed a variety of repairs, and we present a brief discussion of those here as a summary of repair types for sequence constraints. We first give a general overview of his cluster production and repairs, then list relevant constraints, and finally show constraint rankings for the various repairs. (Dylan's data in §8.6 provide an overall review of constraints, including some sequence constraints.)

In his assessment sample, Charles produced 17 out of 47 possible clusters. Because he was capable of producing clusters, the major constraints appeared to be sequence-related, rather than due to **NotComplex(Onset)**. Clusters were avoided through a variety of repairs (deletion, assimilation [double linking], epenthesis, and flop) and those repairs varied, both over time and according to cluster type. At initial assessment (age 5;10), the predominant repairs were deletion (26/47 tokens) and assimilation (15/47). Obstruent-sonorant and /s/-stop clusters were subject to deletion, particularly /l/-clusters and /s/-clusters with (oral or nasal) stops as the second consonant (/sm/, /sp/, /sn/, /st/).

black	/blæk/	[bæk]
snowing	/snoʊɪŋ/	[nowɛ̃n]
star	/stɑɹ/	[θaə]

The pattern of deletion for /st/ differed from other /s/-[-continuant] clusters, in that the fricative rather than the oral or nasal stop was maintained; nondefault [+continuant] survived (§6.1.6.4.1).

Clusters with [w] as the second element (whether as a substitution or as a matching phone) often showed assimilation, resulting in a [fw] or [vw] cluster:

| brush | /bɹʌʃ/ | [vwʌθ] |
| dress | /dɹɛs/ | [vwʌθ] |

Doubly linked place of articulation was also seen in the few words with more faithful realization of the clusters:

| snake | /sneɪk/ | [θneɪk] |
| bread | /bɹɛd/ | [bwʌd] |

Over time, deletion and assimilation became much less common, and epenthesis increased in frequency for obstruent-approximant clusters (from 3/47 tokens at 5;10, to 15/53 at 6;0). The increasing use of epenthesis did not reflect increasing ability to produce initial weak syllables (which he was able to do before the data collection process began). However, the fact that he was capable of producing multisyllabic words with initial weak syllables allowed him to use epenthesis successfully for clusters.

| black | /blæk/ | [bʊlæk] |
| dress | /dɹɛs/ | [dʊwɛs] |

Flop was rare in clusters (see below).
The following sets of constraints were relevant, particularly at Point 1.

1. Sequence constraints prohibited two consonants in a cluster with different values for place features or for [continuant].

NoSequence(ArticA...ArticB)   (both usually high-ranked)
NoSequence(-continuant... + continuant)

2. Faithfulness constraints for nondefault place features were generally high-ranked: most of the time for [Labial], but less so for [Dorsal] at Point 1 (5;10).

Survived(Labial)   (always high-ranked)
Survived(Dorsal)   (variably ranked, but always lower than
                        Survived(Labial))

3. **SinglyLinked** was often low-ranked at Point 1. Assimilation occurred primarily in the pre-treatment sample (decreasing to 8/53 tokens at 6;0) (See §7.3.1.8.1).

SinglyLinked(Labial)   (both usually high-ranked, but not always)
SinglyLinked(+continuant)

4. **Survived(Link)** was usually high-ranked, preventing flop, but occasionally, flop did occur (1/47 tokens at 5;10; 3/53 at 6;0). A surviving feature usually had to appear in its original segment:

Survived(Link)   (usually high-ranked, but not always)

5. **Not(V-Root)** was high-ranked at first, but less so after **Survived(C-Root)** became higher-ranked. Vowel epenthesis in clusters was rare at first, and consonants were often deleted from clusters.

Not(V-Root)   (usually high-ranked)
Survived(C-Root)   (usually low-ranked)

The variable ranking of these constraints led to a number of different output patterns, summarized below.

7.5.1. PATTERN 1: CLUSTER REDUCTION: SEGMENT DELETION

As noted, all clusters were subject to deletion at Point 1. Often the stop was retained (as it frequently is in child speech), but in /tw/ and /st/, the default Coronal /t/ was often deleted:

| twenty | /twɛnti/ | [wɛnti] |
| star | /stɑɹ/ | [θaə] |

The nondefault features tended to survive (in this case, either [Labial], or [+continuant]). We present the ranking for /tw/ as [w] below. The Root survived for /w/, winning out over the default /t/.

NoSequence(ArticA . . . ArticB)	**Survived(C-Root)**
NoSequence(-continuant . . . + continuant)	
Not(V-Root)	
Survived/LinkedUpwards(Labial)	
SinglyLinked	
Survived(Link)	

This ranking prohibits the cluster *[tw], and resolves it by deleting one of the segments. The sequence constraints (on articulator features and [continuant]) prevented the cluster. **Not(V-Root)** prevented vowel epenthesis. The high ranking of **Survived(Link)** prevented fusion (and flop; see below): [Labial] could not be delinked, and relinked to the /t/, to yield *[p]. High ranking of **Survived(Labial)** and **Survived(Link)** caused the /w/ to survive in its original segment: [wɛnti].

The tendency for nondefault [Labial] to win out over default [Coronal] has been discussed elsewhere (§6.1.6.4.1, and §7.4.2).

7.5.2. PATTERN 2: CLUSTER PRODUCED WITH ASSIMILATION

Assimilation was also frequent at Point 1. **SinglyLinked** constraints were unstably ranked at that point. When they were ranked lowest of all, C-Root could survive because of assimilation. In order to resolve *both* sequence constraints, both [Labial] and [+continuant] spread from the /w/ to the initial consonant slot (see §7.3.1.8.1). Both default ([Coronal], [-continuant]) and nondefault ([Dorsal]) features were targets of assimilation.

| twenty | /twɛnti/ | [fwɛnti] | (2/4 tokens) |
| crayons | /kɹeɪ(j)ɑnz/ | [fweɪjɔ̃nð] | |

Constraint rankings for *twenty* are similar to those above for deletion, but with low rankings of **SinglyLinked** and **Survived(Link)** and high rankings of **Survived(C-Root),** allowing spreading of [Labial] and [+continuant]. For *crayon*, in addition, **Survived(Dorsal)** was ranked lower than **Survived(Labial)**; thus, /k/ surfaced as [f]. (For the sake of clarity, we ignore the feature co-occurrence constraints prohibiting *[ɹ].)

7.5.3. PATTERN 3: LONG-DISTANCE FLOP

Long-distance flop was an (infrequent) repair. It showed up twice for the word *crayon* (at 5;10 and 6;0):

| crayon | /kɹeɪ(j)ɑn/ | [kɛwɔ̃n] |

This resulted from a low ranking of **Survived(Link)** and **Survived(C-Root)**, and a high ranking for **SinglyLinked**, **Survived(Labial)**, and **Survived(Dorsal)**. The sequence constraints were resolved via the deletion of a consonant (rather than assimilation), but neither [Dorsal] nor [Labial] could delete. The low ranking of **Survived(Link)** allowed [Labial] to survive in a different location. [Labial] flopped from /w/ (which could then be deleted, allowing [Dorsal] and [k] to survive) to /j/ (replacing default [Coronal]).

7.5.4. PATTERN 4: EPENTHESIS (ADDITION)

Epenthesis became a more frequent repair over time.

| crayon | /kɹeɪ(j)ɑn/ | [kəweɪjɔ˞n] |

As in the flop repair, faithfulness for the place features was high-ranked. Both [Labial] and [Dorsal] survived in their original segments, respecting high ranking of the linking constraints. The sequence constraints were still high-ranked, but in this case, **Not(Root)** was ranked lowest, allowing interruption of the sequence. This change was not correlated with any change in words with initial unstressed syllables, which were correct before the study began. This change is a trade-off regression: increased faithfulness to the number of consonants is bought at the price of decreased faithfulness to the number of vowels. Our view of learning (§4.12) can handle such regressions. However, Tesar and Smolensky's (in press) approach to learning cannot handle trade-off regressions *unless* they occur for independent reasons (§4.12.2). Tesar and Smolensky could handle this regression only if it were a byproduct of the development of word-initial unstressed syllables. Since it was not, this regression constitutes evidence against their approach to learning.

7.5.5. PATTERN 5: CLUSTER (ALBEIT OFTEN WITH AN UNRELATED SEGMENTAL SUBSTITUTION!)

At 5;10, a few clusters were produced without assimilation, epenthesis, or flop. These included [bw] for /bɹ/, [gj], and [θn], all with shared place of articulation (double linking). At 6;0, there were a number of different clusters with matching places of articulation and values of [continuant] ([pw], [bw], [kw], [gw], [pj], [bj], [kj], [gj], [θn], [θm], θk]). Cluster production occurred when **Survived(Dorsal)**, **Survived(Labial)**, **Survived(Link)**, and **Not(V-Root)** were all ranked higher than the **NoSequence** constraints. The two articulator features had to survive, in their original segments. No vowel could be epenthesized between the two consonants. Interestingly, clusters with coronals were most resistant to change, showing longer persistence of deletion, assimilation, and epenthesis. No constraints forced the default feature [Coronal] in the output. The last two-element cluster to appear with two segments was /st/, showing strong effects of high-ranked **Not Twice(Coronal)** (preventing two coronals from surfacing), and high-ranked **SinglyLinked** and **Distinct** (preventing merger into one doubly linked token of [Coronal]).

For Charles, a few key constraints were unstable in relative ranking. Over time, these rankings and their resulting repairs progressed in the direction of feature and structure faithfulness for consonants. Articulatory timing of the cluster was the last parameter to be sacrificed, with varying lengths and types of epenthetic vowels allowing production of the two consonants (see Eveson, 1996). Over time, the epenthetic vowels reduced in length, until adult-like clusters were produced.

If we used solely a process/rule-based analysis, variability would be the unifying theme for Charles's analysis. However, the constraint-based analysis provides a different type of data unification. Although there were different repairs, they all were responses to the same underlying constraints on feature sequences. The differences derive from constraints on feature faithfulness and on double linking. The constraint-based analysis allows us to provide a deeper level of explanation for the variable surface patterns.

7.6. CONCLUDING REMARKS

This chapter has examined the effects of sequence constraints on output in child phonology, with the variety of repairs that appear in response: deletion or addition of features, elements, or links between constituents. We emphasize the following points:

1. Similar types of constraints and repairs affect contiguous and noncontiguous sequences, although frequency of repair types depends on constituent type, sequence constraint, and word position.

2. Sequence constraints operate at various levels of the phonological hierarchy, although place features are most often involved in the constraints.

3. Repairs may vary within and across children, at one point in time or across time.

4. Disambiguation of complexity constraints (e.g., **NotComplex(Onset)**) and sequence constraints is not always possible, but we have attempted to find the clearest examples possible.

5. The status of features as defaults or nondefaults is often relevant to the constraint and the repair.

6. Sequence constraints and repairs may also be sensitive to the prosodic prominence of elements. The concept of tier interaction is complex, because of its multidimensionality. However, it is a strength of the multilinear approach to phonological analysis that we have mechanisms to describe phonological phenomena which take interactive effects of features and word/syllable structure into account.

7. For several analyses, standard phonological analysis fell short of being able to account fully for the patterns.[16] Incorporating activation levels, as in our version of OT, often led to better explanatory power in those cases. We return to this discussion in §10.2.

8. Surface variability does exist, but may mask a more coherent and consistent set of underlying constraints.

Finally, as we have commented throughout the book, there is a great need for larger and more carefully collected and annotated data sets.

---

[16] In discussion of word-final clusters, we noted that Elsen's (1991) subject Annalena paused between cluster elements, apparently in order to facilitate production of both elements. We called that a type of addition repair. Jeremy also used pausing in production of the word *funny*. This word was usually pronounced as [fʌɪ]. One of the spontaneous productions of the word *funny* at assessment had two separate equal stress syllables with an intermediate pause, suggesting that a conscious and nonphonological strategy enabled him to produce all elements of the word.

    funny   /fʌni/   [fʌi]~[fʌn<PAUSE>ni]

These examples emphasize that faithfulness to underlying form can be manipulated consciously as well as unconsciously, and that not all explanations of surface phenomena are captured through purely phonological analyses.

8

THEORY AND APPLICATION: NOT JUST FOR THE CLINICIAN

This chapter examines data from children with protracted phonological development, partly to focus on clinical application, but also to tie together various threads from the preceding chapters as a review. The discussion and examples thus pertain to a general readership, and not just to those with a clinical interest.

Speech-language pathology has benefited from the advances in phonological theory in the past 25 years.[1] Phonological theories provide frameworks for identifying patterns in speech output. For children with disorders severe enough to warrant intervention, the analysis of such patterns provides a basis for an intervention program. The more coherent, transparent, and psychologically real the theory, the more useful it can be for analysis and program planning. Both phonological process analysis and standard generative phonology have served as tools for clinical practice in the past twenty years (see, for example, M. Edwards & Bernhardt, 1973a; Shriberg & Kwiatkowski, 1980; Ingram, 1981; Grunwell, 1985; Elbert & Gierut, 1986; Hodson & Paden, 1991). More recently, multilinear frameworks have been utilized as a basis for setting up phonological intervention programs (Bernhardt, 1990, 1992a,b; Von Bremen, 1990; S. Edwards, 1995; Major & Bernhardt, 1996. See also Bernhardt & Stoel-Gammon, 1994, for an introductory tutorial on the application of nonlinear theory to intervention.). Constraint-based analyses as presented in this book have not yet been systematically applied to analysis of disordered data or to intervention planning (although Stemberger & Bernhardt, 1997, provide a modified constraint-based approach for one child). In

---

[1] Phonological intervention assumes a close interrelationship between phonology and phonetics. The speech-language pathologist works in real time, structuring input, and providing feedback on a child's *phonetic* productions. This process is conducted in an attempt to induce permanent *phonological* change which in turn will result in more advanced (and stable) *phonetic* output. The successful application of phonological theory to the analysis of disordered speech in the last 25 years suggests that this assumption is tenable.

this chapter, we bring both multilinear and constraint-based frameworks to bear on data from children with different types of phonological disorder profiles. The final detailed case profile allows us to review many of the issues and analyses brought up in the preceding data chapters, but within one phonological system.

As a prelude to the analysis profiles, we review similarities and differences between typical and protracted phonological development. This comparison also serves as a summary of developmental phenomena in terms of constraint-based analyses and multilinear theories.

8.1. CHILDREN WITH TYPICAL AND PROTRACTED PHONOLOGICAL DEVELOPMENT: SIMILARITIES AND DIFFERENCES

In §1.4.2, we commented that the similarities between typical and protracted phonological development outweigh the differences. Given that a child has normal oral and perceptual mechanisms, the main distinguishing characteristics of a phonological disorder are the extra time required for acquisition, and the prolonged effect of early high-ranked constraints. One possible effect of protracted development is "chronological mismatch": relative advances in one part of the phonological system compared to others (Grunwell, 1987). For example, an English-learning child with a phonological disorder may master use of [l] and [ɹ] (typically acquired later), before having mastered codas (typically acquired earlier). Whether this is only true of children with protracted development, we are not sure. A minority of children with typical development may also have such patterns, but a faster rate of acquisition may make the "mismatches" less obvious. While the majority of phonological patterns are similar in the two groups, unusual patterns do appear in the speech of a small proportion of children with phonological disorders. However, the children who show these unusual patterns have many typical developmental patterns as well. (The existence of one unusual pattern may result in special attention, such as therapy, even if no other problems are apparent. See Bedore et al., 1994).

This section outlines major similarities and differences between the groups, indicating relevant constraints. This is not an exhaustive list, but highlights the most frequently observed phenomena. Note that most of these comparisons are more impressionistic than statistical, although Bernhardt and Stoel-Gammon (1996) and Grunwell (1987) have made some quantitative comparisons. We follow the order of the earlier chapters, beginning with features, then proceeding to prosodic structure, and finishing with effects involving sequences of segments.

8.1.1. PLACE FEATURES: SIMILARITIES

1. All places of articulation may be realized early (Bernhardt & Stoel-Gammon, 1996).

2. If not all places of articulation are realized, the most frequent place features for consonants are [Coronal] and [Labial]. However, [Dorsal] is sometimes more common than [Coronal] (Bernhardt & Stoel-Gammon, 1996; Colin, §8.3).

3. Across children, vowels develop early, with the possible exception of /ɛ/ and some diphthongs (Otomo & Stoel-Gammon, 1992). Some children may experience delays in acquisition of rounded vowels (§5.6.2.4.2).

4. Child default place features and values may differ from those of adults (Bernhardt & Stoel-Gammon, 1996; §5.5.1, §8.3). The following ranking leads to the expected [Coronal] default:

Not(Labial)   ‖‖‖   **Not(Coronal)**
Not(Dorsal)   ‖‖‖
Survived/LinkedUpwards(C-Place)   ‖‖‖

A less-typical [Dorsal] default derives from the following ranking:

Not(Coronal)   ‖‖‖   **Not(Dorsal)**
Not(Labial)   ‖‖‖
Survived/LinkedUpwards(C-Place)   ‖‖‖

8.1.2. PLACE FEATURES: DIFFERENCES

Place features may appear in disordered speech that are not in the target language, especially if there are perceptual differences (e.g., hearing loss) or vocal tract anomalies (e.g., cleft palate or motor weakness), but even in the absence of such physical differences (S. Edwards, 1995).

A particular "phonetic setting" may result in these place feature differences (Laver, 1994). For example, if a person has a generally retracted tongue position, pharyngeals, uvulars, and/or palatals may be prevalent. We refer the reader to Tia's case profile in §8.5.2 for a detailed discussion of such patterns.

8.1.3. LARYNGEAL FEATURES: SIMILARITIES

1. Acquisition of voicing contrasts appears to differ across language groups and across children (Edwards & Shriberg, 1983). Some of these differences are undoubtedly attributable to maturational differences with respect to control of the glottis. Others may be experimentally induced, and result from transcribers' perceptual biases with respect to Voice Onset Time (VOT).

2. For some children, laryngeals [h] and [ʔ] serve as default consonants (Bernhardt, 1990; Stemberger, 1993a; §5.5.3.2, §7.4.1.2, §7.4.4.3). The glottal substitutions may arise because of prosodic constraints (Dylan, §8.6), feature constraints (§5.5.3.2), or sequence constraints (§7.4.1.2, §7.4.4.3).

8.1.4. LARYNGEAL FEATURES: DIFFERENCES

1. In reports by Ingram (1990) and by Gierut, Simmerman, and Neumann (1994), subjects with phonological disorders showed acquisition of voicing con-

trasts (at least in onset) before place contrasts. Ingram noted that the opposite appeared to be true for children with normal development. This probably reflects the difficulty that some children with disorders encounter in acquisition of place contrasts, rather than a relative difference between groups in the acquisition of voicing. When the children with disorders were the same age as the younger normals in the study, they may very well have had difficulty with voicing also.

2. Proportionally more children with phonological disorders may encounter difficulty in acquisition of [+s.g.]. In Gierut et al. (1994), 4 of the 30 children did not use [h] contrastively (even though each of them used other fricatives and glides contrastively). In Bernhardt (1990) three of the six subjects with disorders lacked [h] (and again, all three children used other fricatives, although one used them only in codas). DE (§7.4.1.3) and Terry (§7.3.4.5) had particular difficulty combining the feature [+s.g.] with [-continuant] in onsets (for aspiration of word-initial voiceless stops), which resulted in unusual phonological patterns.

3. On the other hand, proportionally more children with phonological disorders may use glottals to replace other segments (Smit et al., 1990). Glottals are useful default segments when timing units must be preserved, but oral articulation is difficult.

8.1.5. MANNER FEATURES: SIMILARITIES

1. Stops, nasals, and glides are more common in early development than liquids or oral fricatives (Stoel-Gammon & Dunn, 1985; Dinnsen, 1992). Typical rankings for constraints are as follows:
High-ranked constraints:

NotCo-occurring(-sonorant, + continuant)   Result: No Fricatives
Not(+ lateral)   Result: No [l]
NotCo-occurring(Labial,Coronal)   Result: No [ɹ]
Survived(+ nasal)   Result: Nasals ✔

Low-ranked constraints:

Not(-continuant)   Result: Stops and nasals ✔
Not(V-Place)   Result: Glides ✔

The low ranking of **Not(-continuant)** indicates that [-continuant] is often the default value for consonants.

2. Order of development for particular segments within a manner category varies across children (M. Edwards & Shriberg, 1983; §5.5.3).

3. Manner defaults may differ from those of adults, although they appear to do so less commonly than place defaults (§5.5.3). If **Not(-continuant)** is high-ranked, stops may be prohibited. High ranking of **Survived(TimingUnit)** and **Survived(-sonorant)** may result in the replacement of a stop (the usual default) with a fricative (low ranking of **Not(+ continuant)**).

Not(-continuant)	‖‖	**Not(+ continuant)**
Survived(TimingUnit)		**Co-occurring(+ continuant→ + sonorant)**
Survived(-sonorant)		**Survived(-continuant)**

If **Co-occurring(+ continuant→ + sonorant)** is also high-ranked, a sonorant may replace a stop.

Not(-continuant)	‖‖‖	**Not(+ continuant)**
Survived(TimingUnit)		**Survived(-sonorant)**
Co-occurring(+ continuant→ + sonorant)		**Survived(-continuant)**

8.1.6. MANNER FEATURES: DIFFERENCES

1. Fricative substitutions for stops may occur more often in disordered speech than in typically developing speech (Bernhardt & Stoel-Gammon, 1996). This is more likely a result of enduring contextual effects (e.g., rime co-occurrence constraints) than a result of feature default differences, and is discussed further in §8.1.8 below.

2. Lateral sibilants and affricates are uncommon developmentally, and are generally considered aberrant productions if not in the target language (Smit et al., 1990; see Darryl, §8.5.1.2).[2]

Co-occurring(Coronal, + continuant→ + lateral)   Result: [ɬ] for sibilants

3. Rare reports of ingressive airflow productions (Ingram & Terselic, 1983), clicks (Bedore et al., 1994), and trilled coronals (Bernhardt, p.c.) have been made clinically. (See §5.5.1.2.1 for an analysis of click substitutions for stridents.)

4. Voiceless nasals (sometimes referred to as nasal snorts, if they are loud) can occur in disordered speech as substitutions for singleton fricatives or stops.[3] When the nasal cavity cannot be occluded, there is insufficient intraoral air pressure to produce obstruents. This pattern is therefore most common when the velum is structurally or functionally inadequate (absolute high ranking of **Not(-nasal)**). It can occur even if there is no velopharyngeal insufficiency, however (see §5.5.3.4). See the case profile of Tia, a cleft palate speaker, for further discussion (§8.5.2).

8.1.7. PROSODIC STRUCTURE: SIMILARITIES

1. Early syllable and word structure is characterized by open monosyllables or disyllables: CV and CVCV (Ingram, 1989b; Stoel-Gammon, 1993; see §6.1.4, §6.2.3). Codas are generally prohibited (deleted).

Not(Coda)   ‖‖‖   Survived/LinkedUpwards(Root)

---

[2] Children with typically developing speech sometimes use lateral fricatives, but only in the realization of /sl/-clusters.

[3] Children with typically developing speech may use voiceless nasals, but only in the realization of /sm/ or /sn/. See §6.1.6.4.

2. Early syllable and word structure rarely contains consonant sequences or clusters (Ingram, 1989b; Stoel-Gammon, 1993; see §6.1.6, §6.1.7). Again, deletion is common.

> **NotComplex(Onset)**   ‖‖   **Survived/LinkedUpwards(Root)**
> **NotComplex(Coda)***

8.1.8. PROSODIC STRUCTURE: DIFFERENCES

Some children with protracted development may develop onset clusters before codas or intervocalic consonants: CCV becomes established before CVC or CVCV (Dylan, §8.6; Bernhardt & Stoel-Gammon, 1996). This may be an example of a chronological mismatch. Typically developing children tend to overcome **Not(Coda)** before **NotComplex(Onset)**.

8.1.9. CONTEXT-SENSITIVE PATTERNS: SIMILARITIES

Context-sensitive patterns can reflect effects of word position (§6.1.12) and/or sequences (Chapter 7).

1. Fricatives and dorsal consonants frequently appear word finally first (Bernhardt, 1990; Dinnsen, 1996; M. Edwards, 1996; §6.1.12.2). This usually indicates high ranking of at least one of the following rime co-occurrence constraints:

> **Co-occurring(σ-Rime→Dorsal)**
> **Co-occurring(σ-Rime→ + continuant)**

2. Voiced obstruents tend to appear later in codas (M. Edwards & Shriberg, 1983; Bernhardt, 1990; see §6.1.12.1). This reflects low ranking of faithfulness in codas (a weak prosodic position); **Not(+ voiced)** is ranked above **Survived (+ voiced)** in codas. It may also reflect a specific constraint against voicing in codas: **NotCo-occurring(Coda, + voiced,-sonorant)**.

3. Sequence constraint effects between consonants and/or vowels are found in the speech of children with typical and protracted development (Menn, 1983; Stoel-Gammon, 1983; Macken, 1992; Levelt, 1994; §7.3.4). Place sequence constraints such as the following may be more common than other sequence constraints.

> **NotTwice(C-Place)**
> **NoSequence(DefaultArtic...NondefaultArtic)**

4. In cluster reduction, the least sonorous element is usually retained, although either element may be retained (Ingram, 1989b; §7.3.1.5, §7.3.2.2). Even if [l], [ɹ], or fricatives are produced as singletons, they may be absent from cluster contexts.

8.1.10. CONTEXT-SENSITIVE PATTERNS: DIFFERENCES

Metathesized word-initial /s/-stop clusters have been reported for disordered speech (Lorentz, 1976; Bernhardt, 1994a; Chin, 1996). (They may also occur in normally developing speech, but no reports have been found.) Sonority effects are probably responsible for the pattern (rising sonority from the vowel outwards, as discussed in §4.7.1.6). The following high-ranked constraint (which reflects the [-continuant]...[+continuant] sequence in clusters such as [pl]) leads to stops appearing before fricatives (e.g., [ks]) rather than after the fricative as in adult English ([sk]):

NoSequence(+ continuant...-continuant)

8.1.11. SUMMARY: SIMILARITIES AND DIFFERENCES BETWEEN TYPICAL AND PROTRACTED DEVELOPMENT

There are many similarities between typical and protracted development. Differences may include chronological mismatches in disordered speech, or (occasionally) unusual segments or repair patterns. But overall, similarities outweigh differences. Even for children who exhibit one of the observed "differences," most developmental patterns are the same as for typically developing children.

8.2. PHONOLOGICAL PROFILES: OVERVIEW

Throughout the book, we have presented many small data sets exemplifying phenomena at various levels of the phonological hierarchy. In doing so, we have been unable to give a more complete picture of any one child's phonological systems. This section presents a more in-depth exploration of data from individual children, in order to demonstrate how multilinear and constraint-based frameworks characterize phonological systems. We have chosen children with different types of phonological profiles. A full analysis of one child's system is included in the final section (§8.6).

The profiles presented illustrate the following aspects and benefits of multilinear and constraint-based analysis for describing phonological systems.

1. *Analyzing phonological data in terms of a number of different hierarchical levels provides an opportunity to observe the strengths of a child's phonological system in addition to the needs.* Children may have reasonably well-established word and syllable structure but strong constraints on features (Colin). Alternatively, they may have few constraints on features but strong constraints on word and syllable structure or feature sequences (Jeremy). Equally strong constraints may exist at all levels (Dylan).

2. *The multilinear concept of default and the OT concept of constraint rank-*

ings account for many observed phenomena. In early phases of phonological development, nondefault features are less likely to appear in the output, and defaults are more common. Low ranking of faithfulness constraints for nondefault features is typical. Defaults may be *pervasive* (Colin), *positional* (Jeremy), or *specific to certain feature groups* (Charles, Tia, Darryl). Defaults can be adult-like in terms of which features are the defaults, or *child-specific* (with different defaults from those in the adult language).

3. *Phonological defaults can be affected by articulatory-phonetic settings (Laver, 1994). These can result from structural or functional abnormalities of the oral mechanism, or perceptual differences (hearing or visual impairment).* Charles had a forward-thrusting tongue pattern which affected coronal defaults. Darryl had lateralized airflow for sibilants. Tia had a repaired cleft palate which affected general substitution patterns and defaults. Dora had a severe hearing loss and tended to use visible segments (labials or alveolars) for other (less visible) segments.

4. *Constraint interactions typically apply across the whole system.* Dylan's system shows strengths and needs at all levels, and has many phenomena typical of early phonological development. His case study is presented in detail as an overall summary of phenomena discussed in the book.

The short profiles begin with Colin's, which shows pervasive constraints and defaults (§8.3). We then present Jeremy's profile, which shows more specific positional constraints and defaults (§8.4). The final section includes brief discussions of profiles that reflect specific functional and/or structural abnormalities (Charles's, Darryl's, Tia's, Dora's: §8.5).

8.3. PERVASIVE DEFAULTS

In early phases of phonological development, some children show the use of pervasive segmental defaults across word positions and for a wide variety of segments, with no apparent phonetic or perceptual conditioning of these patterns. These can take a number of different phonetic shapes, although they are usually among the typically minimally specified segments, such as glottals (Chrissie: Bernhardt, 1990, *S6*, §5.5.3.2) or [t] (Sally: Bernhardt, 1994b). "Systematic sound preferences" or "favorite sounds" have been noted previously both for normally developing speech (Farwell, 1977) and disordered speech (e.g., Weiner, 1981; Stoel-Gammon & Dunn, 1985; Yavaş & Hernandorena, 1991). Multilinear and constraint-based approaches provide a more coherent analysis of this phenomenon. Defaults and nondefaults are a part of all phonological systems. If many things are impossible, the system is more likely to show pervasive use of defaults, and minimal use of nondefaults.

8.3.1. COLIN (AGE 5;0): OVERVIEW

Colin's profile exemplifies the phenomenon of pervasive default use. His system also demonstrates a chronological mismatch between the prosodic and segmental tiers, favoring the prosodic tier.

Colin had a very severe phonological disorder: at assessment, matches with adult targets were as follows: 13% for singleton consonants, 25% for vowels, and 22% for word shapes. (Words generally had the correct number of syllables. CVC word shapes matched the target 69% of the time, and CVCV 72% of the time.) We focus particularly on his consonantal defaults, because his vowels and word and syllable structure were "well developed' in comparison.[4] (See Table 8.1.)

TABLE 8.1   Colin's Consonantal Inventory at Assessment[a]

	Initial	Medial		Final
		Onset	Coda	
Nasals	m[b]	(m)[b]	*(m)*	**(m)**
	n			(n)
				(ŋ)
Stops	<u>p</u> (ʰ)	(pʰ)		p
	<u>b</u>	b		*(b)*
	<u>k</u> (ʰ)	k (ʰ)		<u>k</u>
	<u>g</u>	g		*(q)*
Fricatives				*(θ)*
		s		s
		ʃ		
		(ç)		
Glides/				
/l/	j			
		(ɹw)[a]		
	h	<u>h</u>		
		(ʔ)		ʔ

[a] Rounded /ɹ/ (one token)
[b] Only in word *mommy*
Bold: Both a match and a substitution; *Italics:* Substitution only; Underline: 75% + match; Parentheses: 1–10% match.

In the 170-item single-word assessment elicitation, 155 words had default segments. Typical outputs were [gak], [bap], (or reduplications or combinations of those), [gahə], or [bahə]. Sometimes a feature of the target was realized in his productions (for example, [-continuant], [Labial]), but often no connection between the default word and the target word was apparent. Interestingly, although default features were prevalent in his spontaneous speech, he succeeded in imitat-

[4] The major vowel default was the [+low] [a].

ing all segments of English (in words) except diphthongs and /l/ at least once
during the assessment.

8.3.2. COLIN'S PERVASIVE DEFAULTS

Colin typically produced a velar stop in place of other consonants. Primary
default features were [Dorsal] and [-continuant]. Although [-continuant] is an expected default, stops do not usually replace *all* manner categories, particularly at
age 5. [Dorsal] is less expected than [Coronal] as a default. (Coronal stops were
missing from his inventory.)

daddy	/dædi/	[gahi]
snow	/snoʊ/	[gaː]
laugh	/læf/	[gaʊ] (S); [gak] (E)
thumb	/θʌm/	[gaːʔ]
Santa Claus	/sæntəklɑːz/	[gagagak] (E)

Timing units needed to be preserved and filled with segmental material (because
of high-ranked prosodic faithfulness constraints), but **Not** constraints for nondefault features were also high-ranked, prohibiting nondefault features. Low-ranked
Not constraints for default features allowed production of pervasive defaults.

Survived(C-TimingUnit)	**Not(Dorsal)**
LinkedDownwards(C-Timing Unit)	**Not(-continuant)**
Not(Nondefault)	**Survived(Nondefault)**

8.3.3. COLIN'S CONTEXTUALLY CONDITIONED DEFAULTS

Colin also had context-bound (positional) defaults (like Jeremy, §8.4), although these were not as prevalent as the velar stops. Default onsets were [h]
(intervocalically) and [n] (word initially, for vowel-initial targets). In word-final
codas, [ʔ] was the default. Positional constraints, particularly **Co-occurring
(σ-Margin→-continuant)** and **Uninterrupted(+continuant)**, overrode other
constraints.

Glottals were frequent defaults. Intervocalically, [h] was a frequent default onset. Word finally, [ʔ] appeared (somewhat less frequently) as a default coda.

fishing	/fɪʃɪŋ/	[bahʌʔ]
thumb	/θʌm/	[gaːʔ]
radio	/ɹeɪdijoʊ/	[gaha] (S); [bəhə] (E)
yellow	/jɛloʊ/	[nə̃hõ]

In intervocalic position, there was a plateauing effect of the feature [+continu-
ant] from the surrounding vowels, that is, a high ranking of **Uninterrupted
(+continuant)**. This was driven by a higher ranking of **Not(+ continuant)** than

Distinct(+ continuant). In plateauing, the intervening consonant links to the single token of [+continuant], to avoid an interrupted gesture. The number of tokens of [+continuant] in the output is minimized by merging adjacent tokens of [+continuant]. The glottal [h] has no place features and requires few resources. Thus, it was an optimal default segment for realization of [+continuant]. (See §7.4.4.3 for an in-depth discussion of this phenomenon.)

Generally, stops appeared in word margins because of high ranking of **Survived/LinkedDownwards(C-TimingUnit)** and **Co-occurring(σ-Margin→ -continuant).** The general default [k] was relatively frequent word finally. However, coda position was still developing (69% coda realization). Unlike [k], the glottal stop has no place features. Requiring fewer resources than [k], glottal stop thus was a useful default word finally.

Survived(C-TimingUnit)	
LinkedDownwards(C-TimingUnit)	
Co-occurring(σ-Margin→-continuant)	**Co-occurring(Rime→ + continuant)**
	Not(-continuant)
Not(Nondefault)	**Survived(Nondefault)**
	Not(+ c.g.)

The nasal [n] appeared as a default onset for most vowel-initial words (although velar stops also appeared in this context occasionally).

	egg	/(ʔ)ɛg/	[nã]	
	itch	/(ʔ)ɪʧ/	[naɪs]	(E)
	off	/(ʔ)ɑf/	[nɑk]	(E)
BUT:	itchy	/(ʔ)ɪʧi/	[kɪʧi]	(E)

The unusual default onset [n] derives from the interaction of a number of constraints. As noted above, **Co-occurring(σ-Margin→-continuant)** was high-ranked. Colin had to produce a [-continuant] consonant in onset position, and often produced [k]. However, in the context of vowel-initial words, the more prevalent substitution was [n] (also [-continuant]). This was unexpected. The only other coronals in his speech were fricatives, produced imitatively in non-word-initial positions. Furthermore, velars or glottals were typical defaults, and few sonorants were produced in margins overall. Velar stops are [-sonorant]; thus, the default value for [sonorant] in margins was [-sonorant].

How did a sonorant then surface in a margin in the context of vowel-initial words? Perhaps Colin perceived the adult form as starting with a glottal stop (see §6.1.3), and was trying to remain faithful to the features of that consonant. Since /ʔ/ is [+sonorant] (see Appendix B), a high ranking of **Survived(+ sonorant)** would lead to a word-initial sonorant in the output of these words. Sonorant glides never occurred word initially, however, indicating high ranking of **Co-occur-ring(σ-Onset→ + consonantal)** (see §6.1.12). Since nasals are the only consonants that are [+sonorant], [+consonantal], and [-continuant], nasals appeared in the output.

But why [n], when Colin's default place was [Dorsal]? In English **NotCo-occurring(+nasal,Dorsal)** prohibits [ŋ] in onsets. (/ŋ/ is only possible in codas because **Co-occurring(Rime→Dorsal)** is ranked even higher; see §4.7.1.3 & §6.1.12.2.1.) Most children are sensitive to this adult constraint. As a result, [Dorsal] was not possible. It seems that [Coronal] was the next-most-optimal place feature. (Labials only appeared if in the target word, that is, they responded to **Survived** constraints, but could not be inserted as defaults.)

RESULTS

Survived(+sonorant)	**Sonorant**
Co-occurring(σ-Onset→+consonantal)	**Consonant in onset**
Co-occurring(σ-Margin→-continuant)	**Stop in margins**
NotCo-occurring(+nasal,Dorsal)	**No [ŋ]**
Not(Labial)	**No insertion of [Labial]**
Not(Coronal)	**Insertion of [Coronal] due to higher-ranked Not-Co-occurring(Dorsal,+nasal)**
Not(Dorsal)	**General default insertion of [Dorsal]**
Not(+nasal)	**Insertion of [+nasal]**

A complication for this analysis is that underlying /n/ rarely survived in the output. Although there was an [n] in the frequent word *no*, word-initial /n/ surfaced as [g] in other words. Thus, [+sonorant] did not always survive. This is an example of a chain shift: /n/ > [g], but /ʔ/ > [n]. OT does not handle such chain shifts well (see §10.2.1).

Colin's system, although simple on the surface, shows complex interactions of a number of constraints, some of which applied across word positions, and some of which were contextually bound. Generally, when very specific constraints need to be posited, the analysis appears contrived and not sufficiently explanatory. One part of a phonological system may have its own idiosyncratic patterns, but that is not common. We return to this issue in the final chapter (§10.2.3).

8.3.4. COLIN'S INTERVENTION PROGRAM AND OUTCOMES

The major goal of Colin's program was to reduce the use of child-specific pervasive defaults and enable him to produce words with the nondefault and default features of English. Over a 10-month period, the following were set as intervention targets (16 weeks of therapy three times a week and weekly therapy for 4 subsequent months):

1. Accurate vowel production and elimination of the /n/ onset to vowel-initial words through practice with diphthongs /aʊ/ and /aɪ/ (Intervention blocks 1 and 2)
2. [Coronal, +anterior] to replace dorsal and glottal defaults: onset /d/, /s/ (first in non-word-initial positions), then onset /t/, /l/, /θ/ (Blocks 1–5).
3. Use of labials other than stops: postvocalic /f/, then /w/, then onset /m/, then onset /f/ (Blocks 1–5)

By the end of Block 1, vowel matches increased notably, epenthetic [n] onsets disappeared, and he began to use coronal fricatives anywhere except in word-initial position. By the end of Block 2, he was beginning to change the place default to [Coronal, +anterior], both appropriately (e.g., for coronal targets), and occasionally for other segments. Over the next three intervention blocks, the default use of medial [h] disappeared, and dorsal stops became much more restricted in their default use. The nondefault features [-consonantal] (onset glides) and [+lateral] became established. Prosodic structure continued to improve with consistent production of CVC, CVCV, and CVCVC, and the emergence of clusters. Within that time period, the least improvement was noted for establishment of typically later-developing /ɹ/ and the interdentals, and for word-initial fricatives and /m/. Thus, there was a general circumscription of the unusual default features, and more consistent realization of nondefault features. General inventory constraints were more typical of his age, but some of the specific context-bound constraints were still operative. A mild dysfluency became apparent. At age 9 (after virtually no treatment from age 6) he had not yet completely mastered word-initial /s/-stop clusters, /ɹ/, or the interdentals, was moderately dysfluent, and was experiencing some difficulty with academic subjects. The lack of change in the non-treatment period indicates that the intervention program had a direct positive influence on his speech development. The multilinear concepts of autonomous features, underspecification, and child defaults were useful in explaining the strengths of his system and his intervention needs. An intervention program was developed which targeted the elimination of pervasive child-specific defaults, and facilitated the realization of nondefault features through the already well-established word structure. In the primary grades, his skills were not considered sufficiently different from those of other children, and thus he was not a candidate for speech therapy in a rural community with limited services. At age 9, he again became a candidate for intervention because of the plateauing of speech development, the deterioration in fluency, and his academic needs.

8.4. CONTEXTUALLY CONDITIONED DEFAULTS

Specific context-bound defaults were noted as a secondary set of patterns to Colin's general pervasive velar stop defaults. Jeremy's profile further exemplifies context-bound defaults in response to several general syllable structure, rime,

TABLE 8.2   Jeremy's Consonantal Inventory at Assessment[a]

	Initial	Medial		Final
		Onset	Coda	
Nasals	<u>m</u>	m	(m)	<u>m</u>
	<u>n</u>	**(n)**	(n)	**n**
			(ŋ)	
Stops	**p** [(h)]	(p)		(p)
	b	**(b)**		
	t[(h)]	(t)		(t)
	d	**(d)**		
	(kʰ)			
	g			
Fricatives	**f**	(f)		
	v			
				<u>s(ʃ)</u>
Glides/				
/l/	**w**	**(w)**		
	<u>j</u>			
	(l)			
	(h)			(ɚ)
	ʔ	(ʔ)		

[a] **Bold:** Both a match and a substitution; *Italics:* Substitution only; Underline: 75%+ match; Parentheses: 1–10% match.

and sequence constraints. (For further detail on Jeremy, see Bernhardt, 1990, *S3*; Bernhardt & Gilbert, 1992; §7.3.1.6.1, §7.3.1.7, §7.3.2.1, §7.4.1.1.)

8.4.1. JEREMY'S FEATURE PRODUCTION

Jeremy also had a chronological mismatch between word structure and feature development, but in his case, segmental development was advanced in comparison with prosodic structure development. Stops, fricatives, and nasals were frequent, and all other segments of English (except affricates) were present at least once in imitation in an assessment sample. On the other hand, feature output was often compromised by syllable and word structure and/or sequence constraints. A contextually conditioned default [s] coda often appeared as a response to such constraints.[5] Before discussing the major prosodic constraints, we note the following about his feature production and limitations. (See Table 8.2.)

1. Manner: Nasals were the only sound class to appear frequently in both onset and coda.

mine	/mɑɪn/	[mɑĩn]
thumb	/θʌm/	[pʌ̃ˀm]
combing	/koʊmɪŋ/	[komĩn]~[bõwĩn] (E)

[5] Leonard and Brown (1984) describe a child with a similar word-final [s] default.

Stops were frequent in word onset, but rare in codas.

up	/ʌp/	[ap]	
toy	/tɔɪ/	[tʰɔɪ]	
cake	/keɪk/	[kʰeˡsˀ]	(E)
hug	/hʌg/	[ʔaˀs]	
see	/siː/	[diː]	

Fricatives appeared frequently both in onset and coda.

laugh	/læf/	[ʔaʊs]	(E)
five	/faɪv/	[faɪç]	
van	/væn/	[væ̃s]	(E)
jump	/dʒʌmp/	[daˀs]	(E)
buzz	/bʌz/	[bʌs]	(E)
rabbit	/ɹæbɪt/	[wɛˀs]	

However, there were contextual effects on place of articulation for fricatives in terms of word position: labiodentals appeared in onset only, and [s] appeared in codas only (a pattern also reported by Gierut, 1986, for another child with a phonological disorder). Note that manner was preserved for labiodentals in all contexts, whereas only (default) place was preserved for the coronal fricatives in onset.

Onset:	/f/	>	[f]
	/v/	>	[v]
	/s/	>	[d]~[tʰ]
Coda:	/f/	>	[s]
	/v/	>	[s]~[ç]
	/s/	>	[s]

2. Place and voicing. Place of articulation and voicing also showed positional differences.[6] The most frequent place of articulation word finally was coronal, primarily in combination with [+continuant] ([s]). Voiceless obstruents appeared in all word positions except medial coda position. Voiced obstruents appeared only in onset (compare *see* and *buzz*).

8.4.2. JEREMY'S DEFAULT CODAS

Of 431 target words in the assessment sample, only 153 matched the adult target in terms of syllable number and timing unit realizations (36%). Clusters were absent. Overall, less than half (55/115) of his attempts at disyllabic adult targets had two syllables. (Weak syllables were often deleted.) No words of three or more syllables were produced. Deletion repairs were more common for multi-

---

[6] There were also occasional CV interactions between dorsals and back vowels and between coronals and front vowels in onsets, suggesting a sequence constraint involving to the consonants and vowels: **NoSequence(Dorsal...Coronal)** and **NoSequence(Coronal...Dorsal)**.

syllables than monosyllables, although the same type of constraints and repairs affected all words.[7]

mommy	/mʌmi/	[mʌmi]
monkey	/mʌŋki/	[mãŋ.'dɪs]
wagon	/wægn̩/	[ʷæs]
Bandaid	/bændeɪd/	[mɛˡs]

The following constraints were high-ranked, and cause the reduction of clusters within onsets and codas and the deletion of extra syllables:

NotComplex(Foot)
NotComplex(Onset)
NotComplex(Coda)

Not(Coda) was also high-ranked, but was gradually losing its power (i.e., was variably ranked lower). Due to default [s] insertion, 81% of tokens for (C)VC targets had codas.

eat	/iːt/	[is]~[i] (C)
van	/væn/	[vãs]
tub	/tʌb/	[bʌs]
milk	/mɪlk/	[ŋÃs]

Binary(σ,μ) was also a high-ranked prosodic constraint implicated in the production of default [s] codas. This leads to a state of affairs where (a) a syllable is limited to two moras (**Binary(σ,μ)**), (b) every timing unit in a rime must be a mora (**Co-occurring(Rime→μ)**), and (c) a mora can link downwards to only a single Root node (**NotComplex (μ)**). This constraint affected production of codas and diphthongs (the latter being primarily limited to open syllables).

	now	/naʊ/	[naʊ]
	way	/weɪ/	[weɪ]
BUT:	down	/daʊn/	[daˢn]
	page	/peɪdʒ/	[bɛˢs]

Given a high ranking of **Binary(σ,μ)**, rimes are limited to two weight units. If margin constraints outrank rime constraints, the coda consonant is produced rather than the glide portion of the diphthong. Thus, prosodic-segmental interaction constraints were also relevant.

Co-occurring(σ-Margin→ + consonantal) ⫴ **Co-occurring(Rime→-consonantal)**

But how did [s] arise in particular? Additional constraints are implicated, primarily **Co-occurring(Rime→ + continuant)** and **NoSequence(Artic...Ar-**

---

[7]The prosodic structure limitations appeared to extend to the phrasal level. He seldom combined words into phrases at the outset of the study (age 3;4). Phonological intervention appeared to influence his morphosyntactic development. At the end of the study (age 3;10) he consistently produced word combinations (Bopp, 1995).

tic_{Nondefault}). In early development, the rime often has [+continuant] elements only (§6.1.12.2.2). Furthermore, nondefault articulator features are less likely to appear in weak prosodic positions (such as codas), especially following segments with other features on the same tier (§6.1.12.1). Labials and dorsals were generally prohibited after coronals (although labials were possible in codas when no other features were in the word). (See §8.4.1 and §8.4.3 for more detail on his sequence constraints.) The [s] served a general function in the system: to realize all and any phonological material after the first vowel of a word, using default features for both margins *and* rimes.

Margin:	[+consonantal], [-voice]
Rime:	[+continuant]
ArticB in a sequence:	Default Place (Coronal)

8.4.3. JEREMY'S INTERVENTION PROGRAM AND OUTCOMES

The CV[s] structure was a strength of the system, in that it allowed codas to be realized and impossible sequences to be avoided, but it also negatively affected intelligibility because of its pervasive use in a variety of both monosyllabic and multisyllabic targets. In order to reduce use of CV[s], intervention strategies targeted both CVC and CVCV words in the first therapy period, with a variety of stops and nasals as in C_1 and C_2. Two segmental targets, /l/ and /h/, complemented the prosodic targets. In spite of the much stronger prosodic structure constraints, Jeremy made rapid gains in prosodic structure development by the end of the first subblock of treatment (nine sessions over 3 weeks). The default [s] segment disappeared, and codas and multisyllabic words became common. (See Bernhardt & Gilbert, 1992, or Bernhardt, 1990, for details.) Some sequence, rime, and complexity constraints continued to be present at Week 6, in addition to constraints on the features. By the end of Week 12, he had mastered [l] and [h], eliminated sequence and rime constraints, and started to produce word-final clusters. By the end of Week 18, a variety of clusters emerged, reducing the impact of prosodic complexity constraints, and making his speech fully intelligible. He went on to develop the remaining word shapes and segments on his own. Language skills improved significantly throughout the phonology project. Although he received further short periods of language intervention at age 4 and again at ages 5 and 6, testing at age 11 revealed no apparent speech or language difficulties and above-average academic achievement.

8.5. PHONETIC SETTINGS AND DEFAULTS: PERCEPTUAL DIFFERENCES

Perceptual or oral mechanism abnormalities can result in articulatory-phonetic delays/deviance, although there is no one-to-one correspondence between speech production and either the type/degree of hearing loss or the structure/function of the oral mechanism. In the case of hearing impairment, output may be faithful to the established underlying representation, but that representation may be different from the ambient target language, because of a different auditory perceptual basis. If underlying representations are adult-like, phonological contrasts may or may not be maintained in phonetic output. Howard (1993) describes a child with a repaired cleft palate who maintained many phonological contrasts, even though few productions matched the adult targets phonetically. She maintained a contrast within the labial class between stops (produced as bilabial clicks or glottal stops) and other labials. A voicing contrast was also apparent (at least acoustically): aspiration followed glottal stops that replaced voiceless stops, but not voiced stops. However, a place distinction was not always maintained between /p/ and lingual stops and affricates, since glottal stops replaced all of those targets. Thus, mechanism differences may or may not lead to general faithfulness to underlying distinctions. Even where general faithfulness is maintained, surface differences may be noted, either because perceptual differences result in different underlying representations or because a particular structure or dysfunction of the oral mechanism makes certain articulations impossible. One particular subset of segments may be affected, as we show below for Charles and Darryl, or a larger part of the system may be affected, as we show for Tia and Dora.

8.5.1. CORONAL DEFAULTS

As we discussed in detail in §5.5.1.2.1, children can have different defaults for coronal fricatives. Dentalized coronals are common, whether or not people have delayed speech development. In fact, some never modify their "lisps." Lateralized productions are less common and are typically not considered normal developmental phenomena (Smit et al., 1990). Here we present brief profiles of both types of patterns for two children with phonological disorders: Charles (Bernhardt, 1992b), who had a "frontal lisp," and Darryl (Bernhardt, p.u.d.), who had a "lateral lisp."

8.5.1.1. Charles: [-grooved], [+distributed] Defaults

Charles had a forward-thrusting tongue pattern during speaking and swallowing and a pronounced open bite (wide space between top and bottom front teeth during occlusion). Coronal fricatives and some coronal stops (primarily word-initial /t/) were produced as ungrooved dentals or interdentals. Note the variability between fricative and affricate production word initially, independent of whether the target was a fricative, affricate, or voiceless stop (although /t/ usually surfaced as a stop or affricate).

two	/tuː/	[tʰuː]	Alveolar stop ✔
tub	/tʌb/	[tʌbᵊ]	Dental stop
TV	/tiːviː/	[ˈθiviʲᵊ]	Dental affricate
tells	/tɛlz/	[θɛʊð]	Dental fricative

dog	/dɑg/	[dɔˀg]	Alveolar stop ✔
dog	/dɑg/	[dɔːg]	Dental stop
Dad	/dæd/	[d̪æd̪]	Dental stops
sis	/sɪs/	[θɪˀθ]	Dental fricative
see	/siː/	[ˈθi]	Dental affricate
zoo	/zuː/	[ðuwˀ]	Dental fricative
shoe	/ʃuː/	[θuː]	Dental fricative
chicken	/tʃɪkən/	[θɪkə̃n]	Dental fricative
cherries	/tʃɛɹiz/	[ˈθɛwið]	Dental affricate
jump	/dʒʌmp/	[ðʌmp]	Dental fricative
thing	/θɪŋ/	[θɪŋ]	Dental fricative ✔
thumb	/θʌm/	[fʌm]	Labiodental fricative
the	/ðə/	[ðə]	Dental fricative ✔
		[d̪ə]	Dental stop

Before examining the patterns for coronals, we note here other characteristics of his segmental system:

1. All major articulator features were established.
2. Both values of the feature [continuant] were established for labials and dorsals in all word positions, and for coronals in non-word-initial position.
3. Voicing contrasts were established, although word-initial stops were seldom aspirated.
4. Neither /l/ nor /ɹ/ were established. (/l/ > [j] in onset; /ɹ/ > [w] in onset. In codas, the liquid either surfaced as a vowel or was deleted).

Coronals were particularly problematical. The terminal features of [Coronal] reflected an advanced and ungrooved tongue tip setting, which resulted in both adult-like and non-adult-like default/nondefault values.

1. [anterior]: The nondefault feature [-anterior] was not yet established, and hence [+anterior] was an expected adult-like default (applying to both [dento]alveolars and palatoalveolars).

Not(-anterior) ‖ **Not(+anterior)**
‖ **Survived(-anterior)**

2. [grooved]: The feature [-grooved] was an expected default for stops, but it applied also to the fricatives, and hence was the system default. Occasionally, his dental sibilants had a strident acoustic quality, suggesting that there was inconsistent realization of [+grooved].

Not(+grooved) ‖ **Not(-grooved)**
‖ **Survived(+grooved)**

3. [distributed]: The adult nondefault feature [+distributed] appeared as a match for the interdental targets /θ/ and /ð/, but was probably a child default feature, since many coronals surfaced as dentals. (Additionally, some words with /θ/

surfaced with [f], usually in assimilatory contexts.) Voiced and postvocalic stops appeared to surface more often as alveolars ([-distributed]), although phonetic transcription may be less reliable at least for the voiced segments. (Recently, Bernhardt, Loyst, and Muir, 1996, reported a discrepancy in transcription and palatometric data for voiced alveolars with the palatometric data showing less accurate production.) If the transcriptions were reliable, the particular difficulty with [t] may have been a result of trying to produce the [+s.g.] feature for aspiration, with an affricate or fricative resulting instead. (DE, who had a similar problem regarding [+continuant] in onset, had high-ranked co-occurrence constraints regarding [-continuant] and [+s.g.]. See §7.4.1.3.) This would account for the affrication/frication. Once Charles produced an affricate, the only possible [+anterior] fricative was dental, resulting in more dentalized productions for the voiceless stop.

Not(-distributed) ||| Not(+distributed)
	Survived(-distributed)

As we noted in §5.5.1.2.2, children often have dental ([+distributed]) anterior coronals, at least in part because of the size of the tongue relative to the oral cavity. Many children produce these dentalized coronals with a flat ungrooved tongue, as Charles did. Detailed analyses of the types of patterns observed for Charles are presented in §5.5.1.2.1. Palatoalveolars were absent. Producing any grooved sibilant was very difficult.

Although we are primarily concerned with the terminal features of [Coronal] here, the lack of manner contrast between word-initial coronal fricatives, affricates, and voiceless stops is also interesting. In English, Coronal is the only place category which allows a 3-way contrast between stops, fricatives, and affricates; potentially, this freedom makes learning the various values for [continuant] more challenging. Mowrer and Burger (1991) report that, in Xhosa, which has a whole series of (lingual) affricates, interdental fricatives are frequent substitutions for all but velar affricates (which surface as [k]). Thus, Charles's difficulties and general substitution patterns are not unique to him, nor to English, with its one set of affricates. What is possibly more intriguing with respect to Charles's data is that he did maintain a distinction for [continuant] in non-word-initial positions. (See also §7.4.1.3 for DE.)

eat	/iːt/	[it]
eating	/iːtɪŋ/	[itʰĩn]
quarter	/kwɔɹtɹ/	[korʊː]
ice	/ʌɪs/	[ʌɪθ]
icy	/ʌɪsi/	[ʌɪθiˈ]
clothes	/klouz/	[koð]
itch	/ɪtʃ/	[ɪtθ]
watch	/wɑtʃ/	[wɔtθ]

Why was it more difficult for him to maintain an obstruent contrast in word-initial position? High-ranked margin and rime constraints generally promote a [-continuant] onset, the opposite of what was happening for the /t/. Furthermore, onset is a strong prosodic domain in which it is possible to make more feature distinctions. For Charles, there may have been an articulatory basis for the phonological pattern. When initiating articulatory gestures with a rapid forward-thrusting tongue movement, it may be difficult to control the tongue tip sufficiently in order to make a precise distinction between occluded and unoccluded segments, particularly with coarticulatory anticipation of the [+continuant] vowel.

The segmental component of Charles's intervention program first targeted (successfully) nondefault features [-anterior] for palatoalveolar fricatives and affricates, and [+lateral] for /l/. (There were also successful prosodic goals targeting clusters.) The palatoalveolars require a more retracted tongue position than interdentals, and thus a movement opposite to that of the forward thrust was facilitated, while setting up a phonological contrast. Interestingly, in the first four intervention sessions, he produced the palatoalveolars as [-grooved] alveopalatals. However, by the second treatment cycle (1 month later, with no intervening focus on them), he produced them as [+grooved] palatoalveolars. The /l/ provided an opportunity to introduce a new manner feature, but also to target alveolar rather than dental placement (although either type of production was accepted initially). Both of these segmental targets were mastered in the second cycle of treatment (after 18 sessions distributed over 3 months, and with intervening cluster targets in the other 18 sessions). The alveolars /s/ and /z/ and the postalveolar /ɹ/ were the next targets. The earliest successful contexts for /s/ and /z/ were word-final position and /sk/ clusters (end of the third cycle). In both of these contexts tongue position is retracted, either in anticipation of the velar /k/ or because the tongue is already in retracted position after vowel production. Short therapy blocks (with weekly appointments) were provided once or twice a year between ages 6 and 8 for maintenance of the grooved sibilant production, stabilization of the target interdentals, and production of /ɹ/. With the advent of the secondary dentition, /s/ and /z/ stabilized completely for Charles. Some attention was paid to his swallowing pattern with a view to maintaining stability of the alveolar productions, although only for a short period of time. (He required orthodontic braces at age 12 for a continuing open bite.) Prevocalic /ɹ/ became successfully incorporated into his system by age 7 (prior to final stabilization of the sibilants), but he elected to continue speaking without rhotacized vowels most of the time (at least in part because his parents do not use them in their dialects).

In summary, for Charles, coronal production for sibilants and word-initial /t/ was associated with a forward thrusting tongue movement pattern. This was first addressed by focusing on alternative nondefault values for coronals ([-anterior], [+lateral]), to provide phonological and phonetic contrasts. Phonological contrasts were further facilitated through introduction of /ɹ/ and by systematically narrowing in on the adult default sibilant features ([+grooved], [-distributed]), beginning with the more retracted palatoalveolars and then carefully monitoring context for /s/ and /z/. The phonological contrast strategy facilitated early change. Coarticulatory practice with back vowels and consonants helped stabilize a nondentalized placement for the coronals.

Charles's profile shows that a default can result from observable articulatory-phonetic constraints or settings, and can affect one particular subset of the phonological system. These settings can be changed by establishing nondefault features, and thereby new phonological contrasts. Choosing stimuli that maximize phonetic context can facilitate production. (See Bernhardt, 1992b, for a detailed case study of Charles.)

8.5.1.2. Darryl: Lateral Substitutions

In §5.5.3.4, we noted that /l/ sometimes replaces fricatives in normally developing speech. In this section we give an example in which laterals replaced a number of different segments (particularly word finally).[8]

For Darryl, laterals appeared for all fricatives and affricates, except word-initial labiodentals and /θ/. (No data were available for /ð/.) Voicing of the target was generally maintained: [l] replaced voiced fricatives/affricates and [ɬ] replaced voiceless targets. If the target was palatoalveolar, the lateral often had a palato-alveolar quality.

fish	/fɪʃ/	[fɪɬ ˀ]	Initial f: ✔
thumb	/θʌm/	[θɐ̃m]	Initial θ: ✔
mouth	/mʌʊθ/	[mʌʊɬ]	
soap	/soʊp/	[ɬaoʊp]	
shoe(s)	/ʃuː(z)/	[ɬ ˀul]	
watch	/wɑtʃ/	[wɑɬ ˀ]	
page	/peɪʤ/	[pɛɪl]	

Word finally, [ɬ] also replaced /k/. (No data are available for word-final /g/.)

| rock | /ɹɑk/ | [wɑɬ] |
| fork | /fɔɹk/ | [fɔɹ̩ɬ] |

Word-initial singleton velars, on the other hand, were produced as coronal stops (except in *candle*). (Labial and coronal stops matched the targets.)

	cowboy hat	/kaʊbɔɪhæt/	[taboʊhæt]
	crayon	/kreɪjɑn/	[teɪ.ɑn]
	gun	/gʌn/	[dʌn]
BUT:	candle	/kændl̩/	[kæni]

Among the sonorants, /l/ and /w/ matched the adult targets, but /j/ was lateralized. Prevocalic /ɹ/ surfaced as [w] but postvocalic /ɹ/ surfaced as [l] or a vowel. Nasals

---

[8] M. Edwards and Bernhardt (1973b) present data for another child, John, who used [ɬ] for fricatives and /k/, but in word-initial position. Unlike Darryl, John had few codas.

generally matched the adult target unless there was a preceding cluster with a sonorant in the target, in which case /n/ surfaced as [l].

star	/stɑɹ/	[ɫ⁾ɑl]
sweater	/swɛtɹ̩/	[wældə]
leaf	/liːf/	[liɫ]
yoyo	/joʊjoʊ/	[ʎoʊʎoʊ]
yellow	/jɛloʊ/	[lɛloʊ]

Clusters with approximants had variable patterns (see *sweater, star, crayon*). When there were two sonorants in the word, the obstruent often deleted, and at least one lateral appeared in the child's output.

queen	/kwiːn/	[wil]
glove	/glʌv/	[ɫ⁾ʌl]
green	/gɹin/	[wil]

There are insufficient data and space to comment accurately on all of Darryl's patterns. We will focus on the following:

1. The greater prevalence of lateral substitutions in codas
2. The lack of velars
3. The presence of coronal stops in codas

Darryl had difficulty controlling tongue configurations. Coronal continuants require the creation of a central channel, narrow for [+grooved] segments, broad for [-grooved] continuants. The sides of the tongue must be high, and stiff enough that a good seal is formed. The greater the airflow (and it is greatest in [+grooved] segments), the tighter that seal must be. If the seal is insufficient, there will be lateral airflow, and this is most likely with [+grooved] segments. However, this is not the whole story, because it does not account for the fact that "lateral lisps" have central tongue tip contact at the teeth for most young children with this phenomenon. It appears that a lateral articulation is being *substituted* for an articulation with central airflow, not being *added* to it at a late phonetic level. For this reason, we regard this pattern as phonologically based, deriving from the following (phonetically grounded) constraint:

Co-occurring(Coronal, + continuant→ + lateral)

Of course, **Not(+ lateral)** must be ranked lower than this constraint, so that violations can be avoided by inserting **Not(+ lateral)**. Most speakers who show the effects of this constraint substitute a lateral articulation only for [+grooved] fricatives and affricates. The lower airflow in flat-tongued [θ] and [ð] allows central articulation. This suggests that **Co-occurring(Coronal, + strident→ + lateral)** may be the relevant constraint for many speakers (and that some speakers use the feature [strident] rather than [grooved]; see §5.5.1.2.1). (Some speakers retain the effects of this constraint into adulthood.)

Darryl's use of laterals additionally involved more complex interactions with other constraints. In codas, all fricatives, affricates, and voiceless velars became laterals. However, in onsets, only the grooved fricatives and /j/ were lateralized. The difference between onsets and codas derives from the fact that onsets are strong prosodic positions (in which faithfulness tends to be high) but codas are weak prosodic positions (with low faithfulness). The labiodental fricatives were labiodentals in onsets, and thus [+lateral] was not a possible articulation (high ranking of **Survived(Labial)**). The flat-tongued [θ] showed survival of [-grooved] and [+distributed] in the strong onset position. The substitution of [l] for /j/ may have been partially related. The glide [j] was not possible in the child's system (as has been observed for other children; see §5.5.1.5.1), and **Not(+ lateral)** was low-ranked. Producing [l] allows faithfulness to the [+continuant], [+sonorant], and [Coronal] features of /j/ (without requiring central airflow for a coronal continuant in a consonantal position).

In codas, the labiodentals and [θ] also became laterals. This derives from the low level of faithfulness in coda position. **Survived** constraints are ranked low. High-ranked **NotCo-occurring(Labial, + continuant)** can cause /f/ and /v/ to become nonlabial in codas (§5.5.4.3). High-ranked **Co-occurring(Coronal, + continuant→ + lateral)** can cause *all* coronal fricatives to become lateral. This is a standard interaction between faithfulness and syllable position that we have seen elsewhere.

The sole remaining puzzle is why word-final /k/ surfaced as a lateral fricative, but only in codas and even though coronal stops did not become laterals in codas. Basically, it appears that /k/ (but not [t]) became a coronal fricative, but only in codas; as such, it had to be [+lateral], like all coronal fricatives in codas.

1. **Not (Dorsal)** was higher-ranked than **Not(Coronal)** and **Survived(Dorsal)**. Underlying [Dorsal] deleted, and default [Coronal] was inserted. This was especially likely in codas (§6.1.12.1).

2. Coda consonants were subject to **Co-occurring(Rime→ + continuant)**, which sometimes leads to fricative substitutions for stops in codas (§6.1.12.2.2). Thus, /k/ was realized as a fricative; and since it was also coronal, it was [+lateral]. But why were [-continuant] /t/ and /p/ not subject to this rime co-occurrence constraint? In §6.1.12.2, we noted that it is something of a problem for us that *any* stop fails to become a fricative when this rime co-occurrence constraint is high-ranked. We suggested that the facts require one of two solutions. (a) Default features such as [-continuant] are specified in underlying representations, or (b) the constraint **Lexical(+ continuant)** specifically prevents *insertion* of [+continuant] (independent of the effects of **Not(+ continuant)**). Either solution prevents /t/ and /p/ from becoming a fricative in a coda in Darryl's speech, but neither solution explains why /t/ and /p/ were treated differently from /k/.

The phoneme /k/, unlike /t/ and /p/, was unfaithful to the target place of articulation. This is an instance in which lack of faithfulness to one feature ([Dorsal]) led to lack of faithfulness to another feature ([-continuant]). We have seen such phenomena elsewhere (§6.1.6.1.1; DE, §7.4.1.3). This is awkward for most versions of OT, but has a possible solution within ours. It appears to derive from differences in activation levels between segments. We return to this topic in §10.3.6.

Darryl was not followed as a research subject in the phonological intervention studies. However, his program targets included /f/ and /θ/ in coda position (building on their strength in onset), along with /k/ and nasal clusters in codas. These successfully circumscribed his defaults, and resulted in much greater intelligibility. He retained his lateralized production for some time, but final outcomes for that problem are not known.

8.5.2. CONSTRAINTS AND DEFAULTS IN CLEFT PALATE SPEECH

Surgical repairs of cleft palate do not always result in resolution or prevention of speech problems. Inadequate closure or habitual oral musculature patterns can result in either obligatory or compensatory substitutions, often involving glottals, pharyngeals, or nasals. Typical developmental substitutions frequently compound the intelligibility problem.

We give some examples here from Tia, who had insufficient velopharyngeal closure even after secondary surgery had been performed at age 4;5 to narrow the velopharyngeal port (pharyngoplasty). She was fitted with a speech bulb at age 5;10 (a dental appliance with a velar extension) at age 6 to occlude the nasal cavity. This was gradually reduced in size to encourage her to use her pharyngeal and lateral walls to aid in closure. Some of her patterns continued to persist, however, due to continuing inadequate velopharyngeal closure and to habit.

Tia, like many other cleft palate speakers, had a variety of substitution types. Some of these were a direct result of structural differences, and others were developmental, such as use of the glide [w] for /l/ and /ɹ/, and cluster reduction. We will concentrate here only on the structurally related patterns for manner and place of articulation.

8.5.2.1. Tia: Manner of Articulation

In the sonorant class, (nasalized) vowels, glides, and nasals were present. Obstruents were infrequent, particularly when she was not wearing the speech bulb, because she then had insufficient velopharyngeal closure and intraoral air pressure.

wagon	/wægn̩/	[weĩŋĩn]
zipper	/zɪpɹ̩/	[n̥ɪʔn̩]
scissors	/sɪzɹ̩z/	[n̥ɪʔn̩]
telephone	/tɛləfoʊn/	[n̥ɛfoũn]

Nasals or glottals often substituted for the obstruents. We will concentrate here on the nasal substitutions, discussing glottals under place of articulation below. Fully nasal substitutions were common, but sometimes (particularly with labials) she produced only partially nasalized obstruents, as in *bath* as [æ]. Such partially nasalized obstruents are not uncommon in cleft palate speech (and, in fact, Laver notes that even normal speakers vary in oral/nasal balance [1994:413].) Note that a contrast was maintained only some of the time between fricatives and stops, as in the word *bath*.

The use of nasals for oral consonants is obviously phonetically grounded in cases such as this. However, the patterns of nasalization are interesting, in terms of the variation in voicing, degree of nasalization, and nasal turbulence. In *wagon*, a segment with oral place and nasal airflow replaced /g/: [ŋ]. In *bath*, there was more oral than nasal airflow on both obstruents. But in *scissors* and *zipper*, the consonants had only voiceless (turbulent) nasal airflow. This is similar to the pattern of nasal snorts reported for a child without a cleft palate (Carolyn) in §5.5.3.4. The default was [+nasal], and almost all segments were fully or partially nasalized. When the target phoneme was [+s.g.], that feature survived in the output, so that the nasal was voiceless (a "nasal snort"). The nasal was also voiceless for voiced target phonemes that are high-amplitude fricatives. In §5.5.3.4, we suggested that the feature [+strident] might be best here, and that the turbulent airflow of the nasal snort allows the [+strident] feature of the grooved fricatives and affricates to survive. However, [+strident] segments had to be voiceless in Tia's speech. The following constraint ranking derives the observed patterns:

		RESULTS
Not(-nasal)	Survived(-nasal)	Nasal replacement of
NotCo-occurring(+ nasal, + continuant)	Not(+ nasal)	of oral consonants
	Survived(+ continuant)	
	Not(-continuant)	
Survived/LinkedUpwards(+ s.g.)	Not(+ s.g.)	"Fricatives" must be
Survived/LinkedUpwards(+ strident)	Not(+ strident)	produced, even if
		[+ nasal].
NotCo-occurring(+ strident, + voiced)	Survived(+ voiced)	Only [-voiced] nasals
	Not(-voiced)	can be [+ strident].

8.5.2.2. Tia: Place of Articulation

In Tia's speech the place feature that most often matched the target was [Labial] (like Howard's, 1993, subject), whether for stops, fricatives, or the glide [w] (see *wagon* and *bath* above).

fishing   /fɪʃɪŋ/   [fɪn̥ĩŋ]

However, even labials were subject to substitution patterns. Insufficient palatal closure resulted in manner changes: nasalization or nasal emission, as in *bath*. The /p/, like other stops, sometimes surfaced as a glottal stop, losing oral place altogether.

Coronal place had the fewest matches. Before the speech bulb was used, a variety of compensatory substitutions appeared for sibilants and affricates: nasals (see *zipper* above), glottals, or pharyngeals.

| sleeping | /sliːpɪŋ/ | [hiʔmĩŋ] | (Glottal [h]) |
| church | /ʧɹʧ/ | [tʊʕʕ] | (Pharyngeal affricate) |

Even with the speech bulb in place, coronals were often produced in a postalveolar (midpalatal) region, or as glottals.

| the | /ðə/ | [ɟə]~[ðə] |
| sit | /sɪt/ | [çɪt] |

The postalveolar (palatalized) substitutions usually distinguished coronals from velars and labials, although velars sometimes surfaced as palatals.

Although dorsal place was often maintained, velars sometimes surfaced as glottals ([h]), uvulars ([q], [ɢ]), or palatals ([c], [ɟ]), both before and after the introduction of the speech bulb.

Christmas	/kɹɪsməs/	[hɪhmʌ]
go	/goʊ/	[ɢoʊ]
goodbye	/gʊdbaɪ/	[ɟʊdbaɪ]

With the bulb in, dorsal matches unfortunately decreased (perhaps because of discomfort with the pressure of the wire on the velum).

8.5.2.3. Cleft Palate Speech: General Comments

The structural and functional aspects of Tia's oral mechanism predisposed her to use articulators not often used in English. Tia's substitution patterns are not uncommon for cleft palate speech. Posterior and nasal defaults are much more common than [+anterior] coronals. The larynx, the pharynx, and the nasal cavity are not subject to the same air pressure requirements as the oral cavity, and hence are optimal cavities for compensatory output. The feature [+nasal] is the default (**Not(-nasal)** ranked higher than **Not(+nasal)**). If a child wants to produce oral consonants, but cannot, pharyngeals and laryngeals (and to some extent, uvulars) are logical compensatory substitutions because they are produced below the level of the velopharyngeal port, and thus cannot be nasal. Such substitutions allow underlying [-nasal] to survive, but only with the help of co-occurrence constraints that allow glottals and pharyngeals to be nonnasal. Rankings for place differ from those of typical speech, in order to accommodate those high-ranked manner constraints. Constraints are ranked such that [Dorsal] and [-high] are the defaults (rather than [Coronal] and [+anterior]). **Survived(C-Place)** is ranked low enough that glottals often result.

For some speakers, compensatory patterns disappear after secondary surgery (pharyngoplasty). In such cases, the underlying phonological system may have been intact throughout, with phonetic implementation compromised by the mechanism. For other speakers (like Tia) surgery does not result in automatic improvement. Oral place consonants may be possible, but a retracted tongue position may persist, with concomitant posterior or even nasal substitutions continuing. A retracted tongue position and lack of velar closure may persist either because of "habit" (the ranking of the constraints) or because of predisposing physical conditions such as alveolar fistulae, scar tissue, maxillary abnormalities, or muscular atrophy, etc. Additional intervention is then needed. Sometimes speech therapy alone is sufficient. In Tia's case, secondary surgery and speech therapy were insufficient, both because of inadequacy of the mechanism and because of "habitual" patterns. The use of a speech bulb appliance helped her occlude the nasal cavity and extinguish some of her habitual patterns. She was most successful in producing a fricative/stop contrast, suggesting that faithfulness constraints had perhaps always been high-ranked for production of that contrast, but that mechanism inadequacy made it impossible phonetically. Place contrasts were less affected by use of the speech bulb, although coronals improved, and dorsals deteriorated (discomfort?). An additional pharyngoplasty resulted in decreased nasal emission, and, along with speech therapy, resulted in more consistent place and manner contrasts. However, she continued to have a retracted tongue position, ` with palatal placement for alveolar targets. Thus, she became a candidate for intervention using palatometry (computerized visual feedback).

8.5.3. HEARING IMPAIRMENT AND DEFAULTS

In the cases presented above, the assumption is that, for the most part, the children perceive the adult targets accurately and form underlying representations that are essentially adult-like. However, if a child has a significant hearing loss, underlying representations may or may not be like those of the target language, unless training or visual input (including text) teaches otherwise. Because consonants produced at the front of the mouth are most salient visually, defaults may be conditioned by visual perception in place of or in addition to auditory perception.

For example, for place, Stoel-Gammon (1988) notes a preponderance of labials in the babbling of deaf infants. Dora, a 9-year-old with a severe hearing loss and a cochlear implant, also showed a number of labial substitutions (Bernhardt, p.u.d.). The voiced labial stop [b] appeared for a variety of other segments (many of which were also labial, but not all).

on	/ɑn/	[ʔɑb]
no	/noʊ/	[boʊ]
la	/lɑ/	[bɑːo]
red	/ɹɛd/	[bɛːʔ]
wagon	/wægn̩/	[bæᵊdĩn]
mom	/mʌm/	[b̃ʌ̃b̥m]
throwing	/θɹoʊɪŋ/	[bɹ̃õʊ̃bĩn]

Syllabic [m̩] appeared (most unusually) for the vowel /iː/.

eat	/iːt/	[m̩t]
key	/kiː/	[hm̩]
leaf	/liːf/	[m̩f]
noisy	/nɔɪzi/	[bɔɪʑʔhm̩]

Dora did produce some coronal stops, fricatives, and nasals, but the less visible dorsals were absent (and coronals often replaced them, as in [dãm] for *gum*). The **Not(Labial)** constraint was lowest-ranked, allowing default insertion of [Labial]. **Not(Coronal)** was lower-ranked than **Not(Dorsal)**, allowing insertion of [Coronal] in some circumstances.

Not(Dorsal) ||| **Not(Coronal)** ||| **Not(Labial)**

In terms of manner, there were both typical and atypical developmental patterns. A typical pattern was the use of stops for some fricatives ([-continuant] being a typical default). The use of stops for all other categories is less expected, however, particularly at age 9. High ranking of **Co-occurring(σ-Margin→-sonorant)** prohibited sonorant consonants; underlying sonorants became obstruents, especially stops. Obstruents are rarely nasalized in any language, due to the high ranking of **Co-occurring(-sonorant→-nasal)**. Thus, when nasals became obstruents, they were fully or partially denasalized (as in *mom* and *no*). This requires a low enough ranking of **Survived(+nasal)** that [+nasal] can be deleted; if **Survived(+nasal)** were to be ranked too high, then [+nasal] would survive, leading either to a nasalized obstruent or to the additional survival of [+sonorant]. Since some nasalized obstruents did occur, there must have been some instability to the ranking of **Survived(+nasal)**. Nasal sonorants did occur in codas or when syllabic, due to high ranking of **Co-occurring(Rime→+sonorant)**.

We are unsure why syllabic [m̩] substituted for /i/, however. The restriction to /i/ suggests that /i/ was the default vowel (with no place features specified underlying). Unlike other vowels, there were no **Survived** constraints for place features to protect /i/. Perhaps V-Place deleted, and C-Place was inserted. Default C-Place was [C-Labial] (see above). The [+sonorant] feature of the vowel survived (high ranking of **Co-occurring(Rime→+sonorant)**), and so the output had to be a sonorant consonant. In English, that means a nasal or [l], but *[l] was not possible in this child's system. Thus, [m̩] resulted. This is derived via the following constraint ranking:

LinkedUpwards(V-Artic)	**Not(V-Place)**	**Survived(V-Place)**
Survived(V-Artic)		**Not(C-Place)**
Co-occurring(Rime→+sonorant)		**Not(C-Labial)**
Survived(+sonorant)		**Not(+nasal)**
Not(+lateral)		

Another unusual characteristic of her speech was the increased intensity and tenseness noted on coronal obstruent productions. (Sometimes the stops were produced as ejectives.) These segments were difficult for her to hear and produce, and perhaps she could only articulate them by using extra force. Such differences are not uncommon for deaf speakers, particularly after speech therapy (Ling, 1976).

Whether because of auditory or visual perceptual influences, or some other cause, deaf speakers may show alternate phonetic settings, such as shown above. Tongue position may be excessively retracted (Dagenais & Critz-Crosby, 1992) or advanced, or both (advanced tongue tip, retracted tongue body), resulting in unexpected defaults for vowels and consonants. Oral-nasal contrasts may be absent or inconsistent, as may sonorant-obstruent contrasts. Some deaf speakers may have a combination of unusual default patterns. Sharon, an adult with a severe hearing loss, had a retracted tongue position for velars ([k˃] and vowels), an often fronted (dental) articulation for coronals, hypernasality, and suprasegmental differences (Bernhardt et al., 1996). By using visual feedback from the palatometer, she was able to retract her tongue tip sufficiently to produce an accurate place difference for all of the sibilants, and to advance her tongue body sufficiently for the velars, thereby bringing the vowels forward, and modifying the pharyngeal resonance.

All of the speakers discussed in this section have had multiple constraints on speech production. We have attempted to focus on major aspects of their phonological and phonetic systems, in order to illustrate key differences and similarities. For the remainder of the chapter, and as a final example for the book, we present a full analysis of one child's speech.

8.6. DETAILED CASE PROFILE: DYLAN (AGE 4;6−5;0)

Dylan was a subject in Bernhardt's (1994b) study of nonlinear (multilinear) phonological intervention. At the beginning of the study, Dylan had moderate to severe delays in all aspects of phonological development, and at the end of the 16-week intervention period (48 sessions) he had age-appropriate intelligible speech. By presenting his case profile, we can therefore provide a comprehensive review of many of the aspects of multilinear constraint-based analysis presented in this book.

At assessment, Dylan had a severe phonological disorder. Overall, singletons matched the targets only 39% of the time. He had become withdrawn socially because of his feeling of embarrassment in communicative situations. Standard tests of hearing, language comprehension, and production showed average or above-average performance, and there were no structural or functional oral mechanism anomalies. Metaphonological skills were variable. He was able to segment sentences and disyllables into constituents. However, he was unable to segment monosyllables, or provide rhyming or alliterative words on request, at an age where at least some children (with or without phonological disorders) can perform such tasks. (See Bernhardt, Edwards, & Rempel, 1996.)

For phonological analysis, a standard set of objects and pictures provided stimuli for four primarily spontaneous single-word samples (of at least 164 words each). General conversation during the recording session provided extra words for analysis, many in connected speech contexts. Harminder Dhillon, the speech-language pathologist who conducted the intervention, elicited the samples at the beginning of the study and at the end of each of the three treatment blocks. The audiocassette tapes were narrowly transcribed at the University of British Columbia using International Phonetic Association (IPA) (1989) and supplemental diacritics. Point-to-point agreement between two independent transcribers for the single-word sample was 81% on the first pass. A third transcriber helped resolve differences, until 100% agreement was reached. For the connected speech sample, there was over 95% agreement between two transcribers on the first pass.

It is difficult to talk about one part of Dylan's phonological system without making reference to other parts, but of course we cannot discuss all parts simultaneously. Thus, we present a brief summary here as a background. In overview, Dylan's speech at assessment (age 4;6) was both typical and atypical of early phonological development. His most frequent word and syllable shape was CV(V). Where syllable codas were present, they were typically sonorants (primarily nasals). All basic places of articulation were realized. However, fricatives and liquids were rare, except for a few tokens of labiodentals and [l] (and the glottal [h]). When a target word had a coronal onset and a labial coda, the feature [Labial] migrated or assimilated from coda to onset. Those aspects of his system are typical of early phonological development. A more atypical characteristic of his speech was the use of onset clusters and multisyllabic words at a time when he had multiple restrictions on codas and features. Thus, his profile is another example of "chronological mismatch," both within the prosodic domain, and between the prosodic and segmental domains. (See Tables 8.3 and 8.4.)

The profile that follows primarily concerns the assessment analysis. We first describe the "framework" of the system (i.e., the word and syllable structure), and then proceed to discuss the details of feature production, finishing with the specific pattern of labial migration/assimilation. An overview of the intervention program and results completes the profile.

8.6.1. DYLAN: WORD AND SYLLABLE STRUCTURE AT INITIAL ASSESSMENT

Detailed analysis of prosodic structure typically begins at the level of the word. However, phrasal level influences on word production are also observable through separate analyses of connected speech and single-word structures. The connected speech samples provide an opportunity to observe any aberrations in prosody (in rate, rhythm, pitch, volume), plus any pervasive phonetic characteristics, such

TABLE 8.3   Dylan's Segmental Inventory at Assessment[a]

	Initial	Onset	Medial Coda	I.V.	Final
Nasals	$\underline{\text{m}}$	m	m	m	**$\underline{\text{m}}$**
	$\underline{\text{n}}$	n	n	(n)	**$\underline{\text{n}}$**
			ŋ		$\underline{\text{ŋ}}$
Stops	**pʰ**				
	p				
	b	**b**		b	
	tʰ	**(t)**			
	d	**d**		**d**	
	kʰ				
	g	**g**		**(g)**	
/l/	**l**		**(1)**		**1**
Glides				(ɹʲ)	
	$\underline{\text{w}}$	**$\underline{\text{w}}$**		**$\underline{\text{w}}$**	
	$\underline{\text{j}}$			**$\underline{\text{j}}$**	
	$\underline{\text{h}}$	**$\underline{\text{h}}$**			
			(ʔ)	(ʔ)	(ʔ)

[a] **Bold:** Both a match and a substitution; *Italics:* Substitution only; Underline: 75%+ match; Parentheses: 1–10% match. I.V. = Intervocalic.

TABLE 8.4   Dylan's Clusters at Assessment

Initial	Medial onset
mj[a]	
	kj[a]
pw	pw
bw	bw
ʙw	
tw	
dw	
kw	
gw	gw
(ɸw)[b]	
(vw)[b]	

[a] The only clusters matching adult target
[b] 2 tokens in sample

as hypernasality, hyponasality, excessive use of glottal fry, or unusual tongue position.

Throughout the study, Dylan had normal prosody in connected speech. Glottal fry was evident on many single word utterances in the first sample, but was less evident in connected speech, and decreased notably in subsequent samples. The

initial creakiness presumably reflected nervousness during the single-word elicitation, rather than any voice aberration.

8.6.1.1. Dylan: Word Length, Word Shapes, and Stress Patterns

Dylan's most frequent word type was a monosyllable of the CV(V) type. However, multisyllabic words with a variety of shapes, lengths, and stress patterns
appeared in both single-word and connected speech samples (imitated or spontaneous). In multisyllabic words, the most common syllable was also CV(V). Multisyllabic words in the sample can be characterized as follows:

1. Maximal word in terms of length: 4 syllables (5 tokens)

   elevator   /(ʔ)ɛləveɪtɹ̩/   [ʔɛ.wə.beɪ.ə]   S'-W-S-W

2. 3-syllable words: 16 tokens (including 10 compounds)

   Stress patterns: S'WS (9); S'SW (2); WSW (3), SWW (2)

3. Complexity of word shape: CVC.CV.CCV

   Santa Claus   /sæntəklɑz/   [dæntəkwɑː]

   Possible constraint: Binary(PrWd,Foot) (a maximum)

Dylan may have been able to produce words with more than four syllables, but
none occurred in the sample. In the connected speech sample (conceivably more
representative of his typical performance than the elicited single word sample),
91% of the words (309/340) were monosyllabic. The higher proportion of monosyllables in connected speech may have reflected the sampling context or the prag-
matics of attempting to make oneself understood, but may also have resulted from
interactive effects of phrasal length and word length.[9]

Coda and onset constraints (elaborated below) did not appear to be dependent
on word length, but rather, on more pervasive systemic constraints.

8.6.1.2. Dylan: Syllable Structure

Proceeding "down" the prosodic hierarchy, we examine

1. Maximum and typical onsets, both word initially and medially
2. Maximum and typical rimes, both word initially and medially
3. Context-free and context-sensitive onset and rime constraints, both for features and for prosodic structures.

8.6.1.3. Onsets

Dylan's words contained both singleton and cluster onsets. Percent Consonants
Correct (PCC) for word-initial singletons was 60%, which was high in compari-

---

[9] Crystal's (1987) bucket theory of language disability describes the interactive effect of various
levels of representation on each other for language processing. As the complexity of phrase structure
increases, phonological form may be simplified. Panagos and Prelock (1982) have demonstrated this
phenomenon experimentally for children with language and phonological disorders.

son to PCC for medial singletons (30%) and word-final singletons (24%). Onsets were obligatory. High-ranked constraints were:

σ►Onset
LinkedDownwards(Onset)

8.6.1.3.1. Simple Onsets

All consonants which he could produce appeared in word-initial onset position (with word-initial position being a strong prosodic position; see §4.7.1.4), given the following ranking: [10]

Survived/LinkedUpwards(Feature) ||| Not(Feature)

Glottal stop onsets occurred word initially and word medially. (The expected glottal stop onset to vowel-initial words was also present, as in adult English.) Glottal stop substitutions appeared frequently word medially. In this weaker prosodic position (noninitial position), **Not(C-Place)** was high-ranked in comparison with **Survived(C-Place)**, so only placeless (glottal) consonants were possible; all other features were lost, yielding [ʔ]. Underlying Root nodes survived, and so medial consonants were not deleted:

open   /(ʔ)oʊpn̩/   [ʔoʊʔĩn]

Survived/LinkedUpwards(C-Root)					Survived(C-Place)
Not(C-Place)		Survived(Features)
		Not(+ c.g.)
		Not(-continuant)

NotCo-occurring(Rime,C-Place) may also have been involved in suppression of medial consonants. (At least some word-medial consonants had coda properties, as we show in subsequent sections.)

8.6.1.3.2. Complex Onsets

Cluster production depended on rankings of sequence constraints and **Not** constraints for features. Stop-glide clusters were frequent, and fricative-glide clusters were rare. (No other clusters were produced.)

Stop-glide sequences were possible, whether as matches with the adult target or from substitutions.

flying	/flaɪɪŋ/	[bwaɪjẽŋ]
glovey	/glʌvi/	[gwʌʔʔi]
music	/mjuːzɪk/	[mjuʔɪ]
train	/tɹeɪn/	[tweɪn]

Sequence constraints prohibited a sequence of two continuant consonants (fricative-glide) or a sequence of two true consonants (obstruent-/l/). No consonants

---

[10] The onsets of the second syllable of compounds were also realized all of the time (e.g., *airplane* as [ʔɛ²pʲweɪn], and *bubblegum* as [bʌbʌgãm]).

could be deleted (high-ranked faithfulness to Root nodes and higher structure), nor could vowels be epenthesized to break up the consonant sequences. Fricatives that began clusters became stops. Liquids in second position in clusters became glides.

Survived(C-Root)	NotTwice(+ continuant)	Survived(+ cont)
Survived(Place)	NotTwice(+ consonantal)	Not(-cont)
LinkedDownwards(Place)		Not(+ cons)
Not(V-Root)		Survived(+ lateral)

The only underlying /s/-clusters to surface with two elements were /sl/ and /sw/, with [w] as the second consonant, and a bilabial stop or trill as the first consonant (double linking of [Labial]).

| sweater | /swɛtɹ/ | [ʙwɛtə] |
| sleeping | /sliːpɪŋ/ | [bwiʔĩn] |

These fit the general pattern for allowable clusters. (The assimilation in *sleeping* is discussed further in §8.6.2.4 below. Note that in this case only the [Labial] feature, and not the [+continuant] feature, showed assimilation, unlike in *three* and *flower*, discussed below.) On occasion, the /s/ deleted even before [w]:

| swim | /swɪm/ | [wɪm] |

This suggests some variability of ranking, in which [+continuant] cannot be deleted from /s/, but a fricative cannot be the first consonant in a cluster. Consequently, the feature is floating in the output, not linked to any syllable (and hence is not pronounced).

The /s/-stop clusters showed cluster reduction. The /s/ could not become a stop (yielding outputs like *[dnoʊ]), because of the high ranking of **NotTwice(-continuant)** in onset clusters; one consonant had to delete. The surviving consonant was [-continuant] (due to high ranking of **Co-occurring(σ→-continuant)**); this is a common pattern in child phonology (§6.1.6.1.2).

smaller	/smɑlɹ/	[mɑwɛ]
sticker	/stɪkɹ/	[dɪʔə]
snow	/snoʊ/	[noʊ]

Fricative-glide clusters were possible, but rare. Three clusters with labial fricatives and [w] appeared in the assessment cluster data.

| three | /θɹi/ | [vwi]~[ɸwi] | but also [wi] |
| flower | /flaʊwɹ/ | [ɸwaʊwɪʊ] | |

There may have been a single token of [+continuant] shared between the fricative and the glide. The two underlying singly linked tokens of [+continuant] in the fricative and the glide may have been merged into one doubly linked token. This occurs when **Distinct(+ continuant)** is ranked lower than **Not(+ continuant)**, with the result that the number of tokens of [+continuant] are minimized. Because there is just a single token of [+continuant], there is no violation of **Not-Twice(+continuant)**. However, it appears that **Distinct** was usually high-ranked, and so this was rare; it only occurred at all because of a slight instability in the ranking of **Distinct**. (See §7.3.1.7.1 and §7.3.1.2 for further discussion of this phenomenon in clusters.) The emergence of fricatives in word-initial clusters was considered an important goal in the intervention planning (see below).

8.6.1.4. Dylan: General Rime Characteristics

Rimes included long and short vowels and diphthongs, and some sonorant codas. Glottal stop codas were frequent.

8.6.1.4.1. Vowels

Lax (short) and tense (long) vowels and diphthongs were acquired.

sister	/sɪstɹ/	[dɪʔʔɪ]
dollhouse	/dɑlhaʊs/	[dɑl.haʊ]
tooth	/tuːθ/	[tʰuː]

Syllable weight was definable in terms of vowel moras, two for long vowels and diphthongs, and one for short lax vowels. (Diphthongs also have two V-Root nodes in a sequence; long vowels have only one Root node.) The child was faithful to the adult targets. The following ranking is indicated:

Survived(μ)	‖‖	**Not(μ)**
Survived(V-Root)	‖‖	**NotTwice(V-Root)**

Moras survived and could be inserted (for diphthongs). V-Roots survived.

8.6.1.4.2. Codas

Postvocalic consonants were limited to sonorants: nasals, a few instances of [l], and glottal stops. In single-word productions, 20% of monosyllable coda targets were realized. In the connected speech sample, 27% of codas were realized in monosyllabic words. (Nasals matched the target 16/19 times in single-word targets, and /l/, 3/8 times. In the connected speech sample, nasals matched 20/20 times, and /l/, 3/4 times.)

	gum	/gʌm/	[gʌm]
	sun	/sʌn/	[dɑ̃n]
	song	/sɑŋ/	[dɑ̃ŋ]
	all	/(ʔ)ɑl/	[ʔɑl]~[ʔɑː]
BUT:	tooth	/tuːθ/	[tʰuː]
	cake	/keɪk/	[kʰeɪʔ]
	eight	/(ʔ)eɪt/	[ʔeɪ]

Sonorant consonants are often preferred in codas (via high ranking of **Co-occurring(Rime→ +sonorant)**; see §6.1.12.2). However, obstruents could not be changed into sonorants ([+sonorant] could not generally be inserted), and so they deleted instead:

Co-occurring(Rime→ +sonorant) ||| **Not(+sonorant)** ||| **Survived(C-Root)**
Survived(+sonorant)

This constraint applied in multisyllabic words also. For word-final codas, there was a 45% match for consonant realization. Word medially, there was a 35% match. (We temporarily ignore the status of potentially ambisyllabic intervocalic consonants, and focus only on those consonants that appear first in cross-syllable sequences.)

flying	/flaɪɪŋ/	[bwaɪjɛ̃ŋ]
chipmunk	/tʃɪpmʌŋk/	[pʰɪʔmʌ̃ŋ]
broken	/bɹoʊkn̩/	[bwɔʊʔĩn]
seven	/sɛvn̩/	[dɛᵊm]
candle	/kændl̩/	[kʰændoʊ]
meatball	/miːtbɑl/	[miʔbɑl]
baseball	/beɪsbɑl/	[beɪʔbɔ]
dollhouse	/dɑlhaʊs/	[dɑlhaʊ]
numbers	/nʌmbɹ̩z/	[bʌ̃mbə]
finger	/fɪŋgɹ̩/	[bɪŋgɛᵊ]

Codas were proportionally more frequent in multisyllables than in monosyllables in the sample. This is probably due to sampling bias rather than particular constraints, however. There was a larger number of nasal targets in the multisyllabic words (particularly the morpheme -*ing*). Nasals appeared as word-final codas 44/48 times, and as word-medial codas 15/17 times. (The /l/ appeared as a coda 2/4 times word-finally, and 1/10 times word-medially.)

8.6.1.4.3. Coda Substitutions

Various compensatory patterns allowed surface realization of coda slots or features some of the time when target codas were not produced. Use of compensatory patterns increased surface realizations (SR) of coda slots to over 70% in monosyllables across both single word (77%) and connected speech samples (73%) (compared with 27% and 20% coda matches for actual target consonants).[11]

Compensatory patterns included vowel lengthening, glottal stop insertion, and labial feature migration (in forms such as *tub*). Sometimes more than one com-

---

[11] When codas are not realized, vowel lengthening and glottal stop insertion may or may not indicate marking of the coda slot with some phonetic material. Open syllables can be produced in different ways phonetically. Vowels can be lengthened as the syllable "trails off," or glottal stops can be inserted to bring an open syllable to an abrupt end for some phonetic or pragmatic reason. Consistent use of lengthening or glottal stop insertion in connected speech may be more indicative of compensatory patterns, however.

pensatory pattern appeared. For example, in *tub*, there was compensatory lengthening and migration of [Labial] to the onset.

bed	/bɛd/	[bɛˑ]	Diphthongization
big	/bɪg/	[bɪː]	Vowel lengthening
snake	/sneɪk/	[neɪə]	Vowel "lengthening" (V-Root insertion)
bath	/bæθ/	[bæʔ]	[ʔ] insertion
eat	/(ʔ)iːt/	[ʔiːʔ]	[ʔ] insertion
tub	/tʌb/	[pʰʰʌː]	[Labial] migration; Vowel lengthening
dive	/daɪv/	[pˈaɪ]	[Labial] migration

We are concerned here with vowel lengthening, diphthongization, and the insertion of glottal stop; see §8.6.2.4 for details on labial migration.

An obstruent coda consonant did not always disappear completely. It sometimes was replaced by a glottal stop. We do not think that the obstruent was
changed into a glottal stop. That would require insertion of [+sonorant], and we
noted above that that did not seem to happen. If it had happened, we would have
expected the consonant to show up as a nasal or lateral, and they never did. We
believe instead that the consonant's underlying timing unit survived; since this did
not happen every time, the ranking of **Survived(C-TimingUnit)** must have been
unstable. Since that timing unit must be linked to a segment (**Linked-
Downwards(TimingUnit)**), the deletion of the coda consonant caused a problem.
This problem could be resolved via the insertion of a sonorant consonant with no
C-Place (though underlying C-Place in nasals and /l/ was tolerated). Glottal stop
was inserted.

RESULTS

Survived(C-TimingUnit)	**Not(Coda)**	**Survival of coda timing unit**
LinkedDownwards(TimingUnit)		
Co-occurring(Rime→+sonorant)	**Not(+sonorant)**	**Rime = [+son], but not [+cons]**
NotCo-occurring(Rime,C-Place)		
Survived(C-Root)	**LinkedUpwards(C-Root)**	**Floating C-Root**
Survived(C-Place)	**Not(+c.g.)**	**Glottal stop inserted**
	Not(-continuant)	

This is not the only way to provide a segment to fill the timing unit. A glide
could be inserted, as it was in *bed* above. This would result from a similar ranking
as for Glottal Stop Insertion, but with **Co-occurring(Rime→V-Place)** also high-
ranked. The following detail needs to be added to that constraint list:

Co-occurring(Rime→V-Place)	**Not(V-Place)**
Survived(V-Place)	

This would cause V-Place to be inserted, and a glide with default vowel features
would result. This was unusual; this constraint was normally ranked low, but there

was some instability in the ranking. In general, no V-Place was inserted, and a glottal resulted.

There is no reason why a segment has to be inserted here, however. The timing unit could link downwards to an existing segment: the preceding vowel. That vowel would then be linked to two timing units, and would thus be long. This would result from the same ranking as for Glottal Stop Insertion, with the following detail added:

Not(C-Root) ||| **SinglyLinked(V-Root)**

If **SinglyLinked** is ranked lowest, then the vowel lengthens. If **Not(C-Root)** is ranked lowest, then a glottal stop is inserted.

These compensatory patterns were more frequent in monosyllables and in medial coda position of multisyllabic words than in word-final position of multisyllabic words: 13% more word-final codas in monosyllables, and 33% more word-medial codas. Compare *chipmunk* and *baseball* above, to *dollhouse* or *numbers*. The higher proportion of compensatory patterns may be a consequence of constraints on metrical structure: stressed syllables should be heavy (with a long vowel, diphthong, or coda), and unstressed syllables should be light (with a short monophthong and no coda); see §6.2.4. The following detail needs to be added to the above constraint listing:

Heavy(Stressed) ||| **Survived(C-TimingUnit)**
Light(Unstressed) |||

This made survival of the timing unit especially likely in stressed syllables, and especially unlikely in unstressed syllables. This also predicts an interaction with vowel length. Since long vowels and diphthongs make a stressed syllable heavy without a coda, there is less reason for the coda timing unit to survive; see §8.6.1.5 below.

Overall, word length and syllable stress constraints restricted the realization of coda obstruents. Sonorants, however, were less affected, even in multisyllabic words; this suggests that the difficulty underlying the deletion of coda consonants was related to features, not to whether a coda could be present (due to **Not(Coda)**). In the next two sections, we examine contextual influences on coda production further.

8.6.1.5. Dylan: Contextual Influences on Monosyllabic Coda Realizations

Monosyllables in the single-word sample were examined to determine contextual influences on coda production: (a) vowel length and (b) target consonant features. All types of substitutions and omissions appeared in the context of all vowel lengths and consonant features. However, some proportional differences suggested an influence of vowel length and target consonant features on realization of obstruents.

Glottal stop substitutions were more frequent after short lax vowels than after long vowels and diphthongs. Final consonant deletion was more common af long vowels and diphthongs than after short lax vowels. For monosyllables with short lax vowels, 14 out of 19 nonmatching forms had glottals (with only 5 deletions). For monosyllables with long vowels or diphthongs, only 4 out of 20 nonmatching forms had glottals (with 16 deletions). This is a significant difference ($\chi^2(1) = 8.24$, $p < .005$, Yates corrected).[12] Long vowels and diphthongs have two timing units, and thus already satisfy high-ranked **Heavy(Stressed)**. Codas were not necessary to make the stressed syllable heavy. Indeed, the presence of a coda after a long vowel or diphthong actually leads to the violation of another constraint: **Binary(σ,μ)**, prohibiting more than three moraic timing units in a syllable. If coda timing units must be moraic (**Co-occurring(Rime$\rightarrow\mu$)**), an output such as [buːʔ] violates **Binary(σ,μ)**. This leads to the full deletion of coda consonants after a long vowel or diphthong.

However, when monomoraic lax vowels were in the target, some kind of phonetic material was needed to fill the empty timing unit. Glottal stops were inserted for that purpose.

8.6.1.6. Dylan: Intervocalic Singletons

Word-medial onsets show patterns observed for both onsets and codas. In monomorphemic English words, intervocalic singletons preceding unstressed syllables are ambiguous as to coda or onset status (see §6.1.13). In Dylan's assessment sample, intervocalic singletons behaved differently depending on context. They always appeared before stressed vowels, even when stress was secondary. In these cases, they were behaving as onsets.

| sewing machine | /ˈsoʊɪŋməˌʃiːn/ | [ˈdoʊwinmæˌdin] |
| elevator | /ˈɛləˌveɪtɹ̩/ | [ʔˈɛwəˌbeɪə][13] |

Some of the same constraints and repairs noted for codas applied to intervocalic singletons, suggesting that they were acting at least partly as codas. Only ?% of intervocalic targets were realized as (nonglottal) consonants, a proportion ?ivalent to that for coda consonants in monosyllables. The nasal /m/, in con-?, always matched the target, just as it did in codas.

?ottal stop insertion was the most frequent repair pattern intervocalically. ?ix percent of the nonmatching forms had glottal stops. This compensatory ? was even more frequent than in word-final position (which had 21% glottal ? x vowels and long vowels were equally frequent before glottal stops (un-?as considered a lax vowel, in which case lax vowels were more frequent ?ttals). Because of the ambiguous status of /æ/, it is not clear whether ? ? vowel length effect, as there was in codas, or whether the glottal ?nore as a syllable divider (ambisyllabic) than a coda. Consonant de-

?quivalent numbers of tense vowels and diphthongs among the 16 words with deleted

?ial assimilation in *elevator* is also relevant here, but we return to that under the ?ation.

letion (with or without compensatory vowel lengthening) was much less frequent for intervocalic targets than for monosyllable coda targets. Glottal stops do separate the two syllables, preventing sequences of two vowel nuclei (**NotTwice (Nucleus)**).

There were other divergences between intervocalic consonants and word-final codas. Unlike in codas in monosyllabic words, intervocalic /n/ was missing in three of six tokens. A more notable divergence was the developing use of consonants other than sonorants intervocalically, particularly voiced stops [b] and [d] (and occasionally, [g]).

bubble	/bʌbl̩/	[bʌbə]
rabbit	/ɹæbɪt/	[wæbɪʔ]~[wæːʔɪʔ]
table	/teɪbl̩/	[pʰɛboʊ]
together	/tugɛðɹ̩/	[gɛdʊ]~[təgɛˀ]~[tʊgɛdɪ] (one after the other)
feather	/fɛðɹ̩/	[bʔɛdɪ]

It appears that [+voiced] was critical for medial consonant realization. Voiceless stops (other than [ʔ]) and fricatives did not appear word medially. (See *glovey*, *soapy*, *toothy*). There is a reason why [+voiced] might survive between vowels: plateauing. The two tokens of [+voiced] in the vowels may be merged into one doubly linked token (if **Not(+voiced)** is ranked higher than **Distinct(+voiced)**). To avoid an interrupted gesture (**Uninterrupted(+voiced)**), any intervening consonant must also link to that token of [+voiced]. In Dylan's system, assimilation was not permitted; a link could not be added from [+voiced] to a voiceless consonant. However, the underlying [+voiced] of a voiced obstruent could be merged into the single token of [+voiced] in the vowels. This allowed the voiced obstruent to survive and link to a syllable (which was impossible in codas); and the other features of the stop then also survived. The following ranking is indicated:

Survived(C-TimingUnit) ‖	**Not(+voiced)** ‖	**Co-occurring(Rime→+sonorant)**
Survived(+voiced)		**Distinct(+voiced)**
Uninterrupted(+voiced)		
Survived(Features)		
Not(Link)		

Although the glottal stop patterns discussed above suggested that intervocalic consonants were acting as codas, the voiced stops may have been acting primarily as onsets (or at least as ambisyllabic consonants). However, there was another pattern more consistent with coda than onset patterns (the use of glottal stops for all fricatives except /ð/). In word onset, fricatives were realized as (usually voiced) stops; but in codas, they deleted or were replaced with glottals. The replaceme of voiceless fricatives with glottals was consistent with the pattern for voicele stops in intervocalic position. However, it is not clear why medial voiced fricatiᵥ could not appear as [+voiced] stops, since voiced stops were possible wⁱ medially (and occurred as substitutions for voiced fricatives word initially). ꓕ

may reflect the relationship between faithfulness and activation levels (§4.7.1.5). In strong word-initial position, when [+continuant] deleted from the voiced fricatives, the segment was able to survive. In weak word-medial position, where the survival of consonants was marginal, the deletion of [+continuant] lowered the activation level of the segment so that it did not survive. Thus, when one feature was deleted, even the Root node was deleted. We have noted in several places that this is possible in our version of OT, but not in standard OT. We return to this issue in §10.2.3 and §10.3.6.

A final aspect of voiced stop production concerns the labials. As we discuss in §8.6.2.4, labials often survived via spreading (with assimilation violating **SinglyLinked(Labial)**, or with flop violating **Survived(Link)**). Although we have insufficient data to prove this definitively, it may be relevant that the tokens with intervocalic [b] also had labial word onsets, whereas [d] and [g] occurred in nonreduplicative contexts. (Compare *bubble*, *rabbit*, and *table* above with *together*, for example.) Double linking of [Labial] may have helped facilitate realization of intervocalic [b], a pattern we have seen before (particularly in Chapter 7, see e.g., §7.3.1.8.2).

In summary, intervocalic consonants generally had the same types of compensatory patterns and omissions as codas. The most important differences were the low survival rate of /n/ word medially, and the high survival rate of voiced stops. The voiced stops may have been behaving as onsets. Realization patterns for intervocalic consonants in Dylan's sample demonstrate that contextual factors and feature types play a role in the realization of consonants in this position (see also Bernhardt & Stemberger, forthcoming).

8.6.2. DYLAN: SEGMENTAL SYSTEM
AT INITIAL ASSESSMENT

In this section, focus is specifically on the feature system and its constraints, though we have already referred to a number of those constraints while discuss-
prosodic structure. Segmental inventories, substitution patterns, and feature
tories served as a basis for the following analysis. (Table 8.3 shows a seg-
inventory.)

Dylan: Manner Features

, glides, and stops were common. Fricatives, [l], and [ɹ] were rare. High-
ture constraints were as follows:

(+nasal)
-consonantal)   (for glides)
+sonorant)   (for glide and nasal targets; for substitutions for /l/)
rring(+continuant,-sonorant)   (no fricatives)
l)   (unstable)

ental patterns were present. Where prosodic structure con-
ult in deletion or glottal stop insertion, fricatives surfaced as

stops with the same place of articulation (when there was no labial assimilation). Both /l/ and /ɹ/ surfaced as glides.

1. Fricatives: Constraints for Stopping repair

NotCo-occurring(+ continuant,-sonorant)	Survived(+ continuant)
Not(+sonorant)	Not(-continuant)

   a. Delink [+continuant].
   b. Insert default value [-continuant] (yielding a stop).

2. Onset /l/ (underlyingly /ɬ/): Constraints for Gliding repairs

Not(+ lateral)	Not(-consonantal)
Survived(+ sonorant)	Not(V-Labial)
Survived(V-Dorsal)	Survived(Coronal)
Co-occurring(V-Dorsal, + back,-low→V-Labial)	

   a. Delink [+lateral].
   b. Insert default [-consonantal], [V-Labial] (yielding [w]).

3. Onset /ɹ/: Constraints and repairs

NotCo-occurring(Labial,Coronal)	Survived(Coronal)
Survived(Labial)	

   a. Delink [Coronal]. (This is the standard order of the **Survived** constraints; §4.6.1.)

8.6.2.2. Dylan: Laryngeal Features

1. [+spread-glottis]: Aspirated stops and [h] were present in the system. Hence this feature was established. The [+s.g.] feature may have been underlying rather than an inserted (allophonic) feature, because word-initial stop *substitutions* for fricatives were not aspirated. (See also §8.6.1.6.)

Underlying [+s.g.] could survive, but, because the system default was [-s.g.], [+s.g.] could never be inserted:

Survived(+ s.g.)	Not(+ s.g.)	Not(-s.g.)
		Not(-voiced)

Word initially, voiceless fricatives surfaced as voiced stops (high ranking of **NotCo-occurring(+ continuant,-sonorant)**). Voiceless fricatives are (allophonically) [+s.g.] in adult languages, and there are two possible ways that this could be brought about. First, the fricatives might be [+s.g.] underlyingly (as we posited for aspirated stops). However, since this would lead us to expect the fricatives to surface as aspirated stops, we believe that this is incorrect for Dylan's system. Second, the feature [+s.g.] could be absent underlyingly, and inserted in the output, due to high ranking for **Co-occurring(+ continuant,-voice→ + s.g.)**. Because [+continuant] did not survive in Dylan's fricatives, [+s.g.] was not inserted. The resulting stop received default [-s.g.]. In English, word-initial unaspirated stops are transcribed as voiced [b], [d], [g]; it is possible that Dylan produced these stops without true (pre)voicing. If they were truly voiced, it would have been due to another constraint: **Co-occurring(-s.g.→ + voiced)**. The following constraint ranking is indicated.

RESULTS

NotCo-occurring(+ cont,-son)		Survived(+ cont)	No fricatives
Not(+ sonorant)		Not(-continuant)	Stop inserted
Co-occurring(+ cont,-voice→ + s.g.)			If no [+ cont], no [+ s.g.].
Survived(+ s.g.)	Not(+ s.g.)	Not(-s.g.)	
Co-occurring(-s.g.→ + voiced)	(+ voiced)	Not(-voiced)	[-s.g.] and [+ voiced] inserted.

2. [+voiced]: The feature [+voiced] survived for adult stop targets word initially and medially. However, voicing features did not always survive (refer to §8.6.1.5). When [+continuant] and [+grooved] deleted medially, so did [+voiced]] (along with the rest of the segment).

3. [+constricted-glottis], [-spread-glottis]: The **Not** constraints for both of these features were low-ranked, allowing default insertion.

8.6.2.3. Dylan: Place Features

1. [Labial]: Labial nasals were present in all word positions. Labial stops survived in onsets. **Survived(Labial)** was high-ranked. **SinglyLinked(Labial)** was low-ranked (unstably), allowing assimilation of [Labial] from coda to onset.

2. [Dorsal]: Velar stops were present in onsets. The velar nasal inconsistently appeared in codas. (Occasionally, [n] appeared in its place.) **Survived(Dorsal)** was high-ranked. However, **NotCo-occurring(Dorsal, + nasal)** was variably ranked even higher (reflecting the difficulty of combining two nondefault features; see §5.5.4). Since the coda consonant had to be a sonorant, [Dorsal] deleted in /ŋ/.

3. [Coronal]: [Coronal,+anterior] was the default. **Not(-anterior)** was high-ranked, and **Not(+ anterior)** was low-ranked (although palatoalveolars were also prohibited by constraints on [+continuant]). Coronal stops appeared initially and medially (whether underlying stops or fricatives). Coronal nasals appeared finally and (variably) medially. However, [Coronal] could be replaced in labial assimilations, reflecting higher ranking for **Not(Coronal)** than for **SinglyLinked(Labial)**.

Survived(Labial) ‖ **Not(Labial)** ‖ **Not(Coronal)** ‖ **SinglyLinked(Labial)**
                                                       Not(Link)

This ranking shows that [Coronal] was the default place. However, the system preferred to spread [Labial] rather than to have [Coronal] in the output.

8.6.2.4. Dylan: Labial Migration/Assimilation

Only the feature [Labial] migrated or assimilated. All assessment sample utterances demonstrating [Labial] assimilation or migration are reported in Table 8.5.[14]

---

[14] One lexical item in the assessment sample did not show the typical pattern of labial assimilation (*them* as [dɛm]).

TABLE 8.5   Dylan: Labial Migration or Assimilation at Assessment

Assimilation: /m/ trigger

time	/taɪm/	[paɪ̃m]
thumb	/θʌm/	[bẽm]
sometimes	/sʌmtaɪmz/	[bẽmpaɪ(m)]~[bẽmpaɪ]
numbers	/nʌmbɹ̩z/	[bãmbə]

Labial migration: Labial stop trigger

tub	/tʌb/	[pʰʰʌː]~[pʰʌ']
tubby	/tʌbi/	[pʰʌʔi]
drip	/dɹɪp/	[bwɪᵊ]
sleep	/sliːp/	[bwiː] (2)
sleeping	/sliːpɪŋ/	[bwiʔɛ̃ŋ]~[bwiʔɛ̃n]
soapy	/soʊpi/	[boʊʔ.ʔi]
zipper	/zɪpɹ̩/	[bɪʔʔɪ] (2)
chipmunk	/tʃɪpmʌŋk/	[pʰɪʔmʌ̃ŋ]

Labial migration: Labiodental fricative trigger

twelve	/twɛlv/	[pwɛʊ]~[pʰwɛʊ]
dive	/daɪv/	[p'aɪ]
diving	/daɪv+ɪŋ/	[baɪ.ĩŋ]

Cluster assimilation: [w] trigger[b]

threw/through	/θɹuː/	[bwu]~[bwiu]
throw	/θɹoʊ/	[bwɔʊ]
throwing	/θɹoʊ+ɪŋ]	[bwowĩŋ]
sweater	/swɛɹɹ̩/	[bwɛʔdʊ]~[ʙwæ^dʊ]

[a] In number ([bãmbə]) the nondefault feature [+nasal] deleted, when [Labial] assimilated. This is somewhat unexpected since there were no obvious constraints against co-occurrence of [Labial] and [+nasal]. The presence of [b] in medial onset may have promoted a type of reduplication in this case.

[b] The [b] for /θ/ may have been an independent feature-based change rather than assimilation of [Labial]. However, *thing* was [dĩŋ], suggesting that the [b]'s did result from spreading.

When other constraints prevented [Labial] from linking medially and finally, the high ranking of **Survived(Labial)** caused it to link up to an initial coronal consonant. **SinglyLinked(Labial)** and **Not(Link)** were low-ranked, as shown in §8.6.2.3 above.

Labial migration/assimilation was directional (right-to-left) and only targeted coronals.

1. Directionality: The restriction on directionality indicated ill-formedness for [Labial] only in second position (weak prosodic positions). This would derive from high ranking for **NoSequence(Coronal...Labial)** (which is also high-ranked in adult English; see §7.4.1.3).

van	/væn/	[bæ̃ː]	(*[bæ̃m])
money	/mʌni/	[mʌi]	(*[mʌmi])

As mentioned earlier, labial nasals survived in codas (except in *game*). However, [Labial] spread to onset position to replace [Coronal] to avoid violation of the sequence constraint on place features.

2. Targets limited to coronals: Only (default) coronals were targets of labial assimilation or migration. Dorsals were immune.

	tub	/tʌb/	[pʰʰʌː]~[pʰʌˈ]
BUT:	glove	/glʌv/	[gwʌ]
	cup	/kʌp/	[kʌ]
	gum	/gʌm/	[g̃ʌm]
	game	/geɪm/	[geɪ]

Survived(Dorsal) was higher-ranked than **Survived(Labial)**. Thus, [Labial] could never replace [Dorsal]; migration and assimilation were not possible for dorsal targets.

Additional constraints are needed to account for other aspects of patterns involving [Dorsal]. [Dorsal] did not spread, even when the velar was deleted and a coronal was in the onset.

truck   /tɹʌk/   [twʌ]

The following ranking is indicated:

SinglyLinked(Dorsal)	‖	**Not(Coronal)**	‖	**SinglyLinked(Labial)**
LinkedUpwards(Labial)	‖		‖	**LinkedUpwards(Dorsal)**

The feature [Labial] could not be floating. If the segment that it was in deleted, [Labial] linked up to unspecified C-Place in onset (migration). The feature [Labial] could also be doubly linked between coda and onset (consonant harmony/ assimilation/spreading). The feature [Dorsal] could not be doubly linked, and so Velar Harmony was never observed; the system preferred to insert default [Coronal] rather than to spread [Dorsal]. Floating [Dorsal] was tolerated, and so [Dorsal] did not link to C-Place in onset even if the segment it was in deleted.

8.6.3. DYLAN: PHONOLOGICAL INTERVENTION IN BLOCK 1

As a subject in an intervention outcomes study, Dylan's intervention program was subject to a certain extent to random assignment of conditions. For each goal, there were four sequential sessions of therapy in a given treatment cycle (about 45 minutes each). The first two treatment blocks of the program had 16 treatment sessions (i.e., four goals), and the last, 12 sessions. Treatment sessions were three times a week for 16 weeks total. Given the short time frame and success of the program, Dylan's progress appeared not to be hindered in any way by constraints of experimental design.

Following the principles suggested by multilinear frameworks, intervention was targeted separately for segmental (feature) development and prosodic structure (with half of each cycle devoted to the two types of goals).

8.6.3.1. Dylan: Feature/Segmental Targets in Block 1

At assessment, Place and Laryngeal features were established at least at a basic level. Thus, Dylan's greatest needs were for fricatives, [l], and [ɹ]. Spreading of [Labial] was also a concern in terms of features, but was not addressed directly (see prosodic targets below).

1. /l/ and /ɹ/: According to the views held at the onset of the study, /l/ and /ɹ/ were considered members of the liquid sound class and therefore two variants of the same target. Because of the study design, treatment methodology included awareness and perceptual contrast activities only, with no elicited production or feedback for productions. (In a nonresearch situation, production activities may or may not have been included.)

2. Fricatives: One labial fricative (/v/) and one coronal fricative (/s/) were selected as targets (thereby including exemplars with different nondefault and default features). Because he could produce some clusters (stop-glide clusters), clusters were considered viable prosodic structures for practising fricative production. Thus, /s/ was targeted in CCV words, whereas /v/ was targeted in CV(/m/) words. Treatment methodology for fricative targets utilized imitation, attention to production cues, and feedback on attempts.

8.6.3.2. Dylan: Prosodic Structure Targets in Block 1

Dylan's greatest need for prosodic structure at assessment was coda production, both word finally and word internally. By strengthening non-word-initial positions, it was also hypothesized that labial migration might decrease (if it partially reflected weakness in prosodic structure). Intervocalic and word-final position were targeted separately, and with different treatment methodologies, in accordance with the overall design.

1. CVCV with focus on C_2 as a mora: C_2 targets = /n/ and [ɾ]; V_1 = short lax: Words with short lax vowels in the stressed syllable served as stimuli, and the second consonant was considered moraic (i.e., a coda). Treatment techniques drew attention to the same segment in monosyllabic codas (*pen, penny; Bet, Betty*). Rhythmic support was given to emphasize both the short lax vowel and the moraic coda consonants. The /n/ was an optimal segment, because it was already established in monosyllabic codas, and was partially established in intervocalic contexts. The flap [ɾ] was partially established, but /t/ and /d/ were not used word finally. Although he did not have to produce the CVC words with final stops, he was exposed to them in the context of the treatment sessions. (For further elaboration of treatment techniques, see Bernhardt, 1994c).

2. CVC with focus on C_2 as rime element: C_2 targets = /p/ and /k/; V=long or diphthong: Stimulus items contained long vowels in this condition; consequently, the coda consonant was not treated as moraic. Paired stimuli such as *ache/cake, oak/coke*, were used. Activities focused on word segmentation at the onset-rime division. VC units (rimes) were presented in alternating sequences: VC-VC-VC, which eventually formed CVC words (VCV to CVC). Other strate-

gies included lengthening of onsets prior to articulation of VC (rime) units ("*mmmmmmmmmm-ake*").

Across the two prosodic structure conditions, all available places, manners, and voicing contrasts were included. The variety of segments and contrasting methods created maximal opportunities for development of a coda and production of the labial [p] in second position.

8.6.3.3. Dylan: Results of Block 1 Intervention for Segmental Targets

There was a difference between liquids (awareness training) and fricatives (imitation/feedback training) favoring the fricatives.

1. Liquids: The only change was production of [l] in medial (intervocalic) position some of the time (3/10 matches).

television	/tɛləvɪʒn̩/	[tʰɛləbɪʔm̩]
yellow	/jɛloʊ/	[jɛloʊ]

2. Fricatives: Fricatives appeared in all word positions, even though they were targeted only in word-initial position. The proportion of matches for all fricatives was 39% (41/105), and for the targeted word-initial position, 32% (19/60). The segments which primarily contributed to these matches were the targeted phones [v] and [s], but also [ʃ] occasionally (as a substitution for /tʃ/ and /dʒ/), and (slightly devoiced) word-final [z] (as a substitution for /dʒ/).

The /s/ appeared in the (targeted) word-initial cluster slot 27% of the time (9/33), with matches for /sn/ (3/6), /sw/, (5/10), and /st/ (1/8). Where not a match, the /s/-slot was still vacant in clusters except in two cluster words with labial codas, *sleeping* ([bwipɪ̃ŋ]) and *sleep* ([bwi]). (For example, *snake* was optionally [s:neɪʔ] or [neɪ]; *slipper* was [wɪpə].)

Singleton coronal fricatives also appeared in word-initial position, showing generalization from the cluster training. Two tokens of singleton [s] appeared word-initially in *see* (2/7 attempts at /s/), and three in cluster realizations of /s/ and /z/ (undoubtedly artifacts of the clinical training which focused on clusters).

soap	/soʊp/	[s:boʊːp]	
zoo	/zuː/	[s:tu]~[s:du]	(2/4 attempts at initial /z/)

Otherwise, the stop substitution [d] continued. Minimal transfer was noted to medial position: four [s] tokens appeared, two as apparent metatheses.

icy	/(ʔ)ʌɪsi/	[ʔʌɪsːʔiː]
cagey	/keɪdʒi/	[kʰeɪːsʔi]
snaky	/sneɪki/	[neɪsːʔi]
starry	/staɹi/	[dɑsʔi]

Again, patterns of deletion and substitution were similar to those in the assessment sample, with the exception of more frequent use of [d] for medial coronal fricatives.

Generalization was most apparent word finally, even though fricatives had not been targeted in that position. (This is consistent with the general affinity of codas for fricatives; see §6.1.12.2.2.)

brush	/bɹʌʃ/	[bɹʌsᐠʃ]	½
buzz	/bʌz/	[bʌsː]	(½ attempts had [s])
facecloth	/feɪsklɑθ/	[beɪʔkwɑs]	
star(s?)	/stɑɹ(z)/	[dɑs]	(2/3)

The affricates were particularly noticeable, being produced as [+continuant] and [Coronal] 82% of the time (9/11). Although affrication was not yet emerging for the affricates, [-anterior] was developing, and voicing was inconsistent.

itch	/(ʔ)ɪtʃ/	[ʔiːʃː]~[ʔiːʃː]	
watch	/wɑtʃ/	[wɑʃ]~[wɑʔ]	(3 tokens with [ʃ])
church	/tʃɹɪtʃ/	[duːɪsː]	
page	/peɪdʒ/	[peɪː]	
cage	/keɪdʒ/	[kʰeɪːs]	
judge	/dʒʌdʒ/	[dʌz]	

The [+continuant] feature appeared 12 times for the other word-final coronal fricative targets (seven times for plurals).

eggs	/(ʔ)ɛgz/	[ɛɪz̬]~[ɛɪts]	
ice cubes	/(ʔ)ʌɪskjubz/	[ʌɪʔkʰjuːbs]	(1/3 had the cluster.)
papers	/peɪpɹz/	[peɪːʊˈz̬]	(2 tokens)
pages	/peɪdʒəz/	[pʰeɪdɪs]	
coins	/kɔɪnz/	[kʰɔĩːŋs]	

In summary, all coronal fricative and affricate targets except /ð/ had some realization as coronal fricatives in word-final position in this block. Where no fricative appeared, substitution/deletion patterns were similar to those in the assessment sample.

For the labial fricative /v/, only one token was present word-initially in the word/syllable "V". Medially, four of eleven targets matched, although only for one word (*TV*), with [b] used four times as a substitution, [w] once, and glottals twice. A [v] appeared in *glove* once word finally (1 out of 4 matches, with 3 omissions). Generalization did not occur for /f/, although stop substitutions appeared for /f/ word medially and word finally, suggesting a change in the right direction.

coffee	/kɑfi/	[kʰɑʔbi]	
laughing	/læfɪŋ/	[wæʔbĩŋ]	
leafy	/liːfi/	[sːwipʰʔi] (2)	
microphone	/maɪkɹəfoʊn/	[maɪʔəbouwə]	
leaf	/liːf/	[wiːpʰ]	
laugh	/læf/	[wæpʰ]	

In *leafy*, [+continuant] may have migrated from medial to initial position, but the [s] may also have been a mere overgeneralization of the /s/-cluster pattern (an artifact of therapy).

8.6.3.4. Dylan: Results of Block 1 Intervention for Prosodic Structure Targets

Notable gains were made in consonant realization for C_2 in both CVC and CVCV (50% gain for CVC, and 40% gain for CVCV). The proportional gain for prosodic structure was greater overall than for segmental targets (similar to outcomes in Bernhardt, 1990; Bernhardt et al., 1993).

1. Disyllabic targets with /n/ and [ɾ]: Disyllabic words had consonants rather than glottal stops for C_2 80% of the time. Including only intervocalic obstruents and /l/, consonants were produced 67% of the time (60 out of 90 tokens), compared with a 23% match at assessment. No mismatches were noted for treatment targets /n/ or [ɾ]. Other untargeted segments also appeared as C_2: more frequent use of [b] and [d] substitutions for fricatives, plus "new" phones [p], [s], [v], and [g]. Two of these transferred from the segmental condition ([s], [v]) and two from the CVC condition ([p], [g] from /k/). Coronal onsets appeared with labial intervocalic consonants, showing that labial assimilation and migration were decreasing.

tubby	/tʌbi/	[tʰʌʔi]~[tʰʌʔbi]
TV	/tiːviː/	[tiv(ː)i] (4 tokens)
diving	/daɪvɪn/	[daɪbĩŋ]
zipper	/zɪpɹ̩/	[dɪʔbə]~[dɪʔbʊ]
soapy	/soʊpi/	[doʊpʔiː]
chipmunk	/tʃɪpmʌŋk/	[pʰɪʔmʌ̃ŋ]
jumping	/dʒʌmpɪn/	[bwʌmʔĩŋ]

2. CVC with /p/ and /k/: For obstruent targets, 54% were realized with consonants in this block compared with none in the assessment sample. Thus **Co-occurring(Rime→ + sonorant)** was becoming lower-ranked. Treatment target /p/ matched 5 out of 6 times, and /k/ matched 5 out of 14 times. The only missing [p] was in *sleep* ([bwi]), still showing labial migration and coda deletion. Glottal stops usually replaced /k/ targets. Generalization was noted to voiced cognates /b/ (with a [p] substitution twice in three attempts) and /g/ (1 out of 3 tokens), but also to the CVCV target /t/ (5 out of 15 tokens), and to the segmental condition fricative targets [v], [s], and [ʃ] (see above). Again, labial assimilation was less frequent (*tub*: [tʰʌ]~[tʰʌp]), although still evident in test items *sleep* and *soap*.

8.6.4. DYLAN: THE CONTINUING PROGRAM

In a busy clinical practice, Dylan may have been dismissed at the end of Block 1 because of his significant gains. However, because he was in a study, and was soon to move to a remote community, the program was continued.

Block 2 had some of the same intervention targets and some new ones. Segmental targets included /l/, /ɹ/, palatoalveolars (/dʒ/, /ʃ/) and, for one session, labiodentals. Although /s/ was developing in some word positions, it was still weak or absent in others, and hence, another goal was the strengthening of /s/ across word positions. A new prosodic structure was CVCC (with nasal-stop and stop-/s/ clusters). The CVCC shape was considered a useful structure for promoting further development of codas, including complex codas.

By the end of Block 2, he showed mastery of CVCC, palatoalveolars except for untargeted /ʧ/, and word-initial [l]. Although not at mastery level, [s] was used in more contexts, and [ɹ] was produced word initially in 2 out of 8 tokens. He did not yet produce the interdentals. Block 3 (12 sessions) included a review of liquids, /ʧ/, and interdentals. Although he did not achieve 100% mastery for those targets, it was felt that he would continue to show progress on his own. (Block 3 also included metaphonological goals with respect to rhyming and alliteration. He still had difficulty with these tasks at the end of the study.) Two years later (with no intervention in the interim), the only residual errors were inconsistent use of [l] and [ɹ] in clusters. His literacy skills, on the other hand, were 3 years in advance of his grade level.

8.7. MULTILINEAR PHONOLOGICAL INTERVENTION: GENERAL COMMENTS

Dylan was one subject in a study designed to assess the utility of intervention in a clinical setting based on multilinear theories. The program was effective for Dylan as it was for all the children in the study (Major & Bernhardt, 1996). We cannot say whether Dylan and the others would have responded the same or better to a treatment program based on another theory or another type of application of multilinear theories, due to limitations of the study design. Future studies will address the comparative questions.

Application of the new theories builds on what has been learned over the last 20 years with previous applications. Recasting Dylan's intervention targets in phonological process terminology, processes targeted for elimination were:

Block 1:
    Segmental processes: Stopping (Stridency Deletion)
                         Gliding
    Structural processes: Final Consonant Deletion
                         Glottal Replacement
                         Labial Assimilation and Migration
                         Cluster Reduction (or Stridency Deletion)
Block 2:
    Segmental processes: Stopping (Stridency Deletion)
                         Gliding
                         Depalatalization
                         Deaffrication
    Structural processes: Cluster Reduction
                         Stridency Deletion

Block 3:
    Segmental processes: Gliding
                            Depalatalization
                            Deaffrication
                            Labialization
    Structural processes: Cluster Reduction

While those processes can describe his intervention program, the relationships between them are not transparent, nor do they give a comprehensive picture of his total phonological system. Multilinear constraint-based theories provide a deeper understanding of the patterns in his speech and the interactions in the system. For example, in terms of the feature system, underspecification theory provides an explanation for the asymmetries in his labial migration/assimilation. The default feature [Coronal] was vulnerable when the nondefault [Labial] had to survive (and codas were impossible). But [Dorsal] was not subject to labial assimilation because it too was a nondefault feature. This is a common pattern in assimilation (Stemberger & Stoel-Gammon, 1991). To give an example in terms of the prosodic system, mora theory provides an explanation for the related patterns in medial and word-final position relative to syllable weight.

Having a deeper understanding of the child's system facilitates intervention in a variety of ways, from target selection and program organization, to actual intervention techniques (word selection, strategies, activities).

8.7.1. PROGRAM ORGANIZATION

The intervention program can be systematically organized to target different parts of the system independently (capitalizing on strengths in one part of the system while bolstering weak areas in other parts of the system). This may involve a cycle of goals (as promoted by Hodson and Paden, 1991), or some specific type of sequence suitable to the particular child (easy-difficult sequences; alternations of prosodic and segmental goals, etc.). For children in the multilinear studies, feature and prosodic structure targets were independently targeted (and alternated) during each treatment block. Targets included "new" features and word shapes, new co-occurrences of features, and new word positions for existing features and segments.

Targets can be more precisely defined using multilinear terminology. For example, "cluster reduction" is a broad term, and does not delineate which particular clusters should be targeted. More specific goals name the different word shapes, for example, /s/CV, CVCC. Similarly, "final consonant deletion" is a broad term, whereas specific word shapes such as VC, CVC, CVCVC, etc., define more precisely what type of codas shall be targeted. Note that goals are also expressed positively. Rather than "undeleting" stridency deletion, targets are new nondefault features [+continuant] or [-anterior].

8.7.2. INTERVENTION TECHNIQUES

During intervention itself, word selection can also be sensitive to the particular goals. If there is a tendency to spread [Labial] from codas, and developing codas is the main goal, the clinician should probably not include labial-final words among the first words chosen for treatment.

Treatment strategies and activities can be and have been developed that exploit theories of syllable structure (onset-rime, mora), stress patterns, and feature combinations (Bernhardt, 1994c; Bernhardt, Ruelle, & Edwards, 1995), and provide the child with different ways to "break the code."

8.7.3. A NOTE ON CONSTRAINT RANKINGS AND DYLAN'S INTERVENTION

Constraint rankings may appear formally daunting but they are no more so than the complex ordered rules or processes of generative phonology. They do help determine the interaction of constraints in the system. Although Dylan's intervention program was not designed as an application of Optimality Theory (OT), we can reconsider the prosodic structure targets of the program in the context of that framework.

The two prosodic targets were CVCV and CVC with true consonants in the C_2 position. The stops /p/ and /k/ were specific C_2 targets for CVC word shapes, and the coronal stops (flap [ɾ]) and /n/ were targets for C_2 in the CVCV word shapes. The CVCV therapy targets had default place features; thus, concentration was on the survival of Root nodes with low demands for C-place. The coda consonants for CVC had nondefault place features; thus, concentration was divided between survival of nondefault features and C-Root, and inhibition of [Labial] migration or spreading (higher ranking of **SinglyLinked(Labial)**).

In retrospect, several factors may have converged on the successful outcomes:

1. Inclusion of both CVC and CVCV target word shapes in the same block, since both involved survival of C-Root nodes in nononset positions;

2. Inclusion of all C-Artic features in the C_2 position, since survival of C-Artic interacted with coda constraints, and [Labial] had some special properties of its own; and

3. Using an onset-rime approach to treatment for CVC with [Labial]. The stimuli presented for imitation were VC units; thus [Labial] could not spread to onset without violating the obligatory onset constraint (glottal epenthesis), which was highest-ranked. This facilitated coda realization.

Although there has as yet been no intervention application based on constraint ranking, future applications might benefit from further interpretation of this analysis framework. (See Stemberger & Bernhardt, 1997.)

8.8. CONCLUSIONS

Applying the complex theories we have been discussing in this book is not a straightforward task. Being able to learn new theories means having access to them, and time to digest the concepts and formalism. The complexity of linguistic and psycholinguistic theories appears to be increasing, as constructs from computer logic and information processing are incorporated into the analysis of human language. Even if a clinician has access to relevant linguistics and psychology journals, time and opportunities are limited for advancement in linguistic and psycholinguistic theories.

Those of us who have had the opportunity to apply multilinear theories have been very excited by the enterprise. Some of the particular reasons for our enthusiasm are the following:

1. The utility of organizing intervention programs in terms of well-defined prosodic structure and segmental targets and time periods
2. The match between therapy cycles (Hodson & Paden, 1991) and autonomous tiers
3. The concepts of underspecification and defaults which explains much of the data we see in child phonology, particularly those with protracted use of certain segments and pervasive substitution patterns
4. The detailed theories for prosodic structure at the subsyllabic, foot, and word levels, suggesting types of goals and types of approaches to intervention
5. The concept of feature hierarchy and co-occurrences as ways of thinking about segments and setting therapy goals that address different parts of the hierarchy, and combine features that do not yet co-occur
6. The concepts of constraints and repairs, and ranking of constraints
7. The positive framing of most goals, supporting a concept of additive learning

In conjunction with multilinear frameworks, we are excited by the concept of on-line processing from lexical representations. We see the introduction of OT as a step in bridging the gap between formal linguistic theory and psychological processing. For those of us working "on-line," but acknowledging the contributions of linguistic theory, any step in that direction is welcome.

9

ACQUISITION OF ADULT
ALTERNATIONS

Throughout this book, we have focused primarily on phenomena that are present in the child's speech but not in adult speech. We have principally addressed the acquisition of aspects of the adult system that do not alternate in the adult speech: the elaboration of prosodic structure, the acquisition of features, and the mastery of constraints on sequences. This focus takes us to those parts of the child's system where the ranking of faithfulness constraints is lower than the adult ranking, leading to faithfulness violations in the child's speech that are not present in the adult speech. Over the course of development, the child must rerank the faithfulness constraints higher, so that there are fewer and fewer faithfulness violations, until the adult system is reached.

However, there is more to phonology than nonalternating forms. Adult forms may involve alternations: the presence or absence of a schwa in the plural -s (*wash-es* /wɑʃ-əz/ vs. *walk-s* /wɑk-s/), or alveolar stops vs. taps (*sit* [sɪt] vs. *sitting* /sɪɾɪŋ/). Wherever alternations occur in adult speech, there is an accompanying lack of faithfulness with respect to some aspect of the morpheme's pronunciation. In the adult system, faithfulness constraints must be ranked low enough that they can be violated. The child must learn the rankings that lead to the same alternations and faithfulness violations that are observed in adult speech.

This raises an interesting possibility for acquisition: that the child's ranking of faithfulness constraints might sometimes be higher than the ranking in the target adult language. In some instances, the child might be *more* faithful to the underlying representation than adults are. In other instances, the child and the adult might both be unfaithful, but to different aspects of the pronunciation. In either circumstance, to reach the adult system, faithfulness constraints must be reranked *lower*, so that faithfulness can be violated more often.

Based on our discussions in previous chapters, the reader may have reached the conclusion that children tend to be less faithful to the underlying representation than adults do. This is partly an artifact of our focus on aspects of pronunciation that do not alternate in the adult system. If the child ranks faithfulness constraints as high as they are ranked in adult speech, or higher, the pronunciations will be adult-like. Many faithfulness constraints are in fact ranked high, and children remain faithful to some aspects of the phonology (such as the survival of [+nasal] in onsets) from the very beginning. Only when the faithfulness constraints are ranked *lower* than in adult speech can we observe a deviation from the standard adult pronunciation. Similarly, only when adults rank the faithfulness constraints low can the child's pronunciation deviate from the adult pronunciation by being *more* faithful.

The possibility that children's speech can show greater faithfulness than adult speech does not arise in all approaches to acquisition within Optimality Theory (OT). However, it is a prediction of the approach taken in this book, in which constraints are initially ranked in a semirandom fashion. Although faithfulness constraints are usually ranked lower than in adult speech, the semirandom ranking of the initial system leads to some faithfulness constraints being ranked higher than in the target adult language, for some children. However, a different approach is conceivable, in which the faithfulness constraints are always ranked low at first, and come to be ranked higher only if there is evidence for that higher ranking (Smolensky, 1996b). Within such an approach, we predict that children can never be more faithful to the underlying representation than adults.

Too little is known about children's acquisition of the alternations that are present in the target adult language. One reason for this is that most research on the acquisition of phonology has been done on English, which has relatively few phonological alternations. Even for English, however, we have insufficient data. Researchers studying phonological development tend to focus on the many interesting phenomena that are restricted to the child's speech. Researchers studying morphological development tend to ignore or control for alternations, without making them the subject of inquiry. Most of the emphasis of crosslinguistic work has been on morphology and syntax. Few of the papers in Slobin (1985) mention phonological alternations, even when they must have been prevalent in the data. Aksu-Koc and Slobin's (1985) paper on Turkish, for example, does not mention vowel harmony, which is integrally involved with the inflectional morphemes and particles that they study.

Although this is pure speculation at the present, we have certain expectations about which alternations should be acquired early by children. The easiest alternations to learn should be those that make use of the phonological tendencies of most young children (MacWhinney, 1978). If most children begin with a particular faithfulness constraint being low-ranked, and that same constraint is low-ranked in the target adult language, then the alternation should be acquired early by most children. A minority of children may learn it later, if that particular faithfulness constraint begins with too high a ranking. On the other hand, if an adult alternation requires low ranking for a constraint that is generally high-ranked in the speech of young children, the alternation should tend to be learned later.

We speculate that alternations involving deletion of an element should be acquired early and possibly without error. **Survived** constraints tend to be ranked relatively low in early child speech, leading to extensive deletion for most children. If the relevant **Survived** constraint tends to start out low-ranked, the alternation should appear early without any reranking. Since constraints are never reranked unless the adult language requires them to be reranked, those **Survived** constraints that are *correctly* low-ranked will never change. A child's early system should be a combination of correctly low-ranked **Survived** constraints and incorrectly low-ranked **Survived** constraints; only the incorrectly ranked constraints are ever reranked.

Similarly, assimilation is common in early child phonology (§7.4.2) and thus should be acquired early. A large proportion of English-learning children show reduplication (§6.1.4.2; §7.4.2), which can even resemble grammatical reduplication (§6.2.5.3.2). Consequently, grammatical reduplication might be expected to show up early when it occurs in the adult language; Maratsos (personal communication, 1994) has observed that young Tagalog-learning children seem to make use of reduplicating affixes early on in acquisition.

We first explore several alternations of English, about which the most is known. We then present short sections on the other languages for which information (albeit very limited information) is available.

9.1. ENGLISH

Despite all the research that has been done on English, relatively little is known about the acquisition of alternations that appear in adult English. We address the following alternations, beginning with ones that are (mostly) phonologically conditioned (palatalization, tapping, schwa insertion, and cluster reduction), and ending with ones that more lexically conditioned (suppletive allomorphy in closed class lexical items, and alternations associated with derivational affixes).

9.1.1. BETWEEN-WORD PALATALIZATION

In English, word-initial /j/ shows an alternation after the stops /t/ and /d/. Kaye (1988) notes that this is mostly limited to forms of the pronoun *you*: *you, your, yours, yourself,* and *yourselves*.[1]

you	/juː/	[juː]
need you	/niːdjuː/	[niːdʒuː]
want you	/wʌntjuː/	[wʌɲtʃuː]
found your football	/faʊnd jɹ fʊtbɒl/	[faʊɲdʒɹ fʊtbɒːɫ]

[1] And, in some dialects, *y'all* [jaɫ], *you'uns* [jʊnz], and *youse* [juːz].

The usual analysis of this alternation is that the alveolar stop and the palatal glide fuse into a palatoalveolar affricate, preserving the underlying voicing (or voicelessness) of the stop. (See §6.1.6.4 for discussion of the mechanisms underlying fusion.) The fused segment has most of the features of the /t/ or /d/, plus [Coronal,-anterior] (and possibly [+continuant]) from the /j/. In English, a nonanterior coronal stop must be a grooved palatoalveolar affricate; the required features are filled in automatically (due to **Co-occurrence** constraints).

Note, however, that the adult facts are ambiguous with other interpretations. We could use slightly different transcriptions, to reflect a different analysis:

need you   [niːd ʒuː]
want you   [wʌnt ʃuː]

In this analysis, the palatal glide becomes a palatoalveolar fricative, with voicing assimilated from the preceding alveolar stop. There are two segments in the output (faithful to the input), and the syllable boundary coincides with the word boundary (the usual case). This would involve the spreading of [-sonorant] from the stop:

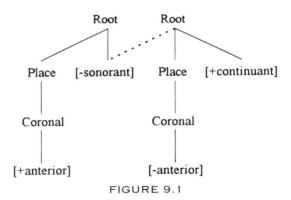

FIGURE 9.1

An alveolar stop spreads [-sonorant] to a following nonanterior coronal continuant (the glide [j]). The glide thereby becomes an obstruent: a nonanterior coronal fricative [ʃ] or [ʒ]. This assimilation is further accompanied by the assimilation of [voiced], since the resulting fricative is voiced after voiced obstruents but voiceless after voiceless obstruents. This may not be an accurate analysis of the adult pronunciation, which sounds like a (syllable-final) affricate. However, the phonetic difference between an affricate [ʤ] and a cluster [dʒ] is subtle: the stop and fricative portions are shorter in a true affricate than in a cluster. It cannot be taken for granted that young children acquiring English always are aware that an affricate is present here.

For either analysis, the alternation is motivated by constraints on sequences. The restriction to forms of the word *you* suggests that it occurs only in a weak prosodic domain, in which faithfulness constraints are often low-ranked: closed class lexical items (see §4.7.1.5). The affricative analysis may derive from the following ranking:

NotTwice(Coronal)	‖	Survived(Root)
Survived(-anterior)	‖	
SinglyLinked	‖	

Two consecutive tokens of [Coronal] are not permitted, whether singly or doubly linked. Instead, one segment deletes; the /j/ deletes, because faithfulness is ranked lower in weak prosodic domains. However, [-anterior] survives and links to /t/ or /d/, causing it to become a palatoalveolar afficate. The less adequate assimilation analysis derives from high ranking of **NoSequence(-sonorant... + sonorant)** and **NoSequence(-voiced... + voiced)**, along with low-ranked **Survived** constraints for [sonorant] and [voiced] in the weak prosodic domain; **Survived(Root)** is high-ranked, resulting in two segments in the output ([dʒ]). The restriction to /t/ and /d/ is unclear; it appears to be an instance in which assimilations occur only when other features are shared (see §4.6.1; §7.2).

Stemberger (previously unpublished data [p.u.d.]) found that Morgan did not initially produce this alternation. Faithfulness was greater than in adult speech. The sequence /dj/ surfaced faithfully as [dj]. Faithfulness constraints can be ranked higher than in adult speech.

When palatalization finally appeared in Morgan's speech, it appeared in a skewed way. As in adult English, it primarily affected variants of the pronoun *you*, though other /j/-initial words were occasionally affected. Unlike adult English, it occurred after all obstruents:

need you	/niːd juː/	[niːd ʒuː]
love you	/lʌv juː/	[lʌv ʒuː]
hug you	/hʌg juː/	[hʌg ʒuː]
want you	/wʌnt juː/	[wʌnt ʃuː]
like you	/laɪk juː/	[laɪk ʃuː]
keep you	/kiːp juː/	[kʰiːp ʃuː]

Palatalization was never observed after sonorant consonants like /m/ and /n/.

| comb you | /koʊm juː/ | [kʰoʊm juː] |
| spin you | /spɪn juː/ | [pʰɪn juː] |

Apparently, the child interpreted the adult alternation as the spread of [-sonorant] and [voiced], and generalized it to all obstruents (rather than just to /t/ and /d/). The process overapplied like this for about 2 months, then narrowed to the same environment as in adult speech. We do not know whether this overgeneralization is widespread or unique because of the lack of reports in the literature on acquisition of palatalization.

9.1.2. INTERVOCALIC TAPPING

In North American English, /t/ and /d/ are realized as the tap [ɾ] between vowels, except when the second vowel is stressed. Although [t] and [d] are possible in very slow or formal pronunciations of words like *water* [wɑtɹ] and *read* [ɹɛdi], pronunciations with a tap are far more common. In fact, evidence that words like *water* contain /t/ in the underlying representation (or even a stop rather than a tap) is limited to occasional formal pronunciations. Similarly, in words like *needed* and *waited*, stops are rarely used except in slow formal speech. There is evidence that /t/ and /d/ are underlying in words like *waited* and *needed*, because [t] and [d] are present in other variants of the morpheme, such as *need, needs, wait,* and *waits,* including the base form, which is in general the form with the greatest frequency (Francis & Kučera, 1982). Little is known about the acquisition of tapping, especially in morphologically complex words.

Formal discussions of this process are rare in the ·phonology literature. We assume that /t/ and /d/ become taps via the assimilation (plateauing) of [+sonorant][2] from the surrounding vowels:

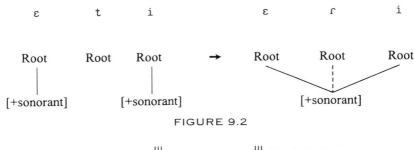

FIGURE 9.2

NotTwice(+ sonorant) ‖‖ **Not(-sonorant)** ‖‖ **SinglyLinked(+ sonorant)**
Not(+ sonorant)
Uninterrupted(+ sonorant) ‖‖‖

The low ranking of **SinglyLinked** allows assimilation to occur, and makes assimilation more optimal than inserting [-sonorant], in some circumstances. The two tokens of [+sonorant] in the vowels are fused into one doubly linked token, either to avoid repetition of [+sonorant] on the vowel plane (**NotTwice**) or to minimize the number of tokens in the output (**Not**). The high ranking of **Uninterrupted** does not allow this fusion unless the intervening consonant also becomes [+sonorant]. **NotCo-occurring** constraints restrict this spreading to the intervening consonant with only default place ([Coronal,+anterior]) and manner ([-continuant,-nasal]) features. Since sonorants are voiced (**Co-occurring(+ so-**

---

[2]This alternation cannot be viewed as just the spreading of [+continuant], since fricatives do not result.

norant→ + voiced)), the resulting tap is voiced. This makes the stop a nonnasal nonlateral sonorant consonant: the liquid [ɾ].

From 2;0 to 3;8, Gwendolyn (Stemberger, p.u.d.) produced all taps in monomorphemic words as [d], as in *water* ([waːdoʊ]). This is expected if adult taps in monomorphemic words are taken to be underlying /d/'s. However, she realized "taps" in bimorphemic words as either [t] or [d], depending on which appeared in other inflected forms:

| sitting | /sɪtɪŋ/ | [sɪtɪn] |
| needed | /niːdəd/ | [niːdəd] |

In bimorphemic words, a /t/ or /d/ is underlying in the base form, and the addition of the *-ing* and *-ed* affixes creates a sequence to which tapping applies in adult speech. The constraints were clearly not ranked in the adult ordering. If [-sonorant] were underlying in /t/ or /d/, we could say that faithfulness prevented the alternation from occurring. However, we assume that [-sonorant] is underspecified in stops. Instead, it appears that **Not(-sonorant)** is ranked lower than in adult speech: it is more optimal to insert [-sonorant] in /t/ and /d/ than to spread [+sonorant] from the surrounding vowels. This allows /t/ and /d/ to surface as stops, as in most other phonological environments. (In older, process-based theories, it would have been assumed that the child had simply not acquired the tapping rule. In the framework that we assume, our analysis appears superficially different, but it contains the same insight: there is only one treatment for /t/ and /d/, in all environments.)

Gwendolyn's pronunciations like [sɪtɪn] represent pronunciations that are rarely produced by adults. Thus, she did not likely copy adult pronunciations for these words. Instead, the /t/ and /d/ from other inflected (and unsuffixed) forms of these morphemes probably generalized to these forms. This demonstrates that different inflected forms of a morpheme are not stored as completely separate and noninteracting words.

By 4;0, Gwendolyn produced all intervocalic /t/'s and /d/'s as [d]:

| water | /wɑɾɹ̩/ | [wɑːdow] |
| sitting | /sɪtɪŋ/ | [sɪdɪn] |

One portion of tapping in adult speech was acquired: voicing. There was plateauing of the feature [+voiced] from the vowels. That this affected only /t/ reflects the effects of complexity: [+voiced] could not be combined with any nondefault feature unless that combination was present underlyingly (as in underlying /z/ or /b/). Gwendolyn's system still did not tolerate the liquid [ɾ], and consequently a stop was produced.

We might expect that children would differ on when "tapping" was acquired. Morgan also reduced taps in monomorphemic words to [d]. From the first attempts at words like *sitting* and *patted*, the /t/ was realized variably as [t] or [d] (just as it varies between [t] and [ɾ] in adult speech). This suggests that the voicing portion of tapping (plateauing of [+voiced]) had already been acquired by the time that bimorphemic words were produced. The variability between [t] and [d] in such words reflects an unstable ranking of the relevant constraints, however.

Despite the common status of taps in adult North American English, the acquisition of tapping has received no attention, especially in inflected forms. How most children acquire taps, in general and in inflected forms, is unknown.

9.1.3. SCHWA INSERTION

In English, schwa is inserted before -*s* and -*ed* suffixes in certain environments: between a strident (/s, z, ʃ, ʒ, ʧ, ʤ/) and -*s*, and between an alveolar stop (/t, d/) and -*ed*. This derives from the following ranking:

NotTwice**(C-Root)** **Survived(C-Root)** **NotTwice(+grooved)** **SinglyLinked**	**Not(V-Root)** **Not(σ)**

NotTwice$_{\text{Dependents}}$(C-Root)
Survived(C-Root)
NotTwice(+grooved)
SinglyLinked

Not(V-Root)
Not(σ)

Since there is voicing assimilation in these suffixes, the sequences /tt/, /dd/, /ss/, and /zz/ would result from suffixation, but geminates are prohibited by **NotTwice(C-Root)**. Additionally, a sequence of two strident consonants is prohibited. Neither consonant may be deleted, however. Nor may the two consonants be reduced to a single long segment. The low ranking of the **Not** constraints allows a vowel to be epenthesized between the two consonants, thereby eliminating the violations of the **NotTwice** constraints by making the consonants nonadjacent.

As noted in §6.12.1.4.1, children rarely produce more syllables than in the adult form: epenthesis of vowels is relatively rare. This suggests that young children might also have difficulty acquiring an adult process that involves the epenthesis of a vowel. Although the information is limited, we can say the following about the acquisition of Schwa Insertion. (a) Schwa Insertion is often absent in early speech. (b) Schwa Insertion is sometimes overgeneralized to forms that should not have it. (c) Schwa insertion can be present and interact with the deletion of the suffix consonant in ways that are difficult to account for within OT. We address each of these observations in turn.

9.1.3.1. Absence of Schwa Insertion

Just as Palatalization and Tapping may be absent from a child's speech, Schwa Insertion may be absent. MacWhinney (1978), for reasons internal to the theory that he was using, referred to this phenomenon as *affix-checking*; since this is the most commonly used term for this phenomenon, we will use it here. English-speaking children have difficulty with past tense forms when the base word ends in /t/ or /d/, and with plurals and present tense forms when the base ends in /s/ or /z/. Rather than producing target forms like *needed* and *kisses*, children often simply use the base forms *need* and *kiss* (Berko, 1958; MacWhinney, 1978; Derwing & Baker, 1980; Bybee & Slobin, 1982). The insight behind the term "affix-checking" rests on the observation that the phonological material of the suffix is similar to the final consonant of the base morpheme. It has been suggested that children do not add the suffix to these forms because the words already *seem* to end in that suffix. MacWhinney (1978) made this insight explicit, by including a mechanism in his model of acquisition and production that checks a word for affixes, before adding an affix; that mechanism prevents double-marking errors such as *walkeded* and *rockses*, in which the affix is added twice.

We suggest an alternative analysis. Children generally rank **Not(V-Root)** higher than in adult speech: a schwa may not be epenthesized. However, a consonant may delete.

dishes	/dɪʃ-z/	[dɪʃ]
bridges	/bɹɪdʒ-z/	[bɹɪdʒ]
needed	/niːd-d/	[niːd]
wanted	/wʌnt-d/	[wʌnt]

As noted in §6.4, across children, the suffix often deletes. The following ranking is relevant:

NotTwice_{Dependents}(C-Root)	‖	**Survived(C-Root)**
NotTwice(+grooved)		
Not(V-Root)		
Not(σ)		
SinglyLinked		

It is preferable to delete one of the consonants than to epenthesize a vowel between them.

Alternatively, **Survived(C-Root)** may be ranked high, as in adult speech. If **Not(V-Root)** is also ranked higher than the **NotTwice** constraints, a consonant cluster results:

dishes	/dɪʃ-z/	[dɪʃs]	needed	/niːd-d/	[niːdd]
bridges	/bɹɪdʒ-z/	[bɹɪdʒz]	wanted	/wʌnt-d/	[wʌntt]

Berko (1958) reports that 5-year-old children sometimes produce such forms, but it is unknown how commonly they occur (especially in spontaneous speech in nonexperimental elicitation). Faithfulness can apparently be more important in child phonology than in adult phonology, preventing the epenthesis of a vowel, even at the cost of consonant clusters that are highly unusual in English.

This analysis thus predicts that alternatives will exist and that not all children will do affix-checking (contra MacWhinney, 1978; Bybee & Slobin, 1982). Affix-checking would be universal among very young children only if **Not(V-Root)** were *always* ranked very high, preventing epenthesis from occurring. We assume that constraints are ranked differently by different children. Some children will begin with a relatively adult-like ranking of **Not(V-Root)**, allowing epenthesis to occur.

Just as some children use epenthesis to rescue unsyllabifiable final consonants from deletion (§6.1.4.2), some children acquire Schwa Insertion quite early. Amahl (Smith, 1973) showed early acquisition of Schwa Insertion, as did Gwendolyn and Morgan (Stemberger, 1994b). In Gwendolyn's speech, the -*ed* and -*s* affixes were first used during a period in which all of the following were deleted: word-final fricatives, unstressed closed syllables, and one member of a consonant cluster; see §6.1.12.1.3.1, §6.2.4.1, and §6.1.7.1 for discussion. Consequently, the -*ed* suffixes were used before the -*s* suffixes, but even -*ed* was used only after a vowel; it was phonetically impossible everywhere else (§6.4.1.5). The developmental sequence for -*ed* was the following:

		Point 1	*Point 2*	*Point 3*
cried	/kɹaɪd/	[tʰaɪd]	[tʰaɪd]	[tʰaɪd]
kissed	/kɪst/	[tʰiː]	[tʰɪs]	[tʰɪst]
needed	/niːdəd/	[niːd]	[niːdəd]	[niːdəd]
side	/saɪd/	[saɪd]	[saɪd]	[saɪd]
first	/fɹ̩st/	[foʊ]	[foʊs]	[foʊst]
bucket	/bʌkət/	[baː]	[bʌtət]	[bʌtət]

Since [d] was allowed in the coda as a singleton consonant only in stressed syllables at the earliest age, the -*ed* suffix was initially used in that environment (by 2;9, 100% of the time in spontaneous speech). In other phonological environments, the past-tense form was homophonous with the base form. The next relevant change in the child's system (at 2;10) was to allow unstressed closed syllables, and the [əd] allomorph of -*ed* appeared, used in an adult-like fashion (only when the base morpheme ended in /t/ or /d/). Only when coda consonant clusters began to appear in monomorphemic words (2;11) did -*ed* begin to appear when the base morpheme ended in some other consonant. Clearly, affix-checking was not involved here. This same developmental progression was observed for Morgan's -*ed* suffixes (Stemberger, 1994b), Gwendolyn's -*s* suffixes (Stemberger, p.u.d.), Morgan's -*s* suffixes (Stemberger, p.u.d.), and Amahl's -*s* suffixes (N. Smith, 1973). These data suggest that Schwa Insertion is used to resolve violations of **NotTwice**, but not to resolve violations of **NotComplex(Coda)**; outputs such as *stopped* [tʰaːpəd] never occurred. See §9.1.3.3 for discussion.

We have been implying that affix-checking is entirely reducible to a special type of cluster reduction, but it also has a more morphological aspect. Many researchers (Berko, 1958; MacWhinney, 1978; Stemberger, 1981, 1984; Menn & MacWhinney, 1984) suggest that the word-final [d] of *needed* [niːd] is doing "double duty." It is the realization of both the base-final /d/ and the /d/ of the suffix. Within OT, this arises because affixes are encoded as constraints (see §4.9):

PastTense(/d/,R)

This constraint requires that past tense forms end in [d]. Since the input form /niːd/ ends in /d/, leading to an output form [niːd] ending in [d], this constraint is satisfied without adding segments. However, the [d] in such an output corresponds to two sources: the affix and the base. Such multiple correspondence is not desirable from the point of view of communicative function because the tense marker in such words is encoded in a less salient way than in most other past tense forms. For communicative reasons, an affix should add phonological material:

Distinct(Base,Affix)

If **Distinct** is ranked high, then affix-checking cannot arise; producing *needed* as [niːd] violates that constraint. Given that a child has the phonological abilities to produce an affix (so that unstressed syllables and codas are possible in the output), a high ranking for **Distinct** prevents affix-checking. A low ranking for **Distinct** permits affix-checking.

Affix-checking may also emerge at a later point in development as a regression (Stemberger, p.u.d.). As noted above, Morgan marked *-ed* and *-s* affixes first after vowels, and then began using the syllabic allomorphs obligatorily in the appropriate contexts. On occasion, she would even produce doubly marked forms, which are possible only when Schwa Insertion applies to the second affix to make it syllabic:

| weareded | [wɛədəd] | trollses | [tʰwoːɬzəz] |
| dresseded | [dwɛstəd] | | |

Beginning at 2;10, as also noted below in §9.1.3.2, Schwa Insertion optionally applied after /s/ and /z/ in words like *kissed* and *used*. Possibly in reaction to both types of nonmatching forms, at 3;3, nonmatches reflecting affix-checking began to occur:

faint(ed)	[feɪnt]
horse(s)	[hɔəs]~[hɔəsəz]
sneeze(s)	[sniːz]~[sniːzəz]

For a period of a few weeks, affix-checking was quite common. In an informal elicitation task with plurals ("there are two . . ."), the affix was present only half the time. The child had been producing two types of forms in which a schwa was erroneously present: (a) after /s/ and /z/ in order to allow both the fricative and the *-ed* suffix to surface, with **NotTwice(Coronal)** ranked too high; and (b) in doubly marked forms, with **SinglyExpressed** ranked too low. Rather than reranking those constraints, however, the child apparently reranked **Not(V-Root)** higher, to prevent schwa from being epenthesized. An undesirable side effect of the reranking was to make Schwa Epenthesis only variably possible in environments where it is required in adult English. When epenthesis was not possible, the affix deleted. This prevented overgeneralization of Schwa Insertion and double marking, but at too high a cost. In a few weeks, affix-checking vanished from Morgan's speech. This regression demonstrates (a) that affix-checking can suddenly arise in systems where it has been absent, and (b) that children do not always rerank the "right" constraint (the one that would allow them to directly reach the adult ranking). Not all approaches to learning allow for the reranking of the wrong constraint (e.g., Tesar & Smolensky, in press), though the approach sketched in §4.12.1 does.

Constraints are initially ranked differently for different children. If they are ranked so that schwa cannot be epenthesized at all, affix-checking is present (though it may sometimes be entirely a phonological phenomenon, not a morphological one, as the name implies). If constraints are ranked so that epenthesis is possible (as they are in adult English), then Schwa Insertion is present in the child's speech, possibly as soon as unstressed closed syllables are allowed in the child's system (as in Gwendolyn's speech). Such variation between children is expected, given our assumption that the initial ranking of constraints is partially random, so that different children begin with different constraint rankings.

9.1.3.2. Overgeneralization of Schwa Insertion

Schwa Insertion is sometimes observed after segments where it would not be observed in adult speech. This most commonly involves the -s suffixes. In general, it appears that Schwa Insertion is generalized to two environments: (a) clusters with /s/ as a nonfinal member, as in *ask*, *wasp*, and *fist*, and (b) nonstrident final fricatives /f, v, θ, ð/. We address each in turn.

We sometimes find children (e.g., Morgan; Stemberger, p.u.d.) producing forms such as the following:

asks	/æsks/	[ʔæskəz]
wasps	/wɑspz/	[wɑspəz]
fists	/fɪsts/	[fɪstəz]

In standard adult English, the schwa is epenthesized to break up a sequence of two strident consonants. In the clusters /sks/, /sps/, and /sts/, the two strident consonants are not adjacent; consequently, no schwa is epenthesized. Why does epenthesis occur in child language? For /sps/ and /sks/, **NotTwice(+ grooved)** could be responsible, given tier-adjacency (rather than the root-adjacency that is relevant in adult English): there is nothing between the two tokens of [+grooved] on the [grooved] tier, since /p/ and /k/ are undefined for [grooved]. However, one must ask why the insertion of [ə], which is also undefined for [grooved], would help separate the two tokens of [grooved]. Further, in /sts/, the two grooved consonants are separated by a [-grooved] consonant. For **NotTwice** to be relevant, we would have to assume that (a) the intervening [t] is underspecified for [grooved] in the output (contra our assumption that all features are specified in the output), and (b) that **NotTwice** holds only within a coda (as a weak prosodic domain). If a schwa is epenthesized, so that the two consonants are no longer in the same coda, perhaps **NotTwice** is no longer relevant. This analysis may not work within OT, however.

A second possibility is that a particular **NoSequence** constraint prohibits sequences of three obstruents: **NoSequence(-son...-son...-son)** ("**NotThrice**"). If so, it is just a coincidence that two tokens of [+grooved] are present. In §9.1.3.1 and §9.1.3.3, we noted that epenthesis in clusters such as /ps/ (e.g., *cups* ?[tʰʌpəz]) is unusual, and that it was unattested in Morgan's speech at an earlier point. However, at the point at which epenthesis was observed for /sps/, /ps/ was faithfully produced as [ps]. Perhaps the constraints had been reranked enough so that epenthesis was used to rescue the suffix in any impossible cluster; since a cluster with three obstruents was the only unmastered type of cluster at that point, epenthesis was observed only there. We are unhappy with such an analysis, since it is our intuition that the repetition of [+grooved] is relevant here. But an analysis using **NotTwice(+grooved)** fails for technical reasons, and this analysis has the advantage of accounting for the facts.

The second common type of overgeneralization of Schwa Insertion is after other fricatives (again using data from Morgan):

baths	/bæθs/	[bæθəz]
giraffes	/dʒɹæfs/	[dʒɹæfəz]
loves	/lʌvz/	[lʌvəz]
breathes	/bɹiːðz/	[bɹiːðəz]

This could be treated as a misinterpretation of the conditioning behind Schwa Insertion in adult speech (after a grooved fricative or affricate). Perhaps the child has inferred that the relevant factor is that the preceding consonant is [-sonorant, +continuant].

Such an analysis does not explain why Schwa Insertion is generally not misanalyzed in this way for the -ed suffixes. We find:

walked	/wɑkt/	[wɑkt]	*[wɑkəd]
hugged	/hʌgd/	[hʌgd]	*[hʌgəd]
slipped	/slɪpt/	[slɪpt]	*[slɪpəd]
rubbed	/ɹʌbd/	[ɹʌbd]	*[ɹʌbəd]

This is just as straightforward a misanalysis: schwa is inserted when the final consonant is a stop. Yet, to our knowledge, no child has ever been observed to overgeneralize Schwa Insertion with -ed in this way. We need to explain why this sort of overgeneralization is unknown between stops and -ed, but common between fricatives and -s.

The answer lies in the types of consonant sequences that can be found in monomorphemic words. When considering which **NoSequence** and **NotTwice** constraints must be overcome to produce consonant clusters in adult English in simple, unsuffixed words, we find an explanation for why Schwa Insertion overgeneralizes in just the way that it does. In adult English, sequences of two stops occur in final and medial position (e.g., in *act*, *doctor*, and *helicopter*). Sequences of two fricatives, in contrast, are very rare in English. The few words that contain such sequences, whether in initial position (*sphere*, *sphinx*, *sthenic*) or in medial position (*asphalt*, *aesthetic*) are generally unknown to young children, and there are no such sequences in final position. Further, some of these sequences have been lost in many dialects: alongside standard *diphthong* /dɪfθɑŋ/, we find dialectal /dɪpθɑŋ/ and /dɪθɑŋ/. Further, the -th suffixes tend to turn into stops after fricatives. The ordinal numerals *fifth* and *sixth* are optionally [fɪft] and [sɪkst] (showing Stopping) in many dialects, or [fɪθ], [sɪkθ] (showing Fricative Deletion).

The only common source of sequences of two fricatives in English within a word is through the addition of the -s affixes to base morphemes that end in fricatives. This creates a sequence that is outside a young child's previous experience with uninflected English words. If the child (before using inflected forms) has had no reason to overcome a high-ranked **NotTwice([-sonorant, + continuant])** constraint, the child cannot produce a cluster such as *[fs]. This accounts for Schwa Insertion after fricatives. Schwa insertion would probably not take place between fricatives if Schwa Insertion were not also used between strident consonants, but the motivation for the particular overgeneralization is the lack of fricative–fricative sequences.

That being said, a child *may* generalize Schwa Insertion at least some of the time before the -ed suffixes. Morgan (§6.4.2.1) generalized Schwa Insertion in past tense forms; the clusters /st/ and /zd/ optionally surfaced as [səd] and [zəd] in inflected forms. In contrast, /st/ was reduced to [tʰ] when there was no suffix (as in *first*). See §6.4.2.1 for our explanation. (This overgeneralization of Schwa Insertion was limited to /st/ and /zd/. There was no epenthesis in /ft/ and /vd/, which were reduced to [tʰ] and [d]. (See §9.1.3.3 for discussion.) Since Schwa Insertion was conditioned by constraints on codas, we predict that it should have disappeared as soon as /st/ became possible in codas in words like *first*. This was the case; both *first* and *kissed* were produced with [st] at the same time, and pronunciations with schwa epenthesis immediately disappeared. Interestingly, /zd/ lagged behind; the same two realizations, [d] or [zəd], were used for another month, until the [zd] cluster emerged. This lag suggests that sequences of two voiced obstruents were impossible; [zd] emerged when **NotTwice([-sonorant, + voiced])** was reranked lower.

Schwa Insertion can be overgeneralized by children, but in a fairly conservative way. It can be used to break up a sequence of two fricatives, or a sequence of two coronal obstruents. In the next section we account for this conservatism.

9.1.3.3. Restrictions on Schwa Insertion: NotTwice

There is a problematical aspect to some of the data discussed in this section. Consider again Gwendolyn's data from §9.1.3.1:

	Point 1	Point 2	Point 3
cried	[tʰaɪd]	[tʰaɪd]	[tʰaɪd]
stopped	[tʰaːp]	[tʰaːp]	[tʰaːpt]
needed	[niːd]	[niːdəd]	[niːdəd]

The difficult aspect of these data occurs at Point 2, when Schwa Insertion is observed after /t/ and /d/ (as in adult English), but not after other consonants, where consonant deletion is observed instead.[3] Some impossible clusters (e.g., /dd/)

---

[3] An alternative analysis is to treat the allomorphs as suppletive. The /d/ and /əd/ allomorphs of -ed are stored independently, as are the /z/ and /əz/ allomorphs of -s. In that case, the child has learned the appropriate environments for the two allomorphs. The /z/ and /d/ allomorphs are often deleted for syllable-structure reasons. The /əz/ and /əd/ allomorphs do not have that difficulty, and so are used in an adult-like fashion.

show vowel epenthesis, but other impossible clusters (e.g., /pt/) show consonant deletion. A similar problem arises with some of Morgan's data in §6.4.2.1:

needed	/niːdəd/	[niːdəd]
kissed	/kɪst/	[tʰɪtʰ]~[tʰɪsəd]
laughed	/læft/	[læːt]

Impossible clusters such as [dd] and [td] show vowel epenthesis. Impossible clusters beginning with /s/ and /z/ show either vowel epenthesis or consonant deletion. Impossible clusters beginning with other consonants only show consonant deletion.

This is not a completely expected result. In general in OT, we expect to find more consistent resolutions of constraints (although see §7.5). If constraint rankings are unstably ranked, different repairs result. If **Not(V-Root)** is ranked higher than **Survived(C-Root)**, consonant deletion occurs. If **Survived(C-Root)** is ranked above **Not(V-Root)**, vowel epenthesis occurs.

In some adult languages (e.g., Berber: Guerssel, 1978), different resolutions of cluster constraints are found. For example, one set of clusters involves a **Not-Twice** constraint, while the other does not. The geminate /tt/ is reduced to [t] via consonant deletion, but /pt/ is resolved to [pət] via vowel epenthesis. The usual explanation (e.g., Hayes, 1986; Yip, 1988) is that the **NotTwice** violation is resolved via double-linking. If epenthesis then applies, we derive the following representation:

FIGURE 9.3

This gapped representation violates **Uninterrupted(C-Root)**. This violation of **Uninterrupted** can prevent epenthesis, leaving deletion as the only option (other than faithfully producing an unusual cluster).

The acquisition data also involve a **NotTwice** violation, as is evident from the repetition of /d/ in /niːd-d/ and /z/ in /roʊz-z/. The child could have resolved this violation by deleting the /d/ of *needed*; but epenthesis could occur in other clusters:

needed	[niːd]
stopped	?[tʰapəd]

To our knowledge, this pattern has never been observed in the speech of English-learning children. Gwendolyn's data is the opposite: epenthesis to resolve a **NotTwice** violation, but deletion elsewhere.

To derive this pattern of data, we must make use of the fact that the apparent "deletion" of an element is ambiguous: it can be absent from the output (and not pronounced) or it can be floating in the output (and not pronounced). The analyses in this section have assumed that elements are deleted outright, and are not floating in the output. We can see no way to derive Gwendolyn's data with outright deletion. However, if the suffix segment is present in the output but floating, epenthesis may occur, but only to avoid a **NotTwice** violation. This would derive from the following constraint ranking:

Expressed(PastTense)	‖	Not(V-Root)	‖	LinkedUpwards(C-Root)
NotTwice([-son,-cont,Coronal])				
NotComplex(Coda)				
Contiguity				

The high ranking of **Expressed(PastTense)** prevents the outright deletion of the suffix consonant, even though it cannot be integrated into the coda because only one consonant is allowed (**NotComplex(Coda)**). The final consonant of the base morpheme is given priority to link to the coda because it is contiguous to the preceding vowel in the input (**Contiguity**). The low ranking of **LinkedUpwards (C-Root)** allows the suffix consonant to be floating in the output, given that the higher ranking of **Not(V-Root)** prevents epenthesis to rescue the consonant. We derive the output:

FIGURE 9.4

However, this output is not optimal for the word *needed*. **NotTwice** constraints are violated by the presence of repeated elements, regardless of whether those elements are linked or floating. The floating /d/ after the linked /d/ of *needed* violates **NotTwice([-son,-cont,Coronal])** (defined on the adjacency of timing units). To avoid a **NotTwice** violation, a vowel is epenthesized to separate the two tokens of /d/, creating a new syllable to which /d/ can link (see Table 9.1):

TABLE 9.1

	/niːd-d/			/stɑp-d/		
	niːdəd	niːd\<d\>	niːd	tapəd	tap\<d\>	tap
Expressed(Past)			*!			*!
NotTwice		*!				
Not(V-Root)	*	*		*!		
LinkedUp(C-Root)					*	

The **NotTwice** violation is what causes epenthesis here, rather than the requirement that there be no floating segments in the output.

This analysis (which is the only one that we have been able derive in our system) crucially assumes that there may be floating elements in the output. As we noted in §4.5.1.1, there is no independent evidence that shows that floating elements can appear in the output. The two types of deletion are entirely theory-motivated, without any way to independently show that the distinction is real. We regard that as nonoptimal. This analysis, like our analysis of nonminimal repairs, may thus be viewed as suspect by some readers. We have not yet found a way around positing these two distinct types of deletion, however.

9.1.3.4. Restrictions on Schwa Insertion: Underlying Contrasts

There is one additional challenging type of data involving Schwa Insertion. Gwendolyn (Stemberger, p.u.d.) did not acquire velars in codas until 4;3. Until that time, velars surfaced as dentals (as did alveolars). The following past tense data were observed:

needed	[niːdəd]	hugged	[hʌdd]	([hʌdː])
hated	[heɪtəd]	worked	[woʊtt]	([woʊtː])
hided	[haɪdəd]	digged	[dɪdd]	([dɪdː])
sitted	[sɪtəd]	breaked	[bweɪtt]	([bweɪtː])

We give two alternative transcriptions for the forms in the column on the right, since the end of the word could be interpreted as long [tː] and [dː] or as the clusters [tt] and [dd]. When the morpheme had an underlying /t/ or /d/, Schwa Insertion was observed in the past-tense forms, as would be expected. This was the case both for words that take the *-ed* suffix in adult speech (and consequently undergo Schwa Insertion in adult speech) and irregular verbs like *hide* and *sit* when the child regularized them rather than producing the irregular forms (*hid*, *sat*). When the morpheme had an underlying /k/ or /g/, no Schwa Insertion was observed, even though these segments surfaced as dentals that sounded (and looked) identical to underlying /t/ and /d/. This was the case both for words that take the *-ed* suffix in adult speech (and consequently do not undergo Schwa Insertion in adult speech) and irregular verbs like *dig* and *break*, when the child regularized them rather than producing the irregular forms (*dug*, *broke*). The regularization data are particularly important, because they constitute forms that are created by the child rather than learned by observation. One could always maintain that *hugged* and *worked* do not contain a schwa because no schwa is present in the adult pronunciation. But that explanation fails to explain why there is no schwa in the regularizations *digged* and *breaked*.

The transcriptions of /k/ and /g/ as [t] and [d] were checked visually, by looking into the child's mouth while she produced these words. While we cannot rule out the possibility that the stops were velarized, they clearly showed full closure at the dental place of articulation. We would thus expect that **NotTwice** would be relevant, and that a schwa should be epenthesized: *digged* *[dɪdəd] and *breaked* [bweɪtəd]. Such pronunciations never occurred, and an explanation is needed.[4] (See Dinnsen et al., in press, for a similar chain shift involving Labial Harmony rather than an adult alternation.)

In rule-based theories, such chain shifts would be accounted for via rule ordering. The underlying sequence /td/ would be resolved via Schwa Insertion (to [təd]), while /kd/ would be unaffected. At a later point in processing, Velar Fronting would occur, and /kd/ would be altered to [td] (which would become [tt] via Voicing Assimilation). In OT, all changes happen in one step; we do not have the option of positing such an ordering of processes.

It seems impossible to explain these data in terms of constraints on output. Since underlying /t/ and /k/ have the same realization in the output, they would have to be treated identically relative to Schwa Insertion. We return to a discussion of chain shifts in §10.2.1.

There is a possible explanation for these data within our variant of OT. We assume that activation levels affect the ranking of faithfulness constraints (§4.7.1.5). The final activation level of [Coronal] may be lower for underlying /k/ than for underlying /t/. For /t/, there is no competition between default [Coronal] and a nondefault articulator, and activation levels can rise relatively unhindered by inhibition from a competitor. For /k/, there is lexical activation of [Dorsal], which competes with default [Coronal]; although [Coronal] wins out, it may pay the price of a lower activation level. If **NotTwice**$_{Dependents}$**(C-Root)** is sensitive to activation levels, perhaps the token of [t] or [d] from /k/ or /g/ may be too low in activation for the constraint to recognize it as a token of [t] or [d]. If that is the case, then **NotTwice** is not violated; consequently, schwa is not inserted. This is highly speculative, however.

This is not the only instance in Gwendolyn's speech in which underlying velars and alveolars were treated differently. We noted in §6.1.10.1 that final velars were deleted in some words (such as *big* and *leg*) at a point when final alveolars were never deleted. Deletion of the velar could also reflect a lower level of activation than for underlying alveolars.

9.1.4. CLUSTER REDUCTION

In a few clusters in adult English, simplification occurs in inflected forms. For example, /d/ is deleted from /ndz/ clusters:

| hands | /hændz/ | [hæːndz]~[hæːnz] |
| friends | /fɹɛndz/ | [fɹɛndz]~[fɹɛnz] |

Little is known about the acquisition of this alternation. However, Stemberger (1988a) reports the following for Gwendolyn at 2;1:

| friend | /fɹɛnd/ | [fɛnd] |
| friends | /fɹɛndz/ | [fɛn] |

---

[4]One unusual token of the word *worked* was observed: [woʊtət]. This involved both epenthesis of schwa and voicing assimilation for the suffix. Because it is a unique pronunciation, we do not provide an analysis of it here.

In words ending in /ndz/, both the /d/ and the /z/ were deleted, even though the /d/ was always present in the singular form. The deletion is due to the following constraint ranking:

NoSequence(-cont...-cont... + cont) ||| **LinkedUpwards(C-Root)**

This causes the outright deletion of the /d/ even in adult English. The ranking is variable in adult speech, but was stable in Gwendolyn's speech. In adult speech, there is a general tendency to simplify many types of complex clusters (e.g., Guy, 1991).

One aspect of these data may at first appear troublesome: the /d/ is deleted even though the /z/ is also deleted. At the time, the /z/ of the suffix could not be integrated into the coda after a true consonant, and so was deleted (§9.1.3.3). Recall, however, that the /z/ was not deleted outright, but was floating. This means that the **NoSequence** constraint can hold on the output, even though the /z/ is floating, since sequence constraints are not sensitive to whether the elements are linked or floating. As a result, the floating /z/ causes the base-final /z/ to be deleted, and neither the /d/ nor the /z/ appears in the pronunciation.

9.1.5. /g/ DELETION

In English, there are three monosyllabic adjectives that end in /ŋ/ and take suffixed comparative and superlative forms in -er and -est: *long*, *strong*, and *young*. (The only other monosyllabic adjective ending in /ŋ/, *wrong*, does not take -er or -est: *more wrong*, **wronger*.) All three adjectives show a medial /g/ in the comparative and superlative forms:

long   /lɑŋ/   longer   /lɑŋgɹ̩/

In some dialects, the /g/ also surfaces in some phrases:

long ago   /lɑŋ əgoʊ/
strong enough /stɹɑŋ ənʌf/

It has generally been assumed that the /g/ is underlying in these morphemes, but deleted in word-final position in most dialects (Chomsky & Halle, 1968).

Morgan (Stemberger, p.u.d.) often produced the /g/ in nontarget environments (at least by 2;11, and for at least a year after that point). The /g/ appeared obligatorily in all four adjectives that end in /ŋ/, before vowels and at the end of a sentence, but never before consonants:

Long, long, long, long ears.   [lɑŋ lɑŋ lɑŋ lɑŋg ɪəz]
Wrong!   [wɑŋg]

The /g/ appeared with the adjective *wrong*, but never with nouns or verbs that end in /ŋ/ (such as *sing*). The child differed from the target dialect (a) in producing [g] at the end of the sentence, and (b) in producing [g] whenever the next word began with a vowel, not just in phrases with *ago* and *enough*. Apparently, the child had determined that the underlying forms of adjectives contained /g/; nouns and verbs show no alternations in adult English, so the child took the underlying form to contain only a nasal (with no /g/). **NoSequence(+ nasal...-continuant, + voiced...C-Root)** was ranked high; this caused deletion of the /g/ before a consonant but not before a vowel. It should be noted that adults typically delete the voiced stop from /nd/ when the next word starts with a consonant (as in *stand beside*), but typically do not delete as often when the next word starts with a vowel (as in *stand around*; Guy, 1991); this **NoSequence** constraint is ranked high in adult speech. It was also ranked high in Morgan's speech. However, by relying on that constraint to delete the /g/, deletion did not occur at the end of the sentence (when no consonant followed). This example illustrates (a) that a child may show greater faithfulness than adults, and produce clusters that are impossible in the adult language (such as sentence-final [ŋg] clusters), (b) that the child may rely on the wrong constraint in order to achieve the adult alternation, and (c) that a child may overgeneralize some element of an underlying form (associating /g/ with the word *wrong*, unlike in adult English).

9.1.6. SUPPLETIVE ALLOMORPHY: MY/MINE

Some alternations are not generally productive, but must nonetheless be learned for particular lexical items. The possessive pronouns show a number of idiosyncratic differences depending on their syntactic environment; the forms are different in pre-nominal position than in a predicate (with the exception of *his* and *its*):

prenominal	predicative
my	mine
your	yours
our	ours
their	theirs
her	hers
his	his
its	its

Studies of early syntactic development often show the word *mine* used in pre-nominal position in phrases like *mine car*. Little is known about when the adult form *my* appears, or about the development of the other possessive pronouns. (Chiat, 1981, presents some information.) These alternations are not sensitive to phonological factors in standard adult English. We discuss them here, because of an instance from phonological development is which phonological factors helped a child produce the forms appropriately.

Stemberger (1993a) reports an interaction between Larissa's phonological constraints and the development of this alternation. At the time (1;10–2;1), the child's constraints prevented most sequences of consonants from appearing in the output, even if they were separated by a word boundary. For most sequences, including sequences of two bilabial consonants, a schwa was epenthesized to separate the consonants (see §7.4.5):

Book me.	/bʊk miː/	[bʊkə miː]
Come, Tony.	/kʌm toːni/	[hʌmə tʰoːni]
Diane's bike.	/daɪænz baɪk/	[daɪanə baɪk]
Come, Morgan.	/kʌm mɔɹgən/	[hʌmə moːi]

Epenthesis was optional when both consonants were dentals in the output (regardless of their place of articulation in the adult pronunciation):

Papa hot, too.	/pɑpə hɑt tuː/	[pʰapa hat tʰuː]~[pʰapa hatə tʰuː]
Run, Gwendolyn.	/ɹʌn gwɛndəln̩/	[wʌn naniːa]~[wʌnə naniːa]

Epenthesis never occurred when the second word began with a glottal stop or [h] (at that point in time), however, nor when the first word ended in a vowel or a diphthong. Stemberger argued that there were constraints against sequences of consonantal articulator nodes, in our terms:

NoSequence(C-Artic...C-Artic)
NotTwice(C-Labial)
NotTwice(C-Coronal)

Constraints on faithfulness (**Survived(Root)**) were ranked higher than these constraints; no consonant could be deleted. The constraint **Not(V-Root)** was ranked lower; consequently, a default unstressed vowel ([ə]) was inserted to separate the two consonants. Since vowels and glottals have no consonantal articulator node, epenthesis did not occur when those were present. The restriction of epenthesis to the coronal context can be explained by assuming presence of only a single [Coronal] node:

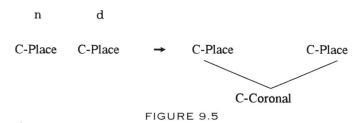

FIGURE 9.5

A single [C-Coronal] is inserted if **Not(C-Coronal)** is ranked higher than **SinglyLinked(C-Coronal)**; it is more optimal to have a single [C-Coronal], even if doubly linked, than to have two [C-Coronal] nodes. This optionality was not present when the two consonants were both bilabials; **SinglyLinked(C-Labial)** was ranked higher than **Not(C-Labial)**, and both underlying [C-Labial] nodes had to survive in the output.

The words *my/mine* showed an alternation. When the consonant at the beginning of the second word was a labial or a glottal, Larissa always used the form *mine* [maɪn], even in prenominal position:

| my horsie | /maɪ hɔɹsi/ | [maɪn hoːi] |
| my bike | /maɪ baɪk/ | [maɪnə baɪk] |

As expected, there was no schwa before the glottal [h], but there was always a schwa before bilabials [p, b, m]. Because *mine* ends in a dental, we would expect variability in the presence or absence of a schwa when the next word began with a dental (as observed for all other words ending in [n], such as *one* and *run*), and this was the case:

my doggie	/maɪ dɑgi/	[maɪn dagi]~[maɪnə dagi]
my snake	/maɪ sneɪk/	[maɪn neɪk]~[maɪnə neɪk]
my kitty cat	/maɪ kɪɾi kæt/	[maɪn tʰɪdi tʰat]~[maɪnə tʰɪdi tʰat]

However, unlike *every* other word that ended in a dental consonant, the word *mine* had one *additional* variant before words that began with a dental consonant (limited to [tʰ], [d], and [n] at the time):

my doggie	[maɪ dagi]
my snake	[maɪ neɪk]
my kitty cat	[maɪ tʰɪdi tʰat]

In this one word, the final /n/ was "deleted." Had this occurred with a word such as *one*, it would have been viewed as a lexical idiosyncracy of unknown cause. Here, however, it appears that the child was using the word *my* rather than *mine*, as is appropriate for the prenominal use of this possessive pronoun.

NotTwice(C-Coronal) allowed Larissa to produce a possessive pronoun that matched the adult target. Following Mester's (1994) OT analysis of suppletive allomorphy in Latin, we treat each of the suppletive allomorphs as a constraint. Mester argues that high-ranked phonological constraints can determine the choice of affixes. Consider Table 9.2:

TABLE 9.2

<MY> /dagi/	maɪn dagi	maɪnə dagi	maɪ dagi
Survived(Root)			
NotTwice(C-Coronal)	*!		
Not(V-Root)		*!	
MINE			*
MY	*	*	

Because the **MINE** constraint was ranked higher than the **MY** constraint, the child used *mine* almost everywhere. However, if **Not(V-Root)** and **NotTwice** were ranked higher than the **MY/MINE** constraints, the *my* allomorph was selected. Since there is no final /n/ in *my*, selecting that allomorph allowed the child to avoid violations of both **NotTwice** and **Not(V-Root)**. The ranking was unstable, however. When **Not(V-Root)** was ranked lowest, the variant [maɪnə dagi] resulted. When **NotTwice(C-Coronal)** was ranked lowest, the variant [maɪn dagi] resulted. Note that this same constraint ranking (instability and all) can never lead to the deletion of the /n/ in the word *one*, because *one* has no morphological variant without the /n/ (see Table 9.3):

TABLE 9.3

/wʌn dagi/	wʌn dagi	wʌnə dagi	wʌ dagi
Survived(Root)			*!
NotTwice(C-Coronal)	*!		
Not(V-Root)		*	
MINE			
MY			

With this ranking, a schwa can be epenthesized, but when **NotTwice(C-Coronal)** was ranked lowest, no schwa was present. Because the word *my/mine* was not present in this phrase, the morphological constraints were not relevant, and the high ranking of **Survived(Root)** prevented the final /n/ from being deleted.

Although there is no information about other children, we suspect that this pattern is infrequent. Larissa's phonology was unusual in that her sequence constraints had an effect on almost all sequences arising at word boundaries. These between-word constraints interacted with morphological constraints to allow adult-like use of the word *my*, but only in the optimal phonological environment. For most children, between-word sequence constraints are lower-ranked, and thus we would not expect this interaction to occur often.

9.1.7. SUPPLETIVE ALLOMORPHY: *THE* AND *A /AN*

In adult English, the articles *a* and *the* have two variants, the distribution of which is partially phonologically determined:

before a consonant:	a dog	[ʔə dɑg]	
	the dog	[ðə dɑg]	
before a vowel:	an apple	[ʔən æpḷ]	(~[ʔə ʔæpɫ̩])
	the apple	[ði æpḷ]	(~[ðə ʔæpɫ̩])

The presence of the /n/ in *an* and the /i/ in *the* are not phonologically predictable; for example, no /n/ is inserted in phrases such as *Laura asked* *[lɔɹən æskt]. There is a special suppletive variant before vowels. It should be noted, however, that the "preconsonantal" allomorphs also occur optionally before vowels (though a glottal stop is generally inserted in the second word, so that the [ə] of the determiner is still technically preconsonantal). Healy and Sherrod (1994) found that college students provide the preconsonantal variant before vowels a large percentage of the time.

Given that the prevocalic allomorph is not obligatory, we may still ask when children begin to use it. The acquisition of the [ðə]/[ðiː] alternation appears to be very late. Stemberger recalls being explicitly taught the alternation in second grade, at a time when it was absent from his own speech and the speech of most of his classmates. Larissa (at 7;5.9) stopped a conversation by ignoring the content of what her father had said to remark (in a very annoyed tone of voice), "Why do you always say [ðiː] instead of [ðʌ]?" To our knowledge, this has never been the subject of an explicit study, but we believe that the alternation is generally acquired between 8–10 years of age. We suspect that *an* is generally acquired much earlier (around 3–4 years of age), but we are not aware of any explicit studies.

Affix-checking can also occur with *a*. Gwendolyn (Stemberger, p.u.d.), at a point when *a* was otherwise used obligatorily as in adult speech and at which initial unstressed syllables were never deleted, produced no article when the noun began with a schwa:

> I have apartment. (*cf.* your apartment)
> You're adult. (*cf.* the adult)

In order to avoid a sequence of two identical unstressed syllables (**NotTwice-**$_{\text{Dependents}}(\sigma)$), the child violated **Distinct(Base,Affix)**, so that the syllable [ə] corresponded to both the article *a* and the first syllable of the base form.

There are also tendencies towards phonological conditioning of allomorphy in other closed class lexical items. The preposition *of* varies between pronunciations with /v/ ([əv]/[ʌv]) and without ([ə]/[ʌ]). Although both variants can appear before both consonants and vowels, our intuitions are that [ə] is statistically more likely before consonants (in phrases such as *a couple of dogs*) while [əv] is statistically more likely before vowels (in phrases such as *a couple of apples*). We are aware of no relevant studies in acquisition.

9.1.8. DERIVATIONAL MORPHOLOGY

Most of the adult phonology literature (e.g., Chomsky & Halle, 1968; Halle & Mohanan, 1985) has focused on alternations that are observed in derivational morphology, such as trisyllabic laxing, which is responsible for alternations such as,

> sane /seɪn/ vs.   sanity /sænɪti/

Some researchers have speculated about the acquisition of such alternations (Kiparsky & Menn, 1977; MacWhinney, 1978), generally with little data, but we will not address them here. Basically, such alternations are not acquired during the preschool years. They appear to be acquired around 10 years of age (B. A. Moskowitz, 1973; Myerson, 1976). The contribution of teaching in schools and of orthography cannot easily be assessed, and it has been claimed (e.g., Jaeger, 1984, 1986) that the alternations are acquired in ways that are quite different from the acquisition of the alternations that we have addressed in earlier parts of this chapter. We thus do not address such alternations, nor other lexically based "alternations" that appear only in irregular inflectional morphology (such as the /iː/ in *sleep* versus the /ɛ/ in *slept*).

9.2. OTHER LANGUAGES

There is limited information about acquisition of alternations in languages other than English. In this section we present information on the acquisition of alternations in the following languages: Hungarian, Sesotho, Spanish, Greek, and Hebrew. We address the languages in an order that reflects how much we know about each language.

9.2.1. HUNGARIAN

MacWhinney (1978) and Fee (1991) address several of alternations in Hungarian. The data are fairly sparse, especially below 30 months. However, something is known about the age at which different alternations are mastered.

One frequently investigated aspect of Hungarian phonology is Vowel Harmony: the vowels within a morpheme generally are all front vowels or all back vowels, and the vowel of a suffix generally has the same value of the feature [back] as the final vowel of the base morpheme. MacWhinney (1978) reports that diary studies show early mastery of vowel harmony. In a "wug"-test with children at various ages, beginning with 30-month-olds, MacWhinney found almost perfect adult-like performance on both known words and nonce words. Thus, this assimilation (motivated by **NoSequence(+ back...-back)** and **NoSequence(-back... + back)**) can be acquired by 2;6. Unfortunately, no data are available for younger children. Assimilation is common for consonants in early child phonology, suggesting that **SinglyLinked** is often low-ranked. Perhaps this makes Vowel Harmony fairly easy to acquire.

MacWhinney also notes that affixes may be subject to Rounding Harmony: the affix has back rounded /o/ after back vowels (*-hoz*), front unrounded /e/ after front unrounded vowels (*-hez*), and front rounded /ö/ after front rounded vowels (*-höz*). MacWhinney reports that children appeared to be using Rounding Harmony consistently by age 2;6, with more than 90% matches with adult targets by age 3;0. Again, nothing is known about younger children. The few errors that occurred usually involved failure of Rounding Harmony when the base vowel was a front rounded vowel:

/mör-höz/   [mör-hez]

This failure reflects a high ranking for **NotCo-occurring(V-Coronal,V-Labial)**; we noted in §5.6.2.1 that front rounded vowels tend to be acquired late. Here, underlying front rounded vowels were possible (high ranking of **Survived(La-**

bial)), but **NotCo-occurring** was ranked high enough to prevent assimilation. We note here that the constraint underlying the adult alternation is unclear, but may be **NotCo-occurring(V-Labial . . .**). A difficulty here is how to state that the second vowel has no [Labial] node. There would be no problem if [Labial] were a binary feature. **Aligned(Labial,R,PrWd,R)** can also account for the spreading, since it does not have to mention anything about the second vowel.

MacWhinney also addresses one pattern of consonant assimilation. In adult Hungarian, /v/ fully assimilates to any preceding consonant: /haz-val/ [hazːal]. This involves deletion of the /v/ but not its timing unit; the preceding consonant links to the stranded timing unit, becoming long. The constraint rankings are as follows:

NoSequence(C-Root...C-Root, + cont,Labial)	LinkedUpwards(C-Root)
Survived(C-TimingUnit)	SinglyLinked(C-Root)
Priority(Left,C-Root)	
Survived(Labial)	

This is nonminimal repair, in which the /v/ deletes; all features of the /v/ must survive, but the consonant is not required to link to a timing unit, and so it is not pronounced. MacWhinney reports that, by 2;6, children in his study showed matches for 88% of tokens, and by 4;9, very few mismatches. Some children occasionally overgeneralized the deletion, so that it occurred also after V-Root: /goː-val/ [goːl]/[goːal]/[goːlal].

In Hungarian, a vowel is inserted between a base-final consonant and a consonantal suffix. This is motivated by **NotComplex(Coda)** (preventing a complex coda) and **Expressed(Affix)** (so that the suffixal consonant may not delete); a low ranking of **Not(V-Root)** allows a vowel to be inserted between the two consonants. MacWhinney reports that children showed matches for 90% of tokens at 2;6, and very few mismatches by 6;8. Unfortunately, MacWhinney does not report what types of errors occur, although we expect they would be parallel to those that occur relative to Schwa Insertion in English (§9.1.3).

Another syllable-structure-related epenthesis involves the insertion of /j/ between two vowels (high ranking of **NotTwice(Nucleus)** or of σ▸**Onset**); this occurs in possessive forms. MacWhinney reports that children were unable to produce possessive forms in his study before 4;9, but inserted /j/ without error at that age.

Interestingly, there are some irregular forms in which /j/ is inserted between a consonant and the vowel of the possessive suffix, for no apparent phonological reason. Children seldom matched the adult target in such forms, simply leaving out the /j/. Alternations that are present solely for lexical reasons are apparently acquired late.

Another alternation that has little phonological motivation is the shortening of vowels that occurs before some (but not all) affixes that start with a vowel. MacWhinney reports that shortening appears to be rare at 2;6. In his samples, long vowels were produced in 20% of tokens even at 6;8. It is a lexical idiosyncracy of some suffixes that vowels shorten before them, and children find lexical idiosyncracies of this sort difficult to acquire.

In opposition to shortening are alternations in which a base-final /a/ or /e/ are lengthened before suffixes that begin with a vowel. Again, there seems to be little phonological motivation for this alternation. MacWhinney reports that children at 2;6 lengthened /e/ on only 59% of tokens, and that children at 6;8 still showed some forms that did not match the adult targets. However, errors did not occur with stem-final /a/, even at the youngest ages. Thus, some arbitrary alternations can be acquired early.

Finally, a medial vowel is deleted in adult Hungarian if (a) it is not base-final, (b) it is in an open syllable, and (c) it follows an open syllable. This is satisfied in (C)VCVC-V(C) forms. This conditioning is common in many languages. It allows a medial vowel to be deleted, provided that no complex onsets or complex codas are created. The constraint underlying the deletion is unclear. It might be one way to minimize the number of syllables. However, word-initial and word-final vowels are not deleted and medial vowels cannot be deleted if they are necessary for the expression of consonants. Vowels must survive in relatively strong prosodic positions (word initially and word finally), but delete in a weak position (word medially) provided that no **NotComplex(Onset)** or **NotComplex(Coda)** violations are created. In medial position, there would be high ranking of **Survived(C-Root)** and **Not(Complex)**, intermediate ranking of **Not(σ)**, and low ranking of **Survived(V-Root)**. MacWhinney reports that children at 2;6 rarely delete the vowel:

tükör-ök   /tykrök/   [tykörök]   (*cf.* base [tykör])

Even at 6;8, children deleted the vowel for only 70% of the adult target tokens. This appears to be another instance in which children ranked a faithfulness constraint (**Survived(V-Root)**) higher than it is ranked in the adult language (possible in our approach, but not for Smolensky, 1996b).

Although we have information about a number of alternations in Hungarian, the information is not as complete as is needed. We need more information about children's nonmatching forms. We need more information from their spontaneous speech. The "wug"-task is imitative, and children's performance may be different (sometimes better, sometimes worse, sometimes just different) on such tasks than in spontaneous speech. Hungarian data are similar to English data in showing that some alternations are acquired earlier than others. Assimilations and syllable-structure-related deletions and epentheses are often learned early. Alternations without clear phonological motivation tend to be acquired late. In some instances, children tend to rank faithfulness constraints higher than in the adult language, so that children show greater faithfulness than adults.

9.2.2. SESOTHO TONE ALTERNATIONS

Demuth (1993) addresses three tonal alternations in Sesotho, for one child sampled at 2;1, 2;6, and 3;0. She investigates the extent to which the alternations are present (and at which age), as well as whether the alternations occur in a different set of environments than in adult speech. The three alternations are Phrase-Final Lowering, High Tone Doubling, and High Tone Delinking.

One alternation is Phrase-Final Lowering, in which the final syllable of a verb carries a simple low tone when the verb appears at the very end of a verb phrase (whether sentence-final or sentence-internal). A verb that always ends in a high tone elsewhere is altered to end in a low tone. Demuth reports that the child produced the final low tone accurately at 2;1, for one environment: utterance-final position. She reports that the child generally did not produce the final low tone when the verb was sentence-internal, even though it was at the end of the verb phrase. Some improvement was seen at 2;6, and the child produced the low tone fairly consistently at 3;0. The alternation was acquired by 2;1, but the environment was incorrect: utterance-final, rather than VerbPhrase-Final.

Another alternation is High Tone Doubling: a high tone spreads to a following toneless vowel:

FIGURE 9.6

Spreading is limited to a single vowel; if there are two or more toneless syllables following the high tone, the H spreads only to the first toneless vowel. Demuth notes that in bisyllabic verbs (which constitute the majority of verbs), the assimilation is ambiguous between spreading to a single vowel versus spreading iteratively to all following toneless vowels; only long forms can differentiate the two analyses. Demuth reports that bisyllabic verbs follow the pattern: the H is linked to both syllables. In longer verbs (which were uncommon in her sample), some forms matched the target, but in other forms the spreading was iterative (and in a few forms there was no spreading at all). The child apparently did have **No-Sequence(H...L)** ranked high enough to motivate the spreading, but did not yet adequately limit the spreading to a single syllable.

A third alternation, High Tone Delinking, involves **NotTwice(H)**:

FIGURE 9.7

When a doubly linked high tone immediately precedes another high tone, the rightmost branch of the high tone is deleted, so that a low-toned vowel separates the two high tones. Demuth reports that the child varied, with some productions matching the adult targets, and some not:

| Match: | [ba^{H}ku^{L}ka^H] | /ba^{H}ku^{L}ka^H/ |
| Nonmatch: | [e^{H}tho^{H}tha^H] | /e^{H}tho^{L}tha^H/ |

This pattern is in conflict with High Tone Doubling. High Tone Deletion defines an environment that is an exception to High Tone Doubling: a high tone spreads to a following toneless syllable, unless the syllable after that has a high tone. The dissimilatory constraint (**NotTwice(H)**) is ranked higher than **NoSequence(H...L)** in the adult phonology. The child's ranking was inconsistent (since there was variation), but the more common ranking was for **NotTwice(H)** to be ranked lower, so that the assimilatory pattern won out over the dissimilatory one.

Demuth also addresses whether children have acquired the correct underlying tone for the verb roots (L versus H) (§5.6.4). Acquisition of the lexical tone is complicated by the alternations discussed here. The child initially showed many mismatches with adult targets; H-tone matched in 73% of tokens, while L-tone matched in only 35% of tokens. Demuth suggests that the child assigned H-tone by default to all verbs, but that does not explain why verbs surfaced with a low tone about a third of the time. It would seem that the alternations make it difficult for the child to sort out which tone is lexically associated with the verb root, leading to many mismatches with adult targets. By the end of the study, the child showed matches most of the time for verbs. Demuth argues that the child's increasing knowledge of the alternations allowed the child to sort out which tones were underlying for particular verb roots, but the details of this process are unclear.

Demuth's study is a preliminary one, based on a single subject, addressing only a few alternations, with limited data. It is not known whether the reported patterns are common or uncommon across Sesotho-learning children.

9.2.3. SPANISH

Kernan and Blount (1966) address the acquisition of Vowel Epenthesis in plurals in Spanish. In adult Spanish, the suffix -*s* is used after vowels, but -*es* is used after consonants. It is generally assumed that only /s/ is underlying, and that [e] is inserted after a consonant. This is similar to Schwa Insertion in English.

Kernan and Blount used a "wug"-task. Children (in three age groups: 5 – 7, 8 – 10, 11 – 12) and adults were asked to supply a particular inflected form for a given nonce word, where the sentential context forced morphemes such as plurals. Three plural forms were elicited:

/tifa-s/
/fepa-s/
/fetor/~/fetores/~/fetors/

Adults produced only the expected forms. Children produced /s/ after a vowel with almost no errors. However, /es/ was produced correctly less than half the time by children under 10 (and on only 53% of tokens at 11–12). The most common response was deletion of the suffix, but there were also many nonmatching forms in which [s] was added without the epenthetic [e].

The high rate of error productions for the /es/ allomorph reflects a high ranking of **Not(V-Root)**, which prevented the epenthesis of /e/. For most children, **Not-Complex(Coda)** was ranked sufficiently high that the suffix simply deleted (violating **Expressed(Plural)**). For a minority of children, **Expressed(Plural)** and **Survived(C-Root)** were ranked higher than **NotComplex(Coda)**. The child could not delete the /r/ of the base and had to express the plural affix. This led to a final consonant cluster that is not possible in the adult language. As noted in §9.1.3.1, English-learning children also show these two error types relative to Schwa Insertion.

9.2.4. GREEK

Drachman (1973) addresses one alternation in Greek. When a clitic that ends in a nasal precedes a noun that begins with a (voiceless) stop, the nasal assimilates to the place of articulation of the stop, and the stop becomes voiced. (Adult Greek does not have underlyingly voiced stops.) Drachman illustrates this alternation using the nominative (*o*) and accusative (*tom*) forms of proper names:

o Petros	/o'petros/	o Kostas	/o'kostas/
tom Petros	/tom 'betro/	ton Gosta	/toŋ'gosta/

Drachman reports that one child (Alexis at 3;4) varied between voiced and voiceless stops:

ton Taso   [to'taso]~[to'daso]

The nasal at the end of the clitic was deleted. This was a general property of nasal-stop clusters for this child. The initial stop variably remained voiceless.

Note, however, that the conditioning environment (the nasal at the end of the clitic) was deleted. In adult Greek, intervocalic stops are always voiceless. The voicelessness of the intervocalic stop after the clitic actually reflects the adult pattern of voiceless intervocalic stops. A second child (Thanasis at 2;6) produced the nasal at the end of the clitic and voiced the stop. However, in morpheme-medial nasal-stop clusters, the nasal was deleted and the stop was voiceless:

/stin kuzina/	[stiŋ guzina]	'in the kitchen'
/somba/	[saˈpa]	'stove'

This child has mastered the adult Greek patterns: voiced stop after a nasal, voiceless stops elsewhere. Since the nasal is deleted morpheme medially, the stop is not (allophonically) voiced.

Drachman reports that Alexis at 3;4 (who did not voice after nasals) nonetheless produced voiced stops when a morpheme-medial nasal was deleted:

dekapende   /ðekapende/   [ðekapeˑde]   'fifteen' (Alexis, 3;4)

Drachman suggests that the child interpreted the stop as underlyingly voiced. However, this could be a fusion: if the (redundant nondefault) feature [+voiced] of the nasal is specified underlyingly, it can survive even when the nasal deletes, so that a voiced stop is present in the output (§6.1.6.4). However,[+voiced] always survived morpheme internally, but survived only variably when the nasal was in a clitic; this may reflect a lower ranking for faithfulness in clitics (a weak prosodic position) than in base forms (a strong prosodic position).[5]

The pattern that would show a strong difference from adult speech would be a nasal followed by a voiceless stop. Drachman does not report such data. Thanasis's data reflect the adult patterns (but do not match the allophonic voicing of stops in particular words). Alexis's data more often preserve the allophonic voicing of the adult target, but this may alternatively be a fusion peculiar to the child's system. The ultimate import of these data are unclear.

9.2.5. HEBREW

Berman (1985) addresses the child's acquisition of several alternations in modern Hebrew. Unfortunately from our point of view, none of the alternations are phonologically predictable in modern Hebrew. They are the modern reflex of phonologically predictable alternations that appear in many Semitic languages, but more recent sound changes have obscured the phonological conditioning.

One alternation is spirantization: short stops after vowels become fricatives, so that /p, b, k/ correspond to [f, v, x]. This is the spread of [+continuant] from the vowel to the consonant and is due to a **NoSequence** constraint that prohibits stops after vowels. Historically, long fricatives were impossible (**NotCo-occurring** ($\mu\mu$,[**-sonorant, +continuant**])), and so the long stops did not spirantize: /pː, bː, kː/ were realized as stops [pː, bː, kː]. Further, the short uvular stop /q/ always remained a stop. The purely phonological conditioning of this alternation has been lost in two ways. First, there are no longer any long consonants in Hebrew, but consonants that were historically long never become fricatives in modern Hebrew. Thus, some /p/'s (historically from short /p/) become [f] after a vowel, but other /p/'s (historically from long /pː/) are always [p]. Second, the uvular stop /q/ is no longer a uvular, but is now a velar stop [k]. Thus, some /k/'s (historically from velar /k/) become [x] after vowels, but other /k/'s (historically from uvular /q/) are always [k]. From the perspective of modern Hebrew, alternations are idiosyncratic, occurring for only certain lexical items and inflectional categories.

---

[5] A third child (Chrisa at 2;3) is not discussed in enough detail to determine patterns. She reduced medial /mb/ to [b]. She had only single-word utterances and used no clitics. Initial stops sometimes voiced (/porta/ [bota] 'door'), but the reason is unclear.

Berman reports that these alternations cause great difficulties for children. There is chaos. Children seem to "settle on one invariant consonantal root for each lexeme, taking a given word as their point of reference—the choice of this word probably being due to input factors of the relative familiarity of this word compared with others from the same root" (1985:282). Thus, the child produces either a fricative or a stop, without alternation in any particular morpheme. Further, when the alternations do begin to be learned, they often overapply to those morphemes that historically involved nonalternating segments.

Because of their phonological opacity, these alternations tell us little about the acquisition of phonological alternations in general. At best, they tell us that any alternation that relies heavily on lexical factors will be difficult to learn. They perhaps have more to say about learning. Children apparently have a tendency to have a single representation for a given morpheme, and will tend to overgeneralize one allomorph when there are phonologically unpredictable alternations. From a detailed study of Hebrew acquisition (which has yet to be undertaken), we might learn something about the acquisition of underlying representations.[6] However, such data tell us little about the acquisition of phonology for speech production.

9.3. SUMMARY AND CONCLUSIONS

As noted at the beginning of this chapter, relatively little is known about how children acquire the alternations that are present in the adult language. The primary focus in research on phonological development has been on the child's lack of faithfulness to adult pronunciations. However, when faithfulness constraints are ranked low in adult speech, leading to alternations, the child may rank faithfulness higher than the adult. Sometimes the alternations (tapping, Schwa Insertion) are simply absent. In other instances, they are overgeneralized. In rare instances, children appear to have *greater* capabilities than adults and to be *more* faithful to underlying representations than adults are, although this is unusual.

Theories of acquisition must be able to account for the fact that a child can show greater faithfulness than adults do. In our approach to OT, we assume that the initial constraint ranking is semirandom. This should lead to instances in which the child's faithfulness constraints are sometimes ranked lower than they are in adult speech, but sometimes ranked higher. We take the data in this section as evidence for our approach, and counterevidence for the alternative (that all children begin with the same initial ranking, in which faithfulness is always ranked lower than in adult speech).

---

[6] Similar suppletion occurs in French (e.g., /bwa-/~/byv-/ 'drink'), and Clark (1985) reports similar variation in terms of which stem is chosen by the child.

10

DISCUSSION
AND CONCLUSIONS

In this book, we have explored the phenomena of phonological development in depth. We have shown how the patterns of child phonology can be accounted for within an approach that makes use of multilinear phonology and Optimality Theory (OT). In this final chapter, we would like to discuss three general topics in an overview of the book. First, we address phenomena that our approach cannot and should not account for (because the phenomena do not concern speech production, which has been our focus). Second, we address phenomena that challenged our approach. Finally, we discuss implications for the phonological system made by the phonological patterns observed in child speech. In Chapter 1, we noted that we view the relationship between child phonology and adult phonology as a two-way street. Phonological development casts some light on various issues (such as the universality of features). Throughout this book, we have traveled that street from phonology to child language; in this chapter, we travel back from child language to phonology.

10.1. BEYOND THE SCOPE OF THE THEORY

A complete picture of the phonological behavior of human beings has many components. In this book, we have focused on only one part of that picture: on speech production. Some phenomena in child phonology have their roots in physiology, in perception, and in other aspects of cognitive processing. In this section, we briefly address some phenomena that we feel our approach does not and *should* not account for.

10.1.1. EASE OF ARTICULATION: PHONETIC GROUNDING

In Chapter 2, we discussed phonetic grounding and how to make constraint rankings sensitive to grounding. This allows us to use a definition of articulatory difficulty that is independent of the phonology, but derives from the anatomy and physiology of the vocal tract. This phonetic grounding is outside any theory of phonology. The theory that we have explored in this book has no explanation for why the vocal tract is the way that it is. However, interactions between the phonology and the motor system strongly shape the nature of the phonology. We bring up ease of articulation here solely to remind the reader of this fact, because other effects discussed in this section have often been attributed to the phonology.

10.1.2. THE ROLE OF PERCEPTION

Braine (1976) argued that some of the patterns observed in child phonology "cry out for a perceptual explanation." Macken (1979) presented some arguments that perception was involved in two phonological patterns that she was analyzing. We agree that some patterns in phonological development must be attributed to perception.

Multilinear phonology focuses on the principles used to construct the pronunciation of words, in a way that is oriented towards production. There is no particular reason why perceptual information should influence this construction. One might argue that it would be relatively easy to build in particular patterns. For example, many aspects of articulation seem to be present to enhance the acoustic consequences of other features. Stevens and Keyser (1989) argue that back vowels are rounded because both rounding and backness lower F2. Palatoalveolars like /ʃ/ are lightly rounded in English, to lower the frequency of their frication, which is already naturally lower than alveolars like /s/, with which they might be confused perceptually. Such redundancies serve to magnify acoustic differences between segments, and one could argue that innate constraints that would cause some features to co-occur would be useful. From the point of view of communicative efficiency for the listener, building in such redundancies in order to exaggerate inherent acoustic differences is quite reasonable. We believe that it belongs to a theory of perception, however, not to phonology per se.

In development, perceptual information can play other types of roles. These roles are also outside the scope of phonology. One such phenomenon is the high frequency of words that begin with labial consonants in the first words of many children with normal vision (e.g., de Boysson-Bardies et al., 1992). There is no phonological reason for such a preference, as witnessed by the fact that blind children show no such preference (Mills, 1988), and the fact that the preference for labials is exaggerated in children who have hearing deficits (Stoel-Gammon, 1988). The common explanation is that labials are preferred in sighted individuals because visual information provides the child with all the information needed to imitate the sounds. Blind children receive no visual information and hence do not prefer labials. Children with hearing deficits rely even more than normals on visual information, and so overuse labials.

In a related vein, we noted in §5.5.4.3.1 that the first fricative to be mastered by many children is [f], even though [s] is more frequent than [f] in adult English and is more widespread than [f] in adult languages in general. We suggested that the child receives visual information about how [f] is made, at a time when the child is still uncertain how alveolar fricatives are made. Visual information increases the salience and clarity of information, and children rely more heavily on it. That information allows low ranking of **NotCo-occurring(-sonorant, + continuant,Labial)**, so that a fricative with a nondefault place feature is possible before a fricative with a default place feature (which is counter to the predictions of our approach). Phonology per se offers no reason why this should be the case. A more general theory of learning and communication is needed for that.

Many of the contextual variants observed for vowels may be perceptually based. For example, some children treat /æ/ differently when it is oral versus nasal. For example, at age 2, Gwendolyn (Stemberger, p.u.d.) observed data such as the following:

| cat | /kæt/ | [tʰat] |
| can | /kæn/ | [tʰiːn] |

The vowel /æ/ had two very different realizations: [a] before an oral consonant, but [iː] before a nasal consonant. None of the constraints that we have addressed in this book would predict such a difference. We believe that this difference derives from the fact that, in the adult pronunciation, /æ/ is oral before an oral consonant but nasalized before a nasal consonant. Beddor, Krakow, and Goldstein (1986) report that the nasal formant in a nasalized vowel (one of the acoustic consequences of vowel nasalization) interferes with the perception of the first formant (the major cue for vowel height). In particular, they show that nasalized [æ̃] sounds higher than [æ] for adult English speakers, even with artificial stimuli for which there is definitely not a real difference in height. If the child takes nasalized [æ̃] to be higher than [æ], it is not hard to explain the child's substitutions, in which the nasalized vowel becomes a higher vowel (front [iː]) but the oral vowel becomes a low vowel (either lower front [a], or central [ɑ]).

Similarly, children often produce /æ/ and /ɛ/ as diphthongs ([æɪ] and [eɪ]) before the velar consonants /g/ and /ŋ/ (and occasionally /k/ and the palatoalveolar /ʃ/). Gwendolyn (Stemberger, p.u.d.) produced such forms:

| leg | /lɛg/ | [jeɪd] |
| bang | /bæŋ/ | [beɪn] |

The back of the tongue is a slow-moving articulator, and hence velars have longer acoustic transitions than labials or coronals; the speed is especially slow for voiced stops and nasals. The F2 of a velar transition is similar to the glide [j], and the glide has an even slower transition. When we compare [ɛg] and [eɪg], the main difference is that the transition is slower in [eɪg]. Rudnicky and Cole (1978) demonstrated that any transition from a vowel to a velar is slow enough to be perceived as a glide in the right context. When the /bɑ/ of the nonsense "phrase" /.'bɑ.'gɑ./ is extracted and spliced before another token of /.bɑ./, listeners often do not hear the expected *[.bɑ.bɑ.], but rather report hearing [.baɪ.bɑ.]. The rising F2 transition before /g/ is slow enough to yield the perception of a palatal glide when it is spliced before a labial consonant (before which F2 should be falling). Only when the slow transitions are before a velar is no glide perceived, because the (adult) listener is accustomed to hearing slow transitions before velars. The transitions must be much longer in order for a palatal glide to be reliably perceived before a velar consonant. Children, with far less experience perceiving English, may misperceive a glide here. This is not predicted by phonology, but by perception and learning.

We noted a similar example in §6.1.6.4.4. Some children fuse clusters such as /gl/ to labial [b], even though neither consonant is labial in the adult pronunciation. We noted that it would be reasonable for the underlying form to be velarized /ɫ/, since that is the most frequent allophone of /l/ in adult English. We also noted that the velarization in [ɫ] has acoustic properties (such as a low F2) that are similar to lip rounding. We suggested that the child may have misinterpreted those cues and perceived [ɫ] as a rounded segment. This is not predicted by phonology, but by perception.

J. Ohala (1974) and Greenlee and J. Ohala (1980) maintain that many historical sound changes have their roots in ambiguities in the acoustic signal. A given piece of acoustic information (such as perceived height of the first formant) may primarily reflect one aspect of articulation (such as tongue height), but may secondarily reflect other aspects of articulation (such as nasalization). A learner must attribute the acoustic information to multiple aspects of articulation. If the learner attributes too much or too little to a particular aspect of articulation, then the child may have an underlying representation that is different from that of adults. That different underlying representation leads to differences in articulation. That is the beginning of a sound change. But it starts with a child's different underlying form and articulation. We have focused on speech production, but this is also a necessary part of a complete theory of phonological behavior.

The role of perception in child substitutions is likely to be important. Multilinear phonology and OT cannot and should not account for such effects. Phonological theory focuses on the production of words. Effects involving speech perception must be accounted for by an independent theory of perception and learning.

10.1.3. INCOMPLETE NEUTRALIZATION

Throughout this book, we have discussed deletions, insertions, and substitutions as if they completely eliminated one element. Many researchers have inferred from this that any apparent neutralizations (e.g., between /t/ and /s/, if both are pronounced as [t]) should be acoustically identical. This is not always the case.

Researchers over the past two decades have reported finding subtle acoustic differences between a correct segment and a perceptually identical error segment. Kornfeld and Goehl (1974) reports that the [w] from /ɹ/ in child speech is often slightly different from the [w] from true /w/. Kewley-Port and Preston (1974) report for child speech that the Voice Onset Time (VOT) of target initial /t/ transcribed as [d] may be systematically different from the VOT of target /d/, even though both may be perceived as [d]. Dinnsen and Elbert (1984) report two children who deleted final stops, but still show very slight transitions after the vowel, in the direction expected on the basis of the consonant that was deleted. Dinnsen and Elbert (1984) have taken this as evidence against a phonological analysis of deletion, devoicing, and so on, and argue that for a different type of analysis, possibly at the phonetic level. McCarthy and Taub (1992) draw similar conclusions from incomplete neutralization in adult speech.

However, such a conclusion rests on the model of performance (and of psychological processing) that is assumed. It depends on a particular (implicit) model in which all operations occur with 100% efficiency. When an element (whether [+voiced] or a whole segment) is deleted, it is deleted completely, so that there is no trace of its existence. Similarly, when an element is present, it is completely present. There are no intermediate states.

Real psychological processing is unlikely to be that efficient. Numerous models assume that elements have some degree of activation, which can range anywhere from a minimum of zero (in which case the element is not there are all) to some maximum (in which case it is completely there). Stemberger (1992a) presents a model of language acquisition of this sort. (See also Dell, 1986; Rumelhart & McClelland, 1986; and Levelt, 1989, among many others, for a similar assumption.) This is relevant, because it is rarely the case that something is 100% present; actual values are slightly lower and variable, between 90% and 96% of maximal activation. Further, absent elements often have slight amounts of activation, between 1% and 10% of maximal activation. All elements with any degree of activation can affect the output, but those with very low levels of activation have only very subtle effects.

The question that such models raise is whether there should be a difference between a segment that is identical in underlying and surface forms, versus one that is different at the two levels. Consider final devoicing. We might have the following:

underlying:	/t/	/d/
surface:	[t]	[t]
activation of [+voiced]:	1%	10%
activation of [-voiced]:	99%	90%

Both segments are well within the acceptable range of voiceless stops. But underlying /d/ is slightly more [d]-like. Basically, the system does not efficiently delete information. Deletion decreases the activation level of an element, but a deleted element may not reach the same low level of activation as one which was under-lyingly voiceless. Thus, we might expect acoustic differences. Indeed, in some models, we might be surprised to find acoustic identity.

A phonological constraint may cause an element to be deleted, but there can still be some subtle articulatory and acoustic effect of the deleted information. Whether such differences are present depends not on the theory of phonology but on the theory of psychological processing. In all probability, actual human pro-cessing is of the inefficient sort that generally leads to subtle influences from "de-leted" information. We thus regard the lack of complete neutralization as irrele-vant to the enterprise that we have undertaken here (but important and interesting in its own right).

10.1.4. LIMITATIONS ON COGNITIVE RESOURCES

Crystal (1987) has argued that limitations on cognitive resources can have an impact on phonology. He bases this proposal largely on the following observation: some children have far more adult-like pronunciations in single-word utterances than in two-word (or multiword) utterances. He argues that such children (most of whom have disordered speech, though some very young normally developing children also show the phenomenon) have strong limitations on the cognitive re-sources that are available for speech. In single-word utterances, there are sufficient resources for the entire task. In two-word utterances, however, lexical access and syntactic processing take too many resources, leaving too little for accurate pho-nological encoding. As a result, phonological encoding is less accurate in two-word utterances than in single-word utterances.

We would like to emphasize that not all less adult-like pronunciations in multi-word utterances are due to resource limitations. We have discussed examples in previous chapters that are due to phonological constraints. Assimilations can oc-cur across words in such a way that the word is pronounced more accurately in isolation (or sentence-finally) than when followed by another word. Vowels can be epenthesized between consonants at word boundaries (§7.4.5). Whole sen-tences can be limited to a single two-syllable foot, so that unstressed syllables are deleted in two-word utterances but not in single-word utterances (§6.3.2.1). Thus, constraints that routinely hold within a word can also pertain to sequences of words. The theory of phonology presented in this book can handle such data.

The types of phenomena that Crystal addressed are not of this type. Resource limitation effects on the phonology tend to be highly variable, so that a given phonological element will be present on one trial but absent on another. For ex-ample, a fricative like /f/ might be correctly pronounced as [f] in a single-word utterance, but regress to [p] in a two-word utterance. In the variant of OT pre-sented here, this is understandable. The ranking of faithfulness constraints is cor-related with activation levels. Resource limitations lead to lower overall activation levels, but those limitations tend to vary from trial to trial, as a function of the overall amount of activity in the child's cognitive system. On some trials, there are sufficient resources, and faithfulness is ranked high. On other trials, there are insufficient resources, and faithfulness is ranked low. Although the variant of OT presented in this book allows for this, most other variants do not, and are unable to account for such effects.

In principle, resource limitation effects might also be found within a single word. They would be apparent when comparing single-syllable words with two-syllable words. Consider the following hypothetical pattern of Fricative Stopping:

| *one-syllable*: | find | /faɪnd/ | [faɪn] |
| *two-syllable*: | finding | /faɪndɪŋ/ | [pʰaɪnɪn] |

Fricatives are pronounced as fricatives in word-initial position in one-syllable words, but as stops in two-syllable words. We can find no phonological reason why such a pattern would exist; both tokens of /f/ are in strong prosodic positions (word-initial position, in stressed syllables) before the same vowels and with the same following consonants. However, this pattern could plausibly derive from resource limitations. A similar conclusion would be drawn from the following pattern with Cluster Reduction:

one-syllable:	stick	/stɪk/	[stɪk]
two-syllable:	sticky	/stɪki/	[sɪki]
	sticker	/stɪkɹ̩/	[sɪkə]

Consonant clusters might be possible in one-syllable words, but not in two-syllable words. Again, we see no phonological reason for such an effect, but it is a plausible effect of resource limitations. Such effects are rarely observed in normal speech, but have been observed in disordered speech, especially in clinical situations.

This brings up the general issue of *attention*: people are capable of better production or perception when attending to a task than when not attending to it. In phonological development, a child may choose to devote more attention to producing a word, and may then pronounce the word better than at other times. This is especially observable in clinical situations, where a child often pronounces words more accurately in the clinic than in natural speech. Normally developing children may also pronounce a word more accurately if it has just been modeled by an adult than if it is produced spontaneously: there *can* be an effect of imitation.

Without doubt, attention and resource limitations affect the developmental process. These mechanisms are entirely independent of phonology, but nonetheless have an impact on phonological encoding. Our theory of phonology has nothing to say about such effects. Nor should it.

10.1.5. PERSONALITY-RELATED FACTORS

Personality factors, such as cooperativeness, perfectionism, and risk taking may also influence phonological development. In clinical situations, a child might be anxious, and therefore less responsive to therapy. Although these can have an effect on the *observed* phonological patterns, they cannot be accounted for *directly* by a theory of phonology.

The most commonly observed effect of this sort is lexical selectivity and avoidance. The phonological system *always* provides an output for any input. However, in a young child's system, that output can be *very* different from the target adult pronunciation of the word. If communication that requires use of a particular word is important enough to the child, the word will be used no matter how much it deviates from the adult form. Some children (who might be described as *pragmatic* or *adventuresome*) do not seem to mind these deviations, and attempt whatever words they need to communicate. Other children (who might be described as *perfectionists* or as less adventuresome), however, may choose to avoid using words if their own pronunciation of the word sounds too deviant. Schwartz and Leonard (1982) examined this experimentally, inspired by the common observation that certain types of words tend not to be attempted by children. For example, when a child can produce at most two syllables in a word, that child may not even attempt to use words with three or more syllables (such as *hippopotamus*), remaining silent when prompted to use the word by an adult.

Phonological theory should be able to derive a pronunciation for all words. However, it should *not* be able to identify the pronunciations that a given child considers too deviant to be usable. Different children have different criteria for determining what is usable and what is not. Some things that have an impact on phonology must remain beyond the scope of phonology. Personality-related factors are one of those things.

10.1.6. OTHER NONPHONOLOGICAL STRATEGIES

Children have occasionally been observed using nonphonological strategies to increase faithfulness to the adult pronunciation. We noted reports from three children who paused within words in order to increase faithfulness. Annalena (§7.3.2.2; Elsen, 1991) disallowed many consonant sequences in codas, but sometimes produced both consonants with a pause between:

Hans   /hans/   [hɑn—θ]

Jeremy (Chapter 7: Footnote 15) usually produced final /n/, but often deleted medial /n/. He occasionally produced data with pauses (and with no adult prompt or model):

funny   /fʌni/   [fʌn—ni]

Chrissie (Bernhardt, 1990: S6) also did this (and for the same word, *funny*). Producing the /n/ as word-final increased faithfulness to /n/, but at the expense of forcing the final vowel into a separate utterance.

This is an unusual strategy. It is beyond the realm of phonology, in that it is not an automatic phenomenon outside the child's conscious control. The children are doing it deliberately, as an attempt to overcome shortcomings in the output of their phonological systems. The closest analog in adult speech is perhaps putting on a foreign accent or speaking very slowly with each syllable separated by pauses. Phonology per se cannot and should not have a way of deriving it.

10.2. WHAT THE THEORY DOES AWKWARDLY

In this book, we have discussed many phenomena in phonological development and shown how they can be derived within the theory employed here. In amongst the workable analyses, there were a few problematic cases. We discuss several phenomena here: (a) chain shifts, (b) the role of segment similarity in assimilation, (c) deletion of entire segments because of constraints on individual features, (d) the special patterns that often affect the low-amplitude voiced fricatives /ð/ and /v/, and (e) cluster harmony. We do not feel that these constitute problems with the theory in principle, but we are unsatisfied with present accounts. We end with a discussion of circularity and power.

10.2.1. CHAIN SHIFTS (COUNTERFEEDING ORDER)

We have followed standard assumptions in OT: (a) that constraints hold over output representations, and (b) that speakers go from the input to the output in a single step during processing. This assumption rules out certain types of analyses that were possible in earlier process-based systems. This is particularly true of patterns that are known as *chain shifts* within historical linguistics, which were handled via *counterfeeding orders* within standard linear generative phonology. These are patterns in which underlying element /A/ is pronounced as [B], but underlying /B/ is pronounced as [C]; [B] is a possible output, but not for /B/ in the input. But if [B] is a possible output, why does underlying /B/ not surface as [B]?

Chain shifts are not common in phonological development. It is in the nature of a book of this kind to collect problematical cases, however. We reported ten instances of chain shifts in Chapters 5–9. We were not able to provide a satisfactory account for most of them.

Some instances may be solvable on the basis of the features that are involved and their default status. In §5.5.1.2.1, we noted that some children produce /s/ as [θ], but /θ/ as [f]. We suggested /θ/ and /s/ may have different feature values than the same segments in adult English: /θ/ may have default place features ([Coronal,-grooved]), while /s/ may be specified as [Coronal,+grooved]. A ranking of **Survived(Coronal)** over **NotCo-occurring(-sonorant,+continuant,Coronal)** allows /s/ to surface as a coronal (albeit as [-grooved] because of low ranking of **Survived(+grooved)**). But the **NotCo-occurring** constraint may be ranked high enough to prevent the *insertion* of default [Coronal] in /θ/, which consequently surfaces as a labial. In §7.3.4.2 and §7.4.1.3, we noted two patterns for Morgan involving [Labial]. [C-Labial] was impossible in a coda in a nasal, but [V-Labial] was shifted out of a rounded vowel into a word-final nasal:

| zoom | /zuːm/ | [ʐwːn] | vs. | shoe | /ʃuː/ | [ɕwːm] |
| gnome | /noːm/ | [nɤːn] | vs. | no | /noː/ | [nɤːm] |

Underlying /m/ surfaced as [n], but underlying rounding surfaced as word-final [m]. It is possible to account for this by assuming that **Survived(V-Labial)** was ranked higher than **Survived(C-Labial)**, so that [m] was possible if it contained [V-Labial], but not if it contained [C-Labial].

Other instances that we discussed are more difficult to explain. In §6.1.6.4.4 (and §4.4.1.3), we noted that Larissa fused /sw/ into [f] (manner and voicing from /s/, place from /w/), but fused /tw/ into [s] (place and voicing from /t/, manner from /w/). If [Labial] had to survive in the fusion for /sw/, why did it fail to survive for /tw/, given that /tw/ was reduced to [s]? In §8.3.3, we reported that Colin produced word-initial /ʔ/ as [n], but initial /n/ was replaced by default [g]. If the features of /n/ could be inserted, why did the same underlying features fail to survive? In §9.1.3.4, we reported that Gwendolyn produced the past tense forms of verbs ending in /k/ with [tt] (Velar Fronting, no Schwa Insertion), but of verbs ending in /t/ with [təd] (Schwa Insertion). (Other chain shifts were reported in §5.5.3.4, §6.2.3.5, §7.3.2.1.1, and §7.3.2.3.)

In §3.3.4, we discussed one way in which such patterns can be derived: stratal ordering. If we assume that phonological processes are grouped into several blocks (strata), and that the blocks are ordered (so that any process on Stratum 1 must apply before any process on Stratum 2), we can derive the sort of chain shifts observed here. One change can occur at Stratum 1 only (spreading of [Labial] from /w/ to /s/; deletion of [+nasal]; Schwa Insertion). The other change can occur at Stratum 2 (spreading of [+continuant] from /w/ to /t/; insertion of [+nasal]; Velar Fronting). If the processes on Stratum 1 cannot reapply to the output of Stratum 2, a chain shift is derived. Goldsmith (1993) and Wheeler and Touretzky (1993) maintain that two levels are needed, to derive data of this type.

There are reasons to be skeptical of such an analysis, however. First, if there are two strata, the problem of learning the constraint rankings becomes much more difficult. In fact, no current proposal for the learning of constraint rankings works unless there is just a single stratum; the learner has to figure out not just the rankings but *which stratum* is relevant, and it is not clear how this is done. Second, it is necessary to justify the existence of two strata in child speech, with justification for why the constraint rankings would be different. As a result, we are reluctant to embrace such an analysis.

Kirchner (1995) and Reiss (1995) propose that compound constraints can solve this problem. For Larissa's /sw/ and /tw/ data, we could assume the following constraint:

Survived(continuant)-OR-Survived(Artic)

The underlying articulator feature *or* the underlying value of continuant had to survive, but the constraint would not be violated if only one of the features survived. Underlying /sw/ can surface as [f] because there is faithfulness to underlying [+continuant]. Underlying /tw/ cannot surface as *[f], because there would be no faithfulness; only [s] (faithful to [Coronal]) and [p] (faithful to [-continuant]) would be possible; this child's constraints were ranked so that [Coronal] survived instead of [-continuant]. This analysis fails for our data, however. For Larissa, underlying /kw/ *also* surfaced as [s]: *quiet* /kwaɪət/ [saɪət]. In /kw/ [s], the output is unfaithful to both [continuant] and [Dorsal]; consequently, it is no better than [f].

For Gwendolyn, the compound constraint would have to be:

Survived(Dorsal)-OR-Not(V-Root)

If underlying [Dorsal] was deleted, then no schwa could be epenthesized. But this is an odd combination of apparently unrelated constraints. Further, Velar Fronting anywhere in the word should have blocked Schwa Insertion, and it did not: the overregularization *getted* /gɛt-d/ [dɛtəd]. Thus, an explanation must be sought elsewhere.

McCarthy (1995) proposes to account for chain shifts by abandoning the assumption that constraints hold only over outputs. We have been assuming that output constraints refer to elements and sequences in the output only. McCarthy proposes that constraints may refer to elements in either the input or the output. He proposes that all constraints come in three variants: one that refers to elements only in the input, one that refers to elements only in the output, and one that refers to elements on either level. This can solve some of the chain shifts that we observed. For Gwendolyn, **NotTwice**_{Dependents}**(C-Root)**, which motivates Schwa Epenthesis in words like *getted*, refers only to *underlying* consonants, not to surface ones. Since the /k/ in *worked* has an underlying segment that is distinct from the /t/ (or /d/) of the past tense suffix, **NotTwice** is not violated, and so Schwa Insertion does not occur. In *getted*, however, the underlying /t/ *does* lead to a violation of **NotTwice**, and so Schwa Insertion occurs. For Larissa, the spread of [Labial] is possible only when the two consonants share [+continuant] *in the input*; since in /tw/ and /kw/ [+continuant] is not shared, [Labial] does not spread. For Colin, if we assume that /n/→[g] is driven by **NotCo-occurring(C-Place,+nasal])**, only *underlying* C-Place causes a problem; epenthesizing C-Place and [+nasal] in the output does not violate the constraint.

There is only one chain shift that we have discussed that seems to be a problem for this approach. In §6.2.3.5, we reported that a Spanish-learning child (Gennari & Demuth, 1997) reduced WSW words to SW, but also reduced WWSW words to WSW. A constraint against initial unstressed syllables should have caused *all* these words to reduce to WS. Gennari and Demuth do report that it was generally the first unstressed syllable that deleted. This would be predicted by a constraint such as:

NotAligned(PrWd,L,Unstressed,L)

This would prohibit an unstressed syllable in word-initial position, but could be restricted to affect only the word-initial unstressed syllable *in the input*.

McCarthy's analysis may be workable. However, it works only at the expense of rejecting one of the most fundamental characteristics of OT: that output constraints are constraints on output. This introduces enough power into the theory that it becomes difficult to falsify. We do not regard this as a satisfactory solution.

In at least some instances, an activation-based account might be possible. In §9.1.3.4, we suggested that the [t] that resulted from underlying /k/ via Velar Fronting might be lower in activation level than the [t] that came from underlying /t/, and that this difference in activation might have avoided a violation of **Not-Twice**; the [Coronal] in the /k/ was too low in activation for **NotTwice** to recognize it as [Coronal]. We are unsure whether such an account would work for other examples of chain shift, however.

We do not regard any of the solutions that we have addressed here as adequate. We leave the resolution of this problem to future research.

**10.2.2. THE ROLE OF SEGMENTAL SIMILARITY
IN ASSIMILATION**

Assimilations are commonly limited to interactions between segments that are very similar, both in adult languages and in phonological development. In §7.4.2.1, we reported that Gwendolyn showed manner harmony between /z/ and /l/, but not between /s/ and /l/: *lizard* /lɪzɹd/ [zɪzowd]) versus *Lucy* /luːsi/ [juːsi]. Only if voicing was shared was Fricative Harmony present. There seems to be a general principle involved here: "like attracts like." Two dissimilar segments do not interfere. Two similar segments attract each other, so that they become even more similar.

Cole and Kisseberth (1994) provide a possible mechanism (and Reiss, 1995, makes a similar proposal): parasitic alignment. They argue that feature domains can be aligned with each other: for example, the left and right edges of a [high] feature domain can be aligned with the left and right edges of a [Labial] feature domain:

Aligned(high,L,Labial,L)

This essentially removes the independence of the two features. If two adjacent high vowels share a single token of the feature [+high], they must also share the feature [Labial] (if it is present). If [Labial] is parasitically aligned with [high], the following sequences would be possible: [i . . . i]/[e . . . e] (same height, neither labial), [u . . . u]/[o . . . o] (same height, both labial), and [e . . . u]/[i . . . o]/[u . . . e]/[o . . . i] (mixed height, mixed labial). Impossible sequences would be [i . . . u]/[e . . . o]/[u . . . i]/[o . . . e] (same height, mixed labial). Given that the two vowels share a single token of [high] (a merger caused by low ranking of **Distinct (+high)** and **Distinct(-high)**), [Labial] must spread to the other vowel. An extension of this is that the spreading of [high] entails the spreading of [Labial]. In §7.3.1.8.1, we reported that Charles spread [Labial] only if [+continuant] spread; that could be an instance of parasitic alignment.

We do not adopt this solution here, because, as we have discussed in earlier chapters, we believe that assimilation should not be analyzed using alignment. However, it is unclear what the alternative should be.

Segmental similarity has a general effect on phonological patterns that extends far beyond phonological theory. In speech errors, segments that differ by one feature tend to be confused and substituted for one another, much more often than segments that differ by multiple features (e.g., Shattuck-Hufnagel & Klatt, 1979; Stemberger, 1991b). For example, a speech error like *Gig girl* (for *Big girl*) is far more likely than an error like *Sig sea* (for *Big sea*), because /b/ shares more features with /g/ than with /s/. Perhaps the same mechanism is involved both in speech errors and in basic phonological patterns. Dell (1986) argues that co-occurring features reinforce each other: each increases the activation level of the other. If [+voiced] is present in both /z/ and /l/, and the [+voiced] in /z/ reinforces [-sonorant], that leads to an increase in activation level for [-sonorant] in /l/ as well, which would make Fricative Harmony more likely (as compared to where /l/ was paired with voiceless /s/). The model of Dell, Juliano, and Govindjee (1993) provides a similar mechanism for the processing of single words in a way that would generalize well to the within-word assimilation patterns of child phonology. We suspect that pursuing this line of inquiry will prove fruitful. However, at the moment, the details of harmony within their system are unclear.

We are not satisfied that phonological theory has yet provided an adequate account of the role of segmental similarity in assimilation. Phonology *should*, and possibly will yet, provide an account of this.

10.2.3. NONMINIMAL DELETION REPAIRS

The majority of repairs in phonological development are minimal: they affect just the element that is responsible for the violation of the relevant constraint. However, nonminimal repairs occur reasonably often. In our approach, we have an analysis which works, from the technical standpoint. There is one constraint type that is violated only if an element is fully integrated into the temporal structure of the word: co-occurrence constraints (**NotCo-occurring** and **Co-occurring**). These constraints refer to *co-occurrence in time*, and only if the segment is fully integrated into the temporal structure (meaning that a pathway can be traced up to a prosodic word) are they violated. Consequently, a segment that contains a feature that is ruled out by occurrence constraints may simply "delete" in its entirety by floating: being present in the output but unintegrated with temporal structure. If the elements are present in the output, **Survived** is not violated; but if they are floating, those elements are not pronounced.

This works, but we are not happy about needing to posit two distinct types of deletion (though the two types are standard in multilinear phonology; for discussion, see Archangeli & Pulleyblank, 1994; Kenstowicz, 1994). It seems unlikely to us that speakers would squander limited cognitive resources on the maintenance of elements that are never pronounced.

McCarthy and Prince (1995) provide an alternative. In our terms, they split **Survived** into two distinct constraints. Their **MAX** constraint (our **Survived (Root)**) is used with reference to whole segments, while **Ident(Feature)** is used for features. **Ident** is a complex constraint that is contingently defined: a feature must survive *if and only if* the segment that it is in survives; otherwise, the feature may freely delete. This more complex definition of survival for features allows us to avoid floating segments in the output: if a co-occurrence constraint is violated by a feature, the whole segment may delete, *without violating survival of the feature*. We are unenthusiastic about constraints with complex definitions and thus have not made use of **Ident** in this book.

McCarthy and Prince's proposal becomes even more complex with respect to data in which a segment apparently deletes, but a feature survives. Gnanadesikan (1995) explores such data for child phonology. It is necessary to assume that a single output segment corresponds to two or more input segments. We showed (§6.1.6.4.5) that this approach makes incorrect predictions about fusions of segments in child phonology. It is necessary to have a simple constraint on the survival of features, independent of the survival of the segment that contains it.

We are unsure of the best resolution of this situation. One possibility is that there are *two* constraints on the survival of every feature. One is defined in a simple way (**Survived**), the other in a complex way (**Ident**). We are unenthusiastic about this alternative, because we believe that there should be as few constraints as possible. The more constraints there are, the more powerful the theory, and the harder it is in principle to test the theory. If a theory cannot in principle be falsified, that is a drawback. If a theory can handle not only the patterns that are observed in the data, but also large numbers of strange and unattested patterns, that is also a drawback. We note again that our approach is technically inadequate, and leave the issue for future research.

10.2.4. STOPPING OF LOW-AMPLITUDE FRICATIVES

In this book, we have been working under the assumption that children with normal hearing perceive the adult pronunciation more or less accurately. For the most part, we have been able to account for substitutions on the basis of the phonological features that should be present if the words and segments were accurately perceived. In this section, we return to that phrase: "more or less" accurate.

There are one or two segments that have consistently proven to be difficult: the low-amplitude fricatives /ð/ and /v/. In a large proportion of children, these two fricatives surface as the stops [d] and [b], respectively. For many children, this is not a problem, since many other fricatives also surface as stops. For some children, however, this constitutes a unique pattern, and makes description difficult. In §8.6.1.6, we reported that Dylan produced most intervocalic fricatives, including /z/ and /v/, as [ʔ] (if they were not deleted outright). Voiced stops most often survived between vowels. Unexpectedly, /ð/ also survived between vowels, surfacing as [d]. We are unable to provide a constraint ranking that would derive this fact.

It is possible that perceptual error was involved here. The amplitude of the frication in /ð/ is very low. Children with any level of hearing problems (including those caused by mild ear infections) may not perceive the frication. In that case, the child perceives the phone as /d/, and treats it in an identical fashion. We are reluctant to make such an assumption in the absence of perceptual tests. However, /ð/ and (to a lesser extent) /v/ often behave exceptionally. We feel that these fricatives are likely to be the "or less" part of the assumption that children perceive adult speech "more or less" accurately.

10.2.5. SEQUENCE HARMONY

One rare type of consonant harmony was not discussed in Chapter 7. Stemberger (1989) reported a few forms like the following for Gwendolyn:

cream cheese   /kɹiːmtʃiːz/   [tʰwiːmtʰiːz]~[tʰiːmtʰwiːz]~[tʰwiːmtʰwiːz]

Only the first variant is expected: the /ɹ/ is realized as [w] where it should be (in *cream*). In the second variant, the /ɹ/ shifts into the second place (into *cheese*). In the third variant, the /ɹ/ is duplicated and appears in both places. Johnson (1995) reports similar data:

camera   /kæmɹə/   [kʰɹæmɹə]

This appears to be "cluster harmony," in which a simple onset becomes a cluster when there is a cluster nearby.

Morgan (at age 1;4, Stemberger, p.u.d.) occasionally produced forms such as the following:

chicken   /tʃɪkn̩/   [tʃɪŋkɪŋ]

This is the creation of a cluster by duplicating a word-final coda consonant as a word-medial coda.

Gwendolyn (Stemberger, p.u.d.) produced similar data involving diphthongs in a number of words:

mailman   /meɪlmæn/   [.ˈmɛʊ.ˌmɛʊn.]   (cf. man   /mæn/   [miːn])
airplane   /ɛɹpleɪn/   [.ˈʔɛʊ.ˌpʰɛʊn.]   (cf. plane   /pleɪn/   [pʰiːn])

A vowel occasionally surfaced as a diphthong near another diphthong, sometimes as an identical diphthong: "diphthong harmony."

There is nothing in our approach to phonology that would predict either type of harmony. Harmony involves the spreading of one or two elements, as low as a feature or as high as a Root node. We suspect that such harmony (which appears to be very rare) is more akin to speech errors (slips of the tongue) than to common phonological processes. "Cluster harmony" is in fact a common type of speech error (Stemberger & Treiman, 1986; Stemberger, 1990). Stemberger (1989) reported that Gwendolyn and Morgan also made speech errors of this sort. Such errors result when there is interference between the phonological forms that are being processed (especially between two words in a sentence or in a compound noun, but also within a word). We believe that the processing difficulties that lead to such errors as occasional slips may be more pronounced for some children, and the slips happen with such frequency that we consider them a standard variant pronunciation. This is outside of the phonology per se, but is an integral part of the child's speech processing.

10.2.6. CIRCULARITY AND POWER OF THE CONSTRAINTS

The last issue that we address is one that we raised in §4.2.2: how we know what the constraints are. We did not create or introduce any new constraints in Chapters 5–9, when we discussed child data; we adhered to the constraints laid out in Chapter 4. However, those constraints were tailored in such a way that we would be able to account for the data in later chapters. In many papers in the OT literature, the constraint set that is being assumed proves inadequate to the task, and changes (often major changes) are introduced. One must ask whether we can make up any constraint that we need, as we need it. If so, then the problem of circularity arises: a constraint causes a certain pattern in the data, and that pattern is the only evidence for that constraint.

Circularity is *always* present in the early stages of building a theory. Abstract principles are empirically based, which makes them circular by definition. However, we can escape from circularity if we can find additional evidence beyond that which originally motivated the constraint. The more tightly we can tie together different phenomena, the less circular the theory.

In this book, we follow several principles that lessen the problem of circularity. (a) Constraints must be as simple as possible. Complexity is to avoided at all costs. (b) Constraints should be as different as possible. Two constraints should *never* have almost identical functions. (c) Constraints should not be arbitrary. They should be grounded in articulation, in perception, in cognitive processing (information processing), or in the needs of communication. We have especially emphasized the role of information processing on the existence of constraints: every element requires cognitive resources, for itself and in order to be combined with anything else. If a factor affects processing in general, it should be encoded as a constraint. If it is unreasonable to expect a factor to affect processing in general, it should not be a type of phonological constraint. (d) As many other ties to processing as possible have been built in, including relating the ranking of faithfulness constraints to activation levels (which we return to in the next section). The "weakness" of a prosodic domain should be supported by evidence of other sorts (such as characteristics of speech errors, the tip-of-the-tongue phenomenon, etc.). We believe that the constraints and the approach laid out here are as noncircular as they can be, given the present state of knowledge.

A related issue is whether OT is simply too powerful. We have noted in this section things that are difficult for us. It is *not* the case that the theory can do absolutely anything. For concreteness, let us examine a phenomenon from §6.2.5.3.1, involving the content of initial unstressed syllables. We noted in that section and elsewhere that "default segments" may arise which have default features. For many children, inserted consonants are coronal stops (such as [d]) or glottal stops ([ʔ]). Sometimes the default is an oral glide (with [w] and [j] being popular, even in adult languages). We also observed that there is often assimilation from the stressed syllable into an initial unstressed syllable. Two children, however, had "dummy syllables" with unusual phonetic content; [ɹi] (Smith, 1973) and [fi] (Gnanadesikan, 1995). We were able to derive these unusual defaults via dissimilation and assimilation. We argued that the "real" syllables should have been *[ji] (Smith) and *[ti] (Gnanadesikan). For Smith's data, **NotTwice**$_{Dependents}$(**V-Root)** led to [Labial] being inserted in the consonant to make the /j/ and /i/ phonetically distinct: [ɹi] (correct). For Gnanadesikan's data **NotTwice(Coronal)** also caused [Labial] to be inserted, and [+continuant] spread from the vowel to the consonant: [fi]. Although this worked, how impressive is it really? Is there anything that could *not* be derived in this fashion? Yes.

The default onset has to have (a) default consonant features if [C-Root] is inserted, or (b) default vowel features if [V-Root] is inserted, or (c) features spread from the vowel to [C-Root], or (d) nondefault features that are motivated via sequence constraints. The last two options allow the default onset to have nondefault features. But note that the nondefault features must be *motivated*. For both of these children, there is independent evidence (from consonant fusion) that [Coronal] is the default place feature for consonants. If both of these children had had schwa as the default vowel, our approach would have predicted the dummy syllables *[jə] and *[sə]. Since schwa has no [Labial] feature, [ɹ] and [f] could not result from assimilation; and we can think of no sequence constraint that would force insertion of [Labial] before schwa. Although a wide range of dummy syllables can be derived in our theory, there are limits to what the theory can derive.

Given the severe limitations that we have placed on the types of constraints that we are willing to posit, and the fact that there are many imaginable phonological patterns that our approach would be unable to account for, we feel that this endeavor has worked remarkably well. There are very few phonological patterns in development that are truly difficult for the theory. The few problematical cases fall into a small number of classes, which we have discussed in this section. A few challenges remain to be overcome, but we have come a fair distance.

10.3. IMPLICATIONS OF CHILD PHONOLOGY FOR PHONOLOGICAL THEORY

One of the purposes of this book was to examine phonological theories in the light of child data. In the previous section, we discussed phenomena in child phonology that current versions of the theory handle awkwardly. In this section, we discuss patterns in child phonology that suggest certain alternatives and directions for phonological theory. Many have been discussed throughout the book. In this concluding chapter, we focus on only a few, in order to address general points about theory development. Some of these concern features and feature geometry. Some concern more general concepts: phonetic grounding, the concept of default, and the sliding scale of faithfulness. We address each of these topics.

10.3.1. OPTIONALITY THEORY: DIFFERENT CHILDREN MAY USE DIFFERENT FEATURES

Within generative grammar there is a strong universalist bent, often combined with nativist views on the development of language. In phonology, this translates into, for example, a set of "universal principles," a set of "universal features," a set of "universal syllable and word structures," and more recently, a set of "universal constraints," that are genetically "hard-wired" into the child. We suggested in §2.4.2 that the question of the origins of language is a separate issue. It is possible to analyze data using formalist models without assuming nativism. But how universal are the features, the principles, the constraints, and so on? As we have noted throughout, child data show trends across languages, but only trends. Universals are often only probabilistic at best (as discussed in §5.3). We exemplify this with particular issues from feature theory.

Children sometimes show patterns that indicate different feature classifications and definitions than would be expected. By allowing a broader definition of features and alternatives for feature systems, the child data become comprehensible. For example, we saw variable interpretations of affricates (§5.5.3.5), fricatives (§5.5.1.2.1 and §5.5.3.4), sonorants (§5.5.1.5, §5.5.3.1, §5.5.3.3, and §5.5.3.6), and consonant and vowel features as they relate to each other (§7.3.4). We discuss each in turn.

10.3.1.1. Affricates—Variable Interpretations

In §3.1.1, we discussed the problem of affricates, which are alternatively analyzed as branching continuants, strident stops, or stops with delayed release. Examination of child data suggests that children also analyze affricates in alternative ways. In English, if affricates surface as alveolar stops or fricatives, children may be treating the affricates as strident stops. High ranking of **NotCo-occurring (+ strident, + continuant)** prohibits their production. If [+strident] ([+grooved]) must survive, a fricative results. If **Not(+ strident)** is high-ranked, a stop results. Once the co-occurrence constraint becomes sufficiently low-ranked, the child then produces affricates. Some children, on their way to producing affricates accurately, first produce highly aspirated stops (e.g., Kendra: Bernhardt, 1994a). For such children, a noisy ([+strident]) stop may be the target, but a stop with a different sort of noise (aspiration) was produced instead. Could this reflect a very different definition of stridency than is usually assumed? Often, children produce affricates that are neither [+strident] (interdental, see Charles, §8.5.1) nor coronal (palatal, velar, or labial). Larissa (§6.1.6.4.4) produced labial affricates for labial-approximant clusters (e.g., /pl/ > [pf] and /bɹ/ > [bv]). Even if the labiodentals were treated as [+strident], how did the feature [+strident] arise from the fusion of /p/ and /l/, both of which are [-strident]? Analyses such as LaCharité (1993) assume that [+strident] pertains to grooved coronal sibilants; thus, for nonsibilants, the strident stop analysis fails. Such data suggest that affricates are complex segments that are both [-continuant] and [+continuant].

Adult languages (e.g., Salish, Xhosa) may also have a series of affricates, only some of which are coronal and strident. The strident stop analysis is problematical in those cases also. Different languages, like different children, may treat affricates alternatively as branching continuants, delayed release stops, or strident stops, depending on their inventories and phonological patterns. It does not appear that there is a single universal representation for affricates in human language.

10.3.1.2. Fricatives—Variable Interpretations

Fricatives may show similar variable interpretations. In §5.5.1.2.1 and §5.5.3.4, we discussed two types of unusual substitutions for fricatives (i.e., clicks and nasal snorts). These cases are unusual, but are striking examples of how segments and features may be alternately interpreted (by children, and, by extension, by language communities).

Fricatives contain high-amplitude noise of long duration, and clicks contain high-amplitude noise of short duration. If a child has **NotCo-occurring(-sonorant, +continuant)** prohibiting fricatives, but wants to produce a high-amplitude phone, a click is a possible substitution (Bedore et al., 1994). A low-level characteristic of the adult target (long duration of high-amplitude noise) is ignored. The feature [+strident] is treated as if it were "[+loud]." In this book, we generally used [grooved] to account for patterns involving the sibilants, partly in order to be consistent in feature use (using all articulator features), and partly because many children find tongue grooving difficult, implying that grooving is relevant to the acquisition process. In the case of clicks, the substitution pattern is best described using an acoustic feature that indicates high-amplitude noise: [+strident]. Just as feature systems differ in whether acoustic or articulatory features prevail, so children's feature systems may be more acoustic or more articulatory.

The feature [+strident] may also be relevant in the case of nasal snort substitutions, but only if it replaces just the strident sibilants. If a child uses nasal snorts for all fricatives, then the feature [strident] is not sufficient. The feature [continuant] could be defined alternatively as concerning both the oral and nasal cavities. Alternatively, a general feature of [+fricative] might be implied. Nasals and fricatives do not pattern together often crosslinguistically or developmentally, but sometimes they do (even in the absence of vocal tract pathology) and hence some flexibility is needed with respect to the relationship between them.

10.3.1.3. Underspecification—Variable Interpretations

Features also show variability in terms of their values as defaults or nondefaults. Underspecification has proven to be a useful concept for describing developmental patterns. Pervasive use of certain segments/features suggests the concept of "default." Nondefaults are often delinked, with default values or features inserted. A number of different "processes" can result in the same substitution: the default voiceless coronal stop, [t]:

> *Defaults: [Coronal,+anterior], [-voiced], [-continuant] inserted*

Velar Fronting:	/k/ > [t]	Nondefault [Dorsal] prohibited
Depalatalization:	/ʃ/ > [t]	Nondefaults [-anterior] and
		[+continuant] prohibited
Backing:	/p/ > [t]	Nondefault [Labial] prohibited
Denasalization:	/n/ > [t]	Nondefault [+nasal] prohibited
Devoicing:	/d/ > [t]	Nondefault [+voiced] prohibited

In all cases, the nondefault features are deleted and replaced with default place features. **Not(NonDefault)** constraints are high-ranked, and **Not(Default)** constraints are low-ranked. Because **Survived(TimingUnit)** is high-ranked, the system defaults are inserted. In process terminology, a number of different and unrelated processes need to be posited. The concepts of nondefault and default unify unrelated repair processes.

In spite of the utility of underspecification in explaining developmental patterns, it is not easy to predict or determine which features will be the defaults in children's phonology. If underspecification derives from *adult* phoneme frequencies, then all children learning a particular language should have the same default values, probably from the beginning of speech production. (Furthermore, if universal frequencies were the most important source, then children *across* languages should have the same defaults.) However, as we showed in many sections in Chapter 5, and for Colin in §8.3, children can have different defaults. Sometimes the difference can be attributed to developmental constraints (such as a forward tongue position, as described in §8.5.1) or vocal tract differences (see §10.3.3), but in other cases, there is no apparent reason/grounding for the difference. This suggests that frequency in the *child's* speech (due at first to random differences in the initial state of the phonological system) is probably more relevant, to the extent that children have different phone frequencies. As phone frequencies change over the course of development, we might expect the default values to shift (as they did for Colin, who eventually started substituting coronal stops for other segments).

Although we derive our assumptions about defaults from frequency and substitution patterns, it is not clear whether type frequency or token frequency are the most relevant for a given child or across children, or whether there are options for underspecification with respect to frequency types. Consider the following from a detailed diary study of Morgan's speech (Stemberger, p.u.d.). (All places of articulation refer to the adult target words.)

1;1.6, 20 words:	11 began with labials (in the adult target)
	4 began with coronals
	4 began with glottals
	1 began with a dorsal: [Dorsal] > [Labial] [baʔ] 'again'

1;4.16, 80 words: 45 began with labials
                    21 began with coronals
                    12 began with glottals
                     2 began with dorsals: [Dorsal] > [Coronal]   [daʔ] 'again'
                                                                  [duʔ] 'goose'

In the earliest words, this child (like many English-learning children) had an emphasis on words beginning with a labial consonant. The high frequency of [Labial] perhaps indicated that [Labial] was the default; and the one word containing a target velar was realized with a labial. Over time the frequency changed, with coronals becoming much more frequent. Additionally, coronals replaced dorsals. If we use frequency as the criterial attribute for assigning default status, [Labial] should have been the default at both points. Based on substitution patterns, at least at Point 2, [Coronal] had more the appearance of a default but [Coronal] had a lower type frequency than [Labial]. Which is the relevant criterion? These data suggest that the *type* frequency (the *number* of words with a certain characteristic) is *not* what determines default values. *Token* frequency may be more important (i.e., the number of times each phone is used in speech). Calculation of token frequency is very difficult, because of the tremendous amount of data collection that is required. Token frequency was not recorded for Morgan's speech (as it is not for the majority of studies), and consequently we will never know whether token frequency correlated with the default status of [Coronal]. Perhaps neither type nor token frequency was important, but some other factor. We do not yet know which are the most important data and how to determine unequivocally that certain values are the default values. However, it is apparent that, as in other areas of feature theory, it is important to consider a number of different possible approaches to that determination, and not to make too many a priori assumptions.

10.3.1.4. Redundant Features—Variable Interpretations

As a further example of variability relative to underspecification, different children treat redundant features in different ways. The feature [voiced] is a prime example. Children differ in whether they maintain the voicing of a sonorant in substitution patterns or not (§5.5.3.3, §5.5.3.6). The feature [voiced] is considered to be a redundant feature of a sonorant. Given common assumptions in underspecification theory, if [+sonorant] fails to surface, [+voiced] should also fail to surface; since there is no underlying specification for voicing in sonorants, the deletion of [+sonorant] removes the factor that normally forces the insertion of [+voiced], and so [+voiced] should not be inserted. In this book, we presented an alternative version of underspecification theory, default underspecification, to account for this type of optionality. The system default may be [-voiced], but the feature [+voiced] is a redundant nondefault (§4.4.2.2). Redundant nondefaults may be specified underlylingly or not, depending on the child. On learning such sounds, a child is faced with a choice: rerank co-occurrence constraints so that the redundant nondefault feature is inserted, or store the nondefault feature in the underlying representation. Either solution is effective in terms of helping the feature to appear in the output. Other examples of this type of optionality include, for example, the [+sonorant] feature of laterals or nasals (§5.5.1.5.1, §5.5.3.3, §5.5.3.6.1), the feature [+labiodental] (§5.5.1.3), and [+s.g.] for fricatives (§5.5.2.2).

Allophonic features are similar to redundant nondefaults in their treatment by children. For example, children sometimes appear to treat all /l/'s as underlyingly velarized, using [w] for a substitution even for /l/'s that are not velarized in adult speech. The aspiration ([+s.g.]) of word-initial stops is sometimes treated as underlying, with fricatives surfacing in place of the word-initial stops, apparently to preserve the 'allophonic' feature (e.g., DE, §7.4.1.3).

In summary, the concepts of defaults and nondefaults are useful in describing patterns in child phonology. However, it is clear that alternate pathways for underspecification are possible, and that theories that allow for such options are preferable to ones that do not.

10.3.1.5. Variable Developmental Paths

In Chapters 5 and 6, we addressed proposals in the literature that attempted to lay out an invariant sequence of stages through which children pass during development. This has been attempted for features, for feature co-occurrence, for syllable structure, and for foot structure. On reviewing the data, we were struck by the high degree of variability across children. No strict stage theory that we have seen can account for all that variability. Children begin with pronunciations that are unfaithful to adult speech in many ways. Nondefault features and structures are a common problem. However, there appears to be little consistency about *which* aspects of faithfulness a given child masters first. If there are universal orders of acquisition, they are very difficult to spot in the data that we currently have available.

10.3.2. PHONETIC GROUNDING

Tied to Archangeli and Pulleyblank's (1994) combinatorial specification theory is the concept of phonetic grounding. Throughout the book, we have reiterated that constraint rankings are most plausible if grounded in phonetics or communicative function. In Chapter 5, we gave many examples of typical constraint rankings for the various features. As we noted in the previous section, [t] is often a default segment, with low-ranked constraints being **Not(-continuant), Not (-nasal), Not(-voiced)** and **Not(Coronal)**. The grounding that underlies the ranking of these particular constraints in unclear (except in terms of the frequency of those particular features). However, there are data which more clearly demonstrate phonetic grounding. In Chapter 8, we presented information about speakers who had vocal tracts with unusual characteristics (§8.5). Anatomical or functional differences sometimes change the "setting" for speech production (Laver, 1994). If someone cannot close off the nasal cavity, **Not(+ nasal)** is obviously very low-ranked. If someone has a forward-resting tongue position, **Not(+ distributed)** is very low-ranked. The ranking of the constraints is predictable, based on the oral mechanism function. Thus, some 'disordered' data can more clearly demonstrate phonetic grounding for the default features.

10.3.3. CONSONANT AND VOWEL REPRESENTATION

In §3.4.3, we argued that consonants and vowels may occupy separate planes. We have made use of that analysis throughout this book. It has proven remarkably useful for explaining the effects of identity on segments. In §7.4.4.3, we discussed several children who had strong constraints on medial consonants, but who allowed any medial consonant if it was identical to the word-initial consonant. It works well to assume that the consonants are on a plane of their own, and that "noncontiguous" consonants separated by vowels nonetheless have adjacent Root nodes that may be merged into a single doubly linked Root node. We also argued that such separation may be true of all adult languages (on the basis of vowel-to-vowel coarticulation effects). Phonetics suggests such a separation for adults, but there is rarely any phonological evidence to support it. Children supply such phonological evidence.

10.3.4. SUCCESS OF INDEXING FAITHFULNESS TO ACTIVATION LEVELS

In this section, we return to the concept of activation level, a concept 'outside' the domain of linguistic theory, but which we have found useful. In §10.1.3, we discussed the interaction of processing and constraints. Several patterns described in the book are simply difficult to explain *without* bringing in the notion of activation levels. OT is a theory that brings together connectionist and traditional linguistic concepts. The child data in this book suggest that further integration of these theories is desirable.

Indexing faithfulness to activation provides an explanation for the loss of co-occurring features, or for the retention of such features. DE (§7.4.1.3) showed survival of [Labial] when it was combined with a feature that was well-established in onsets ([+ voiced]), but loss of [Labial] when it was combined with another feature that was marginal in onsets ([-voiced]). Darryl (§8.5.1.2) showed retention of [Dorsal] and [-continuant] for /k/ in onsets, but loss of both weak features in codas. The other voiceless stops [p] and [t] were viable in codas, because their place features were possible. The impossibility of [Dorsal] also made /k/ susceptible to **Co-occurring(Rime→ + continuant)**, so that it became a fricative (unlike the other stops).

In some connectionist theories of phonological processing (e.g., Dell, 1986), the features of a segment reinforce each other, by increasing each other's activation levels. A well-established (high-activation) feature increases the activation level of a marginal (low-activation) feature, so that the marginal feature can survive. A poorly established feature provides less support, so the marginal feature may fail to survive. Indeed, the low levels of activation may cause *both* marginal features to delete, when they are combined in a single segment. We regard such explanations are inherently interesting, and deserving of further investigation.

In addition to its usefulness in accounting for which domains are strong and which are weak (§4.7.1.5), the concept of activation levels also helps account for lower faithfulness in infrequent and novel words, which also have low activation levels. As noted in §4.10, low-frequency words sometimes show lower degrees of faithfulness in child speech.

Integration of processing theories and linguistic theories is challenging, but each has attributes that can enhance the other through that integration.

10.4. CONCLUSIONS

In this book we took on the task of describing and explaining the full range of the phenomena of child phonology, making use of multilinear phonology and of OT. Both theories provided many new ways of looking at the patterns, and our general perspective after writing the book, is that, yes, they are both very useful for understanding what children do. In this chapter, we have challenged aspects of multilinear phonology and OT. Some things are simply beyond the scope of a theory of phonology. We view this as appropriate. Human behavior is a complex interaction of many domains and general cognitive processing. Phonological processing and the acquisition of phonology are no different. Components of cognition and motor processing must also be taken into account in order to account for the range of phenomena of the acquisition of phonology (and even of adult speech).

Failing to account for phenomena that *should* be accounted for within theories of phonology is more serious. We noted a number of such problems in §10.2. However, none seem to be insurmountable. These theories (like all theories) are still (and always will be) under development. *If and only if* the problems cannot ultimately be resolved, is there a true problem. Multilinear phonology and OT provide a useful framework that resolves many difficult phonological patterns in phonological development. They are worth pursuing even if more work needs to be done.

As we collect data from new children and new languages, our assumptions about what is natural, universal, or expected are constantly undermined. It is *difficult* to give up a set of hypotheses about the organization of the "universe" (narrowly defined as human language). But the data tell us that we *must* be flexible, and allow for options, both for individuals and for languages. Eventually, we *may* know all the possible variation that there can ever be, and at that point can determine what the "universals" might be, and whether we should consider them to be innate, emergent, or acquired. At this point in time, however, we are still discovering what the range of possibilities *are* in child phonology. Many many areas of child phonology have yet to be explored. And thus, we come to the:

END OF PART I . . .

APPENDIX A

INTERNATIONAL PHONETIC ASSOCIATION (1989) SYMBOLS USED IN THIS BOOK

TABLE 1 IPA Symbols[a]

		Bilabial		Labio-dental		Dental/ alveolar		Retro-flex		Palato-alveolar		Alveo-palatal		Palatal		Velar		Uvular		Pharyn-geal		Glottal		Labio-velar	
		vcls	vcd	vcls	vcd	vcls	vcd	vcls	vcd	vcls	vcd	vcls	vcd	vcls	vcd	vcls	vcd	vcls	vcd	vcls	vcd	vcls	vcd	vcls	vcd
stop	oral	p	b			t	d	ʈ	ɖ					c	ɟ	k	ɡ	q	ɢ			ʔ			
	nasal		m		ɱ		n		ɳ		ɲ				ɲ		ŋ		ɴ						
fricative	grooved					s	z	ʂ	ʐ	ʃ	ʒ														
	ungrooved					θ	ð					ɕ	ʑ	ç	ʝ										
	noncoronal	ɸ	β	f	v											x	ɣ	χ	ʁ	ħ	ʕ	h			
affricate						ts	dz			tʃ	dʒ	tɕ	dʑ												
glide					ʋ						ɹ				j		ɰ							w	
lateral	liquid						l		ɭ																
	fricative					ɬ	ɮ								ʎ										
"r"	trill		ʙ				r												ʀ						
	tap/flap						ɾ																		
click		ʘ					ǀ																		

[a] vcls, voiceless; vcd, voiced.

Unrounded vowels				Rounded vowels		
front	*central*	*back*		*front*	*central*	*back*
i	ɨ	ɯ	HIGH	y	ʉ	u
ɪ		ω		ʏ		ʊ
e	ə	ɤ	MID	ø	ɵ	o
ɛ	ʌ			œ		ɔ
æ			LOW	ɶ		ɔ
a	ɑ	ɒ				

DIACRITICS:

aspirated:	Cʰ	dental:	C̬
voiceless:	x̥	prenasalized:	ⁿC
unreleased:	C̚	postnasalized:	Cⁿ
syllabic:	C̩	lateral release:	Cˡ
nasalized:	x̃	glottalized:	x̰
long:	xː	retracted:	x˂
palatalized:	Cʲ	advanced:	x˃
uvularized:	Cˣ	raised:	xˆ
labiovelarized:	Cʷ	lowered:	xˇ

We follow IPA practice with [j] for the palatal glide (rather than [y]), and with the palatoalveolars as [ʃ,ʒ,tʃ,dʒ], rather than [š,ž,č,ǰ].

For the English "r," we use the IPA [ɹ]; it is a palatoalveolar glide, and is rounded in most environments. (Note that [r] is an alveolar trill, and is used for languages such as Spanish in this book.)

For palatoalveolar stops and nasals, we use the palatal symbols ([c, ɟ, ɲ]).

The vowels differ from strict IPA, following standard practice for English:

[ʌ] is used as a mid *central* vowel (not *back*, as in IPA)

[ɑ] is used as a *central* vowel (not *back*, as in IPA)

[ɒ] is used as a back *unrounded* vowel (not *rounded* as in IPA)

[ω] is a lax high back unrounded vowel (no IPA symbol)

[ɔ] is used ambiguously for both the mid rounded and low rounded back vowels, as in British *bought* [bɔːt] (mid) and North American [bɔːt] (low)

We distinguish between two types of diphthongs, in terms of how the glide portion of the diphthong is written. In both types, the glide portion is written as a vowel ([ɪ] or [ʊ]) rather than as a glide ([j] or [w]). Phonetically, the glide portion *is* a glide, making this transcription somewhat misleading; phonologically, however, it is part of a complex nucleus. Thus, the vowel symbol seems appropriate. Since many journals that require the IPA use the vowel symbol for the second portion of the glide, we follow that practice here.

1. When the glide portion is of usual duration, it is written on the line as a separate symbol:

   [aɪ], [aʊ]

2. When the glide portion is extremely short, it is written as a superscript on the preceding symbol:

   [aⁱ], [aᵘ]

APPENDIX B

THE FEATURES USED
IN THIS BOOK

This appendix defines the features used in this book. We use a set of features that are extensively used within phonological theory in linguistics. Features are categorical distinctions that are superimposed on continuous phonetic dimensions. It is not necessarily the case that all languages (or individuals, whether adults or children) place the boundaries between the different categories at exactly the same points along the continuous dimensions. Further, we assume here that features should be defined along *articulatory* dimensions, but it is possible that *acoustic* dimensions might also be relevant. We address some of these points here and in Chapter 5.

B.1. LARYNGEAL FEATURES

For our purposes, we need to deal with only three features that involve control of the larynx.

1. [+**voiced**]: Sounds produced with vocal cord vibration (e.g., /d/, /i/).

How much voicing is necessary for a phone to be [+voiced] is unclear. For prevocalic stops, as little as 10 msec of voicing before release is sufficient. In postvocalic stops, perhaps 25 msec of voicing into closure is needed. For fricatives and sonorants, a certain percentage of the duration must be voiced; how much is unclear. Unvoiced stops (such as [b̥]) in English are frequently treated as [+voiced], but it is unclear whether they might more profitably be treated as [-voiced,-s.g.,-tense].

In traditional views, this is a binary feature. Voiced segments (whether obstruents or sonorants) are [+voiced]; any segment in which the vocal cords are not vibrating is [-voiced]. However, many linguists now regard [voiced] as a privative feature (Mester & Itô, 1989): voiced segments are [voiced], but voiceless segments have no feature (and are voiceless by default).[1] In our view, it is convenient to treat [voiced] as a binary feature. Others (Avery & Rice, 1989) have suggested that the feature [voiced] appears only in obstruents, never in sonorants, on the grounds that voicing is automatic in sonorants, but difficult to sustain in obstruents. However, voicing in obstruents and voicing in sonorants leads to similar patterns in adult phonology (Rice, 1993). There is presently little motivation for using two different features for voicing in obstruents versus sonorants; we use the feature [voiced] for both.

   2.   [+**spread-glottis**] ([**s.g.**]):   The vocal cords are spread wide, leading to low-amplitude noise at the glottis.

Voiceless aspirated stops are [+s.g.], as in English *tip* [tʰɪp]; generally, there must be at least 25 msec of voicelessness after release for a stop to be [+s.g.]. Voiceless fricatives are [+s.g.], as are [h] and [s]. Voiceless sonorants are [+s.g.], as in [m̥] and [n̥] (which often occur in the speech of English-learning children). Breathy voiced (voiced aspirated) phones, such as Hindi [bʰ], are [+s.g.]. All other segments are [-s.g.]. This feature is binary.

   3.   [+**constricted-glottis**] ([**c.g.**]):   The vocal cords are pulled together tightly, so that regular periodic vibration is impossible.

All [+c.g.] segments are [-voiced], by definition. Glottal stop ([ʔ]) is [+c.g.], as are ejectives (as commonly occurs in the word-final allophone of /k/ in English, e.g., *sick* [sɪk']). For our purposes here, all other segments are [-c.g.]. This feature is binary.

B.2. MANNER FEATURES

We treat all manner features as binary.

   1.   [+**sonorant**]:   Sounds in which the pressure above the larynx allows the vocal cords to vibrate continuously, without any rise in pressure above the larynx.

This definition follows Chomsky and Halle (1968). All regularly voiced vowels, glides, liquids (*r*'s and *l*'s), and nasals ([m], [n], [ɲ], [ŋ]) are [+sonorant], because the air that passes through the larynx is quickly vented out through the oral or nasal cavities, and pressure never rises. Obstruents (stops, fricatives, and affricates) are [-sonorant], because the constrictions inhibit airflow; supraglottal pres-

---

[1] By default, a word does not have an /ɹ/ in it unless the /ɹ/ is present in the representation. Thus, unless we specify that /ɹ/ is present in the word *true* (/tɹuː/), the /ɹ/ will not be present. By default, segments are absent unless they are specified. Similarly, if [voiced] is not specified in an obstruent, by default there is an absence of vocal cord vibration: voicelessness. This is part of the parallelism between segments and features.

sure rises during these segments enough to prohibit voicing without special measures to keep voicing going.

The definition provided here is controversial, however, because it ignores what the vocal cords are actually doing; it says only that pressure considerations would allow voicing, not that voicing actually occurs. If a segment is [-voiced], the vocal cords do not vibrate. Yet, voiced [m] and voiceless [m̥] have identical supralaryngeal configurations, supraglottal pressure is low for both, and both are [+sonorant] by the definition used here. Similarly, [h], which is essentially a [+s.g.] vowel, is [+sonorant]. However, many linguists assume that [h] is [-sonorant] (e.g., Hyman, 1975). A similar issue arises with [ʔ], which is [+c.g.] (and hence voiceless), but generally has a supralaryngeal articulation that is the same as that of the following vowel (and hence is [+sonorant] by our definition).

In general, it makes little difference whether [h], [ʔ], and voiceless sonorants are [+sonorant] or [-sonorant]. We assume that they are [+sonorant], but point out data which can be accounted for more easily if they are [-sonorant]. See Chapter 5.

   2.   [+**consonantal**]:   Sounds with a narrow constriction in the oral and/or
                            pharyngeal cavities that significantly impedes the
                            flow of air, either by stopping it, redirecting it, or
                            creating turbulence.

All "true" consonants are [+consonantal], either because they stop the flow of air out of the vocal tract (oral stops and affricates), redirect air out the nasal cavity (nasal stops), narrow the constriction enough to create turbulence (fricatives and affricates), redirect the air around the sides of the tongue (laterals), or briefly block the flow of air (taps and trills). Only vowels and glides have sufficiently wide constrictions that airflow is unimpeded, and these are [-consonantal]. Note that (North American) English "r" (IPA [ɹ]) is a glide, and thus [-consonantal] (Kahn, 1976). The glottal phones [h] and [ʔ] have constrictions only at the larynx, and by definition lack constrictions in the oral or pharyngeal cavities; they are thus [-consonantal] and for this reason have sometimes been called "glides" (Chomsky & Halle, 1968).

There is some difference of opinion about glides in different portions of the syllable. The glide portion of a diphthong is uncontroversially [-consonantal]. Syllable-initial glides are less clear. Evidence suggests that such glides are [-consonantal] in some languages, but are [+consonantal] in others (e.g., Hayes, 1989). Stemberger (1993a) argued that this is the case for at least some English-learning children. It is possible that children may differ on this point, and that different developmental patterns may result.

   3.   [+**continuant**]:   Sounds in which air continues to move through *the
                            oral cavity* (and possibly just over the *constriction*).

Oral stops and affricates, nasal stops, and glottal stop entirely block airflow through the oral cavity and are [-continuant]. All other segments are [+continuant]: vowels, glides, liquids, and fricatives. Note that nasals are [-continuant] even though air continues to be vented through the nasal cavity; nasals pattern with oral stops in adult languages and in language acquisition, not with fricatives. Taps and trills technically block airflow for very brief periods of time, but are nonetheless considered to be [+continuant].

Chomsky and Halle (1968) suggest that the definition might be narrower, focusing on airflow over the constriction. This matters only for laterals like [l], where airflow is blocked at the constriction, but air continues to flow through the oral cavity over the sides of the tongue. Given the redefinition, [l] would be [-continuant]. Languages may differ in the exact definition of this feature, so that [l] is [+continuant] in some languages but [-continuant] in others. For most English-learning children, /l/ patterns with fricatives and glides rather than stops. Thus, we assume that /l/ is [+continuant]; but it is possible that a different assumption is necessary for some children.

We do not use a feature that uniquely identifies fricatives. A feature such as [+turbulent-airflow] would be phonetically justifiable. This would allow nasals with turbulent airflow at the nostrils (such as some versions of [m̥]) to be treated as fricatives. See Chapter 5 for discussion.

4.   [+**nasal**]:   Sounds with the velum lowered so that air moves through the nasal cavity.

Sounds are [+nasal] if air is vented only through the nasal cavity, as in nasal stops, or if air additionally is vented through the oral cavity, as in nasalized vowels, glides, and liquids. All oral vowels, glides, liquids, and obstruents are [-nasal]. Laver (1994:413) notes that there is some slight nasal airflow as "leakage" in all phones. There must be a sufficient amount of airflow for a segment to be [+nasal]; how much is necessary is unclear.

5.   [+**lateral**]:   Sounds in which central airflow is blocked in the oral cavity, but in which air is directed over at least one side of the tongue.

All *l*-type sounds are [+lateral], including "dark" (velarized) [ɫ] and the lateral fricatives [ɬ] and [ɮ]. All other sounds are [-lateral].

6.   [+**tense**]:   Sounds produced with relatively greater "muscular tension."

This feature is vaguely defined. It is primarily used to distinguish tense vowels ([i], [e], [u], [o]) and trilled [r] (all [+tense]) from lax vowels ([ɪ], [ɛ], [ʊ], [ʌ], [ə]) and tap [ɾ] (all [-tense]). Voiceless obstruents are allophonically [+tense], while voiced obstruents are [-tense].

B.3. PLACE FEATURES

The features that govern place of articulation are divided into two different groups: the *articulator* features that determine which major articulator (the lips, the tongue tip, the tongue body, and the tongue root) is used, and the subsidiary features that fine-tune the information provided by the articulator features. The articulator features are privative, and this is reflected by capitalizing the first letter of their names. We treat the other features as binary. The subsidiary features are usually defined in such a way as to be dependent on the articulators with which they are associated. Thus, attendant features can only be present if their associated articulator feature is present. For example, unless the lips are used, the feature [round] is irrelevant, since [round] requires use of the lips.

For those who are primarily familiar with the approach of Chomsky and Halle (1968), this will be a significant change in viewpoint. Chomsky and Halle tried to define subsidiary features in such a way as to cut across all places of articulation. For example, the feature [+anterior] was present for both coronals and labials, even though labials could never be [-anterior] (with the lips reaching back to the hard palate, for example). The features that they employed by-and-large led to odd predictions. The set of [+anterior] segments (labials plus anterior coronals) should be a better natural class than the set of labials alone, because two features are needed for that class ([+anterior,-coronal]); this turns out to be false. As a result, we now restrict features to hold only within major articulators (Sagey, 1986).

B.3.1. THE LIPS

1. [**Labial**]:   Sounds made with some involvement of one or both lips.

For consonants, bilabials ([p], [b], [ɸ], [β], [m]) and labiodentals ([f], [v], [ɱ], [ʋ]) are [Labial]. For both vowels and consonants, all rounded sounds are [Labial]. If there is no involvement of the lips, the segment is blank for this feature, since the feature is privative.

2. [+**round**]:   Sounds involving protrusion of the lips with narrowing at
                         the corners of the mouth.

All rounded vowels (e.g., [u]) and consonants (e.g., [kʷ]) are [+round]. Simple bilabial and labiodental consonants are [-round].

3. [+**labiodental**]:   Labial sounds that are made with only one lip.

All labiodentals ([f], [v], [ɱ], [ʋ]) are [+labiodental]. All bilabial consonants and rounded segments are [-labiodental]. In Chomsky and Halle (1968), the feature label [distributed] was used for this feature, but it referred to additional contrasts for nonlabials (which is no longer considered to be desirable).

B.3.2. THE TIP OF THE TONGUE

1. [**Coronal**]:   Sounds made with raising of the tip or blade of the tongue.

This includes interdentals, dentals, alveolars, palatoalveolars, alveopalatals, retroflexes, and palatals.[2] Because it includes palatals, the palatal glide [j] and at least

---

[2] Palatals are [Dorsal] as well as [Coronal].

high front vowels are also [Coronal]; most researchers treat all front vowels as [Coronal].[3] All other places of articulation are not specified for [Coronal]; the feature is privative.

2. [+**anterior**]:   Coronal sounds made at the alveolar ridge or further
                        forward.

Interdentals, dentals, and alveolars are [+anterior]; palatoalveolars, alveopalatals, retroflexes, palatals, and front vowels are [-anterior]. The feature is binary. Noncoronal consonants are not defined for [anterior].

3. [+**distributed**]:   Coronal sounds made with a wide area of contact
                           between the tip/blade of the tongue and the roof of the
                           mouth or teeth.

Wide constrictions are found for interdentals, dentals, palatoalveolars, alveopalatals, and palatals; these are [+distributed]. Only alveolars and retroflexes are [-distributed]. The feature is binary, and is undefined for noncoronals.

4. [+**grooved**]:   Coronal sounds made with a grooved tongue (a narrow
                       channel at or near the midline).

This is the equivalent of the feature [strident], but given an articulatory definition (Yip, 1988; Laver, 1994:258), rather than an acoustic one as in Chomsky and Halle (1968): strident sounds contain relatively high-amplitude noise. Since all other features are defined in terms of articulation, it is best to define this feature in that way also, for consistency.

A grooved tongue for coronal sounds channels the air and leads to high-amplitude noise. Only fricatives and affricates can be [+grooved]. Palatal fricatives and interdental fricatives are [-grooved]. Alveolar and retroflex fricatives are [+grooved]. Dental fricatives can be either [+grooved] (as with Swedish [ʂ]) or [-grooved] (as in dialectal variants of English [θ] and [ð], which are dental rather than interdental). We distinguish palatoalveolar fricatives as [+grooved] (with a grooved tongue) and alveopalatals as [-grooved] (with a flat tongue).[4] In children learning English, there may be insufficient grooving even of alveolar fricatives, leading to a [-grooved] fricative for which there is no IPA symbol; the ad hoc symbols [sᶿ] (insufficient grooving) and [θˢ] (some grooving, but very little) are often used by speech-language pathologists.

One might also wish to distinguish sounds that have a truly flat tongue (such as [θ]) from those with a broad central channel (such as [j]). It is not clear whether a feature is needed to encode this. It may be a low-level phonetic dimension.

Our treatment of this feature follows Yip (1988) and Laver (1994:261). Chomsky and Halle (1968) treated labiodental [f] and [v] as [+strident], to distin-

---

[3] We question whether it is phonetically defensible to consider mid and low front vowels to be [Coronal].

[4] Some researchers, including Laver (1994:251–252), use "palatoalveolar" and "alveolopalatal" in a way that is opposite to our usage.

guish them from [-strident] [ɸ] and [β]. The feature [labiodental] is used here for that purpose, since it is needed independently for the distinction between [m] and [ɱ], both of which are nongrooved (and clearly nonstrident). In Chapter 5, we note data which might better be accounted for using [strident] rather than [grooved], especially if even short high-amplitude noise as in the bursts of clicks satisfy the definition, so that clicks are [+strident]).

B.3.3. THE TONGUE BODY

These features refer to the exact position of the main body of the tongue, from palatal to uvular places of articulation, including height.

1. **[Dorsal]**:   Sounds made with the back of the tongue.

The [Dorsal] consonants are palatals,[5] velars, uvulars, and pharyngeals. All vowels are also [Dorsal] (at least on the surface), as are the labiovelar ([w]), velar ([ɰ]), and palatal ([j]) glides. [Dorsal] is also present in consonants with a secondary place of articulation involving velarization (such as English "dark" [ɫ]) or palatalization (such as Russian [pʲ]).

2. **[+back]**:   Sounds with the back of the tongue body raised or lowered.

Velar and uvular consonants are [+back], as well as velarized consonants (including English "dark" [ɫ]). The [-back] consonants are the palatals, including palatalized consonants such as [bʲ]. Vowels always have some value of backness; back and central vowels are [+back], while front vowels are [-back]. Backness is not defined for labials, anterior coronals, pharyngeals, and glottals. The feature is binary.

3. **[+high]**:   Sounds where the tongue body is raised.

High vowels and glides, and velar and palatal consonants are [+high]. Uvular consonants and mid and low vowels are [-high]. Nondorsal consonants are blank for [high].

4. **[+low]**:   Sounds where the tongue body is lowered.

Only low vowels and pharyngeals are [+low]. Other dorsal segments are [-low]. All nondorsal segments, including glottals, are blank for [low].

Chomsky and Halle (1968) treated glottal [h] and [ʔ] as [+low]. In Semitic languages, glottals do seem to behave as [+low] (McCarthy, 1991). Glottals do not pattern as [+low] in most languages, including that of English-learning children with normal vocal tracts. In the speech of children with cleft palates, glottals may pattern with pharyngeals. We treat glottals as undefined for [low] for children with normal vocal tracts, but note that they may be [+low] for children with cleft palates.

---

[5] Palatal consonants are [Coronal] as well as [Dorsal].

B.3.4. THE TONGUE ROOT

We mention two features for controlling the tongue root.

1. [**Radical**]:   Sounds in which the root of the tongue is advanced or retracted.

This includes pharyngeal and pharyngealized consonants, and vowels which can be made either with advanced or retracted tongue root. This feature is privative.

2. [**AdvancedTongueRoot**] ([**ATR**]):   Sounds in which the tongue root is advanced.

This feature is binary. Because the main body of the tongue is connected to the root of the tongue, there is some interaction between [ATR] and vowel height. High vowels tend to be [+ATR], because the tongue root is pulled forward when the tongue is raised. Low vowels tend to be [-ATR], because the tongue root is pushed down when the tongue is lowered. The vowels [i], [e], [u], and [o] are always [+ATR]. The vowels [ɪ], [ɛ], [ʌ], [ʊ], and [ɔ] are often [-ATR,+tense]; however, these same symbols are also used for vowels that are [+ATR,-tense], as in adult English; caution is advised. Consonants tend to be blank for this feature.

B.4. OTHER POSSIBLE FEATURES

Some traditional features have not been included here because they are no longer a part of the representation of segments: [syllabic], [long], and [stress]. See Chapter 3.

APPENDIX C

LIST OF THE CONSTRAINTS OF OPTIMALITY THEORY

In this appendix, we provide a quick listing of the constraints that we introduced in Chapter 4. Please refer to Chapter 4 for detailed discussion and illustration of the constraints. Here, we provide the following:

1. our name for the constraint, marked with "☞,"
2. our definition for the constraint,
3. what a violation looks like,
4. any alternative names for the constraint that the reader may commonly come across in the literature, marked with "✄,"
5. what the constraint is used for,
6. the type of grounding (if any).

A constraint name preceded by a question mark is one that may not be needed. It is not useful to present the constraints in the same order as in Chapter 4. We present the constraints in a different functionally related order: whether the constraint purely requires that elements or links be present, purely prevents elements or links from being present, or mixes those two functions.

> *Purely require elements or links*:
> ☞**Survived**
> ☞**LinkedUpwards**
> ☞**LinkedDownwards**
> ☞**WordFinalMassiveness**
> ☞**Affix(/X/,Category,Edge)**
> ☞**Distinct**
> ☞**Expressed**

Purely prevent elements or links:
- ✏**Not**
- ✏**NotCo-occurring**
- ✏**NoSequence**
- ✏**NotTwice**
- ✏**SinglyLinked** = **SinglyLinkedUp**
- ✏**NotComplex** = **SinglyLinkedDown**
- ?✏**Notσ-Peak**
- ?✏**Notσ-Margin**
- ✏**Light(Unstressed)**
- ✏**Binary(σ,μ)**
- ✏**SinglyExpressed**

Require some elements or links, and prevent others:
- Upwards Structure
- Downwards Structure
- ✏**Co-occurring**
- ✏**Contiguity**
- ✏**Uninterrupted**
  - ?✏**UninterruptedDomain**
- ✏**Priority(Direction,X)**
- ✏**Prominent(Foot/PrWd,Left/Right)**
- ✏**Binary(Foot,μ/σ)**
- ✏**Heavy(Stressed)**
- ?✏**Aligned(Category,Edge,Category,Edge)**
- ✏**Size(⟨morph⟩=⟨phon⟩)**

C.1. PURELY REQUIRE ELEMENTS OR LINKS

✏**Survived**: An element in the underlying representation must be present in the surface pronunciation.
It does matter whether the element is linked or floating.
violation: a deleted element (i.e., absent from the output)
old names: ✂Containment; ✂MAX; ✂Corr_{io}(X); ✂Ident; ✂Match
purpose: prevent deletion of underlying elements
delete elements (when violated)
grounding: communicative/functional (maintain lexical information)
A family of constraints, one for every element present in underlying representations
Note: No inherent ranking within the family.

✏**LinkedUpwards**: An element must be linked to an element on the tier above it.
(*An element must be anchored in time relative to other elements.*)

violation: an unlinked (floating) element
Old names: ✂Parse
purpose: prevent floating elements
prevent deletion of elements
float elements (when violated)
grounding: communicative/functional (maintain lexical
information)
*A family of constraints, one for every element except
the highest one (PrWd)*
Note: No inherent ranking within the family.

☞**LinkedDownwards**: Elements must be linked to *all* required elements on
the appropriate lower tier(s).
violation: an element that does not dominate *all* required
elements on tiers below it
old names: ✂Fill
purpose: epenthesis of segments, timing units, etc.
insertion of default features
prevent deletion of underlying elements
grounding: articulatory (to supply all elements needed to
construct the phonetic/motor representation)
*A family of constraints, one for every element
except terminal features (which have no elements
below them)*
Note: No inherent ranking within the family.

☞**WordFinalMassiveness**: Words end with extra *nonprominent* elements.
violation: a vowel-final word
a word ending in a stressed syllable
a word ending in an unstressed syllable in a
right-prominent binary foot
old names: ✂Final-C
purpose: requiring a word to end in extra nonprominent
elements
grounding: word-final lengthening;
?communicative (demarcating word edges)?

☞**Expressed**: An output form expresses a particular morphological feature
contained in the input.
violation: A morphological feature is not overtly expressed.
old names: ✂M-Parse, ✂Subcat
purpose: add affixes (usually segmental material) when called for by the
input (for syntactic, semantic, or pragmatic reasons)
grounding: semantic/pragmatic/syntactic (communicative)
*A family of constraints, one for each morphological affix in the
language*

☞Affix(/X/,Category,Edge): There must be an affix of the specified phonological shape located at the specified edge (left or right) of the specified category.

example: ☞**Plural(/z/,PrWd,R)**

violation: The morpheme is not expressed.

purpose: spelling out the form and location of a particular affix

☞Distinct: Elements that are distinct in the input should be distinct in the output.

violation: An affix is not added when the base already contains homophonous material at the appropriate position in the word.

Two tokens of an element in the input are merged into one token of the element in the output; plateauing to make survival of an element more likely.

old names: ✄Afx, ✄Recov-MCat; ✄*MultipleCorrespondence; affix checking; OCP

purpose: to ensure that an affix is added, even when the base contains homophonous material

to maintain faithfulness to the number of tokens of an element in the input

grounding: communicative/functional (explicit encoding of affix)

C.2. PURELY PREVENT ELEMENTS OR LINKS

☞Not: An element must not appear in the output.

violation: The element is present in the output, *whether it is floating or linked*.

old names: ✄*Struc; ✄NoCoda; ✄*(Element); ✄*Spread; ✄LexFeat; ✄LexLink; ✄DEP; ✄Corr$_{oi}$(X)

purpose: delete elements

prevent insertion of elements

insert elements (when violated)

grounding: cognitive (resources are needed to access any element)

A family of constraints, one for every element

Note: Ranking within the family is based on markedness.

☞NotCo-occurring(A,B): A and B may not co-occur at the same point in time.

Note that A & B are unordered.

Not violated if A & B are contained in a floating element.

violation: A and B co-occur at the same point in time.

old names:	✄PathCond; ✄*Clash; ✄CodaCond; ✄*M; ✄*P
purpose:	cause deletion or flop of an element
	prevent insertion or spreading of an element
	prevent an element from appearing in a particular part of the syllable
grounding:	cognitive (resources are needed to coordinate any two elements at the same point in time)
	Note: Little inherent ranking within the family, except: correlated with the ranking of the Not constraints.

✏**NoSequence(A...B)**:	Given two segments, A cannot be in the first segment if B is in the second segment.
violation:	The sequence A . . . B is present.
old names:	✄ClustCond; ✄Generalized OCP; *(AB)
purpose:	cause deletion or flop of an element
	prevent insertion or spreading of an element
	cause assimilation
grounding:	cognitive (resources are needed to coordinate any two elements in sequence)
	Note: Little inherent ranking within the family, except: correlated with the ranking of the Not constraints.
	There are four variants of the constraints, depending on whether adjacency is defined in terms of tier adjacency, Root adjacency, timing unit adjacency, or syllable adjacency.

✏**NotTwice**:	An element may not appear twice if the two tokens are adjacent.
violation:	two adjacent tokens of an element
old names:	✄OCP
purpose:	cause deletion or flop of an element
	cause fusion of the two elements
	prevent insertion or spreading of an element
	motivate insertion (at a location between the two identical elements)
	cause assimilation, including plateauing
grounding:	cognitive (resources are needed to immediately repeat any element)
	Note: Little inherent ranking within the family, except: correlated with the ranking of the Not constraints.
	There are four variants of the constraints, depending on whether adjacency is defined in terms of tier adjacency,

Root adjacency, timing unit adjacency, or syllable adjacency.
There are two variants of the constraints, depending on whether identity is defined just on the tier, or includes having identical dependent elements.

☞**SinglyLinked**: An element can link upwards to only a single higher element.

       violation: a doubly linked (or multiply linked) element

   old names: none

      purpose: prevent assimilation
               cause degemination
               cause assimilation (when violated)

   grounding: cognitive (resources are needed to extend a gesture beyond its basic duration)
               A family of constraints, one for each element.
               No known inherent ranking within the family.

☞**NotComplex**: An element may link downwards to only one lower element.

       violation: consonant clusters within an onset
               consonant clusters within a coda
               diphthongs (complex nuclei)
               coda (causing a complex rime)
               unstressed syllable (causing a complex foot)
               two stresses in a word (causing a complex prosodic word)
               a Place node dominating two or more articulator nodes
               an affricate (complex Root node)

   old names: ✂*Complex; ✂NoCoda; ✂*Coda

   grounding: cognitive (Resources are needed to coordinate multiple elements.)

?☞**Notσ-Peak**: A segment may not be the peak (head) of the syllable.

       violation: a syllabic segment

   old names: ✂*P

      purpose: preventing a segment from being syllabic
               making a segment syllabic (when violated)
               deleting a segment (occasionally)

   grounding: articulatory and/or perceptual
               A family with one member for each segment that is possible in any human language
               Note: Ranking within the family based on sonority
               Probably not needed. Not used in this book.
               Co-occurring and NotCo-occurring can do the same job.

?☞**Notσ-Margin**: A segment may not be nonsyllabic.
　　　　violation: a nonsyllabic segment
　　old names: ✄*M
　　　purpose: preventing a segment from being nonsyllabic
　　　　　　　　making a segment nonsyllabic (when violated)
　　　　　　　　deleting a segment (occasionally)
　　grounding: articulatory and/or communicative
　　　　　　　　A family with one member for each segment that is
　　　　　　　　　　possible in any human language
　　　　　　　　Note: Ranking within the family based on sonority
　　　　　　　　Probably not needed. Not used in this book.
　　　　　　　　Co-occurring and NotCo-occurring can do the same job.

☞**Light(Unstressed)**: The unstressed syllable of a foot must be light.
　　　　violation: a heavy unstressed syllable
　　old names: ✄RhHrm; ✄WSP
　　　purpose: delete a mora, to make a syllable light
　　　　　　　　cause a heavy syllable to be stressed
　　　　　　　　motivate deletion of a heavy syllable
　　grounding: perceptual (matching phonetic cues for stress)

☞**Binary(σ,μ)**: A syllable is limited to two moras.
　violation: a syllable with three or more moras
old names: none
　purpose: delete extra moras
grounding: unknown (?rhythm in articulation or perception?)

☞**SinglyExpressed**: An element in the input occurs only once in the output.
　　　　violation: An input element appears twice in the output.
　　old names: ✄*MultipleCorrespondence
　　　purpose: prevent deletion of affixes
　　　　　　　　prevent an input segment from appearing with two
　　　　　　　　　　tokens in the output
　　grounding: communicative/functional (maintains lexical
　　　　　　　　information)

C.3. REQUIRE SOME ELEMENTS OR LINKS, PREVENT OTHERS

Upwards structure: ☞**A◂B**: A links upwards to B.
　　　　violation: floating element
　　　　　　　　element linked to the wrong higher element
　　old names: none

> **purpose**: determining which higher element an element links to, in order to satisfy **LinkedUpwards**;
> *therefore, same basic consequences as LinkedUpwards*
>
> **grounding**: unknown
> *a family on constraints, one for each element except the highest*
> *reflects the structure discussed in Chapter 3*
> *Note: may be a part of Gen.*

Downwards structure: ☞**A▸B**: A *must* link downwards to B.

> **violation**: A is present but does not link downwards to B.
>
> **old names**: ✄Ons; ✄Nuc
>
> **purpose**: determining which elements must be present in order for **LinkedDownwards** to be satisfied; *therefore, same basic consequences as LinkedDownwards*
>
> **grounding**: unknown
> *a family on constraints, one for each element except for terminal features*
> *reflects the structure discussed in Chapter 3*
> *Note: may be a part of Gen.*

☞**Co-occurring(A→B)**: If A is present, B must also be present at the same point in time.
> *Note: Ordering of A & B is crucial.*
>
> **violation**: A is present, but B is not present.
>
> **old names**: ✄R-Cond; ✄CodaCond
>
> **purpose**: inserting B
> causing B to spread to the segment containing A
> preventing B from being deleted
> deleting the opposite value of B, if B is a binary feature
> causing a feature to occur in a particular part of the syllable
> preventing a feature from occurring in a particular part of the syllable
>
> **grounding**: articulatory and/or perceptual
> *Note: no inherent ordering to the constraint family*

☞**Contiguity**: Elements next to each other (contiguous) in the UR must be contiguous on the surface.
> **violation**: (a) In associating segments to syllables, a segment is skipped, and so underlyingly noncontiguous consonants become contiguous on the surface.

(b) In associating segments to syllables, a segment is
       epenthesized between two underlying segments, and so
       underlyingly contiguous segments are noncontiguous on
       the surface.
(c) metathesis

old names: none

purpose: determines which of two segments links to a syllable node
       determines position of epenthetic vowel relative to an
         otherwise unsyllabifiable consonant
       prevents metathesis

grounding: communicative (preserving lexical information)

☞**Uninterrupted**:   An element must be linked upwards to all anchors within
         the span of its spread.
       No anchors may be skipped.
       ("Anchor" = the higher element that the element links
         upwards to, as defined by an Upwards Structure
         constraint)

violation: a feature linked to two segments, without being linked to
         a relevant segment that is between them
       crossing association lines

old names: ✄*Gapped; ✄Expression; ✄*Embed

purpose: cause spreading to an intervening segment
       prevent spreading past an opaque segment
       (rarely: motivate deletion of an opaque segment)

grounding: unknown (?articulatory?; ?cognitive?)

☞**UninterruptedDomain**:   equivalent to **Uninterrupted**, but used if feature
         domains are assumed

☞**Priority(Direction,X)**:   Give priority to the token of element X early in
         the word (to the left) or late in the word (to the
         right).

violation: An element in the specified direction is deleted,
           while an element in the opposite direction
           survives and links upward.
       An element in the opposite direction spreads,
           when an element in the specified direction is
           available for spreading.

old names: directionality parameter for spreading

purpose: When a sequence is ruled out by **NoSequence**,
         NotTwice, σ▸**Onset**, **NotComplex**, or other
         constraint, the element in the specified
         direction is preserved in the output, rather than
         the element in the opposite direction.

                    prevents deletion of the element in the specified
                      direction
                    motivates deletion of the element in the opposite
                      direction
                    determines direction of spreading in assimilation

grounding: cognitive (Primacy effect versus Recency effect)

☞**Prominent(Foot,Left)**: The stressed syllable (head) of the foot is on the left. (The foot is trochaic.)

violation: a right-prominent (iambic) foot
a center-prominent (ambibract) foot

old names: ✄RhType=T; ✄FtForm(Trochaic)

purpose: cause feet to be left-prominent
prevent feet from being right-prominent or
center-prominent
can motivate deletion of syllables

grounding: unknown

☞**Prominent(Foot,Right)**: The stressed syllable (head) of the foot is on the right. (The foot is iambic.)

violation: a left-prominent (trochaic) foot
a center-prominent (ambibract) foot

old names: ✄RhType=I; ✄FtForm(Iambic)

purpose: cause feet to be right-prominent
prevent feet from being left-prominent or
center-prominent
can motivate deletion of syllables

grounding: unknown

☞**Binary(Foot,μ)**: A foot has two moras.

violation: a foot with a single light syllable
a foot with three or more moras

old names: ✄FtBin

purpose: cause insertion of a mora
cause deletion of a mora

grounding: unknown

☞**Binary(Foot,σ)**: A foot has two syllables.

violation: a foot with a single syllable
a foot with three or more syllables

old names: ✄FtBin

purpose: cause insertion of a syllable
cause deletion of a syllable

grounding: unknown

✏**Heavy(Stressed)**: The stressed (head) syllable of a foot should be heavy.
violation: a light stressed syllable
old names: ✂RhHrm; ✂WSP
purpose: prevent a light syllable from being stressed
cause insertion of a mora to make a stressed vowel heavy
can be used to motivate deletion of a syllable
grounding: perceptual (phonetic cues for stress)

✏**Aligned(Category,Edge,Category,Edge)**: *Generalized Alignment*
Align the left or right edge of one category (morphological or phonological) with the left or right edge of another category. (The "category" can include phonological elements.)
Edges: L or R
Morphological categories: root, stem, morphological word, prefix, suffix, etc.
Phonological categories: μ, σ, Ft, PrWd, PhPhrase, etc., or any feature or organizing node
violation: Any output form where the edges are not aligned in the stipulated way.
old names: ✂Align; plus many specific names for variants
purpose: causing assimilation
causing deletion of an element
preventing deletion of an element
causing insertion of an element
preventing insertion of an element
determining whether an affix is a prefix or suffix
causing an affix to be an infix (when violated)
preventing elements from linking up to, for example, a particular syllable or foot
many additional uses
grounding: unknown
May not be needed. Not used much in this book.

✏**Size(⟨morph⟩ = ⟨phon⟩)**: A particular morphological category is always of a certain phonological size.
example: ✏**Size(Stem = PrWd)**: A stem is always a prosodic word.
violation: a morphological category that is smaller than the stipulated phonological category
example: a stem that is not a prosodic word (because it has no vowel and hence no syllable or foot)
old names: ✂M-Cat≈P-Cat; ✂Lx≈Pr

purpose: inserting material to bring a morphological
element that is too small up to the proper size
deleting material to bring a morphological
element that is too large down to the proper
size

grounding: unknown (?communicative, as a cue for that
category?)

APPENDIX D

PRACTICAL GUIDELINES
FOR USING CONSTRAINTS

One of the most difficult parts about using any set of constraints is knowing which constraints are relevant to the problem at hand. We observe only the surface pronunciations used by speakers. We must apply knowledge of the phonological system to infer which constraints are relevant and how they are ranked. We have provided many examples of constraint rankings in Chapters 4–9, covering the full range of phenomena that we have observed for phonological development. Readers may be able to apply one of these rankings (directly or with slight modification) for their own purposes. (However, it should be noted, when we presented those rankings, we focused only on the aspects of the data relevant to the point under discussion. Note that the rankings given apply *only* for the aspects of the data that they were intended to cover. To arrive at a full analysis of a set of data, many of our constraint lists and constraint tables have to be merged together.) But there may be times when nothing that we have provided is adequate.

In this appendix, we supply some practical guidelines to help in identifying which constraints are relevant to a particular surface phenomenon. We organize the discussion by the types of surface phenomena that occur. We hope that anyone who is just beginning to use OT will find this a useful guide at first, until, with increasing experience, they develop better intuitions about which constraints are relevant to a given phonological pattern.

No matter how complex the surface patterns, they can always be broken down into simpler subpatterns, which always involve deletion of an element (anywhere from a single feature to an entire foot), insertion of an element (anywhere from a single feature to an entire foot), and/or insertion or deletion of an association line. (Complex constraints, such as [Labial] survives after front vowels in stressed syllables when a dorsal consonant follows, are too specific, and fail to capture general patterns in the phonology. Such patterns derive from the interaction of a number of constraints.) After identifying the more straightforward subpatterns, it is a simpler matter to look for the particular characteristics that betray the workings of the particular constraint that is involved with that deletion or insertion. We emphasize that constraints should be simple.

The very first step is thus to compare the input and the output (or the adult and child forms) and to ask what the differences are. After determining all aspects in which the input and output differ, the relevant constraints can be determined. The beginner may find this to be challenging at first, but will find that it becomes easier with practice.

We divide this appendix into four main sections, providing coverage of all phonological (but no morphological) alternations, with a focus on child phonology patterns.

D.1. deletion of elements and association lines

D.2. insertion of elements (epenthesis, default values)

D.3. insertion of association lines (assimilation, flop)

D.4. building "odd" structures (syllables or feet)

A given phonological pattern may involve all of these sections. There are only a few constraints which, when violated, actually bring about the deletion or insertion. However, many constraints, when high-ranked, can motivate the deletion or insertion. To determine which constraints are important, we need to examine the specific details of the deletion or insertion. We organize our discussion as a series of questions that must be answered, with each answer providing further information about which constraints are involved in the phonological pattern under examination.

We emphasize that determining which constraints are relevant to a given set of data requires that sufficient information be available to answer these questions. When dealing with adult languages, with vocabularies containing thousands of words, sufficient information is usually available. When dealing with the speech of young children, where the child may be using less than fifty words, it is frequently difficult to find enough information to understand the alternations fully. For example, if the child attempts only one word containing a /p/ in a coda (*top*), and pronounces the coda as dental [t], it is difficult to determine whether this is an assimilation (Coronal Harmony), an effect of limitations on the features that may appear in codas, or a constraint on sequences of place features that leads to the insertion of the default [Coronal] feature in the rightmost consonant. In order to determine *exactly* which constraints are involved, it is necessary to have a sufficient number of words which represent diverse phonological environments. The more diversity, the better. Even in adult speech, insufficient diversity in the lexicon can cause uncertainty about which constraints are involved. However, for most phonological patterns, even for young children, there are sufficient data available to allow the researcher to be *fairly* certain about which constraints are involved, given at least a few words with diverse phonological environments. It is important to emphasize, however, that even the most complete data set does not give enough information to rank every constraint with respect to every other constraint. When addressing one particular pattern, often a single division of the constraints into a "high-ranked group" and a "low-ranked group" is sufficient. Rarely is it necessary to divide the constraints into more than four ranked groups.

D.1. DELETION OF ELEMENTS AND ASSOCIATION LINES

Underlying elements and association lines can be deleted in a number of diverse phonological patterns.

1. The deletion of an element always leads to the element being absent in the surface pronunciation.
2. Deletion of an association line *may* lead to an element being absent in the surface pronunciation, but not necessarily: if the element is linked elsewhere, it is still pronounced.

When an underlying element is absent in the surface pronunciation, there are two possible causes:

1. the element has been deleted outright and is not present in the output, or
2. the element is present in the output but floating, so that it receives no phonetic realization.

When an underlying association line is absent, there is only one possibility. It is deleted outright and is not present in the output; there are no floating association lines. Deletion *always* involves the violation of *one* of two constraints (and *never* involves violation of *both* of the constraints):

deletion of element:	**Survived**:	deleted outright
	LinkedUpwards:	floating in output
deletion of link:	**Survived(Link)**:	deleted outright
	Note: It is not necessary to identify the element to which the deleted link is attached. That is determined independently by negative constraints.	

As discussed in Chapter 4, it is often difficult to know whether an element has been deleted outright or is floating. For convenience (and because it strikes us as plausible), we assume that outright deletion is the rule, because then fewer cognitive resources are expended in the access of phonetically unrealized material. Floating elements are unusual, and we are forced to posit them primarily in the case of nonminimal repairs.

In a multilinear representation, deletion can occur at any level in the hierarchy, without necessarily affecting any other element. Thus, a Root node can be deleted (along with most of its dependents), even if the timing unit is not deleted (and is realized as length on an adjacent segment) and the feature [+nasal] is not deleted (and is realized as nasalization on an adjacent segment: e.g., /pan/ [pãː]). Only a single element might be deleted (e.g., only the Root node) or a larger number of elements might be deleted (e.g., the syllable and all lower elements within it). The researcher must determine which element is deleted, and which are still present in the surface pronunciation. Deletion must occur at the *highest* location in the phonological hierarchy at which an element is absent: the foot, the syllable, the timing unit, the Root node, the Place node, and so on. Deletion at *lower* points in the hierarchy depends on whether any lower elements appear in the pronunciation by linking to phonetically realized segments or syllables. If all lower elements vanish without a trace, we assume that they are deleted via a **Survived** violation, although **LinkedUpwards** may really be the culprit. If a lower element survives and links up elsewhere, then of course it is not deleted.

Violations of **Survived** and **LinkedUpwards** are possible only when that violation allows the phonological system to avoid a violation of a higher-ranked negative constraint. The higher-ranked constraint that is the culprit is *always* one that prevents the appearance of some element (at some location) in the output. This means that the culprit is always one of the constraints listed in §C.2 or §C.3 of Appendix C. To repeat them here:

☞**Not**
☞**Co-occurring**
☞**NotCo-occurring**
☞**NoSequence**
☞**NotTwice**
☞**SinglyLinked**
☞**NotComplex**
☞**Contiguity**
☞**Uninterrupted**
?☞**Notσ-Peak** (not used in this book)
?☞**Notσ-Margin** (not used in this book)
☞**Binary(σ,μ)**
☞**SinglyExpressed**
☞**Prominent(Foot,Left/Right)**
☞**Binary(Foot,μ/σ)**
☞**Heavy(Stressed)**
☞**Light(Unstressed)**
?☞**Aligned(Category,Edge,Category,Edge)** (not used in this book)
☞**Size(<morph> = <phon>)**
☞**Priority(Left/Right,X)** (This constraint is important only in determining *which* of two elements is deleted due to *other* constraints.)

One of these constraints prohibits an element. The element can be prevented from occurring anywhere in the word (especially if **Not** is involved), but more often it is prevented in a particular context: in a particular position in a syllable or foot, or given the presence of other features within the segment or in a sequence. In order to determine *which* of these constraints is the culprit, answer the following questions.

Recall also that there is only a single ranking for constraints in most instances, except in two circumstances: (a) when the rankings are unstable, so that *one or more particular words* have more than one pronunciation, or (b) in strong prosodic positions versus weak prosodic positions. It is generally not correct to say that **Not** is ranked higher than **Survived** for some segments, but lower than **Survived** for others. Patterns that would suggest such a state of affairs are more likely to involve some other negative constraint, such as **NotCo-occurring**. When the operative high-ranked constraint is some negative constraint other than **Not**, then **Not** is low-ranked. Similarly, when the operative constraint is some positive constraint such as **Co-occurring**, it may be that **Survived** is low-ranked.

We now pose a series of questions. If the answer is "no" to the question, then just proceed to the next question of the same level (I, II, etc.; or A, B, etc.; or 1, 2, etc.; or a, b, etc.). If we have done our job thoroughly enough, you will eventually answer "yes." When you have answered "yes," then keep on with the questions at the next level down, until you determine which constraint is relevant.

We caution that this presupposes that a single constraint underlies a given phonological pattern. Often *several* constraints conspire in the deletion of an element or association line. In that case, it is necessary to identify each subpattern, and the constraint responsible for it.

In the following descriptions, the constraints listed are the high-ranked constraints that motivate the phenomenon, unless otherwise noted.

If preliminary analysis indicates that more than one segment was deleted:

LEVEL: Foot or syllable.
I. Does the deletion involve a sequence of segments such as a foot or a syllable?
   A. Is a whole foot deleted? Generally, this happens when the word is limited to a single foot.
      All words have just one stressed syllable. This derives either from a **NoSequence** constraint on feet, or from a complexity constraint on prosodic words. Stressed syllables are rarely deleted for any other reason (though a stressed *vowel* can be deleted for other reasons.)
      NotComplex(ProsodicWord): violated whenever there is more than one foot (more than one stressed syllable) in a word.
      Repaired via deletion of all feet except one
      NotTwice(Foot)
   B. Are just *unstressed* syllables deleted?
      1. *All* unstressed syllables? (In all probability, there is a maximum of one syllable per word.)
         Not(σ): a general constraint that keeps words short.
            If ranked higher than **Survived(Root)**, segments are deleted in order to avoid syllables in the word. But every prosodic word

must have at least one foot, and every foot must have at least one syllable, and so one syllable remains in each word: the stressed syllable (head of the foot).

NotComplex(Foot): A foot may link downwards to only one syllable.

2. Only *initial* unstressed syllables?

☞**Prominent(Foot,Left)**: In English, feet are left-prominent. This is violated in words with an initial unstressed syllable.

If **Prominent(Foot,Left)** is ranked high, an initial unstressed syllable is deleted (preferable to making it a single stressed syllable or to inserting a dummy syllable to create a larger foot).

3. Only *heavy* unstressed syllables (with a long vowel, diphthong, or a coda)?

Light(Unstressed): violated when an unstressed syllable is heavy, and can motivate the deletion of a heavy unstressed syllable (nonminimal repair)

4. Only when there are *two consecutive* unstressed syllables in the same foot (as in words like *syllable* or *hippopotamus*, that end in two unstressed syllables)?

Binary(Foot,σ): resulting in the loss of unstressed syllables, so that there is only one unstressed syllable in a foot

NotTwice(Unstressed)

5. Only *final* unstressed syllables?

We are unaware of child data in which this happens. It could reflect high ranking of **Prominent(Foot,Right)**, if the child is treating the feet of English as right-prominent. More likely, it would reflect severe constraints on features late in the word (**NoSequence**), preventing segmental features from appearing late in the word. Initial unstressed syllables are not to the right of anything, and therefore would not be subject to such constraints.

6. Only *medial* unstressed syllables?

When this occurs, it generally reflects the lack of unstressed syllables in feet.

However, the foot on the right edge of the word often is allowed to be larger, with an unstressed syllable:

NotComplex(Foot)   (deletion of all unstressed syllables)

WordFinalMassiveness   (deletion except word finally)

7. Only when particular segments with particular features are present in the syllable?

NotTwice

NoSequence

NotCo-occurring

Constraints on combinations of elements at any level (feature or above), can lead to the deletion of a syllable, as a nonminimal repair. This is *especially* the case if the constraint affects a vowel, and if one of the syllables consists only of a vowel:

NotTwice(V-Labial): *example*: yellow /jɛloʊ/ [jɛʊ] (not *[.jɛʊ.o.])

The vowel /oʊ/ is deleted to avoid a violation.

Deletions of this sort are very unusual, however.

C. Are just *stressed* vowels deleted (without deletion of any unstressed vowels)?

This would be very unusual. If it occurred, it would probably derive from a **NotTwice** or **NoSequence** violation at a lower level, combined with a **Priority(Right)** or **Priority(Left)** constraint that required the unstressed elements to be retained.

There are no constraints on *feet* that would cause such a deletion.

D. Is just the *first* or *last* syllable of the word deleted, regardless of stress?

This would be very unusual. If it occurred, it would probably derive from **NotTwice(σ)** combined with a **Priority(Right)** or **Priority(Left)** constraint that caused the rightmost or leftmost syllable to be retained, regardless of stress.

There are no constraints on *feet* that would cause such a deletion.

If preliminary analysis indicates that just one segment was deleted (such as /CVC/ [CV], or /CCV/ [CV]):

LEVEL: Root node and/or Timing Unit.

II. Does the deletion involve a single segment? (In some cases, a sequence of consonants may be deleted, but that is *usually* the independent deletion of both consonants; we address the few cases which have a different motivation.) Where a segment is present in the underlying representation, there is no segment in the output.

A. Is the deletion limited to a particular position in the syllable (onset vs. nucleus vs. coda)?

1. Are *all* segments in that position in the syllable deleted?

(This is not possible for the nucleus, of course, since all syllables must have a nucleus, although see Shaw, 1996.)

As far as we know, this never happens for onsets.

If it did, it could be due to **Not(Onset)** or **NotComplex(σ)**.

Not(Coda): prevents codas, as do:

NotComplex(Rime)

NotCo-occurring(Rime, + consonantal) (nonminimal repair)

Aligned(σ,R,V,R)

Effect of weak prosodic domain: A coda is deleted, but only in unstressed syllables.

Certain consonants are deleted from the coda of an unstressed syllable, but not from the coda of stressed syllables.

(Note: It is important to examine the *SAME* consonant. A different consonant might be deleted from the coda of an unstressed syllable for reasons that are independent of stress and concern features of manner, place, or voicing.)

Binary(σ,μ): A coda is deleted, but only after a long vowel or diphthong.

If **Co-occurring(Coda→μ)** is so high-ranked that any consonant within the rime must be moraic, and **Binary(σ,μ)** imposes an absolute limit of two moras in syllable, then deletion is possible. Borowsky (1989) and Yip (1988) argue that the vowel generally shortens in this environment, so that the pronunciation is faithful to the features in the consonant but not to the number of timing units in the vowel.

Coda deletion is *possible*, but rare.

2. Are segments deleted only when there are two segments in that part of the syllable?

And segmental content does not affect *whether* a segment is deleted (though it *may* affect *which* segment is deleted)?

a. Is just *one* segment (or rather, *all but one*) deleted?

NotComplex(Onset): All but one segment is deleted from the onset.

NotComplex(Nucleus): One part of a diphthong is deleted, resulting in a simple vowel.

NotComplex(Coda): All but one segment is deleted from the coda.

b. Are *both* (or *all*) segments deleted? This is difficult to derive in standard OT. In our version, in which the ranking of **Survived** is indexed to activation levels, and the competition between the two segments lowers activation levels, the **Survived** constraints are ranked below the **Not** constraints; deletion results. *This is very rare except in the youngest children (or those with severe disorders).*

3. Are only segments containing particular features deleted, but only in one part of the syllable?

This would be a nonminimal repair, in which a whole segment is deleted, due to an ill-formed feature within the segment.

The culprit can be any negative constraint ranked above **Survived** and **LinkedUpwards**. Such deletion is generally in weak prosodic positions (unstressed syllables, final syllables, codas, the second consonant in an onset), where the faithfulness constraints are ranked lower than in strong prosodic positions. The constraints motivating deletion might be:

NotCo-occurring(Rime,X)
Co-occurring(Rime→X)
NotCo-occurring(Coda, + voiced)

NotCo-occurring(<any two features>)
NoSequence
NotTwice
Notσ-Margin

For deletion only in onset position, the same constraints ranked
higher than σ▸**Onset**, plus:

Co-occurring(σ-Margin→X)
NotCo-occurring(σ-Margin,X)

In addition, **Not** can be involved. **Not** can require deletion in an
onset, but be prevented from deleting in a coda by **Co-occur-**
ring(Rime→X). Further, **Not** is ranked higher in weak prosodic
domains such as a coda than in strong prosodic domains such as
an onset.

B. Is deletion restricted to a particular part of the word (initial, medial,
final)?
This is *generally* due to constraints on parts of the syllable or on sequences. It may also involve a prosodically weak position that is defined in terms of the edges of the word.

1. Are only particular sequences involved?
NoSequence
Common: All consonants *except* those that are identical to an earlier segment in the word, or *except* those with mostly default
features.

2. In medial position, is deletion a way to avoid consonant clusters?
NotTwice(C-Root)
NotTwice(C-TimingUnit)
NoSequence(<Features>) (nonminimal repair)
NotTwice(<Feature>), etc. (nonminimal repair)

3. Are all medial consonants deleted, even though word-initial onsets
and word-final codas are permitted?
This would be an unusual pattern. There are two possibilities.
a. It may be that medial position is the weakest prosodic position
(with the beginning of the word being strongest, and the end of
the word being intermediate). **Survived(C-Root)** is ranked
lower than **Not(C-Root)** only in medial position.
b. There is obligatory merger of vowel features such as V-[+con-
tinuant] (low-ranking of **Distinct**). Intervening consonants
would have to also link to the merged features (high ranking of
Uninterrupted). Vowel features may link only to elements on
the vowel plane (high ranking of **V-[Feature]◂V-Element**). If
Survived(C-Root) is ranked low enough, intervocalic consonants delete rather than take part in plateauing.

4. Are codas deleted word finally but not word medially?
(a *very* unusual pattern for children; attested for adult languages)
Aligned(PrWd,R,V,R)

5. Is an element deleted from an onset in word-initial position but *not* deleted from an intervocalic consonant or from a word-final consonant?

The intervocalic consonant may be a coda (or ambisyllabic). If a feature is possible only in a coda, it can also occur in an intervocalic consonant. But a word-initial consonant is solely an onset, and the feature is thus impossible there.

C. Is a vowel deleted only when it has no onset?

σ▸Onset

Such deletion generally only occurs when two vowels are adjacent, which is prohibited by sequence constraints:

NotTwice(V-TimingUnit)

NotTwice(Nucleus)

If the onset preserves the vowel in other contexts, it would be because **Survived(V-Root)** is ranked lower than some negative constraint, but **Survived(C-Root)** is high-ranked; a vowel may not delete if that would cause deletion of a consonant. The high-ranked negative constraint may be **Not(V-Root)** (so that vowels always delete except to preserve consonants or to allow the word to be of some minimum size) or a constraint on the maximum size of a word (such as **Binary(Foot,σ)**; see §6.2.3.3).

D. Does the deletion of a segment with particular feature content take place regardless of position in syllable or word?

Not(<Feature>) (nonminimal repair)

E. Does a neighboring segment become long when the segment is deleted (compensatory lengthening)? The timing unit is not deleted, and spreads to a neighboring Root node.

Survived(TimingUnit)

(**SinglyLinked** as a low-ranked constraint)

If preliminary analysis indicates that all segments are present in the output, but parts of a segment are deleted (such as Glottal Replacement):

LEVEL: Place node; individual features.

III. Does the deletion involve just a part of a segment? There is a segment there, but with feature content different from the underlying segment?

A. Is a long segment shortened without affecting feature content?

Just a timing unit is deleted.

SinglyLinked(Root)

NotTwice(C-TimingUnit)

NotTwice(V-TimingUnit)

Light(Unstressed): shortening only in unstressed syllable

Binary(σ,μ): A vowel is shortened before a coda consonant, *or* a coda consonant is deleted only after a long vowel.

(If **Co-occurring(Coda→μ)** is so high-ranked that any consonant

within the rime must be moraic, and there is an absolute limit of
two moras in a syllable, then deletion of one of the vowel's moras is
an alternative.)

B. Is just the Place node deleted? The consonant then shows up as a glottal [h] or [ʔ] (Glottal Replacement; Debuccalization).

This can derive from any negative constraint that prevents a place
feature

   a. in combination with a manner or voicing feature in the same
       segment,
   b. in sequence with another feature, or
   c. in that part of the syllable.

The culprit would be ranked higher than **Survived(Place)**. It can also
be motivated by a high ranking of **LinkedDownwards(Place)** and
a high ranking of **Not(Coronal)**, preventing default [Coronal] from
being filled in.

Note that this *can* be limited to a particular part of the syllable.

Not(<Articulator>)
NotTwice(<Articulator>)
NoSequence(...<Articulator>...)
NotCo-occurring(<Articulator>,<Manner>)
NotCo-occurring(<Articulator>,<voicing>)
NotCo-occurring(σ-Margin,V-Place)
NotCo-occurring(Rime,C-Place)

C. Is some other feature or node deleted?

This is only possible if a default feature is filled in to replace the deleted feature. See section below on Insertion. Deletion of a feature can
be due to any negative constraint that can refer to features.

   1. everywhere: **Not**
   2. only in a particular sequence: **NoSequence**
       Warning: If it is the right-most element that is deleted, it is pos-
       sible that only coda consonants might be affected, but this may be
       an accident.
   3. only when it appears twice: **NotTwice**
       Warning: If it is the right-most element that is deleted, it is pos-
       sible that only coda consonants might be affected, but this may be
       an accident.
   4. only in combination with other features in the same segment:
       NotCo-occurring, Co-occurring
       Common: [Dorsal] is possible only in a voiceless stop; it is de-
       leted from /g/ and /ŋ/ because it is combined with nondefault
       features. [+continuant] is possible only in [s]; it cannot be com-
       bined with any marked features.
       Warning: Interactions with other constraints might cause deletion
       to be restricted to onsets or codas.

D.2. INSERTION OF ELEMENTS

The insertion of elements *always* involves the violation of the following *low-ranked* constraint, without exception:

Not

Other negative constraints can prevent insertion, though the most common ones are:

NotTwice
NoSequence
NotCo-occurring
Co-occurring
Contiguity
Aligned

Insertion can be caused by many constraints:

LinkedDownwards
NoSequence
NotTwice
NotComplex
Co-occurring
Binary(σ,μ)
Binary(Foot,σ)
Binary(Foot,μ)
Heavy(Stressed)
Aligned
Size(\<morph\>,\<phon\>)

The questions that must be answered are similar to those that must be answered for deletion. Note, however, that there are differences. First, elements above the level of the segment are routinely inserted, in order to provide syllables, feet, and prosodic words to allow underlying segments to link upwards. Second, higher-level elements are rarely inserted unless there is underlying material to support them; insertion of default syllables and feet are uncommon. Most insertion of *segmental* material involves a single Root node (a single segment), or some lower element such as a feature or Place node.

Insertion of structural nodes like σ, Foot, and PrWd is governed by Upwards Structure constraints, driven by **LinkedUpwards(Root)**, plus higher **LinkedUpwards** constraints. We will not deal further with such constraints, but rather address constraints that lead to unfaithfulness in one way or another.

If preliminary analysis indicates that more than one segment was inserted, or a coda was inserted, or vowels were lengthened:

LEVEL: Foot or syllable.

   I. Are syllables or moras or a coda added to make the word or syllable a
      certain minimal size?

A. Is the whole prosodic word made up of inserted material?

In order to be pronounced, a prosodic word must be present, and must dominate a foot. If a foot cannot be constructed on the basis of underlying material, a "default" foot can be inserted. This would be a default word form, identical (or nearly so) on every use, that a child might use to replace large numbers of lexical items. (?[widə], in Bloom, 1973?) Default feet occur only rarely in child phonology.

PrWd▸Foot

B. Is just a single (unstressed) syllable inserted?

One possibility is that the syllable would contain default segments, and be the same in all words.

A second possibility is that the syllable could assimilate segments from the single underlying syllable. (See below on assimilation.)

This usually happens for purely phonological reasons (the foot has a single light syllable) to increase the size up to a minimum (a bimoraic foot).

Binary(Foot,σ)

The minimum size might alternatively be required for morphological reasons: all tokens of a particular morphological category (such as verbs or plurals) must be of a certain (minimum) size (such as a binary foot). Epenthesis would not appear elsewhere. We know of no reports of this for phonological development.

Size(<Morph>,<Phon>)

C. Is a single mora or a coda inserted, when the word would otherwise have just one light syllable? The minimum (bimoraic) size of a foot can be attained by inserting a mora (which would generally be used to make a vowel long), or by inserting a coda.

An inserted coda could be filled via assimilation or via insertion of a default consonant (often [t] or [ʔ]).

Again, this can be for purely phonological reasons (because the foot is made up of a single light syllable) or for morphological reasons.

Binary(Foot,μ)

Size(<Morph>,<Phon>)

D. Is a single mora or a coda inserted, in a word that has two syllables?

This is invariably in a *stressed* syllable. A light stressed syllable is made heavy via the insertion of a mora (which could make a short vowel or an intervocalic consonant long), or via insertion of a coda (with default segmental content).

Heavy(Stressed)

II. Is a vowel added?

A. Is the vowel inserted to rescue a consonant that cannot be made a part of any independently existing syllable?

A vowel is inserted either before or after the extrasyllabic consonant. The particular negative constraint involved determines *why* the consonant cannot be a part of any existing syllable.

1. Is the consonant extrasyllabic because codas are not allowed?
   Not(Coda)
   NotComplex(Rime)
   Aligned(σ,R,V,R)
2. Is the consonant extrasyllabic because the particular feature content includes something that is not allowed in codas but *is* allowed in onsets?
   This could result from the low ranking of faithfulness in weak prosodic positions like codas.
   It may also reflect high ranking for:
   Co-occurring(Rime$\rightarrow$X)
   NotCo-occurring(Rime,X)
   NotCo-occurring(Coda,X)
3. Is the consonant extrasyllabic because it follows a long vowel or diphthong, and the language disallows codas in that environment?
   The syllable maximally has two moras, and coda consonants must be moraic. A vowel is inserted to create a syllable so that the consonant can be in an onset.
   Binary(σ,μ) *plus*   **Co-occurring(Rime$\rightarrow\mu$)**
                          NotComplex(μ)
4. Is the consonant extrasyllabic because the underlying form has two consecutive consonants in a certain position, and complex onsets and codas are disallowed?
   NotComplex(Onset)
   NotComplex(Coda)

B. Is the vowel inserted to separate two consonants that are not allowed to be contiguous via timing unit adjacency?
   By inserting the vowel, the two consonants are no longer contiguous. The negative constraints can refer to Root nodes, or to features.
   NoSequence
   NotTwice_{TimingUnit}

C. Is a default vowel inserted to fill out a timing unit that remains after an underlying vowel is deleted? If the timing unit is filled via assimilation, see below.
   LinkedDownwards(TimingUnit)

III. Is a consonant inserted to give the syllable an onset?
   A. Is the consonant inserted in *any* onset-less syllable?
      $\sigma\blacktriangleright$Onset
   B. Is the consonant inserted only between two vowels?
      This could derive from a restriction that insertion is not possible at the left edge of the word:
      Aligned(Stem,L,PrWd,L)
      Alternatively, it could derive from a constraint on vowel sequences:

NotTwice(V-TimingUnit)
  NotTwice(V-Root)
  NotTwice(Nucleus) (the syllable-level equivalent of stress clash)

C. Is the consonant inserted only in word-initial position?
This is generally because sequences of vowels are dealt with in some other fashion (such as deleting one of the vowels). It is rare for VV sequences to be tolerated, but for a default consonant to be inserted in word-initial syllables.

D. Is the consonant inserted only between two vowels that have some particular feature content?
NotTwice
NoSequence

E. Is the inserted consonant derived via assimilation from a consonant or vowel elsewhere in the word? (See section on assimilation below.)

F. Is a default consonant inserted to fill a timing unit that remains after an underlying consonant is deleted? If the timing unit is filled via assimilation, see below.
LinkedDownwards(TimingUnit)

IV. Is a nononset consonant inserted?

A. Is a word-final coda consonant inserted?
This brings the word or stressed syllable up to a minimum size or
   lengthens out the end of the word.
Heavy(Stressed)
Binary(Foot,μ)
WordFinalMassiveness

B. Is a consonant inserted between two other consonants?
This includes insertion of [t] in /ns/ clusters ([nts]) in adult languages.
NoSequence

C. Is a consonant inserted to absorb a feature that may not survive in its underlying segment? See (D) in the next subsection.

V. Is a feature or other element within the segment inserted?

A. Is an element added to make a coda consonant more vowel-like?
Co-occurring(Rime→X)
NotCo-occurring(Rime,X)

B. Is an element inserted to make an onset consonant more consonant-like?
Co-occurring(σ-Margin→X)
NotCo-occurring(σ-Margin,X)

C. Is a default element inserted to resolve underspecification, either in the underlying form or resulting from the deletion of an underlying element?
LinkedDownwards *plus* lowest-ranked **Not** constraints

D. Is an element inserted because it is required by another element, either because they must co-occur, or because a dominating element is absent?

Co-occurring(A→B)
LinkedUpwards
This includes Node Generation: insertion of a higher element so that a lower element can link upwards to it. Insertion can be up to the level of a timing unit.

E. Is a feature inserted to separate two features that may not appear in sequence?
NoSequence
NotTwice

D.3. INSERTION OF ASSOCIATION LINES

This includes three types of phenomena:

1. assimilation, including harmony and plateauing
2. the linking up of elements that are floating in the input
3. flop (spreading plus delinking)

Assimilation leads to doubly linked or multiply linked elements, and always violates:

Not(Link)   (more violations than if assimilation did not occur)
            Note: It is not necessary to say to which element the inserted link is attached.
            That is determined independently by negative constraints.
SinglyLinked

Linking up underlyingly floating elements does not lead to doubly linked elements, but always violates:

Not(Link)

Flop does not change the number of association lines, but always violates:

Survived(Link)

The insertion of an association line is always motivated by some positive constraint that requires elements to be present. Negative constraints may *additionally* be involved. For example, if **Not(Labial)** leads to an underlying [Labial] feature being deleted, **LinkedDownwards(Place)** might then motivate the assimilation of [Dorsal] from a nearby consonant, thus violating **SinglyLinked(Dorsal)**. The positive constraints that are most commonly involved are:

LinkedUpwards
LinkedDownwards

I. Is a floating element linked up?

The element could be floating in the underlying form.

The element could be floating because the segment in which it appeared in the underlying form is deleted outright in the output.

Survived(<element>) *plus* **LinkedUpwards(<element>)**

If the floating element is not deleted outright, it must be linked upwards to a different segment. Its effect will not always be visible.

II. Is there spreading?

This can be between two consonants, between two vowels, or between a consonant and a vowel.

A. Is there an assimilation?

Assimilation is defined as *adding* a link to an element, so that it is linked to at least two segments in the output.

Assimilation is generally motivated by **LinkedDownwards**.

An element is not linked to a required element on the next tier down. This situation can derive from

a. underlying underspecification,

b. the insertion of the (higher) element due to other constraints (see §D.2), or

c. the deletion of the lower element due to other constraints (see §D.1).

If the **Not** constraint against inserting the appropriate element is ranked higher than **SinglyLinked** and **Distinct**, then assimilation occurs.

Example: /dɑg/ [gag], if **Not(Coronal)** is ranked higher than **SinglyLinked(Dorsal)**.

Reasons for the deletion of an underlying feature that commonly lead to assimilation are **NotTwice(X)**: One X can be deleted.

Some other element can replace the deleted X; AAB changes to ABB.

NoSequence(A...B): Element B may be deleted.

Its place may be filled by spreading A,

or by spreading element C from some other segment.

Resolving violations of **NotTwice** and **NoSequence** can further lead to plateauing, in which the feature spreads to a segment that separates the two segments involved in the negative constraints. Plateauing is caused by:

Uninterrupted (high-ranked), *plus* **Distinct** (low-ranked)

(Note: When two identical elements are merged because **Distinct** is low-ranked, there is no **Survived** violation.)

Further negative constraints that can lead to assimilation are

NotCo-occurring(A,B): Since A and B may not co-occur, one of them may be deleted.

Its place may be filled by spreading Element C from a nearby segment.

Not(A): Element A may be deleted.

Its place may be filled by spreading a nearby Element B.

Spreading may also be motivated by the following constraints, in which case it would be restricted to particular syllable positions:

Co-occurring(Rime→X) (e.g., [+nasal] spreads onto a coda)

NotCo-occurring(Rime,X)

Co-occurring(σ-Margin→X)

NotCo-occurring(σ-Margin,X)

An alternative view of assimilation attributes it to **Aligned** constraints. See Chapters 4 and 7 for discussion.

B. Is there gemination?

A link is added to a Root node that is already linked, making the Root node long.

   1. Is it to provide an onset?

   σ▸**Onset**: The syllable must have an onset.

      a. A link is added to a coda consonant of the preceding syllable, so that the syllable gains an onset. (The affected consonant is now a geminate.)

      b. A link is added to a preceding high vowel ([i], [u]). The portion of the vowel that is linked to the onset is pronounced like a nonsyllabic vowel: a glide. This is *especially* likely after the glide portion of a diphthong:

      flower /.faʊ.ɹ̩./ [.faʊ.wɹ̩.].

   2. Is it to provide a coda?

   Constraints that require heavy syllables may be satisfied by adding an association line to a following onset consonant. This provides a coda for the syllable, which is then heavy. The affected consonant becomes a geminate.

   Possibly relevant constraints are:

   Heavy(Stressed)

   Binary(Foot,μ)

   The coda can be used to increase the heaviness of a foot with a single syllable, when immediately followed by a stressed syllable (stress clash), but the constraint underlying this is unclear; see §6.2.4.

   3. Is it compensatory lengthening?

   A Root node is deleted due to some negative constraint, stranding a timing unit. There is an unassociated timing unit in the underlying form. The timing unit links to a nearby Root node, making it long.

   Survived(TimingUnit)

   LinkedDownwards(TimingUnit)

III. Is there flop?

Flop is defined as a complex operation, in which an underlying association line is *deleted*, and a new association line is *added*. The feature shifts out of one segment and into another. (Or the Root node shifts out of one timing unit or syllable and into another.)

The delinking portion of flop is motivated by the same negative constraints as any deletion. The relinking portion is motivated by the same constraints that cause any insertion of association lines. Some common patterns:

NotTwice(X): One or both elements can be delinked.

Flop may occur, by reassociating the delinked element(s) to (a) nearby segment(s).

If Root adjacency is involved, this resolves the violation.

NoSequence(A...B): Element A or B or both may be delinked.

Flop may occur, by reassociating the delinked element(s) to (a) nearby segment(s).

If Root adjacency is involved, this resolves the violation.

NotCo-occurring(A,B): Since A and B may not co-occur, one or both of them may be delinked.

Flop may occur, by reassociating the delinked element(s) to (a) nearby segment(s) in which **NotCo-occurring** is not violated.

NotComplex(Onset): Instead of deleting, one or both of the consonants (or one of the features in the consonant) flop(s) to elsewhere in the word.

In all cases, adjacency changes and the violation is therefore avoided.

D.4. BUILDING ODD STRUCTURES

In this section, we address instances in which no phonetic material is inserted or deleted, but in which structures are built. For the building of "normal" structure, see discussion in Chapters 3, 4, and 6. Here, we focus on "odd" structures. For child language, this would be any structure that deviates from the target adult pronunciation. For adult language, it would include structures that violate our expectations about what should occur.

I. Is an intervocalic consonant treated as a coda rather than as an onset?

As noted in §3.7, an intervocalic consonant generally is an onset. Syllabifying an intervocalic consonant as a coda violates both σ▸**Onset** and **Not(Coda)**, while syllabifying it as an onset violates neither constraint. However, this constraint can be overridden in particular instances.

A. Is the intervocalic consonant vowel-like (a glide or glottal)?

There are constraints that make the most optimal onset consonant-like and the most optimal coda vowel-like. If the intervocalic consonant is very vowel-like, and these other constraints are ranked higher than σ►Onset, it is preferable to have no onset:

NotCo-occurring(σ-Margin,V-Place)
NotCo-occurring(σ-Margin,-consonantal)
Co-occurring(σ-Margin→C-Place)
NotCo-occurring(Rime,C-Place)
Co-occurring(Rime→-consonantal)

The first three constraints make glides poor onsets, so that inter-vocalic glides might preferentially be codas (or part of a complex nucleus).

The last two constraints make intervocalic [h] or [ʔ] a better coda than an onset.

B. Does the intervocalic consonant follow a short stressed vowel?

Heavy(Stressed)

This constraint requires that a stressed syllable be heavy. If the stressed syllable has an underlying short vowel with no coda, the intervocalic consonant may be treated as a coda in order to make the syllable heavy. This requires low ranking of σ►Onset and **Not(Coda)**, and high ranking of **SinglyLinked(Root)**.

II. Is a different segment made syllabic than in the adult target? (e.g., *music* /mjuːzɪk/ [mɪʊzɪk])

This reflects higher ranking of **NotComplex(Onset)** than of **Not-Complex(Nucleus)** (and constraints on sequences of vowels within the nucleus); a diphthong is preferred to an onset cluster.

III. Is an underlyingly syllabic element made nonsyllabic?

This generally involves high vowels becoming glides. It may be moti-vated by the minimization of the number of syllables, to provide the fol-lowing syllable with an onset, or to avoid sequences of two full vowels:

Not(σ)
σ►Onset
NotTwice(Nucleus)

IV. Do syllable boundaries not coincide with word boundaries?

A word-final consonant may be shifted into the next syllable when the next word begins with a vowel, motivated by high ranking of **Not(Coda)** or **NotComplex(Coda)**. The domain of syllabification is the phrase, rather than the word; or **Aligned(MorphologicalWord,R,σ,R)** is low-ranked.

A word-initial consonant may be shifted into the previous syllable when the preceding word ends with a vowel, motivated by **NotComplex (Onset)**. The domain of syllabification is the phrase, rather than the word; or **Aligned(MorphologicalWord,L,σ,L)** is low-ranked.

V. Is stress placed on a syllable that is different from where stress is placed in adult speech?

This generally results from an excessively high ranking of **Prominent(Foot,Left)**

If this is ranked higher than other constraints, stress can be placed on the first syllable of words such as *balloon* and *giraffe*. This leads either to having two stressed syllables in the word, or to the second syllable being unstressed. If the second syllable is unstressed, the vowel may reduce, in order not to violate **Light(Unstressed)**.

If an underlying stressed syllable becomes unstressed, that violates **Survived(Stressed)**.

REFERENCES

Aksu-Koc, A. A., & Slobin, D. I. (1985). The acquisition of Turkish. In D. I. Slobin (Ed.), *The cross-linguistic study of language acquisition, Vol. 1.* (pp. 839–878). Hillsdale, NJ: Lawrence Erlbaum Associates.

Alderete, J., Beckman, J., Benue, L., Gnanadesikan, A., McCarthy, J., & Urbanczyk, S. (1996). Reduplication and segmental unmarkedness. Unpublished manuscript: University of Massachusetts.

Allen, G. D. (1985). How the young French child avoids the pre-voicing problem for word-initial voiced stops. *Journal of Child Language, 12,* 37–46.

Allen, G. D., & Hawkins, S. (1978). The development of phonological rhythm. In A. Bell & J. B. Hooper (Eds.), *Syllables and segments* (pp. 173–185). Amsterdam: North Holland.

Anderson, J., & Durand, J. (1987). *Explorations in Dependency Phonology.* Dordrecht: Foris.

Anderson, R., & Smith, B. L. (1987). Phonological development of two-year-old monolingual Puerto Rican Spanish-speaking children. *Journal of Child Language, 14,* 57–78.

Applegate, J. (1961). Phonological rules of a subdialect of English. *Word, 17,* 186–193.

Archangeli, D. (1984). *Underspecification in Yawelmani phonology and morphology.* Doctoral Dissertation: MIT. Published by Garland Press, New York, 1986.

Archangeli, D. (1988). Aspects of underspecification theory. *Phonology, 5,* 183–207.

Archangeli, D., & Langendoen, D.T. (1997). *Optimality theory.* Cambridge, MA: Blackwell.

Archangeli, D., & Pulleyblank, D. (1987). Maximal and minimal rules: Effects of tier scansion. In *Proceedings of the North Eastern Linguistics Society, 17,* 16–35. GSLA, University of Massachusetts, Amherst.

Archangeli, D., & Pulleyblank, D. (1994). *Grounded phonology.* Cambridge, MA: MIT Press.

Archibald, J. (1995). The acquisition of stress. In J. Archibald (Ed.), *Phonological acquisition and phonological theory* (pp. 81–109). Hillsdale, NJ: Lawrence Erlbaum Associates.

Avery, P., & K. Rice (1989). Segment structure and coronal underspecification. *Phonology, 6,* 179–200.

Badecker, W. (1988). Representational properties common to phonological and orthographic output systems. Unpublished manuscript: Johns Hopkins University.

Barlow, J. A. (1995). The development of on-glides in American English. In *Proceedings of the 20th Annual Boston university conference on language development.* Boston University, November 1995.

Barton, D. (1980). Phonemic perception in children. In G. Yeni-Komshian, J. F. Cavanagh, & C. A. Ferguson (Eds.), *Child phonology, Vol. 2, Perception* (pp. 97–116). New York: Academic Press.

Barton, D., Miller, R., & Macken, M. A. (1980). Do children treat clusters as one unit or two? *Papers and Reports on Child Language Development (Stanford University)*, *18*, 105–137.

Bates, E., & MacWhinney, B. (1987). Competition, variation, and language learning. In B. MacWhinney (Ed.), *Mechanisms of language acquisition* (pp. 157–193). Hillsdale, NJ: Lawrence Erlbaum Associates.

Beckman, J. (1995). Shona height harmony: Markedness and positional identity. In J. Beckman, L. W. Dickey, & S. Urbanczyk (Eds.), *University of Massachusetts Occasional Papers in Linguistics 18: Papers in Optimality Theory* (pp. 53–76). Amherst, MA: University of Massachusetts.

Beddor, P. S., Krakow, R. A., & Goldstein, L. M. (1986). Perceptual constraints and phonological change: A study of nasal vowel height. *Phonology Yearbook*, *3*, 187–217.

Bedore, L. M., Leonard, L. B., & Gandour, J. (1994). The substitution of a click for sibilants: A case study. *Clinical Linguistics and Phonetics*, *8*, 283–293.

Beers, M. (1991). Phonological acquisition and impairment in Dutch children: Some language-specific aspects. Paper presented at the AFASIC conference, May, 1991, Harrogate, Great Britain.

Beers, M. (1993). The development of consonant clusters in Dutch. Paper presented at the Sixth International Child Language Congress, July, 1993, Trieste, Italy.

Beers, M. (1995). The phonology of normally developing and language-impaired children. *Studies in Language and Language Use, whole number 20*. Dordrecht, Holland: ICG-Printing.

Béland, R., & Favreau, Y. (1991). On the special status of coronals in aphasia. In C. Paradis & J-F. Prunet (Eds.), *The special status of coronals* (pp. 201–221). San Diego: Academic Press.

Béland, R., Paradis, C., & Bois, M. (1993). Constraints and repairs in aphasic speech: A group study. *Canadian Journal of Linguistics*, *38*, 279–302.

Berg, T. (1985). Is voice a suprasegmental? *Linguistics*, *23*, 883–915.

Berg, T. (1988). *Die Abbildung des Sprachproduktionsprozesses in einem Aktivationsflussmodell: Untersuchungen an deutschen und englischen Versprechern*. Tübingen: Niemeyer.

Berg, T, (1990). The differential sensitivity of consonants and vowels to stress. *Language Sciences*, *12*, 65–84.

Berg, T. (1992). Phonological harmony as a processing problem. *Journal of Child Language*, *19*, 225–257.

Berko, J. (1958). The child's learning of English morphology. *Word*, *14*, 150–177.

Berko, J. and Brown, R. (1960). Psycholinguistic research methods. In P. H. Mussen (Ed.), *Handbook of research methods in child development* (pp. 517–557). New York: John Wiley & Sons.

Berman, R. A. (1977). Natural phonological processes at the one-word stage. *Lingua, 43*, 1–21.

Berman, R. (1985). The acquisition of Hebrew. In D. I. Slobin (Ed.), *The crosslinguistic study of language acquisition,Vol. 1.* (pp. 255–371). Hillsdale, NJ: Lawrence Erlbaum Associates.

Bernhardt, B. (1990). *Application of nonlinear phonological theory to intervention with six phonologically disordered children*. Unpublished doctoral dissertation: University of British Columbia.

Bernhardt, B. (1992a). Developmental implications of nonlinear phonological theory. *Clinical Linguistics and Phonetics, 6*, 259–281.

Bernhardt, B. (1992b). The application of nonlinear phonological theory to intervention with one phonologically disordered child. *Clinical Linguistics and Phonetics, 6*, 283–316.

Bernhardt, B. (1994a). Cluster metatheses in phonologically disordered speech: Constraints on sonority sequence, mapping direction or segment composition? *Toronto Working Papers in Linguistics*, University of Toronto, 39–50.

Bernhardt, B. (1994b). Nonlinear phonological intervention: Group and case study results. Paper presented at the Canadian Association of Speech-Language Pathologists and Audiologists Annual Conference, May, 1994, Winnipeg, Manitoba.

Bernhardt, B. (1994c). Phonological intervention techniques for syllable and word structure development. *Clinics in Communication Disorders, 4*, 54–65.

Bernhardt, B. M. (1994d). The prosodic tier and phonological disorders. In M. Yavaş (Ed.), *First and second language phonology* (pp. 149–172). San Diego, CA: Singular Publishing Group.

Bernhardt, B., Edwards, S., & Rempel, L. (1996). Metaphonological skills of typically developing three-year-olds and children with phonological disorders. In T. Powell (Ed.), *Pathologies of speech and language: Contributions of clinical phonetics and linguistics.* (pp. 135–142). International Clinical Linguistics and Phonetics Association, Louisiana State Medical Center, New Orleans, LA.

Bernhardt, B., & Gilbert, J. (1992). Applying linguistic theory to speech-language pathology: The case for non-linear phonology. *Clinical Linguistics and Phonetics, 6,* 123–145.

Bernhardt, B., Loyst, D., & Muir, S. (1996). Palatometry pilot project: Outcomes for a variety of speech disorders. Paper presented at the American Speech-Language-Hearing Association Annual Convention, November, 1996, Seattle, WA.

Bernhardt, B., Miller, M., Barton, M., MacAulay, K., MacKenzie, M., & Wastie, S. (1993). University and clinic in collaboration: Studying efficacy of phonological intervention. Paper presented at the Canadian Association of Speech-Language Pathologists and Audiologists Annual Conference, May, 1993, Charlottetown, P. E. I.

Bernhardt, B., Rempel, L., & Pegg, L. (1994). Bilingual phonological assessment and treatment: Greek-English, German-English examples. Paper presented at the American Speech-Language-Hearing Association Annual Convention, November, 1994, New Orleans, LA.

Bernhardt, B., Ruelle, H., & Edwards, S. (1995). Phonology therapy manual. Unpublished manuscript.

Bernhardt, B., & Stemberger, J. P. (in preparation). Intervocalic consonants in the speech of children with phonological disorders. Unpublished manuscript: University of British Columbia and University of Minnesota.

Bernhardt, B., & Stoel-Gammon, C. (1994). Nonlinear phonology: Introduction and clinical application. *Journal of Speech and Hearing Research, 37,* 123–143.

Bernhardt, B., & Stoel-Gammon, C. (1996). Underspecification and markedness in normal and disordered phonological development. In C. E. Johnson & J. H. V. Gilbert (Eds.), *Children's language, Vol. 9* (pp. 33–54). Mahwah, NJ: Lawrence Erlbaum Associates.

Bernhardt, B. H., & Stoel-Gammon, C. (1997). Grounded phonology: Application to the analysis of disordered speech. In M. Ball & R. Kent (Eds.), *The new phonologies* (pp. 163–210). San Diego, CA: Singular Publishing Group.

Bernstein Ratner, N. (1993). Interactive influences on phonological behavior. *Journal of Child Language, 20,* 191–197.

Bleile, K. M. (1987). *Regressions in the phonological development of two children.* Unpublished doctoral dissertation: University of Iowa.

Bleile, K. (1991). *Child phonology: A book of exercises for students.* San Diego, CA: Singular Publishing Group.

Bloom, L. (1973). *One word at a time.* The Hague: Mouton.

Boas, F. (1911). *Handbook of American Indian Languages.* Bureau of American Ethnology Bulletin 40. Washington: Smithsonian Institution.

Bock, J. K. (1982). Towards a cognitive psychology of syntax: Information processing contributions to sentence formulation. *Psychological Review, 89,* 1–47.

Bopp, K. D. (1995). *The effects of phonological intervention on morphosyntactic development in preschool children with phonological and morphosyntactic disorders.* Unpublished M.A. thesis: University of British Columbia.

Borowsky, T. (1989). Structure preservaion and the syllable coda in English. *Natural Language and Linguistic Theory, 7,* 145–166.

Bortolini, U., & Leonard, L. (1991). The speech of phonologically disordered children acquiring Italian. *Clinical Linguistics and Phonetics, 5,* 1–12.

Bortolini, U., Zmarich, C., Fior, R., & Bonifacio, S. (1995). Word-initial voicing in the productions of stops in normal and preterm Italian infants. *International Journal of Pediatric Otorhinolaryngology, 31,* 191–206.

Braine, M. D. S. (1974). On what might constitute a learnable phonology. *Language, 50,* 270–299.

Braine, M. (1976). Review of N. V. Smith, The acquisition of phonology. *Language, 52,* 489–498.

Bromberger, S., & Halle, M. (1989). Why phonology is different. *Linguistic Inquiry, 20,* 51–70.

Browman, C. P., & Goldstein, L. M. (1986). Towards an articulatory phonology. *Phonology Yearbook*, *3*, 219–252.

Brown, R., & McNeill, D. (1966). The "tip-of-the-tongue" phenomenon. *Journal of Verbal Learning and Verbal Behavior*, *5*, 325–337.

Burton, A. (1980). Phonological systems of aphasic children. *UCLA Working Papers in Cognitive Linguistics*, *2*, 37–187.

Bybee, J. L., & Slobin, D. I. (1982). Rules and schemas in the development and use of the English past tense. *Language*, *58*, 265–289.

Camarata, S. (1989). Final consonant repetition: A linguistic perspective. *Journal of Speech and Hearing Disorders*, *54*, 159–162.

Camarata, S., & Gandour, J. (1984). On describing idiosyncratic phonologic systems. *Journal of Speech and Hearing Disorders*, *6*, 262–266.

Carter Young, E. (1991). An analysis of young children's ability to produce multisyllabic English nouns. *Clinical Linguistics & Phonetics*, *5*, 297–316.

Cazden, C. (1968). The acquisition of noun and verb inflections. *Child Development*, *39*, 433–438.

Chao, Y. R. (1971). The Cantian idiolect: An analysis of the Chinese spoken by a twenty-eight-months-old child. In A. Bar-Adon & W. F. Leopold (Eds.), *Child Language: A book of readings* (pp. 116–130). Englewood Cliffs, NJ: Prentice-Hall Inc.

Chervela, N. (1981). Medial consonant cluster acquisition by Telugu children. *Journal of Child Language*, *8*, 63–73.

Chevrie-Muller, C., & Le Breton, M. T. (1973). Etude de la réalisation des consonnes au cours d'une épreuve de répétition des mots sur des groupes d'enfants de 3 ans et 5 ans ½. *Revue de laryngologie*, *94*, 109–152.

Chiat, S. (1981). Context-specificity and generalization in the acquisition of pronominal distinctions. *Journal of Child Language*, *8*, 75–91.

Chiat, S. (1989). The relation between prosodic structure, syllabification, and segmental realization: Evidence from a child with fricative stopping. *Clinical Linguistics & Phonetics*, *3*, 223–242.

Chiat, S. (1994). From lexical access to lexical output: What is the problem for children with impaired phonology. In M. Yavaş (Ed.), *First and second language phonology* (pp.107–133). San Diego: Singular Publishing Group.

Chimombo, M., & Mtenje, A. (1989). Interaction of tone, syntax and semantics in the acquisition of Chichewa negation. *Studies in African Linguistics*, *20*, 103–150.

Chin, S. (1993). *The organization and specification of features in functionally disordered phonologies*. Unpublished doctoral dissertation: Indiana University.

Chin, S. (1996). The role of the sonority hierarchy in disordered phonological systems. In T. Powell (Ed.), *Pathologies of speech and language: Contributions of clinical phonetics and linguistics*. (pp. 109–117). International Clinical Linguistics and Phonetics Association, Louisiana State Medical Center, New Orleans, LA.

Chin, S. B., & Dinnsen, D. A. (1992). Consonant clusters in disordered speech: Constraints and correspondence patterns. *Journal of Child Language*, *19*, 259–285.

Cho, Y.-M., & Inkelas, S. (1995). Reconsidering [Consonantal]. Unpublished manuscript: Stanford University.

Chomsky, N. (1965). *Aspects of the theory of syntax*. Cambridge, MA: MIT Press.

Chomsky, N. (1986). *Barriers*. Cambridge, MA: MIT Press.

Chomsky, N., & Halle, M. (1968). *The sound pattern of English*. Cambridge, MA: MIT Press.

Chung, S. (1983). Transderivational relationships in Chamorro phonology. *Language*, *59*, 35–66.

Clark, E. V. (1985). The acquisition of Romance, with special reference to French. In D. I. Slobin (Ed.), *The crosslinguistic study of language acquisition,Vol. 1.* (pp. 687–782). Hillsdale, NJ: Lawrence Erlbaum Associates.

Clark, E. V., & Bowerman, M. (1986). On the acquisition of final voiced stops. In J. A. Fishman, A. Tabouret-Keller, M. Clyne, Bh. Krishnamurti, & M. Abdulaziz (Eds.), *The Fergusonian impact, Vol. 1: From phonology to society* (pp. 51–68). Amsterdam: Mouton/deGruyter.

Clements, G. N. (1985). The geometry of phonological features. *Phonology Yearbook, 2,* 225–252.

Clements, G. N. (1988). Toward a substantive theory of feature specification. *Proceedings of the North Eastern Linguistics Society, 18,* 79–93.

Clements, G. N. (1989). A unified set of features for consonants and vowels. Unpublished manuscript: Cornell University.

Clements, G. N. (1990). The role of the sonority cycle in core syllabification. In J. Kingston & M. Beckman (Eds.), *Papers in Laboratory Phonology I: Between the grammar and physics of speech* (pp. 283–333). Cambridge: Cambridge University Press,

Clements, G. N., & Keyser, S. J. (1983). *CV Phonology.* Cambridge, MA: MIT Press.

Clumeck, H. (1980). The acquisition of tone. In G. Yeni-Komshian, J. F. Cavanagh, & C. A. Ferguson (Eds.), *Child phonology, Vol. 1, Production* (pp. 257–275). New York: Academic Press.

Cole, J. S., & Kisseberth, C. W. (1994). An Optimal Domains theory of harmony. Cognitive Science Technical Report UIUC-BI-CS-94-02 (Language Series). The Beckman Institute, University of Illinois, Champaign-Urbana. Rutgers Optimality Archive ROA-22.

Cole, R. A., Jakimik, J., & Cooper, W. E. (1978). Perceptibility of phonetic features in fluent speech. *Journal of the Acoustical Society of America, 64,* 44–56.

Compton, A. J., & Streeter, M. (1977). Studies of early child phonology: Data collection and preliminary analyses. *Papers and Reports on Child Language Development (Stanford University), 13,* 99–109.

Cook, E. (1995). Chipewyan feature acquisition. Paper presented at the UBC international conference on phonological acquisition, June 23–25, 1995, Vancouver, British Columbia.

Cruttenden, A. (1978). Assimilation in child language and elsewhere. *Journal of Child Language, 5,* 373–378.

Crystal, D. (1987). Towards a 'bucket' theory of language disability: Taking account of interaction between linguistic levels. *Clinical Linguistics and Phonetics, 1,* 7–22.

Dagenais, P., & Critz-Crosby, P. (1992). Comparing tongue positioning by normal-hearing and hearing-impaired children during vowel production. *Journal of Speech and Hearing Research, 35,* 35–44.

Davis, K. (1995). Phonetic and phonological contrasts in the acquisition of voicing: Voice onset time production in Hindi and English. *Journal of Child Language, 22,* 275–305.

Davis, B., & MacNeilage, P. (1990). Acquisition of correct vowel production: A quantitative case study. *Journal of Speech and Hearing Research, 33,* 16–27.

Davis, S. (1991). Coronals and the phonotactics of non-adjacent consonants in English. In C. Paradis & J.-F. Prunet (Eds.), *The special status of coronals* (pp. 49–60). Dordrecht, Holland: Foris.

De Boysson-Bardies, B., Vihman, M., Roug-Hellichius, L., Durand, C., Landberg, I., & Arao, F. (1992). Material evidence of infant selection from the target language: A cross-linguistic phonetic study. In C. A. Ferguson, C., L. Menn, & C. Stoel-Gammon (Eds.), *Phonological development: Models, research, and implications* (pp. 369–391). Timonium, MD: York Press.

Dell, G. S. (1985). Positive feedback in hierarchical connectionist models: Applications to language production. *Cognitive Science, 9,* 3–23.

Dell, G. S. (1986). A spreading-activation theory of retrieval in sentence production. *Psychological Review, 93,* 283–321.

Dell, G. S. (1990). Effects of frequency and vocabulary type on phonological speech errors. *Language and Cognitive Processes, 5,* 313–349.

Dell, G. S., Juliano, C., & Govindjee, A. (1993). Structure and content in language production: A theory of frame constraints in phonological speech errors. *Cognitive Science, 17,* 149–195.

Demuth, K. (1993). Issues in the acquisition of the Sesotho tonal system. *Journal of Child Language, 20,* 275–301.

Demuth, K. (1996a). Alignment, stress, and parsing in early phonological words. In B. Bernhardt, J. Gilbert, & D. Ingram (Eds.), *Proceedings of the UBC international conference on phonological acquisition* (pp. 113–125). Somerville, MA: Cascadilla Press.

Demuth, K. (1996b). Prosodic domains and phonological development. Paper presented at the Twenty-First Annual Conference on Language Development, November, 1996, Boston University.

Demuth, K. (1996c). The prosodic structure of early words. In J. Morgan & K. Demuth (Eds.), *From signal to syntax: Bootstrapping from speech to grammar in early acquisition* (pp. 171–184). Hillsdale, NJ: Lawrence Erlbaum Associatiates.

Demuth, K., & Fee, E. J. (1995). Minimal words in early phonological development. Unpublished manuscript: Brown University & Dalhousie University.

Denes, P. B. (1963). On the statistics of spoken English. *Journal of the Acoustical Society of America, 35*, 892–904.

Derwing, B. L., & Baker, W. J. (1980). Rule learning and the English inflections (with special emphasis on the plural). In G. D. Prideaux, B. L. Derwing, & W. J. Baker (Eds.), *Experimental linguistics: Integration of theory and applications* (pp. 247–272). Ghent, Belgium: E. Story-Scientia.

Devers, M., & Broen, P. (1996). Weak syllable deletions: Application of a metrical template. Paper presented at the annual convention of ASHA, November 1996, Seattle, WA.

Diedrich, W., & Bangert, J. (1980). Articulation learning. Houston, TX: College-Hill Press.

Dinnsen, D. (1992). Variation in developing and fully developed phonetic inventories. In C. A. Ferguson, L. Menn, & C. Stoel-Gammon (Eds.), *Phonological development: Models, research, and implications* (pp. 191–210). Timonium, MD: York Press.

Dinnsen, D. A. (1996). Context effects in the acquisition of fricatives. In B. Bernhardt, J. Gilbert, & D. Ingram (Eds.), *Proceedings of the UBC international conference on phonological acquisition* (pp. 136–148). Somerville, MA: Cascadilla Press.

Dinnsen, D. A., Barlow, J. A., & Morrisette, M. L. (in press). Long-distance place assimilation with an interacting error pattern in phonological acquisition. *Clinical Linguistics & Phonetics.*

Dinnsen, D. A., & Charles-Luce, J. (1984). Phonological neutralization, phonetic implementation and individual differences. *Journal of Phonetics, 12*, 49–60.

Dinnsen, D. A., & Elbert, M. (1984). On the relationship between phonology and learning. In M. Elbert, D. Dinnsen, & G. Weismer (Eds.), *Phonological theory and the misarticulating child* (pp. 59–68). (ASHA Monographs Number 22). Rockville, MD: American Speech-Language-Hearing Association.

Donahue, M. (1986). Phonological constraints on the emergence of two-word utterances. *Journal of Child Language, 13*, 209–218.

Drachman, G. (1973). Generative phonology and child language acquisition. *Ohio State University Working papers in linguistics, 15*, 146–159.

Dresher, E. (1994). Child phonology, learnability, and phonological theory. Unpublished manuscript: University of Toronto.

Dresher, B. E., Piggott, G., & Rice, K. (1994). Contrast in phonology: Overview. *Toronto Working Papers in Linguistics, 13.*

Dunlap, E., & Padgett, J. (1990). The representation of Kabardian harmonic clusters. *Univ. of Massachusetts Papers in Phonology, 14*, 91–122.

Dyson, A. (1986). Development of velar consonants among normal two-year-olds. *Journal of Speech and Hearing Research, 29*, 493–498.

Echols, C. (1993). A perceptually based model of children's earliest productions. *Cognition, 46*, 245–296.

Echols, C., & Newport, E. (1992). The role of stress and position in determining first words. *Language acquisition, 2*, 189–220.

Edwards, M. L. (1973). The acquisition of liquids. *Working papers in linguistics, 15*, Ohio State University, 1–54.

Edwards, M. L. (1979). *Patterns and processes in fricative acquisition: Longitudinal evidence from six English-learning children.* Unpublished doctoral dissertation: Stanford University.

Edwards, M. L. (1996). Word position effects in the production of fricatives. In B. Bernhardt, J. Gilbert, & D. Ingram (Eds.), *Proceedings of the UBC international conference on phonological acquisition* (pp. 149–158). Somerville, MA: Cascadilla Press.

Edwards, M. L., & Bernhardt, B. H. (1973a). Phonological analyses of the speech of four children with language disorders. Unpublished manuscript: The Scottish Rite Institute for Childhood Aphasia, Stanford University.

Edwards, M. L., & Bernhardt, B. H. (1973b). Twin speech as the sharing of a phonological system. Unpublished manuscript: The Scottish Rite Institute for Childhood Aphasia, Stanford University.

Edwards, M. L., & Shriberg, L. D. (1983). *Phonology: Applications in communicative disorders.* San Diego, CA: College-Hill Press.

Edwards, S. M. (1995). *Optimal outcomes of nonlinear phonological intervention.* Unpublished M.A. thesis: University of British Columbia.

Eilers, R., Gavin, W. J., & Wilson, W. R. (1979). Linguistic experience and phonemic perception in infancy: A crosslinguistic study. *Child Development, 50,* 14–18.

Eilers, R., & Oller, K. D., & Benito-Garcia, C. R. (1984). The acquisition of voicing contrasts in Spanish and English learning infants and children: A longitudinal study. *Journal of Child Language, 11,* 313–336.

Eimas, P., Siqueland, E. R., Jusczyk, P. W., & Vigorito, J. (1971). Speech perception in infants. *Science, 171,* 303–306.

Elbert, M., & Gierut, J. (1986). *Handbook of clinical phonology.* San Diego, CA: College-Hill Press.

Elman, J., Bates, E., Johnson, M. H., Karmiloff-Smith, A., Parisi, D., & Plunkett, K. (1996). *Rethinking innateness: A connectionist perspective on development.* Cambridge, MA: MIT Press.

Elsen, H. (1991). *Erstspracherwerb: Der Erwerb des deutschen Lautsystems.* Wiesbaden: Deutscher UniverstitätsVerlag.

Everett, D. L. (1995). Quantity, sonority, and alignment constraints in Suruwahá and Banawá prosody. Unpublished manuscript: University of Pittsburgh.

Eveson, M. (1996). *Epenthesis in children's consonant cluster productions: A perceptual and acoustical study.* Unpublished M.A. thesis: University of British Columbia.

Farwell, C. (1977). Some strategies in the early production of fricatives. *Papers and Reports on Child Language Development (Stanford University), 12,* 97–104.

Fee, E. J. (1991). *Underspecification, parameters, and the acquisition of vowels.* Unpublished doctoral dissertation: University of British Columbia.

Fee, E. J. (1994). External evidence for a model of vocalic features. Paper presented at the annual meeting of the Canadian Linguistic Society, June 3–6, 1994, Calgary, Alberta.

Fee, E. J. (1995a). Segments and syllables in early language acquisition. In J. Archibald (Ed.), *Phonological acquisition and phonological theory* (pp. 43–61). Hillsdale, NJ: Lawrence Erlbaum Associates.

Fee, E. J. (1995b). The phonological system of a specifically language-impaired population. *Clinical Linguistics and Phonetics, 9,* 189–209.

Fee, E. J. (1996). Syllable structure and minimal words. In B. Bernhardt, J. Gilbert, & D. Ingram (Eds.), *Proceedings of the UBC international conference on phonological acquisition* (pp. 85–98). Somerville, MA: Cascadilla Press.

Fee, E. J., & Ingram, D. (1982). Reduplication as a strategy of phonological development. *Journal of Child language, 9,* 41–54.

Ferguson, C. A. (1975). Fricatives in child language acquisition. *Proceedings of the Eleventh International Congress of Linguists,* Bologna, Florence, 647–664.

Ferguson, C. A. (1983). Reduplication in child phonology. *Journal of Child Language, 10,* 239–243.

Ferguson, C., & Farwell, C. (1975). Words and sounds in early language acquisition. *Language, 51,* 419–439.

Fey, M. E. (1986). *Language intervention with young children.* San Diego, CA: College-Hill Press.

Fey, M. E., & Gandour, J. (1982). Rule discovery in phonological acquisition. *Journal of Child Language, 9,* 71–81.

Fikkert, P. (1994). *On the acquisition of prosodic structure.* The Hague: Holland Academic Graphics.

Fowler, C. A. (1980). Coarticulation and theories of extrinsic timing. *Journal of Phonetics, 8,* 113–133.

Francis, W. N., & Kučera, H. (1982). *Frequency analysis of English usage.* Boston, MA: Houghton Mifflin.

Freitas, M. J. (1996). Onsets in early productions. In B. Bernhardt, J. Gilbert, & D. Ingram (Eds.),

    Proceedings of the UBC international conference on phonological acquisition (pp. 76–84). Somerville, MA: Cascadilla Press.

French, N. R., Carter, C. W., & Koenig, W., Jr. (1930). The words and sounds of telephone conversations. *Bell System Technical Journal, 9,* 290–324.

Fudge, C. C. (1969). Syllables. *Journal of Linguistics, 5,* 253–286.

Gandour, J., Petty, S. H., Dardarananda, R., Dechongkit, S., & Mukngoen, S. (1986). The acquisition of the voicing contrast in Thai: A study of voice onset time in word-initial stop consonants. *Journal of Child Language, 13,* 561–572.

Garnica, O. (1973). The development of phonemic speech perception. In T. E. Moore (Ed.), *Cognitive development and the acquisition of language* (pp. 215–222). New York: Academic Press.

Gay, T. (1977). Articulatory movements in CVC sequences. *Journal of the Acoustical Society of America, 62,* 183–193.

Geilmann, J. (1993). German schwa in L$_1$ acquisition. *HILP, 01,16,* 1–15.

Gennari, S., & Demuth, K. (1996). Syllable omission in the acquisition of Spanish. In E. Hughes, M. Hughes, & A. Greenhill (Eds.), *Proceedings of the 21st Annual Boston University Conference on Language Development* (pp.182–193). Somerville, MA: Cascadilla Press.

Gerken, L. (1991). The metrical basis for children's subjectless sentences. *Journal of Memory and Language, 30,* 431–451.

Gerken, L. (1994). Sentential processes in early child language. In J. C. Goodman & H. C. Nusbaum (Eds.), *The development of speech perception: The transition from speech sounds to spoken words* (pp. 271–298). Cambridge, MA: MIT Press.

Gierut, J. (1986). Sound change: A phonemic split in a misarticulating child. *Applied Psycholinguistics, 7,* 57–68.

Gierut, J. (1996). An experimental test of phonemic cyclicity. *Journal of Child Language, 23,* 81–102.

Gierut, J., Simmerman, C. L., & Neumann, H. J. (1994). Phonemic structures of delayed phonological systems. *Journal of Child Language, 21,* 291–316.

Gleitman, L., & Wanner, E. (1982). *Language acquisition: The state of the art.* Cambridge, NY: Cambridge University Press.

Gnanadesikan, A. (1995). Markedness and faithfulness constraints in child phonology. Unpublished manuscript, UMass Amherst. Rutgers Optimality Archive ROA-67.

Goad, H. (1996a). Codas, word minimality, and empty-headed syllables. In *Papers & Reports on Child Language Development.* (Stanford University), *28,* 113–122.

Goad, H. (1996b). Consonant harmony in child language: Evidence against coronal underspecification. In B. Bernhardt, J. Gilbert, & D. Ingram (Eds.), *Proceedings of the UBC international conference on phonological acquisition* (pp. 187–200). Somerville, MA: Cascadilla Press.

Goldsmith, J. (1976). *Autosegmental phonology.* Doctoral dissertation: MIT. Published by Garland Press, New York, 1979.

Goldsmith, J. (1990). *Autosegmental and Metrical Phonology.* Oxford: Basil Blackwell.

Goldsmith, J. (1993). Harmonic phonology. In J. Goldsmith (Ed.), *The last phonological rule* (pp. 21–60). Chicago: The University of Chicago Press.

Goldstein, B. (1996). Error groups in Spanish-speaking children with phonological disorders. In T. Powell (Ed.), *Pathologies of speech and language: Contributions of clinical phonetics and linguistics* (pp. 171–177). International Clinical Linguistics and Phonetics Association, Louisiana State Medical Center, New Orleans, LA.

Golston, C. (1996). Direct optimality theory: Representation as pure markedness. *Language, 72,* 713–748.

Gopnik, M. (1990). Feature-blindness: A case study. *Language Acquisition, 1,* 139–164.

Gopnik, M., & Crago, M. B. (1991). Familial aggregation of a developmental language disorder. *Cognition, 39,* 1–50.

Greenberg, J. H. (1965). Some generalizations concerning initial and final consonant sequences. *Linguistics, 18,* 5–34.

Greenlee, M. (1974). Interacting processes in the child's acquisition of stop-liquid clusters. *Papers & Reports on Child Language Development (Stanford University), 7,* 85–100.

Greenlee, M., & Ohala, J. J. (1980). Phonetically motivated parallels between child phonology and historical sound change. *Language Sciences, 2*, 283–308.

Grunwell, P. (1985). *Phonological assessment of child speech*. San Diego, CA: College-Hill Press.

Grunwell, P. (1987). *Clinical phonology*. (2nd ed.) London: Croom Helm.

Guerssel, M. (1977). Constraints on phonological rules. *Linguistic Analysis, 3*, 267–305.

Guerssel, M. (1978). A condition on assimilation rules. *Linguistic Analysis, 4*, 225–254.

Guy, G. R. (1991). Explanation in variable phonology: An exponential model of morphological constraints. *Language Variation and Language Change, 3*, 1–22.

Hale, M., & Reiss, C. (1995). The initial ranking of faithfulness constraints in UG. Unpublished manuscript: Harvard University and Concordia College. Rutgers Optimality Archive ROA-104.

Halle, M. (1959). *The sound pattern of Russian*. The Hague: Mouton.

Halle, M. (1962). Phonology in generative grammar. *Word, 18*, 54–72.

Halle, M., & Mohanan, K.P. (1985) Segmental phonology of Modern English. *Linguistic Inquiry, 16*, 57–116.

Hammond, M. (1995). There is no lexicon. Unpublished manuscript: University of Arizona, Tucson. Rutgers Optimality Archive ROA-43.

Hayes, B. (1986). Inalterability in CV Phonology. *Language, 62*, 321–351.

Hayes, B. (1989). Compensatory lengthening in moraic phonology. *Linguistic Inquiry, 20*, 253–306.

Hayes, B. (1995). *Metrical stress theory: Principles and case studies*. Chicago: University of Chicago Press.

Hayes, B. (1996). Can Optimality Theory serve as the medium for a functionally-guided phonology? Paper presented at the Milwaukee Conference on Formalism and Functionalism, April 1996, Milwaukee, WI.

Healy, A. F., & Sherrod, N. B. (1994). The/Thee pronunciation distinction: A local model of linguistic categories. Paper presented at the 35th Annual Meeting of the Psychonomic Society, St. Louis, MO, November 1994.

Hochberg, J. (1988). First steps in the acquisition of Spanish stress. *Journal of Child Language, 15*, 273–292.

Hockett, C. (1955). *A manual of phonology. IJAL 41(4)*, part 1. Memoir 11.

Hockett, C. (1958). *A course in modern linguistics*. New York: MacMillan.

Hodson, B., & Paden, E. (1981). Phonological processes which characterize unintelligible and intelligible speech in early childhood. *Journal of Speech and Hearing Disorders, 46*, 369–373.

Hodson, B., & Paden, E. (1991). *Targeting intelligible speech*. (2nd ed.) Austin, TX: PRO-ED.

Hoeffner, J. H., & McClelland, J. L. (1993). Can a perceptual processing deficit explain the impairment of inflectional morphology in developmental dysphasia? A computational investigation. In *Proceedings of the 25th annual child language research forum* (pp. 38–49). Stanford, CA: Stanford University.

Hoff, K. L. (1995). *The efficacy of parent-focused language intervention: A case study*. Unpublished M.A. thesis: University of British Columbia.

Hooper, J. (1976). *Introduction to Natural Generative Phonology*. New York: Academic Press.

Hooper, J. (1978). Constraints on schwa-deletion in American English. In J. Fisiak (Ed.), *Recent developments in historical phonology* (pp. 183–207). The Hague: Mouton.

Hopper, P. J., & Thompson, S. A. (1984). The discourse basis for lexical categories in universal grammar. *Language, 60*, 703–752.

Horsley, T. E. (1995). *Spontaneous and imitated utterances of children with phonological disorders*. Unpublished M.A. thesis: University of British Columbia.

Howard, S. J. (1993). Articulatory constraints on a phonological system: A case study of cleft palate speech. *Clinical Linguistics & Phonetics, 7*, 299–317.

Hudson, G. (1980). Automatic alternations in nontransformational phonology. *Language, 56*, 94–125.

Hudson, G. (1986). Arabic root and pattern morphology without tiers. *Journal of Linguistics, 22*, 85–122.

Hulst, H. van der (1989). Atoms of segmental structure: Components, gestures and dependency. *Phonology, 6*, 253–284.

Hyman, L. (1975). *Phonology: Theory and analysis.* New York: Holt.

Hyman, L. (1985). *A theory of phonological weight.* Dordrecht: Foris.

Ingram, D. (1974). Fronting in child phonology. *Journal of Child Language, 1,* 49–64.

Ingram, D. (1980). A comparative study of phonological development in normal and linguistically delayed children. *Proceedings of the first Wisconsin symposium on research in child language disorders, 1,* 23–33.

Ingram, D. (1981). *Procedures for the phonological analysis of children's language.* Baltimore, MD: University Park Press.

Ingram, D. (1988a). Jakobson revisited: Some evidence from the acquisition of Polish. *Lingua, 75,* 55–82.

Ingram, D. (1988b). The acquisition of word-initial [v]. *Language and Speech, 31,* 77–85.

Ingram, D. (1989a). *First language acquisition: Method, description, and explanation.* Cambridge: Cambridge University Press.

Ingram, D. (1989b). *Phonological disability in children.* Second Edition. London: Cole & Whurr and San Diego, CA: Singular Publishing Group.

Ingram, D. (1989c). Underspecification theory and phonological acquisition. Unpublished manuscript: University of British Columbia.

Ingram, D. (1990). The acquisition of the feature [voice] in normal and phonologically delayed English children. Paper presented at the American Speech-Language-Hearing Association Convention, November, 1990, Seattle, WA.

Ingram, D. (1992). Early phonological acquisition: A cross-linguistic perspective. In C. A. Ferguson, L. Menn, & C. Stoel-Gammon (Eds.), *Phonological development: Models, research, implications* (pp. 423–435). Timonium, MD: York Press.

Ingram, D. (1996). The acquisition of prosodic structure in Japanese: A case study. Unpublished manuscript: University of British Columbia.

Ingram, D., Christensen, L., Veach, S., & Webster, B. (1980). The acquisition of word-initial fricatives and affricates in English by children between 2 and 6 years. In G. Yeni-Komshian, J. F. Kavanagh, & C. A. Ferguson (Eds.), *Child phonology, Vol. 1: Production* (pp. 169–191). New York: Academic Press.

Ingram, D., & Terselic, B. (1983). Final ingression: A case of deviant child phonology. *Topics in Language Disorders, 3,* 45–50.

Inkelas, S. (1994). The consequences of optimization for underspecification. Unpublished manuscript: University of California, Berkeley. Rutgers Optimality Archive ROA-40.

International Phonetics Association. (1989). Report on the Kiel convention. *Journal of the International Phonetics Association, 19,* 67–80.

Irwin, O. C. (1948). Infant speech: Development of vowel sounds. *Journal of Speech and Hearing Disorders, 8,* 109–121.

Itô, J. (1986). *Syllable theory in prosodic phonology.* Doctoral dissertation: University of Massachusetts, Amherst. Published by Garland Press, New York, 1988.

Itô, J. (1989). A prosodic theory of epenthesis. *Natural Language and Linguistic Theory, 7,* 217–259.

Itô, J., & Mester, R. A. (1993). Licensed segments and safe paths. *The Canadian Journal of Linguistics, 38,* 197–213.

Itô, J., Mester, R. A., & Padgett, J. (1995). Licensing and underspecification in Optimality Theory. *Linguistic Inquiry, 26,* 517–613.

Ito, K. (1990). *Kodoma no kotoba.* Tokyo: Keiso Shobo.

Iverson, G. K., & Wheeler, D. W. (1987). Hierarchical structures in child phonology. *Lingua, 73,* 243–257.

Jaeger, J. J. (1984). Assessing the psychological status of the Vowel Shift Rule. *Journal of Psycholinguistic Research, 13,* 13–36.

Jaeger, J. J. (1986). On the acquisition of abstract representations for English vowels. *Phonology Yearbook, 3,* 71–97.

Jakobson, R. (1931). Prinzipien der historische Phonologie. *Travaux du Cercle Linguistique de*

Prague, *4*, 247–267. (English version in A. R. Keiler, *A reader in historical and comparative linguistics*, pp. 121–138. New York: Holt, 1972.)

Jakobson, R. (1968/1941). *Child language, aphasia, and phonological universals*. (A. R. Keiler, trans.) The Hague: Mouton, 1968. (Original: *Kindersprache, Aphasie, und allgemeine Lautgesetze*. Uppsala: Almqvist & Wiksell, 1941.)

Jakobson, R., Fant, G., & Halle, M. (1951). *Preliminaries to speech analysis*. Cambridge, MA: MIT Press.

Johnson, C. (1995). Syllable and word similarity in acquisition of pronunciation. Paper presented at the 1995 Child Phonology Meeting, Memphis, TN, May 1995.

Jusczyk, P. (1992). Developing phonological categories from the speech signal. In C. A. Ferguson, L. Menn, & C. Stoel-Gammon (Eds.), *Phonological development: Models, research, implications* (pp. 17–64). Timonium, MD: York Press.

Kahn, D. (1976). *Syllable-based generalizations in English phonology*. Doctoral dissertation: MIT. Published by Garland Press, New York.

Kaisse, E. (1992). Can [consonantal] spread? *Language*, *68*, 313–332.

Kaisse, E. M., & Shaw, P. A. (1985). On the theory of Lexical Phonology. *Phonology Yearbook*, *2*, 1–30.

Kamio, A., & Terao, Y. (1986). Notes on phonological errors in Japanese. Unpublished manuscript: University of Tsukuba.

Kaye, J. (1988). *Phonology: A cognitive view*. Hillsdale, NJ: Lawrence Erlbaum Associates.

Kaye, J., Lowenstamm, J., & Vergnaud, J.-R. (1990). Constituent structure and government in phonology. *Phonology*, *7*, 193–231.

Kehoe, M. (1995). *An investigation of rhythmic processes in English-speaking children's word production*. Unpublished doctoral dissertation: University of Washington.

Kehoe, M. (in press). Stress error patterns in English-speaking children's word productions. *Clinical Linguistics & Phonetics*.

Kehoe, M., & Stoel-Gammon, C. (1997). The acquisition of prosodic structure: An investigation of current accounts of children's prosodic development. *Language*, *73*, 113–144.

Kelly, M. H. (1989). Rhythm and language change in English. *Journal of Memory and Language*, *28*, 690–710.

Kelly, M. H. (1992). Using words to solve syntactic problems: The role of phonology in grammatical category assignments. *Psychological Review*, *99*, 349–364.

Kenstowicz, M. (1994). *Phonology in generative grammar*. Cambridge, MA: Blackwell.

Kenstowicz, M., & Kisseberth, C. (1979). *Generative phonology: Description and theory*. New York: Academic Press.

Kent, R. D. (1981). Articulatory-acoustic perspectives on speech development. In R. E. Stark (Ed.), *Language behavior in infancy and early childhood* (pp. 105–126). New York: Elsevier/North-Holland.

Kernan, K., & Blount, B. (1966). The acquisition of Spanish grammar by Mexican children. *Anthropological Linguistics*, *8*, 1–14.

Kewley-Port, D., & Preston, M. S. (1974). Early apical stop production: A voice onset time analysis. *Journal of Phonetics*, *2*, 195–210.

Kiparsky, P. (1979). Metrical structure assignment is cyclic. *Linguistic Inquiry*, *10*, 421–442.

Kiparsky, P. (1982). From cyclic phonology to lexical phonology. In H. van der Hulst & N. Smith (Eds.), *The structure of phonological representations* (Part 1) (pp. 130–175). Dordrecht, Holland: Foris.

Kiparsky, P. (1985). Some consequences of lexical phonology. *Phonology Yearbook*, *2*, 83–138.

Kiparsky, P. (1994). Remarks on markedness. Paper presented at TREND-2, January 1994.

Kiparsky, P., & Menn, L. (1977). On the acquisition of phonology. In J. MacNamara (Ed.), *Language learning and thought* (pp. 47–78). New York: Academic Press.

Kirchner, R. (1994). Lenition in phonetically based Optimality Theory. Unpublished manuscript: UCLA.

Kirchner, R. (1995). Going the distance: Synchronic chain shifts in Optimality Theory. Unpublished manuscript: UCLA. Rutgers Optimality Archive ROA-66.

Kisseberth, C. (1970). On the functional unity of phonological rules. *Linguistic Inquiry, 1*, 291–306.

Kisseberth, C. (1993). Optimal Domains: A theory of Bantu tone. A case study from Isixhosa. Handout of talk presented at ROW-1, October 22–24, 1993.

Klein, H. (1981). Productive strategies for the pronunciation of early polysyllabic lexical items. *Journal of Speech and Hearing Research, 24*, 389–405.

Klein, H. (1984). Learning to stress: A case study. *Journal of Child Language, 11*, 375–390.

Klein, H., & Spector, C. C. (1985). Effect of syllable stress and serial position on error variability in polysyllabic productions of speech-delayed children. *Journal of Speech and Hearing Disorders, 50*, 391–402.

Kornfeld, J. R. (1971). What initial clusters tell us about a child's speech code. *Quarterly Progress Report, MIT Research Laboratory of Electronics, 101*, 218–221.

Kornfeld, J. R., & Goehl, H. (1974). A new twist to an old observation: Kids know more than they say. In A. Bruck, R. A. Fox, & M. W. La Galy (Eds.), *Papers from the parasession on Natural Phonology* (pp. 210–219). Chicago: Chicago Linguistic Society.

Koutsoudas, A., Sanders, G., & Noll, C. (1974). The application of phonological rules. *Language, 50*, 1–28.

Kuhl, P. K., Williams, K. A., Lacerda, F., Stevens, K. N., & Lindblom, B. (1992). Linguistic experience alters phonetic perception in infants by six months of age. *Science, 255*, 606–608.

LaCharité, D. (1993). *The internal structure of affricates*. Unpublished doctoral dissertation: University of Ottawa.

LaCharité, D., & Paradis, C. (1993). Introduction: The emergence of constraints in generative phonology and a comparison of three current constraint-based models. *Canadian Journal of Linguistics, 38*, 127–153.

Lachter, J., & Bever, T. G. (1988). The relation between linguistic structure and associative theories of language learning—a constructive critique of some connectionist learning models. *Cognition, 28*, 195–247.

Ladefoged, P. (1993). *A course in phonetics*. Fort Worth: Harcourt, Brace, Jovanovich.

Lahiri, A., & Evers, V. (1991). Palatalization and coronality. In C. Paradis & J.-F. Prunet (Eds.), *The special status of coronals* (pp. 79–100). San Diego: Academic Press.

Lakoff, G. (1993). Cognitive Phonology. In J. Goldsmith (Ed.), *The last phonological rule: Reflections on constraints and derivations* (pp. 117–145). Chicago: The University of Chicago Press.

Lamb, S. (1966). *An outline of stratificational grammar*. Washington: Georgetown University Press.

Laver, J. (1994). *Principles of phonetics*. Cambridge, UK: Cambridge University Press.

Leonard, L. B. (1985). Unusual and subtle phonological behavior in the speech of phonologically disordered children. *Journal of Speech and Hearing Disorders, 50*, 4–13.

Leonard, L. B. (1992). Models of phonological development and children with phonological disorders. In C. A. Ferguson, L. Menn, & C. Stoel-Gammon (Eds.), *Phonological development: Models, research, and implications.* (pp. 495–507). Timonium, MD: York Press.

Leonard, L. B., & Brown, B. L. (1984). Nature and boundaries of phonologic categories: A case study of an unusual phonologic pattern in a language-impaired child. *Journal of Speech & Hearing Disorders, 49*, 419–428.

Leonard, L. B., & McGregor, K. K. (1991). Unusual phonological patterns and their underlying representations: A case study. *Journal of Child Language, 18*, 261–271.

Leonard, L. B., MacGregor, K. K., & Allen, G. D. (1992). Grammatical morphology and speech perception in children with specific language impairment. *Journal of Speech and Hearing Research, 35*, 1076–1085.

Leopold, W. (1947). *Speech development of a bilingual child: A linguist's record, Vol. II: Sound-learning in the first two years*. Evanston, IL: Northwestern University Press.

Levelt, C. (1994). *On the acquisition of Place*. Doctoral dissertation. HIL Dissertations in Linguistics. Dordrecht: ICP Printing.

Levelt, C. C. (1996). Consonant-vowel interactions in child language. In B. Bernhardt, J. Gilbert, &

D. Ingram (Eds.), *Proceedings of the UBC international conference on phonological acquisition* (pp. 229–239). Somerville, MA: Cascadilla Press.

Levelt, W. J. M. (1989). *Speaking: From intention to articulation*. Cambridge, MA: MIT Press.

Levin, J. (1985). *A metrical theory of syllabicity*. Unpublished doctoral dissertation: MIT.

Li, C. N., & Thompson, S. A. (1977). The acquisition of tone in Mandarin-speaking children. *Journal of Child Language, 4*, 185–199.

Li, K.-J. (1992). *Topics in the internal structure of phonological representations: With reference to external evidence*. Unpublished doctoral dissertation: University of Minnesota.

Lieberman, P. (1980). On the development of vowel production in young children. In G. Yeni-Komshian, J. F. Kavanagh, & C. A. Ferguson (Eds.), *Child phonology, Vol. 1: Production* (pp. 113–142). New York: Academic Press.

Lightfoot, D. (1992). *How to set parameters: Arguments from language change*. Cambridege, MA: MIT Press.

Ling, D. (1976). *Speech and the hearing-impaired child: Theory and practice*. Washington, DC: The Alexander Graham Bell Association for the Deaf, Inc.

Lisker, L., & Abramson, A. S. (1964). A cross-language study of voicing in initial stops: Acoustical measurements. *Word, 20*, 384–422.

Lleó, C. (1996). To spread or not to spread: Different styles in the acquisition of Spanish phonology. In B. Bernhardt, J. Gilbert, & D. Ingram (Eds.), *Proceedings of the UBC international conference on phonological acquisition* (pp. 215–228). Somerville, MA: Cascadilla Press.

Lleó C., Prinz, M., El Mogharbel, C., & Maldonado, A. (1996). Early phonological acquisition of German and Spanish: A reinterpretation of the continuity issue within the principles and parameters model. In C. E. Johnson & J. H. V. Gilbert (Eds.), *Children's language, 9*, (pp. 11–31). Mahwah, NJ: Lawrence Erlbaum Associates.

Locke, J. (1983). *Phonological acquisition and change*. New York: Academic Press.

Lombardi, L. (1990). The nonlinear organization of the affricate. *Natural Language and Linguistic Theory, 8*, 375–426.

Lorentz, J. P. (1976). An analysis of some deviant phonological rules of English. In D. Morehead & A. Morehead (Eds.), *Normal and deficient child language*. (pp. 29–59). Baltimore: University Park Press.

Loring, A. (1995). English vowel acquisition as vowel feature acquisition. Unpublished M.A. Plan B paper: University of Minnesota.

Lubker, J., & Gay, T. (1982). Anticipatory labial coarticulation: Experimental, biological and linguistic variables. *Journal of the Acoustical Society of America, 71*, 437–448.

Lohuis-Weber, H., & Zonneveld, W. (1997). Phonological acquisition and Dutch word prosody. *Language Acquisition, 5*, in press.

Macken, M. A. (1979). Developmental reorganization of phonology: A hierarchy of basic units of acquisition. *Lingua, 49*, 11–49.

Macken, M. A. (1980a). Aspects of the acquisition of stop systems: A crosslinguistic perspective. In G. Yeni-Komshian, J. F. Kavanagh, & C. Ferguson (Eds.), *Child phonology, Vol. 1: Production* (pp. 143–168). New York: Academic Press.

Macken, M. A. (1980b). The child's lexical representation: The 'puzzle-puddle-pickle' evidence. *Journal of Linguistics, 16*, 1–17.

Macken, M. A. (1987). Learning and constraints on phonological acquisition. In B. MacWhinney (Ed.), *Mechanisms of language acquisition* (pp. 367–397). Hillsdale, NJ: Lawrence Erlbaum Associates.

Macken, M. A. (1992). Where's phonology? In C. A. Ferguson, L. Menn, & C. Stoel-Gammon (Eds.), *Phonological development: Models, research, implications* (pp. 249–269). Timonium, MD: York Press.

Macken, M. A. (1993). Phonological theory and acquisition. Unpublished manuscript: University of Madison, Wisconsin.

Macken, M. A., & Barton, D. (1980a). The acquisition of the voicing contrast in English: A study of voice onset time in word-initial stop consonants. *Journal of Child Language, 7*, 41–74.

Macken, M. A., & Barton, D. (1980b). A longitudinal study of the acquisition of the voicing contrast in American-English word-initial stops, as measured by Voice Onset Time. *Journal of Child Language*, *7*,41–74.

Macken, M. A., & Ferguson, C. A. (1983). Cognitive aspects of phonological development: Model, evidence, and issues. In K. Nelson (Ed.), *Children's language*, *4*, (pp. 255–282). Hillsdale, NJ: Lawrence Erlbaum Associates.

MacWhinney, B. (1978). The acquisition of morphophonology. *Monographs of the Society for Research in Child Development*, *43*, whole no. 1.

Maddieson, I. (1984). *Patterns of sounds*. Cambridge, UK: Cambridge University Press.

Magno Caldognetto, E., & Tonelli, L. (1985). Syllabic constraints on phonological speech errors in Italian. In W. U. Dressler & L. Tonelli (Eds.), *Natural phonology from Eisenstadt* (pp. 73–88). Padua: Clesp.

Major, E., & Bernhardt, B. H. (1996). Relationships between metaphonological skills and disordered phonology: Intervention outcomes. Paper presented at the American Speech-Language-Hearing Association Annual Convention, November, 1996, Seattle, WA.

Marantz, A. (1982). Re Reduplication. *Linguistic Inquiry*, *13*, 435–482.

Marcus, G. F., Pinker, S., Ullman, M., Hollander, M., Rosen, T. J., & Xu, F. (1992). Overregularization in language acquisition. *Monographs of the Society for Research in Child Development*, *57*, whole no. 4.

Marlett, S. (1981). *The structure of Seri*. Unpublished doctoral dissertation: University of California, San Diego.

Marlett, S., & Stemberger, J. P. (1983). Empty consonants in Seri. *Linguistic Inquiry*, *14*, 617–639.

Matthei, E. H. (1989). Crossing boundaries: More evidence for phonological constraints on early multi-word utterances. *Journal of Child Language*, *16*, 41–54.

McCarthy, J. J. (1979). *Formal problems in Semitic phonology and morphology*. Doctoral dissertation: MIT. Published by Garland Press, New York, 1985.

McCarthy, J. J. (1981). A prosodic theory of nonconcatenative morphology. *Linguistic Inquiry*, *12*, 373–418.

McCarthy, J. J. (1986). OCP effects: Gemination and antigemination. *Linguistic Inquiry*, *17*, 207–63.

McCarthy, J. J. (1988). Feature geometry and dependency. *Phonetica*, *43*, 84–108.

McCarthy, J. J. (1989). Linear order in phonological representation. *Linguistic Inquiry*, *20*, 71–99.

McCarthy, J. J. (1991). The phonology of semitic pharyngeals. Unpublished manuscript: University of Massachusetts at Amherst.

McCarthy, J. (1995a). Extensions of faithfulness: Rotuman revisited. Unpublished manuscript, University of Massachusetts, Amherst. Rutgers Optimality Archive ROA-64.

McCarthy, J. (1995b). Remarks on phonological opacity in Optimality Theory. In J. Lecarme, J. Lowenstamm, & U. Shlonsky (Eds.), *Studies in Afroasiatic Grammar*. (Holland Academic Graphics.) Rutgers Optimality Archive ROA-79.

McCarthy, J. J., & Prince, A. (1988). Quantitative transfer in reduplicative and templatic morphology. *Linguistics in the Morning Calm*, *2*, (pp. 3–35). Seoul: Hanshin.

McCarthy, J., & Prince, A. S. (1993a). Prosodic morphology I: Constraint interaction and satisfaction. Rutgers University Cognitive Sciences Center Technical Report-3. Piscataway, New Jersey.

McCarthy, J., & Prince, A. (1993b). Generalized Alignment. In G. Booij & J. van Marle (Eds.), *Yearbook of Morphology*, *1993*, pp. 79–153. Dordrecht: Kluwer.

McCarthy, J. J., & Prince, A. S. (1994). The emergence of the unmarked: Optimality in prosodic morphology. *Proceedings of the North Eastern Linguistics Society*, *24* (pp. 333–379). GSLA, University of Massachusetts, Amherst.

McCarthy, J. J., & Prince, A. S. (1995). Faithfulness and reduplicative identity. In J. Beckman, L. Dickey, & S. Urbanczyk (Eds.), *University of Massachusetts occasional papers in Linguistics 18: Papers in Optimality Theory* (pp. 249–384). Amherst, MA: Department of Linguistics. (Also to appear, in R. Kager, H. van der Hulst, & W. Zonneveld [Eds.], *The prosody-morphology interface*.)

McCarthy, J. J., & Taub, A. (1992). Review of Carole Paradis and Jean-François Prunet, *The special status of coronals*. *Phonology*, *9*, 363–370.

McClelland, J. L., & Elman, J. L. (1986). The TRACE model of speech perception. *Cognitive Psychology, 18,* 1–86.

McHugh, B. (1994). Optimal satisfaction of subcategorization in Hausa plurals. Unpublished manuscript: Temple University.

Menn, L. (1975). Counter example to 'fronting' as a universal in child phonology. *Journal of Child Language, 2,* 293–296.

Menn, L. (1976). *Pattern, control and contrast in beginning speech: A case study in the development of word form and word function.* Unpublished doctoral dissertation: University of Illinois, Champaign-Urbana. Distributed by the Indiana University Linguistics Club, 1978.

Menn, L. (1978). Phonological units in beginning speech. In A. Bell & J. B. Hooper (Eds.), *Syllables and segments* (pp. 315–334). Amsterdam: North Holland.

Menn, L. (1983). Development of articulatory, phonetic, and phonological capabilities. In B. Butterworth (Ed.), *Language production, Vol. 2: Development, writing, and other language processes* (pp. 1–50). London: Academic Press.

Menn, L. (1992). Building our own models: Developmental phonology comes of age. In C. A. Ferguson, L. Menn, & C. Stoel-Gammon (Eds.), *Phonological development: Models, research, implications* (pp. 3–15). Timonium, MD: York Press.

Menn, L., & MacWhinney, B. (1984). The repeated morph constraint: Toward an explanation. *Language, 19,* 519–541.

Menn, L., & Matthei, E. (1992). The "two-lexicon" approach of child phonology: Looking back, looking ahead. In C. A. Ferguson, L. Menn, & C. Stoel-Gammon (Eds.), *Phonological development: Models, research, implications* (pp. 211–248). Timonium, MD: York Press.

Menyuk, P., & Klatt, D. H. (1968). Child's production of initial consonant clusters. *Quarterly Progress Report, MIT Research Laboratory of Electronics, 91,* 205–213.

Menyuk, P. (1972). *The development of speech.* New York: Bobbs-Merrill Studies in Communicative Disorders.

Mester, R. A. (1994). The quantitative trochee in Latin. *Natural Language and Linguistic Theory, 12,* 1–61.

Mester, R. A., & Itô, J. (1989). Feature predictability and underspecification: Palatal prosody in Japanese mimetics. *Language, 65,* 258–293.

Mills, A. (1988). Visual handicap. In D. Bishop & K. Mogford (Eds.), *Language development in exceptional cirucmstances* (pp. 150–164). Edinburgh: Churchill Livingstone.

Mills, A. E. (1985). The acquisition of German. In D. I. Slobin (Ed.), *The crosslinguistic study of language acquisition, Vol. 1.* (pp. 141–254). Hillsdale, NJ: Lawrence Erlbaum Associates.

Mohanan, K. P. (1986). *The theory of lexical phonology.* Dordrecht, Holland: D. Reidel Publishing Company.

Mohanan, K. P. (1991). On the bases of underspecification. *Natural Language and Linguistic Theory, 9,* 285–325.

Morrison, J. A., & Shriberg, L. D. (1992). Articulation testing versus conversational speech sampling. *Journal of Speech and Hearing Research, 35,* 259–273.

Moskowitz, A. I. (1970). The two-year-old stage in the acquisition of English phonology. *Language, 46,* 426–441.

Moskowitz, B. A. (1973). On the status of vowel shift in English. In T. E. Moore (Ed.), *Cognitive development and the acquisition of language* (pp. 223–260). New York: Academic Press.

Moskowitz, B. A. (1975). The acquisition of fricatives: A study in phonetics and phonology. *Journal of Phonetics, 3,* 141–150.

Mowrer, D. E., & Burger, S. (1991). A comparative analysis of phonological acquisition of consonants in the speech of 2½-6-year-old Xhosa- and English-speaking children. *Clinical Linguistics and Phonetics, 5,* 139–164.

Munson, J., & Ingram, D. (1986). Morphology before syntax: A case study from language acquisition. *Journal of Child Language, 12,* 671–680.

Murai, J. (1961). Nyujiki shoki no onsei hattatsu. *Tetsugaku Kenkyu, 474,* 270–292.

Myers, S. (1987). Vowel shortening in English. *Natural Language and Linguistic Theory, 5,* 485–518.

Myerson, R. F. (1976). Children's knowledge of selected aspects of 'Sound Pattern of English.' In

R. N. Campbell & P. T. Smith (Eds), *Recent advances in the psychology of language: Formal and experimental approaches* (377–402). New York: Plenum Press.

Nathan, G. S. (1996). What functionalists can learn from formalists in phonology. Paper presented at the Milwaukee Conference on Formalism and Functionalism, April 1996, Milwaukee, WI.

Nicklas, T. D. (1972). *The elements of Choctaw*. Unpublished doctoral dissertation: University of Michigan.

Ní Chiosáin, M., & Padgett, J. (1993). Inherent V-Place. *Linguistics Research Center Report, 93–09*, Santa Cruz, CA.

Norman, D. A. (1981). Categorization of action slips. *Psychological Review, 88*, 1–15.

Norris, M., & Harden, J. (1981). Natural processes in the phonologies of four error-rate groups. *Journal of Communication Disorders, 14*, 195–213.

Odden, D. (1991). Vowel geometry. *Phonology, 8*, 261–290.

Odden, D. (1994). Adjacency parameters in phonology. *Language, 70*, 289–330.

Ohala, D. (1994). Sonority-driven cluster reduction. Unpublished manuscript: University of Arizona.

Ohala, J. J. (1974). Experimental historical phonology. In J. M. Anderson & C. Jones (Eds.), *Historical phonology II: Theory and description in phonology* (pp. 353–389). Amsterdam: North Holland.

Öhman, S. (1966). Coarticulation in CVC utterances: Spectrographic measurements. *Journal of the Acoustical Society of America, 66*, 1691–1702.

Okrand, M. (1992). *The Klingon dictionary*. New York: Pocket Books.

Olswang, L. B., & Bain, B. A. (1985). Monitoring phoneme acquisition for making treatment withdrawal decisions. *Applied Psycholinguistics, 6*, 17–37.

Orgun, C. O. (1995). Correspondence and identity constraints in two-level OT. *WCCFL*. Rutgers Optimality Archive ROA-62.

Ornelas-Hesse, B. (1989). *Der Erwerb von Verschlußlauten und Frikativen im Deutschen*. Unpublished doctoral dissertation: Universität von München, Deutschland.

Otomo, K., & Stoel-Gammon, C. (1992). The acquisition of unrounded vowels in English. *Journal of Speech and Hearing Research, 35*, 604–616.

Panagos, J. M., & Prelock, P. A. (1982). Phonological constraints on the sentence productions of language-disordered children. *Journal of Speech and Hearing Research, 25*, 171–177.

Paradis, C. (1988). On constraints and repair strategies. *The Linguistic Review, 6*, 71–97.

Paradis, C. (1993). Ill-formedness in the dictionary: A source of constraint violation. *Canadian Journal of Linguistics, 38*, 215–234.

Paradis, J., Petitclerc, S., & Genesee, F. (1996). Word truncation in French-speaking two-year-olds. In E. Hughes, M. Hughes, & A. Greenhill (Eds.), *Proceedings of the 21st Annual Boston University Conference on Language Development* (pp. 441–452). Somerville, MA: Cascadilla Press.

Paradis, C., & Prunet, J. -F. (1989). On coronal transparency. *Phonology, 6*, 317–348.

Paradis, C., & Prunet, J. -F. (1991a). *The special status of coronals*. San Diego: Academic Press.

Paradis, C., & Prunet, J. -F. (1991b). Asymmetry and visibility in consonant articulations. In C. Paradis & J. -F. Prunet (Eds.), *The special status of coronals* (pp. 1–28). San Diego: Academic Press.

Paradis, C., & Prunet, J. -F. (1994). A note on velar nasals: The case of Uradhi. *Canadian Journal of Linguistics, 38*, 425–439.

Paschall, L. (1983). Development at two years. In J. V. Irwin & S. P. Wong (Eds.), *Phonological development in children: 18–72 months* (pp. 73–81). Carbondale: Southern Illinois University Press.

Pater, J. (in press). Minimal violation and phonological development. *First Language*.

Pater, J, & Paradis, J. (1996). Truncation without templates in child phonology. In *Proceedings of the Boston University conference on language development, 20*, 540–552. Somerville, MA: Cascadilla Press.

Peterson, G. E., & Lehiste, I. (1960). Duration of syllable nuclei in English. *Journal of the Acoustical Society of America, 32*, 693–703.

Piggott, G. L. (1992). Variability in feature dependency: the case of nasality. *Natural Language and Linguistic Theory, 10*, 33–77.

Pinker, S. (1984). *Language learnability and language development*. Cambridge, MA: Harvard University Press.

Pinker, S. (1991). Rules of language. *Science*, *253*, 530–535.

Pinker, S., & Bloom, P. (1990). Natural language and natural selection. *Behavioral & Brain Sciences*, *13*, 707–784.

Pinker, S., & Prince, A. (1988). On language and connectionism: Analysis of a Parallel Distributed Processing model of language acquisition. *Cognition*, *28*, 73–194.

Pollock, K., & Brammer, D. (1993). An acoustic analysis of young children's production of word stress. *Journal of Phonetics*, *21*, 183–203.

Pollock, K., & Keiser, N. (1990). An examination of vowel errors in phonologically disordered children. *Clinical Linguistics and Phonetics*, *4*, 161–178.

Poole, I. (1934). Genetic development of articulation of consonant sounds in speech. *Elementary English Rev.*, *11*, 159–161.

Preston, M. S., Yeni-Komshian, G., & Stark, R. (1967). Voicing in initial stop consonants produced by children in the prelinguistic period from different language communities. *Annual Report*, *2*, 305–323, Neurocommunications Laboratory, Baltimore, MD: Johns Hopkins University School of Medicine.

Priestly, T. M. S. (1977). One idiosyncratic strategy in the acquisition of phonology. *Journal of Child Language*, *4*, 45–65.

Prince, A. (1984). Phonology with tiers. In M. Aronoff & R. Oehrle (Eds.), *Language sound structure* (pp. 234–244). Cambridge, MA: MIT press.

Prince, A. S., & Smolensky, P. (1993). Optimality theory: Constraint interaction in generative grammar. Rutgers University Cognitive Sciences Center Technical Report-2. Piscataway, New Jersey.

Pulleyblank, D. (1988). Vocalic underspecification in Yoruba, *Linguistic Inquiry*, *19*, 233–270.

Pulleyblank, D., & Turkel, W. (1995). The logical problem of language acquisition in Optimality Theory. To appear in *Proceedings of the workshop on optimality in syntax: Is the best good enough?* MIT Press and MIT Working Papers in Linguistics.

Pye, C., Ingram, D., & List, H. (1987). A comparison of initial consonant acquisition in English and Quiché. In K. E. Nelson & A. van Kleeck (Eds.), *Children's language*, *Vol. 6* (pp. 175–190). Hillsdale, NJ: Lawrence Erlbaum Associates.

Reiss, C. (1995). Deriving an implicational universal in two theories of phonology. Unpublished manuscript: Concordia University. Rutgers Optimality Archive ROA-102.

Reiss, C., & Hale, M. (1996). The comprehension/production dilemma in child language: A response to Smolensky. Unpublished manuscript: Rutgers Optimality Archive ROA-132.

Rice, K. D. (1993). A reexamination of the feature [sonorant]: The status of "sonorant obstruents." *Language*, *69*, 308–344.

Rice, K. D. (1996). Aspects of variability in child language acquisition. In B. Bernhardt, J. Gilbert, & D. Ingram (Eds.), *Proceedings of the UBC international conference on phonological acquisition* (pp. 1–14). Somerville, MA: Cascadilla Press.

Rice, K., & Avery, P. (1995). Variability in a deterministic model of language acquisition: A theory of segmental elaboration. In J. Archibald (Ed.), *Phonological acquisition and phonological theory* (pp. 23–42). Hillsdale, NJ: Lawrence Erlbaum Associates.

Ringo, C. C. (1985). *The nature of change in phonological development: Evidence from the acquisition of /s/ + stop and /s/ + nasal clusters*. Unpublished doctoral dissertation: Brown University, Providence, R.I.

Rockman, B. K. (1983). *An experimental investigation of generalization and individual differences in phonological training*. Unpublished doctoral dissertation: Indiana University.

Rose, S. (1994). Guttural contrasts. *Toronto Working Papers in Linguistics*, *13*, 147–173.

Ross, A. S. C. (1937). An example of vowel-harmony in a young child. *Modern Language Notes*, *52*, 508–509.

Rubach, J. (1993). Skeletal vs. moraic representations in Slovak. *Natural Language & Linguistic Theory*, *11*, 625–653.

Rubach, J. (1994). Affricates as strident stops in Polish. *Linguistic Inquiry*, *25*, 119–143.

Rudnicky, A. I., & Cole, R. A. (1978). Effect of subsequent context on syllable perception. *Journal of Experimental Psychology: Human Perception and Performance*, *4*, 638–647.

Rumelhart, D., & McClelland, J. (1986). On learning the past tenses of English verbs. In D. Rumelhart & J. McClelland (Eds.), *Parallel distributed processing: Explorations in the microstructure of cognition, Vol. 1* (pp. 216–271). Cambridge, MA: Bradford Books.

Rumelhart, D., & Norman, D. A. (1984). Simulating a skilled typist: A study of skilled cognitive-motor performance. *Cognitive Science, 6*, 1–36.

Sagey, E. C. (1986). *The representation of features and relations in non-linear phonology.* Unpublished doctoral dissertation: MIT.

Sagey, E. C. (1988). On the ill-formedness of crossing association lines. *Linguistic Inquiry, 19*, 109–118.

Samek-Lodovici, V. (1992). Universal constraints and morphological gemination: A crosslinguistic study. Unpublished manuscript: Brandeis University, Waltham, MA.

Sander, E. (1972). When are speech sounds learned? *Journal of Speech and Hearing Disorders 37*, 55–63.

Sanders, G. A. (1974). The simplex features hypothesis. *Glossa, 8*, 141–192.

Schane, S. (1984). The fundamentals of particle phonology. *Phonology Yearbook, 1*, 129–155.

Schein, B., & Steriade, D. (1986). On geminates. *Linguistic Inquiry, 17*, 691–744.

Schwartz, R. G., & Leonard, L. B. (1982). Do children pick and choose? An examination of phonological selection and avoidance in early lexical acquisition. *Journal of Child Language, 9*, 319–336.

Schwartz, R., Leonard, L. B., Wilcox, M. J., & Folger, M. K. (1980). Again and again: Reduplication in child phonology. *Journal of Child Language, 7*, 75–88.

Scobbie, J. M. (1993). Constraint violation and conflict from the perspective of Declarative Phonology. *Canadian Journal of Linguistics, 38*, 155–167.

Scollon, R. (1976). Conversations with a one-year-old. Honolulu: University of Hawaii Press.

Selkirk, L. (1982). The syllable. In H. van der Hulst & N. Smith (Eds.), *The structure of phonological representations*, Part II (pp. 337–383). Dordrecht, Holland: Foris.

Shahin, K. (1995). Child language evidence on Palestinian Arabic phonology. In E. Clark (Ed.), *Proceedings of the twenty-sixth annual child language research forum* (pp. 104–116). Stanford: CSLI.

Shattuck-Hufnagel, S., & Klatt, D. (1979). The limited use of distinctive features and markedness in speech production: Evidence from speech errors. *Journal of Verbal Learning and Verbal Behavior, 18*, 41–55.

Shaw, P. (1992). Templatic evidence for the syllabic nucleus. *Proceedings from the North Eastern Linguistics Society Meeting, 23*.

Shaw, P. A. (1996). Headless and weightless syllables in Salish. Paper presented at the University of Victoria, January.

Shriberg, L., & Kwiatkowski, J. (1980). *Natural process analysis: A procedure for phonological analysis of continuous speech samples.* New York: Wiley.

Shriberg, L., & Lof, G. (1991). Reliability studies in broad and narrow phonetic transcription. *Clinical Linguistics and Phonetics, 5*, 225–279.

Slobin, D. I. (1985). *The crosslinguistic study of language acquisition, Vol. 1.* Hillsdale, NJ: Lawrence Erlbaum Associates.

Smit, A., Hand, L., Freilinger, J. J., Bernthal, J. E., & Bird, A. (1990). The Iowa articulation norms project and its Nebraska replication. *Journal of Speech and Hearing Disorders, 55*, 779–798.

Smith, B. L., & Oller, D. K. (1981). A comparative study of pre-meaningful vocalizations produced by normally developing and Down syndrome infants. *Journal of Speech and Hearing Disorders, 46*, 46–51.

Smith, N. (1973). *The acquisition of phonology.* Cambridge: Cambridge University Press.

Smoczyńska, M. (1985). The acquisition of Polish. In In D. I. Slobin (Ed.), *The crosslinguistic study of language acquisition, Vol. 1.* (pp. 595–686). Hillsdale, NJ: Lawrence Erlbaum Associates.

Smolensky, P. (1993). Harmony, markedness, and phonological activity. Handout from ROW-1, revised. Rutgers Optimality Archive ROA-87.

Smolensky, P. (1996a). On the comprehension/production dilemma in child language. *Linguistic Inquiry, 27*, 720–731.

Smolensky, P. (1996b). The initial state and 'richness of the base' in Optimality Theory. *Technical Report JHU-CogSci-96-4*. Baltimore: Johns Hopkins University Department of Cognitive Science.

So, L. K. H., & Dodd, B. J. (1995). The acquisition of phonology by Cantonese-speaking children. *Journal of Child Language, 22*, 473–495.

Spencer, A. (1988). A phonological theory of phonological development. In M. J. Ball (Ed.), *Theoretical linguistics and disordered language* (pp. 115–151). San Diego, CA: College-Hill Press.

Stampe, D. L. (1969). The acquisition of phonetic representation. *Papers from the fifth regional meeting of the Chicago Linguistic Society* (pp. 433–444). Chicago: Chicago Linguistic Society.

Stampe, D. L. (1973). *A dissertation on Natural Phonology*. Doctoral dissertation: University of Chicago. Published by Garland Press, New York.

Stemberger, J. P. (1981). Morphological haplology. *Language, 57*, 791–817.

Stemberger, J. P. (1984). Length as a suprasegmental: Evidence from speech errors. *Language, 60*, 895–913.

Stemberger, J. P. (1985). An interactive activation model of language production. In A. Ellis (Ed.), *Progress in the Psychology of Language, Vol. 1* (pp. 143–186). London: Lawrence Erlbaum Associates.

Stemberger, J. P. (1988a). Between-word processes in child phonology. *Journal of Child Language, 15*, 39–61.

Stemberger, J. P. (1988b). Underspecification and constraints on geminates. *Linguistic Inquiry, 19*, 154–160.

Stemberger, J. P. (1989). Speech errors in early child language production. *Journal of Memory & Language, 28*, 164–188.

Stemberger, J. P. (1990). Wordshape errors in language production. *Cognition, 35*, 123–157.

Stemberger, J. P. (1991a). Apparent anti-frequency effects in language production: The Addition Bias and phonological underspecification. *Journal of Memory and Language, 30*, 161–185.

Stemberger, J. P. (1991b). Radical underspecification in language production. *Phonology, 8*, 73–112.

Stemberger, J. P. (1992a). A connectionist view of child phonology: Phonological processing without phonological processes. In C. A. Ferguson, L. Menn, & C. Stoel-Gammon (Eds.), *Phonological development: Models, research, implications* (pp. 165–189). Timonium, MD: York Press.

Stemberger, J. P. (1992b). Vocalic underspecification in English language production. *Language, 68*, 492–524.

Stemberger, J. P. (1992c). A performance constraint on compensatory lengthening in child phonology. *Language & Speech, 35*, 207–218.

Stemberger, J. P. (1993a). Glottal transparency. *Phonology, 10*, 107–138.

Stemberger, J. P. (1993b). Rule ordering in child phonology. In M. Eid & G. Iverson (Eds.), *Principles and prediction: The analysis of natural language* (pp. 305–326). Amsterdam: John Benjamins.

Stemberger, J. P. (1993c). Vowel dominance in overregularization. *Journal of Child Language, 20*, 503–521.

Stemberger, J. P. (1994a). Timing units and moras: A synthesis. Unpublished manuscript: University of Minnesota.

Stemberger, J. P. (1994b). Heavy syllable deletion. Unpublished manuscript: University of Minnesota.

Stemberger, J. P. (1995). Phonological and lexical constraints on morphological processing. In L. Feldman (Ed.), *Morphological aspects of processing* (pp. 247–267). Amsterdam: North-Holland.

Stemberger, J. P. (1996a). The scope of the theory: Where does beyond lie? In L. McNair, K. Singer, L. M. Dobrin, & M. M. Aucoin (Eds.), *Papers from the parasession on theory and data in linguistics, CLS 23*, (pp. 139–164). Chicago: Chicago Linguistic Society.

Stemberger, J. P. (1996b). Optimality Theory and phonological development: Basic issues. *Korean Journal of Linguistics, 21*, 93–138.

Stemberger, J. P. (1996c). The dance of the defaults: The acquisition of morphology within phonology. Unpublished manuscript: University of Minnesota.

Stemberger, J. P. (1996d). Syllable structure in English, with emphasis on coda. In B. Bernhardt, J. Gilbert, & D. Ingram (Eds.), *Proceedings of the UBC international conference on phonological acquisition* (pp. 62–75). Somerville, MA: Cascadilla Press.

Stemberger, J. P., & Bernhardt, B. B. (1996). Phonological constraints and morphological development. In E. Hughes, M. Hughes, & A. Greenhill (Eds.), *Proceedings of the 21st annual Boston University conference on language development* (pp.603–614). Somerville, MA: Cascadilla Press.

Stemberger, J. P., & Bernhardt, B. H. (1997). *Optimality Theory*. In M. Ball & R. Kent (Eds.), *The new phonologies* (pp. 211–245). San Diego, CA: Singular Publishing Group.

Stemberger, J. P., & Bernhardt, B. B. (in preparation). Intervocalic consonants in disordered child speech. Unpublished manuscript: University of Minnesota & University of British Columbia.

Stemberger, J. P., Elman, J. L., & Haden, P. (1985). Interference between phonemes during phoneme monitoring: Evidence for an interactive activation model of speech perception. *Journal of Experimental Psychology: Human Perception and Performance, 11*, 475–489.

Stemberger, J. P., & MacWhinney, B. (1984). Extrasyllabic consonants in CV phonology: An experimental test. *Journal of Phonetics, 12*, 355–366.

Stemberger, J. P., & MacWhinney, B. (1986). Frequency and the lexical storage of regularly inflected forms. *Memory and Cognition, 14*, 17–26.

Stemberger, J. P., Pollock, K., & Salck, J. (1990). Initial unstressed syllables in young child speech. Paper presented at the Child Phonology Conference, May 1990, Madison, WI.

Stemberger, J. P., & Setchell, C. M. (1994). Vowel dominance and morphological processing. Unpublished manuscript: University of Minnesota.

Stemberger, J. P., & Stoel-Gammon C. (1991). The underspecification of coronals: Evidence from language acquisition and performance errors. In C. Paradis & J. -F. Prunet (Eds.), *The special status of coronals* (pp. 181–199). San Diego: Academic Press.

Stemberger, J. P., & Treiman, R. (1986). The internal structure of word-initial consonant clusters. *Journal of Memory and Language, 25*, 163–180.

Stengelhofen, J. (1989). *Cleft palate: The nature and remediation of communication problems*. Edinburgh: Churchill Livingstone.

Steriade, D. (1987). Redundant values. *Papers from the twenty-third regional meeting, Chicago Linguistic Society, Vol. 2* (pp. 339–362). Chicago: Chicago Linguistic Society, University of Chicago.

Steriade, D. (1988). Reduplication and syllable transfer in Sanskrit and elsewhere. *Phonology, 5*, 73–155.

Stern, C., & Stern, W. (1907). *Die Kindersprache*. (Reprinted 1975). Darmstadt: Wissentschaftliche Buchgesellschaft.

Stevens, K. N., & Keyser, S. J. (1989). Primary features and their enhancement in consonants. *Language, 65*, 81–106.

Stoel-Gammon, C. (1983). Constraints on consonant-vowel sequences in early words. *Journal of Child Language, 10*, 455–457.

Stoel-Gammon, C. (1985). Phonetic inventories, 15–24 months: A longitudinal study. *Journal of Speech and Hearing Disorders, 53*, 302–315.

Stoel-Gammon, C. (1988). Prelinguistic vocalizations of hearing-impaired and normally hearing subjects—a comparison of consonantal inventories. *Journal of Speech Disorders, 53*, 302–315.

Stoel-Gammon, C. (1993). Phonological characteristics of children's first words: The earliest stages. Paper presented at the Sixth International Congress for the Study of Child Language, Trieste, Italy, July 18–23, 1993.

Stoel-Gammon, C. (1996). On the acquisition of velars in English. In B. Bernhardt, J. Gilbert, & D. Ingram (Eds.), *Proceedings of the UBC international conference on phonological acquisition* (pp. 201–214). Somerville, MA: Cascadilla Press.

Stoel-Gammon & Dunn, C. (1985). *Normal and disordered phonology in children*. Austin, TX: PRO-ED.

Stoel-Gammon, C., & Herrington, P. B. (1990). Vowel systems of normally developing and phonologically disordered children. *Clinical Linguistics and Phonetics, 4*, 145–160.

Stoel-Gammon, C., & Stemberger, J. P. (1994). Consonant harmony and phonological underspecification in child speech. In M. Yavaş (Ed.), *First and second language phonology*. San Diego: Singular Publishing Co.

Stoel-Gammon, C., Williams, K., & Buder, E. (1994). Cross-language differences in phonological acquisition: Swedish and American /t/. *Phonetica, 51*, 146–158.

Straight, H. S. (1980). Auditory versus articulatory phonological processes and their development in children. In G. Yeni-Komshian, J. F. Cavanagh, & C. A. Ferguson (Eds.), *Child phonology, Vol. 1, Production* (pp. 43–71). New York: Academic Press.

Sumio, K. (1978). *Yojikyoiku Sensho ● Ryoiki Hen: Gengo.* Tokyo: Kawashima Shoten.

Suzman, S. (1991). *Language acquisition in Zulu.* Unpublished doctoral dissertation: Witwatersrand University.

Taintutier, M.-J., & Caramazza, A. (1994). The status of double letters in graphemic representations. *Reports of the Cognitive Neuropsychology Laboratory, 94–2.* Hanover, NH: Dartmouth College.

Templin, M. (1957). *Certain language skills in children: Their development and interrelationships.* Institute of Child Welfare Monographs, Vol. 26, University of Minnesota Press, Minneapolis, MN.

Tesar, B. (1995). *Computational Optimality Theory.* Unpublished doctoral dissertation: University of Colorado. Rutgers Optimality Archive ROA-90.

Tesar, B., & Smolensky, P. (in press). Learnability in Optimality Theory. *Linguistic Inquiry.*

Touretzky, D. S. (1986). BoltzCONS: Reconciling connectionism with the recursive nature of stacks and trees. *Proceedings of the eighth annual conference of the Cognitive Science Society.* Amherst, MA, August, 1986. Hillsdale, NJ: Lawrence Erlbaum Associates.

Tranel, B. (1991). CVC light syllables, geminates, and Moraic Theory. *Phonology, 8,* 291–302.

Treiman, R. (1988). The internal structure of the syllable. In G. Carlson & M. Tanenhaus (Eds.), *Linguistic Structure in Language Processing,* (pp. 27–52). Dordrecht, Holland: Kluwer.

Treiman, R., & Breaux, A. M. (1982). Common phoneme and overall similarity relations among common syllables: Their use by children and adults. *Journal of Psycholinguistic Research, 11,* 569–598.

Trigo, R. L. (1988). *On the phonological behavior and derivation of nasal glides.* Unpublished doctoral dissertation: MIT.

Tse, A. C.-Y. (1991). *The acquisition process of Cantonese phonology: A case study.* Unpublished Master of Philosophy thesis: Hong Kong.

Tse, S.-M. (1982). *The acquisition of Cantonese phonology.* Unpublished doctoral dissertation: University of British Columbia.

Tse, J. K.-P. (1978). Tone acquisition in Cantonese: A longitudinal study. *Journal of Child Language, 5,* 191–204.

Tyler, A. A., & Edwards, M. L. (1993). Lexical acquisition and acquisition of initial voiceless stops. *Journal of Child Language, 20,* 253–273.

Ueda, I. (1996). Segmental acquisition and feature specification in Japanese. In B. Bernhardt, J. Gilbert, & D. Ingram (Eds.), *Proceedings of the UBC international conference on phonological acquisition* (pp. 15–27). Somerville, MA: Cascadilla Press.

Velleman, S. L. (1988). The role of linguistic perception in later phonological development. *Applied Psycholinguistics, 9,* 221–236.

Vellemann, S. (1992). Nonlinear representation of 'word recipes'. Paper presented at the annual meeting of the Linguistic Society of America, January 1992, Philadelphia, PA.

Velleman, S. L. (1996). Metathesis highlights feature-by-position constraints. In B. Bernhardt, J. Gilbert, & D. Ingram (Eds.), *Proceedings of the UBC international conference on phonological acquisition* (pp. 173–186). Somerville, MA: Cascadilla Press.

Velten, H. V. (1943). The growth of phonemic and lexical patterns in infant language. *Language, 18,* 281–292.

Vennemann. T. (1972). Words and syllables in natural generative phonology. In T. Bruck et al. (Eds.), *Papers from the parasession on natural phonology* (pp. 346–374). Chicago: Chicago Linguistic Society, University of Chicago.

Vihman, M. (1976). From pre-speech to speech: On early phonology. *Papers and Reports on Child Language Development (Stanford University), 3,* 51–94.

Vihman, M. (1978). Consonant harmony: Its scope and function in child language. In J. H. Greenberg (Ed.), *Universals of human language, Vol. 2: Phonology* (pp. 281–334). Stanford, CA: Stanford University Press.

Vihman, M. (1992). Early syllables and the construction of phonology. In C. A. Ferguson, L. Menn, & C. Stoel-Gammon (Eds.), *Phonological development: Models, research, implications* (pp. 393–422). Timonium, MD: York Press.

Vihman, M. (1996). *Phonological development: The origins of language in the child.* Cambridge, MA: Blackwell.

Vihman, M., & de Boysson-Bardies, B. (1994). The nature and origins of ambient language influence on infant vocal production and early words. *Phonetica, 51,* 159–169.

Vihman, M., Velleman, S. L., & McCune, L. (1994). How abstract is phonology? Toward an integration of linguistic and psychological approaches. In M. Yavaş (Ed.), *First and second language phonology* (pp. 9–44). San Diego, CA: Singular Publishing Group.

Vinson, J. (1915). Observations sur le développement du langage chez l'enfant. *Revue Linguistique, 49,* 1–39.

Von Bremen, V. (1990). *A nonlinear phonological approach to intervention with severely phonologically disordered twins.* Unpublished M.A. thesis: University of British Columbia.

Waterson, N. (1971). Child phonology: A prosodic view. *Journal of Linguistics, 7,* 179–211.

Weiner, F. (1981). Systematic sound preference as a characteristic of phonological disability. *Journal of Speech and Hearing Disorders, 46,* 281–286.

Wellman, B., Case, I., Mengert, I., & Bradbury, D. (1931). Speech sounds of young children. *University of Iowa Studies in Child Welfare, 5(2).*

Werker, J. F., & Lalonde, C. E. (1988). Cross-language speech perception: Initial capabilities and developmental change. *Developmental Psychology, 24,* 1–12.

Werker, J. F., & Tees, R. C. (1984). Cross-language speech perception: Evidence for perceptual reorganization during the first year of life. *Infant Behavior and Development, 7,* 49–63.

Wexler, K., & Culicover, P. (1980). *Formal principles of language acquisition.* Cambridge, MA: MIT Press.

Wheeler, D.W., & Touretzky, D. (1993). A connectionist implementation of cognitive phonology. In J. Goldsmith (Ed.), *The last phonological rule* (pp.146–172). Chicago: University of Chicago Press.

Wijnen, F., Krikhaar, E., & Den Os, E. (1994). The (non)realization of unstressed elements in children's utterances: Evidence for a rhythmic constraint. *Journal of Child Language, 21,* 59–83.

Williams, A. L., & Dinnsen. D. A. (1987). A problem of allophonic variation in a speech disordered child. *Innovations in Linguistics Education, 5,* 85–90.

Yavaş, M., & Hernandorena, C. (1991). Systematic sound preference in phonological disorders: A case study. *Journal of Communication Disorders, 24,* 79–87.

Yavaş, M., & Lamprecht, R. (1988). Processes and intelligibility in disordered phonology. *Clinical Linguistics and Phonetics, 2,* 329–345.

Yip, M. (1987). English vowel epenthesis. *Natural Language and Linguistic Theory, 5,* 463–484.

Yip, M. (1988). The Obligatory Contour Principle and phonological rules: A loss of identity. *Linguistic Inquiry, 19,* 65–100.

Yip, M. (1991). Coronals, consonant clusters, and the Coda Condition. In C. Paradis & J.-F. Prunet (Eds.), *The special status of coronals* (pp. 61–78). San Diego: Academic Press.

Yip, M. (1995). Identity avoidance in phonology and morphology. To appear in *Proceedings of the conference on morphology and its relation to syntax and phonology,* UC Davis, May. Rutgers Optimality Archive ROA-82.

Zipf, G. K. (1935). *The psychobiology of language.* Boston: Houghton-Mifflin.

INDEX

Page references followed by *n*, *f*, or *t* indicate
footnotes, figures, or tables, respectively.

ISBN 0-12-092830-2

9 780120 928309

90051